W9-CBY-092

A SOURCEBOOK FOR BAPTIST HERITAGE

H. Leon McBeth

BROADMAN PRESS
Nashville, Tennessee

© Copyright 1990 • Broadman Press
All rights reserved
4265-89

ISBN: 0-8054-6589-8
Dewey Decimal Classification: 286.09
Subject Heading: BAPTISTS—HISTORY
Library of Congress Catalog Card Number: 89-33091
Printed in the United States of America

Library of Congress Cataloging-in-Publication Data

McBeth, Leon.
  A sourcebook for Baptist heritage / H. Leon McBeth.
    p.   cm.
  Bibliography: p.
  Includes index.
  ISBN 0-8054-6589-8 : $19.95
  1. Baptists—History. 2. Baptists—History—Sources. I. Title.
BX6231.M38   1990
286'.09—dc20   89-33091
                                                                    CIP

Preface

In teaching Baptist history over the past thirty years, I have tried to help my students understand something of the *sources* of history, as well as the major facts and interpretations. Both by precept and, I hope, by example, I have emphasized the need to base one's interpretations upon primary sources.

Over the years when I would share an unusual anecdote, a choice quotation, or a first-hand account of some event in Baptist history, many of the students showed keen fascination. Countless times I have been asked some version of the following question, "Can you tell me the name of the book where you found all of these stories?" Of course, I had to reply that there is no one book that gathers up these first-hand, primary source materials. They are scattered in hundreds of books, letters, diaries, church minutes, court records, wills, Baptist convention and associational records, magazine and newspaper articles, committee reports, sermons, testimonies, private memoirs, journals scholarly and popular, and other repositories. They are found in various libraries, notebooks, attics, cellars, desk drawers, and file folders on several continents and in different languages.

By the time I finish that recital, most of the students are discouraged. How could they ever possibly find all of this Baptist material, or even a fraction of it? And, for all my careful explanation, I often felt that many of them, despite their respectful nods, never quite grasped the difference between *secondary* and *primary* historical sources.

Therefore, in an effort to help my nine o'clock class, and beyond them to assist any interested reader in the field of Baptist history, I began the task of collecting these various source documents. Over the past three decades, I have gathered much more material than could be included here. Hard decisions had to be made in order to keep the book to reasonable length.

The reader is entitled to know the basic principles which guided the final selection of what to include. First, I sought to include data from the major parts of the Baptist family. As to geography, these pages contain documents from Baptists in Britain, the United States, and both Eastern and Western Europe. As to affiliation, most major groups of Baptists are represented, including American, Southern, Free Will, National, Seventh-day, Primitive, Landmark, General, Regular, Duck River, and many others. As to theological complexion, Baptists from the very liberal to ultra-fundamentalists, and all shades in between, are represented here. However, I have not included material from Baptists in Latin America, the Orient, or India, partly because it would have made the book too long, and partly because I lack the language facility to deal with primary sources from those areas.

Second, I have tried to choose documents that represent the Baptist *people,* as well as their leaders. In addition to official reports, the reader will find here some of the most unofficial remarks of ordinary Baptist people. I think that adds balance as well as spice to the story.

Third, I tried to strike some balance between the standard familiar sources and those less known. Often some important sources were omitted because they have been recently published in some other collection and thus are readily available. In such cases, I gave preference to material that is less accessible.

Fourth, I have included fewer selections, but the selections are longer than one finds in some similar collections. In using historical documents over the years, I have concluded that to be useful a primary source must be long enough to carry the message. By using only tiny snippets from here and there, one could include more different sources but the overall collection would, it seems to me, have less value.

Fifth, I resisted the temptation to write lengthy introductions to each document. I wanted to write more, but felt it was more important to use the space to allow the Baptists of the past to speak for themselves. Therefore, my historical introductions are quite brief, just the bare minimum to set the document in context.

If a reader looks for some document in Baptist history that is not included, I can only say that I share the disappointment of having to omit so much. In some cases, helpful documents may not be included for the simple reason that I do not know they exist. In a few cases, permission to republish could not be obtained. In most cases, however, a tough decision had to be made, as in the doctrine of predestination, to include some and exclude others.

One may regard this collection of primary sources as a Siamese twin to my earlier work, *The Baptist Heritage: Four Centuries of Baptist Witness* (Nashville: Broadman Press, 1987). Both books, the narrative history and the source collection, grew out of the same life-long study of Baptist history. The two books follow the same general outline and chapter division and are designed to supplement each other. They are arranged to be used together, but each volume can stand on its own.

Most of the source documents included here are reproduced exactly as they appeared in their original form. Some readers may be distracted by the casual spelling, erratic punctuation, and unpredictable grammar. A colleague who saw this manuscript in early form suggested that I modernize the text. I have resisted that, for it seems important for the reader to see these sources as near their original form as possible. I have tampered with the text only to this extent: In some pieces I omitted excessive punctuation that hampered the flow of thought, and at times I introduced paragraph breaks in huge blocks of material which in their original form offered no relief to the eye.

Though I cannot list all their names here, I thank all of the people who helped in gathering, sifting, preparing, and editing this collection. I am particularly indebted to Carl Wrotenbery, director, Webb Roberts Library, Southwestern Baptist Theological Seminary, Fort Worth, Texas; Ronald Deering, director of libraries, The Southern Baptist Theological Seminary, Louisville, Kentucky; William H. Brackney, then curator, American Baptist Historical Archives, Rochester, New York, and now dean, Eastern Baptist Theological Seminary, Philadelphia, Pennsylvania; Barrington R. White, principal, Regent's Park College, Oxford University, and curator of the Angus Collection of Early English Baptist Materials; Lynn E. May, Jr., director, Southern Baptist Historical Library and Archives, Nashville, Tennessee; and the directors of other Baptist collections in England, Europe, Canada, and the United States. I thank Terry G. Carter, doctor of philosophy graduate in church history from Southwestern Baptist Theological Seminary who lived for several years in Europe, for assistance in locating and translating some documents from European Baptists.

Special thanks go to several of my doctoral students in Baptist history, including Vicki Crumpton, Brad Creed, Ricky McClatchy, Michael D. Gabbert, Richard Blackaby, Michael Barnett, and Dennis R. Wiles. They read and evaluated portions of the collection and no doubt the outcome would have been better if I had listened to more of their suggestions.

I also thank Susan Day and Gloria Wells, loyal secretaries who throughout the project remained pleasant in spirit as well as super-competent in skills.

William B. Tolar, dean, School of Theology of the Southwestern Baptist Theological Seminary, approved my sabbatical leave request which released me from the daily duty of teaching classes and attending faculty meetings in order to complete this project.

Most of all, however, I thank the students in my nine o'clock class who by their interest, curiosity, and willingness to learn about Baptist life and practice provoked me both to begin and to complete this collection of primary sources.

Contents

Andrew Fuller and the Rise of "Fullerism"; William Carey, *An Enquiry* (1792); Abraham Booth, *Commerce in the Human Species* (1792)

Unit III: The Nineteenth Century

Monroe Conference; Basil Manly, Jr., The Sunday School Movement; Report of the First Sunday School Board (1868); The Present Sunday School Board, SBC; The Southern Baptist Theological Seminary; The Whitsitt Controversy; The Landmark Movement; The Gospel Mission Movement; The Role of Women in Southern Baptist Life; Letters from Lottie Moon

Unit IV: The Twentieth Century

Resolutions by Southern Baptists; Southern Baptist Convention Statement on Racial Crisis in America (1968); Southern Baptist Convention "Peace Committee" Report; Virginia Baptist Response to the Denominational Crisis

Unit I
The Seventeenth Century

1
Baptist Beginnings

The Baptists emerged as a distinct denomination out of the left wing of the English Protestant Reformation. Influences from the Continent, particularly from the more biblical groups of Anabaptists, may have played some role in their origin, but Baptist origins and early motifs are primarily British. The English Reformation fostered an intense search for a church that faithfully followed biblical norms in faith and practice. This search led to such successive reform movements as Puritanism and Separatism. From their own reading of the Bible, some of the Separatists concluded that baptism should be applied only to believers. In time they reached the further conclusion that such baptism of believers should be applied by the ancient practice of total immersion. These developments provided the avenue for the emergence of churches that acquired the nickname of "Baptist."

The two groups of Baptists in England had separate origins. The General Baptists, the older of the two groups, as their name implies, held to a "general" atonement. They taught that Christ's death applied to all who would believe and accept it. Their earliest church dates from about 1609, formed by John Smyth while in exile in Amsterdam. The more Calvinistic group, the Particular Baptists, held to a "particular" atonement. They taught that only the elect could be saved. The earliest Particular Baptist church was formed in London by 1638.

The two Baptist groups also differed in ecclesiology; the Particulars were more independent, while the Generals were more connectional. The General Baptists also favored a strict and at times hostile separation from the Church of England, while the Particular Baptists held to milder forms of semiseparation. Differences between the two groups diminished in time, and in the late-nineteenth century they merged.

For the first generation, the Baptists existed only in scattered churches; they did not form anything as cohesive and united as to be called a "denomination." For the Baptists, as for other reform groups in England, religious lines were fluid and everchanging. Gradually through outstanding leaders and through shared confessions of faith, the Baptists found their way to a more united outlook as a cohesive denomination.

The documents in this chapter have been chosen to illustrate the origin of General and Particular Baptists. Many of these documents also show early Baptist beliefs and practices, but selections for later chapters carry these themes further. Since John Smyth formed what is now acknowledged as the first General Baptist church of modern history, several selections from his writings are included. The Jessey Records and the Kiffin Manuscript give valuable, if somewhat incomplete, accounts of the first Particular Baptist churches.

How have other historians viewed these sources on Baptist origins? This chapter includes a brief excerpt from William H. Whitsitt on the introduction of immersion in England. The chapter concludes with a brief selection from J. M. Carroll's well-known *Trail of Blood*, which gives an entirely different perspective on Baptist origins.

13

1.1   John Smyth, *Differences of the Churches of the Separation*, 1608

John Smyth constantly faced the necessity of defending his separation from the Church of England. In several writings, he justified the withdrawal positively by showing that the separated churches restored New Testament patterns in worship, doctrine, and ministry. On the negative side, he argued that the Church of England was a false system from which all true Christians had to separate or risk spiritual contamination. He thus took the position of strict separatism as compared, for example, with the mild semiseparatism of Henry Jacob who wanted to separate only from the corruptions within the Church of England.

In *Differences* Smyth emphasized not only the necessity of separation but also described in detail the manner of worship, governance, financial contributions, and role of ministry in the separated churches. Not all of these emphases are covered in this brief selection, but most of them Smyth later infused into Baptist life. This document is especially notable for revealing Smyth's attitude toward Scripture and the role of translations in preaching and worship. *Source:* John Smyth, *Differences of the Churches of the Separation*, 1608. Reprinted in W. T. Whitley, ed., *The Works of John Smyth*, 2 vols. (Cambridge: Cambridge University Press, 1915), 1:269-292.

To every true lover of the truth especially to the Brethren
of the seperation: Salutations.

Not long since I published a litle methode intituled principles & inferences concerning the visible Church: Wherin chiefly I purposed to manifest the true constitution of the Church, a matter of absolute necessitie & now so cleered by the writings of the late witnesses of Iesus Christ the auncient brethren of the seperation as that it seemeth nothing can further be added. The absolute necessitie of the true constitution appeareth, because if the Church be truly constituted & framed, ther is a true Church: the true spowse of Christ: if the Church be falsely constituted, ther is a false Church: & she is not the true spowse of Christ: Herein therfore especially are those auncient brethren to be honoured, that they have reduced the Church to the true Primitive & Apostolique constitution which consisteth in these three things. 1. The true matter which are sayntes only. 2. The true forme which is the vniting of them together in the covenant. 3. The true propertie which is communion in all the holy things, & the powre of the L. Iesus Christ, for the maintayning of that communion.

To this blessed work of the L. wherin those auncient brethren have labored I know not what may more be added: I thincke rather ther can nothing be added: but now Antichrist is perfectly both discovered & consumed in respect of the constitution by the evidence of the truth, which is the brightnes of Christs comming. Now al though they have also verie worthelie employed themselves in the Leitourgie, Ministerie, & Treasurie of the Church, both in discovering the forgeries & corruptions which the man of synne had intermingled, & also in some good degree reducing them to ther primitive puritie wherin they weere by the Apostles left vnto the Churches.

Yet wee are persuaded that herein Antichrist is not vtterlie eyther revealed or abolished, but that in a verie high degree he is exalted even in the true constituted Churches:
. . .

And lett no man bee offended at vs for that wee differ from the auncient brethren of the seperation in the Leitourgie Presbyterie & Treasurie of the Church: for wee hold not our fayth at any mans pleasure or in respect of persons, neyther doe wee bynd our selves to walk according to other mens lynes further then they walk in the truth: neyther lett the world think that wee approve them in all their practises: let them justifie their proceedinges or repēt of them. wee have (wee willingly & thankfully acknowledge) receaved much light of truth from their writinges, for which mercy we alwayes blesse our God: & for which help wee alwayes shall honour them in the Lord and in the truth. But as Paull withstood Peter to his face & seperated from Barnabas that good man that was full of the holy ghost & of fayth, for just causses: So must they give vs leave to love the truth & honour the Lord more then any man or Church vppon earth. . . .

So desyring the reader to weygh well what I plead & not to bee offended at the manifold quotations which are of necessity that by places compared together the truth which is a mystery may appeare & Antichristianisme which is the mysterie of iniquity may bee discovered, I cease, commending him to the grace of God in Iesus Christ, who in due tyme will bring his people out of Ægypt & Babylon spiritually so called, though for a season they are there kept in Antichristian captivity & greevous spirituall slavery; which the Lord in his due tyme effect, Amen, Amen.

Iohn Smyth

The principall contents of this treatise & our differences
from the auncyent brethren of the Seperation.

1 Wee hould that the worship of the new testament properly so called is spirituall proceeding originally from the hart: & that reading out of a booke (though a lawful ecclesiastical action) is no part of spirituall worship, but rather the invention of the man of synne it beeing substituted for a part of spirituall worship.

2 Wee hould that seeing prophesiing is a parte of spiritual worship: therefore in time of prophesijng it is vnlawfull to have the booke as a helpe before the eye

3 wee hould that seeing singing a psalme is a part of spirituall worship therefore it is vnlawfull to have the booke before the eye in time of singinge a psalme

4 wee hould that the Presbytery of the church is vniforme; & that the triformed Presbyterie consisting of three kinds of Elders viz. Pastors Teachers Rulers is none of Gods Ordinance but mans devise.

5 wee hould that all the Elders of the Church are Pastors: & that lay Elders (so called) are Antichristian.

6 wee hould that in contributing to the Church Treasurie their ought to bee both a seperation from them that are without & a sanctification of the whole action by Prayer & Thanksgiving.

The Differences of the Chvrches of the Seperation, Conteyning a description of the Leitourgie & Ministerie of the visible Church Annexed as a correction & supplement to a litle treatise lately published bearing title principles, & inferences concerning the visible Church.

THE FIRST PART. concerning the Leitourgie of the Church
Chap. 1. of the Kingdom of the Saynts.

The visible Church by the Apostle is called a Kingly preisthood. 1. pet. 2.9. and the Saynts are Kings & Preists vnto God Revel. 1.6.

The Saynts as Kings rule the visible Church. 1. Cor. 5. 12. psal. 149. 9. Mat. 18. 15-17. 1. Cor. 6. 1-9.

The visible Church is Christs Kingdom. Mat. 8. 12. Ioh. 18. 33-37. Act. 1. 3, 1. Cor. 15. 24. 25. Hebr. 12. 28. . . .

In examination of opinions & facts also in conference & disputation evidences of all sorts may be produced for finding out of the truth. Revel. 2. 2. 1. King 3. 25-27.

Evidences are of divers natures: as confessions & lotts: Iosh. 7. 16-21. Oathes: Exod. 22. 10. 11. bookes of all sortes. Dan. 9. 2. 1, King. 14. 19. Act 7. 22. & 17. 28. 1. Cor. 15. 33. Tit. 1. 12. Iude. vers. 14. compared with 1. Timoth. 1. 4. & Luk. 3. 25-27. namly translations, dictionaries, histories, chronicles, commentaries, &c, all which may for evidence of the truth be brought into the Church, by necessary consequence.

Actions of administring the Church or Kingdom are not actions of spirituall worship properly so called, for as the Kingdome and Preisthood of the old Testament were distinct as also their actions severall: Heb. 7. 14. Gen. 49. 10. Deut 33. 8-11. 2. Chron. 26. 18. psal. 122. 4. 5: So are the Kingdom & Preisthood of the new Testament & their actions also: which were typed by the other. Heb. 5. 4. 5. Act. 15. 7-29. with 13. 2, 3. . . . .

Chap. 6. concerning bookes & writing.

Here a question is to be discussed: wither a book be a lawful help to further vs in tyme of spiritual worship. Revel. 10. 10. 11. Ezech. 3. 3. 4.

Bookes or writings are signes or pictures of things signified therby.

Writings are to be considered in the concrete or in the abstract.

In the concrete writings import both the signe & the thing signified therby, that is both the characters & the matter.

In the abstract writings import the signe in relation to the thing signified therby: viz. lettres, sillables, wordes, syntaxe. . . .

Therefore wordes and syntaxe are signes of thinges, and of the relations and reason of thinges.

Hence it followeth that bookes or writinges are in the nature of pictures or Images & therefore in the nature of ceremonies: & so by consequent reading a booke is ceremoniall. For as the Beast in the Sacrifices of the ould Testament was ceremoniall so was the killing of the Beast ceremoniall.

Chap. 7. Of the kindes of bookes or writinges.

Men are of two sortes: Inspired, or ordinary men.

Men Inspired by the Holy Ghost are the Holy Prophets & Apostles who wrote the holy scriptures by inspiration. 2. Pet. 1. 21. 2. Tim. 3. 16. Rom. 1. 2. namely the Hebrue of the ould testament & the greeke of the new Testatment.

The holy Scriptures viz. the Originalls Hebrew & Greek are given by Divine Inspiration & in their first donation were without error most perfect & therefore Canonicall.

Ordinary men write bookes of divers kindes among the rest such as have the word of God or Holy Scriptures for their object are called Theological writinges: among them Translations of the Holy Scriptures into the mother tong are cheifly to be esteemed, as beeing the most principall, yet only as the streame issuing from the fountayne, or as the greatest river of the mayne sea.

No writinges of ordinary men how holy or good soever are given by inspiration, & therefore are subject to error & imperfect & so Apocrypha.

Chap. 8. Of the Originalls of Holy Scripture,
& of the partes of Holy Scripture

Holy Scriptures (as all other writinges whatsoever,) consist of two partes: of the tong & character & of the substance or matter signified by the character.

The tong or character hath apertaining to it the grammar & the Rhethorick wherof the tong or character is the subiect.

The matter or substance of the scripture hath in it, Logick, History, Cronology, Cosmography, Genealogy, Philosophy, Theologie & other like matter.

The principall parte of the matter is the Theologie

A Translation of the holy originalls may expresse very much of the matter contayned in or signified by the originall characters: it can expresse also much of the Rhethorick as Tropes & Figures of sentence.

No Translation can possibly expresse all the matter of the holy originalls, nor a thousand thinges in the Grammar, Rhethorick, & character of the tong.

A Translation so far forth as it doth truly & fully expresse any thing of the originals may be saide inspired of God & no further.

Hence it followeth that a translation be it never so good is mixt with mans devises, imperfect, not equipollent to the originalles in a thousand particulars.

The holy originalle signifie and represent to our eyes heavenly things therfor the book of the law is called a similitude of an heavenly thing Heb. 9. 19-23. . . .

Chap. 9. How the Originalls, or Holy Scriptures are to be vsed.

The Scriptures of the old Testament are commaunded to the Church—2. Pet. 1. 19. 20 & 2. Timoth. 3. 16. as also the Scriptures of the new Testament: 1. Thes. 5. 27. Col. 4. 16. & by proportion.

Heer consider these things,

1. How the Scriptures are to be vsed. 2. How they are not to be vsed.

The Holy Scriptures are the Fountayne of all truth, Ioh. 17. 17. compared with 2. Timoth. 3. 16. 17.

They are the ground & foundacion of our fayth, Ephes. 2. 20. compared with Ioh. 5. 39 & 17. 3.

By them all doctrynes & every Spiritt is to be judged: Esay 8. 20. 1. Ioh. 4. 1. Act. 17. 11.

They are to be read in the Church & to be interp[r]eted: Col. 4. 16. compared with Luk. 24. 27. & 1. Cor. 14. 27. & 12. 10. by proportion 2. Pet. 3. 16.

Neverthelesse the Holy Scriptures are not reteyned as helps before the eye in tyme of Spirituall worship: Reasons are these.

Chap. 10. Reasons proving the Originals not to be given as helps before the eye in worship.

1. Bicause Christ vsed the book to fulfill all righteousnes Mat. 3. 15 & having by the vse of the book fulfilled the law of reading he shut the book in the Synagogue, to signifie that that ceremony of bookworship, or the ministerie of the lettre was now exspired, & finished. Luk. 4. 20. Ioh. 19 30

2. Bicause reading wordes out of a book is the ministration of the lettre, 2. Cor. 3. 6. namely a part of the ministerie of the old Testament which is abolished: Heb. 8. 13: 2. Cor. 3: 11. 13. & the ministery of the new testament is the ministerie of the spirit 2. Cor. 3. 6. . . .

4. Bicause no example of the Scripture can be shewed of any man ordinary or extraordinary that at or after the day of Pentecost vsed a book in praying, prophesying & singing Psalmes: if yea: let it bee done & wee yeeld. . . .

6. Bicause the Churches of the Greekes had no bookes to vse that they might vse lawfully: for they vnderstood not Hebru: & the Septuagints translation ought not to be vsed or made, & the Apostles made no Greek translation: And if the Apostles read the Hebrue an vnknowne tong in the Greek Churches it could not be a lawfull worship, bicause it edified not: if they had the Hebrue before their eyes & intep[r]eted Greek, let it be shewed when & where & wee yeeld vnto it. . . .

9. Bicause vpon the day of Pentecost fyerie cloven tongs did appeare, not fiery cloven bookes. Act. 2. 3. & alwaies ther must be a proportion betwixt the type and the thing typed: vpon the day of Pentecost the fiery law was given in bookes Deut: 33. 2. Exo: 24. 4. 12 vpon the day of Pentecost the fiery gospel was given in tonges Act: 2. 3. Mat: 3. 11. Act: 1. 5. the booke therefore was proper for them, the tonge for vs

Arnold Mr Wilson John Woddin John Milburn Marke Lucar Mr Crafton Mr Granger Henry Parker Mr Jones H. Dod, deceased, a Prisoner Mr Barbone Mr Jacob Mr Lemar.

being ye Lords Day. Just a fortnight after was ye Antient Church so seized upon & two of them comitted to be fellow Prisoners with these. The Lord thus tryed & experienced them & their Friends & foes ye Space of some two Years, some only under Baill, some in Hold: in wch time ye Lord Wonderfully magnified his Name & refreshed their Spirits abundantly, for speak at ye High Comission & Pauls & in private even ye weake Women as their Subtill & malicious Adversarys ware not able to resist but ware asshamed.

2. In this Space ye Lord gave them So great faviour in ye Eyes of their Keepers y^t they suffered any friends to come to them and they edifyed & comforted one another on ye Lords Days breaking bread &c. . . .

4. Their Keepers found so sure in their promises that they had freedom to go home, or about their Trades, or business whensoever they desired, & set their time, & say they would then returne it was enough without the charges of one to attend them.

5. In this very time of their restraint ye Word was so farr from bound, & ye Saints so farr from being scared from the Ways of God that even then many ware in Prison added to ye Church, viz

Jo. Ravenscroft	Sarah	Willm.		Widd. White	
Widd. Harvey	Hump. Bernard	Thos.	⌠ Harris	Ailce	
Mary Atkin	G. Wiffield	Jane	⌡	Eliz	⌉ Wincop
Thos. Wilson				Rebec	⌡

6. Not one of those that ware taken did recant or turne back from the truth, through fear or through flattery, or cunning Slights but all ware ye more strengthened thereby. . . .

After ye Space of about 2 Years of the Sufferings & Patience of these Saints they ware all released upon Bail (some remaining so to this day as Mr Jones &c, though never called on) only to Mr Lathorp & Mr Grafton they refused to shew such faviour, they ware to remain in Prison without release.

At last there being no hopes y^t Mr Lathorp should do them further Service in ye Church, he having many motives to go to new England if it might be granted After the Death of his Wife he earnestly desiring ye Church would release him of y^t office w^{ch} (to his grief) he could no way performe, & that he might have their consent to goe to new England, after serious consideration had about it it was freely granted to him

Then Petition being made that he might have Liberty to depart out of ye Land he was released from Prison 1634, about ye 4th Month called June, & about 30 of the members who desired leave & permission from ye Congregation to go along with him, had it granted to them, namely, M^r Jo: Lathorp, Sam. House, John Wodwin, Goodwife Woodwin, Elder & Younger, Widd: Norton, & afterwards Robt Linel & his Wife, M^r & Mrs Laberton, Mrs Hamond, Mrs Swinerton . . . .

[1633] There haveing been much discussing these denying Truth of ye Parish Churches, & ye Church being now become so large y^t it might be prejudicial, these following desired dismission that they might become an Entire Church, & further ye Comunion of those Churches in Order amongst themselves, wch at last was granted to them & performed Sep^t 12. 1633 viz

Henry Parker & Wife
Widd: Fearne   Marke Lucar   . . . . .Hatmaker
Mr Wilson   Mary Milburn Thos Allen
              Jo: Milburn
              Arnold

To These Joyned Rich. Blunt, Tho: Hubert, Rich. Tredwell & his Wife Kath:, John Trimber, Wm Jennings & Sam Eaton, Mary Greenway———Mr Eaton with Some others receiving a further Baptism.[4]

Others joyned to them, ...

[1638] Other Persecutions besides the Persecutions before^sd

The Good Lord Jesus gave, (Satan still envying ye Prosperity of Zion, stirred up against this Church) several Tryalls afterwards wherein still ye Lord gave occation of Triumphing in him; It's good to record & bring to remembrance our Straights & ye Lords Enlargements, Experience works Hope & Hope maketh not asshamed because ye Love of God is shed abroad in our hearts. to instance in

John Trash was taken by Rag at Mr Digbeys & not Yelding to Rags general warrant, was had to ye L. Mayor . . . . . . & was comitted to ye Poultrey Counter for ten days & then was released upon Bail, wanted his health & was shortly after translated.

11th Month (vulgarly January) ye 21 day at Queenhith (where Mr Glover, Mr Eaton, MrEldred & others ware wth us) after Exercise was done, by means M^r . . . . . the overthwart Neighbour, Officers & others came, at last both ye Sheriffs, & then Veasy ye Pursevant who took ye Names; The Lord gave such Wisdom in their Carriage y^t some of their opposers afterwards did much favour them & bail'd them. The next Day Veasy the Pursevant got Money of some of them, & so they ware dismissed, 4 ware comitted to ye Poultrey Counter viz

R. Smith Mrs Jacob. S. Dry . . . .

2 Month Vulgo Aprill 21. At Tower Hill at Mrs Wilsons where some ware seeking ye Lord wth fasting for ye Parliament (like to be dissolved unless they would grant Subsidies for Warrs against ye Scotish) by procurement of Male ye Arch Prelates Pursevant, Sr Wm Balford Leuetenant of ye Tower sent theither H Jesse (who he found praying for ye King as he told his Mag^ty) Mrs Jones, Mr Brown wth others about 20.

Then S^r W^m asked his Magesties Pleasure concerning them who would have them Released but Dr Laud ye Arch Bishop being Present desired the men might be bound to ye Sessions wch was perform & no Enditement being there against them at their appearance they were freed. . . .

Also 6 Month 22^d day at the L. Nowers house, ye same L. Mayor Sr John Wright came Violently on them, beat, thrust, pinched & kicked such men or Women as fled not his handling, among others Mrs Berry who miscarryed & dyed the same week & her Child. He comitted to ye Counter H. Jessey, Mr Nowel, Mr Ghofton, & that night bound them to answer at ye House of Comons where they appearing he let it fall.

COVENANT RENEWED

[1630] Whilst Mr Lathorp was an Elder here some being greived against one that had his Child then Baptized in ye Common Assemblies,[5] & desireing & urging a Renouncing of them, as Comunion wth them, Mr Can also then walking Saints where he left Mr How (he going wth Some to Holland) He desiring that ye Church wth Mr Lathorp would renew their Covenant in Such a Way, & then he with Others would have Comunion wth them. Mr Dupper would have them therein to Detest & Protest against yᵉ Parish Churches, Some ware Unwilling in their Covenanting either to be tyed either to protest against yᵉ truth of them, or to affirm it of them, not knowing wᵗ in time to come God might further manifest to them thereabout Yet for peace Sake all Yelded to renew their Covenant in these Words

To Walke togeather in all yᵉ Ways of God So farr as he hath made known to Us, or shall make known to us, & to forsake all false Ways, & to this the several Members subscribed their hands.

After this followd several Sheets containing yᵉ Names of yᵉ Members of yᵉ said Congregation & yᵉ time of their admission.

[Notes]

1. Benjamin Stinton, the probable collector of these records.

2. These records must have been written after 1625, since Robinson died in 1624 or 1625.

3. This church is called the JLJ church, from the names of its first pastors Henry Jacob, John Lathrop, and Henry Jessey. It is important to note that it was not a Baptist church at its formation in 1616, though several of the first seven Particular Baptist churches came out of it.

4. This is a very significant statement. Some members felt sufficiently convinced that Church of England baptism was invalid that they sought a new baptism. However, we do not know for sure whether their objection was to baptism from a corrupt church or because it was applied to infants. Some refer to the 1633 schism as the first identifiable Particular Baptist church in England.

5. The "Common Assemblies" were the Church of England. That some members of the JLJ church still attended the state church on special occasions and even had their children christened there is consistent with the moderate separatism of Henry Jacob, founding pastor of the JLJ church. However, over the years the church apparently attracted some more militant members who could not tolerate anything short of total separation.

1.5   Rise of Particular Baptists [the Kiffin Manuscript]

Included among the records of the Gould Manuscript is a paper called the Kiffin Manuscript. Brief as it is, this document gives one of the clearest and most succinct accounts of the rise of Particular Baptists in England through ongoing developments within the JLJ congregation. The schisms of 1633 and 1638 are set out, though one wishes for more details. The conviction of some in 1638 that "Baptism was not for Infants, but professed Believers" is intriguing.

However, perhaps the key importance of this document is its account of how a part of the JLJ church moved beyond baptism of believers instead of infants, to the even more radical position of baptism of believers by total immersion. How they came to the conviction that baptism "ought to be by diping yᵉ Body into yᵉ Water" we are not told, but probably it grew out of continuing study of Scripture, theology, and Christian history. There is no evidence that General Baptists, then numerous in and around London, customarily practiced immersion by 1640-1641. *Source:* Transactions of the Baptist Historical Society (London: Baptist Union Publication Department), 1(1908-1909): 230-236.

An Old MSS, giveing some Accoᵗᵗ of those Baptists who first formed themselves into distinct Congregations, or Churches in London. found among certain Paper given meˡ by Mʳ Adams

[1633] Sundry of yᵉ Church whereof Mʳ Jacob & Mʳ John Lathorp had been Pastors, being dissatisfyed wᵗʰ yᵉ Churches owning of English Parishes to be true Churches desired dismission & Joyned togeather among themselves, as Mʳ Henry Parker, Mʳ Tho. Shepard, Mʳ Samˡˡ Eaton, Marke Luker, & others wᵗʰ whom Joyned Mʳ Wᵐ Kiffin.

[1638] Mʳ Tho: Wilson, Mʳ Pen, & H. Pen, & 3 more being convinced that Baptism was not for Infants, but professed Beleivers joyned wᵗʰ Mʳ Jo: Spilsbury yᵉ Churches favour being desired therein.

[1640] 3ᵈ MO: The Church became two by mutall consent just half being wᵗʰ Mʳ P. Barebone, & yᵉ other halfe with Mʳ H. Jessey Mʳ Richard Blunt wᵗʰ him being convinced of Baptism yᵗ also it ought to be by diping yᵉ Body into yᵉ Water, resembling Burial & riseing again. 2 Col: 2. 12. Rom: 6. 4. had sober conferance about in yᵉ Church, & then wᵗʰ some of the forenamed who also ware so convinced: And after Prayer & conferance about their so enjoying it, none haveing then so so practised in England to professed Believers,[2] & hearing that some in yᵉ Nether Lands had so practised they agreed & sent over Mʳ Rich. Blunt (who understood Dutch) wᵗʰ Letters of Com̃endation, who was kindly accepted there, & returned wᵗʰ Letters from them Jo: Batte a Teacher there, & from that Church to such as sent him.[3]

They proceed on therein, viz, Those Persons yᵗ ware persuaded Baptism should be by dipping yᵉ Body had mett in two Companies, & did intend so to meet after this, all these agreed to proceed alike togeather. And then Manifesting (not by any formal Words or Covenant) wᶜʰ word was scrupled by some of them, but by mutual desires & agreement each Testified: Those two Companyes did set apart one to Baptize the rest; So it was solemnly performed by them.

Mʳ Blunt Baptized Mʳ Blacklock yᵗ was a Teacher amongst them, & Mʳ Blunt being Baptized, he & Mʳ Blacklock Baptized yᵉ rest of their friends that ware so minded,[4] & many being added to them they increased much . . . .

Those that ware so minded had com̃union togeather were become Seven Churches in London.

Mʳ Green wᵗʰ Capᵗ Spencer had begun a Congregation in Crutched Fryers, to whom Paul Hobson joyned who was now wᵗʰ many of that Church one of yᵉ Seven.

These being much spoken against as unsound in Doctrine as if they ware Armenians, & also against Magistrates &c they joyned togeather in a Confession of their Faith[5] in fifty two Articles wᶜʰ gave great satisfaction to many that had been prejudiced.

Thus Subscribed in yᵉ Names of 7 Churches in London.

Wᵐ Kiffin		
Tho: Patience	Tho: Gun	Paul Hobson
Geo: Tipping	Jo: Mabbet	Tho: Goore
John Spilsbury	John Web	Jo: Phelps
Tho: Shepard	Tho: Kilcop	Edward Heath
Tho: Munden		

[Notes]

1. Benjamin Stinton, probable collector of these records.

2. This statement is usually taken as evidence that the General Baptists in and about London were not yet immersing.

3. The document does not specifically say that Blount was immersed in Holland, but that is probably the import of the phrase "Mr Blunt being Baptized."

4. Not all the members were immersed, but only those that "ware so minded," showing that at first this church practiced what later was called "open membership."

5. The First London Confession, issued by seven Particular Baptist churches in 1644, with a revision in 1646. The 1644 edition is included here, pp. 45-53.

1.6 *An Account of Divers Conferences* [in the JLJ Church]

The two previous documents (1.4 and 1.5) establish the basic facts of the emergence of Particular Baptists out of English separatism. They show that baptism discussions in the JLJ church led to schisms in 1633 and 1638 and that at least some members gave up the baptism of infants in favor of applying that ordinance only to professed believers. By 1640-1641 one group that had been members of the original JLJ church went the next step in recovering the ancient practice of applying baptism by total immersion.

However, the adoption of immersion was not unanimous; it included only "such as ware so minded." What happened to those who were not so minded? This document traces continuing baptism discussions in the remnant JLJ congregation after 1641, showing how several leaders including Jessey himself eventually became Baptists. Though their exact origins are not clear, by 1644 at least seven churches in London held and practiced the immersion of believers. Some years later the nickname "Baptist" was tagged on them. *Source:* Transactions of the Baptist Historical Society (London: Baptist Union Publication Department), 1(1908-1909): 239-245.

An Account of divers Conferences, held in ye Congregation of wch Mr Henry Jessey was Pastor, about Infant baptism, by wch Mr H. Jessey & ye greatest part of that Congregation ware proselited to ye Opinion & Practice of ye Antipedobabtists.

being an old M.S.S. wch I^1 rec^d of Mr Adams, supposed to be written by Mr Jessey, or transcribed from his Jurnal.

[1643]   About Baptisme. Qu: Ans:

Hanserd Knollys our Brother not being satisfyed for Baptizing his child, after it had bin endeavoured by ye Elder, & by one or two more; himselfe referred to ye Church then that they might satisfye him, or he rectify them if amiss herein; wch was well accepted.

Hence meetings ware appointed for conference about it at B. Ja: & B. K.: & B. G:^2 & each was performed wth Prayer & in much Love as Christian meetings (because he could not submitt his judgment to depend on wth its power: so yelded to)

Elder^3 The maine Argument was from these fower conclusions

1. Those in Gospel Institutions are so set down to us. those not cleare

2. What ever Privilidg God hath given to his Church as a Church is still given to all Churches.

3. God hath once given to his Church as a Church this Privilidge to have their Children in a Gospel covenant, & to have its token in Infancy. Gen: 17. 7. 10.

4. Baptism appears to be in ye rome of Circumcision
   Conclusion: to be now to Churches Infants

H.K.^4 Ans: To ye third on wch ye weight lyes, that it wants ground & proof from Scripture. That Gen: 17 proves it no more to be given to a Church as a Church, for their Infants to have the token of of Covenant in Infancy, then for the Churches Servants all bought wth money &c without exception of Religion to be Baptized; & y^t not only ye Chil: but Childrens Children to many Generations though neither Father nor Grandfather ware faithfull must be Members, for thus was it wth Abrahams posterity. therefore this was not with it as a Church, but as Jewish or as peculiar to Abrahams Seed Naturall. Unless we may say of the Children of such wretches, that certainly ye Lord is their God & they his People, contrary to 1 Cor: 7. 14.

Elder All such as we ought to judg to be in Gods

Ma:^5 covenant, under promises should have ye token

Mi: of ye Covenant. Thus of ye Infants of Believers especially Church members.

Ans: To ye first proposition or major its not ye Covenant y^t intrests to ye token of itselfe, but Gods Institution, proved thus.

1. The Lords Supper is a token of the New Covenant, it must be to such children as being in Covenant, if Argument good.

2. Enoch, Methusala, Noah, Sem, ware in Covenant, & to be judged So, & Abraham at 75 Years old, & Isaac at two days old; these then must have Circumcision, if major be sound, but not so.

besids being in Covenant there must be a word of Institution touching the time & adjuncts—&c

B.Ki⁶ In Gospell times wherein all these are, New, there are new subjects, Gentiles, a new way of takeing them in; new Ordinances, new time to them, as yᵉ Lords Supper So Bap: As we must not goe to Moses for yᵉ Lords Supper, its time, Persons to pertake &c but to New Testament, so we must for Baptism. now in New Testament is no Institution for Infants baptism.

The being yᵉ Seed of Abraham, of Godly Parents, would not qualify them for Baptism, Matth: 3. This is yᵉ Substance of wᵗ was discussed in all Love for many weeks togeather.

Issue whereof was yᵉ conviction of Bro: Iac: & S. K. B. S.⁷ now against Pedobap: & yᵉ Stagering of more, whereof some searched yᵉ Scriptures, some prayed earnestly for light, & had such impressions on their Spirits against Pedobaptisme, as they told yᵉ Elder upon his enquiry, that he could not but judg there was much of God in it, yet still he then remained in his judgment for it: though thus 16 ware in a weeks space against it: wᵗʰ little or no speach each wᵗʰ other. This was about the 17th of 1 Mo 164 ³/₄ Having had weekly loveing conferance wᵗʰ prayers from yᵉ midst of 11 Mo 1644

[1644] 2. 28: Concluded that to our friends yᵗ then lived in yᵉ Country (about 12) a Letter should be writt from Church to each wᵗʰ tender care, exhortation & consolation.

1ᵈ & 2 Mo. Haveing sought the Lord wᵗʰ fasting for those friends that left us, as not satisfyed we ware baptized as a true Church for our   . And haveing by conference not satisfyed yᵐ

At Mʳ Fountains yᵉ Church considered wᵗ further to do, some judged yᵗ yᵉ Church censure should pass others not

Conclusion was to desire yᵉ Advice of yᵉ Elders & Brethren of other Churches, wᶜʰ was done 1644.3. 27. at Mʳ Shambrookes where ware present These: Mʳ Barbone, Rozer, Dʳ Parker, Mʳ Erbury, Mʳ Cooke, Mʳ Tho: Goodwin, Mʳ Phillip Nye, Mʳ G. Sympson, Mʳ Burrows, Mʳ Staismore,

These by enquiry not Satisfyed that in these absenters was obstinacy but tender Conscience & holyness, & not disturbing us in our proceeds advised us

1. Not to Excoṁunicate, no, nor admonish, wᶜʰ is only to Obstinate.

2. To count them still of our Church; & pray, & love them.

3. Desire conversing togeather so farr as their principles permitt them, so waiting till either (1) some come in, or (2) some grew giddy & scandalous their proceed against them, to this we agreed & so parted. . . .

After that H. Jessey was convinced also, the next morning early after that wᶜʰ had been a day of Solemne Seeking yᵉ Lord in fasting & prayer (That if Infants Baptism were unlawfull & if we should be further baptized &c the Lord would not hide it from us, but cause us to know it) First H. Jessey was convinced against Pedobaptisme, & then that himself should be baptized (notwithstanding many conferences wᵗʰ his honoured & Beloved Brethren, Mʳ Nye Mr Tho: Goodwin, Mr Burroughs, Mr Greenhill, Mr Cradock, Mr Carter, &c, & wᵗʰ Mr Jackson, Mr Bolton, &c) And was baptized by Mʳ Knollys, and then by degrees he Baptized many of yᵉ Church, when convinced they desired it.

Then in time some of those before named returned to communion wth this
Church, as

S. Kenaston	B. & S. Wade
B. Hen Jones	S. Dorrell
S. Buckley	S. Huddel als. Levill.

[Notes]

1. Benjamin Stinton, the probable collector of these records.

2. These initials apparently refer to Brother Jackson, Brother Knowles, and Brother Golding.

3. The elder or pastor was Henry Jessey who, at this point, was still defending infant baptism. However, as a result of this conference "H Jessey was convinced also" as we see near the end of the document.

4. Hanserd Knollys, who here denies that the covenant status of infants in the Old Testament guarantees infant baptism for infants in the church.

5. The "Ma" and "Mi" refer to the major and minor premises of a syllogism. Baptists were often accused, as by Daniel Featley, of being too ignorant to argue by way of syllogism, which was the primary method of scholarly discussion of the time.

6. Brother Kiffin (William), who here argues that baptism and church membership must be determined by New Testament standards, not by anology with the covenant and circumcision in the Old Testament.

7. These initials probably refer to Brother Jackson, Sister Knollys, and Brother and Sister (probably Golding).

1.7 Formation of the Broadmead Church, Bristol

The Broadmead Church in Bristol is important in its own right as a leading Baptist church in Britain from early days to the present. It also illustrates the process by which many congregations went through the successive stages of separating from the Church of England, rejecting infant baptism in favor of believer's baptism, and eventually going the next step to immersion. Although they adopted immersion, the Broadmead Church did not require that ordinance and thus became an open membership church. Of interest in the document is the role of John Cann and Dorothy Hazzard in the origin of this church. *Source:* Roger Hayden, ed., *The Records of a Church of Christ in Bristol, 1640-1687.* (Bristol Record Society, 1974), 90-96. Used by permission.

1640. Soe that in ye year of our for ever blessed Redeemer, the Lord Jesus (1640) one thousand six hundred and forty, those five persons, namely Goodman Atkins of Stapleton, Goodman Cole a Butcher of Lawford's Gate, Richard Moone a Farrier in Wine Street, and Mr. Bacon a young Minister, with Mrs. Hazzard, at Mrs. Hazzard's house, at ye upper end of Broad Street in Bristol, *they Mett together,* and came to a holy Resolution to Separate from ye Worship of ye World and times they lived in, and that they would goe noe more to it, and with godly purpose of heart Joyned themselves together in ye Lord; and only thus Covenanting, *That they would, in ye Strength and assistance of ye Lord, come forth of ye world, and worship ye Lord more purely, persevering therein to their end.*

Thus they having engaged themselves to ye Lord, and one to ye other, to walke before him according to his word, they would goe to hear common prayer noe more; but after ye common prayer was over in ye morning, when ye Psalm was singing, they would goe in to hear Mr. Hazzard preach. Thus they did on ye mornings of ye Lord's day, but in ye afternoones they mett by themselves, and so built up one another. Att their beginning they met usually at Mr. Hazzard's, and sometimes at Mr. Bacon's in Lewin's Mead.

Shortly after this, on a time called Easter, because Mr. Hazzard, eould not in Conscience give ye Sacrament to ye People of ye Parish, he went out of Towne, and tooke that season to visit his kindred at Lyme. And at that Juncture of time ye Providence of God brought to this Citty one Mr. Cann, a *Baptized* man; it was that Mr. Cann that made notes and References upon the Bible. He was a man very eminent in his day for Godlinesse, and for Reformation in Religion, haveing great understanding in ye way of ye Lord.

When Mrs. Hazzard heard that he was come to Towne, she went to ye Dolphin Inn, and fetched him to her house, and entertained him all ye time he staid in ye Citty; who helped them very much in ye Lord, he being a man Skilfull in Gospell order. Like unto Aquila, he taught them ye way of ye Lord more perfectly, and settled them in Church Order, and showed them ye Difference betwixt ye Church of Christ and Antichrist, and left with them a Printed booke treating of ye same, and divers printed papers to that purpose. Soe that by this instrument, Mr. Cann, ye Lord did confirm and settle them; showing them how they should Joyne together, and take in members. And he Exhorted them to waite upon God together, and to Expect ye presence of God with those gifts they had, and to depart from those ministers that did not come out of Antichristian Worship. And when he had staid some time in ye Citty he departed.

And on a Lord's day following he preached at a place called Westerly, about 7 miles from this Citty; and many of ye professors from hence went thither to hear him, with Mrs. Hazzard, willing to enjoy such a light as long as they could; where he had liberty to preach in ye publique place (called a church), in ye morning, but in ye afternoon could not have entrance. Y^e obstruction was by a very Godly great woman that dwelt in that place, who was somewhat severe in ye profession of what she knew, hearing that he was a *Baptized* man, by them called an *Anabaptist,* which was to some sufficient cause of Prejudice; because ye truth of Believers' baptizme had been for a long time buried, yea, for a long time, by Popish inventions, and their sprinkleing brought in ye roome thereof. . . .

But to return to our *Narrative* of ye Lord's carrying on ye Truth of Separation. This godly, honourable woman, perceiving that Mr. Cann was a Baptist, and not in her way, but a step beyond her light, Caused ye publick place to be made fast, whereby they were prevented to Come in. Then he drew forth, with aboundance of people, into a Green thereby, and he sent for Mr. Fowler, ye Minister that lived there, to speake with him, who was a holy good man, of great worth for his Moderation, Zeale, Sincerity, and a sound preacher of ye Gospell, as he approved himselfe since; who, Accordingly, came to Mr. Cann, in ye Green, where they debated ye businesse of Reformation, and ye Duty of Separation from ye Worship of Antichrist, Cleaveing close to ye Doctrine of our Lord Jesus and his instituted worship. To which Mr. Fowler agreed that there was greate Corruption in Worship, and that it was ye duty of People to Reforme from Corruptions in Worship; but he said that at that season, as things Stood, it was not a time, Because they should not be suffered, and should be cast out of all publique places. Mr. Cann answered, that mattered not; though they could not get a publick place or such conveniencyes, they should *Hire a Barne* to meet in, keeping ye Worship and Commands of ye Lord as they were delivered to us. . . .

But Mr. Hazzard being coming home, Mr. Fowler aforesaid, meeting with him tould him his wife was quite gone, and would hear him no more. . . .

Then she, with those few that had joyned themselves together to worship ye Lord more purely (as aforesaid), after Mr. Cann had thus instructed them, and showed them ye Order of God's house, and ye Differenee thereof from Antichristian Worship; then they stept further in Separation, And would not so much as hear any minister that did read Common prayer. Thus ye Lord led them by Degrees, and brought them out of Popish Darknesse into his Marvellous light of ye Gospell.

First of all, yᵉ Lord alone, by his Spirit *(not by might nor by power)* opened their Eyes, and made them cast off yᵉ Body of false Doctrine of yᵉ Church of Rome, that had soe long deceived yᵉ nations, and made them drinke yᵉ wine of her fornication, worshipping under pretence yᵉ true God in a false manner, Wresting yᵉ holy Scriptures to their owne Damnation, saying yᵉ Reall presence of Christ was in yᵉ Sacrament that signified his body by a Transubstantiation, and teaching man's workes merit salvation, and workes of Supererogation, &c.

Secondly, Yᵉ Lord put it into yᵉ hearts of some in Authority in this Nation to cast off yᵉ Body of yᵉ Worship of Rome (as well as their Doctrine), namely, the Nest of Idollaters; even to cast out yᵉ Monks, Friars, Abbots, Priests, Masses, Advocation of saints, with Praying for yᵉ deceased, &c. . . .

Thirdly, It pleased yᵉ Lord in these latter days to raise up a people, and make them come a step further in Reformation, even to come from under yᵉ Skirts of yᵉ Whore; and to cast off Popish Scraps of Doctrine and worship, yᵉ Appendices thereof, namely, Idollatrous Holy dayes, primarily their 3 greate or Cardinal Masses,—viz., Michael's-mass, Christ—or py-masse, thirdly Candles-mass, dayes of their owne invention, like Jeroboam,—together with yᵉ multitude of their saints' dayes soe called, as St. Allsoules, and St. Midsomer. . . .

Fourthly, Yᵉ Lord alone by his Spirit made them to disrelish and cast off Carnal debauched preachers, Idoll shepherds that cared not after yᵉ flock but yᵉ Fleece, lookeing their gaine from every quarter, That did not relish or savour what they preached, nor preach what they savoured. Being thus blinde, others' eyes were opened not to follow them.

Fifthly, Yᵉ Lord made them to embrace and Adhere to, Follow, love, and cleave to Lively and powerful preachers. By giveing yᵉ people a taste of his Spirit they desired more that they might grow thereby, and could not be content with yᵉ abominable Broth that was not poured out by his Spirit.

Sixthly, Yᵉ Holy One, by pouring forth into yᵉ hearts of those that should be saved a more Sanctified Spirit, he made them Cast off; and leaveing yᵉ common roade, they forsooke Prophaning yᵉ Lord's day and hearkening unto Homilies, of which they grew weary.

Seventhly, They left off Superstitious bowing at yᵉ nameing of Jesus, and to yᵉ Altar; which thing was plaine and open Idollatry, Worshipping and Adoring that which there is noe show of Precept for, but a direct and visible breach of yᵉ Second commandment.

Eighthly, They Cast off yᵉ Crosse and other Ceremonies at their Sprinkleing Children; which was a good stepp, though yᵉ people could not see through to Reforme in that particular, to Cast off yᵉ thing of Sprinkling itselfe, which was yᵉ mere invention of men three hundred years after Christ, not mentioned of in Tertullian's time, Yᵉ fruite of Apostacy that yᵉ Church fell into, from one thing to another. Until at last they lost yᵉ Substance of Religion, and kept only a Shaddow thereof. From Baptizing souls, as they entered into yᵉ Church, in a River, they made a *Vaunt,* and placed it in their publique places, near some great door; in all such places signifying or Resembling yᵉ entrance into yᵉ Church. Secondly, From Dipping yᵉ children in yᵉ font they by degrees took up Sprinkleing them. Thirdly, From a Font, in processe of time, they used a Bason in their place called a church. Fourthly, From a bason in their church they brought it to a Bason in yᵉ house. Fifthly, From Men, their parsons, to sprinkle, they allowed women to doe it, in case of necessity, as they called it, to seale their wills, and seale that which they never read by yᵉ party's profession or confession, or saw by their Conversation. Thus leaveing (ye Examples in holy Scripture, and) ye Commands of ye Lord, in vaine doe they worship him, teaching for Doctrines ye Commandments of men, Mark vii. 7, or traditions of men; setting up their posts by ye Lord's.

Ninthly. (Though ye Lord for a time winked at ye times of these ignorances in that thing,) He made them cast off ye use of *Pictures* and Images; and they could not bear to hear any preach or plead for that ould Scrap and relique of Idollatry, soe much like pleading for Baal.

Tenthly. *Y^e Lord wrought soe upon their Spirits, that they would not kneel at ye Sacrament*, because ye Example in Holy Scriptures was Sitting at ye Lord's Supper; though it was pleaded against them,—soe solemne an ordinance was to be done with a greate deale of Reverence, and kneeling was a reverence to God. But a Reverence and decency that God hath not commanded must not be observed, to make void ye Example or command; ye Patterne must be kept. . . .

Eleventhly. They cast off Hearing ye Common prayer—that *Nurse of Formality and Chaine of Security*. Many persons by readeing thereof, (without searching their hearts and leaveing of sinn,) they would lick themselves whole in their thoughts or esteem, like ye Harlott in ye Proverbs said,—I have paid my vows; come, let us Sin and be vaine;—not regarding whether their spirits received any Divine impresse upon it, broken and humbled in ye presence of God, and soe ye Spirit of ye Lord quenched, and no roome to breath, from ye sense of their present miscarriages or wants, whether Consolation or humiliation.

Twelvethly, They were holpen by ye Lord to cast off this alsoe, and to step this further in their Reformation, That at last they would not hear those men that did read Common prayer, that therby did declare themselves to owne or partake in any parte Consentingly to ye Worship of ye Beast.

Thus I have briefly recited Twelve steps that doth compleate a demonstration that they, this Church, in their begining, were truly reformed in a greate measure, in turning from ye Worship of Antichrist. And it is prayed and hoped ye Lord will in his due time, not only turne them from Antichrist, But that he will alsoe turne them perfectly to himselfe, and make them soe to waite upon him untill he Come, Rev. ii. 25; chap. xxii. 20.

1.8   W. H. Whitsitt, On the Recovery of Immersion in England

The importance of the Jessey Records and the Kiffin Manuscript for understanding the emergence of the modern Baptist denomination has been appreciated for only about a century. Perhaps the first historian to see that these primary sources called for a revision of Baptists' understanding of their origins was William H. Whitsitt (1841-1911), professor of church history and later president at The Southern Baptist Theological Seminary in Louisville, Kentucky.

Whitsitt wrote a series of articles as early as 1880 showing that immersion was reintroduced in England in 1640-1641 and dating the emergence of the modern Baptist denomination to that time. In 1896 he published a book on that subject and found himself embroiled in a raging controversy with Baptists who wanted to trace their origin to John the Baptist. The "Whitsitt Controversy," represented elsewhere in this collection, led to the author's forced resignation from the presidency of Southern Seminary. Whitsitt's basic conclusions have long since been accepted by almost all historians, including Baptists. Whitsitt should be read in connection with J. M. Carroll's *Trail of Blood* (selection 1.9), which gives an opposite viewpoint. *Source:* William H. Whitsitt, *A Question in Baptist History* (Louisville: Charles T. Dearing, 1896), 90-100.

EIGHT MONUMENTS OF THE INTRODUCTION OF IMMERSION
INTO ENGLAND IN THE YEAR 1641.

The Jessey Church Records prove that immersion was introduced into England in the year 1641. That was an important change. In all cases where important changes occur it is to be anticipated that historical monuments of some kind will be left behind to indicate that they took place. One of the most prominent monuments of this change is the Fortieth Article of the *Confession of Faith of the Seven Congregations or Churches of Christ in London, 1644,* prescribing immersion as follows: "That the way and manner of the dispensing of this ordinance is *dipping or plunging the body under water;* it being a sign must answer the things signified, which is that interest the saints have in the death, burial and resurrection of Christ; and that as certainly as the body is buried under water and risen again; so certainly shall the bodies of the saints be raised by the power of Christ in the day of the resurrection to reign with Christ."

The *dipping or plunging the body under water* as applied to believers is here for the first time prescribed by an English Confession of Faith, and the year 1644 agrees with the Jessey Church Records, which represent that immersion was first introduced in 1641. If immersion had previously been in use, it is very hard to understand why it should not have been required in any of the previous Confessions. The reason why it was first prescribed in 1644 is to be found in the fact that it was not in use in England until 1641. The Confession of 1644 is an enduring monument to the change that was made in 1641.

The Confession above mentioned, which for the first time prescribes dipping, also carefully specifies the manner in which it shall be performed, as follows: "The word baptizo signifies to dip or plunge (yet so as convenient garments be both upon the administrator and subject with all modesty)." Manifestly this direction about clothing was added because it was to be apprehended that some might administer the ordinance without having convenient garments upon the administrator and subject. . . .

That the name Baptist first came into use shortly after 1641, is another evidence of the fact in question. The name Anabaptist had long been resented. The brethren frequently designated themselves as those who were "unjustly called Anabaptists" (Crosby, vol. 2, Appendix, p. 51). But so long as their contention related merely to the subjects of baptism they could never shake off the name Anabaptists. Their act of baptism being the same as that employed by other Christians, namely, pouring and sprinkling, it was always described as a mere repetition of baptism—as Anabaptism. But when another act was introduced, namely, immersion, it then became possible for the brethren to obtain a new designation. Henceforth they were called "baptized Christians" *par excellence,* and in due time Baptists. The earliest instance in which this name occurs as a denominational designation, so far as my information goes, befell in the year 1644, three years after immersion had been introduced. . . .

Another monument is the baptismal controversy. It began shortly after 1641. Hitherto the Christian world had moved almost together in reference to the act of baptism so that there had been small occasion for a baptismal controversy. For twelve centuries they had stood so unitedly in favor of immersion that the act of baptism was little discussed. For four centuries later Western Christendom had moved so uniformly in the direction of pouring and sprinkling that men seldom contended for the original usage. But now that a body of Christian people had risen up to stem the tide of innovation and sail against the current, there was serious business on hand. When Edward Barber sent forth "A Small Treatise of Baptisme or *Dipping*" a new note had been struck. The man was here asserting against the whole of Western Christendom that baptism is synonymous with dipping; that there is no other baptism but *dipping*. He aimed to show "that the Lord Christ ordained Dipping" and not sprinkling or pouring. The claim that immersion is the *only valid act* of baptism had been a long while unknown in England.

A. R. expressed the idea still more distinctly on the title page of his "Treatise of the Vanity of Childishe Baptism . . . . wherein is also proved that *Baptizing* is Dipping and Dipping is *Baptizing*." In other words he contended that immersion is *the exclusive* act of baptism. For ages before this time that contention had not been urged in England. Here began the earliest notes of that baptismal controversy which is still with us. This controversy opening at least as early as 1642 is a monument of the introduction of immersion, an event, which according to the Jessey Church Records took place in 1641. Prior to that date no English books have been instanced which were written for the special purpose of proving that *immersion alone* is baptism; after that date such works abound in England. Nobody wrote in favor of immersion as the *exclusive act of baptism* prior to 1641, for the reason that nobody in England at that period practiced immersion alone for baptism: divers wrote in favor of it after 1641, for the reason that people began to practice it there in 1641. The case of Leonard Busher does not furnish an exception since it cannot be proven that his work was published in England. Besides it is devoted to another subject, and contains only a brief reference to dipping.

Another evidence of the introduction of immersion 1641 is contained in the fact that before that time no instances are found where churches were divided on this issue. They divided on other issues but not upon this one. After 1641 it was not unusual for churches to divide about immersion. . . . These divisions are indications of the fact that immersion had been introduced as asserted by the Jessey Church Records in 1641. Many of the brethren would refuse to submit to the innovation and these drew away to themselves, leaving the immersion party in control of the ground. Reasons are not wanting to support the conclusion that the separation between the simple Anabaptists and the Dippers was not completed until about the year 1660 (Crosby, 3, 77). In some cases it "broke to pieces the congregation," while in others it resulted in the formation of "Open Baptist" churches, some of which still remain in England as a monument of the introduction of immersion.

Prior to 1641 the followers of Murton and Helwys were in close relations with the Mennonites, and in 1626 a movement was set on foot looking to the organic union of the two parties (Evans, vol. 2, pp. 24-30). After the year 1641 those relations were entirely broken off, and it is claimed by the best Mennonite scholarship that this alienation was caused by the introduction of immersion. The Mennonites being henceforward recognized as unbaptized people were not disposed to continue the fellowship and friendship that had hitherto prevailed. (Scheffer, De Brownisten, p. 156). That separation was one of the striking monuments of the rejection of pouring and sprinkling, which had always been practiced by Mennonites, and of the adoption of immersion.

Another monument of the fact that immersion was introduced into England in 1641 is found in the alarm that was occasioned shortly afterwards respecting the effect of the ordinance upon the health of the people who should submit to it. No records have been produced of the existence of any such feeling prior to the year 1641, for the reason that no such custom as immersion then existed in England: but after 1641 the apprehension was very sincere, even though it was not very just. It was experienced by such men as Richard Baxter and Walter Cradock, and was also considerably prevalent among the common people, who sometimes supposed that the Baptists were a cruel and murderous sect merely because they used immersion. In the year 1646 Mr. Samuel Oates was tried for his life at Chelmsford because Anne Martin died within a few weeks after she had been baptized by him. (Crosby, vol. 1, pp. 236-8.) This was the result of a wild and senseless panic, but it was a panic that occurred because the ordinance was so very new and as yet the public was but little accustomed to it. . . .

An eighth monument of the change from sprinkling and pouring to immersion, is found in the word "rhantise" which appears then to have first come into use in English. When it first began to be denied that sprinkling was baptizing, it became necessary to declare in learned speech just what it might be. The brethren were put upon distinctions; they were compelled to find a name for sprinkling, and since "baptize" was transferred from the Greek language it was natural to look in that direction. Accordingly the word "rhantize" was chosen. The beginning of this movement in philology appears to have been made by A. R[itor] in his "Treatise of the Vanity of Childish-Baptisme," London, 1642, p. 11, where he makes use of the original Greek word as follows: "For a learned and approved Author has noted the Greeke wants not words to express any other act as well as dipping: . . . Much humane authority, both ancient and moderne, might be produced herein, all which would be needlesse, seeing the Scripture itself is so cleere in the point," etc.

Rev. Christopher Blackwood in his "Storming of Antichrist in his strongest Garrisons, of compulsion of conscience and Infants Baptisme," London, 1644, appears to have improved upon the suggestion of A. R. by transferring the Greek word to English. Thereupon an anonymous author speedily issues a work entitled "Mock Majesty, or the Siege of Muenster," London, 1644, and begins the preface as follows: "To the intelligent Reader, Baptized or *Rantized*: Thou must excuse me for this pretty new-stamped word. It is pitty but it should signify something in English. Whether it do so or no, it is not a week since I first met with it, and that in a way of scorn and contempt of the Baptism of our Church (See Christopher Blackwood in his book entitled the Storming of Antichrist in his two strongest holds, etc., very lately published)." There are other indications in literature that the word was then first minted. Thomas Blake, who favored and practiced the rite of pouring, says in his "Infants Baptism freed from Antichristianism," London, 1645, p. 4: "I have seen several dipped; I never saw nor heard of any sprinkled (or as some of you use to speak *rantized,*" (Wall, History, vol. 2, 402). The word "rhantize" is a monument of the change from sprinkling to immersion, that, like the name Baptist, abides with us still.

There are yet other monuments of that great change; but the eight that I have instanced above will suffice to show that it produced an impression. This impression was not confined to the age in which the change occurred, but marks of it still are apparent in our own age and every one of them is in harmony with the Jessey Church Records which represent that immersion was introduced again into England in the year 1641. In particular, as long as the name Baptist shall be uttered anywhere in the world it will point back with unerring certainty to that famous event in that famous "yeare of jubilee," as Edward Barber phrases it. The name was not in use before that period; it has been constantly applied as a denominational designation to our people ever since that date.

1.9   J. M. Carroll, *The Trail of Blood*

Many Baptists felt threatened by the assertions of Whitsitt and others that the Baptist denomination dates back only to the seventeenth century. Following historians like G. H. Orchard[1] of England and D. B. Ray[2] of America, many sought to reaffirm the popular notion that Baptists have existed in unbroken succession back to Jesus, John the Baptist, or to baptizing in the Jordan (hence the "successionist" or "JJJ" theory of Baptist origins).

No writer gave a more popular or more widespread expression of the successionist viewpoint than did James Milton Carroll (1852-1931). In the vivid pamphlet entitled *The Trail of Blood,* Carroll provided material for others who have published sermons, lectures, and giant charts tracing Baptist footprints, stained by the blood of persecution, from the days of the first Baptist (John the) to the present. To some extent, this was an effort to counteract the work of Whitsitt. B. H. Carroll, older brother of J. M. and founder of Southwestern Baptist Theological Seminary in Fort Worth, Texas, led the Whitsitt controversy.

While no reputable historian holds these viewpoints today, this pamphlet is still being published and continues to find strong adherents. *Source:* J. M. Carroll, *The Trail of Blood* (Lexington, Ky.: Ashland Avenue Baptist Church, 1931), 38-45. Used by permission.

Notes

1. *Concise History of Baptists from the Time of Christ Their Founder to the 18th Century.* First published in England in 1638, several times republished in America.

2. *Baptist Successionism* (St. Louis: Baptist Publishing Company, 1883).

FOURTH LECTURE—17th, 18th, 19th Centuries

1. This lecture begins with the beginning of the Seventeenth Century (A.D. 1601). We have passed very hurriedly over much important Christian history, but necessity has compelled this.

2. This three-century period begins with the rise of an entirely new denomination. It is right to state that some historians give the date of the beginning of the Congregational Church (at first called "Independents") as 1602. However, Schaff-Herzogg, in their Encyclopedia, place its beginning far back in the sixteenth century, making it coeval with the Lutheran and Presbyterian. In the great reformation wave many who went out of the Catholic Church were not satisfied with the extent of the reformation led by Luther and Calvin. They decided to repudiate also the preacher rule and government idea of the churches and return to the New Testament democratic idea as had been held through the fifteen preceding centuries by those who had refused to enter Constantine's hierarchy.

3. The determined contention of this new organization for this particular reform brought down upon its head bitter persecution from Catholic, Lutheran, Presbyterian and Church of England adherents—all the established churches. However, it retained many other of the Catholic made errors, such for instance as infant baptism, pouring or sprinkling for baptism, and later adopted and practiced to an extreme degree the church and state idea. And, after refugeeing to America, themselves, became very bitter persecutors.

4. The name "Independents" or as now called "Congregationalists," is derived from their mode of church government. Some of the distinguishing principles of the English Congregationalists as given in Schaff-Herzogg Encyclopedia are as follows:

    (1) That Jesus Christ is the only head of the church and that the Word of God is its only statute book.

    (2) That visible churches are distinct assemblies of Godly men gathered out of the world for purely religious purposes, and not to be confounded with the world.

    (3) That these separate churches have full power to choose their own officers and to maintain discipline.

    (4) That in respect to their internal management they are each independent of all other churches and equally independent of state control.

5. How markedly different these principles are from Catholicism, or even Lutheranism, or Presbyterianism or the Episcopacy of the Church of England. How markedly

similar to the Baptists of today, and of all past ages, and to the original teachings of Christ and His apostles.

6. In 1611, the King James English Version of the Bible appeared. Never was the Bible extensively given to the people before. From the beginning of the general dissemination of the Word of God began the rapid decline of the Papal power, and the first beginnings for at least many centuries, of the idea of "religious liberty. . . ." . . .

8. During all the seventeenth century, persecutions for Waldenses, Ana-Baptists and Baptists (in some places the "Ana" was now being left off) continued to be desperately severe; in England by the Church of England, as John Bunyan and many others could testify; in Germany by the Lutherans; in Scotland by the Church of Scotland (Presbyterian); in Italy, in France and in every other place where the papacy was in power, by the Catholics. There is now no peace anywhere for those who are not in agreement with the state churches, or some one of them.

9. It is a significant fact well established in credible history that even as far back as the fourth century those refusing to go into the Hierarchy, and refusing to accept the baptism of those baptized in infancy, and refusing to accept the doctrine of "Baptismal Regeneration" and demanding rebaptism for all those who came to them from the Hierarchy, were called "Ana-Baptists." No matter what other names they then bore, they were always referred to as "Ana-Baptists." Near the beginning of the sixteenth century, the "Ana" was dropped, and the name shortened to simply "Baptist," and gradually all other names were dropped. Evidently, if Bunyan had lived in an earlier period his followers would have been called "Bunyanites" or "Ana-Baptists." Probably they would have been called by both names as were others preceeding him.

10. The name "Baptist" is a "nickname," and was given to them by their enemies (unless the name can be rightfully attributed to them as having been given to them by the Savior Himself, when He referred to John as "The Baptist"). To this day, the name has never been officially adopted by any group of Baptists. The name, however, has become fixed and is willingly accepted and proudly borne. It snugly fits. It was the distinguishing name of the forerunner of Christ, the first to teach the doctrine to which the Baptists now hold.

Where did these Baptists come from? They did not come out of the Catholics during the Reformation. They had large churches prior to the Reformation.

2
Defining the Faith

What did the early English Baptists believe, and how did they practice their faith? The documents included in this chapter have been chosen to give at least a partial answer to that question. These selections come from various kinds of sources, including confessions of faith, doctrinal treatises, church and associational minutes, and records of the general assemblies of Baptist delegates late in the seventeenth century. From these sources we conclude that Baptists made every effort to base their faith and practice upon Scripture.

Not every Baptist doctrine or practice can be spotlighted here, but major issues in doctrine and worship have been included. Preference is given to materials not readily available elsewhere. The confessions of faith, for example, are prime indicators of emerging Baptist theology, but many of them are readily available in print and thus appear only briefly here.

2.1 A Declaration of Faith of English People, 1611

Primarily the work of Thomas Helwys, these 27 articles form one of the first Baptist confessions of faith and thus one of the earliest systematic expressions of Baptist theology. Helwys (ca.1570-ca.1615) was a layman who helped organize the Smyth exile from England and followed Smyth in forming a Baptist church in Amsterdam. This confession is notable for its irenic spirit, its modifying strict Calvinism without totally embracing Arminianism, and for teaching baptism of believers only (although it makes no mention of immersion). It was probably composed while Helwys and his followers were still in Amsterdam, shortly after they separated from John Smyth. In fact, one purpose was to clarify their differences with Smyth and to try to slow down Smyth's proposed merger with the Mennonites.

These articles were widely circulated in England, where they both shaped and reflected General Baptist doctrine and practice. They reaffirm distinctly Baptist emphases, some of which Smyth was ready to yield in his negotiations with the Mennonites. Thus this brief confession is an important landmark in the preservation and perpetuation of the fledgling Baptist movement. *Source: William L. Lumpkin, ed., Baptist Confessions of Faith* (Philadelphia: Judson Press, 1959), 117-123.

A DECLARATION, ETC.

WEE BELEEVE AND CONFESSE

1.

That there are THREE which beare record in heaven, the FATHER, the WORD, and the SPIRIT; and these THREE are one GOD, in all equalitie, 1 Jno. 5.7; Phil. 2.5, 6. By whome all thinges are created and preserved, in Heaven and in Earth. Gen. 1 Chap.

2.

That this GOD in the beginning created al things off nothinge, Gen. 1.1. and made man off the dust off the earth, Chap. 2.7, in his owne ymage, Chap. 1.27, in righteousnes and true Holines. Ephes. 4.24: yet being tempted, fel by disobedience. Chap. 3.1-7. Through whose disobedience, all men sinned. Rom. 5.12-19. His sinn being imputed vnto all; and so death went over all men.

3.

That by the promised seed off the woman, IESVS CHRIST, [and by] his obedience, al are made righteous. Rom. 5.19. Al are made alive, 1 Cor. 15.22. His righteousness being imputed vnto all.

39

4.

That notwithstanding this Men are by nature the Children off wrath, Ephes. 2.3. borne in iniquitie and in sin conceived. Psal. 51.5. Wise to all evill, but to good they have no knowledg. Jer. 4.22. *The natural mā perceiveth not the thinges off the Spirit off God*. 1 Cor. 2.14. And therefore man is not restored vnto his former estate, but that as man, in his estate off innocency, haveing in himselff all disposition vnto good, & no disposition vnto evill, yet being tempted might yeild, or might resist: even so now being fallen, and haveing all disposition vnto evill, and no disposition or will vnto anie good, yet GOD giveing grace, man may receave grace, or my reject grace, according to that saying; Deut. 30.19. *I call Heaven and Earth to record. This day against you, that I have set before you life and death, blessing and cursing: Therefore chuse life, that both thou and thy seed may live.*

5.

That GOD before the Foundatiō off the World hath Predestinated that all that beleeve in him shall-be saved, Ephes. 1.4, 12; Mark 16.16. and al that beleeve not shalbee damned. Mark 16.16. all which he knewe before. Rom. 8.29. And this is the Election and reprobacion spoken of in the Scripturs, concerning salvacion, and condemnacion, and not that GOD hath Predestinated men to bee wicked, and so to bee damned, but that men being wicked shallbee damned, for GOD would have all men saved, and come to the knowledg off the truth, 1 Tim. 2.4. and would have no man to perish, but would have all men come to repentance. 2 Pet. 3.9. and willeth not the death of him that deith. Ezec. 18.32. And therefore GOD is the author off no mens comdemnacion, according to the saieing off the Prophet. Osæa. 13. Thy distruction O Israel, is off thy selfe, but thy helpe is off mee.

6.

That man is justified onely by the righteousness off CHRIST, apprehended by faith, Roman. 3.28. Gal. 2.16. yet faith without works is dead. Jam. 2.17.

7.

That men may fall away from the grace off GOD. Heb. 12.15. and from the truth, which they have received & acknowledged, Chap. 10.26. after they have taisted off the heavēly gift, and were made pertakers off the HOLY GHOST, and have taisted off the good word off GOD, & off the powers off the world to come. Chap. 6.4, 5. And after they have escaped from the filthines off the World, may bee taugled againe therein & overcome. 2 Pet. 2.20. That a righteous man may forsake his righteousness and perish Ezec. 18.24, 26. And therefore let no man presume to thinke that because he hath, or had once grace, therefore he shall alwaies have grace: But let all men have assurance, that iff they continew vnto the end, they shalbee saved: Let no man then presume; but let all worke out their salvacion with feare and trembling. . . .

11.

That though in respect off CHRIST, the Church bee one, Ephes. 4.4. yet it consisteth off divers particuler congregacions, even so manie as there shallbee in the World, every off which congregacion, though they be but two or three, have CHRIST given them, with all the meanes off their salvacion. Mat. 18.20. Roman. 8.32. 1. Corin. 3.22. Are the Bodie off CHRIST. 1. Cor. 12.27. and a whole Church. 1. Cor. 14.23. And therefore may, and ought, when they are come together, to Pray, Prophecie, breake bread, and administer in all the holy ordinances, although as yet they have no Officers, or that their Officers should bee in Prison, sick, or by anie other meanes hindered from the Church. 1:Pet. 4.10 & 2.5. . . .

14.

That Baptisme or washing with Water, is the outward manifestacion off dieing vnto sinn, and walkeing in newnes off life. Roman. 6.2, 3, 4. And therefore in no wise apperteyneth to infants. . . .

19.

That everie Church ought (according to the exāple off CHRISTS Disciples and primitive Churches) vpon everie first day off the weeke, being the LORDS day, to assemble together to pray Prophecie, praise GOD, and breake Bread, and performe all other partes off Spirituall communiō for the worship off GOD, their owne mutuall edificacion, and the preservacion off true Religion, & pietie in the church Iō 20.19. Act. 2.42 and 20.7, 1. Cor. 16.2 and that ought not to labor in their callings according to the equitie off the moral law, which CHRIST came not to abolish, but to fulfill. Exod. 20.8, &c.

20.

That the Officers off everie Church or congregation are either Elders, who by their office do especially feed the flock concerning their soules, Act. 20.28, Pet. 5.2, 3. or Deacons Men, and Women who by their office releave the necessities off the poore and impotent brethrē concerning their bodies, Acts. 6.1-4.

21.

That these Officers are to bee chosen when there are persons qualified according to the rules in Christs Testament, 1. Tim. 3.2-7. Tit. 1.6-9. Act. 6.3. 4. By Election and approbacion off that Church or congregacion whereoff they are members, Act. 6.3. 4 and 14.23, with Fasting, Prayer, and Laying on off hands, Act. 13.3. and 14.23. And there being but one rule for Elders, therefore but one sort off Elders.

22.

That the Officers off everie Church or congregacion are tied by Office onely to that particular congregacion whereoff they are chosen, Act. 14.23, and 20.17. Tit. 1.5. And therefore they cannot challeng by office anie aucthoritie in anie other congregation whatsoever except they would have an Apostleship.

2.2 Edward Barber, *A Small Treatise on Baptisme, or Dipping,* 1641

The people who came to be called Baptists earned that nickname through their practice of immersion for professed believers in Christ. In their desire for a pure church, they wanted none but believers to receive baptism. Seeking to reduplicate as closely as possible the apostolic practices, they taught that baptism should be by immersion. In the "watery war," as their extensive baptism discussion was called, Baptists denied that infant baptism replaces circumcision and insisted that the New Testament shows no clear examples of infants being baptized. They argued from history that the early church practiced immersion, and from Scripture that the Greek word *baptizo* means to immerse.

Edward Barber's *Small Treatise* of 1641 gives a good example of Baptist views of baptism at that time. Barber was a merchant tailor in London who was imprisoned for almost a year for speaking against infant baptism. He used the prison time to study the Bible further on this question, and the result was this brief but effective treatise to advance the Baptist position. *Source:* Edward Barber, *A Small Treatise of Baptisme, or Dipping, Wherein is Cleerly shewed that the Lord Christ Ordained Dipping for those only that professe Repentance and Faith* (n.p., 1641), original in the Angus Collection, Regent's Park College, Oxford.

The Preface

To all that love the Lord Jesus Christ in sincereity. . . .

Beloved Reader, it may seeme strange that in these times, when such abundance of

Knowledge of the Gospell is professed in the World, there should notwithstanding be generally such ignorance, especially in and amongst those that professe themselves Ministers thereof, of that glorious principle, True Baptisme or Dipping Ephe.4.5 Instituted by the Lord Jesus Christ, which all that look for life and Salvation by him ought to be partakers of, . . . that the Lord should amongst some others, raise up mee, a poore Tradesman, to devlge [sic] this glorious Truth, to the worlds censuring, ...

3. The reports of some, who . . . have reproached us, and so as Saint Jude saith, Speak evill of things they know not. . . .

Lately, It's not unknowne, that the faithfull servants of God, who have indeavored most faithfulnesse, have often gone under reproaches and slanders, as Elijah was counted the troubler of Israel, I Kings.18.17. . . . And Acts 24.5. Paul was counted a pestilent fellow, ...

In like manner lately, those that professe and practice the dipping of Jesus Christ, instituted in the Gospel, are called and reproached with the name of Anabaptists, although our practice be no other then what was instituted by Christ himself, withall desiring, if there be any that from the Word of God can shew that we walke in a false way, or error in denying the dipping of infants, that they would doe it, for wee professe our selves such as desire the glory of God, . . .

By Edward Barber, Citizen and Merchant-Taylor of London; late Prisoner for denying the sprinkling of Infants, and requiring tithes now under the Gospel to be God's Ordinance.

A Small Treatise of Dipping,Wherein is clearly shewed that the Lord Christ ordained Dipping for those onely that profest Faith and Repentance;

 I. Proved by Scripture, and from the Commission of Christ, and practice of the Apostles and Primitive Churches.

 II. By Arguments, with Answers to some objerctions, Psal.119.130. The entrance of thy word giveth light, It giveth understanding unto the simple.

 III. Also a paralell betwixt Circumcision and Dipping, Matth.15.8,9.

 IV. An Answere to some Objections by D. B.

. . . .

Now it follows . . . that the Lord Jesus Christ hath not appointed one Dipping for Jewes, another for Gentiles, one for men, another for women, one for old, another for young; one for the primitive times, another for present and future; one upon manifestation of repentance and faith professed, another upon doing it by God-fathers and God-mothers, much lesse having right thereunto by the faith of their parents . . . For as there is one Body, one Spirit, and beleevers called in one hope of calling, one Lord, one Faith: so also one dipping which was to be administered onely on those that were made Disciples by teaching, and not on those who had it professed by others, which Christ commanded not, Matth. 28.19. Therefore Infants by expresse prohibition are excluded, as is cleare in the following discourse: . . .

1. They onely are to be dipped that are made Disciples by teaching, Matth. 28.19.

Infants cannot be made Disciples by teaching, thefore [sic] Infants are not to be dipt. . . .

3. Againe, if the command of Christ our Saviour for making disciples by teaching before they are dipt, be Evangelicall and perpetuall, as all the Precepts of the Gospel are, then it ought to bee performed and observed in the Church of Christ for ever.

The Major is true, ... Therfore persons upon the manifestation of Repentance and faith onely are to be dipped.

4. None but those that doe expresse that inward Bap.tisme, Matth.3.11. Acts 10.47.48. are to be dipped.

Infants cannot expresse that inward Baptisme, therefore infants ought not to be dipped. . . .

6. We are commanded to stand in the way, and aske for the old pathes, which is the good way and walke therein. . . . The old and good way under the Gospell is the Institution of Jesus Christ . . . . But the dipping of beleevers is that good old way of Christ and Infants is not: . . . .

This is proved. . . They onely are to be dipped in whom repentance and faith is manifested by hearing the Word preached. But in persons of yeares onely is repentance and faith wrought by hearing the Word preached. . . . Therefore onely persons of years [and not infants] are to be dipped.

2.3   Christopher Blackwood, *The Storming of Antichrist,* 1644

Christopher Blackwood was a Cambridge graduate and Anglican priest who converted to Baptist views in the early 1640s. He ministered for a while in Ireland where he was regarded as "the oracle of the Anabaptists." Blackwood is a primary example of the capable ministers brought into the Baptist fold in its early days. The subtitle of this piece names "two last and strongest garrisons" by which Satan maintains his empire, namely compulsion of conscience and infant baptism. Only the latter emphasis is included here. *Source:* Christopher Blackwood, *The Storming of Antichrist, in His Two Last and Strongest Garrisons: of Compulsion of Conscience and Infants Baptisme,* 1644, part II. From the Angus Collection, Regent's Park College, Oxford.

The Storming of Antichrist,   Part II

Question. Whether it be lawfull to Baptize infants?

Answer. It is unlawfull for these arguments. The Baptisme of Christ is dipping. The Baptisme of infants is not dipping, therefore the Baptisme of infants is not the Baptisme of Christ.

I prove the proposition that the Baptisme of Christ is dipping, three waies;

1. From the Greek Lexicon, the Author . . . gives the prime significance to be to Drownd, Dip, or Plunge, and Sometimes to Wash, as he cites Mark.7. Luke 11. . . .

2. From the difference twixt Baptizing and Sprinkling, in Scripture. We see what Sprinkling is, Heb. 9.13, 19. . . . So ver 19 he took the blood of Goates and Hysope and sprinkled both the Book & all the people. . . . Now Baptizing in Scripture is Dipping, Luke 16.24. . . . But especially, Mark 1.9. They were Baptized of John into Jordan, which signifies the word to mean to Dip, not to Sprinkle, and it shews there was an application of the person to the water, not of the water to the person, as it is in Sprinkling. . . .

3. That Baptism signifies no other thing then Dipping, appears from the proportion and lively resemblance twixt dipping into the water and rising up again; Dipping signifieth death, and Buriall with Christ, and rising up above the water, Resurrection with Christ, Rom. 6.24. . . .

Objection. The word Baptize signifieth to sprinkle, 1 Cor. 10.2. They were Baptized unto Moses in the cloud and Sea, and yet there was no water, for they went through the sea, on dry land: Therefore, that Baptisme was the sprinkling of rain From heaven as appeares by comparing Psal.76.17.18 . . . With Exod. 14.21,22.

Answ. 1. Then the Holy Ghost would not have used the word *baptizo* which is never used in Scripture for sprinkling, but the word *rantizo,* which is alwaies used in Scripture for sprinkling. . . .

The Second Argument against Baptizing Infants

1. Ministers who are Christs commissioners ought to cleave close to their commission.

But to make Disciples before Baptizing is the Ministers Commission.

Therefore, Ministers who are Christs commissioners ought to cleave close hereto. . . .

5. *Exception.* Christ saith, baptize all nations; but children are part of the nation, therefore they may be baptized.

Answ. In the proposition there is a fallacie. . . . Christ saith, baptize all nations; but he conjoynes with it, make disciples [of] all nations: which the objector here left out. . . .

3. The Baptisme of Christ is the Baptisme of actuall repentance.

The Baptisme of infants is not the Baptisme of actuall repentance.

Therefore the Baptisme of infants is not the Baptisme of Christ. . . .

4. The Baptisme of Christ requires faith as an inseparable condition or qualification to the right receiving of it, without which it ought not to be administered.

But the Baptisme of infants doth not require faith as an inseparable condition or qualification.

Therefore, the Baptisme of Infants is not the Baptisme of Christ. . . .

It appears that all infants want [lack] faith; For the proof whereof, I will give sundry reasons. . . .

1. They have no knowledge of good nor evill, Deut. 1.39. Cannot discern betwixt the right hand and left, Jon.4.11. How then can they understnd those things that are above the pitch of nature? . . .

3. If they have faith, why are they not after the imitation [initiation?] by baptisme, forthwith admitted to the Lords Supper? . . . .

4. Because not so much as any one of them among so many millions as have been in the world, when he commeth to riper years, giveth any testimony of his faith till he be further taught and instructed. . . .

5. Do all that have received faith in infancy, lose it again when they come to be of more years? It seemeth so. . . .

Object. But though infants have not actuall faith yet they have Seminal faith.

Answ. This is a vain distinction, For 1. There is but one faith. . . . This word (Seminal) doth merely delude men by a Metaphoricall exception to make men think there is a phisickall [sic] grouth of faith as in seeds of vegetive bodies when they are sowen. . . .

Answ. First, the Scripture hath not revealed unto us anything cleerly concerning the salvation or damnation of infants. 2. Forasmuch as there is no name under heaven whereby persons can be saved but by Christ, Acts 4.12, And forasmuch as infants are guilty of originall sin, Rom.5.14. Death reigned from Adam to Moses, and consequently sin over them that had not sinned, after the similitude of Adams transgression, that is to say by actuall sin. It is then most likely that infants as well as others, are saved by the presentment of the satisfaction of Christ to Gods justice for original sin. . . . Without believing, is this satisfaction applyed for dying infants (by vertue of Election and the free grace of God) to the justice of God. Rom.11.7. . . .

Infants Baptisme produces many absurdities;

1. It puts an infant in a state of grace and remission of sins, before calling.

2. It makes them visible members of Christ's church before calling, contrary to 1 Cor.1.2.

3. It upholds a nationall church as Circumcision did. . . .

4. It intayles grace to generation, not to regeneration, contrary to Joh.3.5,6.

5. It goes quite contrary to Christs order, who first bids make disciples, and then baptize after. . . .

6. Hereby carnall seed is taken, and acknowledged to be the spirituall seed of Abram.

7. Whereas the Scripture requires onely persons to be baptized who gladly receive the word, Acts 2.41. and desire baptisme, Acts 8.36. by this infant baptisme all are compelled, they and their children to be made Christians whether they will or no.

8. Christ did never ordain the Sacrament of Baptisme any way to concurre towards grace. . . .

[The treatise has no number 9 at this point.]

10. Infants Bap.tisme is a foundation for the Arminians to maintain falling from grace; If infants be baptized because they are in covenant with God, then it seems they after proving wicked are faln away. . . .

Quest. Whether do you think Baptisme administered in infancy, to be a lawfull Baptisme and sufficient?

Answ. To me it is not; For I think it to be a prophanation of an Ordinance.

2.4 The First London Confession, 1644

One might argue that no confession in Baptist history has been more influential than the one issued by seven Particular Baptist churches in London in 1644. Probably several Baptist leaders had a hand in its composition, among whom John Spilsbery, William Kiffin, and Samuel Richardson were prominent. This confession was no doubt influenced by the famous Westminster Confession of the Presbyterians, framed in London in 1643. Much of the Baptist confession seems to be taken from the Westminster statement, with changes in sensitive areas like baptism.

In this confession Baptists defended themselves against charges of Pelagianism, Anabaptism, anarchism, and immorality. They asserted their adherence to traditional Christian doctrines. While the confession is Calvinistic, it has no trace of the hyper-Calvinism which mars the Second London Confession of 1689.

This is the first Baptist confession issued by a group of churches, and the first to prescribe immersion as the form of baptism. The document includes a strong emphasis upon Christology, the authority of Scripture, and upon preaching. It commits Christians to civil obedience and yet insists upon religious liberty to give primary obedience to God. In ecclesiology, the confession commits Baptists to both local church independence and interchurch cooperation. The marginal note opposite Article XL shows the effort of Baptists to preserve modesty and decorum at public immersions, especially of women. *Source:* William L. Lumpkin, ed., *Baptist Confessions of Faith* (Philadelphia: Judson Press, 1959), 154-171.

To
ALL THAT DESIRE

The lifting up of the Name of the LORD JESUS in sinceritie, the poore despised Churches of God in *London* send greeting, with prayers for their farther increase in the knowledge of CHRIST JESUS.

Wee question not but that it will seeme strange to many men, that such as wee are frequently termed to be, lying under that calumny and black brand of Heretickes, and sowers of division as wee doo, should presume to appear so publickly as now wee have done: But yet notwithstanding wee may well say, to give answer to such, what David *said to his brother, when the* Lords *battell was a fighting,* 1 Sam. 29.30. *Is there not a cause?*

Surely, if ever people had cause to speake for the vindication of the truth of Christ in their hands, wee have, . . . But being it is not only us, but the truth professed by us, wee cannot, wee dare not but speake; it is no strange thing to any observing man, what sad charges are laid, not onely by the world, that know not God, but also by those that thinke themselves much wronged, if they be not looked upon as the chiefe Worthies of the Church of God, and Watchmen of the Citie: . . . . They finding us out of that common road-way themselves walke, have smote us and taken away our vaile, . . . charging us with holding Free-will, Falling away from grace, denying Originall sinne, disclaiming of Magistracy, denying to assist them either in persons or purse in any of their lawfull Commands, doing acts unseemly in the dispensing the Ordinance of Baptism, not to be named amongst Christians: All which Charges wee disclaime as notoriously untrue. . . .

Wee have therefore for the cleering of the truth we professe, that it may be at libertie, though wee be in bonds, briefly published a Confession of our Faith, as desiring all that feare God, seriously to consider whether (if they compare what wee here say and confesse in the presence of the Lord Jesus and his Saints) men have not with their tongues in Pulpit, and pens in Print, both spoken and written things that are contrary to truth; but wee know our God in his owne time will cleere our Cause, and lift up his Sonne to make him the chiefe cornerstone, though he has been (or now should be) rejected of Master Builders. And because it may be conceived, that what is here published, may be but the Judgement of some one particular Congregation, more refined then the rest; We doe therefore here subscribe it, some of each body in the name, and by the appointment of seven Congregations, . . . holding Jesus Christ to be our head and Lord; . . . and wee beleeve the Lord will daily cause truth more to appeare in the hearts of his Saints, . . .

Subscribed in the Names of seven Churches in *London.*

William Kiffin.	*John Mabbatt.*
Thomas Patience.	————————
————————	*John Webb.*
John Spilsbery.	*Thomas Killcop.*
George Tipping.	
Samuel Richardson.	————————
————————	*Paul Hobson.*
Thomas Skippard.	*Thomas Goare.*
Thomas Munday.	————————
————————	Joseph Phelpes.
Thomas Gunne.	Edward Heath.

The
CONFESSION
    Of FAITH, of those Churches
        which are commonly (though falsly)
            called ANABAPTISTS.

I.

That GOD as he is in himselfe, cannot be comprehended of any but himselfe, [1]dwelling in that inaccessible light, that no eye can attaine unto, whom never man saw, nor can see; that there is but [2]one God, one Christ, one Spirit, one Faith, one Baptisme; [3]one Rule of holinesse and obedience for all Saints, at all times, in all places to be observed.

[1] 1 Tim. 6.16.
[2] 1 Tim. 2.5.
Eph. 4.4, 5, 6.
1 Cor. 12.4, 5, 6, 13.
John 14. chap.
[3] 1 Tim. 6.3, 13, 14.
Gal. 1.8, 9.
2 Tim. 3.15.

II.

That God is [1]of himselfe, that is, neither from another, nor of another, nor by another, nor for another: [2]But is a Spirit, who as his

[1] Esa. 44.67 & 43.11.
    & 46.9.
[2] John 4.24.

being is of himselfe, so he gives [3]being, moving, and preservation to all other things, being in himselfe eternall, most holy, every way infinite in [4]greatnesse, wisdome, power, justice, goodnesse, truth, &c. In this God-head, there is the Father, the Sonne, and the Spirit; being every one of them one and the same God; and therefore not divided, but distinguished one from another by their severall properties; the [5]Father being from himselfe, the [6]Sonne of the Father from everlasting, the holy [7]Spirit proceeding from the Father and the Sonne.

3 Exod. 3.14.
4 Rom. 11.36.
  Act. 17.28.
5 1 Cor. 8.6.
6 Pro. 8.22, 23
  Heb. 1.3
  John 1.18
7 Joh. 15.16.
  Gal. 4.6.

III.

That God hath [1]decreed in himselfe from everlasting touching all things, effectually to work and dispose them [2]according to the counsell of his owne will, to the glory of his Name; in which decree appeareth his wisdome, constancy, truth, and faithfulnesse; [3]Wisdome is that whereby he contrives all things; [4]Constancy is that whereby the decree of God remaines alwayes immutable; [5]Truth is that whereby he declares that alone which he hath decreed, and though his sayings may seeme to sound sometimes another thing, yet the sense of them doth alwayes agree with the decree; [6]Faithfulnesse is that whereby he effects that he hath decreed, as he hath decreed. And touching his creature man, [7]God had in Christ before the foundation of the world, according to the good pleasure of his will, foreordained some men to eternall life through Jesus Christ, to the praise and glory of his grace, [8]leaving the rest in their sinne to their just condemnation, to the praise of his Justice. . . .

1 Esa. 46.10
  Rom. 11.34, 35, 36
  Mat. 10.29, 30
2 Eph. 1, 11.
3 Col. 2.3.
4 Num. 23.19, 20.
5 Jere. 10.10.
  Rom. 3.4.
6 Esa. 44.10.
7 Eph. 1, 3, 4, 5, 6, 7.
  2 Tim. 1.9.
  Acts 13.48.
  Rom. 8.29, 30.
8 Jude ver. 4. & 6.
  Rom. 9.11, 12, 13.
  Prov. 16.4.

V.

All mankind being thus fallen, and become altogether dead in sinnes and trespasses, and subject to the eternall wrath of the great God by transgression; yet the elect, which God hath [1]loved with an everlasting love, are [2]redeemed, quickened, and saved, not by themselves, neither by their own workes, lest any man should boast himselfe, but wholly and onely by God of [3]his free grace and mercie through Jesus Christ, who of God is made unto us wisdome, righteousnesse, sanctification and redemption, that as it is written, Hee that rejoyceth, let him rejoyce in the Lord. . . .

1 Jer. 31.2
2 Gen. 3.15.
  Eph. 1.3, 7. & 2.4, 9.
  1 Thess. 5.9.
  Acts 13.38.
3 1 Cor. 1.30, 31.
  2 Cor. 5.21.
  Jer. 9.23, 24.
  Joh. 5.39.
  2 Tim. 3.15, 16, 17.
  Col. 21.18, 23.
  Matth. 15.9.
  Acts 3.22, 23
  Heb. 1.1, 2
  2 Tim. 3.15, 16, 17.
  2 Cor. 1.20.

VII.

The Rule of this Knowledge, Faith and Obedience, concerning the worship and service of God, and all other Christian duties, is not mans inventions, opinions, devices, lawes, constitutions, or traditions unwritten whatsoever, but onely the word of God contained in the Canonicall Scriptures.

VIII.

In this written Word God hath plainly revealed whatsoever he hath thought needfull for us to know, beleeve, and acknowledge, touching the Nature and Office of Christ, in whom all the promises are Yea and Amen to the praise of God.

IX.

Touching the Lord Jesus, of whom [1]*Moses* and the Prophets wrote, and whom the Apostles preached, is the [2]Sonne of God the Father, the brightnesse of his glory, the ingraven forme of his being,

1 Gen. 3.15 & 22.18
  & 49.10
  Dan. 7.13 & 9.24, 25, 26
2 Prov. 8.23
  Joh. 1.1, 2, 3.
  Col. 1.1, 15, 16, 17.

God with him and with his holy Spirit, by whom he made the world, by whom he upholds and governes all the workes hee hath made, who also [3]when the fulnesse of time was come, was made man of a [4]woman, of the Tribe of [5]*Judah,* of the seed of *Abraham* and David, to wit, of *Mary* that blessed Virgin, by the holy Spirit comming upon her, and the power of the most High overshadowing her, and was also in [6]all things like unto us, sinne only excepted.

3 Gal. 4.4
4 Heb. 7.14
　Rev. 5.5 with
　　Gen. 49.9, 10.
　Rom. 1.3. & 9.5
　Mat. 1.16 with
　　Luke 3.23, 26.
　Heb. 2.16
5 Esa. 53.3, 4, 5.
　Phil. 2.8.

X.

Touching his Office, [1]Jesus Christ onely is made the Mediator of the new Covenant, even the everlasting Covenant of grace between God and Man, to [2]be perfectly and fully the Prophet, Priest and King of the Church of God for evermore.

1 2 Tim. 2.15
　Heb. 9.15.
　Joh. 14.6
2 Heb. 1.2. & 3.
　1, 2 & 7.24.
　Esa. 9.6, 7.
　Acts 5.31.

XI.

Unto this Office hee was fore-ordained from everlasting, by the [1]authority of the Father, and in respect of his Manhood, from the womb called and separated, and [2]anointed also most fully and abundantly with all gifts necessary, God having without measure poured the Spirit upon him. . . .

1 Prov. 8.23
　Esa. 42.6 & 49.1, 5
2 Esa. 11.2, 3, 4, 5, &
　　61.1, 2, 3 with
　　Luk. 4.17, 22.
　Joh. 1.14, 16. & 3.34.

XIX.

Touching his Kingdome, [1]Christ being risen from the dead, as-cended into heaven, sat on the right hand of God the Father, having all power in heaven and earth, given unto him, he doth spiritually govern his Church, exercising his power [2]over all Angels and Men, good and bad, to the preservation and salvation of the elect, to the overruling and destruction of his enemies, which are Reprobates, [3]communicating and applying the benefits, vertue, and fruit of his Prophesie and Priesthood to his elect, namely, to the subduing and taking away of their sinnes, to their justification and adoption of Sonnes, regeneration, sanctification, preservation and strengthen-ing in all their conflicts against Satan, the World, the Flesh, and the temptations of them, continually dwelling in, governing and keep-ing their hearts in faith and filiall feare by his Spirit, which having [4]given it, he never takes away from them, but by it still begets and nourisheth in them faith, repentance, love, joy, hope, and all heav-enly light in the soule unto immortality, notwithstanding through our own unbeliefe, and the temptations of Satan, the sensible sight of this light and love be clouded and overwhelmed for the time. . . .

1 1 Cor. 15.4.
　1 Pet. 3.21, 22.
　Matth. 28.18, 19, 20.
　Luke 24.51.
　Acts 1.11 & 5.30, 31.
　John 19.36.
　Rom. 14.17.
2 Mark 1.27.
　Heb. 1.14.
　Joh. 16.7, 15.
3 John 5.26, 27.
　Rom. 5.6, 7, 8 & 14.17.
　Gal. 5.22, 23.
　John 1.4, 13.
4 John 13.1 & 10.28, 29
　　& 14.16, 17.
　Rom. 11.29.
　Psal. 51.10, 11.
　Job 33.29, 30.
　2 Cor. 12.7, 9.
　1 Cor. 15.24, 28.
　Heb. 9.28
　2 Thess. 1.9, 10.
　1 Thess. 4.15, 16, 17.
　John 17.21, 26.

XX.

This Kingdome shall be then fully perfected when hee shall the second time come in glory to reigne amongst his Saints, and to be admired of all them which doe beleeve, when he shall put downe all rule and authority under his feet, that the glory of the Father may be full and perfectly manifested in his Sonne, and the glory of the Father and the Sonne in all his members.

XXI.

That Christ Jesus by his death did bring forth salvation and rec-onciliation onely for the [1]elect, which were those which [2]God the Father gave him; & that the Gospel which is to be preached to all men as the ground of faith, is, that [3]Jesus is the Christ, the Sonne of thee everblessed God, filled with the perfection of all heavenly and

1 John 15.13.
　Rom. 8.32, 33, 34.
　Rom. 5.11 & 3.25.
2 Job 17.2 with 6, 37.
3 Matth. 16.16.
　Luke 2.26.
　Joh. 6.9 & 7, 3 & 20.31.
　1 Joh. 5.11.

spirituall excellencies, and that salvation is onely and alone to be had through the beleeving in his Name.

XXII.

That Faith is the [1]gift of God wrought in the hearts of the elect by the Spirit of God, whereby they come to see, know, and beleeve the truth of [2]the Scriptures, & not onely so, but the excellencie of them above all other writings and things in the world, as they hold forth the glory of God in his attributes, the excellency of Christ in his nature and offices, and the power of the fulnesse of the Spirit in its workings and operations; and thereupon are inabled to cast the weight of their soules upon this truth thus beleeved.

1 Eph. 2.8.
Joh. 6.29 & 4.10.
Phil. 1.29.
Gal. 5.22.
2 Joh. 17.17.
Heb. 4.11, 12.
Joh. 6.63.
Matth. 7.24, 25
John 13.1.
1 Pet. 1.4, 5, 6.
Esa. 49.13, 14, 15, 16.

XXIII.

Those that have this pretious faith wrought in them by the Spirit, can never finally nor totally fall away; and though many stormes and floods do arise and beat against them, yet they shall never be able to take them off that foundation and rock which by faith they are fastened upon, but shall be kept by the power of God to salvation. . . .

XXIV.

That faith is ordinarily [1]begot by the preaching of the Gospel, or word of Christ, without respect to [2]any power or capacitie in the creature, but it is wholly [3]passive, being dead in sinnes and trespasses, doth beleeve, and is converted by no lesse power, [4]then that which raised Christ from the dead.

1 Rom. 10.17.
1 Cor. 1.21.
2 Rom. 9.16.
3 Rom. 2.1, 2.
Ezek. 16.6.
Rom. 3.12.
4 Rom. 1.16.
Eph. 1.19.
Col. 2.12.

XXV.

That the tenders of the Gospel to the conversion of sinners, [1]is absolutely free, no way requiring, as absolutely necessary, any qualifications, preparations, terrors of the Law, or preceding Ministry of the Law, but onely and alone the naked soule, as a [2]sinner and ungodly to receive Christ, as crucified, dead, and buried, and risen againe, being made [3]a Prince and a Saviour for such sinners. . . .

1 Joh 3.14, 15 & 1.12.
Esa. 55.1.
Joh. 7.37.
2 1 Tim. 1.15.
Rom. 4.5. & 5.8.
3 Act. 5.30, 31 & 2.36.
1 Cor. 1.22, 23, 24.

XXXIII.

That Christ hath here on earth a spirituall Kingdome, which is the Church, which he hath purchased and redeemed to himselfe, as a peculiar inheritance: which Church, as it is visible to us, is a company of visible [1]Saints, [2]called & separated from the world, by the word and [3]Spirit of God, to the visible profession of the faith of the Gospel, being baptized into that faith, and joyned to the Lord, and each other, by mutuall agreement, in the practical injoyment of the [4]Ordinances, commanded by Christ their head and King.

1 1 Cor. 1.1.
Eph. 1.1.
2 Rom. 1.7.
Act. 26.18
1 Thes. 1.9.
2 Cor. 6.17.
Rev. 18.18.
3 Acts 2.37 with
Acts 10.37.
4 Rom. 10.10.
Act. 20.21.
Mat. 18.19, 20.
Act. 2.42.
1 Pet. 2.5.

XXXIV.

To this Church he hath [1]made his promises, and given the signes of his Covenant, presence, love, blessing, and protection: here are the fountains and springs of his heavenly grace continually flowing forth; [2]thither ought all men to come, of all estates, that acknowledge him to be their Prophet, Priest, and King, to be inrolled amongst his houshold servants, to be under his heavenly conduct and government, to lead their lives in his walled sheepfold, and watered garden, to have communion here with the Saints, that they

1 Mat. 28.18, 19, 20.
2 Cor. 6.18.
2 Esa. 8.16.
1 Tim. 3.15. & 4.16.
& 6.3, 5.
Acts 2.41, 47
Song, 4.12.
Gal. 6.10.
Eph. 2.19.

may be made to be partakers of their inheritance in the Kingdome of God. . . .

XXXVI.

That being thus joyned, every Church has [1]power given them from Christ for their better well-being, to choose to themselves meet persons into the office of [2]Pastors, Teachers (*a*), Elders, Deacons, being qualified according to the Word, as those which Christ has appointed in his Testament, for the feeding, governing, serving, and building up of his Church, and that none other have power to impose them, either these or any other.

XXXVII.

That the Ministers aforesaid, lawfully called by the Church, where they are to administer, ought to continue in their calling, according to Gods Ordinance, and carefully to feed the flock of Christ committed to them, not for filthy lucre, but of a ready mind.

XXXVIII.

That the due maintenance of the Officers aforesaid, should be the free and voluntary communication of the Church, that according to Christs Ordinance, they that preach the Gospel, should live on the Gospel and not by constraint to be compelled from the people by a forced Law.

XXXIX.

That Baptisme is an Ordinance of the new Testament, given by Christ, to be dispensed onely upon persons professing faith, or that are Disciples, or taught, who upon a [1]profession of faith, ought to be baptized.

XL.

The way and manner of the [1]dispensing of this Ordinance the Scripture holds out to be dipping or plunging the whole body under water: it being a signe, must answer the thing signified, which are these: first, the [2]washing the whole soule in the bloud of Christ: Secondly, that interest the Saints have in the [3]death, buriall, and resurrection; thirdly, together with a [4]confirmation of our faith, that as certainly as the body is buried under water, and riseth againe, so certainly shall the bodies of the Saints be raised by the power of Christ, in the day of the resurrection, to reigne with Christ.

XLI.

The persons designed by Christ, to dispense this Ordinance, the [1]Scriptures hold forth to be a preaching Disciple, it being no where tyed to a particular Church, Officer, or person extraordinarily sent, the Commission injoyning the administration, being given to them under no other consideration, but as considered Disciples.

XLII.

Christ has likewise given power to his whole Church to receive in and cast out, by way of Excommunication, any member; and this power is given to every particular Congregation, and not one particular person, either member or Officer, but the whole.

Margin notes:

1 Acts 1.2. & 6.3. with 15.22, 25; 1 Cor. 16.3.
2 Rom. 12.7, 8 & 16.1. 1 Cor. 12.8, 28; 1 Tim. 3. chap.; Heb. 13.7; 1 Pet. 5.1, 2, 3.

Heb. 5.4.; Acts 4.23.; 1 Tim. 4.14.; Joh. 10.3, 4.; Acts 20.28.; Rom. 12.7, 8.; Heb. 13.7, 17.

1 Cor. 9.7, 14.; Gal. 6.6.; 1 Thes. 5.13.; 1 Tim. 5.17, 18.; Phil. 4.15, 16.

Matt. 28.18, 19.; Mark 16.16.; Acts 2.37, 38 & 8.36, 37, 38 & 18.8.

The word *Baptizo*, signifying to dip under water, yet so as with convenient garments both upon the administrator and subject, with all modestie.
1 Mat. 3, 16.; Joh. 3.23.; Acts 8.38.
2 Rev. 1.5 & 7.14. with Heb. 10, 22.
3 Rom. 6.3, 4, 5.
4 1 Cor. 15.28, 29.

1 Esa. 8.16.; Mat. 28.16, 17, 18, 19.; John 4.1, 2.; Acts 20.7.; Mat. 26.26.

Acts 2.47.; Rom. 16.2.; Math. 18.17.; 1 Cor. 5.4; 2 Cor. 2.6, 7, 8.

XLIII.

And every particular member of each Church, how excellent, great, or learned soever, ought to be subject to this censure and judgement of Christ; and the Church ought with great care and tendernesse, with due advice to proceed against her members.

Mat. 18.16, 17, 18.
Act. 11.2, 3.
1 Tim. 5.19, 20, 21.

XLIV.

And as Christ for the [1]keeping of this Church in holy and orderly Communion, placeth some speciall men over the Church, who by their office are to governe, oversee, visit, watch; so likewise for the better keeping therof in all places, by the members, he hath given [2]authoritie, and laid dutie upon all, to watch over one another.

1 Acts 20.27, 28.
Heb. 13.17, 24.
Mat. 24.25.
1 Thes. 5.14.
2 Mark 13.34, 37.
Gal. 6.1.
1 Thes. 5.11.
Jude ver. 3, 20.
Heb. 10.34, 35. & 12.15.

XLV.

That also such to whom God hath given gifts, being tryed in the Church, may and ought by the appointment of the Congregation, to prophesie, according to the proportion of faith, and so teach publickly the Word of God, for the edification, exhortation, and comfort of the Church.

1 Cor. 14. cha.
Rom. 12.6.
1 Pet. 4.10, 11.
1 Cor. 12.7.
1 Thes. 5.17, 18, 19.

XLVI.

Thus being rightly gathered, established, and still proceeding in Christian communion, and obedience of the Gospel of Christ, none ought to separate for faults and corruptions, which may, and as long as the Church consists of men subject to failings, will fall out and arise amongst them, even in true constituted Churches, untill they have in due order sought redresse thereof.

Rev. 2. & 3, Chapters
Acts 15.12.
1 Cor. 1.10.
Ephef. 2.16. & 3.15, 16.
Heb. 10.25.
Jude ver. 15.
Matth. 18.17.
1 Cor. 5.4, 5.

XLVII.

And although the particular Congregations be distinct and severall Bodies, every one a compact and knit Citie in it selfe; yet are they all to walk by one and the same Rule, and by all meanes convenient to have the counsell and help one of another in all needfull affaires of the Church, as members of one body in the common faith under Christ their onely head.

1 Cor. 4.17. & 14.33, 36.
& 16.1.
Matth. 28.20.
1 Tim. 3.15. & 6.13, 14.
Rev. 22.18, 19.
Col. 2.6, 19, & 4.16.

XLVIII.

That a civill Magistracie is an ordinance of God set up by God for the punishment of evill doers, and for the praise of them that doe well; and that in all lawfull things commanded by them, subjection ought to be given by us in the Lord: and that we are to make supplication and prayer for Kings, and all that are in authority, that under them we may live a peaceable and quiet life in all godliness and honesty.

Rom. 13.1, 2, 3, 4.
1 Pet. 2.13, 14.
1 Tim. 2.2.

XLIX.

The supreme Magistracie of this Kingdome we beleeve to be the King and Parliament freely chosen by the Kingdome, and that in all those civil Lawes which have been acted by them, or for the present is or shall be ordained, we are bound to yield subjection and obedience unto in the Lord, as conceiving our selves bound to defend both the persons of those thus chosen, and all civill Lawes made by them, with our persons, liberties, and estates, with all that is called ours, although we should suffer never so much from them in not actively submitting to some Ecclesiasticall Lawes, which might be conceived by them to be their duties to establish which we for the

present could not see, nor our consciences could submit unto; yet
are we bound to yeeld our persons to their pleasures.

L.

1 Tim. 1.2, 3, 4.
Psal. 126.1.
Acts 9.31.

And if God should provide such a mercie for us, as to incline the
Magistrates hearts so far to tender our consciences, as that we
might bee protected by them from wrong, injury, oppression and
molestation, which long we formerly have groaned under by the
tyranny and oppression of the Prelaticall Hierarchy, which God
through mercy hath made this present King and Parliament wonder-
full honourable, as an instrument in his hand, to throw downe; and
we thereby have had some breathing time, we shall, we hope, look
at it as a mercy beyond our expectation, and conceive our selves
further engaged for ever to blesse God for it.

LI.

1 Acts 2.40, 41. & 4.19, &
5.28, 29, 41. & 20.23.
1 Thess. 3.3.
Phil. 1.27, 28, 29.
Dan. 3.16, 17. & 6.7, 10,
22, 23.

But if God with-hold the Magistrates allowance and furtherance
herein; [1]yet we must notwithstanding proceed together in Christian
communion, not daring to give place to suspend our practice, but to
walk in obedience to Christ in the profession and holding forth this
faith before mentioned, even in the midst of all trialls and afflictions, not accounting our goods, lands, wives, children, fathers,
mothers, brethren, sisters, yea, and our own lives dear unto us, so
we mag finish our course with joy: remembering alwayes we ought

2 Matth. 28. 18, 19, 20.
1 Tim. 6.13, 14, 15.
Rom. 12.1, 8.
1 Cor. 14.37.
2 Tim. 4.7, 8.
Rev. 2.10.
Gal. 2.4, 5.

to [2]obey God rather then men, and grounding upon the commande-
ment, commission and promise of our Lord and master Jesus
Christ, who as he hath all power in heaven and earth, so also hath
promised, if we keep his commandements which he hath given us,
to be with us to the end of the world: and when we have finished our
course, and kept the faith, to give us the crowne of righteousnesse,
which is laid up for all that love his appearing, and to whom we
must give an account of all our actions, no man being able to discharge us of the same.

LII.

Rom. 13.5, 6, 7.
Matth. 22.21.
Titus 3.
1 Pet. 2.13.
Ephes. 5.21, 22.
  & 6.1, 9.
1 Pet. 5.5.

And likewise unto all men is to be given whatsoever is their due;
tributes, customes, and all such lawful duties, ought willingly to
bee by us paid and performed, our lands, goods, and bodies, to
submit to the Magistrate in the Lord, and the Magistrate every way
to bee acknowledged, reverenced, and obeyed, according to godlinesse; not because of wrath onely but for conscience sake. And
finally, all men so to be esteemed and regarded, as is due and meet
for their place, age, estate and condition.

LII [sic].

Matth. 22.21.
Acts 24.14, 15, 16.
John 5.28.
2 Cor. 4.17.
1 Tim. 6.3, 4, 5.
1 Cor. 15.58, 59.

And thus wee desire to give unto God that which is Gods, and
unto *Cesar* that which is *Cesars,* and unto all men that which belongeth unto them, endevouring ourselves to have alwayes a cleare
conscience void of offence towards God, and towards man. And if
any take this that we have said, to be heresie, then doe wee with the
Apostle freely confesse, that after the way which they call heresie,
worship we the God of our Fathers, beleeving all things which are
written in the Law and in the Prophets and Apostles, desiring from
our soules to disclaime all heresies and opinions which are not after

Christ, and to be stedfast, unmoveable, alwayes abounding in the worke of the Lord, as knowing our labour shall not be in vain in the Lord.

1 Cor. 1.24.

Not that we have dominion over your faith, but are helpers of your joy: for by faith we stand.

FINIS

2.5 Thomas Collier, *A General Epistle*, 1651

Thomas Collier (d. 1691) was a leading Particular Baptist pastor, church planter, and theologian in the west of England. He was known for his evangelistic zeal. his skill in organizing the scattered churches into associations, and for trying to moderate the theological differences between General and Particular Baptists. Before his death, Collier issued a Baptist confession, apparently an effort to soften the harsh Calvinism of the Second London Confession.

Collier's lengthy book entitled *A General Epistle to the Universal Church of the First-Born* in 1651, while not in the form of a *systematic* theology, is nevertheless a major expression of Baptist doctrine. In the brief selection given here, Collier defended Baptist views of Scripture against the radical Quakers on the left and the equally radical Rationalists on the right. He insisted that the "divine Originalls" of Scripture are not essential to receiving the authentic biblical message today, since the true Word of God can come through translations. *Source:* Thomas Collier, *A General Epistle to the Universal Church of the First-Born* (London: n.p., 1651), 248-251. From the Angus Collection, Regent's Park College, Oxford.

Chapter X Of the Scripture

Concerning the Scripture, although I shall not question the truth of it, yet I shall propound these three things considerable concerning it.

First, That it is not sufficient in it self as it is a Letter, or word written, to teach or bring any man to the knowledge of God; although God be declared in it, yet that declaration without God powerfully working in the declaration of himself, to and in the spirits of men, they never by this or any other means come to the true and saving knowledge of him: yet,

Secondly, Some make too much of Scripture, setting it up in the room of the Spirit, and so it is indeed become an Idol, not in itself, but through that Idolatry which dwels in the hearts of men: For

First, Some say that it is the Spirit, and that there is no Letter in it; If these make it not an Idol, I know not what an Idol is.

Secondly, Others know no other touch-stone or trial, no other light by which they judge of Truth: thus putting it in the room of the Spirit, who is light, and the greater light to make an Idol of it; for they say, they cannot know Truth untill they bring it to the letter for trial: thus making an Idol of the Letter, setting it up in the room of God, . . .

And this is the reason men are so tost to and fro, because they are led so much by a Letter without them, not discerning Truth in its own light; and so according to the different apprehensions about the Letter, so are men tost to and fro in their judgements: Whereas to know Truth from its own discovery, and to judge of it in its own light, establisheth a soul forever: hence its come to pass that there is so much blindness and darkness in the things of God; so many strange opinions of God, and about the things of God, in taking up rules from, and judging of things according to the letter; . . .

And truly Brethren, its my earnest desire to see souls to live more in the Spirit, and less in the Letter, and then they will see that we judge of the Letter by the Spirit, and not of the Spirit by the Letter, which occasions so much ignorance amongst us; and those who profess themselves to be our teachers, are chief in this trespass; and how then can they teach others, who know not Truth themselves, as they say, but as they reade it without them, and so at the best speak but other mens light? and if they misunderstand what other men have written, then they speak falshood instead of Truth: thus is Scripture abused by many, by most, in making too much of it, making an Idol of it, Yet,

Thirdly, As Scripture is abused by most in making too much of it, so it is by many in making too little of it, looking on it as a thing of nought, as from the flesh, and not as from the Spirit, questioning the truth of it, not acknowledging it to be as it is in it self, a Declaration of God who is Truth: Not that I minde every letter or circumstance in it, but for the substance of it, as it declares purely the God of Truth, so its without question to me a word of Truth; I know right well that it is not the Word of God in the most strict sense, according to what is written in John 1.1. Yet I know it is that Word in which God is declared.

Neither that I am ignorant of the possibility, nay the probability of corruption in it, and in that the Greek and Hebrew too, commonly called the Original; although it be true, no man ever living saw the Original Copies, but as it hath been carried through the hands of Papists: And the truth is, we have all from them; and the greatest Scholars are as far from ever seeing the Original Copies of Scriptures, as any English man, but as their Father preserved them, and their Masters have taught them, so they know them, but no otherwise. . . .

2.6 On the Role of Women in Baptist Life

The proper role of women was a lively topic among Baptist churches in the seventeenth century. Then, as now, one often finds a discepancy between the theory of what women *should* do and the records of what they *actually did*. Various treatises by Baptist leaders, confessions of faith, church minutes, and complaints by their opponents give us our best information about the role of Baptist women. Among both groups of early Baptists, women routinely served as deaconesses and, especially among the General Baptists, they sometimes preached. In *Principles and Inferences*, John Smyth accepted women deacons though he would not allow women to preach. *Source:* John Smyth, *Principles and Inferences concerning the Visible Church* (London, 1607). In W. T. Whitley, ed., *The Works of John Smyth*, 2. vols. (Cambridge: Cambridge University Press, 1915), 1:255-257, 259-261. The Baptist Confession of 1612 accepted women deacons, as did *A Declaration of Faith* of 1611 (see document 2.1, article 20). *Source:* William L. Lumpkin, ed., *Baptist Confessions of Faith* (Valley Forge: Judson Press, 1959), 138. Selection C gives the account of setting aside deaconesses in the Broadmead Church (Particular Baptist) in 1679. The detailed outline of their duties shows that Baptist deaconesses sometimes exercised a speaking/teaching role as well as a one of healing/nurturing. *Source:* Roger Hayden, ed., *The Records of a Church of Christ in Bristol, 1640-1687* (Bristol Record Society, 1974), 208-209. Used by permission.

A. John Smyth, *Principles and Inferences*, 1607

All that have gifts may be admitted to prophecy 1 Cor. 14. 31,

Private persons are 1 men 2. weomen

Private men present at the exercise of prophecy may modestly propound their doubts which are to be resolved by the prophets: Luk. 2, 46, 47, 1 Sam. 19, 20-23. 1 Cor. 14, 30[.]

Weomen are not permitted to speak in the church in tyme of prophecy. 1 Cor. 14. 34. 1 Tim. 2. 12. Revel. 2, 20.

If women doubt of any thing delivered in tyme of prophecy and are willing to learn, they must ask them that can teach them in private, as their husbands at home if they be faithful, or some other of the church. 1 Cor. 14, 35, 1 Tim 2. 12. . . .

The Deacons are officers occupied about the works of mercy respecting the body or outward man. Act. 6, 2.

The Deacons are 1. men 2. or weomen deacons or widowes. Act. 6, 2. Rom. 16, 1.

Men Deacons collect and distribute with simplicity the churches treasury according to the churches necessities, and the Saincts occasions. Rom. 12, 8. 2 Cor. 8, 2-8. 1 Cor. 16, 2. 3. . . .

Weomen deacons or widowes are of 60 yeeres of age, qualified according to the Apostles rule. 1 Tim. 5. 9. releeving the bodily infirmities of the Saincts with cheerfulnes. Rom. 12. 8. and 16, 1. . . .

The widowes cheef office is to visite and relieve the widow, fatherless, sick lame, blind, impotent, weomen with child, and diseased members of the church. 1 Tim. 5. 9 Rom. 12. 8. Mat 25. 35-40.

B.   Statement in Propositions and Conclusions, 1612

76. That Christ hath set in His outward church two sorts of ministers: viz., some who are called pastors, teachers or elders, who administer in the word and sacraments, and others who are called Deacons, men and women: whose ministry is, to serve tables and wash the saints' feet (Acts vi. 2-4; Phil. i. 1; 1 Tim. iii. 2, 3, 8, 11, and chap. v.).

C.   Deaconesses at the Broadmead Church, Bristol, 1679

And this said day [probably March 4, 1679] yᵉ Church chose 4 sisters of yᵉ Church that were widdows, Each of above 60 years of age, to be Deaconesses for yᵉ Congregation, to looke after yᵉ Sick Sisters; namely, S. Smith, yᵉ elder, S. Spurgeon; S. Webb, yᵉ elder, S. Walton; Deaconesses.

UPON yᵉ 18th day of yᵉ first Month, 1679, three of those 4 persons for Deaconesses were, by fasting and prayer, commended to yᵉ work and office, of Widows, or Deaconesses, to this Church: and soe, solemnly, they were sett aparte to that worke of looking after yᵉ sick members of yᵉ Congregation; viz. S. Smith yᵉ elder, S. Webb, yᵉ elder, S. Walton; Deaconesses instituted, all above yᵉ age of 60 yeares, as 1 Timo. v. 9. . . .

Theire worke was further declared to them in these particulars:—

1. To visit yᵉ Sick, to have their Eye and Eare open to hearken and enquire who is sick, and to visitt yᵉ sick sisters in an Especiall manner, to see what they Need, Because it may not bee soe proper for men in severall cases.

2. To visitt not only sick Sisters, but sick Brethren alsoe; and therefore some conceive may be yᵉ Reason why they must be 60 yeares of age, that none occasion may be given; and as 1 Timo. v. 14.

3. Not only to take care of theire sick bodies, of yᵉ Brethren and Sisters, But that theire wants may be supplyed; and therefore to make reports back of theire condition, to yᵉ Elders and Deacons of yᵉ Congregation.

4. It is theire duty alsoe to *speake* a word to their soules, as occasion requires, for support or consolation, to build them up in a spirituall lively faith in Jesus Christ; for, as some observe, there is not an office of Christ *in his Church but it is dipt* in yᵉ blood of our Lord Jesus.

5. Some thinke it is theire duty to Attend yᵉ sick; and if soe, then they are to bee maintained by yᵉ Church.

This being declared, those 3 sisters were set aparte as Deaconesses of this Congregation, by fasting and prayer, said day.

2.7 The Humble Representation and Vindication, 1654

Many who rejected the state church of England also rejected the state government of that nation. Nothing illustrates this better than the rise of the Fifth Monarchy Movement, which taught that God would have Christians put down all earthly government so the "saints" could exercise direct rule in both church and state. Some Particular Baptists were caught up in this movement, though it had less attraction for the General Baptists.

The *Humble Representation* gives a General Baptist response to the Fifth Monarchy Movement. The document is notable for its moderate tone, its firm rejection of apocalyptic religion and politics, and its stance of quiet loyalty both to Baptist churchmanship and to English citizenship. *Source:* W. T. Whitley, ed., *Minutes of the General Assembly of the General Baptist Churches in England, with Kindred Records* (1654-1728) (London: Kingsgate Press, 1909), 1:1-5

The Humble Representation and Vindication Of many of the Messengers, Elders, and Brethren, belonging to severall of the BAPTIZED CHURCHES IN THIS NATION, of and concerning their Opinions and Resolutions touching the CIVILL GOVERNMENT of these Nations, and of their Deportment under the same. London, 1654.

Many of the Messengers, Elders, and Brethren of the Baptized Churches, having from severall parts of this Nation met together in the City of London, to consider how and which way the affairs of the Gospell of Christ, so farre as it concerns them, might bee best promoted and all divisions and offences contrary thereunto removed, or prevented; have also thought it necessary to Publish and Declare their Judgments and consciences touching the Civill Power of the Nation, partly to Vindicate themselves from some aspersions hereabout unduly and without cause cast upon them; And partly to rectify all mens misapprehensions of them.

It hath been, indeed, as well matter of grief to them as of prejudice to the way of Truth professed by them, to hear themselves frequently, and upon all occasions, misreported and misrepresented, so, as if they were no Friends to Magistracy and Civill Government:

Wheras . . . they hold themselves obliged by Gospell Rules, to be subject to the Higher Powers, to obey Magistrates, and to submit themselves to every Ordinance of man, for the Lords sake. And in case the Civill Powers doe, or shall, at any time impose things about matters of religion, which they through Conscience to God cannot actually obey, yet they know no other way in this case, but either patiently to suffer, or humbly to entreat favour. . . .

Nor do they know any ground for the saints, as such, to expect that the Rule and Government of the World should be put into their hands, untill that day in which the Lord Jesus shall visibly descend from Heaven in power and great glory, when . . . the Kingdoms of this World shall become the Kingdoms of the Lord and of his Christ, . . . But till then they rather expect it as their portion, patiently to suffer from the world, as the Scriptures direct them, and as the Saints usually have done, than anywise to attain the Rule and Government thereof. . . .

And in as much as our Saviour Christ hath given this as one sign, not long preceding his next coming, saying, This Gospell of the Kingdom shall be preached in all the world, for a Witness unto all Nations, and then shall the end come. Their hope therefore is, that in these latter daies, at least for a time, God will, by the hands of such Civill Powers as shall favour the Saints, open a door of greater liberty to the Saints, for the spreading of the Gospell in the Nations of the World, than usually hath been injoyed in times past. And [we] do verily beleeve that that measure of liberty this way, which hath of late years been allowed the people of God, hath not contributed a little (God being pleased therewith) towards those marvellous and unwonted Successes, which have been given to those who have been Instruments to procure the same.

Signed by some of the Messengers and Elders of the Baptized Churches, present at this meeting in London, for themselves and in the behalf of the respective Congregations to which they belong.

2.8 Cases of Church Discipline in the Seventeenth Century

General Baptists near Cambridge grouped into congregations that met at Fenstanton, Warboys, and Hexham (and also sometimes in Caxton Pastures). Their church records reveal much about the internal life of early Baptists. Perhaps no aspect of church life is more revealing than the cases of church discipline. In the selections that follow, readers will note the problems Baptists had with Quaker "notions," the difficulty of retaining as well as recruiting a membership, the fluid nature of the Baptist ministry, the cautious practices of church benevolence, and what seems today an unhealthy preoccupation with "casting out" of members. Much of the discipline centered around Quaker rejection of the written Scriptures, water baptism, and the Lord's Supper, all in favor of more "spiritual" authority and practices. *Source:* Edward Bean Underhill, ed., *Records of the Churches of Christ Gathered at Fenstanton, Warboys, and Hexham, 1644-1720* (London: Haddon Brothers and Company, 1854), 86-96, 272-273.

On the 26th day of the twelfth month [1653], at a general meeting held at Caxton Pastures, these ensuing things were declared and taken into consideration:

First, John Denne stood up and said: "Brethren, according to your former order, brother Gilman and myself, on the eighteenth day of this present month, went to Potton, in the county of Bedford, to reprove those persons that have forsaken the congregation and denied the faith. Where, first, after we perceived we could not get them together, we went to John Langhorne, and after some salutations we spake unto him, saying: "The cause of our coming at this time is this; the congregation, taking into their serious consideration how that many persons who formerly joined with us are now turned back, denying the faith, despising the ordinances of God, and followed after vanity, have resolved, according to their duty, to reprove and admonish all such persons, and if they do not repent, to proceed according to the will of God in separating them from the body of our Lord Jesus Christ. And, accordingly, we two were appointed to come unto you, to reprove you for your heinous faults, viz. for denying the faith, and despising the ordinance of God, &c. He said he had been reproved already. We told him it was true he had been so, yet that we might fulfil the will of God we do it again; and withal did earnestly desire him to consider from whence he was fallen and repent. Then he could not believe that Christ died for all. We answered and told him that he did once believe it; but now he said he was better enlightened; and, moreover, he said he was gone beyond those low ordinances which we practise. "For a man," he said, "must not always dwell upon one thing." Then we laboured to prove by the scriptures that the ordinances of God were not low. He confessed that it was true by the letter; but it was the spiritual meaning he said that we must look to; and therefore he said he could not believe as we believed. We told him we did not blame him for not believing as we believed, but for denying the faith which formerly he professed. Then he said: "I believe you hold that God hath given power to all men to believe, but if you do I shall deny it; yet, nevertheless I would, if I were nigh, come and hear you, for I can hear any;" and many other words were spoken which are too tedious here to relate. Whereupon, taking into our consideration his heinous crimes, in—

First, Denying the faith:

Secondly, Forsaking the church of Christ and joining with the church of England:

Thirdly, Despising the ordinances of God:

Fourthly, Contemning all the reproof of the church:—

We excommunicated him.

And then we went to Elizabeth Langhorne, of the same town, and declared to her the cause of our coming, as before. Then she asked whether we had been with any more in the town; we told her that was not an answer to our desires, neither was it anything to the purpose. Then she asked the same thing again; we told her we came not to give her an account of our actions, but to reprove her for her faults, and to know her resolutions. Then she said: "I have received greater dispensations and cannot walk in those low forms which you walk in, for they are ceased. We desired her to prove what she said. She said she could not prove it to us, for what she knew, she said, she knew it by experience (then she began to declare her experiences of God,) and, until we had the same experience, and were gathered up into the same condition, we could not understand it. We told her we would not be guided by her fancy, but if she could prove what she said by the scriptures, we would believe her. She said she could not prove it by the letter, and, she said, we could not understand the mystery. . . . Then taking into our serious consideration her great errors and heinous crimes which she hath committed, in—

First, Denying of the faith:

Secondly, Forsaking of the church:

Thirdly, Denying all the ordinances of God:

Fourthly, Despising all the reproof and admonition of the church:—

We did excommunicate her, and so departed. And being departed we met with William Newgus, of Dunton, to whom we declared the resolutions of the congregation, and reproved him for his faults, in

First, Denying the faith.

Secondly, Forsaking the church of Christ.

Thirdly, Denying all the ordinances of God.

He said he did not deny the ordinances; for, he said, that those that were drawn forth to do them might do them; but for his part they were nothing to him; and as for prayer he said he would be silent, and not pray until he was drawn forth unto it. We asked him what drawing forth he would have? the scripture commanded us to pray continually. He said that was not sufficient. Then company coming unto us our discourse brake off, only we reproved him and exhorted him to repent.

And so we departed and went to the wife of William Austin, unto whom we declared the cause of our coming and the resolutions of the church, as before: which when we had done, she said they were excommunicated already. We told her she was deceived; they were reproved and admonished, but not excommunicated. Then she confessed it and said: " 'Tis true I was reproved by Mr. Denne for denying the faith wherein I was baptized, but I do not deny that Christ died for all, for I say that all shall be saved." . . . We desired her to prove it by the scriptures. She said she looked upon the scriptures as nothing, she trampled them under her feet. We said, we were very sorry to hear her despise and speak evil of the holy scriptures, and desired her to take heed what she said. . . . Then being weary with hearing her utter these, and many more wicked and blasphemous speeches against the Lord God and his Son Jesus Christ, his church, and the holy scriptures, we excommunicated her, . . . And so we departed from her, and went to Robert Langhorne, to whom we declared the cause of our coming, as before. Then he began to speak against the church, and said: "I deny you to be the church of God."

Then we would have proved it, but he would not hear, and said he would not dispute with us; "yet," said he, "I look upon you no otherwise than I look upon the papists, and I had rather join with any people, in any practice whatsoever, than with you." Then we asked him whether he had rather join with drunkards, thieves, and whoremasters than with us? He answered, Yea, he had; and then said he could not talk with us.

Then taking into our serious consideration his abominable errors and heinous crimes which he hath committed, in—

First, Denying the faith:

Secondly, Denying all the ordinances of God:

Thirdly, Forsaking the church and denying them to be the church of Christ:

Fourthly, Slighting the scriptures of truth:

Fifthly, Despising all the reproof and admonitions of the church:—

We delivered him unto Satan, and so departed from him, and inquired for Joan Dunner; but she was not at home, and therefore we could not speak with her.

Then, night drawing near, we returned home; and on the one and twentieth day of the aforesaid month we went to Dunton, in the county of Bedford, to speak with those persons at that town that formerly joined with the congregation. And, after we saw that it was impossible to get them together, we went first to John Harvey and his wife, to whom, after salutations, we said: "The cause of our coming at this time is this; the church of our Lord Jesus Christ, taking into their serious consideration the sad and deplorable estate and condition of many persons that formerly joined with them, but now are turned back and have forsaken the church, denying the faith, and despising the ordinances of God, being like unto the dog that is returned to his vomit, and like the sow that was washed yet returning to her wallowing in the mire, they have resolved, according to their duty, to reprove and admonish all such persons; and (if they shall despise their reproof) to proceed in separating them from the church of God; and, therefore, they have sent us two to you, to reprove you for your faults, viz. for denying the faith and forsaking the church of God, &c..

They said they did not deny the faith. Then I, knowing the cause of their first separation, confidently affirmed they did. The man said again he did not. I told him that what they did now I knew not, but this I was assured they did deny it; for the first cause of their separation was, because we believed that Christ died for all. Then he confessed that he did deny it, but he said: "Now I will not deny it, for as far as I know he might die for all; but this I am assured, that all he died for shall be saved." We desired him to prove what he said. He said he would, and thereupon alleged that the gift was as large as the offence; we granted it, but told him it did not prove what he brought it for, and therefore desired him either to prove it or confess his error; for we did believe that Christ died for some which shall not be saved. . . . Then he would say no more to this, but proceeded to the second thing that we charged him with, viz., forsaking the church, and said: "You blame me for leaving you, but I walked with you as long as I saw any light in those ordinances; but afterwards I was taken into the New Jerusalem, which is the mother of us all, and now am I in the church of God." We answered and said: "We told you before we would not be guided by any man's fancy, and saying that you are in the New Jerusalem will not persuade us that you are so, unless you can make it appear by the scriptures."

Then he asked whether we only were the people of God? We answered: "Whatsoever we are, yet we know none that are accounted the church of God but those that walk in obedience to the ordinances of God." He confessed that, but said they walked in obedience to the ordinances of God. We demanded what ordinances? Then he began to speak, and made a very large discourse touching his discoveries of God (as he called them); declaring how God (as he said) had carried him from one dispensation to another, and that now he was in that condition that he could not sin, being taken up into that new heaven wherein dwelleth righteousness; . . . Then we considering how heinously they have sinned, in—

First, Denying the faith:

Secondly, Forsaking the church of God:

Thirdly, Despising the ordinances of Jesus Christ:

Fourthly, Wresting the holy scriptures:

Fifthly, Despising and contemning all the reproof and admonition of the church:
We excommunicated them; which when we had done, John Harvey said: "Now I will say you have done your duty, although it be long first."

Then we departed from them and went to Will. Newgus and his wife, to whom we declared the cause of our coming, as before. The man said he had told us his mind at Potton, and thereupon waxed very angry, saying, he was confident we would fall to the ground, for we did that we had no power to do; and for his part, he said, he would not join with us again. Some other, words did he utter, but to no purpose; then we reproved him, but he would not hear. Then we turned to his wife who was more mild, and spake unto her, desiring her to declare unto us her mind. Then she said, she saw no light in those ordinances, and she could not walk any longer in them, for she apprehended them to be ceased. We desired her to make it appear by the scriptures, but she refused to do it, and also refused to say any more unto us; wherefore, seeing they refused to join with us, and not only so but also denied the faith, despised all the ordinances of God, as prayer, &c, and despised and contemned all the reproof and correction of the church, we excommunicated them. . . .

[The case of John Ward at Warboys]

Some baptized this year [1656]. The church, considering the long absence of John Ward from the assembly, and sending to enquire the cause found his heart turned from the truth, affirming the scriptures to be a dead letter, also holding baptism with water to be nothing, denying to have fellowship with us. He was admonished the first and second time; at length he was delivered to Satan, for these things:—

Firstly. For affirming the scriptures to be a dead letter.

Secondly. For holding baptism to be of none effect.

Thirdly. For neglecting assembling and refusing admonition; for vindicating that wicked men have the kingdom of God in them, and other strange opinions. . . .

2.9   Baptist Association Records in England

By 1650 both General and Particular Baptist churches had grouped into regional "associations" for mutual encouragement, guidance, and ministry. The following records from various associations were gathered and edited by Barrington R. White of Oxford. They reveal the rationale and activities of associations, and spotlight some of the problems and challenges Baptists faced. These records also show clearly that, from the first, Baptist churches, on doctrinal as well as practical grounds, preferred denominational cooperation over strict independency. *Source:* B. R. White, ed., *Associational Records of the Particular Baptists of England, Wales and Ireland to 1660*, 3 parts (London: Baptist Historical Society, 1971), 1:10-12, 20, 25-26, 28; 3:126-127, 172-177, 184-185.

A.   The South Wales Association, 1654

The sixth General Meeting, 30-31 August 1654

Here the answer was given to the query at the last meeting, respecting the several duties of officers and private members. The following is a copy thereof:

Our Lord Jesus Christ, who is the head of the Church, after he had by himself purged our sins, ascended on high, gave gifts to his church, that each joint in the body might have its peculiar gift, and that thereby unity, peace and order might be preserved for the good of the whole. Eph. 4. 8, 11f., 15f.

1. He gave Apostles, who planted the first churches, and laid down infallible rules of doctrine and discipline, which we are now to observe, in the gathering and building up of churches. Eph. 2. 20f.

2. Prophets who, by divine inspiration, foretold things to come; as John etc.

3. Evangelists, who were the publishers of the Gospel to the world.

4. Miracles.

5. Gifts of healing.

6. Diversities of tongues, for the further publishing and confirmation of the Gospel, by those primitive and extraordinary Apostles, Prophets and Evangelists. All those officers and gifts were extraordinary, and therefore are now ceased; that being effected whereto they were given, only the three first may be said to remain in their writings; as Luke 16.29 and may be said likewise ordinarily to continue, while there are,

1. Apostles or Messengers sent forth to gather churches out of the world.

2. Evangelists, or publishers of the glad tidings, which is only some men's special gift.

3. Prophets, or such as speak to exhortation, etc., of whom hereafter.

Now there are to continue in the Church these officers:

1. Pastors.

2. Teachers.

3. Helps, or those who rule.

These three are called Elders, Bishops, Watchmen, etc., whose joint office is: . . .

1. To take care of the church, Acts 20.17, 28; 1 Pet. 5. 2f.

2. To consult on controversies, Acts 15.1f., 6, 23.

3. To order things in the church, Acts 16.4.

4. To advise in matters of doubt, Acts 21.18f.

5. To govern, 1 Tim. 5.17; Titus 1.5.

6. To visit the sick, if sent for, James 5.14.

7. To care for the distribution of collections, Acts 4.37; 11. 29f.

These were the duties of all the elders, though the greatest charge lay on the pastors, as appears in that, though there were many elders in the church at *Ephesus,* yet the epistle in the Revelation the second chapter, is directed but to one, viz., the angel of the church, and the charge given to, and the account required of him wholly. Now more particularly:

First, the pastor's office is to do all that tends to the feeding of the flock, Jer. 3.15; Mt. 24.45 as to

1. Exhort. Ro. 12.7f; 1 Cor. 12.8.

2. Reprove with all authority. Tit.2.15.

3. Cast out. 1 Tim. 1.20; 1 Cor. 5.1 etc.

4. Lead the sheep, he is to be the mouth of the whole.

5. Watch. 2 Tim. 4.5; Heb. 13.17.

6. Administer all ordinances in the church.

7. Give himself wholly to the word and doctrine, Acts 6.4.

8. Rule well, which consists (1) in the right ordering of questions and disorderly speakings. 1 Cor. 14.33, 40. Col.2.5 etc., (2) in preserving purity of doctrine and discipline, Rev. 2 and 3. The angels are charged with it.

Secondly, the teacher's particular office is, to wait on teaching, to expound scriptures, and confute errors. Tit. 2.7f. 2 Tim.4.2f. And this is no less the pastor's office.

Thirdly, the ruling elder's or helping office is, to oversee the lives and manners of men: to whom also double honour is due, 1. Tim. 5.17; Ro.12.8. He also must take care of God's house, Heb.13.17. 1. Tim. 3.5.

Fourthly, the next officer is a deacon, 1. Tim. 3.8 who is to serve tables, that is, the Lord's Table, and the tables of all others in the church, that shall want his service. He also is to be dedicated to the church's service, as the word deacon imports, Acts 6.1 etc.

Fifthly, for the assistance of the deacons there are widows, of whom, see 1. Tim. 5.16, who are likewise to serve the church, Ro. 16.1 most probably in looking to the poor and sick.

Sixthly, there are, for the further edifying of the church, ordinary prophets, who, though they be not such as wait on the ministry, or are wholly given up to it as yet, are such as being gifted, may speak, as they be permitted, or desired, to edification, exhortation, and comfort, 1. Tim. 4.15; 1 Cor. 14.3, 29f.

Thus far of church-officers with their offices. Now follow the duties of private members, as they are related to their officers and to each other.

B. The South Wales Association, 1656

The fifth General Meeting, 4/6 June 1656.

The conclusions of the messengers of the churches at their meeting at Morton Hinmarsh the 4th, 5th and 6th dayes of the 4th moneth 1656 to certain queries as they follow:

Question 1. Whether baptized believers may joyne in any parte of worship or publike hering the nationall ministers preach or others that are not baptised.

Answer: baptised believers ought not to here the nationall ministers preach nor joyne with them in their publike worship, their pretended ministery being Babilonish, Rev. 18.4. Neither may they soe heare or joyne with unbaptised persones, though hoped to be godly, because they are disorderly in carring one a publick ministery and worship without baptism, Col. 2.5; 2 Thess. 3.6 no, nor with baptised persons neither if not sounde in the faith which is the cause of those that are called free willers, Prov. 19.27.

Question 2. Whether it be the duty of churchmembers allwaies to call each other brother and sister.

Answer: it is the duty of churchmembers allwaies to owne each other in their hearts as brethren and sisters and to manifest the same by calling each other soe when it is expedient and convenient, 1. Pet. 2.17. But, sumtimes, wee know it may lawfully be forborne as divers Scriptures' exampl doe manifest, Col. 1.2; 1. Tim. 1.12; Titus 1.4.

C. The Abingdon Association, 1652

The first General Meeting

Wormsley, 8th day, 8th month (vulgarly, October) 1652.

At a meeteing of chosen members of the churches, viz., of Henly, Reading and Abingdon, it was concluded as followeth;

1st. That perticular churches of Christ ought to hold a firme communion each with other in point of advice in doubtfull matters and controversies, Acts 15.1f., 6, 24, 28; 16.4f. Which scriptures, compared together, shew that the church at Jerusalem held communion with the church of Antioch affording help to them as they could.

2ly. In giving and receiveing in case of want and poverty, 1 Cor. 16.3.

3ly. In consulting and consenting to the carrying on of the worke of God as choosing messengers, etc., 2 Cor. 8.19. And, in all things else, wherein perticular members of one and the same perticular church stand bound to hold communion each with other for which conclusion we render these scripture reasons:

1st. Because there is the same relation betwixt the perticular churches each towards other as there is betwixt perticular members of one church. For the churches of Christ doe all make up one body or church in generall under Christ their head as Eph. 1.22f.; Col. 1.24; Eph. 5.23ff.; 2 Cor. 12.13f. As perticular members make up one perticular church under the same head, Christ, and all the perticular assemblys are but one Mount Syon, Is. 4.5; Song 6.9. Christ his undefiled is but one and in his body ther is to be no schisme which is then found in the body when all the members have not the same care one over another. Wherfore we conclude that every church ought to manifest its care over other churches as fellow members of the same body of Christ in generall do rejoice and mourne with them, according to the law of theire nere relation in Christ.

21y. From that which is a maine ground for perticular church communion, viz., to keepe each other pure and to cleare the profession of the Gospell from scandale which cannot be done (1 Cor. 5.5) unless orderly walking churches be owned orderly and disorderly churches be orderly disowned, even as disorderly walking members of a perticular church, yea, the reason is more full in respect of the greater scandale by not witnessing against the defection (2 Cor. 7.11) of a church or churches.

31y. For the proofe of their love to all saints, perticular church communion being never appointed as a restraint of our love which should be manifest its selfe to all the churches.

41y. The worke of God, wherein all the churches are concerned togather, may be the more easily and prosperously carried on by a combination of prayers and endeavors.

51y. From need they have or may have one of another to quicken them when lukewarme, to helpe when in want, assist in counsell in doubtfull matters and prevent prejudices in each against other.

61y. To convince the world, for by this shall men know by one marke that we are the true churches of Christ. In order thereunto we unanimously agreed at our next meeting to declaire the principles and constitutions of the respective churches to which wee belong.

These things to be offred to the churches to be approved.

It was alsoe agreed to give notice to other neighbouring churches of our next meeting which is appointed to be at Wormsley one the 3rd day of the 9th month and that a coppie hereof should be transmitted to them with our desire for theire concurrence in order to that communion before specified.

D. The Abingdon Association, 1657

The seventeenth General Meeting.

At the meeting at Tetsworth the 20th, 21st and 22nd of the 3rd moneth 1657. . . .

It hath bene for some time sadly observed by us that there hath appeared a great neglect in the churches in taking care to provide a maintenance for the comfortable supply of a [spiritual] ministerie, according to what the rule doth require, which hath brought some to pinching povertie, run others upon desperate temptations and occasioned some to fall into sinfull disorders to the dishonour of their high and holy calling. And, we feare, made the work of the ministrie not onely uncomfortable to the teachers but unprofitable to the hearers. We shall not name particular persons nor instance particular cases, supposing they cannot be unknowne unto you. Onely in generall we have this account to give you, that as the conditions of severall nearer to us which we have had some knowledge of, doth call for reliefe and assistance, so also we have lately received an account from our brother Abraham Chayer of the poore and low condition of severall brethren employed in the worke of the ministrie in the westerne churches which, although modestly and sparingly expressed by our brother yet, from what was said, we could not but gather that their want is very great. And the want of a comfortable supply for themselves and their families is a great discouragement to them in the work of the Lord and an obstruction to the propagation of the Gospell among the churches and to the world. . . .

And because we find in the apostolike times the churches did hold an association together in their contributions that so it might be done by an equalitie and not some eased whiles others are burdened we thought it our dutie to commend it unto you and desire you to commend it to the severall churches to which you belong that they would consider:

1. Whether they take care for the maintaining of those which are their pastours or elders whose setled abode is with them and which are taken off from their civill employments to serve the Lord and the church in the worke of the ministrie.

2. What they can spare (their owne ministrie and poore being provided for) towards the maintenance of a publike ministrie to preach the Gospell to the world and for the reliefe of those where the churches to whom they doe belong are not able to maintaine them. And to put it into a joynt stock to be issued forth according as the conditions of persons employed in the work of the ministrie shall require.

We shall not use many arguments to excite you to a worke [of] this nature. Onely we desire you would consider two things (i) your duty (ii) the necessitie of the case. . . .

But these things we hope are knowne to you as well as ourselves and therefore we shall not enlarge but commend both you and this worke to the blessing of the Lord, leaving ourselves as your patterne and example, hoping that the Lord will enlarge your bowells and the churches' in generall towards the maintenance of his poore ministers, knowing that he that giveth to a prophet in the name of a prophet shall receive a prophet's reward and your charitie in this respect will be not onely acceptable to the saints but an odour of a sweet smell, a sacrifice acceptable and well-pleasing to God who, we desire, may supply all your need out of his riches in glorie by Christ Jesus and remaine,

Your affectionate brethren in Gospell faith and order,

> Richard Deane, John Cox, Thomas Paul, Edward Grainge, Richard Mariman, Henrie Jackson, George Gosfright, John Sowdin etc. . . .

2.10 The Controversy on Singing

To sing or not to sing as a part of worship; that question troubled English Christians, including Baptists, during the seventeenth century. Some regarded singing as worldly and carnal, while others argued that it was both biblical and appropriate for worship. The talented Baptist layman, Isaac Marlow, was an outspoken opponent of singing. His several works against singing were directed mostly against Benjamin Keach, the London pastor who was Particular Baptists' most effective spokesman for singing. *Source:* Isaac Marlow, *The Controversie on Singing Brought to an End* (London: n.p. 1696), 1-13. Copy in the Angus Collection, Regents Park College, Oxford.

Benjamin Keach (1640-1704) is important in Baptist history for many reasons. He was an outstanding Particular Baptist pastor, held and practiced advanced views on denominational organization, was a writer and theologian of note, and pioneered in religious education and literature for children. However, he is best remembered as the man who taught Baptists to sing. Against stout opposition he led his church to adopt singing as part of worship, collected and published early Baptist hymnals, and offered a most cogent and convincing defense of singing. Of Keach's several works on the subject, perhaps the most important is *The Breach Repair'd in God's Worship* (1700). What seems a mere historical curiosity today was a burning issue at that time. *Source:* Benjamin Keach, *The Breach Repair'd in God's Worship: or Singing of Psalms, Hymns, and Spiritual Songs proved to be an Holy Ordinance of Jesus Christ*, 2nd ed. (London: n.p., 1700), Epistle Dedicatory, 3-12. From the Angus Collection, Regent's Park College, Oxford.

A. Isaac Marlow, *The Controversie on Singing Brought to an End.*

The Author's Epistle.

Christian Reader,

While Truth and Righteousness, Errors and Unfaithfulness are on Earth, there is like to be continual Differences in the Minds and Sentiments of Men: But our Grievance is the present Troubles that have risen from some Elders and Ministers of our own Profession, who have held such Notions as are repugnant to the light of Scripture, the known Principles of the body of the Baptized Churches, and that strike at a Foundation principle of Ours, and the Protestants Reformation more in general, as may be seen in the Sequel of this Treatise.

Therefore, considering they have laboured to vindicate the common way of Singing in Gospel-worship, and have manifested their minds, that a Church of Christ has liberty as it shall judge most for Edification to Order many Modes of Divine Worship that are not particularly prescribed in the Word, and also so far for a mixed Church-Communion as to give us ground to fear they design to alter our Churches Foundation-principles of Separation, and of holding the Sacred Scriptures to be our only Rule to determine many Modes of Divine Worship, I think it is but reasonable to enquire of them, Whether they have found a Medium between holding and not holding Communion with false Modes of Worship? And, Whither if they shake down the Churches Settlement, without proposing some other Form of Constitution, they leave it not doubtful to us whether they mean to rebuild them on other Constitutive Principles, or leave them waste for their own pleasures?

So that being sensible of the need there is to appear for the Baptized Interest in these parts, I have drawn up several things, with a Breviate of the Scripture-grounds and reasons for rejecting that way of Worship, and the rather because my Principles about it have been grossly abused in Mr. Keach's Breach Repaired, unto which I have made a large Reply: Yet considering that but few of them has been seen in our Churches about London, I have published the following Discourses, hoping my Brethren will seriously peruse them, impartially to judge thereof, and to escape the mischiefs of Seductions.

The Question between us and our Brethren is not, Whether any such thing as vocal melodious Singing is exhorted unto in the New Testament, for this we freely own; but the Controversie lyes herein, viz. 1. Whether the Saints were moved to the exercise of it in the Apostles time, only as an extraordinary Spiritual Gift, depending on Divine Inspiration, as some other Gifts did, or that it was appointed as a constant Gospel-Ordinance in the Church, in an Ordinary Administration also. 2. In what External manner it was then exercised, whether in a prestinted form of words, made in Artificial Rhimes, or as the Spirit by his more immediate dictates gave them utterance. And, 3. Who it was that sung; whether the Minister sung alone, or with him a promiscuous Assembly of Professors and profane Men and Women, with united Voices together.

Now to resolve these Questions, we must either refer them for determination to the Authority of God's Word, or of Mens Traditions: If we refer them to humane Authority, we may quickly find enough of it for all the Superstitious Ceremonies in the Christian World: But if we refer them to the Word of God, they have lost their Cause, and their own express Confessions and silent Concessions has barred their setting up their practice of Singing by any Authority of the Holy Scriptures. For tho' there's a plain Rule and Directions for Singing in the New Testament, yet it being repugnant to their practice, they have refused to sing by it, and said that there is no other way prescribed or laid down how they should sing, but as God's People sang under the Law.

We might have thought therefore that their Mode of Singing had been after the Legal Pattern; but we find their Practice is contrary to this also, for it was an Office under the Law to sing in Public Worship, and it was confined to the Order of Singers among the Levites; and our Brethren are not able to cite us one Text of Scripture in the whole Bible, to shew that ever the Ministers and People sang with conjoined Voices in the Instituted Worship of God under the Law: Nor can they maintain their Mode of Singing as being a moral Duty, unless they can prove that men have a Natural Gift most aptly to sing their Praises together in metrical Rhimes. And therefore seeing their Practice can neither be justified by the Scriptures, nor as the simple Gift of Nature (as you will find it clearly manifested in the following Treatise) it has nothing else to support it but Humane Art, for it's neither Scriptural, Spiritual, nor simply Natural, but Artificial Worship, that pleaseth Nature and not God; and if our People will have it, right or wrong, they must answer for it at the Judgment-seat of Christ, where I expect to stand the tryal of these Controversies with our Brethren.

London, Aug. the 4th, 1695.

I.M.

The Controversie of Singing Brought to an End.

A Tract on Singing.

That prelimited Forms of praising God, vocally sung by all the Church together, is no Gospel-Ordinance, I have proved already in my former Treatise, ... Therefore this little Tract, or partly Abstract, is chiefly designed to reach those Members of our Churches, especially about London, that have not seen my larger Treatises. To proceed therefore on the Subject matter before us.

First, I do on good ground affirm, There is no Example nor Command for such a Practice in the Worship of God under the Law: There is no such thing in the Old Testament, that the Church of God, Ministers and People, Men and Women, did ever vocally sing together in instituted Church worship. . . .

Secondly, Neither do our Brethren sing after the Example of the Primitive Christians in the first Gospel Churches: For the matter of their Songs was not in a prestinted form of words, but was then given more immediately to the Gospel-Ministers, by an extraordinary Inspiration of the Holy Ghost. . . .

Thirdly, The singing practised in the primitive Gospel-Churches, differed from the common way of singing now in use, in that the Ministers of those Churches which had the Gift of Singing delivered their New-Testament-Songs in the Church, as they did other Gifts in a ministerial way, by a single voice, and not with the conjoined voices of all the Church together; for the Apostle saith, I (not We) will pray with the Spirit, and I will pray with the understanding also. I (not We) will sing with the Spirit, and I will sing with the understanding also: Else when thou shalt bless with the Spirit, how shall he that occupieth the room of the unlearned, say, Amen, at thy giving of thanks, seeing he understandeth not what thou sayest. . . . Moreover, as the Holy Apostle has there shewed, how Singing and Prayer is to be delivered in the Church, by a single Person, with a single Voice, so in the following part of the same Chapter he has left us a confirmation thereof, by laying down the general Rule for delivering the ministerial Gifts of the Holy Spirit, 1 Cor. 14.16, etc. . . .

Fourthly, The Women's vocal singing in the Church, a practice in common use, is chargeable with breaking the positive and express Laws of Christ, which are so plainly, clearly and fully worded, that I know not how such Women can satisfie their Consciences in this practice, unless it be through ignorance of the Scriptures wherein it is forbidden; nor how any Gospel-Ministers can open their Mouths for it, seeing Women are commanded not to teach, nor to speak in the Church, but to learn in silence, and to be in silence; for the Apostle's Words imply, that for Women not to learn in silence in the Church, but to break their silence there, by teaching or speaking in proper Church-worship, is a usurpation of Authority, and Disobedience to the Law, 1 Cor. 14.34, 1 Tim. 2.11, 12.

B.   Benjamin Keach, *The Breach Repair'd in God's Worship*

The Epistle Dedicatory to all the
Baptized Congregations in England and Wales,

Who are in God the Father, and in our Lord Jesus Christ, Grace, Mercy and Peace be multiplied,
Particularly to the Church of Christ, meeting on Horselydown.
Holy and Beloved,

It cannot but rejoice my Soul, when I consider of the exceeding Grace and abounding Goodness of the Holy God towards you his poor and despised Church and People, in respect of that clear Discovery he hath given you of most of the glorious Truths of the Gospel, and of the true Apostolical Faith and Practice thereof. You have not made Men, General Councils, nor Synods, your Rule, but God's Holy Word: your Constitution, Faith, and Discipline, is directly according to the Primitive Pattern; God hath made you (in a most eminent manner) to be the Builders of the old Wastes, and Raisers up of the former Desolations, and Repairers of the waste Cities, the Desolations of many Generations, Isa. 61.4.

You have laboured to sever the Gold from the Dross, and to build with proper and fit Gospel-Materials, viz., Spiritual and Living Stones, well hewed and squared by the Hammer of God's Word and Spirit, and will not take one Stone of Babylon for a Corner; you will go forth (as far as you have received Light) by the Footsteps of the Flock, and feed your Kids beside the Shepherds Tents, Cant. 1.8.

And God of a small People hath graciously made you a Multitude; you have been helped, and so born up by everlasting Arms, that you have held fast your Holy Profession in the Day of Trial, and exposed all that you have had in the World to spoil and loss, for the sake of Jesus Christ, when many turned their Backs, and exposed the Holy Name of God to Reproach; and to our further Joy, many of you have of late, more especially in your General Assemblies, shewed your great Zeal for the Name of God, and Care of his Church, in a more than usual manner; and particularly you have endeavoured to revive our hopes, for the continuation of a faithful and laborious Ministry for the time to come, by striving to promote such Learning and Studies as God's Word directs to; and not require (like Israel's Task-Masters) poor Ministers, as I may so say, to make Brick and allow them no Straw; but you do now more fully see that Gospel-Ministers ought to have a Gospel-Maintenance, . . . and then, Brethren, what can or will be wanting to make you compleat in the whole Will of God? Truly, according to my small Light, I know not, unless it be a restoration of this lost and neglected Ordinance of Singing Psalms, Hymns and Spiritual Songs, which I fear, and partly understand, some of you want light in. I have therefore made bold to dedicate this small Treatise to you all, hoping you will take it from me in good part, and well weigh what is here said, before you judge and condemn it for an Errour. . . .

I have been provoked by our Brother [Isaac Marlow], who wrote against Singing, to set Pen to Paper, and not only by him and his Book, but I have been induced by Multitudes, for several Months, to give him an Answer, so that I hope you will not be offended with me in what I have done. I have much Peace in the doing of it; and truly, Brethren, the loss of this Ordinance doth, I am afraid, more obstruct the increase of our Churches than many are aware of. What a Multitude are convinced of Christ's true Baptism, and yet refuse to have Communion with our Churches when baptized, because they say, if they should, they must lose this Ordinance of Singing, which they have an equal Esteem for: And how doth it open the Mouths of our Godly Brethren of other Persuasions, to speak against us for being so zealous for one Gospel-Ordinance, and so careless about another, that very few Christians, who have had the greatest Light, Zeal and Piety in any Age of the Church, ever doubted of? It grieves me to think there should be a Breach made in God's Worship among you, to whom God hath given so much Light in other Cases. And, O that what is here said, might through the Blessing of God prove a Means to repair it.

In a Word, Singing is injoyned: Some thing it is: If we have it not (but 'tis with you) we would willingly know what your Singing is, or what you call singing: For we do say and testify, we believe you are wholly without Singing in any proper Sense at all. The Lord give us Moderation; don't let us be bitter one against another.

I shall beg a part in your Prayers, and intreat you to look over what Weakness you may see in this small Tract, for I am, you know, but a Babe in Christ's School, and know but in part.

And now to you, my Beloved Brethren and Sisters, . . . I am persuaded 'tis for want of Consideration, for you have no new thing brought in among you. Hath not the Church sung at breaking of Bread always for 16 or 18 Years last past, and could not, nor would omit it in the time of the late Persecution? And have not many of the honest Hearers (who have stayed to see that Holy Administration) sung with you, at that time, and yet none of you ever signified the least trouble? And have we not for this 12 or 14 Years sung in mixt Assemblies, on Days of Thanksgiving, and never any offended at it, as ever I heard? What is done more now? 'tis only practiced oftner: and sure if it be God's Ordinance, the often practising of it, by such who find their Hearts draw out so to do, cannot be sinful.

And on that Solemn Day, when the Church would have it put up, to see how the Members stood affected about Singing, almost every ones Hand was up for it, or to give Liberty to the Church at such times to sing. And when put up in the Negative, but about 5 or 6 at most (as I remember) were against it. Did any one of you, at that time say, if we did proceed to sing at such times, you could not have Communion with us? which if you had, I perceive the Church, nay every one of us who had born our Burden for many Years, would have born it a little longer? Besides, did not the Church agree to sing only after Sermon, and when Prayer was ended? And if those few Brethren and Sisters who were not satisfied, could not stay whilst we sung, they might freely go forth, and we would not be offended with them; so far was the Church, or my self, from imposing on the Consciences of any. . . . The matter of Difference that is at present between the Church and some few of our dear and beloved Brethren and Sisters, is not about Singing itself, nor singing with others, for that has been all along the practise of the Church for many Years (as before I hinted) but only about singing on the Lords Day, unless it be one Member, except the Judgments of any other are lately changed. . . .

If any of you should say, How can we be satisfied to have Communion with the Church, when we believe 'tis an Innovation? (that's a hard word.) Are you Infallible? Is there not ground for you to fear you are mistaken, or to think in the least 'tis a doubtful case, since so much is to be said for it, and has been so generally received from the beginning by most enlightned Saints, and you your selves with the Church for so long a time been in the Practice of it at other times?

Besides, can you find any ground from God's Word, that will warrant you to separate your selves from the Church upon this account? and also may not the same or like Scruple rise in our Spirits against having Communion with you, who we believe lie short of a plain Gospel-Ordinance, and so, through want of light, diminish from God's Word, as you say we add thereto be doing of it? But far be it from us to have a thought to act that way towards any of you. Moreover, will not such a practice, or a Separation from the Church upon this account, justify other Godly Christians, who are Members of such Churches who do not sing, (that are convinced as well as we it is their Duty) to separate from those Congregations, to joyn with such Churches as are in this practice? . . .

I shall conclude with the words of the Holy Apòstle, Finally, Brethren, farewell: be Perfect, be of good Comfort be of one Mind, live in Love and Peace, and the God of Love and Peace shall be with you. 2 Cor. 13.11.

Which is the Prayer of him who is, Your unworthy Brother, fellow Servant, and poor Labourer in God's Harvest,

B. Keach. From my house near Horselydown, Southwark, April 3rd, 1691.

2.11   *Heart Bleedings for Professors Abominations,* **1650**

In 1650 the "Churches of Christ in London, Baptized" issued a treatise emphasizing the authority of Scripture in an effort to counteract the "inner light" teaching of the Quakers who downgraded the Bible as a "meer history." *Heart Bleedings* bears the mark of William Kiffin, one of several Particular Baptists who signed it. This is the earliest known example of Baptists using the term *infallible* to describe the Bible. *Source: Heart Bleedings for Professors Abominations* (London, 1650), 11. Copy in the Angus Collection, Regent's Park College, Oxford.

If we search the Scriptures we shall see cleerly that Jesus Christ was not a figure or shadow of a substance . . . but the true substantial good itself, the true mediator God and man . . . Hence we may safely conclude,

First, That if Christ be a substantial Mediator, truly spiritual, his Gospel then, which he and his Apostles hath declared, is not a bare outward Relation, History, or carnal Letter, but a spiritual and substantial truth and Mystery, containing the whole Minde, Will, and Law of God for us and all Saints to believe and practice throughout all ages.

Secondly, It must needs be as durable as the Mediator is, for the Law of Christs Priesthood is as durable as the Priesthood itself. . . .

Thirdly, It must be granted, That the Scriptures which do declare this great mystery of Jesus Christ and his Gospel, be the holy Scriptures, and the infallible Word of God, for it could never have entered into the heart of man to have known or manifested those hidden mysteries, had not God himself by his own Word revealed them from heaven; now the Scriptures are Gods Word, declaring his Minde, making known his Counsel, being able to make the people of God wise unto salvation through faith which is in Jesus Christ, being given by inspiration of God . . . and therefore not to be slighted and undervalued, as a dead Letter, a bare History, a carnal empty Story.·

3
Defending the Faith

Excerpts from several different treatises are included in this chapter to illustrate the English Baptist struggle for religious liberty. These documents express the major ideas from Scripture, history, and daily life that Baptists used to advance their argument that religious liberty for all is the best policy.

In addition to treatises and arguments, selection 3.5 is taken from the records of a church in Bristol to show how religious restrictions affected one congregation, and how the people responded. No doubt, countless other churches, most of which left no such detailed records, went through similar experiences.

The chapter concludes with an excerpt from relevant sections of the Act of Toleration of 1689. While this legislation did not bring what we know today as full religious liberty, it did allow the greatest degree of toleration known at the time. In the next chapter we will see that these Baptist arguments for religious liberty, first developed and expressed in England, also had an impact in colonial America.

3.1 John Smyth, On Religious Liberty

In his confession of 1612 John Smyth addressed the issue of religious liberty in article 84. Despite its brevity, this is one of the most complete statements of religious liberty of that generation. Smyth and early Baptists advocated complete liberty for all. Although the confession does not use the terms "separation of church and state," that concept is clearly present. *Source:* William L. Lumpkin, ed., *Baptist Confessions of Faith* (Philadelphia: Judson Press, 1959), 140.

84. That the magistrate is not by virtue of his office to meddle with religion, or matters of conscience, to force or compel men to this or that form of religion, or doctrine: but to leave Christian religion free, to every man's conscience, and to handle only civil transgressions (Rom. xiii), injuries and wrongs of man against man, in murder, adultery, theft, etc., for Christ only is the king, and lawgiver of the church and conscience (James iv. 12).

3.2 Thomas Helwys, *The Mistery of Iniquity,* 1612

Thomas Helwys (c.1570-c.1615) helped John Smyth form a Baptist church in Amsterdam in 1609, and brought a remnant back to England in 1611 to preserve the Baptist witness. His major book, *A Short Declaration of the Mistery of Iniquity,* had apocalyptic overtones as the title clearly reveals. In this book Helwys identifies the Roman Church as the first beast of Revelation, and he indicts the Anglican Church for aping the first beast, the Puritans for their compromise, and the Separatists for their incomplete separation. However, the most enduring emphasis is the insistent and sometimes eloquent plea for complete religious liberty for all.

Apparently Helwys tried to present a copy of the *Mistery* to King James and, failing that, sent a copy to the king with a personal note in the flyleaf. *Source:* Thomas Helwys, *A Short Declaration of the Mistery of Iniquity,* 1612. Reprinted by Kingsgate Press, London, 1935.

To the Reader

The feare of the almighty . . . having now at last overweyed in us the feare of men, wee have thus farr by the direction of Gods word and spirit stretched out our harts and hands with bouldness to confesse the name of Christ before men, and to declare to Prince and People plainly their transgressions, that all might heare, & see their fearefull estate and standing, and repent, and turne unto the lord. . . . in this writing wee have with all humble bouldness spoken unto our lord the King, and our defence for this is, that wee are taught of God especially to make supplications, praiers, intercessions, and give thankes for our lord the King: . . .

Now as wee have . . . thus farr confessed Christs name before men by writing, so wee shall (the lord assisting us) be ready, as wee hold our selves bound to confesse Christ before men by word of mouth, not fearing (through Gods grace) them that kill the body and after that are not able to do anie more. . . .

Tho. Helwys.

The Principal matters handled in the Booke.

A Declaration with proofe, that these are the days of greatest tribulation, spoken of by Christ.Mat.24. wherein the abomination of desolation is seen to be set in the holy place.

That there hath bene a generall departing from the faith, and an utter desolation of all true Religion.

That the Prophecie of the first Beast. Revel.13. is fulfilled under the Romish spirituall power and goverment.

That the Prophecie of the Second Beast is fulfilled under the spirituall power & Goverment of Arch-Bishops & lord Bishops. . . .

That God hath given unto the K. an earthly kingdome with all earthly power against the which, none may resist but must in all thinges obey, willingly, either to do, or suffer.

That Christ alone is K. of Israel, & sitts upon Davids Throne, & that the K. ought to be a subject of his Kingdome.

That none ought to be punished either with death or bonds for transgressing against the spirituall ordinances of the new Testament, and that such Offences ought to be punished onely with spirituall swords and censures.

That as the Romish Hyrarchy say in words they cannot err: so the Hyrarchy of Crch-Bs. & lord Bs. shew by their deeds, they hold they cannot err: & herein they agree in one.

The false profession of Puritan-isme (so-called) & the false Prophets thereof discovered. . . .

The false profession of Brownisme (so-called) plainely laid open with their false Prophetts, and with their false supposed seperation from the world. . . .

Some perticular errors in Mr. Robinsons book of justification of Separation, laid open. . . .

The Mistery of Iniquity

If you [church and state authorities] wil yet justifie your selves in these things and make shewe of your selves to bee the servants off the Lambe, and not the servants of the Beast, then stand forth and defend your Kingdome and cause, with the spiritual swerd of the Lambe, which is the word of God. . . . And if you can prove by Gods word that wee ought to say prayers, as you command us, we wil both sing and say as you bid us. . . .

Our lord the King hath power to take our sonnes & our daughters to do all his services of warr, and of peace, yea all his servile service whatsoever, and he hath power to take our lands & our goods of what sort or kind soever, or the tenth thereof to use at his will: and he hath power to take our men servants, and our maid servants, and the chiefe of our yong men, and Cattle, and put them to his worke: and wee are to be his servants. . . .

Also he hath power to make all manner [of] Governors lawes and ordinances of man

1.Pet. 2.13.14. Thus doth God give our lord the King power to demaund and take what he will of his subjects, & it is to be yeilded him and to comaund what ordinance of man he will, and wee are to obey it. And in all these things we acknowledge before God & men we ought to be subject. . . .

Doth not the King knowe that the God of Gods, and lord of Lords, . . . hath reserved to himself a heavenly kingdom, . . . & that with this kingdome, our lord the King hath nothinge to do . . . but as a subject himself: and that Christ is King alone, . . .

. . . Our lord the King will easily see that as Queene Mary by hir sword of Justice had no power over her subjects consciences (for then had she power to make them all Papists, and all that resisted hir therein suffered justly as evil doers) neither hath our lord the King by that sword of justice power over his subjects consciences: . . . .

And we bow our selves to the earth . . . beseeching the K. to judg righteous judgment herein, whether there be so unjust a thing, and of so great cruel tyranny, under the sunne, as to force mens consciences in their religion to God, seeing that if they err, they must pay the price of their transgression with the losse of their soules. Oh let the K. judg, is it not most equall that men should shuse their religion themselves seeing they onely must stand themselves before the judgment seat of God to answere for themselves, when it shalbe no cause for them to say, wee were commanded or compelled to be of this religion, by the King, or by them that had authority from him. . . .

Let our lord the K. in all happiness & prosperity sitt in his owne Princes throne of that mighty Kingdome of Great Britanne, Which God hath given to the King and to his posterity. . . . And let our lord Jesus Christ in power and Majesty sitt upon Davids throne, the throne of the Kingdome of Israell, which his father hath given unto him, & let Christ according to his owne wisdome judg his people Israel [the church], and let our [lord] the K. be his subject. . . .

Will our lord the K. being him self but a subject of Christs Kingdome, take upon him by his Kingly power to make Primates, Metropolitans, Arch Bishops, and lord Bishops to be lords in the Kingdome of Christ, and over the heritage of God! And will our lord the K. do this against the whole rule of Gods word wherein this is no one tittle to warrant our lord the K. thertoo. Will not our lord the K. be supplicated by the humble petition of his servants to examine his power & authority herein! Farr is it from the harts of us the Kings servants to move the King to depart from the least tittle of his right that belongs to his Royall Crowne & dignity: and farr be it from the King to take from Christ Jesus anie one part of that power & honor which belongs to Christ in his Kingdome.

Wee still pray our lord the King that wee may be free from suspect, for haveing anie thoughts of provoking evil against them of the Romish religion in regard to their profession, if they be true & faithfull subjects to the King, for wee do freely professe, that our lord the King hath no more power over their consciences then ours, and that is none at all: for our lord the King is but an earthly King, and if the Kings people be obedient & true subjects, obeying all humane lawes made by the King, our lord the King can require no more. For mens religion to God, is betwixt God and themselves; the King shall not answer for it, neither may the King be judg betwene God and man.

Let them be heretikes, Turks, Jewes, or whatsoever, it apperteynes not to the earthly power to punish them in the least measure.

3.3 Leonard Busher, *Religion's Peace*, 1614

Whether Busher was English or Dutch is unknown, but he was apparently a part of the Baptist beginnings in Amsterdam. He issued *Religion's Peace: or A Plea for Liberty of Conscience* in 1614, and though it may have been published in Amsterdam, the book was widely circulated in

England. It was the first Baptist treatise devoted entirely to religious liberty, and Busher makes a strong and reasonably objective case. For years this treatise was known only in a 1646 reprint, but recently a copy of the 1614 edition has surfaced. Busher's sixteen reasons against religious persecution form the heart of the book. *Source:* Leonard Busher, *Religion's Peace: or A Plea for Liberty of Conscience* (London: n.p., 1646). Reprinted in Edward Bean Underhill, ed., *Tracts on Liberty of Conscience and Persecution,* 1614-1661 (London: J. Haddon, 1846), 1-81.

To the High and Mighty King JAMES, *by the grace of God King of Great Britain, France, and Ireland, and to the Princely and Right Honourable Parliament,* LEONARD BUSHER *wisheth the wisdom of Solomon, the zeal of Josias, and the mercy of Christ, with the salvation of your spirits in the day of the Lord Jesus.*

Forasmuch as your majesty and parliament do stand for the maintenance of the religion wherein you are born, and for the same do most zealously persecute with fire and sword; I have thought it good, and also my duty, most royal sovereign, to inform your majesty and parliament thereof. In all humility, therefore, I give you to understand, that no prince or people can possibly attain that one true religion of the gospel, which is acceptable to God by Jesus Christ, merely by birth.

For Christ saith, *Except a man be born again, he cannot see the kingdom of God.* . . . Therefore Christ commanded this word to be preached to all nations, that thereby they may attain the new birth. . . .

But your majesty and parliament may please to understand, that the scriptures do teach, that the one true religion is gotten by a new birth, even by the word and Spirit of God, . . . Seeing, then, the one true religion of the gospel is thus gotten, and thus defended and maintained—namely, by the word preached only; let it please your majesty and parliament to be intreated to revoke and repeal those antichristian, Romish, and cruel laws, that force all in our land, both prince and people, to receive that religion wherein the king or queen were born, or that which is established by the law of man. . . .

Therefore may it please your majesty and parliament to understand that, by fire and sword, to constrain princes and peoples to receive that one true religion of the gospel, is wholly against the mind and merciful law of Christ, dangerous both to king and state, a means to decrease the kingdom of Christ, and a means to increase the kingdom of antichrist; . . .

And no king nor bishop can, or is able to command faith; *That is the gift of God, who worketh in us both the will and the deed of his own good pleasure.* Set him not a day, therefore, in which, if his creature hear not and believe not, you will imprison and burn him. Paul was a blasphemer and also a persecutor, and could not be converted by the apostles and ministers of Christ; yet at last was received to mercy, and converted extraordinarily by Christ himself, . . . And as kings and bishops cannot command the wind, so they cannot command faith; . . . You may force men to church against their consciences, but they will believe as they did afore. . . .

Your majesty and parliament shall understand, that all those *that confess,* freely, without compulsion, *that Jesus is the Messiah,* the Lord, *and that he came in flesh,* are to be esteemed the children of God and true Christians, seeing such are *born of God;* and *no man can say that Jesus is the Lord, but by the Holy Ghost,* therefore not to be persecuted. . . .

I read that a bishop of Rome would have constrained a Turkish emperor to the Christian faith, unto whom the emperor answered, "I believe that Christ was an excellent prophet, but he did never, so far as I understand, command that men should, with the power of weapons, be constrained to believe his law; and verily I also do force no man to believe Mahomet's law." Also I read that Jews, Christians, and Turks, are tolerated in Constantinople, and yet are peaceable, though so contrary the one to the other.

If this be so, how much more ought Christians not to force one another to religion? AND HOW MUCH MORE OUGHT CHRISTIANS TO TOLERATE CHRISTIANS, WHEN AS THE TURKS DO TOLERATE THEM? SHALL WE BE LESS MERCIFUL THAN THE TURKS? OR SHALL WE LEARN THE TURKS TO PERSECUTE CHRISTIANS? IT IS NOT ONLY UNMERCI-FUL, BUT UNNATURAL AND ABOMINABLE; YEA, MONSTROUS FOR ONE CHRISTIAN TO VEX AND DESTROY ANOTHER FOR DIFFERENCE AND QUESTIONS OF RELIGION. And though tares have overgrown the wheat, yet Christ will have them let alone till harvest. . . .

Now, therefore, I humbly beseech you, suffer not your bishops and ministers any longer to persuade [you] to force your subjects, or any others, to their faith and church by persecution; neither suffer them therewith to defend their faith and church against their adversaries. If they have not any thing from God's word against us, let them yield and submit themselves. If they think they have any thing against us, let them betake themselves only to God's word, both in word and writing. . . . With which scripture, and not with fire and sword, your majesty's bishops and ministers ought to be armed and weaponed. And whosoever shall not hear the words of such bishops and ministers, then such bishops and ministers are commanded by Christ, not to imprison, burn, banish, and hang them; but *to shake the dust of their feet against them, for a witness,* . . . And this commandment of Christ did his bishops and ministers obey, as you may read. By which, and by that which follows, your gracious majesty and princely and honourable parliament, may perceive the will and mind of our Lord and Saviour Christ: unto whose mercy I commend you, . . . Amen.

Your faithful and loving subject,

LEONARD BUSHER.

CERTAIN REASONS AGAINST PERSECUTION.

First—Because Christ hath not commanded any king, bishop, or minister to perse-cute the people for difference of judgment in matters of religion.

Secondly—Because Christ hath commanded his bishops and ministers to persuade prince and people to hear and believe the gospel, by his word and Spirit, . . . and not, as tyrants, to force and constrain them by persecution. . . .

Seventhly—Because if persecution be not laid down, and liberty of conscience set up, then cannot the Jews, nor any strangers, nor others contrary-minded, be ever converted in our land. For so long as they know aforehand, that they shall be forced to believe against their consciences, they will never seek to inhabit there. . . .

Ninthly—Because if persecution continue, then the king and state shall have, against their will, many dissemblers in authority and office, both in court, city, and country. Yea, no man of any degree shall know, whether they are all faithful and true Christians that are about him, and with whom he hath to do: seeing most men will conform them-selves for fear of persecution, although in their hearts they hate and detest the religion whereto they are forced by law. . . .

Tenthly—Because if there be many religions in the land, as it is well known there are, then it will come to pass, through the continuance of persecution, that many religions will be continued in the church; seeing all are forced to church, who bring their reli-gions with them as well as their bodies. Whereby all their devotion is against their consciences, and all the church is a confused Babel, . . .

Eleventhly—Because Christ foretold, that *many false Christs and false prophets should arise, and deceive many; yea, if it were possible, the very elect.* . . . Therefore if persecution be not laid down and liberty of the gospel set up, you may persecute the true Christians instead of the false, as your predecessors have done. . . .

Twelfthly—Because persecution of such as do preach and teach Christ, is a great hindrance to the liberty of the gospel. FOR THEREBY ARE THE JEWS, TURKS, AND PAGANS OCCASIONED AND ENCOURAGED TO PERSECUTE LIKEWISE ALL SUCH AS PREACH AND TEACH CHRIST IN THEIR DOMINIONS . . .

Fourteenthly—Because the burning, banishing, hanging, and imprisoning of men and women by protestants, for difference of religion, do justify the burning, banishing, and imprisoning of men and women, by the papists, for difference of religion; even as the papists do justify the Turks and pagans in such like cruelty and tyranny. Wherein now are the protestants more merciful than the papists, or the papists than the Turks? . . .

Fifteenthly—Because his majesty and parliament would not willingly themselves be forced against their consciences, by the persecution of the bishop of Rome and his princes. So, I beseech them, according to the law Christ hath enjoined Christians, not by persecution to force other men's consciences against their wills, by the irritation [provocation] of the bishops of our land. . . .

Therefore persecution for difference in religion is a monstrous and cruel beast, that destroyeth both prince and people, hindereth the gospel of Christ, and scattereth his disciples that witness and profess his name. But permission of conscience in difference of religion, saveth both prince and people; for it is a meek and gentle lamb, which not only furthereth and advanceth the gospel, but also fostereth and cherisheth those that profess it. . . .

3.4   John Murton, *Persecution for Religion Judg'd and Condemn'd*

No author is listed for the following treatise, but most attribute it to John Murton, an associate and successor of Thomas Helwys as leader of General Baptists in London. The treatise first appeared in 1615, with revised editions in 1620 and 1662. In fact, these subsequent editions contained so much new material that they could be considered separate treatises. The title also changed; the title listed above was attached to the 1662 edition which is used here. *Source*: [John Murton], *Persecution for Religion Judg'd and Condemn'd in a Discourse between an Antichristian and a Christian* (n.p., printed 1615, 1620, and reprinted 1662). Also reprinted in Edward Bean Underhill, ed., *Tracts on Liberty of Conscience and Persecution, 1614-1661* (London: J. Haddon, 1846), 85-180.

To all that truly wish Jerusalem's prosperity and Babylon's destruction; wisdom and understanding be multiplied upon you.

In these days, if ever, that is true which the wise man said, *There is no end in making many books, and much reading is a weariness to the flesh:* yet considering how heinous it is in the sight of the Lord to force men and women by cruel persecutions, to bring their bodies to a worship whereunto they cannot bring their spirits; we thought it our duty, for God's glory, and the reformation thereof in this our own nation, to publish this little writing following, wherein is manifestly proved by the law of God, the law of our land, and his Majesty's own divers testimonies, that no man ought to be persecuted for his religion, be it true or false, so they testify their faithful allegiance to the king.

What shall men do striving about matters of religion till this be ended? For, if this be a truth, that the kings of the earth have power from God to compel by persecution all their subjects to believe as they believe, then wicked is it to resist, and the persecutions of such are justly upon them, and the magistrates that execute the same are clear from their blood, and it is upon their own heads: but if the kings of the earth have not power from God, to compel by persecution any of their subjects to believe as they believe, seeing faith is the work of God, then no less wicked is it in the sight of God to disobey, and the persecutions of such are upon the magistrates, and the blood of the persecuted crieth unto the Lord, and will be required at the magistrates' hands. . . .

Oh! that all that are in authority, would but consider by the word of God, which shall judge them at the last day, what they do, when they force men against their souls and consciences to dissemble to believe as they believe, or as the king and state believe: they would withdraw their hands and hearts therefrom, and never do as they have done, partly through inconsideration, and partly to please lord bishops being in favour with the king. . . .

And of the lord bishops we desire, that they would a little leave off persecuting those that cannot believe as they, till they have proved that God is well-pleased therewith, and the souls of such as submit [are] in safety from condemnation. Let them prove this, and we protest we will for ever submit unto them, and so will thousands: and therefore if there be any spark of grace in them, let them set themselves to give satisfaction, either by word or writing, or both. But if they will not, but continue their cruel courses as they have done, let them yet remember that they must come to judgment, and have their abominations set in order before them, and be torn in pieces when none shall deliver them.

And whereas they have no other colour of ground out of the scriptures, than that they have canonized a law, viz. "That whosoever shall affirm that the king's majesty hath not the same power over the church that the godly kings of Israel had under the law, let him be excommunicated *ipso facto*." The unsoundness of which ground is manifested in this dialogue following, wherein is showed their palpable ignorance, in that they know not the mystery of God; and therefore have they made this canon in flattery to the king, only to support their pride and cruelty. . . .

Oh! that any thing would prevail with them, to make them leave off these cruel courses, of persecuting poor souls that desire truly to fear God, and are most faithful subjects to the king, . . . And if it be a law for all Christians, that in indifferent things one must not offend another, but the strong [to] forbear rather than offend his weak brother, otherwise he *wounds the weak conscience, and sins against Christ;* then how much less hath any man power to be lord over the weak conscience, forcing it to practise that it hath not faith in, bringing it thereby unto sin, and unto condemnation.

We do unfeignedly acknowledge the authority of earthly magistrates, God's blessed ordinance, and that all earthly authority and command appertains unto them; let them command what they will, we must obey, either to do or suffer upon pain of God's displeasure, besides their punishment: but all men must let God alone with his right, which is to be lord and lawgiver to the soul, and not command obedience for God where he commandeth none. . . .   By Christ's unworthy Witnesses,

His Majesty's faithful Subjects:

Commonly (but most falsely) called

Ana-Baptists.

3.5   Persecution in the Broadmead Church, Bristol

Under laws of the Clarendon Code, persecution against Baptists in England took some new turns. Baptists suffered especially from the Conventicle Act (1664), which outlawed unauthorized religious gatherings of more than five persons beyond the immediate family. Records of the Broad-mead Church show how harshly this law was applied. The Baptists had to fear not only the authorities, but also religious bounty hunters who were paid to find and inform on illegal worship gatherings. One notes in the records the courage and constancy of both pastors and people, and various strategies they adopted to preserve their church life even in the midst of persecution. Their references to "the Bishops' men," the "tything men," and the "steeple houses" reveal the depth of Baptist antipathy to the state church system. During this time Baptists usually designated the days of the week and month by number, making it a point of conscience to avoid their pagan names. *Source:* Roger Hayden, ed., *The Records of a Church of Christ in Bristol, 1640-1687* (The Bristol Record Society, 1974), 128, 148-154. Used by permission.

7. This, our Seventh Persecution, in Sr Robert Yeaman's year, began 10 day, 3d mo. 1670.

Yᵉ first Lord's day after said 10th of 3d month, yᵉ Informers from yᵉ Bishop, (that was then one *Ironsides*) came upon us; and because we did not know which way they would begin upon us, we shutt our Publique Meeting-house door when we understood they were coming. Then they fetcht Constables and broake open yᵉ door, came in and tooke our names, for which some of us were brought before yᵉ Magistrates and Convicted. Then, against yᵉ next Lord's day, we broake a wall up on high for a window, and put yᵉ speaker in yᵉ next house to stand and preach, wherby we heard him as well as if in yᵉ roome with us. The Bishop's *Informers* come in againe, take our names; for which we were again brought before yᵉ Mayor, and Convicted. So they did yᵉ 3d Lord's day. And yᵉ fourth Lord's day, yᵉ Mayor himselfe, with his officers and some Aldm came upon us, and turned us out; but seeing they could not make us refraine our Meeting they Raised yᵉ Traine Bands every last day of yᵉ weeke in yᵉ Evening, one band to keep us out of our places, and Nailed up our doors, and putt locks upon them; so they kept us out by force and power, That we were faine to meet in yᵉ Lanes and highways for severall months. . . .

But though we had many good words from yᵉ Courte, gieveing hopes of continuing our Libertyes longer, yett in yᵉ 12 Month, Feb. Anᵒ 1674, yᵉ King, (somewhat before yᵉ Parliament's sitting, then coming nigh,) he sett forth a Proclamation (as) against Papists, but in yᵉ latter end of it Declared that all yᵉ Lycenses formerly given to yᵉ Dissenters were made void.

Then yᵉ Bishop and his clergy greately rejoiced that now they should have their wills on us; for now our foundation Plea at Law, by Lycenses, was taken away. Therefore yᵉ Bishop, being come home, and his Tribe, very speedily begin vigorously to bestir themselves, and lose no time: for yᵉ very same weeke this Proclamation came down to make void yᵉ Lycenses, yᵉ Bishop, with divers of his clergy, gott some of yᵉ Aldermen and some of yᵉ Military Officers together, and goes to Mr. Thompson's meeting, in yᵉ Castle, upon yᵉ 4th day of yᵉ weeke, his Lecture in yᵉ Middle of yᵉ weeke, being yᵉ 10th day of yᵉ 12 Month, Feb. 1674; where findeing of him preaching, they after search mett with him, (where yᵉ People had conveighed him away, in another parte of yᵉ house, against yᵉ freenesse of his owne minde). And soe they laid hands on him, and brought him before yᵉ Mayor, to his Mansion house, where, after long Examination and discourse, about Nine of yᵉ Clock at night, yᵉ Mayor, Bishop, and some Aldermen Commit *Mr. Thompson* to Newgate Prisson for 6 months. Then, as follows, they Imprisson other Ministers. . . .

Then UPON yᵉ 14th day of said 12th month, Feb. 1674, yᵉ next Lord's day following Mr. Thompson's commitment, yᵉ Mayor, Ralph Ollive, with Alderman Hicks and Alderman Lawford, and yᵉ Mayor's serjeants, came to Mr. Weekes' meeting, and to our Meeting; and they finding Mr. Hardcastle preaching, as alsoe Mr. Weekes,.they Carryed them both away, and committed them to yᵉ Custodie of a Chief constable untill yᵉ Morrow. Then Mr. Hardcastle and Mr. Weekes were brought before yᵉ Mayor, to yᵉ Towlzy, where yᵉ Oathes in yᵉ Corporation Act were tendered them. But they no wayes embracing it were againe committed to yᵉ Constable untill yᵉ Evening, and then sent to

Newgate Prisson, to Mr. Thompson. And when Sheriff Fielding, about 10 o'Clock at Night, had brought them to yᵉ Prisson door, he deridingly bid Mr. Weekes take his leave of all his *holy Brethren.*

Now, three of our Ministers being Imprissoned, some of Each congregation, of yᵉ Brethren, mett together to Consult how to Carry on our meetings, that we might keepe to our duty, and Edify one another now our Pastours were gone. Some even were ready of thinking to give off, viz., of yᵉ Presbyterians; that they could not carry it on, Because of their Principle was not to hear a man not bred up at yᵉ university, and not Ordained. But yᵉ Lord appeared, and helped us to prevaile with them to hold on, and keep up their meetings. And for yᵉ first, and some time, we concluded this; to Come and Assemble together, and for one to Pray and read a Chapter, and then sing a Psalme, and after conclude with Prayer; and soe two Brethren to carry on yᵉ Meeting one day, and two another, for a while,—to try what they would doe with us. Soe we did, and Ordered one of yᵉ doors of our meeting place to be made fast, and all to come in at one, but open it when we goe forth; And to appoint some youth, or two of them, to be out at yᵉ door every meeting, to Watch when Hellier or other informers or officers were coming, and soe to come in, one of them, and give us notice thereof. Alsoe, some of yᵉ hearers, women and Sisters, would Sitt and Crowde in yᵉ Staires, when we did begin yᵉ Meeting with any Exercise, that soe yᵉ Informers might not too Suddainely come in upon us; by reason of which they were prevented divers times. . . .

UPON yᵉ 28th of yᵉ 12 Month, 1674, yᵉ Informers come to our meetings again. And at Br. Gifford's meeting, Hellier, with yᵉ Officers, finds him preaching againe; and now haveing a Warrant for him, they Carry him away before yᵉ Mayor, who bindes him to appear yᵉ next day; which being yᵉ 1st of March, or yᵉ first Month, yᵉ Mayor committs Mr. Gifford to prisson, to yᵉ Three Ministers before, for 6 months.

BUT one of yᵉ Ministers, namely *Mr. Thompson* who was first imprissoned, was very Sick when he came in, And although divers persons of note in this Citty, in yᵉ Compassion of their hearts for this sick Minister, did goe to yᵉ Mayor and Sheriffs, and to Sr John Knight, to gett leave that he might be permitted to goe home; but they could not prevaile. And his Physician Interceded that he might be removed out of that Stincking prisson, to some convenient house for Aire, and to Administer somewhat more conveniently to him, and he shewed yᵉ Danger of his condition; Yett notwithstanding they hardened their hearts, and would not graunt it, Because yᵉ Bishop would not give leave.

SOE THAT UPON yᵉ 4th of March, 1674 following, at 12 of yᵉ Clock in yᵉ night, Mr. Thompson, yᵉ said Imprissoned Minister for Jesus Christ, he *Departed* this life, in Newgate Prisson. He was a Corpulent, tall, big man; haveing layen in Prisson but about Three weekes 2 dayes; of that he was Sick about one weeke. Wherefore, being gross, could not keepe him; soe that yᵉ next day, being yᵉ 5th of March, he was Honourably Interred at Phillips's; Being Carryed from yᵉ Prisson to his grave; . . .

Now all yᵉ foresaid Churches, our Ministers being taken from us, one dead, and yᵉ rest Imprissoned, and we feared their death likewise in such a Bad Prisson, and we being pursued closely every meeting, hardly one Escaped, but we were followed by yᵉ Bishop's men, Hellier, or other informers, and officers from yᵉ Mayor. For our Partes, at our Meeting, we presently made use of our ministering gifts in yᵉ Church, (as we did in former persecutions, Contenting ourselves with meane gifts and coarse fare in yᵉ want of Better). Wherefore we considered which way to Maintaine our Meetings, by preserving our Speakers.

In order to which, at our owne Meeting, to prevent Spies that might come in yᵉ Roome as hearers,—and yet that noe strangers, or persons we knew not, might be hindered from coming into our Meeting, whether good or Bad, to hear yᵉ Gospell,—*we*

Contrived a Curtaine to be hung in yᵉ Meeting place, that did inclose as much roome as above 50 might sitt within it, and among those men, he that preached should stand; that soe if any Informer was private in yᵉ Roome as a hearer he might hear him that spake, but could not see him, and thereby not know him. And there were brethren without yᵉ Curtaine, that would hinder any from goeing within yᵉ Curtaine, that they did not know to be friends: . . . And soe all yᵉ People begin to sing a Psalme, that at yᵉ Beginning of yᵉ Meeting we did alwayes name what Psalme we would sing, if yᵉ Informers, or yᵉ Mayor or his Officers come in; thus still when they came in we were Singing, that they could not finde any one preaching, but all Singing. And, at our Meeting, we ordered it soe, that None read yᵉ Psalme after yᵉ first line, but every one bring their bibles, and soe read for themselves; that they might not lay hold of any one for preaching, or as much as reading yᵉ Psalme, and so to imprisson any more for that, as they had our Ministers. . . .

3.6   The Act of Toleration, 1689

By the time of the accession of William and Mary of Orange to the English throne in 1688 it was obvious that the policy of enforced religious uniformity had not worked. Therefore in 1689, as much from practical necessity as from any change of convictions, the Parliament passed an Act of Toleration. While the Act did not grant anything like full religious liberty in the modern sense, it did allow Baptists and other dissenters the freedom to exist, to meet for worship without fear, and to hear and heed their own ministers. However, Baptists still had to pay taxes for support of the state church, they could not serve in government or military posts, and they could not attend Oxford or Cambridge. However, the value of the limited toleration granted in this landmark document must not be minimized. *Source:* Henry Gee and William J. Hardy, eds., *Documents Illustrative of English Church History* (London: Macmillan and Company, 1896), 654-664.

Forasmuch as some ease to scrupulous consciences in the exercise of religion may be an effectual means to unite their majesties' Protestant subjects in interest and affection:

Be it enacted by the king's and queen's most excellent majesties, by and with the advice and consent of the Lords spiritual and temporal, and the Commons, in this present Parliament assembled and by the authority of the same, that [several laws restricting religion and prescribing penalties for those who dissented from the Church of England, laws spelled out in detailed legal language in this Act] . . . shall be construed to extend to any person or persons dissenting from the Church of England, that shall take the oaths mentioned in a statute made this present Parliament, entitled, 'An Act for removing and preventing all questions and disputes concerning the assembling and sitting of this present Parliament;' and shall make and subscribe the declaration mentioned in a statute made in the thirtieth year of the reign of King Charles II, entitled, 'An Act to prevent papists from sitting in either House of Parliament;' which oaths and declaration the justices of peace at the general sessions of the peace, to be held for the county or place where such person shall live, are hereby required to tender and administer to such persons as shall offer themselves to take, make, and subscribe the same, and thereof to keep a register: and likewise none of the persons aforesaid shall give or pay, as any fee or reward, to any officer or officers belonging to the court aforesaid, above the sum of sixpence, nor that more than once, for his or their entry of his taking the said oaths, and making and subscribing the said declaration; nor above the further sum of sixpence for any certificate of the same, to be made out and signed by the officer or officers of the said court. . . .

And be it further enacted by the authority aforesaid, that all and every person and persons that shall, as aforesaid, take the said oaths, and make and subscribe the declaration aforesaid, shall not be liable to any pains, penalties, or forfeitures, mentioned in an Act made in the five-and-thirtieth year of the reign of the late Queen Elizabeth, entitled, 'An Act to retain the queen's majesty's subjects in their due obedience;' nor in an Act made in the two-and-twentieth year of the reign of the late king Charles II, entitled, 'An Act to prevent and suppress seditious conventicles;' nor shall any of the said persons be prosecuted in any ecclesiastical court, for or by reason of their nonconforming to the Church of England.

Provided always, and be it enacted by the authority aforesaid, that if any assembly of persons dissenting from the Church of England shall be had in any place for religious worship with the doors locked, barred, or bolted, during any time of such meeting together, all and every person or persons that shall come to and be at such meeting shall not receive any benefit from this law, but be liable to all the pains and penalties of all the aforesaid laws recited in this Act, for such their meeting, notwithstanding his taking the oaths and his making and subscribing the declaration aforesaid.

Provided always, that nothing herein contained shall be construed to exempt any of the persons aforesaid from paying of tithes or other parochial duties, or any other duties to the church or minister, nor from any prosecution in any ecclesiastical court or elsewhere, for the same.

And be it further enacted by the authority aforesaid, that if any person dissenting from the Church of England, as aforesaid, shall hereafter be chosen or otherwise appointed to bear the office of high-constable, or petit-constable, churchwarden, overseer of the poor, or any other parochial or ward office, and such person shall scruple to take upon him any of the said offices in regard of the oaths, or any other matter or thing required by the law to be taken or done in respect of such office, every such person shall and may execute such office or employment by a sufficient deputy, by him to be provided, that shall comply with the laws on this behalf. . . .

And be it further enacted by the authority aforesaid, that no person dissenting from the Church of England in Holy Orders, or pretended Holy Orders, or pretending to Holy Orders, nor any preacher or teacher of any congregation of dissenting Protestants, that shall make and subscribe the declaration aforesaid, and take the said oaths [shall be restricted]. . . .

And whereas some dissenting Protestants scruple the baptizing of infants; be it enacted by the authority aforesaid, that every person in pretended Holy Orders, or pretending to Holy Orders, or preacher, or teacher, that shall subscribe the aforesaid Articles of Religion, except before excepted, and also except part of the seven-and-twentieth Article touching infant baptism, and shall take the said oaths, and make and subscribe the declaration aforesaid, in manner aforesaid, every such person shall enjoy all the privileges, benefits, and advantages which any other dissenting minister, as aforesaid, might have or enjoy by virtue of this Act.

And be it further enacted by the authority aforesaid, that every teacher or preacher in Holy Orders, or pretended Holy Orders, that is a minister, preacher, or teacher of a congregation, that shall take the oaths herein required, and make and subscribe the declaration aforesaid, and also subscribe such of the aforesaid Articles of the Church of England as are required by this Act in manner aforesaid, shall be thenceforth exempted from serving upon any jury, or from being chosen or appointed to bear the office of churchwarden, overseer of the poor, or any other parochial or ward office. . . .

And whereas there are certain other persons, dissenters from the Church of England, who scruple the taking of any oath; be it enacted by the authority aforesaid, that every such person shall make and subscribe the aforesaid declaration, and also this declaration of fidelity following, viz.

I, *A. B.*, do sincerely promise and solemnly declare before God and the world, that I will be true and faithful to King William and Queen Mary; and I do solemnly profess and declare, that I do from my heart abhor, detest, and renounce, as impious and heretical, that damnable doctrine and position, that princes excommunicated or deprived by the pope, or any authority of the see of Rome, may be deposed or murdered by their subjects, or any other whatsoever. And I do declare that no foreign prince, person, prelate, state, or potentate, hath or ought to have any power, jurisdiction, superiority, pre-eminence, or authority ecclesiastical or spiritual within this realm.'
[And shall subscribe a profession of their Christian belief in these words:

'I, *A. B.*, profess faith in God the Father, and in Jesus Christ His eternal Son the true God, and in the Holy Spirit, one God blessed for evermore, and do acknowledge the Holy Scriptures of the Old and New Testament to be given by Divine inspiration.' . . .

Provided always, and it is the true intent and meaning of this Act, that all the laws made and provided for the frequenting of divine service on the Lord's day commonly called Sunday, shall be still in force, and executed against all persons that offend against the said laws, except such persons come to some congregation or assembly of religious worship, allowed or permitted by this Act.

Provided always, and be it further enacted by the authority aforesaid, that neither this Act, nor any clause, article, or thing herein contained, shall extend or be construed to extend to give any ease, benefit, or advantage to any papist or popish recusant whatsoever, or any person that shall deny in his preaching or writing the doctrine of the blessed Trinity, as it is declared in the aforesaid Articles of Religion.

Provided always, and be it enacted by the authority aforesaid, that if any person or persons, at any time or times after the tenth day of June, do and shall willingly and of purpose, maliciously or contemptuously come into any cathedral or parish church, chapel, or other congregation permitted by this Act, and disquiet or disturb the same, or misuse any preacher or teacher, such person or persons, upon proof thereof before any justice of peace, by two or more sufficient witnesses, shall find two sureties to be bound by recognizance in the penal sum of fifty pounds, and in default of such sureties shall be committed to prison, . . .

Provided always, that no congregation or assembly for religious worship shall be permitted or allowed by this Act, until the place of such meeting shall be certified to the bishop of the diocese, . . .

4
Baptist Beginnings in America

The earliest Baptist church in America was that formed by Roger Williams in Providence, Rhode Island, in early 1639. For most of the seventeenth century, the Baptist presence in the new world was sparse. Most of the churches known to exist in America before 1700 were in New England, with only a few scattered congregations in the middle and southern colonies.

During these days of gaining a foothold in the new world, Baptists struggled to define their faith, defend themselves against both physical and doctrinal assaults, and work out their own internal tensions about various aspects of faith and practice. Their confessions, treatises, letters, church minutes, and other sources reveal something of how Baptists met these challenges.

The founding of the Kittery Church (4.8) has a double importance, in that it illustrates Baptist origins in two areas, Maine and South Carolina.

4.1 John Winthrop's *Journal* on Roger Williams

Governor John Winthrop kept a careful diary of daily events in and around the early Massachusetts Bay Colony. Since Winthrop knew Roger Williams, his comments on Williams's change of religious views are of more than passing interest. From this diary we gather that Williams held "divers dangerous opinions" which, when listed, hardly seem radical today. We also learn from this credible source that sometime before March 16, 1639, Williams was rebaptized at Providence and that he baptized several more persons to form a new church. This church has been recognized as the earliest Baptist church in America. *Source:* James K. Hosmer, ed., *Winthrop's Journal, 1630-1649*, 2 vols. (New York: Charles Scribner's Sons, 1908), 1:154, 168, 297.

Mo. 5 (*July*) 8. [1635] At the general court, Mr. Williams of Salem was summoned, and did appear. It was laid to his charge, that, being under question before the magistracy and churches for divers dangerous opinions, viz. 1, that the magistrate ought not to punish the breach of the first table, otherwise than in such cases as did disturb the civil peace; 2, that he ought not to tender an oath to an unregenerate man; 3, that a man ought not to pray with such, though wife, child, etc.; 4, that a man ought not to give thanks after the sacrament nor after meat, etc.; and that the other churches were about to write to the church of Salem to admonish him of these errors; notwithstanding the church had since called him to [the] office of a teacher. Much debate was about these things. The said opinions were adjudged by all, magistrates and ministers, (who were desired to be present,) to be erroneous, and very dangerous, and the calling of him to office, at that time, was judged a great contempt of authority. So, in fine, time was given to him and the church of Salem to consider of these things till the next general court, and then either to give satisfaction to the court, or else to expect the sentence; . . .

11 mo. January. [1635-1636] The governor and assistants met at Boston to consider about Mr. Williams, for that they were credibly informed, that, notwithstanding the injunction laid upon him (upon the liberty granted him to stay till the spring) not to go about to draw others to his opinions, he did use to entertain company in his house, and to preach to them, even of such points as he had been censured for; and it was agreed to send him into England by a ship then ready to depart. . . . Whereupon a warrant was

sent to him to come presently to Boston, to be shipped, etc. He returned answer, (and divers of Salem came with it,) that he could not come without hazard of his life, etc. Whereupon a pinnance was sent with commission to Capt. Underhill, etc., to apprehend him, and carry him aboard the ship, (which then rode at Natascutt;) but, when they came at his house, they found he had been gone three days before; but whither they could not learn. . . .

[Mo. 1.16. March 16, 1639] At Providence things grew still worse; for a sister of Mrs. Hutchinson, the wife of one Scott, being infected with Anabaptistry, and going last year to live at Providence, Mr. Williams was taken (or rather emboldened) by her to make open profession thereof, and accordingly was rebaptized by one Holyman, a poor man late of Salem. Then Mr. Williams rebaptized him and some ten more. They also denied the baptizing of infants, and would have no magistrates.

4.2   Roger Williams, *The Bloudy Tennent of Persecution,* 1644

Roger Williams (c.1603-1684) is remembered primarily as a spokesman for religious liberty and as founder of the earliest Baptist church in America at Providence, Rhode Island, in 1639. Though he remained a Baptist for only a short time, Williams helped shape continuing Baptist life in the new nation. Of the many books Williams wrote, perhaps *The Bloudy Tennent* made the greatest continuing impact upon American religion and politics. In this magnificent treatise Williams sets out with clarity and force the case for complete religious liberty for all, a soul freedom safeguarded by separation of church and state. Some have claimed that America's founding statesmen, particularly Thomas Jefferson, not only adopted basically these same concepts but may have been directly influenced by Williams. Be that as it may, through the later work of Isaac Backus it is certain that Williams helped form the concepts of religious liberty and separation of church and state as held by Baptists in America. *Source:* Roger Williams, *The Bloudy Tennent of Persecution for Cause of Conscience Discussed* (London: n.p., 1644. Reprinted by the Hanserd Knollys Society, London, 1848), 1-2, 7-12, 19-21, 36-39, 41-45, 117-119, 126-127, 130-131.

. . . First. That the blood of so many hundred thousand souls of protestants and papists, spilt in the wars of present and former ages, for their respective consciences, is not required nor accepted by Jesus Christ the Prince of Peace.

Secondly. Pregnant scriptures and arguments are throughout the work proposed against the doctrine of persecution for cause of conscience.

Thirdly. Satisfactory answers are given to scriptures and objections produced by Mr. Calvin, Beza, Mr. Cotton, and the ministers of the New English churches, and others former and later, tending to prove the doctrine of persecution for cause of conscience.

Fourthly. The doctrine of persecution for cause of conscience, is proved guilty of all the blood of the souls crying for vengeance under the altar.

Fifthly. All civil states, with their officers of justice, in their respective constitutions and administrations, are proved essentially civil, and therefore not judges, governors, or defenders of the spiritual, or Christian, state and worship.

Sixthly. It is the will and command of God that, since the coming of his Son the Lord Jesus, a permission of the most Paganish, Jewish, Turkish, or anti-christian consciences and worships be granted to all men in all nations and countries: and they are only to be fought against with that sword which is only, in soul matters, able to conquer: to wit, the sword of God's Spirit, the word of God.

Seventhly. The state of the land of Israel, the kings and people thereof, in peace and war, is proved figurative and ceremonial, and no pattern nor precedent for any kingdom or civil state in the world to follow.

Eighthly. God requireth not an uniformity of religion to be enacted and enforced in any civil state; which enforced uniformity, sooner or later, is the greatest occasion of civil war, ravishing of conscience, persecution of Christ Jesus in his servants, and of the hypocrisy and destruction of millions of souls.

Ninthly. In holding an enforced uniformity of religion in a civil state, we must necessarily disclaim our desires and hopes of the Jews' conversion to Christ.

Tenthly. An enforced uniformity of religion throughout a nation or civil state, confounds the civil and religious, denies the principles of Christianity and civility, and that Jesus Christ is come in the flesh.

Eleventhly. The permission of other consciences and worships than a state professeth, only can, according to God, procure a firm and lasting peace; good assurance being taken, according to the wisdom of the civil state, for uniformity of civil obedience from all sorts.

Twelfthly. Lastly, true civility and Christianity may both flourish in a state or kingdom, notwithstanding the permission of divers and contrary consciences, . . .

TO EVERY COURTEOUS READER

WHILE I plead the cause of truth and innocency against the bloody doctrine of persecution for cause of conscience, I judge it not unfit to give alarm to myself, and to [all] men, to prepare to be persecuted or hunted for cause of conscience.

Whether thou standest charged with ten or but two talents, if thou huntest any for cause of conscience, how canst thou say thou followest the Lamb of God, who so abhorred that practice? . . .

Two mountains of crying guilt lie heavy upon the backs of all men that name the name of Christ, in the eyes of Jews, Turks, and Pagans.

First. The blasphemies of their idolatrous inventions, superstitions, and most unchristian conversations.

Secondly. The bloody, irreligious, and inhuman oppressions and destructions under the mask or veil of the name of Christ, &c. . . .

Who can now but expect that after so many scores of years preaching and professing of more truth, and amongst so many great contentions amongst the very best of protestants, a fiery furnace should be heat, and who sees not now the fires kindling? . . .

. . . Yet in the midst of all these civil and spiritual wars, I hope we shall agree in these particulars,

First. However the proud (upon the advantage of a higher earth or ground) overlook the poor, and cry out schismatics, heretics, &c., shall blasphemers and seducers escape unpunished? Yet there is a sorer punishment in the gospel for despising of Christ than Moses, even when the despiser of Moses was put to death without mercy, Heb. x. 28, 29. *He that believeth shall not be damned,* Mark xvi. 16.

Secondly. Whatever worship, ministry, ministration, the best and purest, are practised without faith and true persuasion that they are the true institutions of God, they are sin, sinful worships, ministries, &c. And however in civil things we may be servants unto men, yet in divine and spiritual things the poorest peasant must disdain the service of the highest prince. *Be ye not the servants of men,* 1 Cor. vii. [23].

Thirdly. Without search and trial no man attains this faith and right persuasion. 1 Thes. v. [21], *Try all things.*

In vain have English parliaments permitted English bibles in the poorest English houses, and the simplest man or woman to search the scriptures, if yet against their souls persuasion from the scripture, they should be forced, as if they lived in Spain or Rome itself without the sight of a bible, to believe as the church believes.

Fourthly. Having tried, we must hold fast, 1 Thes. v. [21], upon the loss of a crown,

Rev. iii. [11]; we must not let go for all the fleabitings of the present afflictions, &c. Having bought truth dear, we must not sell it cheap, . . .

SCRIPTURES AND REASONS,
WRITTEN LONG SINCE BY A WITNESS OF JESUS CHRIST, CLOSE PRISONER IN NEWGATE,
AGAINST PERSECUTION IN CAUSE OF CONSCIENCE;
AND SENT SOME WHILE SINCE TO MR. COTTON

Whether persecution for cause of conscience be not against the doctrine of Jesus Christ, the King of kings. The scriptures and reasons are these.

1. BECAUSE Christ commandeth, that the tares and wheat, which some understand are those that walk in the truth, and those that walk in lies, should be let alone in the world, and not plucked up until the harvest, which is the end of the world. Matt. xiii. 30, 38, &c.

2. The same commandeth, Matt. xv. 14, that they that are blind (as some interpret, led on in false religion, and are offended with him for teaching true religion) should be let alone, referring their punishment unto their falling into the ditch.

3. Again, Luke ix. 54, 55, he reproved his disciples who would have had fire come down from heaven and devour those Samaritans who would not receive Him, in these words: *"Ye know not of what Spirit ye are; the Son of man is not come to destroy men's lives, but to save them."*

4. Paul, the apostle of our Lord, teacheth, 2 Tim. ii. 24, *that the servant of the Lord must not strive, but must be gentle toward all men; suffering the evil men, instructing them with meekness that are contrary minded, proving if God at any time will give them repentance, that they may acknowledge the truth, and come to amendment out of that snare of the devil*, &c.

5. According to these blessed commandments, the holy prophets foretold, that when the law of Moses concerning worship should cease, and Christ's kingdom be established, Isa. ii. 4; Mic. iv. 3, 4, *They shall break their swords into mattocks, and their spears into scythes.* And Isa. xi. 9, *Then shall none hurt nor destroy in all the mountain of my holiness*, &c. And when he came, the same he taught and practised, as before. So did his disciples after him, for *the weapons of his warfare are not carnal* (saith the apostle), 2 Cor. x. 4.

But he chargeth straitly, that his disciples should be so far from persecuting those that would not be of their religion, that when they were persecuted they should pray, Matt. v. 44; when they were cursed, they should bless, &c.

And the reason seems to be, because they who now are tares, may hereafter become wheat; they who are now blind, may hereafter see; they that now resist him, may hereafter receive him; they that are now in the devil's snare, in adverseness to the truth, may hereafter come to repentance; they that are now blasphemers and persecutors, as Paul was, may in time become faithful as he; they that are now idolaters, as the Corinthians once were, 1 Cor.vi. 9, may hereafter become true worshippers as they; they that are now no people of God, nor under mercy, as the saints sometimes were, 1 Pet. ii. 10, may hereafter become the people of God, and obtain mercy, as they. . . .

THE ANSWER OF MR. JOHN COTTON,
OF BOSTON, IN NEW ENGLAND, TO THE AFORESAID ARGUMENTS AGAINST PERSECUTION FOR CAUSE OF CONSCIENCE, PROFESSEDLY MAINTAINED

PERSECUTION FOR CAUSE OF CONSCIENCE.

The question which you put is, whether persecution for cause of conscience be not against the doctrine of Jesus Christ, the King of kings?

Now, by persecution for cause of conscience, I conceive you mean, either for professing some point of doctrine which you believe in conscience to be the truth, or for practising some work which in conscience you believe to be a religious duty.

Now in points of doctrine some are fundamental, without right belief whereof a man cannot be saved; others are circumstantial, or less principal, wherein men may differ in judgment without prejudice of salvation on either part.

In like sort, in points of practice, some concern the weightier duties of the law, as, what God we worship, and with what kind of worship; whether such as, if it be right, fellowship with God is held; if corrupt, fellowship with him is lost.

Again, in points of doctrine and worship less principal, either they are held forth in a meek and peaceable way, though the things be erroneous or unlawful: or they are held forth with such arrogance and impetuousness, as tendeth and reacheth (even of itself) to the disturbance of civil peace.

Finally, let me add this one distinction more: when we are persecuted for conscience' sake, it is either for conscience rightly informed, or for erroneous and blind conscience.

These things premised, I would lay down mine answer to the question in certain conclusions.

First, it is not lawful to persecute any for conscience' sake rightly informed; for in persecuting such, Christ himself is persecuted in them, Acts ix. 4.

Secondly, for an erroneous and blind conscience, (even in fundamental and weighty points) it is not lawful to persecute any, till after admonition once or twice; and so the apostle directeth, Tit. iii. 10, and giveth the reason, that in fundamental and principal points of doctrine or worship, the word of God in such things is so clear, that he cannot but be convinced in conscience of the dangerous error of his way after once or twice admonition, wisely and faithfully dispensed. And then, if any one persist, it is not out of conscience, but against his conscience, as the apostle saith, ver.11, He *is subverted, and sinneth, being condemned of himself;* that is, of his own conscience. So that if such a man, after such admonition, shall still persist in the error of his way, and be therefore punished, he is not persecuted for cause of conscience, but for sinning.

But if a man hold forth, or profess, any error or false way, with a boisterous and arrogant spirit, to the disturbance of civil peace, he may justly be punished according to the quality and measure of the disturbance caused by him.

A REPLY
TO THE
AFORESAID ANSWER OF MR. COTTON,
IN A CONFERENCE BETWEEN TRUTH AND PEACE.
CHAP. II

Truth. Sweet Peace, what hast thou there?

Peace. Arguments against persecution for cause of conscience.

Truth. And what there?

Peace. An answer to such arguments, contrarily maintaining such persecution for cause of conscience.

Truth. These arguments against such persecution, and the answer pleading for it, [are] written, as Love hopes, from godly intentions, hearts, and hands, yet in a marvellously different style and manner—the arguments against persecution in milk, the answer for it, as I may say, in blood.

The author of these arguments against persecution, as I have been informed, being committed by some then in power close prisoner to Newgate, for the witness of some truths of Jesus, and having not the use of pen and ink, wrote these arguments in milk, in sheets of paper brought to him by the woman, his keeper, from a friend in London as the stopples of his milk bottle.

In such paper, written with milk, nothing will appear; but the way of reading it by fire being known to this friend who received the papers, he transcribed and kept together the papers, although the author himself could not correct, nor view what himself had written. . . .

Peace. The answer, though I hope out of milky pure intentions, is returned in blood—bloody and slaughterous conclusions—bloody to the souls of all men, forced to the religion and worship which every civil state or commonweal agrees on, and compels all subjects to, in a dissembled uniformity:—

Bloody to the bodies, first of the holy witnesses of Christ Jesus, who testify against such invented worships:—

Secondly, of the nations and peoples slaughtering each other for their several respective religions and consciences.

CHAP. III.

Truth. In the answer, Mr. Cotton first lays down several distinctions and conclusions of his own, tending to prove persecution.

Secondly. Answers to the scriptures and arguments proposed against persecution.

Peace. The first distinction is this: by persecution for cause of conscience, "I conceive you mean either for professing some point of doctrine which you believe in conscience to be the truth, or for practising some work which you believe in conscience to be a religious duty."

Truth. I acknowledge that to molest any person, Jew or Gentile, for either professing doctrine, or practising worship merely religious or spiritual, it is to persecute him; and such a person, whatever his doctrine or practice be, true or false, suffereth persecution for conscience.

. . . So thousands of Christ's witnesses, and of late in those bloody Marian days, have rather chosen to yield their bodies to all sorts of torments, than to subscribe to doctrines, or practise worships, unto which the states and times (as Nebuchadnezzar to his golden image) have compelled and urged them. . . .

CHAP. IV.

Peace. The second distinction is this:—

"In points of doctrine some are fundamental, without right belief whereof a man cannot be saved; others are circumstantial and less principal, wherein a man may differ in judgment without prejudice of salvation on either part."

Truth. To this distinction I dare not subscribe, for then I should everlastingly condemn thousands, and ten thousands, yea, the whole generation of the righteous, who since the falling away from the first primitive Christian state or worship, have and do err fundamentally concerning the true matter, constitution, gathering, and governing of the church. . . .

CHAP. V.

Peace. With lamentation, I may add, how can their souls be clear in this foundation of the true Christian matter, who persecute and oppress their own acknowledged brethren, presenting light unto them about this point? But I shall now present you with Mr. Cotton's third distinction. "In points of practice," saith he, "some concern the weightier duties of the law, as what God we worship, and with what kind of worship; whether such, as if it be right, fellowship with God is held; if false, fellowship with God is lost."

Truth. It is worth the inquiry, what kind of worship he intendeth: for worship is of various signification. Whether in general acceptation he mean the rightness or corruptness of the church, or the ministry of the church, or the ministrations of the word, prayer, seals, &c. . . .

First, concerning the ministry of the word. The New English ministers, when they were new elected and ordained ministers in New England, must undeniably grant, that at that time they were no ministers, . . . I apply, and ask, will it not follow, that if their new ministry and ordination be true, the former was false? and if false, that in the exercise of it, notwithstanding abilities, graces, intentions, labours, and, by God's gracious, unpromised, and extraordinary blessing, some success, I say, will it not according to this distinction follow, that according to visible rule, fellowship with God was lost?

Secondly, concerning prayer. The New English ministers have disclaimed and written against that worshipping of God by the common or set forms of prayer, which yet themselves practised in England, notwithstanding they knew that many servants of God, in great sufferings, witnessed against such a ministry of the word, and such a ministry of prayer.

Peace. I could name the persons, time, and place, when some of them were faithfully admonished for using of the Common Prayer, and the arguments presented to them, then seeming weak, but now acknowledged sound; yet, at that time, they satisfied their hearts with the practice of the author of the Council of Trent, who used to read only some of the choicest selected prayers in the mass-book, which I confess was also their own practice in their using of the Common Prayer. But now, according to this distinction, I ask whether or no fellowship with God in such prayers was lost? . . .

CHAP. VI.

Peace. The next distinction concerneth the manner of persons holding forth the aforesaid practices, not only the weightier duties of the law, but points of doctrine and worship less principal:—

"Some," saith he, "hold them forth in a meek and peaceable way; some with such arrogance and impetuousness, as of itself tendeth to the disturbance of civil peace."

Truth. In the examination of this distinction we shall discuss,

First, what is civil peace (wherein we shall vindicate thy name the better),

Secondly, what it is to hold forth a doctrine, or practice, in this impetuousness or arrogancy.

First, for civil peace, what is it but *pax civitatis,* the peace of the city, whether an English city, Scotch, or Irish city, or further abroad, French, Spanish, Turkish city, &c. . . .

Peace. Hence it is that so many glorious and flourishing cities of the world maintain their civil peace; yea, the very Americans and wildest pagans keep the peace of their towns or cities, though neither in one nor the other can any man prove a true church of God in those places, and consequently no spiritual and heavenly peace. The peace spiritual, whether true or false, being of a higher and far different nature from the peace of the place or people, being merely and eessentially civil and human.

Truth. Oh! how lost are the sons of men in this point! To illustrate this:—the church, or company of worshippers, whether true or false, is like unto a body or college of physicians in a city—like unto a corporation, society, or company of East India or Turkey merchants, or any other society or company in London; which companies may . . . wholly break up and dissolve into pieces and nothing, and yet the peace of the city not be in the least measure impaired or disturbed; because the essence or being of the city, and so the well being and peace thereof, is essentially distinct from those particular societies; . . .

CHAP. XLIV.

Peace. The next scripture produced against such persecution is 2 Cor. x. 4, *The weapons of our warfare are not carnal, but mighty through God to the pulling down of strongholds; casting down imaginations, and every high thing that exalteth itself against the knowledge of God, and bringing into captivity every thought to the obedience of Christ: and having in a readiness to avenge all disobedience,* &c.

Unto which it is answered, "When Paul saith, *The weapons of our warfare are not carnal, but spiritual,* he denieth not civil weapons of justice to the civil magistrate, Rom. xiii., but only to church officers. . . .

Truth. I acknowledge that herein the Spirit of God denieth not civil weapons of justice to the civil magistrate, . . .

Yet withal, I must ask, why he here affirmeth the apostle denies not civil weapons of justice to the civil magistrate? of which there is no question, unless that, according to his scope of proving persecution for conscience, he intends withal that the apostle denies not civil weapons of justice to the civil magistrate in spiritual and religious causes: the contrary whereunto, the Lord assisting, I shall evince, both from this very scripture and his own observation, and lastly by that thirteenth of the Romans, by himself quoted.

First, then, from this scripture and his own observation. The weapons of church officers, saith he, are such, which though they be spiritual, are ready to take vengeance on all disobedience; which hath reference, saith he, amongst other ordinances, to the censures of the church against scandalous offenders.

I hence observe, that there being in this scripture held forth a twofold state, a civil state and a spiritual, civil officers and spiritual, civil weapons and spiritual weapons, civil vengeance and punishment and a spiritual vengeance and punishment: although the Spirit speaks not here expressly of civil magistrates and their civil weapons, yet, these states being of different natures and considerations, as far differing as spirit from flesh, I first observe, that civil weapons are most improper and unfitting in matters of the spiritual state and kingdom, though in the civil state most proper and suitable. . . .

CHAP. XLV.

. . . 2. I observe that as civil weapons are improper in this business, and never able to effect aught in the soul: so although they were proper, yet they are unnecessary; for if, as the Spirit here saith, and the answerer grants, spiritual weapons in the hand of church officers are able and ready to take vengeance on all disobedience, that is, able and mighty, sufficient and ready for the Lord's work, either to save the soul, or to kill the soul of whomsoever be the party or parties opposite; in which respect I may again remember that speech of Job, *How hast thou helped him that hath no power?* Job xxvi. 2. . . .

[*Truth*.] Will the Lord Jesus (did He ever in his own person practise, or did he appoint to) join to his breastplate of righteousness, the breastplate of iron and steel? to the helmet of righteousness and salvation in Christ, a helmet and crest of iron, brass, or steel? a target of wood to His shield of faith? [to] His two-edged sword, coming forth of the mouth of Jesus, the material sword, the work of smiths and cutlers? or a girdle of shoe-leather to the girdle of truth? &c. . . .

CHAP. XLVIII.

Peace. I pray now proceed to the second argument from this scripture, against the use of civil weapons in matters of religions, and spiritual worship.

Truth. The Spirit of God here commands subjection and obedience to higher powers, even to the Roman emperors and all subordinate magistrates; and yet the emperors and governors under them were strangers from the life of God in Christ, yea, most averse and opposite, yea, cruel and bloody persecutors of the name and followers of Jesus: and yet unto these, is this subjection and obedience commanded. . . .

Now then I argue, if the apostle should have commanded this subjection unto the Roman emperors and Roman magistrates in spiritual causes, as to defend the truth which they were no way able to discern, . . .

Or else to punish heretics, whom then also they must discern and judge, . . . I say, if Paul should have, in this scripture, put this work upon these Roman governors, and commanded the churches of Christ to have yielded subjection in any such matters, he must, in the judgment of all men, have put out the eye of faith, and reason, and sense, at once. . . .

CHAP. L.

Peace. Which is the third argument against the civil magistrates' power in spiritual and soul-matters out of this scripture, Rom. xiii.?

Truth. I dispute from the nature of the magistrates' weapons, ver. 4. He hath a sword, which he bears not in vain, delivered to him, as I acknowledge from God's appointment in the free consent and choice of the subjects for common good.

We must distinguish of swords.

We find four sorts of swords mentioned in the New Testament.

First, the sword of persecution, which Herod stretched forth against James, Acts xii. 1, 2.

Secondly, the sword of God's Spirit, expressly said to be the word of God, . . .

Thirdly, the great sword of war and destruction, given to him that rides that terrible red horse of war, . . .

None of these three swords are intended in this scripture.

Therefore, fourthly, there is a civil sword, called the sword of civil justice, which being of a material, civil nature, . . . cannot extend to spiritual and soul-causes, spiritual and soul-punishment, which belongs to that spiritual sword. . . .

CHAP. LI.

Truth. A fourth argument from this scripture, I take in the sixth verse, from tribute, custom, &c.: which is a merely civil reward, or recompence, for the magistrates' work. Now as the wages are, such is the work; but the wages are merely civil—custom, tribute, &c.: not the contributions of the saints or churches of Christ, proper to the spiritual and Christian state. And such work only must the magistrate attend upon, as may properly deserve such civil wages, reward, or recompence.

Lastly, that the Spirit of God never intended to direct, or warrant, the magistrate to use his power in spiritual affairs and religious worship, I argue from the term or title it pleaseth the wisdom of God to give such civil officers, to wit, ver. 6, *God's ministers.* . . .

Truth. I conclude . . . that the Christian church doth not persecute; no more than a lily doth scratch the thorns, or a lamb pursue and tear the wolves, or a turtle-dove hunt the hawks and eagles, or a chaste and modest virgin fight and scratch like whores and harlots.

4.3 John Clarke, *Ill Newes from New-England,* 1652

In 1651 John Clarke (1609-1676), then pastor at Newport, Rhode Island, was arrested and put on trial in Boston for preaching against infant baptism. Had not someone paid his substantial fine, no doubt Clarke would have been whipped as was his colleague Obadiah Holmes on the same occasion. Clarke wrote a full account of the Boston incident, along with other data on religious coercion in America, in *Ill Newes*. In the selection below, Clarke explains the circumstances of his arrest and outlines the major points of his theology which he was willing to debate publicly. His dedication of this work to Parliament insured that it would have maximum impact in Old England as well as New England. *Source::* John Clarke, *Ill Newes from New-England: or A Narrative of New-Englands Persecution, Wherein is Declared, That while old England is Becoming new, New-England is become Old* (London: n.p., 1652), 1-4, 9-10.

A Faithfull and True Relation of the Persecution of Obediah Holmes, John Crandall, and John Clarke, meerly for Conscience toward God, by the principall Members of the Church, or Commonwealth of the Mathatusets [sic] in New-England, which rules over that part of the World; whereby is shewn their discourteous Entertainment of Strangers, & how that Spirit by which they are led, would order the whold world, if either brought under them, or should come in unto them: Drawn forth by the aforesaid John Clarke, not so much to answer the Importunity of Friends, as to stop the mouthes, and slanderous reports of such as are Enemies of the Cross of Christ. Let him that readeth it consider, which Church is most like the Church of Christ (that Prince of Peace, that meek and gentle Lamb, that came into this World to save Mens lives, not to destroy them) the Persecuted, or Persecuting.

It came to pass that we three, by the good hand of our God, came into the *Mathatusetts* Bay upon the 16 day of the 5th Moneth, 51 [July, 1651], and upon the 19th of the same, upon occasion of the businesse, we came unto a Town in the same Bay called *Lin,* where we lodged at a Blind-mans house neer two miles out of the Town, by name *William Witter,* who being baptized into Christ, waits, as we also doe, for the Kingdom of God, and the full consolation of the *Israel* of God: Upon the 20th day, being the first day of the week, not having freedom in our Spirits for want of a clear Call from God to goe unto the Publike Assemblie to declare there what was the mind, and counsell of God concerning them, I judged it as a thing suitable to consider what the councell of God was concerning our selves; and finding by sad experience that the hour of temptation spoken of was coming upon all the World (in a more eminent way) to try them that are upon the Earth, I fell upon the consideration of that Word of Promise, made to those that keep the Word of his Patience, which present thoughts, while in Conscience towards God and good will unto his Saints, I was imparting to my Companions in the house where I lodged, and to 4 or 5 strangers that came in unexpected after I had begun, opening and proving what is meant by the hour of Temptation, what by the Word of his patience, and their keeping it, and how he that hath the Key of *David* (being the Promiser) will keep those that keep the word of his Patience from the hour of Temptation; while I say I was yet speaking, there comes into the house where we were, two Constables, who with their clamorous tongues made an interruption in my Discourse, and more uncivilly disturbed us than the pursuivants of the old *English* Bishops were wont to doe; telling us tht they were come with Authority from the Magistrate to apprehend us; I then desired to see the Authority by which they thus proceeded, whereupon they pluckt forth their Warrant, and one of them with a trembling hand (as conscious he might have been better employed) read it to us; The substance whereof was as followeth:

By virtue hereof, you are required to go to the house of William Witter; and so to search from house to house, for certain erroneous persons, being Strangers, and them to apprehend, and in safe custody to keep, and tomorrow morning by eight of the Clock to bring before me. Robert Bridges

When he had read the Warrant, I told them, Friends, there shall not be (I trust) the least appearance of a resisting of that authority by which you come unto us; yet I tell you, tht by virtue hereof, you are not so strictly tyed but if you please you may suffer us to make an end of what we have begun. . . to which they answered they could not. . . .they apprehended us and carried us to the Ale-house, or Ordinary, where after Dinner one of them said unto us, Gentlemen, if you be free I will carry you to the Meeting; to whom was replyed, Friend, had we been free thereunto we had prevented all this, nevertheless, we are in thy hand, and if thou wilt carry us to the Meeting, thither will we goe; to which he answered, then will I carry you to the Meeting. . . .

[At the meeting] Their Pastor answered by way of Quaery, Whether I was a Member of a Church? &c. Before I could give an answer Mr. *Bridges* spake, saying If the Congregation please to give you leave, well, if not, I shall require you silence, for, said he, we will have no Objections made against what is delivered, &c. To which I answered, I am not about for present to make Objections against what is delivered, but as by my gesture at my coming into your Assembly I declared my different [sic] from you, so lest that should prove offensive unto some whom I would not offend, I would now by word of mouth declare the grounds. . . . I could not judge that you are gathered together, and walk according to the visible order of our Lord; which when I had declared, Mr. *Bridges* told me I was done. . .and so commanded me silence: when their meeting was done, the Officers carryed us again to the Ordinary, where being watched over that night, as Theeves and Robbers, we were the next morning carried before Mr. *Bridges,* who made our *Mittimus* [warrant or indictment], and sent us to the Prison at *Boston.* . . .

The Testimony of *John Clarke* a prisoner of Jesus Christ at *Boston,* in behalf of my Lord, and of his people is as followeth.[1]

1 I Testifie that Jesus of Nazareth, whom God hath raised from the dead, is made both Lord and Christ; this Jesus I say is the Christ, in English, the Anointed One, hath a name above every name; He is the Anointed Priest, none to or with him in point of atonement; The Anointed Prophet, none to him in point of instruction; the Anointed King, who is gone unto his Father for his glorious Kingdom, and shall ere long return again; . . .

2 I Testifie that Baptism, or dipping in Water, is one of the Commandments of this Lord Jesus Christ, and that a visible beleever, or Disciple of Christ Jesus. . .is the only person that is to be Baptized, or dipped with that visible Baptism, or dipping of Jesus Christ in Water, and also that visible person is to walk in that visible order of his House, and so to wait for his coming the second time. . . .

3 I Testifie or Witness that every such believer in Christ Jesus that waiteth for his appearing may in point of liberty, yea ought in point of duty to improve that Talent his Lord hath given unto him, and in the Congregation may either aske for information to himself; or if he can, may speak by way of Prophecie for the edification, exhortation, and comfort of the whole, and out of the Congregation at all times upon all occasions, . . .

4 I Testifie that no such believer, or servant of Christ Jesus hath any liberty, much less Authority, from his Lord, to smite his fellow servant, nor yet with outward force, or arme of flesh, to constrain, or restrain his Conscience, no nor yet his outward man for Conscience sake, or worship of his God, where injury is not offered to the person, name or estate of others, every man being such as shall appear before the judgment seat of Christ, and must give an account of himself to God, and therefore ought to be fully persuaded in his own mind, for what he undertakes, because he that doubteth is damned if he eat, and so also if he act, because he doth not eat or act in Faith, and what is not of Faith is Sin.

[Note]

1. Clarke thought he had been challenged to debate his faith, and so drew up these "Conclusions" as a framework for his arguments. However, the ministers were less eager to debate than the magistrates had implied and no debate took place.

4.4   The Whipping of Obadiah Holmes, 1651

Obadiah Holmes (1607-1682) apparently left England to escape religious persecution, but found more of the same in America. He was active among Baptists in Newport, Rhode Island, and served for about twelve years as pastor of that church while John Clarke was absent in England. Holmes was noted for courage under persecution, for spiritual depth, and for doctrinal stability despite his lack of academic credentials. He was brutally whipped in Boston in 1651 for his denial of infant baptism. His courage on that occasion, as told in vivid detail by John Clarke in *Ill Newes from New-England* (1652) and by Isaac Backus in *A History of New England with Particular Reference to the Baptists* (1777) helped make this perhaps the most familiar case of Baptist persecution in America. *Source:* John Clarke, *Ill Newes from New-England: or A Narrative of New-Englands Persecution, Wherein is Declared, That while old England is Becoming new, New-England is become Old* (London: n.p., 1652), 16-22.

The Sentence of Obediah Holmes of Seacuck, the 31 of the 5th M.1651 [July].

Forasmuch as you Obediah Holmes, being come into this Jurisdiction about the 21 of the 5th M. did meet at one William Witters house at Lin, and did hear privately (and at other times being an Excommunicate person did take upon you to Preach and to Baptize) upon the Lords day, or other dayes, and being taken then by the Constable, and coming afterward to the Assembly at Lin, did in disrespect of the Ordinance of God and his Worship, keep on your hat, the Pastor being in Prayer, insomuch that you would not give reverence in veiling your hat, till it was forced off your head to the disturbance of the Congregation, and professing against the Institution of the Church, as not being according to the Gospell of Jesus Christ, and that you the said Obediah Holmes did upon the day following meet again at the said William Witters, in contempt to Authority, you being then in the custody of the Law, and did there receive the Sacrament, being Excommunicate, and that you did Baptize such as were Baptized before, and thereby did necessarily deny the Baptism that was before administered to be Baptism, the Churches no Churches, and also other Ordinances, and Ministers, as if all were Nullity; And also did deny the lawfullness of Baptizing of Infants, and all this tends to the dishonour of God, the despising the ordinances of God among us, the peace of the Churches, and seducing the Subjects of this Commonwealth from the truth of the Gospel of Jesus Christ, and perverting the strait waies of the Lord, the Court doth fine you 30 pounds to be paid, or sufficient sureties that the said sum shall be paid by the first day of the next Court of Assistants, or else to be well whipt, and that you shall remain in Prison till it be paid, or security given in for it.

By the Court, ENCREASE NOWELL

And now because of his sufferings, . . . the sence which his Soul felt of the Lords Support, according to promise, is affectionately set forth, . . . in a Letter written with his own hand, and sent unto those that have obtained like precious faith in *London*. . . . The words of his Letter followeth.

Unto the well beloved Brethren John Spilsbury, William Kiffin, and the rest that in London stand fast in that Faith; and continue to walk stedfastly in that Order of the Gospell which was once delivered unto the Saints by Jesus Christ: Obediah Holms an unworthy witness, that Jesus is the Lord, and of late a Prisoner for Jesus sake at Boston, sendeth greeting.

Dearly Beloved and longed after,

My hearts desire is to hear from you, and to hear that you grow in grace, and in the knowledge of our Lord and Saviour Jesus Christ, . . . I shall the rather import unto you some dealings which I have had therein from the Sons of Men, and the gracious support which I have met with from the Son of God, my Lord and yours, that so like Members you might rejoyce with me, and might be encouraged by the same experiment of his tender mercies, to fear none of those things which you shall suffer for Jesus sake.

I had no sooner separated from their assemblies [the state church], and from Communion with them in their worship of God, . . . but immediately the adversary cast out a flood against us, and stirred up the spirits of men to present myself and two more to *Plymouth* Court, . . . whereupon the Court straitly chargeth us to desist, . . . yet it pleased the Father of mercies (to whom be the praise) to give us strength to stand, & to tell them it was better to obey God rather than man. . . .

Not long after these troubles I came upon occasion of business to the Colony of the Mathatusets, with two other Brethren as Brother *Clark* being one of the two [the other was Thomas Crandall] can inform you, where we three were apprehended, carried to the prison at *Boston,* and so to the Court, and were all sentenced. . . . Upon pronouncing of which as I went to the Bar, I exprest my self in these words: I blesse God I am connted [sic] worthy to suffer for the name of Jesus; whereupon *John Wilson* (their Pastor as they call him) strook me before the Judgment Seat, and cursed me, saying, The Curse of God, or Jesus goe with thee; so we were carried to the Prison where not long after I was deprived of my two loving Friends; at whose departure the Adversary stept in, and took hold on my Spirit, and troubled me for the space of an hour, and then the Lord came in, and sweetly releeved me, . . .

I betook my self to my Chamber, where I might communicate with my God, commit my self to him, and beg strength from him; I had no sooner sequestered my self, and come into my Chamber, but Satan lets flie at me, saying, Remember thy self, thy birth, breeding, and friends, thy wife, children, name, and credit but as this was sudden, so there came in sweetly fronm the Lord as sudden an answer, 'tis for my Lord, I must not deny him before the Sons of men. . . . But then came in the consideration of the weaknesse of the Flesh to bear the strokes of a whip, though the Spirit was willing, and hereupon I was caused to pray earnestly unto the Lord, that he would be pleased to give me a spirit of courage and boldnesse, a tongue to speak for him, and strength of body to suffer for his sake, . . .

And when I heard the voyce of my Keeper come for me, even cheerfulnesse did come upon me, and taking my Testament in my hand, I went along with him to the place of execution, and after common salutation there stood; there stood by also one of the Magistrates, by name Mr. *Encrease Nowell,* who for a while kept silent, and spoke not a word, and so did I, expecting the Governours presence, but he came not. But after a while Mr. *Nowell* bad the Executioner doe his Office, then I desired to speak a few words, but Mr. *Nowell* answered, it is not now a time to speak, whereupon I took leave, and said, *Men, Brethren, Fathers, and Countrey-men, I beseech you give me leave to speak a few words, and the rather because here are many Spectators to see me punished, and I am to seal with my Blood, if God give me strength, that which I hold and practice in reference to the Word of God, and the testimony of Jesus; that which I have to say in brief is this, Although I confesse I am no Disputant, yet seeing I am to seal what I hold with my Blood, I am ready to defend it by the Word, and to dispute that point with any that shall come forth to withstand it.*

Mr. *Nowell* answered me, now was no time to dispute, then said I, then I desire to give an account of the Faith and Order I hold, and this I desired three times, but in comes Mr. *Flint,* and saith to the Executioner, Fellow, doe thine Office, for this Fellow would but make a long Speech to delude the people; . . .

And as the man began to lay the stroaks upon my back, I said to the people, though my Flesh should fail, and my Spirit should fail, yet God would not fail; so it pleased the Lord to come in, and so to fill my heart and tongue as a vessell full, and with an audible voyce I brake forth, praying unto the Lord not to lay this Sin to their charge, and telling the people, That now I found he did not fail me, and therefore now I should trust him for ever who failed me not; for in truth, as the stroaks fell upon me, I had such a spirituall manifestation of Gods presence, as the like thereto I never had, nor felt, nor can with fleshly tongue expresse, and the outward pain was so removed from me, that indeed I am not able to declare it to you, it was so easie to me, that I could well bear it, . . . when he had loosed me from the Post, having joyfulnesse in my heart, and cheerfulnesse in my countenance, as the Spectators observed, I told the Magistrates, you have struck me as with Roses. . . .

[Some weeks later] And now being advised to make my escape by night, because it was reported that there were Warrants forth for me, I departed; and the next day after, while I was on my Journey, the Constable came to search at the house where I lodged, so I escaped their hands, and was by the good hand of my heavenly Father brought home again to my neer relations, my wife and eight children, the Brethren of our Town and *Providence* having taken pains to meet me 4 miles in the woods, where we rejoyced together in the Lord.

4.5   Confession of Faith, First Baptist Church of Boston, 1665

The origin of the First Baptist Church in Boston in 1665 centers around Thomas Gould and his wife, with a small circle of friends in Charlestown (an area we would call a suburb of Boston).

The earliest Baptist confession adopted in America was put forth by this church in 1665. For all its brevity, this bold declaration of faith, written primarily by Gould, announces the Baptists' intention to preach and practice their faith. *Source:* Nathan E. Wood, *The History of the First Baptist Church of Boston* (Philadelphia: American Baptist Publication Society, 1899), 65-66.

The church being gathered mett with great opposition from the government of the place, upon which they drew up and delivered to the Court this confession as followeth to let the world know there faith & order proved from the word of God.

Wee believe with the heart & confess with the mouth that there is but (a) one god (b) Creator & governor of all things (c) distinguished into father, Son, & holy spirit (d) & that this is life eternall to know the only true god & Jesus Christ whom hee hath sent . . . & that the rule of this knowledge faith & obedience concerning the worship & service of god & all other christian duties is the written word of god contained in the bookes of the old & new testaments . . . (f) wee believe Christ is the foundation laid by the father (g) of whom moses and the prophets wrote & the apostles preached (h) who is that great prophet whom wee are to heare in all things (i)who hath perfectly revealed out of the bossom of his father the whole word and will of god which his servants are to know believe and obey . . . (k) Christ his commission to his desciples is to teach & baptise (l) And those that gladly received the word & are baptised are saints by calling & fitt matter for a vissible church (m) And a competent number of such joyned together in covenant & fellowship of the gosple are a Church of Christ . . . (o) wee believe that a church thus constituted are to walk in all the appointments of Christ (p) And have power from him to chuse from among themselves there owne officers whom the gosple allowes to administer in the ordinances of Christ among them whom they may depute or ordaine to this end . . . (q) And this church hath power to receive into there fellowship vissible

believers (r) & if any prove scandelouse obstenate & wicked to put forth such from
amongst them (s) when the church is mett together they may all propesie one by one that
all may all learne & all may be comforted (t) & they ought to meete together the first
day of the weeke to attend upon the Lord in all his holy ordinances continuing in the
Apostles doctrine & fellowship & breaking bread & praise . . . (v) wee acknowlidge
majestracy to bee an ordinance of god & to submitt ourselves to them in the lord not
becawse of wrath only but also for consience sake . . . (w) thus wee desire to give unto
god that which is gods & unto ceasere that which is ceaseres & to every man that which
belongeth to them (x) endeavoring alwaise to have a cleare consience voide of offence
towards god & towards men having hope in god that the resurection of the dead bee of
the just unto life & of the unjust unto condemnation everlasting (y) if any take this to bee
heresie then doe wee with the apostles confess that after the way which they call heresie
wee worship the father of our Lord Jesus Christ believing all things that are written in
the law & in the prophets & in the psalms . . . . This was delivered to A Court of
Assistants on the . . . of the seventh month *1665.*

4.6   The First Building, First Baptist Church of Boston, 1679

For over a decade Boston Baptists met for worship in private homes and, when possible, out
of doors. In 1679 they erected their first building, located on a back street to avoid undue attention. However, they found the doors nailed shut and faced an *ex post facto* law forbidding them to
have such a building. The following document tells the story of that first building and how Baptists responded to the resulting crisis. This selection includes a few paragraphs of explanation
from Nathan E. Wood, who included the document in his history of the Boston church. *Source:*
Nathan E. Wood, *The History of the First Baptist Church of Boston, 1665-1899* (Philadelphia:
American Baptist Publication Society, 1899), 65-66.

In ye beginning of ye year 1679 haveing erected A howse to meet in to worshipp ye
lord, there being y^n noe law to prohibitt such a thing, butt soone After (viz) in ye 3^d
month of said year att A generall Court we were called in Question for building s^d
howse, & forthwith A Law was enacted Against such howses to meet in, without license from ye Court on penalty of forfeiting such howses when mett in 3 days after
conviction of breach of ye law: whereupon we did forbear to meet in our howse. . . . &
ye generall Court being called and not voteing a nonconcurrence we proceeded to make
use of our howse butt after we had mett in itt fower dayes, we were summonsed to ye
Court of Assistants held in boston in ye beginning of ye year 80 to Answer for our
breach of the Afores^d law: the Court calling us in private (as itt was usual) Required to
give them A possitive Answer whether we would Ingage for ye whole in generall or for
our^{r}selves in particular to desist meeting in s^d howse untill ye gen^{ll} Court satt ye next
may. we Answered we were incapable to give A possitive Answer by reson we knew not
ye mind of our Church butt desired some time to speak with our brethren concerning itt,
which was then denyed us, butt ye next morning we sent in this our former request in a
few lynes humbly Intreating ye favo^r y^t we might have liberty to Answer these Questions
till ye beginning of ye weeke following, which was y^n granted, and one ye 2^d day of ye
weeke we had A Church meeting where we did seriously consider of ye matter & did
with one consent Agree not to turn ourselves out from our howse, but concluded to send
A humble Request for our liberty as our Answer . . . .

Imp^{e}m [In primum] that whereas ye onely wise god haveing by his p^{r}ovidence led us
into y^t ord^e & way of ye gospel of gathering into Church fellowshipp, we doe hereby
confess y^t what we did was not out of opposition to or contempt of ye Churches of
Christ in New England, butt in a holy Imitation meerly for ye better enjoym^{tt} of ye

liberty of our conshiences, ye great motive to this removeall att first into this wilderness.

2ᵈ That ye building A Convenyent place for our publique Church Assembly was noe thought of Affronting Authority, there being noe law in ye Country Against any such practise att ye erecting of this howse, . . .

3ᵈ That there being a Law made in May last Against our meeting in ye place built we did Accordingly submitt to ye same, untill we did fully undᵉstand by letters from severall in London yᵗ itt was his Majestyes pleasure & command . . . yᵗ we should enjoy ye liberty of our meetings in like manner as other of his protestant subjects, and ye generall Court att their last meeting not having voted A nonconcurrence.

4ᵗʰˡʸ As therefore ye two tribes & halfe did humbly and meekly vindicate themselves upon ye erecting of there Alter when Challenged for itt by Eleazer and ye messengers of ye tenn tribes, soe doe we hereby confess in like manner yᵗ we have not designed by this Act Any Contempt of Authority nor Any departing from ye living god or change of his worshipp, excepting our owne opinion, . . .

Yᵒʳ peticioners therefore haveing noe designe Against ye peace of this place butt being still as redy as ever, to hazard our lives for ye defence of ye ruelers of ye people of god here, doe humbly request that this our Confession & declaration may find acceptance with this honoᵉble Court, . . .

Signed by us in ye name & consent of ye Church

ISAACK HULL
JOHN RUSSELL
EDWARD DRINKER
THOMAS SKINNER

Butt notwithstanding this our Answer they had upon the 6ᵗʰ day before ordered, If we would not leave our howse to nayle up ye dores and According Impowered ye Marshall by warrant and sent him the same weeke to doe itt, who performed his office by A forcible Entry through Phillipp Squires ground to come to sd howse by reson ye gates were lockt, we required a Coppy of his warrant butt were denyed itt & two of our Brethren went to the secretary desireing we might have a Coppy of ye warrant who Answered he was not to lett us have any. Our dores being now shutt we were Expected the next lords day to meete out In ye yard Itt being a cold wind yᵗ day . . . .

Itt is to be observed that in ye year 79 there was A Synod called who in ordᵉ to bring us to ruing Published in print our practise to be one Cause of ye judginᵗᵗˢ of god upon ye land & alsoe in ye beginning of ye year 80 in March Mʳ Mather teacher of ye north Church in Boston putt forth a Book against us wherein did endevoᵉ (by casting all ye Dirt & filth possible) to render us odious declareing our opinion to come from Satan & that they had noe more love for us than Christ hath for Antichrist. Butt to returne our Dores being nayled up we provided A shedd which we made Against ye howse with bords, butt comeing ye next lords day expecting to meete under our shedd, we found our dores sett open & consulting by ouʳselves whether to goe in, we considered the Court had not donn itt legally Acting by noe Law, & yᵗ we were denyed a Coppy of ye councells ordᵉ & marshalls warrant. Whereupon we Concluded to goe into ye howse itt being our owne haveing A Civell right to itt & accordingly did & mett with noe disturbance yᵗ day.

[Nathan E. Woods explanation] I have given in full this exact transcript from our records because of its intrinsic interest and because it has often suffered from inexact quotation.

In 1679 a law was passed, and made retroactive, "that no persons whatsoever, without the consent of the freemen of the town, where they live, first orderly had and obtained at a public meeting, assembled for that end, and license of the County Court, or, in defect of such consent and license, by the special order of the General Court, shall erect or make use of any (meeting) house," on penalty of forfeiting both the house and the land on which it was built. This was intended to give the sanction of law to action against the Baptists for having built this meeting-house. There had been no specific statute before under which the Court could act, and in order to meet this case (for the house was already built) the law was made.

4.7   John Russell, *A Brief Narrative*, 1680

For many years the leading Baptist church in America was First Baptist in Boston, founded by Thomas Gould in 1665. A later pastor, John Russell, in 1680 compiled an account of the origin and early experiences of that historic church. An important part of the *Narrative* is Russell's defense of the Baptists against eight major charges. Excerpts from that document are presented here not just for the light they shed upon one church, but for the portrayal of conditions faced by most early Baptist churches in America. *Source:* Nathan E. Wood, *The History of the First Baptist Church of Boston, 1665-1899* (Philadelphia: American Baptist Publication Society, 1899), 149-172.

A brief Narrative of some Considerable Passages, concerning the first gathering, and further progress, of a Church of Christ, in Gospel Order, in Boston in NEW EN-GLAND, for clearing their innocency from the Scandalous things laid to their charge.

It pleased God to move the Hearts of some of his dear and precious Servants in this Wilderness, whom he had by his good Word and Spirit taught, and instructed in the Way and Order of the Gospel, to agree together to enter into Fellowship as a particular body, or Church, engaging one to another in a solemn Covenant, in the name of the Lord Jesus Christ, to walk in fellowship and communion together, in the practice of all the Holy Appointments of Christ, which he had, or should further make known unto them. And thus they became a visible Church of Christ, Walking in the Practice, and performance of the holy Ordinances of Christ, according to Divine Institution. . . .

No sooner were these Servants of Christ entered upon this work of the Lord, but they met with great troubles and afflictions, as has always befallen those whom the Lord hath been pleased to single out from others to bear witness to his Truth; Much Scandal and reproach hath been cast on them, their troubles, and temptations followed, one upon the neck of another, like the waves of the sea; but these precious Servants of the Lord having in some good measure counted the Cost before hand, were not moved for any of these things, but were cheerfully carried on by the good hand of the Lord upon them, through all the Afflictions, and Reproaches they met with; And are the most of them now at rest with the Lord, having served the will of God in their Generation.

And now we who survive, . . . think ourselves concerned and obliged, for the sake of Christ, and his truth that we do profess and bear witness to, to give some brief account of things, for the clearing ourselves of those heinous things laid to our charge. . . .

CHARGE 1.

That we are a Schismatical Company, who have rent ourselves from the Churches of Christ, and do receive into our society such who have, through discontent, disorderly left the Churches with whom they have walked.

Ans. To which we answer, That this is a mistake in those that so charge us. For,

First, As to the first Beginners, who are before named, three of them, viz. Richard Goodal, William Turner, and Robert Lambert were persons who had walked in the same way and order, in the Churches in Old England, who were by the Providence of

God, brought into this Land, and had letters of Recommendation from the Churches to whom they did belong. . . .

4. As to our receiving into our Society such who have disorderly rent themselves from the Church, we answer; That there have bin since the beginning of this Church, about 4 or 5 persons that have left the Churches they had walked with, joyned themselves unto us, the most of them being Persons of good repute for Godliness, both before, and since, that could never be justly charged with anything of a Scandalous Nature. . . .

CHARGE 2.

That we are Scandalous persons, and that in these three respects; (1) That the foundation was laid with excommunicate Persons. (2) In that we called such to Administer the holy things of God among us, who were justly for Scandal cast out of the other Churches. And (3) for receiving such into our Society.

Ans. This is a gross mistake; for first, as to those who were the first beginners of this Church, who were seven in number, all of them Men of good repute for Godliness among their Neighbours, but two of them were excommunicate Persons, viz. Thomas Gold, and Thomas Osburne, . . .

The third thing for which we are rendered Scandalous, is, the receiving into our Society those, who for moral Evils have bin justly cast out of the Churches.

Ans. To which we answer, That since the first gathering of this Church, which was on the 28th of the 3d Mon. 1665. there have bin added about sixty Persons or more, of which number, there have bin but two, that were cast out of other Churches, . . .

CHARGE 3.

Another thing laid to our Charge is, That we are disorderly persons, and walk disorderly.

Ans. This is also a mistake: for our practice, and walking, is according to, and agreeable with the Orders of the Lord Jesus Christ, therefore orderly: . . .

CHARGE 4.

Another thing we are Charged with is, That we are Disturbers of the Publick Peace.

Ans. We have never yet been found making any disturbance, by raising any tumults, or causing any Sedition, either in Church or Commonwealth; nor are those that accuse us, able to prove the things whereof they do accuse us. . . .

CHARGE 5.

We are charged to be underminers of the Churches.

This is also a great mistake: we never designed, neither do to this day design any such thing, but heartily desire and daily pray for the well being, flourishing, and Prosperity of all the Churches of Christ, . . .

CHARGE 6.

Another thing we are charged with, is, neglecting the Publick Worship of God on the Lord's Day.

Ans. This is utterly untrue; Though this hath bin the crime that we have usually from time to time presented to Court, and have by Courts been punished for. But it is well known that we do constantly meet on the first Day of the Week, to worship the Lord, and attend on him in all his holy Ordinances, and therefore why we should be so charged, and dealt withal, there is no reason. If it be said that we do absent from the

Publick Assemblies, and meet by ourselves in private houses, and therefore it is not Publick Worship.

We answer, That we do meet together by ourselves, and ought so to do, being an intire Church, and body by ourselves, and therefore cannot meet in their Assemblies. And there was a necessity of congregating together by our selves; Because they would not admit of us to Communion with them in all the Ordinances of God, but shut us out, and would allow us no more priviledge among them than they would allow to a Heathen, or Publican, viz. to come and hear in their Assemblies. . . .

CHARGE 7.

That we are Idolaters, and therefore not to be suffered, . . .

Ans. The Lord God of Gods knows, and Israel shall know that we are innocent in this matter, . . .

CHARGE 8.

We are charged to be enemies to Civil Government.

Ans. We know no reason why we should be charged with this, not in the least degree. (1) It is directly against our Principles, . . . (2) Our continual Prayers to God for them, . . . (3) Our constant subjection and obedience to all their laws, both actively (as far as we can with a good Conscience) and wherein we could not Actively, there we have been Passively obedient; . . .

Fourthly. In paying all due demands whatsoever; not being desirous to withhold from Cæsar at any time, any of his dues. . . .

Thus have we bin vilified, and greatly reproached, and are still to this day. It being without any just reason laid on us, that we are one chief cause of all the Judgments of God on the Countrey. We do not excuse ourselves, as not to have share, or part in many of the Sins that have provoked the Lord against Poor New-England; Neither have we been freed from having our part with others in the general Calamities that God hath brought on this poor place. Yet it is observable how graciously the Lord hath dealt with us; that in the time of great Mortality by the Smallpox, when so many hundreds dyed, though many of us were visited with that visitation, yet no one of our Society was removed by it. . . .

4.8   William Screven, Founding of Kittery Church, 1681-1682

William Screven (1629-1713) became a Baptist in England, and helped establish that faith in the New World, both in Maine and South Carolina. He was ordained by the Boston church and received dismissal from that congregation to form a separate church in Kittery in 1682. The following document traces the origin of the Kittery church, and gives a copy of their deeply moving church covenant. Screven later removed this church to South Carolina, where it became the nucleus of the First Baptist Church of Charleston, the earliest Baptist church in the South. *Source:* Nathan E. Wood, *The History of the First Baptist Church of Boston, 1665-1899* (Philadelphia: American Baptist Publication Society, 1899), 181-182.

A similar attempt at church planting took place in Piscataqua (Kittery), Province of Maine. "William Screven & his wife & Humphrey Churchwood were baptized the 21st of 4mo 1681." In the following February a number more from Piscataqua came to Boston and were baptized. A few months later these brethren and sisters sent word through one of their number to the church in Boston,
that here are a competent number of well established people whose hearts the Lord hath opened insomuch that they have gladly received the word and do seriously profess their hearty desire to the

following of Christ and to partake of all his holy ordinances, according to his blessed institutions and divine appointment: therefore I present my ardent desire to your serious consideration, which is, if the Lord see it fit, to have a gospel church planted here in this place: and in order hereunto, we think it meet that our beloved brother William Screven, who is, through free grace, gifted and endued, with the spirit [ ] to preach the gospel shall be ordained.

[To this request the church made immediate response and sent the following letter:] "A Coppy of A writing given to Brother Screeven in answer to A Request by letter from A Brother and others. Agreed upon att A Church meeting the 11th of 11mo *1681*. From the Church of Christ in Boston the 11th of 11mo *1681*. To all whome itt may concerne these are to Certify that our beloved Brother William Screeven is A member in Comunion with us and haveing had tryall of his gifts Amongst us and finding him to be A man whome god hath quallifyed & furnished with the gift of his holy spiritt and grace, enabling him to open and Apply the word of god which may be through the blessing of the lord Jesus usefull in his hand for the begitting and building up soules in the knowledg of god, doe therefore Appoint & Approve & alsoe encourage him to Exercise his gift in ye place where he lives or else where as the providence of god may cast him & soe the lord help him to by his glory in all things and to walk humbly in ye.fear of his name.

signed by us in the behalf

of ye rest   ISAACK HULL.

JOHN FARNUM.

Elder Screven seeme to have exercised his gifts with very gracious results, for in a few months the Baptists in Kittery so increased that they desired to be set apart as a separate church. They sent therefore a formal request to the church of which they were members:

Upon serious & Solemn Consideration of the Church About A motion or Request made by severall members that lived att Kittery, yt they might become A Church & that they might p-ceed therein provided they were such as should be Approved for such A Foundacon work, the Church gave there grant and att ye time Appointed did send severall messengers to make yt strict Inquiry & Examinaṡon as they ought in such A case who att there Returne brought ye Coppys here Inserted 26th of 7mo *1682*.

The Church of Christ att Boston yt is baptized upon profession of faith haveing taken into serious consideration ye Request of our Brethren att Kittery Relateing to there being A Church by themselves yt soe they might Injoy the precious ordinances of Christ which by reson of distance of habitaṡon they butt seldome could injoy have therefore thought meet to make Choice of us whose names are undᵉwritten as Messengers to Assist them in ye same and coming up to them we have found them A Competent Number and in ye same faith with us for upon carefull examination of them in matters of Doctrine & practise & soe finding one with us by there (we hope) Conshienċous Acknowledgmᵗᵗ of ye Confession of faith putt forth by ye Elders & Brethren of ye Churches in London and ye Contry in England dated in ye year *1682*.

And they haveing given themselves up to ye lord & too one Another in A Solemn Covenant to walk as said Covenant may Express & alsoe haveing Chosen theire officers whome they with us have Appointed & ordained, we doe therefore in ye name of ye lord Jesus & by the Appointmᵗᵗ of his Church deliver them to be A Church of Christ in ye faith and order of ye Gospel,

ISAACK HULL

THOMAS SKINNER

PHILLIPP SQUIRE.

signed by us in ye name
of ye Church in the 25 of 7mo *1682*.

A Coppy of there said Covenant.

Wee whose names are here undᵉwritten doe solemnly & on good Consideration god Assisting us by his grace give up our selves to ye lord & to one another in Solem Covenant, wherein wee doe Covenant & promise to walk with god & one with another In A dew and faithfull observance of all his most holy & blessed Commandm.ᵗᵗˢ Ordinances Institutions or Appointments, Revealed to us in his sacred word of ye ould & new Testament and according to ye grace of god & light att present through his grace given us, or here after he shall please to discover & make knowne to us thro his holy

Spiritt according to ye same blessed word all ye Dayes of our lives and this will wee doe, If ye lord graciously please to Assist us by his grace and Spiritt & to give us Divine wisdome, strength, knowledg, & understanding from Above to p-forme ye same without which we cann doe nothing John 15:4 2 Corinthians 3:5.

Signed by

Wᵐ SCREEVEN, Elder

HUMPHREY CHURCHWOOD, Deacon:

[and eight others]

Unit II

The Eighteenth Century

5

General Baptists in England

This chapter illustrates the story of General Baptists in England during the eighteenth century. Long before 1700 the General Baptists had developed a nationwide structure, which they called the General Assembly. The inherent centralizing tendencies in General Baptist life, evident from the first, surfaced as the General Assembly at times assumed prerogatives usually reserved to the churches.

Doctrinal controversy and spiritual decline marked General Baptists during the first half of the century. The conversion of Dan Taylor and formation of the New Connection represent the spirit of the Wesleyan revival in Baptist form, and for a time brought a measure of renewal to General Baptists. After 1770 Dan Taylor and his New Connection reform movement largely dominated General Baptist life in England. The Old Connection, as those who refused to go along with Taylor are called, eventually declined to the verge of oblivion. Taylor's dissertation on singing is included because it reveals much of the emphases of General Baptist life at that time in addition to the issue of singing as a part of worship.

5.1 The Conversion of Dan Taylor to Baptist Views

No General Baptist leader of the time cast a longer shadow, at least figuratively, than did Dan Taylor (1738-1816). He led the conservative reaction against doctrinal changes among General Baptists, and founded the New Connection in 1770. It would not be too much to say that he virtually carried the new organization on his back for two generations. A coal miner's son, Taylor was first attracted to the Wesleyan movement but left the Methodists when he became convinced of believer's baptism. During his extensive ministry Taylor founded churches, schools, and magazines. He traveled, preached, and wrote extensively and with amazing energy. The following document traces the circumstances of his conversion to Baptist views. *Source:* Adam Taylor, *The History of the English General Baptists,* 2 vols. (London: n.p., 1819), 2:69-74.

The General Baptist' cause, in the northern district of the kingdom, commenced, in the year 1762, in the neighbourhood of Halifax, in the West Riding of Yorkshire. There were then but few professors in that town: a church of the old presbyterians, and a small independent interest, being the only dissenting societies that existed. The particular baptists were, indeed, attempting to gather a congregation; but, it was not till long after this period, that they succeeded in establishing a church. The methodists, also, had, for several years, maintained a small society in the town; and were actively employed, in its vicinity. With these, Mr. Dan Taylor, who was afterwards the instrument of founding the general baptist cause in those parts, had been, for some time, connected. He was then a young man, being born in 1738: but possessing good natural abilities and an intrepid temper, and being zealous in the cause of religion, he had, for more than a year, engaged in visiting the sick, and in leading prayer-meetings.

In these exercises he was so acceptable, that he was urged to attempt to preach. He yielded to the wishes of his friends; and delivered his first sermon in a dwelling-house at Hipperholme, not far from Halifax, in Sept. 1761. His occasional labours were highly encouraged, by the leading men among the Yorkshire methodists; and they were very anxious that he should visit Mr. Wesley, and enter regularly into the ministry, as a travelling preacher. But he did not approve of many things in their order and discipline; and was not satisfied with their manner of explaining some points of doctrine which he thought of essential importance. He, therefore, declined forming any closer engagements: and, towards the Midsummer of 1762, entirely broke all connection with them.

About the same time, four persons in the neighbourhood of Heptonstall, a village nine miles west of Halifax, left the methodists, for nearly the same reasons which had induced Mr. Taylor to forsake them. Their names were, John Slater, John Parker, William Crossley, and a female whose sirname cannot be recovered. These seceders, knowing Mr. Taylor's state of mind, invited him to preach for them; with which he readily complied. . . .

Though these young professors had left the methodists through dissatisfaction with their discipline and doctrine, yet they had not formed any system for themselves. They now found it necessary to determine upon some plan of church order, and some principles of doctrine, on which they could unite to support the cause of their Redeemer. Among other things that became the subject of enquiry, on this occasion, was baptism. Mr. Taylor had occasionally paid some attention to this important branch of christian duty, in the previous years of his religious course; but he now seriously endeavoured to learn the will of his divine Master respecting it. With this view, he read the scriptures carefully, and consulted the best authors on both sides of the controversy. The result was, a complete conviction, that believers' baptism by immersion was the appointment of Christ, and the practice of his apostles. John Slater, also, became decidedly of this opinion: and several other of the friends inclined to adopt it.

Mr. Taylor immediately resolved, without consulting with flesh and blood, to obey what he believed to be the command of his Saviour. He applied to several particular baptist ministers for baptism: but, though they expressed their firm persuasion of his real christianity, and even were well satisfied of his call to the ministry, yet they all declined to baptize him. They knew that he openly maintained, that the Lord Jesus tasted death for every man, and made a propitiation for the sins of the whole world: and this circumstance, in their judgment, rendered it improper for them to comply with his request. One of these ministers, however, kindly informed him of some baptists, at Boston, in Lincolnshire, under the pastoral care of a Mr. Thompson, who, as he believed, were nearly of Mr. Taylor's sentiments.—This appears to have been the first intimation that he received of the existence of any other general baptists besides himself and his few friends.

Though the distance was great, not less than one hundred and twenty miles, and many serious obstacles presented themselves, this ardent searcher after truth, who was not easily frightened, determined to visit Mr. Thompson: and his friend, J. Slater, with equal affection and zeal, resolved to accompany him. They accordingly set out, on foot, on the morning of Friday, February 11th, 1763; and travelled on till night overtook them; when they found themselves in a field surrounded with water, and unable to discover their way. Perceiving a hay-rick near, they took shelter under it: and having commended themselves to the divine protection, in solemn prayer, they laid down and slept securely till the morning. They arose refreshed; and going forwards arrived, towards night, at a place about eight miles beyond Gamston in Nottinghamshire; where they stopt for some refreshment. Making inquiries here on the subject of their journey, they were agreeably surprized to learn, that there was a society of general baptists at Gamston, and that a deacon of that church dwelt in the village where they then were. To him they immediately went; and, informing him of the object of their journey, requested some information respecting the church at Gamston: but he received them very coolly, gave short answers to their questions, and directed them to a neighbouring public-house.

The next morning, being the Lord's day, they returned to Gamston; and arrived at the meeting-house just as the morning service was concluding. In the afternoon, Mr. Dossey preached; and, when he came down from the pulpit, the travellers introduced themselves to his notice. He entered into friendly conversation with them and invited them to his house. Here they spent the three following days; and had much discourse with Mr. Jeffries the pastor, and other principal members of the church. This gave them an opportunity of giving that minister full satisfaction respecting their character and views: and on the Wednesday, he baptized Mr. Taylor in the river, near Gamston. Mr. Slater declined being baptized, at the same time, out of affection for his fellow traveller; choosing to receive the ordinance from him, rather than from any other minister.

After their return to Wadsworth, Mr. Taylor resumed his great work of preaching the gospel, with increased zeal and success. He delivered several public discourses to explain and enforce believers' baptism; and stood ready to defend his principles against all opposers. In a short time, he baptized his friend Slater with several others: and a great degree of attention to the subject was excited throughout the country.

5.2 Formation of the New Connection, 1770

Dan Taylor and his close friends like William Thompson and John Slater came into General Baptist life in 1763 with zeal, energy, and with evangelical ideas shaped largely by the Wesleyan movement out of which they had come. Upon becoming a Baptist Taylor straightway affiliated with the Lincoln Association, led by the venerable Messenger, Gilbert Boyce. Taylor was soon disillusioned with the association and its moribund churches; he was frustrated with their antiquated methods, bored by their obsession with trivial concerns, and offended by their denial of the Deity of Christ. He first set about to change the association and, failing that, decided to pull out and form a new grouping of Baptist churches. This led to the New Connection in 1770, as described in the document below. *Source:* Adam Taylor, *The History of the English General Baptists,* 2 vols. (London: n.p., 1819), 2:133-138.

The Formation of the New Connection.

We have distressing evidence, . . . that a great diversity of opinion respecting some important parts of christian doctrine, caused, for a long series of years, very unpleasant altercations among the [General Baptists]. . . . This was especially the case, soon after the middle of the last century, with the churches and ministers which composed the Lincolnshire Association. Some of them adhered to the principles which had distinguished the English General Baptists, in their best days; and asserted the Divinity of the Saviour—the Atonement made for sin by his death—Justification by Faith alone—and Regeneration by the Holy Spirit. Others either denied these doctrines entirely, or explained them in a manner which their friends thought detracted from their dignity, and opposed the oracles of truth. . . . Such a difference in sentiment naturally produced discussions when the ministers assembled; and the result was, too frequently, an unpleasant degree of altercation.

During these disagreeable contests, Mr. Taylor became acquainted with the societies in the midland counties, . . . and he was much pleased to find that they esteemed the doctrines, which were the subject of debate, as absolutely essential to christianity. This union in opinion, and the general excellence of their character, made him and his friends desirous of a closer connection with them. Several attempts were made, to induce them to join the Lincolnshire association: . . . But the Leicestershire friends declined all these overtures; and steadily declared that they would never have any connection with persons who maintained the opinions which, as they believed, were held by many of the Lincolnshire general baptists. . . .

In the year 1769, disputes ran so high, both at the Lincolnshire association and the general assembly, and some circumstances of so disagreeable a nature took place, that many of the friends of the great truths already mentioned were led to conclude that a separation was necessary, . . . A meeting was accordingly held, at Lincoln, about Michaelmas, 1769; which was attended by Messrs. Taylor and Thompson, from the old connection, and . . . several other of the Leicestershire ministers. It was then resolved that a New Connection should be formed, of such as were assertors of the doctrines which had been so warmly debated: and that the first association of this New Connection should be held in London, June 7th. 1770: . . .

This resolution of separating from their former friends, was not adopted by these good men without considerable reluctance. They considered the mischievous effects of all divisions, and hoped that, by patient endeavours, things might be brought into a better state: and, when they found that a separation was necessary for the peace and prosperity of the churches, they did not venture on that measure, before they had spent a considerable time in deliberation, correspondence, and prayer for divine direction. And several ministers and churches, who agreed in doctrinal points with the seceders, fearing the consequences of dividing, continued, for many years, in the old connection.

On the other hand, the most pious and worthy ministers, who favoured the opposite doctrines, were most earnest in opposing a measure, which, by dividing their strength, and distracting their efforts, would, they feared, prove very injurious to the general baptist cause. Mr. G. Boyce, the messenger of the baptized churches in Lincolnshire, appears to have laboured zealously to prevent the separation. . . . In a letter to Mr. Taylor, dated Feb. 10th. 1770, he observes, "We separate from others, for very just causes and reasons; but for *us* to separate one from another, what will the world say? What a reproach and scandal will it bring upon us all, and upon our holy profession, and the Author of it! O! let it never be. My dear brother, let us take care what we do. Let us make use of every precaution, and take every necessary step that is possible to be taken, to prevent a separation. . . ."

But the breach was now too wide to be closed by persuasion. To all this rhetoric the seceders calmly replied: "It is not to be doubted, if we regard the bible, that some of the vilest errors are, in this age, maintained by some of the general baptists, with as much warmth and zeal as they have ever been by any party of men, in former ages. It behoves us, therefore, to take the alarm; and, with all the little might we have, to militate against these pernicious tenets, which our forefathers so much abhorred, and the word of God so expressly condemns." With such sentiments as these, no reconciliation could be expected: and the discontented party adhered to their resolution.

5.3 *Articles of Religion,* New Connection, 1770

The New Connection is best understood as a Baptist expression of the Wesleyan movement, with overtones as a conservative reaction against the growing liberalism in the Old Connection of General Baptists. At the formation of the New Connection in 1770 Taylor led the new body to adopt a brief statement of their faith. This is by no means a complete confession, but rather a brief state-ment on the issues most at dispute among General Baptists. The Articles emphasize the sinfulness of humans, the need for salvation through faith, the necessity of baptism by immersion, and, above all, the full Deity and humanity of Jesus Christ. *Source:* Adam Taylor, *The History of the English General Baptists,* 2 vols. (London: n.p., 1819), 139-143; also in William L. Lumpkin, ed., *Baptist Confessions of Faith* (Philadelphia: Judson Press, 1959), 342-344.

After solemn prayer to the Father of lights, for his direction and blessing, an union was formed under the designation of The New Connection of General Baptists, formed in 1770; with a design to revive Experimental Religion or Primitive Christianity in Faith and Practice. And, in order that it might be known what they considered as the faith and practice of primitive christianity, six Articles of Religion were proposed, agreed upon, and signed: not as a perfect creed of the new party; but principally as a declaration of their views on those points which had been the chief subjects of debate between them and their former associates. These articles are thus expressed, in the original record.

ARTICLE 1. *On the Fall of Man.* We believe that man was made upright in the image of God, free from all disorder natural and moral; capable of obeying perfectly the will and command of God his Maker; yet capable also of sinning: which he unhappily did, and thereby laid himself under the divine curse; which, we think, could include nothing less than the mortality of the body and the eternal punishment of the soul. His nature also became depraved; his mind was defiled; and the powers of his soul weakened—that both he was, and his posterity are, captives of Satan till set at liberty by Christ.

ARTICLE 2. *On the Nature and perpetual Obligation of the Moral Law.* We believe that the moral law not only extends to the outward actions of the life, but to all the powers and faculties of the mind, to every desire, temper and thought; that it demands the entire devotion of all the powers and faculties of both body and soul to God: or, in our Lord's words, to love the Lord with all our heart, mind, soul and strength:—that this law is of perpetual duration and obligation, to all men, at all times, and in all places or parts of the world. And we suppose that this law was obligatory to Adam in his perfect state—was more clearly revealed in the ten commandments—and more fully explained in many other parts of the bible.

ARTICLE 3. *On the Person and Work of Christ.* We believe that our Lord Jesus Christ is God and man, united in one person: or possessed of divine perfection united to hu-man nature, in a way which we pretend not to explain, but think ourselves bound by the word of God firmly to believe:—that he suffered to make a full atonement for all the sins of all men—and that hereby he has wrought out for us a compleat salvation; which is received by, and as a free gift communicated to, all that believe in him; without the consideration of any works done by us, in order to entitle us to this salvation.—Though we firmly believe, that no faith is the means of justification, but that which produces good works.

ARTICLE 4. *On Salvation by Faith.* We believe that as this salvation is held forth to all to whom the gospel revelation comes without exception, we ought in the course of our ministry, to propose or offer this salvation to all those who attend our ministry: and, having opened to them their ruined wretched state by nature and practice, to invite all, without exception, to look to Christ by faith, without any regard to any thing in, or done by, themselves; that they may, in this way alone, that is, by faith, be possessed of this salvation.

ARTICLE 5. *On Regeneration by the Holy Spirit.* We believe that, as the scriptures assure us, we are justified, made the children of God, purified and sanctified by faith:— that when a person comes to believe in Jesus (and not before) he is regenerated or renewed in his soul, by the spirit of God, through the instrumentality of the word, now believed and embraced; which renewal of his soul naturally produces holiness in heart and life:—that this holiness is the means of preparing us for the enjoyments and employments of the heavenly world; and of preserving in our souls a comfortable sense of our interest in the Lord, and of our title to glory; as well as to set a good example before men, and to recommend our blessed Redeemer's cause to the world.

ARTICLE 6. *On Baptism*. We believe that it is the indispensible duty of all who repent and believe the gospel, to be baptized, by immersion in water, in order to be initiated into a church state; and that no person ought to be received into the church without submission to that ordinance.

SIGNED, Dan Taylor [and 18 others]

5.4 Dan Taylor, *Dissertation on Singing*, 1786

By the time of this treatise, Particular Baptists who favored singing had long since carried the day in their group. Many General Baptists also favored the practice, but some of the Old Connection leaders refused to budge on what they considered a worldly and carnal practice. On the question of singing, as on everything else, Dan Taylor represented an open, progressive, and eminently sensible viewpoint. In this work one can detect the influence of Benjamin Keach upon Taylor. The "Mr. B" addressed here is Gilbert Boyce, messenger of the Lincoln Association, who opposed singing and all other lively practices. *Source:* Dan Taylor, *A Dissertation on Singing in the Worship of God: Interspersed with Occasional Strictures on Mr. Boyce's late Tract, Entitled, "Serious Thoughts on the present Mode and Practice of Singing in the Public Worship of God"* (London: n.p., 1786). Copy in Angus Collection, Regent's Park College, Oxford.

To sing is to pronounce musically, by modulating the voice, and proportioning the sounds of the syllables to one another; in such a manner as may be harmonious, and pleasant to the hearer. And to sing the praises of God, is to pronounce the praises of God in this harmonious manner. Thus it is different from speaking; from prayer; from giving thanks; from joy and thankfulness of heart; and from every other operation both of mind and tongue in which there is no such melody. . . .

Thus it appears, that singing to the Lord, and singing his praises, is frequently and warmly recommended in that book [the Bible], which I readily allow, as well as Mr. B. is "the only rule of our faith and practice in all things of a purely religious nature."

Mr. B. takes much pains to persuade us that this practice is of no use: But he must allow us to prefer the judgment of an all-wise God, to that of fallible men. He very gravely tells his singing brethren, that he, "don't see wherein they are more holy, more heavenly-minded" [than non-singers]. . . .

I venture to add, that what the blessed God here declares to be the excellency of singing his praises, great numbers have happily proved by experience; and thousands now alive can, without any hesitation set their seal to it, as well as in former ages. Not a few have known it to contribute greatly to their conversion to God.

SINGING the praises of God is an ancient practice, and so far as we can find, has been continued from age to age; though it may not have been universally practiced. . . .

The practice of "singing psalms, and hymns, and spiritual songs," not only was recommended by the apostles, and abundantly enforced by precept and example in the Old and New Testament, but was received from the apostles, and practiced in the first ages of the Christian church fifteen hundred years before Mr. Keach and Mr. Allen came into existence. . . .

Mr. B. seems sometimes to object absolutely against all singing in publick worship. Sometimes he appears only to militate against "such a sort of singing as we practice in our churches." He frankly allows that singing Psalms and Hymns was practiced in the apostles' days; and seems to admit that, 1 Cor. xiv. 15. refers to singing in the Church. This indeed is undeniably manifest to any one who reads the chapter attentively over. And therefore I take it for granted that our author has no objection to "singing in public worship," if it be performed as it ought to be.

But still he objects against our manner of singing in three or four respects. Against our joint singing; singing the compositions of other men; and all sorts of persons singing promiscuously. And here he objects to carnal people, and women, joining in the song.

FIRST. With respect then to the first objection. Against "singing with joint voices." It is so manifest that this was done in the Old Testament Church, . . . Now why should there be any change made in the New Testament church, unless we had some intimation given us that our great master designed, and appointed such a change. But instead of that, it is at least evident, that we have one instance of this joint singing in the practice of our Lord, and his apostles. Matt. xxvi.30. Mark. xiv.26.

SECONDLY. As to "singing promiscuously." It is not to be denied that this was admitted in the Old Testament Church; and if then, why not now, unless forbidden in the New Testament? . . .

Mr. B. apprehends that promiscuous singing is wrong on two accounts. "It admits carnal people to join in it," "and women take their part in the service."

Yet again, our author still vehemently insists upon it, that women ought not to join in singing the praises of God in public worship; and says a great deal indeed in order to expose this practice and dissuade from it. I think the whole of what he has said on this subject, that is properly argumentative, is reducible to these two heads: "We have no scripture authority to encourage women thus to sing." And, "Singing is speaking, and teaching; but women are not to speak or to teach in the church and therefore not to sing."

As to "scripture authority," if by this be meant, no scripture enjoins in so many words that "women in public worship shall join with men in singing;" it need not be asserted. Where is it expressly enjoined that women should attend public worship at all? Where are women expressly commanded to sit down at the Lord's table? where we are expressly commanded to preach, or to pray, or to read the scriptures in public worship? I might ask the same questions on multitudes of other subjects: but this would be trifling.

Women as well as men have rational capacities; they, as well as men, have immortal souls; they, as well as men, are made for eternal duration; they, as well as men, are the creatures of God. If singing the praises of God be a moral duty, which I think has been proved already, they, as well as men, are under an obligation to perform it; they, as well as men, have received many blessings from God, which they ought to praise him for. Consider singing as proper and useful on any subject; praise, prayer, narration, or precept, as we have considered it above; women, as well as men, are interested in all these subjects; they, as well as men, can understand them all; and they can profit by them all. They, as well as men, have capacities to sing on them all. They have the organs of speech, and [are] "the daughters of musick," as well as men. They can therefore enjoy the advantages of singing, and experience the goodness of it, and the pleasantness of it; and be edified, and taught, and admonished by it; as well as men. Nothing is more common in scripture, nor more freely allowed by grammarians, . . . than to include the woman in the man: and when directions are given to men, to understand those directions as also binding on women. The instances are innumerable; but needless to be here given. The scripture, however, sufficiently informs us that women have joined with men in singing; and that in public worship too: and we have no evidence that the blessed God disapproves of it; . . .

When a church undertakes any thing of peculiar importance or difficulty in which the women may have occasion to be concerned, or to the expences of which they may have a call to contribute, or in the good or bad effects of which they may be at least as much interested as the men are, it is right they should give their voice in it and their advice concerning it; and it appears to be intolerant not to allow them this privilege. Besides there may be, and I am persuaded there are many things which some of the women understand better than some men. But they are denied this privilege and treated in a very intolerant manner if they be not permitted on any account to speak in the church. This may be applied particularly to the admission of new members, and the choice of officers, pastors, or deacons in the church; on which occasions, for several most obvious reasons which need not be here mentioned, it is not only right but even necessary for women to have liberty to speak as well as men. . . .

SECONDLY. To attempt the solution of some difficulties or cases of conscience, that appear important to some persons, respecting the manner of singing.

I. Is it right to sing Anthems or Songs in prose, in public worship?

I answer, however profitably a single person, or a few persons together may sing these, I cannot think them a proper part of the public worship of Almighty God; for such reasons as the following. All the members of churches are directed to join in singing, as we have seen above; and it is evidently incumbent on them, so far as they can. But few can join in the singing of Anthems; nor have they sufficient time or skill to learn them. And therefore, if Anthems be sung, many of the brethren will generally be deprived of their privileges, and of an opportunity of doing their duty in the worship of God. One capital rule is, "Let all things be done to edifying." . . .

Q.2. Ought Organs, and musical Instruments to be used in Christian Worship?

I answer, I am persuaded they ought not; for they are not once mentioned in the New Testament. . . .

Q.3. Is it right to learn to sing by Notes?

I answer; To me it appears quite proper and laudable, for those who have time and capacity for it. . . .

Q.4. Ought carnal people, or our own children, to join with us in singing the praises of God?

Ans. To me it is clear that they ought. . . . it is binding on all men, converted and unconverted. . . .

Q.5. Is it right to sing in parts? And if so, in how many parts?

Ans. I know of no scripture, nor any rational argument, which militates against singing in parts, admitting it be done in love, and appear to be most for the spiritual edification of the church, . . .

Thus I have dropped a few thoughts freely, though briefly, "on SINGING in the Worship of God." May He "who inhabits the praises of ISRAEL," command his blessing on those who read them!

6

Particular Baptists in England

During the eighteenth century the Particular Baptists rode the same spiritual roller coaster that swept along most of English Protestantism of the time. Like others, the Baptists dipped to devastating spiritual lows and later in the century rose to exciting new peaks. After losing the early generation of great pioneers like William Kiffin and Benjamin Keach, Particular Baptists had difficulty in replacing them with leaders of comparable spirit and vision. The decline of Particular Baptists into the more exaggerated forms of Calvinistic determinism is identified with such names as John Brine and John Gill, both of whom are represented in this chapter.

The spiritual renewal of Particular Baptists after midcentury is connected with such names as Robert Hall, Andrew Fuller, and William Carey. The system of theology which took the name of "Fullerism" retained its Calvinistic base, but allowed human initiative in preaching, missions, and gospel invitations. Acting upon this theology, William Carey led in forming the Baptist Mission Society, an organization which captured the attention and enthusiasm of English Baptists and extended its influence also to Europe and to colonial America. Selections are included here from the writings of Hall, Fuller, and Carey. The minutes of the Baptist Missionary Society of 1792 are included to show the beginning work of that important Baptist organization.

6.1   Hercules Collins, *The Temple Repair'd*, 1702

The long subtitle identifies this essay as an effort to lead the English Baptists to provide an adequate ministry for the churches. By the turn of the century many of the university-educated pastors who had been swept into Baptist life in the halcyon days of the 1640s and 1650s had passed off the scene, and the churches had not yet perfected any plan for replacing them. Hercules Collins, a Particular Baptist, put the responsibility squarely on the churches for enlisting, training, and supporting an adequate ministry. He affirmed that every church should be a seminary. His practical suggestions on biblical hermeneutics to arrive at the meaning of Scripture passages, sermon preparation and delivery, proper behavior for a pastor in the pulpit, and the dangers of lengthy sermons still bear careful reading today. *Source:* Hercules Collins, "The Temple Repair'd. Or, An Essay to revive the long neglected Ordinances, of exercising the Spiritual Gift of Prophecy for the Edification of the Churches; and of ordaining Ministers duly qualified. With proper Directions as to Study and Preaching, for such as are inclin'd to the Ministry" (London: n.p., 1702). Copy in Angus Collection, Regent's Park College, Oxford.

To the Churches of Christ, with all their Pastors and Teachers, and others who have a promising Gift for the edifying the Church; Grace and Gifts be multiplied upon you, through the Knowledg of God, and our Saviour Jesus Christ.

Dearly Beloved; The substance of the Matter contain'd in this Book was deliver'd at a Meeting designed for the promoting Spiritual Gifts in the Churches of Christ, but since that I have seen cause to make some considerable Additions to what was then preached. There are three principal things which induc'd me to publish these my poor Labours in this sad and careless day, wherein there is so little Provision made in the Churches of Christ for a future Ministry; and the first thing is this, That the Churches which are the Schools of Christ may be stir'd up to see what Spiritual Gifts God hath given them, and put them into their proper Exercise. 2. That all Pastors and Teachers would look upon it as their Duty to instruct those Members who are most capable into the knowledg of Gospel Mysteries: . . . My third end in making this publick is, That the Members of Churches, especially those to whom God hath given a good degree of Spiritual Knowledg, would not always content themselves to be only Hearers, but to stir up those Gifts in an humble manner, and put them in use for the Churches Edification; and in order to a regular proceeding and managing that Work, I have given some few plain Directions in this Book.

And let such seriously consider the Apostle Paul's Reproof to the Church of the Hebrews, who tells them, they had need be taught again the first Principles of the Oracles of God, even those very Persons who for the time ought to have been Teachers of others. Pray hear what the late Reverend Dr. Owen saith to this place in his Exercitations on the Epistle to the Hebrews. 'The Apostle doth not only say that they had enjoyed such a time and season of Instruction, as they might have been able to instruct others, but this he declares as their Duty, Ye ought to have been Teachers of others, that is, publick Teachers in the Church.' . . . Every Church was then a Seminary, wherein not only Provision was made for the preaching of the Gospel in it self, but for the calling, gathering, and teaching of other Churches also: . . .

From these and many other Texts of Scripture, 'tis manifest that this Primitive Practice was not to restrain the means of Edification, nor make Teaching and Instruction peculiar to Office; but the Privilege of all that God hath enabled, and Providence called to exercise. . . . But tho all gifted Brethren (duly qualified with Ministerial Gifts of Learning and Utterance, called by the Providence of God, and appointed by any Church and People of God to preach and teach) may lawfully and warrantably do it; yet this liberty doth no more make void the use and necessity of settled and standing Officers in particular Churches, than any good Man's care of the Poor makes void the Office of Deacons; . . . And therefore in this matter we ought to magnify the bountiful Care of Almighty God, for the Provisions he hath made for his Churches, in that he would not leave them to the uncertainty of a general Obligation, lest there might be some neglect in those Administrations, but hath instituted and appointed that in his Churches there should be settled standing Officers, whose stated Work, Duty and Business is to teach and exhort, take care and feed those particular Churches to whom they are made Overseers, . . .

Therefore it is greatly desired, and would be a very glorious Work, if all the Elders of the Churches in every City in England would not only be concern'd in their own particular Congregations for a future Ministry, but that the several Elders would set apart some time every Week for the instructing young Men, Members of Churches, inclin'd to Divine Studies; and so in the Country where two or three Churches are not far asunder, that all their Elders would agree to meet once a Month, or oftner, to hear the Gifts that God hath given their Churches. And that their Gifts might be discover'd, they ought first of all to be put upon Prayer, and then to see what Gifts they have for opening the Word of God; and this to be done to the end that some may be able to teach others also, when we put off this Earthly Tabernacle. . . .

INTRODUCTION. We read in the Books of the Kings in several places of the Schools of the Prophets, and the Sons of the Prophets, who were instructed by those called Fathers, or Seers, such as Samuel, Elijah and Elisha: 'tis not probable that they taught them any Languages, for there was no need of that, because God's Revelations to them were in their own Native Tongue; neither could they give them the holy Spirit, that being God's Prerogative alone; but 'tis very likely the aged Prophets did declare their Prophecies which they had from Jehovah, and open'd and explain'd the Law to them, and put them upon exercising themselves in holy Studies, with a frequent reading the Oracles of God, and meditating therein day and night, with Prayer to the Almighty: and this was done, to make them the more fit for Prophetick Revelation. These Sons of the Prophets were very many, and probably increased by the Ministry and Miracles of Elijah and Elisha.

From the Consideration of these things aforesaid, and the little Care that Churches take for a future Ministry, I have been stir'd up to cast in my Mite into the Treasury of Divine Counsel, hoping it may be of some use to those young Persons whose Hearts God hath inclin'd to the Ministry of the Word: And if my Heart do not deceive me, my Ends are purely the Enlargement and Perfection of the Kingdom of Christ.

That Scripture which I shall lay for the Foundation of my Discourse, is 2 Tim. ii. 15. Study to shew thy self approved unto God, a Workman that needeth not to be ashamed, rightly dividing the Word of Truth. . . .

Now I shall sum up all into one Doctrine. Doct. That it is the Duty of every Gospel-Minister so to study as they may approve themselves to God; and so divide the Word of Truth, that they may not be ashamed, but rather have the Honour that belongs to that calling.

In speaking to this Proposition I shall use this Method. 1st. I shall explain the Point. 2dly. Lay down one Proposition. 3dly. Shew who are good Workmen. 4thly. Give the Reasons why they should so study. 5thly. Improve the Doctrine.

I. By way of Explanation. When the Apostle saith rightly dividing the Word of Truth, you must know it is a Metaphorical Expression, a borrowed Saying, whether it be from the Priest's cutting the Sacrifices, so as all had their proper shares; or from the Parents dividing the Dish amongst several Children; or from the Carpenter, who divides his Timber by a right Line: The word imports thus much, that Ministers should so divide the Word of Truth, as to give every one their due Portion. . . .

II. The second General Head is to lay down one Proposition, which is this;

That it's God alone by the Inspiration of his holy Spirit can make Men able Ministers of the New Testament: This is proved by Christ's words to Paul, who said unto him, I have appear'd unto thee for this purpose, to make thee a Minister and a Witness both of those things thou hast seen, and in those things in which I will appear unto thee. And this St. Paul acknowledgeth, when he saith, Christ hath made us able Ministers of the New Testament. And tho it be granted that human Literature is very useful for a Minister, yet it is not essentially necessary; but to have the Spirit of Christ to open the Word of Christ is essentially necessary: For altho it is possible to make an exact Translation of the Scriptures out of many learned Languages, and give an exact Grammatical Construction of the same, yet if this Man can be void of the Spirit of Christ, he cannot know or understand the Mysteries contain'd in God's Word. . . .

V. The Use and Application. 1. By way of Information. If it be the Duty of Gospel Ministers to study to divide the Word of God aright, then we fairly and naturally infer, that it is their Sin that preach and neglect Study. You may easily perceive from the Pulpit whether the Man hath wrought hard at his Study the week before, or not. . . .

2. This Doctrine refutes the Opinion of those that think it unlawful to study to declare God's Mind, and will contemptuously speak against it, as if we were to preach by Inspiration, as the Prophets and Apostles of old did. What can be a better Confutation of those Men than our Text? which commands Ministers to study to shew themselves good Workmen; and to meditate in God's Law day and night. . . .

3. This affords us a Use of Caution. If it be Ministers Duty to study, then be cautioned against Idleness in the great things of God, and the Concerns of immortal Souls; the Lord hath often reproved idle Shepherds. There is so much precious time spent in the World and Pleasures thereof, that there is a very small remnant of the Week left, I fear by too many, so that they have not sufficient time to improve the Talent God hath

given them; and what can be expected then but a lean Discourse, if not a confused one, when the Sabbath comes?

4. This affords a Use of Consolation. If Shame will attend them that are lazy and idle in the things of God, then Honour and Praise will follow those that are true Labourers in the Lord's Vineyard. . . .

To what I have said I shall add some further helps by way of Direction and Instruction to those that are inclin'd to the Ministration of the Gospel. Consider my whole Method in speaking, 1. To the Penman of the Epistle. 2. To the Time when written. 3. The Occasion. 4. The Scope. Not that there will be always need upon every Subject to take notice of these things, yet upon some Subjects there may be need to take notice of some or all of them. 2dly. Consider how your Text coheres and depends upon what goes before it, but stand no longer upon it than what may make your way plain to the Text. Some have spent so much time upon a Context, that by that time they came to their Text the hour was almost gone, tho they did not know whether they should preach in the same place again. 3dly. Make an exact Division of your Text, if your Text calls you to it, for that will be profitable in the helping of you to Matter. 4thly. Explain any difficult Terms, but spend not time needlessly in Explanation, if things are easily understood without it. 5thly. Raise as many doctrines as the Text will allow, and make what good use you can of every one of them, but insist most on the chief Scope of the place. 6thly. Your Doctrine being laid down, prove it from the Word of God by two or three Scriptures at most; because in the mouth of two or three Witnesses every Truth is established.

After you have prov'd it, then lay down the Reasons and Arguments of the Point why and wherefore it is so. You see that my third General Head is to show what a good Workman is, but that (What) will not come in the handling of every Doctrine. Some Persons lay down Propositions just after their Doctrine; but whatever is done in that, may be done in an Use of Instruction; but that is at your liberty, whether you will do it in Propositions, or an Use of Instruction. And then, what Use you make, let it be always natural from the Doctrine, and draw as many Inferences from it as it will bear; for they are generally very divine things. . . .

Additional Directions and Instructions. 1st. Know ye that the Scriptures are the Best Expositors of themselves; no Man, nor no Church can explain God's Word better than it doth it self: . . .

2dly. Give your selves to reading, above all, the holy Scriptures. . . .

3dly. Let all you deliver be according to the Analogy of Faith; never interpret one Text so as to thwart another; abandon all private Opinions, tho they are never so taking. . . .

4thly. Let your Speech be plain, as Paul's was, Not with enticing Words of Man's Wisdom, but in demonstration of the Spirit, and of Power. Use sound Words that cannot be condemned. Rhetorical Flourishes are like painted Glass in a Window, that makes a great show, but darkens the Light; . . . Let us never speak Words we do not understand ourselves, nor they which hear us. The Prophets and Apostles generally spoke in the vulgar and common Languages which the ordinary People understood: They did not only speak to the Understanding of a King upon the Throne, but to the Understanding of the meanest Subject.

5thly. Watch against vain Tautologies, and repeating the same thing over and over in other words, unless it be when you are more than ordinarily affected with what you are upon from the movings of God's Spirit, and that is hardly ever burdensome to the Hearers; for if the Minister be affected, generally the People are affected; and if the Minister be dull, generally the people are dull. . . .

7thly. Let your Carriage and Habit in a Pulpit be grave and sober, let us have no indecent Behaviour, nor uncomely Garb. It hath been lamented by many to see Ministers, who were set by God for Ensamples to the Flock, with their Hair and Shoulders covered with Pouder, especially when they enter the Pulpit. . . . Our Carriage, Habit and Deportment should be such that we may convince the Consciences of Men that we seek God's Glory and their Good.

And that this may be the better effected, we must speak so loud as our Auditory may hear us, or else both the End of Preaching and Hearing is lost. . . . And take heed of an affected Tone in preaching; let your Voice be natural, or else sound Doctrine may be liable to Contempt.

8thly. We should get the Substance of our Sermons if possible for the Lord's day before Saturday, or else we may be at a loss, and have very poor and lean Discourses: . . . Let the last day of the Week be for the better digesting your Discourses, and treasuring them up in your Memory, and turning to your best Annotators to see what they say upon the Proofs of every Head, as well as upon the Text; and on the Lord's-day before you preach, either Forenoon or Afternoon, spend one half hour in running over your Sermon, either as written in your Study, or as it is laid up in your Memory, or as in both: in so doing it will be profitable both to Minister and People; . . .

14thly. If thou hast much of God's Presence in preaching, be not over confident that that Sermon shall do most good; and if thou art in a dull frame in preaching, so long as you preach God's Word, do not despair of a good Effect; for some have experienced some Sermons blest which they thought were lost, and have heard nothing to their Comfort of that Sermon they expected most from, and this is done that no Flesh might glory in God's Presence.

15thly. Let us preach and prophesy according to the proportion of Faith and Knowledg, speak experimentally and feelingly; that which comes from the Heart is generally carried to the Heart, then it is we preach to Edification; and to that end let not your Sermons in common be very long; it is better to leave the People longing than loathing. Get your Hearts sincerely affected with those things you perswade others to, that your Hearers may see that you are in good earnest, and that you deliver nothing to the People but what you are willing to practice your selves, and venture your Salvation upon. . . .

Be exhorted ever more to maintain, and not lose that blessed Ordinance of Ordination, and calling those to Office who are fit for it. Some have been Probationers all their days, and it is matter of Lamentation, that some Churches have imploy'd Persons in Preaching and administring Ordinances ten or twenty years, tho fitly qualified, and yet never call'd them to Office. And tho in my Epistle I have prov'd the lawfulness, yea and the necessity of preaching in ordinary before Ordination, yet I did never intend by that to destroy a Gospel-Ordinance, viz. a solemn Ordination to Office: Tho it is most true that the Holy Ghost makes Men Overseers of the Church, and that Gifts and Graces are from Christ (which is his internal Call) yet he ought to have an external Call by the Church, to ordain him to Office. . . . Ever retain and never part with that Rite and Ceremony in Ordination of Imposition of Hands, with Prayer, on the Person ordained. . . .

Finally, be exhorted that as your Ministers take care of your Souls, you would take care of their Bodies and Families: The same Shepherd that watches over the Flock is clothed and fed by the Flock. They are bound to take care of your Souls, which is the greater; you ought to take care of their Bodies, which is the lesser.

6.2   John Brine, *A Defense of the Doctrine of Eternal Justification,* 1732

In the eighteenth century the Particular Baptists, who had always been Calvinistic, tended to move toward hyper-Calvinism. Many of them refused to apply the gospel to sinners, abandoned and even ridiculed evangelistic invitations, and severely limited human ability to respond to the gospel. John Brine (1703-1765) helped to fix upon Particular Baptists a withering form of hyper-Calvinism. His treatise argues, as the title suggests, that justification is *eternal*, that the elect are justified from eternity past long before their response of faith. Or, to use Brine's own words, "I shall here endeavour to prove, that Justification by faith has no causality in this affair [salvation]." Brine was influenced by John Skepp (d. 1721) and, in turn, influenced the great John Gill (1697-1771). Brine's theology allowed no room for evangelistic preaching and thus, not surprisingly, his church declined severely. *Source:* John Brine, *A Defense of the Doctrine of Eternal Justification* (London: n.p., 1732). Copy in the Angus Collection, Regent's Park College, Oxford.

The doctrine of Eternal Justification has been lately objected to by Mr. Bragge, in some sermons of his on that subject, published with some other sermons preached at Limestreet, by several ministers; wherein they propose, according to the general title, to state and defend the great doctrines of the gospel, and to answer such objections as are usually advanced against them.

As I have reason to believe Justification from Eternity to be a scriptural doctrine, I think my self under obligation to appear in its defence; and therefore have determined to communicate my thoughts on that subject in this public manner. . . .

First, I am to enquire what it is to be justified by faith. Very great controversies have been moved concerning this. Some affirm, that we are so, in a proper sense; or that faith is the matter and cause of our Justification, as the Arminians and Socinians. This others justly deny; and assert, that Christ's righteousness alone is the matter and cause of our Justification. I shall here endeavour to prove, that Justification by faith has no causality in this affair; it is not the impulsive, material, nor instrumental cause thereof.

1. Faith is not the impulsive or moving cause of Justification. It is an act of pure and free grace, without any motive in the creature. Therefore the Apostle saith, "being justified freely by his grace, through the redemption which is in Jesus Christ." But this benefit would not be of grace, but of works, was our faith the impulsive cause of it; because faith is a work or acts of ours, as we learn from the words of Christ: This is the work of God, that ye believe on him whom he hath sent. Salvation is not of works, in any branch of it; "for by grace are we saved, through faith; that not of our selves, it is the gift of God: not of works, lest any man should boast." From whence it is evident that Justification, which is a considerable part of salvation, cannot be by works. . . . No other cause can be assigned why sinners are justified in the sight of God, than his free favour and sovereign pleasure, as the effect of which he determined to justify them in the righteousness of his Son.

2. Neither is faith the matter of our Justification; which appears by these arguments.

(1.) Because that righteousness, by which we are justified before God, is not our own. . . . It is manifest, that the Apostle excluded every thing from the business of his Justification which might be accounted his own; and, consequently, faith it self, which though it is a fruit of special grace, may properly be reckoned our own, . . .

Faith is an act and work of ours, and therefore cannot be the matter of our Justification. . . .

5. We are justified by the obedience and sufferings of Christ, and consequently not by faith. . . .

Faith is not so much as *causa sine qua non* in this affair, as appears by the eternal Justification of the elect. It has not the least concern herein, if Justification is properly taken.

Secondly, I now proceed to mention those arguments, by which the truth of eternal Justification is confirmed. And,

1. Justification is an immanent, and consequently an eternal act. This argument must be allowed conclusive, unless it can be proved that Justification is a transient act.

2. The elect were by God considered and viewed in Christ from everlasting; . . .

3. The elect were blest with all spiritual blessings in Christ before the foundation of the world; and therefore with Justification, for that is a spiritual blessing. . . .

4. When Christ, as a surety, engaged for the elect, they were justified. . . .

Therefore why may it not be concluded that the elect were justified from everlasting, since God had the atonement of Christ then in his eye?

Justification is God's act, not ours. He only justifies the ungodly by imputing Christ's righteousness to them. Therefore Justification by faith is not to be understood properly, i.e. the being of Justification is not designed; for that has no dependance on faith but the knowledge of this benefit is intended when it is said we are justified by faith. . . .

Object. 2. "If the elect are justified without faith, they may be saved without faith."

I answer: It is very bad logic to argue from a part to the whole; that which is true of the whole, is of a part, but not on the contrary; that which is true of a part, may not be so of the whole. Again: It may justly be said, that in some sense the elect are saved before they believe, and consequently without faith, as appears by these words: "who hath saved us, and called us with an holy calling not according to our works, but according to his own purpose and grace, given us in Christ before the world began." . . .

Thus I have considered all the objections which I have met with, that seem to have a weight in them against the doctrine of eternal Justification; and have, as I hope, fully answered them.

6.3 John Gill, *A Body of Doctrinal Divinity,* 1769

Most historians consider John Gill the major English Baptist example of hyper-Calvinism. Gill (1697-1771) was reared in Kettering, and in 1719 began a pastorate in London that lasted for over fifty years. He spent little time in pastoral ministry, but devoted himself to study, lecturing, and writing. His Thursday lectures drew a cross section of leading citizens of London, from all denominations, to hear the brilliant Dr. Gill lecture on the Bible. His writings were prolific and profound, if not always clear. Gill's *Body of Divinity* (1769) is usually considered his greatest work. Gill maintained that redemption does not apply to all people, but only to the elect who are chosen before the foundation of the world. There is no way, in his system, for the elect to be lost or for the nonelect to be saved. The following is excerpted from *A Body of Divinity,* chapter II (God's election of some) and chapter III (God's rejection of others). *Source:* John Gill, *A Body of Doctrinal and Practical Divinity* (London: n.p., 1769). Reprinted in 1815, and republished in 1977 by Primitive Baptist Library, Streamwood, Illinois. The latter edition is used here, 125 *ff.*

CHAP. II
OF THE SPECIAL DECREES OF GOD, RELATING TO RATIONAL CREATURES, ANGELS, AND MEN; AND PARTICULARLY OF ELECTION.

The special decrees of God respecting rational creatures, commonly go under the name of *predestination;* though this sometimes is taken in a large sense, to express every thing that God has predetermined; and so it takes in all that has been observed in the preceding chapter; which some call eternal providence, of which, temporary providence is the execution; for with God there is not only a provision of things future, but a provision for the certain bringing them to pass; and the counsel and will of God is the source and spring of all things, and the rule and measure according to which he works, Eph. i. 11. but predestination is usually considered as consisting of two parts, and including the two branches of election and reprobation, both with respect to angels and men; for each of these have place in both. Angels; some of them are called *elect* angels,

2 Tim. v. 21. others are said to be *reserved in chains,* in the chains of God's purposes and providence, *unto* the *judgment* of the great day, 2 Pet. ii. 4. Men; some of them are vessels of mercy, afore-prepared for glory; others vessels of wrath, fitted for destruction; some are the *election,* or the elect persons, that obtain righteousness, life, and salvation; and others are the *rest* that are left in, and given up to blindness. Rom. ix. 22, 23. and xi. 7. Though sometimes predestination only respects that branch of it called election, and the predestinated signify only the elect; for who else are called, justified, and glorified, enjoy adoption and the heavenly inheritance? not, surely, the non-elect. Rom. viii. 29, 30. Eph. i. 5, 11. This branch of predestination, election, must be considered first; I shall begin with,

I. The election of angels; of this the scriptures speak but sparingly, and therefore the less need to be said concerning it: that there are some angels that are elect is certain, from the proof already given: there is a similarity between their election and the election of men; though in some things there appears a little difference. . . .

II. The election of men to grace and glory, is next to be considered; and it may be proper in the first place to take some notice of the election of Christ, as man and mediator; who is God's first and chief elect; and is, by way of eminency, called his elect; . . .

But what will now be chiefly attended to, and what the scriptures speak so largely of, is the election of men in Christ unto eternal life.

Some are of opinion that this doctrine of election, admitting it to be true, should not be published, neither preached from the pulpit, nor handled in schools and academies, nor treated of in the writings of men; the reasons they give, are because it is a secret, and secret things belong to God: and because it tends to fill mens' minds with doubts about their salvation, and to bring them into distress, and even into despair; and because some may make a bad use of it, to indulge themselves in a sinful course of life, and argue, that if they are elected they shall be saved, let them live as they may, and so it opens a door to all licentiousness: but these reasons are frivolous and groundless; the doctrine of election is no secret, it is clearly and fully revealed, and written as with a sunbeam in the sacred scriptures; . . .

I proceed then,

First, To observe the phrases by which it is expressed in scripture, whereby may be learnt what is the true meaning of the words *election* and *elect,* as used in scripture with respect to this doctrine. It is expressed by being ordained to eternal life, Acts xiii. 48. *As many as were ordained to eternal life, believed;* by which ordination is meant no other than the predestination, choice, and appointment of men to everlasting life and salvation by Jesus Christ; . . .

This act of God is also expressed by the *names* of persons being *written in heaven,* and in the *book of life,* called, *the Lamb's book of life;* . . . But the more common phrases used concerning it, are those of being *chosen* and *elected;* hence the objects of it are called God's *elect,* and the *election;* that is, persons elected, . . . Wherefore the election treated of is not,

1. An election of a nation to some external privileges, as the people of Israel, who were chosen of God to be a special people, . . . And so this nation of ours is selected and distinguished from many others, by various blessings of goodness, and particularly by having the means of grace; yet all the individuals of it cannot be thought to be the objects of election to special grace, and eternal glory.

2. Nor of an election to offices; . . . and though Christ chose twelve to be his apostles, one of them was a devil: so that though those were chosen to offices, and even to the highest offices in the church and state, yet not to eternal life.

3. Nor of an election of whole bodies and communities of men, under the character of churches, to the enjoyment of the means of grace: . . .

5. This is to be understood of the choice of certain persons by God, from all eternity, to grace and glory; it is an act by which men are chosen of God's good will and pleasure, before the world was, to holiness and happiness, to salvation by Christ, to partake of his glory, and to enjoy eternal life, as the free gift of God through him, . . .

Secondly, The next thing to be considered is, by whom election is made, and in whom it is made: it is made by God, and it is made in Christ. 1. It is made by God, as the efficient cause of it; God, who is a sovereign Being, who does and may do whatever he pleases in heaven and in earth, among angels and men; and has a right to do what he will with his own; as with his own things. temporal and spiritual blessings; so with his own creatures, Shall he be denied that which every man thinks he has a right unto and does? do not kings choose their own ministers; masters their servants; and every man his own favourites, friends, and companions? And may not God choose whom he pleases to communion with him, both here and hereafter; or to grace and glory? . . . And this now being the act of God, it is for ever; for whatever God does in a way of special grace, it is for ever; it is unchangeable and irrevocable; men may choose some to be their favourites and friends for a while, and then alter their minds, and choose others in their room; but God never acts such a part, he is in one mind, and none can turn him; his purpose, according to election, or with respect to that, stands sure, firm, and unalterable.————
2. This act is made in Christ, *according as he hath chosen us in him,* Eph. 1. 4. Election does not find men in Christ, but puts them there; it gives them a being in him, and union to him; which is the foundation of their open being in Christ at conversion, . . .

. . . the reasons why men are elected, are not because Christ has shed his blood, died for them, redeemed and saved them; but Christ has done all this for them because they are elect; . . . now it is not Christ's laying down his life for them makes them sheep, and elect; they are so previous to that; but because they are sheep, and chosen ones in Christ, and given him by his Father, therefore he laid down his life for them. . . .

Thirdly, The objects of election are to be next inquired after, who are men; for with such only is now our concern; and these not as under such and such characters, as called, converted, believers in Christ, holy and good men, and persevering in faith and holiness unto the end; for they are not elected because they are called, converted, &c. but because they are elected they become all this; and if they are not elected, especially until they have persevered unto the end, I can see no need of their being elected at all; for when they have persevered unto the end, they are immediately in heaven, in the enjoyment of eternal life, and can have no need to be chose to it: and all these characters put together, only amount to such a proposition, that he that believes, and endures to the end, shall be saved. But God does not choose propositions, but persons; not characters, but men, nakedly and abstractly considered; and these not all men, but some, . . . they are distinct from the rest of mankind; vessels of mercy, in distinction from vessels of wrath; a seed, a remnant, according to the election of grace; and election itself, as distinguished from the others, called the *rest;* whilst some are given up to believe a lie, that they might be damned, others being beloved of God, are chosen from the beginning to salvation by Christ; for certain it is, that all the individuals of mankind, neither partake of the means fixed in the decree of election, sanctification of the Spirit, and belief of the truth; nor attain to the end of it, which, with respect to men, is eternal life and happiness; . . .

And here is the proper place to discuss that question, Whether men were considered, in the mind of God, in the decree of election, as fallen or unfallen; as in the corrupt mass, through the fall; or in the pure mass of creatureship, previous to it; and as to be created? There are some that think that the latter, so considered, were the objects of election in the divine mind; who are called supralapsarians; though of these some are of opinion that man was considered, as to be created, or creatable; and others, as created, but not fallen. The former seems best; that of the vast number of individuals that came up in the divine mind, that his power could create, those that he meant to bring into being, he designed to glorify himself by them in some way or another; the decree of election, respecting any part of them, may be distinguished into the decree of the end, and the decree of the means. The decree of the end, respecting some, is either subordinate to their eternal happiness, or ultimate; which is more properly the end, the glory of God; and if both are put together, it is a state of everlasting communion with God, for the glorifying the riches of his sovereign grace and goodness, Eph. i. 5, 6. The decree of the means, includes the decree to create men, to permit them to fall, to recover them out of it through redemption by Christ, to sanctify them by the grace of the Spirit, and completely save them; and which are not to be reckoned as materially many decrees, but as making one formal decree; or they are not to be considered as subordinate, but coordinate means, and as making up one entire complete medium; . . . Again, they argue that the end is first in view, before the means; and the decree of the end is, in order of nature, before the decree of the means; and what is first in intention, is last in execution: now as the glory of God is the last in execution, it must be first in intention; wherefore men must be considered, in the decree of the end, as not yet created and fallen; since the creation and permission of sin, belong to the decree of the means; which, in order of nature, is after the decree of the end: and they add to this, that if God first decreed to create man, and suffer him to fall, and then, out of the fall chose some to grace and glory; he must decree to create man without an end, which is to make God to do what no wise man would; for when a man is about to do any thing, he proposes an end, and then contrives and fixes on ways and means to bring about that end: and it cannot be thought that the all-wise and only-wise God should act otherwise; . . .

On the other hand, those who are called sublapsarians, and are for men being considered as created and fallen, in the decree of election, urge, John xv. 19. *I have chosen you out of the world.* Now the world is full of wickedness, it lies in it, is under the power of the wicked one; the inhabitants of it live in sin, and all of them corrupt and abominable; and therefore they that are chosen out of them must be so too: but this text is not to be understood of eternal election, but of effectual vocation; by which men are called and separated from the world, among whom they have had their conversation before conversion, and according to the course of it have lived. They further observe, that the elect are called *vessels of mercy;* which supposes them to have been miserable, and so sinful, and to stand in need of mercy; and must be so considered in their election: but though through various means the elect are brought to happiness, which are owing to the mercy of God; such as the mission of Christ to save them, the forgiveness of their sins, their regeneration and salvation; and so fitly called *vessels of mercy;* yet it follows not that they were considered as in need of mercy in their choice of happiness. It is also said, that men are chosen in Christ as Meditator, Redeemer, and Saviour; which implies, that an offence is given and taken, and reconciliation is to be made, and redemption from sin, and the curse of the law broken, and complete salvation to be effected by Christ; all which supposes men to be sinful, as it does: but then men are chosen in Christ, not as the meritorious cause of election, but as the means, or medium, of bringing them to the happiness they are chosen to. . . . These are some of the principal arguments used on both sides; the difference is not so great as may be thought at first sight; for both agree in the main and material things in the doctrine of election; as,———1. That it is personal and particular, is of persons by name, whose names are written in the Lamb's book of life.———2. That it is absolute and unconditional, not depending on the will of men, nor on any thing to be done by the creature.———3. That it is wholly owing to the will and pleasure of God; and not to the faith, holiness, obedience, and good works of men; nor to a foresight of all or any of these.———4. That both elect, and non-elect, are considered alike, and are upon an equal foot in the decree of predestination; as those that are for the corrupt mass they suppose that they are both considered in it equally alike, so that there was nothing in the one that was not in the other, which was a reason why the one should be chosen and the other left; so those that are for the pure mass, suppose both to be considered in the same, and as not yet born, and having done neither good nor evil.———5. That it is an eternal act in God, and not temporal; or which commenced not in time, but from all eternity; for it is not the opinion of the sublapsarians, that God passed the decree of election after men were actually created and fallen; only that they were considered in the divine mind, from all eternity, in the decree of election, as if they were created and fallen; wherefore, though they differ in the consideration of the object of election, as thus and thus diversified, yet they agree in the thing, and agree to differ, as they should, and not charge one another with unsoundness and heterodoxy; for which there is no reason. . . .

Fourthly, The date of election is next to be considered. And certain it is, that it was before men were born; . . .

And that this act of election is an eternal act, or from eternity, may be concluded,———1. From the foreknowledge of God, which is eternal; God from all eternity foreknew all persons and things; there is nothing in time but what was known to him from eternity, . . . 2. The eternity of election may be concluded from the love of God to his people; for it is to that it is owing; *electio præsupponit dilectionem,* election presupposes love; . . . 6. From the nature of the decrees of God in general, it must appear that this is eternal; for if God's decrees in general are eternal, as has been proved from his foreknowledge of whatever comes to pass; which is founded upon the certainty of his decrees, that so they shall be; and from his immutability, which could not be established if any new thoughts and resolutions arose in him, . . .

Fifthly, The impulsive, or moving cause of this act in God, or what were the motives and inducements with God to take such a step as this: and these were not—1. The good works of men; for this act passed in eternity, before any works were done; . . . 2. Neither is the holiness of men, whether in principle or in practice, or both, the moving cause of election to eternal life; it is an end to which men are chosen; . . . 3. Nor is faith the moving cause of election; the one is in time, the other in eternity: . . . 4. Nor is perseverance in faith, holiness, and good works, the moving cause of election; but the effect of it, and what is ensured by it: the reason why men persevere is, because they are the elect of God, . . .

In short, these maxims are certainly true, and indisputable, that nothing in time can be the cause of what was done in eternity; to believe, to be holy, to do good works, and persevere in them, are acts in time, and so cannot be causes of election, which was done in eternity; . . .

Sixthly, The means fixed in the decree of election, for the execution of it, or in order to bring about the end intended, are next to be inquired into; which are, the principal of them, the mediation of Christ, and redemption by him, the sanctification of the Spirit, and belief of the truth. The mediation of Christ; Christ, as God, is the efficient cause of election; in his office-capacity as an Head, the elect are chosen in him, as members of him; and though his mediation, bloodshed, sufferings, and death, are not the meritorious cause of election, yet Christ in them is the medium of the execution of it; that is, of bringing the chosen ones, through grace, to glory, . . .

Seventhly, The ends settled in the decree of election are both subordinate and ultimate; the subordinate ones have indeed the nature of means with respect to the ultimate one: there are many things to which the elect of God, predestinated or chosen, both with respect to grace and glory, which are subordinate to the grand end, the glory of God. So God is said to *predestinate* them *to be conformed to the image of his Son,* to be made like unto him, not so much in his sonship, nor in his sufferings, as in his holiness: . . . and that in order to another end, that Christ *might be the first-born among many brethren;* the brethren are the predestinated ones, who are brethren to each other; and these are many, the many sons Christ brings to glory; and he is the first-born among them; and that he may appear to be so, he is set up as the pattern of them, to whose image they are predestinated to be conformed, . . .

Now all these ends, both respecting grace and glory, are subordinate ones to the grand and ultimate end of all, the glory of God; for as God swears by himself, because he could swear by no greater, so because a greater end could not be proposed than his own glory, he has set up that as the supreme end of all his decrees; he has *made,* that is, has appointed, *all things for himself,* for his own glory, . . .

Eighthly, The blessings and benefits flowing from election are many, indeed all spiritual blessings; it is as it were the rule, measure, and standard according to which they are communicated; the several chains in man's salvation are connected with it, and hang and depend upon it, Eph. i. 3, 4. Rom. viii. 30. they need only be just named in order, since they have been suggested under the former heads.———1. Vocation. *Whom he did predestinate, them he called;* all the predestinated, or chosen ones, are in time called, and are called according to the eternal purpose and grace of God in election, Rom. viii. 30. 2 Tim. i. 9.———2. Faith and holiness, and indeed every grace of the Spirit. Holiness is both an end and a mean in this decree, as before observed, and made certain by it; faith follows upon it as a free gift of grace, and so hope and love, and every other grace.———3. Communion with God. *Blessed is the man whom thou choosest, and causest to approach unto thee,* Psalm lxv. 4. to come into his presence, and enjoy it in his house, his word, and ordinances.———4. Justification; which is secretly a branch of it, and openly as to the manifestation of it, flows from it; *Who shall lay any thing to the charge of God's elect? it is God that justifieth,* that is, the elect; who because they are chosen in Christ, they are justified in him, Rom viii. 33.———5. Adoption; to which the elect are predestinated, and are denominated the children of God, being given to Christ as such when chosen in him, before the incarnation of Christ, redemption by him, or having the Spirit from him, Heb. ii. 13, 14. John xi. 52. Gal. iv. 6.———6. Glorification; *Whom he did predestinate—them he glorified,* Rom. viii. 30. the elect, the vessels of mercy, are *afore prepared for glory,* for eternal glory and happiness; and are chosen and called to the obtaining of the glory of Christ, which the Father has given to him to bestow upon them, and which they will most certainly enjoy. Rom. ix. 23. 2 Thess. ii. 13, 14.

Ninthly, The several properties of election may be gathered from what has been said of it; as,———1. That it is eternal; it does not commence upon believing, and much less at perseverance in faith and holiness; but it was an act in God before the foundation of the world, Eph. i. 4.———2. It is free and sovereign; God was not obliged to choose any; and as it is, he chooses whom he will, and for no other reason excepting his own glory, but because he will; *what if God willing,* &c. and the difference in choosing one and not another is purely owing to his will, Rom. ix. 18, 22, 23.———3. It is absolute and unconditional; clear of all motives in man, or conditions to be performed by him; for it *stands not of works, but of him that calleth,* the will of him that calls, Rom. ix. 11.———4. It is complete and perfect; it is not begun in eternity and completed in time, nor takes its rise from the will of God, and is finished by the will of man; nor is made perfect by faith, holiness, obedience, and persevering in well-doing, but has its complete being in the will of God at once.———5. It is immutable and irrevocable; God never repents of, nor revokes the choice he has made; some choose their friends and favourites, and alter their minds and choose others; but God is in one mind, and never makes any alteration in the choice he has made; and hence their state is safe and secure.———6. It is special and particular; that is, those who are chosen are chosen to be a special people above all others, and are particular persons, whose names are written in the book of life; not in general, men of such and such characters, but persons well known to God, and distinctly fixed on by him.———7. Election may be known by the persons, the objects of it; partly by the blessings flowing from it, and connected with it, before observed, bestowed upon them; for to whomsoever such blessings of grace are applied, they must be the elect of God, . . . indeed no man can know his election of God until he is called; it would be presumption in him to claim this character, until he is born again; nor should any man conclude himself a reprobate because a sinner, since all men are sinners; even God's elect, who are by nature, and in no wise better than others, but children of wrath, even as others.

There are many things objected to this doctrine of election; but since it is so clear and plain from scripture, and is written as with a sunbeam in it, all objections to it must be mere cavil. . . .

CHAP. III
OF THE DECREE OF REJECTION, OF SOME ANGELS, AND OF SOME MEN.

I make use of the word *rejection* in this article, partly because it is a scriptural phrase and ascribed to God, and partly because it is that act of God which gives the name of reprobate to any; and is the foundation of that character, *reprobate silver shall men call them, because the Lord hath rejected them,* Jer. vi. 30. and stands opposed to election, 1 Sam. xv. 26. and x. 24. but chiefly because the other word *reprobation,* through wrong and frightful ideas being affixed to it, carries in it with many a sound harsh and disagreeable; or otherwise they are of the same signification, and no amendment is made in the doctrine or sense of it, by using the one instead of the other. This doctrine of rejecting some angels and some men from the divine favour, is spoken of but sparingly in scripture, yet clearly and plainly; though chiefly left to be concluded from that of election, and from whence it most naturally and rationally follows. I shall begin with,

I. The rejection of some of the angels, which consists of two parts:———1. A non-election, or preterition of them, a passing over them or passing by them, when others were chosen; . . . for if some were elect, others must be non-elect; if some were chosen, others were not; . . .

II. The decree concerning the rejection of some of the sons of men. It may be observed, that we can hear and read of the non-election and rejection of angels, and of their preordination to condemnation and wrath, with very little emotion of mind: the devils may be cast down to hell, to be everlastingly damned, and be appointed thereunto, and it gives no great concern; no hard thoughts against God arise, no charge of cruelty, want of kindness to his creatures and offspring, and of injustice to them; but if any thing of this kind is hinted at, with respect to any of the apostate sons of Adam, presently there is an outcry against it; and all the above things are suggested. What is the reason of this difference? It can be only this, that the latter comes nearer home, and more nearly affects us; . . .

First, I shall prove that there is a non-election, or rejection of some of the sons of men, when others were chosen; and, indeed, from the election of some, may fairly be inferred, the non-election of others. Common sense tells us, that of persons or things, if some are chosen, others must be left: if there is a remnant of the sons of men, according to the election of grace, then there are others not included in it, which are left unchosen, and are called the *rest. The election,* that is, elect men, *hath obtained it,* righteousness and eternal life; *and the rest are blinded,* Rom. xi. 5, 7. Our Lord says, *I speak not of you all; I know whom I have chosen,* John xiii. 18. plainly intimating, that all were not chosen, and it is certain one was not, and whom he calls *the son of perdition;* one, not only deserving of it, but appointed to it; for though chosen to an office, as an apostle, yet not to grace and glory, John xvii. 12. and how many such there be, no man can pretend to say; but it is evident there are some, and who are generally described by negative characters; as *not known* by God and Christ; the elect are God's people, whom he knows; they are elect, according to his foreknowledge; which carries in it love and affection to them; but of others Christ says, *I never knew you;* he knew them by his omniscience, but not with such knowledge as he knows the elect of God; he never knew them as the objects of his Father's love, . . . they are frequently described, as not having their names written, and *not* to be *found written* in the Lamb's book of life, Rev. xiii. 8. and xvii. 8. and xx. 15. Now as election is signified by the writing of names in the book of life, non-election is expressed by not writing the names of some there; and if those whose names are written there, are the elect, then those whose names are not written there, but are left out, must be non-elect: . . .

Moreover, from the effects of election not having place in some persons, it may be concluded, that there are such who are non-elect. Vocation is a certain fruit and effect of election; *Whom he did predestinate, them he also called,* Rom. viii. 30. not only externally, but internally, with an holy and heavenly calling, to grace here, and glory hereafter. But are all called in this manner? No; there are some who have not so much as the outward call by the ministry of the word, have not the external means of grace; but as they sin without law, perish without it, Rom. x. 14. and ii. 12. Those who are chosen, are predestinated to be conformed to the image of Christ; they are chosen to holiness, and through sanctification of the Spirit. But are all made like to Christ, and conformed to his image? do not many bear the image of Satan, imitate him, and do his lusts? are all men made holy, or have they the sanctification of the Spirit? Whom God predestinates he justifies, by the righteousness of his Son. But are all men justified? No; for though he justifies some of all sorts and nations; as the circumcised Jews by faith, and the uncircumcised Gentiles through faith, yet not every individual; yea, there is a world that will be condemned, and consequently not predestinated to life, 1 Cor. xi. 32. . . . Moreover, whom God has predestinated, or chosen to life and happiness, these he glorifies . . . . But are all glorified? do not some go into perdition, even into everlasting punishment? and therefore must be considered as non-elect, . . . All this put together most clearly and fully proves, that there are some who are not chosen of God, but rejected by him.

Secondly, The parts of this decree, concerning the rejection of men, are commonly said to be preterition and pre-damnation.

1. Preterition is God's passing by some men, when he chose others: and in this act, or part of the decree, men are considered as in the pure mass of creatureship, or creability; in which state they are found, when passed by or rejected, and in which they are left, even just as they are found, nothing put into them; but were left in the pure mass, as they lay, and so no injury done them; nor is God to be charged with any injustice towards them. . . .

2. Pre-damnation is God's appointment, or preordination of men to condemnation for sin; . . . God hardens some mens' hearts, as he did Pharaoh's, and he wills to harden them, or he hardens them according to his decreeing will; *Whom he will he hardeneth,* Rom. ix. 18. this he does not by any positive act, by infusing hardness and blindness into the hearts of men; which is contrary to his purity and holiness, and would make him the author of sin; but by leaving men to their natural blindness and hardness of heart; for the understanding is naturally darkened; and there is a natural blindness, hardness, and callousness of heart, through the corruption of nature, and which is increased by habits of sinning; men are in darkness, and choose to walk in it; and therefore God, as he decreed, gives them up to their own wills and desires, and to Satan, the god of the world, . . .

Thirdly, The causes of this act.————1. The efficient cause is God; it is the Lord, that makes all things for his own glory, and the wicked for the day of evil; it is God that appoints to wrath, and foreordains to condemnation; . . .

2. The moving, or impulsive cause of God's making such a decree, by which he has rejected some of the race of Adam from his favour, is not sin, but the good pleasure of his will: sin is the meritorious cause of eternal death, wrath, and damnation; wrath is revealed from heaven against all unrighteousness and ungodliness of men, and comes upon the children of disobedience, whom God leaves in it; the wages, or demerit of sin, is death, even death eternal: but then it is not the impulsive cause of the decree itself; not of preterition, because that, as election, was before good or evil were done, and irrespective of either; nor of pre-damnation, God, indeed, damns no man but for sin; nor did he decree to damn any but for sin; but yet, though sin is the cause of damnation and death, the thing decreed, it is not the cause of the decree itself: it is the cause of the thing willed, but not the moving cause of God's will; for nothing out of God can move his will; if it could, the will of God would be dependent on the will and actions of men; whereas, his purpose, whether with respect to election or rejection, stands not on the works and wills of men, but on his own will and pleasure: . . .

3. The final cause, or end of this decree, is his own glory; this is the ultimate end of all his decrees and appointments, and so of this, appointing the wicked for the day of evil; it was for this purpose he raised up Pharaoh, and decreed all he did concerning him, that he might shew his power in him, his sovereignty and dominion over him, and that his name and glory might be declared throughout all the earth: . . .

Fourthly, The date of this decree is as ancient as eternity itself; wicked men are *before of old,* said to be *ordained to condemnation,* . . . If men were chosen from the beginning, that is, from eternity to salvation; then those that were not chosen, or not ordained to eternal life, were foreordained as early to condemnation; . . .

And, indeed, there can be no new decree, appointment, or purpose, made by God in time; if the decree of election was from eternity, that of rejection must be so too; since there cannot be one without the other; . . .

Fifthly, The properties of this decree will appear to be much the same with those of the decree of election, and need be but just mentioned: as,————1. That it is an eternal decree of God. . . . 2. That it is free and sovereign, owing to his own will and pleasure, . . . 3. It is immutable and irrevocable; . . . 4. It is of particular persons; it does not merely respect events, characters, and actions; but the persons of men; as they are persons who are chosen in Christ, and appointed, not to wrath, but to obtain salvation by him; so they are persons who are foreordained to condemnation, whose names are left out of the book of life, whilst others are written in it.————5. It is a most just and righteous decree; and no other but such can be made by God, who is righteous in all his ways, and holy in all his works.

6.4   Robert Hall, *Help to Zion's Travellers,* 1781

Robert Hall, Sr. (1728-1791) was one of a growing group of Particular Baptists who felt that "Gillism," as they sometimes called John Gill's hyper-Calvinism, made too little room for human response to the gospel. Hall preached a sermon from Isaiah 57:14 ("take up the stumblingblock out of the way of my people") at the Northampton Association in 1779. He urged the removal of theological stumblingblocks that prevented sinners from coming to Christ. That sermon was later expanded and published in 1781 under title of *Help to Zion's Travellers,* often referred to in verbal shorthand simply as "Hall's Help." This was an important milestone for Particular Baptists in overcoming hyper-Calvinism. *Source:* Robert Hall, *Help to Zion's Travellers: Being An Attempt to Remove Various Stumbling Blocks out of the Way, Relating to Doctrinal, Experimental and Practical Religion,* 1781. Reprinted in Philadelphia: American Baptist Publication Society, 1851, 158-163.

THE DOCTRINE OF ELECTION.

ELECTION or choice always implies freedom of will in the persons who choose or elect. Constraint or compulsion is opposite to choice, which must be voluntary or not at all.

Every elector has an end in view, in respect of which he makes his choice, or for the accomplishment of which the choice is made.

The person chosen is always considered as passive, being entirely at the will of the elector, so far as relates to the act of choosing.

These three ideas are inseparably connected with election, whatever kind of election we refer to, whether made by God or man. But some Christians have confused or discouraging ideas of the doctrine now under consideration, for the want of attending to the different senses in which the Scriptures speak of persons being the chosen, or the elect of God. Of this ignorance or inattention the opposers of sovereign grace take the advantage; and in order to perplex or prejudice their minds, produce Scripture instances of some who were *elected,* and nevertheless perished in their sins, as there is reason to think Saul and Judas did, and yet both of them were chosen of God. Hence it is inferred, that as some are lost who were elected, therefore election does not secure the salvation of those who are chosen, but is of such a nature as to leave their future happiness entirely precarious. . . .

For the relief of serious inquirers after truth, it may be proper to observe, that by Election, in Scripture, is sometimes intended God's setting apart, or choosing a people, to the enjoyment of peculiar external privileges; in that sense he chose the Jewish nation, and, therefore, they, as a nation, notwithstanding their wickedness, are frequently called the Lord's elect, or chosen people. Again, the Lord hath elected, or chosen, particular persons to act in office capacity; as Samuel, Saul, David, and many more under the Old Testament; and Peter, James, Judas, and others, were chosen, or elected in like manner under the New. Hence, Jesus said to his disciples, "Have not I chosen you twelve? and one of you is a devil."

But the election of grace, of which I am treating, is of a different nature, and consists in God's choosing persons in Christ Jesus, or setting them apart as in connexion with him, to salvation, through sanctification of the Spirit, and belief of the truth. Salvation was the end God had in view;—to bring his chosen to the possession and enjoyment of *salvation,* not only as consisting in a deliverance from punishment, but from all iniquity. Therefore, in the definition the apostle gives of the doctrine, sanctification by the Spirit, and a true faith, were what these persons were chosen to be the subjects of, through which only, salvation could be enjoyed. This choice was from the beginning, or ever the earth was. They were not chosen, because they were viewed as holy, and deserving to be God's favorites, on account of their obedience or personal purity, but that they *should* be holy. . . .

Another stumbling-block in the way of many inquirers, next to the doctrine of election, is *reprobation,* which is generally but improperly considered as the counterpart of election, and related to it as its direct opposite; as a negative, is related to a positive idea. But if it be understood as the negative of election, is it not strange it should change its nature, and, in controversy, become a positive idea? And yet as such it has been both opposed and defended with great warmth; for the adversaries of sovereign grace scarcely ever directly encounter the doctrine of election; but artfully file off to reprobation, as if they were conscious that election was itself invulnerable, and could not possibly be reduced. But from the mountain of reprobation they attack the doctrine intended to be demolished, and charge it with the most horrid consequences. These consequences the defenders of sovereign grace have repeatedly proved to be not in the least inferable from the doctrine of God's sovereign choice of his people to grace and glory. But perhaps their defence of the doctrine of reprobation has not been equally successful. And no wonder;—they have unwarily admitted it to be the opposite of election; and this admission has been stumbling to many inquirers after truth, and encouraging to its opposers. Election or choice, indeed, implies a negative, or that some are not chosen; which the Scripture calls the *rest:* this is readily allowed, but reprobation as mentioned in Scripture is never opposed to election. To the doctrine of election it does not seem related, but stands in a quite different situation in the system of scriptural divinity.

1. If reprobation conveyed the idea of non-election, by a person being reprobated, we should understand one not elected; but how will such an idea comport with the apostle's reasoning, when he says, "Know ye not that Jesus Christ is in you except ye be reprobates?" 2 Cor. xv. 15. To suppose him to mean they were not elected if Christ was not in them, is supposing him to contradict his own experience, and oppose self-evident facts; for there was a time when Christ was not in Paul himself; during which period he was exceeding mad against those who professed the name of Jesus. "But," says he, "it pleased God to reveal his Son in me." Before this happy change took place he was in a state of reprobation, for Christ was not in him, and yet he was never in a state of *non-election,* but was one chosen in Christ before the world was. . . .

2. That reprobation is not the opposite of election will appear evident, if it be considered that election is an act of divine sovereignty, arising merely from the will of God, without any fitness in creatures deserving to be so distinguished; but reprobation, whenever the word is used in Scripture, respects a comparative deficiency, or an essential defect in those who are reprobated. . . .

3. Reprobation in Scripture always stands opposed to, and is the natural negative of, approbation, whether it respect the state of a person, the frame of his mind, or the nature of his actions. Hence, vile professors are compared to the alloy or dross frequently mixed with metal. . . .

. . . From the above considerations it is evident that election and reprobation are not inseparably connected, nor even so much as related as *kindred* ideas, and that reprobation does not intend an appointment to eternal misery, for such may still find mercy as Paul did; but that is the opposite to divine approbation, whether it respect persons, principles, or proceedings.

. . . The sober opposers of the doctrine in question, generally charge it with implying three things: 1. An appointment to inevitable destruction of those who are not elected; therefore, 2. That the doctrine of election is injurious to those not included in it; and consequently, 3. Is a reflection on the justice or moral character of God. These reasons, it is confessed, if well founded, would be quite sufficient to justify a dissent from the doctrine, or an opposition to it. But whether these awful inferences are the genuine offspring of election let us now examine.

1. The first objection is, Whether election be an appointment of any creature to destruction? . . . It could not have such a tendency, because election is an act absolutely sovereign, or a gracious act arising simply from Jehovah's will. But punishment does not arise from divine sovereignty. If it did, it would be *causeless!* God never punished (therefore never intended to do so) without a criminal cause in the creature. . . .

3. It is not contrary to the moral character of God. In election there is no connivance at sin implied. By it, sin in the chosen was not rendered less odious, nor justice partially administered in their favour, but a surety was graciously substituted in their stead, who bore their sins, and was wounded for their transgressions, and by whose obedience the law of God was magnified, and through his death impartial justice shone with tremendous lustre. . . .

This doctrine is not discouraging in its own nature, (however it may be represented,) to any sincere seeking sinner. Such are not called to produce evidences of their election, in order to warrant their application to Jesus for salvation. No, my dear friends, your present concern is now to have guilt and pollution removed, that you may stand accepted before Jehovah's bar. To you there is a fountain opened, the blood of Jesus, which cleanseth from all sin. Your desire of coming to Christ, under a sense of the absolute need you are in of a Saviour, is a hopeful sign that you shall know, if you follow on to know the Lord. None but the chosen of God do ever heartily choose religion as the one thing needful; and the language of the compassionate Saviour is, "all that the Father giveth me shall come to me; and him that cometh to me I will in nowise cast out." John vi. 37. . . .

The election and redemption of men are inseparably connected in Scripture as distinct links in the grand chain of gospel truth. The personal objects and end are the same in each; and Christ's claim to his people is founded on both: "Thine they were, and thou gavest them me." . . .

When God choose his people, he foreknew that man would fall, and the whole human race would lose their purity, and become transgressors from the womb. Isaiah xlviii. 8. He therefore chose them to complete salvation and purity, that they might be "without blame before him in love." Eph. i. 4. . . .

Such a redemption is suitable to Christians of every rank, and discouraging to none, if its nature be known properly, or what is included in it be duly considered.

6.5   Andrew Fuller and the Rise of "Fullerism"

Andrew Fuller (1754-1815) grew up among hyper-Calvinists near Cambridge. As a youth he doubted that strict system, and as a young pastor rejected it in favor of a more moderate theology which in time took the name of "Fullerism." Though still a Calvinist, Fuller preached evangelistic sermons, offered invitations to the unsaved to accept the gospel, and favored missionary work. A friend and confidant of William Carey, Fuller helped form the Baptist Missionary Society in 1792, and until his death served as its secretary/treasurer.

Fuller deserves to be better known, and therefore selections from his *Memoir* are included in section A. *Source:* Joseph Belcher, ed., *The Complete Works of the Rev. Andrew Fuller: with a Memoir of His Life by Andrew Gunton Fuller,* 3 vols. (Philadelphia: American Baptist Publication Society, 1845), 1:1-17. In 1783 Fuller accepted the pastorate at Kettering and, upon that occasion, wrote out a confession of his faith which included his determination to "offer the gospel to sinners." Two years later he expanded that confession into a book, published as *The Gospel Worthy of All Acceptation*. This book played a major role in breaking the shackles of hyper-Calvinism among

Particular Baptists. *Source:* Andrew Fuller, *The Gospel Worthy of All Acceptation* (Preface to 2d Ed., 1801) in Joseph Belcher, ed., *The Complete Works of the Rev. Andrew Fuller,* 2:328-332.

A. Andrew Fuller, *Memoir*

My father and mother were Dissenters, of the Calvinistic persuasion, and were in the habit of hearing Mr. Eve, a Baptist minister, who being what is here termed *high* in his sentiments, or tinged with false Calvinism, had little or nothing to say to the unconverted. I therefore never considered myself as any way concerned in what I heard from the pulpit. Nevertheless, by reading and reflection I was sometimes strongly impressed in a way of conviction. My parents were engaged in husbandry, which occupation, therefore, I followed to the twentieth year of my age. I remember many of the sins of my childhood, among which were lying, cursing, and swearing. . . .

I think I must have been nearly fourteen years old before I began to have much serious thought about futurity. The preaching upon which I attended was not adapted to awaken my conscience, as the minister had seldom any thing to say except to believers, and what believing was I neither knew, nor was I greatly concerned to know. I remember about this time, as I was walking alone, I put the question to myself, What is faith? there is much made of it, What is it? I could not tell, but satisfied myself in thinking it was not of immediate concern, and I should understand it as I grew older. . . .

Sometimes I was very much affected, in thinking of the doctrines of Christianity, or in reading such books as Bunyan's *Grace abounding to the Chief of Sinners,* and his *Pilgrim's Progress.* One day, in particular, I took up Ralph Erskine's *Gospel Sonnets,* and opening upon what he entitles *A Gospel Catechism for Young Christians, or Christ All in All in our Complete Redemption,* I read, and as I read I wept. Indeed I was almost overcome with weeping, so interesting did the doctrine of eternal salvation appear to me; yet, there being no radical change in my heart, these thoughts passed away, and I was equally intent on the pursuit of folly as heretofore.

Notwithstanding various convictions and transient affections, I was pressing on in a lamentable career of wickedness; but about the autumn of 1769 my convictions revisited me, and brought on such a concern about my everlasting welfare as issued, I trust, in real conversion. . . .

One morning, I think in November, 1769, I walked out by myself with an unusual load of guilt upon my conscience. The remembrance of my sin, not only on the past evening, but for a long time back, the breach of my vows and the shocking termination of my former hopes and affections, all uniting together, formed a burden which I knew not how to bear. . . .

. . . I was like a man drowning, looking every way for help, or rather catching for something by which he might save his life. I tried to find whether there was any hope in the Divine mercy—any in the Saviour of sinners; but felt repulsed by the thought of mercy having been so basely abused already. In this state of mind, . . . I thought of the resolution of Job, 'Though he slay me, yet will I trust in him.' I paused, and repeated the words over and over. Each repetition seemed to kindle a ray of hope mixed with a determination, *if I might,* to cast my perishing soul upon the Lord Jesus Christ for salvation, to be both pardoned and purified; for I felt that I needed the one as much as the other.

I was not then aware that *any* poor sinner had a warrant to believe in Christ for the salvation of his soul, but supposed there must be some kind of qualification to entitle him to do it; yet I was aware I had no qualification. . . .

. . . I must—I will—yes, I will trust my soul—my sinful lost soul in his hands. If I perish, I perish. However it was, I was determined to cast myself upon Christ, thinking peradventure he would save my soul; and, if not, I could but be lost. In this way I continued above an hour, weeping and supplicating mercy for the Saviour's sake (my soul hath it still in remembrance, and is humbled in me); and as the eye of the mind was more and more fixed upon him, my guilt and fears were gradually and insensibly removed.

I now found rest for my troubled soul; and I reckon that I should have found it sooner, if I had not entertained the notion of my having no warrant to come to Christ without some previous qualification. This notion was a bar that kept me back for a time, though through divine drawings I was enabled to overleap it. . . .

I had then relinquished every false confidence, believed my help to be only in him, and approved of salvation by grace alone through his death; and if at that time I had known that any poor sinner *might* warrantably have trusted in him for salvation, I conceive I should have done so, and have found rest to my soul sooner than I did. I mention this because it may be the case with others, who may be kept in darkness and despondency by erroneous views of the gospel much longer than I was. . . .

In March, 1770, I witnessed the baptizing of two young persons, having never seen that ordinance administered before, and was considerably affected by what I saw and heard. The solemn immersion of a person, on a profession of faith in Christ, carried such a conviction with it, that I wept like a child on the occasion. . . . I was fully persuaded that this was the primitive way of baptizing, and that every Christian was bound to attend to this institution of our blessed Lord. About a month after this I was baptized myself, and joined the church at Soham, being then turned of sixteen years of age. . . .

In the autumn of the same year [1770] an unhappy affair occurred in the church, which occasioned a breach between our pastor, Mr. Eve, and the people, which terminated in his leaving them; and, what rendered it the more afflicting to me, I was much concerned in it. The case was this: one of the members having been guilty of drinking to excess, I was one of the first who knew of it. I immediately went and talked to him, as well as I could, on the evil of his conduct. His answer was, 'He could not keep himself; and that, though I bore so hard on him, I was not my own keeper.' At this I felt indignant, considering it as a base excuse. I therefore told him that he *could* keep himself from such sins as these, and that his way of talking was merely to excuse what was inexcusable. I knew not what else to say at that time; yet the idea of arrogating to be my own keeper seemed too much. He, however, was offended, and told me that I was young, and did not know the deceitfulness of my own heart. Well, I went and told my pastor, who highly commended me, and said, 'We certainly could keep ourselves from open sins. We had no power,' he observed, 'to do things spiritually good; but as to outward acts, we had power both to obey the will of God and to disobey it.'

The business soon came before the church, and the offender was unanimously excluded: the excuse which he had made, too, was considered by all, I believe, as an aggravation of his offence. But, this affair being disposed of, the abstract question of *the power of sinful men to do the will of God, and to keep themselves from sin,* was taken up by some of the leading members of the church. . . . They readily excused me, as being a babe in religion; but thought the pastor ought to have known better, and to have been able to answer the offender without betraying the truth. They alleged that the greatest and best of characters, as recorded in Scripture, never arrogated to themselves the power of keeping themselves from evil, but constantly prayed for keeping grace; that, were it not for the restraining goodness and constraining grace of God, earth would be a hell, and the best of men incarnate devils; in short, that though we are altogether blameworthy for our evil propensities, yet, if they were restrained or conquered, it was altogether to be ascribed to God, and not to us.

On the other hand, the pastor distinguished between internal and external power. He allowed that men had no power of themselves to perform any thing spiritually good; but contended that they could yield external obedience, and keep themselves from open acts of sin. In proof of this he alleged a great number of Scripture exhortations; asking, If we had no power to comply with them, why were they given us? The opponents did not deny our being exhorted to do good and to avoid evil, nor that it was our duty to do both, and our sin to act otherwise; but they denied that this implied our being sufficient of ourselves to do any thing, even to think a good thought.

In these disputes I continued for some time on the side of my pastor; but after a few months I felt difficulties on the subject which I could not answer, and which rendered me unhappy. . . .

. . . But though, during these unpleasant disputes, there were many hard thoughts and hard words on almost all hands, yet they were ultimately the means of leading my mind into those views of divine truth which have since appeared in the principal part of my writings.

[One] morning, as I was walking by myself to meeting, expecting to hear the brethren pray, and my friend Joseph Diver expound the Scriptures, I was met by one of the members whom he had requested to see me, who said, 'Brother Diver has by accident sprained his ancle, and cannot be at meeting to-day; and he wishes me to say to you, that he hopes the Lord will be with *you*.' 'The Lord be with *me!*' thought I, 'what does brother Diver mean? He cannot suppose that I can take his place, seeing I have never attempted any thing of the kind, nor been asked to do so.'

We walked on to the meeting, and took our places, when, after singing, one of the brethren went to prayer. After which the eldest deacon asked me if I would read some part of the Scriptures, and, if I found liberty, drop any remarks as I went on, which might occur. At first I was startled, but, conscious of what had passed in my mind the day before, I thought as brother Diver was absent it might be my duty to try, and therefore making no objections, which as it appeared to me would have been mere affectation, I rose and spoke from Psal. xxx. 5, for about half an hour, with considerable freedom. . . .

In January, 1774, an elderly lady, a member of the church, died, and left a request that, if the church did not think it disorderly, I might be allowed to preach a funeral sermon on the occasion. As the members were nearly of one mind respecting me, they agreed to set apart the twenty-sixth of that month, which was previous to the funeral, for fasting and prayer; and they then called me to the ministry. From that time I exercised from the pulpit. . . .

With respect to the system of doctrine which I had been used to hear from my youth, it was in the high Calvinistic, or rather hyper Calvinistic, strain admitting nothing spiritually good to be the duty of the unregenerate, and nothing to be addressed to them in a way of exhortation, excepting what related to external obedience. Outward services might be required, such as an attendance on the means of grace; and abstinence from gross evils might be enforced; but nothing was said to them from the pulpit in the way of warning them to flee from the wrath to come, or inviting them to apply to Christ for salvation. And though our late dispute had furnished me with some few principles inconsistent with these notions, yet I did not perceive their bearings at first, and durst not for some years address an invitation to the unconverted to come to Jesus. I began, however, to doubt whether I had got the truth respecting this subject. This view of things did not seem to comport with the ideas which I had imbibed concerning the power of man to do the will of God. I perceived that the will of God was not confined to mere outward actions, but extended to the inmost thoughts and intents of the heart. The distinction of duties, therefore, into internal and external, and making the latter only concern the unregenerate, wore a suspicious appearance. But as I perceived this reasoning would affect the whole tenor of my preaching, I moved on with slow and trembling steps; and, having to feel my way out of a labyrinth, I was a long time ere I felt satisfied. . . .

In the spring of 1775 I accepted the invitation of the church at Soham, and was ordained their pastor. The pastors of the other churches, who attended the ordination, took that opportunity to inquire into the controversy which had divided us from our former minister, and requested me to state the difference. Mr. Robert Hall, of Arnsby, who was one of them, expressed his satisfaction in the statement, but recommended *Edwards on the Will* to my careful perusal, as the most able performance on the power of man to do the will of God. Not being much acquainted with books at that time, I confounded the work of Dr. John Edwards, of Cambridge, an Episcopalian Calvinist, entitled *Veritas Redux,* with that of Jonathan Edwards, of New England. I read the former, and thought it a good book; but it did not seem exactly to answer Mr. Hall's recommendation. Nor was it till the year 1777 that I discovered my mistake. Meantime, however, I was greatly exercised upon the subject, and upon the work of the Christian ministry.

The principal writings with which I was first acquainted were those of Bunyan, Gill, and Brine. I had read pretty much of Dr. Gill's *Body of Divinity,* and from many parts of it had received considerable instruction. I perceived, however, that the system of Bunyan was not the same with his; for that, while he maintained the doctrines of election and predestination, he nevertheless held with the free offer of salvation to sinners without distinction. These were things which I then could not reconcile, and therefore supposed that Bunyan, though a great and good man, was not so *clear* in his views of the doctrines of the gospel as the writers who succeeded him. I found, indeed, the same things in all the old writers of the sixteenth and seventeenth centuries that came in my way. They all dealt, as Bunyan did, in free invitations to sinners to come to Christ and be saved; the consistency of which with personal election I could not understand. It is true, I perceived the Scriptures abounded with exhortations and invitations to sinners; but I supposed there must be two kinds of holiness, one of which was possessed by man in innocence, and was binding on all his posterity—the other derived from Christ, and binding only on his people. I had not yet learned that the same things which are required by the precepts of the law are bestowed by the grace of the gospel. Those exhortations to repentance and faith, therefore, which are addressed in the New Testament to the unconverted, I supposed to refer only to such external repentance and faith as were within their power, and might be complied with without the grace of God. The effect of these views was, that I had very little to say to the unconverted, indeed nothing in a way of exhortation to things spiritually good, or certainly connected with salvation.

But in the autumn of 1775, being in London, I met with a pamphlet by Dr. Abraham Taylor, concerning what was called *The Modern Question.* I had never seen any thing relative to this controversy before, although the subject, as I have stated, had occupied my thoughts. I was but little impressed by his reasonings till he came to the addresses of John the Baptist, Christ, and the apostles, which he proved to be delivered to the ungodly, and to mean spiritual repentance and faith, inasmuch as they were connected with the remission of sins. This set me fast. I read and examined the Scripture passages, and the more I read and thought, the more I doubted the justice of my former views. . . .

In 1776 I became acquainted with Mr. Sutcliff, who had lately come to Olney, and soon after with Mr. John Ryland, jun., then of Northampton. In them I found familiar and faithful brethren; and who, partly by reflection, and partly by reading the writings of Edwards, Bellamy, Brainerd, &c., had begun to doubt of the system of false Calvinism to which they had been inclined when they first entered on the ministry, or rather to be decided against it. But as I lived sixty or seventy miles from them, I seldom saw them, and did not correspond upon the subject. I therefore pursued my inquiries by myself, and wrote out the substance of what I afterwards published under the title of *The Gospel worthy of all Acceptation; or the Obligations of Men cordially to believe whatever God makes known.*

My change of views on these subjects never abated my zeal for the doctrine of salvation by grace, but in some respects increased it. I never had any predilection for Arminianism, which appeared to me to ascribe the difference between one sinner and another, not to the grace of God, but to the good improvement made of grace given us in common with others. Yet I saw those whom I thought to be godly men, both among Arminians and high, or, as I now accounted them, hyper Calvinists.

B. Andrew Fuller, *The Gospel Worthy of All Acceptation*, 1781

PREFACE.

When the following pages were written, (1781), the author had no intention of publishing them. He had formerly entertained different sentiments. For some few years, however, he had begun to doubt whether all his principles on these subjects were Scriptural. These doubts arose chiefly from thinking on some passages of Scripture, particularly the latter part of the second Psalm, where kings, who "set themselves against the Lord, and against his Anointed," are positively commanded to "kiss the Son;" also the preaching of John the Baptist, Christ, and his apostles, who he found, did not hesitate to address unconverted sinners, and that in the most pointed manner—saying, "Repent, for the kingdom of heaven is at hand.". . .

Reading the lives and labours of such men as Elliot, Brainerd, and several others, who preached Christ with so much success to the American Indians, had an effect upon him. Their work, like that of the apostles, seemed to be plain before them. They appeared to him, in their addresses to those poor benighted heathens, to have none of those difficulties with which he felt himself encumbered. These things led him to the throne of grace, to implore instruction and resolution. . . .

From this time, his thoughts upon the subject began to enlarge. He preached upon it more than once. From hence, he was led to think on its opposite, faith, and to consider it as *a persuasion of the truth of what God has said;* and, of course, to suspect his former views concerning its not being the duty of unconverted sinners. . . .

He had also read and considered, as well as he was able, President Edwards's *Inquiry into the Freedom of the Will*, with some other performances on the difference between natural and moral inability. He found much satisfaction in this distinction; as it appeared to him to carry with it its own evidence—to be clearly and fully contained in the Scriptures—and calculated to disburden the Calvinistic system of a number of calumnies with which its enemies have loaded it, as well as to afford clear and honourable conceptions of the Divine government. If it were not the duty of unconverted sinners to believe in Christ, and that because of their inability, he supposed this inability must be natural, or something which did not arise from an evil disposition; but the more he examined the Scriptures, the more he was convinced that all the inability ascribed to man, with respect to believing, arises from the aversion of his heart. They *will not* come to Christ that they may have life; *will not* hearken to the voice of the charmer, charm he never so wisely; *will not* seek after God; and *desire not* the knowledge of his ways.

He wishes to avoid the error into which we are apt to be betrayed, when engaged in controversy—that of magnifying the importance of the subject beyond its proper bounds; yet he seriously thinks the subject treated of in the following pages is of no small importance. To him, it appears to be the same controversy, for substance, as that which in all ages has subsisted between God and an apostate world. God has ever maintained these two principles: *All that is evil is of the creature, and to him belongs the blame of it;* and *all that is good is of himself, and to him belongs the praise of it.* The acquiesce in *both* these positions is too much for the carnal heart. The advocates for free-will would seem to yield the former, acknowledging themselves blameworthy for the evil; but they cannot admit the latter. Whatever honour they may allow to the general grace of God, they are for ascribing the preponderance in favour of virtue and eternal life to their own good improvement of it. Others, who profess to be advocates for free grace, appear to be willing that God should have all the honour of their salvation, in case they should be saved; but they discover the strongest aversion to take to themselves the blame of their destruction in case they should be lost. . . .

The following particulars are premised, for the sake of a clear understanding of the subject:—

First, There is no dispute about the doctrine of election, or any of the discriminating doctrines of grace. They are allowed on both sides; and it is granted that none ever did or ever will believe in Christ but those who are chosen of God from eternity. . . .

Secondly, Neither is there any dispute concerning who ought to be encouraged to consider themselves as entitled to the blessings of the gospel. Though sinners be freely invited to the participation of spiritual blessings; yet they have no interest in them, according to God's revealed will, while they continue in unbelief; nor is it any part of the design of these pages to persuade them to believe that they have. On the contrary, the writer is fully convinced that, whatever be the secret purpose of God concerning them, they are at present under the curse. . . .

Fifthly, It is no part of the controversy whether unconverted sinners be able to turn to God, and to embrace the gospel; but what kind of inability they lie under with respect to these exercises; whether it consists in the want of natural powers and advantages, or merely in the want of a heart to make a right use of them. If the former, obligation, it is granted, would be set aside; but if the latter, it remains in full force. They that are in the flesh *cannot* please God; but it does not follow that they are not obliged to do so; and this their obligation requires to be clearly insisted on, that they may be convinced of their sin, and so induced to embrace the gospel remedy.

Sixthly, The question is not whether faith be required of sinners as a virtue, which, if complied with, shall be the ground of their acceptance with God, or that on account of which they may be justified in his sight; but whether it be not required as the appointed *means* of salvation. The righteousness of Jesus believed in is the only ground of justification, but faith in him is necessary to our being interested in it. . . .

Finally, The question is not whether unconverted sinners be the subjects of exhortation, but whether they ought to be exhorted to perform spiritual duties. It is beyond all dispute that the Scriptures do exhort them to many things. If, therefore, there be any professors of Christianity who question the propriety of this, and who would have nothing said to them, except that, "if they be elected they will be called," they are not to be reasoned with, but rebuked, as setting themselves in direct opposition to the word of God. The greater part of those who may differ from the author on these subjects, it is presumed, will admit the propriety of sinners being exhorted to duty; only this duty must, as they suppose, be confined to merely natural exercises, or such as may be complied with by a carnal heart, destitute of the love of God. It is one design of the following pages to show that God requires the heart, the whole heart, and nothing but the heart; that all the precepts of the Bible are only the different modes in which we are required to express our love to him; that, instead of its being true that sinners are obliged to perform duties which have no spirituality in them, there are no such duties to be performed; and that, so far from their being exhorted to every thing excepting what is spiritually good, they are exhorted to nothing else. The Scriptures undoubtedly require them to read, to hear, to repent, and to pray, that their sins may be forgiven them. It is not, however, in the exercise of a carnal, but of a spiritual state of mind, that these duties are performed.

6.6   William Carey, *An Enquiry,* 1792

William Carey's *Enquiry* ranks as one of the most influential Baptist books of all time. Carey (1761-1834) became a Baptist in 1783, and labored as an obscure pastor-teacher-shoe cobbler at Moulton. His wide reading, study of geography, and perhaps influence from his seafaring uncle turned Carey's keen mind to consider the wider world. Against formidable odds, both personal and ministerial, he became convinced that God wants Christians to share the gospel with the whole world. Like many writings of the time, Carey's long title carries the gist of the book, which includes a survey of religious conditions in the world, a brief history of Christian missions, an assessment of the measure of success modern missionary efforts might reasonably expect, and the biblical mandate for missions. Unlike many of his contemporaries, Carey interpreted the Great Commission of Matthew 28:18-20 as still binding on Christians today. *Source:* William Carey, *An Enquiry into the Obligations of Christians to use means for the Conversion of the Heathens* (Leicester: n.p., 1792).

INTRODUCTION

As our blessed Lord has required us to pray that his kingdom may come, and his will be done on earth as it is in heaven, it becomes us not only to express our desires of that event by words, but to use every lawful method to spread the knowledge of his name. In order to this, it is necessary that we should become, in some measure, *acquainted with the religious state of the world;* and as this is an object we should be prompted to pursue, not only the gospel of our Redeemer, but even by the feelings of humanity, so an inclination to conscientious activity therein would form one of the strongest proofs that we are the subjects of grace, and partakers of that spirit of universal benevolence and genuine philanthropy, which appear so eminent in the character of God himself. . . .

In order that the subject may be taken into more serious consideration, I shall enquire, whether the commission given by our Lord to his disciples be not still binding on us,—take a short view of former undertakings,—give some account of the present state of the world,—consider the practicability of doing something more than is done,—and the duty of Christians in general in this matter.

SECTION I
AN ENQUIRY WHETHER THE COMMISSION GIVEN BY OUR LORD TO HIS
DISCIPLES BE NOT STILL BINDING ON US

Our Lord Jesus Christ, a little before his departure, commissioned his apostles to "Go, and teach all nations"; or, as another evangelist expresses it, "Go into all the world, and preach the gospel to every creature." This commission was as extensive as possible, and laid them under obligation to disperse themselves into every country of the habitable globe, and preach to all the inhabitants, without exception or limitation.

They accordingly went forth in obedience to the command, and the power of God evidently wrought with them.

Many attempts of the same kind have been attended with various success; but the work has not been taken up, or prosecuted of late years (except by a few individuals) with that zeal and perseverance with which the primitive Christians went about it. It seems as if many thought the commission was sufficiently put in execution by what the apostles and others have done; that we have enough to do to attend to the salvation of our own countrymen; and that, if God intends the salvation of the heathen, he will some way or other bring them to the gospel, or the gospel to them. It is thus that multitudes sit at ease, and give themselves no concern about the far greater part of their fellow sinners, who to this day are lost in ignorance and idolatry. . . . To the consideration of such persons I would offer the following observations.

First, If the command of Christ to teach all nations be restricted to the apostles, or those under the immediate inspiration of the Holy Ghost, then that of baptizing should be so too; and every denomination of Christians, except the Quakers, do wrong in baptizing with water at all.

Secondly, If the command of Christ to teach all nations be confined to the apostles, then all such ordinary ministers who have endeavored to carry the gospel to the heathens, have acted without a warrant, and run before they were sent. . . .

Thirdly, If the command of Christ to teach all nations extend only to the apostles, then, doubtless, the promise of the divine preference in this work must be so limited; but this is worded in such a manner as expressly precludes such an idea. Lo, I am with you always, to the end of the world. . . .

It has been said that we ought not to force our way, but to wait for the openings, and leadings of Providence; but it might with equal propriety be answered in this case, neither ought we to neglect embracing those openings in Providence which daily present themselves to us. What openings of Providence do we wait for? We can neither expect to be transported into the heathen world without ordinary means, nor to be endowed with the gift of tongues, etc., when we arrive there. These would not be providential interpositions, but miraculous ones. Where a command exists nothing can be necessary to render it binding but a removal of those obstacles which render obedience impossible, and these are removed already. Natural impossibility can never be pleaded so long as facts exist to prove the contrary.

It has been objected that there are multitudes in our own nation, and within our immediate spheres of action, who are as ignorant as the South Sea savages, and that therefore we have work enough at home, without going into other countries. That there are thousands in our own land as far from God as possible, I readily grant, . . . Our own countrymen have the means of grace, and may attend on the Word preached if they choose it. They have the means of knowing the truth, . . . but with them the case is widely different, who have no Bible, no written language, (which many of them have not) no ministers, no good civil government, nor any of those advantages which we have. Pity therefore, humanity, and much more Christianity, call loudly for every possible exertion to introduce the gospel amongst them. . . .

SECTION V

AN ENQUIRY INTO THE DUTY OF CHRISTIANS IN GENERAL, AND WHAT
MEANS OUGHT TO BE USED, IN ORDER TO PROMOTE THIS WORK

If the prophecies concerning the increase of Christ's kingdom be true, and if what has been advanced, concerning the commission given by him to his disciples being obligatory on us, be just, it must be inferred that all Christians ought heartily to concur with

God in promoting his glorious designs, for he that is joined to the Lord is one Spirit.

One of the first, and most important of those duties which are incumbent upon us, is fervent and united prayer. However, the influence of the Holy Spirit may be set at nought, and run down by many, it will be found upon trial, that all means which we can use, without it, will be ineffectual. If a temple is raised for God in the heathen world, it will not be by might, nor by power, nor by the authority of the magistrate, or the eloquence of the orator; but by my Spirit, saith the Lord of Hosts. We must therefore be in real earnest in supplicating his blessings upon our labors. . . .

With respect to our own immediate connections, we have within these few years been favored with some tokens for good, granted in answer to prayer which should encourage us to persist, and increase in that important duty. I trust our monthly prayer-meetings for the success of the gospel have not been in vain. It is true a want of importunity too generally attends our prayers; yet unimportunate, and feeble as they have been, it is to be believed that God has heard, and in a measure answered them. The churches that have engaged in the practice have in general since that time been evidently on the increase; some controversies which have long perplexed and divided the church, are more clearly stated than ever; there are calls to preach the gospel in many places where it has not been usually published; yea, a glorious door is opened, and is likely to be opened wider and wider, by the spread of civil and religious liberty, accompanied also by a diminution of the spirit of popery; a noble effort has been made to abolish the inhuman slave trade, and though at present it has not been so successful as might be wished, yet it is to be hoped it will be persevered in, till it is accomplished. . . .

We must not be contented however with praying, without exerting ourselves in the use of means for the obtaining of those things we pray for. . . .

Suppose a company of serious Christians, ministers and private persons, were to form themselves into a society, and make a number of rules respecting the regulation of the plan, and the persons who are to be employed as missionaries, the means of defraying the expense, etc. This society must consist of persons whose hearts are in the work, men of serious religion, and possessing a spirit of perseverance; there must be a determination not to admit any person who is not of this description, or to retain him longer than he answers to it.

From such a society a committee might be appointed whose business it should be to procure all the information they could upon the subject, to receive contributions, to enquire into the characters, tempers, abilities and religious views of the missionaries, and also to provide them with necessaries for their undertakings. . . .

If there is any reason for me to hope that I shall have any influence upon any of my brethren, and fellow Christians, probably it may be more especially amongst them of my own denomination. I would therefore propose that such a society and committee should be formed amongst the particular Baptist denomination.

I do not mean by this, in any wise to confine it to one denomination of Christians. I wish with all my heart, that every one who loves our Lord Jesus Christ in sincerity, would in some way or other engage in it. But in the present divided state of Christendom, it would be more likely for good to be done by each denomination engaging separately in the work, than if they were to embark in it conjointly. . . .

In respect to contributions for defraying the expenses, money will doubtless be wanting; and suppose the rich were to embark a portion of that wealth over which God has made them stewards, in this important undertaking, perhaps there are few ways that would turn to a better account at last.

Nor ought it to be confined to the rich; if persons in more moderate circumstances were to devote a portion, suppose a tenth, of their annual increase to the Lord, it would not only correspond with the practice of the Israelites, who lived under the Mosaic economy, but of the patriarchs Abraham, Isaac, and Jacob, before that dispensation commenced. Many of our most eminent forefathers amongst the Puritans followed that practice; and if that were but attended to now, there would not only be enough to support the ministry of the gospel at home, and to encourage village preaching in our respective neighborhoods, but to defray the expenses of carrying the gospel into the heathen world.

If congregations were to open subscriptions of one penny, or more per week, according to their circumstances, and deposit it as a fund for the propagation of the gospel, much might be raised in this way. . . .

Many persons have of late left off the use of West India sugar on account of the iniquitous manner in which it is obtained. Those families who have done so, and have not substituted anything else in its place, have not only cleansed their hands of blood, but have made a saving to their families, some of sixpence, and some of a shilling a week. If this, or a part of this were appropriated to the uses before-mentioned, it would abundantly suffice. We have only to keep the end in view, and have our hearts thoroughly engaged in the pursuit of it, and means will not be very difficult.

6.7   Abraham Booth, *Commerce in the Human Species,* 1792

By background and training, Abraham Booth was hardly the sort of pastor one would expect to take a strong and progressive stand on moral and social issues, and yet that is exactly what we find. A General Baptist who quite early converted to Particular views, Booth was a staunch conservative who nevertheless by his *Reign of Grace (1768)* helped break the hold of hyper-Calvinism upon Particular Baptists. He preached and published on several moral issues, but is best remembered for *Commerce in the Human Species,* a hard-hitting sermon against slavery delivered at a time when not all Baptists shared these views. *Source:* Abraham Booth, *Commerce in the Human Species, and the Enslaving of Innocent Persons, Inimical to the Laws of Moses and the Gospel of Christ* (A sermon preached January 29, 1792). Copy in the Angus Collection, Regent's Park College, Oxford.

COMMERCE IN THE HUMAN SPECIES, AND THE ENSLAVING OF INNO-CENT PERSONS, INIMICAL TO THE Laws of Moses and the Gospel of Christ. A SERMON PREACHED IN LITTLE PRESCOT STREET, GOODMAN's FIELDS, January 29, 1792. By Abraham Booth

For this end are we now assembled; and to plead the cause of moral justice, of true benevolence, and of compassion, relative to the poor oppressed Africans, I have read that part of sacred writ which is now before us. Yes, my brethren, I now stand to bear a public testimony against that diversified iniquity which is inseparable from a commerce in the human species—that commerce which is called the Slave Trade, together with its numerous and horrid consequences. . . .

In pursuance of my design, I shall now show, That the law in our text, [Exodus 21:16] though given to the ancient Hebrews as a body politic, proceeds on a moral ground—That God, in certain cases, permitted the Israelites to purchase their fellow-creatures for servitude; yet that purchase and servitude were intended with such restrictions, as rendered them essentially different from the European Slave Trade and its consequences—That supposing God had permitted the Israelitish people to traffic in the human species, and to enslave Gentiles in a much greater degree than he did; it would not have warranted the conduct of Europeans toward the Africans—And, that the European commerce in man, and the slavery consequent upon it, are absolutely inimical to the precepts of Jesus Christ, and the whole scope of his doctrine.

FIRST, The law in our text, though given to the ancient Hebrews as a body politic, proceeds on a moral ground.

That no great labour of proof is necessary to evince the truth of this proposition, a small degree of reflection will show. For though the divine law before us was manifestly given to the Israelites, as part of their judicial code, and was intended to regulate their conduct one toward another; yet it no less apparently proceeds on the same principle with that prohibition of the decalogue, Thou shalt not steal. . . . Manstealing is here classed with such crimes as are most detestable in the sight of God, most pernicious to society, and most deserving of death by the sword of the civil magistrate. Manstealing, therefore, must be considered as a moral evil—universally evil, in every age and in every nation. Nor is it only an evil, but one of the first magnitude against our neighbour. If he who pilfers any one's property, steals a sheep, robs on the high-road, or commits a burglary, be considered and treated as a thief, a robber, a pest of society; of what enormous villany must he be guilty, who kidnaps my honest neighbour, my faithful servant, my dutiful child, or my affectionate wife, to transport the one or the other to a country entirely unknown, and never thence to return! This outrage on the sacred rights of liberty, of justice, and of humanity, is greatly enhanced, if that worst of thieves intend, either to treat them himself as the most abject of slaves, like those in the British West Indies; or to sell them for that most infamous and cruel purpose.

SECONDLY, That though God, in certain cases, permitted the Israelites to purchase their fellow-creatures for servitude; yet that purchase and servitude were attended with such restrictions, as rendered them essentially different from the European Slave Trade and its consequences.

There were two cases in which an Israelite himself might, according to divine law, be sold into a state of servitude. These were, theft, and indecency. Here it is manifest the laws of the Hebrews had such a regard for personal freedom, that even a thief was not considered as a proper subject of sale and servitude, except he was unable to make the appointed restitution.

The Mosaic statutes permitted insolvent debtors to be sold for the benefit of their creditors; but then the servitude to which such debtors were obliged, was far from being oppressive and cruel. . . .

On this divine statute may be remarked, that it did not require, but only permit, the Israelites to purchase Heathens for a lower degree of servitude than that in which any Hebrew might be employed. That is, if they held bond-servants at all, those meanest of servants must be had from among the Gentiles.—This law did not warrant the Israelites to go by sea or land to a far-distant country, as the slave-merchants now do.

THIRDLY, That supposing God had permitted the Israelitish people to traffic in the human species and to enslave the Gentiles in a much greater degree than he did, it would not have authorized the conduct of Europeans toward the Africans.

To prove and illustrate this position, the following particulars may not be impertinent. The Israelites, as a body politic, were the peculiar people of God, in distinction from all other nations then upon the earth. But this is not the case with any people now in the world. While the Mosaic Dispensation continued, that singular and high prerogative was exclusively enjoyed by the Jews; but when the Christian Economy was established, that prerogative ceased; nor did any other nation succeed to the honour. If the English, for instance, the Dutch, the French, or the Spaniards, were to claim the privilege; it would behove them to produce the divine charter by which it was granted. . . .

It follows, therefore, that if the lawfulness of purchasing innocent persons for the most degrading and cruel slavery exist among men, it must be a common right, and equally possessed by all nations: nor can the exercise of it have any limitation from principles of a moral nature. No limits can be assigned, except those of power, of policy, or of inclination. It would, consequently, be quite as equitable, benevolent, and humane, for the Africans, laden with produce of their own country, annually to visit our English ports, as we do theirs, and for similar purposes. Yes, they might, if it were in their power, with equal justice, and with less dishonour, fit out a hundred and eighty, or two hundred ships, for the port of London, of Bristol, and of Liverpool—ships adapted to stowage of man, and furnished with a frightful apparatus to render the confinement of Britons completely miserable, as well as perfectly secure. When this commercial, this man-trading fleet arrived, if cargoes of men, women, and children were not prepared; the officers belonging to each vessel might practise all their arts, to excite a spirit of covetousness and of cruelty in our governors and fellow-subjects: in order that, by an armed force, the peaceable inhabitants of whole villages might be captured—that, in our courts of justice, innocent persons, for the advantage of their judges, might be convicted—that private individuals might kidnap whomsoever they could, and thought saleable—that, by all these infamous means the ship might be freighted, at every returning season, with forty thousand Britons—and, finally, that all who survive their miserable confinement while on board, might be taken to the best market for the human species; exposed, in the most indecent manner, to public sale; handled and examined, like so many head of cattle, by their purchasers; consigned over, with their unborn posterity to the most abject and cruel slavery, from generation to generation; and all for—what? Here let humanity blush, let mercy weep, and let justice be roused into indignation; but let no Britons forget, that this is a picture, in miniature, of their own behaviour toward the Africans!

FOURTHLY, That the European Commerce in Man, and the slavery consequent upon it, are absolutely inimical to the precepts of Jesus Christ, and to the whole scope of his doctrine.

To the precepts of Jesus Christ. For instance: Love your enemies. Do good to them that hate you. Now, is not the whole of that system against which I plead, at irreconcileable enmity with the spirit of these divine precepts? . . . Yet such are the Negro Trade and its consequences, that the most diabolical malice, which ever existed in the heart of man against his bitterest enemy, could scarcely contrive or wish more aggravated misery to befall him in this life, than that under which many thousands of innocent, captured, and enslaved Africans groan.

Again: All things whatsoever ye would that men should do to you, do ye even so to them, is another of our Lord's precepts. This admirably just and comprehensive command, requires each of us to treat every man, as we might reasonably wish every one to treat us, were situations and circumstances reversed. It considers every man as a man, and requires that he be so treated. It impartially views every man, as having capacities, feelings, and rights, peculiar to his own species; and it forbids those capacities to be insulted by degradation, those feelings by unmerited pain, and those rights by injustice. But is not the horrid man-trade, and the detestable connections in which it stands, a manifest outrage on this most salutary precept? Do not that inhuman commerce, and the consequent cruel slavery, treat vast multitudes of human creatures, as if they had no share in the capacities, the feelings, or the rights of men? as if they were mere brutes, made to be taken and sold, enslaved and destroyed? He, therefore, who dares to vindicate such conduct might, on his own principles, be justly kidnapped, bought, and sold for a similar state of slavery. Because whatever arguments prove that any innocent man has an inviolable claim to personal freedom, will equally prove the same thing respecting every one of that character.

Having discussed my subject according to the plan proposed, I shall now conclude with a few exhortations relative to our own duty. As being professedly the followers of Christ, and the friends of mankind, I would exhort you, my brethren earnestly and frequently to pray for the interposition of Providence to abolish the detestable traffic in man. That it is our indispensable duty to pray for the enlargement of our Lord's visible kingdom among men, is plain; that the despised Africans are naturally as capable of being made the spiritual subjects of Jesus Christ as ourselves, ought not to be questioned; and that the Slave Trade, is at present, an effectual bar to the propagation of Christianity among them, appears with decisive evidence. Nay, it is an insuperable obstruction to the progress of civilization among them, and to an honourable commerce with them. Zeal for the honour of Christ and love to our fellow-creatures, ought therefore to inspire us with ardent prayer, that the horrid impediment may be removed, and that Christ may be glorified among them.—Nor ought we to pray merely that God would abolish the infamous commerce in man, on the shores of Africa; but also for the gradual emancipation of oppressed Negroes in the West India islands; that the slavery of innocent persons may cease to exist, and sink under the detestation of all Europe. For what must the enslaved Africans in those islands think of Christians, of Christianity, and of Christ, under the tuition of their oppressors?

Again; Let your ardent and frequent prayers be accompanied with prudent, peaceable, and steady efforts, in order to procure the total abolition of that criminal traffic, and of the cruel slavery consequent upon it. This is manifestly enjoined by that law of the Lord, Thou shalt love thy neighbour as thyself.

As it is our design at this time to make a collection for promoting the general design of that worthy Society, which has existed for some years in this metropolis, in order to effect the Abolition of the Slave Trade, I would earnestly exhort you to make a liberal contribution for their assistance. The members of that benevolent Society have done worthily. They deserve the assistance and the thanks of every friend to moral justice, and to humanity. Let us therefore endeavour to strengthen their hands, and to promote the righteous cause in which they are united; not doubting but the wisdom, the rectitude, and the benevolence of our British legislature will ere long be manifested, in totally abolishing the English commerce in man; and in providing for the gradual emancipation of Negro Slaves in our West India islands.

7

Revival Fires: Baptists in America

In 1700 Baptists in America numbered no more than twenty-four scattered churches, with only 839 members.* By 1800, according to some calculations, they had become the largest denomination in America. Influences that led to such an incredible turn in Baptist conditions in the New World include such factors as the impact of the Great Awakening, the improved social status of Baptists, the winning of religious liberty, Baptists' willingness to form associations to strengthen the churches and lead in planting new ones, and Baptist preference for a style of theology and worship that encouraged evangelism and church growth.

The First Great Awakening birthed churches, such as Second Baptist Church of Boston (7.1), and colleges. Rhode Island College, founded in 1764, helped transform Baptists in America. The struggle for the soul of the college (7.2) sets the stage for similar conflicts throughout Baptist history in America.

No organization for early Baptists in America is more important than the Philadelphia Baptist Association, formed in 1707. Its *Essay* of 1749 helped shape and solidify the concept of the role and function of the denomination among Baptists in America, and its minutes for various years highlights issues and challenges facing Baptists in those distant times.

Baptists in England and America maintained a close relationship during colonial times, as illustrated by efforts of the General Baptists of England to supply the needs of their brethren in the New World (7.7). The Charleston Baptist Association proved formative among Regular Baptists in the South (7.8), as did the Sandy Creek Association among the Separate Baptists (7.11). Toward the end of the century, Regular and Separate Baptists in the South merged (7.12).

7.1 Second Baptist Church, Boston, 1743

In the early 1740s the historic First Baptist Church of Boston faced disaffection, and eventually a split, over the First Great Awakening. A small group of members embraced the Awakening, with its revival theology and fervent emotions, and they tried to bend the First Church in that direction. Pastor Jeremiah Condy and the majority, however, cared little for the Awakening and preferred to continue with the conservative traditions of the church. Tensions increased, an ultimatum was ignored, and schism resulted. The "awakened" withdrew and in 1743 formed the Second Baptist Church of Boston, one of the earliest Separate Baptist churches in America. *Source:* David Benedict, *A General History of the Baptist Denomination in America* (New York: Sheldon, Lamport & Blakeman, 1855), 391-393.

The Second in Boston.

The history of this church, I shall extract entirely from a centennial discourse delivered by its pastor, Rev. Baron Stow. And as it is a recent, well-written account, I shall adopt it without alteration, except it must be greatly abridged.

In the month of September, 1740, the Rev. George Whitefield made his first visit to Boston. His preaching in this town, whether in the old South, or in Brattle Square, or on the Common, was attended by immense throngs, drawn together by the captivations of his eloquence; and the result, by the blessing of God, was a powerful revival, such as

---

*Robert G. Gardner, *Baptists of Early America: A Statistical History, 1639-1790* (Atlanta: Georgia Baptist Historical Society, 1983), 63.

New England had never witnessed. The work was opposed with great vehemence; and no impartial reader of the history of those extraordinary scenes can question, that much of the hostility was provoked by improprieties of both speech and action, that would at any time be offensive to those who love good order and christian decorum. But after making liberal allowance for all that was truly exceptionable, it is cheerfully admitted by the candid christian, that the excitement was, in the main, the product of the Holy Spirit, and that its fruits were eminently favorable to the advancement of true religion. A torpid community was aroused as by the trump of God, from its long and heavy slumber; ministers and people were converted; the style of preaching and the tone of individual piety were improved; a cold, cadaverous formalism gave place to the living energy of experimental godliness; the doctrines of the gospel were brought out from their concealment, and made to re-assert their claims to a cordial, practical credence, and all the interests of truth and holiness received new homage from regenerated thousands.

At this period, the baptist denomination on this continent was exceedingly limited, numbering only thirty-seven churches, and probably less than three thousand members. The preaching of Mr. Whitefield and others who had caught from heaven the same hallowed fire, and the great awakening consequent upon their sanctified labors, gave currency to principles which wrought undesigned changes, and conducted to results that were neither anticipated nor desired. Little did those men of God who were such efficient agents in the 'New Light Stir,' as it was opprobriously called, and who pushed their measures with almost superhuman vigor, amidst a tempest of opposition and obloquy, imagine that they were breaking up the fallow ground of their own ecclesiastical system, and sowing seed from which a sect that was every where spoken against, would reap a bountiful harvest.

The Rev. Jeremiah Condy was at this time the pastor of the First Baptist church in Boston.

He seems not to have participated, either personally or relatively, in any of the good effects of the revival whose gracious fruits were multiplied around him. But a few of the more spiritual members of his church, became 'partakers of the benefits,' and experienced such a deepening of the work of grace in their own hearts, as made them discontented under his ministry. They regarded his preaching as grievously defective in the exhibition of christian doctrine, and took occasion repeatedly to express to him their decided dissatisfaction. But as he was sustained by a large majority of his church, and doubtless considered them as meddlesome enthusiasts, infected with the 'New Light mania,' their remonstrances, however sincere and modest, were utterly unavailing. On the 29th of September, 1742, they addressed to him and to the church a letter, in which they very respectfully and very explicitly, stated their whole difficulty. They complained of Mr. Condy, as denying 'original sin,' or 'explaining away the corruption and depravity of human nature;' as denying the 'doctrine of regeneration,' or improperly 'intermixing it with man's free-agency and co-operation;' as denying 'the operations of the Holy Spirit' as distinct from the operations of the human mind; as denying 'election and predestination;' and as 'holding to falling from grace.' This letter was signed by four individuals, who, in connection with a few others, soon afterwards withdrew, and commenced a separate meeting in a private house. They continued thus to worship by themselves for nearly a year, when, finding that no notice was taken of their communication, and that nothing was likely to be done to make their return either feasible or desirable, they regarded the path of duty as sufficiently obvious, and proceeded to make arrangements for a separate and independent organization.

7.2   The Founding of Rhode Island College

The earliest Baptist College in America was founded in Rhode Island in 1764, and flourishes today in Providence as Brown University. From the first, Rhode Island College resembled Bristol Baptist College and for good reason; its primary founder, Morgan Edwards, was a Bristol graduate. The first Baptist college in America played a crucial role in providing trained ministers, serving as a center of Baptist unity and cooperation, and forming a positive image which furthered the transformation and growth of Baptists in the new nation. The following document, from the writings of Morgan Edwards, traces the foundation of the college, along with a candid account of the struggle between more liberal and conservative Baptists for control of the school. *Source:* Morgan Edwards, *Materials towards a History of the Baptists,* Eve B. Weeks and Mary B. Warren, eds., 2 vols. (Danielsville, Ga.: n.p., 1984), 1:191-196. Used by permission.

Mention was made of the college in Rhode Island government; with a reference to this appendix for its history. Young indeed the institution is, and therefore short would its history be, had it received its existence, locality, endowment and permanency like other institutions of the same nature; but contrarywise, some peculiar circumstances attend each which infer the interposition of Providence, and bespeak it to be a thing of God and not of man only.

The first mover for it in 1762 was laughed at as a projector of a thing impracticable. Nay, many of the baptists themselves discouraged the design (prophesying evil in the churches in case it should take place), from an unhappy prejudice against learning, and threatened (not only non-concurrence but) opposition. Nevertheless, a young Jerseyman (who is now at the head of the institution) went to Rhode Island government and made the design known.

The reason of his attempt in this province was (as has been observed) that the legislature is here chiefly in the hands of baptists, and therefore the likeliest place to have a baptist college established by law. The remainder of what I intend to say on this head, shall be in the words of President Manning, to which I shall add the history of the first charter by Daniel Jenckes, Esq., who both (for obvious reasons) think it necessary to have them published. President Manning's narrative is as follows:

"In the month of July, 1763, we arrived in Newport, and made a motion to several gentlemen of the baptist denomination (whereof Col. Gardner, the deputy governor was one), relative to a seminary of polite literature, subject to the government of the baptists. The motion was properly attended to, which brought together about fifteen gentlemen of the same denomination at the deputy's house, who requested that I would draw a sketch in the design against the day following.

That day came, and the said gentlemen, with other baptists, met in the same place, when a rough draft was produced and read. The tenor of which was that the institution was to be a baptist one; but that as many of other denominations should be taken in as was consistent with the said design. Accordingly the Hon. Josias Lyndon and Col. Job Bennet were appointed to draw a charter to be laid before the next General Assembly, with a petition that they should pass it into a law. But the said gentlemen pleading unskillfulness touching an affair of the kind, requested that their trusty friend, Rev. Ezra Styles (now Dr.), might be solicited to assist them. . . .

The trustees were presumed to be the principal branch of authority, and as 19 out of 35 were to be baptists, the baptists were satisfied without sufficient examination into the authority vested in the fellowship (which afterward appeared to be the soul of the institution while the trusteeship was only the body), and placing an entire confidence in Dr.

Styles, they agreed to join in a petition to the Assembly to have the charter confirmed by authority.

The petition was preferred and cheerfully received, and the charter read, after which a vote was called for and urged by some to pass it into a law. But this was opposed by others, particularly by Daniel Jenckes, Esq., member for Providence, alleging that the Assembly required more time to examine whether it was agreeable to the design of the first movers for it, and therefore prayed the house to have the perusal of it while they adjourned for dinner. This was granted with some opposition. Then he asked the governor (who was a baptist), whom they intended to vest with the governing power in said institution? The governor answered the baptists, by all means. Then Mr. Jenckes showed him that the charter was so artfully constructed as to throw the power into the fellows hands, whereof 8 out of 12 were Presbyterians, (usually called Congregationalists) and that the other four might be of the same denomination for aught appeared in the charter to the contrary.

Convinced of this, Gov. Lyndon immediately had an interview with Dr. Styles (the Presbyterian minister of Newport) and demanded why he had perverted the design of the charter? The answer was, 'I gave you timely warning to take care of yourselves, for that we have done so with regard to our society;' and finally observed that he was not the rogue. When the assembly was convened again, the said Jenckes moved that the affair might be put off to the next session, adding that the motion for a college originated with the baptists, and was intended for their use, but that the charter in question was not at all calculated to answer to their purpose; and since the committee (entrusted by the baptists) professed they were misled, not to say imposed upon, that it was necessary the baptists in other parts of the colony should be consulted previous to its passing into a law, especially as few (if any of them except himself) had seen it, and prayed that he might have a copy for the said purpose, which he promised to return. All of which were granted.

When the charter came to be narrowly inspected, it was found [to] be by no means answerable to the designs of the agitators and the instructions given to the committee. Consequently application was made to the Philadelphia Association, (where the thing took its rise) to have their mind on the subject, who immediately sent two gentlemen hither to join the baptists of this colony in making what alterations and amendments that were to them specified before their departure.

When they arrived, Dr. Ayres, of Newport, was added to the committee, and they happily draughted the present charter, and lodged it, with a new petition, in proper hands. The most material alterations were appointing the same number of baptists in the fellowship that had been appointed (of Presbyterians) by Dr. Styles, settling the presidency in the baptist society; adding 5 baptists to the trustees, and putting more Episcopalians than Presbyterians in the corporation."

Thus the baptists narrowly escaped being jockied out of their college by a set of men in whom they reposed entire confidence. . . .

7.3 An *Essay* on the Power of an Association, 1749

From the first, Baptists have preferred *cooperation* over exaggerated *independency*. Therefore, when they reached a sufficient number in an area, and sometimes before, they grouped their churches into *associations*. In England, Particular Baptist associations leaned over backwards to avoid any hint of superintendency over the churches, but the General Baptist associations frankly assumed and exercised some power over the churches. The earliest continuing association in America, the Philadelphia Association, was formed in 1707. In its early years, the Association played its role by ear, so to speak, but some feared it might assume some church prerogatives. In 1749 the association adopted a formal *Essay,* written by Benjamin Griffith, which defined the powers of an association as compared to the rights reserved to the churches. *Source:* A. D. Gillette, ed., *Minutes of the Philadelphia Baptist Association from A.D. 1707 to A.D. 1807* (Philadelphia: American Baptist Publication Society, 1851), 60-63.

At our annual Association, met September the 19th, 1749, an essay on the power and duty of an Association of churches, was proposed, as above hinted, to the consideration of the Association; and the same, upon mature deliberation, was approved and subscribed by the whole house; and the contents of the same was ordered to be transcribed as the judgment of the Association, in order to be inserted in the Association book, to the end and purpose that it may appear what power an Association of churches hath, and what duty is incumbent on an Association; and prevent the contempt with which some are ready to treat such an assembly, and also to prevent any future generation from claiming more power than they ought—lording over the churches.

ESSAY.

That an Association is not a superior judicature, having such superior power over the churches concerned; but that each particular church hath a complete power and authority from Jesus Christ, to administer all gospel ordinances, provided they have a sufficiency of officers duly qualified, or that they be supplied by the officers of another sister church or churches, as baptism, and the Lord's supper. &c.; and to receive in and cast out, and also to try and ordain their own officers, and to exercise every part of gospel discipline and church government, independent of any other church or assembly whatever.

And that several such independent churches, where Providence gives them their situation convenient, may, and ought, for their mutual strength, counsel, and other valuable advantages, by their voluntary and free consent, to enter into an agreement and confederation, as is hinted in our printed Narrative of discipline, page 59, 60, 61.

Such churches there must be agreeing in doctrine and practice, and independent in their authority and church power, before they can enter into a confederation, as aforesaid, and choose delegates or representatives, to associate together; and thus the several independent churches being the constituents, the association, council or assembly of their delegates, when assembled, is not to be deemed a superior judicature, as having a superintendency over the churches, but subservient to the churches, in what may concern all the churches in general, or any one church in particular; and, though no power can regularly arise above its fountain from where it rises, yet we are of opinion, that an Association of the delegates of associate churches have a very considerable power in their hands, respecting those churches in their confederation; for if the agreement of several distinct churches, in sound doctrine and regular practice, be the first motive, ground, and foundation or basis of their confederation, then it must naturally follow, that a defection in doctrine or practice in any church, in such confederation, or any party in any such church, is ground sufficient for an Association to withdraw from such a church or party so deviating or making defection, and to exclude such from them in some formal manner, and to advertise all the churches in confederation thereof, in order that every church in confederation may withdraw from such in all acts of church communion, to the end they may be ashamed, and that all the churches may discountenance such, and bear testimony against the defection.

. . . A godly man may, and ought to withdraw, not only from a heathen, but from such as have the form of godliness, if they appear to want the power of it, 2 Tim. iii. 5, by the same parity of reason the saints, in what capacity soever they may be considered, may withdraw from defective or disorderly churches or persons; but excommunicate they cannot, there being no institution to authorize them so to do. But in the capacity of a congregational church, dealing with her own members, an Association, then, of the delegates of associate churches, may exclude and withdraw from defective and unsound or disorderly churches or persons, in manner abovesaid; and this will appear regular and justifiable by the light and law of nature, as is apparent in the conduct and practice of all regular civil and political corporations and confederations whatsoever; who all of them have certain rules to exclude delinquents from their societies, as well as for others to accede thereunto.

And further, that an Association of the delegates of confederate churches may doctrinally declare any person or party in a church, who are defective in principles or disorderly in practice, to be censurable, when the affair comes under their cognizance, and without exceeding the bounds of their power and duty, to advise the church that such belong unto, how to deal with such, according to the rule of gospel discipline; and also to strengthen such a church, and assist her, if need be, by sending able men of their own number to help the church in executing the power vested in her by the ordinance of Jesus Christ, and to stand by her, and to defend her against the insults of such offending persons or parties.

7.4 *Minutes,* Philadelphia Baptist Association

What was it like to be a Baptist in America in the eighteenth century? What issues did the churches face, and how did they deal with those issues? The minutes of the Philadelphia Association help answer these questions. Through the window opened by these ancient records we glimpse the churches dealing with doctrinal problems (especially universalism), trying to help the churches obtain suitable pastors, planning for the religious education of children in the days before the Sunday School, sponsoring home missions and Christian education, debating whether to accept non-Baptist immersion, and puzzling whether women should speak out or have a vote in church affairs. The "queries" sent to the association provide an interesting barometer of conditions in the churches, spiritual and otherwise. *Source:* A. D. Gillette, ed. *Minutes of the Philadelphia Baptist Association from A.D. 1707 to A.D. 1807* (Philadelphia: American Baptist Publication Society, 1851.

AN ACCOUNT
OF THE AFFAIRS THAT CAME TO BE CONSIDERED BY THE ASSOCIATION OF THE AFOREMENTIONED CHURCHES, SINCE THEY HELD AN ASSOCIATION, AS FAR AS ANY RECORDS OF THE SAME CAN BE FOUND.

1707.

THERE is no track or footsteps of any regular association, agreement, or confederation, between the first churches in these colonies of Pennsylvania and the Jerseys, that I can find, before the year 1707, when we have, in the records of the church of Pennepek, this account, viz:—Before our general meeting, held at Philadelphia, in the seventh month, 1707, it was concluded by the several congregations of our judgment, to make choice of some particular brethren, such as they thought most capable in every congregation, and those to meet at the yearly meeting to consult about such things as were wanting in the churches, and to set them in order; and these brethren meeting at the said yearly meeting, which began the 27th of the seventh month, on the seventh day of the week, agreed to continue the meeting till the third day following in the work of the public ministry. It was then agreed, that a person that is a stranger, that has neither letter of recommendation, nor is known to be a person gifted, and of a good conversation, shall not be admitted to preach, nor be entertained as a member in any of the baptized congregations in communion with each other.

It was also concluded, that if any difference shall happen between any member and the church he belongs unto, and they cannot agree, then the person so grieved may, at the general meeting, appeal to the brethren of the several congregations, and with such as they shall nominate, to decide the difference; that the church and the person so grieved do fully acquiesce in their determination.

1710.

In the year 1710, several able men, ministers and elders, and in the year following also, came over from South Wales and the West of England—as the Rev. Mr. Nathaniel Jenkins, Mr. John Burrows, Mr. Abel Morgan, and some that had been ruling elders in the churches they came from—all of them men long concerned in the affairs of churches and associations in their own countries.

1712.

One Thomas Selby made a disturbance and rupture in the church at Philadelphia and Pennepek; and application having been made to the Association, the Association did nominate persons from among themselves, to hear and determine of and concerning the said difference. And both parties consenting, the said nominated men proceeded to hear and determine of the same, and brought in their judgment and determination, confirmed under their hands, as followeth, . . .

"With respect to the difference between the members and others, some time belonging to the Baptist church at Philadelphia, as it hath been laid before us, persons chosen by both sides, they having referred the whole of their difference to our determination; we, doing what in us lies for the glory of God, and the peace of the whole church, in regard of the transactions past, and what may be best for the future, for the interest of the gospel, upon due consideration of what hath been laid before us, as followeth, viz:— We do find the way and manner of dealing and proceeding with each other hath been from the rule of the Gospel, and unbecoming Christians in many respects, and in some too shameful here to enumerate the particulars.

"And first, we judge it expedient in point of justice, that Mr. Thomas Selby be paid the money subscribed to him by the members of this church, and he discharged from any further service in the work of the ministry; he being a person, in our judgment, not likely for the promotion of the Gospel in these parts of the country; and considering his miscarriages, we judge he may not be allowed to communion.

"And secondly, as to the members of this congregation, we do apprehend the best way is, that each party offended do freely forgive each other all personal and other offences that may have risen on this occasion, and that they be buried in oblivion; and that those who shall for future mention or stir up any of the former differences, so as to tend to contention, shall be deemed disorderly persons, and be dealt with as such. . . .

1723.

At our Association, convened September 23, 1723, a query from the church at Brandywine came, viz., which way they might improve their vacant days of worship, when they have no minister among them to carry on the public work.

Solution. We conceive it expedient that the church do meet together as often as conveniency will admit; and when they have none to carry on the work of preaching, that they read a chapter, sing a psalm, and go to prayer and beg of God to increase their grace and comfort, and have due regard to order and decency in the exercise of those gifts at all times, and not to suffer any to exercise their gifts in a mixed multitude until tried and approved of first by the church.

Agreed, that the proposal drawn by the several ministers, and signed by many others, in reference to the examination of all gifted brethren and ministers that come in here from other places, be duly put in practice, we having found the evil of neglecting a true and previous scrutiny in those affairs. . . .

1728.

In the year 1728, the Association met the sixth day of the week.

1. Query from Hopewell: What course to take in choosing a ruling elder in the church? We answer, that a church wanting ruling elders or deacons, as in other cases, should set a day apart, and by fasting and prayer, seek the guidance and direction of God, and then unanimously pitch upon one or more of their brethren to act upon trial in the office of ruling elder or deacon; and our judgment is, that persons called upon trial in the said offices, may act by authority of the church, with as full power as if completely qualified; but not so teaching elders or ministers of the word and ordinances.

2. A query from the church at Montgomery: Whether a church is bound to grant a letter of dismission to any member to go to another church, while his residence is not removed?

Answered in the negative, we having neither precept nor precedent for such a practice in Scripture. . . .

1731.

The elders, ministers, and messengers, of the baptized congregations in Pennsylvania and the Jerseys, met in Association at Philadelphia, September 24th, 1731. To the respective congregations we represent, send greeting:—

Dearly beloved and highly esteemed brethren, our joy and our crown, at the appearing of our Lord Jesus Christ, we cannot but rejoice to see your care and diligence, in maintaining this our annual communion, in sending your messengers to associate with us. We met together in love, admitted your messengers, perused your letters, and had cause to bless God that we find the churches in peace among themselves, without distraction, schism or division, or destructive errors, and that in most churches there hath been some addition this last year; for which we bless the great Husbandman, who gives success to the labours of his poor servants. Yet we find the old complaint of dullness, coldness, and indifference in the things of God. . . .

The harvest is great and the labourers are few; pray mightily for more, and treat honourably the few you have left. Your neglect of hearing them may provoke the Master of the vineyard to call home from you those labourers you have, as of late he hath many of our reverend brethren. See what gifts you have among you: if there be any hopeful youths, let them exercise themselves, and be kind to them and tender of them; take heed that you do not discourage them you have, lest you should be made to lament your imprudent and inconsiderate management. . . .

Agreed to the request of the church of Philadelphia, setting forth that they have been at a great charge in building a meeting-house, which is to be very heavy, unless the rest of the churches of the same order will find in their hearts to contribute towards the defraying of the same.

1734.

The elders, ministers, and messengers, of the congregations holding believers' baptism, in Pennsylvania and the Jerseys, met in Association at Philadelphia, on the 21st, 22d and 23d of September A. D., 1734, to the several congregations we represent, send Christian salutation. . . .

Several queries from Middletown came to the Association, viz.—

1. Whether we may accept and take in a minister of a different persuasion at our appointed meetings.

Answered in the negative; unless the church see cause, upon some particular occasions.

2. Whether it may not be more convenient for us to keep up our meetings, as usual, by reading the Scriptures, singing of psalms, and prayer, than to admit men of different persuasions?

Answered in the affirmative.

3. Whether it be justifiable for our members to neglect our own appointed meetings, and at their pleasure go to hear those differing in judgment from us?

Answered in the negative. Heb. x. 25.

Brother Joseph Eaton to preach the Association sermon the next year; and in case of his failure, brother Benjamin Griffith to preach the same.

Minutes of the case between the Association and William Davis, considered September 30, 1734:—

Respecting the crimes alledged against him, of selling two books sent him, and of representing us in a wrong light to Mr. David Rees and Mr. Hollis. He, upon confession of his faults, was pardoned by the Association.

1735

Query. If any member, or members, of a congregation grow scrupulous about matters merely indifferent in themselves, such as the mode of administration, as is usual in our churches, or the quality of the bread or wine, or the manner of serving, as the cup upon a plate, or without, making the same a matter of conscience, and thereupon totally refrain their communion. What is best to be done in such a case?

Solution. That such persons, contending, quarreling, and so refraining church communion upon such light grounds—since such things are left undetermined by our great Lawgiver—are much to be blamed; and a church is nowise obliged to yield to such vain humours, but may continue their order, according to the rules of expediency and harmless decency, and deal according to the word with such delinquents; for it is to be doubted that such person or persons have not a design to make a rupture, seeing the matter in debate is so trivial.

2. Upon a motion moved by some members of the Association: Whether a person that is a well-wisher to us, and desires to be admitted a member into a church far distant from the place of his abode; whereas a church of the same order is nearer to him than the church that he proposes to join with; whether it be orderly for the distant church to receive such an one? Yea or nay?

Resolved in the negative, there being substantial reasons to the contrary. Such practice is contrary to the intendment, in instituting particular churches.—*See Confession of Faith, chap.* xxvii. *See also our Treatise of Discipline,* 28, 29. . . .

1740

A query from Cohansie: Whether a pious person, of the number of Pedo-Baptists, who forbears to have his own children sprinkled, may be admitted in to our communion without being baptized? And doth not the refusing admittance to such an one, discover want of charity in a church so refusing?

Given to vote, and passed all in the negative. *Nemine contradicente.*

Query 2, from Piscataqua: Whether it is regular to baptize persons proposing for baptism, upon the plea that they may be at liberty to communicate where they please?

Answered in the negative. . . .

Added to the several churches belonging, in gospel love, to this Association, by baptism, the past year, one hundred and eleven souls.

1742

A motion was made in the Association for reprinting the Confession of faith, set forth by the elders of baptized congregations, met in London, A. D. 1689, with a short treatise of church discipline, to be annexed to the Confession of faith. Agreed, that the thing was needful and likely to be very useful; and in order to carry it on, it is ordered to send it to the several churches belonging to this Association; to make a trial of what sums of money can be raised, and to send an account to Mr. Jenkin Jones, to the intent, that when the several collections are computed, if it be found sufficient to defray the charges of the work, that then it shall go on; if not, then to drop it for this year; and if it be carried on, that then an addition of two articles be therein inserted: that is to say, concerning singing of psalms in the worship of God, and laying of hands upon baptized believers. Ordered, also, that the said Mr. Jones and Benjamin Griffith do prepare a short treatise of discipline, to be annexed to the said Confession of faith. . . .

1743.

The elders, ministers, and messengers of the several congregations, baptized on profession of faith, meeting at Philadelphia, the 24th of September, 1743, and continued by adjournment to the 28th of the same month. . . .

Tuesday, the house met according to appointment, at 8 o'clock, A.M., to consider further the affair begun yesterday, touching the differences at Montgomery. After some time spent in debate thereon, brother Joseph Eaton stood up, and freely, to our apprehension, recanted, renounced, and condemned all expressions, which he heretofore had used, whereby his brethren at Montgomery, or any persons elsewhere, were made to believe that he departed from the literal sense and meaning of that fundamental article in our Confession of faith, concerning the eternal generation and Sonship of Jesus Christ our Lord; he acknowledged with grief his misconduct therein, whether by word or deed. We desire that all our churches would take notice thereof, and have a tender regard for him in his weak and aged years, and in particular, of that great truth upon which the Christian religion depends; without which it must not only totter, but fall to the ground; which he confesses he was sometimes doubtful of. . . .

1746.

The elders and messengers of the congregations baptized upon profession of faith, in Pennsylvania and the Jerseys, met at Philadelphia, the 24th day of September, 1746. . . .

1. Query from the church of Philadelphia: Whether it be lawful or regular for any person to preach the gospel publicly without ordination?

Answer: that which we have both rule and precedent for in the word of God, is, and must be, both lawful and regular, . . .

Seeing men are called teachers, as Paul and Barnabas are in Acts xiii. 1, and did undoubtedly teach profitably in the church of Antioch, before and without ordination, what reason can be given why there may not be in churches men of useful gifts, and profitable to teach all the days of their life without ordination? It is very probably that the Apostle Paul, seeing he occupied such a station himself a long time, speaks of such gifted brethren, Ephes. iv. 11, by the name of teachers. Seeing they are mentioned besides the pastors, or that such useful men may be the helps the same apostle mentions, 1 Cor. xii. 28, for helps cannot be more useful in any thing than in teaching. Our churches have had such teachers very frequently, as we might instance in many of them by name, if need were as well as the church of Antioch.

2. Query: Whether it is regular for any to use the office of deacon, or to exercise the office of a ruling elder in a church, without ordination?

Solution. As touching ruling eldors or deacons; if there had been no other rule but mere parity of reason, it would appear necessary to have a proof of the persons delegated to those offices by a trial in the office itself; for experience teacheth that some very regular members cannot become useful officers when tried, and if persons, likely to bear the ministerial function, may be found unfit for the office when tried, though sound in the faith, and of approved conversation, so may well minded and well respected persons be found, when tried, to be unfit for inferior offices. If it be objected that we have a precedent for choosing and ordaining deacons, without any proof or trial, it may be sufficient to answer, that the precedent in Acts vi. is very proper to inform us of the nature and property of the deacon's office; but cannot reasonably be pleaded to be imitable in future times, in that particular, in debate; because, 1, that was an extraordinary time, and done by extraordinary persons; and therefore not imitable in ordinary times nor ordinary persons, unless we could bring extraordinary times and persons to be alike, which we cannot. 2. Because the Holy Ghost, since that precedent, hath given us a positive rule to direct the church in ordinary times, which we are bound to follow, 1 Tim. iii. 10; from which the church in after ages ought not to deviate. Ordinarily it is improbable we should find the qualifications of a man for office without a trial; therefore, to ordain men to office in the church of God, without first being proved and approved, is against both rule and reason, and is therefore unlawful to be done by any church of Christ. . . .

3. Query: Whether women may or ought to have their votes in the church, in such matters as the church shall agree to be decided by votes?

Solution. As that in 1 Cor. xiv. 34, 35, and other parallel texts, are urged against their votes, as a rule, and ought, therefore, to be maturely considered.

If, then, the silence enjoined on women be taken so absolute, as that they must keep entire silence in all respects whatever; yet, notwithstanding, it is to be hoped they may have, as members of the body of the church, liberty to give a mute voice, by standing or lifting up of the hands, or the contrary, to signify their assent or dissent to the thing proposed, and so augment the number on the one or both sides of the question. But, with the consent of authors and casuists, such absolute silence in all respects cannot be intended; for if so, how shall a woman make a confession of her faith to the satisfaction of the whole church? or how shall the church judge whether a woman be in the faith or no? How shall a woman offended, after regular private proceeding with an offending member, tell the church, as she is bound to do, if the offender be obstinate, according to the rule, Matt. xviii. 17? How shall a woman do, if she be an evidence to a matter of fact? Shall the church grope in the dark for want of her evidence to clear the doubt? Surely not. Again, how shall a woman defend herself if wrongfully accused, if she must not speak? This is a privilege of all human creatures by the laws of nature, not abrogated by the law of God.

Therefore there must be times and ways in and by which women, as members of the body, may discharge their conscience and duty towards God and men, as in the cases above said and the like. And a woman may, at least, make a brother a mouth to ask leave to speak, if not ask it herself; and a time of hearing is to be allowed, for that is not inconsistent with the silence and subjection enjoined on them by the law of God and nature, yet ought not they to open the floodgate of speech in an imperious, tumultuous, masterly manner. Hence the silence, with subjection, enjoined on all women in the church of God, is such a silence as excludes all women whomsoever from all degrees of teaching, ruling, governing, dictating, and leading in the church of God; yet may their voice be taken as above said. But if a woman's vote be singular, her reasons ought to be called for, heard, and maturely considered, without contempt. . . .

1787

Received a very agreeable letter from the Virginia Association, by their messenger, our esteemed Brother William Fristoe, in which we note two things particularly:

First, That a happy union has taken place between the Regular and Separate Baptists in Virginia of which we also had information by a letter from our Brother John Leland, by order of the committee of Regular and Separate Baptists. In this union we sincerely rejoice.

Secondly, They warn us to beware of a certain Duncan M'Clean, late one of their ministers, who has embraced the doctrine of universal salvation.

In a postscript, Brother Leland informs us, that about twelve hundred persons have been baptized, and added to their churches, within about two years.

4. A letter from the Charleston Association was received, with their minutes, containing very agreeable information of the state of religion in some of their churches.

5. A letter from the Warren Association was read, and their messenger, Brother Manning, entered into a particular detail of the progress of the gospel in various parts of New England. Brother William Wood, of Kentucky, did the same with respect to the interest of religion in that place: and some of the brethren present gave us the like intelligence from Redstone and Georgia. By all which, we were made to rejoice in the prosperity of Zion throughout this continent: and encouraged to believe that the purity of the doctrines and ordinances of the gospel of Christ, are prevailing more and more. . . .

1788

October 7th, three o'clock, P. M.—Brother Elkanah Holmes preached, by appointment, from 2 Cor. iv. 5, "For we preach not ourselves, but Christ Jesus the Lord; and ourselves your servants for Jesus' sake."

2. Brother Samuel Jones was chosen moderator, and Brother Thomas Ustick, clerk. Letters from thirty-four churches were read.

October 8th, 8½ o'clock, A .M.—Met according to adjournment.

3. Proceeded to read the letters from the respective corresponding Associations. Doctor Manning presented a letter from the Warren Association as their messenger, which, with their minutes, contained agreeable intelligence. Brother Stephen Gano, as messenger from Shaftsbury Association, gave in their letter and minutes, which contain comfortable tidings. The Charleston minutes, and a letter also from that Association, came to hand, by which it appears that their circumstances are prosperous and their numbers increasing. A letter was likewise received from the Ketockton Association, giving accounts of a marvellous revival; that in one particular church three hundred had

been added. They further add, that the harmony of their assembly was such, that there did not appear to be among the watchmen, as they beautifully express it, "one discordant note." . . .

11. The church at Cape May query: "Whether a member, who professes that Christ died for all mankind, and that every individual of the human race will finally be saved, ought to be excommunicated?"

Agreed, That every such person, upon conviction, and after proper steps have been taken, ought to be excluded. . . .

Our aged and venerable Brother Kelsay preached in the evening, from Acts viii. 35. His address to the young ministers gave them great pleasure. He advised them, First. To study, with earnest prayer, as if all depended on their own endeavors; but, in preaching, to depend upon Divine assistance, as though they had not studied at all. Second. To be concise in preaching, and to conclude when done. Third. To pray for a blessing on their labors immediately after preaching: and Fourth. To embrace every seasonable opportunity of conversing with precious souls, and not to forget such as were in menial circumstances. . . .

This Association, taking into consideration the ruinous effects of the great abuse of distilled liquors throughout this country, take this opportunity of expressing our hearty concurrence with our brethren of several other religious societies, in discountenancing the use of them in future; and earnestly entreat our brethren and friends to use all their influence to that end, both in their own families and neighborhood, except when used as medicine.

1790

In answer to a query from the church at Stamford, accompanied with a number of quotations from certain authors, holding what is called the new system of divinity: Whether we hold them as Scripture truths, and whether such persons as hold them, and endeavor to promote them, are to be held in fellowship in a gospel church? We reply, that we apprehend danger, lest by these fine spun theories, and the consequences which are drawn from them by some, the great doctrines of the imputation of Adam's sin, Christ's proper atonement, imputed righteousness, &c., should be totally set aside, or, at least, the glory of them sullied. We therefore advise, that great care should be taken to guard against innovations not calculated to edify the body of Christ. But that the individual churches must judge for themselves, when any of their members so far deviate from that system of doctrine held by the churches of this Association, as to require their exclusion.

This Association lament they have occasion again to call the attention of that part of Zion we represent, to another awful instance of departure from the faith once delivered unto the saints. Mr. Nicholas Cox, late a brother in the ministry, having espoused, and artfully, as well as strenuously endeavored, to propagate the fatal notion of the universal restoration of bad men and devils from hell. As such, we caution our churches, those of our sister Associations, and Christian brethren of every denomination, to be aware of him. . . .

1791

Doctor Rogers read a paragraph of a letter from the Rev. Abraham Booth, of London, directed to himself, in which was intimated the expediency of our reconsidering the decision of this Association, in 1788, respecting "the invalidity of Baptism when administered by an unbaptized person."

Agreed to refer it to the next meeting of the Association. . . .

1792

A query respecting the validity of baptism by an unordained and unbaptized administrator, referred in the sixth section of October 5, in our minutes of last year, was taken up, and determined in the negative. . . .

Queries from the church at Great Valley: Are the words bishop and elder of the same meaning in the writings of the apostles?

Yes. This Association, therefore, recommend that the terms pastors, bishops and elders, as used in our Confession of faith, be adopted.

17. Query from the church at West Creek: Is the washing of feet a gospel ordinance?

This Association consider the washing of feet, as mentioned in the New Testament, only as a pattern of humility; nevertheless have no objection to those practising it who think it a duty.

7.5 Universalism Among Baptists in America

By far the most serious doctrinal problem facing Baptists in America in the eighteenth century was universalism or, as some called it, "hell redemptionism." At about the same time this doctrine of "the larger hope," or the idea that eventually all souls will be redeemed and none eternally lost, also spread among English Baptists. Elhanan Winchester, pastor at First Baptist in Philadelphia, turned universalist and in the 1780s tried to pull the church with him. The Philadelphia Association repeatedly warned the churches about the "leprosy of universalism" in their midst. Baptist churches never showed much interest in doctrinal unitarianism, but for several reasons they were powerfully attracted to universalism. In 1790 Samuel Jones wrote the Circular Letter on universalism for the Philadelphia Association. Excerpts are given below. *Source:* A. D. Gillette, *Minutes of the Philadelphia Baptist Association from A.D. 1707 to A.D. 1807* (Philadelphia: American Baptist Publication Society, 1851), 257-260.

CIRCULAR LETTER.
BY REV. SAMUEL JONES, D. D.

The elders and messengers of the several churches met in Association, in the city of New York, October 5th, 1790.

To the several churches in union with this Association, send greeting.

Dearly beloved,—We are happy, at the close of our annual meeting, that we can say, it was agreeable and comfortable through the whole. We had refreshing news from several churches in our connection, as well as from the Associations that correspond with us. It is matter of joy, and calls for acknowledgment and giving of thanks, that peace and good order so generally prevail, and that the work of the Lord is carried on with power in many places. We have, however, to lament, that there are some appearances, in two or three of our churches, of the leprosy of universal salvation, which, perhaps, the Lord may permit to spread, that they which are approved may be made manifest. But, when we see such an Achan, such a troubler of Israel, in the camp, we may well suspect the Lord has a controversy with us. It behoves us, then, to humble ourselves, to implore the divine mercy, and to do our endeavor to prevent the spreading of so dangerous a plague. To this end we have concluded to address you at this time on the aforesaid subject.

The notion of universal salvation, as now propagated, is explained two ways. Some of them say that there is no hell, or, if there be, that there shall not any of the human race be sent there, but that all, good and bad, shall be taken to heaven together. Others say, that though there be a place of future punishment, and though some of the human race are sent thither for a time, yet that they all finally shall be released, and brought safe to heaven.

We doubt not, dear brethren, but it will seem strange to such of you as may not have heard these things before, that any who pretend to be the ministers of Christ, should advance such dangerous notions. Yet so it is. He who, in the beginning, gave divine revelation the lie, when he said to the woman, "Ye shall not surely die," has ever since been going about, like a roaring lion, seeking whom he may devour; and endeavoring, by various means, to deceive and lull asleep, and among others, by endeavoring to evade the force of divine truth.

As for the first of these notions, namely, that not any of the human race are ever sent to a place of future punishment, but that all, good and bad, are taken to heaven, we shall say but little to it; not only because we have no room, but also because we deem it unnecessary. The Scripture, on the one hand, is so express, particular, and positive, and, on the other, the methods they take to evade these Scriptures are so disingenuous, and their endeavors to accommodate other Scriptures to their own views so trifling, that it is hard for any one to believe that they believe themselves, or that they can be serious and in earnest, when the Scriptures positively and without equivocation say, "the wicked shall be turned into hell, and all the nations that forget God," Ps. ix. 17. "That the whole body should be cast into hell," Matt. v. 29. "To be cast into hell fire," Matt. xviii. 9. "How can ye escape the damnation of hell," Matt. xxiii. 33. "To be cast into hell," Mark ix. 45, 47. "And in hell he lift up his eyes, being in torment," Luke xvi. 23; besides a number of other places. What need we more, not to mention the dissolute manners which might be expected to attend, and which actually have been the consequences of so licentious a tenet, as that of which we are speaking.

The other way of explaining this notion, namely, that, though some of the human race are sent to a place of future punishment for a time, yet that they shall all finally be released, and brought safe to heaven; this merits more attention, because it is more plausible, though not more true.

Here we shall consider,

I. That the Scripture is express against it.

II. That there are no Scriptures for it.

III. That there can be none, since it would be likely to do much hurt, but could do no good.

IV. And lastly, that if the notion was in some degree likely to be true, yet that it would be safest to reject it.

I. The Scripture expressly says that future punishment will be for ever, 2 Pet. ii. 17; Jude, verse 13; for ever and ever, Rev. xx. 10; xiv. 11; xix. 3.

And we read of "eternal damnation," Mark iii. 29; "eternal judgment," Heb. vi. 2; "eternal fire," Jude, verse 7; "everlasting fire," Matt. xxv. 41; xviii. 8; "everlasting punishment," Matt. xxv. 26; and of one sin that "it shall not be forgiven, neither in this world, neither in the world to come," Matt. xii. 32. In this absolute manner is expressed the endless duration of the awful denunciations of the wrath of God; and to cut off all pretence of every possible evasion, there are three things remarkable:

1. That the eternal duration of the punishment of the wicked, is expressed in the very same words as eternal duration in general, Dan. ii. 20.

2. In the very same words also, whereby the eternal duration of the happiness of the righteous is expressed, Dan. xii. 2; Rev. xxii. 5; John iii. 16; Matt. xxv. 26.

3. Nay, in the very same words whereby the eternal duration of God himself is expressed, Gen. xxi. 33; Psalm xc. 2; Dan. vii. 27; Lam. v. 19; Deut. xxxii. 40.

II. Since the awful subject before us is so clearly revealed in the word of God, it may seem trifling to undertake to show that there is no Scripture in favor of a release from future punishment, as if it might be possible for Scripture to say and unsay, to speak for and against the same thing. Nevertheless, it may be of use to mention the principle Scriptures that are pretended to hold forth a redemption from hell, in order to show, that beside the foregoing reason, there are generally reasons sufficient, arising out of the texts themselves and contexts, to show that they mean no such thing as they are brought to prove. Thus, for instance, the "all men" in 1 Tim. ii. 4, can never mean every individual of the human race, for there are some "who were before ordained unto condemnation," and are "vessels of wrath fitted for destruction," (Jude 4; Rom. ix. 22;) but rather all sorts of men, as ver. 1, kings and peasants, rich and poor, bond and free, male and female, young and old; and who are therefore to be prayed for: nor can 2 Pet. iii. 9, admit of such an interpretation; for this means, not any of the *us* mentioned before, or the *beloved* in the first verse; nor 1 John ii. 2, which means that the benefits of Christ were not to be confined to the Jews only, but to be extended to the Gentiles also; nor Rom. v. 18, for here the first and second Adams, and their respective offspring are put in opposition, showing that as the offspring of the one was lost by his sin, the offspring of the other shall be saved by his grace; the one offspring condemned for one offence, the other saved from many; nor Col. i. 20, for *all* here must be understood in a limited sense; for it cannot include angels in heaven, who could not be reconciled to God, since they never had been in a state of irreconciliation: all the elect of God then are meant, who are spoken of as reconciled by the blood of the cross. Nor Eph. i. 10, which only says, that all *in* Christ shall be brought together, but not those who never were in him, and die in their sins; nor 1 Cor. xv. 22; for this speaks of the resurrection of the body from natural death, not of a resurrection from spiritual death. Nor Rom. xi. 32, which speaks of having mercy on all, that is, on all that believe, as in the parallel place, Gal. iii. 22. Nor Zech. ix. 11, for these are the words of Christ to the Jewish church, comforting them in the prospect of the favor that should be shown them by Cyrus, and comparing their distressed situation in the Babylonish captivity, to the situation of one in a pit, wherein was no water: and it is said this deliverance should be wrought in virtue of the covenant made in their behalf, which is therefore called *their* covenant. Nor Rev. xx. 13; for this speaks of gathering them from all quarters to the general judgment, who in the next verse are said to be cast into the lake of fire. Nor Heb. xii. 23; for here all the saved are said to be the *first born,* to denote their excellency, high privileges, right of priesthood, and large inheritance. Nor James i. 18; for the *first fruits* here means all the saved, as in the last, who are separated and distinguished by grace from others, as the first fruit was wont to be from the crop, and consecrated to God as that was. Nor 1 Cor. xv. 25, 28, and Phil. ii. 10; Rev. v. 13; for these are only expressive of the universal dominion of Christ, and of homage and adoration paid him on that account. Nor Ezek. xvi. 53, 55; for, if Sodom was to be restored, it must be to its former state, which was a very bad one. If restored should be understood in an improper sense, then by Sodom may be understood the Gentile nations, who were like unto Sodom in practice, Deut. xxxii. 32; Isa. i. 10; Jer. xxiii. 14; Rev. xi. 8; and Israel, by Samaria, who shall be restored when all the Jews, with the fulness of the Gentiles, shall be brought in at the time of the latter day glory. Or that when Sodom and Samaria should return to their former state, then the Jews should to theirs: as much as to say, they never should, as they never were. For, though many of them returned from the Babylonish captivity, yet they were never restored to their former state and glory. And besides, it is expressly said, with respect to "Sodom and Gomorrah, and the cities about them," that they "are set forth for an example, suffering the vengeance of eternal fire," Jude, verse 7.

Thus, brethren, we have cited the principal passages brought in support of this wild notion of universal salvation, and you see how little they are to the purpose. Thus it is that people in a strait will catch at any thing.

III. Further, it is not only manifest that there is no text to support such a notion, but that there cannot be such a text. It cannot be that the Divine being has published any thing that would be, not only contrary to those plain texts, that speak positively of the eternal duration of future punishment, but that it would also be perfectly useless, and at the same time dangerous. If the wicked were ever to be released from hell, time enough to let them know it after they get there, and not before, to encourage them in sin. To give them so much as a hint of it in this life, would be exactly the same as if the Divine Being, when he prohibited the use of the forbidden tree, had told Adam, that if he should eat of that tree, he would contrive a way for his escape, of which we know that not the least item was given before the fall, and indeed than which nothing could be more unworthy the Divine Being. So that if there was any passage within the lids of the Bible that gave information of a release from hell, we might be sure, such a text could never be the word of God.

IV. We only add, that if the notion of restoration from hell was in some degree probable, which it is not, yet it would be much safest to reject it altogether; for if those who place dependence on it should at last find themselves mistaken, awful will be the disappointment. On the other hand, those who place no dependence on it, but seek to avoid future punishment, by placing their dependence on a better hope, if they should be mistaken, they will nevertheless share equal benefit with others.

Let us, therefore, carefully avoid a notion so unscriptural, so useless, and at the same time so dangerous. But, beloved, of you we hope better things, though we thus speak. We do not apprehend much danger, but judge it seasonable, and that it might be of use to give a word of caution.

"Now unto him that is able to keep you from falling, and to present you faultless before the presence of his glory, with exceeding joy, to the only wise God our Saviour, be glory and majesty, dominion and power, both now and ever. Amen."

JAMES MANNING, Moderator.
WILLIAM VANHORN, Clerk.

7.6   A Contract Between Church and Pastor

In the eighteenth century much misunderstanding arose between Baptist churches and their pastors. Many pastors had a hard time collecting what salary the church promised, or even in getting the church to acknowledge they had promised anything. A few churches drew up formal contracts to show what church and pastor expected of each other. A typical such contract is that between the Salem church of New Jersey and Pastor Isaac Skillman, drawn up in 1791 and witnessed by members of the Cohansey and Wilmington churches. *Source:* Minutes, First Baptist Church of Salem, December 12, 1791, as cited in Norman H. Maring, *Baptists in New Jersey* (Valley Forge: Judson Press, 1964), 85-86. Used by permission.

Be it remembered that on the 16th day of November 1791 the following agreement was entered into between the Revd Mr. Isaak Skillman and the Baptist Church and Congregation . . . The said Mr. Skillman covenants and agrees to be the pastor or minister of the Church and Congregation, to execute all the duties that a minister ought to perform in a church, agreeably to the Baptist Confession of Faith, preaching all funerals that he may be called upon to preach for said Congregation, preaching two sermons a day in the summer season, visit the said congregation twice a year formally, and not leave or absent himself from the necessary services of said congregation. And said Congregation and their trustees doth covenant and agree to and with the said Mr. Skillman to pay him for his labours and services . . . the sum of one hundred and twenty five pounds per year to commence on the 14th day of August last. And further the said parties agree and promise each to the other that if any discontent on the part of the said Mr. Skillman, whereby he should wish to be dismissed from serving said Church and Congregation, and if any discontent should arise on the Church and Congregation's part, that they should wish to have said Mr. Skillman dismissed from being their minister, in either case they may, if either of them see meet—call the ministers and some of the members from Cumberland and Wilmington Baptist churches to judge between them and their determinations shall be binding on each party.

7.7   English General Baptist Contact with South Carolina

The General Baptists in England took special interest in South Carolina, and did what they could to extend the Baptist witness in the new land. On several occasions they responded to requests from Carolina Baptists who asked them to send preachers and books. The English brethren found it easier to send the latter than the former. The following excerpts reveal something of the extent of English interest in Baptist work in what is now South Carolina. *Source:* W. T. Whitley, ed., *Minutes of the General Assembly of the General Baptist Churches in England,* 2 vols. (London: Kingsgate Press, 1910). Selected citations from both volumes, as indicated by the dates.

[1702] Whereas our Brethren of the Baptist perswation and of the Generall Faith who haue their aboad in Caralina haue desierd us to Supply them with a Ministry or with books, we being not able at present to doe the former haue collected ye Sum of Seuen pounds twelve Shillings wch wth wt can be farther obtain'd we haue put into the hands of our Bror. S Keeling to Supply ym wth ye latter. & yt ye sd Bror Keeling doe wright a letter to them in the name of this Assembly. . . .

[1757] It was agreed by the Assembly to take into further Consideration the Request of the Baptist Church at South Carolina that the Assembly here would endeavour to assist them with a Learned & Pious Minister and a Letter Lately Recd. by Mr. Grantham Killingworth was read wherin they offer as an Encouragement 100£ a year Sterling & have also Remitted a Bill for 50£ Value to the Said Mr. Grantham Killingworth to assist and enable a Qualified person to go over and assist them in that Character and it was Recommended to every Individual of the Assembly to find out a Proper Person & Acqnt the sd. Mr. Killingworth Directed to him at Norwich or to be Left at Mr. Hezekiah Philips Shad Thames Southwick. . . .

[1758] On Reading the Minutes of the Last Assembly the first of which relating to the Request of the church at South Carolina for a Learned and Faithful Minister Bror Grantham Killingworth Inform'd this Assembly That he had Apply'd to Brother Danil. Wheeler who had Accepted the Invitation and he had Rec'd Information that our said Bror Danl. Wheeler was safely Arrived amongst our Brethren there. . . .

7.8   The Charleston Baptist Association

Baptist work in the South emerged first in Charleston, South Carolina. The first Baptist church in the South was there, and in 1751 the Charleston Baptist Association became the first such organization in the South and the second in America. This small group of churches adopted the patterns of the Philadelphia Association and, like their model, sponsored home missions, Christian education, and encouraged religious training for children. This organization played a central role in shaping early Baptist life in the South. The historian David Benedict gives an informative account of the origin and early life of this influential association. *Source:* David Benedict, *A General History of the Baptist Denomination in America,* 2 vols. (Boston: Manning & Loring, 1813), 2:134-142.

Mr. Hart, who was now the pastor of the church in Charleston, had seen, in the Philadelphia Association, the happy consequences of union and stated intercourse among churches maintaining the same faith and order. To accomplish similar purposes, an union of the four churches before mentioned was contemplated and agreed on. . . .

The object of the union was declared to be the promotion of the Redeemer's kingdom, by the maintenance of love and fellowship, and by mutual consultations for the peace and welfare of the churches. The independency of the churches was asserted, and the powers of the Association restricted to a council of advice. It was agreed to meet again in Charleston, November, 1752. At that time the delegates from Ewhaw attended, and the proceedings of the first meeting were ratified. The instrument of union bears the following signatures: John Stephens, Oliver Hart, Francis Pelot, John Brown, Joshua Edwards, ministers; James Fowler, William Screven, Richard Bedon, Charles Barker, Benjamin Parminter, Thomas Harrison, Philip Douglas, and John Mikell, messengers.

In 1755, the Association, taking into consideration the destitute condition of many places in the interior settlements of this and the neighbouring States, (then provinces) recommended to the churches to make contributions for the support of a missionary to itinerate in those parts. Mr. Hart was authorized and requested, provided a sufficient sum should be raised, to procure, if possible, a suitable person for the purpose. With this view he visited Pennsylvania and New-Jersey in the following year, and prevailed with Rev. John Gano to undertake the service, who attended the annual meeting, and was cordially received. . . . He devoted himself to the work: it afforded ample scope for his distinguished piety, eloquence and fortitude; and his ministrations were crowned with remarkable success. Many embraced and professed the gospel. The following year he received from the Association a letter of thanks for his faithfulness and industry in the mission. At the same time, the expediency of raising a fund to furnish suitable candidates for the ministry with a competent share of learning, was taken into consideration; and it was recommended to the churches generally to collect money for the purpose. The members present engaged, in behalf of their constituents, to furnish one hundred and thirty-three pounds to begin the fund; and Messrs. Stephens, Hart, and Pelot were chosen trustees. In 1759, Mr. Evan Pugh was proposed by Mr. Gano as a candidate for the ministry. He was examined, approved, and put on a course of studies. Having gone through them, he preached before the Association in 1762 with acceptance, and was soon after ordained. . . .

In 1767, the Association having previously called the serious attention of the churches to the subject, formally adopted the confession of faith, published by the London Assembly of 1689. This had been previously held by the churches in their individual capacities, particularly that of Charleston, from the beginning of the eighteenth century. The church at Ashley-river adopted it March 18, 1737. Messrs. Hart and Pelot were appointed to draw up a system of discipline agreeable to Scripture, to be used by the churches. This they brought forward in 1772, and Rev. Morgan Edwards and Mr. David Williams were requested to assist the compilers in revising it. In 1773, it was examined by the Association, and adopted. That and the confession of faith were printed under the inspection of Mr. Hart. . . .

The object of having a respectable and permanent fund established for the education of pious young men, candidates for the ministry, having been seriously contemplated and earnestly wished by several members of the Association, it was this year [1755] taken up, and particularly recommended to the churches. At the following meeting a draft of a plan for the purpose was brought forward by a committee, consisting of Messrs. Furman, S. Mercer, Mosely, and Holcombe, and adopted by the Association. . . .

The Circular Letter, drawn up by Mr. Holcombe, urges the hearty adoption of this plan.

7.9 Morgan Edwards, Baptist Beginnings in North Carolina

The pioneer historian for Baptists in America was Morgan Edwards (1722-1795). A graduate of Bristol Baptist College, Edwards served as pastor of First Baptist Church in Philadelphia. He was a primary founder of Rhode Island College, and after leaving the Philadelphia pastorate served as an "evangelist at large," or a sort of traveling home missionary, for the Philadelphia Association. On his extensive travels Edwards made it a point to collect historical data about Baptists. His manuscripts were not published in his lifetime, and are referred to not as a completed history but as "materials towards a history of Baptists." However, these first-hand primary documents have been used by all Baptist historians since that time. Edwards divided his materials by states. The following excerpts are from his materials on North Carolina. *Source:* Morgan Edwards, *Materials towards a History of the Baptists in the Province of North Carolina*, 1772. Reprinted by Eva B. Weeks and Mary B. Warren, *Materials Towards a History of the Baptists*, 2 vols. (Danielsville, Ga.: Heritage Papers, 1984), 2:79-81. Used by permission.

MATERIALS TOWARDS A HISTORY OF THE BAPTISTS IN THE PROVINCE OF NORTH CAROLINA
1772

Next to Virginia, southward, is North-Carolina; a poor and unhappy province, where superiors make complaints of the people, and the people of their superiors; which complaints, if just, show the body politic to be like that of Israel in the time of Isaiah. "From the sole of the foot to the crown of the head without any soundness, but wounds and bruises and putrifying sores."

These complaints rose to hostilities at Almance-creek (May. 16. 1771) where about 6000 appeared in arms and fought each other, 4000 Regulators killing three Tryonians; and 2000 Tryonians killing twelve Regulators, besides lodging in the trees an incredible number of balls which the hunters have since picked out, and therewith have killed more deer and turkies than they killed of their antagonists.

In this wretched province have been some baptists since the settlement in 1695; but no society of them till about the year 1742, when one was formed about Quehuky: these came hither from Isle-of-wight-county in Virginia, having one William Sojourner to their minister. In 12 years this society had spread her branches through the north and north-east parts, and become 16 churches.

They were all General-baptists. But about 1751 they began to embrace the sentiments of the Particular-baptists, and have since come into those sentiments, except Mr. Parker and his church, and some others. The cause was, partly the preaching of Rev. Robert Williams of Pedee, partly the conversation of a lay-man, commonly called the Clay-maker. His name was William Wallis; but chiefly, a visit which Mr. Gano paid them in 1753.

On his arrival he sent to the ministers, requesting an interview, which they declined, and appointed a meeting among themselves to consult what to do; Mr. Gano, hearing of it, went to their meeting, and addressed them in words to this effect, "I have desired a visit from you which, as a brother and a stranger, I had a right to expect; but as ye have refused, I give up my claim, and am come to pay you a visit." With that he ascended into the pulpit, and read for his text for the following words, "Jesus I know, and Paul I know but who are ye?" this text he managed in such a manner as to make some afraid of him, and others ashamed of their shyness. . . .

In 1755 a small company from Connecticut came and settled in the forks of Cape-fear river at a place called Sandy-creek. They were 16 souls in number, having Shubal Stearns to their minister; these were the beginning of what are commonly, tho' improperly, called "Separate-baptists", who soon spread thro' the province, to South-Carolina and Georgia, and northward, to Virginia, as we have already seen.

7.10 A Description of Early Separate Baptists

The rise of Separate Baptists reshaped Baptist life in the South after the 1750s. Influential persons like Shubal Stearns, Daniel Marshall, and Martha Stearns Marshall popularized a new and fervent form of Baptist life in the South. The Separates tended to be informal, evangelistic, emotional. In their churches women as well as men prayed and exhorted in public, served as deaconesses and elderesses, and sometimes preached. Benedict's description of the early Separate Baptists, and especially of Stearns and Marshall, is quite informative. *Source:* David Benedict, *A General History of the Baptist Denomination in America,* 2 vols. (Boston: Manning & Loring, 1813), 1:37-42.

The appellation of Separates first began to be given to a set of Pedobaptist reformers, whose evangelical zeal was produced by the instrumentality of the famous George Whitefield, and other eminent itinerant preachers of that day, and who began their extraordinary career about the year 1740. Soon after these reformers, who were at first called New-Lights, and afterwards Separates, were organized into distinct Societies, they were joined by Shubael Stearns, a native of Boston, (Mass.) who, becoming a preacher, laboured among them until 1751, when he embraced the sentiments of the Baptists, . . .

Mr. Stearns and most of the Separates had strong faith in the immediate teachings of the Spirit. They believed, that to those who sought him earnestly, God often gave evident tokens of his will. . . . Mr. Stearns, listening to some of those instructions of Heaven, as he esteemed them, conceived himself called upon by the Almighty to move far to the westward, to execute a great and extensive work. Incited by his impressions, in the year 1754, he and a few of his members, took their leave of New England. He halted first at Opeckon, in Berkley county, Virginia, where he found a Baptist church under the care of the Rev. John Garrard, who received him kindly. Here also he met his brother-in-law, the Rev. Daniel Marshall, who was also a Separate, and of whom much will be said in the history of the southern Baptists, just returned from his mission among the Indians, and who, after his arrival at this place, had become a Baptist. They joined companies, and settled for a while on Cacapou, in Hampshire county, about 30 miles from Winchester. Here, Stearns not meeting with his expected success, felt restless. . . . He and his party once more got under way, and travelling about 200 miles, came to Sandy-creek, in Guilford county, North Carolina. Here he took up his permanent residence. . . .

As soon as they arrived, they built them a little meeting-house, and these 16 persons formed themselves into a church, and chose Shubael Stearns for their pastor, who had, for his assistants at that time, Daniel Marshall and Joseph Breed, neither of whom were ordained.

The inhabitants about this little colony of Baptists, although brought up in the Christian religion, were grossly ignorant of its essential principles. Having the form of godliness, they knew nothing of its power. Stearns and his party, of course, brought strange things to their ears. To be born again, appeared to them as absurd as it did to the Jewish doctor, when he asked, if he must enter the second time into his mother's womb and be born. Having always supposed that religion consisted in nothing more than the practice of its outward duties, they could not comprehend how it should be necessary to feel conviction and conversion; and to be able to ascertain the time and place of one's conversion, was, in their estimation, wonderful indeed. These points were all strenuously contended for by the new preachers. But their manner of preaching was, if possible, much more novel than their doctrines. The Separates in New England had acquired a very warm and pathetic address, accompanied by strong gestures and a singular tone of voice. Being often deeply affected themselves when preaching, correspondent affections were felt by their pious hearers, which were frequently expressed by tears, trembling, screams, and acclamations of grief and joy. All these they brought with them into their new habitation, at which the people were greatly astonished, having never seen things on this wise before. Many mocked, but the power of God attending them, many also trembled. In process of time, some of the inhabitants became converts, and bowed obedience to the Redeemer's scepter. These uniting their labours with the others, a powerful and extensive work commenced, and Sandy-creek church soon swelled from 16 to 606 members.

Daniel Marshall, though not possessed of great talents, was indefatigable in his labours. He sallied out into the adjacent neighbourhoods, and planted the Redeemer's standard in many of the strong holds of Satan. At Abbot's creek, about thirty miles from Sandy creek, the gospel prospered so largely, that they petitioned the mother church for a constitution, and for the ordination of Mr. Marshall as their pastor. The church was constituted; Mr. Marshall accepted the call, and went to live among them. His ordination, however, was a matter of some difficulty. It required, upon their principles, a plurality of elders to constitute a presbytery. Mr. Stearns was the only ordained minister among them. In this dilemma, they were informed, that there were some regular Baptist preachers living on Pedee river, (S. C.). To one of these, Mr. Stearns applied, and requested him to assist him in the ordination of Mr. Marshall. This request he sternly refused, declaring that he held no fellowship with Stearns's party; that he believed them to be a disorderly set; suffering women to pray in public, and permitting every ignorant man to preach that chose; and that they encouraged noise and confusion in their meetings. Application was then made to Mr. Leadbetter, who was then pastor of the church on Lynch's-creek, Craven county, South-Carolina, and who was a brother-in-law of Mr. Marshall. He and Mr. Stearns ordained Mr. Marshall to the care of this new church. . . .

The gospel was carried by Mr. Marshall into the parts of Virginia, adjacent to the residence of this religious colony, soon after their settlement. He baptized several persons in some of his first visits. Among them was Dutton Lane, who, shortly after his baptism, began to preach. A revival succeeded, and Mr. Marshall at one time baptized 42 persons. In August, 1760, a church was constituted, and Mr. Lane became their pastor. This was the first Separate Baptist church in Virginia, and in some sense the mother of all the rest. . . . They endured much persecution, but God prospered them, and delivered them out of the hands of all their enemies.

Soon after Mr. Lane's conversion, the power of God was effectual in the conversion of Samuel Harris, a man of great distinction in those parts. But upon being honoured of God, he laid aside all wordly honours, and became a labourer in the Lord's vineyard. In 1759, he was ordained a ruling elder. From the commencement of his ministry, for about seven years, his labours were devoted chiefly to his own and the adjacent counties. Being often with Mr. Marshall in his ministerial journies, he caught the zeal, diligence, and indeed the manners of this zealous evangelist. His labours were crowned with the blessing of Heaven wherever he went. . . .

7.11   The Sandy Creek Baptist Association

In 1758 several Separate Baptist churches in North Carolina formed the Sandy Creek Baptist Association. Their work had begun three years earlier when Shubal Stearns and his group formed the Sandy Creek Church in what is now Randolph County. The Sandy Creek Association quickly became the center for a vast outreach of Separate Baptist activity that blanketed the South. This was only the third such association in America, and the second in the South. Their "Principles of Faith" and "Rules of Decorum" show what the Separate Baptists believed and how they conducted their work. *Source*: George W. Purefoy, *A History of the Sandy Creek Baptist Association* (New York: Sheldon & Co., Publishers, 1859), 104-107.

Elder Luther Rice was invited to a seat in the association as "a representative of the Board of Foreign Missions."

Elders L. Rice, Hezekiah Harman, and Brethren James Bostick, B. Boroughs, William Waddill, the moderator and clerk, were appointed to prepare Articles of Faith, a constitution, and Rules of Decorum, for this association. On Monday the following Articles of Faith, &c., were read and adopted:

PRINCIPLES OF FAITH.

Art. I.   We believe that there is only one true and living God; the Father, Son, and Holy Ghost, equal in essence, power and glory; yet there are not three Gods but one God.

II.   That the Scriptures of the Old and New Testaments are the word of God, and only rule of faith and practice.

III.   That Adam fell from his original state of purity, and that his sin is imputed to his posterity; that human nature is corrupt, and that man, of his own free will and ability, is impotent to regain the state in which he was primarily placed.

IV.   We believe in election from eternity, effectual calling by the Holy Spirit of God, and justification in his sight only by the imputation of Christ's righteousness. And we believe that they who are thus elected, effectually called, and justified, will persevere through grace to the end, that none of them be lost.

V.   We believe that there will be a resurrection from the dead, and a general or universal judgment, and that the happiness of the righteous and punishment of the wicked will be eternal.

VI.   That the visible Church of Christ is a congregation of faithful persons, who have obtained fellowship with each other, and have given themselves up to the Lord and one another; having agreed to keep up a godly discipline, according to the rules of the Gospel.

VII.   That Jesus Christ is the great head of the church, and that the government thereof is with the body.

VIII.   That baptism and the Lord's Supper are ordinances of the Lord, and to be continued by his church until his second coming.

IX.   That true believers are the only fit subjects of baptism, and that immersion is the only mode.

X.   That the church has no right to admit any but regular baptized church members to communion at the Lord's table.

RULES OF DECORUM.

I.   The association shall be opened and closed by prayer, by the moderator, or some person at his request.

II. The names of the several members of the association shall be enrolled by the clerk, and called over as often as required.

III. One person only shall speak at a time; who, when about to speak, shall rise from his seat, and address the moderator.

IV. The person speaking shall not be interrupted, unless he deviate from the subject in debate, or cast reflections on some brother member; in which cases he shall be called to order by the moderator, or by any member of the association.

V. No member, without permission, shall speak more than twice to one subject.

VI. No member may depart from the association without permission.

VII. No member of the association shall address another by any other appellation than that of brother.

VIII. The moderator shall have the same privilege of speech as another member, provided the chair be filled, and when requisite, shall give the casting vote.

IX. It shall be the duty of this association to attend to the request of churches aggrieved; and shall give advice, or send committees, especially appointed, to their assistance.

X. Queries, introduced by the churches, or select committees, shall be twice read before debated.

XI. A motion being made and seconded, shall be taken under consideration, unless withdrawn immediately by the person who made it.

XII. Finally, it shall be the duty of the moderator to correct all impropriety of conduct, such as laughing, talking, whispering, &c., and to keep good order in time of session.

7.12 Union of Regular and Separate Baptists

The Regular Baptists in the South were found along the coastal areas and in the major cities, while the Separates occupied land further inland along the frontier. The Regulars followed the Philadelphia Confession of Faith, favored strict theology and orderly worship, sang formal hymns, preferred educated pastors, and kept their women mostly in silence and subjection. The Separate Baptists, on the other hand, cared little for human confessions, worshiped in a spontaneous and usually quite noisy fashion, sang simple gospel songs, distrusted education, and expected their women to take considerable leadership in church, including serving as deaconesses, praying and exhorting in public, and sometimes preaching. However, in time these differences receded, and the struggle for religious liberty and the rise of the foreign mission movement pulled these two sorts of Baptists closer together. The following account shows how they eventually merged in Virginia and is representative of what occurred in other areas. The union of Regular and Separate Baptists combined diverse strains that prevail to this day in the Southern Baptist Convention. *Source:* David Benedict, *A General History of the Baptist Denomination in America* (Boston: Manning & Loring, 1813), 60-62.

The schism which took place among the Regular and Separate Baptists in 1766, soon after their rise in Virginia, had continued, without being completely healed, for about 20 years, although a very friendly intercourse had been occasionally [sic] kept up amongst them. But in 1787, the happy period arrived, in which all the disputes between these two bodies were compromised, buried, and forgotten. The adjustment of these disputes was conducted by the General Committee on the part of the Separates, and on that of the Regulars by delegates for the purpose from the Ketockton Association; and took place at the fourth session of the General Committee, which was held at Dover meeting-house, in Goochland county. At this meeting, delegates from six Associations of the Separates, and a number from the Ketockton, were assembled, when, pursuant to a previous appointment, the subject of the union between the Regulars and Separates was taken up, and after a brief and temperate discussion of their differences, a happy and effectual union was formed, and their party names dismissed and buried.

The objections on the part of Separates related chiefly to matters of trivial importance, such as dress, &c. and had been for some time removed, as to being a bar of communion. On the other hand, the Regulars complained, that the Separates were not sufficiently explicit in their principles, having never published or sanctioned any confession of faith; and that they kept within their communion many who were professed Arminians. To these things it was answered by the Separates, that a large majority of them believed as much in their confession of faith, as they did themselves, although they did not entirely approve of the practice of religious societies binding themselves too strictly by confessions of faith, seeing there was danger of their finally usurping too high a place: that if there were some among them, who leaned too much to the Arminian system, they were generally men of exemplary piety, and great usefulness in the Redeemer's kingdom; and they conceived it better to bear with some diversity of opinion in doctrines, than to break with men, whose Christian deportment rendered them amiable in the estimation of all true lovers of genuine godliness. Indeed, that some of them had now become fathers in the gospel, who, previous to the bias which their minds had received, had borne the brunt and heat of persecution, whose labours and sufferings God had blessed, and still blessed, to the great advancement of his cause—to exclude such as these from their communion, would be like tearing the limbs from the body.

These and such like arguments, were agitated both in public [sic] and private, so that all minds were much mollified, before the final and successful attempt for union was made. The terms of the union were entered on the minutes in the following words, viz.

"The committee appointed to consider the terms of union with our Regular Brethren, Reported, That they conceived the manner in which the Regular Baptist confession of faith has been received by a former Association, is the ground-work for such union." The manner of this reception was, that they should retain their liberty with regard to the construction of some of its objectionable articles.

After considerable debate, as to the propriety of having any confession of faith at all, the report of the committee was received with the following explanation:

"To prevent the confession of faith from usurping a tyrannical power over the conscience of any, we do not mean, that every person is bound to the strict observance of every thing therein contained; yet that it holds forth the essential truths of the gospel, and that the doctrine of salvation by Christ, and free and unmerited grace alone, ought to be believed by every Christian, and maintained by every minister of the gospel. Upon these terms we are united, and desire hereafter, that the names Regular and Separate be buried in oblivion; and that from henceforth, we shall be known by the name of the United Baptist Churches, in Virginia."

This union took place at a time when a revival of religion had commenced which soon burst forth on the right hand and on the left, throughout the State, "and nothing," says Mr. Semple, their historian, "could be more salutary than this conjunction of dissevered brethren, and the accommodating temper of the parties by which it was effected; and they have, from that period to the present time, most fully demonstrated, that it was an union of hearts as well as parties."

7.13 A Description of the Second Great Awakening in Kentucky

The wave of revivals that historians have named the "Second Great Awakening" took different forms in different places. In the East the revivals usually centered in churches, were led by pastors, rarely showed outbursts of emotion, and led to the formation of many social and benevolent societies. By contrast, the western wing of the awakening often centered not in churches but in freewheeling camp meetings, were led by traveling evangelists, and were marked by extreme emotionalism. To this day, evangelical Protestantism in the West and South has been greatly influenced by the fervor of those camp meetings. This lends importance to Benedict's insightful description of the Second Great Awakening in Kentucky. *Source:* David Benedict, *A General History of the Baptist Denomination in America,* 2 vols. (Boston: Manning & Loring, 1813), 1:251-257.

Some Account of the great Revival in Kentucky and other Parts.

As this peculiar work prevailed to a greater extent in Kentucky than elsewhere, it seems proper under this head to give some account of it.

From 1799 to 1803, there were, in most parts of the United States, remarkable outpourings of the Divine Spirit, among different denominations; multitudes became the subjects of religious concern, and were made to rejoice in the salvation of God. The revival among the Baptists in the southern and western States, has already been frequently referred to, and accounts of the astonishing additions to their churches have been given. This great revival in Kentucky began in Boone county on the Ohio River, and in its progress extended up the Ohio, Licking, and Kentucky Rivers, branching out into the settlements adjoining them. It spread fast in different directions, and in a short time almost every part of the State was affected by its influence. It was computed that about ten thousand were baptized and added to the Baptist churches in the course of two or three years. This great work progressed among the Baptists in a much more regular manner than people abroad have generally supposed. They were indeed zealously affected, and much engaged. Many of their ministers baptized in a number of neighbouring churches from two to four hundred each. And two of them baptized about five hundred a-piece in the course of the work. But throughout the whole, they preserved a good degree of decorum and order. Those camp-meetings, those great parades, and sacramental seasons, those extraordinary exercises of falling down, rolling, shouting, jerking, dancing, barking, &c. were but little known among the Baptists in Kentucky, nor encouraged by them. They, it is true, prevailed among some of them in the Green River country; but generally speaking, they were among the Presbyterians and Methodists, . . .

. . . These meetings were sometimes bid up a month beforehand; great preparations were made for them, and all went expecting to hear much crying out, see much falling down, &c. In these meetings there assembled, in the opinion of spectators, from four to ten or twelve thousand, and at one of them eight hundred fell down under religious impressions, and five hundred communicated. The falling down exercise needs no description, as it is presumed every reader will understand what is meant by it. There was also in these meetings, what was called the *rolling exercise,* which consisted in a person's being cast down in a violent manner, turned over swiftly like a log, &c. These *rolling* disciples often met with mud in their way, and got up from their devotions in a sorrowful plight. Dancing was a very common practice; many pleaded they could not help it, and others justified themselves from David's dancing before the ark, and other passages of scripture. The most singular exercise of all was the *jerks.* "Nothing in nature could better represent this strange and unaccountable operation, than for one to goad another, alternately on every side, with a piece of red-hot iron. The exercise commonly began in the head, which would fly backward and forward, and from side to side, with a quick jolt, which the person would naturally labour to suppress, but in vain; and the more any one laboured to stay himself, and be sober, the more he staggered, and the more rapidly his twitches increased. He must necessarily go as he was stimulated, whether with a violent dash on the ground, and bounce from place to place like a football; or hop round, with head, limbs, and trunk, twitching and jolting in every direction, as if they must inevitably fly asunder. And how such could escape without injury, was no small wonder to spectators. By this strange operation, the human frame was commonly so transformed and disfigured, as to lose every trace of its natural appearance. . . .

There was among these enthusiastick people one more exercise of a most degrading nature, called the *barks,* which frequently accompanied the jerks. Many persons of considerable distinction, in spite of all the efforts of nature, as it was said, were "forced to personate that animal, whose name, appropriated to a human creature, is counted the most vulgar stigma. These people would take the position of a canine beast, move about on all-fours, growl, snap the teeth, and bark in so personating a manner, as to set the eyes and ears of the spectator at variance." Some might be forced to these degrading exercises, but it is certain that many turned dogs in a voluntary manner. A minister in the lower parts of Kentucky informed me, that it was common to hear people barking like a flock of spaniels on their way to meeting. . . . But enough has been said of these frantick scenes. The above accounts are not fabulous tales, but they are real and melancholy facts. In the upper counties in Kentucky, where the revival was the greatest among the Baptists, they were not at all affected with these delirious exercises. In the Green River country and in East-Tennessee, they prevailed considerably amongst them. . . .

7.14 Constitution and Rules of the Beaver Creek Church, 1798

The Beaver Creek Baptist Church in Kentucky was probably typical of scores of small churches on the frontier. Composed of sincere but largely unlettered members, these churches could not turn to learned ministers or established church conventions to guide them. In the time-honored way of Baptists, they formed their own church, defined their own doctrinal beliefs, and set out their own reasonable rules of conduct. Churches like this brought a measure of social as well as religious stability to communities that as yet had no civil structures for law and order. Perhaps none would nominate this as a crucial document, but it does add its bold brushstroke to the overall Baptist mural. *Source:* W. W. Sweet, *Religion on the American Frontier: The Baptists* (New York: Cooper Square Publishers, 1964), 258-260.

A Covenant of a baptist Church on Beaver Creek entered into the 5th of November 1798 (with seven members)

And Constituted by Elders, William Hickman, Carter Tarrant, and Alexander Davidson.

Agreed to be constituted on the essential doctrines of the Gospel viz.

first, We believe in one only true and living God and that their are three persons in the God-head. the Father Son and Holy Spirit.

2nd. We believe that the Scriptures of the old and new Testaments, are the word of God, and the only rule of faith and practice.

3rd We believe that we are saved by grace thro faith and that not of ourselves it is the gift of God.

4th We believe in the doctrine of original sin.

5th We believe in mans impotency to recover himself from the fallen state he is in by nature.

6th We believe that sinners are justiyd in the sight of God, only by the imputed righteousness of Christ.

7th, We believe that the saints shall persevere and never finally fall away.

8th We believe that baptism and the Lord's Supper are ordinances of Jesus Christ, and that true believers and them only are the fit subjects of these ordinances, and we believe that the true mode of baptism is by immersion.

9*th* We believe in the resurrection of the Lord and universal Judgement,

10*th* We believe the punishment of the wicked will be everlasting and the Joys of the righteous will be eternal.

RULES AND REGULATIONS TO BE OBSERVED IN CHURCH DECIPLIN

First, In all Church meetings, it is the duty and place of the Minister or Elder to keep good order, and be forward in carrying on business, and that no member leave their seat without leave,

Second, In all cases touching fellowship the Church shall act by a majority of two thirds, and in case a majority cannot be had the member shall be debar,d from Church privileges untill a majority of 2 thirds can be had, and should any individual shew obstinacy the Church may deal with him or her, as appears right on the case,

Third, In Temporal matters, or such as do not immediately touch fellowship they may decide by a majority.

Fourth, Any motion made and seconded shall be put to the Church and no motion, or question shall be put without a second,

Fifth, Any member making a motion, or speaking in the Church shall rise from his seat, and stand and address the Elder and direct his discourse to him,

Sixth, In all debates the members shall direct their discourse to the elder and not to the contending party,

Seventh, No member shall speak more than three times upon the same subject without leave from the Church,

Eighth. If two shall rise at once to speak the Elder shall determine which rose first, and give him leave to speak first, and afterwards the other may speak,

Ninth, All members shall be receiv,d by experience, letter, or information of a member of our union, or Recantation, the member who may be receiv,d upon information shall be bound to produce his or her letter within twelve months.

Tenth, All offences must be dealt with in gospel order, but publick offences or such as does not come under the denomination of trespass against an individual ought to be dealt with in a publick manner in Church,

Eleventh, From Scripture authority we count it a duty for all members to attend each Church meeting unless providentially hinder,d and especially the Male members, therefore if any member neglect this duty, we count it a breach of good order and agree that all such must be dealt with as the Church direct,

8
Baptists in Colonial America:
The Struggle for Religious Liberty

The Baptist struggle for religious liberty in America can be viewed almost as two separate stories. Political and religious laws varied widely between New England and the Southern colonies, with the middle colonies from the first forming a buffer zone of religious toleration.

In New England the Congregational Church was established by law and supported by public taxation. Baptists there struggled against popular prejudice and against the various Exemption Laws that at times regulated the terms of their payment of taxes to support their opponents' church. Their primary spokesman was Isaac Backus, a Massachusetts pastor who drew insights from such diverse sources as John Locke and Roger Williams to develop his views for religious liberty.

In the South Baptists faced popular prejudice everywhere, and pressures from the Anglican Church in areas where that Church had any real establishment. John Leland of Virginia became the most prominent Baptist spokesman for religious liberty; excerpts from his writings are included in this chapter. Baptists in the South faced nothing comparable to the Exemption Laws of New England, but they did face other laws whose intent was to restrict their freedom of worship and preaching, and to coerce taxes for support of the Anglican Church.

This chapter also contains some human interest anecdotes, drawn largely from the pioneer historian David Benedict, to illustrate the course of persecution of Baptists and Baptist response thereto. The means to end religious persecution in America came with adoption of the First Amendment to the Federal Constitution in 1791.

8.1   Religious Exemption Laws in Massachusetts

Beginning in 1728 Massachusetts passed a series of laws to exempt dissenters, under specified conditions, from paying taxes to support the official church (Congregational). These Exemption Laws varied over the years; they expired, were renewed with revisions, and at times lapsed without being renewed for a period of years. The interpretation and application of the laws also varied, and their limitations even when fairly applied seemed to most Baptists entirely too restrictive. The Baptists also objected to being referred to in the laws as "Anabaptists." Isaac Backus later led Baptists of the Warren Association to challenge the laws entirely. The following document gives excerpts from the Exemption Laws. *Source:* Reuben Aldridge Guild, *Chaplain Smith and the Baptists* (Philadelphia: American Baptist Publication Society, 1885), 82-85.

The first enactment of the General Court of the Province of Massachusetts, exempting both Baptists and Quakers from the payment of ministerial taxes or rates, dates back as far as the year 1728. The preamble and first section of this act read as follows:

Whereas some of the inhabitants of this Province, called Anabaptists, and others called Quakers, refuse to pay any part or proportion of such taxes as are from time to time assessed, for the support of the ministry in the several towns whereto they belong, alleging a scruple of conscience for such their refusal; and thereupon frequent application has been made to this Court for their relief,—

Be it therefore enacted by the Lieutenant Governor, Council, and Representatives in General Court assembled, and by the authority of the same,

Sec. 1 That from and after the publication of this Act, none of the persons commonly called Anabaptists, nor any of those commonly called Quakers, that are or shall be enrolled or entered in their respective Societies as members thereof, and who allege a scruple of conscience as the reason of their refusal to pay any part or proportion of such taxes as are from time to time assessed for the support of the minister or ministers of the churches established by the laws of this Province in the town or place where they dwell, shall have their polls taxed towards the support of such minister or ministers; nor shall their bodies be at any time taken in execution to satisfy any such ministerial rate or tax assessed upon their estates or faculty; provided that such persons do usually attend the meetings of their respective Societies assembling upon the Lord's Day for the worship of God, and that they live within five miles of the place of such meeting.

[Similar laws remained in effect until] . . . In 1753, says Backus, the Legislature "broke in upon their own law, and enacted that the minister, with two principal members of the Baptist Church, should sign their certificates for the future, and also that no minister or church should have any power to give lawful certificates, until they should have obtained from three others churches, commonly called Anabaptists, in this or the neighboring provinces, a certificate from each respectively, that they esteem such church to be of their own denomination, and that they conscientiously believe them to be Anabaptists."

As those, adds Backus, who had lately become Baptists, were not in full fellowship with the old Baptist churches, this act was passed to prevent their being exempted from taxes. It also required them to certify a conscientious belief of a point which they never did believe, viz., that they were Anabaptists (Rebaptizers) a name of reproach cast upon them by their persecutors. This additional act was to continue in force for five years, or until January 6, 1758. It reads as follows:

An Act in addition to an Act passed the thirteenth year of his present Majesty's reign, entitled "An Act further to exempt persons commonly called Anabaptists within this Province from being taxed for and towards the support of ministers."

WHEREAS, Notwithstanding the provision already made by an Act made and passed in the thirteenth year of his present Majesty's reign, entitled "An Act further to exempt persons commonly called Anabaptists within this Province from being taxed for and towards the support of ministers," in order to ascertain and make known what persons are of that persuasion which denominates them Anabaptists, and who shall enjoy the privileges, and be esteemed as entitled to the Exemption from taxes, etc., in said Act mentioned, many doubts have already arisen thereon, and, in many cases, the said exemption has been extended to many persons to whom the same was never designed to extend; for preventing whereof for the future, and in order to ascertain more effectually what persons shall be esteemed and accounted as Anabaptists, and to whom the said exemptions shall be hereafter extended,—

Be it enacted by the Lieutenant Governor, Council, and House of Representatives,

Sec. 1. That no person for the future shall be so esteemed to be an Anabaptist as to have his poll or polls and estate exempted from paying a proportionable part of the taxes that shall be raised in the town or place where he or they belong, but such whose names shall be contained in the lists taken by the assessors, as in said Act provided, or such as shall produce a certificate, under the hands of the minister and of two principal members of such church, setting forth that they conscientiously believe such person or persons to be of their persuasion, and that he or they usually and frequently attend the public worship in such church on Lord's Days.

And be it further enacted,

Sec. 2. That no minister, nor the members of any Anabaptist Church as aforesaid, shall be esteemed qualified to give such certificate as aforesaid other than such as shall have obtained from three other churches commonly called Anabaptists, in this or the neighboring provinces, a certificate from each respectively, that they esteem such church to be one of their denomination, and that they conscientiously believe them to be Anabaptists; the several certificates aforesaid to be lodged with the town clerk, where the Anabaptist, desiring such exemption, dwells, some time betwixt the raising or granting of the tax and the assessment of the some of the inhabitants.

8.2   Persecution of Baptists in Sturbridge, Massachusetts

Isaac Backus (1724-1806) led the struggle of Baptists in New England in their struggle for religious liberty. To this end he focused new attention upon the pioneer contributions of Roger

Williams in laying the groundwork for religious freedom in America. In his own history of Baptists, published in three volumes beginning in 1777, Backus put great emphasis upon the freedom struggle. His vivid description of the persecution of Baptists at Sturbridge, cited below, is an example of his apologetic use of history to advance his viewpoint. We see that Backus made use of firsthand information and primary documents, including a letter from his own mother about her imprisonment. *Source:* Isaac Backus, *A History of New England with Particular Reference to the Denomination of Christians Called Baptists,* 2d ed., 2 vols. (Newton, Mass.: The Backus Historical Society, 1871), 2:94-101.

The exempting law for Baptists had again expired in 1747, when it was revived and continued for ten years. In order that the benefit of it might be extended to that society, two principal members of the second Baptist church in Boston wrote a certificate in their favor to Sturbridge assessors, January 23, 1750. In May following, two principal members of the Baptist church in Sturbridge gave in a list of their society according to law; yet they were all again taxed to Mr. Caleb Rice, a minister in that town. And, only for this and the following year, five men were imprisoned at Worcester, three oxen and eight cows were taken away, and a great deal of other property, for such taxes. Aaron Allen was the collector who did it for 1750, and Jonathan Mason for 1751. The first took a good cow from David Morse, a ruling elder in said Baptist church, for a tax of one pound, one shilling and four-pence; and the other took a pair of oxen from him, valued at eleven pounds, for a tax of less than five dollars. Such havoc did they make of their neighbors' goods, under religious pretences!* . . .

Among the many instances that discovered how tenacious our oppressors were of their taxing power to support worship, take the following. Esther White, of Raynham, had a small interest left her, for which she was taxed *eight-pence* to the parish minister, from whom she had withdrawn four years; and she seriously declared that it was against her conscience to pay it. Therefore, for no more than that sum, she was seized on February 28, 1752, and was imprisoned at Taunton until March, 1753, when said minister's own people were constrained to go and release her, without her paying any acknowledgment to that taxing power. She soon after became a Baptist, and continued to give abiding evidence of true piety, until she died in peace in 1774. . . .And Connecticut still kept pace with the Massachusetts in oppression, of which the place of the author's

---

*From Henry Fisk's "Testimony" we extract the following record of oppressions of Baptists in Sturbridge:—"They stripped the shelves of pewter, of such as had it; and of others that had not they took away skillets, kettles, pots and warming-pans. Others they deprived of the means they got their bread with, viz., workmen's tools, and spinning-wheels. They drove away geese and swine from the doors of some others; from some that had cows; from some that had but one they took that away. They took a yoke of oxen from one. Some they thrust into prison, where they had a long and tedious imprisonment. One brother was called from us and ordained a pastor of a Baptist church, and came for his family; at which time they seized him and drew him away, and thrust him into prison, where he was kept in the cold winter till somebody paid the money and let him out. A. Bloice had a spinning wheel taken away in 1750, and was imprisoned in 1751. D. Fisk had five pewter plates taken away from him in 1750, and a cow in 1751. John Cory imprisoned. 1750. J. Barstow imprisoned, 1750. J. Pike, a cow taken, 1750. A cradle in 1750, and a steer in 1751, were taken from J. Perry. Trammel, andirons, shovel and tongs were taken from J. Blunt in 1750, and he was imprisoned the next year. John Streeter had goods taken in 1750 and 1751; Benjamin Robbins, household goods and carpenter's tools. Household goods and a cow were taken from H. Fisk in 1750 and 1751. Josiah Perry was imprisoned in 1750, and a cow taken from him in 1751. Nathanniel Smith was imprisoned in 1750. David Morse was imprisoned and a cow taken away in 1750, and a yoke of oxen in 1751. Goods were taken from Phinehas Collier in 1750 and 1751. John Newel, goods taken 1750 and 1751. John Draper imprisoned. 1751." ED.

nativity now exhibited a striking example. A widow who had withdrawn from their worship seven years, and steadily attended and supported worship in another church, gives so clear an account of it, that her letter is here presented to the reader, without adding or diminishing a word:—

Norwich, November 4, 1752.

MY DEAR SON: I have heard something of the trials amongst you of late, and I was grieved, till I had strength to give up the case to God, and leave my burthen there. And now I would tell you something of our trials. Your brother Samuel lay in prison twenty days. October 15, the collectors came to our house, and took me away to prison about nine o'clock. in a dark rainy night. Brothers Hill and Sabin were brought there the next night. We lay in prison thirteen days, and then set at liberty, by what means I know not. Whilst I was there a great many people came to see me; and some said one thing and some another. O the innumerable snares and temptations that beset me, more than I ever thought on before! But, O the condescension of heaven! though I was bound when I was cast into this furnace, yet was I loosed, and found Jesus in the midst of the furnace with me. O then I could give up my name, estate, family, life and breath, freely to God. Now the prison looked like a palace to me. I could bless God for all the laughs and scoffs made at me. O the love that flowed out to all mankind! Then I could forgive as I would desire to be forgiven, and love my neighbor as myself. Deacon Griswold was put into prison the 8th of October, and yesterday old brother Grover, and [they] are in pursuit of others; all which calls for humiliation. This church hath appointed the 13th of November to be spent in prayer and fasting on that account. I do remember my love to you and your wife, and the dear children of God with you, begging your prayers for us in such a day of trial. We are all in tolerable health, expecting to see you. These from your loving mother,

ELIZABETH BACKUS.

Some time after, her brother, Mr. Isaac Tracy, was imprisoned for the same cause, while he was a member of their Legislature; and they furiously went on, in imprisoning of persons and spoiling of goods, to support State worship, for eight years, till the spiritual weapons of truth and love vanquished those carnal weapons; and they have not been so used in Norwich for these many years past. As great a victory was also gained in Canterbury. . . .

8.3   Isaac Backus, *An Appeal to the Public for Religious Liberty,* 1773

In 1773 Isaac Backus, head of the Grievance Committee of Warren Association, asked the churches in New England to adopt a policy of noncompliance with the Exemption Laws. Not all of the Baptists were ready for such a bold step of civil disobedience, even in a good cause. Backus needed every persuasion at his command. A part of that persuasion was his hard-hitting treatise, *An Appeal to the Public*. Here Backus pinpoints the problems of the certificate system, and makes his strongest and most cogent defense of religious liberty and separation of church and state. To present his case Backus used insights from both Scripture and reason. Some readers think that in *An Appeal* they hear echoes of John Locke, while others point out that Backus's understanding of "true government" differs from Locke's theory of natural rights and social contract. *Source:* William G. McLoughlin, ed., *Isaac Backus on Church, State, and Calvinism: Pamphlets, 1754-1789* (Cambridge: Harvard University Press, 1968), 309-343.

INTRODUCTION

Inasmuch as there appears to us a real need of such an appeal, we would previously offer a few thoughts concerning the general nature of liberty and government and then show wherein it appears to us that our religious rights are encroached upon in this land.

It is supposed by multitudes that in submitting to government we give up some part of our liberty because they imagine that there is something in their nature incompatible with each other. But the word of truth plainly shows, that man first lost his freedom by breaking over the rules of government and that those who now speak great *swelling words* about *liberty*, while they *despise government,* are themselves *servants of corrup-*

tion. What a dangerous error, yea, what a root of all evil then must it be, for men to imagine that there is anything in the nature of true government that interferes with true and full liberty! . . .

. . . And those who do not thus *know the truth* and have not been *made free* thereby, yet have never been able in any country to subsist long without some sort of government. Neither could any of them ever make out to establish any proper government without calling in the help of the Deity. However absurd their notions have been, yet they have found human sight and power to be so short and weak, and able to do so little toward watching over the conduct and guarding the rights of individuals, that they have been forced to appeal to Heaven by oaths, and to invoke assistance from thence to avenge the cause of the injured upon the guilty. Hence it is so far from being necessary for any man to give up any part of his real liberty in order to submit to government that all nations have found it necessary to submit to some government in order to enjoy any liberty and security at all. . . .

Having offered these few thoughts upon the general nature of government and liberty, it is needful to observe that God has appointed two kinds of government in the world which are distinct in their nature and ought never to be confounded together, one of which is called civil the other ecclesiastical government. And though we shall not attempt a full explanation of them yet some essential points of difference between them are necessary to be mentioned in order truly to open our grievances.

SECTION I
Some essential points of difference between civil and ecclesiastical government

1. The forming of the constitution and appointment of the particular orders and offices of civil government is left to human discretion, and our submission thereto is required under the name of their being the *ordinances of men* for the Lord's sake, 1 *Pet.* ii, 13, 14. Whereas in ecclesiastical affairs we are most solemnly warned not to be *subject to ordinances after the doctrines and commandments of men, Col.* ii, 20, 22. And it is evident that He who is the only worthy object of worship has always claimed it as his sole prerogative to determine by express laws what his worship shall be, who shall minister in it, and how they shall be supported. . . .

2. That as the putting any men into civil office is of men, of the people of the world, so officers have truly no more authority than the people give them. And how came the people of the world by any ecclesiastical power? They arm the magistrate with the *sword* that he may be a minister of God *to them for good* and might execute wrath upon *evil doers.* And for this cause they pay them *tribute;* upon which the apostle proceeds to name those divine commandments which are comprehended in love to our neighbor, and which work *no ill to him.* Surely the inspired writer had not forgotten the first and great command of love to God; but as this chapter treats the most fully of the nature and end of civil government of any in the New Testament, does it not clearly show that the crimes which fall within the magistrates' jurisdiction to punish are only such as work ill to our neighbor? *Rom.* xiii, 1-10, while church government respects our behavior toward God as well as man.

3. All acts of executive power in the civil state are to be performed in the name of the king or state they belong to, while all our religious acts are to be done in the *name of the Lord Jesus* and so are to be performed *heartily as to the Lord and not unto men.* . . . It is often pleaded that magistrates ought to do their duty in religious as well as civil affairs. That is readily granted but what is their duty therein? Surely it is to *bow to the name of Jesus* and to serve him with holy reverence. And if they do the contrary they may expect to *perish from the way, Phil.* ii, 10; *Psal.* ii, 10-12. But where is the officer that will

dare to come in the name of the Lord to demand, and forcibly to take, a tax which was imposed by the civil state! . . .

4. In all civil governments some are appointed to judge for others and have power to compel others to submit to their judgment, but our Lord has most plainly forbidden us either to assume or submit to any such thing in religion, *Matt.* xxiii, 1-9; *Luke* xxii, 25-27. . . . And it appears to us that the true difference and exact limits between ecclesiastical and civil government is this, That the church is armed with *light and truth* to pull down the strongholds of iniquity and to gain souls to Christ and into his Church to be governed by his rules therein, and again to exclude such from their communion, who will not be so governed, while the state is armed with the *sword* to guard the peace and the civil rights of all persons and societies and to punish those who violate the same. And where these two kinds of government, and the weapons which belong to them are well distinguished and improved according to the true nature and end of their institution, the effects are happy, and they do not at all interfere with each other. But where they have been confounded together no tongue nor pen can fully describe the mischiefs that have ensued of which the Holy Ghost gave early and plain warnings. . . .

SECTION II

A brief view of how civil and ecclesiastical affairs are blended together among us to the depriving of many of God's people of that liberty of conscience which he has given them

We are not insensible that an open appearance against any part of the conduct of men in power is commonly attended with difficulty and danger. And could we have found any way wherein with clearness we could have avoided the present attempt we would gladly have taken it. . . . And things appear so to us at present that we cannot see how we can fully obey this command without refusing any active compliance with some laws about religious affairs that are laid upon us. And as those who are interested against us often accuse us of complaining unreasonably, we are brought under a necessity of laying open particular facts which otherwise we would gladly have concealed. . . .

1. Our legislature claim a power to compel every town and parish within their jurisdiction to set up and maintain a pedobaptist worship among them although it is well known, that infant baptism is never expressed in the Bible, only is upheld by men's reasonings that are chiefly drawn from Abraham's covenant which the Holy Ghost calls *The covenant of circumcision, Acts* vii. 8. And as circumcision was one of the handwriting of ordinances which Christ has *blotted out* where did any state ever get any right to compel their subjects to set up a worship upon this covenant?

2. Our ascended Lord gives *gifts unto men* in a sovereign way as seems good unto him, and he requires *Every man, as he has received the gift, even so to minister the same.* And he reproved his apostles when they forbid one who was improving his gift because he followed not them, 1 *Pet.* iv, 10, 11; *Luke* ix, 49. But the Massachusetts legislature, while they claim a power to compel each parish to settle a minister, have also determined that he must be one who has either an academical degree, or a testimonial in his favor from a majority of the ministers in the county where the parish lies. . . .

3. Though the Lord hath *ordained that they which preach the Gospel shall live of the Gospel* or by the free *communications to them* which his Gospel will produce, 1 *Cor.* ix, 13, 14; *Gal.* vi, 6, 7, yet the ministers of our land have chosen to *live by the law.* And as a reason therefor, one of their most noted writers, instead of producing any truth of God, recites the tradition of a man who said, "Ministers of the Gospel would have a poor time of it, if they must rely on a *free contribution of the people* for their maintenance." . . .

Now who can hear Christ declare that his kingdom is NOT OF THIS WORLD, and yet believe that this blending of church and state together can be pleasing to him? . . .

How essentially and how greatly does this [state] constitution differ, and from the institutions established in God's word, both in their nature and effects?

1. In their *nature*. Here you find that every religious minister in that constitution is called the king's minister because he is settled by direction of the king's laws and the tax for such a minister's support is raised in the king's name and is called the king's dues, whereas no man in the Jewish church might approach to minister at the holy altar but such as were *called of God as was Aaron*. And the means of their support were such things as God required his people to *offer and consecrate to Him*, . . .

2. The *effects* of the constitution of our country are such that as it makes the majority of the people the test of orthodoxy so it emboldens them to usurp God's judgment seat, and (according to Dr. Mather's own account which we have often seen verified) they daringly give out their sentence that for a *few* to profess a persuasion different from the *majority*, it must be from bad motives, and that, they *know in their conscience* that they do not act by the universal law of equity if they plead to be exempted from paying the *money* which the *majority* demand of them! And though in OUR CHARTER the king grants to all Protestants *equal liberty of conscience*, yet for above thirty years after it was received the Congregationalists made no laws to favor the consciences of any men in this affair of taxes but their own sect. . . .

These evils cleaved so close to the first fathers of the Massachusetts as to move them to imprison, whip, and banish men only for denying infant baptism and refusing to join in worship that was supported by violent methods. Yet they were so much blinded as to declare that there was this *vast difference* between these proceedings and the coercive measures which were taken against themselves in England, viz., We compel men to "God's institutions," they in England compelled to "men's inventions." . . .

Many try to vindicate their way by that promise that kings shall become nursing fathers and queens nursing mothers to God's people. But as the character carries in its very nature an *impartial care and tenderness for all their children*, we appeal to every conscience whether it does not condemn the way of setting up one party to the injury of another. Our Lord tells us plainly that *few* find the narrow way while *many* go in the *broad way*. Yet the scheme we complain of has given the *many* such power over the *few*. . .the *many* are *prepared* with such instruments of *war against them* as to seize their goods or cast their bodies into prison where they may starve and die for all that the constitution has provided for them. In cases of common debts the law has provided several ways of relief, as it has not in the case before us, for here the assessors plead that they are *obliged* to tax all according to law, and the collector has the same plea for gathering of it. And the minister says, I agreed with the society for such a sum, and it is not my business to release any. So that we have had instances of serious Christians who must have died in prison for ministers' rates if Christianity and humanity had not moved people to provide them that relief which neither those ministers nor the law that upholds them have done. . . .

SECTION III

A brief account of what the Baptists have suffered under this constitution and of their reasons for refusing any active compliance with it

Many are ready to say, the Baptists are exempted from ministerial taxes, therefore why do they complain? Answer: We would be far from forgetting or undervaluing of our privileges but are willing thankfully to acknowledge that our honored rulers do protect our societies so as not to allow them to be interrupted in their worship. And as the taking cognizance of marriage belongs to them, we take it as a favor that they grant our ministers power to administer it so that we may have marriage solemnized among ourselves. Many other liberties we also enjoy under the government that is set over us for which we desire to be thankful both to the Author and to the instruments of them. Yet if our opponents could once put themselves into our place, we doubt not but they would think it was high time to seek for more full liberty than we have hitherto enjoyed. . . .

Our charter, as before observed, gives us equal religious liberty with other Christians. Yet the pedobaptists, being the greatest party, they soon made a perpetual law to support their own way but did nothing of that nature to exempt our denomination from it for thirty-six years. . . .

Here note the inhabitants of our mother country are not more of a party concerned in imposing taxes upon us without our consent than they have been in this land who have made and executed laws to tax *us* to uphold *their worship*. . . .

In civil states the power of the whole collective body is vested in a few hands that they may with better advantage defend themselves against injuries from abroad and correct abuses at home, for which end a few have a right to judge for the whole society. But in religion each one has an equal right to judge for himself, for we must all *appear* before the judgment seat of Christ, that *every one* may receive the things *done in his body* according to that *he hath done* (not what any earthly representative hath done for him), 2 *Cor.* v, 10. And we freely confess that we can find no more warrant from divine truth for any people on earth to constitute any men their representatives to make laws, to impose religious taxes than they have to appoint Peter or the Virgin Mary to represent them before the throne above. We are therefore brought to a stop about paying so much regard to such laws as to give in annual certificates to the other denomination [i.e., the Congregational or Standing Churches] as we have formerly done.

1. Because the very nature of such a practice implies an acknowledgement that the civil power has a right to set one religious sect up above another, else why need we give certificates to them any more than they to us? . . .

2. By the foregoing address to our legislature and their committee's report thereon it is evident that they claim a right to tax us from *civil obligation* as being the representatives of the people. . . . How came the kingdoms of *this world* to have a right to govern in Christ's kingdom which is *not of this world!*

3. That constitution not only emboldens people to *judge the liberty of other men's consciences* and has carried them so far as to tell our General Assembly that they conceived it to be a *duty they owed to God* and their country not to be dispensed with, . . . And only because our brethren in Bellingham left that clause about the *conscience* out of their certificate last year a number of their society who live at Menden were taxed, and lately suffered the spoiling of their goods to uphold pedobaptist worship.

4. The scheme we oppose evidently tends to destroy the purity and life of religion, for the inspired apostle assures us that the church is *espoused as a chaste virgin to Christ* and is obliged to be *subject to him in everything* . . .

5. The custom which they want us to countenance is very hurtful to civil society, for by the law of Christ *every man* is not only allowed but also required to judge for himself concerning the circumstantials as well as the essentials of religion and to act according to the *full persuasion of his own mind,* . . .

CONCLUSION

And now dear countrymen, we beseech you seriously to consider of these things. The great importance of a general union through this country in order to the preservation of our liberties has often been pleaded for with propriety, but how can such a union be expected so long as that dearest of all rights, equal liberty of conscience, is not allowed? Yea, how can any reasonably expect that HE who has the hearts of kings in his hand will turn the heart of our earthly sovereign to hear the pleas for liberty of those who will not hear the cries of their fellow subjects under their oppressions? . . .

Suffer us a little to expostulate with our fathers and brethren who inhabit the land to which our ancestors fled for religious liberty. You have lately been accused with being disorderly and rebellious by men in power who profess a great regard for order and the public good. And why don't you believe them and rest easy under their administrations? You tell us you cannot because you are taxed where you are not represented. And is it not really so with us? You do not deny the right of the British Parliament to impose taxes within her own realm; only complain that she extends her taxing power beyond her proper limits. And have we not as good right to say you do the *same thing?* And so that wherein you judge others you condemn yourselves? . . .

. . . And as the present contest between Great Britain and America is not so much about the greatness of the taxes already laid, as about a submission to their taxing power, so (though what we have already suffered is far from being a trifle, yet) our greatest difficulty at present concerns the submitting to a taxing power in ecclesiastical affairs. . . .

Thus we have laid before the public a brief view of our sentiments concerning liberty of conscience and a little sketch of our sufferings on that account. If any can show us that we have made any mistakes either about principles or facts, we would lie open to conviction. But we hope none will violate the forecited article of faith so much as to require us to yield a *blind obedience* to them or to expect that spoiling of goods or imprisonment can move us to *betray* the cause of true liberty.

8.4   John Leland, *The Rights of Conscience Inalienable,* 1791

What Isaac Backus did in New England, John Leland (1776-1860) did in the South: he motivated, enlisted, and led Baptists in that region in their struggle for full religious liberty. Backus worked through the Grievance Committee of the Warren Association, while Leland worked through the General Committee of Baptists in Virginia. Leland made effective use of humor in his preaching and writing, traits which sometimes offended friend and foe alike. He is often credited with having influenced James Madison to introduce the Bill of Rights as amendments to the Federal Constitution. *Source:* L. F. Greene, ed., *The Writings of the late Elder John Leland* (New York: G. W. Wood, 1845), 179-186.

Suppose a man to remove to a desolate island, and take a peaceable possession of it, without injuring any, so that he should be the honest inheritor of the isle. So long as he is alone, he is the absolute monarch of the place, and his own will is his law, which law is as often altered or repealed as his will changes. In process of time, from this man's loins ten sons are grown to manhood, and possess property. So long as they are all good men, each one can be as absolute, free, and sovereign as his father: but one of the ten turns vagrant, by robbing the rest. This villain is equal to, if not an over-match for any one of the nine: not one of them durst engage him in single combat. Reason and safety both dictate to the nine the necessity of a confederation, to unite their strength together to repel or destroy the plundering knave. Upon entering into confederation, some compact or agreement would be stipulated by which each would be bound to do his equal part in fatigue and expense. It would be necessary for these nine to meet at stated times to consult means of safety and happiness. A shady tree, or small cabin, would answer their purpose, and, in case of disagreement, four must give up to five.

In this state of things, their government would be perfectly democratic, every citizen being a legislator.

In a course of years, from these nine there arises nine thousand: their government can be no longer democratic—prudence would forbid it. Each tribe, or district, must then choose their representative, who, for the term that he is chosen, has the whole political power of his constituents. These representatives, meeting in assembly, would have power to make laws binding on their constituents, and while their time was spent in making laws for the community, each one of the community must advance a little of his money as a compensation therefor. Should these representatives differ in judgment, the minor must be subject to the major, as in the case above.

From this simple parable, the following things are demonstrated: First, that the law was not made for a righteous man, but for the disobedient. Second, that righteous men have to part with a little of their liberty and property to preserve the rest. Third, that all power is vested in, and consequently derived from the people. Fourth, that the law should rule over rulers, and not rulers over the law. Fifth, that government is founded on compact. Sixth, that every law made by legislators, inconsistent with the compact, modernly called a constitution, is usurping in the legislators, and not binding on the people. Seventh, that whenever government is found inadequate to preserve the liberty and property of the people, they have an indubitable right to alter it so as to answer those purposes. Eighth, that legislators, in their legislative capacity, cannot alter the constitution, for they are hired servants of the people to act within the limits of the constitution.

From these general observations, I shall pass on to examine a question which has been the strife and contention of ages. The question is, *"Are the rights of conscience alienable, or inalienable?"*

The word *conscience,* signifies *common science,* a court of judicature which the Almighty has erected in every human breast: a *censor morum* over all his conduct. Conscience will ever judge right, when it is rightly informed, and speak the truth when it understands it. But to advert to the question, "Does a man, upon entering into social compact, surrender his conscience to that society, to be controlled by the laws thereof; or can he, in justice, assist in making laws to bind his children's consciences before they are born?" I judge not, for the following reasons:

First. Every man must give an account of himself to God, and therefore every man ought to be at liberty to serve God in a way that he can best reconcile to his conscience. If government can answer for individuals at the day of judgment, let men be controlled by it in religious matters; otherwise, let men be free.

Second. It would be sinful for a man to surrender that to man, which is to be kept sacred for God. . . . How painful then must it be to an honest heart, to be bound to observe the principles of his former belief, after he is convinced of their imbecility? And this ever has, and ever will be the case, while the rights of conscience are considered alienable.

Third. But supposing it was right for a man to bind his *own* conscience, yet surely it is very iniquitous to bind the consciences of his children—to make fetters for them before they are born, is very cruel. . . .

Fourth. Finally, religion is a matter between God and individuals: the religious opinions of men not being the objects of civil government, nor in any way under its control.

The state of Rhode Island has stood above one hundred and sixty years without any religious establishment. The state of New York never had any. New Jersey claims the same. Pennsylvania has also stood from its first settlement until now upon a liberal foundation; and if agriculture, the mechanical arts and commerce, have not flourished in these states, equal to any of the others, I judge wrong.

It may further be observed, that all the states now in union, saving two or three in New England, have no legal force used about religion, in directing its course, or supporting its preachers. And, moreover, the federal government is forbidden by the constitution, to make any laws, establishing any kind of religion. If religion cannot stand, therefore, without the aid of law, it is likely to fall soon, in our nation, except in Connecticut and Massachusetts.

The evils of such an establishment, are many.

First. Uninspired, fallible men make their own opinions tests of orthodoxy, and use their own systems, as Pocrustes used his iron bedstead, to stretch and measure the consciences of all others by. Where no toleration is granted to non-conformists, either ignorance and superstition prevail, or persecution rages; . . .

Second. Such establishments not only wean and alienate the affections of one from another, on account of the different usage they receive in their religious sentiments, but are also very impolitic, especially in new countries; for what encouragement can strangers have to migrate with their arts and wealth into a state, where they cannot enjoy their religious sentiments without exposing themselves to the law? . . .

Third. These establishments metamorphose the church into a creature, and religion into a principle of state, which has a natural tendency to make men conclude that *Bible religion* is nothing but a *trick of state;* . . .

Fourth. There are no two kingdoms and states that establish the same creed and formalities of faith, which alone proves their debility. In one kingdom a man is condemned for not believing a doctrine that he would be condemned for believing in another kingdom. Both of these establishments cannot be right, but both of them can be, and surely are, wrong. . . .

If these, and many more evils, attend such establishments, what were, and still are, the causes that ever there should be a state establishment of religion in any empire, kingdom, or state?

The causes are many—some of which follow:

First. The love of importance is a general evil. . . .

Second. An over-fondness for a particular system or sect. . . .

Third. To produce uniformity in religion. . . .

Is uniformity of sentiments, in matter of religion, essential to the happiness of civil government? Not at all. Government has no more to do with the religious opinions of men, than it has with the principles of mathematics. Let every man speak freely without fear, maintain the principles that he believes, worship according to his own faith, either one God, three Gods, no God, or twenty Gods; and let government protect him in so doing, i.e., see that he meets with no personal abuse, or loss of property, for his religious opinions. . . .

Fourth. The common objection, "that the ignorant part of the community are not capacitated to judge for themselves," supports the Popish hierachy, and all Protestant, as well as Turkish and Pagan establishments in idea.

But is this idea just? Has God chosen many of the wise and learned? Has he not hid the mystery of gospel truth from them, and revealed it unto babes? Does the world by wisdom know God? . . .

Fifth. The groundwork of these establishments of religion is, *clerical influence.* Rulers, being persuaded by the clergy that an establishment of religion by human laws, would promote the knowledge of the gospel, quell religious disputes, prevent heresy, produce uniformity, and finally be advantageous to the state; establish such creeds as are framed by the clergy; and this they often do more readily, when they are flattered by the clergy; that if they thus defend the truth, they will become nursing fathers to the church, and merit something considerable for themselves.

What stimulates the clergy to recommend this mode of reasoning is:

First. Ignorance, not being able to confute error by fair argument.

Second. Indolence, not being willing to spend any time to confute the heretical.

Third. But chiefly covetousness, to get money, for it may be observed that in all these establishments, settled salaries for the clergy, recoverable by law, are sure to be interwoven; and was not this the case, I am well convinced that there would not be many, if any religious establishments in the Christian world.

8.5   David Benedict, Persecution of Baptists in the South

A number of Baptist writers, especially Isaac Backus and John Leland, present arguments in favor of religious liberty. Their writings, whether lengthy or brief, describe conditions that *should* prevail in America. The historian Benedict, however, offers not arguments but a vivid description of conditions as they actually did prevail. In a chatty and anecdotal style, Benedict helps complete the picture of the Baptist struggle for religious liberty in America. *Source:* David Benedict, *A General History of the Baptist Denomination in America*, 2 vols. (Boston: Manning & Loring, 1813), 1:64-77.

When the Baptists first appeared in North Carolina and Virginia, they were viewed by men in power as beneath their notice; none, said they, but the weak and wicked join them; let them alone, they will soon fall out among themselves, and come to nothing. In some places this maxim was adhered to, and persecution in legal shape was never seen. But in many others, alarmed by the rapid increase of the Baptists, the men in power strained every penal law in the Virginia code, to obtain ways and means to put down these disturbers of the peace, as they were now called.

It seems by no means certain, that any law in force in Virginia authorized the imprisonment of any person for preaching. The law for the preservation of peace, however, was so interpreted as to answer this purpose; and, accordingly, whenever the preachers were apprehended, it was done by a peace-warrant.

The first instance of actual imprisonment, we believe, that ever took place in Virginia, was in the county of Spottsylvania. On the 4th of June, 1768, John Waller, Lewis Craig, James Childs, and others, were seized by the Sheriff, and haled before three magistrates, . . . At Court they were arraigned as disturbers of the peace; on their trial, they were vehemently accused by a certain lawyer, who said to the Court, "May it please your worships, these men are great disturbers of the peace; they cannot meet a man upon the road, but they must ram a text of Scripture down his throat." Mr. Waller made his own and his brethren's defence so ingeniously, that they were somewhat puzzled to know how to dispose of them. They offered to release them, if they would promise to preach no more in the county, for a year and a day. This they refused, and therefore were sent into close jail. . . . After four weeks confinement, Lewis Craig was released from prison, and immediately went down to Williamsburg, to get a release for his companions. He waited on the deputy-governor, the Hon. John Blair, stated the case before him, and received the following letter, directed to the King's Attorney, in Spottsylvania:

"Sir,—I lately received a letter signed by a good number of worthy gentlemen, who are not here, complaining of the Baptists; the particulars of their misbehaviour are not told, any farther than their running into private houses, and making dissensions. Mr. Craig and Mr. Benjamin Waller are now with me, and deny the charge. They tell me they are willing to take the oaths, as others have. I told them I had consulted the Attorney-General, who is of opinion, that the General Court only have power to grant licenses, and therefore I referred them to the Court; but, on their application to the Attorney-General, they brought me his letter, advising me to write to you: That their petition was a matter of right, and that you may not molest these conscientious people, so long as they behave themselves in a manner becoming pious Christians, and in obedience to the laws, ...

"I am, with great respects to the gentlemen, Sir, your humble servant,

JOHN BLAIR.

"Williamsburg, July 16, 1768."

When the letter came to the Attorney, he would have nothing to say in the affair. Waller and the others continued in jail forty-three days, and were then discharged without any conditions. . . .

We have already observed the spread of the gospel in the county of Goochland, and that certain promising young preachers were thrust into the work. . . . In December, 1770, Messrs. William Webber and Joseph Anthony, two zealous young preachers, passed James-river, into Chesterfield, having been previously invited by some of the inhabitants. They, however, met with rigid treatment. The magistrates, finding that many were turning to righteousness, (to madness, as they would have it) and that these young labourers were likely to do them much harm, issued warrants, and had them apprehended and cast into prison. . . . While in prison they did much execution by preaching through the grates; many people attended their ministry, . . .

When Webber and Anthony were let go, they returned to Goochland, to their own company, and resumed their great work: Mr. Webber, however, enjoyed his liberty only a few months. He consented to travel with John Waller, on a course of meetings, to Middlesex, to the upper end of which place they arrived on the 10th of August, 1771. They soon found, however, there was no chance to proceed in their work. While Webber was preaching from these words, *"Shew me thy faith without thy works, and I will shew you my faith by my works,"* a magistrate pushed up, and drew back his club, with a design to knock him down; some person behind him caught the club, and prevented the mischief. Having a warrant to apprehend all who preached, and being backed by two Sheriffs, he seized William Webber, John Waller, James Greenwood, and Robert Ware. On the same day, Thomas Waford, who had travelled from the upper country with the preachers, though no preacher himself, was severely beaten by one of the persecutors with a whip, the scar of which he will probably carry to his grave; he with the four above-named preachers, were tried by James Montague. . . . Waford was discharged, not being a preacher; the other four were ordered to prison, and being conducted by two Sheriffs, they were safely lodged in close jail that night, about 9 o'clock. . . . They gave notice that they would preach every Wednesday and Sunday. Many came to hear them, insomuch that their enemies began to be enraged, and would frequently beat a drum while they were preaching.

On Monday the 24th, being Court day, they were carried to the court-house to be tried. A guard attended them, as if they had been criminals. They were not allowed to speak for themselves, but peremptorily required to give bond and security for good behaviour, and not to preach in the county again for one year. These terms they expressly refused, and were remanded to prison, and orders given that they should be fed on bread and water; accordingly the next day they had nothing else, and not enough of bread. Thus it continued for four days, until the brethren and friends found it out; after that, they were furnished so plentifully that they bestowed much upon the poor inhabitants of the town. . . . The Lord daily opened the hearts of the people: the rich sent many presents, things calculated to nourish them in their sufferings, and alleviate their sorrows. Mr. Webber fell sick; this excited the sympathy of their friends in a higher degree, and they paid him great attention. The persecutors found that the imprisonment of the preachers tended rather to the furtherance of the gospel; for they preached regularly in their prison, crowds attended to hear, and their preaching seemed to have a double weight when coming from the jail; . . . Accordingly, on the 26th day of September, after having been thirty days in close confinement, and sixteen days in the bounds, they were liberated, upon giving a bond for good behaviour.

The rage of persecutors had in no wise abated; they seemed, sometimes, to strive to treat the Baptists and their worship with as much rudeness and indecency as was possible. They often insulted the preachers in time of service, and would ride into the water, and make sport, when they administered baptism. They frequently fabricated and spread the most groundless reports, which were injurious to the characters of the Baptists; and when a Baptist fell into any improper conduct, it was always exaggerated to the utmost extent. . . . Notwithstanding these severe oppositions, the word of the Lord grew and multiplied greatly. Young preachers were ordained, and churches constituted; . . . These new churches, filled with young and inexperienced members, were visited frequently by John Waller, accompanied sometimes by one, and sometimes by another of the preachers of his own vicinity. His ministrations, on the one hand, were exceeding salutary and comfortable to his friends; but on the other, highly displeasing to the enemies of the Baptists. They viewed Waller as the ring-leader of all the confusion and disturbance that had befallen them. . . . Not unfrequently, their leading men would attend the Baptist meetings, and would enter into arguments with the preachers: . . .

To these arguments, Waller and the other preachers, boldly and readily replied, that if they were wolves in sheeps' clothing, and their opponents were true sheep, it was quite unaccountable that they were persecuted, and cast into prison; it is well known that wolves would destroy sheep, but never, until then, that sheep would prey upon wolves; that their coming might, indeed, interrupt their peace; but certainly, if it did, it must be a false peace, bordering on destruction; . . .

Foiled in their arguments, and galled by the reproaches cast upon them, which, doubtless, were often done with too much acrimony, they again resorted to the civil power. In August, 1772, James Greenwood and William Loveall were preaching, not far from the place where Bruington meeting-house now stands, in the county of King and Queen, when they were seized by virtue of a warrant, and immediately conveyed to prison. . . . They preached regularly while in prison, and to much purpose.

On March 13th, 1774, the day on which Piscataway church was constituted, a warrant was issued to apprehend all the Baptist preachers that were at meeting. Accordingly, John Waller, John Shackleford, Robert Ware, and Ivison Lewis, were taken and carried before a magistrate. Ivison Lewis was dismissed, not having preached in the county; the other four were sent to prison. . . . Ware and Shackleford gave bond, and went home; Waller, being always doubtful of the propriety of giving any bond whatever, determined to go back to jail.

From the beginning, the Baptists were unremitting in their exertions to obtain liberty of conscience; they contended that they could not be imprisoned by any existing law; that they were entitled to the same privileges that were enjoyed by the dissenters in England: their judges, however, decided otherwise; and as there was no regular appeal, the propriety of that decision has not been legally ascertained. The prevailing opinion in the present day is, that their imprisonment was unlawful. When they could not succeed in this way, they resorted to the General Court, for the purpose of obtaining licensed places for preaching, &c. agreeably to the toleration law in England.

In the mean time, every thing tended to favour their wishes; their persecution, so far from impeding, really promoted their cause; their preachers had now become numerous, and some of them were men of considerable talents. Many of the leading men favoured them, some from one motive, and some from another; their congregations were large, and when any of their men of talents preached, they were crowded. The patient manner in which they suffered persecution, raised their reputation for piety and goodness, in the estimation of a large majority of the people. Their numbers annually increased in a surprising degree. Every month, new places were found by the preachers, whereon to plant the Redeemer's standard. In these places, although but few might become Baptists, yet the majority would be favourable. Many, who had expressed great hostility to them, upon forming a more close acquaintance with them, professed to be undeceived. . . .

Unit III

The Nineteenth Century

9

Baptists in England

In many ways the nineteenth is the great century for English Baptists. During that halcyon era they cast off remnants of ancient religious restrictions, saw their numbers and public influence grow, advanced many of their pastors to prominent religious leadership in the nation, and benefited from the general upsurge of evangelical church life in England. In the midst of these changes, English Particular Baptists formed a national assembly in 1813, extended the work of their famed Baptist Missionary Society and, toward the end of the century, merged with remnants of the General Baptists.

However, not all was well in the English Baptist Zion. Toward the end of the century the Baptists found themselves caught up in a storm of theological conflict which took the name of the "Down Grade Controversy." Led by such London Baptist giants as Charles Haddon Spurgeon and John Clifford, the Down Grade Controversy threatened the fragile unity which some leaders hoped to achieve through the merger of Particular and General Baptists in 1891. Whether the Down Grade really shattered Baptist life, or merely exposed foundations that were already crumbling, is still debated.

Documents included in this chapter are chosen to illustrate Baptist thought and action in England during the nineteenth century. The rigid demands of space, regretfully, disallow selections from Baptist life in Greater Britain.

9.1 Formation of the Baptist Union, 1813

From their beginning, the Particular Baptist churches preferred a decentralized ecclesiology. Therefore, they were somewhat slower to form general denominational bodies than were their more centralizing General brethren. Though they formed associations quite early, Particular Baptists had no enduring General Assembly until 1813. They did hold general meetings in 1689-91, but no continuing organization resulted. The following document traces the formation of the Baptist Union of 1813. It also gives some reasons for that action, and sets out some of the objectives the founders hope the new organization will achieve. *Source: The Baptist Magazine,* 4 (1812): 356-358.

GENERAL ASSOCIATION
of Baptist Churches.

For several years past it has been thought desirable, that a more general Union of the Baptist Churches than has hitherto, (at least, for the last 130 years) existed in this country, should be promoted. Our readers will recollect that several papers, tending to bring about this measure, have appeared in our Magazine during the past year, and we now cordially congratulate the friends of the Measure, that a basis has been laid for a general and beneficial Union of our churches.

As our work is designed to be a register of passing events in the denomination, we shall give the history of this Subject somewhat in detail. The Society of Associated ministers in London, consisting of the pastors of 17 churches, and other ministering brethren, being desirous of bringing about this object, which they had been requested by ministers in the country to undertake, appointed a Committee of seven persons to arrange the plan. They accordingly appointed a meeting to be held at Dr. Rippon's Vestry, Carter Lane, at 8 o'clock on Thursday the 25th of June, and invited all the Baptist Ministers and Messengers of the churches to attend and take into consideration the proposed measure. . . .

Dr. Rippon being called to the chair, the meeting was opened with prayer, by Dr. Ryland.

After which the Chairman, having congratulated his Brethren who formed this pleasing and respectable Assembly, proceeded to observe, that for many years an Union Meeting of the representatives of the Particular or Calvinistic Baptist Churches in Town and Country had appeared to be an object of considerable importance—that of late the consideration of the subject had been resumed; and as it had been asked, What business would probably engage the attention of such an Assembly? He suggested, it had been thought,—

That one of the first and most important duties of it would no doubt be solemn Prayer to the God of all grace for the eminent out-pouring of his Holy Spirit on the Churches, and the whole world . . . . That at such meetings our Missions in the East Indies would necessarily present a signal object of regard; when we should be able to recommend Auxiliary Societies, or Annual Collections for its support, in the far greater part of our Congregations.

That the yearly Accounts of the state of religion transmitted from the Associated Churches, and others, would create an endless variety of claims, either on our sympathy, our gratitude, or our benevolence; and, some of them, on the united exertions of the whole body.

That our Academies, the larger and smaller, would have their demands on our attention. How can they be more effectually supported? Can any other assistance be given to such whose views are towards the ministry?

That here suitable methods might be proposed by which the talents and influence of the most valuable members of every church might be brought into action, for the good of the whole.

That it would be natural to consult on the best methods of Catechising, and to recommend the same to our families and churches.

That such an Assembly might deliberate on the most effectual means of supporting, all through the kingdom, aged respectable ministers—and on the provision which might be made for the education of the children of our Ministers deceased, as among the United Brethren, and other denominations of Christians.

That such an assembly would afford the best opportunities to concert plans for the encouragement and support of Village preaching—of Sunday Schools—and for the establishment of Penny, and also of Mite Societies, resembling those of our Brethren in various parts of America.

That here an opportunity would be given of recommending interesting publications, and of selecting, and disseminating through the country, such small tracts, and pamphlets, as the general state of religion, and of our own denomination might require.

That the Brethren assembled from the various districts would be able to advise where it is proper that New Meeting-houses should be erected; and of determining that, henceforward, no Case for building, enlarging, or repairing any place of worship, shall be countenanced, unless it has, previously to such erection or alteration, obtained, in writing, the direction, encouragement, and recommendation of the principal Ministers of their own district.

The Chairman then took a rapid glance at the state of the Baptist Churches in foreign parts; and closed with remarking that what he had been saying presented but a few articles, out of a vast multitude, which would press themselves on the consideration of such an Assembly, in which whatever relates to the real interestes of the denomination at home and abroad, would engage the general attention. . . .

9.2 John Howard Hinton, *The Nature and Purpose of a Baptist Union,* 1812

One of the founders of the Baptist Union, and certainly one of its most important early leaders, was John Howard Hinton. Since he had for some years advocated such a union, it is not surprising that at the consultative meeting of 1812 Hinton was called upon to bring a major address. His address bears reading today not only for its interpretation of the nature and function of Baptist denominational bodies, but also for its incisive analysis of English Baptist life early in the nineteenth century. *Source: The Baptist Magazine,* October 1812, 407-414.

Christian Brethren,

I am requested to address you, in a few words, on the subject of the resolutions which I have now read; and I accept the office allotted to me with the greatest cheerfulness, since in the discharge of it I am persuaded I have little or no difficulty to encounter. I am confident that the cause which I plead has an advocate in each of your hearts; and I feel justified in applying to you, without material alteration, the declaration of the Apostle respecting the church at Thessalonica—"As touching brotherly love, ye need not that we should use many arguments to urge on you its necessity and excellency; for ye yourselves are taught of God to love one another."

The first of our resolutions, which is the basis of the rest, by stating that "a MORE general union is desirable," assumes as an acknowledged truth (what, as far as my own knowledge and information extend, I am happy to confirm) that a general spirit of union already exists among our churches; . . .

I submit to you, brethren a few remarks which may serve to illustrate the character by which, I trust, our intended Union will ever be distinguished.—

I first observe that, if it be durable or profitable, it must be marked by a harmony in Religious Principles. It must be an Union of those ministers and those churches who mutually and cordially agree in all the leading truths of Divine Revelation; . . . If these sentiments are, as we humbly trust, taught of God and contain the mind of Christ, then, so far as we are united in them, we are likely to form a Christian Union; and one that will be durable and profitable.

Our intended Union, brethren, should also bear the character of strong and disinterested affection. . . . Our Union should be cemented by a holy delight in each other "for the truth's sake that is in us," for the relation we respectively bear to our common Lord; and for the honor which he has put upon us by employing us in our several posts as it hath pleased him. . . .

I thirdly observe, that if this General Association of our churches prosper, there must be in it a Unity of Exertion. We must set before us some great and common objects of pursuit, and direct to these our unremitted attention. . . .

An unity of faith in the great doctrines of the gospel, of holy affection towards each other, and steady exertion in duty, is highly desirable as it respects our churches individually; but what an accession of strength is derived to the Redeemer's interest, when many churches combine their counsels, their prayers, their property, and their talents of every kind, in breaking up the fallow ground; in planting wholly a right seed; in furnishing aid to churches otherwise too weak to support a stated ministry; in erecting new temples for God; in raising up those which have fallen into decay; in stretching forth the arm of mercy to distant lands; in executing the testament which the divine Redeemer sealed with his blood, and entrusted to the care of his disciples; in conveying his unspeakable gift to the ignorant and benighted nations of the earth. In these exertions, I observe with the sincerest pleasure, we act in concert with many other Christian societies, who, though they do not rank in the same denomination with ourselves, and are also distinguished from each other by various professional shades, yet cordially receive and zealously disseminate those leading doctrines of our holy faith which have ever been "the power of God unto salvation." . . . Our exterior form is indeed different, but we have one glorious leader and commander. We have different stations, but they are all in the same field of exertion: and we should regard each others progress with an emulation from which envy is for ever excluded. . . .

. . . Other denominations have set us an example which I think we do well to follow. Our brethren the Calvinist Methodists have formed a Union; our Independent brethren have done the same; and with nearly the same views as they profess, we are about to form a Union of the Baptist denomination. But could I for a moment believe that a closer union of each class within its own boundary would in the least degree promote a spirit of dis-union between the denominations respectively, become the secret cause of jealousy, and thus diminish their friendly intercourse, I should sincerely deprecate these measures. . . .

. . . If a spirit of humility, spirituality genuine candour, and holy zeal is found amongst us, we may rest assured that God hath not forsaken us; and that other ministers and other churches shall arise from whom a greater revenue of praise shall be gathered than has yet been offered by us to the divine throne. And who that reflects on the commencement, and surveys the progress of our Mission in the East, can forbear to exclaim, "What hath God wrought?" Little more than twenty years ago a few christian ministers, in one of our country associations, in number I believe about twelve, were impressed with an earnest desire to do something for the conversion of the heathen; and after solemn prayer to God for his blessing, they subscribed about thirteen pounds for the commencement of the work. They gave willingly and to their ability; and had their gift consisted but of as many pence, it would with similar dispositions, have been equally acceptable to God. One of them published a small work exhorting his brethren, and especially those of the Baptist denomination, to which he belonged, to come forward with a Mission to the Heathen world. I well remember the flood of contempt that was poured on this design by the leading literary Journals of the day; and I confess I was surprised to find that they would take so much pains to crush an attempt of which they entertained so despicable an opinion. But the great enemy of the gospel had learned by experience not to despise small beginnings. . . .

You have proved your attachment to this work, brethren, by the liberality of your contributions, and you have chearfully avowed your determination that it shall not fall to the ground or be impeded for want of any support that Providence may enable you to render it. God has heard and accepted your vows, and his grace will enable you to fulfil them. . . . When I behold around me a number of respectable young men and young ministers, I cannot help believing that they will consider themselves as receiving from heaven this day a sacred charge that they should make it one great object of their future lives to sustain this Christian Mission, in the same spirit and with the same diligence, with which it has been hitherto conducted. . . .

Christian Brethren who reside in the Metropolis,—We rejoice that this Mission holds out one great and specific object in which we who reside in the country have one common interest with yourselves, and in this we have a pledge that our Union shall be permanent. Assembled to promote its interests, other concerns, which, though secondary, are little inferior in their importance, will present themselves to our notice. The pressure of the times bears heavy on very many of our smaller country churches, and a stated ministry among them is in danger of being annihilated for want of timely aid—such aid as other evangelical denominations afford to their weaker churches, with far greater promptness than we have done. Many of these churches have exerted themselves beyond their strength in support of public institutions. Let not their own safety be forgotten, since if the root be not healthy, it cannot long sustain the more extended branches of the vine.

We return to our respective churches highly gratified, and we hope profited, by this interview. We have entrusted to your Ministers for the present year, the care of collecting and arranging whatever may be thought worthy of attention at our next annual meeting. God alone can determine which of us shall make part of that assembly; but "whether we live we live unto the Lord, or whether we die we die unto the Lord;" and so "living or dying we are the Lord's."

9.3   A Discussion about Baptist Pastors, 1812

The ongoing need for a good supply of capable ministers has occupied the concern of Baptist groups around the world. Particular Baptists in the nineteenth century shared this concern, and offered various plans to meet the need. In their first decades, Baptists converted a number of ministers from the state church. However, that supply soon dried up, and the religious lethargy of the eighteenth century left English Baptists, along with other denominations, suffering not only a shortage of quantity but also, some said, a lowered quality of ministry. One reason for forming the Baptist Union in 1813 was to provide for the training of ministers. It seems significant, therefore, that in 1812 the *Baptist Magazine* carried an extensive correspondence on the need for more and better Baptist ministers. Part of that discussion is reproduced here. *Source: The Baptist Magazine,* September 1812, 234-235, 366-371.

Deficiency of Pastors.

IT is a lamentable fact, that many of our Churches are destitute of Pastors; perhaps a greater number than at any former period. As many of the survivors are far advanced in life, and cannot be expected to continue long in the service of the Redeemer on earth; it is certainly desirable that suitable persons should be raised up among us to fill these important stations in the Church of Christ. . . .

The writer will be greatly obliged if any of the judicious correspondents of the Baptist Magazine will turn their attention to this subject, and furnish answers to the following enquiries.

1. Are there fewer young men of established piety, of improveable talents, and of ardent zeal, in our Churches than in those of other denominations?

2. Is proper attention paid by the Pastors of our Churches to find out suitable gifts? and do the Churches to the extent of their power encourage such persons to devote themselves to the work of the Ministry?

3. Is there any thing in the constitution and government of our Churches, which presents a discouraging aspect to persons who wish to apply themselves to this work?

4. Is the plan adopted by the Deacons of our Churches to provide suitable means for the Pastor's support, the cause of deterring many, who are in comfortable circumstances, from leaving their secular concerns, lest they should incur the sentence pronounced by the Apostle 1 *Tim.* v, 8?

5. Does the number of our churches so much increase that the persons among us who are blest with suitable gifts, are insufficient to supply them?

ATOI.

REPLY TO THE ENQUIRIES OF ATOI,
Respecting the Deficiency of Pastors.
To the Editor of the Baptist Magazine.

Sir,

If you will accept a few general remarks upon the inquiries of Atoi in yours for June, concerning a deficiency of pastors, they are at your, his, and your readers' service.— The first enquiry, "Are there fewer young men of established piety, of improveable talents, and of ardent zeal, in our churches than in those of other denominations?" I should be unwilling to answer in any other way than in the negative, both for honor and truth's sake. . . . If catechising enters into the plan of ministers, or the system of the private tuition of parents, (both are best,) we need fear no competition as it respects the younger parts of our societies. If this is neglected, we need not wonder if, *in some instances,* our youths are not equal to others. . . . It is a most certain fact, that if a child is trained up as a catechumen, his knowledge of divine truths will be very considerable at a very early age.

2. "Is proper attention paid by the Pastors of our Churches to find out suitable gifts? and do the Churches to the extent of their power encourage such persons to devote themselves to the work of the Ministry?" This probably may be answered negatively, at least in some instances. I have heard it repeatedly mentioned, that some ministers and members of churches have manifested the contrary disposition; and so far from encouraging persons having suitable gifts, have discouraged them. Some indirect sarcastical sentences have been indirectly bandied about, especially if a gifted brother has been a little of the *lower class;* such as these, "he is very forward—he is growing conceited— he wants to be a parson." When, probably, his very heart faints within him at the thought of so awful an employment. That some members of churches should do this, is not wonderful, because very few can bear another to move in a higher station than themselves. It is natural enough, *as nature is;* but it is comtemptibly mean in a christian, and abominably base in a minister, to indulge such a conduct for a moment. . . .

3. "Is there any thing in the constitution and government of our Churches, which presents a discouraging aspect to persons who wish to apply themselves to this work?" If by this is intended, the calling of young men to exercise their gifts before the church, or the elder members of the church, that they may give their opinion whether the great Shepherd of the sheep has called such to feed his lambs, (where this judgment is given in love, without any party consideration,) I should think no young man, diffident of himself, and desirous of knowing the will of God, would object to such an ordeal. Young men, who enter into the ministry, will find great consolation in referring back to the opinion of a church of Christ, when they become pastors. Probably, some of their people will suspect they were never *called* to the ministry; perhaps they may be overwhelmed by their own thoughts upon that very subject. But that an idle, prating professor, who can see clearly *his own gifts,* and wonders that others do not perceive *their brilliancy,* should very much dislike such an examination, is by no means strange. . . .

4. "Is the plan adopted by the Deacons of our Churches to provide suitable means

for the Pastor's support, the cause of deterring many, who are in comfortable circumstances, from leaving their secular concerns, lest they should incur the sentence pronounced by the Apostle, 1 *Tim.* v, 8?" Here, Mr. Editor, I think, is a very serious obstacle, without any animad-versions upon Deacon's orders, or disorders. If a young Baptist thinks of getting a handsome genteel living by becoming a Minister, he will find what he ought to find, if such are his motives, a grievous disappointment. There are no ministers that are so ill-provided for as baptist ministers. If a young man has a prospect of obtaining by his industry or ingenuity, either by his business or profession, a comfortable competency for himself and family, he must *venture,* if not *sacrifice,* such prospects, should he take upon him the ministry. The meanest mechanic, if he is clever, has a greater prospect in this world. . . .

5. "Does the number of our churches so much increase that the persons among us who are blest with suitable gifts, are insufficient to supply them?" The Christian world will have reason to hail that time with unspeakable delight, when our churches shall be so numerous as this inquiry in the former part supposes. The prosperity necessary to a great increase of our churches will naturally produce precious souls desirous of helping the glorious work of God. . . . We live in the times when the fields are white for the harvest, let every mean, every encouragement, be used to bring hopeful useful men into the ministry, always remembering that the *good* (generally speaking) are such as must be *sought out;* those who cannot be *kept out of the Pulpit,* seldom last so well as those whom you can *scarcely get into it.* But wisdom is profitable to direct.

S. K. L.

9.4   Letter from William Ward about the Serampore Mission, 1811

No endeavor captured the imagination and support of English Baptists as did the foreign mission to India, led by the great missionary "triumvirate" of William Carey, William Ward, and Joshua Marshman. To Baptists then (and now) few kinds of literature are more fascinating than well-written letters from a missionary describing conditions of life and ministry on a foreign field. William Ward's letter of December 5, 1811, tells much about Baptist missions in India, and response to the letter tells much about Baptists in England. *Source: The Baptist Magazine,* October 1812, 443-444.

BAPTIST MISSION.
DESCRIPTION OF THE PRINTING-OFFICE, SERAMPORE.
Extract of a Letter from Mr. Ward, in India, to the Rev. W. Fletcher, Swannick, Derbyshire.

Scrampore, Dec. 5, 1811.

My dear Cousin,

I was very glad to receive a letter from you; it came also at a very suitable time when I was much distressed with the news of the death of my dear mother and eldest brother. I thank you for this mark of attention to one so unworthy. In looking over the scenes that are past, I sometimes retrace my journies to Losege with much pleasure. I rejoice that you have been preserved in the vineyard till now, and that you do not labour in vain. I should like to see you in the flesh again, but I do not feel distressed that this is impossible; the appointments of God are the best: if we may but meet in heaven, our interview there will have nothing in it painful; then all will be well. This time cannot be far distant, unless, (as I sometimes fear) I should be at last a cast-a-way. I see nothing worthy of our notice, but God's kingdom. I am in the very work, beyond which I have nothing to wish for, except more success in it. No place on earth presents itself in which I should be likely to be doing more good.

Could you see your cousin in his printing-office, surrounded by forty or fifty servants, all employed in preparing the Holy Scriptures for the nations of India, you would, I am sure, be highly pleased. One man is preparing the Book of God for the learned Hindoos, in the Shanskrit language; another for the people of Bengal; another for those of Hindoosthan; another for the inhabitants of Orissa; another for the Mahrattas; another for the Sikhs; another for the people of Assam; and for the Musselmen in all parts of the East, in the Persian and Hindoosthanee languages; others for the Chinese; others for the Talingas; and others are soon to begin in the Cingalese, Tamul, and Malayalim languages.

As you enter the office, you see your cousin, in a small room, dressed in a white jacket, reading or writing, and at the same time looking over the whole office, which is 174 feet long. The next persons you see, are learned natives translating the Scriptures into the different languages, or correcting the proof-sheets. You walk through the office, and see laid out in cases *types* in Arabic, Persian, Nagaree, Talinga, Sikh, Bengalee, Mahratta, Chinese, Orissa, Burman, Carnata, Keshemena, Greek, Hebrew, and English. Hindoos, Musselmans, and converted Natives are all busy. Some composing, others distributing, others correcting. You next come to the presses, and see four persons throwing off the sheets of the Bible in different languages; and on the left are half a dozen Musselmans employed in binding the scriptures for distribution; while others are folding the sheets and delivering them to the Store-keeper to be placed in the Store-room till they can be made up into volumes. This Store-room, which is 142 feet long, is filled with shelves from side to side; upon which are laid, wrapped up, the sheets of the bible before they are bound. You go forward, and in a Room adjoining to the office, are the Type-casters, busy in preparing the types in the different Languages. In one corner, you see another busy grinding the printing ink; and in a spacious open place, walled round, you see a Paper Mill, and a number of persons employed in making paper for printing the Scriptures in all these languages. Added to this, I have to preach several times a week in English and Bengalee, and an almost endless number of other things to do belonging to the mission—the Out-stations—the Family, &c. I think you will acknowledge that I am at my post, and where I ought to be. Pray for me, that I may make full proof of my ministry, and then all will be well. I am, my dear cousin,

thine most truly,

_____ *W. WARD.*

9.5 The Serampore Controversy

One of the unhappiest episodes in English Baptist history is the Serampore Controversy. The relationship between the missionaries on the field, and Andrew Fuller, the general secretary, at home, had always been cordial and cooperative. The missionaries largely set their own priorities and policies, decided their own fields of work, and, in general, conducted the mission as they thought best. Letters from Fuller contained encouragement and occasional counsel, but no official directives. However, things changed. In India, the mission grew in personnel and resources. In England, the Society expanded, moved its headquarters to London, and elected leaders who did not know the missionaries personally and who took a far more managerial approach to the work. Controversy arose about who had final authority to direct the work, and specifically about whether property bought out of missionary earnings belonged to the missionaries or to the mission. As a result, the missionary "triumvirate" of Carey, Marshman, and Ward split off from the Baptist Missionary Society in 1827 and formed their own group. The schism endured until 1837. The following account is sympathetic to the missionaries. *Source:* Two letters to a Member of the Committee of the Baptist Missionary Society. By an Old Subscriber (R. Nichols), London, 1829, 2-4.

The names of Carey, Marshman, and Ward, have been so long publicly eminent for disinterested, persevering, and apostolic devotion of themselves and their property, to the extension of divine truth amongst the idolatrous nations of India, as to render unnecessary in the present instance, a detail of the exertions by which under the divine blessing they have been enabled to accomplish so much. Those labours, and their consequent success, have been published with accompanying praises, in the Periodical Accounts of the Baptist Missionary Society, and during a period of many years have amply supplied materials for the eloquence of committee men, secretaries, and itinerant speakers at the numerous public meetings which have been holden from time to time, for the laudable design of increasing subscriptions to the funds for missionary purposes. Till within the last few months, the religious public were comparatively ignorant of any differences existing between the pious and learned brethren at Serampore, and the Committee in England, who regulated the expenditure of the sums derived from popular contribution. At length, however, those differences (which had existed for many years,) assumed a stronger character and could no longer be concealed.

The Serampore Missionaries originally left England with the express intention of endeavouring *to support themselves* among the people they hoped to benefit, and thus leave whatever sums might be collected to be entirely appropriated to that purpose for which they were immediately contributed; . . . In conformity with these notions of the duties upon which they entered, the brethren in a very short time found the means not only of supporting themselves, but also of devoting a very large amount annually to the expences of missionary labour, and translating, printing, and circulating the sacred Scriptures amongst nations to whom they came, indeed, as "light shining in darkness."

So unusual an instance of lofty resolution and pious disinterestedness did not fail to make a deep and favourable impression on the friends of these distinguished men in England, and on the public generally. The late secretary to the Society, the Rev. Andrew Fuller, the personal friend of Carey, and who was also one of the earliest supporters of the Baptist Mission, was greatly elated and filled with overflowing zeal for the promotion of those objects which the missionaries recommended. . . . When Fuller died, however, "there arose up a new king which knew not Joseph," and the communications with the missionaries took a new complexion. Instead of being, as formerly, the simple, clear, and confidential vehicles of ardent zeal and sincere co-operation, they assumed the frigid gravity and formal precision which belong to the dispatches of "a secretary of state," rather than to the letters of the organ of communication between pious subscribers to missionary funds and the zealous men, the reputation of whose labours had been the means of exciting those subscribers "to throw in their mites." But this was of small importance, though it necessarily had a chilling influence. From a mistaken notion of that compact into which the Serampore brethren had entered among themselves, it was presumed by those who had been lately elevated to official consequence, that Carey and his brethren intended, by that agreement, to make over themselves and all the property they might thereafter acquire to the sole government and disposal of a committee in England, . . . In consistency with their Christian character, the brethren mildly expostulated, and explained that the transaction which had led the committee to assert a right to the property which they (the brethren) had produced, was only meant to divest *themselves* of property, and devote it to the furtherance of their mission, and was never intended to give any foreign committee (who could not of course be competent) a right to interfere in the disposal of funds so originated. These unpleasant things led on to others. . . . Malignant criticism violently assailed them, and they suffered deeply from "the spurns that patient merit of the unworthy takes." But above all, ingratitude stung them—"their own familiar friends in whom they trusted, which did eat of their bread, lifted up the heel against them." So the breach was widened between the committee and the brethren, till at length, they publicly separated and announced themselves independent of each other. How this will be overruled for good, as we trust it shall be, we are unable to decide; . . .

9.6 Samuel Cox, *Salvator Mundi,* 1877

Some Baptists have long had a fascination for the doctrine of universal salvation. Samuel Cox (1826-1893) was certainly not the first to embrace "the larger hope," the doctrine that eventually all souls will be redeemed. However, few statements of this doctrine have had such an impact as his book *Salvator Mundi* in 1877. In the preface to an 1889 edition Cox noted the rapid change among Baptists on the doctrine of eternal destiny, and wrote that "I cannot but rejoice to believe that I have taken a humble part in producing it." He concluded that "no minister now gloats over hell fire as many once did." Although in the Down Grade Controversy Charles H. Spurgeon refused to name specific ministers he regarded as heretical, it was well known that Cox and his book upset Spurgeon mightily. In his *Sword and Trowel,* Spurgeon referred to Cox's universalism as "post-morten salvation." Cox was a graduate of Stepney College, the school that later became Regent's Park, Oxford. He served as pastor in Nottingham for twenty-five years. *Source:* Samuel Cox, *Salvator Mundi: Or, Is Christ the Savior of All Men?* (London: Henry S. King Company, 1877).

PREFACE

The main object of this book is to encourage those who "faintly trust the larger hope" to commit themselves to it wholly and fearlessly, by shewing them that they have ample warrant for it in the Scriptures of the New Testament. . . .

Of all branches of theology Eschatology is perhaps the least attractive to sober and thoughtful students of the Inspired Word, especially if they have discovered that the New Testament predictions of ages and things to come can only be safely approached through the long and winding avenue of Old Testament prophecy. But that section of it which relates to the conditions of men after death is one which so profoundly affects our whole conception both of the character of God and of the salvation wrought by Christ, that even those who most shrink from the interpretation of prophecy are compelled to study it. Indeed I cannot but think it a binding duty on all preachers of the Word that they should not only come to some well-considered conclusion on this point, but that they should also publish and enforce that conclusion, whatever it may be. Few of the more thoughtful and cultivated preachers of the Gospel now hold the dogma of everlasting torment; in a large circle of acquaintance I hardly know one: and yet how few seek to replace it, in the mind of the Church, with any doctrine which they hold to be more in accordance with "the mind of the Spirit." . . .

Of those teachers and preachers who honestly retain the dogma which attaches an endless torment to the sins of time no man can ask more than that, while they preach it with sincerity, they also keep their minds open to any more light which may break out upon them from God's holy Word; but of those who have seen that light and yet will not suffer it to shine through their teaching, what can one say but that they are less worthy of their high calling than those who still walk in darkness? . . .

IV.—HELL.

In my last Lecture I shewed you what I hope you found to be good and conclusive reasons for expunging the verb "to damn," with its cognates, from our translation of the Bible; and I am now to shew you, if I can, equally good and conclusive reasons for expunging the word "hell." . . .

Now in this theological sense, the sense in which we naturally take the word when we meet it in the Bible, I am bold to say that the word "hell" is never once used in the Original, though it is so frequent in our translation of it, and that we have no longer any sort of excuse for retaining it on the sacred page. There is no word at all answering to it whether in the Hebrew or in the Greek. *We,* however, are not concerned with the whole Bible; we have agreed to confine our search for light on the future conditions of men to the Gospels and the Epistles. In our Authorized Version of *these* Scriptures, then, the word "hell" occurs eighteen times, and is used to render the three Greek words, *Tartarus, Hades,* and *Gehenna;* at each of which we will look in turn. . . .

1. The word *Tartarus* occurs but once in the whole New Testament, or, indeed, in the whole Bible. You will find the passage in 2 Peter ii. 4, and a very singular passage it is. . . . Our plain duty to the passage is to read it in English as it reads in the original Greek, "God spared not angels who sinned, but cast them into *Tartarus.*"

2. The word *Hades* occurs five times in the Gospels and Epistles; and in every instance our translators render it by the word "hell." That the translation is an inaccurate one, and at times even a grotesquely inaccurate one, it will be easy to shew.

. . . For whereas our word "hell" denotes the final and everlasting torment of the wicked, there is not a single instance in which the word "Hades" is used in that sense. Where it applies to the lot of the wicked at all, it denotes simply that intermediate and preparatory state of punishment, or discipline, which precedes "the last judgment;" while at least, in some cases, the word obviously covers *Paradise* as well as *Gehenna,* and denotes the tranquil and happy intermediate estate of the good, that rest-full region or condition in which the righteous await the Resurrection, and into which Christ Himself entered, although He was not "left" in it.

3. There is but one other word in the New Testament which is rendered by "hell," the word *Gehenna.* This word occurs twelve times in the Gospels and Epistles. And how inadequately the word "hell" translates it you will see if we consider (1) the derivation of the word; (2) the sense in which it was used and understood in the time of our Lord and his Apostles; and (3) the meaning of the several passages in which it is found. And as these passages are those on which the popular dogma is very largely based, we must examine them with some patience and care.

. . . And the result of the search . . . is that, without a single exception, or with only one very doubtful exception, these writings lend no countenance to, that they positively discountenance, the modern dogma of everlasting torment. That is to say, the uninspired Jewish writings for the six centuries nearest to Christ know nothing, absolutely nothing, of "hell." . . . Obviously they [Jewish Fathers] thought of Gehenna as the state in which the wicked would be reserved for judgment, as an intermediate, not the final, state. . . . and I do not see how we are to escape the conclusion that among the Jews it was taken to denote a punishment, or discipline, which did not extend beyond a definite, and probably a very short, period of time. Christ was a Jew, and spoke to Jews; and in what but their Jewish sense can we fairly and reasonably interpret his words? . . .

We have now examined every passage in the New Testament in which the word Gehenna occurs. We have found that for the most part it is used in a purely figurative sense; that, so often as it is used in a literal sense, it denotes the punishments executed on criminal Jews in this present world: and that, in the one or two cases, in which it veils a reference to the punishments of the world to come, it would be understood by those who heard it as denoting that brief agony which, as they thought, would precede the entire destruction of the wicked. And, therefore, the word "hell," in the sense in which we use it, is in every case a monstrous mistranslation of the word "Gehenna," and should be replaced by it.

VIII.—UNIVERSAL REDEMPTION.

I MAY now assume, I think, that the main conclusions at which we have arrived are tolerably familiar to you, or that they may be recalled to your memories by a mere touch.

We have seen, then, that the English verb "to damn" is used to translate two Greek words which never mean more than "to condemn," and commonly mean only "to judge;" that our English noun "hell" is employed to render three Greek substantives—Tartarus, Hades, Gehenna, each of which, so far from indicating an endless state of torment, indicates only an intermediate and temporary condition of the soul. . . .

For the present I must be content with carrying the argument to a close, by adducing those Scriptures which either expressly affirm or obviously imply *the universality of the redemption* wrought by God in and through Christ Jesus our Lord. . . .

From the dawn of Revelation down to its latest recorded utterance we find the very widest scope assigned to the redeeming purpose and work of God our Saviour. Even in those early days when one man, one family, one nation were successively chosen to be the depositories of Divine Truth; when, therefore, if ever we might expect to find the redemptive purpose of God disclosed within narrow and local limitations, when unquestionably it was in much fettered and restrained by personal promises and by national and temporary institutions, that Divine purpose is for ever overleaping every limit, every transient localization and restraint, and claiming as its proper sphere "all the souls that are" and shall be. . . .

IX.—WHAT WE SHALL BE.

WHEN we were commencing our study, at the very outset of these Lectures, I forewarned you that, in all probability, we should find in the Word of God no clear and detailed disclosures of the final estate whether of the good or of the bad; . . . My warning has been abundantly verified. Although we have now studied most of the leading passages in the Gospels and Epistles which relate to the future life of the human race, we have found none as yet which carries us beyond the aeons of time. While the New Testament has much to tell us of our future conditions, it has nothing, or nothing definite, to say of our final estate, but compels us, in so far as that is concerned, to "*trust* in the living God who is the Saviour of all men," and in a very special sense the Saviour of all who believe in Him. And, indeed, there hardly can be a *final* estate for finite creatures such as we are. We must ever be reaching forth to things before and beyond us, ever rising through grade after grade of being and of attainment, ever approaching yet never reaching that infinite perfection which we name God.

The Scriptures, then, have much to teach us of the *future,* though not much of the *final,* estate of men. And what they teach, in so far at least as we have been able to gather it up, comes to this. No man is wholly good, no man wholly bad. Still some men may fairly be called good on the whole, although much sin and imperfection still cleaves to them; and others may fairly be called bad on the whole, although there is still much in them that is good, and still more which is capable of becoming good. When we die, we shall all receive the due recompense of our deeds, of all our deeds, whether they have been good or whether they have been bad.

If, by the grace of God, we have been good on the whole, we may hope to rise into a large and happy spiritual kingdom in which all that is pure and noble and kind in us will develop into new vigour and clothe itself with new beauty; in which also we shall find the very discipline we need in order that we may be wholly purged from sin and imperfection; in which we may undo much that we have done wrongly, do again and with perfect grace that which we have done imperfectly, become what we have wished and aimed to be, achieve what we have longed to achieve, attain the wisdom, the gifts and powers and graces to which we have aspired: in which, above all, we may be engaged in errands of usefulness and compassion by which the purpose of the Divine love and grace will be fully accomplished.

If we have been bad on the whole, we may hope—and we ought to *hope* for it—to pass into a painful discipline so keen and searching that we shall become conscious of our sins and feel that we are only receiving the due reward of them; but, since there has been some good in us, and this good is capable of being drawn out and disentangled from the evil which clouded and marred it, we may also hope, by the very discipline and torment of our spirits, to be led to repentance, and, through repentance, unto life: we may hope that the disclosures of the spiritual world will take a spiritual effect upon us, gradually raising and renewing us till we too are prepared to enter the Paradise of God and behold the presence of the Lord and the glory of his power: we may hope that our friends who have already been redeemed will pity us and minister to us, bringing us not simply a cup of cold water to cool our tongue, but words of instruction and life. And as for the great mass of our fellowmen, we may hope and believe that those who have had no chance of salvation here will have one there; that those who have had a poor chance will get a better one: that those who have had a good chance and lost it will get a new but a severer chance, . . .

This, on the whole, I take to be the teaching of Scripture concerning the lot of men in the age to come,—a teaching which enables us to see "beneath the abyss of hell a bottomless abyss of love." And if it clash with some dogmas that we have held and some interpretations which are familiar to us, it nevertheless accords, not with "the mind of Christ" only, but also with the dictates of Reason and Conscience, the voices of God within the soul. It presents no such sudden break in our life as, in the teeth of all probability, we have been wont to conceive; no heaven for which we feel that even the best of us must be unfit, no hell which is a monstrous offence to our sense of justice. It promises to every man the mercy of justice, of a due reward for all he has been and done; and, while it impresses on us the utter hatefulness and misery of sin, it holds out to every one of us the prospect of being redeemed from all sin and uncleanness by that just God who is also a Saviour. Nor does it less accord with the demands of Science than with the dictates of Reason and the Moral Sense; for it carries on the evolution of the human race through all the ages to come. And, therefore, let others think as they will, and cherish what trust they will: *"but"* as for us, with the Apostle of the Gentiles, our own Apostle, *"we trust in the living God who is the Saviour of all men."*

9.7 Charles Haddon Spurgeon, Articles on the Down Grade

By any standard of measurement, Charles Haddon Spurgeon (1834-1892) was a giant among English Baptists. For almost forty years he was pastor of New Park Street, London, a small congregation which he built into one of the largest and most influential churches in the world. Spurgeon was known not only for his powerful preaching, but also for his Pastor's College, orphanage, sermons published on two continents, and a widely circulated religious monthly, *The Sword and Trowel*. Reared in the Puritan tradition, Spurgeon was quite conservative in theology. Apparently the publication of Samuel Cox's *Salvator Mundi* (see document 9.6) crystallized Spurgeon's growing conviction that dangerous doctrinal liberalism was eroding Baptist life. In 1887 the growing tensions about theology among Baptists erupted into a major controversy, called the Down Grade. Spurgeon entered the fray with his usual energy, publishing several articles in *The Sword and Trowel*. Frustrated that no more of the Baptists rallied to his banner, and cut to the quick by a censure by the Baptist Union, Spurgeon withdrew from the Baptist Union, thus severing his already tenuous ties to organized Baptist life in England. *Source: The Sword and Trowel*, August 1887, November 1887, February 1888.

A. Charles Haddon Spurgeon, *Another Word Concerning the Down-Grade*

No lover of the gospel can conceal from himself the fact that the days are evil. We are willing to make a large discount from our apprehensions on the score of natural timidity, the caution of age, and the weakness produced by pain; but yet our solemn conviction is that things are much worse in many churches than they seem to be, and are rapidly tending downward. Read those newspapers which represent the Broad School of Dissent, and ask yourself, How much farther could they go? What doctrine remains to be abandoned? What other truth to be the object of contempt? A new religion has been initiated, which is no more Christianity than chalk is cheese; and this religion, being destitute of moral honesty, palms itself off as the old faith with slight improvements, and on this plea usurps pulpits which were erected for gospel preaching. The Atonement is scouted, the inspiration of Scripture is derided, the Holy Spirit is degraded into an influence, the punishment of sin is turned into fiction, and the resurrection into a myth, and yet these enemies of our faith expect us to call them brethren, and maintain a confederacy with them!

At the back of doctrinal falsehood comes a natural decline of spiritual life, evidenced by a taste for questionable amusements, and a weariness of devotional meetings. At a certain meeting of ministers and church-officers, one after another doubted the value of prayer-meetings; all confessed that they had a very small attendance, and several acknowledged without the slightest compunction that they had quite given them up. What means this? Are churches in a right condition when they have only one meeting for prayer in a week, and that a mere skeleton? Churches which have prayer-meetings several times on the Lord's-day, and very frequently during the week, yet feel their need of more prayer; but what can be said of those who very seldom practise united supplication? Are there few conversions? Do the congregations dwindle? Who wonders that this is the case when the spirit of prayer has departed?

As for questionable amusements—time was when a Nonconformist minister who was known to attend the play-house would soon have found himself without a church. And justly so; for no man can long possess the confidence, even of the most worldly, who is known to be a haunter of theatres. Yet at the present time it is matter of notoriety that preachers of no mean repute defend the play-house, and do so because they have been seen there. Is it any wonder that church members forget their vows of consecration, and run with the unholy in the ways of frivolity, when they hear that persons are tolerated in the pastorate who do the same? We doubt not that, for writing these lines we shall incur the charge of prudery and bigotry, and this will but prove how low are the tone and spirit of the churches in many places. The fact is, that many would like to unite church and stage, cards and prayer, dancing and sacraments. If we are powerless to stem this torrent, we can at least warn men of its existence, and entreat them to keep out of it. When the old faith is gone, and enthusiasm for the gospel is extinct, it is no wonder that people seek something else in the way of delight. Lacking bread, they feed on ashes; rejecting the way of the Lord, they run greedily in the path of folly. . . .

Alas! many are returning to the poisoned cups which drugged that declining generation, when it surrendered itself to Unitarian lethargy. Too many ministers are toying with the deadly cobra of "another gospel," in the form of "modern thought." As a consequence, their congregations are thinning: the more spiritual of their members join the "Brethren," or some other company of "believers unattached"; while the more wealthy, and show-loving, with some of unquestionable devoutness, go off to the Church of England. . . .

The case is mournful. Certain ministers are making infidels. Avowed atheists are not a tenth as dangerous as those preachers who scatter doubt and stab at faith. A plain man told us the other day that two ministers had derided him because he thought we should pray for rain. A gracious woman bemoaned in my presence that a precious promise in Isaiah which had comforted her had been declared by her minister to be uninspired. It is a common thing to hear working-men excuse their wickedness by the statement that there is no hell, "the parson says so." But we need not prolong our mention of painful facts. Germany was made unbelieving by her preachers, and England is following in her track. Attendance at places of worship is declining, and reverence for holy things is vanishing; and we solemnly believe this to be largely attributable to the scepticism which has flashed from the pulpit and spread among the people. Possibly the men who uttered the doubt never intended it to go so far; but none the less they have done the ill, and cannot undo it. Their own observation ought to teach them better. Have these advanced thinkers filled their own chapels? Have they, after all, prospered through discarding the old methods? Possibly, in a few cases genius and tact have carried these gentry over the destructive results of their ministry; but in many cases their pretty new theology has scattered their congregations. In meeting-houses holding a thousand, or twelve hundred, or fifteen hundred, places once packed to the ceiling with ardent hearers, how small are the numbers now! We would mention instances, but we forbear. The places which the gospel filled the new nonsense has emptied, and will keep empty. . . .

The other day we were asked to mention the name of some person who might be a suitable pastor for a vacant church, and the deacon who wrote said, "Let him be a converted man, and let him be one who believes what he preaches; for there are those around us who give us the idea that they have neither part nor lot in the matter." This remark is more commonly made than we like to remember, and there is, alas! too much need for it. A student from a certain college preached to a congregation we sometimes visit such a sermon that the deacon said to him in the vestry, "Sir, do you believe in the Holy Ghost?" The youth replied, "I suppose I do." To which the deacon answered, "I suppose you do *not,* or you would not have insulted us with such false doctrine." . . .

It now becomes a serious question how far those who abide by the faith once delivered to the saints should fraternize with those who have turned aside to another gospel. Christian love has its claims, and divisions are to be shunned as grievous evils; but how far are we justified in being in confederacy with those who are departing from the truth? It is a difficult question to answer so as to keep the balance of the duties. For the present it behoves believers to be cautious, lest they lend their support and countenance to the betrayers of the Lord. It is one thing to overleap all boundaries of denominational restriction for the truth's sake: this we hope all godly men will do more and more. It is quite another policy which would urge us to subordinate the maintenance of truth to denominational prosperity and unity. Numbers of easy-minded people wink at error so long as it is committed by a clever man and a good-natured brother, who has so many fine points about him. Let each believer judge for himself; but, for our part, we have put on a few fresh bolts to our door, and we have given orders to keep the chain up; for, under colour of begging the friendship of the servant, there are those about who aim at robbing THE MASTER.

We fear it is hopeless ever to form a society which can keep out men base enough to profess one thing and believe another; but it might be possible to make an informal alliance among all who hold the Christianity of their fathers. Little as they might be able to do, they could at least protest, and as far as possible free themselves of that complicity which will be involved in a conspiracy of silence. If for a while the evangelicals are doomed to go down, let them die fighting, and in the full assurance that their gospel will have a resurrection when the inventions of "modern thought" shall be burned up with fire unquenchable.

B.   Charles Haddon Spurgeon, *A Fragment upon the Down-Grade Controversy*

By this time many of our readers will be weary of the Down-Grade controversy: they cannot be one-tenth so much tired of it, or tried by it, as we are. . . .

Hitherto (and this matter is now merely in its beginning), the chief answer has come from the public teachers, and as far as their public answer is concerned, it amounts, at its best interpretation, to the admission that there may be a little amiss, but not enough to speak about. They are sorry that a few brethren go rather too far, but they are dear brethren still. Many good men lament the fact that liberty is, in certain instances, degenerating into license, but they solace themselves with the belief that on the whole it is a sign of health and vigour: the bough is so fruitful that it runs over the wall. At any rate, denominational peace must be kept up, and there must be no discordant charge of defection to break the chorus of mutual congratulation.

The intense desire for union has its commendable side, and we are far from undervaluing it. Precious also is the protest for liberty, which certain valorous souls have lifted up. We rejoice that our brethren will not submit their consciences to any man; but the mercy is that we do not know of any man who desires that they should. Specially is the object of their brave opposition as free from a desire to rule over them as from the wish to be ruled by them. It is a pity that such loyalty to liberty could not be associated with an equally warm expression of resolve to be loyal to Christ and his gospel. It would be a grievous fault if the sons of the Puritans did not maintain the freedom of their consciences, but it will be no less a crime if they withdraw those consciences from under the yoke of Christ. . . .

As a matter of fact, believers in Christ's atonement are now in declared religious union with those who make light of it; believers in Holy Scripture are in confederacy with those who deny plenary inspiration; those who hold evangelical doctrine are in open alliance with those who call the fall a fable, who deny the personality of the Holy Ghost, who call justification by faith immoral, and hold that there is another probation after death, and a future restitution for the lost. Yes, we have before us the wretched spectacle of professedly orthodox Christians publicly avowing their union with those who deny the faith, and scarcely concealing their contempt for those who cannot be guilty of such gross disloyalty to Christ. To be very plain, we are unable to call these things Christian Unions, they begin to look like Confederacies in Evil. Before the face of God we fear that they wear no other aspect. To our inmost heart this is a sad truth from which we cannot break away.

It is lawful to unite with all sorts of men for good and benevolent and necessary purposes, even as at a fire. Pagan and Papist and Protestant may each one hand on the buckets, and in a sinking ship, heathen and Christian alike are bound to take turns at the pumps. For useful, philanthropical, and political purposes, united action is allowable among men of the most diverse views in religion. But the case before us is that of a distinctly religious communion, a professed fellowship in Christ. Is this to be made so wide that those who contradict each other on vital points may yet pretend to be at one? . . .

The largest charity towards those who are loyal to the Lord Jesus, and yet do not see with us on secondary matters, is the duty of all true Christians. But how are we to act towards those who deny his vicarious sacrifice, and ridicule the great truth of justification by his righteousness? These are not mistaken friends, but enemies of the cross of Christ. There is no use in employing circumlocutions and polite terms of expression:— where Christ is not received as to the cleansing power of his blood and the justifying merit of his righteousness, he is not received at all.

It used to be generally accepted in the Christian Church that the line of Christian communion was drawn hard and fast at the Deity of our Lord; but even this would appear to be altered now. In various ways the chasm has been bridged, and during the past few years several ministers have crossed into Unitarianism, and have declared that they perceived little or no difference in the two sides of the gulf. In all probability there was no difference to perceive in the regions where they abode. It is our solemn conviction that where there can be no real spiritual communion there should be no pretence of fellowship. *Fellowship with known and vital error is participation in sin.* Those who know and love the truth of God cannot have fellowship with that which is diametrically opposed thereto, and there can be no reason why they should pretend that they have such fellowship.

We cheerfully admit that among men who possess the divine life, and a consequent discernment of truth, there will be differences of attainment and perception; and that these differences are no barriers to love and union. But it is another matter when we come to receiving or rejecting the vicarious sacrifice and the justifying righteousness of our Lord. We who believe Holy Scripture to be the inspired truth of God cannot have fellowship with those who deny the authority from which we derive all our teaching. We go to our pulpits to save a fallen race, and believe that they must be saved in this life, or perish for ever: how can we profess brotherhood with those who deny the fall of man, and hold out to him the hope of another probation after death? They have all the liberty in the world, and we would be the last to abridge it; but that liberty cannot demand our co-operation. If these men believe such things, let them teach them, and construct churches, unions, and brotherhoods for themselves! Why must they come among us? When they enter among us at unawares, and are resolved to stay, what can we do? The question is not soon answered; but, surely, in no case will we give them fellowship, or profess to do so.

During the past month many have put to us the anxious question, *"What shall we do?"* To these we have had no answer to give except that each one must act for himself after seeking direction of the Lord. In our own case we intimated our course of action in last month's paper. We retire at once and distinctly from the Baptist Union. The Baptist Churches are each one of them self-contained and independent. The Baptist Union is only a voluntary association of such churches, and it is a simple matter for a church or an individual to withdraw from it. The Union, as at present constituted, has no disciplinary power, for it has no doctrinal basis whatever, and we see no reason why every form of belief and misbelief should not be comprehended in it so long as immersion only is acknowledged as baptism. . . . A large number have this state of things in admiration, and will go on with it; we have no such admiration, and therefore have ceased from it. But we want outsiders to know that we are in nowise altered in our faith, or in our denominational position. As a baptized believer, our place is where it has ever been.

Why not start a new Denomination? This is not a question for which we have any liking. There are denominations enough. If there were a new denomination formed the thieves and robbers who have entered other "gardens walled round" would climb into this also, and so nothing would be gained. . . . Since each vessel is seaworthy in herself, let the hampering ropes be cut clean away, and no more lines of communication be thrown out until we know that we are alongside a friend who sails under the same glorious flag. In the isolation of independency, tempered by the love of the Spirit which binds us to all the faithful in Christ Jesus, we think the lovers of the gospel will for the present find their immediate safety. Oh, that the day would come when, in a larger communion than any sect can offer, all those who are one in Christ may be able to blend in manifest unity! This can only come by the way of growing spiritual life, clearer light upon the one eternal truth, and a closer cleaving in all things to him who is the Head, even Christ Jesus.

C.   Charles Haddon Spurgeon, *The Baptist Union Censure*

The censure passed upon me by the Council of the Baptist Union will be weighed by the faithful, and estimated at its true value. "Afterwards they have no more that they can do." I brought no charges before the members of the Council, because they could only judge by their constitution, and that document lays down no doctrinal basis except the belief that "the immersion of believers is the only Christian baptism." Even the mention of evangelical sentiments has been cut out from their printed programme. No one can be heterodox under this constitution, unless he should forswear his baptism. I offered to pay the fee for Counsel's opinion upon this matter, but my offer was not accepted by the deputation. There was, therefore, nothing for me to work upon, whatever evidence I might bring. What would be the use of exposing myself to threatened law-suits to gain nothing at all? Whatever may be said to the contrary, if we go to its authorized declaration of principles, it is clear that the Union is incompetent for any doctrinal judgment, except it should be needful to ascertain a person's views on baptism. I decline to submit to it any case which would be quite beyond its powers. Would any rational man act otherwise? I have rather too much proof than too little; but I am not going to involve others in litigation when nothing is to be gained.

I do not complain of the censure of the Council, or feel the least care about it. . . . Nevertheless, I would like all Christendom to know that all I asked of the Union is that it be formed on a Scriptural basis; and that I never sought to intrude upon it any Calvinistic or other personal creed, but only that form of belief which has been accepted for many years by the Evangelical Alliance, which includes members of well-nigh all Christian communities.

To this it was replied that there is an objection to any creed whatever. This is a principle which one may fairly discuss. Surely, what we believe may be stated, may be written, may be made known; and what is this but to make and promulgate a creed? Baptists from the first have issued their confessions of faith. Even the present Baptist Union itself has a creed about baptism, though about nothing else. . . . Certain members of the Council talk about having expelled Unitarians: does not this admit that they have already an unwritten Trinitarian creed? Why not print it? Possibly "modern thought" has methods of getting over this which have never occurred to my unsophisticated mind.

To say that "a creed comes between a man and his God," is to suppose that it is not true; for truth, however definitely stated, does not divide the believer from his Lord. So far as I am concerned, that which I believe I am not ashamed to state in the plainest possible language; and the truth I hold I embrace because I believe it to be the mind of God revealed in his infallible Word. How can it divide me from God who revealed it? It is one means of my communion with my Lord, that I receive his words as well as himself, and submit my understanding to what I see to be taught by him. Say what he may, I accept it because he says it, and therein pay him the humble worship of my inmost soul.

I am unable to sympathize with a man who says he has no creed; because I believe him to be in the wrong by his own showing. He ought to have a creed. What is equally certain, he has a creed—he must have one, even though he repudiates the notion. His very unbelief is, in a sense, a creed. . . .

Every Union, unless it is a mere fiction, must be based upon certain principles. How can we unite except upon some great common truths? And the doctrine of baptism by immersion is not sufficient for a groundwork. Surely, to be a Baptist is not everything. If I disagree with a man on ninety-nine points, but happen to be one with him in baptism, this can never furnish such ground of unity as I have with another with whom I believe in ninety-nine points, and only happen to differ upon one ordinance. To form a union with a single Scriptural ordinance as its sole distinctive reason for existence has been well likened to erecting a pyramid upon its apex: the whole edifice must sooner or later come down. . . .

To alter the foundation of a building is a difficult undertaking. Underpinning is expensive and perilous work. It might be more satisfactory to take the whole house down, and reconstruct it. If I had believed that the Baptist Union could be made a satisfactory structure, I could not then have remained in it; because to do so would have violated my conscience. But *my* conscience is no guide for others. Those who believe in the structure, and think that they can rectify its foundation, have my hearty sympathy in the attempt. Let them give themselves to it earnestly and with firm resolve: they will have need of all their earnestness and resolution. In the Assembly, in the Associations, and in the churches they can urge their views, and make it plain that they mean to make the Union an avowedly Evangelical body on the old lines of faith. This they must do boldly, and without flinching. I have no very assured hope of their success, for the difficulties are exceedingly great; but let them combine, and work unitedly, and persistently, year after year, and they may do something, if not everything. It is not for me to lead in a work which I have been forced to abandon; but there are other men who are less known, but not less resolute, and these should take their turn. The warfare has been made too personal; and certain incidents in it, upon which I will not dwell, have made it too painful for me to feel any pleasure in the idea of going on with it. It might even appear that I desired to be reinstated in the Union, or wished to head a party in it, and this is very far from my mind. But let no man imagine that I shall cease from my protests against false doctrine, or lay down the sword of which I have thrown away the scabbard. However much invited to do so, I shall not commence personalities, nor disclose the wretched facts in all their details; but with confirmatory evidence perpetually pouring in upon me, and a solemn conviction that the dark conspiracy to overthrow the truth must be dragged to light, I shall not cease to expose doctrinal declension wherever I see it. With the Baptist Union, as such, I have now no hampering connection; but so far as it takes its part in the common departure from the truth, it will have to put up with my strictures, although it has so graciously kicked me under pretext of deliberation.

Will those who are with me in this struggle remember me in their constant prayers to the Lord, whom in this matter I serve in my soul and spirit?

10
United for Mission: Baptists in America, 1800-1845

The first half of the nineteenth century proved to be a time of unprecedented growth for Baptists in America. In 1814 they formed the General Missionary Convention of the Baptist Denomination, commonly called the Triennial Convention, their first organization of national scope. However, national cooperation in common tasks proved more an ideal than a reality, and the fragile unity was broken in 1845 with formation of the Southern Baptist Convention.

Since the foreign mission movement was a driving force among Baptists at the time, it is not surprising that much of this chapter centers around that movement. An account of the conversion of the Judsons to Baptist views, and especially the vivid letters of Mrs. Judson, are included because they did so much to shape the Baptist identity of the time.

John Mason Peck and the home mission work claim attention and space (10.10), and could justifiably claim more. The pros and cons of theological education are illustrated from the writings of Richard Furman, Jesse Mercer, and Robert Semple (10.12). The "anti-everything" spirit of some Baptists of the time is illustrated through the writings of John Taylor and Daniel Parker (10.13).

The Alexander Campbell movement had a profound impact upon Baptists in the nineteenth century. Various aspects of that movement are illustrated by documents drawn from various associations and from the insightful analysis of J. H. Spencer (10.14). Baptist involvement in the slavery controversy is explored at some length (10.19).

The schism of 1845, out of which came the Southern Baptist Convention, looms much larger in Baptist history now than it may have appeared at the time. Several documents are included to show some of the causes, the painful process, and the continuing impact of that schism (10.28).

10.1 The Boston Female Society

The awakening of women to their potential in the church was an important part of the rise of the foreign missions movement in American religion early in the nineteenth century. In churches throughout the country "female societies" began to appear, raising awareness of as well as funds for missions. These local organizations led in time to regional and national women's societies. Among Baptists, the Boston Female Society proved influential both in the North and the South. Its energetic secretary, Mary Webb, by her letters and personal example helped to arouse a generation of women to their potential, not only for missions, but also for greater involvement in church and society. The original printing used a character similar to our "f" to represent "s." For technical reasons and for clarity's sake, "s" is used here. *Source: Massachusetts Baptist Missionary Magazine,* March 1813.

An ADDRESS from "the Boston Female Society, for Missionary Purposes," to Females professing godliness.

IT will probably be recollected by the female readers of this Magazine, that in March laft, a letter appeared, addressed "to the female friends of Zion," ("from the Boston female society for Missionary purposes;") recommending to female religious societies, to set apart the first Monday afternoon of every month for special prayer; and likewise soliciting a correspondence with them by letter. It was with much trembling and diffidence, we took this public step; but from the success which has attended our feeble efforts, we have reason to believe we were directed to it by unerring wisdom.

Understanding it to be the desire of some of our friends to know what encouragement we have met with, and believing it will not be wholly uninteresting to others, we are happy to announce, that letters have been received from a number of societies of different denominations expressing their warmest approbation of our proposals, and their determination to unite in concert with us. [A postscript in the letter at this point shows that reports had been received from 21 societies, 17 in Massachusetts, 2 in Rhode Island, and one each in New Hampshire and Connecticut.]

By this means we have come to the knowledge of societies and individuals, which before we did not know existed; and we trust we shall have increasing occasion to rejoice, that this channel of intercourse has been opened. . . . We are aware, that by thus coming out, we lay ourselves open to the remarks of the enemies of religion; but believing the path of duty to be guarded on the right hand and on the left, we feel safe. Our object is not to render ourselves *important,* but, *useful.* We have no wish to go out of our province, nor do we undertake to become teachers in Israel; it is our *pleasure* to see our brethren go before, and we are content to be permitted "to glean after the reapers," and follow with our earnest prayers, their more extensive labours: *this* privilege we *must covet.* We cannot be willing to remain in a state of neutrality in a cause which demands so much zeal and activity; nor can we feel satisfied with being made partakers of the grace of the gospel ourselves, without desising to be instrumental of conveying the knowledge of it to others.

We have no doubt, our sisters feel with us, that it is our duty on these occasions, particularly to bear on our hearts the ministers of the gospel; especially our *Missionary* brethren. When we consider how much wisdom, prudence, faith, patience and grace they need, to qualify them for the office; how much they need the supports and comforts of religion in their own souls, in order to render them faithful to the souls of others; and how necessary the influences of the Holy Spirit, to accompany their labours, we must feel culpable if we are not engaged in "holding up their hands." Let us then, unitedly plead for them, and though seas may roll, and mountains and vallies intervene between them and us, they will *feel* that their Father's children are praying for them. . . .

May we not here be permitted, to entreat our dear sisters to take into consideration the important work, in which our afflicted brethren in India are engaged, viz. the translation of the Scriptures into the various languages of that country. Should every Christian in the United States contribute the inconsiderable sum of 25 cents per year to this purpose, some thousands of dollars would be annually devoted to aid a work of the greatest magnitude in which it is possible for mortals to be engaged. And whoever bestows a mite to that object, will no doubt be instrumental of conveying a blessing to the latest posterity. . . .

In behalf of the Society,

Boston, Dec. 7, 1812.   MARY WEBB, *Secretary.*

10.2   Adoniram Judson, Pioneer Baptist Missionary

Adoniram Judson (1788-1850) sailed in 1812 as one of the first appointed foreign missionaries to go out from America. Judson and his wife, Ann, converted to Baptist views aboard ship and, upon their arrival in India, received immersion as Baptists. This conversion triggered a chain of events in America that led to the formation of the General Missionary Convention in 1814, the first national body of Baptists in America. Judson thus helped inaugurate the great era of Baptist missionary organizations in America. Perhaps the spirit of this pioneer missionary is best perceived through his letters. The following three letters by Judson deal with his conversion to Baptist views and his desire to see a Baptist missionary work formed. *Source:* Francis Wayland, *A Memoir of the*

Life and Labors of the Rev. Adoniram Judson, 2 vols. (Boston: Phillips, Sampson and Company, 1854), 1:109, 110, 111-112.

A. Letter to English missionaries requesting immersion

CALCUTTA, August 27, 1812.

TO THE REV. MESSRS. CAREY, MARSHMAN, AND WARD.

As you have been ignorant of the late exercises of my mind on the subject of baptism, the communication which I am about to make may occasion you some surprise.

It is now about four months since I took the subject into serious and prayerful consideration. My inquiries commenced during my passage from America, and after much laborious research and painful trial, which I shall not now detail, have issued in entire conviction, that *the immersion of a professing believer is the only Christian baptism.*

In these exercises I have not been alone. Mrs. Judson has been engaged in a similar examination, and has come to the same conclusion. Feeling, therefore, that we are in an unbaptized state, we wish to profess our faith in Christ by being baptized in obedience to his sacred commands.

B. Letter of Resignation to Dr. Worcester, Corresponding Secretary, American Board of Commissioners for Foreign Missions

REV. AND DEAR SIR: My change of sentiments on the subject of baptism is considered by my missionary brethren as incompatible with my continuing their fellow-laborer in the mission which they contemplate on the Island of Madagascar; and it will, I presume, be considered by the Board of Commissioners as equally incompatible with my continuing their missionary. The board will, undoubtedly, feel as unwilling to support a Baptist missionary as I feel to comply with their instructions, which particularly direct us to baptize *"credible believers with their households."*

The dissolution of my connection with the Board of Commissioners, and a separation from my dear missionary brethren, I consider most distressing consequences of my late change of sentiments, and indeed, the most distressing events which have ever befallen me I have now the prospect before me of going alone to some distant island, unconnected with any society at present existing, from which I might be furnished with assistant laborers or pecuniary support. Whether the Baptist churches in America will compassionate my situation, I know not. I hope, therefore, that while my friends condemn what they deem a departure from the truth, they will at least pity me and pray for me.

With the same sentiments of affection and respect as ever,

I am, sir, your friend and servant,

ADONIRAM JUDSON, JR.

C. Letter to Lucius Bolles about forming a Baptist mission society

CALCUTTA, September 1, 1812.

REV. SIR: I recollect that, during a short interview I had with you in Salem, I suggested the formation of a society among the Baptists in America for the support of foreign missions, in imitation of the exertions of your English brethren. Little did I then expect to be personally concerned in such an attempt.

Within a few months, I have experienced an entire change of sentiments on the subject of baptism. My doubts concerning the correctness of my former system of belief commenced during my passage from America to this country; and after many painful trials, which none can know but those who are taught to relinquish a system in which they had been educated, I settled down in the full persuasion that the immersion of a professing believer in Christ is the only Christian baptism.

Mrs. Judson is united with me in this persuasion. We have signified our views and wishes to the Baptist missionaries at Serampore, and expect to be baptized in this city next Lord's day.

A separation from my missionary brethren, and a dissolution of my connection with the Board of Commissioners, seem to be necessary consequences. The missionaries at Serampore are exerted to the utmost of their ability in managing and supporting their extensive and complicated mission.

Under these circumstances I look to you. Alone, in this foreign heathen land, I make my appeal to those whom, with their permission, I will call *my Baptist brethren* in the United States.

With the advice of the brethren at Serampore, I am contemplating a mission on one of the eastern islands. They have lately sent their brother Chater to Ceylon, and their brother Robinson to Java. At present, Amboyna seems to present the most favorable opening. Fifty thousand souls are there perishing without the means of life; and the situation of the island is such that a mission there established might, with the blessing of God, be extended to the neighboring islands in those seas.

But should I go thither, it is a most painful reflection that I must go alone, and also uncertain of the means of support. But I will trust in God. He has frequently enabled me to praise his divine goodness, and will never forsake those who put their trust in him. I am, dear sir,

Yours, in the Lord Jesus,

ADONIRAM JUDSON, JR.

10.3 Ann Hasseltine Judson, Letters to Family and Friends

Perhaps no one did more to arouse American interest in foreign missions than did the beautiful daughter of Deacon Hasseltine. Ann Hasseltine (1789-1826) was married to Adoniram Judson in 1812 and sailed with him for India. She shared her husband's conversion to Baptist views, howbeit reluctantly, and also shared his trials and triumphs as a pioneer missionary. Her newsy letters to family and friends told vivid and interesting details about day-to-day life among the "heathen." Perhaps her letters did as much to create interest and raise funds for missions as did her husband's more formal missionary writings. *Sources:* Francis Wayland, *A Memoir of the Life and Labors of the Rev. Adoniram Judson,* 2 vols. (Boston: Phillips, Sampson and Company, 1854), 1:105-106. Also in *Massachusetts Baptist Missionary* Magazine, May 1813. *The Latter Day Luminary,* February 1820).

A. Letter to a friend about becoming a Baptist

September 7, 1812.

Can you, my dear Nancy, still love me, still desire to hear from me, when I tell you I have become a Baptist? If I judge from my own feelings, I answer, you will, and that my differing from you in those things which do not affect our salvation will not diminish your affection for me, or make you unconcerned for my welfare. You may, perhaps, think this change very sudden, as I have said nothing of it before; but, my dear girl, this alteration hath not been the work of an hour, a day, or a month. The subject has been maturely, candidly, and, I hope, prayerfully examined for months.

An examination of the subject of baptism commenced on board the Caravan. As Mr. Judson was continuing the translation of the New Testament, which he began in America, he had many doubts respecting the meaning of the word *baptize.* This, with the idea

of meeting the Baptists at Serampore, when he would wish to defend his own sentiments, induced a more thorough examination of the foundation of the Pedobaptist system. The more he examined, the more his doubts increased; and, unwilling as he was to
admit it, he was *afraid* the Baptists were right and he wrong. After we arrived at Calcutta, his attention was turned from this subject to the concerns of the mission, and the
difficulties with government. But as his mind was still uneasy, he again renewed the
subject. I felt afraid he would become a Baptist, and frequently urged the unhappy
consequences if he should. But he said his duty compelled him to satisfy his own mind,
and embrace those sentiments which appeared most concordant with Scripture.

I always took the Pedobaptist side in reasoning with him, even after I was as doubtful
of the truth of their system as he. We left Serampore to reside in Calcutta a week or two,
before the arrival of our brethren; and as we had nothing in particular to occupy our
attention, we confined it exclusively to this subject. We procured the best authors on
both sides, compared them with the Scriptures, examined and reexamined the sentiments of Baptists and Pedobaptists, and were finally compelled, from a conviction of
truth, to embrace those of the former. Thus, my dear Nancy, we are confirmed Baptists,
not because we wished to be, but because truth compelled us to be. We have endeavored
to count the cost, and be prepared for the many severe trials resulting from this change
of sentiment. We anticipate the loss of reputation, and of the affection and esteem of
many of our American friends. But the most trying circumstance attending this change,
and that which has caused most pain, is the separation which must take place between
us and our dear missionary associates. Although we are attached to each other, and
should doubtless live very happily together, yet the brethren do not think it best we
should unite in one mission. These things, my dear Nancy, have caused us to weep and
pour out our hearts in prayer to Him whose directions we so much wish and need. We
feel that we are alone in the world, with no real friend but each other, no one on whom
we can depend but God.

B. Letter about first convert in Burma, 1819

Rangoon Mission-house, June 2d, 1819.

MY DEAR MRS. S———,

In my last, I mentioned Mr. Judson's commencing public preaching in a building
which we had erected for that purpose, and which you will in future know by the name
zayat. Little did I think, when I last wrote, that I should so soon have the joyful intelligence to communicate, that one Burman has embraced the Christian religion, and given
good evidence of being a true disciple of the dear Redeemer. This event, this single
trophy of victorious grace, has filled our hearts with sensations hardly to be conceived
by Christians in Christian countries. This event has convinced us that God can and does
operate on the minds of the most dark and ignorant, and that he makes his own truths,
his own word, the instrument of operation. It serves also, to encourage us to hope that
the Lord has other chosen ones in this place.

As Mr. Judson has given some account of the first impressions of this man, and as I
have had him particularly under my instruction since his conversion, I will give you
some of his remarks in his own words, with which you will be much interested. "Beside
Jesus Christ, I see no way of salvation. He is the Son of the God who has no beginning,
no end. He so loved and pitied men that he suffered death in their stead. My mind is sore
on account of the sins I have committed during the whole of my life, particularly in
worshipping a false god. Our religion, pure as it may be, does not purify the minds of
those who believe it: it cannot restrain from sin. But the religion of Jesus Christ makes
the mind pure. His disciples desire not to grieve him by sinning. In our religion there is

no way to escape the punishment due to sin; but, according to the religion of Christ, he himself has died in order to deliver his disciples. I wish all the Burmans would become his disciples; then we should meet together as you do in your country; then we should all be happy together in heaven. How great are my thanks to Jesus Christ for sending teachers to this country, and how great are my thanks to the teachers for coming! Had they never come and built that zayat, I should never have heard of Christ and the true God. I mourn that so much of my life passed away before I heard of this religion. How much I have lost!"

It is peculiarly interesting to see with what eagerness he drinks in the truths from the scriptures. A few days ago, I was reading with him Christ's sermon on the mount. He was deeply impressed, and unusually solemn. "These words (said he) take hold on my very liver; they make me tremble. Here God commands us to do every thing that is good in secret, not to be seen of men. How unlike our religion is this! . . ."

We have taken him into our employ for the present, as a copier, though our primary object was to have him near us, that we might have a better opportunity of knowing more of him before he received baptism, and of imparting to him more instruction than occasional visits might afford. Mornings and evenings he spends in reading, and scriptures, and when we all meet in the hall for family worship, he comes and sits with us; though he cannot understand, he says he can think of God in his heart.

10.4   Richard Furman, Address at Formation of the Triennial Convention, 1814

At a time when many Baptists either feared or ignored organization beyond the local church, Richard Furman (1755-1825) advocated the formation of a national convention to lead the churches to work together in foreign missions, Christian education, home missions, and church planting. The Triennial Convention, formed in 1814, embodied many of Furman's ideas. This long-time pastor of First Baptist Church, Charleston, South Carolina, advocated a unified, cooperative approach that would enable the churches to do together what they could not do separately. Furman's organizational ideas also appear in the Baptist State Convention in South Carolina in 1821, and the Southern Baptist Convention in 1845. *Source: Proceedings of the Baptist Convention for Missionary Purposes* (Philadelphia: n.p., 1814), 38-43.

Beloved Brethren and Friends,

In what manner and to what extent it has pleased the blessed God, of late, to direct the attention of many among us, to the interests of the Redeemer's Kingdom, some of you are already sensible, and others will learn from the preceding pages. Under the smiles of a propitious Providence, a Convention has assembled in Philadelphia, consisting of delegates from parts of our union, various and remote, to devise a plan, and enter into measures, for combining the efforts of our whole denomination, in behalf of the millions upon whom the light of evangelic truth has never shone. The result of their serious and affectionate consultations, you have an opportunity of perusing. . . .

Within the last few years, it has pleased the good spirit of our God to awaken in his churches a serious concern for the diffusion of the Saviour's cause. Numerous, and in some instances large associations of Christians have been formed for the purpose: considerable sums of money have been collected; bibles and religious tracts are extensively and gratuitously circulating, and the hope which thousands cherish that the glory of the latter days is at hand, is as operative as it is joyous. The blessing which has succeeded the efforts of our denomination in India, demands our gratitude. In a few years, the word of life will probably be translated into all the languages of the East. The change of sentiment relative to the subject of baptism that has lately occured in the minds of two respectable characters, who were sent out as Missionaries by another denomination of our christian brethren, [Adoniram Judson and Luther Rice] appears to have been of the Lord and designed as a means of exciting the attention of our churches to foreign Missions. . . . The brevity of life, the value of immortal souls, the obligations under which divine mercy has laid us, our past inactivity, . . . and the incalculable blessings that may follow our endeavours, form a body of motive which we hope will kindle in many of our youth an ardent desire to enter on Missionary services, and in you the holy resolution to minister of your abundance to all who shall go forth in the name of the Lord.

But, while we call your attention to the spread of evangelic truth, we would impress on your minds that many other and most important advantages may arise to the interests of Christ among us from our acting as societies and on the more extended scale of a Convention, in delightful union. . . . Is it not a fact that our churches are ignorant of each other to a lamentable degree? But for the labours of one or two individuals, it is probable that whole Associations might have assembled in different parts of our Union without being known or knowing that others existed. . . .

The efforts of the present convention have been directed chiefly to the establishment of a foreign Mission; but, it is expected that when the general concert of their brethren and sufficient contributions to a common fund shall furnish them with proper instruction and adequate means, the promotion of the interests of the churches at home will enter into the deliberations of future meetings.

It is deeply to be regretted that no more attention is paid to the improvement of the minds of pious youth who are called to the gospel ministry. While this is neglected the cause of God must suffer. . . . Other denominations are directing their attention with signal ardour to the instruction of their youth for this purpose. . . . While we avow our belief that a refined or liberal education is not an indispensible qualification for ministerial service, let us never lose sight of its real importance, but labour to help our young men by our contributions, by the origination of education Societies, and if possible, by a general theological seminary, where some at least may obtain all the advantage which learning and mature studies can afford, ...

RICHARD FURMAN, President

10.5 Application of Charlotte H. White, 1815

With the application of Charlotte H. White in 1815, the Baptist Board faced for the first time the question of appointing single women as foreign missionaries. Not for another two generations would such appointments become common. Mrs. White, a widow, was appointed with some reluctance to join the household of Mr. and Mrs. George Hough, who had recently been appointed to India. Much to the relief of Adoniram Judson, who feared the mere appearance of bigamy in that polygamous land, Mrs. White soon married an English widower and moved away. Her letter of application reveals a woman of sensitivity and conviction. *Source: Second Annual Report of the Baptist Board of Foreign Missions* (Philadelphia: n.p., 1816), 112.

The determination of the Board to send out brother Hough and his wife to the assistance of brother and sister Judson, was announced in their Report last year. Shortly after its publication, Mrs. Charlotte H. White solicited permission and patronage to attach herself to the mission. Extracts from her letter, making application to this effect, follow, to wit:

Philadelphia, June 13, 1815.

TO THE BAPTIST BOARD OF FOREIGN MISSIONS,

Rev. Sirs,

Having suggested to Mr. Hough my wish to join him and Mrs. Hough in going to India, he has advised me to adopt this method in stating my views to the Board, on whose approbation or disapprobation, will depend my future conduct respecting it.

The Board will naturally inquire into my motives and expectations. Permit me to represent them. It is now about ten years since I was led to search the Scriptures in order to find assurance that Jesus Christ is the son of God; in doing which, I was blessed with a desire to be converted from darknes [sic] to light; the Holy Spirit rousing me to repent, and enabling me to confess Christ as my Lord and Saviour. A farther search after the path of duty to be pursued in openly avowing my hope in Christ, led me to adopt believer's baptism as the scriptural mode of initiation into the visible church. In 1807 I was baptised by the Rev. William Batchelder, of Haverhill, Mass. and received into full communion with the baptist church in that place: a testimonial of which, by a transfer of my standing, is, I believe, on the records of the Sansom-street church in this city, in which I now stand as a regular member.

Since the date of my conversion, I humbly hope my desire has been to do good, and glorify my Redeemer: and especially since missionary endeavours have come within my knowledge I have felt myself deeply interested in them; and their success has been the constant subject of my prayers. Hitherto I have been excluded from rendering any service to the mission; but I now rejoice that God has opened a way, and directed my mind to missionary exertions. On the coming of Mr. and Mrs. Hough to this city, and my being made acquainted with them and their missionary views, my ardour has been revived, and a desire produced to accompany them to India; and I now wait for the Board to approbate my design. My wishes are to reside in their family in the character of a sister to Mrs. Hough and a sister in the Lord;—with them to pursue such studies as are requisite to the discharge of missionary duties;—with them to suffer the hardships of such an undertaking, and with them to enjoy in common the favours of that God whom we would jointly serve; . . .

Having found no period of life exempt from trials, I do not expect to leave them on leaving my native land, but rather to add to their weight and number. . . .

That the Lord may influence the decision of the Board concerning me, and strengthen and enlighten me with his Holy Spirit, that I may be enabled to submit to his will, is the humble prayer of yours in christian love,

CHARLOTTE H. WHITE.

10.6   Luther Rice, Letter to Adoniram Judson, 1823

Early in his work as traveling agent for the Triennial Convention, Luther Rice came to the conviction that Baptists in America needed to do more than foreign missions. They needed an overall, unified plan of denominational ministries, including home and foreign missions, theological education, and Christian literature. Rice saw these related ministries not as rivals to foreign missions, but as integral to the overall Baptist effort. Not all Baptists favored this unified approach. Some opposed it because they feared it would detract from the central task of foreign missions. In the following letter to Adoniram Judson, Rice took pains to defend the unified approach. He particularly wanted Judson to understand the pressing need for theological education among Baptists. *Source:* William H. Brackney, ed., *Dispensations of Providence: The Journal and Selected Letters of Luther Rice* (Published jointly by the American Baptist Historical Society, Rochester, N.Y.; the George Washington University, Washington, D.C.; and The Historical Commission, Southern Baptist Convention, Nashville, Tenn., 1984), 154-156.

Washington, Jan.6. 1823

Most dear brother,

Long have I wanted time to give you a distinct and detailed narrative of the events and circumstances through which the Divine Hand has conducted me, since the never-to-be-forgotten hour of separation from you at Port Louis! To accomplish both these objects—to do away, from this time, the unfrequency of communication between us, and to supply the aforesaid narrative — although I find myself as intensely occupied as ever, and the demands on every effort in my power to make as urgent as ever—I have determined to write to you a letter of some length, *on the first Monday of every month,* and forward the same whenever opportunity for it occcurs. While dear sister Judson remains in this country, I shall transmit these letters to her, to be taken out to you on her return.

Soon after beginning the career which opened before me, and which I have consigned it my duty to pursue, in this country, my mind became impressed with the importance of a general combination of the whole baptist interest in the United States, for the benefit alike of the denomination here, and the cause of missions abroad. . . .

A great difficulty has constantly existed, & great deal of loss has been sustained, for want of a more efficient force at head quarters, and a more systematic and steady application of energy to the business at that point. . . .

In the progress of the business it became obvious that a Theological Institution was indispensably necessary to the attainment of the great objects contemplated, and after a while it was believed that a College would facilitate the purposes of the Theological Institution; and both these came at length to be combined in the Columbian College in the District of Columbia.

At this point, connected with the General Convention, and the Columbian College, it is believed, the foundation is laid, deep and substantial and durable, and strong, for that combination of the baptist interest in this country, and those great evangelical and missionary results, so devoutly to be wished and so fervently to be prayed for. Dr. Staughton, Secretary of the General Convention, is President of the College, and will soon remove from Philadelphia to this place. . . .

Of the arrival and movements of sister Judson, I need say nothing, as she will herself impart to you fully the information.

Your last letter to me is dated the 6th February 1822, and has been in hand several months. I have just read it afresh. I seldom weep, and almost never in sight of any one— but your letters I can never read without tears. I still cherish some hope of seeing you again even in this world, as well as of spending a blessed eternity with you in heaven!

Ever most affectionately
Yours
Luther Rice

10.7   Investigation of Luther Rice, 1826

Luther Rice's vision of a great unified, cooperative denomination that sponsored many forms of ministry was too bold for many Baptists of that time. Rice soon aroused opposition and in his conduct, unfortunately, left ample room for criticism. Rice was completely honest, but he often exceeded his authority. He purchased lands and erected buildings for Columbian College, all on notes or borrowed funds, and often without proper authorization from the Board. His financial records were unclear, his reports vague. He further alienated powerful New England Baptists by expanding the work of the Convention to include more than foreign missions, and by his plan to locate the central denominational offices and institutions in the South. The result was a painful and public investigation of the character and conduct of Rice. Although he was exonerated, after 1826 Rice's influence in the denomination continued to diminish. The following document comes from the report of the committee that investigated Rice. The committee was headed by Lucius Bolles, who was no friend of Rice. *Source:* Proceedings of the Fifth Triennal Meeting of the Baptist General Convention, N.Y., 1826.

Friday, May 5th

Convention met.

Prayer by Rev. Mr. Knowles . . . .

The Report of the Committee on the conduct of Mr. Rice was read and accepted. . . .

Resolved, That no charge against Luther Rice as to immoral conduct has been substantiated.

Resolved, That many imprudencies are properly attributable to him, for which, however, the urgent embarrassments of the College furnish at least a partial apology.

Resolved, That from the various developements it appears that Mr. Rice is a very loose accountant, and that he has very imperfect talents for the disbursement of money.

Adjourned to half past 7 this evening. . . .

Conduct of Mr. Rice

Your Committee, according to the resolution of the Convention entered into a lengthy investigation of the conduct of the Rev. Luther Rice, and what relates thereto in regard to his private responsibilities as a man, his conduct as agent of the Convention, and as agent of the Board of Trustees of the College, and Treasurer of said Board. They had a number of witnesses upon the various charges exhibited against him, and gave him an opportunity of refuting them. After this tedious and unpleasant examination, they have come to the following conclusions.

Your Committee are happy to report, that nothing affecting the moral character of Mr. Rice, has been proved against him, unless a want of punctuality in complying with his contracts be considered of that nature; and to that he pleads inability.

Many imprudences have been laid to his charge, some of which he acknowledges, and your committee hope that a sense of past indiscretions may render him more wise in future. Your Committee however think a short history of the course he has pursued in regard to these transactions, may place the matter more fully before you.

Mr. Rice, upon his own responsibility, and that of a few friends, purchased a piece of land in the vicinity of Washington for the purpose of erecting a College and Theological School, and forthwith commenced the building now standing. In the year 1820, he proposed the business to the Convention assembled in Philadelphia, and requested them to accept the premises and take the College and all its future operations under their superintendence. This was accepted by the Convention under the condition that no debts should be contracted, but that the building should proceed no faster than funds could be obtained to meet the expenses. . . . The injunction of the Convention not to increase the debt was so far disregarded, as to go with the business upon subscriptions instead of the money in hand. As the subscriptions were not collected as fast as money was wanting, a debt of fearful amount was contracted which has since accumulated. . . .

Since that period, various transactions have been entered into by Mr. Rice in conjunction with the Board of Trustees of said College, some of which appear to your Committee to be exceedingly imprudent. In all these transactions Mr. Rice seems to have been the acting man, but not to have done any thing without the final sanction of the Board. On his own private responsibility, certain houses were purchased of Col. R. M. Johnson to a large amount, and which were afterwards received by the Board of Trustees as College property, which have heretofore yielded very little profit to the College, while it has burdened it with a debt of fourteen thousand dollars. Through him a claim of Mr. McKenny against the United States government was taken up, amounting to eleven thousand dollars. This also failed in affording funds to any considerable amount, while it loaded the College with the whole debt of eleven thousand dollars.

Your Committee view these transactions as great indiscretions; and although the

Board of Trustees gave their sanction to them, yet as it was at the instance of Mr. Rice, he is, in our estimation, highly reprehensible. But to this he pleads the necessities of the College. . . . In all these transactions, however, your Committee take pleasure in stating that they can see nothing like corruption, or selfish design; and although he has fallen into imprudences of very distressing tendency, he does not seem to have had any other object in view than the prosperity of the College. In the detailed statements of Mr. Rice's conduct in his monied transactions, the committee have found it difficult to fix upon particular facts, upon which to place a censure, yet by a general view of his whole course, they must say he has been too loose in all his dealings, and that in many of his transactions, in which it was proper he should be governed by the Board and the Committee on education, he seems to have too much followed his own plans, counting upon an easy acquirement of their sanction, and thus abusing their high confidence in him.

All which is respectfully submitted.

LUCIUS BOLLES, Chairman.

10.8   Francis Wayland, Apostle of Baptist Independence

Francis Wayland (1796-1865) graduated from Union College and also studied at Andover Theological Seminary. He served for some years as a college professor, then was called in 1821 as pastor of the First Baptist Church of Boston. He resigned that pulpit in 1826 to assume the great work of his life, the presidency of Brown University. During his twenty-eight years at Brown, Wayland achieved renown for his scholarship, churchmanship, and overall wisdom. He became almost an oracle, a leader whose judgment on every subject was sought and usually followed. He helped shape the organizational concepts of Baptists in America, particularly in the North.

Wayland wrote widely. Several of his eighteen books were required reading in most universities in America, and he also wrote countless articles for journals and papers. In his early years he published a series of letters in *The American Baptist Magazine and Missionary Intelligencer* under the pseudonym of "Backus." Selection A includes excerpts from Letters V and VI. *Source: American Baptist Magazine and Missionary Intelligencer,* May 1824, 324-328. Later in life he wrote several articles under the pseudonym of "Roger Williams," published first in *The Examiner* and later reprinted in *Notes on the Principles and Practices of Baptist Churches. Source:* Francis Wayland, *Notes on the Principles and Practices of Baptist Churches* (New York: Sheldon, Blakeman, & Co., 1857), 177-195.

These two sets of articles under different pseudonyms, coming from different periods of Wayland's life, express quite different views on Baptist organization. The "Backus" articles advocate denominational organization, point out its advantages, and suggest ways to make the denomination function more effectively. By the time of the "Roger Williams" articles, however, Wayland had changed his mind entirely. Under the doctrine of complete church independence, he opposed any idea of the churches forming any kind of denominational structures. The most he would allow was for *interested individuals* to form independent missionary, educational, or other benevolent societies. He insisted, however, that these societies did not involve the churches at all. Thus he would move all missionary and other benevolent ministries outside the church.

The early Wayland advocated a unified cooperative *denominational* approach to Baptist life; the later Wayland retreated to the *independent society* approach. These contrasting concepts have been crucial in Baptist history. As long as Wayland advocated the denominational approach, the Triennial Convention developed as a unified denomination. When he changed his mind, such was his influence that the Triennial Convention reverted to the society approach. This paved the way for the withdrawal of Baptists in the South, who from the first preferred the denominational approach.

A.   Letters on Associations

LETTER V.

To the Editor of the Am. Bap. Magazine.

Dear Sir,

IN some former letters I submitted to your consideration, some remarks on the subject of Baptist Associations. I then noticed the advantages and defects of the system as it now exists among us. . . .

I shall now proceed to consider the most striking defect with which, in my opinion, our system is chargeable. It is, that at present, our whole plan is unfinished. We have the *basis* of a system of perfect representation throughout the whole United States, and here the thing has remained for half a century at a stand. To me it resembles the foundation of a house which had been accurately planned, and judiciously located, for which the materials had been all procured, and brought to the place of building, and then the whole business suspended. . . . We have no concert of action. We have never agreed upon any general plan of union. We have no means of general information. Each Association is an insulated body, destitute of any regular connexion with any other part of the denomination. Each church knows its own Association, but it knows not, nor can it know, definitely and accurately, any thing beyond it. We resemble an army, of which the companies have never been united into regiments, nor the regiments into brigades. No means exists for bringing the whole force to bear upon a single point. Every part is weak because all are divided.

Let us consider what would be the result of such a state of things in our general or state governments. Suppose every county were an independent body, disconnected except by casual correspondence with every other. The necessary result would be, the weakness of the whole. All plans of general improvement must cease, for you could never unite the whole in any co-operation. In fact, the force of the whole, would be precisely the force of one single division, for you could never bring more than the power of a single part into action. And the same result would take place if our system of representation were confined to our state sovereignties. We should be equally incapable of carrying forward improvements in peace, or of uniting our energies in war. Each State would be exposed to any enemy that chose to attack it. It could never be sure of any support beyond its own individual strength. Hence we see the wisdom of the motto of the Father of our country, "UNITED WE STAND, DIVIDED WE FALL."

Now it is evident that the same principles apply to us as a denomination. It is the duty of each of us as individuals, to do all in our power to promote the interests of the Redeemer's kingdom. It is also our duty to do it collectively as a branch of the general church of Christ. But to do this, we must act in concert. We do not wish to bind the consciences of our brethren. We do not want to abridge the liberties of any individul church. These we hold sacred, and we always shall so hold them; but we want them to assist us, and want to assist them, in all the plans that they or we may devise for promoting the salvation of our fellow men. . . . We have one Lord, one faith, one baptism. Why should we not unite all efforts together, and thus do our utmost to promote the cause of Christ in the United States, and throughout the world? . . . We all in substance have the same articles of belief. Why should we not compare them together and publish them to the world? In no other way can we escape the reproach which justly falls upon many who call themselves Baptists, and at the same time hold articles of belief the very reverse of our own. . . . We would see them embodied in a visible shape, so that innovations in doctrine and practice may be hereafter prevented.

Let it not be supposed for a moment that we wish any creeds or articles to be imposed on ourselves, or our brethren. The bible is our only standard, and it is a sufficient standard of faith and practice. But the fact is, we all understand the bible alike, and we understand it in a manner somewhat different from any other denominations of Christians. Why should we not then take some means to ascertain the articles which we generally believe, and thus bind ourselves more closely together?

These ends it will be considered are desirable. But it will be asked, How can they be accomplished? We shall consider this question in the next letter. In the mean time,

I am yours, most sincerely,

BACKUS.

LETTER VI.

Dear Sir,

MY last letter closed with the question, How may a general union of our churches throughout the United States be accomplished? I shall now suggest the answer to it. . . .

First, then, it should be distinctly recognized that each church is distinct and independent. No body which ever can be created, should have any power to control its belief or its practice. The only object of combination should be the good of the whole, and the promotion of the general interests of the cause of Christ amongst us.

Let us begin then with Associations. An Association is a meeting of ministers and messengers from all the churches within a certain district. All the Associations together, therefore, comprise the whole of our church. Any plan of representation which may be devised for combining them all together, would give us the voice of every man in our connexion. And moreover, every Association is well acquainted with the state of all the churches in its own limits. . . .

We see then that the Associations are in possession of all the information we could desire, if it could only be regularly collected. We see they are representative bodies, and could declare the faith and practice of their churches. And moreover, they are representative deliberative bodies, and are empowered to devise means for the promotion of the cause of Christ, not inconsistent with their received rules of faith and practice. The question then returns, in what manner can they be so combined as to effect these valuable purposes?

The model of our system of general and state governments will at once suggest itself to every American. The Associations in one state could easily send delegates to a state convention. This would embody all the information, and concentrate the energies of a state. These state conventions could send delegates to a general convention, and thus the whole denomination might be brought into concentrated and united action.

But it will be asked, perhaps, when these conventions are formed, what is there for them to do? We will answer. It would be the duty of a state convention to ascertain correctly the condition of the churches within its own limits. . . . Another part of their duty would be to encourage the churches to systematic exertion in the cause of Christ. This might easily be done through the means of the Associations whom they represent. Each Association should therefore appoint a treasurer, who should receive the missionary and education contributions of the churches. These contributions the treasurer might pay over to the delegate to the state convention. And the money thus collected, might be appropriated as the convention might advise. A part of it would be doubtless retained for missionary labour within the state, and the rest sent on to the general conventions for the foreign missions.

Again, to carry forward this object, it would be proper that every state convention should appoint a Board of domestic missions for conducting missionary exertion within their own boundaries. The special object of this board would be to assist destitute churches, and supply places with the preaching of the gospel, whenever a promising door was opened for usefulness. . . .

The state conventions might send delegates, who, when assembled, would form the general convention. Under this body might be placed the general missionary and education concerns of the denomination. These objects are dear to us all; and they have become so important as to deserve and require the general superintendence of all our churches. . . .

Thus, then, the superintendence of the missionary and education concerns of our denomination, would be one important business of the general convention. And it cannot but be observed, that whatever was conducted under the direction of such an assembly, would gain the fullest confidence of all our churches. The convention would appoint and locate the different boards, hear their reports, credit their accounts, and censure or approve of their proceedings, as their wisdom should direct.

Another of their duties might be, by delegates, to correspond with our brethren in England, . . . Another of their duties might be to originate and superintend a general book system, by which a vastly greater mass of intelligence might be circulated among our brethren, and a very considerable sum be raised for the propagation of the gospel. Another might be the devising of some plan for collecting and publishing our articles of faith and order, . . . Besides these, and many more which might be named, it will at once be seen, how great an opportunity would be presented to such an assembly, for exciting all our churches to every laudable exertion for the extension of religion. Whatever they recommended, would, by their minutes and by the delegates, be carried home to each state convention, and from thence, by their delegates to each Association, and by the messengers of each Association, to every church; and thus an impulse would be communicated in a few months to every individual of our communion in the United States. . . .

Let it not be said that this is impossible. What denomination in our country except our own is without it? And what others do, we can do. Let it not be considered visionary. . . . Let us recollect it is the cause of our Redeemer that calls for our exertions; and if it shall seem that this can be promoted by such an arrangement as has been proposed, or by any other of a similar nature, let us lose no time in striving to effect it.

I am yours truly,
BACKUS.

B. Independence of the Churches.—Can a Church Properly Be Represented?

BEFORE closing my remarks on the dangers to which we are exposed from following the examples of other denominations, I desire to offer a few remarks on our ecclesiastical organization. We are liable in this respect to swerve from our principles, and of this liability it is well to be aware.

The Baptists have ever believed in the entire and absolute independence of the churches. By this, we mean that every church of Christ, that is, every company of believers united together according to the laws of Christ, is wholly independent of every other; that every church is perfectly capable of self-government; and that, therefore, no one acknowledges any higher authority, under Christ, than itself; that with the church all ecclesiastical action commences, and with it it terminates, and hence, that the ecclesiastical relations proper, of every member, are limited to the church to which he belongs. . . .

The doctrine of the independence of the churches rests upon a few plain and well-established principles. Some of these I take to be the following:

1. Religion is a matter which concerns exclusively the relations between an individual man and his Maker. . . .

2. The manner in which we may acceptably serve God must be made known to us by God himself. . . .

3. In the New Testament, God has therefore in mercy furnished us with a perfect rule of duty. . . .

4. This revelation being a communication from God to every individual, every individual is under obligation to understand it for himself. Aid, sufficient to guide every candid inquirer, is promised to all who will ask for it. . . .

5. Men who, by such an examination of the New Testament, arrive at the same conclusions respecting its requirements, unite together in churches for the sake of promoting holiness in each other, and subduing the world to obedience to Christ. In doing this, however, they neither assume on the one hand, nor concede on the other, any power of original legislation over each other. . . .

6. Such being the nature of a Christian church, I do not see how it can possibly be *represented*. Representation always supposes that there are certain rights, duties, obligations, etc., in which the individual agrees to be governed by the majority. The various constituencies unite in sending certain persons of their own number, who represent their sentiments in these respects, and they agree to obey such laws as these representatives, when assembled together, shall enact. . . .

7. Such being the nature of representation, I ask how can a church of Christ be *represented?* The matters which could be committed to representatives are clearly but two: First, those which Christ has *not* commanded, but which are properly left to the decision of individual conscience; and secondly, those which *have been commanded* by Christ or his apostles. Concerning the first class, these, not being commanded, but being left to the decision of individual conscience, are already without the jurisdiction of the church, and, of course, the church can commit jurisdiction concerning them to no representation. It can not transfer to another a power which by concession it does not possess. But take the other class of duties, or obligations, those commanded by Christ. Can it commit the commands of Christ to any human tribunal? Can a church, or can churches commit the precepts of Jesus to a representation, thus acknowledging their power to add to, to abolish, or to modify what the Master has enacted? Or again: can it concede to any representation the right *to interpret for* us the precepts of Christ? This would be to abolish the right of private judgment, and convert us into Romanists. Nor, lastly, can we commit the *execution* of these laws to representatives, since the power to enforce the laws of Christ rests with each church itself.

It would seem, from these simple principles, impossible that a church of Christ can be *in any proper and legitimate sense represented.* . . . It is as truly a violation of the independence of the churches, and the right of private judgment, when several hundred brethren meet in some public convention, and manufacture public opinion, and adopt courses which their brethren are called upon to follow, on pain of the displeasure of the majority, as when they establish a formal representation, to whose decisions all the constituency must submit. . . .

XXXI.
ATTEMPTS TO FORM A BAPTIST REPRESENTATION HAVE FAILED.—BAPTIST GENERAL CONVENTION.—MISSIONARY UNION.—NO ONE OF ALL OUR BENEVOLENT ASSOCIATIONS REPRESENT THE BAPTIST DENOMINATION.

I HAVE referred to the doctrine of the independence of the churches, and the grounds on which we suppose it to rest. It is a belief to which the vast majority of our brethren have adhered with a most commendable and consistent tenacity.

Notwithstanding this, attempts have been made, at sundry times, among us, to establish some kind of informal representation. They have never met with favor, and have obtained influence among us only through ignorance of their real character. To some of these I will briefly allude.

When State Conventions were first proposed, it was by many believed—and of these I freely confess myself to have been one—that through them we might establish a general Baptist organization. If the churches sent delegates to the Association, the Association sent delegates to the State Convention, and the State Convention sent delegates to the General Convention of the Baptists in the United States, or to the Triennial Convention then existing, it would seem that all this might easily have been accomplished. I now rejoice exceedingly that the whole plan failed, and that it failed through the sturdy common sense of the masses of our brethren. . . .

The Triennial Convention was really a representative assembly, composed, however, not of representatives of *churches* as such, but of representatives chosen by the contributors to Foreign Missions. These contributors were sometimes individuals, sometimes Mission Societies, sometimes churches, sometimes Associations, and sometimes State Conventions. Any Baptist organization whatever, which contributed a given amount annually to the funds of the Convention, had a right to send its representative. Hence it was a very common thing, at its meetings, to hear members tell about their *constituents*. An attempt was made, pretty early in the history of this organization, to give it the control over all our benevolent efforts. It was proposed to merge in it our Education Societies, Tract Societies, Home Mission Societies, and our Foreign Mission Societies, so that one central Board should have the management of all our churches, so far as their efforts to extend the kingdom of Christ were concerned. After a protracted debate, this measure was negatived by so decided a majority that the attempt was never repeated, and this danger was averted. We look back, at the present day, with astonishment that such an idea was ever entertained. . . .

Things had arrived at that point, that every member who loved the cause of missions, or even the peace of our Zion, looked forward to the meetings of the Convention with fear and apprehension. Our best men were becoming glad of an opportunity to be absent from its meetings. When the separation between the North and the South took place, every one saw that a totally different organization had become absolutely indispensable. The Constitution of the present Missionary Union, which is formed on entirely different principles, was unanimously adopted. This was the end of the only representative organization ever attempted among us. The result showed it to be utterly alien from all our principles, and calculated to work nothing but division and dissension among us.

The Constitution of the "Union" excluded all semblance of representation. It was originally composed entirely of life-members, who became such by the payment of $100, though this feature has since been slightly modified. The life-members elect a Board, who hold office for three years, one third being elected every year. The Board elect an Executive Committee for the special management of the concerns of missions. Here, then, every man speaks for himself, and for himself alone. He can throw the blame of his actions on no constitutents, but must stand up and answer to the public for himself. This has been a great advantage, and has tended to save us from many a useless, angry, and partisan discussion. The membership is also much more permanent, and so much time is not occupied by brethren, who, for the first time, have attended a general missionary meeting, and are wholly ignorant of the subject of missions.

Still it is ever to be borne in mind that the Missionary Union, together with the various Associations that frequently meet at the same place, and nearly at the same time, is no *representation* of the *Baptist denomination,* that is, of the Baptist churches, which are in truth the denomination. This is so important a fact, that it deserves a word or two in explanation.

In point of numbers, the members of our Societies, meeting at any one time, are a very inconsiderable fragment of the denomination. Or take the whole membership of these Societies together—and they are, in fact, generally the same persons over again—and they would amount not to a twentieth, probably not to a fiftieth, of our whole number. But whether many or few, they come not as representatives of churches, for the churches have never sent them nor commissioned them; they come together on their own motion, merely as members of the Union, or of the Home Mission, or Bible, or any other Society. The limits of their action are fixed by the Constitution of the Society to which they belong. When they have cared for its interests, they have nothing further to do, and have no more right, at such a time, to act *for the denomination,* . . .

But suppose, it may be said, that every member of a Baptist church was a member of these Societies for Christian benevolence, would not the delegations sent by the churches to the meetings of these Societies, represent the churches? I reply, by no means. The constitution and laws of the church are found in the New Testament. . . . I will take the plain and obvious case of foreign missions. No church has any right to oblige any member to *give* to foreign missions, any more than to *go upon a foreign mission.* The same may be said of a Bible Society, a Home Mission, or any other Society. A church may demand of every member the consecration of himself and his property to Christ, and may very properly exclude him for covetousness, just as it would for lying, profanity, lewdness, or any other sin. But as to the *manner* in which the individual shall exercise his liberality, the church can not direct. . . .

XXXII.

LOVE TO THE SAVIOUR THE BOND WHICH MUST UNITE BAPTISTS TO EACH OTHER.—ERRORS TO BE AVOIDED IN CONDUCTING BENEVOLENT ASSOCIATIONS.—THE SPECIAL OBJECT OF A CHURCH MUST NOT BE TRANSCENDED.—INFANT DEDICATION.—CONCLUDING REFLECTIONS.

THOSE who agree with me in the suggestions which occupy some of my last numbers, will readily see that the representation of churches, in any legitimate sense, is at variance with the first principles to which we have always adhered, . . . The more steadfastly we hold to the independence of the churches, and abjure every thing in the form of a denominational corporation, the more truly shall we be united, and the greater will be our prosperity. If it be asked, What is there then to unite us? I answer, love to Christ and adherence to principle. . . . If the piety and zeal of the Baptist churches become extinct, the denomination will be absorbed into other sects and be no more known. This is to me one of the strongest evidences that we are on the true foundation. A church organized after the manner of a civil commonwealth may retain its form long after the last vestige of piety has vanished, and continue for ages an enemy to Christ as a persecutor of the saints. The soil of Christendom, at the present day, is covered with the festering carcasses of churches, from which the Spirit has for generations departed. The moral atmosphere is rendered pestilential by their presence, and neither piety nor humanity can breathe it and survive.

Let us, then, ever bear it in mind that the Baptist denomination, that is, the Baptist churches, is one thing, and the benevolent associations formed or sustained by individual Baptists are another and a very different thing. Individual members of our churches have a right to form such associations, not at variance with the precepts of the Master, as they choose. . . . This, however, imposes no obligation on those who are not like-minded. They are just as free to let it alone as to unite in it. They may be as good Baptists in letting it alone as in joining it. . . .

And where such associations are formed, they have each one its appropriate office, whether it be foreign or domestic missions, the circulation of Bibles, or tracts, or any other good design. This object is exclusive. It may not properly be transcended or mingled with any other. . . .

. . . Let each stand separately on its own merits, and gain the favor of the whole, not by partisan management, but by good works. The latter course leads to harmony, independence, and mutual love; the other to intrigue, dissension, tyranny, and disaffection. Unless these principles be observed, our general associations will prove a curse rather than a blessing, and a voluntary association which is found to be a curse, will soon cease to exist.

I have spoken above of the distinctive character of the church of Christ. On this subject let me add a single word. I think we should be careful to bear this in mind in all our arrangements. For instance, I have known a church form itself into a Temperance Society, and oblige every member on entering it to take the Temperance pledge. Now, God forbid that I should say a word against temperance, but still, a church is not a Temperance *Society*. A church may very properly, nay, it *must of necessity,* require of every member that whether he eat or drink, he must do it to the glory of God. It may enforce the direct precepts of the New Testament, and the indirect precept of the apostle Paul, in respect to causing a brother to offend; and it may inform every member that this is required of him, and will be enforced accordingly. Nay, further, if a brother has ever been liable to this sin, it may require of him specifically total abstinence on account of his peculiar temptation. But I think that it can go no further. The difference here is important. In the one case, it is a promise of a moral duty made to man; in the other, it is submission to the revealed will of God. The value of this difference must be evident to every one.

So I have known churches to take the Sabbath-school under their care, as it is called, and constitute themselves, in fact, a Sunday-school Society. I do not see how this can be, unless every member is required to teach in a Sabbath-school. No one, however, would believe this to be correct. Under this view, the Sabbath-school scholars are sometimes called "children of the church." I always supposed that the church had none but regenerate children; for if she have unregenerate children of one age, why not of another? Would it not be more in accordance with our principles to consider the Sabbath-school an association of Christians uniting for this purpose under their own laws, and subject to their own arrangements?

These may seem matters of small moment. They may not be great in themselves, but they are of importance if we consider the principles which they involve. If brethren united in church fellowship have the right to take matters not strictly belonging to the church under their legislation, what is there that may not be taken under the cognizance of the church? Where shall the line be drawn? and when a member joins a Baptist church how shall he know to how many things, not commanded by Christ, he commits himself?

10.9 The American Baptist General Tract Society

Americans in the early-nineteenth century developed an insatiable hunger for printed materials. Just at this time the Sunday School made its appearance, adding its vast numbers to the market for the printed word. Baptists responded to these challenges by forming the American Baptist General Tract Society in 1824. This small beginning ultimately became one of the major religious literature and publishing houses in America. *Source: The Columbian Star.* Washington City, 21 Feb. 1824. Photostat in Daniel G. Stevens, *First Hundred Years of the American Baptist Publication Society* (Philadelphia: American Baptist Publication Society, n.d.), 1.

For the Columbian Star. BAPTIST TRACT SOCIETY, MR. EDITOR,

My attention was seriously arrested by your suggestions in the last number of the Star, relative to the formation of a Baptist Tract Society. The subject may be somewhat novel to our denomination, but cannot fail to meet the decided approbation of all who wish well to the interests of Christianity. . . .

It is unnecessary to use any argument to prove the usefulness of Tracts. Containing nothing sectarian, they convey in a cheap form and in a plain style, the great truths which are revealed in that gospel, "worthy of all acceptation." In the accounts of revivals, we see numerous instances, where a tract of six or eight pages was made the happy instrument of introducing the solemn realities of religion to some poor sinner. . . .

The eastern states can be amply supplied by their numerous societies,—but how shall the wants of the southern and western states be gratified? Where shall the work begin? Who will go forward? Let a Society be soon formed in this city [Washington, D.C.] to make a commencement—Let a few numbers of evangelical tracts be immediately published—Let agents be appointed in different places in the neighboring states, who shall form auxiliary Societies and collect funds for publishing more tracts. The expense will be trifling compared with the probable good which must be the unavoidable result, if the concerns of the society should be rightly conducted.

. . . It is time for the Baptists to show themselves equal to other denominations in evangelical effort. And, Sir, as numbers of respectable gentlemen are ready to cooperate in the good work, permit me to hope that a Tract Society will soon be set in operation, under the direction of judicious men, and governed by such regulations as shall foretoken good to thousands.

10.10   John Mason Peck, Baptist Home Missionary

John Mason Peck (1789-1858) became perhaps the most outstanding home missionary Baptists in American ever produced. He was born in Connecticut where he grew up in nominal affiliation with the Congregational Church. In 1811 Peck and his wife, Sally, became convinced of believer's baptism by immersion, and joined the Baptist church of New Durham, New York, where they had recently moved. Soon after his baptism Peck felt he should preach, a decision with which the church fully agreed. Peck's diary reveals the spiritual struggle of the young couple, some of the religious and social customs of churches of that time, and some of Peck's reflections upon the qualifications and preparation of ministers. Selection A tells of his early interest in missions. His 1817 appointment as a missionary to Missouri Territory is recounted in selection B. *Source:* Rufus Babcock, ed., *Forty Years of Pioneer Life. Memoirs of John Mason Peck* (Carbondale: Southern Illinois University Press, 1965), 37-38, 48-49, 49-51, 67-68. Used by permission.

A.   John Mason Peck, Early Interest in Missions

Diary entry for June 25, 1813

Friday Evening, June 25, 1813. Received the last number of the Baptist Missionary Magazine. The missionary accounts from India are very interesting. How many thousands of the poor benighted heathen there are who worship the idol of Juggernaut and adore the river Ganges, but are ignorant of the way of salvation through Jesus Christ! How can Christians in this land of high privileges sit easy and unconcerned, without contributing out of their abundance to spread the gospel in distant pagan lands! My soul is grieved for them in their ignorance. Oh, how I wish I was so circumstanced in life as that I might be able to bear the gospel into some distant pagan lands where it never yet has shined! A large part of the American continent is also involved in darkness. Yes, under the immediate Government of the United States, there is an abundant field for missionary labor. How I should rejoice if Providence would open a door for my usefulness and labors in this way!

But alas, how idle and vain are my thoughts! In this place I am too faithless, too prone to wander. Oh, that I might first learn to perform the duties which come within my reach, and not presume to think I should be more faithful in another part of the vineyard!

Letter to William Staughton, January 5, 1816

For more than two years past I have had my mind frequently exercised about the situation of the perishing heathen, and have ardently longed to be the humble instrument of imparting to some of them the word of life. My situation in life, and the want of requisite qualifications have precluded the hope of ever entering that field until a few months past. The difficulties in the way do not seem quite insurmountable, since I have had opportunity of becoming more attached to the missionary interest and learning the wants of the poor heathen. By communications from Brother Rice I learn that it is in contemplation to establish a mission in the Missouri Territory. On this subject I found in my own mind such a correspondence of feeling and sentiment that I could not forbear opening my mind to him. Ever since I have thought upon the subject of missions, I have had my eye upon the people west of the Mississippi, particularly the Indian nations, and have often wondered why no attempts were made to send the gospel to them. I have often thought that if it was my lot to labor among the heathen, the Louisiana-purchase, of all parts of the world, would be my choice. . . .

Luther Rice, letter to John Mason Peck, in response to inquiry about missions, 1815
To the Rev. John M. Peck.

Very Dear Brother:—Your very kind and highly interesting letter, of October 12th, came duly to hand, and I intended to answer it shortly, but have not found time till now. Brother James E. Welch was with me when I received it, and at my request he wrote to you immediately. He thinks of undertaking a mission to the West, should it be thought advisable. Possibly you may be fellow-laborers in this great field. . . . In answer to your inquiries:

1st. Is it contemplated to form a permanent mission-station in the West? Yes; certainly.

2nd. Would it be best to have schools connected with the mission? Yes.

3d. Any particular place in view for the seat of the mission? St. Louis, probably.

4th. What literary attainments would be indispensable? A good English education, to say the least, so as to be able to conduct a school to advantage. In addition it would be very desirable to possess an acquaintance with the Latin and Greek, if not the Hebrew; and indeed it would be desirable that the missionary should be a graduate of some college, though this should not be considered indispensable. A thorough acquaintance with grammar, rhetoric, geography, and history, are of very great importance.

5th. Would it be thought necessary for some person to accompany you in this Western tour? Should some suitable person find his heart moved to offer himself to the service of the Board, as a missionary to the West for life, it might be very proper for him to travel with me some time in the country for the purpose of ascertaining the best position for the seat and commencement of his missionary labors. . . .

From these observations you will receive the idea that I think it not improper to encourage you in the consideration of undertaking a Western mission. This is done by me on the ground that you possess an education amply sufficient to enable you to conduct an English school to advantage, as well as from the very pleasing impression, relative to your talents, piety, industry, and zeal, left on my mind by my short acquaintance with you last spring. You have at least shown yourself faithful over a few things, and I cannot but cherish the hope that the Head of the Church designs in his providence and grace to make you ruler over many things. . . .

I beg you will write me as soon as convenient, and let me know if you would like to engage in the contemplated Western mission for life, and whether you would like the business of teaching a school; and whether you would be willing to offer to the Board next spring, and would be ready to set out next season distinctly to engage in the mission itself. It would afford me great satisfaction to see you in Philadelphia next spring; and I believe you might be highly useful in this Western country, whether as a missionary or otherwise.

Luther Rice.

B. Appointment of John Mason Peck, 1817

Thursday, 8th [1817]. The convention heard the report of Brother Rice, their general agent. It was very interesting. Oh, how much does the zeal and activity of this devoted servant of the Redeemer reprove the slothfulness of others in this holy cause? Communications were then read from our brethren in India, both from the Serampore missionaries and our own missionaries in Rangoon. A church has been formed at the latter place, and all things prosper. Were it not for some particular circumstances, I should think it my duty to devote my life to that region. The Board made a report in part, in which they express their desire that a Western mission be entered upon. . . .

Saturday, 10th—Heard the report of the committee to whom that part of the report of the Board concerning alterations in the constitution had been committed. Considered the recommendations in committee of the whole, and reached this result:

1. Incorporated with the foreign field certain portions of our own country under the denomination of a Domestic Mission. This secures the great object of a Western mission.

2. Directed the Board to raise a fund for the establishment of one or more classical and theological seminaries to educate missionaries and others.

This, also, I view as a most important object, nearly concerning the welfare of the mission. To qualify young men as missionaries is a preliminary to sending them out. . . .

Friday, 16th. The Board still in session. Messrs. Coleman and Wheelock were accepted, and appointed missionaries to Rangoon. The subject of a domestic mission in the Southwest was brought forward. A letter from Rev. Mr. Ronaldson, of New Orleans, was read, and an appointment given him with the provision of five hundred dollars per annum for his support.

The business relating to myself was then brought forward. [Peck had presented a written document, fully explaining his views and feelings, offering himself as a candidate for appointment in the Western mission.]

The business was not taken up in a manner quite satisfactory to me; and the views of the Board seemed rather discordant on the question, What should the Domestic Mission embrace? Some seemed to entertain the idea that it must only embrace an itinerant mission among destitute churches and such places as are already Christianized. The business was finally deferred till to-morrow.

This view of the case brought a heavy trial on my mind. Indeed I see no way to obtain my object in the mission, but either to engage as a mere itinerant for a limited time, or to go exclusively among the Indians. The first I do not think my duty under existing circumstances; the last does not seem expedient. What will be the result I know not. But I feel to trust in a gracious God who will do all things well. . . .

Saturday, 17th. This day, I suppose, will decide my future prospects. How solemn the thought that a few hours must decide not only with respect to what I have been pursuing for two years past, but what relates to my whole life in the future? I feel a degree of resignation to the hand of God in whatever he may please to appoint. To Him will I commit the whole concern, believing that he will order what is best for his kingdom and glory. At ten o'clock met the Board of Missions. After some business of minor importance, Brother Welch made his communication to the Board. I made some further explanations, and then we withdrew. The decision is now pending. What will be the issue I know not.

Six o'clock. The long agony is over. The Board have accepted Mr. Welch and myself as missionaries to the Missouri Territory during our and their pleasure; and have appropriated the sum of one thousand dollars to defray our expenses in getting to St. Louis and for the support of the mission. In this I think I see the hand of God most visibly. From this moment I consider myself most sacredly devoted to the mission. O Lord, may I live and die in the cause!

10.11   Report from Home Missionary Jacob Bower, 1830s

Official minutes at the home office and actual reports from missionaries on the field often read differently. The reports of Jacob Bower in the 1830s fall into the latter category. They are candid, newsy, and uninhibited. This brief excerpt is included to give a glimpse of home mission work as it appeared to an active participant. *Source:* Annual Report, American Baptist Home Missionary Society, 1835, 13-14.

Rev. Jacob Bower labours in Morgan Co. Ill. Under date of June 11, 1833, he writes, "I have spent much time and laboured incessantly to get the people to throw away their prejudices against missions, and to begin to do a little for the good cause: but they have gone far off, and it will require a tedious time for them to return. It is like putting different kinds of metal into a crucible over a slow fire: they are a long time warming, and then a long time heating, before they will melt and run together. A Missionary must be possessed of a good share of patience and fortitude. Three churches have united in an Association: the last article of its constitution is in these words. 'Each church and member shall be left free to act according to their views of duty on the subject of Missions, B. Societies, Temperance measures, &c. and that the supporting, or not supporting either of these, shall be no bar to fellowship.' We are a feeble band and few in number. I have recently made a tour in Pike Co. a thinly settled region,—where in 16 days, I preached 27 times. Sometimes I would ride 8 or 10 miles and meet about a dozen hearers, who in general seemed to be thirsting for the waters of life. . . .

"The cause of Missions within the range of my travels is not flattering. I have not been able to do much in the field for some time back. The Cholera, that dreadful scourge, has visited Illinois; many towns have been almost evacuated. It was found necessary to suspend our preaching, except twice on Saturday and Sabbath.

"Some people love much in word and in tongue, but not in deed and in truth. They say, 'we like to hear you preach—we are fond of you—come and preach for us.' but only mention their duty,—that the labourer is worthy of his hire, and they will be offended, and say, money-hunter, beggar, missionary, &c. Under these circumstances, the poor missionary must wear out his clothes, his horse and saddle, his body, lungs, and voice, and spend his whole living, and get no help from those who pretend to love him so well. These things are very discouraging . . . Since May 19, I have rode 372 miles, preached

42 sermons, and baptized one—and there are 4 hopeful converts—making in all since the date of my commission, 1247 miles, 191 sermons and 43 baptized.—Sunday Schools suffer greatly for want of competent superintendents and teachers . . . ."

Feb. 24, 1834. After noticing the severe winter as interrupting active operations, he says. "Meetings have been full, and I think I may venture to say that there is a good state of feeling among my hearers in several places, which is truly encouraging to my heart. The good cause is evidently gaining ground, though its progress is slow; it is like the morning dawn; darkness imperceptibly withdraws, and the light approaches. Opposers are not so saucy and violent as they were two year ago: it will be a great work to get professors properly into their duty. In 81 days, I have ridden 634 miles, preached 75 times, baptized one, and aided in the ordination of one preacher. I have cheering prospects of communicating to you some good news in my next. I have sat down and wept with a mixture of sorrow and joy, when thinking over the distressing situation of Zion in Illinois, and how God has remembered her in mercy."

10.12   Documents on Baptist Theological Education

Next to foreign missions, no cause aroused more Baptist effort and opposition in the early-nineteenth century than theological education. Many Baptist leaders saw clearly that the churches could not grow beyond the vision of their pastors; they warned that limited pastors would limit the churches. Baptists in New England gave fewer speeches on the subject, but quite early they formed numerous schools that offered excellent training opportunities. However, these appealed mostly to a regional or even local clientele.

Baptists in the South, who had few such local schools, tried against considerable opposition to get the Triennial Convention to sponsor a theological school for all Baptists of every region. They had strong advocates in Luther Rice, Richard Furman, and W. B. Johnson of South Carolina, Jesse Mercer of Georgia, and Robert Semple of Virginia. They also had outspoken opponents, of whom John Taylor of Kentucky serves as an example. Selection A gives Richard Furman's resolutions on theological education in 1817. *Source: The Latter Day Luminary,* February 1820, 22-24. Selection B gives a defense of Christian education from the 1818 report of the Convention Board. *Source:* Fourth Annual Report of the Baptist Board of Foreign Missions for the United States 1818, 193-195. Both of these voice strong support for theological education. Selection C goes beyond advocacy and proposes a practical plan for the operation of a Baptist school. *Source:* Proceedings of the Baptist General Convention at their Second Triennial Meeting, 1820, 325-327.

Not everyone approved these plans. To some Baptists, ministerial education seemed at best a lack of faith and at worst a human effort to displace God. John Taylor, who opposed almost everything the Triennial Convention did, spoke out strongly against theological education. A sample of his antieducation arguments are included in selection D. *Source:* John Taylor, *Thoughts on Missions* (n.p., 1819), 23-24.

A.   Richard Furman, Resolutions on Theological Education, 1817

Proposed Resolutions, including a scheme of Education, having for its object the assistance of pious young men designed for the gospel ministry, which were laid before the Baptist Convention at Philadelphia, in May, 1817.

I. Resolved, That it be recommended by this Convention, to the Baptist churches throughout the United States, and their adherents, to form themselves into education societies, for the purpose of aiding pious young men of their connexion, who appear on good evidence to be called of God to the gospel ministry, in obtaining such education as may best fit them for extensive usefulness in the cause of our Redeemer, and enable them to appear as workmen who need not be ashamed, rightly dividing the word of truth: And likewise for assisting poor ministers, who have families, and have not obtained the advantages which are derived from a suitable education, by gratuitously furnishing them with the most necessary and useful books, to aid them in their endeavours to obtain mental improvement. For the accomplishment of which design the following scheme is submitted to the consideration of the churches.

1st. Let a charity sermon be preached once a year, at least, in each church, and a collection made expressly for the purposes above specified; and let the monies so collected together with any other collections, donations or bequests obtained for such purposes, be conveyed by the hands of a person specially appointed as a representative to attend the meeting of the association to which such church belongs, and there to be deposited in a common fund, under the direction of a body of delegates similarly appointed by other churches belonging to that association: or to a number of associations uniting in the same measure as a common cause: excepting always such part of the monies, (say a third part) as shall be appropriated to the establishment and support of a Theological Seminary, in our connexion, to be hereinafter described; which last sum shall be conveyed to the general fund, and be placed under the care and direction of the Board of commissioners connected with this Convention, or such part of them as shall be intrusted with the superintendence of the education department.

2d. Let the Body formed by the coalition of churches, as above recommended, be styled the General Committee, or Trustees of the churches united in Association or Associations, ...

3d. Let this committee of the churches be invested with full power to examine applicants for the churches' bounty, with respect to their qualifications, according to the sentiment before expressed; to wit, that ministers must be the subjects of renewing grace, be called of God to the office, and receive gifts of Jesus Christ, the great prophet of the church, to fit them for the work.

4th. Let the committee by their proper officer, or officers, contract for the education of the young men so taken under their care, at some convenient seminary; superintend their education and morals, that the former may be promoted by due excitement, and the latter preserved in purity; a departure from which shall be considered as incurring censure and the loss of privilege. It shall also be considered as the object of their care, to secure the return of money to the fund which may have been expended at any time on the education of persons who do not, in a reasonable time after they have completed their studies, enter on the work of the ministry to the satisfaction of the committee.

5th. After young men thus provided for, have finished their classical studies, or obtained a proper acquaintance with general science, let it be the concern of the churches to place them in a situation favourable to the study of divinity. While in circumstances which prevent their obtaining more ample assistance, let the students come under the care of some pious, well informed, and judicious minister; but when a divinity college shall have been established, according to the provision made in the constitution of this Convention, let as many of them as the respective funds of the societies, or churches, can support, be sent to said seminary; expecially those who possess superior talents, together with a desire and aptness for study.

6th. As it is possible that some churches belonging to the associations may refuse or neglect to make contributions, and that embarrassments may arise from this cause, let the exclusive right of managing the business of the fund be vested in the delegates of those churches which regularly contribute to its support.

II. Resolved, That as soon as a sufficient fund shall be obtained for this purpose, the Board of commissioners shall take measures for establishing, at some convenient and central situation, a Theological Seminary and Library, under the care of learned, pious professors; in which theology shall be studied in its various branches, church history, the Hebrew language, and other oriental languages, the knowledge of which is favourable to a right understanding of the sacred scriptures, as far as the same may be found practicable and convenient, together with biblical criticism and pulpit eloquence.

III. Resolved, That the agents, or missionaries, which may be appointed by the Board of missions to travel in our own country, shall be particularly charged with the important concern of giving information to the churches of our denomination, and the public at large, concerning the true nature and design of the scheme in which the foregoing articles are comprehended, of recommending it to their serious regard, and of affording assistance to those who may be disposed to bring it into operation, in what relates to a right beginning and organization.

B.   A Defense of Christian Education, 1818

AMID the range of interesting efforts recommended by the baptist Convention to the Board of missions, the education of youth destined for the work of the ministry, is one of the highest importance. It is demanded by the improved state of society; it supplies to the young minister himself numerous and solid advantages, and is, with the blessing of God, in every case useful; but as relates to the business of translation, it is of indispensable value to the foreign missionary. The manner in which this duty was pressed upon the Convention by the venerated President, [Richard Furman] at its last session, will not soon be forgotten. . . .

It may be thought unnecessary in the present state of society to assign any reasons to prove the utility and importance of education in assisting the minister of the sanctuary in the discharge of the public and solemn duties of his office. When, however, it is recollected that the most valuable principles fail in their effect unless frequently reviewed, "line upon line" may be found advantageous.

The bible in its popular translation ought unquestionably to engage the laborious attention of the candidate for pulpit labours. The saints of God are accustomed to its phraseology, and find in its words a savoriness which accords with the most gracious exercises of their hearts. It has become venerable for its antiquity, and is received among christians as their guide to heaven.

It is our happiness that as a translation the scriptures are most excellent; but still they are a translation. They supply the best remedy for the evils which the confusion of tongues has created, but the words are not those which the Holy Ghost first employed in conveying revealed truth to man. An acquaintance with the original scriptures qualifies the minister of Christ for contemplating the sentiments delivered in the sacred volume in a variety of lights. It enables him to correct errours which mistaken friends or avowed enemies of divine truth may have introduced. . . .

Besides the oracles of God in their translated and original forms, the public speaker ought to become familiar with the grammar of his own language. Logic will assist him to reason with accuracy, and rhetoric to convey the result of his investigations and the fervours of his heart with acceptance. Without an acquaintance with profane history he can never explain the prophecies which are on record; and ignorant of ecclesiastical, he can never trace to their sources the mischievous errours that prevail. Geography, ancient and modern, is of importance; the former will aid him in his public expositions, and the latter serve to animate and direct the enlarged zeal of his heart, for the extension of the Mediator's kingdom.

The able minister is made such by the Holy Ghost, and only those who in the judgment of the churches are subjects of grace will be admitted to the benefits of the institution. . . .

The same blessed Spirit who assisted the apostles to speak with tongues, employs and blesses human acquisitions to the honour of the divine name. . . . The divine Spirit in employing our English bible for the conversion and sanctifying of the people of God, condescends to make use of the instrumentality of human learning. Had our translators been ignorant of gender and case, of mood and tense, of syntax and government, the bible in the vernacular tongue had never been ours. . . .

That there are in the church eminent ministers of Christ whose opportunities of mental improvement have been small, furnishes occasion for holy joy. Never let human acquirements be regarded as indispensably necessary for pulpit duties. Should it however be inferred that mental improvement is of no moment, the inference is no more correct than that because sometimes God converts men by a thunder storm the ministry of the gospel may be laid aside. Ask those excellent men who, without literary aid, have become great in the church of Christ, their ideas of the value of education, and without an exception you will hear them deplore the want of it. If their eminence and usefulness have been great without learning, what would they have been had they possessed it . . . ?

But learning makes men proud! Alas, such is the frailty of the human heart, that pride will spring as a noxious plant, whether the soil in which it grows be cultivated or not. Pride is not the associate of wisdom only. The most unlettered professors may sometimes be classed among the proudest. The preacher may be as proud, while from the pulpit he is inveighing against that learning which he does not possess, as he who before his congregation opens a thousand of its stores. Superficial literature may produce vanity; but sound learning, sanctified attainments, originate and maintain unaffected humility.

It is hoped that the churches of our denomination are becoming more and more convinced of the duty of assisting pious youths in their education; and do we need arguments to strengthen this conviction? Had ancient prophets their schools for the edification of their youth, and shall we not endeavour to have Naioths and Bethels now? Enemies of christianity are employing learning for its overthrow, and shall not the champions of the Cross be assisted to meet them on equal ground? Did not much of the superstition and folly of the dark ages of the church arise from an unlettered ministry? Has not the reformation, under God, sprung from the intrepidity of men who have been as eminent for learning as for zeal and piety? Is it not the interest of the churches that their spiritual guides possess every possible qualification for advancing their knowledge of divine subjects? Have not the churches, already, realized many important advantages from the literary institutions which exist in our connexion? And ought not such considerations to animate to new and continued exertions?

The cause is the Lord's. Its aim is the prosperity of the churches; and its supporters will find ample consolation in committing the whole to the protection of the Supreme Head of the church, and in a holy and resolute perseverance to expend their talents and substance to the praise of his glory.

C. Plan of Operation, Baptist Theological Seminary, 1820

IMPRESSED with the importance of an extended course of education to the pious minister of the gospel, but aware, at the same time, that, owing to difference of age and circumstances, all who are called to the ministry, and can devote some time to preparatory studies, cannot spend in them the same number of years,—the general Convention of the Baptist denomination in the United States, in instituting a seminary devoted to the service of our Lord, in helping to cultivate the talents which he commits to those whom he calls to labour in the word and doctrine, have thought it their duty to give it such an organization as to afford suitable instruction both to graduates of colleges, and to others possessing those qualifications which are in this Plan required.

The Institution is to be open for the admission of those persons only who give evidence of their possessing genuine piety, with suitable gifts and attainments, and who, moreover, present certificates from the churches of which they are members, approving of their devoting themselves to the work of the ministry.

Those who have received a collegiate or a liberal education, are to enter immediately upon the studies most intimately connected with the ministry. Provision is to be made for the instruction of students in this course two years; and they are to be divided accordingly into two classes—the *Junior* and the *Senior*.

Other candidates, upon being admitted, are to pursue those academical studies which are the most important to a person preparing for the ministry; and are to be divided into two classes—the *First-year* and the *Second-year*—and then be in readiness to enter the *Junior*. It is, however, distinctly to be understood, that persons whose age and other circumstances may render it improper for them to spend the time requisite for attaining the learned languages, shall be afforded means of pursuing such a course of improvement in the English, as may conduce in the highest degree to their usefulness.

At an early period, they are also to devote some of their attention to those subjects which particularly belong to them as students of the Bible, and candidates for the ministry. They likewise, as also and especially those in the two higher classes, are to exercise their gifts in public speaking, so often, and in such places, as in the judgement of the Professors, it shall, in the case of each individual, be expedient, and most conducive to his improvement.

While the students are thus, with meekness and diligence, to strive for the acquisition of useful learning, '*it is required above all, that they make the* BIBLE *the object of their most attentive, diligent, and prayerful study.*'

The Professors in this Institution are to take precedence of each other according to seniority; they are to be men of piety and learning, members of a Baptist church, and advocates for that system of evangelical doctrine, which maintains that it is "God who hath saved us, and called us with an holy calling, not according to our works, but according to his own purpose and grace, which was given us in Christ Jesus before the world began." They are also to be ordained ministers of the gospel; but this requisite is not to be indispensable with regard to those instructers who are employed chiefly in the academical course; . . .

It shall be the duty of the Professors to aid the students in the acquisition of a radical and adequate knowledge of the sacred Scriptures in the original languages; to guide them to correct principles of interpretation, and bring to their assistance, in endeavouring to understand the various parts of the Bible, all those helps which may be derived from an acquaintance with Jewish customs and Oriental literature; to give lectures on the formation, preservation and transmission of the sacred volume; on the languages in which the Bible was originally written; on the Septuagint version of the Old Testament, and on the peculiarities of the language and style of the New Testament, resulting from this version and other causes; on the history, character, and use of the ancient versions and manuscripts of the Old Testament, and of the New; on the canons of biblical criticism; on the canonical authority of the several books of the sacred code; on the Apocryphal books; on modern translations of the Bible, more particularly on the history and character of our English version; and also on the various readings and difficult passages in the sacred writings.

It shall be their duty to give lectures on divine revelation; on the inspiration and truth of the Old and of the New Testament, as proved by miracles, internal evidence, fulfilment of prophecies, and historic facts; on the nature, interpretation, and use of prophecy; on the great doctrines and duties of the Christian religion, together with the objections made to them by unbelievers, and the refutation of such objections: more particularly on the revealed character of God, as Father, Son, and Holy Ghost; on the fall of man, and the depravity of human nature; on the covenant of grace; on the character, offices, atonement, and mediation of Jesus Christ; on the character and offices of the Holy Spirit; on the Scripture doctrines of regeneration, justification, and sanctification; on evangelical repentance, faith, and obedience; on the nature and necessity of true virtue or gospel holiness; on the future state, the immortality of the soul, the resurrection of the body, and the eternity of future rewards and punishments, as revealed in the gospel; and on the positive institutions of Christianity; and, in a word, on all the important subjects of experimental and practical religions. They shall also give the requisite instruction in sacred rhetoric and ecclesiastical history.

It shall also be their duty to have frequent recitations, and other appropriate exercises in the different branches of study; to devote their time and talents to accelerating the progress of their pupils in the acquisition of those attainments which shall be most conducive to their usefulness in the gospel ministry, to communicate instruction adapted to their different capacities and attainments; to point out the course of study to be pursued, with the approbation of the Board; to furnish the students with a list of such books as may be perused by them with the greatest profit; to assist them in studying the Bible and other writings to the best advantage; to animate their pursuits by frequent inquiries and examinations relative to their progress in books and knowledge: to assign them proper subjects for their first compositions, and suggest a proper manner of treating them; to devote special attention to the improvement of their style and delivery, favouring them with free and affectionate remarks on their productions and their public speaking; to watch over their health with paternal solicitude; to teach them how they may distribute and employ their time to the greatest advantage; to give them friendly advice respecting their intercourse with persons in various stations and circumstances;—above all, to confer with them freely and frequently on those subjects, and to take those measures which are best calculated to promote their growth in grace, and warm their hearts with love to God and the souls of men.

While the general Convention adopt the preceding as the basis of their Institution, they confidently commit to the wisdom of the Board the occasional emending of its internal organization, and the assigning of the various departments of instruction to the different Professors that may be appointed.

D. John Taylor, Opposition to Theological Education, 1819

I did signify in the early part of this essay, that part of the distresses of my old age, was the plan now set on foot by some of the Baptists, for patrimonial, theological education; and the object of all this is to make preachers, preachers of a certain grade, Missionary preachers. And this produces a new clue for begging or teasing the people for more money, with this pretext, *we will make more preachers for you,* as if Jesus Christ did not know how to make preachers for his own use among men. Though the plea is, the state of society calls for it, this is an old error, old as the days of Origen, and one of the first mediums to corrupt the religion of Jesus Christ. Was not the state of society, when Christ was on the earth, as to refinement, equal to what it is now? What kind of men did he make choice of, to bear his name to all the world? . . . What theological school did he apply to for any of all these? But now money is wanting to make preachers, and prayer is but little talked of for that purpose. The Savior asks no man's consent to be a Christian, and he prepares their minds by necessity, to preach the gospel, money or no money; so that, woe is me, if I preach not. When Jesus Christ needs a scholar in his harvest field, he calls whom he will, as Saul of Tarsus; but mostly uses those who were neither prophets nor the sons of one, as he did Amos. . . .

Nothing is more absurd than to say, that a man cannot understand the Scriptures, but by a knowledge of the original languages in which they were written. This is some of the doctrine of those Theologians, by which they would destroy our confidence in all translations, and thereby take our Bible from us. This, to be sure, is much allied with the old man of sin, or the mother of Harlots. This I have elsewhere called hoodwinking the people. Nothing can offer a greater insult to the Baptists, than to beg of them money, and thereby send them a new race of preachers; such as they have not been used to. . . . But these great men would have us think that our homespun preachers have only been converting the vulgar part of the community; but by a more refined kind of preaching, the rich and wise will become converted. What a pity, that these great men cannot be of the same mind of Christ, who rejoiced in spirit that these things were hid from the wise and prudent, and revealed unto babes; and with Paul, who says, not many mighty, wise or noble after the flesh, are called, and God delights to take the wise in their own craftiness, to destroy the wisdom of the wise, and bring to nothing the understanding of the prudent, which will be the fate of these money hunters, if I mistake not; for the people will find out the trick. But this new style of preachers is to be educated on patrimony. When they leave the school, they will of course be poor, and always be looking and holding out hands for patrimony. Their hands are too delicate either to make tents, or pick up a bundle of sticks, to make a fire to warm themselves as Paul did; and of course, must be the same kind of shameless beggars, that all Missionaries that I have seen, now are. . . .

10.13 The Antimission Movement

The rise of foreign missions transformed Baptists in the early-nineteenth century. Out of the dynamic of foreign missions arose the women's movement, home missions, theological education, and even, to some extent, the Sunday School movement. However, not all Baptists favored the new missionary emphasis. Some merely held aloof, while others actively opposed the movement. Motives behind this opposition included theological, personal, financial, and regional factors.

John Taylor (1752-1835) was a prominent farmer/pastor in Virginia. Unschooled himself, Taylor distrusted schools. He also feared that the financial basis of missions would undercut Christian spirituality and that the New York headquarters of the Home Mission Society would somehow undercut the independence of churches elsewhere. Excerpts from his *Thoughts on Missions* form selection A. *Source:* John Taylor, *Thoughts on Missions* (n.p., 1819), 3-21. Daniel Parker (1781-1844) sowed seeds of discord wherever he went, principally in Illinois, Tennessee, and Texas. Excerpts from his familiar *Views on the Two Seeds* are given in selection B. *Source:* Daniel Parker, *Views on the Two Seeds,* taken from Genesis 3d chapter, and part of 15th verse (Vandalia, Ill.: Republished by S. L. and C. J. Clark, 1923). The Black Rock Address (1832, selection C) gives a classic statement of Baptist opposition not only to mission societies but also to such agencies as tract and Bible societies, Sunday Schools, colleges and seminaries, and revival meetings. *Source:* B. L. Beebe, ed., *The Feast of Fat Things* (Middletown, N.Y.: G. Beebe's Son, n.d.), 3-30. More recently reprinted in W. J. Berry, comp., *The Kehukee Declaration and Black Rock Address* (Elon, N.C.: Primitive Publications, n.d.), 24-41.

No Baptist leader in the West saw more clearly the devastation wrought by Baptist "anti" forces than did R. B. C. Howell (1801-1868). Howell served as pastor of the First Baptist Church of Nashville while under appointment from the Home Mission Society. He also founded the paper that became the *Tennessee Baptist,* favored theological education, served as president of the Southern Baptist Convention, and waged determined resistance to the divisive Landmark movement that grew up in Nashville around J. R. Graves. Howell's assessment of the damage of antimissionism to Baptist life in Tennessee (selection D) is marked by keen insight, clear expression, and missionary loyalty. *Source: The Baptist Memorial,* New York, November 1845.

A. John Taylor, *Thoughts on Missions,* 1819

Through my infirmity this year, I have only been to five Baptist associations; though I have been in the habit for many years of going to from six to eight of those great annual meetings, and found some considerable degree of pleasure at those councils. But I must agree, for a number of years past, many things attending these great councils, throw an awful shade over them; some of which I will name. First.—A number of the messengers are members of the Legislature of the state, and filling some of the highest offices in the commonwealth. But to the praise of a number of those great men, they seem much more humble than many others of common rank, and who labor hard, and perhaps a year before hand, to carry some favorite point, and aim at parliamentary exactness, and with all the cunning of the bar; so that whether by hard working, or overwriting, or especially overtalking their opponent, they seem much to exult when the vote is carried on their side. Judge ye, is this from Heaven or of men?

But great as this evil may be in religious society, there is another in my belief much greater, . . . The deadly evil I have in view, is under the epithets or appellations of *Missionary Boards, Conventions, Societies,* and *Theological Schools,* all bearing the appearance of great, though affected sanctity, . . .

. . . There can be but very little doubt, when Judson and Rice were baptized by the English Missionaries in Calcutta, that they would cheerfully have received them as fellow labourers in the field of Missions.—Neither do we suppose, from the people who first sent them on a mission, they would have had any aversion to the English government. But equality in labour, I apprehend, did not suit those aspiring gentlemen. Nothing short of a large empire would answer their ambitious views. Therefore, Rice receives his furlough, as Judson terms it, to return and seek his fortune among the American Baptists, and succeeds, to be sure, far above his most sanguine expectation. . . .

The same year [1815] . . . Mr. Rice made his first appearance in Kentucky, at Elkhorn association, near Lexington. . . . When Luther rose up, the assembly of thousands, seemed stricken with his appearance. A tall, pale looking, well dressed young man, with all the solemn appearance of one who was engaged in the work of the Lord, and perhaps he thought he was. He also being a stranger, every eye and ear was open; . . . For my own part I was more amused with his ingenuity than edified by his discourse, and more astonished at his art in the close, than at any other time. He had the more pathos the nearer he came getting the money, and raising his arms as if he had some awfully pleasing vision, expressed without a hesitating doubt, that the angels were hovering over the assembly, and participating in our heavenly exercise, and just ready to take their leave, and bear the good tidings to heaven of what we were then about, in giving our money for the instruction and conversion of the poor heathens; . . . Though I admired the art of this well taught Yankee, yet I considered him a modern Tetzel, and that the Pope's old orator of that name was equally innocent with Luther Rice, and his motive about the same. . . .

Money and power are two principal members of the old beast. That both these limbs are found in this young beast is obvious, and exemplified in the great solicitude of correspondence with all the Baptist associations. Power is acquired by connection with a hundred associations, a fine nest egg of gold to answer their future ambition.

Perhaps I might not use the freedom I do, but for two tours I have taken in the Missouri country within a year past. The marvellous tales, coming from that country, about the mission there, were some inducement to my enterprize. To read, or hear the

Reports of Peck and Welch, it would seem as if the whole country was almost a blank as to religion. But the fact of the case contradicts their Reports. From their statements, one would think, there was not surely a preacher in the country that deserved the name, and hardly a church there that was in good order, whereas the fact is, there are three Baptist associations in the territory, and as many preachers, perhaps, as there are in Kentucky according to the number of the people, and many of them respectable. . . .

Why this mighty solicitude in these men to constitute churches? The motive is obvious. In the first place, these will be fine tales to write to the great board; and secondly, every church thus set up by themselves, will be under their own immediate control. Suffice it to say, that in Missouri the Missionaries pursue all the shameful measures to get money, that they do in other countries, though it is a new frontier country, many of the people poor, and all of them straitened for necessaries. It would be thought, being sent on the patrimony of the board, that they would be sparing as to donations among the poor backwoods people; but even there it is . . . *give, give.*—Their shameful trade of begging, disgusts the people wherever they go. They will beg for money for the interest of the mission; they will beg for money to print the Luminary; they will beg for money to build and finish their fine meeting house, when half the churches in the country have no house of any sort to worship God in; they will beg for money to educate young men in Dr. Stanton's Theological school, to make more Missionaries; they will beg for supplies in their own families, both in food and furniture; in short, their whole trade is begging. . . .

B. Daniel Parker, *Views on the Two Seeds,* 1826

Much has been said upon the doctrine of Election and Non-Elect. If we could correctly understand the light afforded us, in this part of the curse levied on the serpent, for what he had done, it perhaps would afford us as much information as any part of Divine Writ. . . . I shall first show a distinction in the natural existence of these two seeds; and secondly, the two covenants by which they are distinguished.

First. The natural existence of these seeds appear first in our text—yet they are sources from whence they sprung. The seed of the woman was no doubt Christ in the prime or true sense of the word. Yet, as Christ and his church are one, He the head and the church the body, we shall find the seed to be the members of the body.

A Trinity appears in the one only true and living God. . . . thus as the Father, Word and Holy Ghost are all one, and in one, so was the man, seed, and the woman: God the Father, Christ the Seed, and the Holy Ghost the instrument of their spiritual existence. So as we bore the image of our natural father, from our natural birth, we shall bare the image of our Heavenly Father by this spiritual birth. . . .

We shall now return to man in his first formation. When Adam stood with his wife and seed in him, I cannot believe that there stood any in him but the church of Christ— therefore all that stood and fell in Adam, were the elect of God, chosen in Christ before the world began. Some of my reasons are these, (weigh them well), there are two settled points with me. First, that God never created a set of beings, neither directly nor indirectly, that he suffered to be taken from him, and made the subjects of his eternal wrath and indignation; (think how would this be consistent with the Divine Creator?). Second, that God, as God, in no case possesses more love and mercy than power and wisdom. If he does, oh, think, the pain and distress the great I AM must feel and bear, to see the objects of his love and mercy to sink to woe and misery for the want of power and wisdom in himself to save (where would be the glory now?).

As there is a third point equally settled in my mind, which is that the Universalian doctrine is false, and that the unbelievers, dying in their sins, will sink to eternal woe—

it now devolves on me to show from what source the Non-elect has sprung. So at it we go.

I shall first take another view of Adam; for as he bore the name, and was the head and sovereign, not only of his own seed and wife, but of all creation which was put under him, and they all were effected by his standing, or falling. So he was the figure of Christ, which was to come, who was the head of all principalities and powers, and all things were to be affected by his standing or falling in the work of redemption. As there can be no living head without a body, there can be no Christ without a church; and Christ was from everlasting to everlasting, ere the earth was, by and for whom the world was made. And as there can be no shadow without a substance, I view Adam with the seed and woman in him, the complete figure of the Lord Jesus Christ, with the church in him, before all worlds was: therefore, while he was in the world, could look to his Father to glorify him, with the same glory he had with the Father before the world was.

Thus when the church was beguiled and had sinned, Christ was not deceived, but his love, relationship, and union to, and with her, was such that he could not be glorified without his bride, therefore he resolves to die with her, or that she should live with him; for it was impossible to separate them—his love was stronger than death. He takes upon himself, not the nature of angels, but the seed of Abraham, marries her human nature, owns the debt of his bride. . . . He bore our sins in his own body on the tree; dies for her sins: rises again for her justification, redeems her from the curse of the law, and brings life and immortality to light through the Gospel; washes her spiritual seed with his own blood, and fits them for eternal glory with himself. . . . This law required nothing to be done by Adam to preserve his standing, or making him any better—it was a law of prohibitions, (though a finite being) was able to perform. The act of doing became the sin. Thus we see where the spirit and principle of doing came from. The serpent distilled it into the woman, and set her to doing that which God had forbid, with a spirit of pride and unbelief, with a view of making herself something more than her God had made her; thus the spirit and principle of the works of the law for justification became instilled in the human heart, and has been at war with the sovereignty of God from that day to this. . . .

This brings us to the text—here God, as a curse to the Serpent for what he had done, lays the foundation of war between the Serpent and the woman, and the Serpent's seed and the woman's seed. The woman here is certainly a figure of the church of Christ. The enmity of the Serpent against the church has plainly appeared through the persecutions in the different ages of the world, while she standing opposed to the works of darkness, has proved her enmity to the Serpent. And the woman's seed here spoken of, I think was Christ and his elect in him, which was created in Adam, and by ordinary generation God designed should be brought into a natural existence in the world. And as Christ and his people are one, wherever I find one of this seed, distinguished in their natural birth, I shall feel authorized to notice it as the seed of the woman. The Serpents seed here spoken of, I believe to be the Non-elect, which were not created in Adam, the original stock, but were brought into the world as the product of sin, by way of sin, by way of a curse on the woman, who by means of sin, was made susceptible of the seed of the Serpent, through the means of her husband, who had partook with her in the transgression, and thereby became the medium through which the Serpent's seed was, and is communicated to the woman, and she became the mother of this seed, which is evidently the curse God laid upon her, when, "Unto the woman he said, I will greatly multiply thy sorrow and thy conception, in sorrow shalt though bring forth children, and thy desire shall be to thy husband, and he shall rule over thee." . . .

. . . It is evident that there are that two seeds, the one of the Serpent, the other of the woman; and they appear plain in Cain and Abel, and their offsprings. The Serpent's seed is first spoken of, and Cain first appears, although Eve owns him as a man from the Lord, yet she does not claim him her seed; . . . Eve claims Abel as her seed, and can say at the birth of Seth, that God had appointed her another seed, instead of Abel, whom Cain slew.

Thus the enmity between the two seeds appears, and the wickedness on the part of the Serpent's seed, when Cain slew Abel. . . .

I am apprized that unbelieving critics will try to believe (notwithstanding what I have said on the subject) that agreeable to my views the Devil has created a great set of beings; this is not my view; for if the Devil had the power of creating, he would be almighty. There is a great difference between creating and begetting. A man may beget, but he cannot create. Which is most reasonable to believe, that Satan had power to beget a principle and nature in man (which is admitted on all sides) or to believe that he, by permission, possessed power to beget material existence through or by the beings God had made, and in whom he had begot his own principle and nature. . . .

Another point of inquiry arises, did the Serpent's seed, or Non-Elect, stand or fall in Adam? I answer, No, the elect of God only was created, stood, and fell in Adam, partook of the serpentine nature, and were by nature the children of wrath, even as others; and therefore the original sin is in, or entailed on them, while the Serpent's seed. Although they did not receive it by the fall of man, yet they received this wicked nature immediately from the same corrupt source, which had involved the elect of God; thus in the nature of the two seeds no difference appears; for Satan had wholly captivated the elect, and engraved his image in their hearts.

And though Satan's seed had not fell in Adam, with the elect, under the curse of the divine law, yet they were sin in the abstract, flowing from the fountain of corruption. . . .

Come, my reader, let us reason together a moment. You may think my doctrine wretched—but think again, is it scripturally and experimentally reasonable to believe, but that there are sinners lost? Are these lost sinners the creatures of God by creation? Is it not more reasonable to believe they sprung from Satan, than from the Divine Being? As I think you believe with me, that God never created any one for destruction, is it not more to the glory and honor of God, to believe that he will punish Satan in his own seed, than in beings, which he himself had made, and Satan had got possession of? Does God possess more love and mercy than wisdom and power? Does he, as God, want to save more than he will or can save? How can these things be, and he be a God of infinite power and wisdom? . . .

. . . For although God did not create the Serpent's seed, or non-elect, in Adam, yet he had given man the power of begetting, and the woman of conceiving; and Satan, by sin, through the man, begets his seed in the woman, while God, for sin by the woman, multiplies her conception; and thus the Serpent's seed comes through the original stock, and yet God not their creator in the original stock.

C. The Black Rock Address

Minutes of the Proceedings and Resolutions, Drafted by the Particular Baptists, convened at Black Rock, Maryland, September 28, 1832. A meeting of Particular Baptists of the Old School convened agreeable to a previous appointment at the Black Rock meeting-house, Baltimore, Md., on Friday, 28th September, 1832. Resolved, That a committee of seven brethren, viz: Trott, Healy, Poteet, Barton and Beebe, together with the Moderator and Clerk, be appointed to prepare an Address expressive of the views of

this meeting, touching the object for which it was convened. The committee appointed to prepare an Address, submitted the following, which was unanimously adopted.
To the Particular Baptist Churches of the "Old School" in the United States.

BRETHREN:—It constitutes a new era in the history of the Baptists, when those who would follow the Lord fully, and who therefore manifest a solicitude to be, in all things pertaining to religion, conformed to the Pattern showed in the mount, are by Baptists charged with antinomianism, inertness, stupidity, &c., for refusing to go beyond the word of God; but such is the case with us.

We will notice severally the claims of the principal of these modern inventions, and state some of our objections to them for your candid consideration.

We commence with the Tract Societies. These claim to be extensively useful. Tracts claim their thousands converted. They claim the prerogative of carrying the news of salvation into holes and corners, . . . and they claim each to contain gospel enough, should it go where the Bible has never come, to lead a soul to the knowledge of Christ. . . .

If we were to admit that tracts may have occasionally been made instrumental by the Holy Ghost for imparting instruction or comfort to inquiring minds, it would by no means imply that tracts are an instituted means of salvation . . . we cannot admit the propriety of uniting with or upon the plans of the existing Tract Societies, even laying aside the idea of their being attempted to be palmed upon us as religious institutions. . . . They [those who join societies] thus become accustomed to receive everything as good which comes under the name of religion, whether it be according to the word of God or not; and are trained to the habit of letting others judge for them in matters of religion, and are therefore fast preparing to become the dupes of priestcraft. Can any conscientious follower of the Lamb submit to such plans? If others can, we cannot.

Sunday Schools come next under consideration. These assume the same high stand as do Tract Societies. They claim the honor converting their tens of thousands; of leading the tender minds of children to the knowledge of Jesus; of being as properly the instituted means of bringing children to the knowledge of salvation, as is the preaching of the gospel that of bringing adults to the same knowledge, &c. Such arrogant pretensions we feel bound to oppose. First, because these as well as the pretensions of the Tract Societies are grounded upon the notion that conversion or regeneration is produced by impressions made upon the natural mind by means of religious sentiments instilled into it; and if the Holy Ghost is allowed to be at all concerned in the thing, it is in a way which implies his being somehow blended with the instruction, or necessarily attendant upon it; all of which we know to be wrong.

Secondly, because such schools were never established by the apostles, nor commanded by Christ. . . .

Thirdly. We have exemplified in the case of the Pharisees, the evil consequences of instructing children in the letter of the Scripture, under the notion that this instruction constitutes a saving acquaintance with the word of God. We see in that instance it only made hypocrites of the Jews; and . . . we cannot believe it will have any better effect on the children in our day.

We pass to the consideration of the Bible Society . . . The idea of giving the Bible, without note or comment, to those who are unable to procure it for themselves, is in itself considered, calculated to meet the approbation of all who know the importance of the sacred Scriptures. But under this auspicious guise, we see reared in the case of the American Bible Society, an institution as foreign from anything which the gospel of Christ calls for, as are the kingdoms of this world from the kingdom of Christ. . . . We see united in this combination all parties in politics, and all sects in religion; and the distinctive differences of the one, and the sectarian barriers of the other, in part thrown aside to form the union. At the head of this vast body we see placed a few leading characters, who have in their hands the management of its enormous printing establishment, and its immense funds, and the control of its powerful influence, . . .

We will now call your attention to the subject of Missions. Previous to stating our objections to the mission plans, we will meet some of the false charges brought against us relative to this subject, by a simple and unequivocal declaration, that we do regard as of the first importance the command given of Christ, . . . to "Go into all the world, and preach the gospel to every creature," . . . We also believe it to be the duty of individuals and churches to contribute according to their abilities, for the support, not only of their pastors, but also of those who go preaching the gospel of Christ among the destitute. But we at the same time contend, that we have no right to depart from the order which the Master himself has seen fit to lay down, relative to the ministration of the word. We therefore cannot fellowship the plans for spreading the gospel, generally adopted at this day, under the name of Missions; because we consider those plans throughout a subversion of the order marked out in the New Testament. . . .

Brethren, we cheerfully acknowledge that there have been some honorable exceptions to the character we have here drawn of the modern missionary, and some societies have existed under the name of Mission Societies which were in some important points exceptions from the above drawn sketch; but on a general scale we believe we have given a correct view of the mission plans and operations, and of the effects which have resulted from them, and our hearts really sicken at this state of things. . . .

Colleges and Theological Schools next claim our attention. In speaking of colleges, we wish to be distinctly understood that it is not to colleges, or collegial education, as such, that we have any objection. We would cheerfully afford our own children such an education, did circumstances warrant the measure. But we object, in the first place, to sectarian colleges, as such. The idea of a Baptist College, and of a Presbyterian College, &c., necessarily implies that our distinct views of church government, of gospel doctrine and gospel ordinances, are connected with human sciences, a principle which we cannot admit: . . . In the second place, we object to the notion of attaching professorships of divinity to colleges; because this evidently implies that the revelation which God has made of himself is a human science on a footing with mathematics, philosophy, law, &c., . . . Thirdly. We decidedly object to persons, after professing to have been called of the Lord to preach his gospel, going to a college or academy to fit themselves for that service.—1st. Because we believe that Christ possesses perfect knowledge of his own purposes, and of the proper instruments by which to accomplish them . . . 2nd. Because we believe that the Lord calls no man to preach his gospel, till he has made him experimentally acquainted with that gospel, and endowed him with the proper measure of gifts suiting the field he designs him to occupy. . . .

We now pass to the last item which we think it necessary particularly to notice, viz: four-days or protracted meetings . . . Therefore, whenever circumstances call a congregation together from day to day, as at an association or the like, we would embrace the opportunity of preaching the gospel to them from time to time . . . but to the principles and plans of protracted meetings, distinguishingly so called, we do decidedly object. The principle of these meetings we cannot fellowship. Regeneration, we believe, is exclusively the work of the Holy Ghost, performed by his divine power, at his own sovereign pleasure, according to the provisions of the everlasting covenant; but these meetings are got up either for the purpose of inducing the Holy Spirit to regenerate multitudes who would otherwise not be converted, or to convert them themselves by the machinery of these meetings, . . .

Brethren, we have thus laid before you some of our objections to the popular schemes in religion, and the reasons why we cannot fellowship them. Ponder these things well. Weigh them in the balances of the sanctuary; and then say if they are not such as justify us in standing aloof from those plans of men, and those would-be religious societies, which are bound together, not by the fellowship of the gospel, but by certain money payments. If you cannot for yourselves meet the reproach by separating yourselves from those things which the word of God does not warrant, still allow us the privilege to obey God rather than man.

D.   R. B. C. Howell, *Missions and Anti-Missions in Tennessee,* 1845

The following questions have been proposed to me, by a distinguished and beloved brother, residing in a distant part of the United States, and I have been requested to answer them in the pages of the Memorial.

"1. Would not the statistics of the last quarter of a century show, that in Tennessee many churches and associations, which in the earlier portion of this period, were missionary in their feelings and tendencies, and partially so in their action, have since gone over to the other side? Why is this?"

"2. Anti-mission Baptists in Tennessee now bear a larger proportion to mission Baptists, than in the other states. Why is this?"

"3. Anti-mission Baptists have been annually diminishing elsewhere, for some time; here they seem to increase, or, at least, to maintain their relative numbers. Why is this?"

The task here assigned me is rather a difficult one, but I shall address myself, without any formality, to its performance. To the first question I give an affirmative reply. The original churches in Tennessee were all missionary in their feelings and tendencies, and partially so in their action, and they continued to maintain this attitude until about a quarter of a century ago. Their sympathies appear to have been peculiarly elicited by the condition of the Indians, by whom, on all sides, they were surrounded. . . .

A quarter of a century ago, therefore, the feelings, and tendencies, and action of the Tennessee churches were missionary, and they would have continued so, had the interests of truth been properly superintended; and any tolerable resistance been offered to the evil influences, which were brought to bear upon them, and which proved so disastrously successful in their overthrow. Many churches and associations, "then missionary," have since gone over to the other side. The causes that produced this revolution, I will now attempt to designate and illustrate.

About that time the noted Daniel Parker began to attract attention. He was, as is well known, the author of the "Two Seed Doctrine," as it is usually called, and then, and for some time after, resided in Middle Tennessee; from whence he removed to Illinois, and finally to Texas, where, last autumn, he paid the debt of nature. Several circumstances combined to give him and his doctrine extraordinary influence. Our Methodist brethren had, from the first settlement of the country, been very numerous and strong. Here the Cumberland denomination arose, and it swept over the land like a whirlwind. Both these classes of christians were ultra-arminian, and they and the Baptists were perpetually at war. It is not surprising, that in these circumstances, the Baptists became insensibly ultra-predestinarian. Of this doctrine Parker was the champion, and therefore, the general favorite. In his person, dress, and manners, he was plain, approximating to vulgarity. This also added to his popularity. And, withal, he was a man of astonishing ability, and untiring industry. . . .

Mr. Parker set in motion the means that overthrew missions in Tennessee, and to which he was induced by the following considerations.—He was ambitious to be a writer, and sought, as the medium of his communications with the public, the columns of the Columbian Star, then published in Washington City. His essays, setting forth his own peculiar opinions, were rejected by that paper, and his doctrines ridiculed as equally immodest and preposterous. This was too much for a man of his unbounded pride and self-confidence tamely to endure. The offence given him was unpardonable. The conductors of the Star he knew to be associated in the conduct of the missionary enterprise, and of ministerial education. From that hour he conceived the most implacable hatred against the men, and all their pursuits. . . .

Meantime, no agent, or other friend of missions, visited the state, who might have corrected these false impressions, and set all these matters, and missions particularly, in their proper light. No Baptist paper existed in the south, and none was taken, except, perhaps, by one in a thousand of our brethren. Moreover, some of the prime friends of missions became converts to Mr. Alexander Campbell's system, and joined him. Thus missions became beyond measure odious. . . .

The second inquiry is this:—"Anti-mission Baptists in Tennessee now bear a larger proportion to Mission Baptists, than in the other states. Why is this?"

It grows out of the facts already detailed, and the circumstances under which the re-organization of our missionary associations were made. I will explain.

The light which had been driven from the state gradually returned. Another race of men, better informed, was rising up. . . . A small number advised with each other, and determined to meet at an appointed time and place, and decide what they would do. . . . They were, however, soon taught, and that, too, in the most painful manner, that they had committed two errors,—they had organized before they had disabused and enlightened the members of the churches generally, and consequently, before they were prepared to co-operate in the work; and they had not consulted a large number of brethren, lay and ministerial, who considered themselves thereby undervalued and abused. . . .

Correctness of theological principle, as well as resistance to selfish schemes, was also pleaded as a reason for opposition. God, it was maintained, would surely save his people, in his own time and way,—not one of the elect would ever be lost. . . . therefore, no orthodox Baptist could be either a missionary or a friend of missions. The whole was denounced as a scheme of arminianism, as to doctrine, and prompted only by a desire for money, and the hope of fame, on the part of its advocates. . . .

These measures, prosecuted with ceaseless industry, were not without corresponding results. The cause of missions was brought almost to an entire pause. . . .

The last question is as follows—"Anti-mission Baptists have been annually diminishing elsewhere, for some time; here, (in Tennessee) they seem to increase, or, at least, to maintain their relative numbers. Why is this?"

I doubt much whether anti-mission Baptists in Tennessee are increasing, or do maintain their relative numbers. Their numbers, however, are very respectable, and they frequently have important additions. This arises from two causes; the character and circumstances of the nominally anti-missionaries, and the weakness of the missionaries.

In the first place, when the lines were drawn, many . . .warm-hearted and active ministers and people were included with the opposition, and still remain in their ranks. . . .

The weakness of the missionary party is the second cause. They are composed of a host of as noble spirits as I have ever known, and they do all they can; but they have not been able to occupy the state. To do so they would require fifty times the amount of men and means that they can now command.

This is my answer to the third inquiry. I will add a few observations.

Since the recommencement of missionary efforts in Tennessee, the cause has been slowly but steadily progressing. In East Tennessee, where, I think, they have more religion, and in the western district, where they have more information, greater advancements have been made than in Middle Tennessee. The denominational state paper is now exerting great influence. An institution has been commenced, and successful efforts are being made to secure fifty thousand dollars for educational purposes. A few young men are studying at various points, with a view to the ministry. Something has been done for the distribution of the bible, and to support foreign missions, and some few thousand Baptist books have been distributed. The Convention has been changed into a General Association, with auxiliaries in the two extremes of the state, and ten or a dozen missionaries, on an average have been kept constantly in the field, whose labors have been blessed with extraordinary success. Some very strong and influential churches have arisen in prominent positions, and it is believed that the state can never be thrown back into its former darkness. Tennessee presents a most promising field of labor. The great impediment to the success of the principles which we believe to be scriptural and true, is the want of a sufficient number of well instructed, humble, and laborious ministers, devoted to their appropriate work.   H.

10.14   The Alexander Campbell Movement

Alexander Campbell (1788-1866) led a major schism in Baptist life in the 1830s. This schism produced the Church of Christ movement of today. Alexander and his father, Thomas Campbell, came from a Presbyterian background in Ireland, whence they immigrated to America in the early 1800s. After an intense period of Bible study, the Campbells in 1812 adopted immersion of believers and the next year affiliated with the Redstone Baptist Association in western Pennsylvania. This was an uneasy alliance. Time would reveal that between the Campbells and the Baptists the similarities were shallow, while the differences were deep. From 1816 onward Alexander Campbell agitated such issues as Old Testament authority, the role and status of the ministry, the nature of saving faith, and the place of baptism in the salvation experience. He opposed missionary societies, ministerial titles, and, especially after acquiring substantial property, ministerial salaries. Campbell engaged in widely publicized debates, published a popular paper, and preached throughout several states. While many Baptists were attracted to his reforming ideas, others opposed them as undercutting historic Baptist practices and beliefs. *Sources:* Minutes of the Franklin Association of Baptist Churches, held at Buffalo Lick, Shelby County, Kentucky, August 1826. J. H. Spencer, *A History of Kentucky Baptists,* 2 vols. (For the author, 1886), 1:610-611. Minutes of the Franklin Association of Baptists, Frankfort, Kentucky, July 1830. In American Baptist Historical Society, Rochester, New York

A.   American Baptist Association (Kentucky)
Circular Letter on Campbellism's Objection to Confessions, 1826

TO THE CHURCHES COMPOSING THE FRANKLIN ASSOCIATION,

. . . In this annual address we propose to consider this question. Is it lawful and expedient to adhere to a Creed, in the admission of members into the fellowship of the Church, and particularly in the admission of candidates into office?

Creeds formed or enforced by the civil authority, are usurpatious, leading to persecution and to despotism; while those formed by voluntary Associations of Christians, enforced by no higher penalty or sanction, than exclusion from membership in the society are not only lawful, but necessary, in the present state of the religious world. To deny to any religious society the privilege of expressing their views of the Bible in their own words and phrases, and of denying admission to those who reject their views, is a violent interference with the rights of conscience—it is tyranny. . . .

By a creed we mean an epitome, or summary exhibition of what the Scriptures teach. Are we to admit members into the church and into office, are we to license and ordain preachers, without enquiring for their creed? . . . There are but two methods of admitting members into church, and into office. It must be done either with or without respect to a Creed.

We cannot conceive of any third method. If the church rejects a candidate because he holds Sabellian Arian or Socinian principles, she then has respect to a Creed. She insists upon her own interpretations of the Bible, upon fundamental points. She does not deny him the liberty of interpreting the Bible for himself; this would be usurpation—it would be tyranny. But while he contemns and reviles her views of the Bible, she claims to herself the right of denying to him her fellowship. . . . Yes without respect to a Creed, she is reduced to the cruel necessity, of harboring under her wings, the vilest heresies that now disgrace the Christian name. Can she do this and incur no guilt? Can she do this and yet preserve her unity, purity, and harmony? Is there communion between light and darkness, fellowship between righteousness and unrighteousness, concord between Christ and Belial?

If the modern adversaries of all creeds and confessions, should say, that they will not go thus far, that they will not admit into the church, and much less into the ministry, or rather the bishops office, one holding Socinian principles, they evidently yield the question. . . . For if they can make one article to exclude a Socinian, they may make another to exclude the Arian, and a third to exclude the Pelagian, and a fourth to exclude the Armenian, &c &c adding article to article, untill they get as many as they conceive the exigencies of the church requires. . . .

We do not propose to enquire, how long, or how short, a church covenant, or creed shall be. Nor will we examine, now, into the merits or defects of any existing summary of Faith. These questions do not enter into the present controversy. Is it lawful and expedient for a church to adopt any articles of Faith, whatever, as a test of union and a fence against corruption? This is the enquiry to which the attention of the christian world, has been recently summoned, and to which we respond.

It has been said, that to adopt a creed as a religious test, "is to supercede the Bible, and to make a human composition instead of it, a standard of Faith. That when we do this, we offer a public indignity to the sacred volume, as we virtually declared either, that it is not infallible or not sufficient." In reply to this, we use the language of a distinguished divine, who in a few words has exposed its fallacy and swept it from the arena of eclesiastical controversy. The whole argument which this objection presents, is founded on a false assumption. No Protestant ever professed to regard his Creed, considered as a human composition, as of equal authority with the Scriptures, and far less as of paramount authority. Every principle of this kind, is with one voice disclaimed by all the Creeds, and defences of Creeds, that have appeared in ancient, or modern times, so far as we are informed. And whether, notwithstanding this, the constant repetition of the charge, ought to be considered as fair argument or gross calumny, the impartial will judge. A Church Creed professes to be deduced from the Scriptures, and to refer to the Scriptures, for the whole of its authority. Of course when any one subscribes to it, he is so far from dishonouring the Bible, that he does public homage to it. He simply declares by a solemn act, how he understands the Bible, in other words, what doctrines he considers it as containing. . . .

But still, we are asked, "if the Scriptures are not plain and easy to be understood, can we make them plainer than the author has done? Why "hold a candle to the Sun &c?"

This objection amounts to nothing, while the fact remains undisputed, that thousands who profess to receive the Scriptures, by their false and spurious glosses, do virtually deny the radical doctrines contained therein. The lamentable act, that the enemy (even now,) comes in like a flood and it devolves upon every religious society, who would bear witness to the truth, the imperious duty, of lifting up a standard for truth.

Let those who oppose the use of Creeds, answer these questions. Has the Head of the Church made no qualifications, necessary for the admission of members into the Church? Has he made no qualifications necessary for admission into office? Has he established no tribunal on earth, to judge of these qualifications? Is an Arian, Socinian, or Universalist, qualified for either membership, or office? Can it be said, they are not without respect to a Creed? Strip the point in issue of all the tawdry guise, which the ingenuity of modern times has cast over it, and there is scarcely room for controversy. The common sense of every man revolts at the idea of assembling in the same church, and around the same board, everything that now bears the name of Christian; . . . Must those who maintain the true Gospel, walk together in Church fellowship, with those who are accursed for preaching another gospel, and who espouse damnable heresies? Is this the New Testament plan? If you say, (as doubtless you will,) that it is not; that such a Society would not be the Church of Christ—the result is this, "If there be any divine warrant, for a Church (in this day,) there is a divine warrant for a Creed, as a test of union, a bond of fellowship, a fence against error, and a shield against that spirit of restless inspiration, which esteems every novelty, an improvement." What shall be its dimensions, its height, or depth, its length or breadth, is not now the topic of enquiry. But one thing is certain, it should be large enough, to meet the exigencies of the Church, by preserving her, while in the wilderness, exposed to trials, in peace, purity and love; And it should be small enough, to find a lodgment in the heart, of the weakest lamb, sound in the faith. . . . Upon this interesting subject, the history of near eighteen centuries should admonish us. To live, as a society, without a Confession of Faith has been often attempted—but we have yet to be informed of the first instance of its succeeding. We understand that the Congregational churches of Massachusetts, have made the dangerous experiment, and like those who have embarked before them in the same presumptuous enterprise, they have fallen a prey to dissention and heresy, to a degree equally instructive and mournful. . . .

Note—The above Circular Letter was written by S. M. Noel.

James Ford, Clerk   S. M. Noel, Moderator

B. Beaver Baptist Association (Pennsylvania) against Campbellism, 1829

In August, 1829, Beaver Association, a small Baptist fraternity in Pennsylvania, met at Providence meeting-house, near Pittsburg, and, after discussing the subject of Mr. Campbell's teaching, resolved to withdraw fellowship from Mahoning Association, on account of its maintaining, or countenancing, the following sentiments, or creed:

1. They maintain that there is no promise of salvation without baptism.

2. That baptism should be administered to all who say that Jesus Christ is the son of God, without examination on any other point.

3. That there is no direct operation of the Holy Spirit, on the mind, prior to baptism.

4. That baptism produces the remission of sins and the gift of the Holy Spirit.

5. That the Scriptures are the only evidence of interest in Christ.

6. That obedience places it in God's power to elect to salvation.

7. That no creed is necessary for the church but the Scriptures as they stand.

8. That all baptized persons have a right to administer the ordinance of baptism.

This is believed to have been the first official declaration of nonfellowship for Mr.

Campbell and his followers. The other associations corresponding with Mahoning, withdrew fellowship from it, during the same, and the following month. The Appomattox Association in Virginia, at its meeting, in May. 1830, recorded the following item:

"Whereas, there is satisfactory evidence, that the writings of Alexander Campbell have exerted what we consider a mischievous influence upon numbers of churches, fomenting envy, strife and divisions among those who had before lived in fellowship and peace. Therefore, *Resolved,* That this association most cordially approves the course pursued by the Beaver and her sister associations in withdrawing from Mahoning."

C. Franklin Baptist Association (Kentucky)
Report and Warning about Campbellism, 1830

To the Churches composing the Franklin Association.
Dear Brethren:

You will learn from our Minutes, the results of this called session of our association. Before Alexander Campbell visited Kentucky, you were in harmony and peace; you heard but the one gospel, and knew only the one Lord, one faith and one baptism. Your church constitutions were regarded, and their principles expounded and enforced, by those who occupied your pulpits. Thus you were respected by other denominations, as a religious community. . . . Have not these happy days gone by? In place of preaching, you now may hear your church covenants ridiculed, your faith, as registered upon your church books, denounced, and yourselves traduced; while the more heedless and unstable, abjure the faith, and join with the wicked, in scenes of strife, schism and tumult. The fell spirit of discord stalks in open day through families, neighborhoods and churches. If you would protect yourselves as churches, make no compromise with error; mark them who cause divisions; divest yourselves of the last vestige of Campbellism.

As an Association we shall esteem it our duty to drop correspondence with any and every Association, or Church, where this heresy is tolerated. Those who say they are not Campbellites, and yet countenance and circulate his little pamphlets, are insincere: they are to be avoided. . . .

. . . And that you may know the full extent of our objections, we herewith send you several articles gathered from his Christian Baptist, and Millenial Harbinger, with a reference to the pamphlet and to the page, where you can read and judge, whether they are, or are not, the reformation tenets.

It may be said that these scraps are garbled from many volumes. Verily, they are but scraps; but each scrap embodies an opinion easily understood; so that this may, with some propriety, be called a Confession of Opinions. We are not obliged to re-publish his pamphlets. Were we, however, to do it, the nature and bearing of these opinions would not be changed.

THE THIRTY-NINE ARTICLES!!

or

A new edition of old errors, extracted from Alexander Campbell's Christian
Baptist and Millenial Harbinger.

1. "That there has been no preaching of the gospel since the days of the apostles."
2. "That the people have been preached to from texts of scripture until they have been literally preached out of their senses." . . .
5. "That all the faith that men can have in Christ, is historical . . ."
8. "That baptism, which is synonymous with immersion, and for which every such believer is a proper subject, actually washes away sin, and is regeneration . . ."

9. "That in the moral fitness of things in the evangelical economy, baptism or immersion is made the first act of a Christian's life, or rather the regenerating act itself; in which the person is properly born again—born of water and spirit—without which, into the kingdom of heaven he cannot enter." . . . C. B. vol. 5, p. 223. . . .

12. "That by the mere act of a believing immersion into the name of the Father, Son, and Holy Spirit, we are born again, have all our sins remitted, receive the Holy Spirit, and are filled with joy and peace." C. B. vol. 5, p. 213. "Query. Is a believer in Christ not actually in a pardoned state, before he is baptised? Answer. Is not a man clean before he is washed!! . . . And, blessed be God! he has not drawn a mere artificial line between the plantations of nature and of grace. No man has any proof that he is pardoned until he is baptized. . . ." Ch. Bap. vol. 6, p. 188.

13. "That christian immersion is the gospel in water. The Lord's supper is the gospel in bread and wine." C. B. vol. 5, p. 158. As water saved Noah, so baptism saves us. . . ." C. B. vol. 7, p. 125. . . .

16. "All the sons of men cannot show that there is any other faith, but the belief of facts either written in the form of history or orally delivered. Angels, men, or demons, cannot define any thing under the term faith, but the belief of facts or of history; except they change it into confidence. . . ." C. B. vol. 6, p. 186. . . .

18. Millions have been tantalized by a mock gospel, which places them as the fable places Tautalus, standing in a stream parched with thirst, and the water running to his chin, and so circumstanced that he could not taste it. There is a sleight of hand, or religious legerdemain, in getting around the matter. To call any thing grace, or favor, or gospel, not adapted to man, as it finds him, is the climax of misnomers. To bring the cup of salvation to the lips of a dying sinner, and then tell him for his soul he cannot taste it, without some sovereign aid beyond human control, is to mock his misery and to torment him more and more." C. B. 6 vol. p. 187. . . .

26. "I have not spent, perhaps, an hour in ten years in thinking about the Trinity. It is no term of mine. It is a word which belongs not to the bible, in any translation of it I ever saw. I teach nothing, I say nothing, I think nothing about it, save that it is not a scriptural term, and consequently, can have no scriptural ideas attached to it." C. B. 7 vol. p. 208. . . .

28.   "Come, Holy Spirit, Heavenly Dove,
                With all thy quick'ning powers!
          Kindle a flame of sacred love
          In these cold hearts of ours."

"In the singing this hymn, which is very ingeniously adapted to your sermon and prayer, you have very unfortunately fallen into two errors. First—you are singing to the Holy Spirit, as you prayed to it, without any example from any one of the old saints, either in the Old or New Testament; and without the possibility of ever receiving an answer to your prayer. The second error into which you have fallen, is this: you acknowedge [sic] your church to be the church of Christ; and if the church of Christ, its members of course have the spirit of Christ."—Ch. Bap. vol. VII, p. 129. . . .

32. "THE BELIEF OF ONE FACT, and that upon the best evidence in the word, is all that is requisite as far as faith goes, to salvation. The belief of this one FACT, and submission to ONE INSTITUTION, expressive of it, is all that is required of Heaven to admission into the church. The one fact is, that Jesus, the Nazarene, is the Messiah. The evidence upon which it is to be believed, is, the testimony of twelve men, confirmed by prophecy, miracles, and spiritual gifts. The one institution is, baptism into the name of the Father, and of the Son, and of the Holy Spirit. Every such person is a christian, in the fullest sense of the word." C. B. vol. 1, p. 221.

33. "Revivals. Enthusiasm flourishes, blooms, under the popular systems. This man was regenerated when asleep by a vision of the night. That man heard a voice in the woods, saying, 'Thy sins are forgiven thee.' A third saw his Saviour descending to the tops of the trees at noon day. A thousand form a band, and set up all night to take heaven by surprise. Ten thousand are waiting for a power from on high, to descend upon their souls; they frequent meetings for the purpose of obtaining this power." C. B. 1 vol. p. 187 . . .

35. Some look for another call, a more powerful call than the written Gospel presents. They talk of an inward call, of hearing the voice of God in their souls. This special call is either a lie or it makes the general call a lie. This is where the system ends. The voice of God, and the only voice of God, which you will hear, till he calls you home, is his written Gospel." Mil. Har. No. 3, p. 126-7. . . .

38. "In the natural order of the evangelical economy, the items stand thus:—1st, Faith; 2d, Reformation; 3d, Immersion; 4th, Remission of sins; 5th, Holy Spirit; 6th, Eternal Life." C. B. 6 vol. p. 66. "There are three Kingdoms; the Kingdom of Law, the Kingdom of Favor, and the Kingdom of Glory; each has a different constitution, different subjects privileges, and terms of admission. The blood of Abraham brought a man into the Kingdom of Law, and gave him an inheritance in Canaan. Being born, not of blood, but through water and the spirit of God, brings a person into the Kingdom of favor; which is righteousness, peace, joy, and a holy spirit, with a future inheritance in prospect. But if the justified draw back, or the washed return to the mire, or if faith die and bring forth no fruits, into the Kingdom of Glory he cannot enter. Hence good works through faith, or springing from faith in Jesus, give a right to enter into the holy city." C. B. 6 vol. 255.

39. Vol. 5, p. 122. "There is no democracy nor aristocracy in the governmental arrangements of the church of Jesus Christ. The citizens are all volunteers when they enlist under the banners of the Great King, and as soon as they place themselves in the ranks, they are bound to implicit obedience in all the institutes and laws of their sovereign. So that there is no putting the question to vote, whether they shall obey any particular law or injunction. Their Rulers or Bishops have to give an account of their administration, and have only to see that the laws are known and obeyed."

[Truly, this is not democracy; nor is it a moderate aristocracy. What is it, short of Episcopacy or Papacy!]

BRETHREN: Can you read this, and say or think that it is not, even now, high time to "march out of Babylon?" Doubtless you cannot hesitate. In February, 1825, Mr. Campbell denounced reformation. "The very name, (he said), has become as offensive as the term "Revolution" in France." He is now in a paroxism about Reformation. In all the extravagance of unbridled fanaticism, he fancies that he has already introduced the Millenium, as far as his tenets, have prevailed. The Millenium, he dreams, has bursted in upon South Benson, Versailles, Clear Creek, David's Fork, and Shawnee Run. Who besides himself, and those who have sold their birth right—who have commuted the heads and hearts for reformation pottage, can indulge in a conceit so silly and ridiculons. [sic] From such frenzy and quackery, and above all from such a Millenium, may a kind Providence deliver us. Amen.

10.15　Call for a Baptist State Convention in South Carolina, 1820

The earliest Baptist state convention in America was formed in South Carolina in 1821. In 1820 a committee of Baptists, led by Richard Furman of Charleston, issues a *Call* to the various associations in South Carolina to send delegates to consider forming a statewide body. That *Call*, with its analysis of the most pressing Baptist needs of the time, forms an important document in Baptist history. Furman had long advocated cooperative organization to allow Baptists to maximize their ministry efforts. The Charleston Association had already begun to work in a limited way in ministerial education and home missions, but Furman and others saw an opportunity for greater efforts in those areas. The objects of the proposed state convention would be primarily twofold: to sponsor ministerial education, and to promote missions, both foreign and domestic. A related convention endeavor would be the formation of Sunday Schools. This state convention provided a pattern of organization which influenced the Southern Baptist Convention in 1845. *Source:* A Call for a State Convention in South Carolina, 1820, issued as part of the Minutes of the Charleston Baptist Association, 8 Nov. 1820.

Call for a State Convention in South Carolina
To the Different
Baptist Associations
In the State of South-Carolina.

BELOVED BRETHREN,

There are two portions of Scripture which minister a serious alarm to Churches, as well as to Individuals. One is in Malachi, "Cursed be the deceiver who hath in his flock a male, and voweth and sacrificeth to the Lord a corrupt thing:" the other is in the Epistle of James, "To him that knoweth to do good, and doeth it not, to him it is sin." The first requires that our best offerings should be presented to the Lord, when we engage in his service; the second shows, that by keeping back from the performance of duty and promotion of good, when that duty and good are known, we incur guilt, and consequently suffer the righteous displeasure of the Lord. . . .

These remarks are intended to be introductory to certain considerations respecting the present state of our Churches, in which it is believed defects or deficiencies exist, which are injurious to the cause of God, by preventing its progress, and by presenting it, too often, in an unfavorable light before men of discernment. They are also designed to be introductory to a plan for improvement; by the regular operation of which these evils, through the blessing of God, may be removed, and the Churches assisted to come forth in their strength, under the approving smiles of the Almighty, to perform their part in the great work of evangelizing the world. . . .

The evils, defects, or deficiencies referred to above, or which will be principally considered here, consist partly in practice, partly in sentiment, and partly in disposition: but may be summed up under the character of neglect. . . .

The neglect of giving education to Ministers; of affording support to those who are already employed in the ministry; of providing convenient, decent houses, in many instances, for the public worship of God; of educating children carefully and religiously; and of taking proper measures for sending the gospel abroad among the unenlightened and destitute, may all be traced up to this cause. And these are evils which exist less or more among a great part of our Churches, and in some places to a high degree. On each of these we might insist with advantage; but as what relates to the assistance of Ministers, by giving them education, is a subject of the first importance in our estimation; and as with the want of it, all the other defects we have noticed, are ordinarily more or less connected, we shall insist principally on this. And here it is natural to ask; is it not certain, that Ministers who have failed to obtain some good share of education, are not fitted to take that station in society, or exert that influence which would properly belong to them if they had? Is not this apparent to persons of common discernment; and are not their defects in language and knowledge, lamented by their friends, while they become the matter of scoff and derision to their enemies? Do not even children, who have obtained a tolerable portion of regular education, see these defects in them; and when they have made a little advance in knowledge and experience, do they not begin to discover them themselves; and feel embarrassed and discouraged, especially when they have to speak before an enlightened audience? But if they remain insensible to these defects in themselves, which every discerning eye discovers; are bold and confident of their knowledge and abilities, and venture upon subjects to which they are unequal, in language which is not proper, and with reasoning which is not just (all of which is too common,) how necessarily as well as certainly do they become the objects of censure and ridicule. They may in these cases think the disapprobation arises from men's dislike of religion and truth, and so be disposed to glory in it; when, in truth, it is on account of that for which, if it is the effect of choice, or the consequence of neglect, they ought to be sorry and ashamed.

Another evil growing out of this state of things is often found to be of great magnitude, and essential injury. It is this—When entrance into the ministry is made so easy, that every person with warm passions, apparent piety, and a little fluency of speech, can readily get encouragement to enter on the ministerial character and work, just as he is, persons of a forward spirit, and unworthy motives, often get admittance; and those too, who profess essential qualifications, come in this case under strong temptations to reject, or neglect the means of improvement, which would be of the highest importance, in rendering them workmen who need not be ashamed, and in making them extensively useful in the cause of God. And it operates still further as an evil, in leading them to think that religion, in its spirituality, requires them thus to act. The consequence of these sentiments and their influence in practice is, that in a very large proportion of our Churches, our ministers have but little of that improvement which is to be obtained by rational means: and the Churches with the gifts of Providence in their possession, by which those means might be provided, not only fail to improve them to this purpose, but remain careless and secure, in their neglect; and are even confident, in many instances, that they are pursuing the right course, and that all will be well. A state of weakness, therefore, seems to be entailed on our Churches on this plan: advantages placed in our reach by a kind Providence are not secured; and usefulness, which might be arrived at, is not attained:—And we will add that most serious disadvantages are about to be suffered, beyond any thing we have heretofore experienced, unless a serious and thorough reformation shall speedily take place. . . .

The plan of assisting pious young men in obtaining education for the ministry, which used to be considered as exclusively belonging to the Baptists, has been adopted by [other] denomiantions [sic], and with great activity, zeal and perseverance, they are forming funds and uniting Societies for the permanent support of this scheme: and many young men are now actually receiving education for this purpose; some indeed have already come out on this plan. We, therefore, may reasonably expect, that a large number of zealous advocates for sentiments which we do not consider Scriptural, possessing talent, zeal and piety, will soon be actively employed in every part of our country, propagating not only the gospel in general, in which we must wish them success, but their peculiar sentiments too, and forming congregations in support of them, where Baptists now exist. According to the common course of events, therefore, it may be expected that these Preachers will collect about them many of the enlightened and leading characters in the country where they go, who have any respect for religion, and are not decidedly Baptists in sentiment; and with them a large proportion of the multitude, whose knowledge is very imperfect, their principles lax, and their minds disposed to come under the influence of any who by them are considered as influential and honorable. Thus we think there is great reason to apprehend that such Churches as we have described, and their Ministers with them (they continuing in their present state,) will love their influence in society where they now possess it, and be thrown into the back ground.

Another consideration of great weight presents itself to the mind here. It is this: unitarianism is exerting itself with ingenuity, vigor and address, to make proselytes and acquire permanence. Many who were considered as orthodox and even pious christians, have by its adherents been won over to their sentiments. In the Northern States they have made considerable progress, and acquired extensive influence; even Baptist Ministers and Churches (though blessed be God not many) have been corrupted. In Charleston, also, they have made an impression, and there is reason to apprehend the fermenting influence of the leaven will extend into the country. Now by this scheme the proper divinity of our Divine Lord is denied, together with the merit of his atoning blood, the necessity of his renewing grace, and the reality of regeneration. The personality of the Holy Ghost is also denied; and we are taught to understand nothing more by his character, than of an undefined power or influence, sometimes exerted on the human mind. To support all which sentiments, and others connected with them, we are told that the scriptures have been wrongly translated or corrupted, and that some parts of them are not of divine authority: A copy is made out professing strict conformity to the original, in favor of these sentiments; and notes are added to give confirmation to this meaning. Tracts controversial and didactic, are written with ingenuity and address, and with a great show of learning and reason, and industriously circulated, especially among the higher circles of society, in order to win over to the scheme as many as possible. Now how can it be expected that successful opposition can be made to such a scheme, and to such measures, without the instrumentality of learned men, on the spot, where the attack on truth and righteousness is made, and that in so formidable a manner. . . .

We, therefore, propose that a united general meeting of all the Baptist Associations in this State be held, as soon as the subject can be brought regularly before them, for their consideration; and that a delegation be made of a suitable number of their most enlightened and influential members; men who are governed by the fear and love of God, to concert measures in favor of these general interests, in which the cause and honor of God are so deeply concerned; and particularly with a view to the work of collecting and establishing funds in favor of educating ministers, and of sending the gospel to the destitute.

Each of these subjects embraces two important objects: The first of which respects the immediate assistance of pious young men designed for the gospel ministry, by giving them a knowledge of languages and general science; the second, for the establishment of the Theological Seminary, proposed by the Convention . . . [Second, for missions] contributions are proposed—First, for sending the gospel to the Heathen—secondly, to the destitute in our own country. The whole to be conducted in strict connection with the General Convention, in which we consider the interest of the Baptists in America, virtually and happily combined.

We propose further, that the Assembly which may be formed on this plan, shall be called The State Convention of the Baptists in South-Carolina: that the place of meeting be Columbia; and that the meeting be held on the first Tuesday in December of the ensuing year [1822].

In the beginning of our Address we have noticed the obligations Christians are under to render their best offerings to God, and of doing good when it is in the power of their hand, the subject known, and the opportunity afforded:—We now add that the subject before us, though of great magnitude and high concern, is practicable; and if there is but a willing mind, may with the common blessing of Divine Providence be effected with ease. To make which appear evident, let it be considered, that according to the returns made to the different Associations in this State, the Churches they represent contain from fourteen to fifteen thousand members. Persons uniting with them in worship, many of whom are generously disposed, and many fully Baptists in sentiment, are probably three times that number: this will give a total of sixty thousand. Now, if but one fourth part of this number should contribute but one dollar a year, to a general fund, for these pious and beneficent purposes, there would be fifteen thousand dollars. . . .

With respect to the Theological Seminary, or College, and the Missionary measures, it ought also to be remembered, that they are objects of attention to the Baptist denomination throughout the United States: that very considerable contributions have been already made in their favor; and that there is reason to believe, that as the public mind becomes more generally enlightened concerning their nature and design, and roused to action, these contributions will become much more considerable.

We wish to suggest, that the formation of Societies in the respective Congregations connected with the Churches, both of male and female members, either separate or united, is a measure that bids fair to be useful in the work of collecting funds; and has been known to be of excellent use to those who have adopted it; among which are several Churches in our immediate connection. In the British and Foreign Bible Society, which expends more than four hundred thousand dollars yearly, in translating, printing and distributing the blessed word of God, among almost all the nations of the earth, a great part of the funds is collected in this way. But public collections, connected with annual Charity Sermons, should not, we conceive, be overlooked. Nor should the benevolent fail to receive information, that donations and legacies made for such purposes, would be faithfully and religiously applied to the proper objects.

Should the union here contemplated be formed, we trust the Convention will turn its attention with peculiar regard to the institution of Sunday Schools, for the gratuitous instruction of the ignorant, so far as to enable them to read the Scriptures; and to the instruction of children and youth who can read, in religious knowledge. These have been found to be of excellent use; having been the blessed means of bringing about the conversion of many children; and frequently of young persons who have been assistant teachers in them, of both sexes.

We are not without apprehension, that some of our brethren, at the first view, may feel backward to engage in this undertaking, under an impression that it originates too much in carnal motives, and has worldly advantages in view, more than the interests of the Redeemer's Kingdom; and that its tendency is to depreciate the persons, gifts and labors of valuable Ministers of Christ, who have borne the burden and heat of the day in their Master's cause, and have been owned by him, as well as esteemed by his people, as Ministers of the New Testament, worthy of acceptation, though destitute of human learning; or possessing it only in a small degree.— Should such ideas exist in the minds of any, we hope they will not be cherished there. What our motives are is known to God, who tries the heart and reins: we trust it will be found in the great day of final accounts, to have originated in a concern for his glory, and the best interests of the Church. But we are free to declare, that we do not consider human learning as an essential requisite for the gospel ministry; nor that any man is qualified by its possession, without grace and ministerial gifts, for the service. We know that there are men who possess it to a high degree, and have taken on them the office of Ministers by profession, who are by no means well qualified for it; and that there are others who possess but very little of such learning, and yet are useful and excellent Ministers of Christ. Yet such labor under certain disadvantages; and there are important, and often most necessary services called for in the cause of God, which they are not qualified to perform. Many of us know this feelingly; and if by private exertion, some obstacles have been surmounted, and some attainments arrived at; yet we have had in such circumstances, and still have in a manner, to creep, where we might have run, or have mounted upon wings like the eagle toward Heaven.

The learning also which we wish to promote is not that which a man of a vain mind would wish to pursue, and which would enable him to appear in gaudy colors before an ill-judging multitude; but solid knowledge, which will qualify the man of piety and uprightness to labor with advantage in the cause of righteousness; and to appear before the children of wisdom and of God, as a workman, who need not be ashamed, rightly dividing the word of truth: who may be able to stand in the front of the battle where truth and righteousness are the subjects of contest, and by whom the mouths of gainsayers may be stopped, when they contradict and blaspheme.

To learning of this character, and to measures well calculated to obtain it, we trust, every loyal subject of Zion's glorious King will give his cordial approbation, and vigorous support . . .

Yours affectionately in gospel bonds.

Signed in behalf of the Charleston   RICHARD FURMAN,
Baptist Association, and by their order,   JOHN M. ROBERTS,
November 8th, 1820.   JOSEPH B. COOK.

10.16   The Slavery Controversy Among Baptists

The controversy over slavery proved divisive for Baptists, as it did for the entire nation. At first the controversy was more ideological than geographical, with both opponents and defenders of the slave system found in both North and South. However, after 1800 opposition to slavery came to be more identified with the North, while the South turned more to the defense of that system. This controversy provoked a major schism among Baptists in 1845, out of which the Southern Baptist Convention was formed.

In selection A, Richard Furman defends slavery. This Charleston pastor was one of the most influential Baptists of his day. His treatise, addressed to the governor, was authorized by the Baptist State Convention of South Carolina and expresses the views of most Baptists of that time. Though strongly proslavery, Furman's tone is moderate; he does not succumb to the depths of "Negrophobia" known at some places in the South. This treatise was prompted by the attempted slave uprising in 1822 in South Carolina under the leadership of Denmark Vesey. Vesey, a former slave who had purchased his own freedom, was a Baptist in Charleston who earned his living as a carpenter. Uneasy blacks learned of his plans and informed authorities who put down the uprising with considerable cruelty. This treatise is one of the most important Baptist defenses of slavery. *Source:* Richard Furman, *Exposition of the Views of the Baptists Relative to the Coloured Population of the United States* (Charleston, S.C.: A. E. Miller, 1823).

By 1840 the subject of slavery had become so controversial that some churches had stopped supporting the foreign mission work. To avert such defections, the acting board of the General Convention (the foreign mission agency) adopted a policy of neutrality on slavery (selection B) and urged continued cooperation by churches both North and South. At its triennial meetings in 1841 and again in 1844 the full Convention adopted a similar neutrality statement, and the Home Mission Society adopted a like policy. This was an effort, unsuccessful as it turned out, to prevent the slavery controversy from disrupting the missionary work. The document cited is from the acting board of the foreign mission society in 1840, but is substantially the same as that adopted the next year by the general meetings of both foreign and home societies. *Source:* Minutes, Tenth Triennial Meeting of the Baptist General Convention for Foreign Missions, 1841, Boston. Copy in American Baptist Historical Society, Rochester, New York.

A. Richard Furman, Treatise on Slavery, 1822

Exposition

of

The Views of the Baptists

Relative To The

Coloured Population

Of The United States

In

A Communication

To The Governor of South Carolina

Charleston, 24th December 1822

Sir,

When I had, lately, the honour of delivering to your Excellency an Address, from the Baptist Convention in this State, requesting that a Day of Public Humiliation and Thanksgiving might be appointed . . . protection. . . . I took the liberty to suggest, that I had a further communication to make on behalf of the Convention, in which their sentiments would be disclosed respecting the . . . lawfulness of holding slaves—the subject being considered in a moral and religious point of view.

You were pleased, sir, to signify, that it would be agreeable to you to receive such a communication. . . . I now take the liberty of laying it before you. . . .

The Convention are aware, that very respectable Citizens have been averse to the proposal under consideration; the proposal for appointing a Day of Public Thanksgiving for our preservation from the intended Insurrection, on account of the influence it might be supposed to have on the Black Population—by giving publicity to the subject in *their view,* and by affording them excitements to attempt something further of the same nature. These objections, however, the Convention view as either not substantial, or overbalanced by higher considerations. . . .

But the Convention are persuaded, that publicity, rather than secrecy is the true policy to be pursued on this occasion; . . . It is proper, the Convention conceives, that the Negroes should know, that however numerous they are in some parts of these Southern States, they yet are not, even including all descriptions, bond and free, in the United States, but little more than one sixth part of the whole number of Inhabitants, estimating that number which it probably now is, at Ten Millions; and the Black and Coloured Population, according to returns made at 1,780,000: That their destitution in respect to arms, and the knowledge of using them, with other disabilities, would render their physical force, were they all united in a common effort, less than a tenth part of that, with which they would have to contend: . . . That, however in some parts of our Union there are Citizens, who favour the idea of general emancipation; yet, were they to see slaves in our Country, in arms, wading through blood and carnage to effect their purpose, they would do what both their duty and interest would require; unite under the government with their fellow-citizens at large to suppress the rebellion, . . .

On the lawfulness of holding slaves, considering it in a moral and religious view, the Convention think it their duty to exhibit their sentiments, . . . because they consider their duty to God, the peace of the State, the satisfaction of scrupulous consciences, and the welfare of the slaves themselves, as intimately connected with a right view of the subject. The rather, because certain writers on politics, morals and religion, and some of them highly respectable, have advanced positions, and inculcated sentiments, very unfriendly to the principle and practice of holding slaves; . . . These sentiments, the Convention, on whose behalf I address your Excellency, cannot think just, or well founded; for the right of holding slaves is clearly established in the Holy Scriptures, both by precept and example. In the Old Testament, the Israelites were directed to purchase their bond-men and bond-maids of the Heathen nations; except they were of the Canaanites, for these were to be destroyed. . . .

In the New Testament, the Gospel History, or representation of facts, presents us with a view correspondent with that, which is furnished by other authentic ancient histories of the state of the world at the commencement of Christianity. The [ancient empires] were full of slaves. Many of these with their masters, were converted to the Christian Faith, and received, together with them into the Christian Church, while it was yet under the ministry of the inspired Apostles. In things purely spiritual, they appear to have enjoyed equal privileges; but their relationship, as masters and slaves, were not dissolved. . . .

Had the holding of slaves been a moral evil, it cannot be supposed, that the inspired Apostles, who feared not the faces of men, and were ready to lay down their lives in the cause of their God, would have tolerated it. . . . If they had done so on a principle of accommodation, in cases where the masters remained heathen, to avoid offences and civil commotion; yet, surely, where both master and servant were Christian, as in the case before us, they would have enforced the law of Christ, and required, that the master should liberate his slave in the first instance. But, instead of this, they let the relationship remain untouched, as being lawful and right, and insist on the relative duties.

In proving this subject justifiable by Scriptural authority, its morality is also proved; for the Divine Law never sanctions immoral actions. . . .

[Slaves] become a part of his [the master's] family . . . and the care of ordering it, and of providing for its welfare, devolves on him. The children, the aged, the sick, the disabled, and the unruly, as well as those, who are capable of service and orderly, are the objects of his care: The labour of these, is applied to the benefit of those, and to their own support, as well as to that of the master. Thus, what is effected, and often at a great public expense, in a free community, by taxes, benevolent institutions, bettering houses, and penitentiaries, lies here on the master, to be performed by him, whatever contingencies may happen; and often occasions much expense, care and trouble, from which the servants are free. Cruelty is certainly, inadmissible; but servitude may be consistent with such degrees of happiness as men usually attain in this imperfect state of things.

If the above representation of the Scriptural doctrine, and the manner of obtaining slaves from Africa is just; and if also purchasing them has been the means of saving human life, which there is great reason to believe it has; then, however the slave trade, in present circumstances, is justly censurable, yet might motives of humanity and even piety have been originally brought into operation in the purchase of slaves, when sold in the circumstances we have described. If, also, by their own confession, which has been made in manifold instances, their condition, when they have come into the hands of humane masters here, has been greatly bettered by the change; if it is, ordinarily, really better, as many assert, than that of thousands of the poorer classes in countries reputed civilized and free; and, if, in addition to all other considerations, the translation from their native country to this has been the means of their mental and religious improvement, and so of obtaining salvation, as many of themselves have joyfully and thankfully confessed—then may the just and humane master, who rules his slaves and provides for them, according to Christian principles, rest satisfied, that he is not, in holding them, chargeable with moral evil, nor with acting, in this respect, contrary to the genius of Christianity.—It appears to be equally clear, that those, who by reasoning on abstract principles, are induced to favour the scheme of general emancipation, and who ascribe their sentiments to Christianity, should be particularly careful, . . . that they do not by a perversion of the Scriptural doctrine . . . not only invade the domestic and religious peace and rights of our Citizens, but, also by an intemperate zeal, prevent indirectly, the religious improvement of the people they design . . . to benefit; and, perhaps, become . . . the means of producing in our country, scenes of anarchy and blood; and all this in a vain attempt to bring about a state of things, which, if arrived at, would not probably better the state of that people; which is thought, by men of observation to be generally true of the Negroes in the Northern States, who have been liberated. . . .

. . . It is, therefore, firmly believed, that general emancipation to the Negroes in this country, would not, in present circumstances, be for their own happiness, as a body; while it would be extremely injurious to the community at large in various ways. . . . If a man has obtained slaves by purchase, or inheritance, and the holding of them as such is justifiable by the law of God; why should he be required to liberate them . . . ?

Should, however, a time arrive, when the Africans in our country might be found qualified to enjoy freedom; and, when they might obtain it in a manner consistent with the interest and peace of the community at large, the Convention would be happy in seeing them free: . . . But there seems to be just reason to conclude that a considerable part of the human race, whether they bear openly the character of slaves or are reputed free men, will continue in such circumstances . . . while the world continues. . . .

And here I am brought to a part of the general subject, which, I confess to your Excellency, the Convention . . . wish it may be seriously considered by all our Citizens: This is the religious interests of the Negroes. For though they are slaves, they are also men; and are with ourselves accountable creatures; having immortal souls, and being destined to future eternal award. Their religious interests claim a regard from their masters of the most serious nature; and it is indispensable. Nor can the community at large, in a right estimate of their duty and happiness, be indifferent on this subject. . . .

The Convention are particularly unhappy in considering, that an idea of the Bible's teaching the doctrine of emancipation as necessary, and tending to make servants insubordinate to proper authority, has obtained access to any mind; . . . the idea is an erroneous one; . . . the influence of a right acquaintance with that Holy Book tends directly and powerfully, by promoting the fear and love of God, together with just and peaceful sentiments toward men, to produce one of the best securities to the public, for the internal and domestic peace of the state.

It is also a pleasing consideration, . . . that in the late projected scheme for producing an insurrection among us, there were very few of those who were, as members attached to regular churches, . . . who appear to have taken a part in the wicked plot, . . . It is true, that a considerable number of those who were found guilty and executed, laid claim to a religious character; yet several of these were grossly immoral, and, in general, they were members of an irregular body, which called itself the *African Church,* and had intimate connection and intercourse with a similar body of men in a Northern City, among whom the supposed right to emancipation is strenuously advocated.

The result of this inquiry and reasoning, on the subject of slavery, brings us, sir, if I mistake not, very regularly to the following conclusions:—That the holding of slaves is justifiable by the doctrine and example contained in Holy writ; and is, therefore consistent with Christian uprightness, both in sentiment and conduct. That, all things considered, the Citizens of America have in general obtained the African slaves, . . . on principles, which can be justified; . . . That slavery, when tempered with humanity and justice, is a state of tolerable happiness; equal, if not superior, to that which many poor enjoy in countries reputed free. That a master has a scriptural right to govern his slaves so as to keep them in subjection; to demand and receive from them a reasonable service;

and to correct them for the neglect of duty, for their vices and transgressions; but that to impose on them unreasonable, rigorous services, or to inflict on them cruel punishment, he has neither a scriptural nor a moral right. . . . That it is the positive duty of servants to reverence their master, to be obedient, industrious, faithful to him, and careful of his interests; and without being so, they can neither be the faithful servants of God, nor be held as regular members of the Christian Church. . . . That masters having the disposal of the persons, time and labour of their servants, and being the heads of families, are bound, on principles of moral and religious duty, to give these servants religious instruction; or at least, to afford them opportunities, under proper regulations to obtain it: And to grant religious privileges to those, who desire them, and furnish proper evidence of their sincerity and uprightness: Due care being at the same time taken, that they receive their instructions from right sources, . . . It is, also, believed to be a just conclusion, that the interest and security of the state would be promoted, by allowing, under proper regulations, considerable religious privileges, to such of this class, as know how to estimate them aright, and have given suitable evidence of their own good principles, uprightness and fidelity; . . . All which is, with deference, submitted to the consideration of your Excellency.

With high respect, I remain, personally, and on behalf of the Convention,

Sir, your very obedient and humble servant,

RICHARD FURMAN

President of the Baptist State Convention

B. Policy of Neutrality on Slavery

Policy of Neutrality

APPENDIX.

Address of the Board, adopted Nov. 2, 1840.

The Board of Managers of the Baptist General Convention for Foreign Missions have observed, with painful interest, indications of a tendency on the part of some of their beloved brethren and co-adjutors, to withdraw from the missionary connection in which they have been happily associated for many years. And they are constrained by their sense of duty to the interests entrusted to their care, by their love to the Redeemer and the souls for whom he died, and by their affectionate regard toward all who at any time have extended their aid to the Foreign Missionary cause, to remind their brethren of the design of their association and the principles on which it was formed and has been conducted.

The primary and exclusive object of the founders of the General Convention, as expressed in the preamble to the constitution, was to "send the glad tidings of salvation to the heathen, and to nations destitute of pure gospel light." . . .

Corresponding with the oneness of the object for which the Convention was organized, is the simplicity of the terms on which cooperation for its accomplishment may be proffered and received. Our venerated fathers who constituted the original Convention, contemplating in the new organization the prosecution of the Foreign Missionary enterprize alone, and justly appreciating the vast extent of the work . . . were careful to lay no obstruction in the way of any individual who might be disposed to communicate to its funds, nor any restriction on the liberty of counsel or direction in its concerns, further than was judged indispensable to their efficient and safe administration. . . .

Such being the design of the organization of the Convention, and such the principles on which co-operation may be tendered and accepted, the Board are unable to discover any sufficient reason for the withdrawal of support on the part of any of their contributors, in view of facts or considerations wholly extrinsic and irrelevant.

There is still another subject to which the attention of the Board has been called by some of their respected contributors—lying yet more widely aside from the sphere of their appropriate operations; and if in alluding to it they break the silence of their neutrality, it is only that by "defining their position" they may relieve the embarrassing uncertainty of brethren, northern and southern, and secure to themselves, through the divine blessing, their wonted freedom from extraneous anxieties in the furtherance of their own peculiar work. We refer to the continuance of Christian fellowship between northern and southern churches.

The view entertained by the Board as to the relevancy of this subject to the work of Foreign Missions, has already been indicated. It does not come under their cognizance in any form; nor, they may be permitted to add, within the scope of the General Convention, with its present constitution. There is, in fact, no body, ecclesiastical or civil, empowered to act in this particular on behalf of the churches interested. The churches are independent communities; they can exercise no authority over one another; they have delegated no power to individuals or associations, within the knowledge of the Board, to act for them. The members of the Board are also members of many different churches. In their respective churches they act, or may act,—and as individuals also,— in reference to this and other matters pertaining to church relations; but as a Board of the Convention for Foreign Missions, they can say and do nothing. Such is the position assigned to them in their appointment to the Board; as such they acceded to it; and from it they have never, in any form, nor in any degree, swerved. They have desired and have sought to keep distinct, things that are disconnected; and, as men faithful to themselves, and as a Board faithful to their constituents, neither to use their official influence to give weight and currency to their private opinions, nor, on the other hand, through the unseasonable and unseemly obtrusion of personal feelings do treachery to the sacred interests committed in good faith to their charge.

In conclusion, the Board affectionately and earnestly entreat their brethren and fellow-helpers to remember, that the enterprize in which we are engaged, for the dissemination of the Gospel in foreign lands, asserts a claim on the sympathies, and prayers, and benefactions of us all, which cannot with safety, nor consistently with our avowed faith and confessed obligations, be set aside. . . .

The Board look forward to the approaching anniversary of the Convention with mingled solicitude and hope;—with hope, for we shall greet on that high day of our solemnities endeared brethren and friends, from the north, from the south, and from the west, with whom we have often taken sweet counsel, and of whose affections and confidence, we trust, no disastrous influences shall have despoiled us, as none will have estranged them from ours;—with solicitude, lest by the unseasonable diversion of our thoughts to irrelevant subjects, the unity of the design of our confederation be infringed, and the harmony of our counsels disturbed.

10.17   Home Missions and the James Reeve Case

Disruption of work in the Home Mission Society centered around the case of James Reeve of Georgia, also known as the "Georgia Test Case." Troubled by rumors that the Home Mission Society would not appoint a slave owner as a home missionary, the Baptists of Georgia devised a test case to determine if the rumors were true. They nominated James Reeve, a slave owner, and raised the money for his salary. They frankly identified Reeve as a test case to "stop the mouth of gainsayers." In its triennial sessions the Home Mission Society had adopted an official policy of neutrality on the slavery issue, and the acting board evidently tried to abide by that policy. They felt that they could *neither* appoint nor refuse to appoint Reeve, since he was a test case, without violating neutrality. Therefore, they simply declined to receive the nomination, thus avoiding any action on the appointment. While the acting board apparently acted with integrity, Georgia Baptists nevertheless interpreted the action as proof that no slaveholder would be appointed. *Source: From Minutes of the Meetings of the American Baptist Home Mission Society and of its Executive Committee,* 7 Oct. 1844 book 2, 303.

American Baptist Home Mission Rooms,
New York, Oct. 7, 1844.

The Executive Board of the American Baptist Home Mission Society, having examined the application of the Executive Committee of the Georgia Baptist Convention for the appointment of Eld. James E. Reeve, feel it their duty to state that, in addition to the information required of applicants, this communication contains a statement that Mr. Reeve is a slaveholder, and that fact is offered as a reason for his appointment, in the following terms: "We wish his appointment so much the more, as it will stop the mouths of gainsayers. I will explain. There are good brethren among us, who, notwithstanding the transactions of your Society at Philadelphia, are hard to believe that you will appoint a slaveholder as a Missionary, even when the funds are supplied by those who wish such an appointment." The application, therefore, is an unusual one.

We disclaim attributing to our Georgia brethren a design to *disturb the deliberations of the Board* by introducing the subject of slavery through the medium of their application, but such, evidently, is its tendency. In the opinion of several members of the Board, the application seeks the appointment, not in the usual manner, merely of a Missionary, but of a slaveholder, and is designed as a test whether the Board will appoint a slaveholder as a Missionary, . . .

The appointment of Missionaries, constitutionally eligible, and recommended according to our established rules, without the introduction of extraneous considerations calculated to disturb our deliberations, this Board are during the period of their appointment, sacredly bound in equity and justice, to make, to the extent of their pecuniary ability—keeping in view a fair distribution throughout the field, of the funds, committed to their trust. But when an application is made for the appointment of a slaveholder, or an abolitionist, or an anti-slavery man, *as such,* or for appropriations to fields where the design of the applicant is apparently to test the action of the Board in respect to the subjects of slavery or anti-slavery, their official obligation either to act on the appointment or to entertain the application, ceases. Therefore,

Resolved, That in view of the preceding considerations it is not expedient to introduce the subjects of slavery or anti-slavery into our deliberations, nor to entertain applications in which they are introduced.

Resolved, That taking into consideration all the circumstances of the case, we deem ourselves not at liberty to entertain the application for the appointment of Rev. James E. Reeve.

Resolved, That the Corresponding Secretary transmit a copy of the foregoing views and resolutions to the Chairman of the Executive Committee of the Georgia Convention.

By order of the Executive Board.
BENJAMIN M. HILL, Cor. Sec'y.

10.18　Foreign Missions and the Alabama Resolutions

Troubled by rumors that no slaveholder could be appointed as a foreign missionary, and stung by the Georgia Test Case (10.17), Baptists of Alabama issued a militantly worded challenge to the acting board of the foreign mission society. Instead of a concrete case like James Reeve in Georgia, the "Alabama Resolutions" asked a series of hypothetical questions with a "demand" that they be answered satisfactorily or Alabama Baptists would withhold their missionary offerings. The board, unlike their counterparts in the home mission society, made no pretense of abiding by neutrality, and answered bluntly that they would not appoint a slaveowner. This blunt exchange helped precipitate the division of Northern and Southern Baptists. *Sources: The Baptist Memorial,* New York, May 1845. Minutes, Acting Board of the General Missionary Convention, 24-25 Feb. 1844.

A. The Alabama Resolutions and a Reply

We lay aside every thing else prepared for this department, to insert, by request, for convenient reference, and permanent preservation, the documents connected with the threatened division of the South and North, in the work of Foreign Missions. The first item consists of

THE ALABAMA RESOLUTIONS.

Whereas, the holding of property in African negro slaves has for some years excited discussion, as a question of morals, between different portions of the Baptist denomination united in benevolent enterprise: and by a large portion of our brethren is now imputed to the slaveholders in these southern and southwestern states, as a sin at once grievous, palpable, and disqualifying:

1. *Resolved,* By the Convention of the Baptist denomination in the State of Alabama, that when one party to a voluntary compact among christian brethren is not willing to acknowledge the entire social equality with the other, as to all the privileges and benefits of the union, nor even to refrain from impeachment and annoyance, united efforts between such parties, even in the sacred cause of Christian benevolence, cease to be agreeable, useful, or proper.

2. *Resolved,* That our duty at this crisis requires us to demand from the proper authorities in all those bodies to whose funds we have contributed, or with whom we have in any way been connected, the distinct, explicit avowal that slaveholders are eligible, and entitled, equally with non-slaveholders, to all the privileges and immunities of their several unions; and especially to receive any agency, mission, or other appointment, which may run within the scope of their operations or duties. . . .

5. *Resolved,* also, That the Treasurer of this body be, and he is hereby instructed, not to pay any money intended to be applied without the limits of his state, except at the written order of the President of this Convention, with the concurrence of the Board of officers before mentioned; and this body, profoundly sensible of the vast issues dependent on the principles herein advanced, will await, in prayerful expectation, the responses of our non-slaveholding brethren.

REPLY OF THE FOREIGN MISSION BOARD TO THE ALABAMA CONVENTION.

Dear Sir: We have received from you a copy of a Preamble and Resolutions, which were passed by the "Baptist State Convention of Alabama." And as there is a "demand" for distinct and explicit answers from our Board, to the inquiries and propositions which you have been pleased to make, we have given to them our deliberate and candid attention.

Before proceeding to answer them, allow us to express our profound regret, that they were addressed to us. They were not necessary. We have never as a Board either done, or omitted to do any thing, which requires the explanation and avowals that your Resolutions "demand." They also place us in the new and trying position of being compelled to answer hypothetical questions, and to discuss principles; or of seeming to be evasive and timid, and not daring to give you the information and satisfaction which you desire. . . .

We need not say, that slaveholders, as well as non-slaveholders, are unquestionably entitled to all the privileges and immunities which the Constitution of the Baptist General Convention permits, and grants to its members. We would not deprive either of any of the immunities of the mutual contract. In regard, however, to any agency, mission, or other appointment, no slaveholder or non-slaveholder, however large his subscriptions to Foreign Missions, or those of the church with which he is connected, is on that account entitled to be appointed to any agency or a mission. The appointing power, for wise and good reasons, has been confided to the "Acting Board," they holding themselves accountable to the Convention for the discreet and faithful discharge of this trust.

Should you say, "the above remarks are not sufficiently explicit; we wish distinctly to know, whether the Board would or would not appoint a slaveholder as a missionary;" before directly replying to this we would say, that in the thirty years in which the Board has existed, no slaveholder, to our knowledge, has applied to be a missionary. And, as we send out no domestics or servants, such an event as a missionary taking slaves with him, were it morally right, could not, in accordance with all our past arrangements or present plans, possibly occur. If, however, any one should offer himself as a missionary, having slaves, and should insist on retaining them as his property, we could not appoint him. One thing is certain, we can never be a party to any arrangement which would imply approbation of slavery.

In regard to our Board, there is no point on which we are more unanimously agreed, than that of the independence of churches. We disclaim all and every pretension to interfere with the discipline of any church. We disfellowship no one. Nevertheless, were a person to offer himself as a candidate for missionary service, although commended by his church as in good standing, we should feel it our duty to open our eyes on any facts to the disadvantage of his moral and religious character, which might come under our observation. And while we should not feel that it was our province to excommunicate, or discipline a candidate of doubtful character, yet we should be unworthy of our trust, if we did not, although he were a member of a church, reject his application. . . .

We have, with all frankness, but with entire kindness and respect, defined our position. If our brethren in Alabama, with this exposition of our principles and feelings, can co-operate with us, we shall be happy to receive their aid. If they cannot, painful to us as will be their withdrawal, yet we shall submit to it, as neither sought nor caused by us.

There are sentiments avowed in this communication, which, although held temperately and kindly, and with all due esteem and Christian regard for the brethren addressed, are, nevertheless, dearer to us than any pecuniary aid whatever.

> We remain yours, truly,
> In behalf of the Board,
> DAN. SHARP, President.

BARON STOW, Rec. Sec'y.

REV. JESSE HARTWELL, President Alabama Baptist State Convention.

B.   Solomon Peck, Where to Draw the Dividing Line

The Board then took up the communication in reply to the resolution of the Alabama Baptist Convention. Two of the ammendments proposed at the last meeting were adopted and the remainder was withdrawn, the For. Sec. stating in writing the reasons why he withdrew them as follows:

"In giving my vote on the adoption of the letter to the Baptist State Convention of Alabama, I beg leave to state to the Board, briefly, my position and grounds of action. . . . The case has associated with it, in the course of discussion, *another element* which changes its character and aspect, and I feel bound to consider the question under this new aspect, disclaiming at the same time all responsibility for its being so presented.

It has become manifest, in the course of debate, that there is a decided *contrarity of views,* as to the policy proper to be pursued, both *in* and *out* of the Acting Board; and that, if the inquiry of the Alabama State Convention be not answered explicitly, those who dissent from the views above expressed, *will retire,* the most if not all, from their present relations to the Board and the General Convention; and the Acting Board, itself reduced perhaps to a minority of its present members, will be left with a minority of northern supporters and contributors to cooperate with southern contributors in sustaining our missionary operations. And the inevitable consequence of this would be either a speedy and lamentable reduction of our missions and stations, or the early transfer of most, if not all of them, to a new missionary organization. In other words, the question before my mind, under this new aspect, is not whether a course shall be adopted which would threaten a dismemberment of the General Convention by severing the South from the North, but which of too (sic) divisions would be least disastrous to the Missions; a division between the North and South, or a division in the North, leaving, as already intimated, an ever-diminishing minority at the North to cooperate with the South. This, as it appears to me, is the alternative now presented. I regret that it is so; *I disclaim all responsibility for its being so:* I have done what I could to prevent it. But *being presented,* it is necessarily taken into account in determining what is best to be done; and constrains me to *accede* to a measure in its *own* light and on its *own* merits I should deem unnecessary and unwise. . . .

10.19   Documents of the Baptist Schism of 1845

In 1845 Baptists in the South formed the Southern Baptist Convention, thus dividing Baptists in America along regional lines. Whether Southern Baptists withdrew, or were, in effect, pushed out from national cooperation, is still debated. In response to two final straws, the Georgia Test Case (10.17) and the Alabama Resolutions (10.18), Baptists of Virginia issued a call for a consultative convention in Augusta for May 1845. Not all Baptists in the South agreed on what that consultative convention should do. Some advocated immediate separation from the national mission societies, while others urged delay and caution. From a wealth of documents which remain, only representative selections can be included here. *Sources: The Religious Herald* (Va.), 13 March 1845, 2-3. *Baptist Banner and Pioneer* (Ky.) John L. Waller, ed., 1 May 1845, 2-3. H. L. Morehouse, ed., *Baptist Home Missions in North America,* 1832-1882 (New York: Baptist Home Mission Society, 1883), 391-395.

A.   *Religious Herald* (Virginia), Advocating Immediate Separation

BOARD OF THE TRIENNIAL CONVENTION. We last week stated that the Board of the Baptist Triennial Convention, after mature deliberation, had decided that they could not, and would not appoint a slaveholder, a missionary. A decision so adverse to the rights of the Southern portion of the Baptist church could not fail to attract immediate attention, and decided action. As soon, therefore, as suitable notice could be given, the Board of the Virginia Baptist Foreign Missionary Society, met at the Second Baptist Church in this city, and the result of their deliberations our readers will perceive from the accompanying documents.

We have no doubt but that their course will be approved by the great body of the Southern and South Western Baptists. We have for some time felt apprehensive, that union could not be much longer maintained. The altered tone of the Baptist periodicals in New England, and in some of the Western states, since the meeting of the Convention in April; their constant and unremitted denunciations of slaveholders—the frequent annunciation that the Board was becoming daily more pro-slavery; the passage of anti-slavery resolutions at the annual meeting of the Boston and Salem associations gave strong premonitory symptoms of the existence of a feverish excitement, which would probably at a distant period, exhibit itself in some overt act which would compel the South to withdraw.

At the last meeting the Convention decided that they had no control over slavery or anti-slavery—that these questions should have no bearing on their acts as a missionary body.—Acting on this principle, slaveholders as well as anti-slavery members, were placed on the Board. If the Convention had not been willing to recognize the equality of their Southern brethren; to admit them to all offices, agencies, and appointments, as readily as non slaveholders, that would surely have been the proper time to have laid down the rule of future action. But they, voluntarily and freely elected, several slaveholders as members of the Board, selected to conduct its operations until the next annual meeting.

In this course they but carried out the principle strictly adhered to from the first organization of the Society. . . . Several of the delegates, and members of the first Board, were slaveholders. . . . Without the co-operation of Southern Baptists, it would probably not have been formed; at least its ability to do good must have been seriously curtailed. Slaveholders, then, formed an essential part of the social compact. . . .

The course of the Convention has been uniform and decided on the subject. There has been no exhibition of doubt or hestitation. On every suitable occasion, the right of the South to a full participation of all the offices and privileges in the gift of the Society, was fully and freely admitted. Slavery was declared to be a subject over which it had no cognizance—which it would not entertain nor discuss.

If the Convention was thus precise and guarded in its action on this subject, it certainly intended that the Board to which the direction of its business was intrusted during the interim betwixt one meeting and another, should be equally cautious. It had laid down the principle and it had a right to expect that it should be a rule of action to the Board. The Board surely had no right to adopt a course which the society had disclaimed. . . . If any one thing was clearly laid down as a part of its policy, a maxim from which it would not depart, at its last meeting, it was that the subject of slavery and slaveholding, as connected with the rights of southern members, should not be entertained. The Board, therefore, had no right to impose a test which the Convention by its uniform course had rejected. . . . no authority was given to the Board, or could be intended to be conferred upon it, to nullify the acts of their principal by saying—you have appointed slaveholders to office, you have recognized their equality, but you will not give them our sanction—we will not appoint them missionaries.

But it seems they wished to show their disapprobation of slavery. . . . If an alteration was deemed expedient it was the province of the Convention to change the existing relation, not theirs. They were allowed to entertain their own views, elsewhere, but not in the Convention, and of course not in the Board. . . . As agents they ought to have said to the Alabama brethren—this is a question we must leave to the Convention—they have decided that no difference shall be made, betwixt the friends and opponents of slavery, . . .

At each session of the Convention a Board of Managers is chosen, consisting of eighteen vice presidents, and forty managers, besides the officers, scattered throughout the different states of the Union which send delegates to the Convention. A portion of these members living in and around Boston, are termed the Acting Board. Now, all these members have a right to meet with the Acting Board, and to participate in its proceedings. In any difficult case, they can be called on to attend, and afford to the Acting

Board the aid of their counsel. Seventeen of these members reside in the slaveholding states, and a majority of them would probably have been opposed to the decision of the Board. Why, on such a momentous question, were not the other members consulted? . . .

There was a portion of the Baptists in the New England states, who were not willing to join the Free Baptist Foreign Missionary Society, believing that they could influence the Board to do some act which would cause a rupture with the South. The Reflector, their organ, was constantly boasting, that the Board was becoming more pro-slavery. It confidently asserted that no slaveholder would be appointed as a missionary. It was asserted as a fact that the Home Secretary, Dr. Pattison, was corresponding with Jesse Bushyhead, one of its missionaries, and a slaveholder, to induce him to resign. His death occuring removed this difficulty. These intimations probably induced the Alabama Convention to propose the enquiry to the Board. To secure apparently the good will of this fraction of the Baptist church, the Board have decided to disfranchise the South. . . .

Of 707,942 Baptists in the United States in 1844, by the returns in the Baptist Almanack, 391,211, considerably over one half are in the slaveholding states. If according to an admitted principle, the majority ought to govern, the opinions of that majority ought to have been ascertained and respected by the Board. . . .

A Southern Convention had been suggested some months ago, by the Editor of the Christian Index. We have no doubt that it will be generally approved, and we trust unite in harmonious co-operation the South. The time and place are simply suggested, and may be altered if deemed expedient. Under present circumstances, we deem further co operation no longer expedient, nor desirable. To be consistent, the Board must reject slaveholding agents, and slaveholding members of the Board. . . .

TO THE BAPTIST CHURCHES OF VIRGINIA. Dear Brethren: Accompanying this communication you will find a letter addressed by the Board of the Baptist Triennial Convention to the Rev. Jesse Hartwell, President of the Alabama State Convention, in reply to a preamble and resolutions recently adopted by this body. . . . But the letter of the Board has dissipated all misconception on this subject. From it we learn that no slaveholder, under any circumstances, would be appointed by the Board as a missionary, or even as an agent, (this is plainly implied,) to collect funds from slaveholding churches. Concerning this unexpected resolution of the Board, we wish to speak with candor and courtesy, but we must also speak with frankness and firmness. It is an outrage on our rights. This will clearly appear for the following considerations:—

1. The decision of the Board is unconstitutional. The Triennial Convention was formed and, from its organization, it has been sustained by slaveholders and non slaveholders. They have met and acted in the Convention itself, and in its Board, on terms of perfect social and religious equality. No man, who is at all acquainted with the history of the Convention, can entertain any doubt that the Southern Baptists would have indignantly refused to co-operate with it on any terms implying their inferiority. . . .

2. The decision of the Board is a manifest violation of the compromise resolution adopted at the last meeting of the Convention. This is the resolution—

"Resolved, That in co operating together as members of this Convention in the work of Foreign Missions, we disclaim all sanction, either expressed or implied, whether of slavery or of anti slavery; but, as individuals, we are perfectly free both to express and to promote, elsewhere our own views on these subjects in a Christian manner and spirit." . . .

. . . The Convention resolved that the views certained of slavery or of anti-slavery should no bar to harmonious effort;

3. The decision of the Board is inconsistent with admissions made by the letter under consideration. . . .

4. The decision of the Board is unjust to the Southern supporters of the Convention.

From the organization of the Convention to the present time, the Baptists of the South have contributed cheerfully, and in some cases, liberally, to its treasury. But, can any man believe they would have made these contributions, had they known, or even suspected, that the Board would have refused to appoint a slaveholder, under any circumstances, as a missionary or agent? . . .

5. The decision of the Board, supposing not intended to produce division, is as unwise as it is unjust.

A slaveholder would not be likely to apply for an appointment as a missionary to the East—and certainly he would not think of carrying slaves with him on such a mission. But suppose a slaveholder should desire an appointment as a missionary among the Indians,—he might be eminently qualified for the office; intelligent, pious, humane to his slaves, held in high estimation by his brethren; such a minister in a word, as has heretofore been cheerfully admitted into Northern pulpits; his slaves might earnestly desire to accompany him, and there might be no law to prevent it, and no prejudice against slavery in the proposed field of his labor to diminish his usefulness; and yet, under the decision of the Board, he would be ineligible to the appointment. . . .

In view, brethren, of these considerations, we feel that we have been injured by the decision of the Board. For their conscientious opinions on the subject of slavery, we censure them not. If they are unwilling to co-operate with slaveholding Christians in the Missionary enterprize, we have no right to complain. We have cherished a sincere sympathy with them in their delicate and embarrassing situation.—We have vindicated their conduct and their motives. We have cherished no unfavorable suspicions against them. But we are disappointed, and pained at their decision—a decision which tramples alike on the constitution and the rights of Southern members.

And now brethren, in this exigency, what shall we do? To remain united with the Board is impossible. Self respect forbids it. All hope that the Board will revoke their decision is vain. They have acted, so we learn from the Christian Reflector, deliberately and unanimously. They have examined the ground, and taken their position.

In view of the considerations above presented, the Board of the Virginia Foreign Mission Society have adopted the following resolutions:

1. Resolved, That this Board have seen with sincere pain the decision of the Board of the Baptist Triennial Convention, contained in a recent letter addressed to Rev. Jesse Hartwell, of Ala. and that we deem the decision unconstitutional, and in violation of the rights of the Southern members of the Convention; and that all farther connexion with the Board, on the part of such members is inexpedient and improper.

2. Resolved, That the Treasurer of this Board be required to deposit in one of the Savings banks of the city, any funds which may be in hands or which may come into them, to be disposed of as the Society, at its annual meeting, may direct.

3. Resolved, That this Board are of opinion, that in the present exigency, it is important that those brethren who are aggrieved by the recent decision of the Board in Boston, should hold a Convention to confer on the best means of promoting the Foreign Mission cause, and other interests of the Baptist denomination in the South.

4. Resolved, That in the judgment of this Board, Augusta, Geo., is a suitable place for holding such a Convention; and that Thursday before the 2nd Lord's day in May next is a suitable time.

5. Resolved, That while we are willing to meet our Southern brethren in Augusta, or any other place which may be selected, we should heartily welcome them in the city of

Richmond—and should it be deemed proper to hold it in this city, the Thursday before the 4th Lord's day in June next will be a suitable time.

On motion,

Resolved, That churches and associations of the State be recommended to appoint delegates to the proposed Convention.

Resolved, That the proceedings of this meeting be published under the direction of brethren Taylor, Jeter, Walker, and Smith.

J. B. TAYLOR, Pres't Board.

C. WALTHALL, Sec'y.

For the Religious Herald. NEW ENGLAND, Feb. 27th, 1845

Mr. Editor:

The die is cast. The Board of the General Convention have passed a resolution, that a slaveholder shall not be appointed a missionary. Is not this virtually saying, that the Baptist Denomination of these United States, shall no longer be one? That it is, may be readily inferred from the fact that what the Board have done, they have not done rashly. They have weighed their position well. They have felt the pulse of the people here, and they know full well the sentiment of the brethren at the South. They knew that the churches here were prepared to go with them, and they knew full well that the churches at the South were not thus prepared. Is not this act of theirs then, a virtual decision that our Convention is no longer to be one? . . .

But what shall we do? We who live on the other side of Mason and Dixon's Line? . . . Shall we continue to act with those who think us unworthy to share with them the honor and privileges of spreading the Gospel throughout the world? No, not we. This can never be. I spurn the thought. We can never do it. We must stand on free and equal grounds, or we cannot stand at all. We have now to act for ourselves and alone. The time has fully come when we must take a stand on this subject, when we must speak our sentiments, plainly, fully, manly, and decidedly. . . . We must withdraw ourselves from them. We must organize and act separate and distinct from such. . . .

They may talk of the expediency of not appointing a slaveholder as a missionary as much as they please, but at the bottom of it all, is the principle that we are sinners, and I might add, "sinners above men," for even Dr. Wayland declares slavery to be as "great a sin as can be conceived of." . . . They are determined to act on the principle, that slavery is a sin (right or wrong) let the brethren at the South do as they please. And that the churches here will go with the Board, there is not the shadow of doubt. . . .

But this is not all. I have somewhat further to tell thee of. The Board of the Home Mission Society will not appoint a slaveholder as a missionary. This I have known long since, but refrained from informing you, on the ground that I thought we might possibly, after a while, settle that difficult question in some way satisfactory to both sides. . . .

But to show you that I am not alone in the sentiments above expressed in relation to the propriety of a decided action on the part of the South, I will mention that I have called on some four or five brethren from the South who are pursuing a Theological course at Newton, who are decidedly of opinion that they can no longer remain at that place. Besides being in a region where abolition sentiments are constantly stuffed down their throats whether they will or will not, they feel a positive difficulty since this action of the Board they had not felt before. . . . But the churches here (if this act of the Board be an index to their views) do not believe slaveholders are suitable persons to be missionaries; and if not missionaries then not ministers; so that to act consistently, they cannot admit slaveholders in their Theological Institutions. And the Ed. Society will have to pass such a regulation if they act consistently. . . . These brethren are decidedly of the opinion that they must leave that institution and seek one in a southern clime, or enter immediately into the field. . . . I can add nothing to this; it speaks its own language. The time has come not only when we ought to act, but when we must act.

Yours truly,

S.C.C. [Probably Samuel Cornelius Clopton]

B. *Banner and Pioneer* (Kentucky), Opposing Immediate Separation

Our views of a Southern Convention seems not to be understood by our worthy brother of the Religious Herald. He seems to think that we are opposed to a Southern Convention, and that we would oppose a Southern organization under any circumstances. In this he wholly mistakes us. . . . He . . . thinks that no one can be in favor of a Southern Convention unless he is the advocate of an immediate, State-line, separation of the South from the North, and an organization of the South separate and apart from the Triennial Convention. . . . Whereas, we think a Convention of all, (not a part only,) the Southern Baptists and the friends of Baptist Union in the United States, should be called; not for the inevitable purpose of effecting a separation, but for the purpose of ascertaining whether the causes of difficulty cannot be removed and the union of the denomination preserved. . . .

Brother Sands [William Sands, editor, *Religious Herald*] is of the opinion and so is our correspondent "A Baptist," that all the North will sustain the Board, and that the Triennial Convention will, of course, sustain it; the North having the majority in the body. This supposition, of our brethren, may turn out to be true, but we are not yet convinced that it will: . . .

In reply to all this, and every thing else which may be urged of the same kind, we offer the following remarks:

In the first place, if a Convention of all the South and the friends of union in the North can be convoked within twelve months from this time, they will be in possession of all the information, as to the state of the abolition and union parties, which would enable them to decide, not only upon the relative strength of the parties, but upon the probable disposition of the Triennial Convention, and of the best method of preparing for the event.

. . . A called meeting of the Triennial Convention will be composed of the members which composed that body in 1844, and will have full power to remove the Board or adopt any other measure to secure the harmony of the denomination and the rights of the South. If this is done the abolitionists will be compelled to retire from the Convention and organize to themselves, instead of driving away the South. If, however, such a called meeting of the Triennial Convention should sustain the present Board and refuse to do justice to the South, the South would then be consolidated and ready, as one man, to organize, without either loss of time or funds.

The above is a mere outline of what our views are, as to what measures are necessary, previous to a final separation of the South from the North—we cannot say every thing necessary to a fair exhibition of our views, upon this subject, in a single article: we intend however to be understood upon this question, before we let it rest.

We here briefly state our objections to an immediate separation of the South from the North, by State lines, and an organization of the South, versus the Triennial Convention, by such lines.

In the first place, we object to it, because, it is the policy of the abolitionists of the North to effect such a State-line separation, in order to compel those who oppose them, in the free States, to unite in their ultra measures. They know that if the South does not withdraw, the North will divide, and the abolitionists must go to themselves: hence their solicitude to drive off the South. . . .

In the second place, we object to this State line division, because, it will not only separate those brethren, churches and Associations, that now hold sweet intercourse and fellowship, across these lines, but it will tend to gender sectional strifes and divisions; it will produce alienation of heart, and lead to contentions, turmoil and warfare, along the whole line of division: and who can contemplate this state of things without pain and trepidation?

We object, in the third place, to a State line division of the South from the North, because we believe that the union of these States, and the perpetuity of our happy government, can only be secured by preserving, undivided, the ligaments which bind the parts together. The political, mercantile and social relations of the people of this country constitute these ligaments; the strongest of which are those of the social class. Let the three great denominations of christians be divided, by State lines, upon the subject of abolitionism, and who does not see that all social intercourse between the parties will be sundered, and the parts continually recede? . . . Who does not see, therefore, that if the religious and consequently the social interests of the country are divided by State lines, that more than half of the bonds which hold the political compact in harmony are dissolved, and that the ground work is laid for the ultimate dissolution of the union, and the destruction of the fairest fabric of civil and religious liberty the world ever saw? . . .

That such a result is not only possible, as a consequence upon such a division of the religious bodies of this country by State lines, but that it is desired and aimed at by the ultra-Abolitionists of the North, no one can doubt who has read their papers, conventional proceedings, resolutions, &c., to say nothing of the official, renunciation of American citizenship, by their leaders, in an address to the President.

WE WISH TO PRESERVE THE UNION.—Hence, we say, let its friends cohere; and if the Abolitionists cannot be still in such company let them withdraw. We prefer that the North should be divided rather than that the whole denomination and the nation should be sundered in order to preserve the Abolitionists from the trouble of a separate organization. Our plan is, therefore, to interlink the parts, where the Abolitionists would produce division—to strengthen, if possible, the bonds which unite the good and the true men of our denomination, and let those restless factionists go to themselves. But if it should be found, after a fair trial, that the South have nothing to hope for from the North—if all the North should prove opposed to Union: we shall be found heart and hand with the South—WE ARE SO NOW, but we are desirous to hold on to as many Northern men as possible in order to frustrate the schemes of ultra-Abolitionists and to preserve the Union of the denomination and of the country. BUT IN NO EVENT WHATEVER, will we ever consent that the Board of Foreign Missions with which we co operate, in future, SHALL BE LOCATED IN BOSTON.

NORTHERN PAPERS.—All the Baptist papers in the North, except the Christian Watchman and the Baptist Advocate, are decidedly in favor of the act of the Board and are desirous that the South should withdraw. The Watchman is the only Northern paper which has ventured openly to oppose the Board. The Advocate seems to be equivocal in its course; . . .

SOUTHERN PAPERS.—The Religious Herald and the Christian Index concur in the opinion that the South should immediately withdraw from the North and organize to themselves. The Biblical Recorder of North Carolina, and the Baptist of Tennessee, occupy, as we understand them, somewhat similar ground to our own. They are fully determined on sustaining the rights of the South; but think this can be better done by frustrating the designs of the abolitionists in the North, and holding on to as much interest on that side of the line as possible. As the Alabama Baptist has been withheld from us since its former editor made his unfortunate attack upon us, we do not know its position in relation to this question.

Our Southern correspondents seem to be divided in opinion about in the same way that the Southern editors are: But, we trust, that however divided as to incipient measures, all will be united in their ultimate plans.

C.   The Schism of 1845, A Northern Perspective

In 1832, the great anti-slavery contest in England culminates in the introduction and passage of a bill for the abolition of slavery, throughout the wide domains of Great Britain, after 1834. The effect of this in America is to strengthen the hands of those who for years had been agitating the abolition of slavery here. . . .

In 1844, at the annual meeting of the Society, in Philadelphia, the subject is introduced for the first time in the form of a resolution by Rev. S. Adlam, of Me., to the effect that slaveholding should not debar a minister from appointment as a missionary of the Society. He explains that his resolution is put in a negative form purposely, but he and others who are opposed to the appointment of slaveholding missionaries, want an unequivocal answer to the question. Rev. Richard Fuller, of S.C., offers an amendment to the effect that, as the constitution of the Society allows auxiliary Societies the right of appointment and designation of funds, any action concerning slavery or anti-slavery is unconstitutional, as well as unwise; that the Society is only an agency to receive and disburse funds committed to it according to the wishes of contributors, and should not meddle with this matter. The subject is warmly discussed Friday forenoon, Monday afternoon and Tuesday forenoon, when the amendment of Dr. Fuller prevails by a vote of 123 to 61. Immediately, Rev. J. S. Maginnis, of N.Y., moves the appointment of a committee consisting of three from the North, three from the South, and three from the West, together with the chairman, "to take into consideration the subject of an amicable dissolution of this Society, or to report such alterations in the constitution as will admit of the co-operation of brethren who cherish conflicting views on the subject of slavery." . . .

At Providence, in 1845, the majority report of the committee, appointed the year before, is adverse to any alteration of the constitution or plan of operation. A counter report is brought in by Dr. Colver. . . . It is evident that separation is inevitable. The special committee submit the following report:

"As the existing Society was planted at the North, has its Executive Board there, and there received a character of incorporation, which it seems desirable to preserve, and as a separation seems to many minds inevitable, owing to the strong views of Churches and individuals against the appointment of slaveholders to serve the Society, and a such views prevail principally at the North, therefore in case of such separation, we recommend the adoption of the following resolutions:

1st. *Resolved,* Should such separation among the former friends and patrons of the Society be deemed necessary, that the existing charter be retained by the Northern and other Churches, which may be willing to act together upon the basis of restriction against the appointment of slaveholders.

2d. *Resolved,* That the Executive Board be instructed, in such case, to adjust, upon amicable, honorable and liberal principles, whatever claims may be presented by brethren who shall feel, upon the separation, unable further to co-operate with the Society, or disposed to form a separate organization at the South."

After much discussion, the report is adopted. The Society takes no action on the appointment of slaveholders, or in any other respect which can be used as a reason for separation; but leaves the responsibility of separation with those who choose to take the step; it being well understood, however, that it will doubtless come, and provision being made for the contingency. Hence the separation takes place, not as the result of positive action by the Society, but by the logic of events.

Southern brethren withdraw and organize the Southern Baptist Convention in 1845. Though an attempt is made in 1846 to engraft upon the constitution some anti-slavery restrictions, yet in the circumstances, this is felt to be unnecessary. In 1849 Dr. Colver secures the appointment of a committee to investigate representations "that this Society is in some way fraternally connected with American slavery." This committee, consists of Drs. Nathaniel Colver, John Peck, and Edward Lathrop, after full examination, present a detailed report, the conclusion of which is:

"That in so far as your committee are able to ascertain there is no relation or action of the Society which involves directly or indirectly the countenance and fellowship of slavery."

So ends the controversy.

11

Going Separate Ways: Baptists in America, 1845-1900

After the schism of 1845, Baptists in America went their separate ways and, in time, tended to develop somewhat different outlooks upon church and denominational life. This chapter seeks to trace the progress of Baptists in America, both North and South, from their unhappy division in 1845 to the end of the century.

Documents are included to spotlight major trends and developments among Baptists, such as the Northern occupation of the Southern home mission field after 1863 and Southern reaction leading up to the Fortress Monroe Conference of 1894. In the North, such diverse developments as the work of the three great societies, the formation of the University of Chicago, and the provocative thought of Francis Wayland are cited. In the South, attention is given to the founding of the Baptist Sunday School Board in 1891, the far-reaching Landmark movement led by J. R. Graves, and Landmark-related issues like Crawfordism and the Whitsitt controversy. The chapter concludes with selections from the letters of Charlotte "Lottie" Moon, who would probably be shocked to know that she has become the patron saint of Southern Baptist foreign missions.

11.1 Report on Missions in Africa, ABMU, 1882

The American Baptist Missionary Union, successor to the Triennial Convention, maintained a continuing commitment to missions in Africa. Their annual report for 1882 included a section entitled "Report on Missions in Africa," which cited mission challenges and strategies for that land. This report recommends greater involvement of black Baptists, both North and South, in African missions. Though their motives might bear further consideration, the Baptists did recommend that more black missionaries be appointed. *Source:* Sixty-Eighth Annual Meeting, American Baptist Missionary Union. As printed in *The Baptist Missionary Magazine,* July 1882, 182.

Rev. Thomas Armitage, D.D., of N.Y., presented the report of the Committee on Missions in Africa.

REPORT ON MISSIONS IN AFRICA.

The Committee to whom was referred so much of the Annual Report as relates to Africa, together with the preamble and resolutions offered by Dr. Wayland, ask permission to report,—

1. That this vast region, peopled by unknown millions of Negroes, Kaffirs, and Moors, where Islamism and Paganism have struggled for supremacy for nearly a thousand years, leaving it more degraded and superstitious with every new contest, is now ready for the saving efficacy of the gospel, being open on nearly every side, rendering it one of the most promising fields on the globe for redemption to Christ Jesus.

2. That it is the duty of the Missionary Union to strengthen and enlarge our mission in Liberia, and to establish new missions in the interior of Africa, as soon as we can, especially amongst those large and approachable tribes where the climate is most endurable to men of American birth, whether white or colored.

3. That, as pestilence is the chief obstruction to the establishment of missions in Africa, constantly proving fatal to those apostles of science, philanthropy, and religion who are born in other lands, it is proved by long experience that our colored brethren, though natives of America, are, by nature and constitution, better adapted to endure the

trials of its climate, and to become more readily acclimated, than men of other races. We should, therefore, as far as possible, selection missionaries from their ranks,—men of piety and sound judgment, of zeal and learning, who will be able to acquire the vernacular tongues, to formulate them, to teach and translate therein, and to establish gospel churches on an enlightened and solid basis.

4. That, inasmuch as our colored brethren in the Southern States are deeply interested in the evangelization of Africa, and have already sent out missionaries there, we recommend that the Executive Board correspond with these brethren on the subject, tendering sympathy and aid in the work, and inviting their co-operation with the Missionary Union in the attempt to win Africa to Christ. We think, also, that if our Southern colored brethren need assistance in collecting funds for this object, it would be wise for our Board to assist them by sending a district secretary or agent to visit their churches, associations, conventions, and other bodies, as far as may be, without expense to them, it being understood that all moneys so collected, shall be faithfully expended in African mission-work, and that all funds specially designated for that work, from whatever sources, shall be so used.

Respectfully submitted by Committee.

11.2   Northern Baptist Home Mission Reports

No denomination in America made a more valiant attempt to win America to faith in Christ than did Northern Baptists in the nineteenth century. Henry L. Morehouse (1834-1917), who headed the American Baptist Home Mission Society 1879-92, was perhaps the most dynamic Baptist leader of his generation, and he made the ABHMS the most dynamic Northern Baptist agency during his time.

Selection A recounts the ABHMS decision to send missionaries to work in the South in 1862. Their failure to send missionaries to Southern states in the 1840s was alleged as one reason for the schism of 1845. *Source:* H. L. Morehouse, ed., *Baptist Home Missions in North America, 1832-1882* (New York: Baptist Home Mission Society, 1883), 397. Selection B describes general conditions among the black freedmen as of 1863 (*Source:* Ibid., 398), while selection C gives specific conditions of one worker among freedmen in Louisiana in 1875. *Source:* Forty-Second Annual Report, American Baptist Home Mission Society, Washington, 1875, 50. Selection D cites home mission work among the Chinese on the West Coast. *Source:* Ibid., 34-35.

These representative documents confirm that Northern Baptists, through their ABHMS, conducted aggressive home mission work in different areas and among different kinds of people.

A.   Decision to Occupy the Southern Field, 1862

"*Whereas,* We recognize in the recent abolition of slavery in the District of Columbia, and in the setting free of thousands of bondmen by the advancement of our national armies into the insurgent States, a most impressive indication that Divine Providence is about to break the chains of the enslaved millions in our land, and thus furnish an unobstructed entrance for the Gospel among vast multitudes who have hitherto been shut out from its pure teachings; and

"*Whereas,* We see in the entire reorganization of the social and religious state of the South, which must inevitably follow the successful overthrow of the rebellion, the Divine Hand most distinctly and most imperatively beckoning us on to the occupancy of a field broader, more important, more promising than has ever yet invited our toils; therefore

"*Resolved,* That we recommend the Society to take immediate steps to supply with Christian instruction, by means of missionaries and teachers, the emancipated slaves—whether in the District of Columbia or in other places held by our forces—and also to inaugurate a system of operations for carrying the Gospel alike to free and bond throughout the whole southern section of our country, so fast and so far as the progress of our arms, and the restoration of order and law shall open the way."

The recommendations, after full discussion, are adopted at the second session. June 25th, 1862, the Board vote—

"That immediate measures be taken for the occupation by our missionaries of such Southern fields as in the Providence of God may be opened to our operations.

B. Conditions Among the Freedmen, 1863

"The distinguishing traits of humanity are nearly effaced. We had, before, no idea of how near human beings may approximate to the brutes. Most of them have no more self-reliance, or capacity for self-help, than children. They have no idea of economy or accumulation.

"In some sense these contrabands are very religious people. They are excitable, impressible, seemingly devout in a very high degree; and there is, no doubt, much real piety among them. But it often has with it a strange inter-mixture of ignorance and superstition and downright immorality. The moral feelings are benumbed. As to *conscience,* to use the language of one of the superintendents, the whole thing seems *rubbed out.* They are most religious; but it is a religion entirely destitute of morality! Such is the influence of slavery! This is the religion which we have been told the institution fosters!

"Helpless, hopeless, friendless, these poor creatures appeal to us most loudly for assistance! Not a man in the whole camp to care for their souls! Not a teacher to instruct them even in the lowest branches of learning!

"Few, if any, missionary fields, as we believe, make a stronger demand upon our denomination to-day than that here indicated. Difficult indeed is the problem. What are we to do for the freedom which are being thrown in increasing numbers upon our hands? One thing is certain, *they must not be neglected.* And upon whom else so clearly rest this obligation as upon Northern Baptists?"

C. Joanna P. Moore, Report on Work Among Freedmen in Louisiana, 1875

"I have had about seventy on my list, but some got discouraged in a few days, others were compelled to leave and go to work, and it has required a great amount of perseverance to keep them in school. They are so easily discouraged, or perhaps I ought to say, their position makes it discouraging, beginning so late in life, with homes and children to care for. But I do feel that the effort they have made has done them great good. There is here a very bad class of young girls from sixteen to twenty-five years of age that I have been trying to reach, but I fear that I have not done them much good. Perhaps the good seed will grow sometimes. I have a meeting for the little girls in which they are taught to sew and do various other things. My programme for the day has been women's school from 8 to 10 A. M., followed by children's sewing till 12 M. Then, in another part of the town, I meet a class of women from 1 to 3, immediately followed by children's school. Now that the weather is warmer, I fear I shall not be able to accomplish so much in the future. I attend three Sunday-schools each Sabbath. Have not been absent from any one of them since I organized them. The average attendance in two of them is about fifty, sometimes seventy-five are present. The other school averages about thirty. It is very hard work to get the older ones into the Sunday-school. It is too tame work for them to quietly sit down and listen to the reading of the Bible; but we are making a great effort in that direction, and gradually they are coming in, especially the women that I teach during the week."

D.   E. Z. Simmons, Report on Chinese Mission, 1875

"We have a prosperous mission here [San Francisco], with twelve members. Four of these joined last year. These converts are live, working Christians. We have a good school, with an average attendance of fifty-five every evening. There are three Chinese Sunday-schools in our different churches. And we have a flourishing school in Portland, Oregon, and one Chinese preacher there—all supported by the Baptist church in Portland.

"With the aid of my members there are preached here, on an average, about ten sermons a week in Chinese. The Chinese preach about six times each week, and all without any money remuneration. This will do a great deal of good if faithfully continued. But most of this work is done under very unfavorable circumstances. Much of the preaching is done in the streets, and the wind is so strong that it makes it very laborious, and I am afraid that my strength will not permit me to continue long.

"Our school is full, and we could have one hundred just as well as fifty-five, if we had the room and the teachers. We must have more room. Our mission would not near accommodate our Sunday-school, which is now held in the First Baptist Church, and they are going to move soon to another part of the city, and then we will be obliged to provide for ourselves. We ought to have this church for our mission. It is the cheapest that can be bought (that would do for a mission house). I wish some of the Lord's rich stewards would give us $30,000 to buy this or some other property for our mission. We must have a place if we continue the mission. And I do hope the Baptists will never disgrace themselves by giving it up. We can't give it up without being recreant to a God-imposed duty and responsibility. God in His wise providence has brought these Chinese here and enabled us to commence this good work. But we can't stay where we are, for we have to labor under too many difficulties. We are losing good men for the want of better accommodations. The Methodists, who are right near us, have a splendid property, just such as we need. It cost them over $30,000. And the Presbyterians are well prepared and equipped for the work, compared to us. They have an appropriation of $30,000 in addition to their present property, for a new mission house. They see the importance of this work, and are acting accordingly.

"Last year seven thousand Chinese returned to China. If one out of every one hundred of these had been truly converted, who could estimate the good these seventy missionaries would do, as they would preach in their own towns and villages, and all at their own charges. O, brethren, think of the possibilities of this work. I think we can't well overestimate the importance of it. Pray for us, and do all you can for us in giving."

11.3   Annual Report, American Baptist Publication Society, 1846

The American Baptist Publication Society was the successor of the Baptist Tract Society, formed in 1824. Its report in 1846 shows an aggressive program of printing and distribution of Baptist literature. The report shows a Baptist market for a wide variety of literature, ranging from brief tracts to major books, like the *Complete Works of Andrew Fuller*. They also provided reading material suitable for older youth, as well as catechisms and Sunday school lessons for children.

This report in 1846 is remarkable for the absence of any reference to the formation of the Southern Baptist Convention the year before. In fact, that schism was at first limited to the two mission societies and did not extend to the ABPS. The publication society printed materials from both Northern and Southern Baptist authors (note the two works by R. B. C. Howell of Nashville) and distributed materials to Baptists in all sections.

The Society also published more copies of *The Psalmist*, a church hymnal that helped to shape the worship styles of Northern Baptists. This hymnal, however, never won wide acceptance in the South. The Society also provided a hymnal for Indian churches.

This report illustrates the wide range of materials offered by this growing Baptist agency. It also shows the growing maturity of Baptists in America who could provide a market for such a variety of materials. *Source:* Seventh Annual Report, American Baptist Publication Society, Philadelphia, 1846, 11-13.

The measures and operations of the Society during the last year have been prosecuted with efficiency and success.

PUBLICATIONS ISSUED.

The Board have issued the "COMPLETE WORKS OF ANDREW FULLER," of the commencement of which mention was made in the last Annual Report. The second and third volumes contain a larger number of pages, and consequently were issued at a greater expense than the first volume. The three volumes include 2420 octavo pages, and are sold for $7,50. "The writings of few men have exerted, and are still exerting a wider influence than those of Fuller. They have an originality, depth and pathos, that will in all coming time give them a place among standard theological writings. . . ."

Such is the recently expressed opinion of the Boston Recorder, the oldest weekly religious periodical in our country. It is earnestly hoped that no *Baptist* minister will remain long unprovided with a copy of this great work.

The Board have stereotyped "TERMS OF SACRAMENTAL COMMUNION, by R. B. C. Howell, D. D." This work has already secured a wide circulation in this country, and has been re-published in England. Its present attractive form, with the price reduced, will secure for it a still wider circulation. It makes a 12mo. of 271 pages, and will be ready for sale, next month.

An original and valuable work on "THE DEACONSHIP, by R. B. C. Howell, D. D.," has been stereotyped and an edition printed, which is now in the binder's hands. It examines critically the New Testament authority on the Office, Qualifications and Duties of Deacons. This is a work, which it is hoped, will find circulation in every church; for in it principles are discussed no less important to each member of the body than to its officers. It contains 154 pages, 18mo. . . .

"MARRIED LIFE, A WEDDING GIFT, by Joseph Belcher, D. D.," has been stereotyped, and will soon be issued. It is the first of a series of miniature volumes, with gilt edges. It contains 128 pages, 32mo.

"THE BAPTIST MANUAL," has been revised and a new edition issued.

A new edition of "BAPTISM IN ITS MODE AND SUBJECTS, by Alexander Carson, L. L. D.," has been published. It contains 502 closely printed octavo pages. . . .

The Board have ordered, "A HISTORY OF BAPTISM BOTH FROM THE INSPIRED AND UNINSPIRED WRITINGS, by Isaac Taylor Hinton," to be stereotyped. About seventy pages have been stereotyped at the time of presenting this report. Five thousand copies have been sold by this Society. The work has been re-published in England, and the present stereotype edition will be from a revised copy of the English edition.

Having a large stock of "THE PSALMIST" on hand, at the last Anniversary, then recently issued, the Board have printed only 5000 copies during the year. The introduction of this Manual of Psalmody into the churches in every state, is making steady progress, and is gradually but effectually taking the place of all older compilations, while many churches that never before used a book in this branch of congregational worship have already adopted the Psalmist. The sound piety, good sense and good taste of the people, will do much to extend its usefulness.

During the year, 3,000 copies of our small CATECHISM, for the use of Families and Sunday Schools, have been published.

INDIAN HYMN BOOK.—Rev. James N. Cusick, a Baptist Missionary of the Tuscarora tribe of Indians from the State of New York, having compiled a Hymn Book in their language, chiefly translations of some of our best and most popular hymns, and the necessary funds having been raised in Philadelphia, the compilation was approved by the Publishing Committee, and an edition of 500 copies published. It contains 128 pages, 32mo., and is entitled, *Ne Kororon Ne Teyerihwahkwatha Igen Ne Enyontste Ne Yondatteskos Yagorihwiyoghstonh Rotinensyonih Kaweanondahko Ne Sorwatagwen.* Translated as follows—"The Collection of Sacred Songs, for the use of the Baptist Native Christians of the Six Nations. Revised by James N. Cusick." This band of aborigines, most of whom are Baptists in principle, and civilized, are about to remove to the Indian Territory, west of Missouri. There is a Baptist Church of this tribe in Canada of nearly 100 members, with a pastor, to whom a portion of the books are to be sent.

11.4   The University of Chicago

Two documents are cited here from the founding of the University of Chicago in 1890. This represents by far the most ambitious educational project of Northern Baptists to that time. This has become a world-class university, though it no longer sustains any significant ties to Baptists. The founding of the University of Chicago was the first major project of the newly formed American Baptist Education Society and, as it turned out, also the last.

Selection A recounts the facts of the founding of the university, along with some of the reasons for that action. Selection B includes excerpts from an address by F. T. Gates, corresponding secretary of ABES. This address is important not only for its summary of reasons for founding of the university in Chicago, but also for its general survey of the needs and prospects of Baptist education in America. *Source:* First Annual Meeting, American Baptist Education Society, Tremont Temple Baptist Church, Boston, 1889, 14-16, 23-31.

A.   Founding of the University of Chicago

ESTABLISHMENT OF A BAPTIST INSTITUTION OF LEARNING AT CHICAGO.

The Board has decided to undertake the establishment of a Baptist institution of learning in the city of Chicago. In July last, a convention of western pastors and laymen met in Chicago to consider the propriety of accepting a conditional offer of lands and buildings for a college to be located at Morgan Park. It was unanimously resolved that the offer ought to be accepted. A provisional committee, constituting of prominent pastors and laymen, was appointed to secure if possible the fulfillment of the conditions. After inquiry and consideration, this committee laid before your Board a full statement of the facts, and invited the counsel and the co-operation of the Society. . . . The communication of the provisional committee at Chicago was carefully considered by the Board at its December meeting, and the following resolutions were unanimously adopted:

Resolved, That the establishment of a thoroughly equipped institution of learning in Chicago is an immediate and imperative denominational necessity.

Resolved, That we rejoice in the powerful sentiment favorable to such an institution, that prevails not only in Chicago and the West, but also throughout the denomination at large.

Resolved, That we invite brethren of means to unite in an endeavor to found such an institution, and pledge the hearty co-operation of this Board, and that the Corresponding Secretary of the Society be directed to use every means in his power to originate or encourage such a movement. . . .

The scope of instruction to be proposed, the location to be chosen, whether in the city or in a suburb, the funds required form substantial foundation, the extent to which the Society may wisely co-operate in the undertaking, these and other important questions the Executive Committee of the Board referred at a later meeting to a committee of eastern brethren, consisting of Drs. Andrew, Hovey, Weston, Elder, Duncan, Moorehouse, Taylor, Harper and Hon. Chas. L. Colby. The very carefully considered report of this committee has been laid before your Board. So much of this report as relates to minor details of the organization of the institution has been reserved for future consideration. So much of it as sets forth the conditions and scope of endeavor on which the Society should seek subscriptions has, with some modifications and additions, been adopted by the Board. This action of your Board is set forth in the following preamble and resolutions, on which, as a basis, the hearty co-operation of the denomination in this great enterprise is invoked.

(1) *Resolved,* That this Society take immediate steps toward the founding of a well equipped college in the city of Chicago.

(2) *Resolved,* That the institution be located in the city of Chicago and not in a suburban village.

(3) *Resolved,* That the privileges of the institution be extended to persons of both sexes on equal terms.

(4) *Resolved,* That for a suitable site for the proposed institution there be provided at least ten acres of land.

(5) *Resolved,* That the Board proceed to raise one million dollars as a financial foundation for the proposed institution. . . .

(7) *Resolved,* That at least $600,000, and as much more as possible, of the million or more subscribed shall be an endowment fund, the principal of which shall remain invested and the income used only so far as shall be necessary for the expenses of conducting the institution, and shall not be used in the purchase of lands or in erecting or repairing buildings.

(8) *Resolved,* That the Board shall secure the incorporation of the proposed institution as early as practicable; that the Board of Trustees shall consist of twenty-one members, divided into three equal classes, with terms of service expiring respectively in one, two and three years; that the choice of persons for the first Board of Trustees shall be subject to the approval of the Executive Board of this Society, and that the President of the institution and two thirds of the Board of Trustees of the same shall always be members of Baptist churches.

B. F. T. Gates, Address upon Founding of University of Chicago, 1889

This paper, as originally prepared, contained a general survey of the condition and needs of organized Baptist education throughout the entire land. The country was divided into sections, and each of these sections, the East, the South, the Central West and the Pacific Slope, was studied separately and in comparison with the others. But it was found that any just presentation, however condensed, of areas so vast and conditions so varied and so complicated, must trespass upon the time of the Society. In selecting, therefore, a single field of our territory for survey I have chosen that one which for the next twelve months, as appears in the report of the Board, is destined to receive the special heed of the Society and of the denomination. I shall invite your attention, accordingly, to the condition and needs of the upper Mississippi Valley, or, as it may be termed, the Central West.

I mean the region that lies between Ohio and the Rocky Mountains, north of the Ohio River and north of the southern limits of Missouri and Kansas. This vast area, popularly called the West, is, in fact, the eastern central portion of the continent. . . . This vast empire, destined early to sustain the heaviest weight of population on this continent, is united, homogeneous, indivisible, knit together in living unity, with arteries of life clearly defined and permanent, all radiating from and returning to the City of Chicago as the centre and heart. Comprising four-fifths of the territory of the Baptists of the North, it already contains nearly half their number. To be exact there are 384,000 Baptists in the States enumerated, to 444,000 east of Indiana, a ratio of 9 to 11. The western Baptists will soon greatly preponderate in numbers. With four-fifths of the most fertile territory of the North, it is not unreasonable to suppose that ultimately the Central West will also contain four-fifths of our numbers.

Such is the field of our present survey. For brevity and clearness let me present what I may say in a series of numbered statements:

1st. The educational needs of the West cannot be supplied by our Colleges in the East, however celebrated or well equipped. Distributed among our seven eastern colleges, there were last year, all told, forty-one students, Baptists and otherwise, attracted from homes west of Ohio. This number is four per cent. of the attendance of these colleges. They derived ninety-six per cent. of their students from their local territory east of the Indiana line.

We need in the West, as elsewhere, one centrally located college in each populous State. . . .

2d The financial resources and equipment of our Colleges in the West are meagre and inadequate. Omitting colleges that are such in name only, we have ten institutions between Ohio and the Rocky Mountains, all of which give instruction more or less thorough and extended in collegiate studies. Five, or half of these, have practically no endowment whatever.

Distributed somewhat unequally among the remaining five is an aggregate of about five hundred thousand dollars in invested funds. Certainly our eastern colleges are not amply endowed; but all the western colleges together have not as much productive endowment as has Rochester or Hamilton; not half as much as Brown; not one-sixth as much as our eastern colleges in the aggregate. . . .

In the last thirty years great progress has been made in educational architecture, but that progress has not been recorded in western Baptist colleges. Our buildings are for the most part suggestive of an earlier day, when they marked the limits of an advancing civilization that has long since swept past them. . . .

The scanty means at hand have not made possible the purchase of many books or of much illustrative apparatus. Such libraries as that of Brown, with its sixty-four thousand volumes, or that of Rochester, with it twenty-five thousand carefully selected purchased books, are unknown among our colleges in the West. . . .

The average salaries paid the professors in our western colleges are not such as high character and competence ought to command. The nominal salary averages $1015.00; and this is not always paid. The highest average afforded by any one institution is $1300.00—about half the usual salary of eastern professors. . . . The ablest Baptist teachers have in general been claimed by institutions of other denominations capable of affording them a larger field and a remuneration more equitable.

3rd. Comparatively feeble as they are, none of our western colleges has been able to attract and retain any considerable number of collegiate students. Nearly four-fifths of the whole number of students enrolled are in the preparatory and primary departments. In all the West, with its three hundred and eighty-four thousand Baptists, we gave instruction last year to fewer male classical students than were at the same time matriculated in Colby University in Maine from a Baptist constituency of less than twenty thousand.

4th. We are not raising up in the West an educated ministry. It is true that a very large number of ministerial students receive temporary and partial instruction in our colleges or in their preparatory departments. . . . In all our western colleges only twenty-five young men were brought to graduation last year, and of these nine only were students for the ministry. This is one ministerial graduate for each six hundred churches in the West. . . .

5th. Other denominations, wiser than we to forecast or better organize to promote culture, are far in advance of Baptists in western education and are diverting from us many of our most promising youth. . . .

6th. Our western Baptist colleges are not so evenly distributed or so centrally located as to supply the present or afford promise of supplying the future and permanent needs of Baptists of the West. . . . Our present colleges, therefore, while redundant in some localities, are not so distributed as ever to supply our needs, however thoroughly equipped they might ultimately become. Only one-eighteenth of the West is within the area of their present effective attractions. . . . Seventeen-eighteenths of the West lies then without the attraction of any Baptist College. And yet I must qualify the impression this appalling statement is likely to give. Our western colleges are located in the more populous States, and by computing the Baptist population within the attraction of our colleges I find that one-fifth of our people live within the territorial boundaries of the colleges. It is therefore substantially true that four-fifths of our Baptist youth in the West live outside the range of our colleges. Their names do not appear in our catalogues. The sections in which they live are not represented at our colleges. They are being educated, if educated at all, under care of other denominations or of the State universities. This explains, in part, why we graduate so few students for the ministry—seven to nine a year. We touch only a fifth of our people. . . .

We are accustomed to contemplate the city chiefly as a centre for the collection and distribution of material products over a mammoth mid-continental territory. But Chicago is not less preeminent in its vast field as a moral, intellectual and spiritual centre of exchange. To-day the news, the literature, the medical and legal science of the West is disseminated from Chicago. With its five divinity schools, enrolling more than six hundred students, Chicago is the seat of western Theological learning. The city of Chicago will lift so far aloft a Baptist college as an intellectual and religious luminary that its light will penetrate every State and illumine every home from Lake Erie to the Rocky Mountains. . . .

Nothing great or worthy can be done for education in the West until this thing is done. . . .

11.5 Francis Wayland, Thoughts on the Missionary Organization of the Baptist Denomination, 1859

Francis Wayland (1796-1865) was a major theologian and philosopher among Northern Baptists in the nineteenth century. As pastor in Boston and later president of Brown University, he shaped Baptist thought and conduct for generations. Wayland was also perhaps the major architect of Northern Baptist ideas of what a denomination is and how it ought to work.

At first Wayland favored a unified Baptist denomination in which a cooperative convention of delegates from churches worked together to plan and carry out benevolent ministries. In this he agreed with Richard Furman of Charleston, and the Triennial Convention formed in 1814 represented the unified concept. However, Wayland later changed his mind. He came to believe that any convention composed of church delegates somehow compromises the independence of the churches. He concluded that any benevolent work beyond the local church should be conducted not by a convention of church delegates, but by completely independent societies. Interested individuals who joined such societies could carry on whatever work they preferred without any relationship to the churches. In this way Wayland believed the independence of the churches could be protected, while, at the same time, the autonomy and economy of benevolent work could also be maintained. Following these views, Wayland provided the rationale that dismantled the expanded Triennial Convention in the 1820s and returned that body to its single purpose society approach.

Some have compared this ecclesiology to Landmarkism in the South, even describing Wayland's views as "landmarkism" with a little "l." Wayland and Southern Landmarkers like J. R. Graves might have agreed on the primacy of the local church, but there were other significant differences between their doctrinal and denominational views.

The document cited here comes from 1859, late enough to represent Wayland's mature thought. Following his views would mean that Baptists could exist in local churches, but could not form any true *denomination* at all. Baptists in the North have been greatly influenced by Wayland, while Southern Baptists have more nearly adhered to the unifying concepts of Richard Furman. *Source:* Francis Wayland, *Thoughts on the Missionary Organizations of the Baptist Denomination* (New York: Sheldon, Blakeman & Co., 1859), 4-36.

THE present condition of our Missionary work manifestly demands the prayerful consideration of every true-hearted Baptist. Our numbers are increasing. Our aggregate wealth is sufficient for the most extended system of Christian enterprise. Our sentiments are better than ever understood; and their agreement with the principles of the New Testament is more generally admitted than at any previous period. In all the prominent articles of belief and practice we are united. No denomination of Christians has greater advantages than ourselves for laboring successfully to extend the Redeemer's Kingdom. . . .

Our efforts for the extension of the Kingdom of Christ are directed to two objects—Domestic and Foreign Missions. What is now the condition of these agencies among us?

Our Home Mission has done a noble work. It has planted pastors in the churches throughout the West, and, at a very moderate expense, has been the instrument of incalculable good. Probably by no other means which we have employed, have we done so much to extend the Kingdom of our Lord. But the amount contributed to this society has been wholly unworthy of us. . . .

In the foreign field our case is yet more to be deplored. God gave us at the beginning Missionaries, whose praise is in all the churches. He sent them to a most inviting field of labor, and gave them souls for their hire in great measure. In no portion of Missionary ground has the Word of God been attended with a richer blessing.

With all this encouragement; with all the additions that have been made to our numbers and material power, for many years we have made no progress; nay, we have gone backward. For the last seven years, the number of laborers in the foreign field has been diminishing; . . .

Nor is this all. Our Missionaries are not agreed among themselves. . . . When we meet to consult concerning missions, missions are almost the last thing thought of, and, in fact, frequently can hardly obtain a hearing. Our time is spent in unfortunate disputings; and we contend so earnestly for the salvation of the Union, that we render it doubtful whether indeed it is at all worth saving. . . .

Now I say that this is a subject which requires the earnest and prayerful attention of every one among us. If we do not as a denomination bear fruit, we shall be cut off as a worthless branch—the Saviour will leave us to our own devices—the Holy Spirit will depart from us and from our assemblies, and God will divide us in Jacob, and scatter us in Israel. . . .

We are pledged to devote ourselves to the extension of the kingdom of Christ at home and abroad, and every organization is to be judged according to its adaptedness to promote this result.

I remark, then, our organizations are *complicated, interfering with each other,* and *expensive.* They should be rendered *simple* and *economical.*

I say they are *complicated,* and *interfering with each other.* Let me illustrate my meaning.

I will commence with the work of Home Missions. Our regular and established organization for the promotion of this work, is our Home Mission Society. This society, in connection with churches, associations, and state conventions, is, so far as we can presume, capable of doing this work, but we have in fact three agencies engaged in it. The Publication Society employs itself in colporteur labor, and makes this the strong ground of its solicitation. The American and Foreign Bible Society has entered to the full extent of its power into the same work, and it also puts forward its claims on precisely the same ground. Either society would undertake to do this work for the whole country, if our State Conventions and other local agencies would surrender it into their hands.

Here, then, we have three distinct societies engaged in the work of Home Missions; three sets of offices, and officers and agents, each interfering with each other, and all doing the same work. The expense of collection and distribution must be almost three-fold, and three times as many ministers as are needed are taken from their appropriate duties to engage in this kind of labor. If it be said the Home Mission Society has not the funds to devote to their kind of service, the answer is apparent, it would have the funds, if we would all unite in it, as our only agency for doing our Home Mission work. . . .

The same complication and interference exist in our labors to extend the Kingdom of Christ among foreign nations.

The legitimate agency among us for the work of Foreign Missions, is the American Baptist Missionary Union. It was constituted for this sole object and to this object we believe it has restricted itself. But both of the other societies to which I have referred, have entered into the same field. The Publication Society has some colporteurs in the north of Europe, the very same work that the Union is carrying on in Germany. It appeals to the public for aid, on the ground of its labor in Foreign Missions. The Bible Society again goes over the very same field from which the Union derives its support, and collects funds for the translation and circulation of Bibles in heathen lands. . . . Three sets of agents are thus employed to collect for Foreign Missions, a work that could far better and less expensively be done by one. The churches are annoyed and harassed by the multiplicity of calls. They become confused by so many applications in different forms for the same objects. They know not which to prefer, and, in the end, lose their interest in all. As the interest in them all declines, more agents become necessary; thus the less there is to be collected, the greater is the expense of collection; . . .

Now, what is the obvious remedy for all this? Is it not the entire simplification of all our organizations? Let our foreign work be confided to one organization, if we have an organization, and let it do this and nothing else. . . .

If we thus simplify our operations, every society will stand exclusively upon its own merits. Every one will know when and how much he gives, either for Home or for Foreign Missions, for the circulation of the Bible at home, or for the publication of religious books. Some cannot give to all, and they can have an opportunity of selection.

It will then be distinctly seen in how far each object is sustained by the affections of the denomination. Those which we choose to foster and encourage will grow, and those which we do not choose to support, will decline and die. To this there can certainly be no objection. . . .

But this is only one of the questions presented for our consideration. There is a general conviction that a change is required in the form of our missionary organizations. . . . We do not wish to change, unless we can change for the better; and if plans are presented which we prefer to those at present employed, we desire from those to select the best. It is with this view I proceed to ask, under what form of organization can we most effectually promote the work of missions, that is, extend the reign of Christ on earth?

I remark in the first place, that there exists quite a general dissatisfaction with the present form of our missionary organizations. . . . This applies particularly to the Foreign Mission organization. For several years past thoughtful members have attended the meetings in constant fear of some measure which would throw everything into disorder. Without the passage of any resolutions, or any legalized change in the constitution, the organization of the Union has been entirely subverted. The Board, which was intended as the deliberative branch of the organization, has been in fact reduced to a nullity, and now there is a motion pending to abolish it altogether. . . .

The Foreign Missionary organization commenced with the Triennial Convention, . . . Mr. Rice, the general agent, was everywhere received with enthusiasm, and contributions, as it seemed, to any amount could be had only for the asking. Soon the attempt was made to render the convention the agent for all our benevolent operations. Home Missions, a Tract Society, a general Education Society, together with the Columbian College, were *consolidated* under its management, and in fact one common treasury was to be used for them all. The Board in the meantime had been removed from Philadelphia to Washington, which was henceforth to be the centre of all these great undertakings. The result may easily be imagined. Confidence in the wisdom of the Board was shaken, the means for carrying on its schemes were withheld, and everything seemed on the verge of destruction. The denomination came to the rescue. These various modes of benevolence were separated from the missionary department, a committee for Foreign Missions was formed in Boston, and under the ministration of the late Dr. Bolles its prospects began to revive. . . . When the slavery question caused a disruption of the South from the North the opportunity was improved to make such changes as experience seemed to have rendered desirable.

For a few years everything seemed to move on prosperously; every one appeared satisfied, and it was hoped that our brethren, without molestation or difference of opinion, would now labor in the work of the conversion of the world. But, before long, we were doomed to meet the former difficulties. . . . The care of Missions was neglected at our annual meetings, in order to consider all sorts of difficulties; our contributions have, consequently, fallen off so much, that, with a greatly reduced force in the field, the call is ever for retrenchment.

We are now convinced that some other change is necessary, and that, unless it be made, our Missionary efforts must dwindle into insignificance, or be abandoned altogether. . . .

I remark, then, in the first place, that centralizing organizations are certainly not in strict accordance with the principles of benevolence made known by our Lord.

Christ always speaks of benevolence as an especial means of grace to the believer. He places it by the side of secret prayer, and He gives the same directions for both. He evidently intends that every individual shall, so far as possible, do his own charity, just as much as he shall do his own praying. . . .

. . . Now, a central organization is at variance with these principles. It keeps the two parties as far apart as possible, by placing between them a vast number of intermediate agencies. We employ a succession of paid almoners instead of being almoners ourselves. We surrender to them all the planning, all the responsibility, all the legislation, and we, ourselves, do nothing but furnish the means. . . .

We consider every church a perfectly independent community, under law to no one but Him who is our Master, even Christ. . . . While every true disciple desires to serve the Master, no one likes to be controlled by his brethren as to the manner in which he shall do it. He must carry out his own conscientious convictions, or he cannot labor with interest; and if this privilege is denied him, he will probably soon cease to labor at all.

Now, with such elements as these strongly developed, it is evidently very difficult to carry on successfully, for any length of time, any extensive central organization. . . .

What then shall be done? It has been proposed that we attempt a system of consolidation, that is, unite several forms of benevolent effort under one organization. This will accomplish one valuable object, it will deliver us from the cost of three or four agencies where only one is needed. The evils of centralization would, however, seem, in this manner, to be increased rather than diminished. Can we not find something better adapted to our purposes? Can we not discover some mode of action more in harmony with the teachings of the New Testament, and better adapted to the views and necessities of our own denomination?

In reflecting upon this subject, it naturally occurs to us that we possess one form of organization which appears perfectly adapted to our character and principles. It is the ordinary Baptist Association. This naturally springs up wherever Baptist churches exist, its principles are everywhere the same, and it continues unchanged from generation to generation. It seems to belong especially to us, and is the offspring of our own individual and ecclesiastical principles. And what is a Baptist Association? It is nothing more than an annual and voluntary meeting of delegates from churches in a neighborhood or district, who come together as independent bodies, to tell each other what the Lord has done for them during the year past, and encourage each other to more earnest efforts for the future. Here we have no collisions, for there is nothing to strive about. . . .

If the association is then especially a Baptist institution, alway acceptable, nay it would seem necessary, always successful and never worn out, might we not in some way use it as a model in the formation of our plans for uniting the whole denomination in missionary labor? Suppose, for instance, in the case of Foreign Missions, all centralizing organization was abandoned, and missions and missionaries were supported directly by individual churches and clusters of churches. Many of our wealthy churches might support a single mission. Others, and there are hundreds of them, nay, individual members, are able to support a single missionary. Churches, unable to do this, might combine together, or might unite in an association for this purpose. . . . Brethren would send out to the heathen just such missionaries as embraced most fully their own particular views, and so long as the missionary and his supporters agreed, there could be no collision. If they disagreed, the matter would rest with themselves, and could affect no other portion of the field or the laborers. . . .

If this could be accomplished we should be at once relieved from all the machinery of boards, committees, secretaries, treasurers, and agents, inasmuch as every church, or cluster of churches, would be all this to itself. Some of these duties might be required in the affairs of each individual organization, but the labor would be so light, that, probably, in every case, it would be performed gratuitously. . . .

. . . The more I have reflected on the subject, the more obvious has it seemed to me, that preaching Christ to the heathen must be a more simple business than is commonly supposed. There were no missionary boards, and no central organizations, in the times of the Apostles, and yet they labored with an efficiency that turned the world upside down; why should we need such organizations now? So far as the Foreign Mission is concerned, I see no difficulty in putting such a plan into immediate operation.

In our Home Missions the case is somewhat different, and our plans would require some modification. Home Mission work is of two kinds: The first is required in the older States, where our churches are numerous, but where there are neighborhoods and districts unblessed with the preaching of the gospel. These destitute places are within the bounds of churches and associations, and State conventions, and to them this part of the work of evangelization is of course to be confided. . . .

But, besides this labor in the older States, there is a distinct field to be cultivated in our new States and frontier settlements. Christians are scattered over these regions, few and far between; and they need to be encouraged, collected together, formed into churches where this is expedient, their children gathered into Sabbath schools and Bible classes, in a word, they need to be blessed, so far as possible, with the same means of grace as ourselves. But they cannot do this without aid from abroad. . . .

But even here the principles previously alluded to should, as far as possible, govern us. Every church, and association, and convention, should do its *own work* just so far as it is able, and we should aid those only who having done all in their power are at present unable to complete their own work of evangelization.

And here let me add a remark suggested by the preceding observations. If such be the condition of our country, should there not be a division of labor among us? Is not the care of the West, at present, all that can be required of the more Western States? Would it not be better if they should specially charge themselves with this work, and for the present, be relieved from any other? We on the Atlantic slope are able to carry on the foreign mission work, and also aid our brethren at home. As our missions increase, and their pecuniary ability enlarges, and the home work becomes less onerous, they will commence the work of Foreign Missions for themselves, . . .

If something like these principles could be adopted, that is, if every church and every local organization, by its own independent action, labored to extend the kingdom of Christ to the utmost of its power, looking to a more general organization for aid, only when the work to be done was too great for its unassisted effort; and if, when the work to be done could be accomplished without any central organization, such organization should be abandoned altogether, such a change would seem to promise many advantages. . . .

It will be said that the support of missionaries would in this manner be rendered more precarious. I do not take this view of the case. In our present manner of support, all are straitened, or all well sustained together; in the other, while some are well sustained, others might be straitened, the condition of the one being unaffected by that of the other. For myself I should prefer the plan which was the most strongly marked by individualization. . . .

11.6 Southern Baptist Attitudes on Race

It is well known that attitudes of Baptists in the South on slavery helped lead to the Southern Baptist Convention, although other factors also played a significant role. The issue of race relations has been a continual concern for Southern Baptists. The documents in this section reflect typical, although not unanimous, attitudes of Baptists in the South on race in the second half of the nineteenth century.

Selection A describes ministry to the black population as carried on by the Charleston Association. This reveals genuine efforts to minister, mixed with paternalistic attitudes. *Source: Minutes of the 115th and 116th Sessions of the Charleston Baptist Association,* 1866, 1867, 10-13.

In 1883 H. H. Tucker, associate editor of the *Christian Index* of Georgia, a leading Baptist paper in the South, took opportunity to set the record straight in a disturbing editorial affirming traditional Southern views on race (selection B). *Source: The Christian Index* (Ga.), 22 March 1883. The annual report of the Home Mission Board of the Southern Baptist Convention in 1891 included a section on "Our work among the COLORED PEOPLE." This report is a strange combination of genuine concern, authentic effort at ministry, and incredible paternalism, racism, and misunderstanding (selection C). *Source: Annual,* SBC, 1891, in Report of the Home Mission Board, xxxvi.

These documents confirm that many Baptists in the South after the Civil War held racial views that were at best paternalistic, and at worst outright racist.

A.   Charleston Association, Ministry to Black Population, 1866

The Committee on the Colored People beg leave to report:

That they have seriously considered the matter, and cannot conceive of any better course to be pursued with these people, under existing circumstances, than that suggested by Dr. J. C. Furman in his report to the Baptist State Convention of South Carolina, on the 238th page of their Minutes; we therefore advise the adoption of that report by this Association.

T. W. MELLICHAMP, Chairman.

The report of the above Committee was adopted, with the suggestion which it makes; and the report "upon the Instruction of the Colored People," adopted by the State Convention, was ordered to be transferred to our Minutes as our report upon that subject, as follows:

The Committee upon the Instruction of the Colored People beg leave to report: That they have given the subject the most serious consideration, and only regret that they cannot perform the duty devolved on them by the Convention, in a manner more satisfactory to themselves. They are compelled, with little experience, to speak upon a point the solution of which requires much experience.

The Churches of our State, as well as of the whole South, find themselves unexpectedly in the midst of one of the greatest social changes which the history of the world presents. While Rome, in the plenitude of her power, judged it for the public safety to restrain with certain limits the exercise by her citizens of the right to emancipate their slaves, and thus allowed this work to go on only by degrees, in our land the fearful experiment of emancipation has been made on the broadest scale, and with the suddenness and violence of an earthquake. The work thus done, whether just or unjust, whether wise or foolish, is finally done. No Southern man now dreams of a reversal of this act of the Government. To us, as good citizens and Christians, the only questions left, are: WHAT ARE THE DUTIES WHICH ARISE OUT OF OUR CHANGED RELATIONS? and HOW MAY WE BEST PERFORM THEM?

To one class of these duties the attention of the Convention has been called by the resolution under which your Committee was appointed, viz: OUR OBLIGATION IN REGARD TO THE INSTRUCTION OF THE COLORED PEOPLE.

In the times gone by, that duty was recognised and acted upon, imperfectly indeed, as all religious duty is in the hands of imperfect man, and under certain disadvantages. These disadvantages arose from laws, in our State at least, which prohibited all but oral instruction, and which were intended to prevent the danger that might spring from inflammatory publications, which fanatical zeal was aiming to circulate among the slave population of the South. These laws were in fact disapproved by many of the best people of the State, as being unwise in policy and liable to still more serious objections; yet, with the law-abiding spirit of our people, they had the effect of diminishing the amount of instruction in letters which the colored people had received, and which they would have continued to receive. Still, many slaves did learn to read, and their instruction of each other, and sometimes by the children of the family, was not unfrequently winked at by their masters, who, but for the law, would themselves have instructed, or would have encouraged their children to instruct their blacks.

As matters now stand, no legal obstructions lie in the way of teaching the colored people; and it is a plain duty of Christians to make efforts, or to foster and encourage efforts made, to enable the colored people to read—especially that they may read that blessed Book whose truths, understood and practised, constitute the only sure basis of the peace and prosperity of society, as they do of the true welfare, present and future of the individual man.

In almost every family, and upon farms and plantations generally, something can be done to teach the younger negroes, and such of the older ones as may be willing to learn. The performance of this labor, as a gratuity, by the former owners of the freed people, or by the junior members of their families, would greatly tend to restore the confidence once felt by the slaves in their masters. We say the former confidence, for in many instances it has been apparent that, as in the case of the Christians of Galatia and the apostle Paul, a rude shock has been given to previously existing confidence, by the perverting instructions of persons claiming indeed to be the special friends of the negro, but with no professed love for the Southern white man, and with little real love for the black.

In many cases, this impression, we have reason to know, has, in a good degree, been corrected. Justice and kindness exercised towards the blacks in their new relations have so far served to dispel a mischievous delusion. To restore that confidence between the employed and their employers, which is so necessary to public quiet and domestic peace, few things would operate more powerfully than a cordial readiness to aid them in gaining the advantages to be derived from the knowledge of letters.

As to the particular modes in which instruction may be imparted to them, it is scarcely necessary to say anything. Of course, the Colored Sunday School will prove a great instrument for accomplishing this work; as to other Schools, and the methods of imparting instruction, the circumstances of each case will have to be considered in determining the best mode. Only let what is done be done in such manner as will enable the pupil to learn, and then let the Scriptures be put into his hands. Let the New Testament be made a text book, and then, while the learner feels that he is enjoying liberty in one of its highest forms, he will also be learning so to use that liberty as not to abuse it.

But much of the instruction of the blacks, as of the whites also, emanates from the pulpit, and therefore, the question before us involves the consideration of the future Church relations of the colored people.

There is reason to believe that in certain localities, and under certain circumstances, they will prefer to be organized into separate Churches. Where this desire is strongly felt, and there is any probability of their being able to maintain public worship among themselves, it seems to your Committee the better plan to give them letters of dismission, to aid them in forming Churches of their own, and then to assist them either by allowing them the use of the house of worship, or helping them to build. In Churches thus formed, there would often exist a need for aid in keeping their records, and this service kindly rendered to them by a white brother would doubtless be appreciated by them. In like manner, they might be induced, in thus setting up for themselves, to share, the services of white ministers. We do not see why, in the same neighborhood, oftentimes at the same house of worship, there might not be two Churches one white and one colored, having the same ministerial supply, but each one transacting its business independently. Unless some such arrangement as this be made, it is to be apprehended that the colored people will suffer greatly; for there are very few of the colored men who are received as preachers, from whom any but very meagre religious instruction can be obtained. Should any of these become infected with a fanatical and disorganizing spirit, it is easy to see how much they might mislead their class, and of what wide-spread mischief they might become the authors.

In other cases it may be found that the colored members of our Churches will prefer to go on as they are. In such cases there would be a manifest propriety in allowing things to proceed in their customary channel, until such time as they themselves shall of their own accord seek separation and a distinct organization.

Should colored Churches be thus formed, it will be very important to have the minds of their members impressed with the necessity of guarding against the hasty admission of members, and especially against the introduction of incompetent and otherwise unsuitable men into the ministry. Let them be taught the qualifications for the sacred office authoritatively laid down in the Word of God, and induced to secure the counsel of judicious white brethren in deciding upon the claims of such as may seek licensure or ordination. It has sometimes been known that colored men licensed to preach, have derived great advantage from occasional instruction afforded them by neighboring pastors. The same thing may be profitably repeated in our present circumstances.

Your Committee beg leave to submit the following resolutions:

RESOLVED, first, That in our present circumstances, there seems to be no one special plan for the general instruction of the colored people, which can be confidently pronounced THE BEST, and that each case must be decided upon its own merits.

RESOLVED, secondly, That where the Colored People prefer to remain in their present Church connections, it will be better for them so to do, provided they studiously avoid occasions of irritation and offence.

RESOLVED, thirdly, That where the colored members become restive from the continuance of such relations, it will be wise regularly to dismiss them for the constitution of separate Churches; to aid them by kind counsels, and, as far as practicable, by other means, and to persuade them to secure for themselves the benefits of an intelligent ministry.

RESOLVED, fourthly, That Colored Sunday Schools, which have for many years been conducted in some parts of the South, ought, in the opinion of the Convention, to be established wherever it is practicable; and that it is a worthy Christian work for white brethren and sisters to engage in the conduct and instruction of such Sunday Schools.

B.   Georgia Editorial on Race, 1883
Are We Orthodox on the Race Question?

Some people seem to hate the Chinese and to worship the Negro, while to the Indian they are indifferent. We hate neither, we worship neither, we are indifferent to neither. We love them all. Not indeed with the love which we feel for the members of our family, nor with the love which we have for our life-long friends, or neighbors, or acquaintances, nor yet with the love which we have for the Caucasian race. There is such a thing as the love of man *as* man; it is the heart-felt recognition of a common humanity and of universal kinship. We wish well to all races, and to all classes and conditions of men. We should be glad to see them all enjoy the blessings of the highest civilization; we should be happy beyond measure, if every human being in the whole world were a disciple of the Lord Jesus, and a large partaker of the grace of God. When we pray, "Thy kingdom come," we are in earnest; we desire it to come *everywhere;* we make no exceptions. Far be it from us to say, "Let this spot be omitted, or let this soul be left out." Nay rather, we are in accord with the Psalmist when he says, "Let the *whole earth* be *filled* with his glory;" and we feel as if our soul were confluent with David's, where in view of the comprehensiveness of his own prayer, he said, "The prayers of David, the son of Jesse, are ended." We are ready, and willing, and more than willing, to aid with heart, and head, and hands, and feet, and fortune, in furthering the real welfare of every race, and of every individual of every race.

Yet we have our preferences. Among his disciples Christ had his. The ties of blood we can not ignore, and race is only another name for blood. In our heart we "provide" a special place for "our own." The fact that we love some more than others does not prove that we have no love for the others. We love the English-speaking people of our own race, and more particularly the *American* English-speaking people of our own race, and still more particularly those known as the "Southern people" of that race, more than we love any other people. Our affection for peoples shades off according as they are more remote from us, either in race, or in nationality, or in geographical position; but is strong enough for African Negroes, (*a fortiori* for our own Negroes) and for Chinese, and for Fijis, to make us a cheerful contributor to their temporal or spiritual welfare.

But we do not believe that "all men are created equal," as the Declaration of Independence declares them to be; nor that they will ever become equal in this world, and perhaps not in the world to come, for even there "one star differeth from another in glory." We believe that some of these various races are inferior to others in physical organization, in intellectual ability, and in capacity for development, political, social, moral, or religious, and that they will so remain until the end of time. Nor does this view interfere with our belief in the original unity of the human race. Things are not as they were. We think that our own race is incomparably superior to any other, and that our distant cousins of the Aryan family in India are next best. The people of Terra del Fuego are perhaps the worst. As to the Indian we accept, (not giving it a construction too literal,) Oliver Wendell Holmes' definition of him: "A few instincts on legs flourishing a tomahawk." As to the Negro, we do not know where to place him; perhaps not at the bottom of the list, but certainly not near the top. We believe that fusion of two or more of these races would be an injury to all, and a still greater injury to posterity. We think that the race-line is providential, and that Providence intended that it should be perpetuated unless a new dispensation should blot it out. It is our opinion that any great intermingling of these races, even without fusion, is a misfortune and an evil, though God may bring good out of it, causing the wrath of men to praise him; for any such great intermingling must have its origin in sin.

We think that any legislation, preaching, teaching, or action, which tends to promote great intermingling, unnecessarily, is unwise and wrong. We have no dealings with other races than our own except to do them good, or for purposes of business, and we prefer to have as little business with them as possible. Yet our feeling of benevolence for them is none the less on this account. We should be prompt to wash the feet of the meanest man of the meanest race, if necessity required, and would feel, that in the act there was no letting down of dignity, but rather an enhancement of it, and our heart would be glad if there was benefit from the deed. But having completed our task, we should gravitate swiftly back to "our own." Instinct is unconquerable; and it *ought* to be. Finally, we believe that the gospel ought to be preached to every creature, and that in the last day all distinctions that sin has made will disappear, and, that Christ will acknowledge his own, out of every kindred, and tongue, and people, and nation.

This is our "Confession of Faith." We think that we are orthodox. If we are not so, we should be glad for some one to point out the heresy.   T.

C.   A Statement on Race Relations, Home Mission Board of SBC, 1891

Our work among the COLORED PEOPLE

has by no means reached the proportions its importance demands. To no people are we more deeply indebted than to them. Our past as well as our present relations to them form weighty obligations which should move us to seek in every way the betterment of their condition, but expecially to give them that religious culture which will fit them both for this life and that which is to come. The race problem, as it is called, has been deemed by statesmen the most perplexing of all questions affecting our society and our political institutions. We venture the assertion that it can and will be found of easy solution.

Nothing is plainer to any one who knows this race than its perfect willingness to accept a subordinate place, provided there be confidence that in that position of subordination it will receive justice and kindness. That is the condition it prefers above all others, and this is the condition in which it attains the highest development of every attribute of manhood. Whenever it shall understandingly and cheerfully accept this condition, the race problem is settled forever.

The only thing needed now on his part is the assurance that he may confidently rely upon the justice and kindness which such a condition always demands and should always receive.

This assurance the Christian men and women of this Southern land ought to give. Not the assurance of words, simply, nor yet of resolutions passed by political or religious conventions; nor simply the enactment of laws that are just and equal, but that higher and stronger assurance which springs from a persistent course of Christian conduct that looks with kindly eye and open hand upon his physical and mental needs, and, above all, upon his soul's necessities. It is perfectly in the power of the Baptist people of the South to do all and give all that is needed to accomplish this end.

With the great mass of the professed Christians among them members of Baptist churches, with three-fourths of this entire population under Baptist influence, we have but to take hold of their religious interests with an earnestness becoming Christian men, and they will respond to such expressions of kindness with an alacrity and a sincerity that will surprise every beholder. If the Baptists of the South will but open their eyes to see their opportunity and open their hearts to the stimulating influences of Christian obligation to these people, they will themselves be amazed and gratified at the ease and rapidity with which the end will be attained. We do not hesitate to affirm our confident belief that an expenditure under the best conditions by our Home Mission and State Boards of fifty thousand dollars a year for the next ten years will settle this race question forever.

What greater good could come to our country, or what grander triumph to Christianity than so easy and perfect a solution of a question which has been and is now the despair of the statesmanship of the world?

11.7   Annual Reports, Southern Baptist Publication Society

When the Southern Baptist Convention was formed in 1845, some wanted to make a complete break with Northern Baptists. The majority, however, limited the schism at first to the two mission societies. The newly formed SBC formed only two general boards, one for foreign and one for home missions. In its early sessions the SBC voted specifically not to form its own publication board, preferring to continue to use church literature from the American Baptist Publication Society of Philadelphia. The ABPS had leaned over backwards to cooperate with Baptists in the South, and no trace of the North/South conflict shows up in its records.

However, some influential Southern Baptists insisted that they needed their own Southern church literature. When the SBC declined to sponsor publication work, they formed their own society for that purpose. This reveals the depth of the desire for Southern Baptist literature, and also how tenacious were the remnants of the old "society" approach to Baptist benevolences.

In 1847 interested individuals formed the Southern Baptist Publication Society, located in Charleston, South Carolina. It was in most respects a mirror image of the ABPS of Philadelphia, except it was *Southern*. Two annual reports of the SBPS, about a decade apart, reveal some challenges and achievements of this early effort to produce a distinctly Southern Baptist literature. *Sources:* First Annual Report, Board of Managers, Southern Baptist Publication Society, 1848, 9-11. Tenth Annual Report, Southern Baptist Publication Society, 1857, 10-13.

A.   First Annual Report, 1848

It may not be inappropriate, on the present occasion, to advert briefly to the circumstances, which led to the formation of the Southern Baptist Publication Society. It is well known that, in portions of the Southern country, a strong feeling has existed for years on the subject. At the time that the dismemberment in our Missionary organizations took place, the question was seriously agitated, and while the majority of our brethren were opposed to immediate action, many were satisfied of the propriety of at once organizing a Southern Institution for the publication and distribution of moral and religious truth. With the Society whose Board is located in Philadelphia, there was no cause for dissatisfaction. That institution had stood nobly aloof from the exciting questions which agitated the Denomination. Engaged in the great work of disseminating religious knowledge, it knew no party. It proclaimed itself neither *for* nor *against* the South. Its position was neutral, and of that neutrality, the South had no reason to complain. . . . But, still, by many it was believed to be both expedient and desirable, that we should have a Southern Organization for Publication purposes. The general confidence of the South in the North had been shaken. Their trust had been wrecked amidst the ravings of Abolition phrenzy; and the common sentiment was, give us a Southern Society, or we will patronize none, the common demand was for a literature adapted to the genius of our own institutions, thriving upon our own soil, fostered and cherished by our own Southern intellect. The time, it was believed, had arrived for us to proclaim our independence of the North, to begin to work for ourselves, to encourage the development of Southern talent, and to engage in united, vigorous, and energetic efforts for diffusing light and knowledge through all the waste places of our Southern Zion. Other influences were operating, other denominations were at work—and we alone were doing comparatively nothing towards spreading religious truth, and the cherished principles of our faith, through the mighty influence of the press. It was time for us to awake out of sleep, and come forth in the contest for truth and righteousness. The progress of society, the developments of the age, our growing population and their increasing wants, the encroachments of error, and the alarming destitution of religious knowledge in many portions of our land, and amongst many adherents of our denomination—all, all indicated the desirableness and necessity of combined and efficient action. To slumber on in apathy, and inactivity, would be virtually to abandon the field, to relinquish the triumphs which truth had already won for us, and to proclaim ourselves alike indifferent to the wants of humanity and the claims of religion.

In accordance with a call from the Central Association of Georgia, Delegates from South Carolina, Georgia, Virginia, and Alabama assembled in the city of Savannah, on the 13th of May 1847, and after a full and free discussion of the desirableness and expediency of at once organizing a Southern Baptist Publication Society, the Society was duly organized, . . .

In pursuance of this resolution, the Delegates proceeded to form the Society, and adopted the following Constitution, which they commend to the consideration and acceptance of the Denomination in the Southern and South-western States. They also request the attendance of the Denomination, by Delegates, at the time and place of the next meeting of the Society in 1848, that the measure may be consummated by the concurrence of the whole Denomination in the South and South-west of the United States.

B. Tenth Annual Report, 1857

THE Board of the Southern Baptist Publication Society, in offering their Tenth Annual Report, find a wide field, both in reviewing the past history, and in the present prospects, of this institution. . . .

The first movers for the information of this Society, must have foreseen that the work undertaken by them, would be beset with difficulties. When the preliminary discussions on the movement took place in Virginia, at one of the Baptist anniversaries in that State, the response was soon heard from the Southern part of the country, especially from the States of Georgia and South-Carolina. But there were many among our brethren who at first felt a reluctance to the sundering of relations with the American Baptist Publication Society, inasmuch as that Society had given no adequate grounds of complaint to Southern Baptists, of a sectional or ecclesiastical nature. The other principal Societies, especially those for Home and Foreign Missions, having terminated their connection with the South, and by the formation of the Southern Baptist Convention with its Boards, it was soon regarded as an incongruity to leave the supply of the literature for the denomination in the South, dependent upon and subject to, the local influences which governed the denominational and general organizations at the seat of their operations in the Northern States. But however strongly such views may have been entertained by Southern Baptists, every discerning mind among them could not but foresee, that to build up an important institution from nothing, would demand an arduous and prolonged effort. . . .

In sustaining a book publishing concern at the South, the difficulty in a financial, and manufacturing point of view, was aggravated by the feeling, that Southern Baptists, and the Southern people, had been reproached for not being able to produce or sustain a Southern literature. . . . Southern authorship was obliged to seek for Northern publishers; and the complexion of all our literature as found in the trade at the South, was at the dictation of people controlling book manufacturing, and the book business far beyond our own limits. . . .

Against all these forbidding indications, the projectors of this Society, and those who have since been its conductors, have felt from the beginning, that the interests of the Baptist denomination in the South, as well as the furtherance of a Southern religious literature, imperatively required that this Society should be endowed and sustained to an extent equal to any of the great publishing institutions of the age. It was plain also, that a special vocation was assigned to it, in preparing works suited to the wants of the Sunday Schools in the South, in developing the relative and reciprocal duties growing out of our state of society and our social institutions, and in adapting measures which would lead to a more adequate discharge of our duties in supplying preaching and oral instruction for our colored population.

11.8 Report to Southern Baptist Convention on the Fortress Monroe Conference

After 1862 the American Baptist Home Mission Society of New York sent home missionaries into the South, and by 1870 had about one third of their total force at work in Southern territories. Southern Baptists protested what they regarded as an "invasion" of their field, but Northern Baptists replied that they were impelled by the spiritual needs in the South, especially among the freedmen.

By the 1890s, however, several factors led to a reassessment of Northern Baptist activity in the South. The incoming flood of European immigrants in the Northeast, and the escalating population of the Pacific Coast, challenged the resources of the American Baptist Home Mission Society. Baptists in the South had rebounded somewhat from Reconstruction devastation and felt able to assume more of the burden of ministry in the Southern field, among both blacks and whites. Baptists of both regions saw the problems of duplicate and overlapping ministries in the South.

These factors led to a conference between Northern and Southern Baptist leaders at Fortress Monroe, Virginia, in 1894. The document cited here reveals some of their agreements at that important conference. *Source: Annual,* SBC, 1895, 14-16.

20. T. T. Eaton, Kentucky, from the Committee, presented the following report on

THE CONFERENCE WITH THE
AMERICAN HOME MISSION SOCIETY

Your committee are thankful to be able to report the success with which God has blessed our efforts. After considerable correspondence, a conference with the Committee of the American Baptist Home Mission Society was arranged to be held at Fortress Monroe, Virginia, September 12,1894. . . . The meeting was in all respects delightful. There was full, frank, free discussion on all questions presented; but every vote was unanimous except one, and that one was as to who should preside over the joint meeting. The Northern brethren voted unanimously for a Southern brother to preside, while the Southern brethren voted unanimously for a Northern brother to preside; and we were so urgent in the matter that the Northern brethren yielded the point, and Brother Howard presided over our deliberations. Your committee presented to the Committee of the Home Mission Society the following overture:

"*Resolved,* That, desiring to avoid discussion of past issues, or of matters on which it is known that the views of the brethren North and South are widely divergent, we will in all sincerity address ourselves to the task of securing for *the future* such co-operation as may be found practicable, without attempting at once to adjust all differences. The committee desire to state that in making this overture the Southern Baptist Convention is prompted, not by any necessity of its own work or that of its Home Mission Board, but, believing that the time has come when it should enlarge its work among the colored people of the South, it entertains the hope that a proper co-operation with the Home Mission Society in its work already established would contribute to the efficiency of both."

After deliberations covering a good part of two days, the Joint Committee unanimously adopted the following:

"I. *As to Schools among Colored People.* 1. That the Home Board of the Southern Baptist Convention appoint an advisory local committee at each point where a school controlled by the American Baptist Home Mission Society is, or shall be located, and that this committee shall exercise such authority as shall be conferred upon it from time to time by the American Baptist Home Mission Society. 2. That the control of the school shall remain in the hands of the American Baptist Home Mission Society; but these local advisory committees shall recommend to the American Baptist Home Mission Society any changes in the conduct or in the teaching forces of these schools, including the filling of vacancies, with the reasons for their recommendations. 3. That the Southern Baptist Convention, through its Home Mission Board, shall appeal to the Baptists of the South for the moral and financial support of these schools, and that these local committees shall encourage promising young colored people to attend these institutions. 4. That the joint committee recommend to the respective bodies appointing them the adoption of the foregoing section as unanimously expressing their views as to the work in the schools among the colored people.

"II. *As to Mission Work among the Colored People.* It is unanimously voted by the joint committee to recommend to our respective bodies that the American Baptist Home Mission Society and the Home Mission Board of the Southern Baptist Convention co-operate in the mission work among the colored people of the South, in connection with the Baptist State bodies, white and colored, in the joint appointment of general missionaries, in holding ministers' and deacons' institutes, and in the better organization of the missionary work of the colored Baptists. The details of the plan are to be left to be agreed upon by the bodies above named.

"III. *As to Territorial Limits.* The committee of the American Baptist Home Mission Society, not being instructed to consider any subject except co-operation in labor for the colored race, respectfully refers to the Board of the American Baptist Home Mission Society the proposition of the committee of the Southern Baptist Convention on the subject of territorial limits, and asks for its favorable consideration.

"The following is the text of the proposition referred to: 'We believe that, for the promotion of fraternal feeling and of the best interests of the Redeemer's kingdom, it is inexpedient for two different organizations of Baptists to solicit contributions or to establish missions in the same locality, and for this reason we recommend to the Home Mission Board of the Southern Baptist Convention and to the American Baptist Home Mission Society that, in the prosecution of their work already begun on contiguous fields or on the same field, all antagonisms be avoided; and that their officers and employees be instructed to co-operate in all practicable ways in, the spirit of Christ. That we further recommend to these bodies and their agents, in opening new work, to direct their efforts to localities not already occupied by the other.'"

By direction of the joint committee their action was furnished to the denominational press, and has been widely published. Everywhere there has been hearty approval, and earnest hopes are generally cherished that a brighter day has dawned upon our denominational work among the colored people, and in regard to friction arising and liable to arise in reference to territorial limits. . . . Respectfully submitted.

> T. T. Eaton,
> H. H. Harris,
> T. P. Bell,
> A. J. S. Thomas,
> B. H. Carroll,
> O. F. Gregory,
> W. J. Northen,
> J. B. Gambrell,
> I. T. Tichenor.

11.9 Basil Manly, Jr., The Sunday School Movement

Basil Manly, Jr. (1825-1892) was an outstanding Southern Baptist pastor, seminary professor, hymn writer, and Sunday School pioneer. He insisted that Southern Baptists needed not only college and seminary education for their leaders, but they also needed a strong Sunday School movement for the religious education of children and adults in the churches.

In 1858 Manly issued a treatise (selection A) urging that every Baptist church form a Sunday School. At that time only a minority of Southern Baptist churches had such schools. Manly's long-term advocacy of the importance of the Sunday School had an enormous impact upon Baptists in the South. He lived to see a time when perhaps half of all Southern Baptist churches had Sunday Schools. He also played a major role in leading the SBC to form the Sunday School Board. *Source:* Basil Manly, Jr., *A Sunday School in Every Baptist Church* (Charleston, S. C.: Southern Baptist Publication Society, 1858).

Manly felt that Southern Baptists should provide their own Sunday School literature, and he was a major leader in the Southern Baptist Publication Society. His *Little Lessons for Little People* (selection B) illustrates his effort to provide Sunday School lesson materials for children. The catechism approach was widely used at the time. *Source:* Basil Manly, Jr., *Little Lessons for Little People* (Nashville: Sunday School Board of SBC), 3-17.

A. Basil Manly, Jr., A Sunday School in Every Baptist Church, 1858

Gather the people together, men, and women, and children, and thy stranger that is within thy gates, that they may hear, and that they may learn, and fear the Lord, your God, and observe to do all the words of this law.

AMONG the latest injunctions of Moses, "the man of God," is this command: it was part of the permanent and divinely appointed law of the land. . . . the manner in which the knowledge of true religion was to be kept up among the Jews is here defined to be by assemblies for instruction, including men, and women, and children, and strangers; and that Moses tells them the special object of this regulation was, "that your *children, which have not known any thing, may hear and learn to fear the Lord.*" . . .

These same principles lie at the basis of the Sunday school system. . . . the conviction has grown upon me, until it is now firm and distinct, that there is no new measure which promises greater or more certain success in home efforts, than to establish A GOOD SUNDAY SCHOOL IN EVERY BAPTIST CHURCH.

By a *good* Sunday school, is meant not a more extra, more ornamental than useful, an appendage in which few take an interest, a sort of fifth wheel to a wagon, but one which is the very nursery of the church—one to which the older and better informed members lend the sanction of their attendance, and the aid of their wisdom and skill in its instructions—one in which *the church,* as such, feels interested and participates.

I said "a Sunday school in every *Baptist* church," not because I object to the union principle in suitable cases. The American Sunday School Union has done much good, and I trust will accomplish more. But I am speaking to Baptists of *their* duties and responsibilities, and I believe one of these is to have a Sunday school in every one of their churches. . . .

In considering any enterprise, we estimate its cost and its profits, and if the latter far outweigh the former, we are not deterred by apparent or real difficulties, nor by the novelty or magnitude of the scheme. Let us examine then,

I. THE COST.

Not the pecuniary cost; for it is obvious, at a glance, that the money needed is very little, and that little the donors seem absolutely to be giving to themselves, since it is to be used, under their own eyes, for the benefit of themselves and their children.

Now this ought to be a refreshing idea, that a scheme is presented proposing to accomplish great things and demanding very little money. . . .

The principal item of the cost is the trouble of attendance. Houses need not to be built, nor teachers and apparatus imported from abroad—they are all ready. It is simply necessary for several families to come together at the church, bringing their Bibles with them, and persist in doing so punctually and regularly, and there might be a Sunday school at once.

A collateral advantage, growing in part out of this, is the adaptation of the Sunday school to all classes. It is so cheap and so simple, that it may be easily instituted and managed in the most poverty stricken and ignorant community, while it is the valued ornament of the most polished circles. . . .

We have, almost unavoidably, trenched on the second part of our subject, to which we now proceed, viz.,

II. THE PROFITS.

In estimating these, we have one important advantage. The Sunday school is no new thing. It has been variously and thoroughly tried; and if there is any one institution, of human suggestion, to the benefits of which experience has given a uniform and exalted testimony, it is the Sunday school.

1. *The intellects of many will be stimulated and developed, some of whom, perhaps, no other means could reach.* The absolute amount of mental education obtainable at a Sunday school is not unimportant. It includes those rudiments which open the way to everything else, and which, without any additional aid from others, have enabled many strong minds to push themselves into eminence. But the actual quantity of information

communicated is not the only point to be regarded. The insensible influence of association is great. If you gather the most educated and pious persons in a neighborhood and engage them in the work of instruction, the intellectual elevation and refinement resulting from bringing a mass of young minds into contact and communication with these is not easily estimated. . . .

2. *The union of moral with mental training would be happily exemplified.* "The Sunday school system," remarks a discerning writer, "is the only general system of education which recognizes man in his true character, as an intellectual and moral being, possessed of a never dying spirit, whose capacities for enjoyment or misery must forever expand, and who must dwell forever with angels and the redeemed amid the glories of heaven, or with devils and the damned in the woes of hell."

The minds of the young cannot remain blank a single day; . . . It is of the most inestimable importance that the principles of religion should pervade and give life to all the instruction which a child receives.

If it is said that where ordinary teachers cannot or will not, *parents* ought to give this kind of instruction. I grant it. Nothing can ever supersede parental teaching, nothing should ever usurp its place. But, 1. Many parents are incapable of usefully communicating instruction. 2. Many others are not disposed to take the trouble; and so, from lack either of competency or will, the duty is extensively neglected. 3. Others commence the work, but fail steadily to adhere to it, or err egregiously in their methods of attempting it. 4. A conclusive answer to this objection is, those who most deeply feel the obligation, and who are most competent to discharge the duty, . . . are the very persons who highly appreciate, and warmly promote the Sunday school.

3. *The early conversion of the children is rendered more probable.* I am aware that there is a good deal of latent scepticism in many minds, when the conversion of children is spoken of. To me, however, there is nothing more attractive, nothing more desirable, nothing for which I am willing more ardently to labor, and which I will more eagerly expect, until it is accomplished, than the conversion of children, just as early as they can become subjects of correct moral impression, and of a saving change.

How early may children be truly and thoroughly converted? Who will undertake to fix the limit? There is danger indeed of presuming that they are converted before they are, of crowding the church with the young and uninformed, whose age is too tender, and whose minds are too plastic to be sure that any impression is genuine or permanent, and who are too little accustomed to self-scrutiny to distinguish clearly the exercises of their hearts. This danger should be sedulously guarded against.

But is there no danger on the other hand? . . . Early in life, the advantages for conversion are greater, the mind is retentive of what is taught, the conscience is comparatively unhardened, the heart is tender, prejudices are few and feeble, and they readily yield to, and more permanently retain, the impressions made on them during that period.

If they are not converted while young, they have lost all that time for self-improvement. It was a period in which there might have been growth in grace; instead of that, the opposite principle has been permitted to luxuriate. Let us not esteem lightly so many years of youth saved from the service of Satan, and spent in the service of God. . . .

4. *The establishment of a Sunday School in every church would confer great benefits on the church members.* A Sunday school agent in the West remarked to an intelligent Christian, that if they did not gather the children upon the Sabbath, and give them systematic religious instruction, they would grow wild. "Yes," was the reply, "and we shall grow wild, too." . . .

A Sunday school in a church would make its members Bible students. How little is the Bible read, even by professing Christians! How much less is it studied! Is it extravagant to say that numbers spend twice (or ten times) as many hours over their newspapers as over their Bibles? And even this brief reading, how cursory and inattentive; and their memory of what is read, how faint and indefinite! . . .

But let a church organize itself, as it were, into a Sabbath school; let the older and better informed instruct the younger, each doing what he can; and let all have their attention concentrated on some one portion of scripture or topic of divine truth, instead of being scattered over the whole range of religious knowledge: the result will be, that teacher and scholar will be alike stimulated and interested, and both will learn more in a year than in three years of the ordinary indefinite reading. . . .

A Sunday school in every church would give private Christians healthful spiritual exercise. I believe that God has a work for every one to do, and that our souls cannot prosper except we are engaged in it; . . . But, in the situation in which many of our churches are, what channel of usefulness is open to the private Christian? What personal effort can he ordinarily put forth for the diffusion of the gospel? . . . But here is a method by which all may do something, in which all may engage either as teacher or scholar, which affords mutual improvement to all, gives exercise to the most benevolent and holy dispositions, and is twice blessed in enriching at once the teacher.

It is a thought of no small importance, in this connection, that the Sunday school affords a noble and appropriate sphere for the activity of pious ladies, and that in the very thing for which God has especially fitted them, the training of the young. They can attend to this with more of affection, and simplicity, and patience, and, therefore, of effectiveness, than ordinarily falls to the lot of the other sex. They constitute a large part, probably two-thirds, of our membership. We cannot afford to leave unemployed the hands or hearts of any portion of the church; . . .

5. *A Sunday school in every church would promote the due observance of the Lord's day.* It is fast becoming a question in this country, whether we shall have a Sabbath or not. The increasing press and hurry of business in this busy land; the lax views of some divines concerning the authority and sanctity of the Sabbath; the sanctions already given by custom and public opinion to large encroachments on its holy hours; and, above all, the influx of tens of thousands yearly from lands where practically they have no Sabbath, are powerful influences against which the friends of the Lord's day must contend. . . . Now the Sunday school is obviously one of the most efficient auxiliaries in leading men to remember the Sabbath day to keep it holy.

A Sunday school in every church would further promote the keeping of the Sabbath by tending to introduce worship once a week instead of once a month. When the monthly system was the best that could be had, on account of the rapid increase of churches and the scarcity of preachers, it was perhaps right to be thankful, if not content; but its continuance has, doubtless, been a blight on our churches. It has given rise to, and in turn been nourished by, some of the most serious evils prevalent among us— such as the undue multiplication of feeble churches, too weak to stand alone; . . .

6. *A Sunday school in every church would cultivate and draw out the gifts of many who might, in the providence of God, become ministers of the gospel.* From every side we hear the cry of destitution. The old States and the new, city and country, the cultivated regions and the ruder frontiers, other denominations as well as our own, share in this complaint. It is a growing and increasing deficiency, even here at home; while myriads in heathen lands now opened by the hand of God to receive the gospel, are lifting up to us in vain the wailing cry, "Come over and help us." . . .

Among these Sunday school teachers there would, doubtless, rise up many a one, whose thoughts would be first directed to the ministry, by his humble, prayerful efforts to teach a child the way to Christ, and whose mental and moral preparation for the work would be greatly aided by the advantages of the Sunday school. The work of teaching would be likely under the divine blessing, to develop those very powers, and that identical spirit which may afterwards make an eminently holy and useful minister.

Or suppose that this reasonable expectation should fail, the effect is postponed only a few years, till out of the ranks of the youth gathered into these schools, one and another, yea, scores and hundreds should step forth, who, like Timothy, had "from a child known the holy scriptures," and who would be ready to devote the strength of their manhood to preaching Christ.

. . . A minister is formed by his people almost as much as the people are modified by him. Give him an appreciating audience; give him an active, zealous, praying church; give him a collection of Bible class students to preach to, who will detect errors resulting from ignorance or indolence, while they will receive with gratification the results of earnest study of the Bible, and it will make him learn more and preach better.

There is, moreover, in this system a powerful and vital principle not only of self-perpetuation, but of extension also. . . . true liberality is a matter of training in childhood to a considerable degree. The young must be familiarized with missions, and indoctrinated in their duty, or else they scarcely ever learn it. The habit and the principle of giving, need to be *early* implanted. . . .

7. In conclusion we may say, that *a Sunday school in every church would tend to give permanent and healthful extension to every branch of benevolent effort among us.*

There never was a truer thing said than that "the denomination that takes care of the childern will have the people;"

We shall only say, in conclusion, that if any man among us could, . . . set in motion a train of causes which should result in placing a good Sunday school in every Baptist church in our land, that man might be content to lie down and die, as one who had finished his work.

B. Basil Manly, Jr., *Little Lessons for Little People*

TO TEACHERS AND PARENTS.

The old plans of teaching trained memory alone; and success was counted by the number of pages or verses recited by rote.

A new plan discards memorizing almost altogether, and sets mere infants to reasoning on everything, without materials on which, or skill by which, to arrive at just conclusions.

Both are extremes. The memory is greatly aided by clear, familiar, interesting explanations, and to understand a thing is a higher attainment than a parrot-like recitation. But if children never learn anything which they do not understand, their learning and understanding both will be of very meager dimensions.

Again, pictures, stories, pleasurable appendages of every kind are valuable to enlist the intellect of children. But let us not forget that there is a solid and substantial pleasure, which the child enjoys, independent of all external attractions, who *knows that he knows his lesson;* that he can recite it promptly, without mistake or dread—in short, that it is *his.*

Do not fail, then, to cultivate an exact and ready memory   B. M., Jr.

TO THE CHILDREN.

This little book has been made especially for you, by one who loves children. He has picked out for you, from the choice and precious fruit of the Bible, some things which seemed suited for little people. Here they are. He hopes they will please you; he hopes still more that they will do you good.

While you learn these little lessons, ask God to make you good children, for Jesus' sake; and then, when you grow up, you will be good men and women; and when you die, you will go home to heaven.

LESSON I.
ABOUT THE FIRST THINGS.

1. Who was the first of all beings? God.
2. Was there ever a time when God was not? No.
3. Was there ever a time when there was nothing else but God? Yes.
4. Who was the first sinner? Satan.
5. Where was Satan when he sinned? In heaven.
6. Where was he thrown after he sinned? Into hell.
7. Who was the first man? Adam.
8. Who was the first woman? Eve.
9. Who was the first person born into this world? Cain.
10. Who was the first person that died in this world? Abel.
11. How did he die? His brother Cain killed him.
12. Who was the first man that ever went to heaven? Abel.
13. Who was the first man that went to heaven without dying? Enoch.
14. Who was the first murderer? Cain.
15. Who was the first man that married two wives? Lamech.
16. Who was the first great warrior that we read of? Nimrod.

LESSON II.
HOW THIS WORLD WAS MADE.

1. Who made the world? God.
2. Did he make all the trees and flowers and beasts and people, in the world, also? Yes; he made all things.
3. What did he make them out of? Out of nothing.
4. Did God make all at once, or one thing after another? He made one thing after another.
5. In how many days did God make this world? In six days.
6. What did he make the first day? Light.
7. What did he make the second day? The air or firmament.
8. What did he make the third day? Dry land and plants.
9. What did he make the fourth day? The sun, moon, and stars.
10. What did he make the fifth day? Fishes and birds.
11. What did he make the sixth day? Beasts and creeping things and MAN.
12. What sort of a world was it when God had finished making it? All very good.
13. What did God do on the seventh day? He rested.
14. Why? Was he tired? No; God cannot be tired.
15. Why did he rest? To teach us to rest one day in seven.

LESSON III.
HOW THE WORLD BECAME BAD.

1. You said that the world, when God made it, was all very good. Is it so now? No.
2. What has spoiled the world? Sin.
3. What curse has sin brought upon the ground? Briers and thorns.

4. What has sin brought upon man's body? Pain and death.

5. What has sin brought upon man's soul? Guilt and shame.

6. How did sin enter the world? By Satan, the tempter.

7. Whom did he tempt? Eve.

8. Whom did Eve tempt? Adam.

9. Where had God placed Adam and Eve? In the beautiful garden of Eden.

10. What command did he give them? Not to eat of the forbidden fruit.

11. If they did eat it, what did he say would happen to them? He said: "Ye shall surely die."

12. How did Satan tempt Eve to eat the forbidden fruit? He said "Ye shall not surely die."

13. What did Eve do? She took and ate it.

14. What else did she do? She gave to Adam, her husband.

15. What did he do? He ate it, also.

16. Did he not know it was wrong? Yes; he was not deceived.

17. What was the consequence of Adam's sin? All men have become sinners.

LESSON IV.

HOW THE WORLD IS TO BECOME GOOD AGAIN.

1. Will the world always be bad? No.

2. What did God promise Adam and Eve? That the seed of woman should bruise the serpent's head.

3. Who was the serpent? Satan, the tempter.

4. Who is meant by the seed of the woman? Jesus Christ.

5. When did Jesus Christ come into the world? More than eighteen hundred years ago.

6. What did he do to save poor sinners from sin and Satan? He died for them.

7. Where is Jesus now? He is in heaven.

8. What is he doing there? He is interceding for us.

9. Who will be saved by his death and intercession? All who believe in him.

10. Do little children need to be saved? Yes, because they sin.

11. Can they believe in Jesus? Yes, as soon as they can understand that he is the Savior of sinners.

12. When will the world be good again? When everybody in it loves Jesus.

13. How will that make the world better? Because all who love Jesus will hate sin.

14. Why will they hate sin? Because Jesus hates it.

15. If there was no sin in this world, would it not be a great deal happier? Yes; it would be almost like heaven.

16. What ought we to do to hasten on that happy time? We must all love and serve Jesus ourselves.

17. What else can we do? Try to get everybody else to love him, too. . . .

11.10   Report of the First Sunday School Board, 1868

Before the Civil War, Southern Baptists formed a number of diverse, competing organizations to promote Sunday School work among the churches, and to supply their literature. The Southern Baptist Publication Society (Charleston, 1847-1863) represented the more educated and progressive Southern Baptists of the Southeast, while the Southern Baptist Sunday School Union (Memphis, formed 1857 and abolished during the War) appealed to more conservative Southern Baptists in the West. The Bible Board of the SBC (Nashville, 1851-1863) was at first limited to Bible printing and distribution, but later expanded into Sunday School literature. However, it fell into control of the Landmark faction, lost the confidence of Southern Baptists, and was abolished.

Competition in a limited market, doctrinal conflict, and Civil War devastation pulled all of these organizations under. However, just as the SBPS folded in Charleston in 1863, the Board of Sunday Schools was formed in the same city. In some ways this first Sunday School Board of the SBC was a continuation of the SBPS. Led by Basil Manly, Jr. and John A. Broadus, the new board was largely an extension of the educational work of The Southern Baptist Theological Seminary, then located in Greenville. The Board of Sunday Schools lasted until 1873, when the Home Mission Board assumed what was left of its work. The document below comes from the 1868 report of the Board of Sunday Schools. *Source: Annual,* SBC, 1868, 36-40.

PUBLICATIONS.

KIND WORDS.—The circulation of this Sunday-school paper has steadily increased, and the evidence of its usefulness and popularity has come from all parts of the South. In the aggregate 379,000 copies have been issued and circulated during the year. The deficit between the receipts and expenses of the paper for the year is about $228.08. If the donations to destitute Schools, and our losses through the mails—at least $300—be considered, the paper, even at the low rates of subscription, has fully met the expenses of its issue. . . .

FUTURE OPERATIONS.

Against the prosecution of this work by this Convention it has been urged:

1. That the Sunday-school enterprise is comparatively too unimportant to engage the time and energies of the Convention.

2. That the financial condition of our people affords no promise of adequate means for the successful prosecution of the work.

3. That all needed supplies may be obtained from external sources.

4. That because of the cheapness of the work, no general collection of funds is necessary.

5. That there is a manifest preference for separate State organizations.

6. That the other Boards of this Convention are sufficient instruments for all its purposes.

7. That it is desirable to relinquish our efforts in favor of some wealthy and well-established Society.

It is sufficient here to indicate some considerations on the other side.

1. That it is now too late to re-open the questions of the usefulness or importance of the Sunday-school work; that no labor, adapted to promote the cause of Christ and the interest of souls, is too unimportant for the attention and toil of any combination of Christians, and, especially, when that work is, at least, as directly and abundantly productive as any other enterprise.

2. That our financial depression is equally decisive against every other enterprise; that such depression cannot impair our Christian obligation to do what we are able; that whilst, under the circumstances, we may not expect an extraordinary work, yet, with a proper disposition, a successful work is practicable; that, if now abandoned, this work cannot be easily resumed by us in the future.

3. That, if supplies may be obtained from external sources, yet these are not so certain to be as generally approved, as well adapted to our use, nor so likely to be received with the same confidence as our own; that this would give to others the control of a work which belongs to ourselves; that it removes a stimulus to production by our own competent authors; that it is a condition of unnecessary and humiliating dependence.

4. That whilst no other work is more economical or inexpensive, yet funds are necessary to supply the destitute, to sustain missionaries and others, and provide needful materials; that to publish and circulate books requires capital, and that we may gradually acquire this capital. . . .

6. That division and definiteness of labor promotes skill and success; that, to commit this work to other Boards of this Convention would encumber their present efficiency; that no other existing Board of this Convention can actively prosecute this work.

7. That no external Society can command the hearty sympathy, co-operation or contributions of Southern Baptists; that to thus staunch the flow of the liberality of our people would seriously re-act against all our benevolent enterprises, and impair the piety of our churches; that any foreign Society must act either directly, and thus sow discord among us, or through separate State organizations, and thus at increased expense to ourselves; that equal reason exists for so relinquishing every other general enterprise, and thus destroying the Convention itself; that such Societies are controlled by those not in sympathy of feeling with us, or who are hostile to our convictions; that we cannot be really represented in the management of such Societies. . . .

10. That this work, if not done by ourselves, will not remain undone, but will be prosecuted by Romanists and other Pedobaptists of various creeds, introducing serious errors and evils among our people and our posterity.

We earnestly urge that this Convention will give the questions thus suggested a calm and patient consideration; and, while deferring to the wishes and wisdom of our brethren, and without disposition to screen ourselves from responsibilities under which we have made every effort to be faithful, we respectfully request that this Board be located in some more advantageous and prominent position.

We have done all that we could to forward the work assigned us. This Board has existed only five years. Part of this time, a desolating war raged over all our territory, and the remaining time has witnessed the great poverty and oppression of our people. . . .

We cannot, we must not, as Southern Baptists, withhold our labor and our means from the Sunday-school work. Having seized the plough, dare we look back? As an efficient instrument for winning souls; for promoting the study of the Scriptures, and of religious tracts and books; for implanting and cultivating, in the young and in the mature, a spirit of enterprise and active beneficence; for extending and elevating the intelligence and piety of our churches; for disseminating and impressing religious truths; for securing a more thorough training in doctrine, and for aiding our pastors, we ought to cherish and prosecute this work as not the least of our efficient Convention agents.

11.11   The Present Sunday School Board, SBC

We have seen (document 11.10) that Southern Baptists made four efforts to have their own publication ministry, and by 1873 all four had failed. From 1873, when the first Sunday School Board was abolished, until 1891, the Home Mission Board carried on a limited publication ministry.

By the late 1880s many Southern Baptists felt the time had come to make another effort to produce and distribute their own church literature. Several factors influenced that trend, including the growing economic recovery in the South, a growing market since more churches had Sunday Schools and bought literature for them, the success of the limited printing operations of the Woman's Missionary Union in the South, and growing dissatisfaction with Northern Baptist literature.

James Marion Frost (1848-1916) was the primary founder of the present Baptist Sunday School Board, established by the SBC in 1891. Frost was a pastor in Richmond when he became captivated by the aggressive denominational vision of Isaac Taylor Tichenor (1825-1902). Tichenor, head of the Home Mission Board, felt that Southern Baptists should develop their own indigenous home mission and publication work, without depending upon Northern Baptists. Taking up this vision, Frost led in forming the Sunday School Board in 1891, and served as its secretary 1891-92, 1896-1916.

In selection A Frost traces the origin of the present Sunday School Board. *Source:* J. M. Frost, *The Sunday School Board: Its History and Work* (Nashville: Sunday School Board, n.d.), 7-21. Selection B gives excerpts from the first annual report, showing that the Board got off to a cautious but promising start. *Source: Annual,* SBC, 1892, LV-LVII, LXIII-LXIV, Appendix C.

A.   J. M. Frost, Origin of the Sunday School Board

I.
How the Board Came to Be.

THE Sunday School Board at Nashville was established by the Southern Baptist Convention in the session of 1891, at Birmingham, Ala. It was the final issue of a discussion which ran through several years, was conducted with tremendous energy, and stirred our people profoundly throughout the South. It was the settlement of one of the most vital and momentous questions ever raised in the Convention, and determined the far-reaching policy, that the Baptists of the South would act for themselves, and not depend on others to make their literature or conduct their publication interests or foster their Sunday school work.

The agitation arose first over the question whether the Convention should publish a series of Sunday school helps, and then the issue became more definite and concrete whether the Convention should have a separate and coördinate Board to take care of these several interests. The discussion went through several meetings of the Convention with stirring times intervening, . . . The successive meetings grew, even became crowded in attendance, while the interest became deeper and more intense, and each time the result issued in the same direction as if guided by an unseen hand toward a final goal.

1. FORMER SUNDAY SCHOOL BOARD.

We must needs, however, go further up the stream to find the source. There had been a former Sunday School Board of the Convention; it was created in 1863 at Augusta, and located first at Greenville, S. C.; it was later removed to Memphis, and then discontinued by the Convention in the session of 1873, at Mobile—marking among our people a decade of almost tragic effort, of noble achievement and of memorable history. This early movement was led by Basil Manly, Jr., and John A. Broadus, who had charge of the Board as President and Corresponding Secretary. . . .

Under the management of those men and their associates that former Board founded a Sunday school paper, which was called *Kind Words,* indicative of its spirit and purpose as issued among somewhat conflicting conditions. The paper, of course, went with the Board to Memphis, and when the Board was discontinued the paper was entrusted by the Convention to its Home Mission Board, located then in Marion, Ala., now in Atlanta.

Kind Words abides to this day, having been published successively at Greenville, Memphis, Marion, Macon, Atlanta and now Nashville. Through all this half century of somewhat checkered history the paper has never missed an issue, and has grown from a small monthly as a child's paper to a goodly sized eight-page weekly, very popular with all classes. Dr. Samuel Boykin became its editor at Memphis, and continued with it through all the years until his death at Nashville in 1899.

This paper may be traced like a golden thread through the annals of the Southern Baptist Convention, and is the connecting link between the past and present, between our prosperity of today and the severe struggle of our fathers in those far-away years. . . .

3. A NEW QUESTION IN THE ISSUE.

This narrative is following annual sessions of the Southern Baptist Convention, and in point of time has come into January, 1890. The question concerning *Kind Words* Series was somewhat enlarged, and a new question was brought into the discussion, the question of the Convention creating a new Board to have charge specifically of these publications and to look otherwise after the interests of the Sunday school cause in our churches.

This new question brought me into the very heart of the conflict that was on; indeed, the question of a new Board was of my making, and made the issue more sharp and concrete. Hitherto I had taken no public part in the discussion, though deeply concerned. . . . I was sympathetic with the Publication Society, and appreciated its work, but not as against this new movement of Southern Baptists. . . . when its request came for me to stand with the Society as against the Convention, my duty was plain, and the question had only one side from my point of view. . . .

. . . My first article proposing the new Board was published the latter part of February, 1890, in the *Religious Herald* at Richmond, one of the leading papers among Southern Baptists. It had been adverse to the Home Board movement, and became adverse also to my proposition for a new Board. Though not recalling the date of the paper, the article itself, as I now recall, was signed February 10, 1890—my forty-first birthday; it looked forward and contemplated presenting the proposition to the Convention at Fort Worth the following May.

. . . One night the latter part of January I was awakened from sleep with the thought of a new Board in full possession, and stirring my soul in such way as I make no effort here to describe, and for which I make no unusual claim. It worked itself out in a set of resolutions which I determined while lying there to present to the Fort Worth Convention. . . .

At Fort Worth in May as intended the resolutions as first published were presented to the Convention, and on my motion were referred without debate to a committee consisting of one from each state. . . . The best the committee could do after much effort was to present a majority report, which was adopted, with two members presenting a minority report. But even this majority report was in the nature of a compromise. It named a Sunday School Committee in place of a Board of Publication, to be located in Louisville, with an outline of duties specified. . . .

5. SETTLED AT BIRMINGHAM, 1891.

Then followed another year of anxious waiting, discussion, earnest effort on both sides, for and against the new movement. And at the Convention in Birmingham a year later the Sunday School Committee from Louisville on the first day submitted its annual report. . . . the Committee held its place, and now recommended to the Convention the appointment of a Sunday School Board. On my motion the report was referred to a committee and made a special order for Monday morning. . . . Dr. J. B. Gambrell and I were appointed a sub-committee to formulate a report.

It was a serious task. We represented opposing sides of the issue, but . . . we set ourselves to the task with the best that was in us. . . . After much conferring together, and at the close of a conference which lasted practically all day, he proposed to let me write the report and even name the location of the Board, provided he could write the closing paragraph. When the report was written and he added his words, they were accepted, provided he would let me add one sentence.

He consented, and the task was done so far as the sub-committee was concerned. . . .

The report created a Sunday School Board coördinate with the other two Boards of the Convention, practically followed the lines of my original resolutions of nearly two years before, and named Nashville as the place of its location. It was unanimously adopted by the larger committee after some discussion, and later to the surprise of everyone was adopted in the Convention without discussion. . . .

At the hour of the special order on Monday morning the great hall was crowded to the limit. I reached the hall with the report fresh from the committee, and was unable to enter the building, but was literally lifted in through a window and made my way to the platform as the report was already being called for. The excitement and expectation were intense. The rumor had gone out of a "battle between the giants," like the Battle of Waterloo, but with no one certain as to the outcome. I had scarcely finished reading, with the audience hushed to stillness, and before I could address the President, Dr. John A. Broadus was on the platform and in command of the occasion. And in less time than I can write it, he had brought the Convention to a vote. No one knew how, but all saw it done and acquiesced in the decision.

He did what few men may do once, but perhaps no man would try a second time. He did not move the "previous question," for that would have failed, but he accomplished the same result through the sheer power of his influence, and brought the Convention to vote without debate. I make no effort to reproduce what he said. He made no speech, besought that others would not speak—put a lid on the volcano, and waited to see what would happen—a sublime moment of heroism and faith. It was masterful in the noblest sense. Some thought his action part of a scheme, but not so. He no doubt had his purpose and plan well in mind, but if he ever told anyone, the secret has never become known to me.

So the report was adopted with thirteen dissenting voices. The end had come; the Sunday School Board had been established. . . .

B.   First Annual Report, Sunday School Board (SBC), 1892

Coming with its first report the Sunday-school Board greets the Convention with bright face and cheerful heart. When you created this Board in your session at Birmingham one year ago, and located it at Nashville, Tenn., you entrusted to us as its members a great interest and momentous task. We knew the magnitude of the undertaking and recognized the strain which it would bring. Indeed with some of us there were grave doubts as to the wisdom of creating the Board and serious misgiving as to what would be the result. However, we accepted the trust in good faith as committed to us by the Convention and determined to give it our best administration. In all its actions the Board has been harmonious and unanimous. . . .

Desiring that the management of its trust shall have thorough investigation before the Convention, the Board respectfully asks for three committees, to which shall be referred respectively its business condition, its publications and the sphere of its work with what may be the possibilities of its future influence upon our denominational life and missionary enterprises.

ORGANIZED

At its first meeting after the adjournment of the Convention, the Board unanimously and cordially elected Rev. Lansing Burrows, D. D., of Augusta, Ga., to be its Corresponding Secretary, . . . But he declined to accept the call.

At its next meeting the Board elected Rev. J. M. Frost, then pastor of the Leigh Street Church, Richmond, Va., who, though having said publicly at the Birmingham Convention that he could not consider at all the secretaryship, yielded to the demand that was made upon him, and under a solemn sense of duty to God and a desire to serve his brethren, accepted the position and entered upon the duties of his office July 1st, 1891. . . .

In this report today we take up a broken thread in the history of the Southern Baptist Convention, reviving a work begun and fostered more than twenty-five years ago by some of the best men God has ever given to the denomination. Basil Manly, Jr., was then President of the Sunday-school Board, and John A. Broadus its Corresponding Secretary. It is something significant that this work originated with the same men who laid the foundations of our Theological Seminary, and at the same time when great plans were being thought out for the future work of the Baptists of the South. Their only publication was the paper *Kind Words*. . . . Out of *Kind Words* came in 1886 a complete series of Sunday-school periodicals which are now published by the Southern Baptist Convention. Notwithstanding the intervening chasm of years, and the seasons of trial and vicissitude, we stand, brethren, in a royal line. . . . In this Convention series of Periodicals there are eight different publications which came to the Board from the Sunday-school Committee of last year, and were received by that committee the year before from the Home Mission Board.

The Teacher—a monthly magazine, adapted especially to the needs of teachers and families. . . . In each issue there are editorial notes, able articles, book notices, expositions of the lessons by persons who, as able expositors and practical workers, know the needs of our people; blackboard exercises specially prepared for each lesson; "talks with primary teachers and mosaics for primary classes—the wants of every department being provided for. . . .

The Quarterlies—*The Primary, The Intermediate* and *The Advanced* are graded to suit the different classes as designated in their titles. Each is adapted to the wants of its own grade. Illustrated with maps and pictures, and prepared by our best scholars, they fully fill their place.

Kind Words, our Sunday-school paper for young people, is published in three editions, Weekly, Semi-monthly and Monthly. . . .

Lesson Leaflets—single sheets, containing only the exposition of the lesson as heretofore and issued each week. The expositions are specially prepared and in no way inferior to the best in the series. . . .

The Child's Gem—a small weekly paper, beautifully illustrated, and specially adapted to small children; contains brief and simple stories, each notes of the Sunday-school lesson with questions and answers; and is very popular with the little folks.

The Lesson Cards—adapted to the scholars of the infant department, printed in beautiful colored designs. . . . Questions and answers in the simplest language to suit the little ones. . . .

Bible Lesson Pictures an elegant picture for each Sunday printed in colors, representing the principal event or leading thought of each lesson, with the Topic and Golden Text. . . .

In addition to these, the Board furnishes such other things as are needed in the equipment of a Sunday-school, such as reward cards, collection envelopes, question books, record books and a good line of catechisms, etc. This is done as a convenience to those ordering periodicals without additional cost to them, and a small margin of profit to the Board.

The Periodicals though much in advance of what they were, will be improved from time to time, both in literary merit and mechanical excellence. We are glad to report that they are in growing demand with our people, and their circulation is steadily and rapidly increasing. Increase of circulation means increase of value and power for good. . . .

Furthermore, in a way entirely different but not less effectual, will our work bear with great force upon the Convention's Foreign Mission interests. Our field is among the children, and through the Convention literature we will endeavor to develop in them the missionary idea and missionary spirit. This is of immense importance; for in the Sunday-schools of today are the missionaries of the future for the home and foreign fields, also the future pastors who will determine the character of our churches in the future, and even future members who are to support all our work at home and abroad. The Sunday-school therefore must be in touch with the Convention in all its missionary enterprises; and the Convention must lay its foundations among the children. . . . To put your hand upon the Sunday-school is surely to put your hand upon the future movements and energies for bringing in the kingdom of the Lord Jesus. . . .

It is manifest that the Sunday-school Board, through the power of its periodicals, may become a great factor in our denominational machinery second indeed to no other force in its influence upon our denominational life. It becomes a missionary power on home fields and foreign fields through its missionary literature. Who can foretell the results simply in increased contributions to the Boards of the Convention, when you shall have two, and three, and four generations of men and women who almost from their cradle have been trained to think missionary thoughts, pray missionary prayers and make missionary sacrifices in contributions laid at the Master's feet? But there is another way which in its far-sweeping influence surpasses all money considerations, and is simply immeasurable in its power to tell upon succeeding generations, namely, the cultivating and growing in thousands of children, not only the missionary idea and spirit, but the missionary himself, who shall tell the wondrous story of redeeming love among the nations of the earth. Brethren, this great enterprise which you have entrusted to the Sunday-school Board is not a scramble and squabble for literature, but something in every way high and noble, and with your endorsement and support in Convention assembled and in your churches and Sunday-schools the Board may do a work of which the ages will be proud. Of course the literature is essential, but only as a means to an end—a powerful means to a noble end.

And, moreover, if the leadings of Providence can ever be read and interpreted, God's hand is surely in this movement, his favor has surely been upon the work. He has turned the hearts of the people as no other power could have turned them; and instead of the Board's being distractive and a stirrer-up of strife, it now promises to be a unifying element in our denominational life and enterprises. All opposition and strife and discord are gone—or seem going. It is marvellous in our eyes and has filled our hearts with exceeding joy. God is opening a great door to the future for the Baptists of the South, and laying upon them immense responsibilities. He has thrown difficulties aside and bids the great Baptist host to a forward movement—trained in one school, and having one Lord, one faith, one baptism, one great heart and purpose for bringing in the kingdom of the Lord Jesus, and sharing in the joy and glory of his coronation. . . .

11.12   The Southern Baptist Theological Seminary

A supply of trained ministers has always been a need of Southern Baptist churches. From the early 1800s, Baptists in the South had colleges but their pastors either went North for theological training or, more commonly, simply went without it. From the time of the schism of 1845, some Baptists advocated formation of a theological seminary for the South.

Several barriers delayed such a school. Not all Baptists in the South saw the need for a seminary. Others felt that the college Bible departments could supply this need. Among the colleges, sectional rivalries prevented any one of them from winning acceptance throughout the South. However, by the 1850s, there emerged a growing sentiment for a Southwide theological school. The Bible Department of Furman University was separated from the university in 1859 and expanded to become The Southern Baptist Theological Seminary. First located in Greenville, South Carolina, the seminary moved to Louisville, Kentucky, in 1877.

The primary founder of Southern Seminary was James Petigrew Boyce (1827-1888). His inaugural address at Furman University in 1856 (selection A) is a formative document in Southern Baptist theological education. The three principles which Boyce laid out in that address have guided Southern Baptist theological education to the present. *Source:* James P. Boyce, *An Inaugural Address to the Board of Trustees of The Furman University* (Greenville, S.C.: C. J. Elford's Book and Job Press, 1856).

From his mentor Francis Wayland, Boyce had learned the importance of a confession of faith to which the faculty of a theological school should be committed. The Abstract of Principles (selection B), drawn up primarily by Basil Manly, Jr. in 1858, became the theological standard of the seminary. These articles also constitute the first confession of faith formally adopted by any Southern Baptist group. *Source:* William A. Mueller, *A History of Southern Baptist Theological Seminary* (Nashville: Broadman Press, 1959), 238-241.

A. James P. Boyce, Inaugural Address, 1856
Proposed Changes in Theological Education

Gentlemen of the Board of Trustees
of the Furman University:

I congratulate myself that I address to-night a body of men pledged to the interests of Theological Education, . . . we hold the Education of the Ministry a matter of the first importance to the Churches of Christ.

Indeed, did we think otherwise, we could no longer justly stand forth as exponents in any sense of the opinions upon this subject which prevail in our denomination. The Baptists are unmistakably the friends of education, and the advocates of an Educated Ministry. . . .

I would see the means of Theological Education increased, I would have the facilities for pursuing its studies opened to all who would embrace them, I would lead the strong men of our Ministry to feel that no position is equal in responsibility or usefulness to that of one devoted to this cause, and I would spread among our Churches such an earnest desire for Educated Ministers as would make them willing so to increase the support of the Ministry as to enable all of those, who are now forced from want of means to enter without the fullest preparation upon the active duties of the work, so far to anticipate the support they will receive, as to feel free to borrow the means by which their education may be completed.

The mind of the whole denomination has been awakened to the want of success under which we have suffered in our past efforts, and the best intellects and hearts in all our Southern bounds are directed to the causes of our failure, and to the means by which success may be attained.

In the efforts to establish the Common Theological Institution, proposed as a remedy for this evil, I heartily concur. I do not think that the demand for Theological Education calls at present for more than one Institution. . . .

. . . In performing the duty assigned me, I find myself irresistibly forced from other subjects which might have been appropriate, and led to suggest to you THREE CHANGES IN THEOLOGICAL INSTITUTIONS, which would enable them to fulfil more adequately at least, if not completely, the hopes of their founders. These changes are intended to meet evils which, in one case by the many, in the others by the few, have been already experienced, and they are suggested as furnishing ample remedies for the existing evils.

The first evil to which I would apply a remedy, is one which has been universally experienced—which, more than anything else, has shaken the faith of many in the value of Theological Institutions, . . . I refer to the failure of the Theological Institution to call forth an abundant Ministry for the Churches, and supply to it adequate instruction. . . .

. . . The Theological Seminary has not been a popular Institution. But few have sought its advantages. But few have been nurtured by the influences sent forth from it. And while our denomination has continued to increase, and our principles have annually been spreading more widely, it has been sensibly felt that whatever ministerial increase has accompanied, has been not only disproportionate to that of our membership, but has owed its origin in no respect to the influence of Theological Education. . . .

In ascribing this evil for the most part to our Theological Institutions, I would not appear unmindful of other circumstances upon which an increase of the Ministry in our Churches depends. Never would I consent to lift my voice upon such a subject as this, without a distinct recognition of the sovereignty of God working his own will, and calling forth, according to that will, the many or the few with whose aid he will secure the blessing. Never could I proceed upon any assumption that would seem to take for granted that there is not the utmost need of more special awakening to devotion and piety in our Churches, and a more fervent utterance of prayer for the increase of the laborers. Neither would I have it supposed that all that the Theological Institution can effect will be fully adequate to our wants, while our Pastors neglect to search out and encourage the useful gifts which God has bestowed upon the members of their Churches, or the Churches themselves neglect the law of God which provides an adequate support for the Ministry. But while due prominence is given to all of these circumstances, it yet appears that the chief cause is to be found in our departure from the way which God has marked out for us, and our failure to make provision for the education of such a Ministry as He designs to send forth and honor.

Permit me to ask what has been the prominent idea at the basis of Theological Education in this country? To arrive at it we have only to notice the requisitions necessary for entrance upon a course of study. Have they not been almost universally that the student should have passed through a regular College course, or made attainments equivalent thereto?

The idea which is prominent as the basis of this action, is, that the work of the Ministry should be entrusted only to those who have been classically educated—an assumption which singularly enough is made for no other profession. It is in vain to say that such is not the theory or the practice of our denomination. It is the theory and the practice of by far the larger portion of those who have controlled our Institutions, and have succeeded in engrafting this idea upon them, contrary to the spirit which prevails among the Churches. They have done this without doubt in the exercise of their best judgment, but have failed because they neglected the better plan pointed out by the providence and word of God. . . .

In His word and in His providence, God seems to have plainly indicated the principle upon which the instruction of the Ministry should be based. It is not that every man should be made a scholar, an adept in philology, an able interpreter of the Bible in its original languages, [but] . . . the opportunity should be given to those who cannot or will not make thorough scholastic preparation to obtain that adequate knowledge of the truths of the Scriptures systematically arranged, and of the laws which govern the interpretation of the text in the English version, which constitutes all that is actually necessary to enable them to preach the Gospel, to build up the Churches on their most holy faith, and to instruct them in the practice of the duties incumbent upon them. . . .

Never has He illustrated that principle more fully than in connection with the progress of the principles of our own denomination. We have had our men of might and power who have shown the advantages of scholastic education as a basis, but we have also seen the great instruments of our progress to have been the labors of a much humbler class. Trace our history back, either through the centuries that have long passed away, or in the workings of God during the last hundred years, and it will be seen that the mass of vineyard laborers have been from the ranks of fishermen and tax gatherers, coblers and tinkers, weavers and ploughmen, to whom God has not disdained to impart gifts, and whom He has qualified as his ambassadors by the presence of that Spirit by which, and not by might, wisdom or power, is the work of the Lord accomplished.

The Baptists of America, especially, should be the last to forget this method of working on the part of their Master, and the first to retrace any steps which would seem to indicate such forgetfulness. . . .

I have spoken of our Ministry in the past, as composed of men whose success illustrates the theory of the need only of Theological Education. And yet it is apparent that they enjoyed none of the advantages for that purpose which are connected with the present arrangements for study. In the absence of these, however, they did attain to the amount of Theological Education which is essential. . . . And if, by any course of training, substantially of the same kind, our Theological schools can restore to us such a mass Ministry as was then enjoyed, the days of our progress and prosperity will be realized to have but just begun. . . .

I believe, gentlemen, that it can be done; and more than this, that in the attempt to do it, we shall accomplish an abundantly greater work. Let us abandon the false principle which has so long controlled us, and adopt the one which God points out to us by His word and His providence, . . .

Let such a change be made in the Theological Department as shall provide an English course of study for those who have only been able to attain a plain English education. Let that course comprise the Evidences of Christianity, Systematic and Polemic Theology, the Rules of Interpretation applied to the English version; some knowledge of the principles of Rhetoric, extensive practice in the development from texts of subjects and skeletons of Sermons, whatever amount of Composition may be expedient, and full instruction in the nature of Pastoral duties—let the studies of this course be so pursued as to train the mind to habits of reflection and analysis, to awaken it to conceptions of the truths of Scripture, to fill it with arguments from the word of God in support of its doctrines, and to give it facility in constructing and presenting such arguments—and the work will be accomplished.

Experience alone can determine the length of time such a course should occupy. It should be so arranged for two years, however, that the better prepared and the more diligent may be able to pass over it in one. Doubtless this would be done by the vast majority, at least of those of riper years.

By the means proposed, the Theological school will meet the wants of a large class of those who now enter the Ministry without the advantages of such instruction—a class equally with their more learned associates burning with earnest zeal for the glory of God and deep convictions of the value of immortal souls, one possessed of natural gifts, capable even with limited knowledge of enchaining the attention, affecting the hearts and enlightening the minds of many who surround them—a class composed, however, of those who, with few exceptions, soon find themselves exhausted of their materials, forced to repeat the same topics in the same way, and finally to aim at nothing but continuous exhortation, bearing constantly upon the same point, or as is oftentimes the case, destitute of any point at all. In their present condition, these Ministers are of comparatively little value to the Churches, having no capacity to feed them with the word of God, affording no attractions to bring a congregation to the house of God, and no power to set before them, when gathered there, such an exposition of the word of God as may, through the influences of His spirit, awaken them to penitence, and lead to faith in the Lord Jesus Christ. . . .

The adoption of the true principle will not only tend, however, to secure for us this education in the masses, which we need, but will also increase five-fold the number of those who will receive a thorough Theological education. It will do this by the change of policy to which it will lead in reference to another class of our candidates for the Ministry.

We have among us a number of men who have enjoyed all the advantages of College life, but who have not been able, or willing, to spend the additional years needed for Theological study. These are possessed of far greater advantages than those of the other class, men of polished education, of well trained minds, capable of extensive usefulness to the cause of Christ, but their deficiencies are plainly apparent, and readily traceable to the lack of a Theological education. . . .

The theory of the Theological school should doubtless be to urge every one to take full courses in both departments; but when this is not possible, it should give to those who are forced to select between them the opportunity of omitting the collegiate and entering at once upon the Theological Course, I see not how any one can rationally question that many, if not all of those who are fitted for the Sophomore, or even the Freshman class in College, are prepared, so far as knowledge of books or languages is concerned, to enter with very great, though not with the utmost profit, upon the study of Theology.

I proceed now to speak more briefly of a second change needed in our Theological Institutions, by which it is to be hoped they will be enabled to produce scholars adequate to the exigencies of our own denomination, and to the common cause of Christianity. . . .

I refer not now to the charge that there has been that want of practical training by which those who have taken a Theological course, have practically but little benefitted immediately thereby. This evil, which I believe may be justly urged against the instruction of every Theological Institution in our country, is to be attributed to the fact that the Professors place the means of instruction in the hands of their students without exercising over their pursuit of those studies the superintendence which is needed. . . . The remedy for this evil is the adoption of that method of instruction which should have marked the previous Collegiate course. The studies should be so pursued as to call forth and improve all the powers of analysis and synthesis in the consideration of the subjects presented, and so to practice the student in the quick production of his thoughts, as well in deriving the appropriate subject from his text, as in forming skeletons of discourses, that he will not only be fully acquainted with the truth, but also able to present it readily and appropriately upon all occasions. If this course be pursued, and the student be encouraged at the same time to engage in every practical work, such as instructing in Sabbath Schools and Bible Classes, conducting Social Meetings in destitute places, preaching where the only ambition will be to present the truth plainly and simply; the complaints about the lack of efficient and practical training in Theological students will no longer be heard.

Neither do I allude to the inability of our Institutions to compel the attendance of those immediately about them who seek the highest attainments. To remove this, the department must also secure a sufficient number of the ablest men, the course must be extended to three years, so as to furnish time for the pursuit of the widest range of study, and the practical training already referred to being then adopted, the superior advantages afforded would soon manifest themselves in the character of the scholarship and the Ministry it would send forth. Under such training, the same material would be made doubly as efficient as under that of any of our present institutions.

Nor is the change here proposed connected with a project which was at one time, perhaps is now, a favorite scheme, for the benefit of Theological Institutions—the establishment of a Professorship devoted to the relations of science and the Bible. There can be no doubt that Christian minds should be devoted to the consideration of this subject. . . . But this seems to be already accomplishing among the many who, having like Christian sympathies with us, . . . occupy such positions in connection with our Colleges and scientific schools, . . .

The dissatisfaction to which I refer, has been awakened by the inadequate extent to which all Theological Institutions have pursued their studies, and the consequent lack among us of the scholarship which prevails in some countries abroad. It has been felt as a sore evil, that we have been dependent in great part upon the criticism of Germany for all the more learned investigations in Biblical Criticism and Exegesis, and that in the study of the development of the doctrine of the church, as well as of its outward progress, we have been compelled to depend upon works in which much of error has been mingled with truth, owing to the defective standpoint occupied by their authors.

And although the disadvantages of American scholars have been realized, arising from the want of adequate Theological libraries, as well as from the inaccessible nature of much other material, it has been felt that it has been in great part due to the limited extent to which the study of Theological science has been pursued among us, that we have been so much dependent upon others so unable to push forward investigations for ourselves, and even so inadequately acquainted with the valuable results of others who have accomplished the work for us. . . .

. . . It is a matter of the deepest interest to all, that we should be placed in a position of independence in this matter, and that our rising Ministry should be trained under the scholarship of the Anglo Saxon mind, which, from its nature, as well as from the circumstances which surround it, is eminently fitted to weigh evidence, and to decide as to its appropriateness and its proper limitations. But the obligation resting on the Baptist denomination, is far higher than this. It extends not merely to matters of detail, but to those of vital interest. The history of religious literature, and of Christian scholarship, has been a history of Baptist wrongs. We have been overlooked, ridiculed and defamed. Critics have committed the grossest perversions, violated the plainest rules of criticism, and omitted points which could not have been developed without benefit to us. . . .

The Baptists in the past have been entirely too indifferent to the position they thus occupy. They have depended too much upon the known strength of their principles, and the ease with which from Scripture they could defend them. They have therefore neglected many of those means which extensive learning affords, and which have been used to great advantage in support of other opinions. It is needless to say, gentlemen, that we can no longer consent to occupy this position. We owe a change to ourselves—as Christians, bound to show an adequate reason for the differences between us and others—as men of even moderate scholarship, that it may appear that we have not made the gross errors in philology and criticism, which we must have made if we be not right—as the successors of a glorious spiritual ancestry illustrated by heroic martyrdom, by the profession of noble principles, by the maintenance of true doctrines—as the Church of Christ, which He has ever preserved as the witness for His truth, . . .

It is scarcely necessary to remark, that any plan which can be devised, must be based upon the presence in the Institution of a good Theological library—one which shall not only be filled with the gathered lore of the past, but also endowed with the means of annual increase. Without this, no Institution can pursue extensive courses of study, or contribute anything directly to the advancement of learning. The Professor is cut off from valuable and necessary books, and the student hindered from making even the least important investigations in the course of study he is pursuing.

The plan I propose to you, supposes the possession of such a library; and this, even if it be such, is its only peculiar item of expense. Taking the idea from the provision made in some of our Institutions for the degree of Master of Arts, it has occurred to me that an additional course of study might be provided for those who may be graduates of Theological Institutions. . . . These and similar studies which should be laid down in a well digested course would bestow accurate scholarship, train the student in the methods of original investigation, give him confidence in the results previously attained, and open to him resources from which he might draw extensively in interpreting the Scriptures, and in setting forth the truths they contain. The result would be, that a band of scholars would go forth from almost every one of whom we might expect valuable contributions to our Theological literature.

It is to be expected that but few would take advantage of this course. Such would certainly be the case at first. The only result would be that but little additional provision will be needed. Two additional recitations a week for each of three or four Professors, would be more than adequate. And though such students should not be more than a twentieth part of those graduated, though not more than one each year, will not their value to the denomination more than counterbalance the little additional attention which will thus be given?

Were the production of this kind of scholars the only advantage to be gained, we might readily rest upon this the advocacy of this change. But there are others connected with it which may still further commend it by an apparently more practical tendency. . . . the Missionary, with his few books, limited time, and weighty responsibilities, will still feel the great importance of the advantages gained from this course, and will be grateful to that Institution which has placed it within his reach. And while from this class we would furnish such instruction abroad, would it not be to them also that our Institutions at home would chiefly look for their Professors? . . .

The change which I would in the last place propose, is not intended to meet an evil existing in our Theological Institutions so much as one which is found in the denomination at large, and which may at some future time injuriously affect this educational interest. It is the adoption of a declaration of doctrine to be required of those who assume the various professorships.

The most superficial observer must perceive that in our day the sound doctrine of our Churches is much imperilled. Campbellism, though checked in every direction in which it attempted to develope itself, has left no little of its leaven among us, and exerts no inconsiderable influence. The distinctive principles of Arminianism have also been engrafted upon many of our Churches; and even some of our Ministry have not hesitated publicly to avow them. That sentiment, the invariable precursor, or accompaniment of all heresy—that the doctrines of Theology are matters of mere speculation, and its distinctions only logomachies and technicalities, has obtained at least a limited prevalence. And the doctrinal sentiments of a large portion of the Ministry and membership of the Churches, are seen to be either very much unsettled, or radically wrong. . . .

The day has already come when it has been made matter of congratulation in a Baptist journal of high standing, that at the examination of perhaps the best endowed and most flourishing Baptist Theological Seminary in America, the technical terms of Theology were no longer heard.

A crisis in Baptist doctrine is evidently approaching, and those of us who still cling to the doctrines which formerly distinguished us, have the important duty to perform of earnestly contending for the faith once delivered to the saints. Gentlemen, God will call us to judgment if we neglect it.

The evil is one which calls for the adoption of a remedy by every Church and every Minister among us. It demands that every doctrine of Scripture be determined and expressed, and that all should see to it, the Churches which call and the Presbyteries which ordain, that those set apart to preach the word be men "whose faith the Churches may follow," "who take heed to themselves and the doctrine," and "are not as many who corrupt the word of God."

Peculiar obligations rest, however, upon those to whom are entrusted the education of the rising Ministry. God in His mercy preserve the instructors from the crime of teaching a single error, however unimportant, and grant unto all our Boards the grace necessary for faithfulness to the trusts devolved upon them, that false doctrine, however trifling, may receive no countenance. . . .

It seems to me, gentlemen, that you owe this to yourselves, to your Professors, and to the denomination at large; to yourselves, because your position as Trustees, makes you responsible for the doctrinal opinions of your Professors, and the whole history of creeds has proved the difficulty without them of convicting errorists of perversions of the word of God—to your Professors, that their doctrinal sentiments may be known and approved by all, that no charges of heresy may be brought against them; that none shall whisper of peculiar notions which they hold, but that in refutation of all charges they may point to this formulary as one which they hold *ex animo,* and teach in its true import—and to the denomination at large, that they may know in what truths the rising Ministry are instructed, may exercise full sympathy with the necessities of the Institution, and look with confidence and affection to the Pastors who come forth from it.

But some one will object that Scripture authorizes no such test in our Churches; and that as Christians, who claim even in matters of Church government, to be guided merely by Scripture example and precept, the Baptists cannot consistently introduce it. Let the objection be admitted. It would operate only against the use of such tests in a Church, and not in any voluntary society or combination into which we enter of our own accord. The Theological School is not a matter of Scriptural regulation, as is the Church; and in arranging its laws, we have only to see to it that the principles upon which they are based, do not violate those of the Scriptures. They may be matters of mere expediency. The Church being a Scriptural institution, receives its laws and its forms from the commands or examples contained in the New Testament; but the Theological Institution receives such laws as human wisdom can best devise, to carry out the laudable designs of its founders. . . .

The adoption of an abstract of doctrine, is but the means taken by a Church to meet these obligations. Perceiving the probability, that at some time such questions must arise, she acts beforehand, when her judgment is perfectly cool, when there are no outward circumstances to warp it, and when she can patiently examine the word of God, and know if these things be so. The time of trial is not the time for legislation. . . .

By the Baptists of all ages, creeds have been almost universally used, and invariably in this two-fold way. To some of other denominations, it has seemed that we have been without them, because the principle of liberty of conscience which we have at the same time maintained, has forbidden the laying of civil disabilities upon those who have differed from us. We have appeared to them, therefore, to put them forth only as declarative of our principles. It is to be regretted that many Baptists in our own day have given countenance to this opinion by misstatements of our practice. . . . Suffice it to state, that we have simply maintained that civil disabilities are not the means of punishing the offending members of the Church of Christ. We have looked to the Scriptures for the rule to govern us in such matters, and we have adopted the truly Apostolic plan by which we have accomplished all at which they aimed. The truth of God, which we have held, has been plainly declared. A confession of faith in Christ and in at least the prominent doctrines of Christianity, has been required of the candidate for baptism. By the principles thus set forth, we have judged the heretical among us, and wherever they agreed not with us, have excommunicated them from our Churches and our fellowship. The ideas which we have held of the spiritual nature of the kingdom of Christ, have developed the principle of liberty of conscience, and debarred us from the infliction of bodily punishment, or the subjection to any civil disability. But the same views of the spirituality of the Church, have impressed upon us the necessity of excluding those who have violated the simplicity which is in Christ.

It is, therefore, gentlemen, in perfect consistency with the position of Baptists, as well as of Bible Christians, that the test of doctrine I have suggested to you, should be adopted. It is based upon principles and practices sanctioned by the authority of Scripture, and by the usage of our people. In so doing, you will be acting simply in accordance with propriety and righteousness. You will infringe the rights of no man, and you will secure the rights of those who have established here an instrumentality for the production of a sound Ministry. It is no hardship to those who teach here, to be called upon to sign the declaration of their principles, for there are fields of usefulness open elsewhere to every man, and none need accept your call who cannot conscientiously sign your formulary. And while all this is true, you will receive by this an assurance that the trust committed to you by the founders is fulfilling in accordance with their wishes, that the Ministry that go forth have here learned to distinguish truth from error, and to embrace the former, and that the same precious truths of the Bible which were so dear to the hearts of its founders, and which I trust are equally dear to yours, will be propagated in our Churches, giving to them vigor and strength, and causing them to flourish by the godly sentiments and emotions they will awaken within them. May God impress you deeply with the responsibility under which you must act in reference to it!

These, gentlemen, are the changes I would propose in Theological Institutions.

B.   Abstract of Principles, Southern Baptist Theological Seminary, 1859

The following is an excerpt from the Fundamental Laws of the Seminary written into its charter on April 30, 1858: "9. Every Professor of the Institution shall be a member of a regular Baptist Church; and all persons accepting Professorships in this Seminary, shall be considered by such acceptance, as engaging to teach in accordance with, and not contrary to, the Abstract of Principles hereinafter laid down."

I. THE SCRIPTURES

The Scriptures of the Old and New Testaments were given by inspiration of God, and are the only sufficient, certain and authoritative rule of all saving knowledge, faith and obedience.

II. GOD

There is but one God, the Maker, Preserver and Ruler of all things, having in and of himself, all perfections, and being infinite in them all; and to Him all creatures owe the highest love, reverence and obedience.

III. THE TRINITY

God is revealed to us as Father, Son and Holy Spirit each with distinct personal attributes, but without division of nature, essence or being.

IV. PROVIDENCE

God from eternity, decrees or permits all things that come to pass, and perpetually upholds, directs and governs all creatures and all events; yet so as not in any wise to be the author or approver of sin nor to destroy the free will and responsibility of intelligent creatures.

V. ELECTION

Election is God's eternal choice of some persons unto everlasting life—not because of foreseen merit in them, but of his mere mercy in Christ—in consequence of which choice they are called, justified and glorified.

VI. THE FALL OF MAN

God originally created man in His own image, and free from sin; but, through the temptation of Satan, he transgressed the command of God, and fell from his original holiness and righteousness; whereby his posterity inherit a nature corrupt and wholly opposed to God and His law, are under condemnation, and as soon as they are capable of moral action, become actual transgressors.

VII. THE MEDIATOR

Jesus Christ, the only begotten Son of God, is the divinely appointed mediator between God and man. Having taken upon Himself human nature, yet without sin, He perfectly fulfilled the law, suffered and died upon the cross for the salvation of sinners. He was buried, and rose again the third day, and ascended to His Father, at whose right hand He ever liveth to make intercession for His people. He is the only Mediator, the Prophet, Priest and King of the Church, and Sovereign of the Universe.

VIII. REGENERATION

Regeneration is a change of heart, wrought by the Holy Spirit, who quickeneth the dead in trespasses and sins, enlightening their minds spiritually and savingly to understand the Word of God, and renewing their whole nature, so that they love and practice holiness. It is a work of God's free and special grace alone.

IX. REPENTANCE

Repentance is an evangelical grace, wherein a person being, by the Holy Spirit, made sensible of the manifold evil of his sin, humbleth himself for it, with godly sorrow, detestation of it, and self-abhorrence, with a purpose and endeavor to walk before God so as to please Him in all things.

X. FAITH

Saving faith is the belief, on God's authority, of whatsoever is revealed in His Word concerning Christ; accepting and resting upon Him alone for justification and eternal life. It is wrought in the heart by the Holy Spirit, and is accompanied by all other saving graces, and leads to a life of holiness.

XI. JUSTIFICATION

Justification is God's gracious and full acquittal of sinners, who believe in Christ, from all sin, through the satisfaction that Christ has made; not for anything wrought in them or done by them; but on account of the obedience and satisfaction of Christ, they receiving and resting on Him and His righteousness by faith.

XII. SANCTIFICATION

Those who have been regenerated are also sanctified, by God's word and spirit dwelling in them. This sanctification is progressive through the supply of Divine strength, which all saints seek to obtain, pressing after a heavenly life in cordial obedience to all Christ's commands.

XIII. PERSEVERANCE OF THE SAINTS

Those whom God hath accepted in the Beloved, and sanctified by His Spirit, will never totally nor finally fall away from the state of grace, but shall certainly persevere to the end; and though they may fall, through neglect and temptation, into sin, whereby they grieve the Spirit, impair their graces and comforts, bring reproach on the Church, and temporal judgments on themselves, yet they shall be renewed again unto repentance, and be kept by the power of God through faith unto salvation.

XIV. THE CHURCH

The Lord Jesus is the Head of the church, which is composed of all his true disciples, and in Him is invested supremely all power for its government. According to his commandment, Christians are to associate themselves into particular societies or churches; and to each of these churches he hath given needful authority for administering that order, discipline and worship which he hath appointed. The regular officers of a Church are Bishops or Elders, and Deacons.

XV. BAPTISM

Baptism is an ordinance of the Lord Jesus, obligatory upon every believer, wherein he is immersed in water in the name of the Father, and of the Son, and of the Holy Spirit, as a sign of his fellowship with the death and resurrection of Christ, of remission of sins, and of his giving himself up to God, to live and walk in newness of life. It is prerequisite to church fellowship, and to participation in the Lord's Supper.

XVI. THE LORD'S SUPPER

The Lord's Supper is an ordinance of Jesus Christ, to be administered with the elements of bread and wine, and to be observed by his churches till the end of the world. It is in no sense a sacrifice, but is designed to commemorate his death, to confirm the faith and other graces of Christians, and to be a bond, pledge and renewal of their communion with him, and of their church fellowship.

XVII. THE LORD'S DAY

The Lord's day is a Christian institution for regular observance, and should be employed in exercises of worship and spiritual devotion, both public and private, resting from worldly employments and amusements, works of necessity and mercy only expected.

XVIII. LIBERTY OF CONSCIENCE

God alone is Lord of the conscience, and He hath left it free from the doctrines and commandments of men, which are in anything contrary to His word, or not contained in it. Civil magistrates being ordained of God, subjection in all lawful things commanded by them ought to be yielded by us in the Lord, not only for wrath, but also for conscience sake.

XIX. THE RESURRECTION

The bodies of men after death return to dust, but their spirits return immediately to God—the righteous to rest with Him; the wicked, to be reserved under darkness to the judgment. At the last day, the bodies of all the dead, both just and unjust, will be raised.

XX. THE JUDGMENT

God hath appointed a day, wherein he will judge the world by Jesus Christ, when everyone shall receive according to his deeds: the wicked shall go into everlasting punishment; the righteous, into everlasting life.

11.13   The Whitsitt Controversy

The name of William Heth Whitsitt (1841-1911) was linked to a major controversy in Southern Baptist life in the 1890s. Whitsitt, as professor of church history and later as president of The Southern Baptist Theological Seminary in Louisville, came to a new understanding of Baptist origins. Influenced by primary historical sources such as the Jessey Records and the Kiffin Manuscript (documents 1.4 and 1.5 above), Whitsitt concluded that Baptists as they are known today came into existence in England in the early-seventeenth century.

Whitsitt published his views first in unsigned encyclopedia articles in 1880, and\later in *A Question in Baptist History* (Louisville, 1896). These views provoked a storm of controversy, led primarily by B. H. Carroll (1843-1914) of Texas. The trustees at the seminary at first resisted pressures to discipline or dismiss Whitsitt. The document cited here comes from an 1897 report, and spells out some of the issues of what was by then known as the Whitsitt Controversy. However, despite an appearance of peace, Whitsitt was forced out of the seminary in 1899. His views on Baptist origins are today almost unanimously accepted. *Source: Annual,* SBC, 1897, 15-16.

23. A communication from the Board of Trustees of the Southern Baptist Theological Seminary was presented as information, by W. E. Hatcher, Virginia. Whereupon it was ordered that the communication be printed in the minutes of the Convention.

The Trustees of the Southern Baptist Theological Seminary, assembled in their annual meeting in Wilmington, N. C., May the 6th, 1897, desire to submit to the Baptists of the South the following statement, in regard to the institution whose interests have been committed to their care and management:

1. That we account this a fitting occasion to reaffirm our cordial and thorough adherence to the fundamental articles adopted at the time when the Seminary was established, and to assure those on whose behalf we hold in trust and administer the affairs of this institution, of our steadfast purpose to require hereafter, as we have in the past, that the fundamental laws and scriptural doctrines embodied in those articles shall be faithfully upheld by those occupying chairs as teachers.

2. That we cannot undertake to sit in judgment on questions in Baptist history which do not imperil any of these principles, concerning which all Baptists are agreed, but concerning which serious, conscientious and scholarly students are not agreed. We can, however, confidently leave to continued research and discussion, the satisfactory solution of these questions.

3. That believing the Seminary to hold an important relation to the prosperity and usefulness of Southern Baptists, we consider it our duty, while demanding of those in charge of the departments of instruction the utmost patience in research and the greatest

discretion in utterance, to foster, rather than repress, the spirit of earnest and reverent investigation.

4. That being fully assured that the tender affection which we cherish for this institution, founded by our fathers and bequeathed by them to us, is shared by the Baptists of the South, we can safely trust them as we ask them to trust us, to guard its honor, promote its usefulness and pray for its prosperity.

Upon the adoption of the foregoing statement, the Trustees appointed a committee to notify Dr. Whitsitt of this action, and to invite him to meet with them and to make any voluntary statements he might desire. Whereupon Dr. Whitsitt appeared before the Board and read the following paper:

WILMINGTON, N. C., May 7, 1897

To the Board of Trustees of the Southern Baptist Theological Seminary:

DEAR BRETHREN:—I beg leave to return sincerest and heartiest thanks for the noble and generous treatment that you have bestowed upon me. I have only words of affection for every member of the Board. After consulting with the committee I have the following to say: . . .

4. That on the historical questions involved in the discussion, I find myself out of agreement with some honored historians; but what I have written is the outcome of patient and honest research, and I can do no otherwise than to re-affirm my convictions and maintain my position. But if in the future it shall ever be made to appear that I have erred in my conclusions, I would promptly and cheerfully say so. I am a searcher after truth, and will gladly hail every helper in my work.

5. That I cannot more strongly assure the brethren that I am a Baptist than by what I have recently declared with regard to the abstract of principles set forth in the Fundamental Laws of the Seminary. I am heartily in accord with my Baptist brethren in every distinctive principle that they hold. My heart and life are bound up with the Baptists, and I have no higher thought on earth than to spend my days in their fellowship and service, in the name of the Lord Jesus Christ.

Respectfully submitted.

WM. H. WHITSITT.

At the conclusion of the reading of the foregoing paper the trustees joined in singing

"How firm a foundation, ye saints of the Lord,

Is laid for your faith in his excellent Word,"

during which, amid flowing tears and many expressions of satisfaction and joy, the members of the Board pressed forward and gave Dr. Whitsitt the hand of fellowship and confidence. The trustees then instructed B. H. Carroll of Texas, and W. E. Hatcher of Virginia, to communicate to the Southern Baptist Convention this action, and also to give it to the public press. Please bear in mind that this statement is made to the Convention for information and not for action.

11.14   The Landmark Movement

No movement in the nineteenth century had a more profound impact in shaping Southern Baptist identity and intense denominational loyalty than the Landmark movement. Led by the great triumvirate of James Robinson Graves (1820-1893), Amos Cooper Dayton (1813-1865), and James Madison Pendleton (1811-1891), Landmarkism embodied a high church ecclesiology that said Baptists have the only true churches in the world. According to this view of the church, Baptists logically have the only true baptism, Lord's Supper, and ministers; all other churches are "human societies," their ordinances mere "nullities," and their pastors hired functionaries rather than true ministers. Landmarkers also believed that Jesus and His apostles established Baptist churches, and that Baptist churches, under whatever name, have an unbroken historic succession from the New Testament to the present.

This movement proved divisive and damaging in Southern Baptist life. Graves and his followers tried to dismantle the SBC, especially its Foreign Mission Board. Through the influential pages of the *Tennessee Baptist,* which he edited, Graves spread ultraconservative doctrines, a rigid spirit of intolerance and denunciation for all who disagreed with him, and an unseemly love for controversy.

Selection A throws light on the background of Graves, who was apparently greatly influenced by the Alexander Campbell "Reform" movement in Baptist life. In the long run Graves did not join the Campbell Reformation, but his rigid spirit and exclusivist views have much in common with Alexander Campbell. *Source: The Southwestern Baptist,* 1 July 1858, 3. Selection B lists a number of Baptist doctrines to which Graves adhered; for years he ran this list regularly as a standing article in the *Tennessee Baptist. Source: The Tennessee Baptist,* 6 Oct. 1857.

Perhaps Graves' most important book was also one of his smallest: *Old Landmarkism: What Is It?* First published in 1880, this popular book carried the Landmark message to the masses of Southern Baptists (selection C). *Source: J. R. Graves, Old Landmarkism: What Is It?* (Texarkana, Tex.: Baptist Sunday School Committee, 1928), ix-xv, 113-119, 121-127. Used by permission of the Baptist Sunday School Committee, Bogard Press. In 1883 Graves published one of his larger books, *The Work of Christ in the Covenant of Redemption* (selection D). This was one of the earliest works by a Southern Baptist to advocate dispensational premillennialism. *Source: J. R. Graves, The Work of Christ in the Covenant of Redemption developed in Seven Dispensations* (Memphis: Baptist Book House, 1883), 379-382, 391, 405.

A. The Background of J. R. Graves

Cogar's Landing. Jassemine Co., Ky.,
June 18, 1858

Elder Henderson:—Dear Sir—I have been asked to answer several questions in regard to Jas. R. Graves, now and for some time past a minister in the Baptist Church; and being satisfied that there exists sufficient reasons for making the inquiries, I answer as follows:

1. Jas. R. Graves boarded with me in Jassemine county, Kentucky, more than a year, about 1841 and 1842. He was teaching school. He was a wild, thoughtless man, full of fun and; entirely too much for a member of the church; unscrupulous in his relation of facts; would tell the truth if insisted on. He always told me he was a member of the Baptist Church; but told my neighbor, W. T. Wilson, that he was a member of the Presbyterian Church.

2. During the time of my acquaintance with Jas. R. Graves there was an extensive revival of religion at Mt. Freedom, near my house, under the preaching of the Rev. T. J. Fisher, a Baptist minister. At that meeting Graves joined the Baptist Church and was ordained a minister. He produced no letter of dismission from any other church and was received on his own statement of his former membership. He was very anxious that my mother-in-law, Mrs. Davenport, my wife and myself, who were members of the Christian (Campbellite) Church would join with him at Mt. Freedom, and stated to us that if we would do so, that he could and would before a great while convert the church at Mt. Freedom, into a Reformed (Campbellite) Church. He said he was satisfied that all the younger members would agree to it, but that a few of the old Hardshells might not. I replied to him that I doubted whether he understood the doctrines of the Reformed Church. He said he did understand them, and believed them to be true, and took me to his room where he exhibited to me a large number of the Millenial Harbinger, (Mr. Campbell's publication) which I was taking at the time. I had enjoyed the meeting very much, and when I ascertained that Graves was in earnest with his proposition, I refused to be a party to any such proceedings.

W. G. Cogar.

[The editor continues following Cogar's statement]

Col. Cogar, in a private note, accompanying the foregoing says: "If any one of the answers or any part of thereof is questioned by Graves, I only request that I shall be informed, and I will not only make them good, but will add as many more of equal importance." Col. C. then refers to the Pastor of the Church at Mt. Freedom, the deacons and several of the elder members, some eight or nine, for proof as to the character of Mr. Graves before he joined the church, and as to the manner of his getting into it, to-wit: "on his own statement of his former membership"—without any regular letter of dismission.

B.   J. R. Graves, A Statement of Landmark Principles, 1857

SIX IMPORTANT FACTS

"1. All scholars, critics, and lexicographers, of any note, unanimously declare that the primary (i. e., first) and leading signification of "Baptizo" is to dip or to immerse, while some of the very best scholars of any age affirm that it has no other meaning— Carson, Anthony, Stuart, etc.

"2. Standard historians unanimously agree that primitive and apostolic baptism was administered by the immersion of the believers in water, in the name of the Trinity.

"3. Nearly all standard Pedo-Baptist commentators admit that the Bible does not furnish one plain command for, or example of, infant baptism, and there is the utmost disagreement and contradiction among them on what grounds for for what purpose it is to be administered.

"4. All standard historians unanimously affirm that the government of the Apostolic churches was purely democratic (i. e., vested in the people or membership), and all the churches independent republics (the Baptist church is the parent of republicanism).

"5. No society, organized upon principles differing from those of the Apostolic churches, having different subjects, ordinances, orders in the ministry, can justly be called a gospel church, or a church of Christ, or a branch of the church of Christ.

"6. All religious societies having legislative powers and clerical or aristocratical governments (i. e., in the hands of the clergy, or a few, as a session), are anti-scriptural and anti-republican tyrannies which no Christian can lawfully countenance, or republican freeman ought to support; consequently, all the acts and ordinances of such irregular bodies are illegal and ought not to be received by us; nor should such societies be, in any way, recognized as scriptural churches or their preachers as official ministers of the gospel."

SIX IMPORTANT PRINCIPLES

"1. The Bible, and the Bible alone, unalloyed with human devices or traditions, is, and ever has been, the religion of Baptists.

"2. Positive laws (as Baptism and the subject of Baptism, etc.) are not left to be inferred, but in all cases require positive and plain commands or examples.

"3. To divide the positive requirements of Christ into essentials and non-essentials, is to decide how far Christ is to be obeyed, and in what points we may safely disobey him. But to refuse one of the least of his positive requirements or to teach others so, it involves one in the guilt of violating all.

"4. Every positive law, ordinance or practice, in the church, not expressly commanded or exampled, is positively forbidden—and these are all human inventions, and traditions, as infant baptism, sprinkling, pouring, etc., now practiced for religious rights, for which no scriptural warrant can be found, and are therefore sinful.

"5. Christ gave no men, society, or church, the authority to traffic with the ordinance or organization of his church or kingdom so as to make, or change his laws, and substitute one thing for another. To surrender what He has established, is treachery—to change them is treason.

"6. Principles can neither be conceited nor compromised.

BAPTIST COROLLARIES

"1. There is no church, but a body of immersed believers, who have been immersed by one who has himself been immersed, after conversion and a hope of salvation.

"2. There are authorized no ministers, but immersed preachers, acting under the authority of a regular church—and who have been ordained by a presbytery of immersed believers.

"3. There is no peculiar sanctity to a house of worship, no special sacredness to a pulpit, nor is one spot or locality, one rostrum, bench, desk or pulpit, more consecrated than another; except as the associations connected with its occupancy, or the purpose to which it is devoted, render it sacred.

"4. Since nothing is more evident than the fact, that we teach more effectively by example than by precept—therefore, so long as we appropriate our pulpit for official preaching of the gospel by those whom we consider duly baptized and ordained to the ministerial office, it is equally evident that it is improper for us to invite those teachers to occupy them, when we know they are neither baptized nor ordained, and especially since they claim it to be, and construe the act on our part into a recognition of their claims, and thus confirm their followers in error.

"Nothing can be more inconsistent than to admit those preachers into our pulpit who hold and teach doctrines, on account of which we would exclude both from our pulpits and our churches, any minister of our own denomination.

"This, we claim, is one of the old landmarks of the Baptist church.

"5. That a body of immersed believers is the highest ecclesiastical authority in the world, and the only tribunal for the trial of cases of discipline; that the acts of the church are of superior binding force over those of an association, convention, council, or presbytery—and no association or convention can impose a moral obligation upon the constituent parts composing them.

"6. That no association or convention has the right to demand support for any project or scheme which they have originated, but may only recommend, advise, and urge the performance of duty in subservience to the great Christian voluntary principle.

"7. That Baptists never dissented from anything but sin—and are not protestants, but have been, in all ages, the Repudiators of Popery."

AXIOMS

"1. That unimmersed bodies of Christians are not churches, nor are any privileged companies of them the church, hence all Pedo-Baptists denominations are only religious societies.

"2. That Baptism and an official relation to a church are prerequisites to a regular gospel minister—hence all ordinances administered by an unbaptized and unordained although immersed minister, are null and void."

BAPTIST POLICY

"1. To be in all things consistent with our principles whether we gain or lose numbers or popularity.

"2. To fulfill our peculiar mission—which is to be the witnesses of Christ's truth against every system of error, and those who originate or advocate them, and above all, by no act to countenance, recognize, aid or abet those who teach error, or to confirm those who are in error.

"3. To employ all the energy of the denomination for the conversion of the world, through the most effectual means and agencies, as our missionary organization, Bible and publication societies, theological seminaries, male and female colleges, and Sunday schools, prayer meetings, and regular periodicals.

"4. To occupy every village and city in the world, with a suitably qualified, faithful, energetic and devoted minister.

"5. To furnish a pastor for every church, and missionaries of the cross for every destitute region and land, at home and abroad, under the whole heaven, and sustain them.

"For the steadfast and uncompromising advocacy of these principles and this policy, this paper is especially devoted.

J. R. GRAVES, *Editor.*"

C.   J. R. Graves, *Old Landmarkism: What Is It?* 1880

1. From the preface

My thoughts were first awakened to the subject discussed in this little book in 1832, upon witnessing the immersion of my mother and sister by a Pedobaptist minister, and the plunging of another subject face forward as he knelt in the water, and the pouring water upon another while kneeling in the water, the sprinkling it upon another in the same position, and the sprinkling upon several others while standing on the banks of the stream, and yet others out of a pitcher in the meeting-house. Those different acts for *"one baptism"* made an indelible impression, and the more so because the administrator seemed to be in ill humor when he immersed, and *dipped his hand in water and laid it upon the heads of the candidates he immersed while he repeated the formula!* The questions started were: "If he did not believe in immersion, was the act at his hands valid? If 'what is not of faith is *sin,*' could his sin be an act acceptable to God?"

Twenty-two years after, that mother applied to the 2d Church in Nashville, of which I was pastor, for membership upon her immersion, which brought the whole matter up afresh as a practical question for serious examination. Being quite young and this my first pastorate, I referred the whole matter and responsibility to Dr. Howell, then pastor of the 1st Church, telling him that I was in serious doubt about the validity of her baptism. He promptly decided it all sufficient and according to the *usage* of the denomination. From this time I commenced the careful study of the question, "Can an unbaptized man administer baptism?" Reason said, No; and I found no example of it in the New Testament after a church had been organized. Soon the question with me assumed a proper form: "Has any organization, save a scriptural church, the right to authorize any one, baptized or unbaptized, to administer church ordinances?" I decided this, by God's Word, in the negative; and subsequently this additional question came up: "Are immersions administered by the authority of a scriptural church with an *unscriptural design* valid?" Such immersions I also decided, by the clear light of the Scriptures, to be null and void; and thus I instructed my church, which, from that day to this, has never been troubled about unscriptural baptisms.

Shortly after I had the pleasure of seeing that mother and sister observe the ordinance as at first delivered.

In 1846 I took charge of "The Tennessee Baptist," and soon commenced agitating the question of the validity of alien immersions, and the propriety of Baptists recognizing, by any act, ecclesiastical or ministerial, Pedobaptist societies or preachers as *churches* and ministers of Christ. This agitation gave rise to the convention, which met at Cotton

Grove, W. T., June 24, 1851, of all Baptists willing to accept and practice the teachings of Christ and his apostles in these matters. In that convention these questions were discussed, and the decisions of that meeting embodied in the famous "Cotton Grove Resolutions," which attracted the attention of Baptists throughout the whole South. As a matter of history, I copy them from the minutes, which were offered in the form of "queries."

"Rev. J. R. Graves offered the following queries:

"1st. Can Baptists, consistently with their principles or the Scriptures, recognize those societies not organized according to the pattern of the Jerusalem Church, but possessing different *governments,* different *officers,* a different class of *members,* different *ordinances, doctrines* and *practices,* as churches of Christ?

"2d. Ought they to be called gospel churches, or churches in a religious sense?

"3d. Can we consistently recognize the ministers of such irregular and unscriptural bodies as gospel ministers?

"4th. Is it not virtually recognizing them as official ministers to invite them into our pulpits, or *by any other act that would or could be* construed into such a recognition?

"5th. Can we consistently address as *brethren* those professing Christianity, who not only have not the doctrine of Christ and walk not according to his commandments, but are arrayed in direct and bitter opposition to them?"

These queries were unanimously answered in the negative, and the Baptists of Tennessee generally, and multitudes all over the South, indorsed the decision.

The name of Old Landmarkers came in this way. In 1854 J. M. Pendleton, of Kentucky, wrote an essay upon this question at my special request, viz: "Ought Baptists to recognize Pedobaptist preachers as gospel ministers?" which I brought out in tract form, and gave it the title, "An Old Landmark Reset." This calm discussion, which had an immense circulation in the South, was reviewed by many of the leading writers, North and South, and they, by way of reproach, called all Baptists "Old Landmarkers" who accepted his conclusions, and the impression was sought to be made that Brother Pendleton and myself were aiming at dividing the denomination and starting a new sect.

From this brief history it will be seen that *we,* who only deem ourselves "strict Baptists," are not responsible for the name, but our opposers. But that we have no reason to be ashamed of it will be seen by every one who will read this little book. Why should *we* object to the name "Old Landmarkers," when those ancient Anabaptists, whom we alone represent in this age, were content to be called Cathari and Puritans, which terms means the same thing as Old Landmarkers?

I put forth this publication now, thirty years after inaugurating the reform, to correct the manifold misrepresentations of those who oppose what *they* are pleased to call our principles and teachings, and to place before the Baptists of America what "Old Landmarkism" really is. Many believe that simple opposition to inviting ministers into our pulpits is the whole of it, when the title to the tract indicated that *that* was only *one* of the landmarks of our fathers. Others have been influenced to believe that we hold to "apostolic succession;" others, that we hold that baptism is essential to salvation, but its efficacy ineffectual unless we can *prove* the unbroken connection of the administrator with some apostle; and yet others, that we hold that any flaw in the qualification of the present administrator, or any previous one in the line of his succession, however remote, invalidates all his baptisms and ministerial acts, as marriages, etc., past, present, and future, and necessitates the re-baptisms and re-marriages of all he has ever immersed or married. It is certainly due to those who bear the name to be vindicated from these hurtful misrepresentations. I think it is no act of presumption in me to assume to know what *I* meant by the Old Landmarks, since I was the first man in Tennessee, and the first *editor* on this continent, who publicly advocated the policy of *strictly* and consistently *carrying out in our practice those principles which all true Baptists, in all ages, have professed to believe.* Be this as it may, one thing is certainly true, no man in this century has suffered, or is now suffering, more than myself "in the house of my friends," for a rigid maintenance of them.

In 1846 pulpit affiliations, union meetings, receiving the immersions of Pedobaptists and Campbellites, and inviting Pedobaptists, as "evangelical ministers," to seats in our associations and conventions, even the Southern Baptist, had become, with but few exceptions, general throughout the South. At the North not only all these customs, but inviting Pedobaptist preachers to assist in the *ordinations,* and *installations,* and recognitions of Baptist ministers, was quite as common. I have noticed that in some of these meetings Universalist, if not Unitarian, ministers affiliated, and delegates were appointed by Baptist associations to meet Pedobaptist associations and Methodist conferences.

At this writing, January, 1880—and I record it with profound gratitude—there is only one Baptist paper in the South, of the sixteen weeklies, that approve of alien immersion and pulpit affiliation ("The Religious Herald"), while already *two* papers in the Northern States avow and advocate Landmark principles and practice. I do not believe that there is one association *in the whole South* that would to-day indorse an alien immersion as scriptural or valid, and it is a rare thing to see a Pedobaptist or Campbellite in our pulpits, and they are no longer invited to seats in our associations and conventions anywhere South.

2. Landmark reasons for refusing communion to non-Baptists

The inconsistencies and evils of intercommunion among Baptists.

"Truth is never contradictory or inconsistent with itself."—*Tombes.*

Baptist churches, with all their rights, have no right to be *inconsistent,* nor to favor a practice unwarranted by the word of God, and productive of *evils.* Under the inflexible law of "usage," which compels the pastor to invite "all members of sister churches present" to the Lord's Supper, the following *inconsistencies* and *evils,* exceedingly prejudicial to our denominational influence and growth, are practiced and fostered.

1. Baptist churches that practice intercommunion have practically no communion of their own. They have church members, church conferences, church discipline, but no church communion; and, therefore, no scripturally observed Lord's Supper, and, therefore, none at all, as I have shown in Chapter VII. The communion of such churches is *denominational,* and not *church* communion.

2. Baptist churches that practice intercommunion have no guardianship over the Lord's Supper, which is divinely enjoined upon them to exercise. They have control of their own members to exclude them from the table if unworthy, . . . but they can not protect the table from such so long as they do not limit it to their membership. . . .

4. There are multitudes—I rejoice to say nearly all our Southern churches outside the cities—who will not receive persons immersed by Catholics or Campbellites, Protestants or Mormons, because they do not regard them as baptized at all; yet by their open denominational invitations they receive all such—and there are many of them in the churches—to their table, as duly qualified. . . .

Consistency.—If each Baptist church had its own communion, with its own members, independent of all others, then each church could receive into membership, or exclude from membership, whoever it pleased, and no other church or communion be injured by it. On the one hand, the church excluding a person would have no power to prevent his uniting with another church made up of members no better than himself;

and, on the other hand, the church receiving the excluded person would not, in so doing, restore him to the communion from which he had been cast out.

THE EVILS OF DENOMINATIONAL COMMUNION.

1. It opens the *door* to the table to all the ministerial impostors that pervade the land. . . . These impostors hold "revival meetings" until all their borrowed sermons are exhausted, and make it a point to do all the baptizing, and have the weakness of some other ministers to keep a record of the number of their baptisms. It is needless to say that the church is often divided by their influence, and left in confusion and disgrace when they are exposed. . . .

The remedy is, let no strange traveling preacher be admitted to the table as participant, nor into our pulpits, until the church has written back and learned that he is in all respects worthy.

2. *Denominational communion* never has been sustained, and never can be, but at the expense of peace. . . .

3. It has encouraged tens of thousands of Baptists, on moving away from the churches to which they belong, to go without transferring their membership to a church where they were going, as they could have the church privileges—preaching and COMMUNION—without uniting with, and bearing the church's burdens. . . . If Baptists could have no such privileges without membership, they would keep their membership with them and enjoy it. . . .

6. We annually lose thousands and tens of thousands of worthy persons who would have united with us, but for what they understand as our unwarranted close-communion. Our practice can never be satisfactorily explained to them as consistent, so long as we practice a partial, and not a general, open communion. Our denominational growth is very materially retarded by our present inconsistent practice of intercommunion. If we practiced strict church communion, these, and all Christians, could understand the matter at once; and no one would presume to blame us for not inviting members of *other* denominations to our table, when we refuse, from principle, to invite members of other Baptist churches—our own brethren.

7. It is freely admitted by reliable brethren who enjoy the widest outlook over the denomination in America, that for the last few decade of years the general drift has been, and now is, setting towards "open communion"—it is boasted of as a "broadening liberalism." There are numbers in all our churches—and the number is increasing, especially in our fashionable city and wealthy town churches—who are impatient of the present restrictions imposed upon the table; because, not being able to divide a principle, they are not able to see the consistency of inviting members of sister churches, and rejecting those whom we admit to be *evangelical* churches, as though all evangelical churches are not sister; nor can they divine why Pedobaptist ministers are authorized to preach the gospel and to *immerse;* are invited to occupy our pulpits, and even to serve our churches as supply pastors for a season—all their ministrations recognized as valid, and yet they are debarred from our table. They work for us, and we refuse to allow them to eat. The only ground upon which we can successfully meet and counteract the liberalizing influences, which are gently bearing the Baptists of America into the slough of open communion, is strict local church communion, and the firm and energetic setting forth of the "Old Baptist Landmarks" advocated in this little book. . . .

3. Landmark views on Kingdom and Church Continuity

Landmark Baptists very generally believe that for the Word of the Living God to stand, and for the veracity of Jesus Christ to vindicate itself, the kingdom which he set up "in the days of John the Baptist," has had an unbroken continuity until now. I say kingdom, instead of succession of churches, for the sake of perspicacity. Those who oppose "church succession" confuse the unthinking, by representing our position to be, that the identical organization which Christ established—the First Church of Judea—has had a continued existence until to-day; or, that the identical churches planted by the apostles, or, at least, *some one* of them, has continued until now, and that Baptist ministers are successors of the apostles; in a word, that our position is the old Romish and Episcopal doctrine of apostolic succession. I have, for full a quarter of a century, by pen and voice, vehemently protested against *these* misrepresentations, as Baptists have, for twice as many more, against the charge of teaching that no one can be saved without immersion, and quite as vainly; for those who oppose us seem determined to misrepresent, and will not be corrected. We repudiate the doctrine of apostolic succession; we do not believe *they* ever had a successor, and, therefore, no one to-day is preaching under the apostolic commission any more than under that which Christ first gave to John the Baptist. They are our opposers who, in fact, hold to apostolic succession; for the majority do believe that, if ministers, they are preaching by the authority contained in that commission! So much for this charge.

Nor have I, or any Landmarker known to me, ever advocated the succession of any particular church or churches; but my position is that Christ, in the very "days of John the Baptist," did establish a visible kingdom on earth, and that this *kingdom* has never yet been "broken in pieces," or given to another class of subjects—has never for a day "been moved," or ceased from the earth, and never will until Christ returns personally to reign over it; that the organization he first set up, which John called "the Bride," and which Christ called his church, constituted that visible kingdom, and to-day all his *true* churches on earth constitute it; and, therefore, if his *kingdom* has stood unchanged, and will to the end, he must always have had true and uncorrupted churches, since his kingdom can not exist without true churches.

The sense in which any existing Baptist church is the successor of the First Church of Judea—the model and pattern of all—is the same as that existing between any regular Masonic Lodge and the first Lodge that was ever instituted. Ten thousand local Lodges may have existed and passed away, but this fact in nowise affects the continuity of Masonry. From the day it was organized as symbolic Masonry, it has stood; and, though it may have decayed in some places, it has flourished in others, and never has had but *one beginning*. Thus it has been with that institution called the Kingdom of Christ; it has had a continuous existence, or the words of Christ have failed; and, therefore, there has been no need of originating it, *de novo,* and no unbaptized man ever had any authority to originate baptism, or a church, *de novo.* I understand that Christ's declaration (Matt. 16: 18), and Paul's statement (Heb. 12: 28), are emphatic commentaries upon the prophecy of Daniel (2: 44).

We do not admit that it devolves upon us more than upon every other lover of Jesus to prove, by incontestible historical facts, that this kingdom of the Messiah has stood from the day it was set up by him, unbroken and unmoved; to question it, is to doubt his sure word of promise. To deny it, is to impeach his veracity, and leave the world with our a Bible or a Christ. We dare not do this. We believe that his kingdom has stood unchanged, as firmly as we believe in the divinity of the Son of God, and, when we are forced to surrender the one faith, we can easily give up the other. If Christ has not kept his promise concerning his *church* to keep it, how can I trust him concerning *my salvation?* If he has not the power to save his *church,* he certainly has not the power to save me. For Christians to admit that Christ has not preserved his kingdom unbroken, unmoved, unchanged, and uncorrupted, is to surrender the whole ground to infidelity. I deny that a man is a believer in the Bible who denies this.

Nor do we admit the claims of the "Liberals" upon us, to prove the continuous existence of the church, of which we are a member, or which baptized us, in order to prove our doctrine of church succession, and that we have been scripturally baptized or ordained. As well might the Infidel call upon me to prove every link of my descent from Adam, before I am allowed to claim an interest in the redemptive work of Christ, which was confined to the family of Adam! We point to the Word of God, and, until the Infidel can destroy *its* authenticity, our hope is unshaken. In like manner, we point the "Liberal" Baptist to the words of Christ, and will he say *they are not sufficient?* When the Infidel can prove, by incontestible historical facts, that *his* kingdom has been broken and removed one year, one day, or one *hour* from the earth, then we surrender our Bible with our position. . . .

I have no space to devote to the historical argument to *prove* the continuity of the kingdom of Christ, but assure the reader that, in our opinion, it is irrefragable. All that any candid man could desire—and it is from Catholic and Protestant sources—frankly admitting that churches, substantially like the Baptists of this age have existed, and suffered the bitterest persecution from the earliest ages until now; and, indeed, they have been the only religious organizations that have stood since the days of the apostles, and are older than the Roman Catholic Church itself.

D.　J. R. Graves, Advocating Dispensational Millennial Views, 1883

CHAPTER X.

The Church of Laodicea Symbolizes the Character of the Churches of Christ in the Last Days of this Dispensation.

Having considered the predicted state of the nations, their political agitations and marshalings for a general conflict, let us now notice the religious aspects of society and state of the churches, given by Christ as signs of his near coming—his being at the door and knocking.

What is the predicted state of the Church of Christ at the close of this dispensation?

The sure word of prophecy on which I rely, for it most certainly is a prophecy, is Christ's message to the last of "the seven churches in Asia."

It is true that various views are entertained by expositors, with respect to these letters, as there is touching the Revelation itself; and, since these letters partake of the character of the book in which they stand, I will briefly state these views as described in Abbott's "Dictionary of Religious Knowledge":

"The first school, that of the Praeterists, embraces those who hold that the whole, or by far the greater part, of the prophecy of this book has been fulfilled. They regard it as intended merely to describe events then passing, and they limit its denunciations to the destruction of pagan and persecuting Rome. This view finds few modern defenders outside of Germany, and may be safely disregarded by the reader.

"The second is that of the historical interpreters, or those who hold that the prophecy embraces the whole history of the church and its foes, from the time of its composition to the end of the world. The expositors of this school, while they differ among themselves in detail, agree in regarding the Book of Revelation as a continuous prophetic history of the church, describing in symbolical language the various phases through which it was ordained to pass; and they look for the proper interpretation of the book largely to the events which have occurred in the history of the church thus far.

"The third view is that of the Futurists, or those who maintain that the prophecy, with perhaps the exception of the first three chapters, relates entirely to events which are to take place at or near to the coming of the Lord."

The second of these views is that held, though in different forms, by the greater number of evangelical scholars, and is the one I fully adopt, the reasons for which I will briefly lay before the reader.

1. These letters containing messages, like all the other parts of the book, were by an angel dictated to John in ecstatic vision when an exile in the Isle of Patmos. In this respect they are like the revelations made to Daniel by the angel, and must be explained by the same laws of interpretation—*i. e.,* those governing symbols.

2. The messages to these churches are all **prophetic.**

This revelation was given by Christ to show unto his servants what things must shortly come to pass (ch. i. 1). These messages, as well as the book, must be interpreted by the same rules—**symbolically.**

The simple explanation upon this view is: The seven cities bearing these names were all the churches then existing on the peninsular, which the Isle of Patmos overlooked, called Proconsular Asia. Since these seven churches were then the sole representatives of Christianity in all Proconsular Asia when he wrote this, and because the inditing spirit knew there never would be any others, the Saviour selected them to symbolize all his churches that would exist until the close of the Dispensation. Each church, with the characteristics and trials given it, was designed to symbolize the characteristic and trials of all his churches during the period it represented. In this respect they partake of the character of the seven seals, trumpets and vials, for these divided all prophetic time into periods—*i. e.,* each one characterized by its own peculiar characteristics and trials. Thus, in the history of the seven symbolic churches, we have presented a complete panoramic history of Christianity from the first century until, in answer to the prayers of a long-waiting Bride, the Lord shall come. . . .

Admitting that the symbolic view is the correct one, and that these churches represent church periods, as the trumpets do State periods, and admitting that the universal belief of the Jews is correct, viz., that six thousand years closes the world's week, and the seventh introduces the world's grand Sabbatism, there remained about two thousand years from the First to the Second Advent of Christ, and this divided by seven, the number of church periods, the average length of these periods would be about three hundred years.

But the blasts of the trumpets were some longer and some shorter, so the periods symbolized by the churches, or "lampstands," varied in duration. One period may have been only one hundred, another one hundred and fifty, and yet another three hundred or more years. . . .

CHAPTER XI.
THE COMING OF CHRIST FOR HIS SAINTS.
The Second Coming of Christ under two Aspects—He Comes "into the Air" for his Saints—The "Resurrection of the Just"—The Translation or Rapture of Living Saints—They meet their Lord in the Air and Receive their Glorified Bodies.

The Second Advent of Christ manifestly has two aspects or comprises two events:

1. His coming into the air **for** all his saints, and

2. His visible appearing in glory to the whole world **with** all his saints.

The first is that aspect of his coming which relates to the resurrection of all the righteous dead and the translation of all the then living saints, and the second is that aspect which relates to the unbelieving Jews and Gentiles—the world. He comes not in the same manner to his friends and his foes. . . .

I have thus proved by the Word of God, by the best scholarship of this age, and **concensus** of the best scholarship—

1. That the first resurrection, which will be of **all the saints** only, will be a literal resurrection, and **pre**-millennial.

2. The second coming of Christ, which also is a literal appearing, will be in connection with the first resurrection. This rising of the just dead and rapture of the living souls "to meet the Lord in the air," will be prior to the tribulation period, which is before the coming of Christ.

3. **Therefore, that the coming of Christ must be pre-millennial.**

I feel warranted in declaring that the doctrine of the **pre**-millennial coming of Christ is one of the old landmarks of primitive Christianity, and should be received and held fast by all Christians of this age.

Unless this doctrine is clearly apprehended by the reader, it will be quite useless for him to pursue these chapters further. The Scriptures will present an inextricable maze of inconsistency and contradictions. The doctrine of the **pre**-millennial and personal coming of Christ is the ground and pillar of my theory of Eschatology.

11.15   The Gospel Mission Movement

One spin-off from Landmarkism among Southern Baptists was the "Gospel Mission Movement." Led by Tarleton Perry Crawford (1821-1902), a veteran Southern Baptist missionary to China, this movement sometimes took the name of "Crawfordism."

After years of service in China, Crawford found himself out of agreement with the Foreign Mission Board about mission strategy, support, and administration. He came to feel that missionaries should draw only a bare subsistence allowance, and seek to become self-supporting so as not to require even a stipend. His views on nonsupport from the sponsoring Board became more pronounced after his shrewd and sometimes questionable investments in China allowed him financial independence.

Following the influence of J. R. Graves, Crawford came to believe that missionaries should be sent out only by local churches, not by mission boards. This, he believed, was the *gospel* method, hence the name of the movement. He felt that for a mission board to appoint, set salaries, and give directions for missionaries was tantamount to an episcopal function. After years of conflict, the Board severed its relations with Crawford.

In 1892 Crawford expressed his views in a hard-hitting booklet, entitled *Churches, To the Front!* Excerpts are included in selection A. *Source:* T. P. Crawford, *Churches, To the Front!* (China: n.p., 1892). Selection B, probably written by H. H. Harris, former president of the board and interim secretary between Tupper and Willingham, summarizes the Gospel Mission controversy from the standpoint of the Foreign Mission Board. *Source: Foreign Mission Journal*, Sept. 1893, 37-41.

A.   The Gospel Mission Movement

ON reading a recent letter from a Baptist pastor in one of our American county towns, saying that his Church had resolved to support a missionary in China, I felt like exclaiming, Is this the beginning of a new era among our Baptist Churches? Are they, at last, about to rise in their individual capacity and do their own work? About to carry out the commission of Christ in harmony with the independent, self-acting principles of their time-honored constitution? What a glorious movement this! How it will revive their waning sense of responsibility, deepen their devotion, develop their energies and clothe them with salvation as with a garment! It will also effectually counteract that dangerous tendency of our times towards centralization by closing the door against those "outside organizations" which encourage it through taking control of their work, their workers and their contributions. To take control of these, or any part of them, is so far to take control of the Churches, so far to overthrow their independence and self-respect, so far to reduce them to the position of mere "tributary appendages."

These organizations, beginning in 1814 with foreign missions alone, have gone steadily on enlarging the sphere of their operations until they have now come to embrace almost every kind of religious work. Not content with this, they have added many enterprises of a secular character and also placed them upon the Churches for support, in direct violation of our time-honored principles. According to these principles, Baptist Churches are self-acting religious bodies, constituted for religious purposes only; each one being directly responsible to Christ for the faithful execution of its sacred trust. Hence it can never abdicate nor transfer any part of its work to the control of an outside body. Neither can it permit any encroachment upon its appropriate sphere or any extension of it into the secular realm. . . . But this does by no means preclude individuals from co-operating with those organizations which do not intrude upon the appropriate sphere of the Churches.

This "organization craze" has gone to great extremes, and the time has come for our people "to call a halt." . . . We have had enough of General Conventions, National Societies, Central Boards, Executive Committees and other like agencies "for doing Church work"—or rather, for preventing it; "for pushing our principles"—or rather, for overthrowing them; "for promoting union among brethren"—or rather, for keeping up rivalries among themselves. . . . A revolution towards simplicity or local action and responsibility in mission matters, is imperatively demanded. Any co-operation of Baptist Churches in work requiring the employment of men and money, to be efficient, must necessarily be limited in its range and definite in its aim.

The notion that union is strength under all conditions is a great mistake. It is strength only to the extent required for the accomplishment of any given purpose. Beyond that point it is worse than weakness. . . . For instance, should a hundred distant men unite in raising a log cabin when eight or ten neighbors can raise it with perfect ease? If not, why should thousands of our Churches unite in supporting a missionary when one, two or a few adjoining ones can do it very much more readily and cheaply, as well as better for themselves and the Master's cause? Then, let Boards, pastors, editors, every one encourage them singly, or in groups smaller or larger according to circumstances, to choose, support and look after the work of their missionary evangelists, wherever sent, in the same direct manner that they now choose, support and look after the work of their pastors. If they be competent for the one, they ought to be competent for the other. . . .

If I read the signs of the times aright, local co-operation is the coming method of mission work among Baptist Churches. In this way every one of a group can readily act as a body in choosing a missionary, selecting a field, fixing a salary, electing a committee-man, and in deciding other important matters connected with the undertaking. . . . How simple, convenient, inexpensive, efficient and Baptistic the proposed mode of procedure in comparison with the present complicated, inconvenient, expensive, inefficient and unBaptistic system—wheel within wheel, delay, friction and waste everywhere! . . .

The general impression that Churches, as such, are incapable of conducting missions—largely growing out of erroneous conceptions of the work to be done—casts reproach not only upon them but also upon Christ and the Apostles, their original founders. The truth of the matter is this: the work of foreign missionaries, when freed from the care of "subsidy money," its accompanying host of "native employés," "schools" and other "worrying adjuncts" and confined to Gospel or spiritual things as it should be, is comparatively simple. . . . Yet, painful to say, these erroneous conceptions gave origin to our two great Conventions. Their very existence and course of action throw discredit upon the Churches by taking the work out of their hands and by claiming superior managing ability for the Boards of their appointment. However, the unwritten history of their operations fails to sustain the claim, or to free them from the charge of serious blunders in the selection of men, the adoption of measures and the expenditure of funds. Not only so. Our foreign missions, relatively to the growth of the denomination, are weaker to-day than they were thirty years ago. These results—without any reflections upon individual men—show clearly that the system is not adapted to our people. . . .

The Church, or group of Churches, that supplies the funds and the missionary that does the work should together settle these matters according to the circumstances of the case, and under Christ assume the whole responsibility of the undertaking. An outside party should no more come between a Church and its missionary than between a Church and its pastor. All ministerial gifts belong to the Churches, to be employed by them in furthering the Master's cause.

Baptists are a Gospel-loving, Gospel-preaching people, and it will be well for them to adhere to their calling. . . . Centralization and ring-government may suit the policy of other denominations. They do not suit ours, but are deadly hostile to it. Yet, strange to say, this dangerous element was introduced among us with the first session of the Old Triennial Convention in 1814; and, stranger still, the Northern Baptist Union and the Southern Baptist Convention have continued it down to the present day. . . . These permanent Boards, by taking in hand the missionary work of our Churches and mixing it up with various enterprises of a popular kind, have now come to control a vast amount of labor, money, property, credit and patronage, all professedly in the name of the Baptist denomination, as if it were an actual entity capable of doing work by employing men and means like the consolidated denominations around us! . . .

If ever our Churches, North and South, had cause for protecting their freedom against encroachments, they have it now. This they may readily do by casting off this incongruous system with all its expensive adjuncts at home and aboard and, taking up their evangelistic work, singly or in groups, after the simple manner above suggested. By so doing, they will be able not only to preserve their autonomy and spirituality, but also to save on foreign missions alone fifty to sixty cents in the dollar, and, without increasing their present contributions, be able to send from their midst more than double as many missionaries into foreign fields. In my opinion, $650 per individual, or $1,400 per family, is amply sufficient to cover, on an average, all necessary expenses, including passage, children, work—everything. Many missionaries will doubtless require much less.

Please do not misunderstand the origin of these views. They do not spring from any personal grievance or sudden impulse, but from many years of observation in connection with mission operations, and from deep-seated Baptist convictions; . . .

Again, I am not opposed to the existence of Conventions, Societies, Boards or Committees of the proper kind, in the proper place, and for the proper purpose; but I am deeply opposed to all those which intrude themselves and their enterprises upon the Churches—to all those which take any part of their work, their workers, or their funds away from their control. To this class—without mentioning others here—clearly belong the Northern Baptist Union, the Southern Baptist Convention and their Boards. These Boards, though not subject to the Churches, both *originate* and carry on such enterprises as they think proper—whether religious or secular, wise or otherwise—at the expense of the Churches. They are, therefore, unlawful bodies within the Baptist fold and should disband. . . .

While opposing all intruding bodies, I could readily sanction General and State Conventions for mutual acquaintance, for interchange of views on matters of common concern, . . . But these Conventions should collect no funds, employ no men, hold no property and exercise no authority over the government or the work of the Churches.

CHURCHES, AS SUCH, TO THE FRONT!

B.   SBC Response to Gospel Missionism, 1893

OUR BOARD AND THE "GOSPEL MISSION"

Numerous requests have come for information in regard to the withdrawal of brethren Crawford, Herring, Bostick and League from connection with the Foreign Mission Board. It does not undertake, of course, to bring out all the facts contained in over a hundred letters and papers now on file. Indeed, the differences below indicated soon become complicated with personal and pecuniary questions into which I am unwilling to enter. One of the brethren withdrew informally, we hardly know when or how, two voluntarily tendered their resignations, and one was requested to resign. Sharp things have been said about the tryanny and lavish expenditures of the Board, but we trust to the common sense of the average Baptist not to be misled by statements that are obviously extravagant, and in all controversies with our brethren we deem it better to endure in silence rather than to retort unkindly. What is written may seem to lack the spice of personality. It will probably be unsatisfactory to the advocates of the "Gospel Mission;" perhaps equally unsatisfactory to the most ardent supporters of the Board. Extremists have a great advantage in any public discussion—they see only one side and can state that clearly and forcibly. But the interests of truth are better subserved by trying honestly to look at both sides, and thus compare schemes, though both be faulty in so far as they are human.

There are, as it seems to me, two radical differences in principle and several resultant differences in policy, between the brethren above named and the Board.

DIFFERENCES IN PRINCIPLE

1. *Church Independence*—They hold that a local church or group of churches ought to select appoint and sustain its own missionary, and that he should be responsible and should report his work only to the appointing body. We also believe in the complete independence of the churches in all local matters, but claim that, according to the New Testament teaching, there should be fraternal cooperation between then in all matters of wider concern. Hence arise councils, Presbyteries, District and General Associations, and the Southern Baptist Convention. If the Convention, through its Board, should accept the ideas advanced in Dr. Crawford's tract entitled "Churches to the Front," it would simply commit suicide, and in its fall would crush other organizations of Baptists. Indeed, the good Doctor's common sense has saved him from a rigid application of his own theory and compelled him to give it up by saying "church, or group of churches." The group of churches, with a committee to represent them, differs in size but is precisely the same in principle as the Convention with its Board. . . .

2. *Aim of Missions*—On this there are two diverse views. One set of learned and very pious interpreters emphasize the work of *evangelizing* and *proclaiming as a herald*. They regard Matt. 24:14 as prophetic of a time now near at hand, and propose to prepare for the coming of the Lord by heralding the gospel among the nations. They do not expect to gain many converts, but to evangelize the world in preparation for the

millenium. These are the Premillenarians, and furnish not a few of the most zealous laborers for missions, including such men as Drs. Gordon and Pierson. Another set of expositors are chary about attempting exact interpretation of prophecy until it has been fulfilled, but stand firmly upon the plain terms of the Great Command (Matt. 28:19, 20) and its practical exemplification in Acts and in the Epistles, in which *preaching and teaching* are regularly combined. These labor to save souls, to train converts, to establish churches as centres of influence—candlesticks in the midst of darkness. Now it seems to me that our brethren above named, without being fully committed, lean strongly towards the former theory, while we adhere rather to the latter. . . .

DIFFERENCES OF POLICY

Out of these different views on matter of principles necessarily arise differences in practice, of which I may mention:

1. They claim the fullest personal liberty as servants of the Lord and of his churches (a) to do their own work in their own way, which we fully and freely concede and have always conceded; (b) to remove from place to place or to return to this country at pleasure, which we hold to be inconsistent with reasonable rules to which they have personally subscribed, and (c) to criticize publicly the work of our missionaries in other fields, which seems to us unbrotherly. . . . We think that they have no right, while drawing support from the treasury of the Board, to do and say what will necessarily, so far as believed, seriously impede the flow of contributions into the treasury.

2. They are entirely opposed to the appropriation of any mission money for schools. This Board has never gone so far in school work as some other denominations, nor so far as our brethren of the Missionary Union. . . . but it seems to us that schools for the instruction of promising young men and women in the doctrines of the Bible, and even for secular instruction of the children of converts from heathenism or Romanism are almost essential to the establishment of self-supporting, self-propagating churches. . . .

3. They hold that it is wrong to pay natives for any religious work, claiming that such payment subsidizes them and leads them to profess Christianity for the sake of gain. It seems to us that the troubles of which they complain have existed in all countries and at all times since the days of Christ and his apostles, (Matt. 7:22; Phil. 3:18, 19) and that the proper way to avoid them is to observe the utmost care in the selection of native helpers. To hold that all natives who are willing to preach have been subsidized, is not only to distrust them, but to distrust the grace of God. If we show utter want to confidence in converts from heathenism, they will hardly deserve confidence. We hold, therefore, that self-sustaining churches will be established earlier by giving such help as may be needed to men who seem most worthy and most consecrated and who give evidence of being called of God, and by gradually diminishing this help as the churches thus formed become able to support their own preachers. This is the plan pursued by our State Mission Boards. This is the plan which has already borne good fruit in and around Canton, our oldest and in many respects most successful mission field.

4. Bro Herring, as I understand him though I am unable to say that the other brethren agree, thinks that the missionaries sent out by a church or group of churches should be allowed to endure hardship, and even death, when their supporters fail to furnish means in due time. . . . There is unquestionably more of romance, more of what is commonly called heroism, in the new plan than in the old, but we believe that as "faith without works is dead," so a bare trust in God without the use of means suggested by sound common sense, is fanaticism. . . .

5. The brethren insist on the economy of wearing native dress, living in native houses, subsisting on native food. We say, very well, where it can be done without

injury to influence or to health. The plan works satisfactorily in Italy, fairly in Japan, Brazil and Mexico, but how would it do among the naked denizens of mud huts in Africa? Cheap, certainly, in money, but at terrible cost of health and life. As to China, we judge that there are some sections of the vast empire in which it is wise to adopt partly or fully the native mode of living, others in which it would be unwise. On these matters each of our missionaries is allowed the fullest liberty. . . .

Let me say, moreover, that there seems to be a very general impression that the Board, like a great corporation, pays certain fixed salaries, which employees have a right to draw whether they need it or not. Such is not at all the case. We undertake to furnish a comfortable support and name $50 a month as a "general rule," with deviation, more or less, "for good and sufficient reasons." A wise economy in the administration of missions funds is unquestionably a duty of the highest importance but the sacrifice of health or life to save dollars is not wise economy.

11.16   The Role of Women in Southern Baptist Life

The role of women in Southern Baptist churches has stirred controversy in the twentieth century. The documents cited here show that this is no new controversy; Baptist men and women debated this issue long before the present generation.

In 1846 R. B. C. Howell (1801-1868), a prominent pastor and writer in Nashville, published his book on *The Deaconship* (selection A). One chapter advocates a role for Baptist deaconesses, justifying that concept by ancient Scripture and modern need. *Source:* R. B. C. Howell, *The Deaconship: Its Nature, Qualifications, Relations, and Duties* (Philadelphia: American Baptist Publication Society, 1846), 98-107. Selection B reproduces a speech by Sarah Ann Chambers given at the Alabama Baptist Convention in 1882. Interestingly, a granddaughter of Mrs. Chambers was ordained to the ministry by a Southern Baptist church in Dallas in the 1970s. *Source:* Handwritten copy of unpublished paper read at the Alabama State Convention, 1882, provided by Martha Gilmore of Dallas, granddaughter of Mrs. Chambers.

The ultraconservative Kentucky pastor, James Boardman Hawthorne (1837-1910), published a sermon on "Paul and the Women" in which he advocated a severely limited role for women in church and society (selection C). *Source:* J. B. Hawthorne, *Paul and the Women* (Louisville: Baptist Book Concern, 1891), 2-17. Many Southern Baptists during the suffragette movement of the late-nineteenth century became extremely anxious about the issue of women speaking in public. We see that concern reflected in an article by an unidentified pastor in the *South Carolina Baptist* in 1898 (selection D). *Source: South Carolina Baptist,* 21 Sept. 1898, 1. R. W. Sanders and J. W. Perry, eds.

A.   R. B. C. Howell, The Role of Baptist Deaconesses, 1846

CHAPTER VII
DEACONESSES

Female assistants to the Deacons existed in the primitive churches.—References to them by Ecclesiastical Historians.—By early Christians writers.—By the Scriptures.—Are they necessary?—Their qualifications.—Their duties.—They are virtually employed in our own churches.—Practical conclusions.

FEMALE assistances to the deacons, usually called DEACONESSES, existed in the primitive churches. They were ladies of approved character and piety; and their duty required them to minister to females, under circumstances in which it would have been manifestly improper that the other sex should have been employed. Their services were regarded as of very great importance, if not entirely indispensable. Ecclesiastical historians, the early Fathers, and other writers, refer to them frequently and familiarly.

Mosheim, for example, in his "History of the First Century," introduces them thus: "The Eastern churches elected *deaconesses,* and chose for that purpose, matrons, or widows, of eminent sanctity, who also ministered to the necessities of the poor, and performed several other offices, that tended to order and decency in that church."[1] All the other writers of his class, of distinction, have stated the same thing in similar terms.

Clemens of Alexandria,[2] who wrote in the *second* century, treats extensively of deaconesses, advocates their legitimacy, and appeals, as authority, to Paul's first epistle to Timothy. Jerome, who flourished in the *fourth* century, speaks of them,[3] as generally found in the churches. The book of "Apostolic Constitutions" prescribes their election, and publishes forms for their ordination.[4] We may indeed appeal, on this topic, even to the enemies of the Christians. Pliny, the distinguished Roman Governor of Bithynia, in his well-known letter to the Emperor Trajan,[5] regarding their affairs, describes two females whom he ordered to be put to the torture, and says of them, *quaae ministrae dicebantur,* "who were called *ministresses,* or female deacons."

There can be, therefore, no doubt as to the matter of fact: It is conceded, on all hands, that deaconesses were employed, and that constant resort was had to their ministry in the first churches of Christ. The only question to be decided is whether the word of God authorizes, or in any manner enjoins their appointment. This infallible authority is our unerring guide. When we have ascertained its teachings, we comply without further inquiry. Let us, then, "to the law and to the testimony." "What saith the Scriptures?"

In his address to the church in Rome, Paul thus appeals to his brethren of that city: "I commend unto you Phoebe, our sister, which is a [διάχονον, a *Deaconess,* in our version] *servant* of the church in Cenchrea; that ye receive her in the Lord, as becometh saints; and that ye assist her in whatsoever business she hath need of you; for she hath been a *succorer of many,* and of me also."[6] Phoebe is, therefore, by an apostle, called expressly a *Deaconess* of the church; and we are assured that she had honorably and effectually exercised that office, in the *succors* she had extended to many, and, either directly or indirectly, to the apostle himself among the number. Two facts are implied in this passage, both of which are worthy of our attention. The first is, that the apostle speaks of this excellent lady *in her official character,* in terms of high approbation, and commends her, not only as a sister, but as a *Deaconess,* to his brethren in Rome. This he never could have done, if *he* had not regarded the office as legitimate. And the second is, the strong probability, that, as the church at Cenchrea had deaconesses, they were also found in all the other churches. Uniformity, no doubt, prevailed in their organization. This passage, therefore, must be regarded as conclusive of the Scripture warrant for deaconesses.

But this is not all. *Three* other passages are supposed to allude to the deaconesses. To these I will refer, however, only as collateral testimony in the premises.

Speaking of a class of persons called "Χήρας," (Cheras), the apostle says: "Let not a *widow* be taken *into the number* under threescore years old; having been the wife of one man; well reported of for good works; if she have brought up children; if she have lodged strangers; if she have washed the saints' feet [ministered the usual rites of hospitality]; if she have relieved the afflicted; if she have diligently followed every good work."[7] The nature, or the privilege of this *class,* into which only widows, of the character described, were to "be taken," I shall not now attempt to determine. It is very certain, however that they were not, as has been so generally supposed, to be "taken into the number" of those who were *supported by the church.* "It can hardly be imagined that a widow, unless she had considerable property, could have done the things enumerated, some of which would occasion no small expense."[8] She could not, therefore, have been very poor. Would it not, also, have been a strange prohibition, if the benevolence of the church had been denied to a woman, however helpless and afflicted, unless she was *sixty years old?* How singular, too, the condition that she must have had *children,* to entitle her to this bounty! If a woman have children, she is thought on that account to be less dependent. Indeed, in a previous injunction, in immediate connection with this passage, the apostle says: "If any widow have children, or nephews, let them learn first to show piety at home, and to requite their parents, for that is good and acceptable before God."[9] In other words, such widows are to be supported by their children, or nephews, and not by the church. Who, then, were these "Χήρας?" *(Cheras.)* The qualifications required of them singularly resemble those of a deacon. Their age, however, was too great to suppose that they were capable of much active service. Many of our best Biblical expositors presume that they were those who had been deaconesses, and now, in the evening of their days, enjoyed some kind of peculiar immunities.

A second passage speaks of them, as is believed, under the general name of "WOMEN." Addressing some unnamed brother and friend at Philippi, Paul says: "I entreat thee also, true yokefellow, [colleague] help *those women* who labored with me in the gospel."[10] How did they labor with him in the gospel? It cannot be that they *preached,* since the same apostle says, in another place, "I suffer not a woman to teach nor to usurp authority" in the church. Yet they labored with Paul, and were so distinct from all others, that they were known by the simple description, *"those women."* Why should we withhold our assent from the almost unanimous opinion of commentators, that they were the deaconesses of the church?

To the last passage I had occasion before to refer, when treating of the qualifications of deacons, and then promised that I would, in a future chapter, consider it more at large. In our common version it has the following reading: "Even so must their [the deacons'] wives be grave, not slanderous, sober, faithful in all things."[11] We have already seen, I trust, satisfactorily, that no reference is here had to the wives of deacons. But does not the apostle say, "Even so must *their wives* be grave?" In our translation he does; but when you turn to the original, you find no such thing! The reading is γυναῖκας ὡσαύτως σεμνάς literally, "Let the *women* also be grave." This strikingly resembles the last passage noticed, "Help those *women."* The wives of the deacons, as we have before seen, are spoken of in the next verse, and not in this. These *"women,"* then, were some other *"women,"* and not the deacons' wives. What women were they? Clemens, Jerome, and other ancient writers, say they were the *Deaconesses,* and so say our best writers of modern times. The conclusion is most natural. No one supposes they were the deacons' wives. Paul, in other places, speaks of them. He was here describing the qualifications of deacons, and what is more consonant than to suppose, that, in passing, he adds a few words regarding the qualifications of deaconesses. As the *Deacons,* so the *Deaconesses* must be grave, not slanderers, sober, faithful in all things. Such, I confess, appears to me to be the true sense of the apostle.

Take all these passages together, and I think it will be difficult for us to resist the conclusion that the word of God authorizes, and in some sense, certainly by implication, enjoins the appointment of deaconesses in the churches of Christ.

Were they, in ancient times, and are they now, "requisite and necessary"? . . .

We cannot but reply in the affirmative, if we consider what has been, in all ages, and what is now, the condition of females in the East. . . . In Oriental countries, therefore, deaconesses were, and are, beyond question, indispensable.

And are they altogether useless among us? Do we not know that they might have admission to multitudes of their own sex with very great advantage to the interests of religion, under circumstances in which, otherwise, they must remain unvisited? Gentlemen cannot administer to their wants. And further, when ladies are to be baptized, they may be left, and frequently are, in the most painful manner, unattended, unless there are some persons specially designated for that duty; or they may be accompanied by those of very unsuitable character. Deaconesses, therefore, are everywhere, as necessary as they were in the days of the apostles.

When we look around us we see, indeed, in effect, deaconesses in nearly all our well-regulated churches. In most of the other denominations, the office is rendered unnecessary, partly by their having abolished baptism, partly by their aristocratic propensities, on account of which, as we have seen in another place, they themselves confess that they have almost "no poor among them"; and partly by their having instituted, in opposition to the gospel, female orders, as with the Roman Catholics, who have their troops of *"Sisters of Charity,"* and other sisters rather too *charitable;* but in the true church, in which are maintained primitive principles, all the original institutions of religion are indispensable. There are ladies, self-appointed, I admit, but whose intelligence and piety have led them to see that such offices ought to be performed, and, governed by a just sense of propriety, who voluntarily undertake to discharge them. Thus they become substantially deaconesses, and in some degree make amends for the want of proper ecclesiastical action. Our churches thus far, consequently, have the benefit of the deaconesses.

We have now seen, with as much brevity as the nature of the case would admit, that female assistants to deacons, or deaconesses, existed in the primitive churches; we have considered the passages in the word of God, in which they are named and described; we have proved their necessity at the present day, as well as in former times, where the duties and ordinances of religion are administered in their original and lawful forms; we have examined their qualifications, and shown that they are sill found, substantially, in all our best-regulated churches.

[Notes]

1. Vol. I. pp. 90, 91.
2. *Stromat.,* Lib. 3, p. 443.
3. Comm. in 1 Tim. 3:11.
4. Lib. 8, ch. 19, 20.
5. A. D. 106.
6. Rom. 16:1, 2.
7. 1 Tim. 5:9, 10.
8. Clark's Com in loc.
9. 1 Tim. 5:4.
10. Phil. 4:3.
11. 1 Tim. 3:11.

B.   Sarah Ann Chambers (Alabama), Woman's Work in the Church, 1882

It is not the object of this paper to show what woman has done in the church, nor to dictate what she ought to do. Some good people seem to think that women are not called on to do anything in the church, except, as one sister quaintly remarks, "Go to meeting, sing, and make pies for the preacher." These things I think we ought to do, and do them heartily, as unto the Lord; and most of us find such duties to be very pleasant ones. But there are other services in which we should love to engage, although they involve greater sacrifices.

In the history of our Savior's life on earth, and in the writings of His apostles, Woman has an honored place. Her love for her Redeemer and his Servants, and her zeal and diligence in good works, are clearly shown forth in the characters of the women whose names we find there.

We believe that it is the duty, and the privilege of woman to work not only for the good and prosperity of the church of which she is a member, but also for the advancement of the Redeemer's kingdom in the world. We claim this as our duty, because Christ commands it. He says, "follow me," to every one of us today, as plainly as he said it to the fishermen of Galilee. If we follow him, we will labor with him for the salvation of a world for whose redemption he left the shining courts of Heaven, and the glory that he had with the Father before the world was. And we claim it as our privilege, because He died for us, and we love him. He refused not the offering of precious ointment which Mary's love prompted her to bestow upon him, but said that wherever his name should be spoken, in time to come, this act of hers should also be told as a memorial of her. It is the nature of woman to work for what she loves; and it is with us as with all of Christ's people—the more we work for His cause, the more we love it.

But some of us good sisters, who are quite active in what is called "church work" are inclined to prescribe rather narrow limits for their labors. They are ready to help furnish and adorn the meeting house—to buy lamps, stoves, etc, or even to raise money for building the house. But talk to them of organizing a *Missionary Society,* and they "are not able to do anything"—or they are "in favor of attending to house duties first." They seem to feel that they have done their part, when they have toiled, and begged, and scolded, and denied themselves, until they have got their church-house ceiled painted and perhaps carpeted, the pulpit cushioned and furnished with seats, and the building warmed and lighted with stoves and chandeliers; while millions of immortal souls walk in darkness to the grave, with none to show them the way to heaven. Is this the "good part" which Mary chose, which should not be taken from her? Our house will crumble and decay, even as these frail bodies will: but a single soul, saved from death, will shine as the stars forever and ever, around the throne of God. We love to labor with our hands for these temples where we worship God. We love them; we want to see them rise, fair and comely, all over our beautiful land; we want them comfortable and decent within, as, alas! they often are *not*. All honor to our sisters who do their part in keeping the sanctuary of the Lord. But let us not do this, and leave the other undone. We must not wait until every church is lighted with an elegant chandelier before we send the lamp of God's word to the nations that sit in darkness.

Having concluded that it is our duty to work for missions, we should inquire what is the best way in which we can do it. Experience and common sense teach that in this as in all other undertakings, it is best to have some system by which to work. In the present undeveloped condition of most of our churches, Ladies' Missionary Societies seem to be the most successful means of enlisting the women of the church to labor for Christ. Some good people oppose these Societies. I am not competent to argue the question with these persons, but we will take it for granted that they admit it to be the duty of Christian women to do what they can for the spread of the gospel of Christ. If so, then perhaps it is the idea of women organizing themselves into an independent Society that is objectionable to them. Then I will say that in my view they ought not to be *independent,* so for as their relation to the churches are concerned. They should not be separate bodies, but rather a committee in the church, and responsible to it. And when our churches are fully alive to their duty in evangelizing the world, and with pastors who will lead them in the work, I think there will be no need of (Women's Missionary Societies) as they now exist. But there must be some obligation brought to bear in order to bring our people up to their duty in contributing of their time and means to the cause of Missions, and if there is in your church no plan or system by which each member is influenced to contribute regularly toward the spread of the gospel, then, my sister, you should consider whether it is not your duty to persuade others to join you in a society that will supplement, as it were, the work of the church. A Missionary Society may be a very simple thing. If Mrs. A. and Mrs. B. agree together that they will give so much each month for Missions, or will devote a certain part of their time to work to obtain money for Missionary purposes, that is a Missionary Society—that is, if they *do* what they agree to do. . . .

As an evidence of what Women's Missionary Societies have accomplished in our own denomination, we learn from the Handbook of the American Baptist Missionary Union, that of the 192 American Missionaries employed by that body, 44 are supported by the Women's Societies of the North and West. These Societies working through two central organizations—the "Woman's Baptist Missionary Society," (Boston) and "The Woman's Baptist Missionary Society of the West," (Chicago) contributed to the Missionary Union, during the year ending with March, 1882, more than $60,000. In the face of such facts, we cannot but thank God for Woman's Missionary Societies.

The Sunday School offers a wide field where woman may work for her Master. Let none despise it for the work of teaching our young people the truths of God's Word, in the Sunday School, is only second in importance to that of proclaiming it from the pulpit. Indeed, there is reason to believe that souls are brought to Christ through this means, that might never be reached from the pulpit. In this way the most timid woman may imitate the illustrious example of Priscilla, whose name, traced by the inspired pen, shines down through the ages as one who "taught the way of the Lord." When the Lord shall come to make up His jewels, how many thousands of them will be gathered from the classes in our Sunday Schools, taught from week to week by faithful, modest, consecrated women! In that day, they shall have their reward.

Dear Christian sister, what are *you* doing for Christ, who died for you? Let us pause a moment, amid the wearying routine of toil for the things that perish with the using; let us lift our thoughts above these, and see what treasures we may lay up in heaven. See that we strive for in this world—all that we fill our lives with care and anxiety to win— will by and by slip from our hands; what are they worth, compared to one soul, which it takes the blood of Jesus to buy? . . .

If there be one here who has ever listened to the cry from heathen shores—"Come over and help us!" and has felt it in her heart to say "Lord, send me!" let me solemnly entreat her to give heed to the impulse. God speaks to men no more by signs and miracles. The known need of laborers in a field—the desire to go there, and the opportunity of fitting yourself for the work may be the "call" which ought to summon you from your quite fireside in this Christian land, to the white fields of China, or Burmah, or Africa, there to do for our heathen sisters a work that our brethren can never do. It is woman that must bear the gospel to woman in some heathen lands: and while other states are sending their best and brightest daughters, shall Alabama have no share in the glorious harvest?

S. A. Chambers

C.   J. B. Hawthorne, Sermon on "Paul and the Women," 1891

In the providence of God I have been placed in the position of spiritual adviser and teacher to this congregation of Christian men and women. I am called by the spirit of God and the suffrages of this people to expound to them the teachings of the sacred Scriptures. My commission requires me to instruct, to exhort, to comfort, and rebuke. This is what God demands, and what you have a right to expect of me. Occupying this responsible and sacred position, I claim your respectful and devout attention this morning, while I attempt to set before you the teachings of the divine Word upon a subject of vital importance to the order, peace, and welfare of the churches of Jesus Christ.

The question which you have requested me to discuss is, "Do the Scriptures Forbid Women to Speak in Mixed Assemblies?" By mixed assemblies is meant public gatherings composed of men and women.

I feel that I owe to this congregation and community an explanation of my conduct in reference to this important matter. No man is more indebted to Christian women than I. No man in the gospel ministry has been more helped by them. They have understood me better than men. They have never misinterpreted my motives. They have always appreciated the difficulties and embarrassments connected with my work, and have given me their profoundest sympathy in every conflict with error and ungodliness. When the whisky rings and their hirelings sought to destroy me, the Christian women of this land stood by me with dauntless devotion.

Remembering these things, my sympathies have been with the women whenever they have met the opposition of men in any of their undertakings. I have almost assumed that in any conflict between men and women, the women were right.

If through God's infinite mercy I am ever permitted to see the face of the apostle Paul, I shall feel that I owe him an humble apology for having many times tried to believe, that in some unaccountable way he had made a prodigious mistake, and inflicted upon woman a cruel injustice in forbidding her to speak in the church. My sympathies, my prejudices, and three-fourths of my reading and thinking have been on the woman's side of this question. But the conflict is over. After a long and painful struggle I have made an unconditional surrender to conscience, and Paul, and the Holy Ghost.

What do the Scriptures teach upon this subject? The discussion must be limited to this single question. Your feelings, the opinions of men, and the spirit of the nineteenth century cannot be admitted into this controversy. It is a subject upon which God has spoken, and we cannot array human opinion or human feeling against his truth without aligning ourselves with Robert Ingersoll and his followers. . . .

On the question now before us we find in this "Book by inspiration given" a thus saith the Lord. "Let the women keep silence in the churches, for it is not permitted unto them to speak." By these words Baptists have stood through all the centuries of their existence, and by them they will continue to stand "till time's last thunder shakes the world."

I will state briefly some of the objections which are urged against the most obvious meaning of Paul's command.

1. It is claimed by some, not many, that the apostle did not intend to forbid women to take part in any SERIOUS discussion, but to prohibit them from indulging in IDLE CHATTER. It was the habit of women then, and it is in some places now, when they got together in a public meeting, to indulge in a great deal of chit chat or small talk. It is claimed by a few hard-pressed champions of a feeble cause, that it was this that Paul meant to forbid. . . .

2. Others claim that Paul's prohibition is limited to speaking in the church, and that while it would be unlawful for a woman to speak in a church, it is permissible in a prayer-meeting. In answer to this it is sufficient to say, that a meeting of this congregation for prayer is just as much a meeting of the church as a meeting to hear the preaching of the gospel. The word church was applied by the New Testament writers to meetings in private houses. It is not necessary for us to come into this building to have a meeting of the First Baptist Church of Atlanta. The same persons gathered together in any private house of this city for religious worship would be the First Baptist Church.

3. There are some who contend that Paul could not have forbidden women to speak

upon religious subjects in meetings of the church, because there were prophetesses in those days, and such were allowed to speak.

That there were females among the early Christian churches who corresponded to those known among the Jews as prophetesses is admitted; but there is no conclusive evidence to show that either practice is itself right, but to condemn the manner of the performance as a violation of all the rules of propriety and subordination.

On another occasion, in this very epistle, he fully condemns the practice in any form, and enjoins silence on the female members of the church in public meetings. . . .

Let us suppose that Paul did permit women to deliver their prophecies before mixed assemblies. We know that he did not permit them to TEACH on such occasions. He wrote to Timothy: "Let the women learn in silence in all modesty. But I suffer not a woman to teach, nor to usurp authority over the man, but to be in silence." If he permitted them to prophesy, but not to TEACH, there must have been some radical difference between the office of the prophet and that of the teacher. What was that difference? The prophet was a revelator. He revealed things concerning the past, the present, or the future, which were hidden from the world. He was simply a mouth-piece for God. He said nothing on his own responsibility. He simply uttered what God had spoken to him.

The function of the teacher was to expound what had been revealed, to explain, to make clear to the church the meaning of God's revealed will.

Now, sometimes the two offices were performed by the same person; but if women were forbidden to TEACH, it follows that the function of the prophetess was limited to revealing mysteries.

We cannot fail to see the conclusion to which this brings us. If Paul permitted women to speak in the churches of his day, the privilege was limited to those who had the gift of prophecy—those to whom God made known secrets that hitherto were hid in the great deep of His own mind. And if the speaking of women in meetings of the church was confined to those who had the gift of prophecy, then women of THIS day are not scripturally qualified to speak to the church because they have not the gift of prophecy.

Do the women of this day who go into mixed assemblies and speak claim to be prophets? Do they claim that what they say is a revelation from God? If they do, and their claim be true, their utterances should be written down and incorporated with the other Sacred Scriptures. If they are indeed prophets, inspired and accredited as Isaiah, Jeremiah, Daniel, Peter, Paul and John were, then we have abundant material to make a new Bible every week.

But are they prophets? They cannot be if Paul has spoken the mind of God. What does he say? In immediate connection with these words forbidding women to speak in the church, he says: "If any man think himself to be a prophet or spiritual let him acknowledge that the things which I write unto you are the commandments of the Lord."

But that is just what the women-preachers will not acknowledge. They stubbornly declare that what Paul wrote upon this subject is not "the commandment of the Lord." Some of them say that he was a dissatisfied and crabbed old bachelor who was prejudiced against women, and imposed this restriction upon them only to show his dislike of them. . . .

Now where there is this conflict between Paul and the women what shall I do? What ought I to do? The Lord knows how distressful it is to me not to go with the women. Without their sympathy and friendship this world would be to me a solitude. But having Adam's experience before me, how foolish it would be for me to follow these daughters of Eve in violating a law as simple and legible as God could make it?

4. The position on which the advocates of this new doctrine and practice rely more than any other, and to which they cling with the greatest persistence, is that the law which Paul lays down in his letter to the Corinthians was intended only for the Corinthian church—that it was purely a local regulation made necessary by a peculiar and exceptional state of things among the Christians of Corinth.

This position is utterly untenable. Any one can see at a single glance that Paul did not make this law for the Corinthian women only. He wrote the same thing to Timothy that he might apply it to the churches in the region about Ephesus.

In his letter to Timothy he assigns two reasons for not permitting women to teach and pray in a mixed assembly.

1. "For Adam was first formed, then Eve." Now the Corinthians were not the only people in the world who had descended from Adam and Eve. All nations, kindreds, tongues and tribes have descended from Adam and Eve. I trust that the people of Atlanta, and especially the members of the First Baptist Church, have not ceased to believe that even they are descendants of Adam and Eve. I entreat these female apostles of the new Gospel and new dispensation to permit us to hold on to that much of the old Bible.

If we have descended from Adam and Eve, then Paul's law forbidding women to speak before mixed assemblies was not local, and is binding on the women of the First Baptist Church of Atlanta.

"Adam was first formed." The man was formed out of the dust of the earth. The woman was formed out of the man. She was formed for him, for his help and companionship. Here lies the strength of the reason which the apostle gives for the divine law that the woman shall be in subjection to the man. She is to be in subjection to the man not so much because she was made after the man, for she and the man were both created after the beasts of the field, but because she was made out of the man and for him.

So the woman's subjection to the man is according to the laws of nature and creation.

Now, Paul says that when a woman goes into a church and teaches or preaches in the presence of men, she reverses God's order and violates the laws of her own nature and creation. "I suffer not a woman to teach, nor usurp authority over the man." Teaching implies authority over those who are taught, and as a woman has not, according to God's economy, authority over man, she is not permitted to stand up in a public assembly and teach him. God knows that millions of women have the ability to teach men; but he does not permit them to do it, at least in a public way, because it has the appearance of authority.

2. The second reason which Paul had for prohibiting women from speaking in mixed assemblies was "That Adam was not deceived: but the woman being deceived was in the transgression." . . .

D. Essay on Women Speaking in Public, 1898

> • Is It a Blessing to Them, or to the Men Who Listen?
>
> BY A NORTHERN PASTOR

It is known that women in the North, in large numbers, maintain as "a right" their liberty to speak before mixed assemblies. So far as these women are concerned, the question before us hardly admits of debate—indeed, does not. Men have looked upon the question in the midst of real mental conflict, some to answer it in the negative some to answer in the affirmative, some to say, "We must submit to the inevitable."

If Baptists of the North have erred in encouraging women to speak in public, they not only continue to commit that error, but are undoubtedly confronted by a serious problem connected with woman's place and work in the Redeemer's kingdom. If it is a sin for woman to long for this kind of publicity, she stands not alone in her sin—the preachers of the North must share it with her. And when the time comes to take a stand either for or against woman's addressing mixed assemblies, in answer to the question as to her having the necessary qualifications for the pastorate, there will be "great searchings of heart." If things progress in the North for twenty-five years more in the present direction, this question will surely come, What then? But, out of strict fairness to the question, let us present two sides. Let us look at this, first, from the view-point of the women who advocate this "right."

In the first place, the claim of woman's intellectual equality with man is asserted, and from it is drawn the inference that what woman can do let her do it. If God has endowed woman with natural gifts equal to man's who dare set a limit to her exercising these gifts? Now that the great colleges and universities afford women the same opportunity of self-culture that men enjoy, and now that it is demonstrated beyond all question that the average woman at college does better work than the average man, the conclusion seems inevitable that woman is not only man's intellectual equal (if not superior), but should also enjoy with him a common field of labor, being debarred from nothing open to men.

Then, too, taking woman's interest in humanity—has she not an equal share in the destiny of the race? Has not every human now living cost some woman a great price in birth and nature? Shall man say to woman: "Now stand aside; let me use my gifts in this way; there is no place for you in public life?" Shall woman not be a reformer? And if a reformer, shall she not preach? And if she preaches, shall she not be pastor? Coming more directly to the church life, are not the majority of our church-members women? Two-thirds of the members of Baptist churches in the North are women! Is it in keeping with reason to suppose that women shall keep silence in the churches when the burden of church support falls on them? The conclusion is—no!

But when the teaching of scripture is dealt with by women, as they confront the question of their "right" to speak before mixed assemblies, there is a diversity of method. Some women allow themselves to indulge in comments on Paul's teaching, which show that they have lax views of inspiration, or a spirit of irreverence. So they speak against Paul as unfit to take an impartial view of the subject. Others, more guarded, seek to show that Paul on this, as on some other points in his writings, must have dealt with questions and customs peculiar to his own times; and, as times have so greatly changed, and woman's condition has changed with them, the inference is that what he says about women keeping silence in the churches is not to be regarded as of permanent force.

Here, then, is a fair statement of the case, so far as women, who favor their sex speaking in public, are concerned.

Let us now turn to the other side of the question.

Granting all that woman's mental equality may demand, the question might be asked: Is it simply a question of mental equality? The weightier elements that enter into the discussion are to be found elsewhere. And so far as woman's education at the same schools with men is concerned, that admits of debate in spite of the position of eminent teachers of to-day. We are not to be too hasty in asserting that there is no place for women's colleges, and that the training of women should be identical with the training of men. Such questions can only be settled by appeals to facts, and the facts do not all fall on one side.

Woman's place and work in the church presents a question of no small magnitude. We have already stated that two-thirds of the members of our churches in the North are women; and no doubt the proportion of men is on the decrease. You will at once see that the immediate outlook is not bright for our churches in the North. It simply means that multitudes of men who have been brought up in homes nominally Christian, have no faith in religion. But to the argument: If women have such a numerical preponderance, and if they bear in such large measure the burdens of the churches, why should they not have a voice in the affairs—all the affairs of the church? If she can speak, why not let her do so? The writer at this point wishes to say what he has for some time felt to be the truth: Many men, there is reason to believe, are alienated from our churches by women speaking too much. It is not classing women as weak beings when men decline to be addressed by them in mixed assemblies. If the truth were known, the writer fully believes, many a church is dying in the borders of the North, because the women insist on doing so much of the talking in all kinds of meetings. This public exercise of women, and the numerical disparity, between men and women in the membership, place men at a disadvantage in management of church affairs; and we have yet to know of a strong church which does not have a strong membership of men. . . .

Touching upon the Scripture already reverted to, the writer will not attempt an exegesis; that has been often performed. Of one thing we may rest assured, the Apostle Paul's language is very plain. You do not need to know Greek in order to understand him when he says, "Let your women keep silence in the churches." That may mean the church at Corinth and vicinity, though Paul speaks elsewhere on the subject in writing to Timothy. It may mean that he is speaking for his own times, and not for ours. It may mean, too, that he is speaking for our time, and that he is guided by the Holy Spirit to utter a wise principle whose validity shall not be affected by time. The wisdom of his words may at this very hour be receiving a powerful demonstration in a great many ways. It is certainly true that no man can, in view of the facts, positively limit the meaning of the utterance of Paul to his time or to the conditions of society when he wrote.

It is not hard to see, from what has been said, the leanings of the present writer. For years he has been used to the public work of women in the way we are now discussing. But he feels that having said so much, he should not close without frankly facing the head of this article. Is women's speaking in public a blessing to them, or is it a blessing to the men who listen? Can we answer that question? Perhaps not absolutely with "yes" or "no;" but we believe we can answer it in a way both general and definite—general as to the principle involved, and definite as to its application. One or two general facts deserve attention.

(1) Woman's natural constitution, as a rule, does not fit her for public address. Her nerves are made delicate by her Creator, and civilization has made them more delicate. The nervous strain of public address is certainly more wearing on her than on a man. She is more easily excited, more easily depressed than man, and nature would suggest that she keep her life free from publicity, at least from the publicity of a mixed assemblage.

(2) Another fact which is worthy of notice: The woman who devotes herself to public speaking, as a rule, becomes unwomanly; she becomes, generally speaking, hardened and uninviting in bearing. Can any woman afford to do this, on slight ground?

(3) As a rule, men are not drawn to women who seek a public career. This either means that men do not know what kind of a woman to appreciate, or it means that such women lose one element (or more) of their attractiveness by becoming public speakers.

(4) Back of this whole matter lies a great field of facts, which would require another paper the length of this to so much as outline. The social condition in the north is favorable to womans losing sight of her place. Now understand me, if you please. The outlook for marriage in the case of multitudes of noble women is exceedingly unpromis-

ing. If they have no money, they have unequal chances of marriage. Marriage is becoming to be largely a business transaction. This is one side.

Among many educated women there is an ambition to be independent and pay no attention to the matter of marriage. This ambition may take one of many directions. And be it said with sorrow that many married women, highly trained in our schools, regard a family as an embarrassment, children as a burden, an obstacle in the way of their ambition.

In short, there is a close competition in many fields, between the men and women of the North, especially between young men and young women. And this competition becomes more and more intense.

Are we not warranted in saying that false ideals of womanhood and womanliness are set before many northern women, and that in pursuing these ideals the desire to be before the public at any cost has not been wholly lacking? Can women's public speaking prove a blessing to them or to the men who listen, if these things be true? Southern people can at least reflect on this question.

11.17   Letters from Lottie Moon

Few people have made such an impact upon Southern Baptist life as Charlotte Diggs Moon (1814-1912). Miss "Lottie" Moon served for almost forty years as a missionary in North China. She is said to have mastered the Chinese language and integrated into the Chinese culture more thoroughly than any other Westerner has ever done.

A daughter of privilege and affluence in the old South, Lottie Moon received the best education available at a time when that was unusual for girls. After the Civil War she became a schoolteacher in Georgia. In 1873 she was appointed by the SBC Foreign Mission Board as a missionary in China, where her younger sister Edmonia already served.

Though she was by all accounts an effective missionary in China, Lottie Moon's major impact was upon the Baptists in this country. Stories of her loneliness and hardships drew an emotional response from Southern Baptists. Her letter to H. A. Tupper (selection A) reveals a woman of understanding and insight. *Source:* Handwritten copy, Roberts Library, Southwestern Baptist Theological Seminary, Ft. Worth, Tex. Drawing from the example of Methodist women, Miss Moon suggested that Baptists take up a Christmas offering for missions (selection B). *Source: Foreign Mission Journal,* Dec. 1887, 10. She would no doubt be shocked to learn that the offering so modestly launched in 1888 would a century later approach the sum of $100 million a year and that it would, since 1918, bear her name.

A.   Letter to H. A. Tupper, 1887

Rev. Dr. H. A. Tupper:

My dear Brother,

In reading Williams' Middle Kingdom, one is surprised at the slow steps by which China was opened to the Western world. One is astonished at the gross ignorance of the Chinese officials and at the amazing assumptions of superiority consequent thereupon.

Morrison, the first Protestant missionary to China, was not allowed to go beyond the small space allotted to foreigners outside the city of Canton. He worked on in faith, compiling his dictionary and translating Scriptures, being permitted to see but small fruit of his labors for the conversion of souls. Later, in the providence of God, the first Treaty ports, Canton, Amoy, Aingpo, Toochow and Shanghai were thrown open to commerce and to missionary effort. Still no one was allowed to go into the interior. The longing aspirations of Christian hearts that China should be open to the gospel were still unsatisfied. Another war arose and as its result Peking received Western legations and Christian missions were at once established there. Virtually the whole country was open, but there was still a feeling of insecurity among foreigners. The government had taken no pains to inform the people of the changed state of affairs. An English consular agent, travelling with passport from Peking was brutally murdered. England demanded a large indemnity with the alternative of war. The indemnity was paid and Chinese officials thenceforth bestirred themselves to impress upon the people the fact that foreigners were under government protection. Then came the fearful famine and large sums were contributed, chiefly in England, to aid the starving people. Missionaries laid down their lives in the hard and trying work of distribution to the fever-stricken and starving.

Now, as the result of all these wonder-workings of God's providence, China, once hermetically sealed to Western intercourse, is wide open for residence or for travel. More than that, a mighty change is being wrought in the feelings of the people toward foreigners. No true missionary cares for physical hardships. He endures them without a regretful or discontented thought. But "The iron enters the soul" when all his advances are met by suspicion, coldness, dislike or actual hatred. For many long years, this was what missionaries in China had to endure. Happily that state of things is rapidly passing away. The change is very marked in the prosecution of country work in the Tungchow region. Where of old we were met by cold, averted glances, by violence and dislike, we are greeted now by smiles and words of cordial welcome. The mere idle gaze of curiosity is in many cases exchanged for thoughtful, earnest, respectful attention to the words of life. I have just returned today from a short trip to the country. I was much delighted by the friendliness of the people. I am more and more impressed by the belief that to win these people to God we must first win them to ourselves. We need to go out and live among them, manifesting the gentle and loving spirit of our Lord. But what can we do, so few amid so many? We have four missionaries here in Tungchow. How many can we reach? One missionary could spend months with profit in a circle of a dozen villages. We have in this country some hundreds of villages. By short, hasty visits we might reach them perhaps once a year, but to what profit? We need to make friends before we can hope to win converts. We should have scores of workers for every one that we have now in the field. I have spoken only of the region about Tungchow, but what of the regions beyond? What of Whonghein, with its eight hundred villages and its four missionaries? What of Pingtu where we have pleaded to have missionaries sent? What of that vast region beyond with its teeming millions?

One is amazed that Christians in the West do not bestir themselves to give the gospel to this people. The prayer in former times was that God would open China. God has answered that prayer and now, who goes forth to possess the land? Where are the hundred missionaries that we ought to have today in Shantung if we would even *begin* to reach these people? Where is the silver and the gold that should be in the Lord's treasury to send out those men and women who are asking to be sent to the heathen? Alas! Alas! Some are adding more fields to their broad lands, some are laying up in banks, some are spending in selfish indulgence. So these heathen people go down to death without ever having heard the name of Jesus. In the day of Judgment, at whose door will lie the sin?

L. Moon

Tungchow,
March 19, 1887

B. Letter About Formation of Woman's Missionary Society, 1887

In a former letter I called attention to the work of Southern Methodist women, endeavoring to use it as an incentive to stir up the women of our Southern Baptist churches to greater zeal in the cause of missions. I have lately been reading the minutes of the ninth annual meeting of the Woman's Board of Missions, M. E., South, and find that in the year ending in June, they raised over sixty-six thousand dollars. Their work in China alone involved the expenditure of more than thirty-four thousand dollars, besides which they have missions in Mexico, Brazil, and the Indian Territory. They have nine workers in China, with four more under appointment and two others recommended by the committee for appointment. I notice that when a candidate is appointed, straight way some conference society pledges her support in whole or in part. One young lady is to be sent out by means of the liberal offer of a Nashville gentleman, to contribute six hundred dollars for travelling expenses. A gentleman in Kansas gave five thousand dollars to build a church in Shanghai in connection with woman's work there.

The efficient officers of this Methodist Woman's organization do their work without pay. Travelling and office expenses are allowed the President of the Board of Missions. This money is to be used at her discretion in visiting conference societies that are not able to pay her expenses. Office expenses alone are allowed the Corresponding Secretary and her assistant, and also to the Treasurer. A sum is appropriated for publications, postage, and mite boxes. The expenses for all purposes are less than seventeen hundred dollars. In a word, Southern Methodist women, in one year, have contributed to missions, clear of all expenses, nearly sixty-five thousand dollars! Doesn't this put us Baptist women to shame? For one, I confess I am heartily ashamed.

In the matter of appointments to mission work, extreme care is taken in the selection of candidates, and, judging by the high character and efficient work of Southern Methodist women in China, this care is not exercised in vain. Candidates are sent up by the societies of their respective conferences. There is a standing committee on examination of candidates. Above this is a committee on missionary candidates appointed at the annual meeting. There is also an educational committee, whose duty it is to ascertain if the applicant comes up to the required standard in education. When the candidate has satisfactorily passed these various examining committees the case comes before the Board, and the applicant, if accepted, is recommended to the Bishop for appointment.

I am convinced that one of the chief reasons our Southern Baptist women do so little is the lack of organization. Why should we not learn from these noble Methodist women, and instead of the paltry offerings we make, do something that will prove that we are really in earnest in claiming to be followers of him who, "though he was rich, for our sake became poor?" How do these Methodist women raise so much money? By prayer and self-denial. Note the resolution "unanimously approved" by the meeting above:

"*Resolved,* That this Board recommend to the Woman's Missionary Society to observe the week preceding Christmas as a week of prayer and self-denial." "In preparation for this,

"*Resolved,* That we agree to pray every evening for six months, dating from June 25, 1887, for the outpouring of the Holy Spirit on the Woman's Missionary Society and its work at home and in the foreign fields."

Its "work at home," be it noted, is to arouse an interest and collect money for the foreign field, as also the Indian Territory.

Need it be said why the week before Christmas is chosen? Is not "the festive season, when families and friends exchange gifts in memory of The Gift laid on the altar of the world for the redemption of the human race, the most appropriate time to consecrate a portion from abounding riches and scant poverty to send forth the good tidings of great joy into all the earth?"

In seeking organization we do not need to adopt plans or methods unsuitable to the views, or repugnant to the tastes of our brethren. . . . Power of appointment and of disbursing funds should be left, as heretofore, in the hands of the Foreign Mission Board. Separate organization is undesirable, and would do harm; but organization in subordination to the Board is the imperative need of the hour.

Some years ago the Southern Methodist Mission in China had run down to the lowest water-mark; the rising of the tide seems to have begun with the enlisting of the women of the church in the cause of missions. The previously unexampled increase in missionary zeal and activity in the Northern Presybterian church is attributed to the same reason—the thorough awakening of the women of the church upon the subject of missions. In like manner, until the women of our Southern Baptist churches are thoroughly aroused, we shall continue to go in our present "hand to mouth" system. We shall continue to see mission stations so poorly manned that missionaries break down from overwork, loneliness, and isolation; we shall continue to see promising fields unentered and old stations languishing; and we shall continue to see other denominations no richer and no better educated than ours, outstripping us in the race. I wonder how many of us really believe that "it is more blessed to give than to receive." A woman who accepts that statement of our Lord Jesus Christ as a fact, and not as "impracticable idealism," will make giving a principle of her life. She will lay aside sacredly not less than one-tenth of her income or her earnings as the Lord's money, which she would no more dare to touch for personal use than she would steal. How many there are among our women, alas! alas! who imagine that because "Jesus paid it all," they need pay nothing, forgetting that the prime object of their salvation was that they should follow in the footsteps of Jesus Christ in bringing back a lost world to God, and so aid in bringing the answer to the petition our Lord taught his disciples. "Thy kingdom come."

L. Moon.

Tungchow, Sept. 15, 1887.

12
Baptist Beginnings in Europe

From their beginnings in the early-nineteenth century, European Baptists have had their own distinctive identity and spiritual flavor. This major community among Baptists of the world has both similarities to and differences from the British and American branches of the Baptist family.

Most historians agree that Baptists originated as a separate denomination in the early-seventeenth century. They emerged out of the intense desire for biblical reform in the English Puritan and Separatist movements. However, European Baptists originated over two centuries later, from quite different sources. Baptists on the Continent took their rise from the wave of Pietist awakenings that swept Europe after 1800. These Pietist awakenings emphasized reading of the Bible, personal religious faith, and spiritual disciplines like prayer and meditation. Those caught up in this intense spiritual movement generally adopted a life-style more inward and quietist than was characteristic of those Baptists who stemmed from more activistic forms of British Purtanism. European Baptists have also had to cope with intense persecution, both from hostile civil governments and equally hostile state churches.

The documents included in this chapter are chosen to illustrate the beginnings and spirit of Baptist life in Europe. One is not surprised that Johann Gerhard Oncken shows up prominently in these documents. It would be difficult to overstate his importance in early European Baptist history.

12.1 Baptist Beginnings in Germany

Baptist beginnings in Germany center around Johann Gerhard Oncken (1800-1884), who is known as the "Father of Continental Baptists." Oncken was born in Varel, Germany, but lived for years in Scotland and England. He was influenced by the evangelical Haldane movement in Scotland, and later served as a Bible distributor in England. He was back in Germany by 1823, and in 1834 adopted Baptist views. Oncken proved to be a one-man missionary society. He traveled widely throughout Europe, forming churches and strengthening Baptist work. He served an almost apostolic role among European Baptists.

Two documents are included here describing the work of Oncken. Selection A describes the formation of the church in Hamburg in 1834, the oldest surviving Baptist church in Europe. This also includes an account of Oncken's baptism by Barnas Sears, the American professor. *Source:* Proceedings of the Eighth Triennial Meeting of the Baptist General Convention for Missionary Purposes, Richmond, 1835, 26-27. Selection B gives excerpts from Oncken's 1839 report to the Triennial Convention in America, which had sponsored him as a missionary. *Source:* Proceedings of the Ninth Triennial Meeting of the Baptist General Convention for Foreign Missions, Boston, 1839, 10.

A. Formation of the Church at Hamburg, 1834

God prepared the way for the operations of the Board, by raising up at Hamburg, a man, who seems to be well fitted to be a pioneer. He is thus described, in a letter from Professor Sears, who was requested by the Board to make inquiries in Germany, respecting the religious state and wants of the country:—

"I know not that there is any regular Baptist church in all the north of Germany. Of the Mennonites, I have nothing to say now; but aside from them, there are in Germany not a few individuals who are Baptists in sentiment. On my arrival at Hamburg, I called on Mr. Oncken, whom I found to be in all respects an interesting man. He is a German, a little more than thirty years of age, married in England, has two children, is perfectly master of the English language, (which is spoken much in Hamburg,) and though not a man of liberal education, has a very strong, acute mind, has read much, is a man of much practical knowledge, and is very winning in his personal appearance and manners. From 1823 to 1828, he was a missionary of the Continental Society, and preached in Hamburg and vicinity, with very considerable success. Since that time, he has been agent of the Edinburgh Bible Society, and has more influence than any other man in selecting the publications of the Lower Saxony Tract Society. . . . He has at length become so thoroughly a Baptist, that he cannot be satisfied without being a member of a Baptist church, and the second day after my arrival, he requested me to baptize him; but in consequence of his going to Poland as an agent of the Bible Society, to be absent two or three months, and also of a variety of circumstances connected with the formation of a church, it was deemed advisable to defer it until spring. Six or eight (Mrs. Oncken is one of the number) are wishing to receive the ordinance at the same time. The design at present is, that after his return, I, in connection with some other Baptist minister, if possible, (I know of no one nearer than Switzerland,) should go to Hamburg, administer the ordinance, form a church, and ordain Mr. Oncken pastor. . . .

The Board immediately adopted measures to secure the services of Mr. Oncken, as a missionary, and they placed, in the mean while, at the disposal of Professor Sears, a moderate sum, to be expended, at his discretion, in promoting the cause of religion, in connection with the Baptist churches in Germany.

On the 22d April, 1834, Mr. Oncken and six other individuals were baptized by Professor Sears, and were the next day formed into a church, of which Mr. Oncken was ordained as the Pastor. The present condition of this church, and other particulars relative to the religious condition of Germany, may be learned from the following extracts from a letter of Professor Sears to the Corresponding Secretary, dated Berlin, Nov. 10th, 1834:—

"The church at Hamburg are very happily united, are unmolested by the government, and are in a prosperous state. Thirteen have been baptized in all. Of these, one young brother has recently died of the cholera. His last words, addressed to a friend who was not pious, were, 'O how blessed is religion in the hour of death! I know where I am going.' . . .

"The church hold a meeting by themselves in one place on Sabbath morning, where other serious persons attend, and in another place in the afternoon, public preaching, before a congregation that is constantly increasing. They have also several prayer meetings. Five of the male members have taken different districts of the city, which they visit as missionaries, regularly, once in two weeks. In some cases, two go together, the more and the less experienced being united. If we consider the pagan state of that great city, we must look upon this missionary labor of private brethren as truly apostolical. Great results have not yet been witnessed, but every thing wears an encouraging aspect. . . . The immediate vicinity of Hamburg, especially between there and Bremen, is an inviting field of labor. . . . Truly these disciples are lambs in the midst of wolves, and some of them have been prejudiced against those who have been to them the instruments of so much good. If bro. Oncken could be enabled to make frequent short missionary tours to these and similar places, and then once or twice in a year, to take a longer tour, to hold personal interviews with different individuals scattered over Germany, who begin to see at least trees as men walking, converse with them on the doctrines and discipline of the Christian church, and prepare the way for subsequent correspondence and cooperation, and know what places to direct his traveling brethren to visit, [then we believe Baptist work in Germany would advance rapidly.]

B. Johann Gerhard Oncken, Report on Early Baptists in Germany, 1839

The following summary view of the German mission is given in a letter of Mr. Oncken, under date of Feb. 8, 1839:

The church at Hamburg, the past year, has been sheltered under the wings of the Almighty. No root of bitterness has troubled us; uninterrupted peace and harmony have prevailed. The seed sown has been abundantly blessed, and 25 converts have been added to our number, and with the exception of two, have proved faithful to their profession. We have now 75 members, with 25 catechumens, of whom 10 or 12 have experienced the power of divine grace in the heart, and who will shortly be added to us. Let us raise here an *Ebenezer* to our adorable God. It is now nearly five years when we were first led down into the Elbe, 7 in number, with nothing but contending elements around us, every man's hand being against us. And now this flock is so numerous. Not unto us, O Lord, not unto us, but to thy name be the glory.

From the authorities we have experienced no trouble, though we are still under the same restrictions as before. We baptize generally at some distance from Hamburg, on Hanoverian territory, as we dare not do so on Hamburg ground. The brethren continue to exert themselves in the spread of the truth, and many sinners have through their instrumentality been brought under the sound of the gospel. Several of them have visited different parts of Holstein during the winter, and have distributed tracts and bibles.

But let me proceed to state what God has wrought in the south. I went, the last September, to Stuttgart, where I remained about twelve days; and on the 9th of October, eight dear brethren were baptized, five miles from Stuttgart, in the Neckar. The Lord abundantly blessed his own ordinance, so that they all went on their way rejoicing, and from that day new additions were constantly made. I was constantly engaged in examining candidates, and 23 converts were baptized in the name of the Triune Jehovah, and formed into a gospel church. The blessedness I experienced in those days cannot be expressed. I left Stuttgart with loud hosannas to God on my tongue. But the best still comes. The brethren at Stuttgart soon confessed openly what had taken place, and the whole city was moved. Article after article appeared in the newspapers, which were transferred into other papers, and before I reached home the thing was known throughout Germany. . . .

At Marburg, in Hessia, I also formed interesting connections, and preached there several times; and three brethren have since applied for baptism.

At Berlin, the opposition to the good old way appears to be greater than in any other place, and the prospects are not bright.

To Jever, in East Friesland, I have sent one of our members, as a colporteur, and his labors are blessed. Seven converts are waiting my arrival, and others give pleasing indications, that a good work has been begun in them.

12.2 Johann Gerhard Oncken, Letter to American Baptist Tract Society, 1834

A part of the genius of Johann Gerhard Oncken was his ability to enlist others to aid his evangelistic work in Europe. At different times, and often at the same time, Oncken represented a number of missionary societies in England, Scotland, and America. One of the agencies that assisted Oncken was the American Baptist Tract Society, as the following report shows.

From his youth, Oncken had been impressed by the power of the printed word. Tracts had helped bring about his own conversion, and he had distributed Christian literature as part of his early witness. As a Baptist, Oncken distributed Bibles, tracts, and other types of literature throughout Europe. He valued English-language materials, especially tracts and books dealing with the subject of baptism. He obtained much of this material from the Baptist Tract Society in America. The following letter describes Oncken's activities early in his ministry. *Source:* Eleventh Annual Report, Baptist General Tract Society, Philadelphia, 1835.

Gottingen, 9th mo. 30th, 1834.

My dear Brother,— I feel greatly indebted to the Directors of the Baptist General Tract Society, for the many excellent books sent me, most of which are already in circulation, especially those on baptism—they arrived at a time when they were greatly needed. If I am spared to return to Hamburg, I shall be again under the necessity to apply for a fresh grant. The English language is now much studied, so that I can always make good use of books and tracts in that language.

As the subject of baptism has been, since the recent occurrence at Hamburg, more a point of investigation, and as that holy ordinance is entirely neglected, and instead of it, a mere human invention has taken its place, I would urge the Directors of the Baptist General Tract Society, very warmly, to take into early consideration, the importance of having another tract on that subject translated into German and published as early as possible. The former little tract, 'Scripture Manual,' has already done much good, if not in influencing persons to apply for baptism, at least in causing them to doubt the truth and practice of infant sprinkling, and in leading them to a closer examination of the word of God on these subjects. . . . But the fear of men, and the probable persecution that will arise, unless God prevent it, is a bar to many to come boldly forward and follow their Lord and Master. Should I become connected with the Baptist Missionary Society, I should then have an immense field for the distribution of Tracts. I pray that the great Head of the Church, may direct my beloved brethren in America, and my unworthy self, to adopt such measures as he will own and bless in the extension of pure and undefiled religion.

The state of this country, (Hanover) is truly awful. The gospel is not preached, the Bible is not read, the Sabbath is universally profaned, and the use of ardent spirits, has been and is still increasing to an alarming extent. I heard a sermon last Sabbath at E.——— on account of which I could wish to weep tears of blood. Only here and there I have met with a solitary Christian, or a minister, who holds to something like sound views on the leading doctrines of our holy religion. . . .

The Tract Society at Hamburg is flourishing and doing much good—it issued last year upwards of 300,000 tracts, a considerable proportion of which were sent to Russia, the south of Germany and Switzerland.

I am now reading the memoir of that excellent woman, Mrs. Judson, and by the blessing of God, it has done me already much good. I am very anxious that it should be translated, as by that means it would familiarize many minds with the Baptists, and produce in them a friendly disposition, which cannot be effected by putting works in their hands, that treat exclusively on the subject of baptism. Can you do any thing in furtherance of this object? A considerable number would be sold, but the risk is too great for my means to undertake it alone. . . .

. . . Your unworthy but affectionate brother in Christ Jesus.

J. G. Oncken

12.3   German Baptist Confession of Faith, 1847

Baptists in Germany and, to some extent, throughout Europe had their own origins in the nineteenth century, largely independent of British Baptist origins two centuries earlier. However, later contacts between Baptists in England, America and the Continent were quite extensive, both in personal visits and by the printed word. Therefore it is not surprising that Baptist confessions in Europe should bear similarity to those elsewhere. That is the case with the pioneer German Baptist confession of 1847. The following gives brief excerpts from that confession. Translation is by Terry G. Carter. *Source:* Günter Balders, Theurer Bruder Oncken, *Das Leben Johann Gerhard Onckens in Bildern and Dokumenten* (Oncken Verlag Wuppertal und Kassel, 1978), 89-90, 118.

On Baptism

Baptism is a first fruit of faith and love toward Christ, the entry into obedience toward the Lord and into His church. It is the ceremonial declaration, the confession of the sinner, who has recognized the horribleness of sin and the damnation of his total being; that he should put all his hope alone on the death and resurrection of Jesus Christ, his saviour, and should believe in Him as the saviour from the curse and wages of sin; that he should dedicate himself with body and soul to Christ and should put Him on as his righteousness and strength; that he should surrender his old being to death and should want to walk with Christ in a new life.

But Baptism is also the ceremonial declaration and assurance of God toward the believing candidate for baptism, that he is submerged in Christ Jesus, and therefore with him has died, has been buried, and resurrected; that his sins are washed away, and that he is a beloved child of God with whom the Father is well pleased. Baptism should evoke the conviction of his salvation and eternal bliss more pronouncedly, and such a thing God wants to work through a sealing with the Holy Spirit, however, only there where He previously has brought about through this (His) Spirit the true beatifying belief in the Son of God, in the power of His death and resurrection.

We believe that in these holy symbols (of the Lord's Supper) Christ gives his body and blood to the believers to take in a spiritual way. The communion of the body and blood of Christ in taking the Holy Lord's Supper should be to the believer a godly pledge, whereby the conviction of one's share in Christ and in His sacrifice is exalted and intensified and whereby the pardon of sins which is grasped by him in his belief is continually assured and renewed again and again.

On Oaths and War

We believe that authorities have been ordained by God and that He invests them with power for the protection of the righteous and for the punishment of the evil. We hold ourselves obligated to abide by all their laws unconditionally, if these laws do not restrict the free exercise of the duties of our Christian belief, and through a still and quiet life in all piety to facilitate for them their difficult task. Also we hold ourselves obligated according to God's command to pray for the authority that it might so manage its entrusted power according to His will and under His gracious protection that peace and justice through this would be maintained.

We believe that the misuse of the oath for the Christian is forbidden, but that the oath— . . . the reverential solemn invocation of our God as a witness of truth—[if it is] rightfully demanded and committed, is only a prayer of extraordinary form.

We believe that the authority, which also according to the New Testament, does not carry the sword in vain, has the right and duty according to godly laws to mete out the death penalty and also to use the sword against enemies of the land to protect those entrusted with their care and we therefore hold ourselves obligated if we are ordered by the authority [to do so] to serve in the army in war. However we can also heartily unite with those, who in regard to the oath and war service do not share our conviction.

We see ourselves not hindered through our belief to take on a position of authority.

12.4   Peter Mønster and Baptist Beginnings in Denmark

Judged by the amount of space given in the American religious press, the subject of Baptist beginnings in Europe must have been of great interest in America. The following article, describing local concern at the growth of Baptists in Denmark, is typical. Having cited the concern expressed in the *Fatherland*, this article then traces the conversion of Peter Mønster and early Baptist witness in Denmark. One notices that Baptist beginnings almost anywhere in Europe are directly or indirectly connected with Johann Gerhard Oncken of Germany. The material is here reproduced as it appeared, though some of the sentences are incomplete. *Source: The Christian Review,* xi, 1846, 278f.

The Baptist Controversy

The *Fatherland*, a Danish paper, says: "Are their [Baptists'] doctrines erroneous, [then] let the clergy and schoolmasters prove them to be so to the people. The schoolmaster, Rasmus Sorensen of Vensolv, however, a man whose love of truth and unaffected Christian faith are questioned by no one, has just published a book, entitled, "What is the Holy, Universal Church?" etc., in which he shows that infant baptism is neither evangelical nor apostolic. If it is not possible to refute him, and to render the errors of Baptists obnoxious, by counter arguments and proofs; but if, on the contrary, it must be admitted that their doctrines are confirmed by the word of God and the history of the Christian Church, then, in spite of imprisonments, condemnations, banishments, etc., there will soon be in Denmark as many Baptists as there are now Lutherans. Therefore we now call upon all the zealous disputants amongst the clergy by argument and proofs to refute the statements put forth in Rasmus [sic] Sorensen's book.

[An account of Baptist beginnings] Mr. Mønster, an engraver, and the leader of Danish Baptists, . . . some time since came to the conviction, . . . that neither infant baptism nor sprinkling for baptism was agreeable to the institution of Christ or the practice of the apostles. . . .

In 1839, Mr. Köbner, a Baptist from Hamburg, undertook a journey into Denmark by the suggestion of Mr. [Johann Gerhard] Oncken for the purpose of forming a connection with the awakened Danes. . . . "On the journey," says Mr. Köbner, "I succeeded in forming a friendly acquaintance with many believers, and held numerous and well attended meetings; but the doctrine of adult immersion as opposed to the sprinkling of children, found little acceptance among them. They clung to the latter with much greater firmness and decision than is generally the case in Germany. It happened one evening that a discussion arose on the subject of baptism between myself and a countryman by the name of Rasmus Ottesen, a man endowed with considerable natural abilities and held in great esteem among his fellow believers. He attacked me with violence, directed against me all the force of his wit, and [in] his heat advised me to go to Mønster in Copenhagen, where I should find people of my own stamp and similar taste.

This hostile intimation proved to be the means, appointed by God, for the formation of the present Baptist church in Denmark. Hurt by the bitterness and ill-treatment of my opponent, I became silent and thus terminated the conversation; when the thought occurred to me that the intimation he had given me might possibly be a hint from God, and I determined immediately to act upon it, altered my route, and proceeded directly to Copenhagen, which I had not intended to visit. Here I found a small spot that God himself had prepared, and into which, with trembling hands, I deposited the seed, small indeed as a grain of mustard seed, but which has already become a flourishing plant having put the forth three branches [churches]."

12.5   Grandma Lovegren, Sketch of Swedish Baptist Pioneers, 1950

The following letter was written by a Swedish woman in Oregon identified as "Grandma Love-gren." She was a daughter of Sven C. Nelson, one of the Swedish Baptist pioneers. The letter was sent to her grandson, a Dr. L. A. Lovegren of Fort Worth, Texas, in 1950. The letter contains a homely and ungrammatical, but apparently authentic, account of Baptist beginnings in Sweden. *Source:* Handwritten letter in Barnes-Baker Collection, Southwestern Baptist Theological Seminary, Ft. Worth, Tex.

Cherry Grove, Oregon
June 5th, 1950

Dear August

God bless you and keep you safe. Thank you for your letter of May 27th glad to hear from you. . . .

About the Baptist History. We have a couple of books. One is your Fathers given to him in 1912 by the author J. Bystrom. It is printed in the Swedish Language and I am wondering if you can read Swedish but the Conference may have them in English by now. . . .

A little about the first Baptists in Sweden, that I know about, is my Father and his two Brothers. My uncle F. O. Nelson was Born Aug. 28, 1809 My Father S. C. Nelson Born March 28, 1812 My uncle B. N. Nelson was the youngest but I do not have the date Father as well as Uncle Fred were Sailors or seamen. Fred first as he was older and Sven later. Both were converted first Fred in the Mariners Church in New York later Sven in the same place. Their Morther was a Christian but died while the boys were quite young. their Father wept when he saw that she was going and said What will become of the boys; their Mother answered. God will take care of the boys and they will teach you. After F. O. was converted, he had the opertunity to show his father the way of salvation.

It seems that uncle Ben (as we used to call him) stayed on land but was ready at the time that the others were ready to be Baptized Sep 21st 1848 in the late evening in a bay called Vallers vik (vik means Bay) where the first Baptism on Swedish soil was performed. the candidates were as followes Sofia Ulrika Nelson, F. O.'s wife, Sven Christian Nelson, my Father, Bernt Nicklas Nelson, my uncle, Andreas Wang, Abraham Lindstrom.

Uncle F. O. had been Baptized in Hamburg by J. G. Oncken in [the] Elbe River Aug 1st 1847 so he Joined with those Baptized in organising a church Sep 21st 1848. My mother and Ben's wife witnessed the Baptism from a distance. Another was Baptized feb. 13th 1849. I am not sure of dates but I think my parents came to America in 1853. Now there has crept in a little error, in that my Nephews, August Nelsons boys, are being introduced as direct decendants of F. O. Nelson although this History tells the same thing, that we know that, F. O. Nelson did not have children. Also I found that an old lady had told some visitors how that Bernt Nelsons wife's name was Christina and that she had twin girls that were so alike that the mother tied a red ribbon on one of their arm to know them a part. This is true so far but she had added, that they had early gone to Jesus, meaning that they had died this last is not true these my cousins grew up, came to America were Married and raised families, but their mother died when they were quite young and their father married again and had four children with his first wife and three children with his second wife.

I do not know if this will help you in your History study it is more about our immediate family.

love,   your Grandma Lovegren

12.6   A Description of the Russian Stundists, 1893

Russian Baptists took their rise from several different evangelical movements. Among these sources are: the traditional Baptists of the Johann Gerhard Oncken stamp; the German Mennonites of an Anabaptist heritage; the Russian dissenter sect known as Molokans; the Plymouth Brethren of England; and the Russian Stundists. The document cited below describes the Stundists—their origins, teachings, and practices. They were nicknamed from the German word *Stunde* (hour) because of their practice of meeting often for about an hour for Bible reading, prayer, and testimony. The Stundists' commitment to the Bible conditioned them to be open to Baptist teachings; many of them received immersion and affiliated with Baptist churches in Russia. *Source:* John Brown, *The Stundists: The Story of a Great Religious Revolt* (London: James Clarke & Co., 1893), v-vii, 1-6, 55-57, 62-64, 66-69.

IN the second half of last century [the 18th], and again in the second half of this [the 19th], Southern Russia has been the scene of widespread revolt, the first political, the second religious, both revolts taking place very much in the same latitude, only that one took its rise east of the Volga and the other in the provinces west of that great river. . . .

The great revolt of our own time is that of a people leaving, not the territory, but the religion of the Russian Empire. The story of this second revolt is here told for us with great vividness and power by one who is exceptionally qualified for the task, as being probably better acquainted with the Stundists than any one else who has written about them. . . . Yonder in the neighborhood of Kherson, where our great philanthropist John Howard fell before the plague in 1790, and where he lies buried, the Stundist movement took its rise some five and thirty years ago. The cause of its rise is an old and oft-repeated story in the history of Christianity. The official, State-recognised Church had become corrupt, had sunk into worldliness and death; gross immoralities and sensual lives on the part of the clergy had brought religion into uttermost contempt, when, at length, in the most unexpected way the breath of God began to breathe life among the dead. . . . The Stundist movement, as its name implies, had a German origin. As far back as 1778 the great Empress Catherine had colonised Kherson with peasants from the Suabian land, who brought with them their religion, their pastors, and their industrious, sober ways. . . . Some of the Russian peasants who had been helped in their poverty or ministered to in their sickness by their German neighbours began to attend their services—to keep the *stunden,* or *hours,* of praise and prayer; they learned to read, were furnished with the New Testament in their own language, and eventually some of them found the deeper blessing of eternal life. In this simple scriptural fashion this memorable movement began. . . .

Beginnings

The origin and first beginnings of this movement, which eventually acquired the name of Stundism, are involved in a good deal of uncertainty; but sufficient is known to enable us to form a tolerably accurate notion of the causes which led up to the greatest religious revolt of modern times. These are two-fold—one cause, the utter lifelessness of the Russian Orthodox Church; the other—an external cause—the increased spiritual life among the Germans settled in numerous colonies over the greater portion of Southern Russian.

To get at the real origin of Stundism we must inquire a little into both of these. The Russian Church, which had been galvanised into unhealthy activity by its fratricidal conflict with the Old Believers in the reign of Peter the Great, had, after its victory over these heretics, sunk into utter inanity and empty ceremonialism. Uncontrolled by any effective oversight of their training and conduct, the clergy had ceased to be anything more than dull and extortionate collectors of church fees. They led gross lives of drunkenness and immorality, unredeemed by any spark of religious life. They were despised by the meanest of their flocks, and ignorant to a proverb. . . .

On the other hand, the Russian peasants of the South, a race altogether distinct in sentiment and imagination from the phlegmatic people of the Central and Northern provinces—Little Russians as they are called—had examples before their eyes of men leading upright, God-fearing lives, modelling their conduct on New Testament teachings, cleanly, thrifty, able agriculturists. These were their neighbours, the Germans. The Empress Catherine, who, whatever her faults as a woman, was a great ruler and a far-seeing administratrix, had invited a large number of Suabian peasants, who in their South German homes had been simmering with indignation against the corrupt rule of their time, to settle in her empire on fertile lands, . . . The piety, integrity and steadiness which distinguished them in their Würtemberg homes they transplanted to Russia. Out on the steppe they built their trim houses, surrounded them with fruit trees and flower gardens, and carefully tilled their land, raising splendid crops of wheat and barley. They brought their earnest pastors with them, and built commodious churches and schools. Clean and well dressed, they crowded the churches for the numerous services, and the schools were filled with their eager children. The colonies became little paradises on the steppe, and small wonder that the Russian's heart filled with bitterness when he looked on the brightness, purity, harmony and comparative opulence of the strangers' villages, and compared them with the disorder, dirt, drunkenness and discord in his own.

For many years after the arrival of the Germans in Russia, the two peoples kept rigorously aloof from one another; but little by little the stronger race began to acquire an influence over the weaker. The sick Russian would apply to the German apothecary, the impecunious Russian to the German money-lender, the beggars—and there were thousands of them came to the colonies—for alms, . . . It was with no deep design to effect a Reformation, no presentiment of what was coming, that the pious farmer, the day's work done, would sit side by side with his Russian workman, and German New Testament in hand, or book of German hymns, would laboriously translate for his tattered disciple the words of Christ, or the noble spiritual songs of the *Vaterland.*

This was the attitude of the Germans in the colony of Rohrbach, a flourishing little place near the River Boug, and not very far from the great commercial city of Odessa. The pastor there was a certain Bonekemper, a man full of zeal, who not only laboured for the spiritual welfare of his own Germans, but for the enlightenment of their Russian dependents. He decided on taking two important steps. The Germans were in the habit of meeting together for prayer and praise at stated times. These exercises they called *Stunden,* or "hours." Bonekemper decided to invite the Russian labourers who had acquired a smattering of German to attend the *Stunden.* Here, they first heard Protestant worship, and it was their attendance at these services that first earned for them the title of *Stundists,* a title of opprobrium attached to them by the Orthodox priests of the neighbourhood. Bonekemper's second step was to procure a supply of Russian New Testaments. These he readily obtained from German and English friends in St. Petersburg. To those of the Rohrbach labourers who promised to learn to read the energetic pastor made a present of a New Testament. Classes of Russians were formed; Germans taught them to read their own Russ language; writing was added; German tracts were distributed; there was ferment, and stir, and inquiry, and much searching of heart. This was in 1858, a memorable date, for it was the birth-year of Stundism. . . .

Religious and Social Ideas

"THE Bible, and the Bible alone, is the religion of Protestants," is a saying attributed to an English divine of the last century. The Stundists are probably more circumscribed still. The New Testament, and the New Testament alone, is the religion of Stundists. Theoretically, they pay the same reverence to both Old and New Testaments; practically, the New Testament is their only rule of faith and conduct. . . .

It follows from this that the other great Evangelical doctrine of the right of every man to interpret Scripture for himself is also tenaciously held by the Stundists. Not the Church, not a priest or a commentator, but each individual man has the right and incurs the duty to search the Scriptures for himself. . . .

It will be hardly necessary to go into any detail as to the positive side of the Stundist belief. The Stundists are Evangelical Protestants pure and simple, . . .

The Stundist is a thinking, enlightened man, with clear notions about questions that are at present agitating the world. In this respect he is as different as possible to his Orthodox neighbour, who is generally a bovine-minded man, with brutal instincts and little outlook beyond to-day. The Stundist reads everthing he can lay his hands on—old newspapers and magazines, books on agriculture, cookery books, books of household medicine; and he has formed fairly distinct notions on most things he reads about. If you visit a village where Orthodox and Stundists live together, you can nearly always pick out the Stundist. He is cleaner, brighter, more alert. His clothes look smarter, his hair is cut shorter, his beard is trimmed or shaven. And if you enter their houses the difference is still more marked. Cleanliness and neatness in place of dirt and disorder. The children are tidy, the housewife does not shrink away in terrified bashfulness, but greets you with ease, and as though she had equal rights in the house with her husband. . . .

The position of women and children in a Stundist household is worthy of attention. To a very great extent the patriarchal form of family government still prevails in Russia. It is hardly too much to say that the head of the household rules absolutely and autocratically, or that he possesses the power of inflicting death on child or wife who is disobedient or unfaithful. The children stand around in fear and trembling in the presence of their father, the wife rises on his entrance, is seated only when he permits it, and her portion at meals is what he leaves or refuses. The Stundist has altered all this. His wife is his helpmate and bosom friend, with share in his joy and trouble. She is his sister in the assembly for worship. Her voice may be heard there in praise or prayer. She sits down with him at the same Lord's Table, and, with equal rights acknowledged before God, the Stundist husband would never think of curtailing her rights or slighting her position in his own household. It rarely happens that a Stundist inflicts corporal punishment on his children. The law of love is the law of his home. . . .

12.7   Persecution of Baptists in Russia, 1870s

From the first the Orthodox Church and the civil government in Russia alternated, and sometimes collaborated, in trying to restrict the spread of Baptist witness in Russia. The following letters, written by Russian Baptists from firsthand experience, describes some hardships of the infant churches. These letters originated in response to inquiries from abroad, particularly Johann Gerhard Oncken in Germany, and were published in England. In most cases, the names of the writers were suppressed to avoid placing them in greater danger. From these accounts one notices the importance of Bible distribution and home Bible studies in the growth of Baptist work in Russia. *Source:* Letters to the Editor, *The Quarterly Reporter,* January 1874, 2-5; April 1874, 4-8.

A. Letter to Johann Gerhard Oncken

Odessa, December 10, 1873

Dear Brother Oncken,

Brother _____ has informed me that some friends in England wish an account of the persecutions in Russia, in order to take advantage of the approaching marriage of the Duke of Edinburgh to make as powerful a representation as possible to His Majesty Alexander II. on behalf of emancipation of our afflicted brethren.

I have already written on this subject to one of the Secretaries in London, of the Evangelical Alliance, requesting him to lay the matter before the recent conference at New York and also to Mr. Wurstenberger, in Berne, and gladly comply with your request in the hope that my report may be found suitable for the purpose intended.

1. A considerable religious awakening took place about fifteen years ago, through study of the Scriptures, in several villages in the neighborhood of Odessa, chiefly through the instrumentality of Michael Ratuschus and Alexander Kopustjan. Those who were unable to read assembled together around those who were better instructed, and listened with the greatest eagerness to the reading of the New Testament. The consequence was that they soon became aware of many of the errors of the Greek Church, and spread their new discovery far and wide. Having in this way attracted the attention of the Russian priesthood, they were denounced to the authorities, and a course of imprisonment, corporal punishment, and abuse of every kind was set in operation against them. These severe measures however, only had the effect of driving the people more and more from the church to which they had hitherto belonged, and of which they had been constant adherents. . . .

2. In the year 1866 the Bible was extensively circulated in Elizabethgrad, Lubonirke, and the surrounding district in the province of Kherson. At one place, a Russion named Ivan Kjaboschapka, bought a Testament, and a number of people were led to meet together to hear the gospel. But no sooner did this come to the knowledge of the clergy than the most stringent measures of repression were instantly set on foot. By their orders these people were severely beaten, imprisoned, and persecuted in every conceivable way. While Ivan was so cruelly flogged that the ground was covered with his blood, a priest who was looking on exclaimed, "Beat him to death: he is a son of Satan!" and told the others that they had better have taken [to] horse-stealing than to be engaged in such an affair.

3. A great awakening took place about four years ago among the Russians in several villages in the neighborhood of Nicholaiof, also in the province of Kherson. After suffering a great deal of persecution from the priests and the authorities, a number of these people were attacked by a brutal mob while assembled at a prayer meeting on the 2nd of January, 1872, and were dragged to prison through the miry roads, in the presence of some of the local authorities and the priests. Five men and one woman in particular were thrown down and beaten with rods at intervals during the whole day in so cruel a way that their bodies were almost stripped of the flesh. . . . In the village of Bastanka some of the people received as many as 150 strokes of the rod, so that a few days afterward the splinters of the wood were taken out of their tortured flesh. These sufferers ventured to address the emperor, and sent three petitions to him, in which they gave a full description of the barbarous treatment to which they had been subjected, and begged that they might be permitted to live in peace according to the dictates of God's Word; but all their efforts were in vain, no reply was received, and the meetings are still strictly prohibited. . . .

4. About thirty of our friends at Lubonirka have been lately sentenced by the justice

of the peace to a fine of fifteen roubles each for attending a meeting: and in the village of Pletjano Taschlock several were so dreadfully beaten for reading the Bible that they were not even able to go to the town of Elizabethgrad to get medical treatment.

5. In the district of Taratschka, province of Kiev, several Russians had been brought to the knowledge of the truth through the study of the Scriptures, and were immediately exposed to rigorous persecution. They were imprisoned, loaded with chains, sentenced to hard labour, and suffered not only from hunger, but from other bad treatment. One of the head priests summoned the brethren before him and thus addressed them:—"What has the Gospel brought you to now?" to which one of them replied, "It has caused us to give up stealing and the vicious life we used to lead." "It would have been far better for you to have gone on with your stealing," said the priest, "for the Bible is full of false-hood and heresy, and if we were to allow you to read it, you would spread it every-where." He then ordered the police to take their Bibles away and give them crucifixes and saints' pictures instead. When the brethren refused to take them, he ordered four-teen of them, eleven men and three women, to be flogged and sent to prison, where they were kept in confinement nearly a year. At the present time nineteen men are in prison at Kiev because they refuse to return to the Greek Church. . . .

B.   Letter to Johann Gerhard Oncken from "A brother well acquainted with the facts."

Dear Brother Oncken,

In reply to your letter I beg to say that the brethren in prison are Russians, who have left the Greek church.

The persecution is carried on by the Governor of the Province of Cherson, and was set on foot after a visit was paid by him to the village in which brother _____ lives.

In the province of Kiev the clergy have stirred up the authorities to use their power against our brethren. It is not surprising that the clergy should play the chief part in this. A priest in Kiev has lately published a pamphlet, in which he compares this movement to the cholera, but expresses the opinion that the spiritual disease is far more to be dreaded than the bodily one.

I have already explained to you that the brethren are not persecuted from political reasons, but merely because of their desire to worship God according to their own conscience. The authorities, in general, are very well pleased with them and have often expressed the wish that everybody were like them, but they think that they should go to Church and comply with the general customs. The brethren at Kiev are mostly still unbaptized but in every other point are united with our brethren and are of the same opinions. Those in the province of Cherson are all baptized.

Br. _____ has at last been set at liberty with the four other brethren on bail, but he is not allowed to leave the village until the case has been tried. He told us that for some time he was confined with the greatest criminals, and nearly lost his life in conse-quence. No one knew where he was. In that painful situation he cried to God for deliv-erance and the Lord heard his prayer. The next day, he and his four companions were removed to a more commodious prison where his friends were allowed to visit him occasionally and supply him with food.

C.   J. Wiehler, Letter About Persecution in Odessa

Odessa, Jan. 20, 1874

At the close of last year [1873] I received a summons to appear before the court of enquiry about the Russian persecutions. I have been under sentence of enquiry for the last two years by the Russian government, because it was through my instrumentality that the churches in Odessa were formed. Now that they are so severely persecuted that all Christian intercourse is forbidden, I wished to meet them in a German village not far distant, in order to speak words of comfort to them, as I had done sometimes before. I went accordingly February 6, 1872, to the Protestant colony of Rohrback, six wersts [approximately four miles] from the Russian church at Osnower. We met at the house of a brother and discoursed together on our most holy faith—comforting and edifying one another. We took the Lord's Supper, and the brethren and sisters returned strengthened and refreshed to their homes. This enraged the enemy, and he put it in the hand of an official, who also called himself a brother, to have me arrested and brought before the magistrates. He came to my hotel in the evening and said I was arrested—and because I had formed a new church in their village! I was confined for the night and then sent to Stanowoi, 60 wersts distant; thence on to Odessa, where the magistrate released me on parole. The affair dragged on so long that in the autumn of 1872 I set off for St. Petersburg to lay before the Minister of the Interior my petition that the cause might be tried at once, and explained that I had not interferred with the "true believers," (as the Russians call their Church), but only with those already in our communion. The Minister promised to have the case brought on at once in Odessa, and I was somewhat comforted and came hither at once. But at New Year, 1873, the chief minister of the Greek Church at B. came to tell me that I had to pay 400 roubles, and five others had to be also fined heavily.

Is it possible that anything can be done in England? If so, it should be done quickly, as I have advised the brethren to appeal to the higher court, and if that is in vain, to the Imperial Court at St. Petersburg. . . .

Unit IV

The Twentieth Century

13
British Baptists

The source documents in this chapter come mostly from Baptist life in England. Those Baptists of British heritage and identity outside of England certainly merit notice here, did not the rigors of space squeeze them out.

The restructuring of the Baptist Union and the rise of the General Superintendency system deserve attention. For most of the twentieth century, English Baptists have faced numerical decline. The Baptist Union has made several significant studies of the spiritual condition of English Baptists; perhaps no other Baptist group in the world does such competent analysis of conditions affecting the churches as do the English Baptists. This chapter cites two of those studies, "Speak That They Go Forward" (1946) and "Signs of Hope" (1979).

The Union has also commissioned any number of studies of various doctrines and church practices; one thinks immediately of such things as the doctrine of the church, ordination, the role of children in the church, the charismatic movement, and others. This chapter cites several of these and omits others only with extreme reluctance.

13.1   Doctrinal Basis of the Baptist Union

The Baptist Union of Great Britain and Ireland has never adopted any detailed doctrinal confession. This organization, formed in 1813, has modified its brief statement from time to time but has not resumed the prolific confession making which marked English Baptists in the seventeenth century. In the Down Grade Controversy of the 1890s Charles Haddon Spurgeon urged the Union to adopt a conservative confession, and when they declined, he withdrew. The Declaration of Principle, the theological section of the Baptist Union constitution, is given here, followed by a brief list of the objects for which the Union exists. *Source: The Baptist Union of Great Britain and Ireland* (London: Baptist Church House, n.d.).

(Extracts from the Constitution)
III—DECLARATION OF PRINCIPLE
The basis of this Union is:
1.   That our Lord and Saviour Jesus Christ, God manifest in the flesh, is the sole and absolute authority in all matters pertaining to faith and practice, as revealed in the Holy Scriptures, and that each Church has liberty, under the guidance of the Holy Spirit, to interpret and administer His Laws.
2.   That Christian Baptism is the immersion in water into the Name of the Father, the Son, and the Holy Ghost, of those who have professed repentance towards God and faith in our Lord Jesus Christ who 'died for our sins according to the Scriptures; was buried, and rose again the third day.'
3.   That it is the duty of every disciple to bear personal witness to the Gospel of Jesus Christ, and to take part in the evangelization of the world.

IV—THE OBJECTS OF THIS UNION

The objects of the Union are the advancement of the Christian religion, especially by the means of and in accordance with the principles of the Baptist Denomination (this being the main purpose) and the following objects, but so that these objects are ancillary to the main purpose and not so as to extend the objects of the Union beyond such main purpose.

1. To cultivate among its own Members respect and love for one another, and for all who love the Lord Jesus Christ.
2. To spread the Gospel of Christ by ministers and evangelists, by establishing Churches, forming Sunday-schools, distributing the Scriptures, issuing religious publications, and by such other methods as the Council shall determine.
3. To afford opportunities for conference and for united action on questions affecting the welfare of the Churches, the support of the ministry, and the extension of the Denomination, both at home and abroad.
4. To promote fraternal relations between Baptists in this and in other countries.
5. To obtain and disseminate accurate information respecting the organizations, labours and sufferings of Baptists throughout the world.
6. To confer and co-operate with other Christian communities as occasion may require.

13.2   English Baptist General Superintendents

In addition to local church pastors and deacons, General Baptists in the seventeenth century accepted a third kind of minister called a "Messenger." The messengers were "ministers at large" who traveled among the churches, and whose ministerial leadership was accepted in all the churches. Particular Baptists made only limited use of this office, and by the late-eighteenth century most General Baptists had abandoned it. However, early in the twentieth century that basic concept reappeared under a new name. In 1916 John H. Shakespeare led English Baptists to organize into ten geographical areas, each to be headed by a "General Superintendent." These Superintendents relate to the pastors and churches, and to the Baptist Union, somewhat like a bishop would. The following document comes from a 1978 study of the nature and function of the General Superintendency. *Source:* Report of the Working Group on the General Superintendency to the Baptist Union Council, D. M. Harper, Chairman. Unpublished Study Report, November 1978, 2-13. Used by permission.

INTRODUCTION

The Baptist Union of Great Britain and Ireland comprises inter alia churches and Associations affiliated upon the basis of a single Declaration of Principle. The members of such churches are, therefore, associated together and desire to witness to Christ in the world and believe themselves to be part of the universal Body of Christ, the Church.

Within this association of interdependent churches is a community of ministers. Such a Ministry is the gift of Christ to the Church and the call to exercise the functions of a minister comes from Christ through His church. A person so called and trained is not only a minister of a local Baptist Church but is also recognised as a minister in the larger fellowship of Baptist churches associating together in the Baptist Union.

Since the Ministry is Christ's gift to the Church, the churches have, very properly, a responsibility to test the minister's call, to train him and then to provide continuing care for the minister and his family. The ministry will provide gifted, trained and skilled leadership for the churches and, through the administration of the Word and Sacraments, seek to equip God's people for mission, which means making real and credible the Gospel of Christ in the life of the world to-day.

Within this total Ministry, certain ministers have been called to exercise responsibility for the wider fellowship of ministers and churches. Among the early General Baptists this task was summed up in the office of Messenger. Since 1916 this has been the responsibility of those called by the Baptist Union to be General Superintendents.

The Superintendency took root slowly among the churches of the Baptist Union but it is now widely acknowledged to be for the good of the churches and ministers. It is an essential factor for effective caring by the churches for each other and the Ministry, particularly as it relates to the Home Mission Scheme of the Baptist Union.

At first the General Superintendents were appointed to help in the administration of funds contributed by the churches of the Baptist Union for the support of the Ministry. The Superintendents were also to ensure better spiritual and material standards for ministers, to facilitate the movement of ministers between the churches, to stimulate the churches in common action, spiritual growth and effective mission and generally to promote the interests of the Baptist Union.

Baptists are now organised effectively as a denomination and they participate with other Christians in the Free Church Federal Council, the British Council of Churches and the World Council of Churches. This participation sometimes takes them into areas of Christian concern at the local level where the ecumenical demands create a growing pressure for the representative Baptist person to speak for Baptists as a whole. Hitherto, this has not been Baptist practice, but more and more the Superintendent is being drawn into this representative role in ecumenical activity. Baptists are also involved, like other parts of the Church in Britian, in their own world confessional family, the Baptist World Alliance. Thus those appointed to co-ordinate the mission our churches need to be people with ecumenical insights.

I. *THE PRESENT SITUATION*

The Working Group has sought to establish the dimensions of the Superintendent's task. From the evidence received, we conclude that the Superintendents accept, for the most part, the size of their Areas and have expressed confidence about their ability to know both ministers and churches. Evidence from ministers and churches, however, shows that most of those who view their work from the outside do not share this confidence. Both, ministers and churches, whilst expressing appreciation of the Superintendency, urge a large increase in the number of Superintendents because Areas are considered to be impossibly large. We have, therefore, sought to analyse all the aspects of the work deemed to be within the Superintendent's province before recommending how these tasks may be allocated.

I.A. *THE AREAS*

The Baptist Union has divided the whole of England, parts of West Wales, Gwent and Glamorgan, into ten Areas for the purposes of its Administration. Each of these Areas has a General Superintendent who has responsibility, officially, for the care of accredited ministers and affiliated churches of the Baptist Union in terms which are specified in the Home Mission Fund Scheme, Section II, paragraph 4-7. Appointments are made on a five year basis, renewable by the Baptist Union Council upon the recommendation of the Area concerned. . . .

All these Areas, with the exception of the Metropolitan Area, are geographically large and Superintendents travel an average of 14,000 miles per year by car in addition to journeys undertaken by public transport on Baptist Union business. The Metropolitan Area, though geographically compact, has the largest number of ministers and churches, and traffic density produces physical demands which are just as great as those of distance. . . .

The Superintendents work from their own homes and the house is either provided by the Baptist Union or a Housing Allowance is granted where the Superintendent is providing his own accommodation. Superintendents provide their own cars, the Baptist Union helping with a loan when this is requested. The allowance for travelling (1978) is 10p. per mile for the first 14,000 miles (allowing for depreciation) and then 5p. per mile after this. Committee expenses for travel by rail are met in the same way as other Baptist Union Committee expenses.

I.B. *THE PASTORAL CARE OF THE MINISTRY*

The Superintendent is specifically charged with responsibility for encouraging, advising and guiding ministers and, in practice, the following series of duties and expectations have accrued:

i) *Prospective Candidates* for the ministry usually receive advice from the Superintendent on the correct way to proceed and a good deal of counselling and consultation by the Superintendent with the home church and its minister normally precedes the interview by the Association Ministerial Recognition Committee.

ii) *New entrants to the ministry* resume their contact with the Superintendency when students in the Baptist Colleges are interviewed by the Superintendent in whose Area the college is situated a year before they complete their courses. . . .

iii) *Probationer ministers,* in particular need special care. The First settlement is crucial and there is evidence of students accepting invitations to pastorates that are unsuitable for a minister just beginning his ministry. Much is already done to assist these probationer ministers, but there is a significant measure of disappointment among this group about the support they receive. . . .

vi) *Ministers* are always the pastoral concern of the Superintendent, and the Superintendent seeks to build up his acquaintance with them by visiting them in their homes. Some Superintendents aim to visit every manse in their Areas once a year and claim that they are almost able to achieve this target. Other Superintendents organise their visitation on other patterns and rely more on contacts with ministers at Fraternals and Association meetings. It is recognised that distances vary from Area to Area. Visits by Superintendents to particular localities by prior arrangement to meet with ministers are welcomed but are not to be considered a substitute for visitation of the home.

vii) *Ministers' wives and families* are a part of the Superintendent's pastoral responsibility. Many wives pay tribute to the love, concern and help of their Area Superintendent; on the other hand, many feel a sense of isolation in matters of care, concern and encouragement for the family as a whole on both spiritual and practical levels. Almost 50% of wives who were consulted thought of the Area Superintendent as a remote person whom they are unable to contact or communicate with.

viii) *Retired ministers* and their wives and ministers' widows are included in the Superintendent's pastoral responsibility and it is similarly important that they receive the care which they deserve.

I.C. *MINISTERIAL SETTLEMENT*

i) The procedures for settlement occupy a considerable part of the Superintendent's time. Ministers seeking a settlement are interviewed by the Superintendent to establish basic information about them according to an agreed form of questions. Superintendents also interview the Diaconates of vacant churches to gather information about the life and mission of the church.

ii) August excepted, the Superintendents' Board meets on the first Monday of each month at the Baptist Church House. Four of these monthly meetings extend over a two-day period. Normally the greater part of the time is spent on settlements, which are approached in two ways:

    a) Each Superintendent is allowed to present a special case. This may be a minister with particular problems or a church with special needs and circumstances.

    b) The meeting then deals with the *'Blue Book'*. This has five sections.

        1. The Removal List—a dozen or so names of ministers who must move urgently.

        2. The Confidential List—usually about sixty ministers who think it timely to seek a move

        3. The Students' List—students who will complete their courses in Baptist Colleges during the year.

        4. The Residential Selection Conference List—candidates who have been given permission through the Residential Selection Conference to seek Baptist pastorates.

        5. The Supplementary Ministers List.—In addition to the 'Blue Book' each Superintendent also has a list of the vacant churches. . . . Churches are encouraged to deal with one minister at a time and to invite the minister for an interview as well as to preach on a specific Sunday. Often the interview is entirely separate from the preaching occasion.

iii). Sometimes churches approach their Superintendent about a name not on the Superintendents' list and receive information about this minister from the Superintendent's own knowledge. . . .

I.D. *THE MINISTRY TO THE CHURCHES*

i) The pastoral care of the churches includes encouragement of spiritual growth and outreach in mission. Yet the most frequent cause of contact between the Superintendency and the churches is a pastoral vacancy and for some churches this is the only contact they have. Superintendents welcome the opportunity of conducting worship in the churches within their Areas and sharing in other activities of the fellowship.

ii) Many churches expect the Superintendent to be too busy to be concerned about their situation unless there is a pressing problem. This gives rise to the notion that Superintendency is constantly involved in crisis situations. The wise counsel and spiritual leadership given by the Superintendents at such times is warmly acknowledged, but these same qualities of wisdom and leadership need also to be channelled into situations of opportunity and advance. . . .

I.E. *ADMINISTRATION*

The task of the Superintendent in relation to ministers, churches, Associations, the Area and the Baptist Union involves a considerable amount of administration. . . .

The outline of administrative responsibilities which follow is not necessarily accurate in every case, but reflects the general picture:

i) *Ministers.* The Superintendent needs to record information which relates to settlement matters for the 'Blue Book'. . . .

ii) *Churches*. The Superintendent needs to possess and keep up-to-date a complete list of churches and ministers and church officers; . . .

iii) *Associations*. The Superintendent prepares reports for the Association Committees and Assemblies on a wide range of topics, denominational or inter-church. . . .

iv) *The Area*. The Superintendent prepares agendas and minutes for the Area Committee and deals with ministerial accreditation procedures including the collection of references for, and notices to, candidates. He is usually involved in the planning of Area and Association Ministers' Conferences.

v) *The Baptist Union*. The Superintendent has over-all responsibility for the propagation of information from the various departments of the Baptist Union. . . .

vi) *Committees*. The office of Superintendent carries with it a place on many committees. . . .

vii) *Ecumenical Relationships*. The emergence of local ecumenical projects in the last decade has generated the need for persons to represent the Baptist interests at regional level. The Superintendent is recognised by leaders of other denominations as the person who represents Baptists at this level.

I.F. *ROLE IN ORDINATION AND INDUCTION*

i) *Ordination*. This event usually takes place within the context of the church which has recognised the gift and calling to the Ministry. The Principal of the College which has been responsible for training for ministry usually performs this function. . . .

ii) *Induction*. Much more generally, the Superintendent is expected to officiate at an induction. As the representative person of the wider fellowship of Baptist Churches and often the one who introduced the pastor to the church, the Superintendent is the natural choice. . . .

I.G *THE APPOINTMENT AND THE RE-APPOINTMENT OF SUPERINTENDENTS*

i) When a vacancy occurs in the Superintendency, that vacancy is made known through the columns of the Baptist Times and the Associations and churches within the Area concerned are invited to submit names of those who might be considered for the appointment. A committee of ten, five representing the Area and five representing the Baptist Union, then meet to decide upon the name to be brought before the Baptist Union Council. . . .

ii) The appointment is for a period of five years and the General Superintendent is eligible for re-election at the end of that period, ...

iii) It has been the usual experience that when a man is appointed, he will retain his office until retirement. Some have extended their service as Superintendents beyond the age of sixty-five.

APPENDIX I

I. *Historical origins of the General Superintendent*

The Doctrine of the Ministry Report (1961) traces the historical roots of the Superintendents' office to the Baptist use of the word "Messenger".

There has never been complete agreement between the General and Particular Baptists upon the fundamental relationship between the church and the ministry. The General Baptists, developing their understanding of the Church from the idea of "covenant" theology among the Brownists, held the view that the officers of every church or congregation "are tied by office to that particular congregation only whereof they are chosen". Each congregation was bound to one another and to God by the covenant, but each minister's authority was strictly limited to his own congregation. . . .

Baptist churches in the 18th century were marked by a growing awareness of fellowship which was wider than the local church. Associations were formed and in the Confessions which they issued there was evident a broader connectionalism. The General Baptists developed the General Assembly towards the end of the 17th century as a means for discussing matters of common concern. In 1678 Thomas Grantham had argued that decisions made by such gatherings were in no way binding upon the churches. But in 1696 the Assembly minuted the view that independency was "very dangerous and detrimental to the churches".

It was at this time that the office of "Messenger" was developed among the General Baptists and to a lesser extent among Particular Baptists. Originally he was a person commissioned by a church to preach the Gospel, to form new churches and could be sent by one fellowship to settle a dispute and discuss matters of common concern in another church. The Messenger's office reveals a growing concern for evangelism and association life among Baptists.

The Particular Baptists never made the Messenger a distinct order within the ministry. It was the General Baptist decline into Socinianism and Unitarianism and the retreat of many Particular Baptists into hyper-Calvinism, which resulted in the decay of the office. Churches were less and less prepared to free men for such work and independency re-asserted itself.

It was this growing awareness of the ministry as a clearly defined group, which led J. H. Shakespeare to take action through the Baptist Union. The churches responded magnificently to his appeal for the support of the ministry, with £250,000. It was to administer the fund, and to help ministers and churches achieve better spiritual and material standards, that the Baptist Union appointed the ten General Superintendents in 1916.

"What seemed to some a radical departure in Baptist policy was, in certain respects, a return to the Messenger system, which had been a feature of the life of the General Baptists in the seventeenth century." (E. A. Payne, *The Baptist Union: A Short History*, p. 182). Perhaps the idiosyncratic J. C. Carlisle more accurately reflected the mood of the denomination in 1916 when he wrote, in a chapter headed "When Shakespeare Ruled", that "could they (the old guard on the Council) have read all that was in Shakespeare's mind they would have been more afraid. The scheme went through and for the first time in their history the Baptists became an ecclesiastical body . . . The scheme would not have gone through if it had not been for the Secretary and a few laymen who insisted that the support of the ministry must carry with it some degree of responsibility for efficiency." (*My life's Little Day*, p. 162). . . .

II. *Attempts to clarify the Superintendent's Role*

In the Baptist Union booklet of 1949 already mentioned, Dr. M. E. Aubrey wrote that "The very name superintendent is only a Latin rendering of the Greek *episcopos*, or bishop, or the Anglo-Saxon overseer, as the Quakers named their leaders. The New Testament Church had its bishops and without them it is difficult to see how any church can claim to match the New Testament model" (p.3).

In the 1948 *Baptist Doctrine of the Church* statement, the relationship of Baptist churches to each other was clearly defined. "We believe that the local church lacks one of the marks of a truly Christian community if it does not seek the fellowship of other Baptist churches, does not seek a true relationship with Christians and churches of other communions and is not conscious of its place in the one Catholic Church". But the only statement made about Superintendents was: "they have the care of churches in different areas". . . .

As the *Doctrine of the Ministry Report* noted, the present situation raises issues about

Church and Ministry which did not formerly exist, and which complicate old problems. The development of a nationally organised Baptist denomination; the growth of world confessional bodies like the BWA; and the inter-confessional bodies like the BCC and the WCC; plus the variety of interpretation given to the world ministry today among Baptists all generate new problems.

The Ministry Report claimed that "the whole community of our churches, i.e. within the Baptist Union, is responsible for maintaining the ministry denoted by the doctrine of the priesthood of all believers, together with the spiritual leadership essential to that ministry." (p.35). Three obligations emerge from this responsibility. The churches must prepare adequate spiritual leadership by providing adequate facilities for the guiding and training of those spiritually gifted to be leaders. The churches must also provide adequate material support for those who exercise such a ministry. Third, the churches have the "obligation of arranging means by which spiritual leaders who need or desire counsel, guidance or assistance may receive it. The Baptist Union has endeavoured to fulfil the obligation by the establishment of the Superintendency."

In this situation the local church as a member of the whole community accepts as altogether adequate the spiritual leadership thus provided, which means that Baptist Union churches find their ministers from those so accredited by the Union. It also involves consulting with other churches when a minister is appointed. "This means full consultations with the representatives of the whole of the community, a readiness to accept the counsel sought and a desire to act for the good of the whole community as well as of itself." (p.37). . . .

The constitutional position of the Superintendents' Board was left unchanged when the Union was restructured. It reports directly to the Council and not through any of the Main Committees. This was because the Superintendents may be involved with all the departments in their work. The Superintendents are directly responsible to the General Secretary, as are the other Heads of Departments. When the Board meets the General Secretary and Head of the Ministry Department both regularly attend and participate in the meetings and there is a specific point at which each can bring business.

It is a fact that the denomination has never discussed the Superintendency in depth. The matter has been alluded to often, but never worked out thoroughly. To some extent the prior studies on Church and Ministry have been undertaken. We must now determine the role of the Superintendent and establish ways and means for that role to be fulfilled.

13.3   The Baptist Doctrine of the Church

Baptists emerged as a separate denomination in the seventeenth century largely in an effort to recover a pure church. They have sought to define and achieve a form of church that would approach that original high goal. The following document cites a recent effort by English Baptists to state their view of the church. *Source:* Roger Hayden, ed., *Baptist Union Documents*, 1948-1977 (London: The Baptist Historical Society, 1980), 5-11. Used by permission.

A Statement approved by the Council of the Baptist Union of Great Britain
and Ireland, March 1948

1. The Baptist Union of Great Britain and Ireland represents more than three thousand churches and about three hundred thousand members. Through its membership in the Baptist World Alliance it is in fellowship with other Baptist communities through the world numbering about thirteen million, who have accepted the responsibilities of full communicant membership.

Baptists have a continuous history in Great Britain since the beginning of the seventeenth century. Many of their principles, however, were explicitly proclaimed in the second half of the sixteenth century by the radical wing of the Reformation movement. They claim as their heritage also the great central stream of Christian doctrine and piety through the centuries, and have continuity with the New Testament Church in that they rejoice to believe and seek faithfully to proclaim the Apostolic Gospel and endeavour to build up the life of their churches after what seems to them the New Testament pattern.

THE ONE HOLY CATHOLIC CHURCH

2. Although Baptists have for so long held a position separate from that of other communions, they have always claimed to be part of the one holy catholic Church of our Lord Jesus Christ. They believe in the catholic Church as the holy society of believers in our Lord Jesus Christ, which He founded, of which He is the only Head, and in which He dwells by His Spirit, so that though manifested in many communions, organized in various modes, and scattered throughout the world, it is yet one in Him. The Church is the Body of Christ and a chosen instrument of the divine purpose in history. . . .

THE STRUCTURE OF LOCAL BAPTIST CHURCHES

3. *(a)* It is in membership of a local church in one place that the fellowship of the one holy catholic Church becomes significant. Indeed, such gathered companies of believers are the local manifestation of the one Church of God on earth and in heaven. . . . To worship and serve in such a local Christian community is, for Baptists, of the essence of Churchmanship. . . .

(b) The basis of our membership in the church is a conscious and deliberate acceptance of Christ as Saviour and Lord by each individual. There is, we hold, a personal crisis in the soul's life when a man stands alone in God's presence, responds to God's gracious activity, accepts His forgiveness and commits himself to the Christian way of life. Such a crisis may be swift and emotional or slow-developing and undramatic, and is normally experienced within and because of our life in the Christian community, but it is always a personal experience wherein God offers His salvation in Christ, and the individual, responding by faith, receives the assurance of the Spirit that by grace he is the child of God. It is this vital evangelical experience which underlies the Baptist conception of the Church and is both expressed and safeguarded by the sacrament of Believers' Baptism.

(c) The life of a gathered Baptist church centres in worship, in the preaching of the Word, in the observance of the two sacraments of Believers' Baptism and the Lord's Supper, in growth in fellowship and in witness and service to the world outside. Our forms of worship are in the Reformed tradition and are not generally regulated by liturgical forms. Our tradition is one of spontaneity and freedom, but we hold that there should be disciplined preparation of every part of the service. . . . The scriptures are held by us to be the primary authority both for the individual in his belief and way of life and for the Church in its teaching and modes of government. It is the objective revelation given in scripture which is the safeguard against a purely subjective authority in religion. We firmly hold that each man must search the scriptures for himself and seek the illumination of the Holy Spirit to interpret them. We know also that Church history and Christian experience through the centuries are a guide to the meaning of scripture. Above all, we hold that the eternal Gospel—the life, death and resurrection of our Lord—is the fixed point from which our interpretation, both of the Old and New Testaments, and of later developments in the Church, must proceed. . . .

(e) Although each local church is held to be competent, under Christ, to rule its own life, Baptists, throughout their history, have been aware of the perils of isolation and have sought safeguards against exaggerated individualism. From the seventeenth century there have been "Associations" of Baptist churches which sometimes appointed Messengers; more recently, their fellowship with one another has been greatly strengthened by the Baptist Union, the Baptist Missionary Society and the Baptist World Alliance. In recent years, General Superintendents have been appointed by the Baptist Union to have the care of churches in different areas. Indeed, we believe that a local church lacks one of the marks of a truly Christian community if it does not seek the fellowship of other Baptist churches, does not seek a true relationship with Christians and churches of other communions and is not conscious of its place in the one catholic Church. . . .

THE MINISTRY

4. A properly ordered Baptist church will have its duly appointed officers. These will include the minister (or pastor), elders, deacons, Sunday school teachers and other church workers. The Baptist conception of the ministry is governed by the principle that it is a ministry of a church and not only a ministry of an individual. It is the church which preaches the Word and celebrates the sacraments, and it is the church which, through pastoral oversight, feeds the flock and ministers to the world. It normally does these things through the person of its minister, but not solely through him. Any member of the church may be authorized by it, on occasion, to exercise the functions of the ministry, in accordance with the principle of the priesthood of all believers, to preach the Word, to administer baptism, to preside at the Lord's table, to visit, and comfort or rebuke members of the fellowship. . . .

The Sacraments

We recognize the two sacraments of Believers' Baptism and the Lord's Supper as being of the Lord's ordaining. We hold that both are "means of grace" to those who receive them in faith, and that Christ is really and truly present, not in the material elements, but in the heart and mind and soul of the believer and in the Christian community which observes the sacrament. . . .

Following the guidance of the New Testament we administer Baptism only to those who have made a responsible and credible profession of "repentance towards God and faith in the Lord Jesus Christ". Such persons are then immersed in the name of the Father, the Son and the Holy Spirit. Salvation is the work of God in Christ, which becomes operative when it is accepted in faith. Thus we do not baptize infants. There is, however, a practice in our churches of presenting young children at a service of public worship where the responsibilities of the parents and the church are recognized and prayers are offered for the parents and the child. Baptists believe that from birth all children are within the love and care of the heavenly Father and therefore within the operation of the saving grace of Christ; hence they have never been troubled by the distinction between baptized and unbaptized children. . . .

CHURCH AND STATE

6. Our conviction of Christ's Lordship over His Church leads us to insist that churches formed by His will must be free from all other rule in matters relating to their spiritual life. Any form of control by the State in these matters appears to us to challenge the "Crown Rights of the Redeemer". . . .

It will be seen that in this statement of the doctrine of the Church the emphasis falls time and again upon the central fact of evangelical experience, that when God offers His forgiveness, love and power the gift must be personally accepted in faith by each individual. From this follows the believer's endeavour to walk in the way of the Lord and to be obedient to His commandments. From this follows, also, our traditional defence of civil and religious liberty. It governs our conception of the Church and our teaching on Believers' Baptism. Gratefully recognizing the gifts bestowed by God upon other communions, we offer these insights which He has entrusted to us for the service of His whole Church.

13.4 John Clifford, Address to the Baptist World Alliance, 1911

The Baptist World Alliance was formed in London in 1905, with John Clifford chosen the first president. Clifford's presidential address in Philadelphia in 1911 reveals much about Baptists' attitudes of the time toward themselves and toward the larger world. Clifford defined the nature and functions of the Baptist World Alliance. *Source:* John Clifford, "The Baptist Word Alliance: Its Origin and Character, Meaning and Work." Address before the Baptist World Alliance, Philadelphia, June 1911.

THE BAPTIST WORLD ALLIANCE: ITS ORIGIN AND CHARACTER,
MEANING AND WORK
Address from the Chair of the Baptist World Alliance, Delivered on Tuesday,
June 20th, 1911, in Philadelphia, U.S.A.
By JOHN CLIFFORD, M.A., LL.D., D.D.

DEAR BRETHREN AND FRIENDS:

I cannot enter upon the duties of this office without first of all thanking you with all my heart for the honor you have conferred upon me. Frankly, I must say, it was one of the great surprises of my life when the Baptist World Congress held in London in 1905, elected me to the Presidency of this newly created Alliance. . . .

And now, my brethren, the one subject your President cannot escape from, on this, the first occasion of our meeting as an Alliance, is THE ALLIANCE ITSELF, ITS CREATION AND CHARACTER, ITS MEANING AND WORK. . . .

The novelty of this organization is surprising, partly because it appears in a people delivered over, body and soul, to individualism, and in mortal terror of the slightest invasion of their personal and ecclesiastical independence; and yet to others, who have grasped the intrinsic catholicity of our fundamental principles, it is astonishing that we have been so long arriving at the present stage of our development.

For although this Alliance is a new creation; it is really the outward and visible sign of an inward and spiritual grace that has been working within us, with special energy and vitality, during the last ten or fifteen years; and witnesses to magnetic and cohesive forces operating, though latent, and powerful though silent. . . .

Deep in the soul of us has always dwelt the conviction that we are the possessors of a genuinely universal religion; although it has only found voice here and there. For the most part we have not known one another . . .

But a new day has dawned. The barriers are broken down. The post and the press, the telegraph and the telephone, the rail and the steamboat unite us. . . . So our Alliance is *possible.* Moulded under different conditions, dwelling under different flags, trained in different climes and by different teachers with different methods, we come together rejoicing, that in the new nature, we have received through the grace of God, there is neither Greek nor Jew, Englishman nor American, black nor white, bond nor free, but that all are one in Christ, and Christ is all in each and in all. . . .

II.

What is new is that this is a *World* Alliance of Baptists. We have other unions; but they are restricted. This is all embracing. They unite two or three churches in a locality, a hundred in a county, or thousands in a nation; this represents all, and is really and not factitiously ecumenical.

It is not our immense numbers that creates this union; though we must have more than eight millions of registered members, and a host of adherents; nor is it by the authority of persons that we meet, as of a Pope claiming infallibility, or a body of Patriarchs compelling our appearance; nor is it again, in obedience to the mandate of a church, or the action of the machinery of the State. Our cohesiveness is due to our ideas. They bind us together. They are our driving and inspiring force. . . .

III.

But this organization is a World Alliance of *Baptists,* and that means that the catholic principles on which we base ourselves we derive straight from Jesus, are accepted on His authority, and involve in all who accept them total subjection of soul to His gracious and benignant rule. He is Lord of all, and He only is Lord of all. . . . Jesus Christ holds the first place and the last. His word in final. His rule is supreme.

(2) And now it follows upon that, that the ideas to which we give witness root themselves, first in the teaching of the New Testament, and secondly in the soul's experience of Christ. . . .

IV.

Another cord binding us together in an indissoluble spiritual union, and clothing this Alliance with a true catholicity is our unswerving maintenance of an exclusively regenerated church-membership. . . . On spiritual experience we build; not on creeds; but on "conversion," "a change of heart," the awakening of the soul to God in Christ; regeneration by the Holy Ghost, a conscious possession of the mind and spirit of Jesus, a will surrendered to God, a life dedicated to His service. . . .

Therefore we preach "soul liberty," and contend against all comers that the spirit of man has the privilege of direct conscious relation to God in Christ and through Christ. Nothing may come between the soul and God. . . . The soul must be free. . . .

V.

In speaking of the *work* of this Alliance it is important, at the outset, to recall the limitations imposed upon us by our ecumenical character. From sheer necessity we are not competent to judge one another's local work with accuracy. We lack sufficient data. We miss the special point of view. We are too far apart and we have the enormous difficulty of the "personal equation." Britishers do not know the United States and yet some of them do not hesitate from passing sentence upon the American churches, stating their problems, and showing how they could be solved, even though they have only had the opportunity of paying a flying visit to these climes; and they do it apparently unaware that their verdicts are no more than thinly disguised assertions of their own prejudices and presuppositions. Nor can Americans estimate the weight of the social pressure on Baptists in England, and the enormous resistance we have to overcome in following the light we see. You do not see the diminished returns in the till of the village shop, and the persecution in the village streets consequent upon State patronage and support of one particular church. To know that you must get into touch with our village churches as I have done for more than fifty years. . . .

Besides it avails nothing to make light of the fact that we do not think as Christendom thinks on the vital elements of Christianity. The great historic churches are against us: the Roman Catholic, the Eastern, the Anglican, and some other communions; and against us on subjects that go to the uttermost depths of the soul of the gospel of Christ;

and therefore "Separation" is one of the inevitable conditions of faithfulness to our experience of the grace of God, to our interpretation of the claims of Jesus Christ, and to the principles He has given as the ground and sphere of our collective life. It cannot be helped. We accept the isolation, and all the penalties it involves. . . .

VI.

And now standing upon this eminence, let us ask what is the outlook for the Baptist people all over the earth? What is the position likely to be assigned to us in leading and shaping the religious life of mankind?

To answer that question we need ask first, towards what sea are the deeper currents of thought and action in modern civilization setting? What is the "stream of tendency" amongst the progressive peoples? Is it with our principles or against them?

The reply is unequivocal and complete.

(1) Protestantism is to the fore. The races leading the life of the world are either distinctively Protestant, as in Britain and the United States or they are effectively using Protestant ideas as weapons against Roman Catholicism as in France and Spain. . . . Protestantism is one of the chief factors moulding the coming generations of men.

(2) The leaven of teaching concerning the intervention of the magistrate in religious affairs cast by John Smith and Roger Williams into the three measures of human meal in Holland and England and America, has been doing its work. The United States has established forever the doctrine of the neutrality of the State towards all Christian societies. France has cut the concordat in twain, and State and Church are free of each other. Portugal is doing the same this year. Welsh Disestablishment is at the doors. And though England, as usual, lags behind, yet both within and without the Anglican Church the conviction that separation is just, gains strength, and all that is wanted is the opportunity to translate the conviction into legislative deed.

(3) In like manner the reflective forces of the age make against an exclusive and aggressive priestism. Indeed, it has received its sentence of death, and is only waiting for the executioner. It has to go. . . .

(4) Nor can prelacy stand against the divine right of the democracy. Although the cry of "Increase the Episcopate" is heard, yet the Bishops themselves admit that they must give the laity some share in the administration of the affairs of prelatical churches. The people cannot be excluded from churches or from nations. Their day has dawned; and it will go on to its full noon. Not churches, nor parties, not nations merely, but the people are the legatees of the future; the inheritance is theirs. . . .

(5) But the most outstanding characteristics of our time is the amazing dominance of the idea of social service. The age is permeated with the obligation of brotherhood, the duty of self-sacrificing ministry, to the more needy members of the Commonwealth. We cannot escape it. Social problems are supreme. "The condition of the people" question is everywhere surging to the front. Housing and health, temperance and purity, drill for the body, education for the mind; these and kindred phases of life are never out of sight. The churches have broadened out so as to embrace them. . . .

(6) And all this movement is intensely moral. The illuminated and energized conscience is in it. It is ennobled by a high ethic. The Spirit has "convinced the *world* of sin and righteousness and judgment"; and in the strength of that conviction, a concerted and comprehensive attack is being made by churches and States, by individuals and societies on the strongholds of injustice and misery, and a long stride is taken to that one far-off divine event towards which the whole creation moves.

VII.

Need I trace the parallel between those manifest tendencies of this New Century and the principles which our fathers set forth and which we maintain? Is it not obvious that the ideas and aims are ours, and that whatever becomes of us as churches, this, at least, is certain, that those ideas of ours are working mightily as the formative factors of the future? . . .

For in addition to our ruling ideas we have a freedom as to verbal forms of belief and of organized collective life, though we are so immovably fixed as to principles, that leaves us wholly at liberty to adapt ourselves to the teaching of experience, and the changing needs of societies as continuously living organisms can and must. Biblical criticism does not disturb us, for we do not rest on it, but on personal experience of the grace of Christ. Modes of political government do not affect us; we can accept any, but we fare best under the most democratic; . . .

Let us then humbly accept our responsibility for leadership of the religion of the future and go forward to our place. Pioneers never get the best pay, but they do the best work; . . . Be ready to endure the cross and despise shame. Rise to the courage of your best moments. Push your convictions into deeds. Scorn bribes. Stand true. Be faithful to Christ and His holy gospel, and so help to lead the whole world into the light and glory of His redeeming love.

13.5   English Baptist Response to Ecumenical Proposals

What should be the relation of Baptist churches to other denominations? What about acceptance of baptism, communion, or ordination between Baptist churches and others, especially the Church of England? Since they originated, Baptists have been asking these questions, though the answers have changed slightly over the generations. The following document shows the reaction of the Baptist Union to the Church of England Lambeth Conferences appeal of 1920. From this we see that English Baptists at that time were more interested in interchurch cooperation than in any merger. *Source:* Earnest A. Payne, *The Baptist Union* (London: Carey Kingsgate Press, 1959), 279-282.

Reply of the Churches in Membership with the Baptist Union to the "Appeal to all Christian People" issued by the Lambeth Conference of 1920.

Adopted unanimously by THE ASSEMBLY of the BAPTIST UNION at Leeds on
Tuesday, 4th May 1926

We, the representatives of Churches in membership with the Baptist Union of Great Britain and Ireland, gathered in Annual Assembly, greet in the name of our Lord Jesus Christ all Christian people, and at this time especially those within the Anglican Church.

The "Appeal to all Christian People", issued by the Lambeth Conference of 1920, and transmitted to us by the Archbishop of Canterbury, has stirred deeply our minds and hearts. We received it with the respect and sympathy due to a message from brethren in Christ representing a great historic communion and moved by a spirit of brotherly love toward their fellow-Christians; and we have sought to give it the prayerful consideration which it manifestly deserves. . . .

We recognize fully and gladly the courtesy and lofty purpose of those who made the Appeal. These qualities are manifest not only in the document itself but also in the attitude of their representatives throughout the discussion of the high matters which they brought before us. We associate ourselves with our Anglican brethren in longing and prayer for a larger unity among all who follow and serve our Lord and Saviour Jesus Christ. . . .

We believe in the Catholic Church as the holy Society of believers in our Lord Jesus Christ, which He founded, of which He is the only Head, and in which He dwells by His

Spirit, so that though made up of many communions, organized in various modes, and scattered throughout the world, it is yet one in Him.

We believe that this holy society is truly to be found wherever companies of believers unite as Churches on the ground of a confession of personal faith. Every local community thus constituted is regarded by us as both enabled and responsible for self-government through His indwelling Spirit. . . .

We reverence and obey the Lord Jesus Christ, our God and Saviour, as the sole and absolute authority in all matters pertaining to faith and practice, as revealed in the Scriptures, and we hold that each Church has liberty to interpret and administer His laws. We do not judge the conscience of those who take another view, but we believe that this principle of the freedom of the individual Church under Christ has the sanction of Scripture and the justification of history, and therefore we cannot abandon it without being false to our trust. Moreover, it is plain to us that the headship and sole authority of our Lord in His Church excludes any such relations with the State as may impair its liberty.

This view of the Church determines our attitude towards the special issues raised by the Lambeth Appeal.

The Scriptures, in and through which the Spirit of God speaks, possess for us supreme and unique authority. While we recognize the historic value of ancient creeds, we cannot give them a place of authority comparable with that of the Scriptures.

Christian Baptism and the Communion of the Lord's Supper are duly received by us not only as rites instituted and hallowed by our Lord Himself, but as means of grace to all who receive them in faith.

Because we hold the Church to be a community of Christian believers, the ordinance of baptism is administered among us to those only who make a personal confession of repentance and faith. We baptize by immersion in water in accordance with the mode of baptism received by our Lord and practised by His earliest followers as recorded in the New Testament, and because this symbolic representation guards the thought of that inner baptism of the Holy Spirit which is central in Christian experience. In our judgment the baptism of infants incapable of offering a personal confession of faith subverts the conception of the Church as the fellowship of believers. . . .

The Lord's Supper is observed regularly and devoutly by our Churches. Its value for us depends upon both the presence of our Lord and the faith with which we receive the bread and wine that show forth His redemptive sacrifice; but not upon the official position of a celebrant or upon any change in the elements due to words of consecration. It seems to us contrary to the simplicity that is in Christ that the full effect of the Lord's Supper as a means of grace should be held to depend on episcopal ordination. . . .

Our doctrine of the Church determines our conception of the ministry. We hold firmly the priesthood of all believers, and therefore have no separated order of priests. The ministry is for us a gift of the Spirit to the Church, and is an office involving both the inward call of God and the commission of the Church. We can discover no ground for believing that such commission can be given only through an episcopate, and we hold that the individual Church is competent to confer it. For us there is no more exalted office than a ministry charged with preaching the Word of God and with the care of souls. Those called to devote their whole lives to such tasks are held in special honour. Yet any full description of the ministerial functions exercised among us must also take account of other believers who, at the call of the Church, may preside at the observance of the Lord's Supper or fulfil any other duties which the Church assigns to them.

The deepening sense of friendship and unity between the various parts of the one Church of Christ gladdens us. We thank God that many ancient misunderstandings are passing away, that in our own country hostility and bitterness are giving place to charity and cooperation, and that the Lambeth Appeal by its language and spirit has drawn the Churches nearer to one another.

It will be gathered from this reply that union of such a kind as the Bishops have contemplated is not possible for us. We would say this not only with that frankness which we believe is the highest courtesy among Christian brethren, but with the assurance of our regret that the way in which they would have us to go with them is not open.

Further progress in the direction of Christian unity can be secured, we are convinced, only by unreserved mutual recognition. . . .

We believe that the time has come when the Churches of Christ should unite their forces to meet the need of the world. We therefore are prepared to join the Church of England in exploring the possibility of a federation of equal and autonomous Churches in which the several parts of the Church of Christ would co-operate in bringing before men the will and claims of our Lord.

We assure our brethren of our earnest prayer that the blessing of God may rest upon the Churches of the Anglican Communion, and that He may continue to impart abundantly to its members the riches of His grace.

Finally, we would reaffirm our belief in the real spiritual unity of all who are loyal to Christ and His truth and our eagerness to welcome every means by which, in common action for the spread of His message and the helping and healing of men, that unity may be displayed to the world.

Grace be with all them that love our Lord Jesus Christ in sincerity.

13.6   The Meaning and Practice of Ordination Among Baptists

What is the meaning of ordination among Baptists? That is the basic question addressed in the study paper below. This paper originated as a report to the Baptist Union in 1957, citing Baptist understanding of the biblical and theological meaning of ordination. One valuable part of the study is the review of Baptist statements on ordination in the past. *Source:* "The Meaning and Practice of Ordination among Baptists." A Report submitted to the Council of the Baptist Union of Great Britain and Ireland (London: Carey Kingsgate Press, 1957), 10-42.

ORDINATION AMONG BAPTISTS

39. (i) *Historical evidence*

English Baptists of the seventeenth century held Ordination Services and regarded them as an important element in church order. The word "ordination" was at times used for the Service of setting apart of deacons, but in this statement attention is confined to its use in regard to the pastoral office. . . .

. . . Generally, the pastor was already a member of the local church before his invitation to become its pastor. It was not unusual for the pastoral work to be begun some months before the ordination. The practice suggests that delay was deliberate, perhaps to enable both minister and church to obtain confirmation of the call by the Holy Spirit. Ordination took place at a solemn Service attended by the pastors of nearby churches and the Service included questions regarding the call, together with prayer, sermons and the laying on of hands by the pastors. No unordained persons took part. The appointment was to a specific pastoral charge and was held to be for life. If the pastor removed to another church and was by that church invited to become its pastor, he was re-ordained.

40. During the eighteenth century the practice of the previous century was continued. There is little doubt, however, that the changing pattern of society and the rise of other evangelical groups affected the thinking and polity of Baptist churches. These changes began to emerge towards the end of the eighteenth century and to become of vital importance during the nineteenth century. The Great Awakening in America and the Methodist Revival produced a new spirit within our Baptist life, . . . It is probable that the Methodist emphasis upon lay preaching and upon a circuit system, together with the changing of pastorates every few years, affected indirectly the thought and practice in Baptist churches. By the beginning of the nineteenth century men began to move more frequently from one church to another. The rise of many new towns through industrialism brought another challenge for the promotion of new churches. . . .

42. The new situation at the end of the eighteenth century demanded a revival of the old order of evangelists. In 1797 the Baptist Missionary Society began a home work section and sent an evangelist to Cornwall. As the nineteenth century progressed there appeared a number of evangelists. Some were sent forth by the churches and others were only loosely attached. . . . The growth and spread of Nonconformity during the second half of the nineteenth century was rapid and this led to a further loosening of tradition. Churches became increasingly autonomous and did not always refer to other churches in their call of pastors or in connection with their ordination. During this period there was also a reaction from the Oxford Movement. The use of the title "Reverend", which Baptists had used since the seventeenth century, was now challenged; the laying on of hands was omitted, and then the word ordination dropped out of use. By about 1885 Ordination and Commissioning Services had given place to Welcome Meetings.

43. Towards the end of the nineteenth century Baptists began to express more definitely their fellowship with one another through the Baptist Union, . . . and since 1896 there has been a Committee of the Baptist Union concerned with Ministerial Recognition. The original objects of the Committee were:—

"1. To prevent the unworthy or unfit entering the ministry.

2. To commend those qualified to the denomination.

3. To secure to those recognised eligibility for funds."

But the right of local churches to choose whom they will as pastors has always been expressly recognised. . . . Ministers are now ordained only once. . . .

IV
THE MEANING OF ORDINATION

47. The following form of words is offered as a definition of ordination. The subsequent paragraphs are an elaboration of this definition in which suggestions are made concerning some of its implications.

Ordination is the act, wherein the Church, under the guidance of the Holy Spirit, publicly recognises and confirms that a Christian believer has been gifted, called and set apart by God for the work of the ministry and in the name of Christ commissions him for this work.

48. (i) The Call of God is fundamental.

Consideration of ordination must begin with the recognition that Christian ministry depends upon the call of God and is His gift in Christ to the Church (Ephesians 4, 11-12). . . .

49. (ii) Ordination is an act of the Church.

The work of the ministry is not personal service rendered by the individual in his own right, nor is a minister a free lance "prophet" exercising his ministry in a private capacity. He is a leader within a fellowship, viz. the Church (Acts 14, 23; 15, 22; Romans 16, 1; 1 Cor. 12. 18, 28, etc.). . . .

APPENDIX 1

Baptists and Ordination

There are frequent references to ordination in the early Baptist Confessions, of which the following are examples.

"Every Church hath power given them from Christ, for their better well-being, to choose to themselves meet persons into the office of elders or deacons, being qualified according to the word . . . as those which Christ hath appointed in His Testament, for the feeding, governing, serving and building up of His Church, and that none have power to impose on them either these or any other." (Particular Baptist London Confession, 1644.)

The Confession of the thirty Baptist Congregations which joined together in 1651 declares that "fasting and prayer ought to be used, and laying on of hands, for the ordaining of servants or officers to attend about the service of God" (McGlothlin: *Baptist Confessions of Faith*, pp. 105-108).

"The way appointed by Christ for the calling of any person fitted and gifted by the Holy Spirit into the office of Bishop (i.e. pastor) or Elder in a Church is that he be chosen thereunto by the common suffrage of the Church itself and solemnly set apart by Fasting and Prayer with imposition of hands of the Eldership of the Church if there be any before constituted therein." (Second London Confession, 1677.)

The fullest General Baptist statement on the subject in the early period is that of 1678, in which the officers of the Church are listed as (1) bishops or messengers; (2) elders or pastors; (3) deacons or overseers of the poor. "Bishops" are to be chosen "by the common suffrage of the Church and solemnly set apart by fasting and prayer, with imposition of hands, by the bishops of the same function, ordinarily, and those bishops so ordained have the government of those churches that had suffrage in their election . . . and the particular pastor, or elder, in like manner is to be chosen by the common suffrage of the particular congregation and ordained by the bishop or messenger God hath placed in the church he hath charge of . . ." (McGlothlin, op. cit., pp. 146-7). The Particular Baptists marked appointment both to the pastoral office and the diaconate "with imposition of hands of the Eldership of the Church, if there be any before constituted therein" (1689 Confession, McGlothlin, op. cit., p. 266). . . .

The rise of the Baptist Missionary Society in 1792 was an important development, although its significance in the matter of ordination was not fully appreciated. In 1795 two missionaries were set aside for a Mission to Sierra Leone with prayers and the laying on of hands. Andrew Fuller in 1804 took up some of these issues, urging that missionaries should be commissioned in this country and ordained on the mission field by the churches who called them into the pastoral office. In this country the regular practice of ordination appears to have faded about the middle of the century. . . .

It is well known that C. H. Spurgeon rejected the idea of ordination when it was suggested to him in 1854 at New Park Street, and it may be surmised that about that time we begin to see a reaction to the Oxford Movement. On the other hand, Rogers, the first Principal of Spurgeon's College, insisted on giving what he deliberately called an ordination address, and in the *Sword and Trowel* from 1865 there are occasional references to Services held "in connection with the Ordination of . . . when the former Pastor of the Church or a nearby Pastor asked the question usual upon such occasions and offered the ordination prayer." There is no reference to laying on of hands. By 1880 references to ordination have become infrequent and it was not until after the First World War that they come into prominence. Since that time ordination has gradually become the regular practice with or without the laying on of hands.

APPENDIX 2

Official Baptist Statements relating to Ordination (1896-1953)

Modern English Baptist official statements on ordination (which have often been issued in relation to statements made by other bodies, or by conferences connected with inter-church discussions) are summarised below:—

1923. Adopted by the Annual Assembly of the Baptist Union:—

1. Affirming the doctrine of the priesthood of all believers and the obligation resting upon them to fulfil their vocation according to the gift bestowed upon them:

   By the *Ministry* we mean an office within the Church of Christ (not a sacerdotal order) conferred through the call of the Holy Spirit and attested by a particular or local Church.

   By *Ordination* we mean the act of the Church by which it delegates to a person ministerial functions which no man can properly take upon himself.

2. Inasmuch as the setting apart to the ministry is a matter deeply affecting the welfare of the Church:—

   (i) An ordination should take place in the Church to which the person is called.

   (ii) In order to witness to the unity of the Church, and to safeguard the entrance into the ministry, it is desirable that the ordination should receive the concurrence and approval of the County Association or of its Committee.

   (iii) In regard to anyone called to the exercise of the ministry in spheres other than that of the pastorate of a Church, ordination should take place in the presence of those by whom the person has been called.

   (iv) It is recommended that the ordination or any subsequent induction service should include the observance of the Lord's Supper.

1926. In reply to the Lambeth Appeal of 1920 authorised by the Baptist Union Assembly of 1926 it was affirmed:—

We hold the priesthood of all believers and therefore have no separated order of priests. The ministry is the gift of the Spirit to the Church and is an office involving both the inward call of God and the Commission of the Church . . . . We hold that the individual Church is competent to confer it.

1930. Reply of the Baptist Union to the Report of the World Conference on Faith and Order at Lausanne. (B.U. Council Report).

III. The Nature of the Church.

   We cannot agree that the ministry, as commonly understood, is essential to the existence of a true Christian Church, though we believe a ministry is necessary for its highest effectiveness. We think of the function of the ministry in terms of leadership rather than of government and discipline. We believe that, while we should frankly discuss our differences, at this time it may be a gain to emphasise our agreement on the permanent and essential marks of the Church. . .

V. The Ministry of the Church.

   Under III above, we have already referred to our view of the ministry as not being essential to the very existence of a Church.

   We do not confine the administration of Sacraments to ordained ministers, nor stipulate for the laying on of hands.

   In our thought, the declaration in the Report that the administration of the Sacraments is to be made effective through faith is inconsistent with the practice of administering Baptism to others than believers. . . .

1937. The Second World Conference on Faith and Order, Edinburgh (in which Baptists shared) (Bell, 3rd Series, p. 267) affirmed:—

1. The Ministry was instituted by Jesus Christ and is a gift of God to the Church.
2. It presupposes a royal priesthood of all Christians.
3. Ordination to the ministry according to the New Testament teaching is by prayer and the laying on of hands.
4. It is essential to a United Church that it should have a ministry universally recognised.

"It must be acknowledged, however, that even in connexion with these statements, different interpretations are to be reckoned with.

"For example, while all would agree that the ministry owes its origin to Jesus Christ and is God's gift to the Church, there are differences of judgment regarding the sense in which we may say that the ministry was 'instituted' by our Lord.

"Again, those who agree in accepting the laying on of hands as the form of ordination differ on the meaning to be attached to the rite, or on the question by whom it should be administered."

1938. Reply of B.U. Council to the Federal Council of Evangelical Free Churches on documents for consideration of the Churches by a joint committee of Anglicans and Free Churchmen (B.U. Report 1939, App. IV, p. 56).

It is in accordance with the will of God and in the true interest of the Church that individual Christians, men or women, having suitable gifts should be solemnly set apart by the Church as its ministers; in many cases this is done by the Apostolic practice of prayer and the laying on of hands by the recognised representatives of the Church. . . . Such ordination does not confer a priesthood other than that already possessed by all believers. . . . They regard as fully valid the ministry of any Christian man or woman whom the Christian community may invite to preach, to administer the sacraments or to discharge any other ministerial duty. . . .

II

1948. A Statement approved by the Baptist Union Council on *The Baptist Doctrine of the Church*.

The Ministry

4. . . . Baptists, however, have had from the beginning an exalted conception of the office of the Christian minister and have taken care to call men to serve as pastors. The minister's authority to exercise his office comes from the call of God in his personal experience, but this call is tested and approved by the church of which he is a member and (as is increasingly the rule) by the representatives of a large group of churches. He receives intellectual and spiritual training and is then invited to exercise his gift in a particular sphere. His authority, therefore, is from Christ through the believing community. It is not derived from a chain of bishops held to be lineally descended from the Apostles, and we gratefully affirm that to our non-episcopal communities, as to those episcopally governed, the gifts of the Spirit and the power of God are freely given.

Many among us hold that since the ministry is the gift of God to the Church and the call to exercise the functions of a minister comes from Him, a man who is so called is not only the minister of a local Baptist church but also a minister of the whole Church of Jesus Christ.

Ordination takes place when a man has satisfactorily completed his college training and has been called to the pastorate of a local church, appointed to chaplaincy service or accepted for service abroad by the Committee of the Baptist Missionary Society.

The ordination service is presided over by either the Principal of his college, a

General Superintendent or a senior minister and is shared in by other ministers and lay representatives of the church. Though there is no prescribed or set form of service, it invariably includes either a personal statement of faith or answers to a series of questions regarding the faith. From the seventeenth century onwards, ordination took place with the laying on of hands: in the nineteenth century this custom fell into disuse, but is now again increasingly practised.

1953. Adopted by the Annual Assembly of the Baptist Union.

Whereas for many years the Baptist Union of Great Britain and Ireland has, acting through the Council, prepared lists of Ministers and Probationers accredited by the Union in accordance with a scheme of Ministerial Recognition, and whereas it is desirable that the purposes of the Scheme should be restated:

Resolved as follows:—

1. The purposes of the Scheme are
    (*a*) To encourage candidates for the Baptist Ministry to fit themselves for their vocation by means of suitable courses of study and training, to be undertaken whenever possible in a Baptist College recognised by the Baptist Union.
    (*b*) To accord to those Ministers who have so fitted themselves and whose qualifications are approved, the recognition of the Baptist Union, and to commend them to the Churches.
    (*c*) To encourage Ministers by all possible means to magnify the Ministry and to lay upon themselves the disciplinary ideals of their calling.
    (*d*) To take action in cases of conduct unbecoming to the Ministry.
    (*e*) To facilitate Ministerial settlement.
    (*f*) To meet the requirements of Denominational Schemes, Funds and Trusts.
2. There shall be prepared and maintained a list of
    (*a*) Baptist Ministers in the British Isles who are for the time being accredited for the purposes of the Scheme.
    (*b*) Probationer Baptist Ministers in the British Isles.
3. All Persons who become or remain Ministers or Probationers accredited by the Union are required to accept the Declaration of Principle as contained in the Constitution of the Union.
4. (*a*) The Council is empowered to administer the Scheme and may from time to time make Bye-Laws consistent with the purposes aforesaid.
    (*b*) No such Bye-Laws nor any amendment or repeal thereof shall take effect unless approved by the Council on a resolution carried by the votes of at least two-thirds of the members present at a meeting of the Council.

The Union acknowledges that there are others whose names do not appear on the above-mentioned Accredited Lists who are Ministers of Baptist Churches and may rightly be designated Baptist Ministers.

13.7 The Role of Baptist Deaconesses

In the earliest English Baptist churches women as well as men served in the role of deacon. The role of men deacons has changed over the years, but the role of women deacons (or deaconesses) has changed even more. A shortage of pastors, especially during the two world wars, catapulted deaconesses into more pastoral forms of ministry in English Baptist churches. The changed *functions* of deaconesses led to changes in their *training*, which in turn encouraged further changes in actual service. The document below comments on the role of English Baptist deaconesses about mid century. *Source:* "The Doctrine of the Ministry" (London: The Baptist Union of Great Britain and Ireland), Appendix 4.

In 1919 the Baptist Union assumed responsibility for the work which had been carried on by the Baptist Deaconess Home and Mission, and decided to enlarge its scope. It was agreed to found a college in London, and "to call out and train Baptist women who were qualified and ready to devote themselves to some specialised form of ministry in the Church, and more particularly to the work of deaconesses among the poor, to missionary work, and in positions of leadership in the Church, Institute, Sunday School, and Christian social work."

A Special Committee was set up by the Baptist Union Council to survey the organisation land the function of the Order and the College, and its findings were presented to the Council in March, 1941. Attention was drawn to the variety of work the deaconess was called upon to do. "We do not aim at training Women Ministers, but some deaconesses have been virtually put in the position of Ministers and given the responsibility of organising and maintaining churches. Others act as assistants to Ministers, with special responsibility for the conduct of Women's Meetings, for Sunday School work and the care of young women and children.

By-Laws were drawn up and approved by the Baptist Union Council in 1948, setting forth rules governing the relationship of deaconesses to the Baptist Union on the one hand and to the churches on the other, and dealing with recognition, settlement and sustenance.

At the settlement of a deaconess in a church a Service of Induction and Recognition is usually held.

The fact that deaconesses are increasingly doing the work normally undertaken by a minister raises questions about their status and the training necessary for them, and we would call the attention of the Denomination to these matters.

13.8   A Baptist View of Children in the Church

An insistence that baptism "appertaineth not to infants" helped call Baptists into existence as a separate denomination. However, English Baptists have not always agreed on the status of the child in the church. The following study paper on this subject reveals not only a Baptist view of children in 1978, but also includes a helpful section tracing the development of a theology of children through Baptist history. *Source:* David F. Tennant, *Children in the Church: A Baptist View* (London: Baptist Publications, 1978), 7-33. Used by permission.

Introduction

There are those who have called this the 'age of the evolution of the child'. For us the days when children were an economic necessity have gone. The days when children were playthings, 'seen and not heard', have disappeared also. . . .

It has been said that Baptists have no theology of childhood. The issue has been raised sharply time and time again: does the Baptist view of little children depend on baptism or vice versa? In attempting to answer this question and make a contribution to an ongoing debate we had better go back to the beginning.

Historical Background

1. Double Separation

The first Baptist church was established in 1609 in Amsterdam under the leadership of John Smyth. Members of this community, having previously been exiled in Holland because of their separation from the established church, returned to England in 1612 and founded a church in England under Thomas Helwys. The first Baptists had come to their convictions by way of separatism with its roots in puritanism. They repudiated the notion of an established state church, believed fervently in the gathered church, in the centrality of the scriptures, and the restriction of baptism to believers only. These were the General Baptists whose atonement theology was Arminian in source: Christ died for all men. A group emerged later in London whose theology was Calvinistic in origin with the stress on the sovereignty of God leading to election of the chosen and salvation only for those elected. These were the Particular Baptists.

In accepting the baptism of believers only, *both groups repudiated infant baptism.* . . . But, refusing to baptise their babies, on the grounds of their separation as the gathered church, and refusing to christen or 'name' them was a kind of double separation of the babies, for they were now outside the 'officially constituted spiritual life of the nation'.

2. Problems

Baptists had to fight on two fronts: on the one hand they had certain things in common with the other separatists and could be identified with them. Yet the separatists retained infant baptism in terms of covenant. Infants born into the families of church members were, like the Jews of old; born into covenant community, were heirs of the promise and baptism was a sign of that inheritance. . . .

The other front on which the early Baptists were fighting was in relation to the established church. Baptism in this church grafted a child into the church and was the antidote for original sin and therefore had regenerative power. This baptism was for all, irrespective of the faith of the parents. Here the problem was not merely a theoretical one but was caused by the fact of a high infant mortality rate for which the established church view was both an answer and a solution. It was also a consolation to sad and fearful parents.

So certain issues were raised: the relationship of believing children to the church and gospel; the issue of sin in respect of childhood; the nature of the church; and at the root is the nature of the gospel, God's remedy for sin. Is it actual, to be appropriated by faith, or possible, meaningless without the profession of faith upon which it depends? To these issues Baptists had to turn and have continued to return ever since!

3. Answers that ask Questions

To John Smyth the church was a gathered community called by God, and consisted of those who confessed their faith in Christ and were baptised. . . . It must be added, however, that Smyth was more sympathetic to the status of children than the Particular Baptists, for although he refused to administer baptism to infants, yet he did concede that the children of believers were in some way 'under the gospel'. The questions of the status of the child before God and church were still begged.

The Particular Baptists differed from their General brethren concerning baptism, not in the mode of administration, nor the status of those to whom it was administered, but in regard to its motif. Baptism was not so much initiation into the church as the symbol of the death, resurrection, new birth motif. In common with the other separatists they followed the idea of covenant.

The Particulars now differed from their General brethren in denying any privilege at all to the infants of believers, repudiating any analogy between circumcision and baptism, and placing the covenant not in the context of inheritance and birth, but in the context of repentance, faith and rebirth. . . .

If, then, children are excluded from membership of the church, are they also excluded from the kingdom of God? The Particular Baptists answered by making a distinction between the church visible, membership of which was by faith and repentance followed by baptism, and the invisible church known only to God. The final decision about salvation is with God and the grace of election, and amongst the elect might well be infants whose membership of the invisible church would be secure by virtue of that election. . . .

4. School on Sunday

The rise of the Sunday School Movement was essentially a response to some kind of rudimentary education for children who were in large numbers (50% of the population were children in the 18th century). . . .

Originally the aim was instruction in the Three R's, remembering that the religious education of the child was essentially still in the home and in the church through cate-chetical teaching. . . . Like others, Baptists responded to the Sunday School movement enthusiastically. In character and quality they were no different from others, and this is important because Baptists did 'not take their children into the church immediately after birth' and as a consequence were confronted with certain problems. These prob-lems related to original sin, the status of children, the relationship of children to God and the church.

The Changing Situation

1. The Ceremony of Dedication

The answer of Baptists to questions about childhood and church and ceremonies relating to birth was that no ceremony was needed at all. Yet there is some evidence that . . . even Baptists felt the need for placing at least the children of believers firmly in the church and in the purpose of God at birth. . . . There is also some evidence as early as the 18th century of a dedication service of some kind. Thomas Grantham provided a ceremony of dedication, based on Jesus' example in blessing the children. His wording, however, is ambiguous and it is not at all clear what this ceremony was about or what it meant.

Many attribute the beginnings of the dedication service as we know it to John Clif-ford, though even this has been questioned. . . .

Issues to be Faced

1. Towards a Theology of Childhood

The problems and issues raised in the foregoing discussions are still with us in one way or another. The big question concerns the status of children and their relation to the church and the kingdom of God. . . .

The dedication service was popularised by parents wishing to associate their children with the church immediately at birth. The ecumenical movement has brought Baptists into closer contact with others and their views, and in some cases into partnership. Further, the now almost commonly accepted pattern of worship and instruction called family church has placed children in the church for worship, and in some instances for learning, with adults. . . .

The early Baptist's view of little children was determined by their understanding of the church. We have already shown that certain difficulties were encountered because of the nature of the gospel, sin and little children and they concluded that children were different and outside the notions of responsibility demanded by repentance and faith, simply because they were children. So we have to ask—when does a child cease to be a passive beneficiary of the atoning work of Christ and become a responsible person? In other words, what is the age of discretion, understanding, decision? Can we ever be dogmatic about this? Baptist practice in some parts of the world is more akin to other traditions than to Baptists in Europe. In the Southern States of the United States, for example, Baptists baptise at anything from seven to ten years of age. For all its risk this practice does recognise that in maturity there are certain nodal years (points of significant growth) and this is one such moment. . . .

2. Childhood in the Bible

There is no single picture of childhood in the Bible. There are a number of pictures. Broadly speaking, in the Old Testament children are the gift of God (Psalm 127). Not only are they a gift of God's providence as Psalm 127 makes clear, a part of the divine order, but also they are the 'Israel to be'. . . .

This view of childhood as preparatory held until the time of Jesus, was shared by Paul, and assumed by him in his view of Christ and the Christian life. To Paul the Christian life is one of 'a man in Christ'. Childhood is associated with preparation, as is evidenced by Eph. 3 and 1 Cor. 13. . . . Moreover, with the saying and actions of Jesus about children, we have a highly unusual and original idea of childhood. . . . According to Jesus, in the kingdom of God childhood is the model. . . .

3. What does this say for the Church?

The child belongs to a family and if his family belongs to the church, so does he. He is to be placed in the church at birth and nurtured into faith through the careful partnership of church and home. Baptists must ask whether this placing of the child at birth needs a ceremony and if so what sort of ceremony. Is there a case for baptising or initiating the child into the church because of his special relationship with the church and therefore with God? If then the child belongs to the church with his parents, then the church must be more than just those committed to responsible membership, the fellowship of believers. If baptism is reserved for the moment of conscious personal choice, as most Baptists would say, is it necessary to invent some sort of childhood ceremony—some childhood sacrament even—to demonstrate that relationship of the child with the church by virtue of his birth to Christian parents? If for Baptists the ceremony is dedication then it is a kind of initiation into the process of growth for responsible membership of the church. It is also the dedication of parents and the church to a mutual task. It is also blessing of the child and the occasion of the church's celebration of the mighty acts of God in creation and redemption.

4. Let's Listen!

It is worth pausing now to listen to what those who do baptise infants have to say to us. Counting heads is never a good guide to truth but the fact is that the majority of Christians for many centuries have baptised infants. In so doing certain things are held to be of importance although there is no common agreement amongst all infant baptisers as to the central significance of the rite. However, if we listen, then at least three things are being said that Baptists must take account of, with or without a ceremony!

First, infant baptisers recognise that the grace of God is operative independently of man's response. They recognise that Christian life begins with God's saving acts in Jesus Christ, and the continuance of that life in God is equally dependent on the grace of God, his mercy and forgiveness, and does not depend on the individual's faith or lack of it. ('We love because he first loved.') Further, God's grace can be mediated through church and home, and the child baptised in infancy is firmly placed in home and church as the environment through which the prevenient grace of God can be mediated. Now this is not at all to disparage the importance of individual personal faith, and most infant baptisers will recognise the importance of 'confirming' faith at some stage. . . .

Secondly, following on from the above, infant baptisers stress the special relationship that the children of believers have with the church, a relationship that is different from that of the children of non-believing parents. . . . Infant baptism is saying something important about family and marriage and home, and Baptists could well listen.

Thirdly is the special stress on the family as a unit. This raises the question of Christian marriage, children born of such a union, the growing and extending unity within God's purpose of this family and their place together within God's family. Infant baptism is saying something important about family and marriage and home, and Baptists could well listen.

13.9   Michael Taylor, *A Plain Man's Guide to the Incarnation*, 1977

Since the days of Matthew Caffyn, some English Baptists have struggled with the question of the full Deity of Jesus Christ. Renewed controversy over Christology surfaced at the Baptist Union Assembly in Nottingham in 1971 with Michael Taylor's bluntly stated sermon, "The Incarnate Presence: How Much of a Man Was Jesus Christ?" Taylor offended many Baptists by what they regarded as a denial of historic doctrines about Jesus Christ. The Council, a kind of executive committee for the Baptist Union, thwarted all efforts to have Taylor officially censured. The controversy later subsided somewhat, but not before a number of leading churches and ministers used the occasion to withdraw from the Baptist Union. *Source:* Michael Taylor, *A Plain Man's Guide to the Incarnation* (Loughborough, Leisc.: ONE Publications, 1977), 1-10. Used by permission.

The Myth of God Incarnate

Hard on the heels of the death of God has followed the cutting-down-to-size of Jesus Christ, or so it may seem to many. . . .

A lot has been written in the last ten years about the Christian understanding of the sort of person Jesus was (that is about Christology or the Doctrine of the Person of Christ). If you want to read all about it, there is a long list of books and articles (a bibliography) written up to about 1973 at the back of John Robinson's **The Human Face of God** S.C.M. If you are prepared to sample one or two you could try **Grace and Truth** by Anthony T. Hanson, S.P.C.K. or **Christ for Us Today**, S.C.M. (a collection of short essays) or the relevant parts of Hans Kung's **On Being a Christian,** Collins. The most recent and well-publicised offering to hit the market is **The Myth of God Incarnate** another collection of essays edited by John Hick (S.C.M.). . . . Reading the book has provided the immediate stimulus for what follows, and much of the material.

1. Why must Christianity be something which can be believed?

To get down to business, rumour is rife that certain aspects of Christian belief, in particular belief about Christ, have become unbelievable. What is wrong with that? Why must Christianity be something which can be believed? . . .

You can still argue however that Christianity must be believable and not as has been suggested that the more unbelievable it is the better! What good is it to anyone if it's not? It may present some unpalatable truths which no-one wants to believe but little is to be gained from unbelievable ones which no-one can. Unfamiliar and uncomfortable insights can make sense. What is ruled out is nonsense. For example a growing understanding of how life has evolved and developed on this planet made nonsense of Genesis 1 and 2 as factual accounts of how the world began. A growing appreciation of how the books of the Bible came to be written made nonsense of theories of direct verbal inspiration. As a result Christianity had to make what were painful adjustments at the time. It had to be made believable. The same some suggest must now be done with what it has traditionally said about the person of Christ.

2. And what is it in particular that is unbelievable now?

The short answer is the doctrine of the Incarnation. . . . It is unbelievable that God became a man when Jesus was born in the same matter-of-fact way that the cat sits on the mat, or a chrysalis turns into a butterfly, or a rich man might pretend to be a poor nan, or the frog in the fairy tale changes into a prince; though the transfiguration of God was not quite like any of those because according to traditional Christian belief he wasn't pretending and it wasn't a fairy tale and he didn't exactly change from one to the other but managed to be both at the same time. But it was plain matter of fact.

We must not overdraw the picture. There are plenty of other beliefs, such as the belief that God is deeply mixed up in the affairs of this world and that he was highly active in the life of Jesus, that do not fall with the doctrine of the Incarnation; and of course plenty of people will insist that this doctrine, so central to Christian thought, is not unbelievable at all. They do still believe it, and having thought about it rather carefully, regard it as a perfectly intellectually respectable thing to do. The unbelievers will privately remain convinced that the believers won't be able to believe much longer unless they insist on 'kicking against the pricks of the facts'.

3. Why isn't it believable?

The absurdity of attempting short answers to big questions becomes increasingly apparent. In a sense there is no answer to this one. We start and stop believing for reasons we cannot trace. What was credible simply does become incredible and vice versa. But if I attempted a long answer in the hope of earning decent marks, I think I should have to write something under at least four headings.

The first goes back to what we were saying before. You can't believe one thing because you can't believe another, and we can't believe that God becomes a man in Jesus because we can no longer believe as earlier generations did believe that on that or any other occasion God intervenes in such a tangible way in what goes on in his world. . . . The world we believe we have to deal with is made up of known patterns of cause and effect and if not known then capable, with patience, of being discovered. There are reasons for apparently inexplicable reversals other than the reason that God interferes and causes things to happen like an engineer who tampers with the machine or a gardener who suddenly produces a new rose. Because we don't believe he behaves like that we don't believe in miracles and we don't believe in the intervention to crown all interventions, namely the Incarnation.

Second, if the church believes that God became man or rather was God and man in Jesus at one and the same time, it has never been able to explain what that means. No explanation should clear up all the mysteries but it should make some sort of sense. . . . We notice that in one way or another they fail and end up with a man and no God or God and no man by settling for a paradox and admitting defeat. We have nevertheless swallowed our scepticism and loyally carried on believing that something sensible was still being discussed. Now we have found the courage of our scepticism and can call nonsense by its name.

Third there are moral reasons why the doctrine of Incarnation is unbelievable. It has been too closely identified with unpleasant, authoritarian attitudes and may have been developed to justify them. Since Jesus was God, the church of Jesus had the right to behave in a godlike way, Lording it over people and claiming that since it possessed the absolute truth it had the right to the final word. It became remarkably unlike Jesus himself, . . .

Fourth, the claim that Jesus alone is the final way to know God and find salvation is easy to believe when there is no real alternative because there is no real encounter with the other great religions of the world. Where there is, as in our so-called global village, then it begins to sound rather rude and very unfair. Jesus may be the 'last word' for Christians, but he is not for the majority of mankind. . . . and is it conceivable that the God who acted in Jesus has failed to act in other equally important ways for the good of mankind?

4. Why don't I have to believe it?

This may not be the best question to send in search of an answer, but it does draw attention to a point which is central to the current debate. Someone may object that however unbelievable the doctrine of the Incarnation may be, and however many impressive reasons may be given for not believing it, it will still have to be believed because it is revealed truth or, if you like, God told us and we must accept God's word for it.

This is where the historians have radically altered the picture for us. They have begun to trace how certain ideas such as the Incarnation grew up. They can't do it with complete accuracy but what seems perfectly clear is that it is the product of a great many ingredients. . . . To put it differently, a different person, with a different experience, coming from a different background, such as Asia or Africa for example, would have come up with a different result. This can actually be seen to be happening in the early church where everyone didn't think alike and there is more than one account of what it could mean to say that men had had a decisive encounter with God in Jesus.

Now once you recognise that a doctrine has a history, that it has evolved and been affected by all sorts of factors along the way, that doesn't give you the right to say it isn't true but it does make it hard to regard it any longer as a ready made, timeless truth revealed by God. . . .

5. What is the alternative?

I was always taught that grammatically speaking there is only ever one alternative. In this case however there are several, and they are not, like the normal alternatives, mutually exclusive. I will refer to four of them: you can go on saying the same thing, or you can say something different, or you can allow more than one thing to be said, or you can say very little at all.

First, you can go on saying the same thing. You can go on telling a story about God becoming a man in Jesus but you will not be a fundamentalist about it and take it too literally, just as you can go on telling a story about God busily making a world during the inside of a working week without believing that you are actually giving a blow by blow account of seven days in the life of a Creator. You know the difference between poetry and prose, and that these stories are poetry. . . . The story of the Incarnation, like that of Creation, is a myth in the best technical sense of the word. Myths are not lies but they are not factual accounts of events. They express in story form the inner meaning of events. God did not make the world in a week, but the world is dependent upon God. God did not literally become a man in a way that bears description (but defies explanation), but the events concerning the man Jesus did have a quality which could be described as Godlike.

This ability to distinguish different ways of using language ('my love is like a red red rose' and 'my love is not like my neighbour's wife') is crucial not only when we decide to say the same thing but also, second, when we decide to say something different, for it is not that a new way of stating the doctrine of the Incarnation can be taken literally whereas the old one could not. It is still a way of interpreting what happened rather than describing it, but to many it will be a more satisfactory way. One such restatement, more satisfactory to many, is to say that the Godlike quality about Jesus did not arise from the fact (sorry) that he was God anymore than we are God. It arose from the fact that God acted in Jesus in such a way that all that happened round and through him became the saving events they did. Jesus is different from us not because he is the only God man, but because God did something different in Jesus from what he does in us. God was at work in Christ but God was not Christ.

The third possibility is for Christians to relax a little more than they have in the past over their understanding of what sort of person Jesus was. The church has insisted on everyone toeing the line over the Incarnation. Everyone must believe that God became man. It has never been so fussy about our understanding of what Jesus did or, if you like, the doctrine of salvation. Many different accounts of our salvation have been allowed to exist in the church from the word go. The two (Christologies or theories about the person of Christ and Soteriologies or theories about the work of Christ) are closely tied together as we shall see, and if variety is allowed in one, perhaps it can safely be allowed in the other.

Fourth and finally, some suggest it is possible to say very little. . . . Is it not sufficient merely to recognise, at this distance at least, that Jesus and the events concerning him were the occasion, for reasons that can never now be very clear to us, which sparked off an enormously significant venture of the human spirit into the mystery and reality of God? Who Jesus was (God or man or both) matters less than what he was like and what because of him, has happened since. . . .

6. Does it matter?

There are really two questions here: first does the argument matter that there is good reason for me to get involved (the busy non-theologian must be very tempted to say 'NO') and second, is anything really lost by not believing in the Incarnation? The two are hard to keep apart. . . .

That God became a man in Jesus, and suffered as we do, and turned that suffering from a dead end into a creative new beginning, would be some grounds for taking the more tolerant, hopeful view. In that sense the argument about the Incarnation matters. It matters for my faith in providence whether God became a suffering man. And it matters if he didn't. It is not just idle theological table-talk.

But does it matter in the second sense? Is anything lost if we do not believe rather literally in the Incarnation? Suppose that God did not become a man. Does that prevent us from believing that God is deeply involved in our suffering and suffers with us, and could not the suffering of Jesus still be of such a quality as to awaken in us or strengthen us in that conviction? But need it be the only evidence, and could it taken by itself ever be sufficient evidence; and isn't the evidence more impressive if indeed we experience on more than one occasion a hopeful creative, Godlike quality about certain people's sufferings? And could it not be agreed that far from everything being lost by abandoning the traditional doctrine of Incarnation something is actually gained? If God became man uniquely and therefore but once in Jesus, it is a fantasy to understand him as entering into anything but a very tiny part of human suffering. He suffered once. It is only by modifying and even abandoning such a view that we can say that he suffers all the time: not when one man suffered but as each man suffers.

But let me finish with a different type of example. Presumably it matters to us whether Christianity is true, in which case, it could be argued, it matters if Jesus is God. If he is then Christianity is true because it's God's truth. If he is not, then our grounds for believing are swept away, and we have one more opinion amongst the rest. But our grounds for believing are not swept away if we no longer accept the doctrine of the Incarnation for the simple reason that they were never there. The Incarnation does not provide the grounds for believing anything. It is not a guarantee, it is simply one more belief. It does not answer the question 'Is Christianity true?' with the answer 'Of course it's true because it comes from God'. It has to face the question whether it is true itself. It is not the basis for Christian belief, it is part of some Christians' beliefs.

13.10   Assessing Baptist Spiritual Conditions

For most of the twentieth century English Baptists have faced unrelenting numerical decline. By mid century that downward trend accelerated sharply and included, some feared, spiritual as well as numerical decline. The Baptist Union as well as individual leaders have sought diligently to confront, assess, and above all to reverse these somber trends. Several major studies have analyzed the Baptist situation, making recommendations for improvement. Two such studies are cited here.

Selection A cites an important study of 1946, "Speak—That They Go Forward." This study arose out of conditions just after World War II, and makes a remarkably candid analysis of the Baptist situation. *Source:* Henry Cook, *Speak—That They Go Forward. A Report on Spiritual Welfare in Churches of the Baptist Denomination* (London: The Kingsgate Press, 1946), 5-20. Selection B excerpts "Signs of Hope," a study authorized in 1977 and presented to the Baptist Union in 1979. While candidly facing the discouraging trends, framers of this study found reasons to hope that the worst days were past and that Baptists could look toward a time of recovery. English Baptist life since 1979 has borne out only a portion of this hopeful expectation. *Source:* "Signs of Hope: An Examination of the Numerical and Spiritual State of Churches in Membership with the Baptist Union of Great Britain and Ireland," March 1979. To conserve space these excerpts are presented in paragraph form rather than the detailed outline of the original report.

A. Speak—That They Go Forward. A Report on Spiritual Welfare in Churches of the Baptist Denomination. By Henry Cook, M.A.

I. PRELIMINARY.
1. HOW THE REPORT ORIGINATED.

The Spiritual Welfare of the churches is a matter of constant concern to all of us, and at various times it has come before the Baptist Union Council. A special session was devoted to the subject in March, 1944, when there was some very frank and honest speaking about the present position of the churches, and, as a result, it was decided to ask the Officers of the Union to appoint a group of Council members who would examine the whole situation with a view to submitting a report. . . .

3. WHAT WE CAN DO.

The Report, as will be seen, covers a very wide field and touches on a great many questions. Whole books have been written on points that are now referred to in a paragraph or a sentence. . . .

What we need above everything else to-day is a sense of real concern for the situation before us. How far is it due to our own shortcomings and failures? Are we doing all that we might, or have we grown weary in well-doing because of the lack of response, or, what is worse, have we lost our first love and is our zeal for the winning of the world for Christ a thing of the past? . . .

II. THE PROBLEM.
1. THE SITUATION BEFORE US.

In 1910 Sir George Macalpine delivered his Presidential Address to the Baptist Union, taking as his subject "The Arrested Progress of the Churches." For years there had been steady growth in many directions, Churches and Sunday Schools had been well attended, and there had been constant baptisms and additions to Church-membership. But in 1909 there was no increase in the denomination as a whole, and over the broad area of the Church's work in England there was a slowing-up of momentum. There were signs that conditions were not so favourable as they had been, and hence it became possible to speak of "arrested progress."

Since then, the "arrested progress" has become a definite decline. Congregations and Sunday School attendances are very much smaller, conversions and baptisms in many churches are extremely rare, and, what is even more distressing, do what we will, we seem helpless to bring about a change. . . .

2. CAN WE GO FORWARD?

It is here, at the point where diagnosis ends and remedy begins, that most of us find ourselves in difficulties. We all know what is wrong, but how to put it right, how to deal with the situation that confronts us—"ay, there's the rub." . . . There is, in fact, no simple formula that will guarantee revival. Only God by His Spirit can give us the Pentecost we need, and no one, not even the wisest or best of us, can say when or how it will come. . . .

III. THE PURPOSE OF GOD.

As Christians we have no doubt whatsoever that God's will for the world has been revealed in Jesus Christ. The world is not being left to itself. Christ has made known God's redeeming purpose for our sinful race, and the Cross for ever demonstrates God's readiness to make the uttermost sacifice that men and women may be brought back to Himself. We confront a divided and despairing world with the Gospel of all-sufficient grace, and we are sure that in it we have the remedy for all the ills of our time, both individual and collective.

This general statement is not likely to be challenged. But there are a number of points involved in it, and these seem to gather round four main points—The Message, the Church, the Ministry, and Evangelism.

1. THE MESSAGE.

For convenience in discussion we put down a number of things that we ought always to have in mind.

(1) It should never be forgotten that our message is essentially the declaration of an activity of God as He manifests Himself to men in redemptive grace with a view to their salvation. That activity is disclosed in the historic revelation preserved for us in the Scriptures, beginning with God's dealings with Israel and reaching its climax in the work of Christ accomplished in His life, death, resurrection and ascension to the right hand of God.

(2) That being so, we can, as Paul said, preach the Gospel "in much assurance." Things *can* happen to the men and women before us because God by His Spirit is seeking to bring home the truth as we declare it, and that should give eagerness, gladness and urgency to our speech. . . .

(3) But if this is to be done effectively we must ourselves be perfectly sure of our ground. We must, that means, have an experience of God's power in ourselves, and our own personal conviction should give wings to our words, . . . we can never make a thing plain to our hearers unless we thoroughly understand it ourselves. . . .

(4) The message when fully thought-through must be mediated to ordinary folk, and hence its language must be living and true. . . . We get to know our people, their ways of thinking and speaking, and down the avenues of their own minds we can come to them bearing the Gospel in our hands.

(5) It is important that we relate God's Word to living situations. It is perfectly possible to discuss the great questions of sin and forgiveness in the abstract as philosophical problems that call for intellectual solution, and this is a form of mental discipline that no wise man will despise. But the Church must make men and women see that the Gospel "speaks to their condition" and deals with their actual situation, personal, domestic, business, or social. Sin may be an abstract noun, but sinners are living people, and it is with sinners that we are vitally concerned. Doctrine and conduct are interwoven. . . .

(6) In all this, however, we must never allow ourselves to forget that the Gospel is primarily concerned with man's need of God in his personal life, and our appeal must always be for definite conversions. . . .

(7) The Gospel is an offer of God's forgiving and transforming love, and where it is received there is the entrance into the soul of the joyous power and companionship of the Spirit.

(8) But the Gospel message carries with it consequences that go far beyond the present life, and it is a tragic thing that the Church has allowed its message to lose something of its eternal significance because misguided people have cheapened "the solemn realities" of hell, and judgment, and the final consummation of all things in the Advent of our risen and triumphant Lord. Eschatology is no doubt a more complicated subject than some people imagine. But the facts are in the Gospels, and they provide the background that gives urgency and importance to our message. It would be all to the good if our theologians would help us here. Too long we have neglected vital things in the Gospel because they have been mishandled, and by so doing we have so foreshortened our prespective that the Gospel has largely lost its eternal significance. "It is a fearful thing," says the Epistle to the Hebrews, "to fall into the hands of the living God"; and there is, says Jesus, an outer darkness where there is weeping and wailing and gnashing of teeth. The Scripture maintains on this whole subject a solemn dignity which some preachers have sometimes forgotten, but there can still be an effective appeal based on the need for decision lest we miss our opportunity and find ourselves facing a door that is shut. Let us not eviscerate our message because foolish people misuse what Carlyle calls "the great and solemn realities of death and judgment."

(9) One last point: It is only by a return to a worthy interpretation of the Gospel that we can save the world from its present moral chaos. Multitudes to-day have no standards of any sort except their own immediate self-interest, and there is a consequent widespread increase in drunkenness, immorality, dishonesty, and similar evils. . . . There is no solution for the deterioration in human character except that of the Gospel. We must get man into right relations with God, and that by the acceptance of His will as the dominant fact in their lives. . . .

2. THE CHURCH.

Nothing is easier than to belittle the Church and to dwell on its present difficulties and deficiencies. . . . For much of the defeatist spirit that exists we have ourselves to blame, and we suggest that we set ourselves to exalt the Church. Something is wanted among us akin to a soldier's pride in the regiment. We as Baptists have a great history, and no denomination has made a bigger contribution to the life of the Church as a whole. Why is it that so little of it is known? . . .

We as Baptists are fortunate in having a doctrine of the Church that is thoroughly self-consistent and at the same time capable of adaptation to changing conditions, and we urge that more be made of it in teaching. The following points should be noted:—

(1) *Baptism.*—New Testament Baptism is a vital part of the Gospel, and we should make more of it. This means a good deal more than the refusal to baptise infants; it means that we expound our doctrine of Baptism in relation to the whole fact of the Church, for Baptism is at once an evidence of the believer's union with his Lord and an entrance into the society of those who love and serve the Saviour which in our view is the essential meaning of the Church. In Baptism we "put on Christ" and we publicly identify ourselves with His cause and His people. . . .

(2) *Worship.*—It is hardly necessary to say that this is the vital spot in our Church's life, and everything for the Church's meaning and power is affected by it. . . . We are a

little disturbed at the growing habit of reading prayers in the services. We recognise the value of the great prayers that have come to us sanctified by the usage of many centuries. But our Free Churches have a tradition of their own which under God has been greatly used, and we think that this habit of reading prayers in public worship is alien to our genius and seems to argue a lack of that direct dependence upon the Spirit which leads to the creation of the true devotional quality in our services. . . . Finally on this point a word might be said on hymns. The great hymns of the Church have been steeped in Christian doctrine, and that cannot be said of some of our modern hymns. We should choose hymns that will definitely nourish and express our Christian faith, if our worship is to have the right quality.

(3) *The Prayer Life of our Churches.*—We are disturbed about the condition of things in this respect. It is one of the clearest symptoms of our present lack of spiritual vitality. . . .

(4) *The Communion Service.*—The reference to prayer has relevance here. There seems need to emphasise the fact that the prayers at the Table are supposed to be prayers of thanks for the Bread and Wine. Sometimes they meander vaguely over many topics, and the service suffers in consequence. . . . What is needed is some guidance from the pastor. We think, too, that there is a danger of the Communion Service being regarded as an appendage to the first service. Would it not be good, say quarterly, to have one service centring in the Communion itself? . . .

(5) *Church Membership.*—In recent years the erasure column in our statistical forms has been very much used. . . . Possibly we make church membership too easy, . . .

More serious, however, is the need for emphasising the standards expected in membership, and possibly there is a need for a stronger element of Puritanism among us. The old limitations may be outmoded in some respects, but after all a church member must learn to count the world well lost for the sake of Christ. It seems incredible, but we all know how true it is that there are church members who feel little sense of obligation with regard to public worship. They apparently do not realise that they are part of the witnessing community without which Christ's work in the world is stultified, and their sense of responsibility seems to have faded. . . .

3. THE MINISTRY.

In many ways this is the key to most of our problems. . . . We need the best equipped ministry possible for all our churches. We should never forget that the great leaders of Christ's Church have been men who had received the best training intellectually that their time could furnish. Paul, Augustine, Luther, Calvin, Wesley—is it necessary to extend the list? . . .

But we would stress the need for a constant emphasis on the fact that a minister must be first and foremost and always a man of God, for the quality of his own inner life is the vital thing in his ministry. It is possible for this to be obscured and, while we rightly lay great emphasis on the sermon, we must not forget that a minister's power both in the pulpit and out of it is largely determined by what he is in himself as a sincere, humble and diligent servant of Jesus Christ. Given that a minister is truly a man of God, his ministry, whatever his gifts, will be profitable. The world more than anything else needs men who are the embodiment of the Christlike spirit, and that can only be found where the flame of devotion is kept constantly alive on the altar.

The Baptist view of the ministry rests on the idea that all live servants of Christ are called to share it. The Church itself is in fact meant to be a ministering community, and we think more should be made of this. Deacons, for instance, should feel that they are more than a business executive. They are charged with a spiritual leadership. Deacons in the old days felt that, whatever happened, they must be loyal to the church services, acting the part of Aaron and Hur to the pastor as he ministered the Word of Life. They are meant to be "examples to the flock," and they should aim at being model church members. Times have no doubt changed, but the spiritual demands are greater and not less. Perhaps we fail to give the deacon's office the place it should have by not making it a rule that every one entrusted with it should be as solemnly set apart for his work as a minister is, and the same thing is true of Sunday School teachers. The one thing certain is that we shall never impress the world on behalf of the Church unless we, who are its officers and members, show ourselves keen and sincere.

4. EVANGELISM.

This is unquestionably a matter of prime importance, . . . England has become a mission-field, and we must do our utmost to meet the challenge that comes to us. Several points might usefully be noted.

(1) We are convinced that evangelism must be closely linked with churchmanship, and the motto of our enterprise should be "Through the Church to the Church "—that is to say, the Church must be the active agent, and the purpose of the movement should be definite association with the Church through Baptism and membership. . . . The evangelism that depreciates the Church has not so learned Christ.

(2) This means that there is a close connection between evangelism and the life of the Church: in fact, the one should be interwoven with the other. Any activity of the Church that does not lead to evangelism is misdirected and wasteful, whereas on the other hand if it is to be effective it must have a living Church behind it. . . .

(3) This brings us to what in missionary language is called "the Christian community"—the people, that is, who are all round the fringe of the Church but are still outside its ranks. Let us take three examples of this. (a) Our Sunday Schools. . . . (b) Our women's meetings seem to offer a similar recruiting ground. . . . (c) The youth organisations are a big problem. . . .

IN CONCLUSION.

Everything in a matter of this kind must turn on the enthusiasm of our own hearts. The work will be hard and often discouraging. Many of our churches have lost heart and have ceased to expect great things from God, far less to attempt great things for Him. We that are strong in faith must undergird those that are weak by sympathy and prayer, and in a great venture of the Spirit the denomination must seek to demonstrate its essential unity. But first we must ourselves feel deeply the shame of our own stagnation, and there must be in our own hearts that sense of "concern" that will make us cast ourselves upon God and cry like Jacob at Peniel, "I will not let Thee go except Thou bless me." We need a baptism of repentance in all our churches. The days are heavy with destiny, and God has seen fit to match us against them. He has a purpose for us, as we believe, and in His Name we must seek to realise it.

B.   Signs of Hope, 1979

SECTION 1   The Mandate

The annual Assembly of the Baptist Union held at Nottingham in April 1977 requested the Baptist Union Council "to set up an inter-departmental commission to examine the causes for the numerical and spiritual decline in our denomination. [The Council] . . . agreed to set up a group with the following terms of reference:

1. To analyse our present situation and in particular: (a) the actual pattern of numerical decline and the reasons for it (e.g., the shift of population . . . ; the fact of commu-

nity change; the effects of radio and television on the habits of the population; the charismatic movement; ecumenical commitment. . . . (b) the meaning of the expression "Spiritual Decline" and the reasons for this, if it has occurred, (c) the lessons to be learned from the experience of other denominations.

2. To bring recommendations for any future action in the hope of stimulating numerical and spiritual growth." . . .

SECTION 3 Extension Work: 1945-1978

The recent call that the Denomination should take a long, hard look at itself might seem to suggest that previously little or nothing had been attempted. Such a suggestion would, of course, be misleading. No doubt there have been times when individual churches have been complacent: . . .

This however is not the whole picture. Many of our churches have continually sought the leading of God in reaching men and women among whom they are situated. Some have proceeded along traditional ways of evangelism; others have pioneered new approaches and have explored other means by which the Gospel may be shown to be relevant to contemporary society. . . .

Nor has the Union itself been inactive. Throughout the period under review, there have been presented to the churches various *calls to commitment* and exhortation to evangelism. . . . [Here the report cites several such denominational programs].

SECTION 4 Facts and Figures: Emerging Patterns

The Group recognizes that many factors are involved both in defining and assessing decline and growth. It is aware of the danger of placing too much emphasis on, and overestimating the significance of, figures, but having been required to study "numerical decline" it has necessarily had to devote some attention to membership and other statistics in an attempt to evaluate their implications. . . .

A straight comparison of the figures given in the B. U. Handbook and Directory for the years 1952 and 1977 suggests a staggering loss of members during this period:

> 1952   205,013 members in 2109 churches
> 1977   147,200 members in 1745 churches

This apparent loss of 57,813 members would represent a decline of 28.2% in all. . . .

SECTION 5 Factors Impinging upon the Size and Health of our Churches

The life of discipleship in the church

Any church fellowship at any time must be engaged in the ongoing task of nurturing the spiritual life, always avoiding a merely nominal or formal Christianity. All too easily the living experience of one generation can become a hollow and second-hand form for the next. The life of faith requires us to explore a present day obedience which may involve the costly and disturbing experience of cutting loose from yesterday's securities and achievements. When that price proves too great, there is a danger in our denominational life of holding to out-dated structures and practices instead of learning anew the meaning of gospel obedience.

All too often the *Church Meeting* has failed to direct the life and mission of the local church in dynamic and purposeful planning. In some cases it has become the monopoly of certain interest groups, even families, so that it has been difficult for voices of newer and younger members to be heard. Each local church represents a theocracy rather than a democracy and therefore should expect the Holy Spirit to manifest himself through the whole membership rather than be confined to working exclusively through minister, elders and deacons. . . .

The renewing of our *patterns of worship* in each succeeding generation has often been faulty, and the people of God have come together without a proper sense of expectancy. . . . Prayer needs to be real: our tradition makes it possible for us to use both extemporary and set forms of prayer. . . . New translations have made the reading of Scripture in worship more intelligible but one disadvantage has been the loss of a Common Version.

Some modern forms of hymnology have not always been submitted to as rigorous a testing of their worthiness as the worship of Almighty God demands. . . .

A tradition which puts as high an emphasis on *The Sermon* as does our own must necessarily be particularly vulnerable to weaknesses in preaching. The number of gifted preachers among us is fewer that the regular needs of the denomination require: too few possess the power to arrest a congregation, to stretch their mental and spiritual powers, both of which are God-given, to make contemporary the Eternal Word. . . .

The *teaching function* of the church has also suffered from some neglect, though in recent years more attention to systematic preaching has, in part, righted the indiscipline of earlier years. In particular it may be doubted whether sufficient of our churches given enough attention to the instruction of the new member, both before and after baptism. . . .

The local manifestation of the Body of Christ in *Christian fellowship* is crucial. Care must be taken to integrate new members, to surround them with love and allow them to exercise their gifts in sharing in the common life of the body. . . .

It is important that the churches recognise that they are stewards of a God-given ministry. . . . every congregation, both privately and corporately, needs to uphold its minister in prayer and make certain that he is free to wait upon God. . . . Some congregations have suffered, however, because the minister has tended to assume an autocratic leadership role. . . .

Theology and practice need to be worked out in the area of *lay involvement* in the ministry and service of the local church. The denomination still possesses very considerable untapped resources among lay people that could bring a new diversity to worship, preaching and service. . . .

The Christian Church has too often suffered from a schizophrenia that separates *evangelism . . . from social responsibility.* Both belong together in Christian mission. . . .

Undoubtedly, children's work is hard today and success in this field makes considerable demands upon the energies of church members and ministers alike. Sunday Schools and Family Church children's departments should be competently staffed and imaginatively organised, with teachers zealous, dedicated and willing to give up time in prayer, preparation and the visitation of the children in their homes. . . .

The nature of the society in which the Church is set

The rise and decline of churches has always to be related to the changing character of the societies in which they are set. From the earliest days of Baptist witness, the *outward movement* from the centre of urban communities has, in the captial at least, led to the problem of the once flourishing church whose community has now scattered to other areas. The problem of *downtown areas* and the potential of *new suburbs* continues in the same tradition. . . .

Not only do Baptist churches find it difficult to survive in working class areas, but they have not done as well as they might have hoped in *areas of suburban expansion.* . . . A more affluent society has developed a larger appetite for *leisure,* and this, coupled with a situation in which parents and children are often widely separated geographically, has presented increasing problems to an organisation whose activities are weekend-oriented. . . .

There are also *intellectual as well as social problems* in a world in which television, with great financial resources, is present in most homes. How can Church and Sunday School compete with its communication technique? . . . The pulpit has not always been as helpful as it might have been in equipping the people of God for *the task of living in a world where sinful structures have great power* . . . . Our *colleges* however have not been able to devote sufficient resources in a crammed curriculum to preparing our ministers for equipping their people to live in a secular world, nor has sufficient attention been given to techniques of proclaiming the gospel in a post-Christian society. . . .

Churches, Denominational Structures and the Ecumenical Scene

It has been argued that our denomination has been handicapped in its strategic planning by its being a fellowship of churches rather than a centralised ecclesiastical organisation. The Union accordingly only has such authority as the churches give to it. . . . All its work must therefore proceed on the basis of mutual trust and partnership which makes it particularly and properly vulnerable to anything that brings that trust into question. . . .

It is to be regretted that the Union's *ecumenical involvement* has been the cause of some tension within the fellowship. It is certainly no easy task to discover how to be both faithful to one's own understanding of God's truth, yet open to the insights into that same truth to which others bear witness. . . .

SECTION 6 The Church Growth Movement

A number of speakers [who gave input to the Group] made mention of the "Church Growth" movement and emphasised the value that this had been to churches in this country and the U. S. A. . . .

The Church Growth Movement, while not without its weaknesses, is one of many movements at work at present which are timely in waking us up to possibilities of our times and in matching us to this hour. It is important that such thinking does not become a focal point for more talk but a challenge to new faith and love that overflows into obedience and into joyful, intelligent and effective evangelism.

SECTION 7 Conclusion: Quantity and Quality

The Group were charged with assessing not only numerical but spiritual decline. In its work it has found it impossible to keep these two aspects separate. . . . We need to treat with caution the argument that decline in quantity can be offset by increase in quality. . . .

With such a mandate for discipleship, it would be foolish for any generation to be complacent as to its own achievements: more appropriate as [is] a profound sense of holy discontent. We believe, however, that there are *signs of change* among our people. Negatively, some of our churches have been honest enough to confess a loss of devotional depth, a loss of confidence, and confusion as to the direction in which they should go. . . . Positively, however, there does seem to be a new move towards more openness and less hypocrisy, a greater sense of flexibility and an unwillingness to be bound by precedent, a new concern to proclaim the eternal gospel in terms relevant to the contemporary scene. . . .

The group is concerned neither to whitewash the past nor to encourage euphoria on slender evidence. It does, however, believe that both nationally and denominationally there are *signs of hope* and urges our people to rededicate themselves, with reserve or reservation, to the work of the kingdom in confidence that it is Christ's work that we do and not our own.

14

Northern Baptists

For Baptists in the North, the twentieth century has been a time of restructuring, of struggling with internal tensions over the fundamentalist movement, and of redefining tasks in the world and relationships to other Christian groups. Documents included in this chapter are intended to illustrate these major trends.

In 1908 Baptists gathered up the several independent societies and formed them into a Northern Baptist Convention. That experiment never worked as well as hoped, and, in fact, was never fully accepted by many influential churches and leaders. After some important changes in 1950, Baptists made more radical changes in the structure of the denomination in 1972.

For almost all of the twentieth century, Baptists in the North have struggled with the challenge of fundamentalism. This militant movement arose within Northern Baptist ranks after the turn of the century, and reached epidemic proportions by 1920. Perhaps no denomination in America has been more radically affected by the fundamentalist movement than Northern Baptists. The resulting controversy led to several schisms by mid century, and the parent group has struggled to maintain spiritual balance in the light of these debilitating denominational hemorrhages. This chapter includes sources to trace the rise and impact of fundamentalism among Northern Baptists, but documents relating to the progress of individual schismatic groups are included in Chapter 16.

The blockbuster publication, *Rethinking Missions* (1932), merits space here because it illustrates the effort of Northern Baptists along with other denominations to redefine their world mission task. This chapter concludes with excerpts from the report of the Study Commission on Denominational Structure (SCODS), in 1972. As a result of this study, Baptists in the North abandoned the *convention* concept entirely and made the most radical restructuring of the denomination since formation of the Triennial Convention in 1814.

14.1 Unifying Impact of the American Baptist Publication Society

By the turn of the century, Northern Baptists were seeking more unity in the work of their various national societies. In their report of 1900, the Publication Society claimed to have been a major unifying factor in Baptist work in America. Though their bold claims may have been exaggerated, Baptist history shows that few organizations draw people together and create common outlook and understanding more effectively than the agency that determines what the people read. This report also shows that, as of 1900, some Baptists still held the goal of reunification of Baptists in America. *Source:* "Seventy-Sixth Anniversary of the American Baptist Publication Society, Detroit, 1900," 16.

This Society has been a bond of union for the denomination in America, stronger than popes, bishops, or presbyters, and our unity in faith and practice is due more largely to its influence than to any other earthly power. It works under a union label of the noblest kind, a label that covers more than a hemisphere, for America means more now than formerly. It has never been actuated by sectional impulses and has never seen its duty through partisan eyes. It has refused to restrict its horizon to something narrower than its name signifies. It has been true to the broad purpose of its founders, and has shown equal diligence and liberality in promoting the interests of the denomination in every section of our country. It has also been equal to all the demands, and there has never been a legitimate call from the denomination that it has not been ready and willing to meet. Enlisting the co-operation of the wisest and best men of the nation, it is prepared to-day as ever to give the best service to the denomination as a whole in every portion of our common country.

Mr. President, I am not uttering sentiments manufactured for this occasion, but am expressing the earnest longing of my soul, when I say that my whole being yearns for the day when the Baptists of this land shall not have to place the limiting adjective Northern or Southern, Eastern or Western, before the names of their agencies and enterprises, but when, forgetting the things which are behind and filled with the white fire of zeal for the things to come they shall be one body, actuated by one impulse, and keeping step to the commands of a common Lord, and shall move forward in an unbroken phalanx for the conquest of the world.

For what this Society has done and is doing to that end I devoutly thank God. For its larger and more successful work in the future I devoutly pray.

14.2 Formation of the Northern Baptist Convention

Baptists in America formed their first organization of national scope in 1814, the famed Triennial Convention. However, disagreements surfaced at once about the nature and function of that body. Some Baptists wanted a *unified convention,* made up of representatives from churches and other groups, to pursue different kinds of ministries. Others preferred to work through an *independent society,* made up of interested individuals. The Triennial Convention began basically as a society, then for a few years blossomed into a multifaceted convention, and in the 1820s reverted to its society basis. After that reversion Baptists formed other national societies to pursue other forms of ministry, such as the American Baptist Tract Society in 1824, the American Baptist Home Mission Society in 1832, and the American Baptist Education Society in 1888.

The proliferation of such societies, each with its own budget, agenda, and field of work, spotlighted the need for cooperation and correlation in Baptist denominational life. By the turn of the century many Northern Baptists were ready to give the unified convention plan one more try. The centralizing trends in American society at the time, and the obvious success of Southern Baptists with the convention plan, probably influenced this trend. *Source: Minutes of the Meeting for the Organization of The Northern Baptist Convention, Washington, D.C.,* 16-17 May 1907 (St. Louis: Freegard Press, 1907), 7-14.

(1) In May, 1896, at Asbury Park, N. J., "A Commission on Systematic Beneficence" was created, by the adoption of a series of resolutions presented by the finance committee of the American Baptist Missionary Union. These resolutions were also adopted by the American Baptist Home Mission Society, and the American Baptist Publication Society. Rev. F. M. Ellis, D.D., of Baltimore, Maryland, then declared, "We have unified the denomination at the contribution box, and that is next to the throne of grace."

(2) In May, 1897, the Women's Baptist Home Mission Society adopted resolutions, urging Northern Baptists to combine all their missionary periodicals into one, and pointed out the waste occasioned by the current method of publishing numerous journals. At the Anniversaries the same year, the report of the Commission on Systematic Beneficence called attention to the significant and the suggestive example of the joint efforts which had been made during the previous year by the three general societies to cancel their debts.

(3) In November, 1898, at the meeting of the Baptist Congress in Buffalo, N. Y., Rev. George E. Horr, D.D., then editor of *The Watchman,* declared, "There is a great opportunity for the denomination to harmonize its missionary work.* * * * There is

just as much necessity that the work of the Missionary Union, the Home Mission Society and the Publication Society should be harmonized,—note that I do not use the word *unified,*—should be *harmonized,* as there ever was that our controversies in regard to the Bible question should be adjusted, as they were at Saratoga a number of years ago." This significant deliverance was the subject of much comment. The denominational press, particularly *The Standard,* started discussion which increased the sentiment in favor of a closer relation between the organizations that were conducting our denominational work.

(4) So far the discussion had related principally to the harmonious co-operation of distinct organizations. It was inevitable that such discussions should produce a feeling in the hearts, and a conviction in the minds of many intelligent Baptists that our brotherhood should be more pronounced and an exhibition of it in Christian work more manifest.

(5) In May, 1900, at the Anniversaries in Detroit, Mich., "A Commission on Co-Ordination", composed of representatives of the general societies, including the women's organizations, with Mr. Stephen Greene, of Massachusetts, as chairman, was appointed to consider the better co-ordination of our denominational work. The duties of this commission were: "To consider the relative amounts which the denomination should be asked to furnish for our different benevolent enterprises, and also to consider the practicability of more closely co-ordinating the different departments of our denominational work, and to make such other recommendations as in their judgment they may deem wise."

(6) In May, 1901, in Springfield, Mass., there was held the first of several general meetings of the denomination. This was a mass meeting on "Co-Ordination." The report of Mr. Stephen Greene, of Newton Center, Mass., chairman of the committee, made six notable suggestions. Among them was one that

> "The best interests of our work as a denomination require that the annual gatherings of the American Baptist Home Mission Society, the American Baptist Missionary Union and the American Baptist Publication Society should be representative and delegated bodies, having the same basis of representation, so that the delegates to the three societies shall be, so far as possible, identical.

> "As a step necessary toward this end we recommend that the several societies, at the earliest possible date, and after mutual consultation through their executive boards, change their constitution so as to require the same qualifications of voters at their anniversaries.

> "It is believed that such action is fundamental, and if taken would create an atmosphere in which a 'better co-ordination' would be possible. If the executive officers and boards of our several societies could be brought to realize, as such action would help them to see, that their constituencies were actually one, a distinct advantage would be gained, and if the representatives of our churches could go up to the Anniversaries with the clear conviction that an actual responsibility concerning the entire work of the denomination rested upon them, it is certain that a better co-ordination of the different departments of our work would be the result."

It was at this *general denominational meeting* that many remarks were made upon the need for reforming the method of conducting our Anniversaries, and for improving the existing scheme of representation. Objections to the proposed uniform basis of representation were raised to the effect that it was a step towards consolidation. There were also vague references to an impression that there was competition and rivalry between the societies.

The Women's Home Missionary Society, during these Anniversaries, adopted resolutions favoring co-ordination, and advising that a period of five years be devoted to adjusting existing interests without the injury of any.

At these Anniversaries also, another recommendation of the committee of which Mr. Greene was chairman, was adopted, providing for an annual joint meeting of executive boards or committees of the societies, but a recommendation to publish a joint missionary periodical was rejected.

Another recommendation was adopted to appoint a committee of nine, to consider the matter of district secretaryships of the societies, and the relations of collection agencies.

This was a most notable meeting. It had a marked influence upon the growing desire for co-ordination, and orderly procedure. It is claimed that from this meeting, and from the report presented by Mr. Greene, dates the denominational movement, resulting in the formation of the Northern Baptist Convention.

(7) In December, 1901, in New York City, there was held an important conference of the executive boards and committees of the societies, in accordance with a recommendation adopted at Springfield. At this conference, among the questions discussed was, "What Changes, if Any, are Desirable and Feasible in our Denominational Work?" A committee was also appointed to take into consideration the matter of the relations of the collection agencies of the societies. It was voted to submit the methods involved in the operation of the several societies to a general meeting of the societies to be held in St. Paul.

(8) In May, 1902, at the Anniversaries in St. Paul, Minn., resolutions offered by Dr. Lemuel Moss, at a meeting of the American Baptist Missionary Union, were almost unanimously adopted, providing for a committee of fifteen persons who were to ascertain whether there was any lack of proper adjustment and co-operation between the three societies, including organizations associated with them, as to fields of labor, collecting and other agencies, and methods of work, and whether there could be an improvement in the mutual relations of these agencies. These resolutions were also adopted by the American Baptist Home Mission Society, and the American Baptist Publication Society.

The committee appointed at the mid-year conference in New York City, in December, 1901, reported that, "in view of existing conditions, neither economy nor efficiency would be furthered by the adoption of the method of employing one man to represent the three societies." At a general conference of three societies, during their Anniversaries in St. Paul, the report of this committee was brought up for consideration, and a motion to appoint one district secretary to represent the three societies in a given territory was defeated by a vote of 127 for it, to 135 against. The whole matter was then referred to the committee of fifteen provided for in the resolution offered by Dr. Moss.

At the same general conference of the three societies, the publication of one missionary magazine was also considered, and after opposition to such a consolidation of missionary magazines, it was voted to appoint a committee to investigate and report upon the matter.

(9) In May, 1903, at the Anniversaries at Buffalo, N. Y., the Committee of Fifteen appointed the previous year at St. Paul, reported that consolidation of the three societies was neither practical nor desirable, and left matters practically where they were. However, their report resulted in the appointment of a Committee of Conference, consisting of nine persons, "to which all matters of controversy between the missionary societies should be referred, and which should have authority to settle such controversies in the

name of the denomination." This committee has had no matters brought before it, and indeed has had no existence since the year expired for which it was appointed. No attention has been paid to it, and no appointments have been made to membership upon it since the Anniversaries that created it.

(10) In May, 1904, at the Anniversaries in Cleveland, O., there was another general denomination meeting at which, however, no opportunity was given to discuss general denominational matters. At this meeting, a committee was appointed to represent the Baptists of the North, in co-operation with other committees, in a proposed Baptist World Congress to be held in London. This Congress met in 1905 and was not only suggestive, but decidedly helpful to the movement for denominational solidarity. The same effect was produced by the formation of the General Convention of the Baptists of North America, in Saint Louis in May, 1905.

(11) In September, 1906, the Chicago Baptist Association, after listening to a notable paper entitled, "An Awakening Consciousness of Denominational Unity, What Does it Demand?" adopted the following resolution:

For years there has been a growing belief among our churches that there should be more coherence in our missionary work, and especially that our Baptist Anniversaries should be made more helpful to denominational unity. The splendid work now carried on by our several missionary societies ought to be more widely extended; and there should be some platform from which may be voiced the sentiments of the denomination upon movements and policies which concern the denomination as a whole, and are not germane to the work of any one of our present societies exclusively.

In view of the widespread dissatisfaction with present arrangements for conducting our Baptist Anniversaries, dissatisfaction which in no degree concerns the honored leaders of our denominational societies, but which concerns arrangements and policies and precedents growing out of the nature of the organizations and their history, therefore,

Resolved, That the Chicago Baptist Association, consisting of over 20,000 Baptists, puts upon record its earnest desire for greater effectiveness in the conduct of our great annual meetings, known popularly as the Baptist Anniversaries.

In order that reasonable steps may be taken looking to improvements, this association urges the executives of our national societies to call a joint meeting of all societies in connection with the Anniversaries of May, 1907. That for this meeting a suitable program be provided by the executive boards of the societies; that provision be made for the permanent organization of a general association or convention representing all the northern Baptist churches; that one of the special functions of this association or convention shall be the appointment of a representative committee on arrangement to act in connection with the boards of the societies in unifying and improving the exercises of all the meetings of all the societies whose anniversaries are held each May; that this general association or convention be so organized and its objects be so stated that it shall voice to a large degree the trend of denominational sentiment and policy in such matters as touch the welfare of all the churches, leaving to the societies the management of the great missionary and publication work which they are now conducting.

Resolved, That if no steps are taken by the boards of the societies before April 1, 1907, to call such a general or joint meeting as proposed, that the moderator of this association be empowered to appoint a committee to act in conjunction with other committees and representatives of churches in this and other states to consider the advisability of calling a general convention or association for the purposes specified.

(12) In November, 1906, at a meeting of the Baptist Congress in Saint Louis, Mo., a conference was held in which brethren from different parts of the country participated. It was decided to call the attention of the general societies to the prominent ministers and laymen from all parts of the country, was addressed to the secretaries of the societies:

To the Corresponding Secretaries of

The American Baptist Missionary Union; and

The American Baptist Home Mission Society; and

The American Baptist Publication Society,

Dear Brethren:

In view of the growing desire, most recently shown by state conventions, district associations, and persons, for an organization through which Northern Baptists may consider the manifold interests of the kingdom of God, and express a denominational opinion thereon, we respectfully request you to set apart, during the Anniversaries of the societies in 1907, at least one morning and afternoon, as near the middle of the week as possible, for a meeting to consider the expediency of such an organization.

We suggest that in your call for this meeting, if you consent to issue it, each church be requested to appoint its pastor and two delegates, who shall represent it at this meeting, with power to effect the organization if found desirable.

This request is addressed to you in order to avoid even an apparent expression of any unfriendly attitude towards our heartily appreciated denominational societies or their executive officers.

(13) December 11th, 1906, in compliance with the request of those brethren, the following call was issued for the meeting at which the Convention was provisionally organized:

Whereas, in various quarters a desire has been expressed for a meeting in connection with the Anniversaries at Washington, D. C., in 1907, to consider the question of a general organization of Baptists as represented in the constituencies of the American Baptist Missionary Union, the American Baptist Home Mission Society, and the American Baptist Publication Society; the undersigned acting upon the request of those interested in the subject, and with the approval of their respective boards, and representing their joint committee on the Anniversaries, do hereby formally call a meeting of those who shall be entitled to membership in these societies, and of others who shall be formally appointed by their churches to participate in the deliberations, on Thursday evening, May 16, and Friday forenoon, May 17, at the Calvary Baptist Church, Washington, D. C., for the purpose of effecting a general organization, if it shall be deemed desirable to do so; and suggest that Thursday evening, Rev. W. C. Bitting, D.D., of St. Louis, Mo., address the body for fifteen minutes upon a motion to form such an organization, to be followed by Rev. A. J. Rowland, D.D., of Philadelphia, Pa., in an address of ten minutes in seconding the motion; these to be followed by general discussion in which speakers shall be limited to five minutes each; and that Friday forenoon be devoted to the consideration of the report of the committee on organization with an address of twenty minutes by Prof. Shailer Mathews on the functions of such an

organization, followed by general discussion, speakers being limited to five minutes each.

H. L. MOREHOUSE,

T. S. BARBOUR,

A. J. ROWLAND,

Committee.

14.3   Is Immersion Essential to Baptist Church Membership?

Is immersion essential, preferable, or completely indifferent in relation to Baptist church membership? Baptists in England and America have opted for all three of these positions. The Baptist
Congress, an annual gathering of Baptist leaders from across the nation, met for about a week each
October to hear and respond to papers on various topics of current interest. The conditions of
church membership, and particularly the role of immersion, came in for frequent discussion, as it
did in 1909.

The document is composed of three parts. First, T. O. Conant, editor of *The Examiner,* urged
that Baptists keep immersion as a prerequisite to membership. Next, Elijah Hanley, pastor in
Providence, was to have given a paper on the other side of the issue. Instead, Dr. Hanley declined
to send a paper, but offered a brief note implying that he had been intimidated into silence on this
sensitive issue. This exchange was followed by a brief statement by W. H. P. Faunce, president of
Brown University, who revealed considerable sympathy for Hanley's views. *Source: Proceedings
of the Twenty-Seventh Annual Session of the Baptist Congress, New York, 1909* (Chicago: University of Chicago Press, 1909), 112-125.

RECENT TENDENCIES TO CHANGE DENOMINATIONAL PRACTICE

Mr. Chairman: The first step away from the simplicity of the gospel order was taken
when, very early in the history of the church, the ecclesiastical leaders, arrogating to
themselves powers which did not belong to them, began to substitute their own fanciful
interpretations for the plain precepts of Christ and the apostolic writers. The assumption that they were at liberty to do this lay at the bottom of all those terrible perversions
of the principles of the gospel which transformed the simple brotherhood established by
our Lord into a vast spiritual despotism, pretending to wield supernatural powers and to
control the keys into the Kingdom of Heaven. And the most far-reaching and mischievous of these perversions was the substitution of the doctrine of baptismal regeneration
for that of the baptism of believers. . . .

The Reformation of the sixteenth century, whose spirit had already been for two
hundred years in the air, was a long step backward toward the New Testament ideal; but
alas! it proved a case of arrested development. For various reasons, which cannot now
be specified, infant baptism was retained in the Reformed State churches, and, more
than anything else, became a bar to their complete emancipation from some of the
pernicious errors of Rome. . . . But for their fidelity and zeal in the face of persecution,
and the vital seed they planted and fertilized with their heart's blood, there might have
been no truly evangelical churches in the world today. Now, the vital principle on which
they stood may be summarized in the following propositions, which I present as the
basis of my argument today:

I. There is but one safe guide for Christ's disciples in the organization of a Christian
church—the New Testament.

II. The New Testament, by command, precept, and example, plainly indicates what
a Christian church should be.

III. Any departure, for any reason, from the fundamental principles of this New

Testament pattern is perilous to the spirituality of the church, and a hindrance to the spread of Christ's evangel in the world.

This is the essential spirit, if not the precise words, of our Baptist fathers' message to the men of their time—a message vital still, and worthy of earnest heed.

I. It is not many years since it would have been superfluous to argue for the truth of my first proposition in a Baptist assembly. Every Baptist held it as a sacred and irrefragable article of faith. "The New Testament our only rule of faith and practice," has been our battle-cry for generations. But we have fallen upon other and, as some profess to think, more enlightened days. There are among us those who hold the authority of the New Testament in somewhat light esteem. . . .

II. Since organization is essential to successful work, it ought not to surprise us that God should reveal the kind of organization he desired his church to have. And we find it in the New Testament. It is very simple: A company of believers in Jesus Christ, immersed in his name on confession of their faith, bound together for worship and service by their common love for him and for each other. . . .

III. Since, then, the model is God-given, it is evident that any departure from its essential elements is inadmissible. . . . Ingenious attempts have been made, of late, to show that baptism is no longer obligatory—if, in fact, it ever was—and therefore that subject and mode are of no particular consequence. But there is no foundation for such a plea. . . . To whom has Christ made it known that his disciples need no longer be baptized? Those who presume to set aside his law are bound to give conclusive reason for their presumption. But they have no reason. The commandment stands, unrepealed, unamended.

Today we are confronted with a proposition to exempt certain disciples from compliance with this universal obligation. . . .

It is a plea without basis in sense or reason that asks us to subordinate our hallowed principles, drawn from the New Testament, to the mistaught consciences of some who wish to join with us, not from principle, but for sentimental reasons. If anyone wishes to join a Baptist church, let him conform to the usage of the church, not look to the church to conform its usage, received from the Lord, to his personal preference.

And so, I contend, the new proposition—new at least to this country—to receive to our membership those who have not been scripturally baptized, who have only been subjected—who have not even subjected themselves—to a rite that has not the remotest resemblance to New Testament baptism, is not unwise only, but involves positive disobedience to the law and will of Christ. This objection is fundamental, and should be controlling. But there are practical consequences which would follow its adoption which deserve mention here.

a) It would introduce an element of cleavage into our churches. There would be two classes of members, the baptized and the unbaptized. . . .

b) It would tend, as it has done in England, to confuse the minds of the people, especially our young people—as to the relative importance of the two forms and subjects of the ordinance; and in time the less convenient and agreeable form would be sure to be crowded into the background.

c) It would cause division in the denomination. . . .

d) It would tend to weaken the conception of our people as to the real meaning and importance of believers' baptism. . . . It proclaims the Lord's burial and resurrection, and the believer's burial and resurrection with him—the symbol of a fundamental and glorious fact. Surely our Lord knew when he instituted it whether or not it was needful. Are we wiser than he?

e) Finally, the history of the church from the beginning has demonstrated the peril of changing an ordinance of Christ into a rite teaching a doctrine different from that which he intended it to teach. He left but two—both relating to the solemn facts of his death and resurrection. . . .

But if we should be thus guilty, what then would become of our age-long protest against the error of infant baptism? This ancient rite is not simply a pretty service of dedication; it is the supplanting of a vital ordinance of Christ by a fundamental and pernicious perversion of that sacred ordinance. If now we accept it as valid baptism—as we shall do if we accept for membership those who have been thus "baptized"—we fling our protest to the winds, and no longer have any reason for being. We have committed denominational "hari-kari." . . .

Mr. Chairman, I stand simply for the maintenance of the faith once for all delivered to the saints. The New Testament, plainly interpreted, is our sufficient rule of faith and practice. Let us accept its guidance, loyally follow it, and we shall not go astray.

THE PRESIDENT: I am sorry that a disappointment is in store for the Congress, in that the next speaker is detained, and has sent a letter in place of his paper, which letter the Secretary will now read to us.

THE SECRETARY: Before leaving home I received a letter which I hold in my hand from Dr. Hanley, dated November 5, in which he states he expects to be with us beginning with Tuesday, and to stay throughout the Congress. I have another letter which I will read *verbatim et literatim* in accordance with the request contained in it.

FIRST BAPTIST CHURCH
ELIJAH A. HANLEY, PASTOR
PROVIDENCE, R. I.

November 9, 1909

To the Baptist Congress, Rev. Theodore A. K. Gessler, D.D., Secretary:

Dear Brethren: At the request of your committee, I have carefully prepared a paper on the subject assigned me, setting forth a serious situation before Baptist churches today and pointing out that change in policy which I believe to be required by fidelity to the truth and spirit of Jesus Christ and also by consistency with historic principles enunciated by our fathers.

While I firmly believe that the paper contains a vital message, I have come to feel, on further consideration, that the time has not yet arrived when I can fully declare my views on this subject without bringing grief to many and without arousing controversy which by its emphasis on secondary things would misrepresent my real attitude and would greatly embarrass my present work.

Without the least compromise as to convictions of the truth and ideals for the Baptist church, but with recognition of the law of growth in spiritual progress, I beg to send earnest regrets, after having done my utmost to fulfil all obligations in this matter.

For the sake therefore of service in my own field, more important I believe for the progress of the denomination than anything I could now say at the Baptist Congress, and with the unwavering confidence that a larger policy in our Baptist churches must surely come, I cheerfully forego the privilege of attempting to forecast what course American Baptists must take for the future, if they are to fulfil their mission in the work of establishing the Kingdom of God.

This communication may be read or printed, provided it be used entire.

Very sincerely,

E. A. HANLEY

THE PRESIDENT: We regret the absence of Dr. Hanley, and still more the reason that he alleges for its necessity. Every man is a judge of his own position and his own acts. It is not for us to judge, but I hope and believe that any man in our denomination could fully and freely express his opinion, provided he did it in a courteous and Christian way.

The appointed speakers of the evening are now to address us. I hope that gentlemen who desire to take part in the discussion will be preparing themselves to follow immediately, and without pause, at the close of these two addresses.

The first of these speakers is our honored brother, so long pastor of the Fifth Avenue Church in this city, where he and the editor dwelt together in loving unity, and who is now the honored president of Brown University, Dr. Faunce. *(Applause.)*

W. H. P. FAUNCE, LL.D.: *Mr. Chairman, Ladies, and Gentlemen:* I am certainly in a difficult position. I cannot discuss Dr. Hanley's paper, because it is not here. I cannot very well discuss the paper of my warm friend, Dr. Conant—to be candid—I am so much on the other side. . . .

Dr. Hanley's letter affords us food for thought, even if there should be no discussion whatever. It is not the paper of a coward, of a man who skilfully retreats. On the contrary, it expresses definitely and clearly his view, and any man who wants to know that view in detail can talk with him. I urged him to come here. I saw no reason why he should not come here, why any Baptist should not speak his mind at this Congress. But others urged him very strongly not to come, . . .

The Baptist denomination is today experiencing two great movements: One a movement for organic unity in work; the other a movement for greater freedom from ceremonial restriction. The movement for organic unity has amazed us by its rapidity, its determination, its imperativeness, its success. . . .

The other movement is working as yet under the surface, but working steadily, and in due time will also sweep away all the arguments against it, from whatever source they may be drawn, and will achieve in some way a larger freedom, a genuine exaltation of the spirit above the letter.

I know at least a dozen Baptist ministers in churches as prominent as that of Dr. Hanley's who share his convictions and ought to be heard here tonight. They will be heard in the next ten years, either in the churches that they now serve, or in other churches that will be glad to listen.

Our Baptist churches have drifted into a position at variance with the teachings of our Baptist fathers, . . . Our fundamental principle is the assertion of the human soul, the belief that every soul has immediate access to God, and in his presence can stand erect and fearless before all human authority. The primary Baptist position is the vindication of the individual, not only his right to worship God according to the dictates of his own conscience, but to formulate his own faith, and to interpret Scripture and history for himself. . . .

Now there are two corollaries from this position, both very obvious. One is that religion must be free from state control. Surely we need to say nothing about that tonight. The other is that believers are free from sacramentalism of every kind. . . .

If I wanted to make the Baptist position—and I am a Baptist from the soles of my feet to the crown of my head—if I wanted to make the Baptist position, for which our fathers lived and died, absolutely clear to the Christian world, I would ask a hundred Baptist ministers to preach next Sunday morning from the text, "Jesus himself baptized not, but his disciples." And when they had done that I would ask them to preach on the following Sunday morning from the text: "I thank God I baptized none of you." In all seriousness I say it, if a hundred Baptist ministers were to preach from these two texts on successive

Sundays the original Baptist position, which made personal faith the essential for admission to a regenerate church, would become obviously plain to the whole Christian world.

14.4 Baptists and European Immigration in New England

The story of the floods of European immigration into New England after 1880 is well known. No denomination in America made a more valiant effort to evangelize the new Americans than did Northern Baptists. The following article, published in 1915, discusses this immigration and assesses its impact upon the nation as well as upon Baptists. *Source:* A. B. Coats, "New Americans in New England," *Watchman-Examiner,* 2 Sept. 1915, 1135-1136.

The New American is in New England, and very numerously there. According to the census of 1910 New England had a population of 6,522,681. Of these, 3,877,819, or a little more than fifty-one per cent., were born in foreign lands or of foreign parents—the "New Americans," as we have consented to call them. In fourteen States of the Union these New Americans are in the majority. . . . Within our borders are men and women of more than forty nationalities, the most of them in considerable numbers.

THE EFFECT ON OUR NATIONAL LIFE

It goes without saying that the presence of these multitudes from other lands most powerfully affects our life as a Nation. The earlier immigrants from the northern and western part of Europe were from the same racial stock as ourselves. They did not differ widely from us in laws and customs and habits of thought. But the immigrants of the last twenty-five years are of a different sort. They are for the most part from southern and eastern Europe, from lands where traditions and ideals utterly foreign to us prevail. The intimate intermingling of these people with the old American stock has already profoundly changed established customs and ideas in all departments of life.

The effect first to be felt was economic. The injection of this mass of cheap and unskilled labor into the ranks of the toilers complicated the already strained relations of labor and capital, with resultant strikes and lockouts. The social and civic effect has also been marked. Crime, and especially crime against the person, has had marked increase. So, too, in our political life is more and more felt the power of this new element in our citizenship. In all our cities the naturalized citizen is not only holding the balance of power, but in many instances he is in numerical majority. Every city in Rhode Island but one is under Catholic control. This is true of nearly all the cities of Massachusetts, as it is of the cities of Connecticut. In the last session of the Congress of the United States every Representative from Connecticut was a Roman Catholic Irishman. So much for present conditions. . . .

OUR TASK ALREADY STUPENDOUS

If in the next fifty years not another immigrant should make our land the goal of his ambitions we have all we can do properly to care for those who are already here and who will beyond all peradventure remain to become a vital part of our national life. What sort of citizens will these new Americans become? What will be their ideals and principles? What attitude will they come finally to take toward those ideas of right and justice that have heretofore been the glory of our Nation and the bulwarks of our safety? . . .

These New Americans are everywhere. Not only are they in certain quarters in the large cities, but they are in all the towns and villages and in the rural sections. The whole land is teeming with them, and it is utterly impossible for the missionary organizations, however faithful and efficient, to extend Gospel privileges to them all. There is not only lack of sufficient funds to put one versed in the language wherever a little cluster of one of these nationalities is found, but the workers themselves cannot be obtained. More and more those who have studied this problem are concluding that it can only be solved by the local American church. How do the churches themselves view the matter? What efforts, if any, are they putting forth through the regular services of the church and the Sunday school to reach these people who live in the neighborhood? The matter is important. At the suggestion of the Home Mission Society I made a canvass of the Baptist churches of Connecticut to discover what had already been accomplished by them in this direction. The result of that canvass I now desire to place before you.

There are 154 churches in the State. Nineteen of these are colored churches, eight are Swedish, four German, one Italian, one Hungarian. Twenty other small and pastorless churches were not included in the investigation. To the 101 other churches a letter of inquiry was sent asking how many, if any, of the foreign born and their children were in the membership of the church and Sunday school. Ninety-five churches responded with the desired information. Of these, twenty-one said that neither in the church or in the Sunday school were any of the foreign born or their children. The seventy-four remaining churches report all the way from one to ten different nationalities represented in both the church and the Sunday school. In all twenty-four different nationalities have thus been reached, as follows: Armenians, Austrians, Belgians, Bohemians, Chinese, Danes, Dutch, French, Germans, Greeks, Hungarians, Italians, Japanese, Jamaicans, Jews, Norwegians, Persians, Poles, Portuguese, Russians, Slovaks, Swedes, Swiss, Syrians. . . .

The total of New Americans in the Baptist churches in Connecticut is 2,421, and the Sunday school contingent numbers 2,777. Last year the entire membership of the Baptist churches of the State was reported as 26,286, of which 3,088 were colored, and a Sunday school enrolment of 18,943, of which number 1,360 were in the colored churches. Making these reductions it is seen that the New Americans already constitute ten and a half per cent. of the white membership of the churches, and more than fifteen and a half per cent. of the Sunday school enrolment. If my inquiry had gone further and asked after the facts concerning the church attendance of those of foreign birth it would have revealed a still more hopeful condition.

From these investigations and from what my experience while connected with this work has taught me I make two or three deductions:

First. These people can be reached with the Gospel. New England is one of the most hopeful and promising mission fields in the world.

Second. They can be reached in the ordinary services of the churches with no other means than the local church has at its disposal.

Third. When they are brought under the power of Christ they make a real addition to the working force of the kingdom. As soon as they are converted they manifest the missionary spirit and impulse to a marked degree.

The converted New Americans are excellent Christians. They are not like us in every respect. They have a genius for religion all their own. Some of the things they do shock us. Some of the things we do shock them. They need our patient watchcare and our sympathetic and generous help. They will prove neither ungrateful nor unworthy. The time is coming, and sooner, possibly, than some of us think, when here in New England the high interests of the kingdom will be in the hands of the New Americans.

14.5 Walter Rauschenbusch, *A Theology for the Social Gospel*, 1917

Walter Rauschenbusch (1861-1918) is known as the father of the Social Gospel in America. The Social Gospel movement was an effort to apply the teachings of the gospel to the entire social environment. The Social Gospel grew to some extent out of the immigrant community and addressed the social concerns of Northern industry laborers while largely overlooking social crises of the South such as racism and sharecropping. Rauschenbusch was educated at the University of Berlin and the University of Rochester in New York. During an eleven-year pastorate in the "Hell's Kitchen" area of New York City, Rauschenbusch met firsthand the desperate plight of America's poor working families. Later as professor of church history at Rochester, he sought to articulate a theology that would apply the gospel to daily life as well as to salvation after death.

Rauschenbusch wrote eleven books, of which the best known are *Christianity and the Social Crisis* (1907) and *A Theology for the Social Gospel* (1917). The selection below comes from the latter book. Even this brief excerpt makes clear that the kingdom of God was the central theological concept of the Social Gospel. *Source:* Reprinted with permission of Macmillan Publishing Co. from *A Theology for the Social Gospel* by Walter Rauschenbusch. Copyright 1917 by Macmillan; copyright renewed 1945 by Pauline E. Rauschenbusch.

CHAPTER XIII
THE KINGDOM OF GOD

IF theology is to offer an adequate doctrinal basis for the social gospel, it must not only make room for the doctrine of the Kingdom of God, but give it a central place and revise all other doctrines so that they will articulate organically with it.

This doctrine is itself the social gospel. Without it, the idea of redeeming the social order will be but an annex to the orthodox conception of the scheme of salvation. It will live like a negro servant family in a detached cabin back of the white man's house in the South. If this doctrine gets the place which has always been its legitimate right, the practical proclamation and application of social morality will have a firm footing.

To those whose minds live in the social gospel, the Kingdom of God is a dear truth, the marrow of the gospel, just as the incarnation was to Athanasius, justification by faith alone to Luther, and the sovereignty of God to Jonathan Edwards. It was just as dear to Jesus. He too lived in it, and from it looked out on the world and the work he had to do.

Jesus always spoke of the Kingdom of God. Only two of his reported sayings contain the word "Church," and both passages are of questionable authenticity. It is safe to say that he never thought of founding the kind of institution which afterward claimed to be acting for him. . . .

But the Kingdom was merely a hope, the Church a present reality. The chief interest and affection flowed toward the Church. Soon, through a combination of causes, the name and idea of "the Kingdom" began to be displaced by the name and idea of "the Church" in the preaching, literature, and theological thought of the Church. Augustine completed this process in his *De Civitate Dei*. The Kingdom of God which has, throughout human history, opposed the Kingdom of Sin, is today embodied in the Church. The millennium began when the Church was founded. This practically substituted the actual, not the ideal Church for the Kingdom of God. The beloved ideal of Jesus became a vague phrase which kept intruding from the New Testament. Like Cinderella in the kitchen, it saw the other great dogmas furbished up for the ball, but no prince of theology restored it to its rightful place. The Reformation, too, brought no renascence of the doctrine of the Kingdom; it had only eschatological value, or was defined in blurred phrases borrowed from the Church. The present revival of the Kingdom idea is due to the combined influence of the historical study of the Bible and of the social gospel.

When the doctrine of the Kingdom of God shriveled to an undeveloped and pathetic remnant in Christian thought, this loss was bound to have far-reaching consequences. . . . The atrophy of that idea which had occupied the chief place in the mind of Jesus, necessarily affected the conception of Christianity, the life of the Church, the progress of humanity, and the structure of theology. I shall briefly enumerate some of the consequences affecting theology. This list, however, is by no means complete.

1. Theology lost its contact with the synoptic thought of Jesus. Its problems were not at all the same which had occupied his mind. . . . It claimed to regard his revelation and the substance of his thought as divine, and yet did not learn to think like him. The loss of the Kingdom idea is one key to this situation.

2. The distinctive ethical principles of Jesus were the direct outgrowth of his conception of the Kingdom of God. When the latter disappeared from theology, the former disappeared from ethics. Only persons having the substance of the Kingdom ideal in their minds, seem to be able to get relish out of the ethics of Jesus. Only those church bodies which have been in opposition to organized society and have looked for a better city with its foundations in heaven, have taken the Sermon on the Mount seriously.

3. The Church is primarily a fellowship for worship; the Kingdom is a fellowship of righteousness. When the latter was neglected in theology, the ethical force of Christianity was weakened; when the former was emphasized in theology, the importance of worship was exaggerated. . . . Thus the religious energy and enthusiasm which might have saved mankind from its great sins, were used up in hearing and endowing masses, or in maintaining competitive church organizations, while mankind is still stuck in the mud. . . .

4. When the Kingdom ceased to be the dominating religious reality, the Church moved up into the position of the supreme good. To promote the power of the Church and its control over all rival political forces was equivalent to promoting the supreme ends of Christianity. This increased the arrogance of churchmen and took the moral check off their policies. . . .

5. The Kingdom ideal is the test and corrective of the influence of the Church. When the Kingdom ideal disappeared, the conscience of the Church was muffled. It became possible for the missionary expansion of Christianity to halt for centuries without creating any sense of shortcoming. It became possible for the most unjust social conditions to fasten themselves on Christian nations without awakening any consciousness that the purpose of Christ was being defied and beaten back. . . .

6. The Kingdom ideal contains the revolutionary force of Christianity. When this ideal faded out of the systematic thought of the Church, it became a conservative social influence and increased the weight of the other stationary forces in society. If the Kingdom of God had remained part of the theological and Christian consciousness, the Church could not, down to our times, have been salaried by autocratic class governments to keep the democratic and economic impulses of the people under check.

7. Reversely, the movements for democracy and social justice were left without a religious backing for lack of the Kingdom idea. The Kingdom of God as the fellowship of righteousness, would be advanced by the abolition of industrial slavery and the disappearance of the slums of civilization; the Church would only indirectly gain through social changes. Even today many Christians can not see any religious importance in social justice and fraternity because it does not increase the number of conversions nor fill the churches. Thus the practical conception of salvation, which is the effective theology of the common man and minister, has been cut back and crippled for lack of the Kingdom ideal.

8. Secular life is belittled as compared with church life. Services rendered to the Church get a higher religious rating than services rendered to the community. . . .

Wherever the Kingdom of God is a living reality in Christian thought, any advance of social righteousness is seen as a part of redemption and arouses inward joy and the triumphant sense of salvation. When the Church absorbs interest, a subtle asceticism creeps back into our theology and the world looks different.

9. When the doctrine of the Kingdom of God is lacking in theology, the salvation of the individual is seen in its relation to the Church and to the future life, but not in its relation to the task of saving the social order. . . .

10. Finally, theology has been deprived of the inspiration of great ideas contained in the idea of the Kingdom and in labor for it. The Kingdom of God breeds prophets; the Church breeds priests and theologians. The Church runs to tradition and dogma; the Kingdom of God rejoices in forecasts and boundless horizons. . . . The Kingdom of God is to theology what outdoor colour and light are to art. It is impossible to estimate what inspirational impulses have been lost to theology and to the Church, because it did not develop the doctrine of the Kingdom of God and see the world and its redemption from that point of view. . . .

In the following brief propositions I should like to offer a few suggestions, on behalf of the social gospel, for the theological formulation of the doctrine of the Kingdom. Something like this is needed to give us "a theology for the social gospel."

1. The Kingdom of God is divine in its origin, progress and consummation. It was initiated by Jesus Christ, in whom the prophetic spirit came to its consummation, it is sustained by the Holy Spirit, and it will be brought to its fulfilment by the power of God in his own time. The passive and active resistance of the Kingdom of Evil at every stage of its advance is so great, and the human resources of the Kingdom of God so slender, that no explanation can satisfy a religious mind which does not see the power of God in its movements. The Kingdom of God, therefore, is miraculous all the way, and is the continuous revelation of the power, the righteousness, and the love of God. . . . This doctrine is absolutely necessary to establish that organic union between religion and morality, between theology and ethics, which is one of the characteristics of the Christian religion. . . . Without this doctrine we shall have expositions of schemes of redemption and we shall have systems of ethics, but we shall not have a true exposition of Christianity. The first step to the reform of the Churches is the restoration of the doctrine of the Kingdom of God.

2. The Kingdom of God contains the teleology of the Christian religion. It translates theology from the static to the dynamic. It sees, not doctrines or rites to be conserved and perpetuated, but resistance to be overcome and great ends to be achieved. Since the Kingdom of God is the supreme purpose of God, we shall understand the Kingdom so far as we understand God, and we shall understand God so far as we understand his Kingdom. . . .

3. Since God is in it, the Kingdom of God is always both present and future. Like God it is in all tenses, eternal in the midst of time. It is the energy of God realizing itself in human life. . . . No theories about the future of the Kingdom of God are likely to be valuable or true which paralyze or postpone redemptive action on our part. To those who postpone, it is a theory and not a reality. It is for us to see the Kingdom of God as always coming, always pressing in on the present, always big with possibility, and always inviting immediate action. . . . The Kingdom is for each of us the supreme task and the supreme gift of God. By accepting it as a task, we experience it as a gift. By labouring for it we enter into the joy and peace of the Kingdom as our divine fatherland and habitation.

4. Even before Christ, men of God saw the Kingdom of God as the great end to

which all divine leadings were pointing. Every idealistic interpretation of the world, religious or philosophical, needs some such conception. Within the Christian religion the idea of the Kingdom gets its distinctive interpretation from Christ. (a) Jesus emancipated the idea of the Kingdom from previous nationalistic limitations and from the debasement of lower religious tendencies, and made it world-wide and spiritual. (b) He made the purpose of salvation essential in it. (c) He imposed his own mind, his personality, his love and holy will on the idea of the Kingdom. (d) He not only foretold it but initiated it by his life and work. . . .

5. The Kingdom of God is humanity organized according to the will of God. Interpreting it through the consciousness of Jesus we may affirm these convictions about the ethical relations within the Kingdom: (a) Since Christ revealed the divine worth of life and personality, and since his salvation seeks the restoration and fulfilment of even the least, it follows that the Kingdom of God, at every stage of human development, tends toward a social order which will best guarantee to all personalities their freest and highest development. . . . (b) Since love is the supreme law of Christ, the Kingdom of God implies a progressive reign of love in human affairs. . . . (c) The highest expression of love is the free surrender of what is truly our own, life, property, and rights. A much lower but perhaps more decisive expression of love is the surrender of any opportunity to exploit men. No social group or organization can claim to be clearly within the Kingdom of God which drains others for its own ease, and resists the effort to abate this fundamental evil. . . . (d) The reign of love tends toward the progressive unity of mankind, but with the maintenance of individual liberty and the opportunity of nations to work out their own national peculiarities and ideals.

6. Since the Kingdom is the supreme end of God, it must be the purpose for which the Church exists. . . . The institutions of the Church, its activities, its worship, and its theology must in the long run be tested by its effectiveness in creating the Kingdom of God. For the Church to see itself apart from the Kingdom, and to find its aim in itself, is the same sin of selfish detachment as when an individual selfishly separates himself from the common good. The Church has the power to save in so far as the Kingdom of God is present in it. If the Church is not living for the Kingdom, its institutions are part of the "world." In that case it is not the power of redemption but its object. It may even become an anti-Christian power. If any form of church organization which formerly aided the Kingdom now impedes it, the reason for its existence is gone.

7. Since the Kingdom is the supreme end, all problems of personal salvation must be reconsidered from the point of view of the Kingdom. It is not sufficient to set the two aims of Christianity side by side. There must be a synthesis, and theology must explain how the two react on each other. The entire redemptive work of Christ must also be reconsidered under this orientation. Early Greek theology saw salvation chiefly as the redemption from ignorance by the revelation of God and from earthliness by the impartation of immortality. It interpreted the work of Christ accordingly, and laid stress on his incarnation and resurrection. Western theology saw salvation mainly as forgiveness of guilt and freedom from punishment. It interpreted the work of Christ accordingly, and laid stress on the death and atonement. If the Kingdom of God was the guiding idea and chief end of Jesus—as we now know it was—we may be sure that every step in His life, including His death, was related to that aim and its realization, and when the idea of the Kingdom of God takes its due place in theology, the work of Christ will have to be interpreted afresh.

8. The Kingdom of God is not confined within the limits of the Church and its activities. It embraces the whole of human life. It is the Christian transfiguration of the

social order. The Church is one social institution alongside of the family, the industrial organization of society, and the State. The Kingdom of God is in all these, and realizes itself through them all. . . .

14.6   Rethinking Missions, 1932

Are nineteenth-century motives and methods of foreign missions still valid for modern times? That question confronted laypersons as well as ministers in America early in the twentieth century. Baptists participated in, and were greatly influenced by, a high level reevaluation of the theology and methods of foreign missions undertaken jointly by several denominations after World War I. The report of the "Commission of Appraisal" was subtitled, "A Layman's Inquiry after One Hundred Years." While reaffirming some aspects of foreign missions, this study commission either called into question or bluntly rejected many theological concepts upon which Baptists had based their foreign missions. *Source:* William Ernest Hocking, Chm., "Rethinking Missions: A Layman's Inquiry after One Hundred Years" (New York: Harper and Brothers, 1932), 3-23, 37-44, 325-329.

The Mission in the World of Today

It is no new experience for Christian missions, least of all for Protestant missions in Asia, to be questioned. In the very position of foreign missions, as guests and for the most part uninvited guests, among of people of other ways and faiths, they are used to glances which ask, Why are you here? . . .

There are now other questions being put to them, not by the nationals where their work lies, nor by official visitors from the churches at home, but by the turn of the times. Have these missions in some measure finished their work? Are there new channels for what they have been bringing? Is there a decline in their value to the Far East, in view of vast changes since their early days in the relations peoples and the means of intercourse?

Our Commission has brought to a group of Protestant missions in the Orient questions of this sort—not its own questions, we repeat, but the questions of the time—expressed by laymen of the several churches concerned. This Commission has been instructed to be thoroughgoing in its inquiry, and objective in its attitude. It was asked to consider whether these missions ought any longer to go on. And if they ought, whether it should be with great change, or little change, or none. . . .

As to the first and most searching question put to us, whether these missions should in our judgment any longer go on, we may say that this question has been with us, honestly and objectively entertained, throughout our inquiry. As the inquiry closes, we may confess that this formidable question has not proved to be highly significant. It is somewhat like asking whether good-will should continue or cease to express itself. Like other works, organized by men's hands, missions might conceivably ossify in unadaptable forms and deserve to perish. But at the center of the religious mission, though it takes the special form of promoting one's own type of thought and practice, there is an always valid impulse of love to men: one offers one's own faith simply because that is the best one has to offer. . . . There is in this fact, however, no ground for a renewed appeal for the support, much less for the enlargement, of these missions as a whole in their present form and on their present basis. This Commission makes no such appeal. In our judgment, there is not alone room for change, there is necessity for change, . . .

1. *The Motives of Missions*

The motive of all religious missions is an ardent desire to communicate a spiritual value regarded as unique and of supreme importance. It is an integral part of the passion for "saving" men and peoples, and implies a peculiar sense of the tragedy and danger of the unsaved. . . .

Mingled with this concern for individuals, there was the appealing vision of the world-wide Church. It was well to have many centers from which local extensions might begin. Around this picture of the universal Christian community gathered obscurely all that we now think of as preparation for world unity in civilization. We know that to effect an understanding in religious matters is to pave the way for an understanding in other matters. The world must eventually become a moral unity: to this end, it was necessary that the apparent localism of Christianity should be broken down. It must not be thought of as solely the religion of the West. It was because Christianity is *not* western, but universally human, that it must be brought back to the Orient and made at home there.

Let us add that one further motive always joins subconsciously with any impulse to give to others; that is, the impulse through expression to achieve one's own growth. . . .

The mixture of motives. In the actual practice of missions the motives we have been speaking of are necessarily affected by the instruments through which they operate. There is a human aspect of the mission, which, as in all work which takes the name of religion, stands out sharp against the ideal background and becomes the target for a type of caustic comment. . . . It must be taken for granted that whatever the powers or defects of the individual missionary, they will affect his manner and his capacity to transmit his gift.

If he is imperious, dogmatic, vain, narrow, his love of man may still be genuine, yet it will be colored by personal arrogance. The history of missions has plentiful examples of such mixture of motive. With the legitimate motive have been associated such traits as love of adventure, ambition, the impulse to dominate or to impose one's type of mind on others, the "predatory temper," the will to power. . . .

Personnel. We speak of the aggregate number of missionaries in these countries, as if it were a large total. Dispersed as it is among the vast populations of the East, it is in reality a comparatively small society, so distinctively and absorbingly occupied as to be referred largely to itself for companionship. . . .

Of these thousands of persons, there are many of conspicuous power, true saintliness and a sublime spirit of devotion, men and women in whose presence one feels himself at once exalted and unworthy. It is easier to say this, than to say the rest of the truth; the greater number seem to us of limited outlook and capacity; and there are not a few whose vision of the inner meaning of the mission has become obscured by the intricacies, divisions, frictions and details of a task too great for their powers and their hearts. . . .

With due regard to these considerations it is still necessary to say that the human side of the mission, as we find it today, seems on the whole unduly weak. For there are two things which we may rightfully demand of the mission personnel. First, that in those services where there is a recognized standard of efficiency, as in teaching or medicine, the mission staff shall stand well. Second, that in the essential service of interpreting Christianity to the Orient, it shall not too far fail of its great theme. In neither of these respects can we speak of the total impression with the high enthusiasm we should like to offer. . . .

3. *Changes Affecting Missions*

But the personnel of an enterprise is in all cases a response to the inherent appeal which that enterprise at any time presents. It is useless to call for stronger men unless the task is such as to command the interest of such men. The crucial problem, then, is this: whether the motives which animated the inauguration of the Protestant missions a century or so ago remain in full force, in view of the changes which have taken place since their inception.

Of the many changes in the world during the past century, a century of sweeping changes in the life of the Orient as well as in the life of the West, three are peculiarly pertinent to the mission enterprise, an altered theological outlook, the emergence of a basic world-culture, the rise of nationalism in the East.

a. The altered theological outlook. It would be a poor compliment to our theological insight if a hundred years so full of intellectual development, of advance in scientific thought and of philosophical activity, had brought no progress in the conceptions attending our religious experience. . . .

Of all changes in the world, a theological change will bear most directly upon the missionary motive. If the conception of hell changes, if attention is drawn away from the fear of God's punitive justice in the everlasting torment of the unsaved, to happier conceptions of destiny, if there is a shift of concern from other-worldly issues to the problems of sin and suffering in the present life, these changes will immediately alter that view of the perils of the soul which gave to the original motive of Protestant missions much of its poignant urgency.

Generally speaking, these changes have occurred: Western Christianity has in the main shifted its stress from the negative to the affirmative side of its message; it is less a religion of fear and more a religion of beneficence. It has passed through and beyond the stage of bitter conflict with the scientific consciousness of the race over details of the mode of creation, the age of the earth, the descent of man, miracle and law, to the stage of maturity in which a free religion and a free science become inseparable and complementary elements in a complete world-view. . . .

b. The emergence of a world-culture. At the opening of our period there were many cultures, and the cleft between the Orient and the West was especially deep. . . .

c. The rise of nationalism in the East. While the nationalism of the East is being developed in more or less deliberate reaction against western domination and cultural control, it has ceased to be hostile to the spread of world-culture, and may even be considered a phase of that movement, inasmuch as national distinctness is one of the characters of the modern world. . . .

We conceive, then, a change in the conception of the foreign mission, in which functions and methods appropriate in earlier days shall gradually give place to permanent functions and methods. . . . In the coming era, which might be pictured as an era of foreign service or ambassadorship, it will be natural, rather, to maintain in foreign lands a relatively few highly equipped persons, acceptable to those lands as representing the Christian way of thought and life, holding themselves ready to give advice and counsel whether to the local church or to other leaders of religion and thought, sympathetically concerned with the problems of changing local culture, and trying to minimize the strains of an abrupt breach with tradition. . . .

6. *The Attitude Toward Error*

a. The errors. In all the great religious systems of Asia one learns to make distinctions—and is prepared to find them very wide—between the religion of the people, the religion of the priestly class and of the professional holy men, the religion of the scholars and reformers, and the religion of the intelligent laity. . . . It would be a sad error of judgment if, at the moment of a strong and promising movement of internal renovation, the Christian Church should aim at destroying or displacing the old structure.

It is clearly not the duty of the Christian missionary to attack the non-Christian systems of religion. Nor is it his primary duty to denounce the errors and abuses he may see in them: it is his primary duty to present in positive form his conception of the true way of life and let it speak for itself. . . .

7. *Superstition*

The problem of "superstition" deserves a special note: for to many minds this word summarizes the evils which, in the mission fields, Christianity is especially called to combat. And, unquestionably, if one were to assemble the superstitions of the world the peasantries of Asia, together with the Christian peasantries of Europe, would furnish a rich array. It is important to gain a clear concept of superstition, and then to recognize that superstition is not a peculiarity of any special type or tradition in religion: it is a phenomenon of a low stage of general enlightenment and attends every religion in such stages.

Christianity can aid in the struggle to eliminate superstition from its own and other systems

1. By promoting the scientific habit of mind, and demonstrating its own fearlessness in presence of science;

2. By making clear what the function of religion is, in completing the unfinished world-view of science, adding the element of value and meaning which science, taken alone, would omit;

3. By working with enlightened members of all faiths for a non-superstitious conception of providence and prayer.

SUMMARY OF PRINCIPAL CONCLUSIONS

An effort has been made, in the paragraphs below, to gather together in a summary of succinct statements the principal conclusions of the Commission. . . . It is to be borne in mind that the conclusions here presented confine themselves, in so far as they are findings and recommendations, to the seven Protestant societies whose program in the Orient was studied by the Commission.

I. The continuance of missions. To any man or church, possessed of religious certainty, the mission in some form is a matter not of choice but of obligation. If there is any truth or value in religion at all, it is for all men. To ask whether missions in essence should any longer go on is like asking whether good will should continue or cease to express itself.

But the essential rightness of the mission idea will not save actual missions from decline or extinction unless in spirit and deed they worthily present that idea. There is real danger lest adherence to aims and methods which impede the communication of living insight may not alone thwart the success of Christian missions, but end their usefulness.

II. Their aim. The message of Christianity presents a way of life and thinking which the Christian conceives, not as his way alone, but as a way for all men, entering without violence the texture of their living and transforming it from within. The goal to which this way leads may be variously described; most perfectly, perhaps, in the single phrase, Thy Kingdom come. That is, and always has been, the true aim of Christian missions.

In more literal phrasing, the aim of Christian missions today in our conception would take this form:

To seek with people of other lands a true knowledge and love of God, expressing in life and word what we have learned through Jesus Christ, and endeavoring to give effect to his spirit in the life of the world.

III. Their scope. The point of central importance is this—there must be first of all a new kind of person as the unit of society if there is to be a new society; there is no substitute for the regeneration of the individual units. Nothing can displace, or minimize the importance of, a true and well-qualified evangelism.

But the Christian way of life is capable of transmitting itself by quiet personal contact and contagion, and there are circumstances in which this is the perfect mode of speech. Ministry to the secular needs of men in the spirit of Christ, moreover, *is* evangelism, in the right sense of the word; . . .

We believe that the time has come to set the educational and other philanthropic aspects of mission work free from organized responsibility to the work of conscious and direct evangelism. We must work with greater faith in invisible successes, be willing to give largely without any preaching, to cooperate whole-heartedly with non-Christian agencies for social improvement, and to foster the initiative of the Orient in defining the ways in which we shall be invited to help. . . .

IV. Their attitude toward other faiths. The mission of today should make a positive effort, first of all to know and understand the religions around it, then to recognize and associate itself with whatever kindred elements there are. It is not what is weak or corrupt but what is strong and sound in the non-Christian religions that offers the best hearing for whatever Christianity has to say. . . .

V. The men and women in missions. The task of the missionary is an extremely difficult one. It calls not only for a self-sacrificing spirit and an utter devotion, but for moral courage, a high order of intelligence, and a love of adventure. Perhaps more than for any of these it calls for the capacity truly to understand and genuinely to love and sympathize with the people among whom he works.

The Commission is convinced that a much more critical selection of candidates should be made, even at the risk of curtailing the number of missionaries sent out. Those appointed should have the benefit of a carefully planned training for their work; great pains should be taken in the designation of appointees to specific tasks and locations. Whenever possible, nationals should have a voice in their selection and retention, and if feasible, the early years of their service should be of a probationary nature.

VI. Permeative influence and the wider Christian fellowship. Christians should count among the best results of their endeavor the leavening influence of the spirit of Jesus in the common life of each country.

Ways must be found in which the multitude of those in the Orient who are followers of Christ, but who cannot be brought into the body of the Church as now constituted (and perhaps not for a long time to come), may be reckoned as disciples and may come, with each other and with us, into the wider Christian fellowship.

VII. Concentration of effort. The number of weak Christian institutions and of merely nominal Christians throughout Asia is a reproach to the missionary enterprise. Denominational interests, institutional pride and lack of cooperative planning have contributed to the development of conditions which should no longer be tolerated. We are convinced that one of the most urgent needs in all fields is the rigid enforcement of a policy of concentration of personnel and resources. . . .

VIII. Transition from temporary to permanent character. A mission, by definition, is intrinsically temporary; the time comes when established centers of religious life must be left to develop according to the genius of the place.

Missions should now be preparing for the transition from the temporary work of church planting, pioneer work in medicine, education and the training of leaders—to the permanent function of promoting world understanding and unity on a spiritual level through the ambassadorship of relatively few highly equipped persons, and through institutions for the study of theology and civilization, and the emerging needs of the adopted land.

IX. The transfer of responsibility—devolution. The goal of the mission must be the transfer of its responsibility to the hands of the nationals. Answerable for the integrity of its work, the mission cannot realize the idea of the indigenous church by simply letting go. The desire to make himself unnecessary is a mark of the true missionary; but in achieving that end, the transfer of responsibility must follow thorough training of nationals: devolution should be real—not nominal; and gradual—not abrupt.

X. Administrative unity and cooperation. The Commission believes that the time has come for a plan of administrative unity on a comprehensive scale, and proposes a single organization for Christian service abroad in place of the complex, costly and duplicative machinery which now exists. . . .

Its accomplishment will require a hearty acceptance of the general principles that have been laid down, and a determination to do what is needful without counting the cost of personal and denominational advantage. If these can be attained, the task of perfecting a plan of unification can be undertaken with assurance; it will take time to accomplish, but it can be done.

14.7 Controversy about Northern Baptist Schools

A storm of criticism swirled around Northern Baptist schools by 1920. Accusations of weakening of Baptist teachings or, in some cases, outright heresy became so prevalent that the Northern Baptist Convention at its Buffalo meeting in 1920 felt obliged to appoint a committee to investigate the schools. *Source:* Annual, Northern Baptist Convention, Buffalo, New York, 1920, 48-49. Selection A below traces the origin and assignment of that committee. Selection B cites portions of the Board of Education report in 1921, defending the schools and decrying the investigation. However, the criticism continued and became one of the major issues in fundamentalist schisms from Northern Baptist life over the next generation. *Source:* Tenth Annual Report, Board of Education, Northern Baptist Convention, 1921, 6-7.

A. Investigation of Northern Baptist Schools Authorized, 1920

WHEREAS, There are many rumors and charges concerning the teachings and teachers in the secondary schools, colleges, and theological seminaries in the territory of the Northern Baptist Convention which are supported financially and sponsored morally either by the Northern Baptist Convention, by State Baptist Conventions, or the Baptist churches of the Convention, and

WHEREAS, If the charges be true, then the spiritual integrity of our Christian leadership and the scriptural character of our ministry in the offices of pastor, teacher, evangelist, missionary, and secretary are alike in serious jeopardy, therefore in the interest at once of the denominational harmony and our denominational loyalty to the historic doctrines of Baptists, and the spiritual sanity and security at home and in foreign fields, be it

Resolved, 1. That this conference of Baptists, constituent members of the Northern Baptist Convention, request the Northern Baptist Convention at its session in Buffalo, June 23-30, 1920, to appoint a commission of nine members to investigate the teachings in all secondary schools, colleges, and theological seminaries, seeking either financial support or the moral sponsorship of Baptist churches in the bounds of the Northern Baptist Convention, and to make report at the session of the Convention in 1921.

2. That this commission be specially instructed:

(a) To investigate the statement of beliefs submitted by the schools to the teachers therein upon their employment.

(b) To give special attention to the question of whether these schools and individual teachers are still loyal to the great fundamental Baptist truths as held by the denomination in the past, with particular reference to the inspiration of the Word of God, the Deity of Christ, the atonement, the resurrection, the return of the Lord, the spiritual nature of the church, the necessity for a regenerated, baptized church-membership, the unchanged nature of the obligation of the ordinances of baptism and the Lord's Supper, and the imperative responsibility of carrying out the great commission.

3. That no trustee or member of faculty in any school or seminary shall be eligible to membership on this commission.

4. That the Convention provide all necessary expenses for the Committee covering this investigation.

5. That the Committee be instructed to investigate the method of election or appointment of trustees in all our secondary schools, colleges, and theological seminaries, and that they report upon the entire question of the control of these institutions. . . .

B.   A Defense of Northern Baptist Schools, 1921

THE CHARACTER OF OUR SCHOOLS

Our schools and colleges have been under a severe storm of criticism during the past year. The attacks have had a most serious effect in undermining the confidence of our people at a time when they were beginning to take a new interest in the education of their children. If the attacks prove to be unwarranted incalculable harm has been done to the whole present generation.

It is the business of the Board of Education to know the conditions that obtain in our schools. We believe we do know them. For ten years we have been keeping in intimate touch with our colleges. We know that the charges which have been made are largely false. In order to assure ourselves once more as to the situation we have made another careful personal investigation. We have not depended upon questionnaires sent to students. During the past few months the Executive Secretary and his Associate have visited practically every Baptist college in the North. They have conferred with the presidents, the professors, the pastors of the local churches, the secretaries of the Y. M. C. A. and the Y. W. C. A., and the leading Christian students. They have gathered a mass of most interesting and valuable material.

We wish that out Baptist parents could read it. We do not claim, as a result of our study, that any one of our schools is perfect. We know that in some the situation is better than it is in others. But we also know that if our people could understand the real situation, their hearts would rejoice within them. Our colleges are Christian. They are exerting a Christian influence on their students. They are building the best type of manhood and womanhood. From our intimate knowledge we do not hesitate to assert that they furnish the best and safest environment for our children during the four to six critical years of their adolescent life. We would rather have our children in these colleges during these critical years than in any other place. We know that our Baptist parents can trust their children to their schools.

One of our colleges was singled out for criticism on the floor of the Convention one year ago. Our people ought to know that in that single institution over sixty of our boys and girls are volunteers for service on the foreign field. A Baptist pastor has two sons in that college, both of them volunteers. When he visited them the first time, he had scarcely alighted from the train before the older son said: "Father, this is the easiest place I ever found to live a Christian life. A man has to explain why he is not a Christian here." Another student in that same college was asked what her experience had been. She replied:

"You know, when I first came here, my mind was greatly disturbed about what I really did believe. I was all up in the air." Asked, "What put you on your feet again?" this strong, active Christian girl replied: "The Christian attitude of the professors in their classes and their activities outside. The whole atmosphere here is different from that in any place I have ever been."

It seems to us little less than criminal to undertake to undermine the faith of our people in colleges like this. When the facts are known, they are the glory of the Christian church.

14.8 Documents on Fundamentalist Protests in the Northern Baptist Convention

An extensive fundamentalist movement erupted within the Northern Baptist Convention early in the twentieth century. The resulting schisms produced several new Baptist groups, many of which still endure. These include such groups as the Baptist Bible Union in 1923, the General Association of Regular Baptist Churches in 1932, and the Conservative Baptist Association in 1947. In a major article in the *Watchman-Examiner* in 1925 William Bell Riley traced the course of the fundamentalist controversy, including several primary source documents. The citation below comes from that article. Riley (1861-1947), longtime pastor in Minneapolis, was hardly an impartial observer; he was a major leader of the fundamentalist faction. His commentary must be read in that light. Portions of the article are included here because of the importance of the primary documents. *Source:* William B. Riley, "To All Baptists Who Believe the Bible to be God's Word," *Watchman-Examiner*, 19 Nov. 1925, 1497-1498.

At a great missionary conference of the Baptist Bible Union of North America, held in Chicago, November 1-4, 1925, it was decided to form a new missions department and to adopt as its initial enterprise the Russian Missionary Society, of which Pastor Fetler is the general director.

The executive committee was also authorized to investigate other fields—in China, India, Africa, and elsewhere, with a view to the prosecution of foreign mission work in these and other countries.

This action of the Baptist Bible Union grows out of the action of the Northern Baptist Convention in Seattle, in rejecting a resolution intended to recall modernist missionaries from the foreign field; and in the reaction of orthodox Baptists against the Rockefeller-Fosdick effort to dominate the denomination, and to shape its missionary policy.

Since the publication of the Bible Union's intention to form a foreign mission society, there has been a great response from all parts of the continent and from the foreign field, indicating that the action of the Bible Union, in this case, will create an entirely new situation in the Baptist denomination in America.

The following statement embodying the recommendations of the council of the Union to the Convention, was adopted with anonymity and great enthusiasm. We commend it to the careful and prayerful consideration of all true Baptists in America:

"At the meeting of the Northern Baptist Convention held in Seattle, Washington, June 24-29, a commission, which had been appointed the year before, to investigate the affairs of the American Baptist Foreign Mission Society, presented its report in a lengthy document which referred, among other things, to the announcement of the 'inclusive policy' of the board; and declared that while the majority of the missionaries were true to the faith, others were not so."

Examples of departure from the faith were described in the following statement:

That, however, certain missionaries have laid themselves liable to just criticism and necessary investigation by the board seems to us to be clear from quotations which we now make. These are extracts from statements of certain of the missionaries about whose beliefs formal complaint has been made:

Dealing with the subject of the person of Christ one writes:

But the unique element of Jesus' nature does not lie in his being the "only begotten" Son of God. He is not that by his own teaching. Rather, he is the only perfect one among the countless millions of sons of God who have been born into our heavenly Father's earthly home.

Jesus owes many a debt to men who had not obtained the perfection that he had in his relation to God.

In dealing with the person of Christ as related to his death he writes: "In setting an unbridgeable gulf between the glory of Jesus and our own possibilities, it seems to me that men are opposing themselves diametrically to his teaching and desires, and are to a large degree rendering his sacrificial life and death vain."

On the inspiration of the Scriptures and in arguing to show that they are not infallible he writes:

"Surely it is clear that the Bible, part for part, is not an infallible book. . . . There is many a book, many a sermon, many a poem of our day as God-inspired and as God-filled and helpful as many of the Books of the Bible and more so than some. God is still speaking to his children through the voice of his prophets."

Another writes:

"I wish I might say that I have a firm faith in eternal life. It would be a comforting belief. I have resolved to live as though life were eternal—but I have failed to find convincing evidence that such is the case, or that such is not the case. I must regard Paul's teaching in I Corinthians 15:19 as contrary to Jesus' own ideals. 'If we have only hope in Christ in this life we are of all men most pitiable.' Also verse 32 of the same, 'If the dead are not raised, let us eat and drink, for to-morrow we die.' That is not my philosophy. Whether we are to be raised or whether death ends all, it is still worth while to live the Christ life—to love God and men, to suffer for others, to serve and sacrifice. If death be the end, then, we have lived as sons of God; if death be, as I hope, the entrance to a new life, it is well."

The report of this commission was adopted unanimously, after which the following resolution was moved by Dr. W. B. Hinson, of Portland, and seconded by Dr. W. B. Riley, of Minneapolis:

Whereas, The report of our committee appointed a year ago to investigate the work on our foreign fields reveals both a careful and extensive survey of the same; and

Whereas, The Northern Baptist Convention in its session in Indianapolis adopted the New Testament as our basis of faith; and

Whereas, The New Testament clearly teaches the divine and direct creation of man in the image of God, the plenary inspiration of the Scriptures of both the Old and New Testaments, the certain deity of Jesus Christ, involving, his virgin birth, his sinless life, his sacrificial death, his bodily resurrection, and ascension to the right hand of God and his return;

Whereas, The same Scriptures clearly declare the necessity of the sinful soul's regeneration in order to redemption; the baptism of believers a condition of church membership and involves for all the saved a commission to preach the gospel, baptize into the name of the Lord Jesus, and teach them the observance of all things which he has commanded; therefore

Be it resolved, That this Convention record its keen appreciation of the work of this commission; its exceeding great pleasure that the commission can report a majority of our missionaries loyal to the faith once for all delivered; and its profound conviction that in the interest of peace in our own body and the progress of our cause on foreign fields, and the honor of our Christ who is very God of very God, our foreign mission boards are hereby instructed to immediately recall every representative, whether in evangelistic or educational work, who denies any of the great fundamentals of our faith aforementioned, including especially those appointees found by the commission's investigation to be out of harmony with this faith; and as speedily as possible to fill the places thus vacated by equally competent men and women whose evangelical faith and fervor cannot be questioned; and

Be it further resolved, That it is the conviction of this Convention that no man or woman would accept place on our mission boards who cannot, with whole heart, adopt and advocate the historic Baptist and evangelical faith.

After much discussion, an amendment was submitted, striking out everything after the third paragraph, and substituting the following:

Be it resolved, That we urge our Foreign Mission Board, in the light of the facts reported by the commission, such action as seems to them will best conserve our denominational interests and best serve the kingdom of Christ.

The amendment carried by a vote of 742 to 574.

After the afternoon session of the Convention, a special meeting of the Baptist Bible Union was called for 9:30, and a large building was crowded to the doors. The following resolution was adopted by unanimous vote:

Whereas, The Northern Baptist Convention rejected the following simple statement of the fundamentals of the faith commonly held by Baptists:

"The New Testament clearly teaches the divine and direct creation of man in the image of God, the supernatural inspiration of the Scriptures of both the Old and New Testaments, the certain deity of Jesus Christ, involving, his virgin birth, his sinless life, his sacrificial death, his bodily resurrection, and ascension to the right hand of God and his return.

"The same Scriptures clearly declare the necessity of the sinful soul's regeneration in order to redemption; the baptism of believers a condition of church membership; and involves for all the saved a commission to preach the gospel, baptize into the name of the Lord Jesus, and teach them the observance of all things which he has commanded"; and

Whereas, This statement of the fundamentals of the faith was rejected, in spite of the fact that the commission appointed to enquire into the affairs of the Foreign Mission Board of the Northern Baptist Convention, reported that there are at present upon some of the stations men and women who do not hold to the fundamentals of the Christian faith as historically interpreted by Baptists; and

Whereas, This rejection of the fundamentals of the faith is certain to have the effect of more completely destroying the confidence of Baptists in the Foreign Mission Board, and the general administration of the Northern Baptist Convention; therefore

Be it resolved, That this meeting of the members of the Baptist Bible Union and of fundamentalists in sympathy with the Baptist Bible Union standards of faith, request the executive committee of the Baptist Bible Union, together with such fundamentalists as the executive committee may consider it wise to call into counsel, to take into consideration the advisability of organizing a foreign mission society, founded upon the confession of faith of the Baptist Bible Union; and in the event of the decision being reached by that committee that the exigencies of the present foreign mission situation in the Northern Baptist Convention point to a providential leading towards the founding of such a society, this meeting further requests the executive committee of the Union to call a meeting at a place as central as possible to the territory of the Northern Baptist Convention for the organization of such a society; . . . .

In obedience to these instructions, the executive committee of the Baptist Bible Union met in Toronto, September 1-4, 1925; and after hours of prayer and counsel, unanimously decided to report favorably concerning the organization of a missions department. The action was taken with great deliberation, and even in grief, as it was perfectly understood by the committee that such an organization would create an entirely new situation in Baptist affairs. It was also unanimously agreed, however, that no other righteous way out of our difficulties existed.

This fact is further emphasized by the consideration that very shortly after the Conventional adjourned, it was officially announced by that board that it would continue on the "inclusive policy"—by which was meant, that all different faiths found within the Baptist Convention fellowship should have their representatives on foreign fields, and on equal ground. When it was remembered that practically every official of the Foreign Board voted in favor of seating the delegates from the Park avenue or Rockefeller church, it was perfectly understood that no conceivable reform, such as calling home from the foreign fields those who wore the name of Baptist, but in fact were Unitarian, could be hoped for; since the men who would approve the denial of the full inspiration of the Bible, the virgin birth and deity of Jesus Christ, his bodily resurrection and ascension to the right hand of God, and who would also be willing to throw into discard baptism of believers by immersion in water, in connection with the home church, could never be trusted to emphasize these things as essential on the foreign field. The only conceivable cure for such an un-Biblical and utterly subversive spirit within the denomination, is the creation of a new agency that shall stand for the faith which produced the Baptist denomination, and which will furnish our churches with a channel through which to exercise their divinely-given right to preach at home and abroad the gospel revealed in the Bible.

The decision of the executive committee of last September was widely published through certain papers; and the entire membership of the Baptist Bible Union was circularized, calling this conference for the consideration of the foreign mission problem. Therefore, in view of the foregoing facts, the council now recommends the following:

1. That we establish a department of missions in connection with the Baptist Bible Union of North America, to be conducted through our headquarters in Chicago.

2. That the executive committee of the Baptist Bible Union be given the general oversight of this department, and empowered to conduct the same in strict accord with the Bible Union confession of faith, and in keeping with their best judgment; reporting in full to the annual meeting of the Baptist Bible Union, and as much oftener as occasion shall require. . . .

3. And further, it is the judgment of this conference that the field of our foreign work should be unlimited, different stations being taken up as occasion may arise, and the judgment of the committee may approve. The executive committee, therefore, is hereby authorized to investigate any Baptist foreign mission enterprise which shall seek this Union's sponsorship or support; . . .

4. It is also here laid down as a guiding principle for the conduct of the missions department of the Union, that, for all money received, a receipt shall be given; that money specifically designated as for any country or missionary organization or individual, shall be expended in obedience to the donor's direction; . . .

6. This missionary conference of the Baptist Bible Union also declares that the

Union's objective in foreign missions shall be evangelization first and foremost. If education be undertaken at all, it should be regarded as secondary, and its obligation assumed only insofar as it will aid the program of evangelism; since our object is Christianization and not civilization. . . .

8. Furthermore, we desire here and now to declare to the world, that in entering into this co-operative endeavor to preach the gospel at home and abroad, we affirm our conviction that "The local church has the absolute right of self-government, free from the interference of any hierarchy of individuals or organizations and that the one and only superintendent is Christ, through the Holy Spirit; that it is scriptural for true churches to cooperate with each other in contending for the faith and for the furtherance of the gospel; that every church is the sole and only judge of the measure and method of its co-operation; on all matters of membership, of polity, of government, of discipline, of benevolence, the will of the local church is final."—(Baptist Bible Union Confession of Faith—Article xiii).

9. It is hereby understood and declared that this mission department is not intended to reflect upon any missionary organization that stands for "the faith once for all delivered to the saints," as revealed in the Bible, and as historically held by Baptists.

10. And further, after a first-hand investigation of the work being conducted among Russians, Slava and Lets, by Pastor Fetler, and having thereby satisfied ourselves that the work of the Russian Missionary Society is of God, and is being conducted in accord with the principles of the Word of God, we heartily and without reservation adopt the work of the said Society as the initial foreign mission enterprise of the missions department of the Baptist Bible Union of North America; . . .

14.9   Frank M. Goodchild, *What Fundamentalists Stand For*

In the 1920s, as in a later generation, not all Baptists agreed on what beliefs constituted fundamentalism. Frank M. Goodchild, an outstanding Northern Baptist leader and later president of the Fundamentalist Federation, represented a more moderate form of fundamentalist reform. His spirit was more akin to that of J. C. Massee, who refused to go along with the more militant protests of the radical fundamentalists. Goodchild's article of 1925, "What Fundamentalists Stand For," helped distance moderate fundamentists from radicals like W. B. Riley of Minneapolis, T. T. Shields of Toronto, and J. Frank Norris of Fort Worth. *Source:* Frank M. Goodchild, "Five Planks in the Platform of the Fundamentalists of the Northern Baptist Convention," undated pamphlet reprinted in the *Watchman-Examiner*, 10 Dec. 1925.

THE BIBLE

"For the prophecy came not in old time by the will of man, but holy men of God spake as they were moved by the Holy Ghost" (2 Peter 1:21).

Calvinism had its five points of doctrine. They were predestination, irresistible grace, original sin, particular redemption and the final perseverace of the saints. Controversy over these things is a matter of the distant past. To-day it is not only particular doctrines of Scripture that are called in question but the authority of the Bible itself is denied. Fundamentalists stand where loyal Baptists have always stood. We believe that the Bible is God's Word, that it was written by men divinely inspired, and that it has supreme authority in all matters of faith and conduct.

THE CHURCH

"Christ is the head of the Church" (Ephesians 5:23).

Fundamentalists believe just as strongly in the church as in the Bible. Both the Bible and the church are God-given.

The Bible is God's revelation to men. The church is God's own institution on earth through which he ministers to a needy and sinful world. The members of a church acknowledge that they have been redeemed by the blood of Christ, they are striving to live in obedience to Christ, they are associated for worship of their Lord and for spreading abroad the good news of salvation. Fundamentalists emphasize, as the New Testament does, the importance of the local church. Like our Baptist fathers we are ever watchful against centralization of power in any body outside the churches, and we deplore every effort to set up any organization in authority over local church. Christ is the only head of the church, and to him only his church is responsible.

THE DENOMINATION

"Your fellowship in the gospel" (Phillipans [sic] 1:5).

Fundamentalists believe in the denomination. It is quite impossible for a single church to meet effectively the tremendous obligations that press upon Christian people to-day. The churches have therefore related themselves to each other in associations, state conventions, home and foreign mission societies and the like, that they may meet these obligations with united strength and resources. Fundamentalists have loyally supported all these means of carrying the good news of salvation in Jesus Christ to the ends of the earth, insisting only that the messengers, at home and abroad, shall carry the gospel of the grace of God as given in the New Testament.

SCHOOLS

"Teaching them to observe all things whatsoever I have commanded you" (Matthew 28:20).

Fundamentalists believe in schools. We have a commission to teach from Jesus Christ. We support education liberally at home and in the foreign field. We give self-denyingly for it. The schools we have to-day, in which we take pride, were founded by our Baptist fathers who held precisely the same faith that we hold. We regard them as our schools. That is why we pray and work that they may be saved from false teaching. We believe in education, but we believe that the money given by our churches should be used only to establish and maintain schools in which the education given is unmistakably Christian. Professor William Lyon Phelps said it exactly right when he said "A knowledge of the Bible without a college course is more valuable than a college course without the Bible."

MISSIONS

"Go ye into all the world and preach the gospel to every creature" (Mark 16:15).

Fundamentalists believe thoroughly in missions. We take it as our Lord's last command to his people to preach the gospel to every creature. We believe our missionaries should go everywhere like flaming evangels telling men in the plainest way possible that "in Jesus Christ we have redemption through his blood, even the forgiveness of sins" (Col. 1:14). We believe in foreign mission schools, but only as a means of evangelization, and of training native men and women to go out to evangelize their own people. We realize that education alone has no power to regenerate. That labor delegate in a great meeting in London was right when he said, "As a remedy for our ills you say 'Educate, educate, educate', but I say 'Regenerate, regenerate, regenerate.'," The Holy Spirit alone can regenerate.

14.10 American Baptist Foreign Missionary Society, Response to Fundamentalist Attacks, 1924

Fundamentalist agitation among Northern Baptists quickly escalated beyond the schools and permeated the foreign mission society. Accusations circulated that some missionaries held suspect doctrinal views, and that the mission board's so-called "inclusive policy" included appointment of some who either ignored or denied cherished Baptist doctrine. Frederick L. Anderson, chairman of the mission society, defended the society's policies and practices. In 1924 the society summed up four responses to the crisis, and printed this defense in the convention *Annual*. This document shows various ways Northern Baptist leaders tried to prevent fundamentalism from disrupting the foreign mission work. This defense of the mission board concluded with a warning that continued fundamentalist agitation might lead to a reduction in both spiritual and financial support for foreign missions. *Source: Annual,* Northern Baptist Convention, Milwaukee, 1924, 529-538.

Two years ago the Board, in its Annual Report, called attention to the recent theological agitation. This was not confined to Baptists but had manifested itself among other denominations also. The foreign-mission enterprise was eventually brought into this doctrinal discussion. Communications were widely circulated in America calling in question the theological views of a few missionaries of the Society and claiming that they were teaching and preaching other than evangelical truth. After prolonged consideration the Board felt it necessary to issue an official communication to the constituency, stating that it was prepared to investigate fully any cases in which definite charges were presented. Except in a single case which is now being investigated no definite charges have been presented to the Board.

Notwithstanding this communication and its assurance of serious investigation upon the presentation of charges, this theological agitation has continued. Although the denomination at large and especially recent sessions of the Northern Baptist Convention have not been free from its influence, this agitation among Baptists during the past year has been particularly directed against the work of the Society. In June, 1923, a delegation representing certain members of the constituency of the Society appeared before the Secretaries of the Board and later before the Board itself, requesting the privilege of access to the correspondence files of the Society for the purpose of verifying certain extracts which, without the consent or even the knowledge of the Board, had been copied from letters and placed in their hands. After extended consideration, the Board, for reasons indicated later in this review, felt it to be its duty both to the missionaries and to the denomination to decline this request. Thereupon a number of publications were issued by this delegation and were widely distributed throughout the denomination. These publications attacked the policy of the Board in its administration of the work of the Society, and the teaching and preaching of certain missionaries. Later issues published extracts apparently from the letters for which verification had been sought through the requested access to the files. To the situation which had thus been precipitated, the Board has devoted considerable time, prayerful thought, and serious attention throughout the year. A special Committee of Seven, consisting of Prof. H. B. Robins, Rev. A. C. Baldwin, Pres. E. W. Hunt, Rev. H. J. White, T. Otto, Prof. F. L. Anderson, and Secretary P. H. J. Lerrigo, was appointed to study and report on the various aspects of the matter. The records of the Board show that, although great emergency matters like the Japan earthquake disaster, the financial situation, and other important developments were demanding attention, the Board at every meeting throughout the year has had to reserve time for earnest consideration of reports from this committee. A number of statements were formulated and issued, which for purposes of record are incorporated in this report.

The first was issued under date of October 23, 1923, and read as follows:
To the Northern Baptists:

DEAR BROTHERS AND SISTERS: In view of certain rumors and misunderstandings among our people, the Board of Managers of the American Baptist Foreign Mission Society issues the following statement, on which it humbly asks the blessing of God and for which it craves your sympathetic and prayerful consideration.

Your Board is as anxious as any one of you can possibly be that every officer and missionary of our Society should have the character and faith which the Lord Jesus himself can approve. As often previously announced, it is the intention and practise of the Board to deal with any one, officer or missionary, who may manifestly fall below this standard.

Our Denomination, our Society, and our churches have always given to officers, missionaries, and pastors a considerable degree of liberty of theological opinion. To be sure, we have always insisted on a living Christian experience, on a passion for the salvation of men, on loyalty to our Lord Jesus and his gospel, and on belief in the vital teachings of our religion, but it has not been our Baptist custom to limit too explicitly the form in which these doctrines must be held and expressed.

In spite of the fact that the Northern Baptist Convention in all its elections from its foundation to the present year has acted in accordance with this long-standing denominational policy, which makes for unity and inclusion rather than for dissension and division, certain brethren now ask us to reverse this policy. The Board of Managers frankly and kindly refuses to depart from the custom and usage of the Denomination in this regard, believing that it thus carries out the will of the Denomination, as expressed in all its public acts. The Board, composed, like our churches, of men of diverse opinions, has heretofore included and should include among its officers and missionaries representatives of various elements among our people.

There are, of course, limits to this liberty of theological opinion. Every one gives up a certain amount of his liberty when he joins an organization. A Christian must believe certain things to be a Christian, and a Baptist to be a Baptist. The exact limits of liberty, however, will be decided somewhat differently by the succeeding generations. In the history of our Denomination, they have been constantly, though slowly, changing; for instance, a century since, an anti-mission Baptist was in good standing, but now none dare publicly profess anti-mission sentiments, with the theological views on which they were based.

As fresh areas of knowledge are opened up, as new situations and new questions emerge, these changes are bound to come. It would be unwise and futile for any one generation to try to fix the limits of liberty rigidly. *The only instrument by which these limits can be determined fairly and wisely in the particular cases which arise is the living voice of the Denomination, uttering itself continually through ever-changing executive boards and officers, freely elected by the Denomination in the most democratic manner, guided by the Scriptures and led by the Spirit of Christ.*

The Board of Managers of the Foreign Mission Society is the agency, elected by the Denomination, which voices and executes the mind of the Denomination in its general foreign work. It believes that it has the confidence of the Denomination. Every one of its members has been elected by practically unanimous vote. Many of them have been repeatedly re-elected. The Board also calls attention to the great and ever-increasing spiritual results attained on all our fields as the seal of God's approval on our missionaries and our work.

Our missionaries are noble men and women of the highest Christian character, many of whom have endured great hardships and sufferings for our Lord. Their Christian faith is sincere and strong. Their purpose to bring the world to Christ is unwavering and high. They are in every way worthy of the confidence and support of the Northern Baptists. They are justified in expecting that none of us will desert them.

Engaged in a serious attempt to fulfil the Great Commission of our risen Lord at an unparalleled crisis of the world's history, we, as Northern Baptists, should gird ourselves anew to seize the greatest missionary opportunity ever presented to the Christian

Church. Let us continue to stand undivided on the large area of ground common to us all, and work together heartily and lovingly to save our fellow men from spiritual death and to establish the divine Kingdom of righteousness, joy, and peace in this lost and sin-stained world.

By order of the Board of Managers,

(Signed) FREDERICK L. ANDERSON, *Chairman,*

(Signed) WILLIAM B. LIPPHARD, *Recording Secretary.*

A second statement was issued under date of November 15, 1923. After referring briefly to the origin of the attack against the Board this read as follows:

The charges may be reduced to three: (1) That the Board neglects the work of personal evangelism for education and social service, (2) that the Board permits the teaching of liberal doctrines by its missionaries, (3) that the Board has not been straightforward in its dealings with the Denomination. We now proceed to reply to the charges in order.

1. The Board of Managers of the American Baptist Foreign Mission Society recalls that the corporate object of the Society, as stated in its charter, is "the diffusion of the knowledge of the religion of Jesus Christ by means of missions throughout the world," and now reaffirms that in pursuance of that object the proclamation of the gospel of Christ is its primary aim. . . .

The evangelization of vast Oriental and African populations can never be accomplished by white foreigners alone. It must be the task of capable native Christian leaders, who can be developed only by a thorough Christian education. In more than one instance it has been discovered that where there have been mass movements toward Christianity without trained native leaders to guide the new converts, a reaction toward paganism has followed. The increased emphasis on Christian education has been with a view to wider proclamation of the gospel and also to the training of native leaders capable of developing self-supporting, self-governing, and self-propagating churches and other Christian institutions, and of taking a large part in the direction of affairs in general in their own lands. We have learned from experience that in certain countries the denominations which have neglected Christian education have fallen far behind others in evangelistic results.

Nor should it be forgotten that upon certain fields a large proportion of all the baptisms reported (sometimes more than half) are in the schools, not to mention the large numbers who are reached in the hospitals. It is a mistake to assume that all the evangelistic results are in the work of the so-called evangelistic missionaries. Some of the most successful soul-winners are teachers and physicians. Many of the very best are native Christians. The Board of Managers endeavors to promote a spirit of evangelism in the hearts of all missionaries and in every form of work.

We definitely and positively repudiate the idea that social service is the supreme thing, and so far as we are aware, no one connected with our Society would think of substituting it for salvation. . . . So, far from substituting social service for salvation, we teach that salvation of the individual and the world must be found in Christ, and we point men to him and his cross as the moving power for every form of service.

2. It is charged that the Board permits the teaching of liberal doctrines by its missionaries. Our Board has frankly stated to its constituency that it gives to its officers and missionaries a considerable degree of liberty of theological opinion in accordance with the long standing policy of the Denomination, and that it firmly and kindly declines to reverse that policy. Our Denomination, like our individual churches, is made up of men and women of diverse views, and our Board, most appropriately made up in the same way, thinks it only right, fair, and wise that our missionary force should reflect the

situation in our churches at home. We have no intention of restricting our appointees and missionaries to any one group. We represent the whole Denomination and we treat all our constituency as brothers and sisters in the faith. . . .

Our great foreign work has been done by all kinds of Baptists. It belongs to the whole Denomination, and cannot bear its richest and largest fruits without the hearty cooperation of all. If we are united in heart and in loyalty to the Saviour, whom we all love, diversity of view is an advantage and a blessing, giving our work a balance, a sanity, and a manysidedness, which helps us constantly to rise to higher things. . . .

The exact limits of theological liberty have slowly changed in our Denomination with the years, and will doubtless further change in the future. Our Board represents the *present* feeling of our constituency. Freely elected, it is the Denomination's living voice in its sphere and its decisions are, we humbly believe, made in the spirit of Christ. Future Boards, with new light and facing new conditions, may decide somewhat differently, and doubtless will. We, today, must act as kindly, truly, and wisely as we can. We ask not only the generous consideration of all our brethren, but their prayers that we may be led aright.

3. It is charged that our dealings with our people have not been straightforward, that we have denied plain facts, that "subtle deceit was being employed to hide the real conditions from our constituency." As honest men, we feel these charges most keenly. The answer to them is to be found in the statement in the last paragraph. It has always been the policy of our Society and of our Denomination to allow a certain freedom in theological opinion. We had supposed that every Baptist understood it and would read our statements in the light of it. There is nothing new in what we tell the Denomination in our present statements and no change of procedure whatever.

When, in addressing the Denomination, we expressed confidence in the faith of our missionaries and their loyalty to Christ, we meant that we were sure that they stood on the common ground of faith and loyalty, which we have reached in our Board, as a result of the study of the Scriptures and prayerful examination of the truth found there, and of our own experience of divine grace. We had and have confidence in them, and we believe that the Denomination has a right to have like confidence. Of course, there may be possible exceptions in a large missionary force like ours and we again state that we are ready to investigate any such cases, when charges are made to us in definite form over the names of the accusers. This and this only is fair, and just to the accused and is demanded in every civilized court. . . .

We disclaim any dishonesty of motive or act in dealing with our constituency. We cannot avoid misinterpretation by those who do not understand the inclusive policy pursued by all our Societies and the Northern Baptist Convention for years.

We are lovers of Christ, renewed by his spirit, devoted to his great purposes of salvation for the world, trusting in the power of the Living Saviour to use our missionaries and us to bring the Nations to himself.

We crave the hearty support of the whole Denomination for our work, which God has so greatly blessed.

By order of the Board of Managers,

(Signed)   FREDERICK L. ANDERSON, *Chairman,*

(Signed)   WILLIAM B. LIPPHARD, *Recording Secretary.*

In closing this review of a difficult situation which it was compelled to meet during the year, the Board desires to call attention to the damaging effect which such continued public agitation is likely to bring upon the entire missionary enterprise. One of its distressing results may be a diminution of the hearty support, both financial and spiritual, which the missionaries ought to have, and the life work of hundreds of consecrated missionaries, concerning whom there could be no possible question of disloyalty to Christ and his gospel, may thereby be placed in jeopardy.

14.11   Curtis Lee Laws, "Can the Controversy Be Settled?"

Curtis Lee Laws (1868-1946), longtime editor of the combined *Watchman-Examiner,* was one of the more moderate Northern Baptist fundamentalist leaders. He coined the term "fundamentalist" in an editorial in 1920. He was also among a group who founded Eastern Baptist Theological Seminary as an antidote for other Baptist seminaries in the East which had, the group believed, become too liberal. In the editorial cited here, Laws discussed possible ways to settle this or any other religious controversy. *Source:* Curtis Lee Laws, ed., "Can the Controversy Be Settled?" *Watchman-Examiner,* 29 Oct. 1925, 1389-1390.

Many people are asking how the questions in controversy between the various schools of thought are ever to be really settled. Many answers have been given to the question. We propose in this editorial to review some of them briefly.

One answer is that the questions are to be settled by a sound philosophy. A young man said recently, "My only guide and standard in religion is the pure love of truth." By "truth" he meant the deliverances of human reason unaided by a divine revelation. It is a hopeless attitude. The ages have demonstrated its futility. Hundreds of years before Christ Greek philosophy was broken up into many schools of thought under the guidance of the principle. In the early Christian centuries the non-Christian world was broken up in the same way, and so on through all the centuries. Today there are twenty or thirty schools of philosophy of various intellectual hues and shades. They radically contradict each other on the great ultimate questions. If this is the result of twenty-five centuries of speculation he is a bold young man who hopes to solve the riddle of the universe by the pure love of truth in the abstract.

Others say that science is to be the arbiter and settle our controversies, and the science which is meant is chiefly physical science. Many people get all their intellectual bearings from the various sciences, any science, and all sciences except religion. They fail to realize that in religion they must consult the highest religious authority. . . . How to be saved; how to attain high character; how to acquire moral power for service of God and man; how to grow into an ever-increasing spiritual conquest of sin and attainment of holiness—these are not found by looking through microscope or telescope. They are not learned by the study of chemical reactions or star dust or fossils in the rocks.

Another group holds that the only authority which can settle religious controversies is the Christian consciousness. The man with a spiritual mind and heart is the true judge of truth. But where shall such a man be found? Where is the consciousness that is fully Christian? . . . But the champions of the Christian consciousness as the final authority vary greatly in the degrees of their acceptance of the Gospel records which purport to give us the mind of Christ.

There are those also who say that the true road to a settlement of all our controversies is to adopt a principle of comprehension by which all types of thought shall exist side by side under a system of mutual toleration. Theoretically this is a beautiful thing. Practically it is unworkable. Religious convictions go deepest in the human soul. Convictions about God, and Christ and immortality and the spiritual welfare of the race grip men so powerfully that it is not easy to cooperate harmoniously for the great ends of the kingdom with those who hold antagonistic views. . . .

The true answer to the question we are considering is that the New Testament is the authority to settle modern religious controversies. We do not disparage the Old Testament or under-value it in any way. But the center of all the current issues is the Person and work, the life and teachings of Jesus Christ. He is our final authority. But we learn of him fully only through the New Testament. Hence the New Testament is the storm center of modern controversy.

There is no need to discuss minor points of criticism in connection with the authority of the New Testament. . . . There is ample ground for our doctrine of an inspired and authoritative Bible. . . . We have or we have not an authentic and trustworthy account of Jesus in these records. The New Testament picture of him, as a whole, is harmonious and self-consistent. He was and is the divine Son of the eternal Father. To disintegrate the New Testament is to transfer all religious issues back to the subjective realm. All once more becomes speculation. . . .

The great issues of to-day which can and ought to be settled by the New Testament are as follows: Has God given us a supernatural revelation of himself? Is the Bible the record of that revelation? Was Jesus Christ God manifest in the flesh? Was he born of the Virgin Mary? Did he work miracles? Did he live a sinless life and make a real atonement for sin? Did he really rise from the dead? Did he ascend to the Father? Did he bestow the Holy Spirit at Pentecost? Is he alive forevermore as the Saviour of men and Lord of the Kingdom? Will he come again in God's appointed time? There are other questions, but these are the principal ones. The modern rationalistic world is prejudging all these questions, and settling them, to its own satisfaction, without regard to the evidence. Its conclusions, therefore, cannot stand. . . .

The religious outlook of the world is hopeless apart from the New Testament. A supernatural revelation alone satisfies man's religious needs. Rationalism has borrowed the moral elementary teachings of the New Testament and proclaimed them as the assured results of reason. But if their supernatural foundation is removed they become once more a part of the welter of speculative thought. May God save the world from the reign of the anti-supernaturalism which is attempting to usurp the throne of human thought in our day!

14.12 Financial Impact of the Fundamentalist Controversy

In this brief document, Curtis Lee Laws, editor of the influential *Watchman-Examiner* offers his judgment that the fundamentalist controversy had adversely affected financial support of Northern Baptist causes. Spokesmen on both sides of the controversy agreed on this point, but differed on what needed to be done to regain the confidence of the people. *Source:* Curtis Lee Laws, ed., "Editorial Notes and Comments," *Watchman-Examiner,* 29 Oct, 1925, 1391.

WHY NOT MORE GENEROUS GIVING?

Our various societies, organizations and schools will not receive the free, full and joyful support of the rank and file of our Baptist people until confidence is reassured. The large gifts of a few wealthy people cannot compensate for the loss of innumerable small gifts from the humble people. A denomination cannot thrive ultimately which pays little attention to the mass of its constituency and depends upon a few generous givers for support. Money is important but it is not as important as wide and deep spread interest. These are the sources from which will come, not only the support for to-day, but for to-morrow. Beyond question it is true that many of our people believe and profoundly believe that liberalism controls our denomination. Until it is proved to them that this is not true their gifts will be meager and grudgingly offered. If our societies are not controlled by liberals, they ought frankly and joyfully to prove to our denomination their allegiance to New Testament theology and the long time polity of our Baptist churches and organizations. We candidly believe that this and this only is the solution of our problems.

14.13   Formation of the Conservative Baptist
Foreign Mission Society, 1943

Among the more moderate fundamentalists, many resisted all efforts to entice them to bolt the Northern Baptist Convention. While they sympathized with some concerns of those who pulled out in the Bible Union and General Association of Regular Baptists schisms of 1923 and 1932, they continued to try to work within the Convention. However, by the 1940s even the less excitable among them concluded that separation was inevitable. Continued complaints, and a feeling that their complaints were not taken seriously, led to formation of their own Conservative Baptist Foreign Mission Society in 1943. In a two-part article, selections A and B, Earle V. Pierce defended that action. *Source:* Earle V. Pierce, "Northern Baptist Foreign Mission," *Watchman-Examiner,* Part I, 19 Aug. 1943, 794-796; Part II, 26 Aug. 1943, 818-819. In Selection C, Orrin Judd, outstanding Baptist layman and leader in the foreign mission work, responded to the Pierce articles, maintaining that no adequate reasons existed to justify a schismatic society. *Source:* Orrin C. Judd, "Northern Baptist Foreign Missions," *Watchman-Exqaminer,* 28 Oct. 1943, 1033, 1037.

A.   Earle V. Pierce, Defending formation of the new society, Part 1

In the early part of 1924, a missionary from India by the name of Hartley was called before the Board of the Foreign Missions Society because it had been reported that he was unsound.

In fact, when we were in India in '25, the Canadian missionaries asked us why Hartley was ever sent out by our Board. When he appeared on the mission field, a Canadian sent out by our Board, Canadian missionaries asked him why he did not come out under his own Board, and he replied that they never would appoint him, so he came down and was sent out by the A. B. F. M. S.

When he came before the Board for reëxamination, Henry Bond, president of the American Radiator Company and twice president of the Northern Convention, was a member of the Board and took part in the examination.

When the examination was completed, he came in to Dr. Laws' office and said that something had to be done. He said that Hartley had beaten around the bush, given evasive answers, until he, Bond, got tired of it and said, "Now I want you to answer some very plain questions, yes or no. Do you believe the Bible to be the inspired and authoritative and dependable Word of God?" And when Hartley started off again on a rambling reply he thundered to him, "I want you to answer me yes or no!" Hartley then said, "No, I do not!" "Do you believe in the deity of Christ? yes or no." "No, I do not." "Do you believe in his virgin birth? yes or no." "No, I do not." And so with the vicarious atonement of Christ and his resurrection and other important articles of faith.

Following this categorical denial of the great fundamentals, the Board of thirteen present voted nine to four that Hartley was all right.

The Milwaukee Convention

Of course, the facts got out, and soon after came the Northern Baptist Convention meeting at Milwaukee in 1924. At the time of that meeting, I hunted up the Fundamentalists, who were meeting in a hotel room. This was the first group meeting of the Fundamentalists which I had ever attended. I found there a hundred representative men of the denomination. Dr. Massee was presiding. Dr. Goodchild was there; Dr. Laws, Mr. Bond, Mr. Brock, a layman of Denver, Dr. Floyd Adams, and other men of that grade in the denomination. I especially remember that Dr. Massee said, in the course of the meeting, "Gentlemen, I have been approached by two of the liberals today with a proposition. I think they were sincere, but I do not want to get caught. They said, 'If you

Fundamentalists will agree not to spring the Hartley matter on the floor of the Convention, we will stand with you for an investigation of the entire Foreign Mission situation and personnel, for there's something rotten in Denmark.'" One of those men—the one who did the talking and said, "There's something rotten in Denmark"—was Dr. Wallace Petty. The result of the conference was that Dr. Massee made the motion to appoint a commission to investigate thoroughly the Foreign Mission situation and personnel and Dr. Wallace Petty seconded it. There was a strong minority against it, but it passed. Dr. Laws then made a motion that $25,000 be appropriated to be used, if necessary, for this investigation. This passed. Little of this money was used. . . .

What did the declaration of the "evangelical policy" then mean, and what does it mean now? It was given ostensibly to satisfy the denomination that men like Hartley would not be appointed. But the term "inclusive policy" seemed to compromise that construction. To avoid that misunderstanding, there was the further statement that inclusive meant "inclusive within the gospel," and some defining of the gospel was made. There was the positive statement, which has been reaffirmed, "We will appoint evangelicals, and we will not appoint nonevangelicals." . . .

What Is Meant By Deity?

It is declared in the Board's "evangelical policy" that "gospel" includes "belief in the deity of Christ." It most certainly does for all who use "gospel" in the New Testament sense, but when I hear Foreign Board members and secretaries say that belief in the Biblical account of the supernatural birth of our Lord, "the virgin birth," is not essential in a missionary, I object. . . .

Shall We Authorize Infection?

The church is the body of Christ. We are part of that body. Shall we authorize infection in any part of it? Do you want to set aside one part of your body to infection while keeping the other part in health?

Think, then, what confusion this would make on the foreign fields and in the minds of those who are being evangelized. Do we have two Christs to take to men, two Bibles, two gospels, two ways of salvation? . . . . If it is confusing to have different denominations going to the foreign fields, how much more tragic would be the confusion if there were officially endorsed by the denomination not only *the* gospel but "another gospel which is no gospel." . . .

If the New Testament is to be "the rule of faith and practice" of the Baptist denomination, then it must be, and when it ceases to be, the Bible believers will be ready to move out, for the great majority of our denomination are evangelical, and they know what they mean by that.

B. Earle V. Pierce, Defending Formation of the New Society, Part 2

Missionary Method

The "evangelistic policy" of the Foreign Board commits it to a clear evangelical policy of missionary method as well as personnel, as against an exaggerated social emphasis. The present rift in the denomination was precipitated by the election of a secretary whose emphasis for the past fifteen years has been so overwhelmingly social that it was feared this would be his policy as secretary. Since *Missions* has reported the Board action at Springfield concerning Dr. Fridell, it is not out of place to refer to it here. The Staff Committee of the Board had been warned while they were searching for a successor to Dr. Decker that there would be strong objections to Dr. Fridell's election.

They nevertheless presented his name. The Board itself had this warning pressed earnestly upon them before the election, but it was unheeded. At Springfield, in addition to the coming of a delegation of seven to urge upon the Board the reconsideration of its action in the interests of denominational peace, it was admitted in the discussion that letters of protest and of approval had come in to the Board in about equal numbers. Is it a clear following of the path of peace, when peace is so greatly desired, to go forward with even a fifty-fifty protest? It was also admitted that all the protests came from conservatives and that the most of the approvals were from liberals. This in itself says something. . . .

Democratic Procedure

The recent communication from the Foreign Board declares: "Members are elected by the democratic process as provided for by the constitution of the Northern Baptist Convention. The Board, therefore, is not a self-perpetuating body." One state secretary has written to the pastors in his state protesting the formation of a new Foreign Mission Society and saying that if things are not right they can be changed in a democratic way.

This must be looked into. Just how "democratic" are the practices of the Northern Baptist Convention? How far are Baptists democratically controlled, and how far are they board- and secretary-controlled?

The denomination is 75% to 85% conservative, as will be readily admitted. There is not, however, a board of the Convention that represents this proportion, though it must be admitted that there are theological conservatives and there are conservatives more political than theological who quite readily side with the liberals and will not oppose the "organization." As a matter of fact, there are few who realize how far we are board- and secretary-controlled Baptists.

Every cooperating church is allowed to send its pastor and other delegates to the Northern Convention, but many cannot afford to go. Just why it is we will not say now, but the liberal churches are mostly in the larger cities, and their pastors go. The smaller, more remote village and small-town churches are conservative. Few of their pastors or people get to the Conventions. The secretaries are always there with their expenses paid, and again and again they hold the balance of power in an election.

This is an evil long recognized by many, but it is always hard to take power away from those who control the balance of power. As pastor of a church, I have had the right to vote, but have never exercised it in a church election. I do not believe that the paid servants of a denomination should vote. . . .

Foreign Board Election

As to the Foreign Mission Board, let us come to something concrete, without which unprecedented action I do not believe there would be the present rift in the denomination. At the Cleveland Convention, in the providence of God—for the members of the subcommittees on the nomination committee are chosen by lot—it so happened that of the five who drew the Foreign Mission Board assignment four were thorough conservatives. They did what they had a perfect right to do—named most excellent conservative men well distributed over the country for the vacancies on the Foreign Mission Board. When their report was brought back to the General Committee, someone asked, "Whom did the Foreign Mission Board want to have elected this year?" At that, the representative, I am told, of the Foreign Board stepped up and read a list of names. I know that this list had never been voted by the Foreign Board. How it had been made up I am not certain. Then it was proposed and voted, for the liberals knew that they had a majority, that the whole nominating committee vote upon those two slates—the one presented by the representative of the Foreign Board and the other brought in by this committee duly and democratically chosen. In the vote the entire list of nominees presented by the subcommittee was swept aside, something I believe which never happened before in the Northern Baptist Convention.

Following this action, Dr. W. Brougher, Sr., who was the representative for the General Council, took occasion to say very earnestly to the group that, while they thought they had done a very smart thing, time would prove that they had done a very unwise thing. . . . I am very sure that, if there had not been this unprecedented overriding of a conservative committee which brought in a perfectly fair and good report, we would not now be suffering the rift in our denomination.

Which Is The Way?

Now, brethren, where are we? If liberalism is right, we ought all to be liberals and to send out only liberal missionaries, as the Laymen's Inquiry wanted us to do; but there are not two gospels, but one; there are not two Christs, or two Bibles, or two ways of salvation. . . .

If Fundamentalists are wrong in their stand for the Bible, then all should take up the recent cry of one who exclaimed: *"We must fight these Fundamentalists, we must crush them!"* Yet the majority of Baptist churches in his city are Fundamentalist.

Cause of Division

The cause of the present division which we are all deploring is not to be found in one recent event, but in the accumulation of uneasiness, dissatisfaction, frustration on the part of those who hold to the historic Baptist and Biblical faith that they believe to be absolutely vital to the successful propagation of the gospel and the work of the kingdom of God.

I do not believe that the Baptist denomination can long endure three-quarters conservative and one-quarter liberal, with the one liberal quarter exercising such a dominating influence. During the past twenty years, by actual record, 65% of the missionary appointments have been made from liberal theological seminaries, and while these candidates have been brought to declare a basic belief in most of the fundamentals, many of them have been so taught in the liberal nomenclature and emphasis that what they have lacked in gospel consciousness—rather than anything that they would declare contrary to the truth—makes their message devoid of the gospel vitamins that have been the basis of the great success which Baptist missions have had in the past.

C. Orrin C. Judd, Response to Pierce Articles

The recent articles by Dr. Earle V. Pierce in THE WATCHMAN-EXAMINER dealing with reasons leading up to the proposal for formation of a second foreign mission society deserve careful analysis, both because of their content and because of the high standing of the author, who is familiar with the Foreign Board through twelve years' membership, is the leader of the Fundamentalist Fellowship, and was honored a few years ago with the presidency of the Northern Baptist Convention. Study of those articles gives me hope for continued unity, and seems to afford no real basis for complaint against the present Society.

The only example of improper action charged against the Board is based on the appointment in 1924 of a missionary who denied the authority of the Bible and the divinity of Christ. He was not reappointed and would not be sent to the field by the present Board. I feel certain that a mistake of twenty years ago, which has not been repeated, is no ground for condemning the Foreign Mission Society.

Dr. Pierce discusses the Society's "evangelical policy" (sometimes called the "inclusive policy"), and warns against the possibility of "weasel words" therein. He suggests what appears to be a satisfactory ground of agreement in the dictionary definition of "evangelical," which he quotes with approval:

(1) Of or pertaining to the gospel or the Four Gospels. (2) Holding or conformed to what the majority of Protestants regard as the fundamental doctrines of the gospel, such as personal union with Christ, the Trinity, the fallen condition of man, Christ's atonement for sin, salvation by faith, not by works, and regeneration by the Holy Spirit: spiritually minded: as, evangelical religion. In England the term usually designates the Low-church party, and in the United States the "orthodox" churches.

If Dr. Pierce and the group for which he speaks will stand by his next statement, "Let our Foreign Board hold strictly to that definition and there will be no need of another society," there is no ground left for the proponents of a second society.

In my eight years on the Foreign Board, I have made it a point to read the candidate papers which are circulated before each new missionary is considered. I have not known one to be appointed in that period who did not meet the definition which Dr. Pierce quotes. If any such had been appointed, I am sure the articles would have mentioned him and not confined their criticism to one appointee of twenty years ago.

The Virgin Birth of Our Lord

It should be unnecessary to add to the definition of "evangelical" the doctrine of the virgin birth which the articles go on to discuss. Again, I do not recall any missionary appointed during my time who denied the doctrine. Yet I cannot agree with the implications of the rhetorical question put by Dr. Pierce, "How can one believe in the *deity* of Christ who believes that Joseph was his father?" Did not Jesus say, "God is able of these stones to raise up children unto Abraham?" (Matthew 3:9). If we concede any latitude for private interpretation of the Scripture, we should not refuse fellowship with those who give primary weight to the fact that Christ's Davidic lineage is traced through Joseph and who believe that God could beget a divine son through a human father as well as a human mother.

Surely, Dr. Pierce does not intend the slur on missionary candidates which is discernible in his statement that many "have been brought to declare a basic belief in most of the fundamentals" but that they nevertheless "lacked in gospel consciousness." When a man or woman gives his life to the sacrificial, low-paid work of foreign missions, I doubt that anyone has a right to question the sincerity of his declared beliefs.

Much of the argument for forming a new society seems to be based on a confused use of words. The article refers repeatedly to "liberals" and "literalism," but in such different connotations as to convey an impression of unfairness, which I am sure Dr. Pierce did not intend. At one point, he states that "to be 'liberal' is to deny the historic Biblical faith and substitute for it man's philosophy and way of attempted salvation," although in the same paragraph he mentions a pastor "who calls himself a liberal . . . but who yet has so held to the faith of the fathers in which he was brought up that he believes the New Testament facts concerning our Lord and his salvation." Unless Dr. Pierce is sure of the sense in which the word was used, is it fair for him to reproach the Foreign Board on account of some member's statement that "he believes a man can be liberal and still have the gospel"?

Candidate Sources

Again, I question the fairness of the statement that "During the past twenty years, by actual record, 65% of the missionary appointments have been made from liberal theological seminaries." It is surely not a fact that the majority of our recent appointees come from schools which deny the historic Biblical faith and substitute man's philosophy, if that is the meaning intended. Is it possible that the movement for a new society stems from rivalries between old and new seminaries?

If Dr. Pierce means that most of the denomination believe in the divinity of Christ and the authority of the Bible, then he is right in saying that the "denomination is 75% to 85% conservative," but I am sure he knows that no such proportion agree on every detail of interpretation of the Scriptures. . . .

As for the dissatisfaction with Dr. Fridell's recent appointment as foreign secretary, no doctrinal dispute seems to be involved, but only a criticism of his "social emphasis." There is no suggestion that Dr. Fridell does not meet the approved definition of "evangelical." I can sympathize with the view that the Board's action in Springfield was not calculated to promote peace, but I do not see how the naming of a secretary with true Baptist beliefs but a social emphasis justifies a split in the denomination. . . .

Bureaucracy

The second article complains that Baptists are too far "board- and secretary-controlled," and objects to a recent action of the Convention Nominating Committee. The first charge is one that can be made with equal force against almost every charitable or educational organization with which I am acquainted. The special interest and knowledge of board members and paid executives gives them preponderant weight in many cases; the only real antidote is to have members of the society devote just as much study and interest to its affairs as the officials. However, the particular committee action which is challenged is not adequately set forth. There was no proposal by an unauthorized board representative of names which had never been voted on: a subcommittee reported a slate of nominees who were almost all new men, and a board member who was on the general committee explained the contribution which had been made to the Board's work by the men whom it was proposed to replace, all of whom were eligible to reëlction under the Convention's rules. Surely, it was proper for the general committee to decide not to cause a violent break in continuity of service by throwing valuable men off the Board.

It is heartening to find Dr. Pierce concluding, in spite of the statement to which I have objected, with the statement, "Let the Board now declare that it will strictly follow an evangelical policy in its appointment of secretaries and missionaries as that word evangelical is defined in the dictionary and understood by the average run of people, and the present rift will be healed." The Board's action of June 22 reaffirmed that it will demand that all its missionaries and officers be loyal to the gospel, that the gospel means the good news of the free forgiveness of sin and eternal life, and that it believes "in the deity of Christ in whom we see the Father, a faith founded on the trustworthiness of the Scriptures, and the fact that we have experienced this salvation in our own hearts."

Let us recognize that we are all in agreement on these fundamentals and strive together for the enlargement of the Baptist world mission through the existing Society.

Albany, New York.

14.14 Report of the Study Commission on Denominational Structure (SCODS), 1972

Three times in the twentieth century Northern Baptists made rather thorough changes in their denominational structure: in 1908 when the Northern Baptist Convention was formed, in 1950 when the NBC was changed to American Baptist Convention, and in 1972 when the SCODS report changed the name to the American Baptist Churches, USA. Each of these represents far more than a name change; they have pointed to important new directions for Baptist cooperative witness in America. The SCODS report reveals an effort to achieve greater representation in denominational decisions. It also points toward a more "churchly" approach to Baptist cooperative witness. Perhaps the best analysis of these changes, and what they mean to Baptists in America, is found in Robert T. Handy's article, "American Baptist Polity: What's Happening and Why" (*Baptist History and Heritage,* July 1979, 12 *f*). *Source: Yearbook,* American Baptist Convention, Denver, 1972, 311-318.

I. INTRODUCTION

In this summary our goal will be to convey the basic data concerning the report of the Study Commission on Denominational Structure. The process will be to use some of the recurring concerns and issues of our constituency and indicate how the Commission has sought to provide a better approach to meeting those concerns than the present structure offers.

II. REFERENDUM AND PARTICIPATION IN REPORT DEVELOPMENT

Few things have come to mean more to American Baptists than to be heard and to share in the development of the mission programs, the study reports, and the directions for mission in the ABC. From its inception, SCODS has had this built in as a key facet. . . .

In essence, the SCODS report represents one of the most complete participation processes of our constituency ever achieved. With over 6,300 persons being involved in groups, hearing and making alternate proposals, we have come the closest to a full referendum that our constituency has ever experienced.

III. REPRESENTATION

The growing concern of American Baptists is to be properly and proportionately represented in the work, mission, structure, and decision-making processes of the denomination. No longer is it acceptable to say that all of the churches are represented at annual meetings when reality indicates that we are fortunate if one out of four (25%) of the congregations sends delegates. No longer is it acceptable to say the ultimate authority rests with the delegates in annual session when the unrepresentative nature of this body is analyzed.

It is one thing, in principle, to have some representation provided. It is entirely a different thing not to have that principle realized by the majority of congregations and their members.

Problems to be resolved included:

1. Providing a way to involve more Baptists in selecting those who would represent them nationally.
2. Providing a way of separating the functions of staff (to implement policies) and constituency-board (to make policies).
3. Providing a way to have greater coordination of the mission task through the supporting structure, so the oneness and interlocking dimensions of the mission can be more fully realized.
4. Continuing the excellent national meetings for involvement of the constituency, but becoming more realistic about the business to be conducted at the national meetings, and transferring the rest to a broadly representative and selected Board (General Board).
5. Recognizing that *annual* meetings and continuing education participation work against each other, and devising a biennial meeting which would permit for continuing education opportunities in the alternate year.

6. Providing a procedure to pass resolutions and policies which would be prophetic and at the same time representative of the cross section of the denomination.

SCODS proposals to these concerns are well known.

1. To involve more Baptists in selecting the persons who will represent them nationally, the new structure, known as the *election districts,* consisting of not less than 76 nor more than 225 delegates from local congregations, meeting every four years, would select on a rotating basis the *Representative* for those Baptists. The Representative would be accountable to them and speak for them. According to current statistics, 146 of these election districts are to be created. . . .

The election districts will provide three-fourths of the new General Board's membership. The *balancing* of the General Board in *age, skills, ethnic and language groups* will be done through the one-fourth at-large membership nominated by the National Nominating Committee and elected by the delegates at the proposed biennial meeting.

2. The General Board and the national Related Boards are given the responsibility for creating the *national policies and programs* for the ABC. Therefore, for the first time, elected Representatives are charged with this area of responsibility. The staff members are employed to make policy recommendations, develop budget proposals, do the administration and implementation of policies and programs created by the elected Boards.

3. Baptists have always seen structure as a supporting tool. The structures we have had, and are now proposing, come out of our understanding of what is needed to support the missionaries on the field and the mission we have undertaken at home and overseas. . . . Proposed is a General Board whose membership will be divided primarily among the three national program boards, *Educational Ministries, National Ministries, and International Ministries.* . . .

4. *The annual meeting* of the ABC is a strong issue for a number of persons. They like the feeling that ultimately everything can be done here. At the same time they know it really isn't possible to operate and to make the necessary decisions with a *town-meeting* atmosphere and attendance of 3,249 so that the decisions are representative of the total ABC or even a major part of it. We know that over 70 percent of the delegates at any given annual session are from within 750 miles of the convention city. Less than one out of four (25%) of our congregations is represented. Often only slightly more than half of those who come *actually are voting on the key decisions.*

The more the Commission studied the situation, the more convinced it became that the business of the convention had to be transferred to a more representative, broadly based, and inclusive board which could be deliberative. As a result, the Commission has recommended the creation of the General Board of 200 members to carry primary legislative responsibilities for the ABC. The ultimate control is still left with the delegates, for they decide on the by-laws governing the work of the ABC and, thus, if it is deemed necessary, appropriate by-law changes can be made.

National meetings for the celebration, fellowship, inspiration, information sharing, and action on issues of concern to the delegates are vital. Yet if the annual meeting were retained, continuing education for professional leadership would continue to suffer. Congregations simply cannot provide both in the same year, nor do many pastors feel they can do both in the same year. Thus, a biennial meeting of delegates with these revised functions, primarily nonbusiness, has been proposed. The even-numbered year is now available for national, regional, and individual continuing-education opportunities for our professional leadership, *and no more time nor money is required from the congregations to provide both.*

5. Policies and resolutions—*who should make them?* SCODS believes the most broadly representative body needs to have these functions. Therefore the 200⁺ member General Board becomes responsible for developing the policies which guide our corporate mission and for implementing resolutions which speak to that mission and its relationship to the world of which we are a part.

6. Flexibility is built into the structure which is being proposed. Some 25 persons who will be on the 200⁺ General Board will not have a second assignment initially. . . .

IV. COORDINATION OF MISSION ASSIGNMENTS (ADMINISTRATIVE CENTRALIZATION)

Problems to be confronted:

1. The need for a central group to make program assignments, evaluate their effectiveness, and provide the funding to bring such assignments to a successful conclusion.

2. The need for *programs to be assigned to program units,* and for *centralization of administration and staff relationships through the office of the General Secretary.* . . .

3. The recognition that some current program assignments would be better handled in new units in the proposed structure.

4. *General Board makes program assignments, evaluations, and appropriations of budget.*

SCODS is recommending that the General Board be responsible for determining areas of mission that the Convention should carry out, and for assigning such areas to individual program boards which will succeed the current national societies. It also recommends that the performance of those program boards be regularly evaluated by the General Board and its committees.

Heretofore the General Council could approve a national program and assign it to an agency for implementation, or even to one of its own divisions, but like other groups, the General Council had to go to the Finance Committee to see if budget could be made available. In the new structure, the General Board makes policy and program decisions and, in addition, *it also makes the budgetary decisions* since it is charged with budgetary policies, appropriation, and approval.

The initial step taken by Baptists in May, 1961, in Portland, Oregon, in tying the staff closer to the General Secretary is finalized by SCODS. All national staff are being made accountable to the General Secretary. Each Related Board chief executive is an Associate General Secretary. A new post of Associate General Secretary for Field Operations has been developed for closer coordination, support, and representation of the Region, State, and City administrative units and their executives in national work. . . .

V. NATIONAL STAFF TEAM

Concerns:

1. National decisions affect the work and mission in the administrative units of state conventions, city societies, and regions; yet the executives are not fully involved in the decision-making processes.

2. Better coordination would develop program resources and policies, which would be better accepted by our constituency. . . .

VI. INVOLVEMENT

It has been difficult, with the multi-structure for mission implementation, for our members to know who to contact. That new structure seeks to provide an easier solution. If it is a staff concern, it goes to the General Secretary who is responsible for the national staff. If it is a policy or program concern, your best path is to contact your Election District Representative to the General Board. . . .

VII. CONCLUSION

Each of us knows that structure is not mission. Our mission is clear; our commitment demanding, as we seek to be able and complete disciples of Jesus Christ and spread his good news to a world of his children whose lives and structures must be brought under his control. The structure we have devised is to enhance the carrying out of that mission, but must never be confused as being that mission.

—Harvey A. Everett
Director of Interpretation

15
Southern Baptists

Several major trends have marked Southern Baptists during the twentieth century. The Southern Baptist Convention (SBC) itself has undergone major structural changes, and has added a central Executive Committee to oversee the total denominational work. The Convention has expanded far beyond its original Southern boundaries, and along with this geographical expansion has come large numerical growth. Methods of raising and disbursing funds changed radically with the Seventy-five Million Campaign of 1919-1924 and its spin-off, the Cooperative Program of 1925. A combination of economic prosperity and growing world awareness brought vast increases in the missionary work of Southern Baptists, both domestic and international.

Another major trend affecting Southern Baptists in the twentieth century has been theological conflict. Like Rebekah in the Old Testament who bore two nations in one womb (Gen. 25:23), Southern Baptists have for generations housed diverse doctrinal camps in one denominational house. Doctrinal conflict between these groups has broken out sporadically, especially in the Norris Controversy (1920s), the Elliott Controversy (1960s), the Broadman Bible Commentary (1970s), and the Inerrancy Controversy (1980s).

Twice in the twentieth century (1925 and 1963), and largely in response to these controversies, the Southern Baptist Convention has adopted a confession of faith. Though the Convention took precautions to assure that this would not be misused, in fact, the way the 1963 *The Baptist Faith and Message* has been used makes it the most creedal document in Baptist history.

The source documents in this chapter have been chosen to illustrate these and other major trends affecting Southern Baptists in the twentieth century.

15.1 Changes in the Basis of Representation in the Southern Baptist Convention

The Southern Baptist Convention began in 1845 on a *convention* basis, but remnants of the *society* approach remained. Not until 1931 did the SBC abandon the last vestige of the society plan in determining its membership.

Rapid growth of Convention programs and attendance after World War I spotlighted the need to adjust the way the Convention determined its membership. The Mullins Committee considered several plans for radical restructuring, but its report in 1926 called only for minor changes (selection A). *Source: Annual,* SBC, 1926, 31-34. Agitation for change continued. The Committee on Changes in the Constitution in 1931 recommended further minor adjustments, but the E. C. Routh amendment mandated more radical changes. Henceforth, associations and state conventions could not send messengers as before; only *churches* could send messengers to the SBC. *Source: Annual,* SBC, 1931, 43-44.

A. Report of the Mullins Committee, 1926

REPORT OF COMMITTEE ON CHANGING BASIS OF REPRESENTATION

This committee was appointed without instructions in 1924. The sickness of the chairman and inability to get a meeting of the committee caused its continuance by the Memphis Convention.

The question of changing the basis of representation has grown out of the immensely increased membership, the difficulties of deliberation, and the shortcomings in our procedure and methods. Among these shortcomings, alleged or actual, are the following:

1. The difficulty of handling successfully Kingdom interests in so large a body. In 1895, in Washington, D. C., the Convention had 870 enrolled messengers. In the same city in 1920, or 25 years later, it numbered 8,359 messengers. The average enrollment for the past six years has been 5,559.

2. The difficulty involved in dealing with a great number of reports. At the beginning the Convention considered two or three missionary subjects. At the Memphis meeting there were reports by 54 committees upon a great variety of subjects.

3. The tendency to limit discussion to a few appointed speakers on each subject.

4. The length of the reports themselves which are often essays rather than concise summaries of the vital points involved.

5. The ignorance of the messengers concerning new policies recommended due to the absence of advance knowledge to qualify those who vote to do so intelligently.

6. The shortness of the Convention period, which covers from three to five days only.

7. The preponderance of those coming from the locality near the meeting place of the Convention, and the consequent lack of balanced judgment of the whole body in reaching important decisions.

8. The danger of conflicting decisions growing out of the individual or sectional initiative in introducing new measures which may be lacking in proper co-ordination with other interests and activities.

9. The tendency of Convention boards or other agencies to inaugurate new movements or policies without Convention authorization or in conflict with previous Convention action.

10. The lack of co-ordination of the Convention with State Boards and State Conventions, leading sometimes to conflict and confusion, and even to surrender by the Convention of its own functions and powers.

Your committee does not pass judgment on the merit of these statements of objections and dangers. They should not discourage or make us pessimistic. But there is probably a measure of truth in all and much truth in some of them—enough at least to give us pause and lead to a careful survey of our organization and methods.

Remedies Suggested

We next submit some of the various remedies suggested.

1. The first is to change the basis of representation so that the Convention will consist of a few hundred messengers, with one thousand as the maximum.

2. Divide the body into two or three Conventions with the Mississippi River as one line of the division.

3. Let the Convention proper meet once in three years, with a representation of a few hundred messengers, say 250 or 300. Divide the territory into three parts, and in each part, hold inspirational meetings for consideration of the various interests, but without power of changing existing or inaugurating new policies. Under this plan the smaller body meeting triennially would be authoritative.

4. Let the Convention meet once in three years, and provide that the Executive Committee shall be enlarged and consist of not more than 300 members; that this committee shall meet annually; that boards and other Convention agencies report to it each year; that there be annual publication of minutes to its meetings; that its meetings be open to the public and visitors made welcome; and that it derive all its powers and duties from the Convention, whose servant it is. . . .

5. Extend the period of meeting to cover at least an entire week. Reduce the number of subjects to be considered by the Convention. Reduce greatly the length of reports by

committees, as well as the number of reports. Provide a plan for wide announcement in the denominational papers several weeks in advance of Convention meetings of new policies proposed by boards and other Convention agencies. Provide more time for general discussion. Abolish the present plan of making all committee appointments through the committee on committees. Let this committee nominate members of the various Convention boards. Let all other committees be appointed by the President of the Convention.

The preceding outline of conditions is offered as a suitable background for the suggestions of your committee. We make the following recommendations:

1. We reaffirm our conviction that the financial basis of representation is sound and scriptural. The duty and right of the giver to direct the uses of his gift are unquestioned. The New Testament law of stewardship forbids God's servant to abandon the administration of benevolent funds given by him to others whose interests and convictions have failed to produce sacrificial giving to the causes promoted by the gifts. Any future changes in the basis of representation of the Convention should conserve this principle.

2. We recommend that no essential change be made at the present time in the basis of representation.

3. In order to meet many of the present needs of the Convention and to promote its efficiency we recommend the following changes in the present organization of the Executive Committee of the Convention:

(1) The Executive Committee of the Convention shall consist of the President and Senior Secretary of the Convention, and one member for each co-operating state and District of Columbia, and one additional member for each $100,000 contributed by any state to the work of the Convention during the preceding Conventional year. No paid official of the Southern Baptist Convention, or of any State Convention, shall be a member of the Executive Committee. One-third of the Executive Committee shall be elected at the end of each two-year period of service.

(2) The officers of the Executive Committee shall be a President, Recording Secretary, and Executive Secretary, all of whom shall be elected annually by the Executive Committee itself. The Executive Secretary shall not be a member of the Executive Committee, but an employee.

(3) The duties and obligations of the Executive Committee shall be as follows:

To act for the Convention ad interim in matters not otherwise provided for in its plans of work.

(4) To have oversight of arrangements for the meeting of the Convention with authority to change if necessary the time and place of meeting.

(5) The Executive Committee shall be required to represent the Southern Baptist Convention in all negotiations with state or other co-operating bodies in all matters of common interest.

(6) In order to preserve the autonomy of the Southern Baptist Convention its Executive Committee shall have the authority of the Convention for fixing total objectives for allocating funds to its various agencies and recommending same to the Southern Baptist Convention for adoption. It shall be the authorized agency of the Southern Baptist Convention to conclude all agreements with co-operative State agencies for the conduct of necessary arrangements as to handling of Southwide funds raised in the various States, and all other related matters.

(7) In order that the Convention and denomination may be fully advised as to the total liabilities for each fiscal year, each of the boards and other agencies of the Convention shall be required to submit to the Executive Committee not later than March 1, each year, its proposed budget for the ensuing conventional year, and the same shall not

become operative until reviewed by the Executive Committee, and submitted to the Southern Baptist Convention, and approved by that body.

(8) The Executive Committee shall be charged with the duty and responsibility of adjusting any matters of difference between any agencies of the Convention itself, or between Convention agencies and co-operating State agencies.

(9) The Executive Secretary of the Executive Committee shall head the practical work of the committee and have associated with him a promotional committee. The promotional committee, if practicable shall consist of the State Secretaries and others appointed by the Executive Committee who may be associated with the Executive Secretary to promote the work of the Convention.

4. Messengers shall be appointed to the Convention only by the churches themselves, and certified by the churches to the Convention. Proper credential cards shall be prepared for the use of the churches by the Secretaries of the Convention. Groups of two or more churches shall have the power to appoint a messenger or messengers on the basis of their combined contributions, where the sum is not sufficient for the appointment of a messenger in an individual church.

5. Nominations for membership on Convention Boards and other agencies shall be made by groups of messengers from the various states acting separately as committees at a time designated by the Convention, nominations to be voted on and elected by the Convention. The other committees will be appointed by the President of the Convention, and Bylaw 5, providing for a committee on committees is hereby repealed.

6. We recommend further that the Constitution be so amended as that a call may be made for a vote by states, when sustained by not fewer than 100 votes. In the vote by states, each state shall be entitled to as many votes as it is entitled to messengers. If there is division in any state vote, where there is not full representation from that state, the total vote of said state shall be counted in the same ratio as the vote actually cast by those present.

7. Your committee would recommend that all reports be made as concise and brief as the subject matter may admit, and that reports of boards and other agencies of the Convention be made more specific, and detailed as to its expenditures of money.

We urge upon the messengers also the importance of remaining through the entire session of the Convention.

In conclusion, your committee would recommend that its report be not adopted at the present session of the Convention, but held over for one year for full and frank discussion; that it shall be continued to report again at the next annual meeting of the Convention, basing their report upon the present recommendations or such modificiations as may seem wise in the light of full discussion of the whole matter.

Respectfully submitted,

E. Y. MULLINS
JAMES H. ANDERSON
V. I. MASTERS
C. W. DANIEL
C. E. BURTS
E. C. ROUTH
R. H. PITT.

B.   The E. C. Routh Substitute Motion, 1931

REPORT OF COMMITTEE ON CHANGES IN THE CONSTITUTION, BY-LAWS, AND PROCEDURE OF THE SOUTHERN BAPTIST CONVENTION

(All recommendations are printed in italics; Convention action in brackets.)

Constitution

The messengers from missionary societies, churches, and other religious bodies of the Baptist denomination in various parts of the United States, met in Augusta, Georgia, for the purpose of carrying into effect the benevolent intention of our constituents by organizing a plan for eliciting, combining, and directing the energies of the denomination for the propagation of the gospel, adopted rules and fundamental principles which, as amended from time to time, are as follows: . . .

Art. III. The Convention shall consist (1) of messengers who contribute funds, or are elected by Baptist bodies contributing funds for the regular work of the Convention, on the basis of one messenger for every $250 actually paid into the treasuries of the Boards during the fiscal year ending the thirtieth day of April next preceding the meeting of the Convention; (2) of one representative from each of the District Associations which co-operate with this Convention, provided that such representative be formally elected at the annual meeting of his District Association, and the election certified to the Secretaries of the Convention, either in writing or by copy of the printed minutes.

We recommend that Art. III be so amended and rearranged as to read:

Art. III. The Convention shall consist (1) of one representative from each District Association which co-operates with this Convention, provided that such representative be formally elected at the annual meeting of his District Association, and the election be certified to the Secretaries of the Convention, either in writing or by copy of the printed minutes; and (2) of messengers selected on the basis of moneys actually paid into the treasuries of the Agencies of the Convention during the fiscal year ending the thirtieth of April next preceding the meeting of the Convention and properly certified to the secretaries of the Convention as follows: (a) individual Baptists who have given $500 or more; (b) messengers appointed by individual churches which have given $500 or more, but no church shall have more than three messengers; and (c) messengers from State Conventions whose quota on the financial basis has not been filled by classes (a) and (b).

[In lieu of the Committee's recommendation the Convention adopted the article presented by E. C. Routh, Oklahoma:

Art III. The Convention shall consist of messengers who are members of missionary Baptist churches co-operating with the Southern Baptist Convention on the basis of one messenger for every church contributing to the work of the Convention and one additional messenger for every $250 actually paid to the work of the Convention during the calendar year preceding the annual meeting of the Convention, such messengers to be appointed to the Convention by the churches and certified by the churches to the Convention, provided no church shall be entitled to more than three messengers.]

15.2   The Seventy-Five Million Campaign, 1919-1924

In 1919 the Southern Baptist Convention voted to launch a campaign to raise $75 million for Convention ministries over the next five years. The Seventy-Five Million Campaign grew out of wartime prosperity and optimism, and was comparable to similar funds in other denominations. In a whirlwind campaign Southern Baptists pledged over $92 million, but in the postwar agricultural recession they collected only $58 million. Despite failure to reach the monetary goal and the resulting debts, this campaign represents a great leap forward in Southern Baptist stewardship, promotion, and denominational self-identity. The reports of the campaign emphasize not only the amounts of money raised, but even more the impact of this united effort upon evangelism and denominational unity. *Sources: Annual*, SBC, 1919, 122-123; *Annual*, SBC, 1920, 48-59.

A.   The Seventy-Five Million Campaign Authorized, 1919

148. A. J. Barton, Louisiana, offered the following resolution, which was adopted:

WHEREAS, The report of the Committee on the Financial Aspects of the Enlarged Program only provides that the Executive Committee of this Convention has authority, in conference with the Secretaries of the Boards of the Convention and the Secretaries of the several State Boards, to distribute the funds raised in the campaign among the several objects fostered by the Convention outside of local church work, and to apportion the amount to be raised among the several states; and

WHEREAS, We do not now regard this as adequate provision for the accomplishment of this great task to which we have resolutely set our hands; therefore,

Resolved, (1) That the President is hereby authorized to appoint a commission of fifteen members of the Convention; (2) that the whole matter of laying plans and of launching and conducting this campaign be entrusted to said commission; (3) that the said commission is hereby instructed to meet at the earliest date possible and to proceed with all possible promptness and earnestness to lay plans and to prosecute this campaign, and is authorized to employ any and all agencies which in its judgment may be necessary for the speediest and most successful accomplishment of this great task; (4) that the said commission is authorized and instructed to prepare an address to the denomination calling our brethren to a special season of prayer and heart-searching and summoning them to the united and sacrificial effort without which our great objective will be impossible. . . .

B.   First Annual Report, $75 Million Campaign, 1920

58. With George W. Truett, Chairman of the Commission on Campaign, presiding, the following report was presented by General Director L. R. Scarborough, Texas, and adopted after an addres by George W. McDaniel, Virginia, and a prayer of gratitude led by B. C. Hening, Tennessee, the Assistant General Director of the Campaign:

REPORT OF CAMPAIGN COMMISSION.

The Commission appointed by the Southern Baptist Convention at Atlanta, Georgia, May, 1919, for the purpose of raising 75 million dollars for Missions, Education and Benevolence makes the following report to the Convention. . . .

A Brief Review of the Task Committed.

We set down here briefly the steps in the progress of the accomplishment of the task.

1. On June 4th and 5th in Atlanta, Georgia, in a conference of the Executive Committee, the Campaign Commission, the General Secretaries, the State Secretaries, and other workers, the general outline of the program of the Campaign was set out. Headquarters were established at Nashville and housed, by the invitation of the Sunday School Board, in their building: L. R. Scarborough of Fort Worth, Texas, was chosen as General Director; the quotas to be raised by each state were fixed, and the appropriations were made to the various causes subject to future changes and adjustments by the Executive Committee.

2. At a conference composed largely of the same groups mentioned above, in addition to the W. M. U. Vice-Presidents and Secretaries and the Editors of Baptist papers, at Nashville, July 2nd and 3rd, the Commission submitted and the conference approved a detailed plan and program for the conduct of the Campaign. July was set for Prepara-

tion month, August Information, September Intercession, October Enlistment, November Stewardship, and November 30 to December 7 for Victory Week. September 24 was set for all-day prayer meeting, October 24 for calling out the called in our colleges and the 26th in our churches. At this meeting under the leadership of Miss Kathleen Mallory, W. M. U. Secretary and Mrs. W. C. James, W. M. U. President, the women of the South agreed to raise one-fifth or 15 million of our 75 million objective.

3. The organization had four groups: Central Office, Nashville; State forces around State Secretaries; associational organizations; and local church force—a simple, adjustable and workable system. . . .

4. At a conference of State Secretaries, State Organizers and Publicity Directors in Nashville, July 15th and 16th, the state forces were thoroughly drilled in the plan of the Campaign and final touches were given to the program; and the machinery was set going for the accomplishment of the great task.

5. These state forces went back to their states and in general and sectional conferences organized, instructed and moblized the associational forces and set up the organization in the more than 900 associations in the South. During this time a great campaign was put on for the increase of the subscriptions to the twenty Baptist papers. This campaign resulted in securing more than 60,000 new subscribers to these papers.

6. Intercession Month with its week and day of special prayer was widely observed. The soul of Southern Baptists was brought in humble importunity to the God of power; and the tides of enthusiasm began to rise.

7. Such a campaign of enlistment as was put on during October was never known among our people before. New forces by the thousands, laymen, women, young and old, everywhere were brought into active, aggressive service. . . .

9. November was a mighty month for Southern Baptists. The doctrine of Stewardship was pressed on every heart. Information and indoctrination on this great fundamental were spread in religious and secular press, tracts, books, from pulpits, platforms, and everywhere and great gifts began to come in from individuals which mightily stirred the hearts of our people. More than 22 million separate tracts, with more than 166 million pages were sent out from the General Director's office alone. Around three-fourths of a million columns of Baptist information as put in the secular press. Millions of personal letters and private appeals were sent everywhere. The Baptist papers went full length in carrying their message of the Campaign.

10. Victory Week was probably the most momentous period in Baptist history since the Day of Pentecost. During that week and the few days following there was reported from the states composing the Southern Baptist Convention, including credits on the year's work, the pledges of our foreign mission churches, and some other credits, more than 90 million dollars in cash and pledges for the causes involved in the Campaign. This marvelous victory was brought about at an expense up to December 15, 1919, of $273,000 in the Central Office at Nashville and $415,157 in the offices of the various states, making a total of $688,157 at the expense chargeable to the Campaign in all the South, which is around three-fourths of one per cent, figured on the basis of the 90 million raised.

11. On February 19th another conference of the Commission, Executive Committee, State Secretaries, General Secretaries, W. M. U. State Secretaries, The Editors, and others, in Nashville, was held to plan for a Follow-up Campaign. . . . The effort was made during this Follow-up Campaign to have united effort in soul-winning in all the churches which held their meetings in the spring, reaching with salvation and enlist-

ment in church membership and service as many as possible and distributing as widely as possible the large selection of tracts of soul-winning and indoctrination. It is impossible to state at this time the results of this evangelistic campaign. It is known that tens of thousands have been led to Christ and into the fellowship of Baptist churches. . . .

Financial statement of pledges and cash received as reported by the states:

	Pledge.	Cash.
Alabama	$ 4,200,000	$ 666,942
Arkansas	3,114,407	392,000
District of Columbia	250,000	45,450
Florida	1,375,000	204,169
Georgia	10,100,000	1,559,189
Illinois	912,362	127,293
Kentucky	7,454,387	1,335,366
Louisiana	3,002,163	394,526
Maryland	900,000	172,500
Mississippi	4,209,585	862,196
Missouri	981,756	317,460
New Mexico	732,260	66,000
North Carolina	7,250,000	751,883
Oklahoma	3,144,682	308,127
South Carolina	7,600,000	1,262,000
Tennessee	4,540,003	920,000
Texas	16,560,000	1,750,855
Virginia	8,100,318	1,042,523
Special Hospital, Memphis	712,000	
Special Hospital, Dallas	960,000	
Reasonable estimate of credits not included in above	5,000,000	
Received by Foreign Board, miscellaneous	59,346	
Reasonable estimate for what Missouri will raise for missions and benevolence during the five years	1,500,000	
Totals	$92,630,923	$12,237,827

It will be noticed in the above financial statement that nearly all the states reached and went over their quota. A number of the states went far beyond. The states which have not yet reached their quotas had overwhelming difficulties not experienced in some of the other states. It is believed that before the five years are over all the states will go far beyond their quotas. . . . Your Commission congratulates the Convention and our people of the South upon this marvelous triumph in the cash raised, and we confidently believe that by December 1, the real end of the first year, we will collect far more than one-fifth of the 75 million dollars. . . .

Difficulties.

It must be remembered that this Campaign has been conducted in the face of many interfering and interrupting difficulties and against strong opposing odds. We give some of them:

1. *The Shortness of Time.* From the time the Commission got its central organization set up to Victory Week was around five and one-half months. The entire denomination had to be organized, informed, inspired and mobilized within this brief period. . . .

2. *The world conditions, politically, industrially, military and financial were against us.* Seventeen wars were raging. The mind of the people was disturbed over the League of Nations and the Treaty of Peace. There were strikes, large and small, interfering with production and transportation of all sorts of material. Also, the multiplicity of money drives and campaigns had gotten the people tired of these movements.

3. *Probably our greatest difficulty was in the unprecedented weather conditions.* From September through December and much since it rained and stormed throughout a large part of Southern territory. . . .

The Campaign Assets and Gains.

It is confidently believed by your Commission that the denomination has come out of this year's struggles, labors and accomplishments with an enormously increased profit account. The denominational assets have been greatly multiplied and strengthened. This large sum of money when collected and appropriated to the various causes will mean much to the glory of God and the extension of Christ's Kingdom; but the money is not all the gain of the Campaign. There are many other phases of spiritual and denominational enrichment coming to us out of this South-wide and world-wide victory. We here make record of some of these spiritual gains:

1. The unification of our people. The Campaign has cemented Southern Baptists into a mighty, mobilized spiritual phalanx from Maryland to Mexico and from Florida to Missouri. Our people see eye to eye and walk in the unison of a common faith as never before. . . .

2. The enlarged vision of the task of Christ's churches and people. . . .

3. The widespread and thoroughgoing organization of Baptist forces from the individual church point of view and from the whole denominational point of view. . . .

4. The increased liberality of the people, both on the part of the small and the large giver. Individual churches through the organization of their business men are today undertaking larger programs than were undertaken two years ago by whole state conventions. . . .

5. The deepening of the spiritual life and quickening of the religious zeal are probably the greatest advantages and blessings growing out of the Campaign. . . .

6. The indoctrination of the people on the fundamentals of Bible faith has been greatly increased. The truths taught by Jesus Christ and His apostles, the basal doctrines of faith, have been rendered to the people and consequently their Christian characters have been strengthened and the denominational solidarity greatly increased. . . .

7. The impartation and implantation of the conquering, heroic, martial spirit is one of the chief results of the Campaign. The religious life of the people has been simplified and the heroic element in religion has been magnified and a mighty impelling, conquering power has been given to their faith. . . .

8. A deeper compassion and spiritual concern for the relief of the spiritual, physical and social needs of mankind has grown mightily by the impetus of the Campaign. Southern Baptists have heard and deeply sympathize with the cry of the lost world's needs as never before. . . .

9. The Campaign has brought a new appreciation of the value and effectiveness of the Gospel preacher and Christian teacher. Everywhere increased remuneration for the valuable service of these heroes of the Cross has been manifest by the people; and this is of great advantage to the Kingdom of God. Surely our churches will more greatly reward by a fuller support, the self-sacrificing talent and energies of our preachers and Christian teachers in the days to come.

10. Another of the supreme advantages and blessings of the Campaign has been in

the calling out, development, and strengthening of a new and enlarged leadership among men, women and especially among the young people in all the ranks of our forces. New leaders have been developed with a remarkable efficiency, vision and passion for the right. . . .

11. The Campaign has put a new hunger in the hearts of our people for Baptist literature and a new valuation upon the Baptist press. . . .

12. Your Commission wonders if our greatest asset and blessing in this Campaign has not been a re-enduement from the Divine Spirit and the refillment from the Father's bounteous storehouse of power in the hearts of our preachers and churches everywhere. Surely we have seen pentecosts and our preachers, laymen, and women have gone forward in the unction of the Holy Spirit. . . .

The Task Ahead.

As your Commission views the situation, Southern Baptists have come to a new and an enlarged responsibility and to an unspeakable and meaningful and far-reaching task. . . . We have not won all of the victories of the Campaign. We have but made a good start. We have formed a financial program for strengthening our stakes and lengthening our cords. We must member that denominational pledges are good; but the payment of these pledges in the coin of the realm is the best show of victory. . . . Our ability has not yet been tested. The Campaign is a promise and prophecy of what we can do when thoroughly aroused, completely organized and gloriously enlisted. . . .

Recommendations.

Your Commission submits the following recommendations for the redemption of our Campaign pledges and for the conservation of our complete victory:

1. That the Convention urge the churches and their leaders to persistently press the collection of the pledges already made, the securing of pledges from the unenlisted and from new members as they come into our churches week by week. We recommend that the state and associational organizations continue the campaign for pledges until the thousands of churches not reached in our former campaign are reached and enlisted. Probably twenty-five per cent of our churches have not made campaign pledges. We believe that the Campaign should be continued until all our people are enlisted in the mighty movement and that all the new members of our churches may have a chance to share in our glorious victory.

2. That the Campaign for Evangelism and Indoctrination be continued and pressed right on through the summer and fall until every community in the South has been quickened by the renewed Spirit of God and instructed in the way of the Lord more perfectly. We should make the coming summer a mighty harvest time. All our preachers and leaders and the people generally should go afield for lost souls, distributing tracts, instructing, informing and enlisting the people.

3. That during the summer a double campaign be put on in all the states for the purpose of putting our Baptist papers into every Baptist home and for the purpose of enlisting our Baptist young people in Christian education, turning them into our Baptist schools. Two great tragedies cast their shadow across the life of the denomination. One is that probably 600,000 Southern Baptist homes do not have a Baptist paper; and the other is that tens and even hundreds of thousands of our bright Baptist young people are not being trained in our denominational schools. The whole denominational force should be enlisted to lift this tragical situation.

4. In order that these things and the other needful things may be accomplished, your Commission recommends that a committee of one from each state be appointed to

consider the future program—its organization and plans—and make recommendations early in the session of this Convention. We believe that a unified, well-wrought-out program should be made out and set forward by this Convention for the conservation of the victories already won and the inauguration of plans for the winning of other victories.

With unspeakable thanksgiving to God for His continued and wonderful blessings and with unmeasured gratitude to the brethren and sisters of our churches for their full and consecrated co-operation, your Commission hands back to the Convention the trust committed to us a year ago. We have labored together for the glory of our Master, the salvation of the lost, and the establishment of Christ's Kingdom throughout the whole world.

GEO. W. TRUETT, *Chairman,*

L. R. SCARBOROUGH, *General Director,*

15.3   The Executive Committee of the Southern Baptist Convention

When the Southern Baptist Convention was small, program decisions could be worked out directly on the floor at annual meetings with the Convention acting essentially as a committee of the whole. As the Convention and its programs grew, and as they became responsible for the management and allocation of larger sums of money, they saw the need for more planning and correlation. The Executive Committee was formed in 1917 (selection A). *Source: Annual,* SBC, 1917, 33-34. Its tasks were redefined and enlarged in 1927 (selection B). *Source: Annual,* SBC, 1927, 64-69. The Executive Committee now acts for the SBC between sessions, and provides overall planning and correlation for Convention ministries.

A.   Formation of the Executive Committee, 1917

REPORT OF THE COMMITTEE ON CONSOLIDATION OF THE BOARDS.

The committee appointed at the last Convention to consider and report on a resolution to revise Articles 5 to 10 of the Constitution so as to create one strong executive board which should direct all the work and enterprises fostered and promoted by this Convention, beg leave to report that, obeying the instructions of the Convention, a majority and minority of the committee put forth, through the denominational press, last January tentative statements making certain suggestions covering the matter submitted to the committee. Having further considered the whole question, the committee respectfully submits as their completed report to the following recommendations:

First: In view of the diversity of opinions concerning the best method of conducting our work, and the distressing conditions in our country, resulting from the world-war, we recommend that the Boards of the Convention remain separate as at present.

Second: Recognizing, however, that there is a strong sentiment in favor of greater unity in the general direction of the Convention's affairs, and believing that some improvement in the methods of conducting the work would be attained by the creation of a standing committee of the Convention to act for the body between its sessions in ways hereinafter set forth, we recommend that an executive committee of seven, representing the different parts of the territory of the Convention, be elected annually by the Convention as are its standing committees. No officer or member of any of the Boards of the Convention shall be eligible to membership on the executive committee. The duties of the committee shall be to have oversight of the arrangements for the meetings of the Convention with power to change both the time and place of meeting in case an emergency arises making such change necessary; that this committee shall act for the Convention ad interim on business of the Convention and not otherwise provided for in its plans of work; that this committee shall also be empowered to act in an advisory way on all questions submitted to it on matters arising between the Boards of this Convention, but only on request of one or more of the Boards concerned; that this committee shall have no further duties except as other things may be specifically committed to it by the Convention itself at its annual meeting; that the committee shall hold meetings at such time and places as it may select and its necessary expenses shall be a charge equally divided among the three Boards of this Convention.

B.   Enlargement of the Committee and Redefinition of Its Tasks, 1927

SOME VITAL MATTERS

A Complete Survey Needed.

One of the greatest needs of the convention, at this time, is to have a thorough, detailed and analytical survey made of all the affairs and activities of the convention and of its agencies. Many advantages would come from this. It would reveal whatever overlapping and duplication there may be in the work of the convention's agencies. It would, doubtless, call attention to the fact that important matters are being overlooked or, at least, being given slight attention. . . . It was our desire to make such a survey. But this has been impossible because of the limited amount of time that we could give to the work.

Co-operation of the Southern Baptist Convention with the State Conventions.

It is well known that the Southern Baptist Convention is an independent body, and that the several state conventions are independent bodies. . . .

Co-operation calls for certain things. There must be on the part of both parties an understanding of the needs and an interest in the work of the other party. There must be real sympathy. And there should be clear-cut agreements defining the terms and items of co-operation. Only in this way can the interests of both parties be safeguarded and the possibilities of friction and misunderstanding be removed. It goes without saying that, when the agreement is made, both parties should comply with the terms of the agreement. . . .

Some Financial Problems of the Southern Baptist Convention.

These problems demand solution:

1. The problem of making a workable operating budget. It is imperative that the convention make a consolidated operating budget which shall include all of the agencies of the convention. The budget must, at least, take care of the minimum needs of each agency. And each agency must keep its expenditures within the amount fixed by the convention.

2. The problem of raising sufficient money to take care of the consolidated operating budget. That is to say, if the operating budget calls for $4,000,000.00, then, $4,000,000.00 must be raised. Otherwise, if the agencies expend a total of $4,000,000.00 there will be a deficit. To fix an operating budget authorizing certain expenditures will do no good unless that amount of money is raised.

3. The problem of the allocation of funds. The funds of the convention must be so allocated as to meet the operating budget of each agency. And the convention must have such control over its funds as to insure their distribution according to the allocations fixed by the convention. This is the only way that the agencies of the convention can be sure of receiving the amount of money allocated to them—even when the total objective has been raised. It can readily be seen that, if the total amount set as an objective should be raised, and, yet the allocations be not observed, some one or more of the agencies must report a deficit. To illustrate: In 1925, the Baptist Bible Institute was promised,

"based on goals fixed by the states," $151,460.00, but the Institute actually received from the Co-operative Program only $64,036.67. In 1926, the Institute was promised, "based on goals fixed by the states," $117,689.10, but it actually received only $58,046.99.

4. The problem of providing for the needs of the institutions of the convention. Take the seminaries as an illustration. The seminaries can not wisely reduce their operating expenses to any great extent. . . . In other words, their operating expenses are practically fixed and must be provided for. During the last convention year, as shown by the reports of their auditors, all three of our seminaries showed operating deficits. They are as follows: Southern Baptist Theological Seminary, $12,708.49; the Baptist Bible Institute, $33,554.52; the Southwestern Theological Seminary, $55,545.02. The total operating deficit for the year was $101,808.03.

5. The problem of paying off the indebtedness of the agencies of the convention. The consolidated debt of the convention now amounts to $6,521,756.76. This is a tremendous load to carry. To handle their indebtedness, the agencies of the convention last year had an expense of $290,779.02. This amount was paid for interest and commissions on loans.

6. The problem of increasing the work of the agencies of the convention. It is a difficult thing to stand still in our work. We must advance or, more than likely, we will slip back. Surely, Southern Baptists will not long be satisfied to just hold the present lines.

The financial problems here outlined challenge the fidelity, the business ability, and the liberality of Southern Baptists.

An Operating Budget.

We desire to present this matter more fully than has been done in the outline of financial problems.

It has been widely assumed that the Convention since the inauguration of the 75 Million program has been working upon a budget basis. But the slightest review of the history of our so-called budget system overthrows this assumption. Up to this time the convention has never had a real budget. It has set a goal from time to time as to the total amount of money it hoped to raise. Percentages of this amount have been allocated to the agencies of the convention. At no time, however, has the Convention fixed any limitation upon the amount to be spent by convention agencies before the next meeting of the convention. Such agencies, therefore, have felt at liberty, acting through their own boards and having in mind only their own needs, to use their credit, and incidentally the credit of the Convention in borrowing huge sums of money, which, in the last analysis becomes the indebtedness of the Convention. The magnitude of the financial transactions of this character becomes strikingly apparent when it is noted that the combined debts as of January 1, of all Convention agencies amount to the colossal sum of $6,521,756.76. It is doubtless true that these large debts would never have been contracted if the Convention had been operating under a budget. And it is also apparent that if the present independent and uncontrolled activities of Convention agencies in the matter of making new indebtedness is to continue unabated, the time is not far distant when the Convention will become involved beyond the point of safety and will become practically paralyzed in the performance of its function.

How would the operating budget of the Convention be made?

Each agency of the Convention would make out a proposed budget for itself for the next Convention year. The budget of the agency would show the work it desires to accomplish during the coming year and would also show the cost of doing the proposed work.

The proposed budgets of all the agencies would be presented to the body appointed by the Convention to suggest the operating budget.

The Convention's Budget Committee (by whatever name called) would carefully consider the individual proposed budgets of all the agencies. Then, in view of the total amount of money that could reasonably be hoped to be raised by the Convention for all purposes, it would determine just how much each agency could wisely expend.

The proposed budget would be presented to the Convention for its decision. The Convention would approve the suggested budget or make any changes it desires, but when the Convention had passed upon the budget it then places a control over the expenditures of each agency of the Convention.

Your committee is thoroughly convinced that such a budget is absolutely necessary and that it is the only solution by which the present staggering debt can be reduced. Also, that it is the only way to prevent the tragedy of piling up further debts. If the Convention is to assume the debts incurred by its agencies, then it must control the expenditures of all such agencies. . . .

Enlargement of the Functions of the Executive Committee.

After the most earnest consideration, we are convinced that the Convention should have some agency keeping in close touch with all the work of the Convention and its agencies. The affairs of the Convention and its agencies are too varied and too great to be handled effectively without it. It is evident to us that the affairs of the Convention have suffered greatly in the past from lack of such agency. The logical agency to do this is the Executive Committee of the Convention. Under the head of recommendations, we make specific recommendation for the enlargement of the functions of the Executive Committee. . . .

RECOMMENDATIONS OF THE COMMITTEE
I. An Operating Budget

We recommend that the Convention, at this time, commit itself to the policy of having an Operating Budget as a financial working basis for the Convention and its agencies.

II. The Executive Committee

We recommend that Article 11 of the By-Laws of the Convention be changed to read as follows:

The Executive Committee of the Convention shall consist of the president and senior secretary of the Convention, and one member from each co-operating state and the District of Columbia and nine members at large. Nine members shall constitute a quorum for the transaction of business. No salaried official of the Southern Baptist Convention or of any of its agencies, or salaried official of any state convention, or a salaried official of any state agency, may be a member of the Executive Committee. This rule shall not apply in the case of the president or of the senior secretary of the Convention. No member of any board, or board of trustees, or commission of the Southern Baptist Convention, may be a member of the Executive Committee. This shall not apply in the case of the president or senior secretary of the Convention.

For next year the Executive Committee (excluding the president and secretary of the Convention) shall be divided into three equal groups—one group to serve for one year, a second group for two years, and the third group for three years. After that, one-third of the members of the committee shall be appointed for a term of three years. Any member appointed to fill a vacancy in a group shall serve for the unexpired term of that group.

The Executive Committee shall elect a president, recording secretary, treasurer, executive secretary, who shall be the executive officer of the committee, and such other officers and employes as it may deem necessary for the efficient conduct of its work and business. The compensation of its officers and employes shall be fixed by the committee. But no salaried officer or employe of the committee may be a member thereof. The Executive Committee shall have the books of its treasurer audited annually by a Certified Public Accountant. The Executive Committee shall establish and maintain suitable offices or headquarters in some central city within the bounds of the Southern Baptist Convention.

The duties and functions of the Executive Committee shall be as follows:

1. To act for the Convention ad interim in matters not otherwise provided for in its plans of work.

2. To have oversight of arrangements for meetings of the Convention with authority to change, if necessary, the time and place of meeting.

3. To act in an advisory way on matters of policy and co-operation arising between the agencies of the Convention, or between agencies of the Convention and co-operating state agencies.

4. To represent the Southern Baptist Convention in all negotiations with state conventions, and state boards, and other co-operating bodies in matters of common interest. The Executive Committee shall be the authorized agency of the Southern Baptist Convention to conclude all agreements with co-operating state agencies for the conduct of necessary arrangements as to handling of Southwide funds raised in the various states, and all other related matters.

5. To recommend to the Convention an Operating Budget for the Convention year, and to recommend the percentages of Southwide funds to be allocated to each cause or agency. The Operating Budget shall include all agencies of the Southern Baptist Convention.

6. To present to the Convention a consolidated financial statement of all the agencies of the Convention. The statement shall show the assets, liabilities, and the debts of the agencies.

7. The Executive Committee shall notify the agencies of the Convention of all actions or instructions of the Convention relating to the work or other matters of the agency or agencies involved, and shall report to the Convention whether such agency or agencies have carried out the wishes of the Convention.

8. To hold meetings at such times as may be necessary or advisable for the transaction of the business committed to it by the Convention.

9. To make reports of its proceedings to the Convention at each annual session, and to make any recommendations it may desire concerning the affairs of the Convention, or concerning the affairs of the agencies of the Convention.

The Executive Committee shall have no authority to control or direct any agency of the Convention. But the Executive Committee shall have full authority to study the affairs of the agencies of the Convention, and to make suggestions, when deemed advisable, to the agencies, and to report its findings to the Convention, and to make recommendations to the Convention concerning any matter whatsoever.

The expenses of the Executive Committee shall be borne by the Sunday School Board. The Sunday School Board shall advance to the Executive Committee, from time to time, funds sufficient for the Committee to discharge its duties without financial embarrassment.

15.4   Comity Agreements Between Northern and Southern Baptists

Although the Northern Baptist Convention from 1908 to 1950 had a regional name, Baptists in the North have never held a regional outlook. The motto of the Home Mission Society in 1832, "North America for Christ," reflects the territorial commitment of Northern Baptists. From its beginning in 1845, the Southern Baptist Convention has had a regional name, but for much of its history, especially in the twentieth century, the SBC has also maintained a national outlook and ministry. With two such overlapping Baptist groups, one is not surprised that their history reflects some areas of duplication and tension.

In a series of "comity agreements" beginning with Fortress Monroe in 1894, Baptists North and South have attempted to reduce the overlap and ease the tension. Perhaps the most important comity agreement of this century was that reached at Hot Springs, Arkansas, in 1912 (selection A). *Source: Annual,* SBC, 1912, 46-54. These comity agreements never worked well, and after 1942 they did not work at all, due largely to a new wave of tension caused by admission of California churches into affiliation with the Southern Baptist Convention (selection B). *Source: Annual,* SBC, 1942, 50. By mid century Southern Baptists were engaged in aggressive geographical expansion outside the South. At the San Francisco Convention of 1951, hardly a typical Southern city, they proclaimed the end of comity (selection C). *Source: Annual,* SBC, 1951, 36-37.

A.   The Hot Springs Agreement, 1912

Your Committee, in accordance with your action, entered into an arrangement with the Committee of Nine from the Northern Baptist Convention for a joint meeting at Old Point Comfort, Va., September 27 and 28, 1911. An informal meeting of some members of the two committees was held in Philadelphia in June, and it was resolved to send a brief communication to the Baptists of New Mexico in response to requests which had come from certain pastors in New Mexico, urging immediate action by the joint committee. This letter contained simply an earnest exhortation to unity of spirit, coupled with the request that the brethren of New Mexico await patiently the meeting of the two committees of nine in the early autumn. This action was ratified at the Old Point Comfort conference. . . .

A communication was presented by the committee from the Northern Baptist Convention, setting forth the objects had in view by the Northern Baptist Convention in requesting the appointment of said committee of conference. . . . The committee from the Southern Baptist Convention prepared a reply to the communication from the Northern Convention. In this reply the Southern committee expressed its profound appreciation of the fraternal and courteous tone and comprehensive presentation of the objects of the meeting, and expressed its desire to unite with the committee from the Northern Convention in any such action as would promote the highest welfare of the two great bodies represented. Perhaps no better statement of the spirit of the two committees could be given than that contained in the following paragraph from the communication of the Northern committee:

"This committee believes that the ultimate purposes of the two Conventions which appointed the two committees now in conference are identical—viz: in the words of the report of the Southern Baptist Convention, 'the world-wide spread of the gospel and the world-wide sway of Baptist principles.'"

In the communication of the committee from the Northern Baptist Convention it was suggested that we formulate some basis for the conference by means of a declaration of the principles which should govern Baptist bodies in the conduct of their mission work. A tentative outline of such principles of comity was suggested. These suggestions were referred to a sub-committee from the committee of the Southern Baptist Convention.

After several hours of labor, the sub-committee presented a reply to the communication from the committee of the Northern Convention. There was full, frank and free discussion of the principles set forth, and, while in the main the suggestions toward principles of comity were accepted, various modifications were proposed, and a final agreement was reached, and by unanimous vote the Principles of Comity were adopted.

Another meeting of the joint committee was held in Hot Springs, Ark., January 24 and 25, 1912. At this meeting a committee was appointed to revise the Principles of Comity still further. Much time and labor were expended and a unanimous vote was passed adopting the revised Principles of Comity as hereinafter set forth.

Another important matter which was considered at the meeting at Old Point Comfort related to the conditions prevailing in our Baptist work in New Mexico. A sub-committee of two was appointed by the committee from the Northern Baptist Convention, Brethren J. S. Dickerson and Walter Calley, and a corresponding committee of two was appointed by the committee from the Southern Baptist Convention, Brethren A. J. Barton and E. Y. Mullins. . . .

The sub-committee of four representing the two general committees, in accordance with instructions, visited Clovis and Roswell, N. M., October 27, 28, 29 and 30. . . . The committee felt upon leaving New Mexico that it had obtained all the essential facts. . . . As a result of their deliberations, they recommended to the joint committee of eighteen a plan for the readjustment of the forces engaged in missionary work in New Mexico. . . . As will be seen in the plan adopted by the joint committee, a three-year period was contemplated during which a gradual transfer of the home mission work in New Mexico from the Home Mission Society to the Home Mission Board should be made. All of the four agencies mentioned above, however, agreed in the expression of a desire that the transfer take place at once. Accordingly, the sub-committee recommends the elimination of the three-year transfer period, as will hereinafter be indicated.

In connection with the proposed plan certain differences of opinion regarding matters of detail arose between the Home Mission Board and the Board of the old New Mexico Convention. Owing to the brevity of the time at its disposal prior to the meetings of the two general Conventions, it was impossible to bring about complete unanimity of all minor points.

It was decided also at the Old Point Comfort meeting to send a communication to the various Boards and Societies of the Northern Baptist Convention and Southern Baptist Convention, inviting them to express to the joint committee of eighteen their views regarding the "scope and territorial spheres of their several activities; of their ideas of comity toward the corresponding organizations of the sister Convention; and their views as to what will secure the heartiest coöperation between both general Conventions in the spread of the gospel over the world." . . .

Principles of Comity.—The Principles of Comity adopted by the joint committee, after final revision at Hot Springs, are as follows:

Statement of Principles Adopted by the Committees of Conference of the Northern and Southern Baptist Conventions.

At a meeting of the committees of conference of the Northern and Southern Baptist Conventions held at Old Point Comfort, Va., September 27 and 28, 1911, after mutual correspondence and conference, the following statement of principles and their application was unanimously adopted:

Since the ultimate purposes of the two Conventions are the same and the aims of the two committees, co-laboring as one, are the same, the fresh recognition of some of the simple and fundamental principles for which Baptists stand should help us to eliminate misunderstandings between the constituencies of the two Conventions and more effectively promote their happy coöperation for "the world-wide spread of the gospel and the world-wide sway of Baptist principles."

It is unnecessary to review the last half century of denominational history. The possibility of errors in judgment on the part of individuals or of missionary organizations is freely conceded. We must look to the future to correct the errors and failings of the past.

We recognize the following as fundamental Baptist principles:

Fundamental Principles.

1. The independence of the local Baptist church.

2. The moral interdependence and the coöperation of Baptist churches in promoting the interests of the kingdom of God.

3. The purely advisory nature of all denominational organizations in their relation to Baptist churches.

Organizing Principles.

The voluntary principle should rule in all general organizations among Baptists.

Contiguous Baptists churches should unite in district associations and in State conventions for the promotion of the kingdom of God and their common denominational interests. The ideal organization is one association in a given territory and one convention in a given State. There may be local conditions, however, which make impracticable the immediate attainment of this ideal.

Concerning Comity.

1. Financial aid given to churches by a general denominational body should create gratitude to God and promote Christian fraternity in service, but should not impair in any way the freedom or autonomy of the church or churches receiving such aid.

2. Denominational organizations of every kind should "jealously regard the rights of all sister organizations, and of the churches, being always careful to promote unity and harmony, and to maintain inviolate the highest principles, thus exemplifying the noblest function of liberty, to wit: a proper respect for the liberties of others."

3. No Baptist body should use its influence to disintegrate or injure the work of any other Baptist bodies. Every Baptist organization should be an integrating and constructive force.

Application of the Foregoing Principles.

Because the kingdom of God and its interests are greater than the interests of any organization, whatever its constituency, and because "associations, societies, conventions and boards are expedients and agencies to be created and used by the churches," and because the kingdom of God can be promoted only when its work is conducted and its agencies and personal workers conduct themselves in the spirit of our Lord Jesus Christ, the Northern and Southern Baptist Conventions, putting aside all unholy competitions and realizing their unity in our Lord Jesus Christ, should "work together in the most agreeable and loving manner," each "promising to contribute to our common welfare, assuring one another of the full and abiding desire to work in fullest accord." Coöperative relations should be not only in fraternal feeling and Christian respect for one another's work in territory now exclusively occupied by either Convention, but by both Conventions, which have churches affiliated with them in the same State, should strive to effect the best possible working union of our forces in that State. While this statement sets forth our right attitude in such States, the ideal condition is that in which the entire body of the membership follows the majority in its coöperation with any general body. . . .

Plan for Readjustment in New Mexico.—The plan adopted by the joint committee for the readjustment of the work in New Mexico was as follows:

"We recommend—

"(1) That the members of the two existing State Conventions in New Mexico come together and organize a new Convention under a new name within the sixty-day period hereinafter mentioned.

"(2) That a new constitution be framed, the provisions of which, concerning coöperation, be such as to render impossible misunderstandings at the points where they have hitherto arisen, but would recognize the right of general bodies to ratify or approve all appointments in which they share financial responsibility.

"(3) That a secretary be elected whose salary shall be paid wholly by the new State convention, and that neither of the present secretaries be considered eligible; this not for any personal reason reflecting in any way upon these brethren, but in order to avoid as far as possible all occasion for partisan feeling.

"(4) That after the formation of the new State convention, it coöperate with the home mission agencies of the Northern and Southern Baptist Conventions for a period of three years, in the following manner:

"(a) That all State mission work in New Mexico be under the control of the new State convention through its Executive Board in coöperation with the American Baptist Home Mission Society and the Home Mission Board of the Southern Baptist Convention.

"(b) That for the first year after the organization of the new convention, the American Baptist Home Mission Society and the Home Mission Board of the Southern Baptist Convention shall each contribute to the new State convention a sum at least equal to their appropriation for the current fiscal year of the two general Conventions, to be expended in a manner satisfactory to the three Boards.

"(c) That for the second year the American Baptist Home Mission Society shall give two-thirds of the amount contributed by it during the preceding year for State mission work during that year, and the Home Mission Board of the Southern Baptist Convention the balance, to be expended as above indicated.

"(d) That for the third year the American Baptist Home Mission Society shall give one-half of the amount contributed by it during the year immediately preceding the State mission work, and the Home Mission Board of the Southern Baptist Convention the balance, to be expended as above indicated.

"(e) That at the end of this period of three years the New Mexico Baptist Convention transfer its entire affiliation to the Southern Baptist Convention, and that the Southern Baptist Convention thereafter assume the burdens and responsibilities of Baptist home mission work in New Mexico.

"(f) If in the judgment of the three coöperating bodies there should arise a necessity for increasing the total annual appropriations for the work of New Mexico, said increase shall be provided by the Home Mission Board of the Southern Baptist Convention. If, on the other hand, in the judgment of the three coöperating bodies, circumstances should justify a reduction in the amount of the total annual appropriations, the appropriation of the American Baptist Home Mission Society shall be diminished by such amount.

"(g) That for the three-year period heretofore mentioned the Executive Board of the new convention in New Mexico provide an equitable basis for the distribution of undesignated gifts to the missionary objects of the two general Conventions; and we suggest as such basis the ratio of appropriations to the work in New Mexico by the two general home mission agencies.

"(5) That we request the two existing New Mexico Baptist Conventions to meet within sixty days after action by the two general Conventions for the purpose of considering the question of dissolving the present organizations and of coming together for the adoption of the above plan.

"(6) The plan above outlined is suggested upon the assumption that the Statement of the Principles of Comity and their application as affirmed by the joint committees in conference be adopted by the Northern and Southern Baptist Conventions."

As previously indicated, the Home Mission Society, Home Mission Board, and the two New Mexico Conventions, expressed a preference for the immediate carrying out of the above plan and the elimination of the three-year period. The sub-committee therefore recommend that the three-year period be eliminated and that the above plan be adopted.

The plan we have just presented for settlement of the divisions in New Mexico was unanimously adopted by a representative conference of the Boards of the two New Mexico Conventions. However, in carrying on to completion the plan of the joint New Mexico sub-committee, as above outlined, conditions were proposed by certain New Mexico brethren. Up to the present time it has been impossible to secure entire unanimity as to these conditions. . . .

In the light, therefore, of the desirability of obtaining not only ostensible but real and abiding peace for the Baptists of New Mexico, the sub-committee recommends, and in this recommendation this committee joins, that the Convention reappoint the committee of nine, and that the committee be instructed to continue its efforts permanently and satisfactorily to unify the denomination in New Mexico, and that it be given power to work out an agreement which shall conserve all that has been accomplished thus far, and to make operative the plan already agreed to, it being understood that this committee shall not alter the plan adopted, a plan approved by the Home Mission Society, the Home Board, and the two Boards in New Mexico, its efforts henceforth being directed solely toward the removal of such misunderstandings as still exist. Furthermore, we recommend that the committee be instructed not to concur in new conditions which shall in any way impair the integrity of the plan of settlement already adopted, or which shall interfere with the functions of either the Home Mission Society, the Home Mission Board, the New Mexico Conventions, or of either the Northern or the Southern Baptist Conventions, or which shall in any way invade the rights of the local churches.

In concluding this statement of a plan for the reorganization of the work in New Mexico, we desire to express our profound appreciation of the splendid work done by the Home Mission Society of the Northern Baptist Convention during the many years of its occupancy of New Mexico as a sphere of missionary operations. . . .

The considerations which led the sub-committee on New Mexico to recommend the transfer of the home mission work in New Mexico to the Home Mission Board of the Southern Baptist Convention were various. For one thing, it seemed eminently desirable that there should be one convention, and not two, and affiliation with one general missionary organization. This seemed to the committee essential to the highest unity and efficiency of the work. New Mexico lies South of the parallel of latitude which constitutes the northern boundary of the Southern Baptist Convention. This alone, however, would not have been regarded as a determinative factor in the solution of the problem. The chief consideration in the minds of the committee was the fact that the tide of immigration into New Mexico from Texas and other Southern States in recent years has been so great. The result has been that the population of New Mexico has become largely Southern in tradition and sympathy and preference. This condition, taken in connection with the others which have been mentioned, seemed to the committee a sufficient ground to warrant it in adopting the plan above outlined. . . .

Respectfully submitted,
E. Y. MULLINS,
Acting Chairman.

B. Admission of California Messengers, 1942

58. For the committee on consideration of the petition of California churches, Walter P. Binns, Virginia, in the absence of the chairman because of illness, moved that the committee be continued another year with the addition of three members. The following substitute motion offered by J. B. Rounds, Oklahoma, was adopted after discussion. . . .

After a careful study of the situation and in consideration of the provisions of the Constitution and By-Laws of this Convention, we recommend that the Southern Baptist General Convention of the state of California be admitted to membership in the Southern Baptist Convention.

They have thirty-one cooperating churches with an approximate membership of 3,000, fifteen of these churches have been organized during the past twelve months. They have sent $560.23 during the past twelve months to the Southwide causes. They give 20% of all cooperative program receipts to the Southwide causes.

They will be admitted to representation on only three Boards of this Convention by the provisions of the Constitution till they attain a membership of ten thousand within their state.

C. Acknowledging the End of Comity

13. T. C. Gardner, Texas, brought the report of the Committee on Relations with Other Religious Bodies, with the following recommendations which were adopted, after the report was amended, on motion of L. E. Solomon, Florida, to continue this same committee: . . .

4. We recommend that: Whereas the Southern Baptist Convention has defined its territorial position in reports to the Convention in 1944 and in 1949 by removing territorial limitations, and whereas the Northern Baptist Convention has changed its name so that it is continental in scope, the Home Mission Board and all other Southern Baptist boards and agencies be free to serve as a source of blessing to any community or any people anywhere in the United States.

15.5   Southern Baptists and Religious Liberty

Southern Baptists, like others who bear the Baptist name, have been deeply committed to religious liberty. Two of their most outstanding leaders, Edgar Young Mullins (1860-1928) and George Washington Truett (1867-1944) issued important and widely quotes treatises on that subject. *Sources:* E. Y. Mullins, *The Axioms of Religion* (Philadelphia: Judson Press, 1908), 185-200. George W. Truett, *Baptists and Religious Liberty* (Nashville: Baptist Sunday School Board, 1920), 3-36.

A.   E. Y. Mullins on Religious Liberty

CHAPTER XI

THE RELIGIO-CIVIC AXIOM: A FREE CHURCH IN A FREE STATE

RELATIONS BETWEEN CHURCH AND STATE.

The religio-civic axiom which states the American principle of the relations between Church and State is so well understood and is accepted by the people of the United States so generally and so heartily that it is unnecessary to spend time in pointing out at length what the axiom implies. Mr. Bryce in his "American Commonwealth" remarks: "It is accepted as an axiom by all Americans that the civil power ought to be not only neutral and impartial as between entirely different forms of faith, but ought to leave these matters entirely on one side, regarding them no more than they regard the artistic or literary pursuits of the citizens."[1] In short the entire contents of the axiom is summed up in the statement that the State has no ecclesiastical and the Church no civic function. Mr. Bryce also says: "Of all the difference between the Old World and the New this is perhaps the most salient. Half the wars of Europe, half the internal troubles that have vexed European States, from the Monophysite controversies in the Roman empire of the fifth century down to the Kulturkampf in the German empire of the nineteenth, have arisen from theological differences or from the rival claims of Church and State."[2] In this connection also I give a statement from Buckle. He says in his "History of Civilization": "During almost a hundred and fifty years, Europe was afflicted by religious wars, religious massacres, and religious persecutions; not one of which would have arisen if the great truth had been recognized that the State has no concern with the opinions of men, and no right to interfere even in the slightest degree with the form of worship which they may choose to adopt. This principle was, however, formerly unknown or at all events unheeded; and it was not until the middle of the seventeenth century that the great religious contests were brought to a final close and the different countries settled down to their public creeds."[3] Such quotations might be indefinitely multiplied, but it is needless. Neither of the writers quoted is an American, and yet each states the principle in a manner which is in complete unison with our way of regarding the matter. For many centuries the struggle between Church and State was an unequal one. By a sort of spiritual instinct the church tugged at her chains with various movements of protest against the English and European establishments. It was like the struggle between the eagle and the serpent. The church, as the eagle in the contest, was sometimes dragged down into the dust by the foe. Again, with the serpent's sinewy coils about her body she would rise heavily into the air only to be dragged downward again. At length the eagle, with beak and talons dripping with the blood of her slain foe, mounts upward and builds her nest on a lofty crag forever beyond the serpent's reach. This was when Roger Williams founded the commonwealth of Rhode Island. A new era in man's spiritual history began then.

The leadership of the Baptists of Rhode Island and Virginia in introducing the doctrine of complete separation of Church and State has already been pointed out in a previous chapter. Indeed two great conceptions were formally promulgated by the Baptists of the seventeenth century in their creeds and Confessions, which in a striking manner show that they were far in advance of Christendom in general in their views as to the essential nature of Christianity. One of these is the doctrine of world-wide missions, which is absent from the Westminister and other creeds of the period. It is a well-known fact that Christendom at large was apparently dead to this great obligation until William Carey aroused it. Yet in their "Confession of Faith," issued by churches in and around London in 1660, the Baptists of England promulgated the doctrine and obligation of world-wide missions as we shall see in a later chapter.

ANOTHER GREAT BAPTIST PRINCIPLE.

But we are here more directly interested in the other great Baptist principle in which they antedated others. Their view of soul freedom and separation of Church and State they promulgated in their earliest known creeds and their practice has never parted company with their doctrine. We find the following in the "London Confession," published in 1644. After declaring the duty of obedience to magistrates and all legally constituted authorities in all things lawful the Confession in the forty-ninth article says: "But in case we find not the magistrate to favor us herein, yet we dare not suspend our practice because we believe we ought to go on in obedience to Christ, in professing the faith which is declared in the holy Scriptures and this our confession of faith a part of them; and that we are to witness to the truth of the Old and New Testament unto the death if necessity require, in the midst of trials and afflictions, as his saints of old have done," etc.[4] In the next article it is declared that it is lawful for a Christian to be a magistrate and to take oaths. Under the forty-eighth article the following language occurs: "As we cannot do anything contrary to our understandings and consciences, so neither can we forbear the doing of that which our understandings and consciences bind us to do; and if the magistrate should require us to do otherwise, we are to yield our persons in a passive way to their power, as the saints of old have done."[5]

Of like tenor with the above are all the Baptist creeds. There has never been a time in their history, so far as that history is known to us, when they wavered in their doctrine of a free Church in a free State. Nowhere in the American colonies before the Revolution, save in Rhode Island and among Virginia Baptists and in a few great minds such as Madison and others like him, had this novel and far-reaching conception taken root. Men in general regarded the separation of Church and State as a doctrine of anarchy and chaos, and honestly believed that its practical application would quench the sun of religion in the heaven of man's spiritual hopes.

It is a singular fact, to be noted in this connection, that many writers of great intelligence in other respects even to-day fail to grasp clearly the distinction between religious toleration and religious freedom. Doctor Bacon in his "History of American Christianity" falls into the common error of referring to the Maryland colony under the Calverts as an example of religious liberty; whereas all who are familiar with the distinction know that in Maryland not religious liberty in the modern sense and in the ancient Baptist sense, but only toleration was enjoyed. We find the same error in an address so recent as that of one of the speakers at the Congress of Arts and Science in St. Louis. Americans of to-day would no more rest content under a system of mere religious toleration than they were willing to endure taxation without representation under George the Third. . . .

The American theory of Church and State which the prophetic soul of Roger Williams discerned clearly in the early seventeenth century, which the English Baptists also grasped and put into formal statement a little later in the same century, which Virginia Baptists championed against the established church in the eighteenth century, and which through their influence came to full expression in the first amendment to the Constitution of the United States, is in all respects opposed to the English and European theory. We thus make a real contribution to the world's civilization.

Americans do not deny that the ends for which government exists are moral, but they do deny that those ends are religious. Mr. Bryce is scarcely correct in the statement that our view regards the general government simply as a great business organization created by the people for certain specified purposes which do not include matters of the church or religion. While Americans have spent little time in theorizing about the nature of the State I think it is a fair inference from the Declaration of Independence that in the main they regard our Constitution as grounded in essential moral principles, and that ultimately government is the expression of moral relations which necessarily exist in human society and created by God.[6]

It does not follow, however, that because an institution is the expression of moral relations in one sphere that it is meant to promote moral ends in all spheres. Church and State might in a perfect society coalesce into one; but meantime their functions must be kept separate. . . .

FUNCTIONS OF CHURCH AND STATE DISTINCT.

The functions of Church and State are quite distinct. The American view is based on fundamental facts of human society and of the gospel. The Church is a voluntary organization, the State compels obedience. One organization is temporal, the other spiritual. Their views as to penal offenses may be quite different, that being wrong and punishable in the Church which the State cannot afford to notice. The direct allegiance in the Church is to God, in the State it is to law and government. One is for the protection of life and property, the other for the promotion of spiritual life. An established religion, moreover, subverts the principle of equal rights and equal privileges to all which is a part of our organic law. Both on its political and on its religious side the doctrine of the separation of Church and State holds good. Civil liberty and soul liberty alike forbid their union. As Dr. Newman Smyth remarks: "History has permanently closed these two ways—the way of bringing Christ before the judgment seat of Caesar to be crucified, and the way of putting Christ on Caesar's throne to rule the kingdoms of this world."

Now it is important to keep in mind the meaning of the phrase "a free Church in a free State," if we are to avoid confusion in thought at certain points in our practical application of the principle. If at any point, such as the legal holding of property, the functions of the church carry it over into the civil realm, then we must construe such function as properly pertaining to the church and *vice versa*. But this does not destroy the freedom of either Church or State. The Church is compatible with the State but entirely independent of it. That is to say, it is free. It is a spiritual commonwealth. The citizenship of its members is in heaven, as Paul declares, although at the same time they are citizens of an earthly State. There will, of course, remain a borderland where it will not always be clear how to discriminate and apply the principle correctly.

IMPORTANT ILLUSTRATIONS OF STATEMENT MADE.

We may note before closing this chapter two or three illustrations of the statement made. One is the appropriation of public money for sectarian schools. This is a flagrant violation of the principle and is a long step toward the establishment of one or more denominations in governmental support. Direct gifts of money to religious bodies by the general government is of the essence of union of Church and State. It is not surprising, therefore, that it was when a Baptist, General Morgan, was Commissioner of Indian Affairs that this government, under his leadership, abandoned the practice of appropriating money for sectarian schools.

As to the Bible in public schools also there has been much difference of opinion among Americans. Baptists very generally and consistently oppose the public reading of the Bible in the schools, because they respect the consciences of all others. The underlying question is a difficult one. The State, as it is based on the franchise, and as the franchise implies intelligence, quite properly provides through its educational system for making its citizens intelligent. Can it be said also that the State, as it is based on the franchise, and the franchise implies moral character, quite properly provides through moral teaching in the public schools for making its citizens moral? Religious teaching as distinguished from moral teaching is of course excluded. The answer to the question must be in the affirmative within certain limits. Moral teaching is not objectionable even to atheists. A moral text-book sufficiently elementary and simple, containing extracts from other works containing wholesome moral teaching, might be employed to advantage without violating any man's conscience.

The exemption of church property from taxation is another point which has been much contested. All religious bodies alike have enjoyed the privilege. It has been defended on various grounds as not involving the union of Church and State. The church enhances the value of all other property, adds to the desirability of any community as a place of residence, builds up our civilization in many ways, and is the most efficient of all police forces. It thus gives a *quid pro quo* to the State and more than earns its exemption from taxation. The governor of Montana a few years ago in a message to the legislature made a special request that all church property be exempt from taxation as the best means of advancing the welfare of the entire territory and speeding it on its way to complete civilization.

But others contest the point. They maintain that to exempt churches from taxation is to subsidize religion and to subsidize religion is to subvert our doctrine of a free Church in a free State. They urge also that to tax church property would have a wholesome effect in preventing extravagance in church architecture and in other ways would react favorably upon religion.

Now unquestionably a theoretical justification can be made out for either view, for exemption as well as taxation. It runs thus: To impose a tax is to assert sovereignty; but the State is not sovereign over the Church whose allegiance is to God alone. Moreover, to concede the right to tax involves a concession of the right to confiscate upon proper occasion. Thus the right to tax on the part of the State destroys the freedom of the Church, so that it is no longer a free Church in a free State.

A QUESTION OF INTERPRETATION.

After all, however, the question is one of the interpretation of a principle. If the sovereign State and the sovereign Church agree that a particular practice capable of theoretical justification in opposite directions is not a violation of a general principle of government and of religion then that interpretation must stand. Experience alone will demonstrate the wisdom or unwisdom of the interpretation. Time alone can give the final answer to many questions. Up to the present it cannot be said that time has demonstrated the unwisdom of exempting religious property from taxation. To impose a tax on such property would be a deadly blow to education as well as to religion.

[Notes]
1. "American Commonwealth," Vol. II, pp. 572, 573.
2. "American Commonwealth," Vol. II, p. 570.
3. "History of Civilization," Vol. I, p. 190.
4. Underhill: "Confession of Faith," pp. 45, 46.
5. Underhill, p. 45.
6. *Cf.* Newman Smyth's "Christian Ethics," pp. 263f.

B. George W. Truett, *Baptists and Religious Liberty*, 1920.

FOREWORD

This address was arranged for weeks before the Southern Baptist Convention met in Washington. Washington City Baptists are directly responsible for it. The speaker, Dr. George W. Truett, pastor First Baptist Church, Dallas, Texas, was chosen by a representative group of Baptists to deliver the address. It was delivered to a vast audience of from ten to fifteen thousand people from the east steps of the National Capital, three o'clock Sunday afternoon, May 16, 1920. It was not a Convention session, though the Convention was largely represented in the audience by its members.

Since Paul spoke before Nero, no Baptist speaker ever pleaded the cause of truth in surroundings so dignified, impressive and inspiring. The shadow of the Capitol of the greatest and freest nation on earth, largely made so by the infiltration of Baptist ideas through the masses, fell on the vast assembly, composed of Cabinet members, Senators and members of the Lower House, Foreign Ambassadors, intellectuals in all callings, with peoples of every religious order and of all classes.

The subject was fit for the place, the occasion, and the assembly. The speaker had prepared his message. In a voice clear and far-reaching he carried his audience through the very heart of his theme. History was invoked, but far more, history was explained by the inner guiding principles of a people who stand today, as they have always stood, for full and equal religious liberty for all people.

There was no trimming, no froth, no halting, and not one arrogant or offensive tone or word. It was a bold, fair, thorough-going setting out of the history and life principles of the people called Baptists. And then logically and becomingly the speaker brought his Baptist brethren to look forward and take up the burdens of liberty and fulfill its high moral obligations, declaring that defaulters in the moral realm court death.

His address advances the battle line for the denomination. It is a noble piece of work, worthy the wide circulation it is sure to receive. Intelligent Baptists should pass it on.

A serious word was said in that august presence concerning national obligations as they arise out of a civilization animated and guided by Christian sentiments and principles. As a nation we cannot walk the ways of selfishness without walking down hill.

I commend this address as the most significant and momentous of our day.

J. B. GAMBRELL,
President Southern Baptist Convention.

Baptists and Religious Liberty
By GEORGE W. TRUETT

Southern Baptists count it a high privilege to hold their Annual Convention this year in the national capital, and they count it one of life's highest privileges to be citizens of our one great, united country. . . .

It behooves us often to look backward as well as forward. We should be stronger and braver if we thought oftener of the epic days and deeds of our beloved and immortal dead. The occasional backward look would give us poise and patience and courage and fearlessness and faith. The ancient Hebrew teachers and leaders had a genius for looking backward to the days and deeds of their mighty dead. They never wearied of chanting the praises of Abraham and Isaac and Jacob, of Moses and Joshua and Samuel; and thus did they bring to bear upon the living the inspiring memories of the nobel actors and deeds of bygone days. Often such a cry as this rang in their ears: "Look unto the rock whence ye were hewn, and to the hole of the pit whence ye were digged. Look unto Abraham, your father, and unto Sarah that bare you; for when he was but one I called him, and I blessed him, and made him many."

The Doctrine of Religious Liberty.

We shall do well, both as citizens and as Christians, if we will hark back to the chief actors and lessons in the early and epoch-making struggles of this great Western democracy, for the full establishment of civil and religious liberty—back to the days of Washington and Jefferson and Madison, and back to the days of our Baptist fathers, who have paid such a great price, through the long generations, that liberty, both religious and civil, might have free course and be glorified everywhere.

Years ago, at a notable dinner in London, that world-famed statesman, John Bright, asked an American statesman, himself a Baptist, the noble Dr. J. L. M. Curry, "What distinct contribution has your America made to the science of government?" To that question Dr. Curry replied: "The doctrine of religious liberty." After a moment's reflection, Mr. Bright made the worthy reply: "It was a tremendous contribution."

Supreme Contribution of New World.

Indeed, the supreme contribution of the new world to the old is the contribution of religious liberty. This is the chiefest contribution that America has thus far made to civilization. And historic justice compels me to say that it was pre-eminently a Baptist contribution. The impartial historian, whether in the past, present or future, will ever agree with out American historian, Mr. Bancroft, when he says: "Freedom of conscience, unlimited freedom of mind, was from the first the trophy of the Baptists." And such historian will concur with the noble John Locke who said: "The Baptists were the first propounders of absolute liberty, just and true liberty, equal and impartial liberty." Ringing testimonies like these might be multiplied indefinitely.

Not Toleration, but Right.

Baptists have one consistent record concerning liberty throughout all their long and eventful history. They have never been a party to oppression of conscience. They have forever been the unwavering champions of liberty, both religious and civil. Their contention now is, and has been, and please God, must ever be, that it is the natural and fundamental and indefeasible right of every human being to worship God or not, according to the dictates of his conscience, and, as long as he does not infringe upon the rights of others, he is to be held accountable alone to God for all religious beliefs and practices. Our contention is not for mere toleration, but for absolute liberty. There is a wide difference between toleration and liberty. Toleration implies that somebody falsely claims the right to tolerate. Toleration is a concession, while liberty is a right. Toleration is a matter of expediency, while liberty is a matter of principle. Toleration is a gift from man, while liberty is a gift from God. It is the consistent and insistent contention of our Baptist people, always and everywhere, that religion must be forever voluntary and uncoerced, and that it is not the prerogative of any power, whether civil or ecclesiastical, to compel men to conform to any religious creed or form of worship, or to pay taxes for the support of a religious organization to which they do not belong and in whose creed they do not believe. God wants free worshipers and no other kind.

A Fundamental Principle.

What is the explanation of this consistent and notably praiseworthy record of our plain Baptist people in the realm of religious liberty. The answer is at hand. It is not because Baptists are inherently better than their neighbors—we would make no such arrogant claim. Happy are our Baptist people to live side by side with their neighbors of other Christian communions, and to have glorious Christian fellowship with such neighbors, and to honor such servants of God for their inspiring lives and their noble deeds. From our deepest hearts we pray: "Grace be with all them that love our Lord Jesus Christ in sincerity." The spiritual union of all true believers in Christ is now and ever will be a blessed reality, and such union is deeper and higher and more enduring than any and all forms and rituals and organizations. Whoever believes in Christ as his personal Saviour is our brother in the common salvation, whether he be a member of one communion or of another, or of no communion at all.

How is it, then, that Baptists, more than any other people in the world, have forever been the protagonists of religious liberty, and its compatriot, civil liberty? They did not stumble upon this principle. Their uniform, unyielding and sacrificial advocacy of such principle was not and is not an accident. It is, in a word, because of our essential and fundamental principles. Ideas rule the world. A denomination is moulded by its ruling principles, just as a nation is thus moulded and just as individual life is thus moulded. Our fundamental essential principles have made our Baptist people, of all ages and countries, to be the unyielding protagonist of religious liberty, not only for themselves, but as well for everybody else.

The Fundamental Baptist Principles.

Such fact at once provokes the inquiry: What are these fundamental Baptist principles which compel Baptists in Europe, in America, in some far-off seagirt island, to be forever contending for unrestricted religious liberty? First of all, and explaining all the rest, is the doctrine of the absolute Lordship of Jesus Christ. That doctrine is for Baptists the dominant fact in all their Christian experience, the nerve center of all their Christian life, the bedrock of all their church polity, the sheet anchor of all their hopes, the climax and crown of all their rejoicings. They say with Paul: "For to this end Christ both died and rose again, that he might be Lord both of the dead and the living."

The Absolute Lordship of Christ.

From that germinal conception of the absolute Lordship of Christ, all our Baptist principles emerge. Just as yonder oak came from the acorn, so our many-branched Baptist life came from the cardinal principle of the absolute Lordship of Christ. The Christianity of our Baptist people, from Alpha to Omega, lives and moves and has its whole being in the realm of the doctrine of the Lordship of Christ. "One is your Master, even Christ, and all ye are brethren." Christ is the one head of the church. All authority has been committed unto Him, in heaven and on earth, and He must be given the absolute pre-eminence in all things. One clear note is ever to be sounded concerning Him, even this, "Whatsoever He saith unto you, do it."

The Bible Our Rule of Faith and Practice.

How shall we find our Christ's will for us? He has revealed it in His Holy Word. The Bible and the Bible alone is the rule of faith and practice for Baptists. To them the one standard by which all creeds and conduct and character must be tried is the Word of God. They ask only one question concerning all religious faith and practice, and that question is, "What saith the Word of God?" Not traditions, nor customs, nor councils, nor confessions, nor ecclesiastical formularies, however venerable and pretentious, guide Baptists, but simply and solely the will of Christ as they find it revealed in the New Testament. The immortal B. H. Carroll has thus stated it for us: "The New Testament is the law of Christianity. All the New Testament is the law of Christianity. The New Testament is all the law of Christianity. The New Testament always will be all the law of Christianity." . . .

Infant Baptism Unthinkable.

It follows, inevitably, that Baptists are unalterably opposed to every form of sponsorial religion. If I have fellow Christians in this presence today who are the protagonists of infant baptism, they will allow me frankly to say, and certainly I would say it in the most fraternal, Christian spirit, that to Baptists infant baptism is unthinkable from every viewpoint. First of all, Baptists do not find the slightest sanction for infant baptism in the Word of God. That fact, to Baptists, makes infant baptism a most serious question for the consideration of the whole Christian world. Nor is that all. As Baptists see it, infant baptism tends to ritualize Christianity and reduce it to lifeless forms. It tends also and inevitably, as Baptists see it, to the secularizing of the church and to the blurring and blotting out of the line of demarcation between the church and the unsaved world. . . .

Surely, in the face of these frank statements, our non-Baptist neighbors may apprehend something of the difficulties compelling Baptists when they are asked to enter into official alliances with those who hold such fundamentally different views from those just indicated. We call God to witness that our Baptist people have an unutterable longing for Christian union, and believe Christian union will come, but we are compelled to insist that if this union is to be real and effective, it must be based upon a better understanding of the Word of God and a more complete loyalty to the will of Christ as revealed in His Word.

The Ordinances Are Symbols.

Again, to Baptists, the New Testament teaches that salvation through Christ must precede membership in His church, and must precede the observance of the two ordinances in His church, namely, baptism and the Lord's Supper. These ordinances are for the saved and only for the saved. These two ordinances are not sacramental, but symbolic. They are teaching ordinances, portraying in symbol truths of immeasurable and everlasting moment to humanity. To trifle with these symbols, to pervert their forms and at the same time to pervert the truths they are designed to symbolize, is indeed a most serious matter. Without ceasing and without wavering, Baptists are, in conscience, compelled to contend that these two teaching ordinances shall be maintained in the churches just as they were placed there in the wisdom and authority of Christ. . . .

The Church a Pure Democracy.

To Baptists, the New Testament also clearly teaches that Christ's church is not only a spiritual body but it is also a pure democracy, all its members being equal, a local congregation, and cannot subject itself to any outside control. Such terms, therefore, as "The American Church," or "The bishop of this city or state," sound strangely incongruous to Baptist ears. In the very nature of the case, also, there must be no union between church and state, because their nature and functions are utterly different. Jesus stated the principle in the two sayings, "My kingdom is not of this world," and "Render unto Caesar the things that are Caesar's, and unto God the things that are God's." Never, anywhere, in any clime, has a true Baptist been willing, for one minute, for the union of church and state, never for a moment. . . .

A Free Church in a Free State.

That utterance of Jesus, "Render unto Caesar the things that Caesar's, and unto God the things that are God's," is one of the most revolutionary and history-making utterances that ever fell from those lips divine. That utterance, once for all, marked the divorcement of church and state. It marked a new era for the creeds and deeds of men. It was the sunrise gun of a new day, the echoes of which are to go on and on and on until in every land, whether great or small, the doctrine shall have absolute supremacy everywhere of a free church in a free state.

In behalf of our Baptist people I am compelled to say that forgetfulness of the principles that I have just enumerated, in our judgment, explains many of the religious ills that now afflict the world. All went well with the early churches in their earlier days. They were incomparably triumphant days for the Christian faith. Those early disciples of Jesus, without prestige and worldly power, yet aflame with the love of God and the passion of Christ, went out and shook the pagan Roman Empire from center to circumference, even in one brief generation. Christ's religion needs no prop of any kind from any worldly source, and to the degree that it is thus supported is a millstone hanged about its neck.

An Incomparable Apostasy.

Presently there came an incomparable apostasy in the realm of religion, which shrouded the world in spiritual night through long hundreds of years. Constantine, the Emperor, saw something in the religion of Christ's people which awakened his interest, and now we see him uniting religion to the state and marching up the marble steps of the Emperor's palace, with the church robed in purple. Thus and there was begun the most baneful misalliance that ever fettered and cursed a suffering world. For long centuries, even from Constantine to Pope Gregory VII, the conflict between church and state waxed stronger and stronger, and the encroachments and usurpations became more deadly and devastating. When Christianity first found its way into the city of the Caesars it lived at first in cellars and alleys, but when Constantine crowned the union of the church and state, the church was stamped with the impress of the Roman idea and fanned with the spirit of the Caesars. Soon we see a Pope emerging, who himself became a Caesar, and soon a group of councilors may be seen gathered around this Pope, and the supreme power of the church is assumed by the Pope and his councilors.

The long blighting record of the medieval ages is simply the working out of that idea. The Pope ere long assumed to be the monarch of the world, making the astounding claim that all kings and potentates were subject unto him. By and by when Pope Gregory VII appears, better known as Hildebrand, his assumptions are still more astounding. In him the spirit of the Roman church became incarnate and triumphant. He lorded it over parliaments and council chambers, having statesmen to do his bidding, and creating and deposing kings at his will. For example, when the Emperor Henry offended Hildebrand, the latter pronounced against Henry a sentence not only of excommunication but of deposition as Emperor, releasing all Christians from allegiance to him. He made the Emperor do penance by standing in the snow with his bare feet at Canossa, and he wrote his famous letter to William the Conqueror to the effect that the state was subordinate to the church, that the power of the state as compared to the church was as the moon compared to the sun.

This explains the famous saying of Bismarck when Chancellor of Germany, to the German Parliament: "We will never go to Canossa again." Whoever favors the authority of the church over the state favors the way to Canossa.

When, in the fulness of time, Columbus discovered America, the Pope calmly announced that he would divide the New World into two parts, giving one part to the King of Spain and the other to the King of Portugal. And not only did this great consolidated ecclesiasticism assume to lord it over men's earthly treasures, but they lorded it over men's minds, prescribing what men should think and read and write. Nor did such assumption stop with the things of this world, but it laid its hand on the next world, and claims to have in its possession the keys of the Kingdom of Heaven and the kingdom of purgatory so that it could shut men out of heaven or lift them out of purgatory, thus surpassing in the sweep of its power and in the pride of its autocracy the boldest and most presumptuous ruler that ever sat on a civil throne. . . .

The Reformation Incomplete.

The coming of the sixteenth century was the dawning of a new hope for the world. With that century came the Protestant Reformation. Yonder goes Luther with his theses, which he nails over the old church door in Wittenberg, and the echoes of the mighty deed shake the Papacy, shake Europe, shake the whole world. Luther was joined by Melancthon and Calvin and Zwingli and other mighty leaders. Just at this point emerges one of the most outstanding anomalies of all history. Although Luther and his compeers protested vigorously against the errors of Rome, yet when these mighty men came out of Rome, and mighty men they were, they brought with them some of the grievious errors of Rome. The Protestant Reformation of the Sixteenth century was sadly incomplete—it was a case of arrested development. Although Luther and his compeers grandly sounded out the battle cry of justification by faith alone, yet they retained the doctrine of infant baptism and a state church. They shrank from the logical conclusions of their own theses.

In Zurich there stands a statue in honor of Zwingli, in which he is represented with a Bible in one hand and a sword in the other. That statute was the symbol of the union between church and state. The same statute might have been reared to Luther and his fellow reformers. Luther and Melancthon fastened a state church upon Germany, and Zwingli fastened it upon Switzerland. Knox and his associates fastened it upon Scotland. Henry VIII bound it upon England, where it remains even till this very hour.

These mighty reformers turned out to be persecutors like the Papacy before them. Luther unloosed the dogs of persecution against the struggling and faithful Anabaptists. Calvin burned Servetus, and to such awful deed Melancthon gave his approval. Louis XIV revoked the Edict of Nantes, shut the doors of all the Protestant churches, and outlawed the Huguenots. Germany put to death that mighty Baptist leader, Balthaser Hubmaier, while Holland killed her noblest statesman, John of Barneveldt, and condemned to life imprisonment her ablest historian, Hugo Grotius, for conscience' sake. In England, John Bunyan was kept in jail for twelve long, weary years because of his religion, and when we cross the mighty ocean separating the Old World and the New, we find the early pages of American history crimsoned with the stories of religious persecutions. The early colonies of America were the forum of the working out of the most epochal battles that earth ever knew for the triumph of religious and civil liberty.

America and Religious and Civil Liberty.

Just a brief glance at the struggle in those early colonies must now suffice us. Yonder in Massachusetts, Henry Dunster, the first president of Harvard, was removed from the presidency because he objected to infant baptism. Roger Williams was banished, John Clarke was put in prison, and they publicly whipped Obadiah Holmes on Boston Common. In Connecticut the lands of our Baptist fathers were confiscated and their goods sold to build a meeting house and support a preacher of another denomination. In old Virginia, "mother of states and statemen," the battle for religious and civil liberty was waged all over her nobly historic territory, and the final triumph recorded there was such as to write imperishable glory upon the name of Virginia until the last syllable of recorded time. Fines and imprisonments and persecutions were everywhere in evidence in Virginia for conscience' sake. If you would see a record incomparably interesting, go read the early statues in Virginia concerning the Established Church and religion, and trace the epic story of the history-making struggles of that early day. If the historic records are to be accredited, those clergymen of the Established Church in Virginia made terrible inroads in collecting fines in Baptist tobacco in that early day. It is quite evident, however, that they did not get all the tobacco.

On and on was the struggle waged by our Baptist fathers for religious liberty in Virginia, in the Carolinas, in Georgia, in Rhode Island and Masschusettes and Connecticut, and elsewhere, with one unyielding contention for unrestricted religious liberty for all men, and with never one wavering note. They dared to be odd, to stand alone, to refuse to conform, though it cost them suffering and even life itself. They dared to defy traditions and customs, and deliberately chose the day of non-conformity, even though in many a case it meant a cross. They pleaded and suffered, they offered their protests and remonstrances and memorials, and, thank God, mighty statesmen were won to their contention, Washington and Jefferson and Madison and Patrick Henry, and many others, until at last it was written into our country's Constitution that church and state must in this land be forever separate and free, that neither must ever trespass upon the distinctive functions of the other. It was pre-eminently a Baptist achievement.

A Lonely Struggle.

Glad are our Baptist people to pay their grateful tribute to their fellow Christians of other religious communions for all their sympathy and help in this sublime achievement. Candor compels me to repeat that much of the sympathy of other religious leaders in that early struggle was on the side of legalized ecclesiastical privilege. Much of the time were Baptists pitiably lonely in their age-long struggle. We would now and always make our most grateful acknowledgment to any and all who came to the side of our Baptist fathers, whether early or late, in this destiny determining struggle. But I take it that every informed man on the subject, whatever his religious faith, will be willing to pay tribute to our Baptist people as being the chief instrumentality in God's hands in winning the battle in America for religious liberty. . . .

The Present Call.

And now, my fellow Christians, and fellow citizens, what is the present call to us in connection with the priceless principle of religious liberty? That principle, with all the history and heritage accompanying it, imposes upon us obligations to the last degree meaningful and responsible. Let us today and forever be highly resolved that the principle of religious liberty shall, please God, be preserved inviolate through all our days and the days of those who come after us. . . .

Liberty Not Abused.

It behooves us now and ever to see to it that liberty is not abused. Well may we listen to the call of Paul, that mightiest Christian of the long centuries, as he says: "Brethren, ye have been called unto liberty: only use not your liberty for an occasion to the flesh, but by love serve one another." This ringing declaration should be heard and heeded by every class and condition of people throughout all our wide stretching nation.

It is the word to be heeded by religious teachers, and by editors, and by legislators, and by everybody else. Nowhere is liberty to be used "for an occasion to the flesh." We will take free speech and a free press, with all their excrescences and perils, because of the high meaning of freedom, but we are to set ourselves with all diligence not to use these great privileges in the shaming of liberty. A free press—how often does it pervert its high privilege! . . .

Things Worth Dying For.

When this nation went into the world war a little while ago, after her long and patient and fruitless effort to find another way of conserving righteousness, the note was sounded in every nook and corner of our country that some things in this world are worth dying for, and if they are worth dying for they are worth living for. What are some of the things worth dying for? The sanctity of womanhood is worth dying for. The safety of childhood is worthy dying for, and when Germany put to death that first helpless Belgian child she was marked for defeat and doom. The integrity of one's country is worth dying for. And, please God, the freedom and honor of the United States of America are worth dying for. If the great things of life are worth dying for, they are surely worth living for. . . .

A League of Nations.

. . . Standing here today on the steps of our Nation's capitol, hard by the chamber of the Senate of the United States, I dare to say as a citizen and as a Christian teacher, that the moral forces of the United States of America, without regard to political parties, will never rest until there is a worthy League of Nations. I dare to express also the unhesitating belief that the unquestioned majorities of both great political parties in this country regard the delay in the working out of a League of Nations as a national and worldwide tragedy.

The moral and religious forces of this country could not be supine and inactive as long as the saloon, the chief rendezvous of small politicians, that chronic criminal and standing anachronism of our modern civilization, was legally sponsored by the state. I can certify all the politicians of all the political parties that the legalized saloon has gone from American life, and gone to stay. Likewise, I can certify the men of all political parties, without any reference to partisan politics, that the same moral and religious forces of this country, because of the inexorable moral issues involved, cannot be silent and will not be silent until there is put forth a League of Nations that will strive with all its might to put an end to the diabolism and measureless horrors of war. I thank God that the stricken man yonder in the White House has pleaded long and is pleading yet that our nation will take her full part with the others for the bringing in of that blessed day when wars shall cease to the ends of the earth. . . .

The Right Kind of Christians.

This noble doctrine and heritage of religious liberty calls to us imperiously to be the right kind of Christians. Let us never forget that a democracy, whether civil or religious, has not only its perils, but has also its unescapable obligations. A democracy calls for intelligence. The sure foundations of states must be laid, not in ignorance, but in knowledge. It is of the last importance that those who rule shall be properly trained. In a democracy, a government of the people, for the people, and by the people, the people are the rulers, and the people, all the people, are to be informed and trained.

My fellow Christians, we must hark back to our Christian schools, and see to it that these schools are put on worthy and enduring foundations. A democracy needs more than intelligence, it needs Christ. He is the light of the world, nor is there any other sufficient light for the world. He is the solution of the world's complex questions, the one adequate Helper for its dire needs, the one only sufficient Saviour for our sinning race. Our schools are afresh to take note of this supreme fact, and they are to be fundamentally and aggressively Christian. Wrong education brought on the recent world war. Such education will always lead to disaster. . . .

The Christian School.

The time has come when, as never before, our beloved denomination should worthily go out to its world task as a teaching denomination. That means that there should be a crusade throughout all our borders for the vitalizing and strengthening of our Christian schools. The only complete education, in the nature of the case, is Christian education, because man is a tripartite being. By the very genius of our government, education by the state cannot be complete. Wisdom has fled from us if we fail to magnify, and magnify now, our Christian schools. These schools go to the foundation of all the life of the people. They are dispensable to the highest efficiency of the churches. Their inspirational influences are of untold value to the schools conducted by the state, to which schools also we must ever give our best support. . . .

The one transcending inspiring influence in civilization is the Christian religion. By all means, let the teachers and trustees and student bodies of all our Christian schools remember this supremely important fact, that civilization without Christianity is doomed. Let there be no pagan ideals in our Christian schools, and no hesitation or apology for the insistence that the one hope for the individual, the one hope for society, for civilization, is in the Christian religion. If ever the drum beat of duty sounded clearly, it is calling to us now to strengthen and magnify our Christian schools.

The Task of Evangelism.

Preceding and accompanying the task of building our Christian schools, we must keep faithfully and practically in mind our primary task of evangelism, the work of winning souls from sin unto salvation, from Satan unto God. This work takes precedence of all other work in the Christian program. Salvation for sinners is through Jesus Christ alone, nor is there any other name or way under heaven whereby they may be saved. Our churches, our schools, our religious papers, our hospitals, every organization and agency of the churches should be kept aflame with the passion of New Testament evangelism. . . .

A World Program.

While thus caring for the homeland, we are at the same time to see to it that our program is co-extensive with Christ's program for the whole world. The whole world is our field, nor may we, with impunity, dare to be indifferent to any section, however remote, . . .

A Glorious Day.

Glorious it is, my fellow Christians, to be living in such a day as this, if only we shall live as we ought to live. Irresistible is the conviction that the immediate future is packed with amazing possibilities. We can understand the cry of Rupert Brooke as he sailed from Gallipoli, "Now God be thanked who hath matched us with this hour!" The day of the reign of the common people is everywhere coming like the rising tides of the ocean. The people are everywhere breaking with feudalism. Autocracy is passing, whether it be civil or ecclesiastical. Democracy is the goal toward which all feet are traveling, whether in state or in church. . . .

The Price To Be Paid.

Are we willing to pay the price that must be paid to secure for humanity the blessings they need to have? We say that we have seen God in the face of Jesus Christ, that we have been born again, that we are the true friends of Christ, and would make proof of our friendship for Him by doing His will. Well, then, what manner of people ought we to be in all holy living and godliness? Surely we should be a holy people, remembering the apostolic characterization, "Ye are a chosen generation, a royal priesthood, an holy nation, a peculiar people: That we should shew forth the praises of Him who hath called you out of darkness into His marvelous light, who in time past were not a people but are now the people of God."

Let us look again to the strange passion and power of the early Christians. They paid the price for spiritual power. Mark well this record: "And they overcame him by the blood of the Lamb, and by the word of their testimony; and they loved not their lives unto the death." O my fellow Christians, if we are to be in the true succession of the mighty days and deeds of the early Christian era, or of those mighty days and deeds of our Baptist fathers in later days, then selfish ease must be utterly renounced for Christ and His cause, and our every gift and grace and power utterly dominated by the dynamic of His cross. Standing here today in the shadow of our country's capitol, compassed about as we are with so great a cloud of witnesses, let us today renew our pledge to God, and to one another, that we will give our best to church and to state, to God and to humanity, by His grace and power, until we fall on the last sleep. . . .

15.6 Lawsuit Concerning North Rocky Mount Baptist Church, Rocky Mount, North Carolina, 1954

A Baptist church determines its own doctrine and practice, but when property ownership is contested the civil courts have jurisdiction. Several celebrated court cases involving Baptist churches in America date back to the 1700s, but one of the most important involved the North Rocky Mount Baptist Church in North Carolina in 1954. The court's decision hinged on whether the majority of members had a right to cause the church to withdraw from Southern Baptist affiliation, thus, in effect, changing the denomination of the church. Local courts affirmed that in a Baptist church the majority of members rules, but the state high court reversed that verdict and gave the property to the minority on the grounds that they, no matter how few, continued to constitute the church. This precedent has enormous significance for any litigation involving Baptist churches. *Source:* Advance Sheets of Cases Argued and Determined in the Supreme Court of North Carolina, 241, 3:201-215.

7. Same—Part of congregation which remains true to faith, customs, usages and practices accepted by both factions prior to dissension, is entitled to control and management of church property.

The evidence in this case to the effect that the majority of the congregation of the Missionary Baptist Church in question had ceased to participate in the general programs and activities of the Association and the Baptist Conventions, had resolved that, after ceasing its affiliation with the State and Southern Associations, the Church should continue its ministry as an independent Baptist Church, had ceased to use religious literature furnished by the Convention, had given its pastor exclusive control of the pulpit, had discharged officers and Sunday School teachers who voted against such action, etc., *is held* sufficient to support the conclusion that by such acts the majority had diverted the use of the church property to customs, doctrines and practices radically and fundamentally opposed to the characteristic usages, customs, doctrines and practices recognized and accepted by both factions of the congregation before dissension arose, and judgment that the minority, which had continued to support the usages, customs, doctrines, and practices recognized and accepted by both factions prior to the dissension, were entitled to the control and management of the property, is affirmed. The conclusion of the trial court that the true congregation is that which adheres and submits to the regular order of the Church is modified in accordance with the above.

APPEAL by the defendants from *Paul, Special Judge,* Special December Civil Term 1953 of NASH.

Action brought by plaintiffs for possession and control of the church property of the North Rocky Mount Missionary Baptist Church, and to restrain the defendants from interfering with the use and control of said church and its properties.

Pursuant to G. S. N. C. 1-184 a jury trial was waived. After hearing the evidence and argument of counsel the judge found the facts, stated separately his conclusions of law, and entered judgment as follows: that the individual defendants have ceased to be a part of the true congregation of the North Rocky Mount Missionary Baptist Church, and are not entitled to share in the use and possession of the church property; that the plaintiffs and all other members of said church who adhere and submit to the regular order of the church, local and general, are the true congregation, and entitled to the use and possession of the church property; that the individual defendants be, and they are hereby enjoined from interfering with the use and possession of said church property by the true congregation.

The defendants appealed . . . .

This question is presented for decision upon the Record before us: Have the defendants, and those united with them, as against a faithful minority, diverted the property of the North Rocky Mount Missionary Baptist Church to the support of usages, customs, doctrines and practices radically and fundamentally opposed to the characteristic usages, customs, doctrines and practices recognized and accepted by both factions of the congregation of this particular church before the dissension between them arose?

While it is true the membership of the North Rocky Mount Missionary Baptist Church is a self-governing unit, a majority of its membership is supreme and is entitled to control its church property only so long as the majority remains true to the fundamental faith, usages, customs, and practices of this particular church, as accepted by both factions before the dispute arose. . . .

A majority of the membership of the North Rocky Mount Missionary Baptist Church may not, as against a faithful minority, divert the property of that church to another denomination, or to the support of doctrines, usages, customs and practices radically and fundamentally opposed to the characteristic doctrines, usages, customs and practices of that particular church, recognized and accepted by both factions before the dissension, for in such an event the real identity of the church is no longer lodged with the majority group, but resides with the minority adhering to its fundamental faith, usages, customs and practices, before the dissension, who, though small in numbers, are entitled to hold and control the entire property of the church. . . .

CONCLUSIONS OF LAW.

Property rights being involved, the Court has jurisdiction to hear and determine such rights.

That in the North Rocky Mount Missionary Baptist Church the church property belongs to the true congregation, who are entitled to its possession.

That the true congregation in church organizations is those who adhere and submit to the regular order of the church, local and general, whether a majority or minority of membership.

That the individual defendants in this action have departed from the fundamental usages, customs, doctrine, practice and organization of the North Rocky Mount Missionary Baptist Church and of the denomination, and that said defendants refuse to adhere and submit to the regular order of the church, and are, therefore, not a part of the true congregation of said church.

That the plaintiffs have remained true to the fundamental usages, customs, doctrine, practice and organization of the North Rocky Mount Missionary Baptist Church and of the denomination, and that they do adhere and submit to the regular order of the church, and that they are, therefore, a part of the true congregation.

That the defendants should be enjoined and restrained from interference with the use and possession of the church property by the true congregation.

It is apparent that the Trial Judge has designated certain matters as Findings of Fact, which should be designated Conclusions of Law.

The findings of fact stated above are supported by adequate competent evidence.

The Rev. Samuel H. W. Johnston testifying with respect to the practices, customs, doctrine and usages of Southern Baptists said, p. 411 of the Record: "If what we have seen is significant of what Southern Baptists stand for, I don't want any part of it. I'll never quit preaching the truth. I will fight this till the day I die. I will denounce evil wherever I find it, and the Baptist organization in the South is rotten to the core."

Dr. R. T. Ketcham, a national representative of the General Association of Regular Baptist Churches and editor of their official organ, testified as a witness for the defendants that his association holds to the view of premillennialism, that the millennial question has been made a test of fellowship by virtue of the fact that his association puts a premillennial interpretation of Art. 17 of the Baptist Faith and Message, and that a post millennial church has never applied for fellowship in his association.

The Conclusion of Law made in this case: "That the true congregation in church organizations is those who adhere and submit to the regular order of the church, local and general, whether a majority or minority of membership" is not a correct statement of the law, under the pleadings and facts before us.

In the instant case there is no allegation in the complaint that the North Rocky Mount Missionary Baptist Church has been at all times governed and conducted by the rules, customs and practices of Missionary Baptist Churches in general, nor have the defendants made any such admission. The Record before us discloses that the North Rocky Mount Missionary Baptist Church from the beginning has been a pure democracy and independent of any external control. It is known to all that from the beginning Baptist Churches have retained, and refused to give up their independence.

The proper conclusion of law in this case is that the true congregation of the North Rocky Mount Missionary Baptist Church consists of those members of its congregation who adhere to the characteristic doctrines, usages, customs and practices of that particular church, recognized and accepted by both factions before the dissension between them arose. . . .

The defendants contend in their brief that "an examination of this Record discloses that the only difference that exists between the plaintiffs and defendants in this action is continued cooperation and affiliation with the State and Southern Baptist Conventions." The defendants, therefore, contend that the rule that the majority of an independent or congregational society may not divert the property from the denomination to which the society belongs, or from the fundamental doctrines and tenets to which it originally subscribed, does not prevent such a majority, over the objection of a minority, from severing a voluntary ecclesiastical connection of the society from another body. 45 Am. Jur., Religious Societies, p. 766; Anno. 8 A.L.R. 123; Anno. 70 A.L.R. 86; *Organ Meeting House v. Seaford*, 16 N.C. 453. In the *Organ Meeting House Case* the bill charged a part of the members composing the Lutheran Church adopted a general synod, a form of church government previously unknown to the Lutheran Church. In our opinion, as we view the evidence in the Record, far more serious differences exist.

The defendants, and those united in interest with them, have done the following things:

One. They have ceased to participate in the general programs and activities of the

Roanoke Baptist Association, the North Carolina State Baptist Convention and the Southern Baptist Convention, and have withdrawn their financial support of these agencies and institutions in their Co-operativeProgram, except support of the Baptist Orphanage, contrary to what the North Rocky Mount Missionary Baptist Church did before the dissension in the congregation began.

Two. They have resolved that the North Rocky Mount Missionary Baptist Church, after such cessation of affiliation with the local, State and Southern associations, shall continue its ministry in the community as an Independent Baptist Church.

Three. They have stopped the use of Sunday School and Religious Literature prepared and approved by the Southern Baptist Convention, and are using Sunday School and Religious Literature prepared and published by the General Association of Regular Baptist Churches, an association, which, according to the testimony of Dr. R. T. Ketcham, its national representative and editor of its official organ, holds to the view of premillennialism, and that the millennial question has been made a test of fellowship. This is contrary to what the North Rocky Mount Missionary Baptist Church did before the dispute in the congregation arose.

Four. The Board of Deacons have approved and agreed that the Rev. Samuel H. W. Johnston shall have exclusive control of the pulpit, with power to say who shall, and who shall not, occupy the same, contrary to the custom and practice of this particular church before the dissension began.

Five. They have discharged several of the North Rocky Mount Missionary Baptist Church officers and Sunday School teachers for the reason they opposed and voted against the Resolution adopted on 9 August 1953 by an affirmative vote of 241 members against a negative vote of 144, with 200 abstaining from voting, out of an enrolled membership of approximately 1,300 persons.

Six. The Rev. Samuel H. W. Johnston has done all he could to separate himself as far as possible from the programs of the North Carolina State Baptist Convention and the Southern Baptist Convention, until such time as certain things he called "evils" are rectified.

The plaintiffs, and those united in interest with them, have done these things:

One. Have since 9 August 1953 regularly conducted meetings elsewhere than in the North Rocky Mount Baptist Church, with an ordained minister in the pulpit.

Two. Have continued to use the Sunday School and Religious Literature prepared and published by the Southern Baptist Convention.

Three. Have continued to participate in, operate with, and support the programs and activities of the Roanoke Baptist Association, the North Carolina Baptist Convention and the Southern Baptist Convention.

Four. Have circumspectly and carefully done exactly what the membership of the North Rocky Mount Missionary Baptist Church did before dispute between the factions arose.

The defendants, and those united in interest with them, by resolving that the North Rocky Mount Missionary Baptist Church shall continue its ministry in the community as an Independent Missionary Baptist Church, and by doing the things found as facts by the Trial Judge, as set forth in this opinion, and by being in possession of and using the church property for those purposes and plans have, as against the plaintiffs, and those united in interest with them, who are a faithful minority, diverted the property of the North Rocky Mount Missionary Baptist Church to the support of usages, customs, doctrines and practices radically and fundamentally opposed to the characteristic usages, customs, doctrines and practices recognized and accepted by both factions of the congregation of this particular church before the dissension between them arose.

The defendants contend that the court erred in taxing the costs against the individual defendants, for the reason that the defendants individually are not parties to the action. The court's ruling seems to be correct for it would appear that these parties are sued as individuals, and the title of the positions they hold are merely *descriptio personae*.

The evidence in the Record discloses that the Rev. Samuel H. W. Johnston was the person, who inspired and led the movement, which caused the dissension in the North Rocky Mount Missionary Baptist Church. The evidence clearly shows the purpose of this movement. David Braswell, a member of this church, testified as a witness for the plaintiffs (R., p. 196): "At the last of March or the first of April Mr. Johnston was around at my house. We were discussing the church situation in general, and he made the remark that when he got his business lined up, he was going to pull the church out of the Convention, and run it like he wanted to run it." A. J. Silberhorn, a witness for the plaintiffs and a member of this church testified (R., p. 154): "At a Deacons' meeting a week or two before the actual voting of the withdrawal from the Southern Baptist Convention one of the Deacons asked this question of the Pastor, and I believe I can quote it in his words. He says, 'Pastor, what are we going to do after we withdraw from the Southern Baptist Convention? Don't you think we ought to have something prepared in which to present to the people?' and the Pastor answered, 'Yes, I plan that as soon as the voting is over, that I announce to the congregation that we apply for fellowship in the General Assembly of Regular Baptist Churches.'" David Lewis, a member of the church, testified as a witness for the plaintiffs that G. W. Stoglin, one of the defendants, told him prior to the meeting of 9 August 1953 (R., p. 168): "That their plans were to withdraw from the Southern Baptist Convention and State Baptist Convention, and form a new Independent Baptist Church and affiliate themselves with the General Association of Regular Baptists."

We have carefully examined and considered all the defendants' assignments of error, including the authorities cited in their brief, and the defendants have not shown prejudicial error sufficient to justify another trial of this long and bitterly contested case. The heat of conflict is over, and the time has come in the Rocky Mount Missionary Baptist Church for the exercise of the Christian graces of reconciliation, forbearance, brotherly love and unity, according to the admonition given by the Apostle Paul to the Church at Corinth.

The lower court ordered, adjudged and decreed: "That the plaintiffs and all other members of said church who adhere and submit to the regular order of the church, local and general, are the true congregation." That part of the judgment will be modified to read as follows: "That the true congregation of the North Rocky Mount Missionary Baptist Church consists of the plaintiffs and all other members of the congregation who adhere and submit to the characteristic doctrines, usages, customs and practices of this particular church, recognized and accepted by both factions of the congregation before the dissension between them arose."

We conclude that the court's findings of fact were supported by competent evidence, and that they are sufficient to sustain the judgment, as herein modified, based thereon. *Woody v. Barnett, supra.*

Judgment modified and affirmed.

15.7 Church Music and Worship

Those who assess differences between Northern and Southern Baptists often overlook the diverse worship patterns in the two groups. In the nineteenth century while Baptists in the North issued hymnals and formal hymns based on the music tradition of Lowell Mason, most Baptists in the South sang the informal gospel songs of the Sacred Harp tradition. However, in the 1940s Southern Baptists stepped up efforts to upgrade their church music. They issued the *Broadman Hymnal* in 1940, put new emphasis upon the Convention's Church Music Department, and urged local churches to give more attention to worship. Reports to the Convention on "Church Music and Worship" illustrate these trends in Southern Baptist worship. *Source: Annual,* SBC, 1941, 120-122.

In the Baltimore Convention last year the work of the committee on Church Music was enlarged to include all phases of worship. Specific instruction was given to a new committee of seven "to study not only the subject of Church Music but the approach to, and furtherance of, a deepened spiritual and reverential conception in all phases of worship in the churches and their organized life throughout the Southern Baptist Convention."

This order of the Convention, it will be recognized, is one of great importance. It is to be interpreted as meaning that there is serious and widespread dissatisfaction with present conditions among us, also a deep desire for a more vital, beautiful, dynamical, commanding worship in Baptist churches. The problem, in our judgment, was correctly apprehended by last year's committee, in that they construed it to involve, basically first of all, our conception of true worship itself, and then the expression of sincere reverence and real spirituality in this worship, to be attended by a much larger per centage of our people.

That conditions in respect to the demands of worship among us represent a low ebb must be generally admitted. Mournfully we confess that apparently we are in one of the historic, periodic slumps in true worship. There was such a decline in the time of the Old Testament prophets, again in the days of Jesus, later in Europe at the outbreak of the Protestant Reformation, yet again during the French Revolution, still again most grievously in England prior to the Wesleyan Revival, also notably in Russia beginning with the regime of Lenin, yet again tragically in Germany with the rise of Hitler, and now once more deplorably in America.

Baptists, leading all other groups in the South, have ample cause to view gravely their situation. Perhaps one of the most highly developed and spiritually effective state bodies of our entire eighteen is North Carolina. Secretary Huggins, in cooperation with pastors in that state, is just now conducting a most challenging campaign of three months in behalf of vitalized worship in the churches. He reports: "Baptists in North Carolina number, according to latest information, more than 500,000. Most of these are above twelve years of age. Of our total membership only twenty-five per cent are regular in their attendance upon the worship services of the church. This means that on any given Sunday morning there are *present* in our churches 150,000, *absent* 350,000. . . . There are, perhaps, in North Carolina 500,000 souls to whom God and Christ means little or nothing, with, perhaps, 500,000 in the churches of all other denominations." Can we who live outside North Carolina boast a better showing. No. It is feared that in many of our states the situation is far worse.

Helpful as the enumeration and elaboration of different causes for this deplorable decline in support of church worship might be, we must center our investigation in this report upon one, that of worship itself. Does our worship fail to attract and hold our people because of fatal defects in it? Are the materials used too poor? Does it lack in impressiveness and vitality? Is it deficient in unity, coherence, beauty? Are its shortcomings chiefly musical? Or is the congregational participation short? Or is the whole order unstudied, that is, either a copy of dead traditions or a hodgepodge of prayers, hymns and preachments unrelated to each other or to life as it pulses today? These and other pertinent questions press for intelligent answer.

In seeking the right answer, we consider first what is a sound and Scriptural pattern of true worship. It would seem that an undoubted outline would combine the three elements of Adoration, Communion and Dedication. As to Adoration, the very word "worship" means to adore, to exalt, to bow down to, to deify, to pray to. Our Saviour taught us to begin our prayers with the hallowing of God's name. Adoration, all agree, is a prime essential of true worship. The second element is Communion, that of our surrender to God, of whose presence we become vividly aware in our worship, by which communion God gives himself to us, speaks to us and endures us with his vision and power. The third element is Dedication. After first adoring the living God, then listening to his voice in Scripture, sermon, song, meditation and prayer, we come finally to dedication, wherein we gather the ragged ends of our lives together and say, "From now on, O God, we offer ourselves and pledge ourselves to live and give, that thy Kingdom may come and thy will be done on earth."

In order to realize and achieve to the fullest such meaning in our worship, pastor and people must make the best possible preparation. The preacher will seek by study and prayer to prepare his sermon, which in our conception can never be dispensed with or minimized, for preaching is ordained of God as one of the major means of his grace. Surely we are agreed that the sermon should be no sensation-mongering, no mere jabbering of current comment, no formless, shapeless gruel, peppered with personal anecdotes and sacrilegious use of the Lord's precious name, but an authentic message from God, wrought with the finest art of which the preacher is capable under the Holy Spirit.

But the sermon is not the only part of the worship which should receive careful preparation. In our justifiable recoil from fixed, liturgical forms of prayer prevailing in ritualistic churches, we may yet unconsciously lapse into slovenly habits of prayer-expression which are just as fixed, or else we may fall victims to a sloppy emotionalism. Avoiding these errors, there should be profound spiritual preparation for public prayer.

In like manner much care should be given to the presentation of God's Word, whether it be in the form of responsive reading or by the minister alone. In any case it should be read as it was in the days of Ezra: "They read in the book of the law of God distinctly, and gave the sense, and caused them to understand the reading" (Nehemiah 8:8).

One of the most significant acts of true worship is the offering. Diligent preparation should be made to insure that it will serve as a means of worship. The negligible manner in which the offering is frequently taken tends to play it down miserably. Unashamedly, definitely let us make of the offering a prominent, glorified part of our worship. . . .

Concerning the ordinances, it need only be pointed out that they should be Scripturally interpreted and reverently, beautifully, meaningfully administered. . . .

We come now to the musical part of our worship, a matter which has been the subject of report before this Convention for the past several years. It is heartening to observe that here we have much to record in the way of progress and good ground for hope of improvement. Music occupies from a third to a half of all our church exercises, including the preaching, teaching, training, prayer, missionary and evangelistic services. It is being no longer regarded as a stepchild of the worship. Instead of begrudging time to musical performance, instead of tolerating secular-minded choristers who may have professional training but little understanding of true worship, or else allowing a type of trashy songs which often sadden or anger the thoughtful worshipper, Southern Baptists are awakening to an appreciation of noble, worshipful music. Evidence of this is seen in the fact that ten of our Baptist state conventions now hear annual reports on church music. Just as they have made denominational inquiry into and financial provision for aids to better preaching, Bible teaching, soulwinning, Church training, so they would look into and provide for good music in their worship. In some states, as in the case of North Carolina already cited in this paper, the executive boards are addressing themselves definitely to the task.

Another evidence of progress is the growing revolt against nondescript songbooks which specialize in the sort-of-swing tunes that find the feet and not the heart and utilize words which are neither literary nor Scriptural, such songbooks as are peddled by commercial publishers who for profit victimize many congregations. Our churches are requiring hymnbooks which have been competently edited for supplying the needs of real worship. Still another evidence of this progress is the growing ability of our children to sing the great hymns of the ages, those tried and proven, because they have been taught in the public schools to sing them. Joined with the public school systems in the effort to correct low musical ideals have been our Baptist Training Unions which have incorporated training in religious music in their weekly programs. We hail this wide training as honoring the genius of Baptist churches, which exalt personal religion and congregational participation in worship and all phases of church activities. We do not forget that Catholics very early in their history abolished congregational singing because of unworthy musical execution and have since confined church music to the clergy and choir. Baptists would not wish to do away with noble choirs as an aid to soulful worship, but they would rue the day when their congregations ceased to sing.

More gratifying evidence of progress in respect to church music is noted in the correlation of instruction in our denominational schools with that of our churches, in the training of musical leaders and of religious choirs. Most heartening of all is the fine work of our Sunday School Board in planning for rural church education in church music and in arranging a Music Emphasis Conference at Ridgecrest under the direction of its music editor, B. B. McKinney, scheduled for July 26-August 1. When two years ago this Convention asked the Sunday School Board to make a survey of music in our Southern Baptist churches, it secured beneficial results which will be increasingly realized.

Much, however, remains to be undertaken. Your committee, rejoicing in what has been accomplished, would urge that we press forward toward other highly desirable improvements in our worship and music. Two recommendations seem to us to be advisable:

First, that this Convention, welcoming the response of our denominational schools to the suggestion of correlating their musical instruction with the training undertaken in our churches, call upon them to extend in whatever ways may seem wise this instruction-correlation to the end that our denomination may be furnished with better standards, higher appreciation of good religious music, more general training in rendition, and that it may be equipped with more good musical leaders in the churches.

Second, finding no authorized, strictly Southern Baptist hymnal in existence and believing there would be large advantage in providing our churches with one suited to the needs of our people, wherever they may choose to use it, we recommend that the Sunday School Board through its appointment of a competent, representative committee, take under advisement the creation of the proposed hymnal and report its findings a year hence.

Respectfully submitted,

J. M. Dawson, Chairman	T. Eugene West
R. J. Bateman	E. A. Patterson
Alwyn Howell	H. Grady Daniel
Adiel J. Moncrief, Jr.	

15.8   Statement of Faith, Foreign Mission Board, SBC, 1920

In response to doctrinal agitation, the Foreign Mission Board of the SBC adopted a doctrinal statement in 1920 to guide its mission appointees. Though brief, the confession is fairly complete. Unlike the confession adopted by the SBC five years later, the Board's statement does not follow the New Hampshire Confession. The doctrinal articles are followed by a lengthy statement on Southern Baptist relation to the ecumenical movement, a matter of some concern at that time. *Source: Annual,* SBC, 1920, 196-199.

The Board would submit here a Statement of Belief which was unanimously adopted at its annual meetimg last June for the guidance of young men and women who shall be appointed by this Board to represent the denomination in Christian service and witness-bearing on the fields of our activities. This statement is as follows:

A Statement of Belief.—All missionaries of the Foreign Mission Board of the Southern Baptist Convention are expected to read carefully and subscribe to the following statement of belief before they are appointed to missionary service under this Board.

I believe and am prepared to teach the following:

I.   I believe that the Holy Scriptures of the Old and New Testaments were written by men who were divinely inspired and that they are a sufficient and final authority in all matters of religious faith and practice;

II.   That there is one and only one living and true God who is revealed as Father, Son and Holy Spirit;

III.   That the virgin birth, the deity, the vicarious death, the bodily resurrection and the Second Coming of Jesus Christ are plainly taught in the Scriptures;

IV.   That in his natural state, man is depraved and without true holiness;

V.   That salvation is wholly of grace through Jesus Christ;

VI.   That on condition of personal repentance for sin and faith in the Lord Jesus Christ any man can receive the forgiveness of sin and salvation unto everlasting life;

VII.   That regeneration is necessary to spiritual life in Christ, and that this change is effected by the direct action of the Holy Spirit upon the heart of each individual who exercises personal faith in Jesus Christ;

VIII.   That sanctification is the process by which, between regeneration and glorification, the spiritual life of the believer is deepened, and he grows in grace and the knowledge of our Lord and Saviour Jesus Christ;

IX.   That a church is a company of voluntarily associated baptized believers in Christ, recognizing Him as the only Head of the church, exercising only such administrative and disciplinary authority as He has committed to it, conducting holy worship, observing the ordinances as He has commanded, and seeking by co-operative effort to extend His Kingdom in all the world;

X.   I believe in the evangelical view of the ordinances. They were appointed to show the Lord's death and resurrection. They are not sacraments. They do not expiate sin; they exhibit the atonement. Baptism is not a means of salvation but a symbol of Christ's resurrection. The Lord's Supper is not a social feast, but a memorial of Christ's death. We are not to observe it to show our amiability, but do it in remembrance of Him. I will observe and teach these ordinances in accordance with the views and customs common among Southern Baptists;

XI.   I believe that the Lord's Day or Christian Sabbath should be sacredly observed by all Christian believers everywhere;

XII.   That civil government being ordained of God, due obedience and subjection should be rendered to the government under which I may live and that prayers should be offered for rulers; but that God alone is Lord of the conscience and He has left the soul free to worship after its own dictates;

XIII. That there will be a resurrection and future judgment and that believers in Christ will go to a place of eternal happiness and unbelievers to everlasting condemnation.

I accept the following Pronouncement on Christian union and co-operation which has been adopted by the Foreign Mission Board and the Southern Baptist Convention, and will seek to promote harmony and unity in the denomination at home and in the mission to which I am sent, and will co-operate with my fellow-missionaries in advancing the cause of Christ and the denomination along lines thus fixed for the Board and its Missionaries:

"1. This Board has not and will not enter into nor be committed to any compact by which arbitrary territorial boundaries or divisions are fixed for its missionary operations. Such division of territory being a part of a general program of federation, and it being impossible for this Board to recognize divisions thus arbitrarily made, we must decline participation in such program. The Board and its missionaries will in the future, as in the past, endeavor to exercise wisdom and Christian courtesy as well as conscience in such matters; will seek to conserve economy of labor and money in locating its forces, and with due regard to need, opportunity, and probable results, but cannot consent to have any limitations fixed upon the Commission under which it operates, nor be put in a position which would forbid its loyalty and faithfulness to any company of Christian converts who may now or hereafter profess a "like precious faith with us."

"2. We cannot subscribe to any agreement providing for an interchange of church letters contrary to the recognized custom among the Baptist churches of the South. The churches which are supporting the work of this Board have a well-known standard of qualification for church membership, and we shall seek to foster this standard in every land where this Board sends its missionaries.

"3. This Board will not engage in any form of co-operation, hospital, publication, educational or other missionary activity, which is not fully reported to the Convention, and which does not meet the approval of the convention, under the auspices of which it operates and to the instructions of which it is subject. We esteem it to be a matter of primary importance that this Board be in a position to control, or control jointly with other Baptist bodies, the religious instruction which is given boys and girls entrusted to its care. This is necessary in order to safeguard what we believe to be our message to the world.

"4. To avoid an exhaustive enumeration, and yet to make the statement comprehensive, we add, that we shall seek to foster a policy abroad which is consistent with the denominational policy at home, and no pressure will be allowed to swerve the Board from its course. We make these declarations for the information of our people at home, and with the view of saving the scattered missionaries of this Board all possible embarrassment and confusion from such pressure.

"Again, we would remind all that Southern Baptists are on record by repeated action of the Convention in recognition of that spiritual unity which exists among all believers in Christ, and in favor of their organic union as soon as it can be perfected on New Testament lines. We re-affirm these sentiments. We would have all our people recognize the bonds of brotherhood which unite Christians of every name, cultivate a large spirit of fraternity and strive together with others to secure the closest possible impact of our common Christianity upon the social order for the establishment of righteousness in the earth. We would, however, admonish our people at home and abroad to remain true to New Testament principles of faith and church policy, and by so doing, seek to preserve the unity of the denomination, enlist all our forces for the holy cause of missions, and thus insure the integrity, support and success of this work."

This Statement, though much briefer, will be found to be in accord with the Fraternal Address which was prepared by the Committee of which Dr. Mullins was chairman, and which has had such cordial welcome and approval. It attempts to state only a sort of "irreducible minimum" of truth, a synopsis of the faith which is common among our people. It was adopted unanimously by the full Board in annual session, and with the purpose of promoting unity on the mansion fields. Its value to this end is perhaps as great in what is omitted as in that which is included in the Statement. The Board does not require anyone to sign it, but does present it to all volunteers for mission service before they are appointed to any field by the Board, and it expects all such to respect it in their teaching and practice on the mission field. Those who are sent to the fields are necessarily young and go forth before they are enured to contrary winds of doctrine. They are thrust forth into a strange environment where new and unfamiliar influences are felt, and have need to be fortified against them. Scattered on remote fields where communication with the home constituency is only occasional, they do not have opportunity for conference and the advantage of counsel such as the young enjoy at home. Some such statement as this has been found necessary to facilitate the examination of the frequently large numbers of applicants in the midst of crowded Board sessions, as well as to satisfy the Board that it is not sending to the field those who will inject discord into their stations, or promulgate on the field doctrines which are not acceptable to the churches at home which support the work. This Statement, together with the Fraternal Address, may have value for our Baptist people everywhere as suggestive of the common bonds of faith, and a basis for Baptist federation and a missionary program.

15.9   John Franklyn Norris and Southern Baptists

Few people have had a greater impact upon Southern Baptists than did the "Texas Cyclone," John Franklyn Norris (1877-1952). Pastor of Fort Worth's First Baptist Church from 1909 to 1952, Norris became the major leader of fundamentalism in Southern Baptists life. He teamed up with W. B. Riley of Minneapolis and T. T. Shields of Toronto in what proved to be an unsuccessful effort to unite Baptist fundamentalism into one movement. After Norris was excluded from Southern Baptist life, he formed his own independent denomination, remnants of which still exist.

The following documents illustrate various phases of the life and impact of J. Frank Norris. Selection A includes two letters about his background. E. P. Kirkland knew the Norris family and watched young Frank grow up. This lends a note of authenticity to Kirkland's comments on Norris's background. Kirkland's letter was sent to F. S. Groner, then executive secretary of the Baptist General Convention of Texas, which had suffered much from the disruptive attacks of Norris. The original letter, written in pencil on lined tablet paper, contains many grammatical errors but is reproduced exactly. In his perfunctory reply, Groner was correct in his assessment that Norris would soon split off, but erred in thinking that Norris had little support in Texas. Selection B cites a letter of Norris to his archenemy, Lee Rutland Scarborough, president of Southwestern Baptist Theological Seminary of Fort Worth. *Sources*: Original letters or copies in J. Frank Norris File, A. Webb Roberts Library, Southwestern Baptist Theological Seminary, Fort Worth, Texas.

A.   Letters on the Background of J. Frank Norris

(1) From E. P. Kirkland to F. S. Groner, 1922

J. Frank Norris never in accord with the organized work of the Convention Baptist

J. Frank Norris was a member of the Baptist Church at Hubbard, Hill Co. Texas, and was Licensed by that Church to preach. The Mt. Antiock Church called him to its pastorate, and in a Short time the Church at Mt. Antiock called for his Ordination. At a 5th Sunday Board meeting at Hubbard it was announced that at 3 O'clock Sunday evening J. Frank Norris would be Ordained to the full Ministerial work.

I taken dinner that day with the Pastor Rev. Cat Smith.[1] After dinner the Subject of Ordination was mentioned, and the Pastor Said that he would not take any part in the Ordination, as J. Frank Norris "was too recently from the Campbellites, and that he was a Haydenite,"[2] and did not come to the Church house that evening. I remained at the meeting until the Ordaining Presbytery was organized, and as I was not well I left for home so as to reach home before night fall.

The Ordaining Council was composed of Revs W. T. Compere, R. A. Cox, Moore, and Scott, possibly others, all B. M. A. Preachers.[3]

Very soon after his Ordination Norris entered Baylor University, and the Board of Deacons of the Mt. Calm Baptist Church, who was dominated by Haydenite asked Rev. J. L. Walker the then Pastor to resign, which he did, and the Mt. Calm Church Called J. Frank Norris for fulltime, and he Served them all of the four years that he was a Student in Baylor University.

After this he entered the Baptist Seminary at Louisville Ky. and I heard him preach his first Sermon in Texas, after his graduation at Louisville, and that evening I rode with him for Several miles, and he told me then that Baptists held to, and taught many things that was not contained in the Scriptures.

I write in evidence that the Rev. J. Frank Norris has never been in full accord with the organized work of the Convention Baptist of Texas.

[Signed] E. P. Kirkland
Flomont Texas, Oct. 27th, 1922

PS. In writing the foregoing I have not tried to recall dates as I could not remember them. The events is all that are necessary. I am not writing this for publication, but only to inform you of a part of J. Frank Norris's history. E. P. K.

(2) From F. S. Groner to E. P. Kirkland

11/3/1922

Rev. E. P. Kirkland
Flomont, Texas.
Dear Brother Kirkland:

I wish to thank you for your explanation of Norris and his ecclesiastical lineage in your letter of the 27th. It throws some light on his pedigree. The more we learn of him the more we know he will soon drift to his own place, which is separation from his brethren.

You will be glad to know that he has practically no following in the State.

Thanking you again, I remain

Most cordially yours
[F. S. Groner]

[Notes]

1. The pastor's full name was Catlow Smith.

2. Followers of Samuel A. Hayden, a Texas pastor and editor who had sought to disrupt the work of the Baptist state convention in Texas.

3. The Baptist Missionary Association, as Hayden's splinter group was called.

B.   Norris to L. R. Scarborough, October 28, 1924

My dear Dr. Scarborough:

I have just read with a great deal of amusement mingled with pity, your latest attack on me published in the "Baylor Lariat" and I understand published in two other local papers.

First of all if there are any further favors you and those of like mind as yourself can render me by giving me larger audiences and a wider hearing, I confess that I should express to you my profound appreciation. It is deeply regretted however that you send out your tracts and special publications at the expense of the mission money of the denomination, which thing you have been doing now for the last three years.

You are making yourself a laughing-stock of even your closest friends.

When Dr. Brooks broke faith with the denomination and came out and defended evolution in the Baylor Bulletin in December, 1923, just one month after he had stated that he was "opposed to evolution of every phase and kind," you told him he had made a collossal blunder. Why don't you now stand up to your report that went to the Tarrant County Association which is now in the minutes of the Association, in which you opposed and repudiated the stand of Dr. Brooks and his associates? What are you afraid of? It was pathetic the way you hedged, straddled and compromised to Dr. Brooks when he went after you immediately after he received my telegram concerning the action of the Tarrant County Association. . . .

Your bitter attacks on me have not gotten you anywhere, but on the contrary they have cost you very heavily. You take bretheren into confidence and tell them things that are untrue concerning me and these bretheren sit right down and write me or tell me about them.

Why you have lost your judgment and don't exercise your ordinary common sense and see the "handwriting on the wall".

The Baptist Standard and directors turned you down, have turned you down repeatedly; on an article following the Galveston Convention in which you made a bitter attack on me. Several of the directors told me about it and you had to admit it a short time ago.

You carried a bitter attack down to the Star Telegram on me and they refused to publish it, even for pay. Even the nondescript, irresponsible Tribune said your article was libelous and they had to eliminate portions of it it was so bitter.

Your own faculty are divided against you and your policy, and they have told you so.

I am just mentioning these things so you may know that I know of your course.

I not only have no bitterness for you, but I have come to have a profound pity for you.

You have used everything at your command to injure me, and you have only added to me instead of hurting me.

You lost your temper and blamed me for the discussion concerning your famous "land deal" when you secured a large block of land in connection with the location of the Seminary. I was not the cause of the discussion. The deed records of Tarrant County speak for themselves. A few months ago an auditor, the one who has been auditing the books, in the main for the Baptists of Texas for several years came over from Dallas and checked over this record—I did not have him do it—but certain leading Baptists in Dallas were interested in it.

I have never accused you of any wrongdoing—it was others who criticized you for taking half of your offering that you raised at a certain City in Texas, instead of sending the entire amount in to the headquarters at Dallas. I am not saying anything about it. The records speak for themselves, and the brethren in Dallas have done the talking.

You lost your temper when it was discussed, and continued to be discussed, the fact that you changed the auditor's report of the Seminary. I was not the one that told it. The records speak for themselves. . . .

Therefore, if you can do anything to help me in my next meeting in a similar way, I shall appreciate it. There are quite a number of the best places in Texas that are urging me to come.

For instance, I am going to Arlington in Tarrant County, the largest and best place in the County outside of Fort Worth. They are going to have a large tent or tabernacle. The meeting will be held next spring. I shall appreciate all that you may do similar to your fine work here in Houston. . . .

You dear brethren who have so utterly lost your heads have rendered me as great a favor as the envious brethren of Joseph rendered him. Only a few days ago a great magazine with 2,800,000 circulation sent a member of the staff to write up the full history of me and my work.

It is rather significant that simultaneous with your ardent proposition that your "hat was in the ring" and you were going to put the First Baptist Church and its pastor out of business—I repeat it is rather significant that simultaneous with your threat against me because I exposed evolution, that I should suddenly be given a hearing at the world's greatest pulpits. Excuse me, Dr. Scarborough, for seeming to boast, but I am sure you are generous enough to rejoice in the success and promotion of another. So you have rendered a great service in many ways. . . .

I notice where you indicate or threaten that my seat is going to be challenged at the coming convention in Dallas. In order that you may be thoroughly informed I here now announce that I am going as a messenger of the First Baptist Church, and I challenge you to make your challenge!

Be assured, Dr. Scarborough, I have written you in the finest vein of humor and I quite sympathize with you in the awful predicament that you and others find yourselves. Everybody has laughed at your predicament from start to finish. . . .

Be assured I wish you the very best and greatest possible success and do rejoice and shall rejoice for every soul that is won under your ministry. When you and I get to Heaven, which I am sure the abounding grace of God is sufficient to take care of us both, we will have many good times sitting down and talking all these matters over.

Yours very sincerely,

Dr. L. R. Scarborough,   [Signed] J. Frank Norris
President Baptist Seminary,
Fort Worth, Texas.

15.10   Efforts to Combat Norrisism

Texas Baptist leaders stoutly resisted the efforts of J. Frank Norris to disrupt cooperative Baptist life and work in Texas (see document 15.9). Two examples of this resistance are the anti-Norris pledge of Texas Baptists. *Source:* Copy in J. Frank Norris File, A. Webb Roberts Library, Southwestern Baptist Theological Seminary, Fort Worth, Texas, and the widely circulated pamphlet on "The Fruits of Norrisism" by L. R. Scarborough. These probably come from the 1920s or early 1930s, though neither bears a publication date. *Source*: L. R. Scarborough, "The Fruits of Norrisism" (Ft. Worth: By the author, n.d.). Reprinted in *Texas Baptist History: The Journal of the Texas Baptist Historical Society,* 1 (1981): 89-97.

A.   Texas Baptist Leaders Adopt Anti-Norris Pledge

A STATEMENT AND A PLEDGE

Texas Baptists face in their annual Convention a great issue. It is not a new one. It is as old as the beginning of God's efforts to save men. It is the problem of progress against reaction; of construction against destruction. Moses, Joshua, Nehemiah, John the Baptist, Jesus Christ and Paul encountered in their day the same spirit, method and opposition. All through the centuries reactionaries and hinderers have sought to block progress. Their methods have been largely the same. Nothing has pleased them. They have had plausible excuses and used every trick of demagoguery, misrepresentation and false accusation.

In more recent years, in this country, our great missionary, educational and benevolent programs have met with the same opposition, largely dominated by the same spirit, using the same methods. It is exactly the issue we face in our denominational progress today in Texas. It is construction against destruction. The opposition to our work today is marked by many of the same characteristics as is shown in the history of these ancient enemies of progress.

This movement is divisive, self-centered, autocratic, hypercritical and non-cooperative. The leader of this movement in Texas has shown the same spirit and method for fifteen or twenty years. It was manifested in his conduct when he was a student in Baylor University, pastor in Dallas and editor of the Baptist Standard. Every missionary of his home association, for fifteen years, has felt the sharp blade of his criticism and opposition. Practically no church, large or small, in his neighborhood has been blessed by his cooperation, but has been beaten back by criticism, suspicion and opposition.

His spirit and methods resulted in his expulsion from the Baptist Pastors' Conference of his home town, and after being restored on good promises which he broke, was expelled again, and now stands excluded from the membership of said Conference. Messengers of his church were denied seats in their own association. B. H. Carroll repudiated the mal-administration of his church and withdrew from its fellowship. Every member of the Southwestern Seminary faculty who held membership there has withdrawn long ago, and none others have joined. The great Southwestern Seminary and other denominational enterprises in his home section, have been constantly under his scathing criticism.

Practically all the money raised by his church, for years and years, has been expended on his own church lots and in the expensive publication and free distribution of his iconoclastic paper, carrying every week criticisms, insinuations, inuendoes and open attacks on the workers, institutions and work of Texas and Southern Baptists. He first attacked all the schools in Texas, then narrowed it to Baylor University, and then widened it against the 75 Million Campaign, its methods, policies and leaders. He attacked the Executive Board of this Convention and its trusted Secretary. He regarded the Investigating Committee, appointed by the Convention, as counting for nothing, and ridiculed them as white-washing. The Convention's action settled nothing with him.

At the Galveston Convention after his leadership and methods had been repudiated by 811 to 31, he confessed his wrongs in apparent sincerity, and earnestly promised cooperation, capitalizing on the New Testament doctrine of forgiveness to get back into the counsels of the Convention. He misrepresents Texas and Southern Baptists in his inter-denominational and Pedo-Baptist relationship. Practically all his conferences on fundamental doctrine and in the evangelism of his church, he uses those who are out of sympathy with our denominational work.

What page of THE SEARCHLIGHT, his official paper, during the last five years, shows one uncritical line supporting the causes of this Convention? What page shows an appeal for state missions, home missions, or hospitals? . . .

Upon the foregoing statement of facts we call attention to the following characteristics of this modern, unscriptural and anti-Baptist reactionary movement:

1. It is self-centered, spending practically all its contributions on itself. Hence, it is anti-calvary. The Christ-Spirit begins at Jerusalem but ends with the last lost man.

2. It is prideful and boastful, always magnifying its own deeds and belittling the achievements of others, hence contrary to the Bible teachings of humility.

It is spectacular and sensational in its spirit and method, appealing to prejudices and passions of people, turning away from the logic of facts and the processes of orderly reason to efforts to discredit the private life of those with whom he differs by dragging alleged faults into the glare of publicity and by such indescent exposure intimidate and embarrass and thus triumph in his contentions. This method is hyper-critical, living on the alleged weaknesses and sins of others, holding nothing dear in its blasting widely advertised criticisms of everything and everybody not in agreement with its purposes and leadership. It constantly sends out the poison of suspicion and everywhere breeds division. God says he hates the sowers of discord.

4. It is anti-missionary and omissionary. If the spirit and policy of this cult were followed by all the Baptist churches of Texas and the South, all associational, state and home missionaries and most of our foreign missionaries would have to be recalled and their missions would go to ruin; all our hospitals, our schools and seminaries, would shut their doors for the lack of support, and the whole Baptist program would fall into ruin. Wherever, throughout the South, THE SEARCHLIGHT has been read and believed, campaign pledges have been repudiated and support has been withdrawn, not only from our schools, but from missions and the other causes. This movement is contrary to the commission of Jesus Christ in His three-fold world-saving program.

5. It is non-co-operative, hence unscriptural and un-baptistic. What little co-operation this movement gives to the causes of Baptists is critical, designated and lop-sided, magnifying local situations, and belittling far-reaching, vital denominational enterprises.

6. It is misrepresentative of Texas and Southern Baptists in that it is inter-denominational. Dr. Gambrell, our great southern hero helped lead Southern Baptists away from the unionists and other compromising alliances, and before he died he warned us against the perils of this new destructive and reactionary movement. . . .

7. The leader of this movement failed to keep his promises of co-operation. He did at the Galveston Convention. He did recently in his own home association. These promises have been continually broken, the fight renewed, and always at the time of our semi-annual campaigns for funds.

Based on these and other facts we the following members from co-operative Baptist churches and members of this Convention would call upon this Convention to enter with us into the following pledge.

OUR PLEDGE

1. That we hereby renew our allegiance to our divinely inspired Bible, which brings to us a revelation of our Savior in whose deity, virgin birth, holy life, marvelous teachings, precious doctrines, atoning death, bodily resurrection and expectant return, we most devoutly believe. We reconsecrate ourselves to an unending opposition to materialism, rationalism, modernism and evolution, or any other cult or heresy opposing the Word of God, the deity of Christ or the integrity of His churches. We are opposed to any of these heresies being taught in any of our schools, and we herein record it as our continued purpose to do our best, through the orderly ways of constructive work, to put out of our schools, if there is any, all false teachings or teachers, and to do our best to prevent these heresies being taught in our schools.

2. We herein covenant with ourselves and God to be loyal to our Saviour's work—orphanages, hospitals, seminaries, schools, our paper, all our mission boards, and all our other causes and their appointed and trusted leaders. They shall have our love, our prayers, our tears, our strength, our full-length co-operation, our money, and we trust if need be, our lives in order that we may in a greater fashion carry Christ's three-fold program of saving, teaching, and healing men to all this lost world. We are for these causes and their friends and we are opposed to all who, posing as friends, seek to destroy, hinder, or prevent these causes from bringing their best harvest to the glory of Christ and the salvation of this world.

As members of this Convention of Christ-honoring, truth-loving, co-operating, aggressive, forward-looking, on-going Baptists, we hereby put our emphatic disapproval upon, and our most earnest condemnation on the method and spirit of this destructive reactionary movement against causes dear to us and vital to Christ's whole will, which movement is fostered, and persistently and ruthlessly carried on by THE SEARCH-LIGHT of Fort Worth. For the sake of denominational fellowship, the unity of our people and the progress of the gospel, the very life and effectiveness of our causes and institutions, we hereby with our whole souls, and our whole strength set ourselves against this destructive, reactionary movement. The spirit and method and leadership of this propaganda does not in any sense represent Texas and Southern Baptists, and we are opposed to it, and are hereby recording our opposition. With profound regret but as a matter of imperious duty and necessity for the welfare of our beloved denomination we feel constrained. We are going on with truth-loving, co-operating Baptists to protect our causes, stand by our leaders and put over the kingdom of God at home and around the world, and we most respectfully petition this Convention to join us in this movement to stand four-square for the causes of our Christ.

B. L. R. Scarborough, The Fruits of Norrisism

FOREWORD

This tract is a discussion of some of the fruits of an old cult under a new name. The following are some of the characteristics of this cult—Norrisism:

1. It is toward true religion what socialism and bolshevism are to politics and industry; wholly destructive in spirit and methods.

2. It is anti-missionary and anti-institutional. It gives nothing to associational, state or home missions and only enough to foreign missions to get representation in the convention. It spends most of its money on itself—some times in court trials for perjury, arson and murder, and in sending out free literature seeking to destroy the causes other people try to build.

3. It thrives on sensationalism, misrepresentation and false accusations of good men and true causes. It masquerades under the cloak of anti-evolutionism, anti-modernism, anti-catholicism in order to ride into public favor and cast poisonous suspicion on the leadership of the causes of constructive Christianity.

4. In its chief leadership it is the embodiment of autocratic ecclesiasticism. All the privileges and rights of the church heading up in the pastor.

5. It uses the pulpit, the press, and the radio to create suspicion, to foment class prejudices and to vent its hatred against innocent personalities and institutions.

6. It divides and splits families, churches, associations and strikes its poisonous fangs at the brotherhood of Christianity.

7. It lowers the standards of right conduct, individual righteousness, ministerial

ethics, personal integrity, and gives to the world a false conception of the character, spirit and methods of Christianity.

8. The only people or causes it praises are those who bow down to its dictum or fail in any wise to cross its path.

9. The individual, the preacher or church who joins in sympathy with this cult will sooner or later cease to cooperate with the mission, educational or benevolent enterprises fostered by God's people.

10. It has some noble names upon the escutcheon of its false accusations and public misrepresentation; Carroll, Gambrell, McDaniel, McConnell, Mullins, C. V. Edwards, Brooks, Sampey, Groner, Ray, Robertson, Forrest Smith, Cullen Thomas, Truett and others—multitudes of false accusations such as: infidelity, graft, heresy, theft and such like, and groundless insinuations have gone out against these good men for years. This tract deals with only a few of these false and slanderous charges against these brethren. These are but samples—there are many others which are as groundless as these.

SOME GREAT PRINCIPLES INVOLVED IN RECENT ACTION
OF THE TARRANT COUNTY ASSOCIATION

Since wide publicity has been given in other ways to the recent action of the Tarrant County Association, it is felt that the matter should be accurately set out in the columns of the Baptist press in Texas.

It is generally known that the Tarrant County Association has been the storm-center of a ceaseless and vicious attack upon the boards, institutions, causes and leaders of Texas and Southern Baptists for many years. It began in the days when B. H. Carroll first moved to Fort Worth and has gone on, night and day, with increasing momentum until today. The same source of confusion in Baptist affairs has carried on agitation in every other phase of life in Fort Worth—political, commercial and social. . . . Baptist ministers' conferences have again and again repudiated this presumptuous leadership by expulsion. The Tarrant County Association has denied it fellowship by large and increasing majority. The Baptist General Convention, for three successive years, by practically unanimous vote, refused it membership in its councils. . . .

There are involved in this action of the association

1. **The principles of co-operation.** The church above alluded to in its letter stated, after quoting the Commission in Matt. 28:18-20, "Therefore, we are not in sympathy with the unscriptural institutionalism which has no place or authority in the Great Commission." The constitution of the Tarrant County Association in Article II says, "The object of this association shall be to establish a means of communication between the churches, to project measures for the furtherance of the cause of Christ within its bounds, and to promote among the churches the support of all the general denominational, missionary, educational and benevolent enterprises." That is, the Association's main object is to promote and support the mission boards, schools, hospitals, orphanages and other enterprises and institutions founded by our fathers and which are supported by the Texas General Convention and the Southern Baptist Convention. The pastor and his church in question stated, in accord with the teachings of this old source of trouble in Tarrant County, that they have no sympathy for nor co-operation with these institutions. In other words the association stands for those causes and institutions and the church in question does not.

The other ground on which they were refused seats as stated by the resolution, was: the action by the pastor and the church in question, clearly showing that he and the church were willing to become a part and parcel of a guerilla warfare which for years has plagued the denomination.

The Tarrant County Association clearly recognizes the privilege of this church to refuse co-operation in building our mission causes, our schools, seminaries, hospitals and orphanages, but it denies them the right to come into fellowship of an association which is in favor of all these things and yet at the same time tries to decide the Association's course in supporting these institutions. . . . Isn't it strange that a pastor and a church, that announce both in theory and in practice, that they are opposed to the things you are trying to do, want fellowship with you and seats in your councils for the sole purpose of trying to keep you from doing the things you want to do? This does not look like New Testament co-operation to me.

2. The Principle of Loyalty to the Commands of the Lord Jesus Christ and the Causes and Institutions which these Commands and Teachings Set Up and Set Forward.

This pastor and church state clearly, both in theory and in practice their opposition to the institutionalism of the Commission. He in his argument, the pastor, tried to establish an alibi, by saying that he meant unscriptural "institutions," such as institutions that teach evolution, and so on. But he unfortunately used "unscriptural institutionalism." Now he and the self-assumed leadership which he is following are opposed to institutionalism of Southern Baptists. Their gifts this year, or their lack of gifts, state that this institutionalism which they are opposed to is missions of all sorts, education of all sorts, and benevolences of all sorts. Their action in not giving speaks as loud as their profession on non-co-operation. . . . That leadership gives practically nothing to any of the causes and institutions fostered by Texas and Southern Baptists. It is pure, downright anti-mission, hardshellism, and anti-institutionalism. Wherever that leadership gets a hold on individuals or churches they at once cease to give to the great causes of the Commission. . . . It is the old fight known all through the ages. Its principle method is misrepresentation, inuendo, suspicion, accusation against character and leadership. It does nothing for the causes itself, but seeks to keep others from doing what they want to do for the causes.

3. The third principle involved in this matter is loyalty to the moral laws of God.

God says, "Thou shalt not bear false witness against thy neighbor." The main basis of this notorious opposition is a palpable violation of this plain commandment of God. This opposition to the causes of Tarrant County Association, and Texas Baptist and Southern Baptist Conventions has ceaselessly misrepresented their causes, therefore, the Tarrant County Baptist Association puts itself, again, with overwhelming force and with a solidarity and a conviction that rings to Heaven, against this opposition and its misrepresentations. It is not only a question of co-operation, and a question of loyalty to the teachings of Jesus Christ, but it is a question of veracity, honor and common honesty in denominational relationship. I itemize some cases:

(1) This opposition has published widely that I said "Prof. Meroney and the Medical College at Dallas must go." I never said that nor anything that could be twisted into such a statement.

ABOUT DR. BARNES.

(2) It also published that Dr. W. W. Barnes, Professor of Church History in the Southwestern Seminary, is an evolutionist. There is not a syllable of truth in this statement. . . .

ABOUT DR. BROOKS

(7) This same source of opposition says that Baylor University faculty and President Brooks are against the McDaniel Resolution passed by the Southern Baptist Convention, and ought to be made to sign it.

I want to say, in the first place, that the McDaniel Resolution was the Southern Baptist Convention's request to the institutions and boards owned and controlled by the Southern Baptist Convention, and that resolution did not ask individual signature to the McDaniel Resolution. . . . Baylor University is not owned by the Southern Convention, and the Convention did not ask, and the resolutions do not require, that the state institutions subscribe to resolutions passed by the Southern Baptist Convention.

I wish to say further, that President Brooks was present and voted for the McDaniel Resolution and published his endorsement, and further as everybody knows, the faculty of Baylor University has already passed, voluntarily and unanimously, a signed expression of their belief in the fundamentals of our faith, which articles of faith wholly endorsed in principle the McDaniel Resolution. Now, why is it necessary, when President Brooks voted for the Resolution and the faculty had already endorsed that principle and all the other fundamentals of faith by their personal signature, why nag and raise suspicioss and untrue charges against a great set of honorable, consecrated, orthodox teachers? . . .

ABOUT DR. McCONNELL

(8) It has been charged time and time again that Dr. F. M. McConnell, former Secretary of Missions in Texas and in Oklahoma, noble pastor, College President, successful evangelist, suddenly left Oklahoma because when his books were opened there were suspicious things found therein. There is not the slightest truth in this charge. It is baseless and pernicious. No truer or nobler man walks the earth than F. M. McConnell. . . .

ABOUT GAMBRELL AND TRUETT

(12) This destructive cult and some deceived by its false statements have circulated the report in pulpit, press and over radio as is quoted in a charge recently made by a deacon of a Baptist church, who is under the dominance of Norrisism as follows: "The big trouble is that Drs. Brooks, Truett, Gambrell, Scarborough, Groner and others had misappropriated a considerable amount of the funds of the 75 Million Campaign." . . . Is it not a shame that such men as Gambrell, Truett, Groner and Brooks should be thus publicly held up as thieves and scoundrels. These school men and secretaries accused of all these crimes have every year been unanimously elected to their positions and have never been charged with arson, perjury, or murder. . . .

ABOUT WHAT GOD HATES.

(13) If Norrisism misrepresents and brings false accusations against such causes and men, masquerading under a cloak of orthodoxy and fundamentalism, can such a cult be trusted in anything? Can one afford to believe its reports of its own membership; the size of its own congregations; the additions it has, the numbers it has in Sunday school and its glaring sensational reports of the greatest revivals in the world? An investigation of the facts back of these swelling numbers will more than likely find them greatly exaggerated. God says in His word "Six things doth the Lord hate— a **proud look,** a **lying tongue, hands that have shed innocent blood,** a heart that deviseth **wicked imaginations,** feet that be **swift in running to mischief** and **false witness that speaketh lies** and he that **soweth discord among brethren."**

Will it profit a man if he is sound in his theology on creation according to Gen. 2:27 and yet violates God's command where he says, **"Thou shalt not bear false witness against thy neighbor."** Ex. 20:17. . . .

15.11   W. T. Conner, Two Letters Concerning Biblical Inerrancy

Walter Thomas Conner (1877-1952) was professor of theology at Southwestern Baptist Theological Seminary from the time of the seminary's move to Fort Worth, Texas, in 1910 until his death. Known as the "Baptist theologian of the Southwest," Conner studied under such Baptist luminaries as B. H. Carroll, E. Y. Mullins, and A. H. Strong. His own theology was strongly conservative, with an emphasis upon biblical authority. Conner could scarcely have anticipated the "inerrancy controversy" of a later generation. This lends added interest to his candid comments in two letters on that subject in 1948. These remarks show that Southern Baptists' most conservative theologian attached little significance to the theory of inerrancy of original biblical autographs. The context of the letters show, and Conner's extensive writings confirm, that he remained staunchly conservative on the doctrine of biblical authority. *Source:* W. T. Conner File, A. Webb Roberts Library, Southwestern Baptist Theological Seminary, Fort Worth, Texas.

February 21, 1948

Dr. E. B. Atwood
2110 Grape Street
Abilene, Texas
Dear Dr. Atwood:

I thank you for your letter of February 20. I would not make the value of the Bible to depend on a doctrine of its inerrancy. That is, inerrancy in the ordinary sense of that term. I know that some of our preachers would, but it seems to me that in order to prove its inerrancy you have to assume the very thing that you start out to prove.

If a man asks about the inerrancy of the Bible, then you have to ask, "What Bible?" If he says the original Greek and Hebrew manuscripts, then the only answer is that I have not seen these and could not examine them. If he says the Bible as we have it, then we know that that is not inerrant. So it seems to me that you soon run into questions to which you can give no straight answer.

I remember that Dr. Mullins somewhere says that we cannot make the religious value of the Bible to depend on any certain conclusion that men come to with reference to the date, composition and authorship of the books of the Bible. I do believe in the infallibility of the fundamental teachings of the Bible. I believe we can depend on these and realize them in our own experience and after all, as I see it, that is what we need and all we need. The other is pure theory and is unproveable. I don't think it is best to make the religious value of the Bible depend on an unproveable theory.

I suppose it is not necessary to go further into this matter now. I wish we had the opportunity, as you indicated, to talk more of these things through.

Again thanking you and your good wife for the privilege of being in your home, I am

Cordially yours,
W. T. Conner

April 13, 1948

Dr. E. B. Atwood
2110 Grape Street
Abilene, Texas
Dear Dr. Atwood:

I read your article on the "Infallible Word of God," with a great deal of interest. So far as I can see, I would agree with your position in its fundamental aspects. I do not know about the advisability of publishing your article at present. I would not want to assume the attitude of declining to face an issue but on some of these questions, I feel that instead of a frontal attack, the better method is to undermind [sic] the presuppositions.

That same thing I think is true with reference to premillennialism, I find that in dealing with the question, it is sometimes best to let the presupposition on which premillennialism is based simply disappear as a man studies further in the field of theology. I wonder if that may not be the better method of dealing with the rigid verbal inspiration theory. I think it is true to say that by the time some men get through the Seminary, the question simply disappears. That is better perhaps than trying to convince them of their error at the beginning.

If a man takes a position that the Bible is inerrant in all respects, by the time he gets through answering the questions that will arise, he may find that the question becomes meaningless. Anyway I enjoyed reading your article.

With best wishes, I am

Cordially yours,
W. T. Conner

15.12   The Ralph H. Elliott Controversy

In 1961 Broadman Press published *The Message of Genesis*, by Ralph H. Elliott, the young professor of Old Testament at the newly formed Midwestern Baptist Theological Seminary in Kansas City. No one anticipated the storm of controversy that erupted around this one-volume theological commentary. Elliott took mildly progressive views on textual criticism in Genesis, but his theological interpretations were mostly conservative. However, this book proved a lightning rod for the collected grievances of conservatives among Southern Baptists and almost overnight a major controversy erupted.

Editorials by E. S. James, powerful editor of the conservative Texas paper, the *Baptist Standard*, did much to fan the controversy and nothing to calm it. *Source: Baptist Standard,* 10 Jan. 1962, 4-5. Used by permission. The sensational "Death in the Pot" article by K. Owen White is cited in selection B. White was then pastor of First Baptist Church in Houston. On the wave of publicity stirred by this article, White was elected president of the Southern Baptist Convention in 1962, thus beginning the trend of choosing SBC presidents specifically because of their conservative theological stance. *Source: Baptist Standard,* 10 Jan. 1962, 7. Used by permission. Selection C cites the response of Elliott and the Midwestern trustees to the James editorial. *Source: Baptist Standard,* 10 Jan. 1962, 6-7. Used by permission. Selection D cites a letter supporting Elliott's position. Elliott was dismissed by the Midwestern trustees in 1962, and later served as pastor of American Baptist churches in New York and Illinois. *Source: Baptist Standard,* 10 Jan. 1962, 7. Used by permission.

A.   "Baptist Theologians and Their Books," E. S. James

Last spring the Broadman Press published *The Message of Genesis* by Ralph H. Elliott, a teacher of theology in the Southern Baptist Midwestern Seminary at Kansas City, Mo. We read it immediately and wrote on page after page our disapproval of many statements in it. The first impulse was to condemn it editorially, but in an effort to be fair to everyone involved and avoid unnecessary embarrassment for anyone we waited for some satisfactory explanation as to why the book was written. A personal interview with President Berquist, personal correspondence with the author, and a direct report from the board meeting of the seminary trustees have brought strong testimonies concerning the fine Christian character of Elliott; but there has been no effort to explain why the book was written and sent out for Baptist consumption.

The time has come when we can no longer withhold comment on the book. In an effort to give readers a fair appraisal of it we are publishing on pages 6 and 7 an article by K. Owen White, a critique by Robert H. Craft, and portions of a letter from the author and of the trustee's resolution which was adopted 14 to 7 in their meeting Dec. 28. Each speaks for itself, and readers will make their own conclusions.

We hold in highest esteem the Christian character of Ralph H. Elliott, but we do object to his book. We do not believe it should have been written by a Southern Baptist theologian, and we hold that Broadman Press should not have published it for Baptist readers. . . .

There is one thing, however, that is more disturbing than this book. That is the attitude of many mature Baptists toward it and other books that strive to make the Bible conform to the modern conception of how things might have been in the distant past. Some highly regarded pastors, teachers, and editors have defended Elliott's treatise and condemned White for finding fault with it. Others caution Baptists about the dangers involved in criticising themselves, and some seem to feel that more harm than good will result from a discussion of what our theologians say and write.

When one attacks the content of a book he is not necessarily attacking its author. Most of us believe in academic freedom so long as it is not an abused privilege. No sane Baptist would consent to "witch hunting" today. It is not our business nor prerogative to magnify every word or phrase that seems to be contrary to established beliefs, but readers should be as free to dissent as writers and teachers are to affirm.

Any Baptist who writes anything can expect it to be critically examined by all readers, and if it won't stand the test of public opinion he had better not write it. Oral statements may be denied or explained away, but the written word is a matter of record. Anyone who attempts to write for the public had better be ready to defend his position. He need not expect everyone to agree with it, and he need not be offended when it is condemned.

There is no finer group of men than the Southern Baptist Seminary professors. They are accepted in the pulpits of the convention, and they preach delightful Gospel messages. They teach with ability and mean so much to so many of us; but when they come to the matter of writing, some of them seem to write for their colleagues and forget that we common folk will read what they say. When one of them speaks of miracles as myths he may not mean that they are fictitious, but it means that to the average Baptist. When he speaks or writes of historical records in the Bible as being symbolic rather than historical he may mean that he regards it as God's inspired Word, but he causes others to doubt that it is. . . .

Scarcely a day passes that we do not hear someone quote from the writings of Robertson, Conner, Boyce, or Mullins to prove the Baptist position on the Scriptures. Then why should one suppose that 50 years hence men will not be quoting the Baptist theologians of today on the position of their Baptist forbears? It is not difficult to imagine the result when the theologians of 2012 quote Elliott's statements that Melchisedec was a priest of Baal or that some statements of Genesis 1 to 11 are to be regarded as symbolic rather than historical. Why should we think that our great grandchildren will not read some of the books being written by Baptist theologians today and use them to prove that their Baptist predecessors believed in apostasy, "open communion," and other doctrines which are contrary to Baptist beliefs?

Fifty years from now the voices of most living preachers will be stilled. Few of the many books the modern pastors write will be read in that day. Editorial comments will have been forgotten, and the current position of the average Baptist will be ignored; but the books now being written by Baptist seminary teachers will still be read and accepted. What a tremendous responsibility it is that rests on these men who determine the theology of tomorrow. How careful each of them should be about every word he writes for Baptist posterity, and how great will the damage be from the speculations of those who have been entrusted with the training of Baptist preachers.

Questionable theology is deadly; and if we allow it to be disseminated without the warning label, we then become accessory to the demise of our denomination. Some of us may have to attend the funeral of Southern Baptists distinctives, but we don't have to attend it silently.

B. "Death in the Pot," K. Owen White

"Since the parable includes the historical and the non-historical, one can say with Richardson: 'We must learn to think of the stories of Genesis—the creation, the fall, Noah's ark, the tower of Babel—in the same way as we think of the parables of Jesus; **they are profoundly symbolical** (though not allegorical) **stories, which aren't to be taken as literally true** (like the words of the textbooks of geology), but which yet bear a meaning that cannot be paraphrased or stated in any other way without losing something of their quality of existential truth'."

"'Adam' originally must have meant 'mankind,' not just one person." "The particular problem of Chapter 5 is the longevity of the antediluvians. **It is difficult to believe that they actually lived as long as stated.** In all probability, the Priestly writer simply exaggerated the ages in order to show the glory of an ancient civilization.". . .

"There developed **the tradition** that this was what happened to Lot's wife—perhaps **not exactly historical** . . ."

"Suddenly, what had been a thought of meditation gripped the inner being of Abraham until **he thought he heard it as a clear call from God,** 'Go sacrifice Isaac'."

Does this sound like Boyce, Broadus, Mullins, Robertson, Sampey, Gambrell, Carroll, Scarborough, and other great Southern Baptist leaders? The quotations listed above are from *The Message of Genesis*, written by Dr. Ralph Elliott, now teaching at Midwestern Seminary, Kansas City, Mo.

Being a graduate of Southern Seminary and having served as pastor of Southern Baptist churches for more than 30 years, I love and believe in my denomination and have a burning passion for it to remain true to the Bible as the Word of God. I have a deep concern that our seminaries shall sound a clear, ringing note in their interpretation of the Scriptures and that young preachers shall come from their halls with not an "uncertain sound."

The book from which I have quoted is liberalism, pure and simple! It stems from the rationalistic theology of Wellhausen and his school which led Germany to become a materialistic godless nation. This is "the wisdom of the world" which seeks to find a "reasonable, acceptable" solution to every problem which involves the supernatural.

Several great denominations in the last generation have drifted from the faith of our fathers, have lost their conviction that the Bible is authoritative and dependable, and now have little evangelistic witness. The drift came from liberalism in their seminaries and their literature.

If the appeal is made for "academic freedom," let it be said that we gladly grant any man the right to believe what he wants to—but, we do not grant him the right to believe and express views in conflict with our historic position concerning the Bible as the Word of God **while he is teaching in one of our schools, built and supported by Baptist funds.**

The book in question is "poison." This sort of rationalistic criticism can lead only to further confusion, unbelief, deterioration, and ultimate disintegration as a great New Testament denomination. It has happened to other denominations; it can happen to us! Modernism is insidious, dangerous, and destructive.

What can be done?

• Invite men with such views to find a place of service with groups or denominations of like theological inclinations.

• Ask the trustees of our institutions to consider seriously the dangers involved in such theological views and to exercise caution in their approval of faculty members.

• Urge our Sunday School Board to be alert to any trend in the direction of liberalism in our publications.

This is not an incidental matter. It involves the total responsibility of every one of us individually, of our churches and our denomination, in declaring plainly, positively, and unequivocally "the whole counsel of God."

In this brief statement I have made no attempt to review the book. The quotations speak for themselves. I have merely emphasized certain words and phrases in these quotations to shed light upon the particular doctrinal or historical truth in question. The influence of this sort of teaching would substitute intuition for inspiration, reason for revelation, and futility for faith. It is quite true of course that in our study and interpretation of God's Word we are not to forsake common sense, but we also need to remember the words of Isaiah 55:8, 9. "For my thoughts are not your thoughts, neither are your ways my ways, saith the Lord. For as the heavens are higher than the earth, so are my ways higher than your ways, and my thoughts than your thoughts."

"There is death in the pot!"

C. Response by Elliott and Midwestern Trustees

Seminary trustees vote confidence in book's author

Trustees of Midwestern Seminary, Kansas City, Mo. have voted confidence in Ralph H. Elliott, professor of Old Testament and Hebrew.

The vote resulted from controversy over Elliott's book, *The Message of Genesis*. The book was published in 1961 by Broadman Press, an arm of the Sunday School Board, a sister agency of the seminary in the Southern Baptist Convention.

The trustees' announcement emphasized the school's support of conservative Baptist thought and doctrine. But it also acknowledged differences which exist on points of interpretation. Trustees said they investigated the beliefs and doctrine of Professor Elliott.

Resolution Statement

The resolution adopted stated:

"Whereas, recently criticism has been made of Dr. Ralph W. Elliott and his book, *The Message of Genesis;* and

"Whereas, the board of trustees through the action of a special committee and by direct action of the board in special session has investigated Dr. Elliott's beliefs and doctrinal position;

"BE IT THEREFORE RESOLVED that while there are members of the board of trustees who are in disagreement with some of the interpretations presented by Dr. Elliott in his book, we do affirm our confidence in him as a consecrated Christian, a promising scholar and teacher, a loyal servant of Southern Baptists, and a dedicated and warmly evangelistic preacher of the Gospel."

Elliott Explains Position

In correspondence with Editor E. S. James of the Baptist Standard, Elliott said:

"I would say to you, that like any human interpreter, I may have missed it. However, I have been in the line of true Baptist heritage in trying. **This I know, I love the Bible with my very life and bow before it as inspired, authoritative, and all sufficient guide for life and faith. But I still have to interpret. I would hope that the Holy Spirit would continue to breathe over its pages within the depths of my life that when I am caught in error I may see and admit and better still, that its illumination might guide my heart and head in ways of truth.** (Bold face by the [*Baptist Standard*] editor.)

"I think I follow in the train of E. Y. Mullins, *The Christian Religion in its Doctrinal Expression,* when I think of Christian revelation as 'primarily a revelation of God himself rather than of truths about God' (p. 141). Furthermore, I would say with him:

"The Bible is not a book of science nor of philosophy. It is a book of religion. It only asks that science and philosophy recognize the facts of man's religious life for which it stands (p. 150).

"I wanted you to see what basic principles I have sought to apply in specific situations. Certainly I would not ask all to agree with all of my conclusions. However, I would ask acknowledgement of my tenacious insistence on the inspiration and revelation of the Scripture. Nor would I have one overlook the emphasis on the sinfulness of man and the redemptive grace of God which I have tried to underscore in *The Message of Genesis.* The central core is there. But methodology is as varied as are Baptists."

D. "Help for the Man in the Pew and in the Pulpit: A Critique of Elliott's Book," Robert H. Craft

It has been well said that in his book, *The Message of Genesis,* Dr. Ralph H. Elliott, professor of Old Testament, Midwestern Seminary (Kansas City, Mo.) has probably made the most significant and creative contribution to the field of Biblical scholarship for Southern Baptists since the writings of Dr. H. E. Dana and Dr. A. T. Robertson.

The first clear and unmistakable help the book offers to the minister or layman is to clarify and face squarely and honestly the major problems of authorship, date, anachronisms, and oral tradition in Genesis. Dr. Elliott's answer to these problems demonstrates his academic integrity and pertinent knowledge of the best in Old Testament scholarship. He reasons about Genesis:

". . . some of the material has roots going back to the early Sumerian—Babylonian period (3000-1500 B. C.). The form of its application to divine history perhaps is exilic and post-exilic (500 B. C.). Many human authors, worship circles, and redactors appear to have had a part in shaping Genesis over a long period of time. In a special sense, this underscores the fact that God is the ultimate author" (Page 11).

Draw From History

In various places in the Bible the authors mention drawing upon current history, personal testimony, editorial conclusion, and differing patterns of research to write their particular book or segment of book. The Gospel according to St. Luke is an excellent example. Luke says,

"Inasmuch as many have undertaken to compile a narrative of the things which have been accomplished among us, just time past, to write an orderly account for you, most excellent Theophilus . . ." (Luke 1:1-3 R.S.V.).

A serious and devout consideration of how and why Genesis was written is essential to the discerning student of God's Word. The author leads the reader through an exhilarating and fruitful study of the delicate problems conservative scholars have too long neglected in the study of Genesis.

The second unique help offered in this commentary, and by far the most important, is that the reader is brought face to face with the fact that God, the Creator of man, is successfully and persistently working for man's plenary redemption from the malignancy of sin. . . .

The treatment of the first eleven chapters of Genesis demonstrates man's basic problem—he is a helpless sinner in need of a Redeemer: The book in subsequent chapters demonstrates God's evangelistic grace in answering man's need through a transformed life. The life of Abraham is a demonstration of this aforementioned thesis. . . . This section beginning on Page 75 and ending on Page 154 is the most inspirational, scholastically honest, and emotionally gripping passage in the whole book. . . .

Pilgrimage of Faith

Abraham's pilgrimage of faith from polytheism to monotheism and God's persistent love and loyalty to Abraham as he faltered, failed, and ultimately succeeded is a needed source of strength for men today. Since God can take a man like Abraham who was nothing and, in spite of his human frailties, make something out of him, there is hope for every man today who will hear God's redemptive call and respond as did Abraham.

A number of valuable themes are enunciated and delineated in this book on Genesis. The reader will want to read and re-read the pages of this book to enhance the meaning of his faith in God. Use of this commentary will cause the thoughtful pastor to thrust himself into a new study of the whole Old Testament, a section of the Holy Bible that will provide his congregation and himself with a more intelligent and vigorous faith in God.

15.13   The Baptist Faith and Message

Twice in the twentieth century the Southern Baptist Convention has adopted a confession of faith. In 1925 at Memphis the SBC responded to the fundamentalist movement, particularly the attacks of J. Frank Norris, and framed their first official confession. These "Memphis Articles," later called the "Baptist Faith and Message," included doctrinal articles which basically followed the New Hampshire confession of 1833. The committee to frame the confession, headed by E. Y. Mullins, added several distinctly Southern Baptist articles on religious liberty, Christian education, and Baptist cooperation.

The Elliott Controversy erupted in 1961. The 1962 meeting of the SBC failed in an attempt to ban Elliott's book, but succeeded in calling for an updated confession of faith. A committee headed by Herschel H. Hobbs of Oklahoma City presented in 1963 the document which has become perhaps the most widely used confession in Baptist history. This "Baptist Faith and Message," like its 1925 prototype, follows the New Hampshire confession, with several additional articles. The document below, from the 1963 SBC *Annual*, gives both confessions so they can be compared. The 1963 version reduces the confession from 25 articles to 17; rephrases article I on Scripture; expands article II on God; combines several doctrines into fewer articles; and expands article VI on the church to include both local and universal church concepts. Both confessions reflect a nonmillennial doctrine of last things.

The introductory statement, spelling out the functions and limitations of a Baptist confession, was attached both in 1925 and again in 1963 and specifically adopted as part of the confession. At one time the Convention directed that the confession not be circulated apart from the introduction, a caution that has not been faithfully observed. Despite efforts to preserve its confessional nature, the 1963 statement has in recent years become more creedal in its usage. *Source: Annual*, SBC, 1963, 269-281.

COMMITTEE ON BAPTIST FAITH AND MESSAGE

Your committee thus constituted begs leave to present its report as follows:

Throughout its work your committee has been conscious of the contribution made by the statement of "The Baptist Faith And Message" adopted by the Southern Baptist Convention in 1925. It quotes with approval its affirmation that "Christianity is supernatural in its origin and history. We repudiate every theory of religion which denies the supernatural elements in our faith."

Furthermore, it concurs in the introductory "statement of the historic Baptist conception of the nature and function of confessions of faith in our religious and denominational life . . . ." It is, therefore, quoted in full as a part of this report to the Convention:

"(1) That they constitute a consensus of opinion of some Baptist body, large or small, for the general instruction and guidance of our own people and others concerning those articles of the Christian faith which are most surely held among us. They are not intended to add anything to the simple conditions of salvation revealed in the New Testament, viz., repentance towards God and faith in Jesus Christ as Saviour and Lord.

"(2) That we do not regard them as complete statements of our faith, having any quality of finality or infallibility. As in the past so in the future, Baptists should hold themselves free to revise their statements of faith as may seem to them wise and expedient at any time.

"(3) That any group of Baptists, large or small, have the inherent right to draw up for themselves and publish to the world a confession of their faith whenever they may think it advisable to do so.

"(4) That the sole authority for faith and practice among Baptists is the Scriptures of the Old and New Testaments. Confessions are only guides in interpretation, having no authority over the conscience.

"(5) That they are statements of religious convictions, drawn from the Scriptures, and are not to be used to hamper freedom of thought or investigation in other realms of life."

The 1925 Statement recommended "the New Hampshire Confession of Faith, revised at certain points, and with some additional articles growing out of certain needs . . . ." Your present committee has adopted the same pattern. It has sought to build upon the structure of the 1925 Statement, keeping in mind the "certain needs" of our generation. At times it has reproduced sections of that Statement without change. In other instances it has substituted words for clarity or added sentences for emphasis. At certain points it has combined articles, with minor changes in wording, to endeavor to relate certain doctrines to each other. In still others—e.g., "God" and "Salvation"—it has sought to bring together certain truths contained throughout the 1925 Statement in order to relate them more clearly and concisely. In no case has it sought to delete from or to add to the basic contents of the 1925 Statement.

Baptists are a people who profess a living faith. This faith is rooted and grounded in Jesus Christ who is "the same yesterday, and to-day, and for ever." Therefore, the sole authority for faith and practice among Baptists is Jesus Christ whose will is revealed in the Holy Scriptures.

A living faith must experience a growing understanding of truth and must be continually interpreted and related to the needs of each new generation. Throughout their history Baptist bodies, both large and small, have issued statements of faith which comprise a consensus of their beliefs. Such statements have never been regarded as complete, infallible statements of faith, nor as official creeds carrying mandatory authority. Thus this generation of Southern Baptists is in historic succession of intent and purpose as it endeavors to state for its time and theological climate those articles of the Christian faith which are most surely held among us.

Baptists emphasize the soul's competency before God, freedom in religion, and the priesthood of the believer. However, this emphasis should not be interpreted to mean that there is an absence of certain definite doctrines that Baptists believe, cherish, and with which they have been and are now closely identified.

It is the purpose of this statement of faith and message to set forth certain teachings which we believe.

Recommendation

PROPOSED 1963 STATEMENT	1925 STATEMENT

I. THE SCRIPTURES

The Holy Bible was written by men divinely inspired and is the record of God's revelation of Himself to man. It is a perfect treasure of divine instruction. It has God for its author, salvation for its end, and truth, without any mixture of error, for its matter. It reveals the principles by which God judges us; and therefore is, and will remain to the end of the world, the true center of Christian union, and the supreme standard by which all human conduct, creeds, and religious opinions should be tried. The criterion by which the Bible is to be interpreted is Jesus Christ.

Ex. 24:4; Deut. 4:1-2; 17:19; Josh. 8:34; Psalms 19:7-10; 119:11,89,105, 140; Isa. 34:16; 40:8; Jer. 15:16; 36; Matt. 5:17-18; 22:29; Luke 21:33; 24:44-46; John 5:39; 16:13-15; 17:17; Acts 2:16ff.; 17:11; Rom. 15:4; 16:25-26; 2 Tim. 3:15-17; Heb. 1:1-2; 4:12; 1 Peter 1:25; 2 Peter 1:19-21.

I. THE SCRIPTURES

We believe that the Holy Bible was written by men divinely inspired, and is a perfect treasure of heavenly instruction; that it has God for its author, salvation for its end, and truth, without any mixture of error, for its matter; that it reveals the principles by which God will judge us; and therefore is, and will remain to the end of the world, the true center of Christian union, and the supreme standard by which all human conduct, creeds and religious opinions should be tried.

Luke 16:29-31; 2 Tim. 3:15-17; Eph. 2:20; Heb. 1:1; 2 Peter 1:19-21; John 16:13-15; Matt. 22:29-31; Psalm 19:7-10; Psalm 119:1-8.

II. GOD

There is one and only one living and true God. He is an intelligent, spiritual, and personal Being, the Creator, Redeemer, Preserver, and Ruler of the universe. God is infinite in holiness and all other perfections. To him we owe the highest love, reverence, and obedience. The eternal God reveals himself to us as Father, Son, and Holy Spirit, with distinct personal attributes, but without division of nature, essence, or being.

1. God the Father

God as Father reigns with providential care over his universe, his creatures, and

II. GOD

There is one and only one living and true God, an intelligent, spiritual, and personal Being, the Creator, Preserver, and Ruler of the universe, infinite in holiness and all other perfections, to whom we owe the highest love, reverence, and obedience. He is revealed to us as Father, Son, and Holy Spirit, each with distinct personal attributes, but without division of nature, essence, or being.

Gen. 1:1; 1 Cor. 8:4-6; Deut. 6:4; Jer. 10:10; Isa. 48:12; Deut. 5:7; Ex. 3:14; Heb. 11:6; John 5:26; 1 Tim. 1:17; John 1:14-18; John 15:26; Gal. 4:6; Matt. 28:19.

the flow of the stream of human history according to the purposes of his grace. He is all powerful, all loving, and all wise. God is Father in truth to those who become children of God through faith in Jesus Christ. He is fatherly in his attitude toward all men.

Gen. 1:1; 2:7; Ex. 3:14; 6:2-3; 15:11ff.; 20:1ff.; Levit. 22:2; Deut. 6:4; 32:6; 1 Chron. 29:10; Psalm 19:1-3; Isa. 43:3,15; 64:8; Jer. 10:10; 17:13; Matt. 6:9ff.; 7:11; 23:9; 28:19; Mark 1:9-11; John 4:24; 5:26; 14:6-13; 17:1-8; Acts 1:7; Rom. 8:14-15; 1 Cor. 8:6; Gal. 4:6; Ephes. 4:6; Col. 1:15; 1 Tim. 1:17; Heb. 11:6; 12:9; 1 Peter 1:17; 1 John 5:7.

2. God the Son

Christ is the eternal Son of God. In his incarnation as Jesus Christ he was conceived of the Holy Spirit and born of the virgin Mary. Jesus perfectly revealed and did the will of God, taking upon himself the demands and necessities of human nature and identifying himself completely with mankind yet without sin. He honored the divine law by his personal obedience, and in his death on the cross he made provision for the redemption of men from sin. He was raised from the dead with a glorified body and appeared to his disciples as the person who was with them before his crucifixion. He ascended into heaven and is now exalted at the right hand of God where he is the One Mediator, partaking of the nature of God and of man, and in whose Person is effected the reconciliation between God and man. He will return in power and glory to judge the world and to consummate his redemptive mission. He now dwells in all believers as the living and ever present Lord.

Gen. 18:1ff.; Psalms 2:7ff.; 110:1ff.; Isa. 7:14; 53; Matt. 1:18-23; 3:17; 8:29; 11:27; 14:33; 16:16,27; 17:5; 27; 28:1-6, 19; Mark 1:1; 3:11; Luke 1:35; 4:41; 22:70; 24:46; John 1:1-18,29; 10:30,38; 11:25-27; 12:44-50; 14:7-11; 16:15-16,28; 17:1-5, 21-22; 20:1-20,28; Acts

1:9; 2:22-24; 7:55-56; 9:4-5,20; Rom.
1:3-4; 3:23-26; 5:6-21; 8:1-3,34; 10:4;
1 Cor. 1:30; 2:2; 8:6; 15:1-8,24-28;
2 Cor. 5:19-21; 8:9; Gal. 4:4-5; Ephes.
1:20; 3:11; 4:7-10; Phil. 2:5-11; Col.
1:13-22; 2:9; 1 Thess. 4:14-18; 1 Tim.
2:5-6; 3:16; Titus 2:13-14; Heb. 1:1-3;
4:14-15; 7:14-28; 9:12-15,24-28; 12:2;
13:8; 1 Peter 2:21-25; 3:22; 1 John 1:7-9;
3:2; 4:14-15; 5:9; 2 John 7-9; Rev. 1:13-
16; 5:9-14; 12:10-11; 13:8; 19:16.

3. God the Holy Spirit

The Holy Spirit is the Spirit of God. He
inspired holy men of old to write the
Scriptures. Through illumination he enables men to understand truth. He exalts
Christ. He convicts of sin, of righteousness and of judgment. He calls men to the
Saviour, and effects regeneration. He cul-
tivates Christian character, comforts believers, and bestows the spiritual gifts by
which they serve God through his church.
He seals the believer unto the day of final
redemption. His presence in the Christian
is the assurance of God to bring the believer into the fulness of the stature of
Christ. He enlightens and empowers the
believer and the church in worship, evangelism, and service.

Gen. 1:2; Judg. 14:6; Job 26:13;
Psalms 51:11; 139:7ff.; Isa. 61:1-3; Joel
2:28-32; Matt. 1:18; 3:16; 4:1; 12:28-32;
28:19; Mark 1:10,12; Luke 1:35; 4:1,18-
19; 11:13; 12:12; 24:49; John 4:24;
14:16-17,26; 15:26; 16:7-14; Acts 1:8;
2:1-4,38; 4:31; 5:3; 6:3; 7:55; 8:17,39;
10:44; 13:2; 15:28; 16:6; 19:1-6; Rom.
8:9-11,14-16,26-27; 1 Cor. 2:10-14;
3:16; 12:3-11; Gal. 4:6; Ephes. 1:13-14;
4:30; 5:18; 1 Thess. 5:19; 1 Tim. 3:16;
4:1; 2 Tim. 1:14; 3:16; Heb. 9:8,14;
2 Peter 1:21; 1 John 4:13; 5:6-7; Rev.
1:10; 22:17.

III. MAN

Man was created by the special act of
God, in his own image, and is the crown-

III. THE FALL OF MAN

*Man was created by the special act of
God, as recorded in Genesis. "So God*

ing work of his creation. In the beginning man was innocent of sin and was endowed by his Creator with freedom of choice. By his free choice man sinned against God and brought sin into the human race. Through the temptation of Satan man transgressed the command of God, and fell from his original innocence; whereby his posterity inherit a nature and an environment inclined toward sin, and as soon as they are capable of moral action become transgressors and are under condemnation. Only the grace of God can bring man into his holy fellowship and enable man to fulfil the creative purpose of God. The sacredness of human personality is evident in that God created man in his own image, and in that Christ died for man; therefore every man possesses dignity and is worthy of respect and Christian love.

Gen. 1:26-30; 2:5,7,18-22; 3; 9:6; Psalms 1; 8:3-6; 32:1-5; 51:5; Isa. 6:5; Jer. 17:5; Matt. 16:26; Acts 17:26-31; Rom. 1:19-32; 3:10-18,23; 5:6,12,19; 6:6; 7:14-25; 8:14-18,29; 1 Cor. 1:21-31; 15:19,21-22; Eph. 2:1-22; Col. 1:21-22; 3:9-11.

created man in his own image, in the image of God created he him; male and female created he them" (Gen. 1:27). "And the Lord God formed man of the dust of the ground, and breathed into his nostrils the breath of life; and man became a living soul" (Gen. 2:7).

He was created in a state of holiness under the law of his Maker, but, through the temptation of Satan, he transgressed the command of God and fell from his original holiness and righteousness; whereby his posterity inherit a nature corrupt and in bondage to sin, are under condemnation, and as soon as they are capable of moral action, become actual transgressors.

Gen. 1:27; Gen. 2:7; John 1:23; Gen. 3:4-7; Gen. 3:22-24; Rom. 5:12,14,19, 21; Rom. 7:23-25; Rom. 11:18,22,32-33; Col. 1:21.

IV. SALVATION

Salvation involves the redemption of the whole man, and is offered freely to all who accept Jesus Christ as Lord and Saviour, who by his own blood obtained eternal redemption for the believer. In its broadest sense salvation includes regeneration, sanctification, and glorification.

1. Regeneration, or the new birth, is a work of God's grace whereby believers become new creatures in Christ Jesus. It is a change of heart wrought by the Holy Spirit through conviction of sin, to which the sinner responds in repentance toward God and faith in the Lord Jesus Christ.

Repentance and faith are inseparable experiences of grace. Repentance is a genuine turning from sin toward God. Faith is the acceptance of Jesus Christ and com-

IV. THE WAY OF SALVATION

The salvation of sinners is wholly of grace, through the mediatorial office of the Son of God, who by the Holy Spirit was born of the Virgin Mary and took upon him our nature, yet without sin; honored the divine law by his personal obedience and made atonement for our sins by his death. Being risen from the dead, he is now enthroned in Heaven, and, uniting in his person the tenderest sympathies with divine perfections, he is in every way qualified to be a compassionate and all-sufficient Saviour.

Col. 1:21-22; Eph. 1:7-10; Gal. 2:19-20; Gal. 3:13; Rom. 1:4; Eph. 1:20-23; Matt. 1:21-25; Luke 1:35; 2:11; Rom. 3:25.

mitment of the entire personality to him as Lord and Saviour. Justification is God's gracious and full acquittal upon principles of his righteousness of all sinners who repent and believe in Christ. Justification brings the believer into a relationship of peace and favor with God.

2. Sanctification is the experience, beginning in regeneration, by which the believer is set apart to God's purposes, and is enabled to progress toward moral and spiritual perfection through the presence and power of the Holy Spirit dwelling in him. Growth in grace should continue throughout the regenerate person's life.

3. Glorification is the culmination of salvation and is the final blessed and abiding state of the redeemed.

Gen. 3:15; Ex. 3:14-17; 6:2-8; Matt. 1:21; 4:17; 16:21-26; 27:22-28:6; Luke 1:68-69; 2:28-32; John 1:11-14,29; 3:3-21,36; 5:24; 10:9,28-29; 15:1-16; 17:17; Acts 2:21; 4:12; 15:11; 16:30-31; 17:30-31; 20:32; Rom. 1:16-18; 2:4; 3:23-25; 4:3ff.; 5:8-10; 6:1-23; 8:1-18,29-39; 10:9-10,13; 13:11-14; 1 Cor. 1:18,30; 6:19-20; 15:10; 2 Cor. 5:17-20; Gal. 2:20; 3:13; 5:22-25; 6:15; Ephes. 1:7; 2:8-22; 4:11-16; Phil. 2:12-13; Col. 1:9-22; 3:1ff.; 1 Thess. 5:23-24; 2 Tim. 1:12; Titus 2:11-14; Heb.2:1-3; 5:8-9; 9:24-28; 11:1-12:8,14; James 2:14-26; 1 Peter 1:2-23; 1 John 1:6-2:11; Rev. 3:20; 21: 1-22:5.

V. JUSTIFICATION

Justification is God's gracious and full acquittal upon principles of righteousness of all sinners who believe in Christ. This blessing is bestowed, not in consideration of any works of righteousness which we have done, but through the redemption that is in and through Jesus Christ. It brings us into a state of most blessed peace and favor with God, and secures every other needed blessing.

Rom. 3:24; 4:2; 5:1-2; 8:30; Eph. 1:7; 1 Cor. 1:30-31; 2 Cor. 5:21.

VI. THE FREENESS OF SALVATION

The blessings of salvation are made free to all by the gospel. It is the duty of all to accept them by penitent and obedient faith. Nothing prevents the salvation of the greatest sinner except his own voluntary refusal to accept Jesus Christ as teacher, Saviour, and Lord.

Eph. 1:5; 2:4-10; 1 Cor. 1:30-31; Rom. 5:1-9; Rev. 22:17; John 3:16; Mark 16:16.

VII. REGENERATION

Regeneration or the new birth is a change of heart wrought by the Holy Spirit, whereby we become partakers of the divine nature and a holy disposition is given, leading to the love and practice of righteousness. It is a work of God's free grace conditioned upon faith in Christ and made manifest by the fruit which we bring forth to the glory of God.

John 3:1-8, 1:16-18; Rom. 8:2; Eph. 2:1,5-6,8,10; Eph. 4:30,32; Col. 3:1-11; Titus 3:5.

VIII. REPENTANCE AND FAITH

We believe that repentance and faith are sacred duties, and also inseparable graces, wrought in our souls by the regenerating Spirit of God; whereby being deeply convinced of our guilt, danger, and helplessness, and of the way of salvation by Christ, we turn to God with unfeigned contrition, confession, and supplication for mercy; at the same time heartily receiving the Lord Jesus Christ as our Prophet, Priest, and King, and relying on him alone as the only and all-sufficient Saviour.

Luke 22:31-34; Mark 1:15; 1 Tim. 1:13; Rom. 3:25,27,31; Rom. 4:3,9,12, 16-17; John 16:8-11.

X. SANCTIFICATION

Sanctification is the process by which the regenerate gradually attain to moral and spiritual perfection through the presence and power of the Holy Spirit dwelling in their hearts. It continues throughout the earthly life, and is accomplished by the use of all the ordinary means of grace, and particularly by the Word of God.

Acts. 20:32; John 17:17; Rom. 6:5-6; Eph. 3:16; Rom. 4:14; Gal. 5:24; Heb. 12:14; Rom. 7:18-25; 2 Cor. 3:18; Gal. 5:16,25-26.

V. GOD'S PURPOSE OF GRACE

Election is the gracious purpose of God, according to which he regenerates, sanctifies, and glorifies sinners. It is consistent with the free agency of man and comprehends all the means in connection with the end. It is a glorious display of God's sovereign goodness, and is infinitely wise, holy, and unchangeable. It excludes boasting and promotes humility.

All true believers endure to the end. Those whom God has accepted in Christ, and sanctified by his Spirit, will never fall away from the state of grace, but shall persevere to the end. Believers may fall into sin through neglect and temptation, whereby they grieve the Spirit, impair their graces and comforts, bring reproach on the cause of Christ. and temporal judgments on themselves, yet they shall be kept by the power of God through faith unto salvation.

Gen. 12:1-3; Ex. 19:5-8; 1 Sam. 8:4-7,19-22; Isa. 5:1-7; Jer. 31:31ff.; Matt.

IX. GOD'S PURPOSE OF GRACE

Election is the gracious purpose of God, according to which he regenerates, sanctifies and saves sinners. It is perfectly consistent with the free agency of man, and comprehends all the means in connection with the end. It is a most glorious display of God's sovereign goodness, and is infinitely wise, holy, and unchangeable. It excludes boasting and promotes humility. It encourages the use of means in the highest degree.

Rom. 8:30; 11:7; Eph. 1:10; Acts 26:18; Eph. 1:17-19; 2 Tim. 1:9; Psalm 110:3; 1 Cor. 2:14; Eph. 2:5; John 6:44-45,65; Rom. 10:12-15.

XI. PERSEVERANCE

All real believers endure to the end. Their continuance in well-doing is the mark which distinguishes them from mere professors. A special Providence cares for them, and they are kept by the power of God through faith unto salvation.

16:18-19; 21:28-45; 24:22,31; 25:34;
Luke 1:68-79; 2:29-32; 19:41-44; 24:44-
48; John 1:12-14; 3:16; 5:24; 6:44-
45,65; 10:27-29; 15:16; 17:6,12,17-18;
Acts 20:32; Rom. 5:9-10; 8:28-39;
10:12-15; 11:5-7,26-36; 1 Cor. 1:1-2;
15:24-28; Ephes. 1:4-23; 2:1-10; 3:1-11;
Col. 1:12-14; 2 Thess. 2:13-14; 2 Tim.
1:12; 2:10,19; Heb. 11:39-12:2; 1 Peter
1:2-5,13; 2:4-10; 1 John 1:7-9; 2:19; 3:2.

*John 10:28-29; 2 Tim. 2:19; 1 John
2:19; 1 Cor. 11:32; Rom. 8:30; 9:11,16;
Rom. 5:9-10; Matt. 26:70-75.*

VI. THE CHURCH

A New Testament church of the Lord Jesus Christ is a local body of baptized believers who are associated by covenant in the faith and fellowship of the gospel, observing the two ordinances of Christ, committed to his teachings, exercising the gifts, rights, and privileges invested in them by his Word, and seeking to extend the gospel to the ends of the earth.

This church is an autonomous body, operating through democratic processes under the Lordship of Jesus Christ. In such a congregation, members are equally responsible. Its Scriptural officers are pastors and deacons.

The New Testament speaks also of the church as the body of Christ which includes all of the redeemed of all the ages.

Matt. 16:15-19; 18:15-20; Acts 2:41-42,47; 5:11-14; 6:3-6; 13:1-3; 14:23,27; 5:1-30;16:5; 20:28; Rom. 1:7; 1 Cor. 1:2; 3:16; 5:4-5; 7:17; 9:13-14; 12; Ephes. 1:22-23; 2:19-22; 3:8-11,21; 5:22-32; Phil. 1:1; Col. 1:18; 1 Tim. 3:1-15; 4:14; 1 Peter 5:1-4; Rev. 2-3; 21:2-3.

XII. A GOSPEL CHURCH

A church of Christ is a congregation of baptized believers, associated by covenant in the faith and fellowship of the gospel; observing the ordinances of Christ, governed by his laws, and exercising the gifts, rights, and privileges invested in them by his word, and seeking to extend the gospel to the ends of the earth. Its Scriptural officers are bishops, or elders, and deacons.

Matt. 16:18; Matt. 18:15-18; Rom. 1:7; 1 Cor. 1:2; Acts 2:41-42; 5:13-14; 2 Cor. 9:13; Phil. 1:1; 1 Tim. 4:14; Acts 14:23; Acts 6:3,5-6; Heb. 13:17; 1 Cor. 9:6,14.

VII. BAPTISM AND THE LORD'S SUPPER

Christian baptism is the immersion of a believer in water in the name of the Father, the Son, and the Holy Spirit. It is an act of obedience symbolizing the believer's faith in a crucified, buried, and risen Saviour, the believer's death to sin, the burial of the old life, and the resurrection to walk in

XIII. BAPTISM AND THE LORD'S SUPPER

Christian baptism is the immersion of a believer in water in the name of the Father, the Son, and the Holy Spirit. The act is a symbol of our faith in a crucified, buried and risen Saviour. It is prerequisite to the privileges of a church relation and to the Lord's Supper, in which the members of

newness of life in Christ Jesus. It is a testimony to his faith in the final resurrection of the dead. Being a church ordinance, it is prerequisite to the privileges of church membership and to the Lord's Supper.

The Lord's Supper is a symbolic act of obedience whereby members of the church, through partaking of the bread and the fruit of the vine, memorialize the death of the Redeemer and anticipate his second coming.

Matt. 3:13-17; 26:26-30; 28:19-20; Mark 1:9-11; 14:22-26; Luke 3:21-22; 22:19-20; John 3:23; Acts 2:41-42; 8:35-39; 16:30-33; Acts 20;7; Rom. 6:3-5; 1 Cor. 10:16,21; 11:23-29; Col. 2:12.

the church, by the use of bread and wine, commemorate the dying love of Christ.

Matt. 28:19-20; 1 Cor. 4:1; Rom. 6:3-5; Col. 2:12; Mark 1:4; Matt. 3:16; John 3:23; 1 Cor. 11:23-26; 1 Cor. 10:16-17,21; Matt. 26:26-27; Acts 8:38-39; Mark 1:9-11.

VIII. THE LORD'S DAY

The first day of the week is the Lord's Day. It is a Christian institution for regular observance. It commemorates the resurrection of Christ from the dead and should be employed in exercises of worship and spiritual devotion, both public and private, and by refraining from worldly amusements, and resting from secular employments, work of necessity and mercy only being excepted.

Ex. 20:8-11; Matt. 12:1-12; 28:1ff.; Mark 2:27-28; 16:1-7; Luke 24:1-3, 33-36; John 4:21-24; 20:1,19-28; Acts 20:7; 1 Cor. 16:1-2; Col. 2:16; 3:16; Rev. 1:10.

XIV. THE LORD'S DAY

The first day of the week is the Lord's day. It is a Christian institution for regular observance. It commemorates the resurrection of Christ from the dead and should be employed in exercises of worship and spiritual devotion, both public and private, and by refraining from worldly amusements, and resting from secular employments, works of necessity and mercy only excepted.

Ex. 20:3-6; Matt. 4:10; Matt. 28:19; 1 Tim. 4:13; Col. 3:16; John 4:21; Ex. 20:8; 1 Cor. 16:1-2; Acts 20:7; Rev. 1:1; Matt. 12:1-13.

IX. THE KINGDOM

The kingdom of God includes both his general sovereignty over the universe and his particular kingship over men who willfully acknowledge him as King. Particularly the kingdom is the realm of salvation into which men enter by trustful, childlike commitment to Jesus Christ. Christians ought to pray and to labor that the kingdom may come and God's will be done on earth. The full consummation of the kingdom awaits the return of Jesus Christ and the end of this age.

Gen. 1:1; Isa. 9:6-7; Jer. 23:5-6; Matt.

XXV. THE KINGDOM

The Kingdom of God is the reign of God in the heart and life of the individual in every human relationship, and in every form and institution of organized human society. The chief means for promoting the Kingdom of God on earth are preaching the gospel of Christ, and teaching the principles of righteousness contained therein. The Kingdom of God will be complete when every thought and will of man shall be brought into captivity to the will of Christ. And it is the duty of all Christ's people to pray and labor continually that

3:2; 4:8-10,23; 12:25-28; 13:1-52; 25:31-46; 26:29; Mark 1:14-15; 9:1; Luke 4:43; 8:1; 9:2; 12:31-32; 17:20-21; 23:42; John 3:3; 18:36; Acts 1:6-7; 17:22-31; Rom. 5:17; 8:19; 1 Cor. 15:24-28; Col. 1:13; Heb. 11:10,16; 12: 28; 1 Peter 2:4-10; 4:13; Rev. 1:6,9; 5:10; 11:15; 21-22.

his Kingdom may come and his will be done on earth as it is done in heaven.

Dan. 2:37-44; 7:18; Matt. 4:23; 8:12; 12:25; 13:38,43; 25:34; 26:29; Mark 11:10; Luke 12:32; 22:29; Acts 1:6; 1 Cor. 15:24; Col. 1:13; Heb. 12:28; Rev. 1:9; Luke 4:43; 8:1; 9:2; 17:20-21; John 3:3; John 18:36; Matt. 6:10; Luke 23:42.

X. LAST THINGS

God, in his own time and in his own way, will bring the world to its appropriate end. According to his promise, Jesus Christ will return personally and visibly in glory to the earth; the dead will be raised; and Christ will judge all men in righteousness. The unrighteous will be consigned to hell, the place of everlasting punishment. The righteous in their resurrected and glorified bodies will receive their reward and will dwell forever in heaven with the Lord.

Isa. 2:4; 11:9; Matt. 16:27; 18:8-9; 19:28; 24:27,30,36,44; 25:31-46; 26:64; Mark 8:38; 9:43-48; Luke 12:40,48; 16:19-26; 17:22-37; 21:27-28; John 14:1-3; Acts 1:11; 17:31; Rom. 14:10; 1 Cor. 4:5; 15:24-28,35-58; 2 Cor. 5:10; Phil. 3:20-21; Col. 1:5; 3:4; 1 Thess. 4:14-18; 5:1ff.; 2 Thess. 1:7ff.; 2; 1 Tim. 6:14; 2 Tim. 4:1,8; Titus 2:13; Heb. 9:27-28; James 5:8; 2 Peter 3:7ff.; 1 John 2:28; 3:2; Jude 14; Rev. 1:18; 3:11; 20:1-22:13.

XV. THE RIGHTEOUS AND THE WICKED

There is a radical and essential difference between the righteous and wicked. Those only who are justified through the name of the Lord Jesus Christ and sanctified by the Holy Spirit are truly righteous in his sight. Those who continue in impenitence and unbelief are in his sight wicked and are under condemnation. This distinction between the righteous and the wicked holds in and after death, and will be made manifest at the judgment when final and everlasting awards are made to all men.

Gen. 3:19; Acts 13:36; Luke 23:43; 2 Cor. 5:1,6,8; Phil. 1:23; 1 Cor. 15:51-52; 1 Thess. 4:17; Phil. 3:21; 1 Cor. 6:3; Matt. 25:32-46; Rom. 9:22-23; Mark 9:48; 1 Thess. 1:7-10; Rev. 22:20.

XVI. THE RESURRECTION

The Scriptures clearly teach that Jesus rose from the dead. His grave was emptied of its contents. He appeared to the disciples after his resurrection in many convincing manifestations. He now exists in his glorified body at God's right hand. There will be a resurrection of the righteous and the wicked. The bodies of the righteous will conform to the glorious spiritual body of Jesus.

1 Cor. 15:1-58; 2 Cor. 5:1-8; 1 Thess. 4:17; John 5:28-29; Phil. 3:21; Acts 24:15; John 20:9; Matt. 28:6.

XVII. THE RETURN OF THE LORD

The New Testament teaches in many places the visible and personal return of

Jesus to this earth. "This same Jesus which is taken up from you into heaven, shall so come in like manner as ye have seen him go into heaven." The time of his coming is not revealed. "Of that day and hour knoweth no one, no, not the angels in heaven, but my Father only" (Matt. 24:36). It is the duty of all believers to live in readiness for his coming and by diligence in good works to make manifest to all men the reality and power of their hope in Christ.

Matt. 24:36; Matt. 24:42-47; Mark 13:32-37; Luke 21:27-28; Acts 1:9-11.

XI. EVANGELISM AND MISSIONS

It is the duty and privilege of every follower of Christ and of every church of the Lord Jesus Christ to endeavor to make disciples of all nations. The new birth of man's spirit by God's Holy Spirit means the birth of love for others. Missionary effort on the part of all rests thus upon a spiritual necessity of the regenerate life, and is expressly and repeatedly commanded in the teachings of Christ. It is the duty of every child of God to seek constantly to win the lost to Christ by personal effort and by all other methods in harmony with the gospel of Christ.

Gen. 12:1-3; Ex. 19:5-6; Isa. 6:1-8; Matt. 9:37-38; 10:5-15; 13:18-30,37-43; 16:19; 22:9-10; 24:14; 28:18-20; Luke 10:1-18; 24:46-53; John 14:11-12; 15:7-8,16; 17:15; 20:21; Acts 1:8; 2; 8:26-40; 10:42-48; 13:2-3; Rom. 10:13-15; Ephes. 3:1-11; 1 Thess. 1:8; 2 Tim. 4:5; Heb. 2:1-3; 11:39-12:2; 1 Peter 2:4-10; Rev. 22:17.

XXIII. EVANGELISM AND MISSIONS

It is the duty of every Christian man and woman, and the duty of every church of Christ to seek to extend the gospel to the ends of the earth. The new birth of man's spirit by God's Holy Spirit means the birth of love for others. Missionary effort on the part of all rests thus upon a spiritual necessity of the regenerate life. It is also expressly and repeatedly commanded in the teachings of Christ. It is the duty of every child of God to seek constantly to win the lost to Christ by personal effort and by all other methods sanctioned by the gospel of Christ.

Matt. 10:5; 13:18-23; 22:9-10; 28:19-20; Mark 16:15-16; 16:19-20; Luke 24:46-53; Acts 1:5-8; 2:1-2,21,39; 8:26-40; 10:42-48; 13:2,30-33; 1 Thess. 1-8.

XII. EDUCATION

The cause of education in the kingdom of Christ is co-ordinate with the causes of missions and general benevolence and should receive along with these the liberal support of the churches. An adequate system of Christian schools is necessary to a

XX. EDUCATION

Christianity is the religion of enlightenment and intelligence. In Jesus Christ are hidden all the treasures of wisdom and knowledge. All sound learning is therefore a part of our Christian heritage. The new birth opens all human faculties

complete spiritual program for Christ's people.

In Christian education there should be a proper balance between academic freedom and academic responsibility. Freedom in any orderly relationship of human life is always limited and never absolute. The freedom of a teacher in a Christian school, college, or seminary is limited by the pre-eminence of Jesus Christ, by the authoritative nature of the Scriptures, and by the distinct purpose for which the school exists.

Deut. 4:1,5,9,14; 6:1-10; 31:12-13; Neh. 8:1-8; Job. 28:28; Psalms 19:7ff.; 119:11; Prov. 3:13ff.; 4:1-10; 8:1-7,11; 15:14; Eccl. 7:19; Matt. 5:2; 7:24ff.; 28:19-20; Luke 2:40; 1 Cor. 1:18-31; Eph. 4:11-16; Phil. 4:8; Col. 2:3,8-9; 1 Tim. 1:3-7; 2 Tim. 2:15; 3:14-17; Heb. 5:12-6:3; James 1:5; 3:17.

and creates a thirst for knowledge. An adequate system of schools is necessary to a complete spiritual program for Christ's people. The cause of education in the Kingdom of Christ is coordinate with the causes of missions and general benevolence, and should receive along with these the liberal support of the churches.

Deut. 4:1,5,9,13-14; Deut. 6:1,7-10; Psalm 19:7-8; Prov. 8:1-7; Prov. 4:1-10; Matt. 28:20; Col. 2:3; Neh. 8:1-4.

XIII. STEWARDSHIP

God is the source of all blessings, temporal and spiritual; all that we have and are we owe to him. Christians have a spiritual debtorship to the whole world, a holy trusteeship in the gospel, and a binding stewardship in their possessions. They are therefore under obligation to serve him with their time, talents, and material possessions; and should recognize all these as entrusted to them to use for the glory of God and for helping others. According to the Scriptures, Christians should contribute of their means cheerfully, regularly, systematically, proportionately, and liberally for the advancement of the Redeemer's cause on earth.

Gen. 14:20; Lev. 27:30-32; Deut. 8:18; Mal. 3:8-12; Matt. 6:1-4,19-21; 19:21; 23:23; 25:14-29; Luke 12:16-21,42; 16:1-13; Acts 2:44-47; 5:1-11; 17:24-25; 20:35; Rom. 6:6-22; 12:1-2; 1 Cor. 4:1-2; 6:19-20; 12; 16:1-4; 2 Cor. 8-9; 12:15; Phil. 4:10-19; 1 Peter 1:18-19.

XXIV. STEWARDSHIP

God is the source of all blessings, temporal and spiritual; all that we have and are we owe to him. We have a spiritual debtorship to the whole world, a holy trusteeship in the gospel, and a binding stewardship in our possessions. We are therefore under obligation to serve him with our time, talents and material possessions; and should recognize all these as entrusted to us to use for the glory of God and helping others. Christians should cheerfully, regularly, systematically, proportionately, and liberally, contribute of their means to advancing the Redeemer's cause on earth.

Luke 12:42; 16:1-8; Titus 1:7; 1 Peter 4:10; 2 Cor. 8:1-7; 2 Cor. 8:11-19; 2 Cor. 12:1-15; Matt. 25:14-30; Rom. 1:8-15; 1 Cor. 6:20; Acts 2:44-47.

XIV. CO-OPERATION

Christ's people should, as occasion requires, organize such associations and conventions as may best secure co-operation for the great objects of the kingdom of God. Such organizations have no authority over one another or over the churches. They are voluntary and advisory bodies designed to elicit, combine, and direct the energies of our people in the most effective manner. Members of New Testament churches should co-operate with one another in carrying forward the missionary, educational, and benevolent ministries for the extension of Christ's kingdom. Christian unity in the New Testament sense is spiritual harmony and voluntary co-operation for common ends by various groups of Christ's people. Co-operation is desirable between the various Christian denominations, when the end to be attained is itself justified, and when such co-operation involves no violation of conscience or compromise of loyalty to Christ. and his Word as revealed in the New Testament.

Ex. 17:12; 18:17ff.; Judg. 7:21; Ezra 1:3-4; 2:68-69; 5:14-15; Neh. 4; 8:1-5; Matt. 10:5-15; 20:1-16; 22:1-10; 28:19-20; Mark 2:3; Luke 10:1ff.; Acts 1:13-14; 2:1ff.; 4:31-37; 13:2-3; 15:1-35; 1 Cor. 1:10-17; 3:5-15; 12; 2 Cor. 8-9; Gal. 1:6-10; Eph. 4:1-16; Phil. 1:15-18.

XXII. CO-OPERATION

Christ's people should, as occasion requires, organize such associations and conventions as may best secure co-operation for the great objects of the Kingdom of God. Such organizations have no authority over each other or over the churches. They are voluntary and advisory bodies designed to elicit, combine, and direct the energies of our people in the most effective manner. Individual members of New Testament churches should co-operate with each other, and the churches themselves should co-operate with each other in carrying forward the missionary, educational, and benevolent program for the extension of Christ's Kingdom. Christian unity in the New Testament sense is spiritual harmony and voluntary co-operation for common ends by various groups of Christ's people. It is permissable and desirable as between the various Christian denominations, when the end to be attained is itself justified, and when such co-operation involves no violation of conscience or compromise of loyalty to Christ and his Word as revealed in the New Testament.

Ezra 1:3-4; 2:68-69; 5:14-15; Neh. 4:4-6; 8:1-4; Mal. 3:10; Matt. 10:5-15; 20:1-16; 22:1-10; Acts 1:13-14; 1:21-26; 2:1,41-47; 1 Cor. 1:10-17; 12:11-12; 13; 14:33-34,40; 16:2; 2 Cor. 9:1-15; Eph. 4:1-16; 3 John 1:5-8.

XV. THE CHRISTIAN AND THE SOCIAL ORDER

Every Christian is under obligation to seek to make the will of Christ supreme in his own life and in human society. Means and methods used for the improvement of society and the establishment of righteousness among men can be truly and permanently helpful only when they are rooted in the regeneration of the individual by the saving grace of God in Christ Jesus. The Christian should oppose in the spirit of Christ every form of greed, selfishness,

XXI. SOCIAL SERVICE

Every Christian is under obligation to seek to make the will of Christ regnant in his own life and in human society to oppose in the spirit of Christ every form of greed, selfishness, and vice; to provide for the orphaned, the aged, the helpless, and the sick; to seek to bring industry, government, and society as a whole under the sway of the principles of righteousness, truth and brotherly love; to promote these ends Christians should be ready to work with all men of good will in any good and vice. He should work to provide for the orphaned, the needy, the aged, the helpless, and the sick. Every Christian should seek to bring industry, government, and society as a whole under the sway of the principles of righteousness, truth, and brotherly love. In order to promote these ends Christians should be ready to work with all men of good will in any good cause, always being careful to act in the spirit of love without compromising their loyalty to Christ and his truth.

Ex. 20:3-17; Lev. 6:2-5; Deut. 10:12; 27:17; Psalm 101:5; Micah 6:8; Zech. 8:16; Matt. 5:13-16,43-48; 22:36-40; 25:35; Mark 1:29-34; 2:3ff.; 10:21; Luke 4:18-21; 10:27-37; 20:25; John 15:12; 17:15; Rom. 12-14; 1 Cor. 5:9-10; 6:1-7; 7:20-24; 10:23-11:1; Gal. 3:26-28; Eph. 6:5-9; Col. 3:12-17; 1 Thess. 3:12; Philemon; James 1:27; 2:8.

cause, always being careful to act in the spirit of love without compromising their loyalty to Christ and his truth. All means and methods used in social service for the amelioration of society and the establishment of righteousness among men must finally depend on the regeneration of the individual by the saving grace of God in Christ Jesus.

Luke 10:25-37; Ex. 22:10,14; Lev. 6:2; Deut. 20:10; Deut. 4:42; Deut. 15:2; 27:17; Psalm 101:5; Ezek. 18:6; Heb. 2:15; Zech. 8:16; Ex. 20:16; James 2:8; Rom. 12-14; Col. 3-12-17.

XVI. PEACE AND WAR

It is the duty of Christians to seek peace with all men on principles of righteousness. In accordance with the spirit and teachings of Christ they should do all in their power to put an end to war.

The true remedy for the war spirit is the gospel of our Lord. The supreme need of the world is the acceptance of his teachings in all the affairs of men and nations, and the practical application of his law of love.

Isa. 2:4; Matt. 5:9,38-48; 6:33; 26:52; Luke 22:36,38; Rom. 12:18-19; 13:1-7; 14:19; Heb. 12:14; James 4:1-2.

XIX. PEACE AND WAR

It is the duty of Christians to seek peace with all men on principles of righteousness. In accordance with the spirit and teachings of Christ they should do all in their power to put an end to war.

The true remedy for the war spirit is the pure gospel of our Lord. The supreme need of the world is the acceptance of his teachings in all the affairs of men and nations, and the practical application of his law of love.

We urge Christian people throughout the world to pray for the reign of the Prince of Peace, and to oppose everything likely to provoke war.

Matt. 5:9,13-14,43-46; Heb. 12:14; James 4:1; Matt. 6:33; Rom. 14:17,19.

XVII. RELIGIOUS LIBERTY

God alone is Lord of the conscience, and he has left it free from the doctrines and commandments of men which are contrary to his Word or not contained in

XVIII. RELIGIOUS LIBERTY

God alone is Lord of the conscience, and he has left it free from the doctrines and commandments of men which are contrary to his Word or not contained in

it. Church and state should be separate. The state owes to every church protection and full freedom in the pursuit of its spiritual ends. In providing for such freedom no ecclesiastical group or denomination should be favored by the state more than others. Civil government being ordained of God, it is the duty of Christians to render loyal obedience thereto in all things not contrary to the revealed will of God. The church should not resort to the civil power to carry on its work. The gospel of Christ contemplates spiritual means alone for the pursuit of its ends. The state has no right to impose penalties for religious opinions of any kind. The state has no right to impose taxes for the support of any form of religion. A free church in a free state is the Christian ideal, and this implies the right of free and unhindered access to God on the part of all men and the right to form and propagate opinions in the sphere of religion without interference by the civil power.

Gen. 1:27; 2:7; Matt. 6:6-7; 24:16-26; 22:21; John 8:36; Acts 4:19-20; Rom. 6:1-2; 13:1-7; Gal. 5:1,13; Phil. 3:20; 1 Tim. 2:1-2; James 4:12; 1 Peter 2:12-17; 3:11-17; 4:12-19.

it. Church and state should be separate. The state owes to the church protection and full freedom in the pursuit of its spiritual ends. In providing for such freedom no ecclesiastical group or denomination should be favored by the state more than others. Civil government being ordained of God, it is the duty of Christians to render loyal obedience thereto in all things not contrary to the revealed will of God. The church should not resort to the civil power to carry on its work. The gospel of Christ contemplates spiritual means alone for the pursuit of its ends. The state has no right to impose penalties for religious opinions of any kind. The state has no right to impose taxes for the support of any form of religion. A free church in a free state is the Christian ideal, and this implies the right of free and unhindered access to God on the part of all men, and the right to form and propagate opinions in the sphere of religion without interference by the civil power.

Rom. 13:1-7; 1 Peter 2:17; 1 Tim. 2:1-2; Gal. 3:9-14; John 7:38-39; James 4:12; Gal. 5:13; 2 Peter 2:18-21; 1 Cor. 3:5; Rom. 6:1-2; Matt. 22:21; Mark 12:17.

HERSCHEL H. HOBBS, Oklahoma City, Oklahoma (President of the Southern Baptist Convention), *Chairman*
HOWARD M. REAVES, Mobile, Alabama
ED. J. PACKWOOD, Phoenix, Arizona
C. Z. HOLLAND, Jonesboro, Arkansas
W. B. TIMBERLAKE, Pomona, California
C. V. KOONS, Washington, District of Columbia
MALCOLM B. KNIGHT, Jacksonville, Florida
DICK H. HALL, JR., Decatur, Georgia, *Secretary*
CHARLES R. WALKER, Marion, Illinois
WALTER R. DAVIS, Hammond, Indiana
GARTH PYBAS, Topeka, Kansas
V. C. KRUSCHWITZ, Elizabethtown, Kentucky
LUTHER B. HALL, Farmerville, Louisiana
ROBERT WOODWARD, Frederick, Maryland
DOUGLAS HUDGINS, Jackson, Mississippi, *Vice-Chairman*
PAUL WEBER, JR., Springfield, Missouri
R. A. LONG, Roswell, New Mexico
NANE STARNES, Asheville, North Carolina
C. HOGE HOCKENSMITH, Columbus, Ohio
HUGH R. BUMPAS, Oklahoma City, Oklahoma

DAVID G. ANDERSON, North Charleston,
South Carolina
E. WARREN RUST, Cleveland, Tennessee
JAMES H. LANDES, Wichita Falls, Texas
R. P. DOWNEY, Salem, Virginia

15.14 The Baptist and Message Fellowship

The dismissal of Ralph H. Elliott from the faculty of the Midwestern Baptist Theological Seminary in 1962 did not calm the controversy. Even before the firing of Elliott, informal meetings of the like-minded had been held, including several pre-Convention gatherings. This dissident group organized in 1973 under the name of Baptist Faith and Message Fellowship. The name was intended to affirm their theological commitment to the confession of that name. In function, this organization bore remarkable similarity to the old Fundamentalist Fellowship in the Northern Baptist Convention. Some of the "founding fathers" of the BFMF, like M. O. Owens, Jr. and LaVerne Butler, represented more moderate forms of fundamentalism. However, within a few years they lost control of the movement; several of the founders, including Owens, resigned from the Fellowship. As more militant leaders arose, the Fellowship kept its name, but turned its efforts to change rather than retain the emphases of the 1963 confession. *Source:* Report compiled by M. O. Owens, Jr., from the first issue of *Baptist Faith and Message,* a periodical distributed at the Portland Convention, 1973. M. O. Owens, Jr. to Leon McBeth, 11 Feb. 1984. Used by permission.

MEETING OF BAPTIST FAITH FELLOWSHIP, OCT. 16, 1972

The group met from 1:30 until after 5 p.m. and then again from 7 until 9 p.m. The Steering Committee then met later that night. Not all of the men who attended were able to stay the entire time. Ray and Joe Sadler flew down from Pennsylvania just to attend, and had to leave in the middle of the afternoon in order to be back in York, Pa. for services that night. Laverne Butler flew down from Louisville and left before 6 p.m. in order to be back to preach in his own church that night. Bill Powell had an evening engagement, and stayed for only part of the time. Raymond Moore came in for part of the evening session.—The fellowship was great; there was a feeling of unanimity and a sense of the Spirit's presence.

The problems which led to this meeting were set forth as follows:

(1) The teaching of heresy and false doctrine in some of our colleges and seminaries.

(2) Publishing books and literature containing serious error by our own Board.

(3) The leaning of the Home Mission Board away from evangelism.

(4) The tendency of the Foreign Mission Board, in some areas, to produce a predominantly institutional ministry in place of a preaching ministry.

(5) The feeling of loneliness on the part of those who dare to be a "loyal opposition" to the establishment and its current trends.

(6) The growing tendency of churches, led by strong Bible-believing pastors, to wean themselves away from the Convention and to become independent.

(7) The sickening feeling and awareness that we are watching the work of Satan as he spreads the cancerous and destructive disease of doctrinal apostasy.

It was felt and set forth that such a group as this, greatly enlarged, might be able to provide help in such areas as:

(1) Provide fellowship for those who make no apologies for their convictions.

(2) Encourage pastors and churches not to abandon the Convention, but to join hands in cooperating in many areas of common interest.

(3) Study and sift literature, including Southern Baptist, so that the churches may know what is true to the Bible and what is not.

(4) The group could easily move to provide literature true to the Word if needed.

(5) Channel and coordinate support to the two Baptist seminaries we know stand true to the Word of God—Mid-America and Luther Rice.

(6) The group perhaps could at some future date establish a college that would stand true to the infallible Word.

(7) Plan, promote and support Bible Conferences, Preaching Weeks, Evangelistic Conferences and other inspirational meetings in which the truth of God's Word is affirmed.

(8) Provide an independent Southern Baptist paper, southwide in coverage, that will tell it like it is, giving full information to the Baptist people.

(9) Coordinate the strength of Bible-believers to elect good men to Boards, etc.

(10) To provide base for Fellowship groups in many of the states.

Several matters were discussed as specific ideas for the group to think about and perhaps to adopt as objectives at a later date. The larger meeting to be held next March would give opportunity for all discussion. At this larger meeting, we will use outstanding men to preach and lead in Bible exposition.

(1) The idea of employing a man full-time was mentioned. He would visit with the pastors, rally them around the Book and the fervent preaching of the Gospel and to the support of institutions that stand firm in the truth of the Word. A starting budget of $25,000 or maybe less would begin such a plan.

(2) Gwin Turner is asking the Sunday School Board to consider the publication of a multi-volume 'Conservative' commentary to offset the Broadman Commentary.

(3) There was strong urging that we move toward a strong, southwide news medium to go to pastors and others. This would require effort. It could do for Southern Baptists what the Presbyterian Journal does for Southern Presbyterians.

(4) Using ourselves as a nucleus, we desire to form a much larger group of Bible-believing Southern Baptists unashamed to believe all the Book, who will stand together.

(5) We believe Southern Baptists, at this point, need a group unafraid to say that doctrinal error never won anybody to Christ, nor brought glory to God.

15.15 Controversial Resolutions by Southern Baptists

According to Southern Baptist polity, Convention resolutions are not binding. They are merely an expression of the opinion of those messengers present and voting. Even so, resolutions elicit intense interest; the news media, and probably some Baptist people, regard them as some kind of official voice of the denomination. Resolutions do at least reveal what Southern Baptists have on their minds at any given meeting. For that reason, three resolutions are included here, two from the Southern Baptist Convention and one from the Baptist General Convention of Texas. In 1984 the SBC adopted a resolution against the ordination of women (selection A). *Source: Annual,* SBC, 1984, 65. This passed easily at the Convention, but has proven increasingly controversial among those Southern Baptists who have heard of it. Selection B cites the SBC resolution on the priesthood of the believer in 1988. The thrust of this resolution has been resisted by many who regard it as undermining the priceless Baptist heritage of freedom. *Source: Annual,* SBC, 1988, 68-69. Selection C cites a Texas resolution which seeks to counteract the SBC statement by reaffirming the historic Baptist emphasis upon the priesthood of the believer. *Source: Baptist Standard,* 2 Nov. 1988, 8. Used by permission.

A.   Southern Baptist Convention Resolution Opposing Ordination of Women, 1984

Resolution No. 3—On Ordination and the Role of Women in Ministry

WHEREAS, We, the messengers to the Southern Baptist Convention meeting in

Kansas City, June 12-14, 1984, recognize the authority of Scripture in all matters of faith and practice including the autonomy of the local church; and

WHEREAS, The New Testament enjoins all Christians to proclaim the gospel; and

WHEREAS, The New Testament churches as a community of faith recognized God's ordination and anointing of some believers for special ministries (e.g., I Timothy 2:7; Titus 1:15) and in consequence of their demonstrated loyalty to the gospel, conferred public blessing and engaged in public dedicatory prayer setting them apart for service; and

WHEREAS, The New Testament does not mandate that all who are divinely called to ministry be ordained; and

WHEREAS, In the New Testament, ordination symbolizes spiritual succession to the world task of proclaiming and extending the gospel of Christ, and not a sacramental transfer of unique divine grace that perpetuates apostolic authority; and

WHEREAS, The New Testament emphasizes the equal dignity of men and women (Gal. 3:28) and that the Holy Spirit was at Pentecost divinely outpoured on men and women alike (Acts 2:17); and

WHEREAS, Women as well as men prayed and prophesied in public worship services (I Cor. 11:2-16), and Priscilla joined her husband in teaching Apollos (Acts 18:26), and women fulfilled special church service-ministries as exemplified by Phoebe whose work Paul tributes as that of a servant of the church (Rom. 16:1); and

WHEREAS, The Scriptures attest to God's delegated order of authority (God the head of Christ, Christ the head of man, man the head of woman, man and woman dependent one upon the other to the glory of God) distinguishing the roles of men and women in public prayer and prophecy (I Cor. 11:2-5); and

WHEREAS, The Scriptures teach that women are not in public worship to assume a role of authority over men lest confusion reign in the local church (I Cor. 14:33-36); and

WHEREAS, While Paul commends women and men alike in other roles of ministry and service (Titus 2:1-10), he excludes women from pastoral leadership (I Tim. 2:12) to preserve a submission God requires because the man was first in creation and the woman was first in the Edenic fall (I Tim. 2:13ff); and

WHEREAS, These Scriptures are not intended to stifle the creative contribution of men and women as co-workers in many roles of church service, both on distant mission fields and in domestic ministries, but imply that women and men are nonetheless divinely gifted for distinctive areas of evangelical engagement; and

WHEREAS, Women are held in high honor for their unique and significant contribution to the advancement of Christ's kingdom, and the building of godly homes should be esteemed for its vital contribution to developing personal Christian character and Christlike concern for others.

Therefore, be it *Resolved,* That we not decide concerns of Christian doctrine and practice by modern cultural, sociological, and ecclesiastical trends or by emotional factors; that we remind ourselves of the dearly bought Baptist principle of the final authority of Scripture in matters of faith and conduct; and that we encourage the service of women in all aspects of church life and work other than pastoral functions and leadership roles entailing ordination.

B. Priesthood of the Believer, SBC, June 1988

SAN ANTONIO—Following is the full text of the resolution on the priesthood of the believer passed at the Southern Baptist Convention, June 15:

"WHEREAS, None of the five major writing systematic theologians in Southern Baptist history have given more than passing reference to the doctrine of the Priesthood of the Believer in their systematic theologies; and

"WHEREAS, The Baptist Faith and Message preamble refers to the Priesthood of the Believer, but provides no definition or content to the term; and

"WHEREAS, The high profile emphasis on the doctrine of the Priesthood of the Believer in Southern Baptist life is a recent historical development; and

"WHEREAS, The Priesthood of the Believer is a term which is subject to both misunderstanding and abuse; and

"WHEREAS, The doctrine of the Priesthood of the Believer has been used to justify wrongly the attitude that a Christian may believe whatever he so chooses and still be considered a loyal Southern Baptist; and

"WHEREAS, The doctrine of the Priesthood of the Believer can be used to justify the undermining of pastoral authority in the local church.

"Be it therefore RESOLVED, That the Southern Baptist Convention meeting in San Antonio, Texas, June 14-16, 1988, affirm its belief in the biblical doctrine of the Priesthood of the Believer (1 Peter 2:9 and Revelation 1:6); and

"Be it further RESOLVED, That we affirm that this doctrine in no way gives license to misinterpret, explain away, demythologize, or extrapolate out elements of the supernatural from the Bible; and

"Be it further RESOLVED, That the doctrine of the Priesthood of the Believer in no way contradicts the biblical understanding of the role, responsibility, and authority of the pastor which is seen in the command to the local church in Hebrews 13:17, "Obey your leaders, and submit to them; for they keep watch over your souls, as those who will give an account;" and

"Be it finally RESOLVED, That we affirm the truth that elders, or pastors, are called of God to lead the local church (Acts 20:28).

C. Priesthood of the Believer, Baptist General Convention of Texas, November 1988

WHEREAS the priesthood of the believer is the belief that Christians have direct access to God through Christ without the necessity of other mediators or priests; and

WHEREAS the priesthood of the believer affirms that each Christian has a spiritual ministry to perform (I Peter 2:4-5); and

WHEREAS the priesthood of the believer is one of the most fundamental of Baptist distinctives; and

WHEREAS the priesthood of the believer is deeply rooted in Baptist history from John Smyth and the early seventeenth century English Baptists to E. Y. Mullins and George W. Truett; and

WHEREAS the priesthood of the believer is a necessary corollary to the New Testament teaching that Jesus Christ is our one mediator before God and that through Him alone we have access before God (I Timothy 2:5); and

WHEREAS the priesthood of the believer is a necessary foundation to Baptist congregational church polity in which authority resides in the local congregation:

BE IT THEREFORE RESOLVED that the messengers to the 1988 annual session of the Baptist General Convention of Texas meeting in Austin affirm their belief in the doctrine of the priesthood of the believer; and

BE IT FINALLY RESOLVED that we vigorously undergird the biblical teaching of the priesthood of the believer in Baptist life in local church, associational, and state convention activities.

15.16   Southern Baptist Convention Statement on Racial Crisis in America, 1968

The Southern Baptist Convention has spoken more than once on the issue of race, and with a considerably different tone than in the previous century. The SBC was one of the first major denominations in America to affirm the 1954 Supreme Court decision on school desegregation. In the midst of the racial crises of the late 1960s, the Convention adopted the statement below, and it was signed individually by the major Convention leaders. This is a courageous and prophetic declaration by the most ethnically diverse denomination in America. However, one must not assume that all Southern Baptists agreed with this pronouncement of their Convention. The Convention expresses only the views of those present and voting. Other records show that many individuals, and many of the SBC churches, resisted racial integration and other efforts to move toward racial equity in America. *Source: Annual,* SBC, 1968, 67-69.

A STATEMENT CONCERNING THE CRISIS IN OUR NATION

We recognize that no individual or organization can speak for all Baptists. The following represents the concern, confession, commitment, and appeal by the majority of the messengers meeting in Houston, Texas, June 5, 1968.

We Face a Crisis

Our nation is enveloped in a social and cultural revolution. We are shocked by the potential for anarchy in a land dedicated to democracy and freedom. There are ominous sounds of hate and violence among men and of unbelief and rebellion toward God. These compel Christians to face the social situation and to examine themselves under the judgment of God.

We are an affluent society, abounding in wealth and luxury. Yet far too many of our people suffer from poverty. Many are hurt by circumstance from which they find it most difficult to escape, injustice which they find most difficult to correct, or heartless exploitation which they find most difficult to resist. Many live in slum housing or ghettos of race or poverty or ignorance or bitterness that often generate both despair and defiance.

We are a nation that declares the sovereignty of law and the necessity of civil order. Yet we have had riots and have tolerated conditions that breed riots, spread violence, foster disrespect for the law, and undermine the democratic process.

We are a nation that declares the equality and rights of persons irrespective of race. Yet, as a nation, we have allowed cultural patterns to persist that have deprived millions of black Americans, and other racial groups as well, of equality of recognition and opportunity in the areas of education, employment, citizenship, housing, and worship. Worse still, as a nation, we have condoned prejudices that have damaged the personhood of blacks and whites alike. We have seen a climate of racism and reactionism develop resulting in hostility, injustice, suspicion, faction, strife, and alarming potential for bitterness, division, destruction, and death.

We Review Our Efforts

In the face of national shortcomings, we must nevertheless express appreciation for men of good will of all races and classes who have worked tirelessly and faithfully to create a Christian climate in our nation.

From the beginning of the Southern Baptist Convention, and indeed in organized Baptist life, we have affirmed God's love for all men of all continents and colors, of all religions and races. We have continued to proclaim that the death of Jesus on Calvary's cross is the instrument of God's miraculous redemption for every individual.

Inadequately but sincerely, we have sought in our nation and around the world both to proclaim the gospel to the lost and to minister to human need in Christ's name. Individually and collectively, we are trying to serve, but we have yet to use our full resources to proclaim the gospel whereby all things are made new in Christ.

We Voice Our Confession

"If my people, which are called by my name, shall humble themselves, and pray, and seek my face, and turn from their wicked ways; then will I hear from heaven, and will forgive their sin, and will heal their land" (2 Chron. 7:14).

The current crisis arouses the Christian conscience. Judgment begins at the house of God. Christians are inescapably involved in the life of the nation. Along with all other citizens we recognize our share of responsibility for creating in our land conditions in which justice, order, and righteousness can prevail. May God forgive us wherein we have failed him and our fellowman.

As Southern Baptists, representative of one of the largest bodies of Christians in our nation and claiming special ties of spiritual unity with the large conventions of Negro Baptists in our land, we have come far short of our privilege in Christian brotherhood.

Humbling ourselves before God, we implore him to create in us a right spirit of repentance and to make us instruments of his redemption, his righteousness, his peace, and his love toward all men.

We Declare Our Commitment

The Christ we serve, the opportunity we face, and the crisis we confront, compel us to action. We therefore declare our commitment, believing this to be right in the sight of God and our duty under the lordship of Christ.

We will respect every individual as a person possessing inherent dignity and worth growing out of his creation in the image of God.

We will strive to obtain and secure for every person equality of human and legal rights. We will undertake to secure opportunities in matters of citizenship, public services, education, employment, and personal habitation that every man may achieve his highest potential as a person.

We will accept and exercise our civic responsibility as Christians to defend people against injustice. We will strive to insure for all persons the full opportunity for achievement according to the endowments given by God.

We will refuse to be a party to any movement that fosters racism or violence or mob action.

We will personally accept every Christian as a brother beloved in the Lord and welcome to the fellowship of faith and worship every person irrespective of race or class.

We will strive by personal initiative and every appropriate means of communication to bridge divisive barriers, to work for reconciliation, and to open channels of fellowship and cooperation.

We will strive to become well informed about public issues, social ills, and divisive movements that are damaging to human relationships. We will strive to resist prejudice and to combat forces that breed distrust and hostility.

We will recognize our involvement with other Christians and with all others of goodwill in the obligation to work for righteousness in public life and justice for all persons. We will strive to promote Christian brotherhood as a witness to the gospel of Christ.

We Make An Appeal

Our nation is at the crossroads. We must decide whether we shall be united in goodwill, freedom, and justice under God to serve mankind or be destroyed by covetousnes, passion, hate, and strife.

We urge all leaders and supporters of minority groups to encourage their followers to exercise Christian concern and respect for the person and property of others and to manifest the responsible action commensurate with individual dignity and Christian citizenship.

We appeal to our fellow Southern Baptists to join us in self-examination under the Spirit of God and to accept the present crisis as a challenge from God to strive for reconciliation by love.

We appeal to our fellow Southern Baptists to engage in Christian ventures in human relationships, and to take courageous actions for justice and peace.

We believe that a vigorous Christian response to this national crisis is imperative for an effective witness on our part at home and abroad.

Words will not suffice. The time has come for action. Our hope for healing and renewal is in the redemption of the whole of life. Let us call men to faith in Christ. Let us dare to accept the full demands of the love and lordship of Christ in human relationships and urgent ministry. Let us be identified with Christ in the reproach and suffering of the cross.

We therefore recommend to the messengers of the Southern Baptist Convention that:

1. We approve this statement on the national crisis.

2. We rededicate ourselves to the proclamation of the gospel, which includes redemption of the individual and his involvement in the social issues of our day.

3. We request the Home Mission Board to take the leadership in working with the Convention agencies concerned with the problems related to this crisis in the most effective manner possible and in keeping with their program assignments.

4. We call upon individuals, the churches, the associations, and the state conventions to join the Southern Baptist Convention in a renewal of Christian effort to meet the national crisis.

15.17   Southern Baptist Convention "Peace Committee" Report

Beginning in 1979 the Southern Baptist Convention was embroiled in a divisive controversy. Whether the "inerrancy controversy," as it came to be called, was a new conflict or merely a new phase in the ongoing struggle since the days of J. Frank Norris is still debated. In 1985 the SBC created a "Peace Committee," and charged them with the difficult task of discovering the causes and prescribing the cure for the convulsions which threatened to paralyze the convention. The report in 1987 seemed to favor the conservative side. However, some paragraphs, which stand out in contrast to the main document, express the views of more moderate members of the committee. The report also includes the 1986 "Glorieta Statement" of the presidents of the six SBC-related seminaries. The Convention overwhelmingly adopted the final report of the Peace Committee, largely without discussion. The Peace Committee may not bring peace, but its report is destined to be an important document in Southern Baptist history. *Source: Annual,* SBC, 1987, 232-242.

Introduction

During the 1985 annual meeting of the Southern Baptist Convention in Dallas, June 11-13, 1985, a special committee was created to attempt to determine the sources of the current controversy in the Southern Baptist Convention and to make findings and recommendations to resolve it. The motion, overwhelmingly adopted, says:

"With gratitude for God's bountiful blessings on us as Southern Baptists and with recognition of our unparalleled opportunity to confront every person on earth with the gospel of Christ by the year 2000 and with acknowledgment of divisions among us, which, if allowed to continue, inevitably will impede our progress, impair our fellowship, and imperil our future; and after much prayer, we offer the following motion:

That a special committee be authorized by this Convention, in session in Dallas, June, 1985; and

That this committee seek to determine the sources of the controversies in our Convention, and make findings and recommendations regarding these controversies, so that Southern Baptists might effect reconciliation and effectively discharge their responsibilities to God by cooperating together to accomplish evangelism, missions, Christian education, and other causes authorized by our Constitution, all to the glory of God. "By this shall all men know that ye are my disciples, if ye have love one to another" (John 13:35) (John 17:21); and

That this committee follow the 1963 Baptist Faith and Message Statement in regard to theological issues, and operate within the Constitution and Bylaws of the Southern Baptist Convention; and

That to accomplish its work, this committee shall recognize the role of trustees and shall work with and through appropriate boards, commissions, and agencies of the Southern Baptist Convention. This committee shall report on the progress of its work to each meeting of the Executive Committee. The trustees, boards, and agencies of the Southern Baptist Convention, and their officers and employees, shall fully cooperate with the committee to accomplish the purposes outlined in this motion; and

The staffing and professional advice for this committee shall be in accord with the Business and Financial Plan of the Southern Baptist Convention. Funding shall come from Cooperative Program funds received by the Executive Committee as a priority item before the percentage division and allocation of the Southern Baptist Convention Cooperative Program Allocation Budget; and

That the committee may conduct its business in open sessions, and may hold public hearings, but, the committee may also hold executive sessions to accomplish its work; and

That any vacancy, or vacancies, on the special committee be filled by the Executive Committee at its next meeting after such vacancy occurs. In the filling of any such vacancy, balance of representation shall be maintained; and

That the committee may make its final report and recommendation to the 1986 Southern Baptist Convention and request that it be discharged, or the committee may make a preliminary report to the 1986 Convention and may recommend that the special committee be continued in existence for an additional year, in which instance, the committee shall make its final report and recommendations to the 1987 Southern Baptist Convention; and

That all Southern Baptists be urged to exercise restraint, to refrain from divisive action and comments, and to reflect Christian love, while this committee is doing its work; and

That the following persons be designated to serve on the special committee: Charles G. fuller, Chairman; Harmon M. Born, Doyle E. Carlton, Jr., Mrs. Morris H. Chapman, *William O. Crews, Robert E. Cuttino, Mrs. A. Harrison Gregory, Jim Henry, William E. Hull, Herschel H. Hobbs, Albert McClellan, Charles W. Pickering, William E. Poe, Ray E. Roberts, Adrian P. Rogers, *Cecil E. Sherman, John Sullivan, Daniel G. Vestal, Jerry Vines, Edwin H. Young, *Charles F. Stanley, *W. Winfred Moore,

*NOTE: William O. Crews was elected president of Golden Gate Baptist Theological Seminary October 13, 1986, but was asked to remain as a member; Cecil E. Sherman resigned from the special committee October 22, 1986, and was replaced by Peter James Flamming; Charles F. Stanley and W. Winfred Moore served by virtue of office

as president and first vice-president of the Convention, and were asked to remain after their terms of office expired.

Since its creation, the Peace Committee has met 14 times. Following each meeting, a report was given to Southern Baptists by Chairman Charles G. Fuller through the denominational news service, Baptist Press.

In keeping with its assignment, the Peace Committee has determined what it believes to be the primary sources of the controversy, has made findings in reference to those sources and, in this report, is making recommendations as to possible ways to effect reconciliation.

I. Sources of the Controversy

During its first meeting, the Peace Committee determined the primary source of the controversy is theological differences, but found there are political causes as well.

Theological Sources: In meeting after meeting of the Peace Committee, talk turned to the nature of inspiration of the Scriptures, often to the point of preempting the committee's established agenda. Gradually, it became clear that while there might be other theological differences, the authority of the Word of God is the focus of differences. The primary source of the controversy in the Southern Baptist Convention is the Bible, more specifically, the ways in which the Bible is viewed.

All Baptists see the Bible as authoritative; the question is the extent and nature of its authority. The differences in recent years have developed around the phrase in Article I of the Baptist Faith and Message Statement of 1963, that the Bible "has. . . . truth without any mixture of error for its matter. . . ."

The action which created the Peace Committee instructed it to follow the Baptist Faith and Message Statement of 1963 in regard to theological issues. Although the statement includes a Preamble and seventeen articles, the committee has focused primarily on Article One, "The Scriptures."

"The Holy Bible was written by men divinely inspired and is the record of God's revelation of Himself to man. It is a perfect treasure of divine instruction. It has God for its author, salvation for its end, and truth, without any mixture of error, for its matter. It reveals the principles by which God judges us; and therefore is, and will remain to the end of the world, the true center of Christian union, and the supreme standard by which all human conduct, creeds, and religious opinions should be tried. The criterion by which the Bible is to be interpreted is Jesus Christ."

Herschel H. Hobbs, a member of the Peace Committee and chairman of the committee which wrote the 1963 Baptist Faith and Message Statement, explained the phrase "truth without any mixture of error for its matters. . ." by reference to II Timothy 3:16 which says, "all Scripture is given by inspiration of God." He explained: "The Greek New Testament reads 'all'—without the definite article—and that means every single part of the whole is God-breathed. And a God of truth does not breathe error." Dr. Hobbs made the comments during the 1981 annual meeting of the Southern Baptist Convention in Los Angeles, California.

Using Article I of the Baptist Faith and Message Statement of 1963 as a yardstick, Peace Committee subcommittees visited each of the Southern Baptist seminaries and five other agencies; the Foreign Mission Board, the Home Mission Board, Baptist Sunday School Board, Historical Commission, and Christian Life Commission. Following those visits, the committee adopted a "Statement on Theological Diversity."

"The Peace Committee has completed a preliminary investigation of the theological situation in our SBC seminaries. We have found significant theological diversity within our seminaries, reflective of the diversity within our wider constituency. These divergencies are found among those who claim to hold a high view of Scripture and to teach in accordance with, and not contrary to, the Baptist Faith and Message Statement of 1963.

Examples of this diversity include the following, which are intended to be illustrative but not exhaustive.

(1) Some accept and affirm the direct creation and historicity of Adam and Eve while others view them instead as representative of the human race in its creation and fall.

(2) Some understand the historicity of every event in Scripture as reported by the original source while others hold that the historicity can be clarified and revised by the findings of modern historical scholarship.

(3) Some hold to the stated authorship of every book in the Bible while others hold that in some cases such attribution may not refer to the final author or may be pseudonymous.

(4) Some hold that every miracle in the Bible is intended to be taken as an historical event while others hold that some miracles are intended to be taken as parabolic.

The Peace Committee is working earnestly to find ways to build bridges between those holding divergent views so that we may all legitimately coexist and work together in harmony to accomplish our common mission. Please pray that we may find ways to use our diversity to win the greatest number to faith in Christ as Savior and Lord."

Early in its second year, the Peace Committee continued to discuss theological concerns, including the fact that there are at least two separate and distinct interpretations of Article I of the Baptist Faith and Message Statement of 1963, reflective of the diversity present in the Convention. One view holds that when the article says the Bible has "truth without any mixture of error for its matter," it means *all* areas—historical, scientific, theological and philosophical. The other holds the "truth" relates only to matters of faith and practice.

The Committee discussed whether the faculties of the SBC seminaries adequately reflect the views of many Southern Baptists who believe in the first interpretation. A Peace Committee subcommittee met with the six seminary presidents to communicate the need for the faculties to reflect the beliefs of these Southern Baptists.

In October 1986, the Peace Committee held a prayer retreat at Glorieta Baptist Conference Center near Santa Fe, New Mexico, attended by the Peace Committee and leaders of all national agencies. During that meeting, the seminary presidents presented a statement of their intentions which has become known as the "Glorieta Statement:"

"We, the presidents of the six SBC seminaries, through prayerful and careful reflection and dialogue, have unanimously agreed to declare these commitments regarding our lives and our work with Southern Baptists.

We believe that Christianity is supernatural in its origin and history. We repudiate every theory of religion which denies the supernatural elements in our faith. The miracles of the Old and New Testaments are historical evidences of God's judgment, love, and redemption.

We believe that the Bible is fully inspired; it is 'God-breathed' (II Tim. 3:16), utterly unique. No other book or collections of books can justify that claim. The sixty-six books of the Bible are not errant in any area of reality. We hold to their infallible power and binding authority.

We believe that our six seminaries are fulfilling the purposes assigned to them by the Southern Baptist Convention. Nevertheless, we acknowledge that they are not perfect institutions. We recognize that there are legitimate concerns regarding them which we are addressing.

We commit ourselves therefore to the resolution of the problems which beset our beloved denomination. We are ready and eager to be partners in the peace process. Specifically:

(1) We reaffirm our seminary confessional statements, and we will enforce compliance by the persons signing them.

(2) We will foster in our classrooms a balanced, scholarly frame of reference for presenting fairly the entire spectrum of scriptural interpretations represented by our constituencies. We perceive this to be both good education and good cooperation.

(3) We respect the convictions of all Southern Baptists and we repudiate the caricature and intimidation of persons for their theological beliefs.

(4) We commit ourselves to fairness in selecting faculty, lecturers, and chapel speakers across the theological spectrum of our Baptist constituency.

(5) We will lead our seminary communities in spiritual revival, personal discipleship, Christian lifestyle, and active churchmanship.

(6) We will deepen and strengthen the spirit of evangelism and missions on our campuses while emphasizing afresh the distinctive doctrines of our Baptist heritage.

(7) We have scheduled for Southern Baptists three national conferences.

A Conference on Biblical Inerrancy-*1987

A Conference on Biblical Interpretation-1988

A Conference on Biblical Imperatives-1989

*Note: The first conference, focusing on biblical inerrancy, was held at Ridgecrest Baptist Conference Center May 4-7, 1987, with more than 1,000 in attendance.

We share these commitments with the hope that all Southern Baptists will join us in seeking "the wisdom from above" in our efforts toward reconciliation:

"The wisdom from above is first pure, then peaceable, gentle, open to reason, full of mercy and good fruits, without uncertainty or insincerity" (James 3:17).

The Peace Committee affirmed the Glorieta Statement and ceased its official inquiry, referring unanswered questions and unresolved issues back to the administrators and trustees of Southern Baptist Theological Seminary, Southeastern Baptist Theological Seminary, and Midwestern Baptist Theological Seminary, hoping the results of their actions would be satisfactory to the Convention-at-large.

During the committee's December 1986 meeting, additional questions arose as to the meaning and the implementation of the Glorieta Statement.

The seminary presidents report that their efforts to implement the Statement have included an effort to recruit conservative scholars to fill faculty vacancies, expansion of reading lists, invitations to conservative scholars to address chapel and other events, a commitment to treat all persons fairly, and expanded evangelistic and missions activities on campus.

The question for the majority of the Peace Committee, however, remains not whether there is diversity in the Southern Baptist Convention, but how broad that diversity can be while still continuing to cooperate.

Political Sources: In the opinion of the Peace Committee, the controversy of the last decade began as a theological concern. When people of good intention became frustrated because they felt their convictions on Scripture were not seriously dealt with, they organized politically to make themselves heard. Soon, another group formed to counter the first and the political process intensified.

The Peace Committee, primarily through its Political Activities Subcommittee, has studied charges and counter charges regarding political activity. It has looked at many issues, including:

Restructuring the Constitution and Bylaws of the Southern Baptist Convention to limit the appointive powers of the president; restructuring the way in which the annual meeting is held, specifically shifting the pre-Convention meetings to post-Convention meetings; cooperation between the Pastors' Conference and the SBC Forum; discussing the coverage of personalities and issues in the controversy by the official and unofficial news media outlets; the use of descriptive terms and labels for the various groups; "depoliticizing" the Convention by asking the various groups to "standdown" from political activities; instituting stricter means of messenger registration and voting to prevent misuse of the registration and voting processes at annual meetings.

A primary area of discussion was changing the Constitution and Bylaws of the Convention to restrict the appointive powers of the president. However, the majority of the committee's members feel the basic Convention structure has served Southern Baptists well and should not now be changed.

The Committee investigated numerous charges of political malfeasance and voter irregularity. It heard a detailed report, complete with statistical analysis, on messenger participation at annual meetings, presented by the SBC registration secretary and Convention manager, as well as the chairman of a special study committee appointed by the SBC Executive Committee. Although the reports included isolated instances of registration and ballot abuse, there was no evidence of widespread or organized misuse of the ballot by any political group and no evidence of massive voter irregularities related to annual meetings.

The Political Activities Subcommittee, as well as a special ad-hoc committee, dealt with the question of a parliamentarian for the annual meeting. The matter was deferred in 1986, because then SBC president Charles F. Stanley appointed a certified parliamentarian to assist him at the Atlanta annual meeting. The Committee is recommending a new bylaw be prepared concerning the appointment of a certified parliamentarian and two assistant parliamentarians for the annual meeting.

A special subcommittee also looked into the possibility of "negative designation" or "selective support" of agencies through the Cooperative Program, but concluded that a change in the basic structure of the unified giving plan would not provide significant help in resolving the crisis.

Some of the issues have been brought forward as recommendations from the Peace Committee. Others were not deemed sufficiently significant to warrant recommendations at this time.

II. Findings

The Peace Committee has made findings on Scripture and on politics.

On Theology: The Committee found there is significant diversity in the understanding of Article I "On Scripture" of the Baptist Faith and Message Statement of 1963. The Committee found there are at least two separate and distinct interpretations of the article. One holding "truth without any mixture of error for its matter," means *all* areas—historical, scientific, theological, and philosophical. The other holds "truth" relates only to matters of faith and practice.

The Committee, discussing whether the faculties of the SBC seminaries adequately reflect the views of many Southern Baptists who believe in the first interpretation, found there was not a theological balance represented in the faculties at Southern Baptist Theological Seminary or Southeastern Baptist Theological Seminary.

The committee adopted two statements concerning its findings on theology, one a "foundational" statement, and the other a more elaborate statement.

1. The *"Foundational Statement on Theology:"*—The Committee agreed the following Scripture references should be read as an introduction to the "Foundational Statement on Theology:" Deuteronomy 4:2; Joshua 1:7; Psalm 119:160; Matthew 5:18; II Timothy 3:16; Revelation 22:10.

It is the conclusion of the majority of the Peace Committee that the cause of peace within the Southern Baptist Convention will be greatly enhanced by the affirmation of the whole Bible as being 'not errant in any area of reality.'

Therefore, we exhort the trustees and administrators of our seminaries and other agencies affiliated with or supported by the Southern Baptist Convention to faithfully discharge their responsibility to carefully preserve the doctrinal integrity of our institutions receiving our support, and only employ professional staff who believe in the divine inspiration of the whole Bible and that the Bible is "truth without any mixture of error."

The Committee also adopted the more elaborate statement on Scripture.

2. The *"Statement on Scripture:"* We, as a Peace Committee, affirm biblical authority for all of life and for all fields of knowledge. The Bible is a book of redemption, not a book of science, psychology, sociology, or economics. But, where the Bible speaks, the Bible speaks truth in all realms of reality and to all fields of knowledge. The Bible, when properly interpreted, is authoritative to all of life.

We, as a Peace Committee, reaffirm the Baptist commitment to the absolute authority of Scripture and to the historic Baptist position that the Bible has "truth without any mixture of error for its matter." We affirm that the narratives of Scripture are historically and factually accurate. We affirm that the historic accounts of the miraculous and the supernatural are truthful as given by God and recorded by the biblical writers.

We, as a Peace Committee, have found that most Southern Baptists see "truth without any mixture of error for its matter," as meaning, for example, that

(1) They believe in direct creation of mankind and therefore they believe Adam and Eve were real persons.

(2) They believe the named authors did indeed write the biblical books attributed to them by those books.

(3) They believe the miracles described in Scripture did indeed occur as supernatural events in history.

(4) They believe that the historical narratives given by biblical authors are indeed accurate and reliable as given by those authors.

We call upon Southern Baptist institutions to recognize the great number of Southern Baptists who believe this interpretation of our confessional statement and, in the future, to build their professional staffs and faculties from those who clearly reflect such dominant convictions and beliefs held by Southern Baptists at large.

However, some members of the Peace Committee differ from his viewpoint. They would hold that "truth without any mixture of error" relates only to faith and practice. They would also prefer a broader theological perspective. Yet, we have learned to live together on the Peace Committee in mutual charity and commitment to each other. We pledge our mutual efforts to fulfill the Great Commission, and we call on others within our Convention to make the same pledge.

On Politics: The committee has found that the sources of the political aspect of the controversy are long standing. Historically, informal political groups or coalitions have emerged in Southern Baptist life. Prior to the last decade, most of these groups operated informally by word-of-mouth among mutual acquaintances interested in selecting the leadership of the Southern Baptist Convention. More recently, these groups have developed organized coalitions centered around theological perceptions and committed to electing leadership committed to a particular viewpoint. The effort has been largely successful, but led to the formation of a counter-effort which has increased hostility and turned up the heat on the controversy.

After its investigation, the Peace Committee found "that the extent of political activity . . . at the present time creates distrust, diminishes our ability to do missions and evangelism, is detrimental to our influence, and impedes our ability to serve our Lord."

The committee adopted two statements, one a "foundational" statement and the other a more elaborate statement.

1. The *"Foundational Statement On Politics."*—It is the unanimous conclusion of the Peace Committee that fairness in the appointive process will contribute to peace.

Therefore, we exhort the present and future presidents of the Southern Baptist Convention, the Committee on Committees, and the Committee on Boards to select nominees who endorse the Baptist Faith and Message Statement and are drawn in balanced fashion from the broad spectrum of loyal, cooperative Southern Baptists, representative of the diversity of our denomination.

The more elaborate statement on politics also was adopted.

2. The *"Statement on Politics:"*—Politics are intrinsically a part of congregational polity, i.e., voting, public and private discussions, influencing others to share one's view.

Historically, informal political groups or coalitions have emerged in Southern Baptist life. Prior to the last decade, most of these groups operated informally by word-of-mouth among mutual acquaintances interested in selecting the leadership of the Southern Baptist Convention. More recently, these groups have developed organized coalitions centered on theological perceptions and individual leaders committed to a defined viewpoint. These coalitions have adopted political strategies for electing officers of the Convention, appointing committees, and changing or preserving the character of accepted institutions. These strategies have included extensive travel, numerous informational and idealogical meetings, mailouts, network of representatives who share in this common strategy, and sustained efforts to recruit messengers to attend the Convention.

We as a Peace Committee recognize that these political coalitions and strategies were born in part, at least, out of deep conviction and concern for theological issues.

But, we believe that the time has come for the Convention to move beyond this kind of politics. We find that the extent of political activity within the Southern Baptist Convention at the present time promotes a party spirit; creates discord, division, and distrust; diminishes our ability to do missions and evangelism; is detrimental to our influence; and impedes our ability to serve our Lord.

If allowed to continue unchecked, such political activity in the Convention can have disastrous consequences affecting our ability to serve our Lord and do His work.

Steps have been taken and additional steps are recommended in this report to resolve the theological issues involved in our present controversy. Because of our fear of the consequences of continued organized political activity within our Convention, and since steps have been and will continue to be taken to resolve theological issues, we feel that continued organized political activity within the Southern Baptist Convention is no longer necessary, desirable, or appropriate. We think the continuation of such political activity in the future would be unacceptable and could be disastrous.

We recommend that the Southern Baptist Convention request all organized political factions to discontinue the organized political activity in which they are now engaged. We think the following specific activities are out of place and request all groups to discontinue these specific political activities:

(1) Organized political activity;

(2) Political strategies developed by a group with central control;

(3) Holding information-ideological meetings;

(4) Extensive travel on behalf of political objectives within the Convention; and

(5) Extensive mail-outs to promote political objectives in the Convention.

In 1986, the Southern Baptist Convention adopted the report of the Peace Committee which found:

(1) Some spokesmen on both sides of the political spectrum have used intemperate, inflammatory, and unguarded language, i.e., "going for the jugular," "Holy War," "independent fundamentalists," "flaming liberal," and other pejorative terms.

(2) Some spokesmen on both sides of the political spectrum and the autonomous independent journals on both sides of the issue have labeled and attributed improper motives to people with whom they disagree.

(3) Distribution of news is necessary in a democratic society. There have been instances when news releases have been altered, distorting the intent of the article and oftentimes creating confusion. In some denominational papers and in some autonomous independent journals, there has been prejudice against the conservative political activists and in some autonomous independent journals there has been prejudice against the moderate side.

The Convention in Atlanta adopted the recommendation of the Peace Committee as follows:

—That the Convention deplore the use of the type of intemperate, inflammatory, and unguarded language used by some spokesmen on both sides of the political spectrum.

—That the Convention urge Baptist Press, the state Baptist papers, and the autonomous independent journals to be especially careful to be fair and accurate in reporting events in the Convention and refrain from labeling and attributing improper motives.

Despite these recommendations approved by the Southern Baptist Convention, the Peace Committee finds that some of the state Baptist papers and the autonomous journals—The Southern Baptist Advocate, SBC Today, Baptists United News, and The Baptist Laity Journal—have continued to use intemperate, inflammatory language and have labeled individuals and impugned motives.

We renew again our request to these papers and journals to contribute to the process of reconciliation and the promotion of our cooperative work together as we seek to do the work of Christ. We again call upon all state Baptist papers and the independent autonomous journals to comply with the action taken at the Atlanta Convention and outlined above. We call upon individual Southern Baptists to use their influence to help stop these divisive actions.

We, the Peace Committee, ask Baptist Press, all Baptist state papers, Baptist publications, and independent autonomous journals to refrain from using terms and labels, specifically terms such as fundamentalist, liberal, fundamental-conservative, and moderate-conservative.

III. Conclusions

The enabling resolution of the Southern Baptist Convention at the 1985 Dallas Convention commissioned this special committee to determine the sources of the controversies within the Convention and to make findings and recommendations that would make it possible for Southern Baptists to effect reconciliation and to continue to cooperate in carrying out evangelism, missions, Christian education, and other causes.

Making peace among all Southern Baptists was not to be the work of the committee. *Reconciliation* was, and still is, the key word. Surely, there must be peace; that is, there must be an end to hostility among us, which is peace. Committed Christians must live in peace. No recommendation of the committee is needed to effect peace—it is found in the heart of the believer.

Reconciliation may be a first cousin to peace, but it rests on a different foundation. To reconcile is to harmonize, to cause to be friendly again, to reunite, to accept our differences and to cooperate in all undertakings which enhance our mutual interests and goals. It was only through a subtle process of reconciliation, taking place over 142 years of history, that Southern Baptists have with God's blessing, and His help, achieved a preeminent position in missions, education, and evangelism. We have kept our differences from creating hostility, until recently, and not only have we lived in peace, but with remarkable harmony and cooperation.

We must never try to impose upon individual Southern Baptists nor local congregations a specific view of how Scripture must be interpreted. If such an attempt is made, then reconciliation is not the goal nor is it possible to achieve.

There is but one way for us to survive *intact* as a denomination. It involves the recognition of some basic facts, among which are these:

(1) Changes are now taking place in the leadership of many Southern Baptist Convention boards.

(2) These changes will impact these boards and agencies for years to come.

(3) The role of many who have exercised leadership in the past will change as colleagues of different persuasion will fill leadership roles.

(4) This change will mean that some who have been in general agreement with Convention programs in the past will have less involvement, while those who previously have had difficulty in agreement with certain Convention programs will have more involvement.

(5) We have seen changes in Southern Baptist life in the past and we will see changes in the future. The important issue is that we must continue to be faithful stewards of the opportunities God has given Southern Baptists.

How then can we survive intact or substantially that way?

First, the hostility must cease within the heart of each of us. That brings peace.

Second, our leaders must have and must demonstrate a view of Baptist life that reaches beyond the limits of their own personal theology. No effort should be made or should be permitted to be made which would seek to eliminate from Baptist life theological beliefs or practices which are consistent with the Baptist Faith and Message Statement and which have found traditional acceptance by substantial numbers of our people. Proponents of extreme positions at each end of the current Baptist theological spectrum should be encouraged to major on those things which lead to cooperative efforts and to minimize divisive issues and controversies.

Third, and most important, nothing must be allowed to stand in the way of genuine cooperation in missions, Christian education, evangelism, and our other traditional causes. While different leaders may arise, the nature and work of our Christian cooperative enterprise must continue unabated.

Finally, we should recognize and freely admit that the greatest source of our strength as a denomination lies in the thousands of local church congregations that support our cooperative undertakings. Through long years of experience, they have learned to trust our leaders, our agencies and institutions and, because of that trust, they have provided magnificent support and responded to that leadership.

We have proclaimed this to be God's way of doing His work. Through continued cooperation in His enterprises, we can continue this mighty work. If we insist on having our way, drawing lines which exclude from places of leadership and responsibility those who do not hold our specific viewpoint, we can destroy what God has created in the Southern Baptist Convention. If, however, we can maintain a cooperative spirit and let our sense of Christian love bridge the gap of the diversity among us, we can continue to bear effective witness to His kingdom enterprise throughout all the world.

IV. Recommendations

We make the following recommendations:

1. Although the Baptist Faith and Message Statement of 1963 is a statement of basic belief, it is not a creed. Baptists are non-credal, in that they do not impose a man-made interpretation of Scripture on others. Baptists, however, declare their commitment to commonly held interpretations which then become parameters for cooperation. Therefore, we recommend that we:

(1.) Reaffirm the 1963 Baptist Faith and Message Statement as the guideline by which all of the agencies of the Southern Baptist Convention are to conduct their work.

(2.) Request, respectfully, all Southern Baptists to continue their high view of Scripture as "given by the inspiration of God (II Tim. 3:16), and to diligently teach and proclaim the truthfulness, the reliability, and the authority of the Bible.

2. Although all Southern Baptists do not understand the Baptist Faith and Message Statement on Scripture the same way, this diversity should not create hostility toward each other, stand in the way of genuine cooperation, or interfere with the rights and privileges of all Southern Baptists within the denomination to participate in its affairs.

Because fairness in the process of making committee board appointments is essential to the process of reconciliation and peace, the committee recommends that the present and all future presidents of the Southern Baptist Convention, the Committee on Committees, and the Committee on Boards select nominees who endorse the Baptist Faith and Message Statement, and are drawn in balanced fashion from the broad spectrum of loyal, cooperative Southern Baptists, representative of the diversity of our denomination.

Recognizing the nature of our diversity and the rightful place of biblical interpretation, we believe we can learn from each other and, in the long run, we can protect each other from unwanted extremes.

We, therefore, further recommend that the Southern Baptist Convention continue in every attempt to remain a unified fellowship, rejecting the notion of any official division of our body.

3. We recommend that the Southern Baptist Convention Executive Committee study and report to the Southern Baptist Convention in 1988, a Convention bylaw establishing an office of parliamentarian, and that the study include the following considerations:

(1.) The president and two vice-presidents, acting together, shall annually appoint a chief parliamentarian and two assistant parliamentarians to advise the presiding officer of the Convention on matters of parliamentary procedure.

(2.) The chief parliamentarian shall be a fully certified member of the American Institute of Parliamentarians who has the experience to serve effectively at annual sessions of the Southern Baptist Convention.

4. In view of the fact that the Cooperative Program is the lifeline of all that we are doing

as Southern Baptists, we commend our churches and state conventions for their increased giving through the Cooperative Program and we recommend to our people that they continue their strong support of the Cooperative Program.

We recognize the historic right of each Southern Baptist church to give to the work of the agencies, in keeping with its deeply held convictions, without intimidation or criticism.

We recommend that the Cooperative Program be continued unchanged.

5. We recommend that, in view of the intense public discussions of the last few years, that trustees determine the theological positions of the seminary administrators and faculty members in order to guide them in renewing their determination to stand by the Baptist Faith and Message Statement of 1963, to the Glorieta Statement of their intention to work toward reconciliation of the conflict in the Convention, and to their own institutional declarations of faith as the guidelines by which they will teach their students in preparation for gospel ministry in the churches, mission fields, and service to the denomination.

The Bible is a book of redemption, not a book of science, psychology, sociology, or economics. But, where the Bible speaks, the Bible speaks truth in all realms of reality and to all fields of knowledge. The Bible, when properly interpreted, is authoritative to all of life.

We call upon Southern Baptist institutions to recognize the great number of Southern Baptists who believe this interpretation of Article I of the Baptist Faith and Message Statement of 1963, and, in the future, to build their professional staffs and faculties from those who clearly reflect such dominant convictions and beliefs held by Southern Baptists at large.

We, as a Peace Committee, recognize and respect those in Southern Baptist life whose view of Scripture differs from this one and pledge to continue to cooperate. We pledge the highest regard, charity, and commitment to them in our combined efforts to fulfill the Great Commission and we call upon them to make the same pledge.

6. We recommend that the Southern Baptist Convention request all organized political factions to discontinue the organized political activity in which they are now engaged. At this time, we think the following specific political activity is out of place and we request all groups to discontinue the following specific political activities:

(1) Organized political activity.

(2) Political strategies developed by a group with central control.

(3) Holding information/idealogical meetings.

(4) Extensive travel on behalf of political objectives within the Convention.

(5) Extensive mailouts to promote political objectives in the Convention.

7. We recommend that Baptist Press, all state Baptist papers, independent autonomous journals and individual Southern Baptists to refrain from the use of intemperate and inflammatory language, labeling individuals and impugning motives.

Specifically, we request that all Baptist writers and individual Baptists refrain from characterizing fellow Southern Baptists in terms such as "fundamentalist," "liberal," "fundamental-conservative," "moderate-conservative."

We request all Southern Baptists to take a positive view of Southern Baptist life, to use their influence to help stop the above divisive actions, and to contribute to the process of reconciliation and the promotion of our cooperative endeavors as we seek to do the work of Christ.

8. We recommend that the Southern Baptist Convention request the SBC Committee on Resolutions to continue its policy of not presenting resolutions that are divisive in Southern Baptist life for at least the next three years.

9. We recommend that the leadership of the Pastors' Conference and the SBC Forum take immediate steps to explore the possibility of "getting together" in ways that will enhance and promote our mutually strong beliefs as expressed in the Baptist Faith and Message Statement.

10. We recommend that the Southern Baptist Convention continue the present 22 members of the SBC Peace Committee to serve for up to, but not to exceed, three years for the purpose of observing the response of all agencies, officers, and other participants to the recommendations of the Peace Committee in an effort to encourage compliance and foster harmonious working relationships among all segments of our Baptist family. The Peace Committee would meet once each year at a time of its own choosing and would make an appropriate report to each annual session of the Convention.

V. Acknowledgements

1. The Peace Committee wishes to acknowledge the assistance provided us by the office and staff of Harold C. Bennett, president-treasurer of the Executive Committee of the Southern Baptist Convention. Special appreciation is due Martha T. Gaddis, administrative assistant to Dr. Bennett, and to Dan Martin, news editor of Baptist Press.

2. The Peace Committee expresses gratitude to the host of Southern Baptists and to Christians of other denominations who have faithfully prayed for the work of the committee throughout its existence.

Charles G. Fuller, Chairman
Southern Baptist Convention Peace Committee

15.18   Virginia Baptist Response to the Denominational Crisis

Many Southern Baptists in high places and low became increasingly disturbed by the controversy in the Convention in the 1980s. Many felt their denominational heritage was eroding, and that the Convention and its institutions were falling into the hands of new Baptists who neither built, supported, nor even valued them. While most expressed themselves with handwringing, some Baptists organized to try to preserve what they regard as the Southern Baptist heritage. One such group is the Baptist General Association of Virginia. The report of their "President's Task Force on the Denominational Crisis," proclaims that "Deep distress is evident among Virginia Baptists." The document reviews the origin and progress of the controversy, and makes suggestions, some of them startling, for coping with the deepening crisis in Southern Baptist life. *Source: The Religious Herald,* 3 Nov. 1988, 6-13.

THE PRESIDENT'S TASK FORCE ON THE DENOMINATIONAL CRISIS
PART I: A BRIEF CHRONOLOGY OF ITS WORK

On pages 8-12 of this issue of the *Religious Herald,* readers will find the report of the President's Task Force on the Denominational Crisis.

It is a most important document which potentially could positively affect Virginia Baptists, Baptists in other state associations/conventions and the Southern Baptist Convention. We hope and pray time will reveal it to be so.

On August 3 of this year, Neal T. Jones, current president of the Baptist General Association of Virginia (BGAV), called a meeting of BGAV officers "to examine the impact on Virginia Baptists of the decade-long theological/political controversy in the Southern Baptist Convention" (*Herald,* Aug. 11, 1988, p. 3).

In addition to Jones, those present were Executive Director Reginald M. McDonough; First Vice President Michael J. Clingenpeel; Second Vice President Eva Easley; Treasurer Nathaniel W. Kellum; and Clerk Frederick J. Anderson. This editor was in attendance as an observer.

In a statement released to the *Herald* following the meeting, Jones said he convened the group "to discuss concerns raised by some Virginia Baptists and to anticipate action that might be taken at the annual meeting of the General Association this fall."

He noted several issues had been identified which needed to be addressed and he had been authorized by the officers to name a task force.

The purpose of the task force, Jones stated, would be "to prepare a positive statement to reaffirm the principles that have historically characterized Virginia Baptists and to declare the basis of our cooperation."

Executive Director McDonough said on that same occasion the task force would be ". . . a group of recognized Virginia Baptist leaders who will relate to the president in preparing what might be called a 'covenant of cooperation.'"

Both McDonough and Jones indicated that the task force members would be announced through the *Herald* as soon as they were chosen and encouraged Virginia Baptists to express their comments and suggestions to Jones or to the task force when named. They emphasized the committee's report would be published in the *Herald* prior to the BGAV annual meeting in November.

Executive Director McDonough agreed during the August 3 session to prepare an article for the *Herald* clarifying "how the Cooperative Program works in Virginia and describing the options a church has in its giving patterns." This particularly significant statement was printed in our issue of August 25 (pp. 6-7).

Shortly thereafter, Clingenpeel was named task force chairman (*Herald,* Sept. 1, 1988, p. 3). Jones announced three additional task force members at that time, each of whom has previously served as president of the General Association and chairman of the General Board: William J. Cumbie, Fairfax; Carl W. Johnson, Richmond; and William L. Lumpkin, Norfolk.

Jones and McDonough, ex officio members by virtue of office, have been regular attendants and participants in the work of the task force.

In making the announcement, Jones told the *Herald* it was his hope the task force would emphasize "cooperation with integrity" and "the autonomy of local churches as well as all other involved denominational entities."

"Baptists must be courageous," he stressed, "about the future. Constructive changes need to be made."

When the task force met during the first week of September, all members were present, including Mrs. A. Harrison (Christine) Gregory, Danville, also a former BGAV president and General Board chairman (*Herald,* Sept. 15, 1988, p. 5).

Chairman Clingenpeel informed the *Herald* that his task force would like "Virginia Baptists to know we are working, that we do see a crisis, that we want to respond to it and provide a voice in the midst of crisis." He also encouraged "all Virginia Baptists" to share their concerns with his group.

He submitted a statement of the task force to the *Herald* which consisted of three brief sections: "There Is a Crisis," "Virginia's Uniqueness Is Not New" and "Action Must Be Taken" (*Herald,* Sept. 15, 1988, p. 5).

The group completed its work on Monday, October 31. We commend the report to our readers for careful study and reflection prior to our forthcoming BGAV annual meeting in Virginia Beach, November 15-16.

Please read Part II of this editorial on page 7 and the full text of the task force's report and recommendations which follow, pages 8-12.

PART II: An Overview of the Report

The decision of BGAV President Neal T. Jones to convene his officers for prayer and counsel on August 3 was a mark of perceptive and wise leadership.

He recognized the increasing negative consequences among Virginia Baptists of the 10-year Southern Baptist Convention controversy and he heard the widespread anguished concern of pastors, staff ministers and lay leaders.

The realities with which he was confronted constituted a clear call to action. It was thoroughly appropriate for him to name a task force of mature and experienced Virginia Baptists to study the present situation among us and to recommend needed actions.

Members of the task force have related to this particular assignment as a priority. They have worked diligently both during and between sessions. The same can be stated of President Jones and Executive Director Reginald M. McDonough.

Now their report and recommendations are complete. It is outstanding work in every way: comprehensive in scope, substantive in content and its recommendations are finely tuned. It is a healthy balance between analysis of the problems with which we are beset and realistically proposed approaches for constructively dealing with them.

The report begins with three basic affirmations which date from the group's statement to Virginia Baptists following its September 9 session. Each is precisely accurate: "There Is A Crisis," "Virginia's Uniqueness Is Not New" and "Action Must Be Taken."

In combination, these basic affirmations define the parameters within which the task force has addressed its assignment.

One of many strengths of the report is the forthright manner in which it identifies and interprets the nature of the present crisis. This involves "many [who] feel betrayed" and disenfranchised from SBC involvement; a new and erroneous interpretation of the meaning of Church-State separation; an erosion of historic mutuality which characterized relations in the past between state associations/conventions and the SBC; and the failure to distinguish between structured and fraternal accountability.

Chairman Clingenpeel and his group write with understanding of the uniqueness of Virginia Baptists and give attention to certain specific facets of this uniqueness. We are grateful they included among them "the early demand for an educated clergy, pluralism in the Commonwealth of Virginia, our constant emphasis on religious freedom and soul liberty, and the consistent inclusion of persons of diverse perspectives in Virginia Baptist leadership roles."

The committee is accurate in giving emphasis to specific qualities characteristic of Virginia Baptists including their affirmation of personal competency and freedom; inspiration and authority of the Bible; voluntary cooperation and connectionalism; and religious and civil liberty.

Committee members are no less correct when they declare their abhorence of "denominational imperialism in any form and state the current controversy "has no quick solution." They appropriately see the General Association "as an equal partner with other Baptist constituencies in the support and well-being of SBC agencies and institutions."

A recurring theme throughout the report is cooperation with integrity between the General Association and the SBC, the desire of Virginia Baptists to participate responsibly and contribute generously to convention causes, but clearly underscored is their unwillingness to have their participation limited to providing financial resources.

The fundamental difference between the General Association and the SBC in interpreting what constitutes Cooperative Program gifts is given attention. A proposed recommendation calls for the General Association to take necessary steps to have its Budget Committee "revise the 1989 BGAV Budget to show how the SBC portion is allocated . . . to each of the SBC ministries."

It is our judgment that the task force has given a convincing rationale for its recommendations concerning the relationship of SBC Executive Committee members to the General Board and BGAV representation on the SBC Committee on Committees. We believe both recommendations are sound and will increase the likelihood that Virginians elected for service on SBC boards and agencies will be representative of a majority of Virginia Baptists.

Section VI of the report, "A New Style of Life for Southern Baptists," begins with this strong statement:

A new style of life for Southern Baptists—one of cooperation with integrity, mutual consultation and unity in diversity—is the only way to ensure survival of our unique denominational system.

It introduces the "Memorial" with which the task force concludes its report. The "Memorial" is historically accurate, timely in its focus and irenic in spirit. We believe it should be adopted by messengers at Virginia Beach.

We urge all Virginia Baptists, especially prospective messengers and visitors, to read and study this report. There is at least the possibility it could be the means by which we move towards the reconciliation for which Virginia Baptists deeply yearn.

All of us owe a profound debt of gratitude to the members of this task force and those who worked with them in their sincere effort to help us "continue in our time-honored ways of believing and working in harmony and freedom."

A Memorial

from the messengers of the

1988 Baptist General Association of Virginia

to the messengers of the

1989 Southern Baptist Convention

Since 1845, when our leaders helped organize the Southern Baptist Convention, Virginia Baptists have been in a partnership relationship with our missionary Baptist brothers and sisters throughout the Southern Baptist Convention. This cooperative connection has sustained and expanded the missionary commitment of the Baptists of Virginia.

The Baptist General Association of Virginia (BGAV) elects the ancient Baptist means of formal mutual communication, a Memorial, to address our partner and identify our concerns. A Memorial is defined as an overture to another based on a summary or presentation of facts.

From time to time, as points of tension surfaced, the partnership between the Southern Baptist Convention and the state conventions has been clarified. The present crisis in Southern Baptist life calls for a re-examination of the partnership and requires that serious efforts be undertaken to ensure continuation of the ideals as detailed in the 1928 Report of the SBC Executive Committee on relations between the Southern Baptist Convention and the state conventions. (See the 1928 SBC *Annual,* pp. 32-33.) We see little evidence of the consultation between partners as assumed in 1928.

We see a shift in the SBC from the vision upheld by an esteemed Virginia pastor, Dr. George W. McDaniel, SBC president in 1926. Faced with division as deep as ours, Dr. McDaniel said: "I beg you therefore not to worry about problems; they belong to God. We should content ourselves to work at the tasks to which He has set our hands, remembering that in service we discover unity" (W.W. Barnes, *The Southern Baptist Convention,* p. 257).

We desire to continue to carry out our part of the partnership, to cooperate with integrity, and to support the work generously. But our ability to do so is diminished by the SBC's abandonment of consultation and consensus leadership. The two-party system of recent days has not worked. It does not work because it leads to division and because bipartisan participation has not been permitted by those controlling the SBC.

The redefinition of our partnership will require a continuing process of prayerful dialogue. It will be a lengthy undertaking. We earnestly desire a relationship in which no faction—right or left—can be arbitrary and exclusionary.

Issues for Consideration and Responses

The messengers of the BGAV urge the messengers of the SBC to consider and respond to these issues:

1. That the SBC maintain its historic relationship with the Baptist joint Committee on Public Affairs (BJCPA) and continue to fund its ministries.

2. That the SBC develop a plan that permits a church, on conscience grounds, to choose to omit from its Cooperative Program gifts selected SBC budget items through a carefully developed plan similar to the BGAV "negative designation" procedure.

3. That the SBC foster theological education that is characterized by:
- Serious academic scholarship;
- Openness of inquiry that encourages independent investigation of the truth;
- Balance in theological approach;
- Responsible freedom within the bounds of historic Baptist confessions of faith.

4. That the SBC President appoint to membership on the 1989 SBC Committee on Committees those persons proposed by the BGAV.

5. That a new style of relating be developed on the partnership principle so that genuine healing may take place and advance be achieved in our cooperative mission enterprise. We affirm the principles of autonomy for each body as described in the 1928 document. We request creative and redemptive dialogue with SBC leadership on the issues. We believe that negotiations between the partners are appropriate and urgent.

Questions for discussion include:

How can we best communicate with one another? Most present-day SBC communication seems to operate on a "One-Way Street" model as though promotion is the same as communication. Virginia Baptists allow Virginia SBC Executive Committee members to serve as ex officio on our General Board in the hope that better communication will result. Even though our hopes have not been altogether realized, the idea is working and needs to be more fully utilized.

How can partnership on representation be assured? Is there a way to improve the nominating process so that confidence and mutual trust will be restored, and that the consultation envisioned in the 1928 SBC action will be achieved?

How can resolutions and public pronouncements be safeguarded so that misuse by those inside and outside the fellowship is diminished? SBC resolutions are not binding on Southern Baptist individuals, churches, associations or state conventions. They express the opinions of a majority of those present and voting. How can we overcome the popular assumption that these pronouncements are binding? Must we abandon or limit resolutions? How is the trustee principle for governing the ministries of the SBC affected by SBC resolutions? Can the SBC and its entities refrain from partisan political endorsements and pronouncements which bring division into our fellowship and damage our cooperative mission enterprise?

How can we work together to develop a distribution of Cooperative Program gifts that reflects generous priorities in mission support funding? Neither of our mission boards receives as much support from the Cooperative Program as from the seasonal special offerings. Does this fact demonstrate the need for alteration of the allocation formula? If so, how can the partnership relationship be used to bring the priorities of the Cooperative Program more into line with the vision of the donors—churches and individuals? Can the trend toward promoted designation be halted and undesignated giving magnified as the best way to support our cooperative mission undertaking?

It would be painful beyond description for the Baptist General Association of Virginia to leave the Cooperative Program plan. But cooperation is not a "One-Way Street." We are convinced both the percent of receipts for SBC causes and the priorities of the total Cooperative Program should be scrutinized prayerfully.

We urge that you take this overture seriously and as a beginning point for a continuing discussion. Your timely response will be eagerly and prayerfully awaited, and will affect the future course of our relationship with the SBC.

16

The Larger Baptist Family

Baptists in America form a large family, with an incredible variety of different groups large and small. There is no way in a collection like this to include source documents from all of them, much as one might wish to do so. No adverse judgment is intended concerning those Baptist groups not represented by source documents here.

16.1 Seventh Day Baptist Address to Baptists in America, 1843

Who are the Seventh Day Baptists, and what do they believe? Why do they insist so strongly upon seventh day worship? One of the best sources for answering these questions, especially in the nineteenth century, is their address of 1843. Directed to the Baptists of America, this address spelled out in detail the sabbatarian convictions and conduct. One would be hard put to find a better defense of the sabbath; the address is calmly stated, biblical in emphasis, and fraternal in tone. The authors included an appeal for first day Baptists to adopt seventh day views and, failing that, to show more understanding for their sabbatarian brethren. *Source:* "An Address to the Baptist Denomination of the United States, on the Observance of the Sabbath." From the Seventh-Day Baptist General Conference (New York: J. Winchester, New World Press, 1843), 5-24.

The General Conference of Seventh-Day Baptists was convened at Plainfield, New Jersey, on the 3rd day of September, 1843. The delegates were generally impressed that the time had come when the denomination should make increased and vigorous efforts to promote the doctrine of the Bible concerning the Sabbath. The following resolutions were therefore submitted by Paul Stillman, of New York, and unanimously adopted.

"*Resolved,* in view of the imperious duty devolving upon us to publish the truth of God to the world, that it is advisable to make an appeal to the various orders of Christians, in reference to the Sabbath of the Bible, urging them to a thorough examination of the subject, as one of great importance to the cause of God.

"*Resolved,* in accordance with the object of the foregoing resolution, that a committee be appointed to prepare an address to our brethren of the Baptist Denomination, to be issued under the sanction of the General Conference."

Thomas B. Brown, Paul Stillman, and Nathan V. Hull, were appointed a Committee for the above purpose, who subsequently presented the following address, which was unanimously approved by the Conference; and measures were taken for its publication, and extensive circulation among the order of Christians particularly addressed.

DAVID NUNN, Moderator.

ADDRESS.

THE SEVENTH-DAY BAPTIST GENERAL CONFERENCE, TO THE MEMBERS OF THE BAPTIST DENOMINATION THROUGHOUT THE UNITED STATES, HOLDING TO THE OBSERVATION OF THE FIRST DAY OF THE WEEK AS A DIVINE INSTITUTION.

BELOVED BRETHREN:

When our Divine Redeemer dwelt on earth, he prayed that all his disciples might be "made perfect in one." As this prayer was in harmony with the sure word of prophecy, which instructs us to look for a time when "the watchmen shall see, eye to eye, and sing with united voice," we are sure that it will ultimately be answered. . . .

We rejoice, brethren, that you, as well as ourselves, are looking for this day of glory. Moreover, we have knowledge of your firm persuasion, that this glorious union of the now scattered forces of Israel, can be effected only upon the basis of divine truth. With a single glance you see the fallacy of that reasoning, which calls upon you, for the sake of union, to sacrifice the least particle of God's word. . . .

We know, moreover, that it is the desire of your hearts, that all dissensions between Christians should be for ever ended. . . . Laboring as you do to expound to others the way of the Lord more perfectly, we cannot suppose that you are yourselves unwilling to learn. We, therefore, approach you with confidence, affectionately and earnestly requesting you to take into consideration the subject which is the only ground of difference between you and us. We conceive it to be a subject of great importance; and though some of you may have made it a matter of thought, we are persuaded that the great body of your denomination have dismissed it without any particular investigation. . . .

When we look over your large and influential denomination, we find, that, in reference to the subject upon which we now address you, you are divided into about three classes. I. Those who, acknowledging the perpetuity of the Sabbath-law, enforce the observance of the Sabbath by the fourth commandment, but change the day of its celebration from the seventh to the first day of the week. II. Those who see the impossibility of proving a change of the day, and, therefore, regard the commandment as abolished by the death of Christ. But, at the same time, they consider the first day of the week as an institution entirely new, to be regulated as to its observance wholly by the New Testament. III. Those who consider neither the Old nor the New Testament to impose any obligation upon them to observe a day of rest, and advocate one merely on the ground of expediency.

I. First, we address those of you who acknowledge the obligation of a Sabbath, but change the day of its celebration from the *seventh* to the *first* day of the week. We may be wanting in discernment, but it really appears to us, that in making the *particular day* to be observed to stand upon New Testament authority, and yet deriving all the *obligation* to *sabbatize* on that day from the Law, there is a departure from the great principle contended for by Baptists, that the extent and bearing of a law, both as to the duties it enjoins and the objects on which it terminates, are to be learned from the law itself, and not from other sources. On this principle you reject the logic of Pedobaptists, who, while they find the ordinance of *baptism* in the New Testament, go back to the law of *circumcision* to determine the subjects. You tell them, and very justly too, that the *law* of the institution is the *only rule* of obedience. But do you not fall into the same error, when the argument has respect to the Sabbath? We can see no more fitness in applying the law of the Sabbath to the first day of the week, than in applying the law of circumcision to the subjects of baptism. . . .

In justification of this change of the day, we often hear you plead the example of Christ and his apostles. But where do we find anything to this effect in their example? Did the apostles *sabbatize* on the first day of the week? Did the churches which were organized by them do so? Observe with marked attention, the question between you and us is NOT, Did they *meet together* and *hold worship* on that day? BUT, Did they *sabbatize?* that is, did they REST FROM THEIR LABOR on the first day of the week? Did they observe it AS a Sabbath? This is the true issue. We have often asked this question, but the only answer that we have received has been, *that they assembled for worship.* But this is not a candid way of meeting the point. . . . Your adroit evasion of the real question seems to place you much in the same predicament as were the Pharisees, when

Christ asked them whence was the baptism of John. It appears as if you reasoned with yourselves, and said, "If we shall say they *did* sabbatize on the first day of the week, the evidence will be called for, and we cannot find it; but if we shall say they did *not,* we fear the day will lose its sacredness in the eyes of the people." We do not by any means wish to charge you with a Pharisaic lack of principle, but we put it to your sober judgment, whether your position is not an awkward one. Brethren, reconsider this point, and see if you are not on Pedobaptist ground.

If the apostles did not sabbatize on the first day of the week, then it follows, as a matter of course, that whatever notoriety or dignity belonged to it, they did not regard it as a substitute for the Sabbath. Consequently, unless the Sabbath law was entirely abrogated by the death of Christ, the old Sabbath, as instituted in Paradise, and rehearsed from Sinai, continues yet binding, as "the Sabbath of the Lord thy God."

But more than this. Even if it could be proved, that the apostles and primitive Christians *did* actually regard the first day of the week *as a Sabbath,* it would not follow that the old Sabbath is no longer in force, unless it could be proved that they considered the new as a SUBSTITUTE for the old; or that so far as the particular day was concerned, it was of a CEREMONIAL character. But where do we find proof for either of these? In the whole record of the transactions and teachings of the apostles, where do we find this idea of *substitution?* Nowhere. . . .

The controversy between us and you appears to be brought down to a very narrow compass. *Did the apostles and primitive Christians sabbatize on the first day of the week?* And, *Is the* WORLD OF MANKIND *bound to imitate their example, or only the* CHURCH? If upon a solemn and prayerful consideration of this subject, you are persuaded that there is no proof that the early Christians regarded the first day as a Sabbath, (substituted in place of the seventh,) and will come out, and honestly avow your conviction, we have no fear that the controversy will be prolonged. For should you still be of opinion that some sort of notoriety was attached to the day, and that Christians met for worship, we shall not be very solicitous to dispute the point. The apostolic rule, "Let every man be fully persuaded in his own mind," will then govern us.—(See Rom. xiv. 5,6.) Our concern is not that you keep the first day of the week, but that you keep it *in place of the Sabbath,* thus making void the commandment of God. If once you discover, that Sunday is not the Sabbath by divine appointment, and therefore cannot be enforced upon the conscience, we are persuaded that your deep sense of the necessity of such an institution, will soon bring you to observance of the ancient Sabbath.

II. But we proceed to address those of you who regard the sabbatic law as having been nailed to the cross, and consider the First Day of the Week as an institution entirely new, regulated as to its observance wholly by the New Testament.

You, whom we now address, are exempt from some of the inconsistencies which we have exposed; but your theory labors under very serious difficulties, and is to be regarded, on the whole, as more obnoxious to the interests of religion, than the one we have been considering.

According to your position, the New Testament recognizes no Sabbath at all. Do not start at this charge. That it is repugnant to your feelings, we allow. You have never thought of anything else than *entire abstinence from labor* on the first day of the week. It is your day of *rest,* as well as *worship.* But on what ground do you make it a day of rest? What *example* have you for doing so? What *law* of the New Testament requires you to lay aside all your secular business? . . .

We are persuaded, brethren, that your conscientious scruples about laboring on the first day of the week, never resulted from the mere contemplation of apostolic example. . . . Even to this day a strong impression rests upon your minds, that the fourth

Commandment contains much of moral excellence; too much to be thrown altogether away, notwithstanding your system of theology teaches its abrogation. Such is the true secret of your tenderness of conscience. Apostolic example has in reality nothing to do with it. Following the secret monitions of conscience, your prosperity is promoted in spite of your theological system. But sound reason discovers, that your experience and your theory are in opposition to each other. . . .

Now suppose one of your brethren attends public worship on the first day of the week, and—to make his conformity to what is supposed to be apostolic example as perfect as possible—participates in the breaking of bread. He then goes home, opens his shop, and commences labor, or into the field to drive his plough. By what law will you convince him of sin? Not the law of the Sabbath as contained in the Decalogue, for that you hold to be abolished. Not any law of the New Testament which says "keep the first day of the week holy; in it thou shalt not do any work," for there is no such law. Not the law of apostolic example, for there is no proof that the apostles ever gave such example. The very utmost that you can with any show of reason pretend of their example, is, that they met together for worship and breaking of bread. To this example your brother has conformed to the very letter—who can say, he has not in spirit also? What now will you do with him . . . ?

III. But we must address that class of Baptists who consider neither the Old nor the New Testament to impose any obligation to observe a day of rest, and advocate one merely on the ground of expediency. In some sections of our country, Baptists would consider it almost a slander upon their denomination to intimate that there were persons of such anti-Sabbath principles, wearing their livery. . . .

If there is no day of rest enjoined by divine authority, and the matter rests wholly upon expediency, we see no reason, except that the voice of the multitude is against it, why you cannot as well observe the *seventh* as the *first* day of the week. There would be no sacrifice of conscience in so doing, while it would be a tribute of respect to those who feel that the keeping of the seventh day is an indispensable part of duty. But it is not on this principle particularly that we desire you to change your ground. Feeling that it is not *our party* that must be honored, but rather *divine truth,* and our party only *for the sake of* the truth, we would much rather correct your doctrinal views.

Of course, you do not deny that a day of rest was once enjoined upon God's chosen people. It is only under the gospel that you suppose all distinction of days to be annihilated. . . .

If the New Dispensation actually has abrogated the Sabbath, we do not believe that it is *expedient* to observe it. We cannot believe, however, that an institution so important to the civilization, refinement, and religious prosperity of mankind, has been abrogated. We refer you to our publications, and to the publications of those who have, in common with us, defended the perpetuity of the sabbatic law; and we entreat you to reconsider your ground. The doctrine of expediency! What a fruitful source of corruption has it been to the church of God! Not an anti-Christian, popish abomination, but what pleads something of this kind. Do, dear brethren, let it be expunged from your creed.

BRETHREN OF THE BAPTIST DENOMINATION.—You are a great and growing people. Your influence is felt throughout the length and breadth of our land. We rejoice in your prosperity. "May the Lord make you to increase and abound in love one towards another, and toward all men." In your prosperity we behold, in a measure, our own. Your baptism is our baptism. Your church government is our government. Your doctrinal principles are ours; and there is nothing which constitutes any real ground of separation, except the great and important subject we now urge upon your attention.

The popularity you have gained as a Denomination, however, is not owing to your Sabbath principles. It is founded entirely on your views concerning the initiating ordinance of the gospel. These views are characterized by that perfect simplicity, which markes every divine institution. Hence you have won the affections of the common people, while, if you had attempted to operate on them by a more complicated theory, failure would have been the result.

This induces us to urge upon your notice the *exceeding simplicity* of the Sabbatarian argument, compared with all those theories which stand in opposition to it. It is adapted to persons of weak capacities, of whom there are thousands in the kingdom of Christ. Any illiterate person can open the Bible, and point to chapter and verse saying, "the seventh day is the Sabbath of the Lord thy God." This is plain; he can understand it. . . .

In thus urging the simplicity of the argument for the Sabbath, we are but doing what you do in regard to Baptism. . . .

The extensive operations in which you are engaged for the conversion of the world, render it in the highest degree important, that you should not err on a question like this. If you are right, you ought to be very certain of it. Among the heathen you are extending the observance of Sunday, along with all your other sentiments. If you are thus sowing the seeds of error instead of truth, the evils who can calculate? Hence you cannot too early begin to review your ground. . . .

Our observations, if correct, go to show what a source of danger the Sunday heresy is to the Moral Law. The Sabbath is a most important precept of this law; "the golden *clasp,*" as an old writer quaintly observes, "which joins the two tables together; the *sinew* in the body of laws, which were written with God's own finger; the intermediate precept, which participates of the sanctity of both tables; and the due observance of which is the fulfilling of the whole law." This important precept is either set aside entirely; or its edge, and keenness, and all its power to cut a sinner's soul, so muffled by a transfer to another day, that the united efforts of the church can do little or nothing toward impressing it on the conscience. Here, then, is a relaxation of the standard of morality; and while the standard is relaxed with regard to this one precept, in vain do we look for the Law, as a whole, to appear glorious in the eyes of men.

Brethren, can we hope that the subject on which we have addressed you, will receive your prayerful attention? Almost your entire denomination has slumbered over it; but may we not hope, that you will now awake? May we not hope, that it will be discussed in your private circles, and in your public assemblies; in your Bible classes, and in your Sunday schools:—that it will be studied by your ministers, and by the people in general; and that every one will, in the deep desire of his soul, pray, "Lord, open thou mine eyes, that I may discern wondrous things out of thy Law." . . .

16.2 The Free Will Baptists

The freedom of the will of every person to believe in Jesus Christ gave to Free Will Baptists both their name and major teaching. The Free Will Baptists draw much from the English General Baptist heritage. In this country, their two independent origins centered in North Carolina with Paul Palmer and in New Hampshire with Benjamin Randall. Few of the Free Will Baptists survived the 1911 merger with the Northern Baptist Convention, but after 1916 the group made a comeback especially in the South. Remnants of the older groups merged in Nashville in 1935 to form the National Association of Free Will Baptists. The following documents illustrate the origin of the modern Free Will denomination, along with some of their emphases. *Sources: The Free Will Baptist,* I. J. Blackwelder, ed., 6 Nov. 1935. Used by permission. Minutes, National Association of Free Will Baptists, 1969, 18-20.

A.   The Merger of Free Will Baptists, 1935

A United Church

A "united church" is an expression with which most of us are familiar, but a "divided church" is an expression with which probably we are more familiar. We have talked much about a united church, and we have heard many others talk on the same subject. But in all probability many of us have said more about division in our church, and have heard others say more about division, than we have said and heard said about unity. Consequently, "division" is one of the most popular subjects among the people of the Free Will Baptist Church, and especially is it popular among our preachers. But people get tired of the same old thing over and over, day after day, and long for deliverance from the monotony of repetition. So it is, we trust, with our people who have heard DIVISION! DIVISIIN! [sic] DIVISION! with very little variety for the last—? no one knows how long. Therefore, in this article let us think together of a "United Church" as we consider five things, each of which offers a liberal contribution to such a union among the people of our own denomination.

The first of the five things that are necessary to the unity of the Free Will Baptist Church is the use of our own literature by all of our Sunday Schools and Free Will Baptist Leagues. For various reasons some of our people, quite a few of them, are using other literature than our own in their Sunday Schools and Leagues. Some of these folk say that our quarterlies aren't well adapted to the various departments, some are saying that our literature is not the best, others are saying that other literature is cheaper, while others say that literature is absolutely unnecessary in Sunday School and League work. But it matters not what the excuse is for not using our own literature, it is still true that those who reject it are in a measure disloyal to their church, and are to some extent helping to block a united church. The use of our own literature by all of our people will greatly contribute to unity among our people.

The second essential to unity is one or both of our church papers in as nearly every Free Will Baptist home as possible. The subscription list to the *Free Will Baptist* is steadily increasing, but it is still far short of what it should be. . . . There is no other medium by which the average Free Will Baptist can keep as well posted on the activities of his church as he can through our church papers. . . . And, too, those who are subscribers to one or both of our papers are manifesting loyalty to and interest in their church, and are also making a contribution to unity among our people.

A third requisite to a united church is a general church program. For these many years our people have been working too independently. Small groups of Free Will Baptists here and there over the United States have known entirely too little about their brothers and sisters in other parts of the country. . . . But why is it thus in our church? is a question that these facts raise in our minds. Well, there may be several things more or less responsible for these conditions in our church, but the one thing that is probably most responsible is the lack of a denominational program for our people everywhere. A general program for our church would better acquaint us with one another and with the work of the church in general, would create within us a greater interest in our work as a whole, and would therefore greatly help to bring our people together in one great united body. We need a general program for our church, and may we pray earnestly and work untiringly for it.

Another very important factor in the consideration of a united church is the same treatise of the faith and practice of the Free Will Baptist Church for all Free Will Baptists everywhere. We may talk about a united church, pray about a united church, and work for a united church, but until we become nearly enough alike to accept the same treatise of faith and practice we will never be united. . . . Of course, we will never be identical on every point of doctrine, but we must be nearly enough the same in our doctrinal views to accept the same treatise of faith and practice or we will never have a united church. A general treatise of the faith and practice of the Free Will Baptist Church is absolutely indispensable to a united Free Will Baptist Church.

Finally, our ministers and Christian workers must have the same kind of Christian training if they are expected to believe, preach, and teach the same doctrine. As long as part of our preachers and Christian workers get their training in one school, part of them in another school, and part of them in still another school, and the greater part of them remain without any special training in any school—just that long there will be strife, faction, and division among our people. If we don't care what our preachers believe and preach and teach, we shouldn't care where they receive their training. But if we expect our ministers to present the doctrine of the Free Will Baptist Church, we must see to it that they receive their Christian training in a Free Will Baptist School. . . . WHY ARE FREE WILL BAPTISTS SO DIVIDED IN DOCTRINE AS WELL AS IN OTHER THINGS? The main reason is this: They have no school where their leaders may receive the same kind of thorough Bible training for the work they have been called to do in our church. . . . Therefore, we must have a school in which we can offer our people the training necessary for the work to which the Lord has called them if we are to realize our dreams of a united church.

Before this article will have been read by our people, the National Association will have met in its first session, and we trust that it will have seriously considered some of these things of which we have been speaking. Through this great organization we hope to offer to our people over the United States the same treatise of the faith and practice of our church, a general program of work, and something definite concerning a centralized school. Let us preach, and teach, and pray for a united church.

B. Free Will Baptists and Doctrinal Issues

REPORT OF COMMISSION ON THE STUDY
OF THEOLOGICAL LIBERALISM, 1962

Paul warned that "the time will come when men will not endure sound doctrine." That time came when the visible church became engulfed in the Roman Catholic heresy. Later, after the rise of Protestantism and the revival of New Testament Christianity, the church faced new doctrinal attacks. The climax of these is the attempt of satan to destroy God's work by modernism. This is perhaps his most successful attack because it is his most subtle attempt. It works from within. Like a worm in an apple, modernism eats away at the core of the church leaving a beautiful outside but no heart.

I. REPORT ON OUR WORK

This Commission has studied the foe of theological liberalism. Attention was given to the fact of what constitutes a modernist in church work. The term is used to designate those who believe and teach certain modern theories about scriptural truth. It does not necessarily apply to the use of modern equipment. It does not necessarily refer to a church with a new building of contemporary design. In the most generally accepted sense a modernist is a theological liberal who does not hold to historical Christian truths. The doctrines of the modernist are such errors as the following: The Bible is a human book full of mistakes instead of the inerrant WORD OF GOD; the miracles of the Bible are more myth than miracle; Jesus is the illegitimate son of an unfortunate woman instead of the Virgin Born, sin-less son of the Almighty God; the death of Christ was a martyr's finish to a religious leader's life instead of the substitutionary atonement for the sins of the world; the resurrection of Jesus was a mental hallucination of some misguided zealots instead of the victorious bodily triumph of the King of kings and Lord of lords; the need of the world is psychological adjustment instead of Holy Ghost regeneration; and the mission of the church is more to construct a new social order than to snatch sinners from eternal hell by God's gospel.

Consideration was also given to the new-modernism: neo-orthodoxy. This is the erroneous method of using good old fundamental gospel words to disguise deceptive beliefs. Many who can freely use such terms as "conversion", "Word of God", "inspiration" and "preach the gospel" mean something very different from the preaching of such men as Elder Benjamin Randall and Elder Paul Palmer. . . .

II. APPRAISAL OF OUR DENOMINATION WITH RESPECT TO LIBERALISM.

The Free Will Baptist Denomination is greatly blessed in that we have no great problem over modernism at the present time. Certain factors play a part in this picture.

One characteristic of our churches in the past that has helped us is conservativism. This in itself is no particular virtue, but it has given us the tendency to steer away from the liberal ideas of modernists.

Alignment with the National Association of Evangelicals has helped make us aware of certain dangers. This group of denominations helps alert members to the peril of modernism. It keeps us aware of the trends created by its antagonistic counterpart—the National Council of Churches.

The firm position taken by the Free Will Baptist College on the fundamentals of our faith is strongly in our favor. Current concern over future denominational loyalty to our historic beliefs chiefly arises from this factor. We find that modernism's biggest enemy among Free Will Baptists is the Bible College.

The orthodoxy of our denominational leaders is an encouraging sign. We feel that those now leading the work of the National Association will never betray the cause by being soft on liberalism.

However, as we see it, Free Will Baptists are approaching a crossroads. Within this decade additional measures should be taken to insure our future against modernism or else trends toward liberalism might set the stage for false doctrine in years to come. It is not enough to be relatively free from the peril now. Safeguards should be created against future encroachments. One of our weakest points might be our inevitable drive for progress. All of us must recognize that the only real progress made is spiritual and scriptural progress.

III. SUGGESTIONS FOR THE FUTURE

Free Will Baptists must pray and work for a revival of Bible standards in Christian living. Great stress should be given to the holy heart and separated life of the Lord's people. Worldliness should be defined and churches should call on members to tow the line. High spiritual standards should be maintained in the ministry. Brotherly love should be exercised in dealing with the problems of worldliness.

Separation from modernists in accordance with II Corinthians 6:14 "Be ye not unequally yoked together with unbelievers: . . ." and other scriptures should be maintained. Clear lines of loyalty to Scriptural Brethren should be held. Though one loves the soul of the modernist, his false beliefs should be *exposed*.

Those who have been educated by modernists and have had close association with them should make their alignment with orthodoxy and disapproval of theological liberalism known clearly and unquestionably. Young men should be discouraged from going to liberal institutions, particularly for theological training.

Pastors should doctrinally prepare their people to "give a reason for the hope." Laymen need to be aware of the issues at stake. Doctrinal sermons help teach the Lord's people. Some ministers have brought a series of doctrinal messages for this purpose. The minister should take his stand against evolution and other errors in the public schools.

More care should be taken by ordaining councils in ordination. Furthermore when one's doctrines are questionable this group should examine. A preacher of sound doctrine will *gladly* restate his position.

A survey of liberalism in other denominations reveals that the chief place of entrance is educational institutions. Generally speaking "as a denomination's schools go, so goes the denomination." We must be kept aware that we need more than just education. We need the right kind of education. Therefore, constant vigilance should be kept over all our Free Will Baptist institutions.

All of us need to maintain a strong spiritual witness and testimony. Forceful, effective evangelism and modernism do not mix. "The best defense is often a strong offense." Furthermore, we must remember that a soul-winning church is a doctrinally sound church.

Finally, we appreciate the opportunity of serving this past year. We feel that the job has just begun. This is a continuous task. Such a commission should be in permanent existence. Therefore, we recommend that the Moderator be authorized to appoint a permanent commission.

16.3   The Primitive Baptists

Opposition to the foreign missions movement in the early 1800s gave rise to the Primitive Baptists in America. They exist in several subgroups, most of them following strict Calvinism and going under names like "Absoluters," "Old School," and "Old Liners." Some still show suspicion toward human religious activity, whether in missions, education, or Sunday Schools. However, in the twentieth century some of their earlier strictness has moderated, to the relief of some and the distress of others. In 1926 R. H. Pittman, editor of the *Advocate and Messenger,* reprinted an important article from 1901 outlining the major principles of Primitive Baptists (selection A). *Source: Advocate and Messenger,* 1926, 36–41. In selection B, Elder W. J. Berry compares Primitive Baptist doctrines and practices of 1840 with those of 1960, with a call to return to the strict principles of the past. *Source:* W. J. Berry, "What Were the Old School Baptists in 1840?—In 1960?" (Elon, N.C.: The Old School Contenders, 1960). This is a reprint of an editorial in the *Old Faith Contender,* October 1959. Used by permission.

A.   Primitive Baptist Statement of Faith

THE PRINCIPLES OF THE GOSPEL MESSENGER
(From The Gospel Messenger For August, 1901)
Reaffirmed by the Advocate and Messenger

(These principles are the great truths taught by the prophets, Christ, and His apostles in the Holy Scriptures, affirmed, in regard to eternal salvation, by the early European reformers and martyrs of the 14th and 15th centuries, similarly reaffirmed by the Protestant reformers, including the Episcopalians, of the 16th century, embodied in substance of doctrine with reference to final salvation, in the Articles of Faith of the Presbyterians, Independents or Congregationalists, and Predestinarian Baptists of the 17th century, fully set forth in the London Baptist Confession of Faith of 1689, adopted as an expression of their belief by all the Predestinarian Baptists of the United States in the 18th century, maintained by nearly every Primitive Baptist church of the 19th century; and these principles, exactly as here published, were unanimously approved by the general meetings of Primitive Baptists at Oakland City, Ind., September 17, 1900, and at Fulton, Ky.,

November 14-18, 1900, representing two-thirds of the Primitive Baptists of the United States; and, I believe, that they are the sentiments of nine-tenths of all the Primitive Baptists now living.)

1. The Holy Scriptures of the Old and the New Testaments are the perfectly inspired Word of God, and the only infallible standard of faith and practice; although the light of nature, and the works of creation and providence, so far manifest the goodness, wisdom, and power of God as to leave all men inexcusable for their sins, and yet unable to accomplish their own salvation.

2. There is only one living and true God, who is a pure spirit, selfexistent, perfect, infinite and eternal in all His glorious attributes of holiness, justice, truth, wisdom, mercy, and goodness, the sovereign Creator, upholder, governor, and judge of the universe, and who exists in the three-fold undivided and indivisible subsistences of the Father, Son, and the Holy Ghost.

3. Nothing takes place by chance; but God's fore-knowledge, purpose and providence embrace all things, including grace and holiness, positively and efficiently, and sin permissively and overrulingly—sin proceeding from the will of the creature, and of which God, who is most holy, is neither the author nor approver, but of which He is the fatherly chastiser in His children, and the righteous punisher in His enemies; the Lord, for the former sins of His people, and to make them more humble, watchful and prayerful in the future, clouding their sense of His love, bringing temporal judgments upon them, and leaving them for a while to manifold temptations and the corruptions of their own hearts, and giving over the wicked, for their former sins, to their own lusts and the temptations of the world and the power of Satan, so that they harden themselves under the same circumstances by which God softens the hearts of His people.

4. For the manifestation of His glory, God, before the foundation of the world, predestinated some men and angels to eternal life, through Jesus Christ, to the praise of His glorious grace, and left others to act in their sins to their just condemnation, to the praise of His glorious justice. The Father gave all the elect of the human family to the Son in the eternal covenant of grace; the Son, according to the prophecies and types of four thousand years, became incarnate of the Virgin Mary, and died and rose again to redeem and justify the elect; and the Holy Ghost regenerates the elect, creating in their souls a new spiritual life, and effectually applies to them the holy and everlasting salvation of Jesus, giving them, generally though not always, under the administration of the word and the ordinances of God, true repentance and faith and hope and love, and working in them both to will and to do of His own good pleasure, and infallibly keeping every one of them unto the fullness of salvation which is to be finally revealed to them; and this eternal salvation is for the elect only, and is personal and unconditional on their part, God by His Spirit working in them all the so-called spiritual conditions of repentance, faith, and love, so that the salvation of the elect is all of Divine and unmerited grace and for it God deserves and will receive all the glory; and all who die in infancy are among the elect, and are saved by God's almighty grace.

5. God created man in His own image, very good and upright; and man of his own will, without any compulsion and undeceived, transgressed the law of God, falling from his original innocence and communion with God, and involving all his posterity in death in trespasses and sins, in total depravity, in utter inclination to all evil, from which only the saving grace of God can deliver him, and enable him fully to will and do that which is spiritually good; and this corruption of nature remains during all this earthly life even in the regenerate, who are made perfectly and imutably free to good only in the state of glory.

6. Good works are such only as God hath commanded in His Holy Word, and are the fruits and evidences of a true and lively faith; . . . the best saints do less than God

requires of them; and the best works, being mixed with imperfection, can never merit pardon of sin or eternal life. Works done by the unregenerate, though useful in this life, to themselves and others, yet, not proceeding from faith in God, nor meant for the glory of God, are sinful and can not please God, . . .

7. While the ceremonial law of types and figures was fulfilled and abrogated by Christ, and the judicial and civil law given the Jews was of limited national use, the formal law of the Ten Commandments, written in substance in the heart or conscience of Adam while he was upright and in the image of God, and delivered by God on Mount Sinai, and written in two tables, the first four containing our duty to God and the last six our duty to man, is of universal and perpetual obligation for all persons, both regenerate and unregenerate, . . .

8. The Triune God alone is to be worshipped, and in spirit and in truth, and only through the mediation of Christ, by prayer, reading the Scriptures, preaching, hearing the Word of God, singing spiritual songs, baptism, the Lord's Supper, fasting, and thanksgiving; and one day in seven—which from the creation of the world to the resurrection of Christ was the last day of the week, but since the resurrection of Christ has been the first day of the week, and is called the Lord's Day—should be kept free from worldly employments and recreations, and devoted to the public and private worship of God, and to the duties of necessity and charity.

9. All orderly-walking believers in Christ ought to be gathered in particular churches, having Christ as their only Head, and having power to carry out that order in worship and discipline which He requireth, their officers being Elders (or Bishops) and Deacons, . . . the duty of Deacons being to serve the tables of the Lord, of the pastor, and of the poor; the duty of pastors being to give themselves to the ministry of the word and prayer and watching for souls; and the duty of the church being to communicate of their natural substance according to their ability to their pastor, and to hold communion with other churches of like faith and order, . . .

10. Baptism is a sign of the fellowship of believers in Christ with Him in His death and resurrection, and should be administered only to believers, and by immersion in water in the name of the Father and of the Son and of the Holy Ghost; and the Lord's Supper was not meant by Him to be a sacrifice for sin, but only as a perpetual memorial of that one offering up of Himself by Himself upon the cross for all the sins of the elect; . . .

11. While after death the bodies of men return to dust and corruption, their souls return at once to God who gave them—the souls of the righteous being made perfect in holiness and received into Paradise, . . . and the souls of the wicked are cast into hell, . . . At the last day such of the saints as are found alive shall not sleep, but be changed; and all the dead shall be raised up with the self-same bodies, and none other, although with different qualities, which shall be united again to their souls forever; the bodies of the unjust shall, by the power of Christ, be raised to dishonor, and the bodies of the just, by His Spirit, unto honor, and be made conformable to His own glorious body.

12. God hath appointed a day of general and final judgment, unknown to men, when apostate angels and all persons that have lived upon the earth shall appear before the tribunal of Christ at His second personal coming to the world, to give an account of their thoughts and words and deeds, whether good or evil. . . . and the righteous shall enter into the fullness of everlasting life, while the wicked shall be cast into everlasting torment.

Sylvester Hassell.

B.   Principles of the Primitive Baptists

WHAT IS MEANT here by **Old School Baptist** is, that body or order of Baptists which developed following the division over money-based missions, seminaries, etc. History shows that no religious society or organization remains the same, all claims to the contrary notwithstanding. We are never what our fathers were, nor what we claim to be, but what we actually are and what we practice.

Prior to their settlement in America, the Baptists were historically and essentially heterogeneous, free evangelistic bodies. In any instance where they have organized beyond this characteristic they cease to be Baptists.

The Baptist churches in America rapidly became strong in membership and influence. With this freedom and prosperity came—as it always does—corruption in doctrine and practice. As in the early church, graceless characters filled the churches and the ministry; with the genuine zeal and some, others of "zeal without knowledge" set about to "bring in the kingdom by carnal methods." This meant the certain departure from the ways of God to the ways of men. Just to mention a few of these, it was decided that if ministers were to "go into the world and preach the gospel" they must first be graduates from schools (called seminaries) that would qualify them to preach and properly perform as evangelists in other countries. It was further decided that the best way to teach the children and to build up the churches was to organize and maintain church Sunday Schools. One thing called for another, until it was seen that to accomplish all these things men and women of "learning and talent" must be had; but they could not be obtained without a salary, etc. This great so-called Christian organization continued to develop until it brought a division among the Baptist churches, between those who supported such things, and those who refused to support them.

Now turning to the **Old School Baptists**. The separation between those called "new school" and "old school" Baptists was completed from 1820 to 1840. While the new school or Missionary Baptists were running their band wagon over the country, taking on every new thing, what were the old school brethren doing? In essence they were spending their time opposing everything the new school was doing. The result was two brand new religious organizations; one organization with a positive, but carnal zeal to do something for the Lord; the other with a negative zeal, or effort to oppose those carnal methods, then the epithet "anti-effort" and "anti-means" Baptists. . . . Many of our old school brethren became so zealous in opposing Arminianism with all of its evil trappings, that they left off preaching the gospel, until that **opposition** to Arminianism itself became their gospel; . . . Unconsciously this new religion replaced true religion and the preaching of Christ. It was right then, and it is right now to oppose every error and every false religion, but once we allow that **opposition** to become the theme of our life, we have automatically established a new order, or a new religion,—reason how we may to the contrary. This is exactly what both the new and the old school did.

The question before us is, "What were the Old School Baptists in 1840?" The reader will note that up to now in referring to Old School the lower case "o" and "s" were used, because it is not proper to capitalize common words. Now the whole situation changes. These two "schools" which began only as religious movements now become full-fledged organizations. The "new school" order chose to be called Baptists or Missionary Baptists; the old school order chose to be called Old School, or Anti-means Baptists, later in the south, Primitive Baptists. That was in 1820-40,—just a little over one hundred years ago.

But now, just what **were these Old School Baptists?** What characterized them as churches and as a people? . . . While their new school brethren were adopting an Arminian or works system, the old school brethren, who had in the south been somewhat Arminian, now advocated what is termed Calvinistic doctrine. They especially stressed election and salvation by grace alone, the total depravity of man, and the necessity of the new birth. . . . In short they preached Christ first and last in all He is to sinners. They preached hellfire and damnation and Christ the only Savior. They did not coddle their hearers with a lifeless flattery and false promises of flowery beds of ease after they joined the church. The ministry was free; they went where a door was opened, preaching their own convictions from their own heart,—none forbidding them. . . .

Gilbert Beebe, who established the periodical called the Signs of the Times, in 1832, was undoubtedly one of the ablest defenders of the Old School position, and was the chief author of the famous "Black Rock Address." In an editorial for September 15, 1840, as the Old School Baptist position for marriage and divorce, he gave death only as a cause for re-marriage, that he did not know of a case and hoped never to hear of an instance among the Old School Baptists contrary to this practice. The Old School Baptists were at that time throughout America opposed to their members carrying so-called life insurance, belonging to secret orders, or any other similar institution of men. Our limited space forbids further listing of what the Old School Baptists were in 1840, but those who search will learn many other things.

You will notice in the question the past tense "WERE" is used instead of "ARE," to show that those claiming to be Old School Baptists TODAY are not what they were in 1840. . . . The pathetic truth is—we say it in kindness, and history proves it—that the majority of the membership in all factions of so-called Old School or Primitive Baptists today do not even **know** what the Old School Baptists of 1840 believed and practiced, and it is plainly evident that they do not preach and practice what they did then. What is the same is mostly in the letter only.

Please do no [sic] understand that we are setting up the order of Old School Baptist of 1840 as a standard for us today in 1960. We shall never do that; . . . But we have shown—only very briefly—what the order of Old School Baptists of 1840 was, because there are so many interlopers with us today in high places, deceiving the people, and claiming to be "Old School or Primitive Baptists." The churches of the old school of 1840 did not use these terms as names for their church, but those of you today—if you will boast of the name Old School Baptist—then plain honesty demands that you at least make some attempt to preach and practice what those Old School Baptists did in 1840. . . .

Do we preach the same doctrine they did? Let us see. When they preached election, how did they explain it? Did they preach it in Christ, or as many do today, in Adam? When they talked about the elect and non-elcet, did they spiritualize every text they came to, applying the same pattern to all? Did they call Esau a "disobedient child," etc., or did they not represent those characters from start to finish in the plain words of "reprobate" and "non-elect"? Should any be ignorant of the fact, it was THIS KIND of preaching that distinguished those Old School preachers and made them very unpopular with the Arminian world. The truth is, election cannot be preached as many Primitive Baptists are interpreting scripture, applying everything to the child of God only. They unwittingly destroy their own support of election. . . .

When those Old School preachers of 1840 exponded [sic] the sovereignty of God, did they put it in words that would leave the hearers subconsciously feeling, if not actually so, that, after all, not they, but God was responsible for all they did and said; they couldn't help it, and therefore would not be punished for the same? Or did they not rather preach that God was the supreme Ruler and Sovereign over all times and events, and "hath decreed in Himself from all eternity, by the most wise and holy counsel of His own will, freely and unchangeable, all things whatsoever come to pass; yet so as thereby God is neither the author of sin, nor hath fellowship with any therein, nor is violence offered to the will of the creature"? . . . If you do not preach it that way, you may be professing to be an Old School or Primitive Baptist, but you are not like those of 1840, therefore you are a different order.

When you preach, do you address your words to church members or friends, coddling them in their sins and making false promises to them if they will "join the church," etc.? . . . John Leland was mourning over his "barren ministry," and said that he had baptized "only three hundred that year!" Do you think that he was a Billy Graham style of preacher? Well, what was it? Do you suppose he whipped up his congregation into an emotional frenzy by whining out some graveyard stories, or sing-songings about "dear old Mother and Dad" which is now widely practiced among many Primitive Baptists? Do you think he used some shallow songs jigged up to capture the carnal nature of the young folks, and then coax them into the church under the spell? Many Old School or Primitive Baptists are using all these and many more shameful, carnal methods, and still do well to get **three** rather than Leland's three hundred **without any such work-mongering**. . . .

The Old School Baptists of 1840 believed that if God calls a man, He will also qualify him to preach. If he does not so preach it was evidence that God did not call him. . . .

When God called a man he preached whether man approved or not; whether they ordained or not. . . .

When God called a man to preach in 1840, he preached the preaching God Himself had bidden him, favoring no man and fearing no man. . . .

If some of those Old School Baptist ministers of 1840 could step down and observe the way we "play at church," what do you think they would say? Or would they have the heart to say anything? Would they think we were entitled to the appelation "Old School or Primitive Baptist"?

How ashamed they would be to step in sometime and see how the Old School or Primitive Baptists of 1960 straight-jacket and gag their ministers; how their bosses and their shameful bar-system tell their ministers where they may and may not preach, with whom they may or may not commune and fellowship. . . .

Let us now look to the churches and their housekeeping. First, those Old School Baptist churches of 1840,—were they free local self-governing bodies of believers, or were they in a tight ring of correspondence? They were not all as free as formerly. They were nearly all free from outside dictation and fear of reprisals; communion and fellowship flowed freely throughout America. . . .

The Old School Baptist churches of 1840 believed that the church of Christ was separated from the world, and her members must be regenerated characters who had been killed to the love of sin and the world; that having made such a profession they were expected to walk accordingly. Such gross sins as drunkenness, fornication, divorce, dishonesty, dancing, theatre-going, and general worldliness were not tolerated, and those who fell into lesser worldly practices were lovingly but firmly exhorted to reform. How does this compare generally with the everyday life of 1960 church members? . . .

The heading of this article is not primarily what is right or wrong scripturally, but rather what were the foundation principles which brought into being the Old School

Baptists,—what did they believe, preach and practice? Having established that, are we identical to them today, or are we satisfied with just the NAME?

For those who want to go back to the foundation laid by **Christ** and **the apostles,** that is a different matter. Some say it cannot be done, and we fear that is true, but by the grace of God, we at least want to be found on our **way back** at His coming.

W. J. BERRY

16.4 The Ultimatum of the Arkansas ABA Faction to the Southern Baptist Convention and Response of the SBC, 1905

The Landmark theology of J. R. Graves found ready acceptance among many Arkansas Baptists. By the turn of the century a large number of pastors and churches, led by Ben M. Bogard of Searcy, objected to the work of the Baptist state convention. They preferred a more Landmark style of work that minimized convention boards, both in the state and in the Southern Baptist Convention. For years they had agitated for changes in the SBC, but in 1905 they issued an ultimatum. The Southern Baptist committee appointed to answer the Bogard group, led by W. E. Hatcher of Virginia, in a four-point response refused to yield to the Landmark demands. Thereupon, the Bogard faction withdrew from the SBC. *Source: Annual*, SBC, 1905, 41-45.

Texarkana Convention Memorial.

Your Committee, to whom was referred the Texarkana Memorial, beg respectfully to submit the following report:

1. That we have sought to give to this memorial a patient and fraternal consideration, and we feel that the Convention ought to make reply to its petitions in the spirit of brotherly kindness.

2. We beg to report to the Convention that our study of the subject-matter of this memorial forces us to the conclusion that it would not be for the best interests of the work which the Convention is seeking to do, to accede to the petitions contained in this memorial. These petitions call for action so entirely out of harmony with the principles of our organization, and the methods upon which our work is conducted, that we feel constrained to ask that they shall be denied. We feel the strongest assurance that the principles upon which the work of our Convention is organized and conducted are in accord with the teachings of God's Word, and in harmony with Baptist history, Baptist usage, and Baptist doctrine.

3. Your Committee feels it important, with a view to avoiding all misapprehension, that a statement should be made in this report in regard to the matter of inter-denominational comity. During the past Convention year the Foreign Mission Board was approached with a request that a committee should be appointed from the several denominations to which all questions of inter-denominational comity should be referred. To this request our Board at Richmond unanimously returned a negative reply. It reserves to itself absolutely, subject to the instructions of this Convention, the whole matter of the selection of field appointment and of missionaries.

4. We beg to assure those from whom this memorial has come that we would look upon any possibility of their separation from our organized work with unfeigned regret, and trust that no such unhappy event shall ever occur. We are sure that our Baptist churches throughout the South are cordially united in their doctrinal beliefs, and in their love of our common Lord and Master, and we greatly desire, and earnestly pray, that we may all be one in purpose and one in a movement for advancing the kingdom of our Redeemer.

W. E. HATCHER,
J. H. KILPATRICK,
JNO. T. CHRISTIAN,
B. H. DEMENT,
C. H. NASH,
WM. ELLYSON.

The report was adopted, and the memorial, to which the above was an answer, ordered to be printed in the minutes.

Dear Brethren.—We, the Committee appointed by the preliminary meeting of the General Association of Baptists of the United States of America, to memorialize the Southern Baptist Convention concerning the things to which objections have been made by many churches and individuals, beg your respectful attention and careful consideration of the matters hereinafter mentioned.

We were appointed by the messengers of fifty-two Baptist Churches who met in Texarkana, Ark., March 22, and we feel certain that thousands of churches are in sympathy with what we have done. But if only one church should come with a memorial of this sort, it should be heard and its requests given careful and prayerful attention.

Our sincere desire is for peace and harmony among Baptists, but we want this peace and harmony to be on Bible principles and methods. We love peace, but we love principle better. First pure and then peaceable. Besides, we do not think we are guilty of causing the division which has been troubling our Zion. We have protested against what we honestly believe to be unscriptural principles and methods of work, and we think those who have persistently clung to those objectionable principles and methods are the cause of the division. He that drives the wedge is guilty of splitting the log.

We do not desire that any part of the work of evangelizing the world should stop, but on the other hand want to help in all Scriptural ways in this great work, and we honestly desire to work with the brethren composing the Southern Baptist Convention, and will do so if you will at this session of the Convention make the following changes in your Constitution:

First, we want the money and the associational basis of representation eliminated from the Constitution and a purely church basis substituted instead. We believe in the churches to whom the Lord gave the commission, and that a church which is willing to co-operate should be entitled to a seat in this Convention by messenger, whether it be large or small, rich or poor, without any specified sum of money being fixed as the basis of co-operation. . . . Nothing short of exclusive church representation will satisfy us. We ask that you eliminate all other basis and adopt the church basis of representation.

We object to the power put into the hands of the Boards by the Convention to appoint and remove missionaries at pleasure without giving them the right to appeal to the Convention, . . .

Third, we object to the Boards being influenced or controlled by what is known as denominational comity. We think that our commision is to go into all the world, no matter who may occupy the field. . . . But since denominational comity is not necessary to Baptist success, the Convention can easily right that wrong. If the Foreign Mission Board has not been guilty of this thing it can be made unmistakably plain by that Board being instructed to open mission work in Persia and Syria, and by its obeying its instructions.

Fourth, some of us object to many other matters of detail concerning the methods of the Convention and its Boards, but we are willing for the sake of peace and harmony among Baptists to waive these objections; we are willing to meet you half way, yea, more than half way for the sake of peace and harmony among the Baptist host. Will you do as much? . . .

Fifth, we attach hereto a copy of our statement of principles and methods of work. We do not ask that you adopt these in full, but send it with this communication so that you may see that we, while we ask you to concede two or three points for the sake of harmony and peace, are really conceding more than we ask you to concede. We are not asking you to make all the concessions; we are willing to meet you as brethren on half-way ground. At the same time we are stating the least we can ask of you. If you reject this at this session we shall consider that we have done our duty and shall trouble you no more.

We bid you God speed in every good work, and ask you to prayerfully consider our request.

B. M. BOGARD,
J. B. SELLMAN,
J. K. P. WILLIAMS,
J. T. TUCKER,
A. J. ROBINS,
J. H. KUYKENDALL,
J. Y. FREEMAN.

16.5   Ben M. Bogard, *The Baptist Way Book,* 1946

Ben M. Bogard, pastor in Searcy, Arkansas, led the schism that produced the American Baptist Association in that state in 1902. His movement represented basically a new outbreak of Landmarkism, with ultraconservative overtones for all areas of church belief and practice. Bogard's book on the "Baptist Way," published in 1946 (by Bogard Press), provides an excellent source for understanding the spirit and emphases of the resurgence of Landmark movement among Southern Baptists. The book spells out Bogard's conviction that all "convention" Baptists have lost the Baptist way. His ultraconservative movement calls them back to the "Baptist way," of doing things (i.e. *his* way). *Source:* Ben Bogard, *The Baptist Way Book* (Texarkana: Bogard Press, 1946), 5-6, 11-17, 20-28, 43-45. Used by permission.

PART I
The Scriptural Way

The Bible is the all-sufficient rule of faith and practice and it is as much a rule of practice as it is of faith.

The commission given by our Master in Matt. 28:19, 20, commands the church to "teach all things whatsoever I have commanded you." The specification of one thing in law is the prohibition of everything else. Since what the church is to teach is specified, viz., "all things whatsoever I have commanded," it follows that all things not commanded are forbidden. It follows that the church is shut up to the things commanded. There is therefore no place for the exercise of private opinion except it be in our effort to understand the things commanded. Any doctrine or institution that is outside of the purview of the Scriptures is wrong. . . .

By the Scriptures, the all-sufficient rule of faith and practice, must every doctrine and every truth be tried. If it be allowed that reason or sanctified common sense shall determine in matters of faith and practice, it shall still be an open question as to whose reason and whose sanctified common sense shall make the decision. If reason or common sense shall be the rule of any part of faith and practice then it is certain that we shall see division, contention, strife. Let the Bible be the rule of faith and practice and our only difficulty shall be understanding our rule. . . .

If Baptists forsake this cardinal and fundamental principle, it shall not be long until they shall cease to be Baptists. They shall be at sea without chart or compass.

In the following chapters we shall examine what the Scriptures teach concerning the Way of Salvation, Baptism, the Lord's Supper, Church Policy, Missions, and Providence. While we hear the Word of God on these subjects, let us remember that this Word is the only and all-sufficient rule of faith and practice.

CHAPTER II
The Way of Baptism

The church only having authority to baptize, it follows that all baptisms administered without church authority are null and void. For this reason Baptists have in all ages refused to recognize the baptisms of those who were not baptized by the authority of a Scriptural church. It was to the church the commission was given and the church institution to which the commission was given is in the world today, and if the Lord meant what He said, He is with that church today. The baptisms of that institution are valid and no other is.

Scriptural baptism is the immersion of a saved person by authority of a Scriptural church.

Since God called the forerunner, John the Baptist—the baptizer—called him "Baptist" because he did the baptizing, it follows that, if God made no mistake, that a CHURCH THAT BAPTIZES should be called a Baptist Church; a baptizing church. Since the baptizing church is a missionary church it is perfectly right to call it a Missionary Baptist Church.

CHAPTER III
The Way of the Lord's Supper

The Lord's Supper is a commemorative ordinance to be observed by the church in memory of the broken body and shed blood of the Saviour. I Cor. 11:24: "This do in remembrance of me."

Only baptized believers have a right to partake of the Supper. The commission given by our Master commands that the newly made disciples be baptized and then "teach them to observe all things whatsoever I have commanded you," Matt. 28:19, 20. One of the things the Lord had commanded was the partaking of the Memorial Supper. The new disciples were first to be baptized then taught to observe the other things which had been commanded. To partake of the Supper before baptism is to violate this law, and if we encourage any to thus violate the law of the Lord on this subject we shall be partakers of their sin. To invite unbaptized people to partake of the Lord's Supper is a sin. Open Communion is therefore a sin—a transgression of the Master's law concerning the Supper. . . .

Note the order here indicated:
1. "Gladly received his word"—disciples.
2. "Were baptized"—baptized disciples.
3. "The same day were added—church members.
4. "Continued in apostolic doctrine"—sound in faith.
5. "And in fellowship"—united in faith and love.
6. Lastly, "breaking of bread"—partaking of the Lord's Supper.

This is the Divine order, and no man has a right to change it. If we observe this order we have Close Communion, the doctrine for which Baptists have always contended.

CHAPTER IV
The Way of Church Polity

There are three forms of church government or polity: the Episcopalian, the Presbyterian, and the Congregational. Episcopacy is government by bishops; Presbyterianism is government by presbyters or preachers; Congregationalism is government by the people—a pure democracy.

Baptists are Congregationalists. They do not claim the right to make or repeal laws, but recognize and obey the unchanging law of their King Jesus Christ. But in the execution of these laws of the Lord there is a pure democracy. . . .

In the New Testament we learn the following facts:
1. The congregation received members. . . .
2. The congregations excluded members from their fellowship. . . .
3. The congregations elected their own officers. . . .
4. The congregations elected their own missionaries. . . .

The conclusion is clear. It was to "the church" that the Commission was given. It is therefore the duty of the congregation to do all that the Commission enjoins. The congregation is the unit in all the work contemplated in the Commission. There is not the slightest hint in the New Testament of their being authority on earth above a congregation of baptized disciples. Where we read of "elders that rule well," the literal rendering is the elders that "lead well." The "elder" or bishop, which are the Scriptural terms for pastor, is a leader of his flock over which the Holy Ghost has made him overseer. But he leads by teaching, by example, and not by authority. To exercise authority is expressly forbidden by our Master. Matt. 20:25, 26: "Ye know that the princes of the Gentiles exercise dominion over them, and they that are great exercise authority upon them. But it shall not be so among you." In I Peter 5:3: "Neither as being lords (masters) over God's heritage, but being examples to the flock."

The Episcopal and Presbyterian bodies have men of authority—men in control. The Master said: "It shall not be so among you." The superintendent of missions, so common among Baptists, has authority to superintend the work of missionaries. The Master said: "It shall not be so among you." Baptists should recognize only one Master, even Jesus Christ and only one Superintendent of Missions, even the Holy Spirit.

A gospel church may exist with or without officers. The churches (Acts 14:23) in which elders were elected existed as gospel churches before they had elders, and if they could exist as gospel churches before they had elders, it follows that if the elders should die or move away, the churches could exist again as gospel churches without them. Elders or pastors are not necessary to the existence of a church. A church is a gospel church with them or without them. So with the deacons. The church at Jerusalem was a gospel church (Acts 6) before the deacons were elected. If all the deacons should die or move away, it would continue to be a gospel church. As Pendleton put it in his Church Manual: "Officers are not necessary to 'the being of a church, but they are necessary to its well being.'"

CHAPTER V
The Way of Mission Work

II Tim. 3:16, 17: **All Scripture is given by inspiration * * * that the man of God may be perfect, throughly furnished unto all good works."**

Is missionary work a good work? To ask the question is to answer it. Then the man of God is "throughly furnished" by the Scriptures for this good work. All that we need to know about mission work, all that we need to do in mission work, is necessarily revealed in the Scriptures if the Scriptures "throughly furnish" us unto "every good work."

The commission (Matt. 28:19, 20) was given to the church as such. This has been made clear in the preceding pages of this book. The church as such is, therefore, the unit in missionary operations. Since mission work is preaching the gospel to every creature, it follows that the church must do the preaching. We therefore see the reason why the Jerusalem church "sent forth Barnabas" (Acts 11:22), and why the Antioch church sent Paul and Barnabas (Acts 13:1-6), and we also see why these missionaries returned and reported their work to the church which had sent them out (Acts 14:24-27). Individual church members wherever they go may tell the story of salvation to those with whom they come in contact (Acts 8:4), and whoever even hears the message of salvation should pass it on to others. (Rev. 22:17) "Let him that heareth say, Come." But the only organized effort recognized in the New Testament for the work of missions is the local congregations of baptized believers. . . .

Since the commission to evangelize the world was given to the churches, it follows that the churches are the only organizations authorized to do mission work. Any other organization that may undertake the work is a usurper, a law-breaker, no matter how good the intention of such organization may be. . . .

Congregations may co-operate in the evangelization of the world, but they must do it as churches. The missionary Paul was sent out by the congregation at Antioch (Acts 13:1-6), but the churches co-operated in his support. II Cor. 11:7, 8: "Have I committed an offense in abasing myself that ye might be exalted, because I have preached unto you the gospel of God freely? I robbed other churches, taking wages of them, to do you service." . . .

This is altogether different from a board or committee engaging in a work on their own motion and incurring expenses, acting without instructions and then calling on the churches to pay the bills. This committee was appointed by the churches, and acted under instructions from the churches according to the "declarations of their ready minds." Thus far may we go and no further.

Nowhere in the Scriptures do we read of a convention appointing a board or committee for any purpose whatever. Such a thing as a convention is unknown to the Scriptures. Such a thing is therefore a usurper, a violater of Divine law and should not be tolerated by the churches. It was to the churches the commission was given and these churches themselves are under the law of their Master. The churches are free and independent within the limits of the New Testament law. Short of what the New Testament teaches they dare not stop; beyond what is there taught these churches dare not go, since the Scripture is the all sufficient rule of faith and practice in missionary work as well as other church work.

PART II
The Historical Way

To establish our doctrine and practice by the New Testament is of chief importance. But the New Testament makes some declarations concerning the history of churches. When our Lord established His church He declared He would build it up, edify it, enlarge it, and the gates of hell should not prevail against it. (Matt. 16:18.) The Greek word "oikodomeso," in Matt. 16:18, translated "will build" means "will build up," "enlarge," "edify." His church was already in existence when He uttered these words, as can be proved by numerous passages, hence we are forced to so understand this passage.

When did the company or congregation of baptized believers begin? Peter answers the question in Acts 1:21 "Wherefore of these men which have companied with us all the time that the Lord Jesus went in and out among us, beginning from the baptism of John," etc. This passage affirms that certain men "companied" with Jesus and that this "company" began "with the baptism of John."

If it can be shown that Baptist churches have existed in all ages since Christ, it will confirm our faith in the Lord's words. If, on the other hand, it can be shown that no church institution in existence has come down uncorrupted through the centuries, it will be enough to make infidels of us all; for if the Lord's promise has failed, if His Word be proved false, what confidence could we place in Him as our Saviour?

The Lord's promise has been kept. There has never been a day since He ascended in the presence of His church, that a church just like the one which saw Him ascend could not be found on the earth. History abundantly establishes this position. . . .

CHAPTER VIII
The Way of Mission Work in History

The Apostolic Baptists were Missionary Baptists. This is abundantly proved by the Master's commanding the church to go "teach all nations, baptizing them." It is seen in the Jerusalem church sending out Barnabas and the Antioch church sending out both Saul and Barnabas. But these Apostolic churches were not Convention Baptists. I propose to prove by unquestioned historic records that the Baptists of history were neither Hardshells nor Conventionites. . . .

There never would have been any such things as Hardshell churches or Convention churches if there had not been a departure from the faith and practice of the ancient churches. Hardshellism is a recent invention, and so is Boardism. Both are in error. Hardshellism violates the Master's law my [sic] refusing to go. Boardism violates the law by trying to take the commission out of the hands of the churches, where the Master left it. . . .

The Evils of Hardshellism

1. Hardshellism is a negative. It stands for nothing and opposes everything.

2. Hardshellism repudiates the Great Commission.

3. Hardshellism lives on the converts made by others. It is a religious parasite.

4. Hardshellism logically repudiates baptism, since they repudiate the Commission, and baptism is a part of the Commission.

5. Hardshellism dries up benevolence and fosters covetousness.

6. Hardshellism makes beggars of their preachers. Instead of receiving wages for their preaching they receive it as alms.

7. Hardshellism teaches that the gospel is not necessary to salvation, and, therefore, flatly contradicts the Scriptures.

8. Hardshellism is a schism and should be treated as such.

9. Hardshellism never built an orphan's home for sheltering, protecting and educating helpless orphan children.

10. Hardshellism never led a soul to Christ nor has it ever been instrumental in saving a soul, they themselves being witnesses.

11. Hardshellism was founded by Daniel Parker, and is of man, not of God.

Minutes Kentucky General Association, October 20, 1837, page 11:

"The anti-missionary spirit owes its origin to the notorious Daniel Parker. He was the first person called Baptist that lent a hand to the infidel and papist in opposing the proclamation of the gospel to every creature."

This deliverance was made only five years after the division among Baptists over the mission question. The messengers of the churches who made this deliverance were personal ear and eye witnesses to the controversy which resulted in the split. They could not be mistaken, and if what they say is not true, we have the spectacle of a body of messengers from the churches putting to record for the deception of future generations, a positive and well know (at that time) falsehood. We cannot conceive of such a thing being possible. If this deliverance is true, Daniel Parker was the originator of Hardshellism.

But let us hear Parker himself:

"It makes me shudder when I think I am the first one (that I have any knowledge of) among the thousands of zealous religionists of America, that have ventured to draw the sword against this error, and to shoot at it and spare no arrows." (See Daniel Parker's address, p. 3)

The question is settled. The Missionary Baptists, who were eye witnesses, declare Daniel Parker was the first to advocate Hardshellism, and Parker himself says he was the first.

It is therefore absurd to talk of Hardshellism tracing a line of succession back of Daniel Parker.

Evils of Conventionism

1. Conventionism ignores the law of Christ and sets up rules of its own.

2. Conventionism gives one man authority over another, and the Master said, "It shall not be so among you." (Matt. 20:25, 26).

3. Conventionism tends toward centralization and destroys congregationalism.

4. Conventions are unknown to the Scriptures.

5. Conventionism fosters liberalism and decries orthodoxy.

6. Conventionism is an invention of man and not a revelation of God.

7. Conventionism is a breeder of strife and confusion among the churches.

8. Conventionism is a departure from the faith and practice of the fathers.

9. Conventionism incurs needless expenses, and unjustly calls upon the churches to pay the debts they had no part in making.

10. Conventionism has a bad spirit. Those it can't control it seeks to ruin.

11. Conventionism is responsible in a large measure for Hardshellism, since the extremes of Conventionism drove many into repudiating all mission work.

12. Conventionism is fast becoming a schism, and unless reform or revolution comes speedily it must be treated as such.

13. Conventionism and Hardshellism are both departures from the historic faith and practice of the ancient Baptists.

The great body of Baptists have never gone off with either faction and they never will.

The Baptists through whom our lines of history run were plain Missionary Baptists; neither Hardshells nor Conventionites.

PART III
The Present Way

The Master has not changed His method of work. If He has, it is certain that He has not notified His servants of it, and until He gives notice of a change of methods Baptists should continue to work by the methods revealed in the Scriptures.

The Scriptures are yet, as in the olden time, the only and all sufficient rule of faith and practice. Let us walk by that rule—"to the law and to the testimony." The following pages shall briefly set forth the New Testament way of meeting present conditions. . . .

CHAPTER XIII
The Way Churches May Associate

There is no Scriptural way by which churches may combine, but they may associate as equals. This associating does not consist in meeting at a given place, but the churches associate in the work. They may elect messengers but these messengers are not the association. These messengers represent the churches—the churches themselves constituting the association. The association, properly speaking, never meets. Only the messengers, from the churches composing the association, meet and while it is common it is not proper to speak of the meeting of the messengers as being the association. These messengers are nothing more nor less than a joint committee appointed by the churches for the purpose of consulting about the work which the Master commissioned each of them to do.

Since the commission was given to the congregation as such, it follows that the congregation as such are the units in all associate or co-operative work. They must, therefore, work together on terms of perfect equality. The large church or the rich is only a church and should have no special privileges on account of its size or wealth. Hence the numerical and financial basis of representation and associations or conventions are equally wrong. If the Lord gave the commission to individuals, the number of individuals should, of course, determine the number of messengers sent, or if the commission were given to churches according to their wealth, then the amount of money given should determine the number of messengers. But if the Lord gave the commission to the church, as such, it follows that an equal number of messengers should be sent from all the churches associating. There is no need of rehearsing the Scriptural arguments proving the commission was given to the churches, as such, for that ground has been fully canvassed in the preceding pages.

To contend logically for the convention system of co-operation one must contend that the commission was given to individuals. To argue for the association system of work one must contend that the commission was given to the churches as such. The whole matter rests right here.

What is called the association is not an organization in the common acceptance of the term at all. It is only an intelligent working together of independent organizations. It is only the associated work—working at the same thing at the same time and the same way, but working as individual churches, independent and free. Beyond this they cannot go without violating the law of the Master, who told the individual church, as such, to "go teach all nations, baptizing them," etc. (Matt. 28:19, 20.)

16.6   The Baptist Missionary Association of America (BMAA)

Tensions within the American Baptist Association increased over the years. In 1950 at Little Rock a dissident group, primarily Texans who felt regional as well as theological friction, withdrew to form yet another Landmark splinter group. They took the name of Baptist Missionary Association of America (BMAA). They are best understood as a Texas version of the Bogard movement of Arkansas. Unlike the ABA parent body, however, the BMAA has enjoyed remarkable growth. Their seminary at Jacksonville, Texas, established in 1965, provides a center of spiritual and theological cohesion for the group. The following report, from their 1982-83 *Handbook,* describes the progress and teachings of the BMAA Baptists. *Source: Directory and Handbook,* Baptist Missionary Association of America, 1982-1983 (Jacksonville, Tex.: Baptist News Service, 1983), 7-8, 19-20.

BAPTIST MISSIONARY ASSOCIATION OF AMERICA (formerly the North American Baptist Association) is a group of regular Baptist churches formed in associational capacity by means of duly elected messengers on May 25, 1950. In theology the churches are evangelical, missionary, fundamental, and premillennial. In associational capacity they respect the equality of churches as constituent units and the equal rights and privileges of ministers of the gospel after their understanding of the New Testament order.

The name of the body was changed in April 1969, to the Baptist Missionary Association of America because the term "North" in the original name was misleading and misunderstood by many, especially in the southern part of the United States.

The formative meeting in 1950 was in no sense the founding of a "denomination," neither was it the institution of new principles and practices. It was a reorganization of a national association with common ties of faith and practice of missionary Baptist churches whose lineage runs back to the days of Christ on earth. . . .

The Baptist Missionary Association of America supports missionary families in many foreign countries and missionary families working with ethnic groups and others in the United States. The Association maintains a seminary, a radio and television ministry, an annuity and benefit agency, an Armed Forces chaplaincy committee, a research and public relations department, a modern encampment ground, bookstores, a youth department, office buildings, and publishes a full graded series of Sunday school, training service, Vacation Bible School and study course literature. The Association also publishes books, tracts and several periodicals including its missions magazine, "The Gleaner".

Fifteen state associations and 86 local and district associations that support the Baptist Missionary Association of America have missionaries working on the local and state mission fields. These supporting associations also own and operate orphanages, colleges, Bible schools, bookstores, office buildings, radio and television programs, and publish a number of periodicals, books and tracts. . . .

DOCTRINAL STATEMENT
(Baptist Missionary Association of America)

The churches of this Association heartily subscribe to and agree to defend and promulgate the historic Missionary Baptist Faith and Practice, the interpretation of which is tersely stated as follows:

1. The Trinity of God.
2. The infallible and plenary verbal inspiration of the Scriptures.
3. The Biblical account of creation.
4. The personality of Satan.
5. Hereditary and total depravity of man in his natural state involving his fall in Adam.
6. The virgin birth and deity of Jesus Christ.
7. Christ's blood atonement for fallen men.
8. His bodily resurrection and ascension back to His Father.
9. The person and work of the Holy Spirit.
10. Justification before God by faith without any admixture of works. All such justified persons are in the family of God.
11. Separation of God's children from the world.
12. Water baptism (immersion) to be administered to believers only and by Divine authority as given to missionary Baptist churches.
13. The Lord's Supper a church ordinance to be administered to baptised believers only and in scriptural church capacity.
14. Eternal security of the believer.
15. The establishment of a visible church by Christ himself during His personal ministry on earth; and his churches are not now, nor have they ever been, universal or invisible.
16. World wide missions according to the Great Commission which Christ gave His church. (Matthew 28:19-20).
17. The perpetuity of missionary Baptist churches from Christ's day on earth until His second coming.
18. The right of scriptural churches to be held as equal units in their associated capacities, with equal rights and privileges for all.
19. The subjection of all scriptural associational assemblies and their committees to the will of the churches, so that they shall forever remain as servants of the churches originating them.
20. The separation of the Lord's church from all so-called churches or church alliances which advocate, practice, or uphold heresies and other human innovations which

are not in harmony with the word of God. Open communion, alien baptism, pulpit affiliation with heretical churches, modernism, modern tongues movement, and all kindred evils arising from these practices are unscriptural.

21. The only valid baptism is that administered by the authority of a scriptural missionary Baptist church Any so-called Baptist church which knowingly receives alien baptism, habitually practices this or other evils as those listed in statement 20 cannot be a scriptural Baptist church, nor can its ordinances remain valid.
22. The personal, bodily and imminent return of Christ to earth.
23. The bodily resurrection of the dead.
24. The reality of heaven, involving Divine assurance of eternal happiness for the redeemed of God.
25. The reality of hell, involving everlasting punishment of the incorrigible wicked.
26. The absolute separation of church and state.

NOTE: The following statements are not binding upon the churches already affiliated with this association, nor require adoption by churches petitioning this body for privileges of cooperation, nor to be a test of fellowship between brethren of churches. However, they do express the preponderance of opinion among the churches of the Baptist Missionary Association of America:

1. We believe in the premillennial return of Christ to earth, after which He shall literally reign in peace upon the earth for a thousand years. Rev. 20:4-6.
2. We believe the Scriptures to teach two resurrections: the first of the righteous at Christ's coming; the second of the wicked dead at the close of the thousand year reign. I Thess. 4:13-17, Rev. 20:4-6, 12-15.

16.7   General Association of Regular Baptist Churches (GARBC)

The General Association of Regular Baptist churches, formed in 1932, represents a major grouping of fundamental Baptist churches primarily in northern states. The GARBC originated out of the fundamentalist controversy within the Northern Baptist Convention, and today represents the more ultraconservative forms of Baptist church life. Two organizations preceded the GARBC, serving as "John the Baptist movements" to prepare the way: the Fundamental Fellowship of 1920 and the Baptist Bible Union of 1923. The Fellowship did not satisfy those who wanted militant action, so some withdrew to form the Baptist Bible Union in 1923. The BBU fell on hard times, caused partly by its own aggressive and ill-considered actions, and it was reorganized at its 1932 meeting to become the GARBC. Documents are included here not only from the GARBC itself, but also from its predecessor movements.

The "Call and Manifesto" of 1922 (selection A) led to the formation of the Baptist Bible Union. *Source: The Baptist,* 7 Oct. 1922, 1132. Used by permission. Selection B traces the origin of the GARBC out of the breakup of the old Baptist Bible Union. The "Des Moines University affair" refers to the failure of a fundamentalist school in 1929. In 1927 the Bible Union took over a Baptist college that had existed in Des Moines since 1916. Two years later financial failure, internal strife, the resignation or firing of most of the faculty, and a campus riot involving faculty, students and trustees brought the school to a disgraceful end. *Source:* Joseph M. Stowell, *Background and History of the General Association of Regular Baptist Churches* (Hayward, Calif.: Gospel Tracts Unlimited, 1949), 28-34. Used by permission.

A.   The Baptist Bible Union
The "Call and Manifesto" of 1922

Twenty thousand copies of a "Call and Manifesto" have been sent to the Baptist churches of the United States and Canada, inviting them as churches and individuals to become subscribing and sustaining members of the "Baptist Bible Union of America" which has been organized with a "Doctrinal Basis" and a statement of "Aims."

THE BAPTIST has received a letter from Elyria, Ohio, signed by three of our Baptist brethren, R. E. Neighbor, W. L. Pettingill, and O. W. Van Osdel, enclosing a copy of the "Call and Manifesto" and requesting us to publish the larger portion thereof. Although there is no indication that the movement is designed either to promote the New World Movement or to extend the circulation of THE BAPTIST, we readily accede to the courteous request of our brethren above named, and give ample space to the announcement of their program for a new segregation and realignment of the Baptist churches of the North American continent.

The Signers

The "Call and Manifesto" is signed by 135 men (as far as we can determine there are no women in the list), eleven of whom are laymen, and "the others are pastors, evangelists, and Bible teachers." Of the total who sign, twenty-three are from Michigan and twenty-four from Ohio. A patient study of the list of signers fails to reveal the names of any considerable number of men who have been conspicuous in their advocacy of the world-embracing program of the Northern Baptist Convention as defined in the New World Movement. . . .

The "Call" is printed verbatim herewith:

"Whereas. There has arisen within the bounds of Baptist denominationalism an ecclesiasticism, dominated by modernism, which has turned away from the Integrity, Finality and Sole-Sufficiency of the Bible as the Inspired Word of God and from the simplicity of Apostolic Evangelism—the message and method of our Fathers; and

"Whereas Within the bounds of Baptist denominationalism this ecclesiasticism, dominated by modernism, has forced the Orthodox into an unholy and God-forbidden alliance with the Heterodox; and

"Whereas, There has arisen from every side, both from churches and individual members, a call loud and long for a new fellowship in Christ Jesus wherein those who hold to the Integrity, Finality and Sole-Sufficiency of the Bible as the Word of God, and who hold to the simplicities of Apostolic Evangelism, may meet in communion, apart from unholy collusions which gender strife;

"Therefore, We, the undersigned Baptist Union of America, requesting that all those who stand with us in the Doctrinal Basis and Aims of the Union, and who desire membership therein shall sign the attached membership application as per instructions on another page." . . .

The "Manifesto" provides for a natural or general body and also for state or sectional unions. It is announced that "a call for a national convention will be sent forth in due season." The more essential articles of the "Manifesto" are as follows:

"*Definition:* The Baptist Bible Union of America is a fellowship of Baptist churches and Baptist believers accepting its Doctrinal Basis and Aims.

"*Membership:* 1. All Baptist churches, Baptist ministers or Baptist church members who endorse the Aims and Doctrinal Basis of the Union, as set forth herein, shall be eligible for membership. 2. Churches or individual believers, becoming members of the Baptist Bible Union, may follow their own pleasure as to maintaining other Baptist denominational affiliations."

An executive committee and a council provide the machinery for "carrying forward the policy of the Union, . . . but always in line with and never contrary to the expressed will of the Union."

The "Aims" of the Union are set forth in the following statement which is printed verbatim:

"*Aims:* 1. To 'Contend earnestly for the faith which was once for all delivered unto the saints,' and the presentation of a united witness to the Bible as not only containing and conveying, but as being in itself the Word of God. 2. The maintenance of the Evangelical Faith; and especially of those essential and clearly revealed doctrines which, at the present time, are being assailed, questioned or ignored in certain circles. 3. To promote a deeper fellowship and a closer cooperation amongst Baptist churches and Baptist believers who hold a like precious faith, and who walk together in their conception of the mission of the church. 4. To oppose any federation of Baptist churches or believers upon any basis which involves the sacrifice of principle, or which discredits the Bible and dishonors the Lord Jesus Christ. 5. To promote such missionary, evangelistic and educational work as the Union may feel led to undertake or desire to encourage. 6. The maintenance of the right of each local Baptist church to manage its own affairs, under the sole authority and rule of the Lord Jesus Christ, and apart from any outside demands."

The "Doctrinal Basis"

The "Doctrinal Basis," full and hearty subscription to which is a condition of membership in the Union, is as follows:

"*Doctrinal Basis:* The following does not profess to be a comprehensive Creed, but is merely a Statement of such truths as, in the present circumstances, it is important that Baptists should rehearse and emphasize, in view of their historic witness and of the flagrant ambiguities and omissions of fundamental and vital truths in the Doctrinal Basis of the Modernists. We emphasize, in particular:

"I. The Divine Inspiration, and the Integrity, Finality, and Sole-Sufficiency of the Bible as the Word of God. II. The Holy Trinity of Father, Son and Holy Spirit—Three Persons in one Substance. Power and Eternity in the unity of the Godhead. 1. The Love and Grace of the Father. 2. The Redemption by the Son: a. His Incarnation, Virgin Birth, Sinless Nature and Life, and His Infallibility as Teacher; b. His Substitutionary and Atoning Death; c. His Bodily Resurrection, actual and real; His Ascension into Heaven, invested with all authority; His Mediatorial Intercession, High Priest over the household of God; and His Glorious Second Advent—premillennial, personal and visible. 3. The Regeneration, or New Birth, by the Holy Spirit. III. The Depravity and Sinfulness of Mankind, in consequence of the Fall. IV. Justification and Adoption by grace, through faith in the propitiatory Sacrifice of the Lord Jesus Christ. V. The Baptism of believers by Immersion, and the Memorial Ordinance of the Lord's Supper. VI. Sanctification by the Holy Spirit through faith and the Word, leading to the growth in Spiritual life of God's people. VII. The Resurrection of the body, both of the just and the unjust, but each in his own order, and the final Judgment of the wicked by our Lord Jesus Christ."

It is of interest to note that this most recent movement for a realignment of the Baptist churches of North America is positively and exclusively premillenarian. Mr. Charles R. Brock in his notable and authoritative statement of fundamental views widely published last summer declared: "There is an impression abroad that premillennialism is accepted by the fundamentalists as definite truth. This is not true." The "Doctrinal Basis" of the "Baptist Bible Union of America" includes "His glorious second advent-premillennial personal and visible," as one of the "essential and clearly revealed doctrines" the hearty avowal of which is prerequisite to membership in the Union.

The new movement is also confined exclusively to Baptist churches, and includes in its "Doctrinal Basis" as a fundamental and vital truth "The baptism of believers by immersion." This feature of the movement is of interest in the light of the facts set forth in the article on the opposite page, and in view also of the fact that one of the most eminent advocates of the Los Angeles fundamentalist interdenominational program which Dr. Scarborough reviews, is also one of the most eminent among the signers of the "Call and Manifesto" of the "Baptist Bible Union of America," namely Dr. J. Frank Norris of Texas. . . .

B. General Association of Regular Baptists

The Des Moines University affair, while perhaps not the basic reason for the decease of the Baptist Bible Union, nevertheless sounded the death knell. It seemed that the Union was never to rise above this failure and shame.

However, in the midst of death the Union gave rise to a new and somewhat different movement to be known as the General Association of Regular Baptist Churches. The roots of this separatist fellowship of Baptist Churches, as we have pointed out, were not new but reached back for years to a sentiment which was constantly cropping up which urged complete separation from the Northern Baptist Convention.

This sentiment had been crystallizing locally on several fronts. We select three of the earliest as characteristic.

At the Jarvis Street Baptist Church in Toronto, Ontario, January 11-12, 1927, a society of Regular Baptist Churches and Regular Baptists was formed to be known as the Regular Baptist Missionary and Educational Society of Canada. While this was a move which was later to result in complete separation from the Canadian Convention, yet at the time of inception it was clearly stated that, "It is intended that such organization is to be without prejudice to the churches' status as parts of the Baptist Convention of Ontario and Quebec."

In Michigan in 1909 a group of churches left the Grand River Rapids Association of Baptist Churches because of the liberal views that had crept into some of the churches of that Association. This group of churches formed the Grand River Valley Association, adopted an orthodox confession of faith and elected to stay in the fellowship of the Michigan Baptist Association. In 1920 under the leadership of Dr. O. W. Van Osdel, the new association reaffirmed its orthodoxy and changed its name to The Michigan Orthodox Baptist Association. Many of the churches of this association began to support independent faith missions and to cease to support the Missionary Societies of the Convention. As a result the association was disfranchised by the Michigan Baptist State Convention and became an independent association.

In 1928 the name of this association was changed to The Grand Rapids Association of Regular Baptist Churches.

In the state of Ohio in 1928, a group of the Baptist Bible Union pastors gathered a list of complaints and presented them to the Ohio Baptist Convention. These complaints struck mainly at Rio Grande College and Denison University but also singled out certain phases of denominational life that were objectionable to the Fundamentalists. The state Convention advised the Unionists to go directly to the heads of the schools with their complaints. The Unionists replied that they had tried this with disappointing results. As a result of all this controversy, several of the Bible Union pastors and their churches withdrew from the Ohio and the Northern Baptist Conventions and at the Central Baptist Church of Columbus organized an independent association to be known as the Ohio Association of Independent Baptist Churches.

All three of these early associations have functioned to this day and especially the latter two have been leaders in paving the way for the nation wide General Association of Regular Baptist Churches.

In the Baptist Bible Union, itself, the emphasis was shifting more and more away from the Convention and the original policy of purging from within. By 1927 Dr. W. B. Riley could write, "A large proportion of the Baptist Bible Union (men) are not even members of the Convention, and the organization has never asked recognition from the Convention in any form."

Two months later Dr. Riley wrote concerning the coming Northern Baptist Convention to be held in Chicago and pointed out the possibility of a Fundamental Baptist organization outside of the Convention and the effect the Baptist Bible Union would have upon its organization. Said he, "There will doubtless be controversy in the Chicago Convention. There are yet men within the bounds of the Convention who will not sit through the Convention sessions and see measures railroaded through that look to the triumph of Modernism and seal their mouths. These men are more and more being pushed to one of two points—either to stay in the Convention and fight a definite length of time with little prospect of final success or quit it and organize within the bounds of the Northern Convention a true Baptist body. It must be confessed that the Baptist Bible Union has paved the way for the latter step. If the time comes when it is clear that the denomination has decided deliberately in favor of Unitarianism, then division is inevitable and the existence of the Union will greatly aid in determining the nature and character of the new organization."

By May in 1932 interest in the Baptist Bible Union had been dissipated (mainly by the Des Moines affair) to the extent that when the eighth convocation was held at the Belden Avenue Baptist Church in Chicago, only 34 delegates registered representing eight states. Along with this was the economic depression making it impossible for some to come. Though the group was small, yet it was in the Providence of God to write Baptist history. This meeting was to be both the last gathering of the Baptist Bible Union and the first of the General Association of Regular Baptist Churches. . . .

"A general discussion was engaged in concerning the conditions of membership in the Association, and the suggestion was made that it should be a membership of Churches, but that loyal brethren who were members of churches not in sympathy with the aims of the Regular Baptist Association should be provided for in some way.

"The executive committee was requested to see that the change of name from Baptist Bible Union of North America to the General Association of Regular Baptists should be accomplished in such a way that the General Association of Regular Baptists would appear to be the legal successor of the Baptist Bible Union of North America." . . .

The name "Regular" adopted by this new body is not to be confused with the small group of Regular Baptists in the South. There has never been any connection between the two groups. The name was employed by the new General Association because it was the name already in use by the Fundamental Canadian Baptists and the Grand Rapids Association already mentioned. It is meant to be a mark of distinction between those holding the regular, historic Baptist position and those irregular Baptists who are tainted with Modernism.

The second annual meeting which was to have been held in Toledo was held in Buffalo at the First Baptist Church due to a change of pastorates in the Toledo church. The gathering convened May 16-18, 1933. In the president's address, he outlined the following five objectives of the new Association:

"FIRST—Become an Association of Baptist Churches to maintain a testimony to the supernaturalism of Christianity as opposed to the anti-supernaturalism of modernism.

"SECOND—It is an organization determined to do its work independent of, and separate from, the Northern Baptist Convention and all its auxiliaries.

"THIRD—It does not in any way propose to preserve a denominational order, but rather to re-affirm the truths of Scripture historically believed by Baptists and expressed by the Baptist Confessions of faith of London 1689 or the New Hampshire Confession of Faith or the Philadelphia Confession of Faith or the Baptist Bible Union Confession of Faith or any such which enunciates the same truths though in other words.

"FOURTH—It is an organization designed to promote a Missionary spirit amongst Baptist Churches for the spread of the Gospel in all the world, and to contend earnestly for the faith once and for all delivered to the saints.

"FIFTH—It also proposes to assist churches secure safe, sound and satisfactory pastors for the proclamation of the Gospel and the work of the ministry. And to assist churches in needy places as much as in them is."

16.8   The Conservative Baptist Association of America (CBAA)

Many Northern Baptists who shared some concerns of the fundamentalists did not pull out in the schisms that produced the Baptist Bible Union in 1923 or the General Association of Regular Baptists in 1932. Instead, they remained within the Northern Baptist Convention and tried to nudge that body toward more conservative positions. After several years, however, even the less excitable among them concluded that division was inevitable. The first breach was in 1943, when a separate conservative foreign mission society was formed. Four years later, the break was completed with formation of the Conservative Baptist Association of America. This group consciously rejected the label of "fundamentalism," and chose instead to call themselves "conservative." At the time of their origin, they represented a more moderate and irenic form of fundamentalism, but in later years some within the group have become more strident on some issues, especially millennialism. *Sources:* "Why the Conservative Baptist Association of America?" (Chicago: The CBAA, 1954), 3-12. "The Conservative Baptist Association of America: Its Mission" (Chicago: The CBAA, 1954), 3-10. Used by permission.

A.   Why the Conservative Baptist Association Was Formed

Students of Baptist affairs will always recognize the Grand Rapids meeting of the Northern Baptist Convention as the turning point in the relations between the liberal leadership of the Convention and its organized conservative Baptist group.

In 1920, aware of the steady inroads of modernism, the gradual abandonment of Baptist polity for a centralized system of ecclesiastical authority and the complete capture of its strongest seminaries by liberalism, one hundred and fifty ministers and laymen signed the call which brought forth the Fundamentalist Fellowship of the Northern Baptist Convention at Buffalo in 1920. Then began the long struggle to win the Convention back to Biblical faith and Baptist practice, to simplify its ecclesiastical structure and to educate the candidates for the ministry in the true Baptist faith.

Every year a pre-convention conference on Baptist fundamentals was held in connection with the Convention and various reform steps were attempted. The schools and colleges of the Convention were investigated, but the advance of modernism was not halted in that field. At Indianapolis in 1922 the conservative group attempted to get the Convention to endorse the New Hampshire Confession of Faith as a standard of doctrine, but the Convention liberals with the support of the middle-of-the-road group defeated this. In 1924, due to the rising storm against modernism in the foreign field, a Committee of Investigation was appointed. The Committee served, reported to the

Convention, was discharged and very little came of it. . . . In 1932 the General Association of Regular Baptists came into existence which, in a little more than ten years, was to gather over 500 Convention churches into its fold as a protest against the modernism in the Convention. Undismayed by these losses, many conservatives continued to cooperate and the liberal leadership of the Convention remained entrenched.

1943

In 1943 came the first break in the relationship between the Convention and the organized conservative Baptist group when the Conservative Baptist Foreign Mission Society was organized. For many years (since 1919) Baptists had expressed dissatisfaction with the leadership and the work of the American Baptist Foreign Mission Society. The first full scale criticism of the policies of the Society was launched in 1923 by the Fundamentalist League of New York and vicinity. The Convention investigation failed to cure the evils. The attempt to organize a new society failed, chiefly for lack of support on the part of many fundamentalists still loyal to the convention. **Conservatives resorted to designated gifts but eventually found out that this did not solve the problem, for it only released funds for liberal causes and gave the inclusive policy a solid financial basis, guaranteed by both liberals and conservatives.** This achievement, whereby both conservatives and liberals were united in their support of the inclusive policy, seemed to be a victory for the conservatives, but many soon saw its true nature—a bulwark for the inclusive policy. The long smouldering dissatisfaction came to a climax in the orgainzation of the Conservative Baptist Foreign Mission Society in December, 1943.

This began a new era in the work of the Conservative Baptists. At last it had a sound channel for its missionary funds, and a leadership whose fidelity to the Gospel is unquestionable. It grew by leaps and bounds, amazing its friends and confounding its foes. It was soon apparent that the blessing of God was upon it. It gave new life and vigor to the whole Conservative Baptist movement, and the Conservative Baptist forces were again on the march.

The Convention soon began its program of opposition. A committee on conciliation was proposed and appointed. Its work was fruitless as to reconciliation, but its majority report to the General Council was the basis of the resolution which declared the new Society outside the framework of the Convention. Its ministerial employees were declared ineligible for membership in the Ministers and Missionaries Pension Fund and their contracts cancelled. Its missionaries were also declared to be ineligible. Ministers were blacklisted everywhere who supported the Society and a long warfare by the Convention against the Society began which has not ceased. In spite of it all the Society continued to prosper and expand under the blessing of God.

The Conservative Baptist Fellowship in 1945 girded itself anew for the struggle for the New Testament faith as held by Baptists, opened a national office in Chicago, created a monthly medium of publicity, "The News Letter," and began the publication of papers and pamphlets dealing with the issues in the Convention. With the Convention stirred and the leadership alarmed, the Northern Baptist Convention met at Grand Rapids in 1946, with many people predicting that the long expected division between the conservatives and the modernists was at hand.

GRAND RAPIDS

The Grand Rapids Convention saw a great gathering of conservative Baptists who had come to participate in a great testimony to the faith. The Convention group, anticipating the struggle, had gathered its forces and the great crowd of Baptists taxed the facilities of the city of Grand Rapids.

In this Convention the conservative group battled for their principles. The effort to deprive the secretariat of a vote in the Convention by constitutional amendment failed. This had been a long standing grievance, for it was charged that the secretariat voted as a bloc for all proposals sponsored by the Convention leadership. The effort to adopt a simple confession of faith which would also exclude from the paid secretariat and the mission fields those who reject these New Testament doctrines was lost. The attempt to cut the Federal Council of Churches out of the Unified Budget was unavailing. This long standing grievance was destined to persist. The attempt to elect an all-conservative slate of officers and board members was defeated. These causes were ably presented and defended but the blind loyalty to the Convention and the prejudice created against the organized conservative movement carried the day. Finally, the Convention adopted the principle of proportionate representation, or representation based upon the percentage of the missionary contributions of the local church given to Convention approved objects. Since the conservative group was largely giving its funds through the Conservative Baptist Foreign Mission Society and more and more refusing to support liberal projects, this would seriously decrease the voting strength of conservative churches in future conventions.

Those defeats and the growing dissatisfaction with the leadership of the Convention produced a serious crisis in the affairs of the Conservative Baptist Fellowship. Many felt that the forks of the road had been reached. If these defeats were accepted and the Fellowship continued to struggle, the disillusioned would depart and add to the growing number of churches which had left the Convention. There were open proposals that the Fellowship sponsor a movement of secession from the Convention. There were others who opposed this.

Feeling that the sentiment of the Fellowship was not sufficiently crystallized to adopt a definite policy, a group of men drew up a resolution of policy. This resolution, offered by Rev. Albert G. Johnson of Oregon, and representing the united thought of many leaders was adopted by the Fellowship and became the plan of action for the year 1946-1947. This was indeed a significant act, more significant than any knew. . . .

THE REPORT OF THE COMMITTEE OF FIFTEEN

Following the instructions of the Johnson resolution passed by the Conservative Baptist Fellowship in session at Grand Rapids, Michigan, May, 1946, the Committee of Fifteen met in a three day conference at the Westminster Hotel, Winona Lake, Indiana, September 17-20, 1946. . . .

The following recommendations are presented as a result of the findings of the Committee:

1. That we purpose to continue fellowship with those of like faith and practice both within and without the Northern Baptist Convention.
2. That for the present the Conservative Baptist Fellowship reaffirm its policy of recommending that our churches remain within the Northern Baptist Convention.
3. That the Conservative Baptist Fellowship continue as an organization within the Northern Baptist Convention.
4. That we support any group within the Convention (N.B.C.) whose efforts will be made toward the accomplishment of the objectives which the Conservative Baptist Fellowship has advocated.
5. That the three proposed regional conferences give consideration to the formation of a united conservative Baptist association of America, to which any sovereign

Baptist church may belong regardless of other affiliations, providing that each church subscribes to our (C.B.F.) doctrinal statement. (It is understood that the number of affiliations is not an ethical problem for an autonomous Baptist church.) And that this Committee shall supply each conference with a tentative and specific outline of the scope and activity of such a group.

Respectfully submitted,

The Committee of Fifteen.

The three regional conferences of the Conservative Baptist Fellowship convened at the call of the Committee of Fifteen. . . .

These three conferences adopted a ringing manifesto which was to become a fundamental policy in the Conservative Baptist Fellowship:

"Since the Northern Baptist Convention has resolved:

" 'That we reaffirm our faith in the New Testament as the divinely inspired record, and therefore, the trustworthy authoritative and all-sufficient rule of our faith and practice';

"And since we believe the New Testament teaches the virgin birth, the atoning death and the bodily resurrection of our Lord together with other great truths historically held by Baptists,

"We Conservative Baptists assembled in Regional Conferences, reaffirm the directive submitted to the Board of Managers of the ABFMS, September 21, 1943, now broadening its appeal to the Northern Baptist Convention, to wit:

" '. . . We declare that we will no longer give monies' to the constituent bodies within the Northern Baptist Convention 'which can in any way be appropriated for the support of missionaries,' secretaries, or others having direction of our organization 'who do not affirm faith in the Bible as the inspired Word of God; the deity of our Lord, Jesus Christ, which includes His pre-existence, virgin birth, miracles, and His bodily resurrection from the dead; the substitutionary death of our Lord for sinners in atonement for their sins; His high priestly intercession at the right hand of God; His eternal sovereignty—and His personal visible return in glory. . . .

ATLANTIC CITY, 1947

The annual meeting of the Conservative Baptist Fellowship was held in Atlantic City, May 16-19, 1947. The attendance was large and representative. The decisions reached were the decisions of an overwhelming majority. Those decisions were preceded by lengthly open forums, conducted in a democratic manner, and all questions were freely debated.

The Committee of Fifteen, appointed immediately after the Grand Rapids Convention, unanimously recommended that steps be taken immediately to form The Conservative Baptist Association of America. The reasons for this momentous recommendation are set forth in th preamble to the Constitution.

On May 17, 1947, by the unanimous vote of the Conservative Baptists in session at Atlantic City, the Conservative Baptist Association came into existence. Believing that the times necessitate a reaffirmation of the historic Baptist faith, the Association adopted a Confession of Faith.

By-laws, defining membership, officers and their duties and other matters were adopted.

The six years that have passed have abundantly proved without question that the formation of the Conservative Baptist Association was by the providence of the Lord. . . .

The Conservative Baptist Association has just closed its most prosperous year at the hand of the Lord and is now a formidable company of Bible-believing Baptist churches across the entire nation. These same churches are exercising great influence in their communities, are bulging with activity, are centers of evangelism, are establishing new churches in areas where there is no gospel testimony and are promoting the cause of home and foreign missions with an emphasis that surpasses anything known in Baptist history.

The Conservative Baptist Association has also recognized the need of training for the gospel ministry. There are now two Conservative Baptist schools, namely, Western Conservative Baptist Theological Seminary at Portland, Oregon and The Conservative Baptist Theological Seminary at Denver, Colorado. . . .

The gracious, abundant blessings which the Lord has providentially added have convinced Conservative Baptists that this is just the beginning of greater tokens of the Lord's sovereign grace to follow. The conclusion is, "This IS the Lord's doing; it is marvellous in our eyes." (Ps. 118:23.) . . .

B.   The Conservative Baptist Association of America, Its Mission and Purpose

THE CONSERVATIVE BAPTIST ASSOCIATION OF AMERICA has been brought into existence:

1. To provide a fellowship of churches and individuals upon a thoroughly Biblical and historically Baptistic basis, unmixed with liberals and liberalism and those who are content to walk in fellowship with unbelief and inclusivism;
2. To encourage the spiritual and financial interest of local churches in sound and Biblical Baptist institutions and projects, both at home and abroad;
3. To encourage the creation of agencies and institutions wherever necessary and advisable to fulfill the commission of our Lord in the face of rising apostasy;
4. To provide mutual assistance among conservative Baptist churches for the encouragement of the local church's activities, such as evangelism, missions, and Bible teaching; and
5. To present a positive testimony to the New Testament faith and historic Baptist principles as a body of churches before the world, religious and otherwise; and to oppose departure and deviation from the great foundational truths of the Word of God.

I.   The Conservative Baptist Association: A Confessional Fellowship. . . .

History reveals that in every time of doctrinal uncertainty and desiring to refute spreading heresies, Baptists have frequently confessed their faith, so the Conservative Baptist Association of America gladly sets forth its confession of faith in this time of widespread departure and denial of the faith of our Baptist fathers. Rejecting the authority of creeds over the inspired Word of God, the Conservative Baptist Association of America equally rejects the right of ecclesiastical organizations to set aside the Word of God or to reject the Word of God for the unfounded speculations of men. The Conservative Baptist Association of America, rejecting all creedal authorities, but believing that every Christian body should be ready at all times to declare its stand on the fundamental doctrines of the Christian faith, has adopted a confession of faith so that the world of men may know.

Acknowledging the freedom of the Christian, under the guidance of the Holy Spirit, to interpret the Scriptures, the Conservative Baptist Association of America believes that matters that lie within the field of interpretation are matters for the local church to determine. It rejects, however, any theory of interpretation that denies the authority of the Scriptures, that denies the revealed facts of Scripture, that denies the fundamental doctrines of the Scriptures. The Christian is, under God, the interpreter of the Scriptures, not the master; the pupil, not the critic; rightly dividing the Word of truth but not **denying** the Word of truth; submitting to the Word of truth, not sitting in judgment upon the Word of truth. The Conservative Baptist Association of America recognizes the right of interpretation of the Scriptures, guided by the Holy Spirit. It does not recognize that form of interpretation, which under the guise of interpretation subverts the faith, sets aside the facts of Divine revelation and substitutes human wisdom for the authority of Holy Scriptures.

The Conservative Baptist Association of America affirms the New Testament basis of the Church and its faith. We hold to "the New Testament as the divinely inspired record and therefore the **trustworthy,** authoritative, and all-sufficient rule of our faith and practice." Accepting this record as trustworthy and authoritative we insist upon the inspiration and authority of the Old Testament as set forth by Jesus and the New Testament writers; the virgin birth of our Lord, the deity of Jesus Christ as the second Person of the Godhead; His sinless life and miraculous deeds as set forth in the New Testament; His death on the cross in our stead (II Cor. 5:21; I Cor. 15:3); His bodily resurrection from the grave (I Cor. 15:4-8) and HIS PERSONAL VISIBLE return (Matt. 24:27-30). The Conservative Baptist Association of America accepts the New Testament as the final authority of the churches, confessing clearly and joyfully its great doctrines and saving truths, accepting it as the final court of appeal from all human creeds and human wisdom.

II. The Conservative Baptist Association of America: Its Affiliated Churches

1. **A New Testament church is an independent church.** The Apostles regarded and treated the churches as independent bodies, having the rights of self-government, without subjection to any other authority. . . . The independence, the rights and the responsibilities of the local churches are set forth in the New Testament. Baptists have always recognized this fundamental right of the local church to determine its affiliations. . . .

Resisting the recurring tendency of ecclesiasticism to coerce and destroy the freedom of the local church, the Conservative Baptist Association of America reaffirms the New Testament teachings establishing the independence of the local church. This independence makes all outside bodies purely advisory in character and with no powers whatever over the local church. . . .

2. **A New Testament church holds firmly to the doctrines and principles of the Christian faith as set forth in the New Testament.**

(a) It is composed of responsible individuals who, by faith, have accepted Jesus Christ as Saviour (Rom. 10:9, 10; Acts 4:12), and submitted to the ordinance of baptism, the door into the local church (Acts 2:41). . . . Having been born again of the Spirit of God (John 3:3-6), the Christian individual becomes a new creation in Christ (II Cor. 5:17) with new standards of life as becometh such.

(b) The New Testament church insists upon a pastoral and teaching ministry that obeys the Pauline injunction "Preach the word; be instant in season out of season; reprove, rebuke, exhort with all long-suffering and doctrine" (II Tim. 4:2). . . .

(c) The New Testament church is responsible to preserve and defend the New Testament faith upon which it is based (I Tim. 3:15; Acts 20:31). Paul writes to Timothy, warning him of perilous times which would come when men would depart from the faith, saying they would be "ever learning and never able to come to the knowledge of the truth" (II Tim. 3:1-7). . . .

(d) The New Testament church will seek and use the opportunity for fellowship with those of like precious faith. . . . The Conservative Baptist Association of America, recognizing the need for spiritual fellowship for those of like faith and kindred spirit, knowing that no fellowship is blessed of God that is not based upon fidelity to the faith and sensitiveness to the leadership of the Holy Spirit, came into existence as the expression of this need. . . . A New Testament church will reject all fellowships not based upon faithful adherence to the doctrines of the Christian faith, and the Baptistic doctrine of the autonomy of the local church.

(e) The hope of the New Testament church for the future is not in the "unrealized possibilities of man" but in the faithfulness of God. . . .

III. The Conservative Baptist Association: Its Mission

1. **The Conservative Baptist Association of America was brought into existence to provide a fellowship for churches and individuals who are willing to confess their faith in the fundamentals of the Christian faith, who are willing to live according to the standards of the Christian faith and who will refuse support to the religious movements of the day that will not confess and declare the fundamental doctrines of the Christian faith.** It rejects fellowship with unbelief, it refuses support to religious inclusivism, and reaffirms the New Testament faith that acknowledges no authority greater than the Word of God.

2. **The Conservative Baptist Association of America was formed to furnish a Biblical basis of unity for the scattered Baptist churches, which rejecting theological liberalism have withdrawn from compromising alliances, or which rejecting the inclusivism of modernistic ecclesiastisism have no Scriptural fellowship, no sound channel for their activities. . . .**

The Conservative Baptist Association extends the hand of fellowship to Baptist Churches everywhere who share "the faith once for all delivered," and the Association's convictions regarding liberalism and inclusivism. The Association longs for the day when divisions between Bible-believing Baptists, which bring reproach upon our Lord, and the faith we hold, will no longer exist. To that end the Association is open for any proposal that will no longer make it necessary for Bible-believing Baptists to be divided. When the faith of a body of Baptist churches is the same as that of another group, and their attitudes toward liberalism and inclusivism also correspond, those bodies ought to be brought together. The Association is concerned that this take place and is ready as far as possible, to promote unity among Bible-believing Baptists.

3. **Rejecting such organized ecclesiastical structures that destroy the independence and freedom of the local church to obey the Word of God and the Spirit of God, the Conservative Baptist Association of America will encourage the spiritual and financial interests of local churches in sound Biblical Baptist institutions and projects at home and abroad. The Association will not attempt to dictate to any church which institution, society or project it shall support, insisting only that such object or benevolence be true to the Baptist faith as set forth in the New Testament, . . .**

4. **Believing that the supreme task of the churches is to preach the Gospel of Christ to lost men, bringing them to a saving knowledge of the Lord Jesus Christ, the Conservative Baptist Association of America reaffirms the primacy of evangelism at home and abroad** (Matt. 28:19-20). . . .

16.9   Formation of the Baptist Bible Fellowship, 1950

John Franklyn Norris (1877-1952), colorful pastor in Fort Worth, Texas, became the leader of Baptist fundamentalism in the South. He helped form the Baptist Bible Union in 1923, and along with W. B. Riley and T. T. Shields tried to unite Baptist fundamentalism into one nationwide movement. He was excluded from Southern Baptist life, and after the Bible Union collapsed

Norris formed the Premillennial Baptist Missionary Fellowship in Fort Worth. This was a Southern equivalent of the General Association of Regular Baptists in the North. Norris changed the name of his group to World Baptist Fellowship. Tensions ran high in the group, centering around doctrinal issues and, even more perhaps, around the dictatorial leadership style of the aging Norris. In his prime Norris kept the WBF under control, but in his old age he could not. In the 1950 meeting of the World Baptist Fellowship in Fort Worth, a group of younger pastors confronted Norris and later withdrew to form the Baptist Bible Fellowship. They wanted more responsible leadership than Norris provided, less sensational methods, more biblical doctrines, and a denominational school and newspaper whose witness would be more positive and irenic than they had experienced in recent years under the domination of Norris. Their *Baptist Bible Tribune,* under the leadership of editor James O. Combs, has become one of the leading Baptist papers in America. The first issue of the *Tribune* carried the following article. *Source:* "Reasons for Baptist Bible Fellowship," *Baptist Bible Tribune,* 23 June 1950. Used by permission.

REASONS FOR BAPTIST BIBLE FELLOWSHIP
"That is Final"—It Was

The following statement is self-explanatory—Editor:

It is commonly known among us that there has been for many months a widespread and deep-rooted restlessness among our people, both the ministers and the laity, because of the manner in which the affairs of the World Fundamental Baptist Missionary Fellowship and the Bible Baptist Seminary have been handled.

We have felt that our voice in the conduct of these affairs has not been commensurate with the responsibilities which we have been asked to assume, and for the amount of money which we have contributed to the work of these institutions. We have sensed, and deeply sensed, the absence of the constitutional principles and procedure which should be the basis of representative government, especially the government of Christian institutions into whose treasuries so many people, many of them poor, are constantly asked to put their money.

This accumulated restlessness came to a head at the annual meeting of the World Fundamental Baptist Missionary Fellowship, which was held in the First Baptist Church of Fort Worth the week of May 21.

Tuesday morning, May 23, was Seminary day. Dr. J. Frank Norris was in charge of the Seminary program. Dr. Norris spoke on the history of the Seminary.

In the meantime, as was generally known, Dr. Norris had made revolutionary changes in the management and personnel of the Seminary. Those changes were made without any general notice to the Fellowship, and we believe they were made in violation of every constitutional principle.

Dr. Norris' position was that he had made these changes—including the taking over of the Seminary finances—in accordance with the constitution and by-laws of the Seminary. There was considerable discussion regarding the legality of the by-laws.

Mr. G. Beauchamp Vick, president of the Seminary, pointed out that the changes made by Dr. Norris had stripped him (Vick) of all authority. Mr. Vick also reminded the Fellowship that the 'election' of the new Seminary "trustees," who in turn "elected" Rev. Jock Troup of Scotland as "president," had taken place early Monday morning before hardly any of the messengers to the Fellowship had reached Fort Worth.

Mr. Vick asked how many in the large audience had attended the Monday "session" where the new trustees were "elected." Fourteen hands were raised. Meantime Dr. Frank Godsoe had stated that it seemed to him that 150 had voted for the "election" of the new trustees.

During the discussion, Rev. Wendell Zimmerman, pastor of the Baptist Temple of Kansas City, called the Fellowship's attention to the fact that the by-laws which Dr.

Norris claimed had authorized his acts (copies of them had been distributed among among the audience) were an altogether different set of by-laws from those published in the Seminary's catalog for the year 1948-49.

Mr. Zimmerman raised the question as to which set of by-laws was the official document.

Mr. Zimmerman moved that a committee be appointed to make an investigation and report back to the Fellowship.

The presiding officer, Rev. W. E. Dowell of Springfield, Missouri, held that the motion was open for discussion.

There was little discussion, except by Dr. Norris, Dr. Norris' conduct and defiant language convinced us that he was opposed to an investigation by such a committee. Of course we do not remember his words verbatim, but substantially they were these:

"We are going to follow these by-laws regardless of any investigation. You can appoint all the committees you want to. We are going to follow these by-laws. These are the by-laws on which this Seminary has been recognized. They cannot be changed. They are on record in Austin. And that is final."

We consider the attitude of Dr. Norris and his defiant language on such a basic matter as this, a profound insult to every one of us, and to every man, woman and child whom God has given us the honor of representing. During the last two years our churches have, in addition to raising the $1300 a week for the current expenses of the Seminary, paid approximately $125,000 on the Seminary's indebtedness.

In view of this we believe that we and our people (and all Christian people, for that matter) have a moral (and legal) right to know whether the authority governing an institution involving such huge sums of money, is the authority of a constitution or the emotional whims of a single man. We believe that we have the moral (and legal) right to know whether the by-laws which Dr. Norris claims gave him the authority to make the revolutionary changes he made, are the official by-laws of the Bible Baptist Seminary, or whether they are not the official by-laws of the Bible Baptist Seminary.

Dr. Norris has spoken. "That is final."

For us it is final. We can not, and we will not, ask our hard-working, trusting and generous people to continue to pour their sacrificial gifts into an institution dominated by a man with an attitude like that of Dr. J. Frank Norris.

We and our people have worked for this Seminary. We have given our money into its treasury. We gave this money as an offering to our Lord. We gave it honestly, generously and gladly. We did the best we could. We leave the case with Him.

2

We make no boasts of what we shall accomplish through our new Fellowship, our new College and our new paper. Thus far God has been wonderfully generous to us. We have some $11,000 to begin with. There are many of us, and we have been drawn together in a bond of fellowship which is natural, deep and strong. . . . Whatever we do we shall do it in the open. All of our books will be regularly audited, and detailed reports will be mailed to our constituency. Our constitutions and by-laws, like our books, will always be open to any who care to see them. . . .

3

Our faith and practice is the historic Baptist faith and practice. We believe in an infallible Bible; in the Virgin Birth, in the substitutionary death of the Saviour, in His physical resurrection, in His physical Ascension, in His literal, Premillennial return to the earth. We believe in the autonomy and dignity of the local church. We believe that the fundamental basis of the fellowship of the Apostolic churches was not educational but missionary. We believe in every kind and form of evangelism which is effective in bringing men and women to Christ. We don't for a moment apologize for holding to the faith of our Baptist fathers, but we believe in promoting good will and unity among all the people of God, and especially among those many groups which constitute the great household of our Bible believing Baptist people.

We are in every practical way against the Modernism now rampant in the Northern and Southern Baptist Conventions. For that we have no apology. We are against every form of church union which involves a central ecclesiastical body legislating for all of us and committing us to every kind of socialistic planning. We are against the Federal Council of Churches, and almost everything that organization stands for. We are against Communism, and we are equally against the opposite form of totalitarianism—Roman Catholicism. We believe, and in every practical way, in the American Constitution, and especially in that part of it which demands the separation of Church and State. We have no sympathy for this peculiar kind of Fundamentalism, whether denominational or interdenominational, which is barren of all ethical content. We believe that true Christian faith will profoundly affect what we think, what we say, what we write and what we do. We believe that every American citizen, regardless of race or color, should enjoy all those rights and prerogatives guaranteed to him by the letter and spirit of the Constitution and Bill of Rights. We believe in the "Capitalistic System," in free speech, and a free and unfettered press and radio. . . .

16.10   Early Black Baptists in America

Most historians agree that the Silver Bluff Church in Aiken County, South Carolina, was the earliest definitely identifiable black Baptist church in America. This church was founded, perhaps as early as 1773 or 1775, by George Lisle (sometimes written Liele or Leile). Unfortunately, little information has survived either about the church or its apparently gifted founder. In his pioneer work, *Negro Baptist History U.S.A.,* Lewis Jordan included an account by Walter H. Brooks on the origin and history of the Silver Bluff Church (selection A). *Source:* Lewis G. Jordan, *Negro Baptist History U.S.A.* (Nashville: Sunday School Publishing Board, NBC, n.d. [1930]), 361-372. Jordan also discussed pioneer black preachers, including Lisle (selection B). *Source:* Ibid., 46-48. An account of several early black Baptist churches in America, by the early historian David Benedict, forms selection C. *Source:* David Benedict, *A General History of the Baptist Denomination in America,* 2 vols. (Boston: Manning & Loring, 1813), 2:189-194.

A.   The Silver Bluff (Black) Baptist Church

THE STORY OF THE SILVER BLUFF CHURCH AND INFORMATION ABOUT NEGRO BAPTISTS IN EARLY TIMES
By Walter H. Brooks, D.D.

In speaking of the beginning of Negro churches in the United States, those of the Baptist faith must not be forgotten. Nor must we err, in thinking that the first churches of this faith were planted at the North. It is true there were Negro Baptists in Providence, R. I., as early as 1774, and doubtless a great deal earlier, but they had no church of their own. Indeed, there is absolutely no trace of Negro Baptist churches, at the North, which existed prior to the nineteenth century. The oldest Negro Baptist churches, north of Mason and Dixon's Line, are the Independent or First African, of Boston, Mass., planted in 1805; the Abyssinian, of New York City, planted in 1808; and the First African, of Philadelphia, Pa., planted in 1809.

Negro Baptist churches, unlike other Negro churches, had their beginning at the South, and at a somewhat earlier date.

The first church of Negro Baptists, the very first and oldest, so far as authentic and trustworthy writings of the eighteenth century establish, was constituted at Silver Bluff, on Mr. Galphin's estate, a year or two before the Revolutionary War.

It continued to worship there, in comparative peace, until the latter part of 1778, when the vicissitudes of war drove the church into exile,—but only to multiply itself elsewhere. Moreover, the work at Silver Bluff began afresh with the cessation of hostilities, and was more prosperous than ever in 1791.

But you ask, "Where is Silver Bluff?"

Silver Bluff was situated on the South Carolina side of the Savannah River, in Aiken County, just twelve miles from Augusta, Ga. All there was of it, in September, 1775, seems to have been embraced in what Rev. William Tennett, of Revolutionary fame, styled "Mr. Galphin's Settlement.". . .

Rev. David George, who was one of the constituent members, and the first regular pastor of the Silver Bluff Church, is our authority in regard to the early history of this flock. We make the following extracts from letters of his, which were published in London, England, in connection with other foreign correspondence, during the period 1790-1793:

"Brother Palmer, who was pastor at some distance from Silver Bluff, came and preached to a large congregation at a mill of Mr. Galphin's; he was a very powerful preacher." * * * "Brother Palmer came again and wished us to beg master to let him preach to us; and he came freequently." * * * "There were eight of us now, who had found the great blessing and mercy from the Lord, and my wife was one of them, and Brother Jesse Galphin. * * * "Brother Palmer appointed Saturday evening to hear what the Lord had done for us, and next day, he baptized us in the mill stream." * * * "Brother Palmer formed us into a church, and gave us the Lord's Supper at Silver Bluff." * * * "Then I began to exhort in the church, and learned to sing hymns." * * * Afterwards the church advised with Brother Palmer about my speaking to them, and keeping them together." * * * "So I was appointed to the office of an elder, and received instruction from Brother Palmer how to conduct myself. I proceeded in this way till the American War was coming on, when the ministers were not allowed to come amongst us, lest they should furnish us with too much knowledge." * * * "I continued preaching at Silver Bluff, till the church, constituted with eight, increased to thirty or more, and 'till the British came to the city of Savannah and took it."

The first clear conception of time, which we get from these extracts, in regard to the origin of the Silver Bluff Church, is where Mr. George speaks of being left in sole charge, as Liele and Palmer may no longer visit Silver Bluff, lest in so doing, they should impart to the slaves of the settlement a knowledge, which, in the then prevailing conditions, would result in their personal freedom, and, consequently, in great financial loss to their masters. This undoubtedly was not later than November, 1775, when the Earl of Dunmore issued on American soil a proclamation of emancipation, in which the black slaves and the white indentured bondmen, were alike promised freedom, provided they espoused the cause of England, in its struggle with the colonists. How well these slaves understood and appreciated the preferred boon, may be inferred from a letter, which was written by Mr. Stephen Bull to Col. Henry Laurens, President of the Council of Safety, Charleston, S. C., March 14, 1776. In that letter he says: "It is better for the public, and the owners, if the deserted Negroes who are on Tybee Island be shot, if they cannot be taken." By this means, as he informs us, he hoped to "deter other Negroes from deserting"—their masters. According to Mr. Bull's representation, the Negroes along the Savannah River were abandoning their masters, and going to the British in scores and hundreds, to the detriment of their owners, and the menace of the cause of American Independence.

Rev. George Liele, although not a runaway slave, appears to have had some liking for the Tybee River, as a place of abode, and it is probable that when he could no longer visit Silver Bluff, and was not in camp with Mr. Henry Sharp (who had not only given him his freedom, but also taken up arms against the Revolutionists), he resorted to Tybee Island to preach the gospel of Christ to the refugees there assembled. At any rate, when Liele appears in Savannah, Ga., as a preacher of the gospel, his biographer declares "He came up to the city of Savannah from Tybee River."

Mr. Geo. Galphin—Patron of the Silver Bluff Church

The planter and merchant, on whose estate the Silver Bluff Church was constituted, is deserving of special mention, in connection with the story of that people. We learn from White's history of Georgia, that "George Galphin was a native of Ireland, emigrated soon after manhood to America, and died at Silver Bluff, his residence, on the Savannah River, in South Carolina, on the second of December, 1782, in the seventy-first year of his age." Mr. N. W. Jones, in his history, quotes Mr. William Bartram as saying that Mr. George Galphin was "A gentleman of very distinguished talents and great liberality."

The spirit of justice and kindness, it appears, was manifest in all his dealings with the peoples of the weaker races, who were daily about him. The Red Man and the Black Man alike saw in him a man of kindly soul. David George, who was ever a British subject, described his former master as an "anti-loyalist." Mr. Jones, speaking as an American, pronounced him a "patriot." Neither spoke of him except to praise. A master less humane, less considerate of the happiness and moral weal of his dependents, less tolerant in spirit, would never have consented to the establishment of a Negro church on his estate. He might have put an end to the enterprise in its very incipiency. But he did not. He fostered the work from the beginning. It was by his consent the gospel of Christ was preached to slaves, who resided at Silver Bluff. It was by his permission the Silver Bluff Church was established. It was he who permitted David George to be ordained to the work of the gospel ministry. It was he who provided the Silver Bluff Church with a house of worship, by suffering his mill to be used in that capacity. And it was he who gave the little flock a baptistry, by placing his mill stream at their disposal on baptizing occasions. But we are satisfied that he had no conception of the far-reaching influence of these deeds of kindness. . . .

The Silver Bluff Church in Exile

With the fall of Savannah, at the very close of the year 1778, the Silver Bluff Church completed the first stage in its history. For at that time Mr. David George, the pastor, and about fifty other slaves, whom Mr. Galphin had abandoned in his flight, went to Savannah, to find safety and freedom under the British flag. Later Mr. George returned to South Carolina, and abode for a time in the city of Charleston. Thence, in 1782, he sailed to Nova Scotia, in company with not less than five hundred white persons, who were adherents of the British cause. . . .

In visiting Europe, Rev. Mr. George took with him letters of commendation from persons of recognized standing in England. The Rev. John Rippon, the distinguished London divine, thus speaks of Mr. George, after investigating his standing. "Governor Clarkson, in the most unreserved manner, assured me that he esteemed David George as his brother, and that he believed him to be the best man, without exception, in the colony of Sierra Leone."

Had the Silver Bluff Church done nothing more than produce this one earnest Christian man, this faithful preacher of Christ, this potent factor in the planting of a colony under the English flag, It would not have existed in vain. But it did more.

The Silver Bluff Church Revived

When peace had been restored, and the Revolutionary forces, British and American, had been disbanded or recalled, Silver Bluff began to assume once more the conditions which existed between master and slave in colonial times. Once more, too, the Galphin place became a center of Christian activities, and the Negro Baptists of Silver Bluff were more numerous than ever.

The man whom God used in resuscitating the work at Silver Bluff was the Rev. Jesse Peter, who, according to an old custom of applying to the slave surname of the master, was better known as Jesse Galphin, or Gaulfin. Having been connected with the Silver Bluff Church from the very first, and only separated from it during the Revolutionary War, and the period of readjustment immediately thereafter, Jesse Peter was eminently fitted, at least in one particular, to take up the work at Silver Bluff, which the Rev. David George had resigned in the year 1778. He knew the place, he loved the people: Silver Bluff was his home, and there he was held in high esteem. Moreover, he possessed what is essential to ministerial success everywhere, deep sincerity, seriousness of purpose, knowledge of the Word of God, an excellent spirit, and capacity to deliver, with profit and pleasure, the message of truth and mercy. Mr. Jonathon Clarke, and the Rev. Abraham Marshall, we knew him personally have left on record beautiful testimonials of his work and his worth.

Why this young man, who had obtained his freedom by going to the British at the fall of Savannah, in 1778, remained in America to resume the condition of slave, after the Revolutionary War, is not known. It is known, however, that, unlike Rev. George Liele and Rev. David George, men of adventurous spirit, the Rev. Jesse Peter was not inclined to wander far from the scenes and sounds of his South Carolina home. If, indeed, he ever traveled beyond Kiokee, Ga., in the one direction, and the city of Savannah, in the other, we have failed to note the fact. It is known, too, that he had an indulgent master, and it is possible that he preferred a state of nominal slavery, under his protection, to a fancied state of want and hardship in a foreign land. Or it may be, he was willing to die for Christ, and so deliberately entered again into the old condition of bondage, in order to enjoy the privilege of preaching Jesus, where Liele and George had labored in other days. . . .

Jesse Peter as Resident Pastor

Of Jesse Peter's ministry at Silver Bluff, as a resident pastor, we are not well informed. In a letter written from Kiokee, Ga., May 1, 1793, Rev. Abraham Marshall speaks of him as follows:

"I am intimately acquainted with Jesse Golfin; he lives thirty miles below me in South Carolina, and twelve miles below Augusta. He is a Negro servant of Mr. Golfin, who, to his praise be it spoken, treats him with respect."

Jesse Peter, then, was resident pastor of the Silver Bluff Church in the early spring of 1793.

From another source we learn that the membership of the Silver Bluff Church, at this time, was sixty or more.

The Church at Augusta

Here we lose sight of the Silver Bluff Church, just as the First African Baptist Church, of Augusta, Ga., better known as the Springfield Baptist Church, comes into being. Jesse Peter had secured standing and recognition for the First African Church, at Savannah, Ga., and Henry Francis has been ordained for the Ogeeche Church by him and Andrew Bryan and the Rev. Henry Holcombe, and it is natural that he would wish for his work at Silver Bluff, the standing and recognition which had been secured for the work in and about Savannah, Ga.

In order to obtain this boon, and have his work in touch with that near the seacoast, it would be necessary to transfer its place of meeting from the state of South Carolina, to the state of Georgia, where he had a friend, who was able to bring things to pass. It is in this way alone we account for the beginning of the First African Baptist Church at Augusta at the very time when the Silver Bluff Church disappears. The curtain falls on the Silver Bluff Church, with Rev. Jesse Peter as pastor, when the church is reported as in a flourishing condition. The curtain rises, and again we see a flock of devoted Christians, with Jesse Peter as pastor, but they are twelve miles away from Silver Bluff, South Carolina, receiving the regulating touches of the Rev. Abraham Marshall, white, and another white Baptist minister, which give the body standing and influence, as the First African Baptist Church, of Augusta, Ga.

Here is what Benedict says of the body. "This church appears to have been raised up by the labors of Jesse Peter, a 'black preacher of respectable talents, and an amiable character. It was constituted in 1793, by elders Abraham Marshall and David Tinsley. Jesse Peter, sometimes called Jesse Golfin, on account of his master's name, continued the pastor of this church a number of years, and was very successful in his ministry."

If, as we presume, the Silver Bluff Church is still with us, in another meeting-place, and under a new name, the oldest Negro Baptist church in this country today, is that at Augusta, Ga., having existed at Silver Bluff, S. C., from the period 1774-1775 to the year 1793, before becoming a Georgia institution.

B.   George Lisle, Pioneer Black Baptist Preacher

Pioneer Preachers

The list [of pioneer preachers] is a long and brilliant one. In the antebellum days it includes names which are immortal in our archives. George Lisle. a Negro, who was the first American Baptist foreign missionary, preceding William Carey, the renowned European missionary, by at least fifteen years. Lisle, though handicapped by the chains of human slavery and hampered by law-enforced ignorance, incurring the penalties of being a Negro, rose above all these degrading circumstances and became the chief human factor in the salvation of Jamaica, the most beautiful island in the Carribean Sea. . . . To Lisle belongs the honor of possibly being the first ordained Negro Baptist preacher in the New World. He preached in Georgia during the Revolutionary War, and his ministry was greatly blessed by a number of converts whom he baptized in the Savannah River. At the close of the war he went to Jamaica as the indentured servant of Col. Kirkland, an English officer. On getting settled in his new home on the island, Lisle was so deeply impressed with the sad conditions of superstition and ignorance in which he found the Negroes of Kingston, that he determined to do something to alleviate this state of affairs. He preached first at the race tracks and on the street, but later, hired a room at his own expense and organized a little Baptist church consisting of four persons.

Others joined him in forming a church which grew until in less than eight years he had baptized 500 persons.

In 1789 he built a chapel, and in spite of the rentless storm of persecution which he encountered, during which time he was imprisoned, placed in the stocks and finally tried for his life, for preaching "sedition." From 1805 to 1814, a law forbidding all preaching to slaves was strictly carried out. One man was hung for preaching and baptizing—but their labor bore fruit and when in 1814, Baptists in England were moved by letters of appeal from Lisle and others, to send missionaries, they found the people ready to greet them and cooperate in their work, because of the pioneer mission work established by George Lisle, 35 years before. . . .

Personal Letter of George Lisle (Page 122 N. B. C. Minutes, 1915)

The first Baptist church was orgainzed in 1784, in Kingston. A personal letter written to Dr. Rippen, of London, in 1791, will show more fully the character, work and struggle of this man.

"I cannot tell what my age is, as I have no account of the time of my birth, but I suppose I am about 40 years old. I have a wife and four children. My wife was baptized by me in Savannah, and I have every satisfaction in life from her. She is much the same age as myself. My eldest son is 19 years, my next son, 17, and the third, 14, and the last child, a girl of 11 years. They are all members of the church. My occupation is a farmer, but as the seasons of this part of the country are uncertain, I also keep a team of horses and wagons for the carrying of goods from one place to another, which I attend myself, with the assistance of my sons, and by this way of life have gained the good will of the public, who recommended me to the business and to some very principal work for the government. I have a few good books, some good old authors and sermons, and one large Bible that was given me by a gentleman. A good many of our members can read, and are all desirous to learn. They will be very thankful for a few books to read on Sundays and other days.

"There is no Baptist church in this country but ours. We have purchased a piece of land at the east end of Kingston, containing three acres, for the sum of $775, and on it we have begun a meeting house, 57 feet in length by 37 feet in breadth. We have raised the brick wall eight feet high from the foundation, and intend to have a gallery. . . . The chief part of our congregation are slaves, and their owners allow them, in common, but three or four bits a week to feed themselves, and out of so small a sum we cannot expect anything that can be of service from them; if we did, it would soon bring scandal upon religion. The free people in our society are poor, but they are willing, both free and slaves, to do what they can. As for my part, I am too much entangled with the affairs of the world to go on, as I would, with my design in supporting the cause. This has, I acknowledge, been a great hindrance to the gospel in one way; but I have endeavored to set a good example of good industry before the inhabitants of the land, it has given general satisfaction in another way. And, reverend sir, we think the Lord has put the power of the Baptist societies in England and to help and assist us in completing this building, which we look upon to be the greatest undertaking in this country for the bringing of souls from darkness into the light of the gospel. And as the Lord has put it in your heart to inquire after us, we place all of our confidence in you to make our circumstances known to the several Baptist churches in England, and we look upon you as our father, friend and brother. Within the brick walls we have a shelter in which we worship until our building can be accomplished.

"Your letter was read in the church two or three times, and did create a great deal of love and warmness throughout the congregation, and we shouted for joy and comfort to think that the Lord has been so gracious as to satisfy us in this country, with the same kind of religion of our beloved brethren in the old country, according to the Scriptures, and that such a worthy ——— of London could write so loving a letter to such poor worms as we are. And I beg leave to say that the whole congregation sang out they would, through the assistance of God, remember you in their prayers. They all together give their Christian love to you and all the worthy professors of Jesus Christ in your church at London, and beg the prayers of your churches in general and of our congregation wherever it pleases you to make known our circumstances. I remain, with the utmost love, reverend sir, your unworthy fellow laborer, servant and brother in Christ.

George Lisle.

C. Benedict's Account of Early Black Baptist Churches

CHAP. XIII.

An Account of four Baptist Churches of Africans in Georgia, and of two in the West-Indes; together with some general Observations respecting the Circumstances of the African Slaves in the Southern and Western States.

A MYSTERIOUS Providence has permitted a large portion of the sable sons of Africa to be transported from their native country to this western world, and here to be reduced to a state of absolute and perpetual slavery; but He who can bring good out of evil, has overruled this calamity for their spiritual advantage; and thousands of these poor, enslaved, and benighted people, we have very satisfactory reason to believe, have found gospel liberty in the midst of their temporal bondage, and are preparing to reign forever in the kingdom of God.

There are multitudes of African communicants, in all the Baptist churches in the southern and western States; and in Georgia there are four churches, wholly composed of them. Some brief sketches of their history will now be given.

First Coloured Baptist Church in Savannah.

The origin of this church, according to Rippon's Register and Holcombe's Repository, was in the following manner. About the beginning of the American war, George Leile, sometimes called George Sharp, but more commonly known among his brethren and friends by the name of brother George, began to preach at Brampton and Yamacraw, near the city of Savannah. . . . When the country was evacuated by the British, George, with many others, removed from Georgia to Kingston, in the island of Jamaica. . . .

Previous to George's departure for Jamaica, he came up to the city of Savannah from Tylee-river, where departing vessels frequently lay ready for sea, and baptized Andrew Bryan and Hannah his wife, and two other black women, whose names were Kate and Hagar. These were the last labours of George Leile in this quarter. About nine months after his departure, Andrew began to exhort his black brethren and friends, and a few whites who assembled to hear him. Edward Davis, Esq. permitted him and his hearers to erect a rough wooden building on his land at Yamacraw, in the suburbs of Savannah. Of this building they were, in a short time, very artfully dispossessed. It appears that these poor, defenceless slaves met with much opposition from the rude and merciless white people, who, under various pretences, interrupted their worship, and otherwise treated them in a barbarous manner. Andrew Bryan, and his brother Samson, who was converted about a year after him, were twice imprisoned, and they, with about fifty others, without much ceremony were severely whipped. Andrew was inhumanly cut, and bled abundantly; but while under their lashes, he held up his hands and told his persecutors, that he rejoiced not only to be whipped, but *would freely suffer death for the cause of Jesus Christ.* The Chief Justice, Henry Osbourne, James Habersham, and David Montague, Esquires, were their examinants, who released them. Jonathan Bryan, Esq. the kind master of Andrew and Samson, interceded for his own servants and the rest of the sufferers, and was much grieved at their punishment. The design of these unrighteous proceedings against these poor innocent people, was to stop their religious meetings. Their enemies pretended, that under a pretence of religion, they were plotting mischief and insurrections. But by *well doing* they at length silenced and shamed their persecutors, and acquired a number of very respectable and in-fluential advocates and patrons, who not only rescued them from the power of their enemies, but declared that such treatment as they had received would be condemned even among barbarians. The Chief Justice Osbourne then gave them liberty to con-tinue their worship any time between sun-rising and sun-set; and the benevolent Jonathan Bryan told the magistrates that he would give them the liberty of his *own house or barn,* at a place called Brampton, about three miles from Savannah, and that they should not be interrupted in their worship. From this period, Andrew and Sam-son set up meetings at their master's barn, where they had little or no interruption for about two years. Such was the beginning of the first African church in Savannah, which, after having been the mother of two others, now contains about fifteen hundred members. . . .

Towards the close of the year 1792, they began to build a place of worship in the suburbs of the city of Savannah, which, by the assistance of a number of benevolent gentlemen of different denominations, was finished in due time, and is 42 feet by 49. The plan of building this house, it seems, was projected by Messrs. Jonathan Clark, Ebenezer Hills, and others. The corporation of the city of Savannah gave them a lot for the purpose.

This coloured church, as it is generally called, (for no white person belongs to it) is now a large and respectable establishment. Many of its members are free, and are pos-sessed of some estate. It was one of the three churches which formed the Savannah-river Association; and by its returns to that body in 1812, it contained about fifteen hundred members, many of whom belong to the plantations in the neighbourhood of Savannah, and some are a number of miles out in the country. But their masters give them liberty every Sabbath to meet with their brethren, and the poor creatures, with peculiar de-light, go up to their Jerusalem to worship.

Andrew Bryan, the pastor of this church, is now an old man, and is spoken of by all who know him in terms of peculiar respect. He was born at a place called Goose-Creek, about 16 miles from Charleston, (S. C.) in what year is not known. He was a slave when he began to preach; but his kind master indulged him with uncommon liberties. After his death, he purchased his freedom of one of his heirs. . . .

Since writing the above, I have been informed by Mr. Johnson of Savannah, that this venerable man finished his course in October, 1812. He was supposed to have been about 90 years of age. . . .

Although he was a slave when he began to preach, yet he left an estate worth about three thousand dollars. He is succeeded in the pastoral office by his nephew Andrew Marshall, who is now working his time out, (as they call it) and is said to be a man of promising parts.

Second African Baptist Church in Savannah.

This church was formed in 1802, and now consists of upwards of three hundred members. This church has also a comfortable meeting-house in Savannah, 67 feet by 30. It is under the pastoral care of a very respectable black preacher, whose name is Henry Cunningham. He, like Andrew Bryan, was originally a slave, but is now free, having worked his time out.

*The African Church on the Great Ogechee River, commonly called
the Great Ogechee Coloured Church.*

This body, like the last mentioned, originated from the African church in Savannah, under the care of Andrew Bryan; and was constituted in 1803. But it has not been so prosperous as the two others, and has diminished rather than increased.

African Church in Augusta.

This church appears to have been raised up by the labours of Jesse Peter, a black preacher of very respectable talents, and an amiable character. It was constituted in 1793, by elders Abraham Marshall and David Tinsley.

Jesse Peter, sometimes called Jesse Golfin, on account of his master's name, continued the pastor of this church a number of years, and was very successful in his ministry. I find his character thus given by Mr. Abraham Marshall, in 1793, in Rippon's Register, Vol. I. p.545: "He is a servant of Mr. Golfin, who lives twelve miles below Augusta, and who, to his praise be it spoken, treats him with respect. His countenance is grave, his voice charming, his delivery good; nor is he a novice in the mysteries of the kingdom."

Mr. Peter died about 1806. Their present pastor is Caesar M'Cridy, under whose ministry the church appears to flourish and prosper. They have a meeting-house at Springfield, in the upper end of the city of Augusta.

This church was once upwards of five hundred in number; but it is now reduced, by various means, to a little less than four hundred, who walk together in harmony and love.

This church has belonged to the Georgia Association from its beginning. Abraham Marshall, the friend of black people, lives but a short distance from it; and to his fatherly care they are much indebted for many of their comforts.

There are multitudes of black people in all the churches in the southern States; but I know of no church of the Baptist denomination which is wholly composed of them, except those whose history has been related.

Their white brethren generally do not encourage them to form churches by themselves. Such are their circumstances, their mode of life, and their want of knowledge to regulate church affairs, that it is altogether best, in the present state of things, that they should be connected with their white brethren, who are capable of guiding and instructing them.

16.11   Later Black Baptists in America

Documents in the previous section (16.10) illustrate the history of early black Baptists in America, while this section spotlights later developments. Black churches formed a Baptist association as early as 1836, and efforts at a national body were not far behind. However, not until 1880 did black Baptists achieve a continuing national convention. That convention merged with two others in 1895 to form the present National Baptist Convention, Incorporated. Recent developments may lead to a healing of schisms that divided the National Convention in 1915 and 1961. The very helpful time chart of Sloan S. Hodges traces black Baptist history from 1619 to 1961. *Source:* Sloan S. Hodges, *Black Baptists in America and the Origins of Their Conventions* (Washington, D.C.: Progressive National Baptist Convention, Inc., n.d.).

1619	First ship load of African slaves landed at Jamestown, Va., one (1) year before the MAYFLOWER with Pilgrims landed at Plymouth Rock, Mass., in 1620.
1742	David George was born a slave.
1743	The Newton, Rhode Island Church carried the first recorded instance of a Black Baptist, Quassey, as one of the membership of fifty-one.
1762	Robert Stevens and 18 other Blacks were members of the Providence, Rhode Island, Baptist Church.
1772	The First Baptist Church, Boston, Mass., received Blacks as members.
1750	George Leisle (Leile) was born a slave in Virginia.
1773	George Leisle was converted and began preaching.
1773 or 1775	George Leisle with Wait Palmer, a white deacon, organized the Silver Bluff Baptist Church, Aiken County, South Carolina. This is commonly accepted as the first Negro Baptist Church organized in America and in the World.
1775	George Leisle (Leile) was ordained to preach the Gospel, May 20, and was given the freedom to minister to the other slaves by his master, Henry Sharp, a white deacon in Kiokee Baptist Church, where Leisle (Leile) held membership.
1775	David George and Jesse Peters were converted under the preaching of Leisle (Leile) and shortly thereafter began preaching themselves and traveling with Leisle.
1778	George Leisle (Leile) organized the First African Baptist Church, Savannah, Georgia.
1778	David George pastored a church in Savannah, Georgia.
1780	Lott Carey was born a slave 30 miles south of Richmond, Virginia.
1782	David George went to Halifax, Nova Scotia.
1783	David George with six followers organized a church at Shelbourne, in Canada. In 1792 he led a colonization group of 1,196 Blacks to Sierra Leone, West Africa.
1783	George Leisle (Leile) sailed for Jamaica, B.W.I. Prior to this date, Mr. Sharp, Leisle's master, had emancipated him, but when Mr. Sharp died, some members of the Sharp family attempted to re-enslave Rev. Leisle (Leile). After much intense prayer, two friends came to his rescue. A white man of Savannah loaned him $700.00 to get himself and family out of the country. The other was a British officer, a Colonel Kirkland, who told him of Jamaica, and the large Negro population there who were in deplorable conditions of ignorance and degeneracy.
	In sailing to Jamaica to preach the Gospel, George Leisle became the first foreign missionary in modern times. Long before William Carey left England for India or David Livingston went to Africa; long before the American Baptist Mission Society was organized in Tremont Temple in Boston; before Adoniram Judson went to Burma, this Black Baptist preacher launched out as a trail blazer in modern missions. He organized the First African Baptist Church Kingston, Jamaica, B.W.I.
1775-	In this quarter of a century, preachers were called to preach, converts were

1800   won, churches were organized and built, activities for freedom were initiated and by the turn of the century there were 25,000 Negro Baptists.

1807   Lott Carey joined a Baptist Church in Richmond, Virginia.

1812   John Jasper was born on July 4 in Fluvana County, Virginia.

1813   Lott Carey purchased his freedom and that of his two children for $850.00, which he had saved.

First Effort at Organization

1815   The African Baptist Missionary Society was organized in Richmond, Va. From 1815 to 1845 it contributed through the American Baptist Union, a white northern organization. In 1845, the white Baptists split over the slavery issue and the Southern Baptist Convention was organized. From 1845 to 1880 it contributed through the Southern Baptist Convention.

1821   Lott Carey and Collin Teague, whom he had won to Christ, sailed to Africa from Norfolk, Va., January 16th on the ship, NAUTILUS. They landed in Sierra Leone, West Africa. They were sent by the African Baptist Missionary Society. Lott Carey established the First Baptist Church in Monrovia, Liberia.

Other Missionaries sent out by the African Baptist Missionary Society included Solomon Cosby and W. W. Colley. The Southern Baptists closed their mission stations on the West Coast of Africa in 1875. Rev. W. W. Colley and Rev. W. J. Davis, who were working for the Southern Baptists at that time, continued to work as missionaries in other areas of Africa until 1879 when they returned to America.

National Organizations

1840   The American Baptist Missionary Convention was organized in Abyssinian Baptist Church, New York, N.Y. with Elder John Livingston, Moderator. This was the first Baptist Convention organized by Negroes. It could not operate in the South. Its area of operation was northern and middle western states.

1864   The Western and Southern Missionary Baptist Convention was organized to work in areas beyond which the American Baptist Missionary Convention was working.

1866   The Consolidated American Baptist Missionary Convention was organized in Richmond, Va. This was a merger of the American Baptist Missionary Convention and the Western and Southern Missionary Baptist Convention. Thus, the organized work was under one umbrella.

The Consolidated Convention organized six district conventions, two of which were: The General Association of the Western States and Territories, organized 1873; and The New England Baptist Missionary Convention, organized in 1875. The other four Conventions were overshadowed by state conventions and district associations and soon passed out of existence. The General Association of the Western States and Territories and The New England Baptist Missionary Convention, acting independent of the parent body, caused the parent body to weaken and decline until it ceased to meet after 1877.

1879   Rev. W. W. Colley returned to America from his labors in Africa and determined to arouse his black brethren to the urgent need for missionary work in

Africa. He wrote letters and traveled extensively urging Baptist leaders to meet in Montgomery, Alabama, November 24, 25, 26, 1880.

The Baptist Foreign Mission Convention

1880   Rev. Colley was successful in getting Baptist leaders to meet him in Montgomery. One hundred and fifty-one messengers from 11 States answered the call. There in First Baptist Church, The Baptist Foreign Mission Convention was organized, Rev. W. H. McAlpine of Alabama was elected President. Eleven vice-presidents were elected—one from each state represented. A Board of Directors was organized with Rev. A. Binga, Jr. of South Richmond the first Chairman, and Rev. Colley the first Corresponding Secretary and field agent. The headquarters was Richmond. Inasmuch as this Convention was committed to foreign missions only, the Executive Board was really the Foreign Mission Board.

The American National Baptist Convention

1886   The American National Baptist Convention was born when Rev. W. J. Simmons of Louisville, Ky. sent out a call in the form of a petition for the American National Baptist Convention to be formed. Prominent Baptists throughout the nation signed the petition and 600 delegates representing 17 States met in the First Baptist Church, St. Louis, Missouri, August 25th. One writer, commenting on those present, said, "Among them were graduates in law, medicine and theology; professors of philosophy, German, French, Latin, Greek, and Hebrew; a number of ex-state representatives, ex-senators; two ex-lieutenant governors; editors and teachers, not a few; a Baptist senator from Mississippi and a Baptist Missionary from London, England." W. J. Simmons was elected President. One of the main objectives of the Convention was the unification of all Negro Baptists of America for "mission work in the United States of America, in Africa and elsewhere abroad, and to foster the cause of education." The Baptist Foreign Mission Convention, through its Board in Richmond, continued to do the foreign mission work for the American National Baptist Convention. A united national Baptist convention had not yet been achieved, but the concept was firmly planted and the idea was growing.

The National Baptist Educational Convention

1893   Prior to 1893, educational and missionary work of Negro Baptists was largely directed throughout the United States by the American Baptist Home Mission Society of New York and the American Baptist Publication Society of Philadelphia. These societies had done great work. Schools founded by these societies are well known.

The graduates of the Home Mission Schools began to insist, more and more, that they have a hand in directing the policy of the schools from which they had graduated. The sentiment for Negro Baptists to own and control their own schools grew until it resulted in the founding of numerous schools like Simmons University in Kentucky, Selma University in Alabama, Arkansas Baptist College, Guadalupe College in Texas, Virginia Seminary, Lynchburg, Va., Central City College in Georgia, Morris College in S. C., and scores of other independent Negro Baptist schools.

The National Baptist Educational Convention of the U.S.A., organized in 1893, was the first attempt of Negro Baptists to direct the educational policy for the entire Negro Baptist denomination.

The National Baptist Convention, U.S.A.

1895   The National Baptist Convention, U.S.A. was organized September 24, 1895, in Friendship Baptist Church, Atlanta, Ga. The following three conventions adjourned their meetings in 1894 to meet together in Atlanta, Sep*. 24, 1895:

> Baptist Foreign Mission Convention, organized 1880 in Montgomery Ala. American National Baptist Convention, organized 1886 in St. Louis, Mo. National Baptist Educational Convention organized in 1893.

These three conventions were united and became the National Baptist Convention, U.S.A. Dr. E. C. Morris was elected President. The new Foreign Mission Board took charge of the foreign work previously under the Baptist Foreign Mission Convention. The new Educational Board took charge of the educational work, previously under the National Baptist Educational Convention. Rev. L. M. Luke of Georgia was elected the first Secretary of the Foreign Mission Board. He served only three months before he was taken by death.

Rev. L. G. Jordan, who was Pastor of Union Baptist Church, Philadelphia, Pa. was elected to succeed Rev. Luke as Secretary of the Foreign Mission Board in October 1896. Soon after his acceptance, he transferred the office of the Foreign Mission Board from Richmond to Louisville, Ky. This action was not approved by the eastern brethren, especially those in North Carolina and Virginia.

The Lott Carey Mission Convention

1897   The controversy over moving the Foreign Mission Board from Richmond, Va. to Louisville, Ky., plus other issues, such as the use of American Baptist Literature and cooperation with white Baptists in general, led to the organization of the Lott Carey Foreign Mission Convention in 1897 in Washington, D.C. with Rev. C. S. Brown of North Carolina as first President. A Compact Between The National Baptist Convention, U.S.A., and the Lott Carey Foreign Mission Convention was adopted at the Chicago Convention in 1905. However, the two conventions continued to go their separate ways with each electing its own officers, holding its own meetings and promoting its own program.

The National Baptist Convention of America, Unincorporated

1915   The National Baptist Convention of America, Unincorporated, sometimes referred to as the Boyd Convention was organized September 9, 1915 in Salem Baptist Church, Chicago, Ill. Dr. E. P. Jones of Mississippi was elected President. This Convention was organized as the result of the controversy over the ownership and control of the National Baptist Publishing House. The Publishing Board was incorporated under Tennessee laws, but the National Baptist Convention, U.S.A. was not incorporated and could not legally elect members to the Publishing Board. Therefore, the Convention could not control the Publishing Board. But the Convention could refuse to accept the legal status of the Publishing Board. In such an impasse, the Publishing Board bolted and organized a new Convention.

The Progressive National Baptist Convention, Inc.

1961   The Progressive National Baptist Convention, Inc. was organized November 14, 1961 in Zion Baptist Church, Cincinnati, Ohio.

The question of tenure for officers, especially the President, had been "popping up" in the National Baptist Convention, U.S.A. ever since its beginning. The early Presidents observed a voluntary tenure. From 1880, when the Baptist Foreign Mission Convention was organized, to 1894, when Dr. E. C. Morris was elected President, there had been eight Presidents in the space of 14 years. They were as follows: W. H. McAlpine 1880-82; J. Q. A. Wilhite 1883; J. A. Foster 1884; W. A. Brinkley 1885; W. J. Simmons 1886-90; E. M. Brawley 1891; M. Vann 1892-93; and E. C. Morris, elected in 1894.

17
Baptists in Europe

One overwhelming reality that has vitally affected religion in Europe, East and West, in the twentieth century has been the rise of Communism. Many of the primary sources cited in this chapter reflect that reality. One must remember that the term "Baptist" does not always mean exactly the same in a European context as in England or the United States. In Europe, many Christians who immerse are tagged as "Baptist," though in other ways they may differ significantly from Christians of that name elsewhere. Much of the twentieth-century history of European Baptists and near-Baptists involves religious persecution, and the documents selected here reflect that fact. By far the largest group of European Baptists are those within the USSR and thus they are somewhat overrepresented in the sources cited here.

17.1   West German Baptist Statement on Scripture, 1982

By the 1980s Baptist leaders in West Germany felt a need to reaffirm the authority of the Bible for faith and practice. The situation in Germany, as they saw it, did not call for composing a complete new confession of faith, but simply a reaffirmation of the authoritative role of Scripture in Baptist life. The following statement was approved by the leadership of the Baptist Union and provided to the churches for their guidance. The selection below includes an introduction by the German leaders explaining the origin and purpose of their statement on Scripture. *Source:* Taken from "*Wort der Bundesleitung zum Verstandnis der Bibel,*" issued by the Bundesmissionshaus, 6 Nov. 1982. Trans. by Terry G. Carter.

This statement of the Union leadership about the Bible question was approved at the November meeting in Wildbad and given to the churches as an aid. It is not to be understood in the sense of a written confession, but rather as an acute word for our situation.

Jesus says: "Heaven and earth will pass away; but my Word will not pass away."

This Word of Jesus encounters us today at a time when many things have become uncertain and people are seeking reliable orientation. The testimony of the Bible is this orientation and has the unchanged power to take people into the salvation history of God. The wonder of the Bible is that it confronts us with the living God and presents, for us to recognize, His holy and gracious will.

God leads us through the testimony of Scripture to conversion and renewal. He gives us assurance of salvation in life and death. So He helps us build up the church and witness to and serve the world.

We wonder whether this understanding of Holy Scripture is still binding us within our church or whether we are allowing ourselves to be shaken in our love for it by the frequently encountered relativity of the Scripture. We wonder also whether a too inflexible pre-understanding of the Bible does not narrow the dynamic [or living] quality of the Word of God.

Such considerations and acute problems, as they were discussed at the Union conference in Siegen in 1982, have moved the Union leadership to issue a statement to the churches concerning Biblical understanding. It was prepared by a team of the Union leadership in cooperation with lecturers of the Theological Seminary and has as its purpose the stimulation of renewed discussion of the Bible within the churches.

I. The Authority of the Bible

The Bible is unique, incomparable and irreplaceable. It possesses its own authority and dignity through God himself. The Creator, Saviour and Perfecter of men reveals himself in it. God says everything in the Scripture that is neccessary for us to know with regards to salvation, our faith and life. He has begun his salvation work in us and will complete it. (Phil. 1:6)

Jesus Christ is the central focus of Scripture. He is the incarnation of the Word of God. The Scripture finds its fulfillment in Him, the Son of God. His incarnation, His life and service, His death, His resurrection and future return are the way which leads to eternal life. (Acts 4:12)

God has made provision for our being led into the whole truth through His Spirit. (John 16:13) Inspired by the Holy Spirit, men have written the Biblical Scriptures (II Peter 1:21) and under His leadership put them together. This Spirit gives to Scripture until this day saving and convincing power and makes faith, love and hope grow. Through Him people are being called to a binding imitation of our Lord Jesus Christ and to serve one another. Through the Spirit they are also being enabled and directed toward the completion of the Kingdom of God.

II. Study of the Bible

Jesus himself calls for the exploration of "the Scripture". (John 5:39) It requires no special theological education to understand the clear testimony of the Bible. Each person can perceive in it the message of God, both for himself and for other people. Bible study is for every Christian an indispensable precondition for growth in faith, for cooperation in the church and for witness and service in the world.

The Word of God wants to do more than just inform. It wants to touch our heart. (Acts 2:37) Seizing the gospel means to be seized by it. . . .

The Bible is also an historical book. It bears witness of the activity of God within the history of Israel and in the life of Jesus within his church and its environment. In order to investigate carefully the historical reality of the Bible in the most aspects possible, e.g. languages, religions and cultures, theology makes use of the corresponding sciences and their methods (philologies, historical sciences, social sciences). A comprehensive and consciously responsible interpretation of Scripture will occupy itself with the problems and knowledge of these sciences. In so doing theology must be aware of the temporality and limitation of all science. Theology must also maintain its servant character and never be permitted to exalt itself above the Biblical message. . . .

The churches need shepherds and teachers of the Bible, called by God, who are prepared for preaching and pastoral service. In our theological seminary the students should receive a corresponding education. We advocate a thorough study of all theological subject fields, which includes scientific-theological Bible study.

III. Life with and in the Bible

The path of our churches was from the beginning on a life with the Bible. Spiritual awakenings have always been combined with [connected to] a great love for the Word of God. Our churches have experienced this in their own histories. In living with the Bible they experienced forgiveness, renewal, fellowship, mission and awakening. . . .

Whoever lives in the Bible will gain assurance and strength for life and service, comfort in temptations and sorrow, guidance in ethical decisions and hope for the future. We learn more and more to trust in the guidance and promises of God. "Your Word is a lamp unto my feet and light unto my path." (Psalms 119:105)

So the Holy Scripture remains for us authoritative. We refuse an arbitrary selection of individual parts of Scripture. It is for us binding in its absolute authority. We wish for our churches an increased joy in the intensive study of the Bible which becomes again and again a source of living discipleship.

"Everything that has been written before, has been written for our instruction, so that we have hope through the steadfastness and comfort of the Scriptures." (Rom. 15:4)

Wildbad, 6 November 1982.

17.2 Wolfgang Mueller, Interview About German Baptists, 1983

What is going on among Baptists in West Germany? What issues and challenges do they face? American readers have been intensely interested in such questions since the days of Johann G. Oncken. When Wolfgang Mueller, editor of *Diezemeinde,* the Baptist paper of West Germany, visited the United States, he was often questioned about Baptist life in Germany. The following selection comes from an interview Mueller gave in 1983. *Source:* Interview printed in *SBC Today,* June 1983, 10-11. Used by permission.

What is the size of the Baptist Union in Germany?

There are about 70,000 members within the West German Baptist Union and this includes members from so-called Plymouth Brethren churches which united with the Baptists in 1941. So it's about 61,000 Baptists and the rest are Plymouth Brethren— around 400 congregations.

There are nine associations. They do not always coincide with the states. There is a union in Eastern Germany and in the German Democratic Republic as well.

The local church is autonomous, and once a year we have the convention which elects the union council as we call it and also determines the policies. For example, two years ago the convention voted down a proposal to ordain women for the ministry. It was about three-fourths majority against it. Some churches had threatened to leave the union if we had voted for the proposal. Naturally the Brethren churches would be very much against it because they are very conservative.

Do the churches not have the authority to ordain whom they please?

Not quite, because the pastors have a certain legal status which is given by the union, so whenever we ordain a minister, a representative of the union must be present.

Is the legal status given by the German government?

In a way, yes. The union is responsible for the placing of ministers, so when, for example, a pastor looks for a new church and can't find one the union has to step in and try to place him. And we also are connected with the union by the retirement plan that we have.

Does the union then guarantee an ordained minister a position?

Yes. He must do some very awful things if he is to be excluded, but he has to be heard first and appear for a board hearing.

Germany has a tax for religion?

There is a church tax for the Roman Catholic Church, the established protestant church, the Jewish faith and the old Catholic church. Baptists or Methodists could raise that same church tax from their members if they wanted to but we don't.

Because of your belief in the separation of church and state?

Yes, and we would probably starve if we only had that much money, because it is 9 precent of the income tax, not of the income.

You're doing mission work in Africa?

Yes. This, however, is not only a German enterprise. It is the European Baptist mission. So we cooperate with a number of smaller unions. And the second mission field is

South America, both Argentina and Brazil. But we have only four European missionaries there. All the others are natives of those countries, even though some of them are of German descent.

How large is the European Baptist Federation?

The Federation is approximately 750,000 of whom two-thirds live in Eastern European communist countries. So the Russian or Union Council is by far the largest with about half a million members. The British would be next, then followed by Rumania.

Was the debate on ordaining women primarily on theological grounds?

Yes, they quoted Paul. Some women go to seminary. They can be employed by a church. Many would call it minister of education or so, and if a church chooses it can permit her to preach. In my home church it's no problem. We repeatedly have women who preach. But still they couldn't be ordained as pastors. I'm not happy about that at all.

Are there other theological discussions or tension points?

One was that of possible open membership: would it be possible to accept a person who is not being baptized as a believer into membership? There are some churches in Britain who do it but this has been turned down, too.

It is a problem because in our country there are people who basically believe in believers' baptism. But since they have been baptized or christened as babies they do not want to renounce that as not being baptism at all.

Another problem is the rising tide of ultra-conservatism or fundamentalism. We thought we had been over that for a long time but it's coming in from America. Especially the question, for example, of evolution and creationism and so forth.

What is the position of most of the churches on what we call inerrancy?

Traditionally European Baptists have always been conservative but not fundamentalist. These were phrases and terminologies which were quite unknown to us. We didn't think along these lines. But this is being brought in by Americans.

We would say the Bible is the word of God. However, we would not be dogmatic on certain single issues and there has been a variety of thought. For example, should you take the creation story literally or as a symbol? There's more than one opinion. So far we do not excommunicate one another, which may happen if things get worse.

Have you adopted a statement of faith?

Yes. We call it a confession of faith. It's rather lengthy and a little difficult to read, adopted by both Germanies, Austria and Switzerland.

There is one difference that's rather funny. The German Democratic Republic Baptists differ on the question of baptism. So Baptists agreed on everything but on baptism.

They feel the Western version is a little too sacramental in that it emphasizes the togetherness or the oneness of faith, baptism and church membership and even receiving the Holy Spirit.

They emphasize a little more the old Baptist tradition of baptism being just a confession of faith, whereas we would say it is both a confession of faith and an act of God. We cannot separate baptism from the act of Christ. So the act of the acceptance of Christ, baptism and church membership. You cannot just pull it apart.

One of the big issues is of social and political concern—the question of peace. There is a strong tension between the older and younger generations.

There are exceptions on both sides, but most of the older members tend to be rather conservative politically and they would go along with the policies of the Christian Democratic Union, the conservative party which just won a victory. Whereas a good number of the younger generation tend to a more pacifistic point of view, or at least what we call the "atomic pacifists." They wouldn't be basic pacifists, but they are against nuclear arms and the arms race. About 50 percent of the young men in our churches are conscientious objectors whereas the national average is 10 percent. This would not be the attitude of the generation above 45 years of age.

We have compulsory military service and they have to apply to be recognized as conscientious objectors, and they have to do alternative service in hospitals, old peoples' homes and so forth. It [service for conscientious objectors] is now 18 months but will be raised to 20. Military service is 15 months.

What other forms has the peace movement taken? Has the Baptist union taken a position?

No, the union has not taken a position as usual; nor have the free churches in general and it would hardly be possible because we are so divided. Some of our young people have taken part in demonstrations but not as church groups, as individuals.

In one association we have "Initiative Shalom," and they come together to discuss questions of peace and to educate people how to live peacefully, not only on the large scale but also the small scale. Some people frown upon it: they even found it hard to find churches where they could meet.

How about European Baptists, are they divided on the peace issue?

I would think so. There is going to be a conference in Sweden. As a whole there is a tendency towards a qualified position of pacifism, not in the fundamental sense, perhaps, of the Mennonites, but pertaining to the present arms race and nuclear arms.

17.3 The Situation of Baptists in Romania, 1973

Baptists in Romania have shown remarkable growth and spiritual vitality in recent years. The Baptist leaders in this East European country have been able to maintain considerable contacts with Baptists in the West. Iosif Ton is a Romanian Baptist who studied in Britain and received a theology degree from Oxford before returning to Romania in 1972. The following analysis of the situation in Romania represents his first major report after his return. The report was issued by the Center for the Study of Religion and Communism (CSRC). *Source:* Josef Tson, "The Present Situation of the Baptist Church in Romania," *Religion in Communist Lands*, November 1973, Supplementary Paper No. 1. Used by permission.

This is an attempt at analysis of the present situation of the Baptist Church in Romania in the light of biblical and New Testament principles. It may be shocking to see how far we have erred from these principles—even to the extent that it is questionable whether we can still be called a New Testament church at all.

I must begin by explaining that the Baptist churches sprang up in Romania in a completely spontaneous way. They were founded by men who were seeking a true spiritual life governed by the Word of God as revealed in the Holy Scriptures. There was no organized action from abroad to spread this faith in our country. A few sparks scattered here and there, in Bihor, Ardeal, Bucovina kindled a fire which spread throughout the land. . . .

It is also very important to show that our faith spread and grew without a centralized inter-church organization any more than any impulse from outside. True, the churches maintained strong fraternal relations and very early on formed themselves into "circles", each of which was served by a particualr evangelist or preacher. Almost from the beginning the need was felt of an organization which would represent the churches' interests to the State, and which would be able to arrange certain activities which were outside the capabilities of the individual churches. But this organization, when it came into being, was a product, not the cause, of the growth of the Baptist churches.

The Baptist Union was formed relatively late—in 1920—and from that date until 1955 preserved the character of all other Baptist Unions, namely that of a representative and consultative organ for mutual assistance.

THE 1955 CONGRESS

After the Union's congress, held in the autumn of 1955, this Union changed its fundamental character, although the Constitution of the Baptist Union remained the same as before and although the churches did not give the Union a mandate to change its functions and powers. The 1955 Congress marks the moment when the sacred and essential principles of our faith began to be renounced and deserted.

In 1954 the ministry of Cults had the idea of issuing the **Regularization of Religious Services,** which aimed at substantially reducing the number of services and other church activities. However, the **Regularization** was unusually dangerous not because it reduced the number of services—although this in itself had and continues to have a very harmful effect on the life of our churches. The **Regularization** was harmful because of the way in which it was imposed, according to a new principle, foreign to our denomination and belief. The authorities asked the leaders of the Union to implement the **Regularization** in such a way that it should seem a measure desired by the Union and **imposed by it** on the local churches and not something imposed by the State. Firstly, to accept such a proposition meant that the Union lied, committed a sin: namely that of transmitting as its own a decision which it had in no way made. However, even if the Union could have exonerated itself by affirming before the whole world that it had not acted freely but under pressure, nevertheless its action contained a greater evil—namely the introduction of a principle whereby the Union can take **obligatory** decisions on behalf of the churches and **impose** them upon the churches. Such an idea is quite contrary to Baptist principles. We are not a centralized Union where decisions are taken and then imposed on the churches. We are a Union of free, independent, self-governing churches, and the Union has no statutory, i.e. legal, right to impose any decision which the local churches do not freely choose to accept. . . .

In 1954 the leadership of the Union realized how harmful the **Regularization** was and what disastrous results it would have, and so refused to accept its implementation. As a result the Ministry of Cults announced that it no longer recognized the Union's leaders and asked the denomination to organize a congress and choose another set of leaders. At this congress (referred to above) held in the autumn of 1955, the representative from the Ministry of Cults imposed his choice of leaders on the Union—leaders whom the congress delegates did not want. One should remember that the Secretary General was elected only at the third vote, after the representative of the Ministry of Cults had said categorically that he **must** be chosen since he was the only man whom the State authorities would accept. After such pressure, the Congress delegates hesistantly raised their hands and voted for a man whom they did not want (to vote not according to the dictates of one's conscience is to lie, and so to sin!) At that moment the back of the Union was broken. Those who voted yielded and were inwardly crushed. They started down the slopes of compromise which one after another followed the congress. . . .

. . . If at that congress we had remained true to ourselves, we should have preserved our form unaltered and we should not have found ourselves subsequently in the position of having to renounce, step by step, so many of our essential principles. Many men before us have died for these New Testament principles. But we decided that it was better to survive at any price, even the price of our own true essence. We have forgotten what our Lord says to us, that only the man who loses his life with Him and for Him will gain it!

The leadership chosen in 1955 has shown itself ready to accept without comment any resolution of the Department of Cults (the new name for the Ministry of Cults), regardless of whether it contradicts the doctrines and principles of the Baptists, or even the spirit of our country's laws. We are aware that this is a very grave allegation, but what follows will illustrate and prove it abundantly. We shall illustrate just a few of the resolutions accepted by the Union and passed on to the churches as decisions of the Union.

FORM OF WORSHIP

In the first place they accepted and imposed th **Regularization of Religious Services.** On this point we must add the following. The Baptist churches do not have an obligatory liturgical form. Our principle is that the assembly of the local church decides, under the guidance of the Holy Spirit and in the light of Holy Scripture what form their worship will take, what the church will do when it meets together and how many times it will come together for worship, Bible-study or any other form of religious activity. No one from outside, and in particular the Baptist Union, has the right to restrict this freedom. . . .

STATE CONTROL OF PASTORS' APPOINTMENTS

Another resolution accepted and executed by the Union was the one known as the **Arrondation.** This led to the closure of hundreds of churches. By accepting with resignation a decision which denied thousands of people the freedom to practice the cult—as given in the Constitution and in the Law on Cults (1948)—the Union's leadership showed that it was alienated from the genuine interest of the Baptist churches. Nevertheless this was not the most disturbing aspect of this resolution, for it also led to a departure from another fundamental Baptist principle. Within the framework of this act the Union agreed to create a "scheme of service", which fixed a set number of posts for pastors in the country. Although hundreds of churches had the economic resources and the desire independently to support a pastor, they discovered that they had no right to do so because they were not included in the scheme. The payment of the pastors' salary was also taken out of the hands of the local church and given to the association (a local State organ). Thus the pastor became financially dependent on the association and not on the church. . . .

The choosing of a pastor by the local church without external intervention is an essential aspect of a fundamental doctrine. To renounce it is to renounce New Testament practice and this affects the very being of the church. . . .

Thus, it is our firm belief that any church, even if small and insignificant, is authorized and—under guidance of the Holy Spirit—must be free to decide for itself who will be its pastor. "It seemed good to the Holy Spirit and to us" (Acts 15-28) is the New Testament formula for a decision taken by the church, and this must always be our practice. Now we come to the distrubing question which must be put to all the churches; if the pastor of a church is no longer chosen by the respective church under the guidance of the Holy Spirit, but is named by someone from the centre, can one still say that this church is obeying the Holy Spirit? Or are we in fact rejecting an essential element in our life when we accept an unbiblical principle? When we no longer act under the direct guidance of the Holy Spirit as perceived by the assembled church, whom are we obeying? We must state clearly and bluntly—and the churches need to pay attention to this—

that **when the churches allow others from outside to resolve their problems they lose no less than the Lordship of Christ over His Church!**

This is an essential matter, and in vital matters there can be no room for negotiations or for compromise. When a church renounces the guidance of the Holy Spirit and the Lordship of Christ, the work it does from that time onwards, we can be sure, will be a purely human work and not the work of God. That church has lost its life. . . .

INTERFERENCE IN LOCAL LAY LEADERSHIP

However, the problem of a pastor's election is not the only one of this nature. In recent years, State interference in the life of our churches has been extended to the committee of leaders in a local church. How can a church still say that its committee was chosen under the guidance of the Holy Spirit when the list of candidates for election was first presented to the district inspector of cults for approval? This man can strike whom he likes off the list, and in practice he strikes off those who are the best sons of the church. How can the church still say that it continues to be subject to the Lordship of Christ, when it allows its pastor, or deacon or secretary or any other of its servants, to be dismissed by the inspector of cults (usually the real reason for the dismissal was that these men were very active in the cause and had given themselves wholeheartedly to promoting the work of God), and when it is ready to accept another pastor, another deacon, or another secretary, proposed by someone else from outside?

At this point we must discuss a point of juridical order. There now exists a **Decree for the Organization and Functions of the Department of Cults,** which authorizes this Department to recognise pastors and other church leaders. When this decree was promulgated the the Baptist churches in Romania faced in fact a legal crisis, because this decree infringes one of their principles—namely, that the State must in no way interfere in her internal life. This is the reason why a change in our Union's Constitution was recommended so as to bring it into line with the laws of the State. One of the changes recommended concerns pastors—that they be nominated directly by the Union. . . .

The problem of pastors and the Committees of local churches must be further clarified and discussed here. The State wants to assume the right to authorize and dismiss pastors and members of committees. On what grounds will the State give its authorization? Because these men are sufficiently prepared culturally or intellectually, or have a good theological training, or because they are sufficiently enthusiastic for the work of the church? Or because they are sufficiently clean from a moral point of view? Practice so far does not support such suppositions. On the contrary, it was observed that almost as a general rule the men (proposed as candidates for election to church committees) struck off the lists of candidates presented to the inspectors of cults are those with higher education. The aim was to deprive the church of intellectuals in its leadership. In addition any pastor, zealous for the work committed to him, has a good chance of falling into disgrace and being dismissed by the Department of Cults. So long as the pastor is tame, often consults the inspector of cults, and obeys the resolutions of the Department of Cults, he is more likely to remain in his job even if the church would much prefer to have him replaced. A State, the declared ideology or [sic] which is atheism, cannot pretend to be able to judge who should or should not be a leader of the church. . . .

RESTRICTIONS ON BAPTISM

Another restriction on our religious freedom which has been accepted and imposed on the churches by the Union concerns baptism. This will throw into sharp relief another aspect of the present situation of the Baptist churches.

A few years ago the Department of Cults told the leadership of the Union that from then on any pastor who wished to hold a baptismal service must apply first to the district inspector of cults and present him with a list of those to be baptized for his approval. The Union transmitted this new regulation to the churches **orally,** during the so-called "information meetings" of the associations. From then on any pastor who did not obey this decision would be immediately dismissed because he had broken **a regulation which was not written down** and which no one would ever dare write down as a regulation or decree of law in view of its unconstitutional nature!

On the basis of the Constitution of our country every citizen is free to believe or not to believe, he is free to change or to renounce his religion. No inspector of cults (nor any pastor or priest!) has the legal right to stop a citizen changing his religion, and the inspectors are very careful to avoid any situation in which they could be proved to have broken a law. An inspector of cults, however, does something very different. He strikes off the list of candidates for baptism handed to him for approval by the Baptist pastor all those not born into Baptist families, that is, those who theoretically have another religion and who by baptism want to change that religion and become Baptists. The inspector of cults does not say to the respective citizen that he does not approve of his becoming a Baptist. No, he will not do that, because he does not have the right to approve or stop a change in religious adherence. But he acts more subtly. He says to the Baptist pastor: "If you baptize this citizen, I will dismiss you." The Baptist pastor, knowing that he is now left by his Union in the hands of the inspector of cults, may accept the ban and tell the candidate that he cannot baptize him. Perhaps he might explain humbly and sadly that he cannot do it because he will lose his livelihood. It is evident to all, therefore, that the right of a citizen to decide his own religion is in fact denied by such behaviour. Therefore, to ask approval for a baptismal service is unconstitutional and it is not contained in a written directive because it is illegal.

There is yet another aspect of this restriction which must be a problem of conscience for every pastor and church. We have a command from the Lord Jesus Christ to make disciples and to baptize them, and we believe that this command is as valid today as it was two thousand years ago and that it is our duty by virtue of the divine call. Do we then refuse to obey the command of God because the inspector of cults forbids it? Or, to use the words of the apostles, "Shall we listen to men rather than to God?"

Nor have we yet exhausted the problem. We shall see how sinful this situation is and how it affects us—as do the matters discussed previously—**at the essence of our being,** if we make a comparison with the Orthodox denomination. The Orthodox church believes in seven "mysteries" (sacraments), and considers that its essential function lies in the administration of these sacraments. Now who would ever conceive of a situation where an Orthodox priest would have to ask the approval of an inspector of cults before administering one of the sacraments—a wedding, the eucharist or. . . . . . the baptism of a child? We Baptists have no "mysteries", but we do have two symbols—the Lord's Supper (the Eucharist) and baptism, and they are also absolutely essential to us, forming a basic part of our doctrine and playing a major role in our lives. How can we have sunk so low as to allow, as a church, someone outside the church to decide when and how we may hold a baptismal service, or if we can have it at all? (Why then do we not also ask permission to have the Lord's Supper?) How can we still believe and affirm that this is the work of God and not of men? . . .

INTERFERENCE IN FINANCIAL AFFAIRS

Another area where the Baptist churches have renounced one of their principles is that of financial affairs. The church must be sovereign of its own money: it, and it alone, is capable of deciding, under the guidance of the Holy Spirit, what must be done with its money. Now, however, the State dictates to the church what it is allowed and not allowed to do with its money. We have now reached a situation where should a church, for example, wish to buy a guitar, it must obtain permission from the Department of Cults. Our position must be absolutely clear on this issue: we cannot permit our financial affairs to be controlled by any body other than the church. The State can claim the right to verify the honesty of the way this money is administered by those entrusted with this job by the church, but the State cannot claim to control the church over the way it uses its own money.

DEACONS AND THE LORD'S SUPPER

The interference of the State authorities in the churches' internal affairs does not end there. We must describe another trend which is affecting our New Testament stand. From the beginning of our history in this country, deacons have played a very important role. Where there was no pastor, the deacons carried out every act of the ritual: the Lord's Supper, baptismal services, weddings, funerals, and so on. When the number of pastors was severely reduced in the early '60s (when the "scheme of service", discussed above, was introduced) and when almost every pastor had to look after between five and ten churches, the inspectors of cults also introduced and imposed the idea that deacons did not have the right to administer the Lord's Supper. Many pastors and churches accepted this new "docrine"! But from what Bible did they get it? When this new "doctrine" was applied, some pastors could only administer the Lord's Supper, for—having up to ten churches to look after—they only had time to run from one church to another to administer this service.

A recent event at the First Baptist Church in Timisoara illustrates the dangerous character of this situation. This church refused to accept another pastor after the one they had chosen had been dismissed by the Union at the order of the Department of Cults. The leaders of the Timisoara Association then refused to send this church a pastor who would give the Lord's Supper, and they threatened her deacons, should they dare to administer it themselves. Thus the association leaders put pressure on the church to make it accept another pastor than the one they had chosen.

This is reminiscent of events of the Middle Ages when the Pope placed whole areas under an interdict, commanding the priests not to administer the Eucharist there. This act is yet another illustration of the dangers of centralization of which I have spoken. . . .

UNWRITTEN LAWS

Many "unwritten laws" governing the life of our churches have recently been introduced. One stipulates that a pastor has the right to preach only in his own church and nowhere else. If a pastor wants to preach elsewhere he must get the approval of the inspector of cults for his district, or that of the Baptist Union leaders. Now, does this not limit the freedom of movement and speech which is given to us in the Constitution and by this country's laws?

An even more disturbing and dangerous instruction given by the inspector of cults is the one which allows the pastor and members of the local church's committee to preach from the pulpit. Such an instruction is actually implemented by many pastors and by many churches! How can we reconcile this with our fundamental belief that every Baptist is a priest and that every member of the church has not only the right but also the duty to contribute to the life of the church and to speak at and lead its worship services?

Such State interference in the life of our churches reached a head in the spring of this year. A delegate of the Department of Cults was sent to the town Simeria and, threatening to withdraw permission for that church to function, asked the secretary of the church to receive back into membership a group of men whom that church had excluded a few years ago. If we have reached a point where even the quality of a member of a church can be judged by someone from the outside, then is it not time for us to ask ourselves profoundly and with all seriousness the question: "Whose is this church?"

CONCLUSION

Let us now recapitulate everything the church has lost, because this will enable us to reckon up what we have left and to whom we belong:

1. The church can no longer choose its own pastor, and the pastor is no longer employed by the church, but by a central organisation.
2. The church can no longer choose whom it wants to serve on its committee of leaders.
3. The church's deacons can no longer perform essential ritual acts.
4. The church cannot baptize openly any longer, as its Lord commanded for all who accept Jesus Christ as Lord and personal Saviour.
5. The church cannot invite a guest to speak, and not even its own members, but only those who are acceptable to certain persons outside it.
6. The church can no longer decide what to do with its own money.
7. The church has reached the point where someone from outside can dictate whom it should receive into membership.

We repeat what must be repeated, emphasized and underlined, namely that the thing **which the church has lost through all these compromises is the guiding authority of the Holy Spirit in its life and the Lordship—**which **should be unique and exclusive— of the Lord Jesus Christ over it.** It is time that the church asked itself not only if it can still bear the name of Baptist, but further if it is still a New Testament church, and, in the last analysis, if it is still the Bride of Christ. If not, it must ask whether it has—like the Israel of the Old Testament concerning whom it was said that it committed harlotry with foreign gods—taken upon itself the role of a prostitute. These are hard words, but biblical ones! And the Bible is not a book which spares the feelings of those who fall away from the commandments and from the will of God!

To one church which had departed from the Bible and from its true life, the Lord Jesus Christ writes: "Remember from what you have fallen: repent and do the works you did at first" (Rev. 2:5).

From what have we fallen? We have fallen from the legal position in which the Law of Cults of 1948 had placed us and which is still in force, and from the position of a free and autonomous church given us by the **Statute** and the **Confession of Faith** of our denomination which were accepted by the State in the Decree No. 1203/1951, and which is also still in force.

What we meant to say to the Baptist churches is that through **Regularization, Arrondations,** and unwritten instructions **issued** since 1955, they have been forced into a situation which is neither constitutional, statutory, nor biblical! . . .

It is time to stop and ask ourselves where we are and how we arrived here, and whether it is good that we are here. If we conclude that it is not good, let us have the courage to turn away from the place to which we have fallen and to make afresh the biblical, New Testament stand, as our Lord Jesus Christ asks us to do. Let us repent through the words of the prophet Isaiah who says, "O Lord our God, other lords apart from You have ruled over us, but Your name alone do we acknowledge" (Isa. 26:13).

We emphasize again that the Constitution and the laws of our country give us full liberty. Come then, let us as a free church and as the free men we are, as the Constitution and other basic laws give us the right to do, and as our **Statute** and **Confession of Faith** accepted by the State authorities, instruct us. Come, let us break away from the regularization and instructions of a group of men who in issuing them to us have broken their creed and have exceeded the powers given them by law and by our Statute. Come, then, and ignore every limitation of freedom which has been imposed upon us by the Union since 1955, and in this way let us return to legality and the teaching of the New Testament. We live in a free country with democratic laws; come and live as free men, as these laws teach us. Come, let us ask our pastors not to wait for instructions and permission from the inspector of cults for their work in the church, but to ask for instruction on their knees from our only Master and Lord Jesus Christ.

Let us prove that by the side of our Lord Jesus Christ we have the courage even to die if anyone tries to jeopardize His Lordship over us.

From the authorities of the State we ask the following:

1 The cessation of pressures limiting the number of religious services in our churches.

2 The cancellation of the measures imposed by the **arrondation,** and the reopening of all Baptist churches which are still closed, and permission to form new churches wherever there is a statutory, that is legal, number of Baptist believers who request it.

3 An end to licencing of pastors and of the requirement that pastors be recognised by the Department of Cults, so that every church may choose the pastor it wants.

4 The cessation of the requirement that inspectors of cults approve a list of members from which the church may choose its committee, and also of the requirement that inspectors of cults recognize the leaders chosen by the church.

5 An end to any kind of interference in the life of the church by inspectors of the cults where baptisms and other ritual acts (the Lord's Supper, the preaching of the Gospel) are concerned.

6 An end to any interference in the financial affairs of the church, with the exception of control over the honesty of the financial operations.

Baptists in Romania wish to demonstrate that they are loyal citizens, with a high moral standing, who wish to have a chance to show this. They believe that they can contribute something valuable to building up our socialist life and consequently ask the right to exist as **Baptists** in this society, in every sphere of its activity and at every level. The Romanian State stands only to gain internally and externally if it accords us the right to a free and undisturbed existence.

The Bible teaches us to love the country in which we live, to respect its authorities, and to give to them all which is due to them. However, the Bible futher teaches us that our Supreme master is God. **His authority** demands from us an unconditional and absolute commitment. When this is affected, we prefer to renounce this life on earth, because we believe in eternal life with God our Creator and with Christ our Saviour.

We ask the authorities of the State to understand that we have two sets of loyalties—loyalty to the State and loyalty to God—and if we are faced with a conflict of loyalties, then we will be obliged to put our loyalty to God first.

17.4 Vasili G. Pavloff, Report on Baptists in Russia, 1908

Vasili G. Pavloff, an outstanding Russian Baptist leader, reported to the Baptist World Alliance in 1908 on the origin, growth, and current situation of Baptists in Russia. Pavloff was described as "a Russian pioneer both in testimony and suffering." His paper contains early primary source materials on Soviet Baptists. Modern readers will note Pavolff's optimism concerning Soviet political leadership after the Revolution of 1905 when Baptists enjoyed more religious liberty than they had under the tzars. Unfortunately, events of later years would made this optimism hard to sustain. *Source:* Reports, Baptist World Alliance, Berlin, 1908, 152-160.

THE RISE, GROWTH AND PRESENT POSITION OF THE BAPTIST BODY IN RUSSIA.
Rev. V. PAVLOFF, Odessa.

IT is over 400 years ago that the Reformation took place in Germany, whereas in Russia it may be said to be only now beginning. For the most part the people of the Slavonic race have not up to the present time received the teaching of Christ in its pristine purity, but are still under the influence of either the Romish or the Greek Church. The people of Russia are far behind the other European nations as regards Religion and Civilization, for which fact, as their history will show us, the Mongolian invasion is chiefly responsible—other causes being the pernicious influence of serfdom, and the absence of political and religious liberty. The great merit of the Greek Church as compared with that of the Romanists, is that it has not withheld the Bible from the people, but has allowed it to be translated into the vernacular and read freely.

I will ask my hearers to take with me a brief survey of four things—I. The origin of the Baptist Church in Russia. II. Its growth. III. Its position at the present day, and IV. Our duties and tasks.

I.—THE ORIGIN OF THE BAPTIST CHURCH.

The first Baptist teachings heard in Russia arose in two southern districts simultaneously, namely, the village of Luboirka (in the government of Kherson), and Tiflis the capital of Transcaucasia. The impulse to this great evangelical movement was given in the first instance by German Baptists. In the Khersonese government the first propagator of our principles was a peasant, one Ivan Rjaboschapka, living in the village of Lubomirka, while Transcaucasia first received Baptist doctrines from a German named Martin Kalweit, a native of the village of Taurogeni, in the province of Kovno.

These two streams of Baptist doctrine, quite distinct from each other in their sources, mingled by-and-by, and swelled to a mighty river, which, like the River of Life in Ezekiel's vision, grew ever broader and fuller, satisfying the thirst of all who drank of it. . . .

In Transcaucasia, as aforesaid, the first seeds of Baptist doctrine were sown by the humble German artisan Martin Kalweit, who with his family had settled in Tiflis in 1862. This Kalweit came of a Lutheran family. In his native province of Kovno he had heard of the Baptists and their teaching from a woman who had attended their gatherings in Prussia; and, being desirous of knowing more about them, he crossed the Prussian border and went to Ickschen. Here he heard God's word, believed, and was baptised, together with his sister convert, in 1858, in the village of Kraweli by the Baptist preacher Leuket.

In Tiflis a Russian merchant named Nikita Voronia became acquanted with Kalweit. Voronia had belonged to the sect of Molokani (who, like the Quakers, reject the ordinances of Baptism and the Lord's Supper). He had long felt convinced, however, of the necessity of baptism for believers, but did not know from whom he could receive it, as he failed to find Christians of any real spirituality among either the Lutherans or the members of the Orthodox (i.e., the Russo-Greek) Church, and other professors of evangelical Christianity at that time there were none. Kalweit baptised Voronia on August 20th (September 1st), 1867; after which the latter administered the rite from time to time to various Molokani converts, one of whom was V. Pavloff, then a youth of 16.

This last baptism took place in 1871, by which time the infant Church in Russia numbered 10 members.

II.—THE GROWTH AND DEVELOPMENT.

The two groups of Baptists—the Khersonese and the Transcaucasian—continued each steadfast in the faith and in good works, without knowing of each other's existence until considerably later. Then it was from the newspapers that the little body in Transcaucasia learned of the evangelical movement in the south of Russia (the promoters of which soon after became known as "Stundists"), and not till the year 1876 did the two little bands make each other's acquaintance in person. . . .

The preaching of the reformed doctrines met with resistance at the very beginning from the clergy of the "Orthodox Church." This body, protected by the State, had no better weapons wherewith to make war on the backsliders from their Church than governmental and legal measures: arrest, banishment, and other forms of persecution were employed for the extinction (as it was hoped) of the Divine flame in the hearts of the converts. But all in vain: for vital Christianity is like the "bush which burned with fire and was not consumed." . . .

In Transcaucasia also the Gospel was already finding its way into many Molokani villages. Voronia's work of evangelisation was followed by that of Pastors Ivanoff and Pavloff. The latter was sent by his congregation at Tiflis, in 1875, to study for the Ministry at Hamburg for a year, at the end of which time he was ordained by Brother J. G. Oncken, and returned to Tiflis, where he found his flock increased to the number of forty. . . .

In 1884 the first Baptist Conference in Russia was summoned by John Wiehler, pastor of the "Brüdergemeinde" (New Mennonites) in the village of Novovassievka (province of Taurida). Here was established the Baptist Union in Russia, Brother Wiehler being elected President. From now the Baptists in South Russia and Transcaucasia began to know each other more intimately, and to be associated in the carrying on of the good work in the evangelised districts. During this Conference, eight evangelists were for the first time appointed for a term of a year, to carry on the work of these districts. Brother Wiehler continued to preside over the Baptist Union in Russia till 1886, when the danger of persecution obliged him to fly to Roumania. . . .

The Caucasian Baptists—sectarians born, and having worked for the most part among sectarians like themselves—escaped persecution for a long while. In 1880 the Church at Tiflis was formally established with Pavloff as pastor. But in 1887 the wave of persecution reached this Church also, and her pastor and his co-worker, N. Voronia—together with A. Amirchanianz, a Lutheran preacher from Armenia—were banished for four years to Orenburg, on the borders of Siberia. Soon after three of the most prominent members of the same Church—Brothers M. Kalweit, A. Masajew and A. Leuschkia—were banished for eight years. Yet the Church did not lose heart, but continued to hold services, and to increase in numbers. The persecution now began to spread all through Russia, and the most remote corners of Transcaucasia and Siberia were before long filled with sectarians of every sort and condition. . . .

III.—THE PRESENT POSITION OF THE BAPTIST CHURCH IN RUSSIA.

The Baptist Church in Russia has proved her vitality. Not only has she survived the systematic and long-continued persecution of both Church and State, she has done more—has grown strong, and diffused herself throughout the vast Russian Empire: "from the glowing plains of Colchis to the bleak rocks of Finland"—from St. Petersburg, across the snow-covered deserts of Siberia, to Amur and Manchuria. If a man should travel from Odessa to Churbin—a month's journey by rail—he would find even in the latter remote town a little body of Russian believers. As to the variety of the nations and tribes who up to the present time have embraced our Baptist faith in that land, they comprise: Russians (proper), Armenians, Tartars, Germans, Poles, Esthonians, Livonians, Lithuanians, Letts, Finns and Swedes.

With the year 1906 a new era dawned for Russian Baptists. In that year an Imperial Manifesto was issued concerning religious liberty, by which all exiles in Transcaucasia and Siberia were released. Most of these returned to their native places, and well was it for them that they did so; for soon afterwards, in the very places where they had been spending their term of banishment, a terrible war broke out between the Tartars and Armenians—a war to which vast numbers of people fell victims, and which practically ruined both nations for the time being. Thus the Lord delivered His people at the right moment from the danger which threatened them.

The revolution shook the Russian nation, both as regards politics and religion, to its very foundations. At the same time it showed clearly how false had been the accusations of hostility to the Government, brought against the sectarians by the clergy of the established Church—since with a few exceptions, our brethren remained neutral throughout the Reign of Terror.

After the publication of the manifesto concerning religious liberty, the Baptists lost no time in putting their new rights to use, and now manifested the utmost zeal in mission work. With the permission of the authorities, they instituted meetings in theatres, lecture halls, and tea houses. . . .

I had the privilege of preaching Gods's word at such meetings in three towns: in Balaschov and Berdiansk last year, and this year in Kharkov. As I took my stand on the platform and looked upon the thousands waiting so eagerly to hear the sacred word expounded, I thought of my eight years of exile at Orenburg, for this very same act of preaching the Gospel as understood by us Baptists, and I could hardly trust my senses. I felt that the scene around me must surely be, not a reality, but a dream. Truly "the Lord hath done great things for us, whereof we are glad."

Still, we do not as yet possess entire religious liberty, since all the meetings referred to were held only by permission of either the Minister of the Interior or the Governor of the province; and the local authorities, co-operating with the clergy, have often endeavoured by every possible means to prevent our people from thus assembling. Persecution is not quite a thing of the past, and in many villages our meetings are frequently broken up by the police, while the mob often seriously ill-treat the worshippers. . . .

In May of last year we started a Missionary Society, by which 19 brethren were appointed to be evangelists for the term of a year; and before long a similar Society was formed in Siberia, appointing the same number of men to do evangelistic work. The combined receipts of these two Societies amounted in one year to about £1,800. Beside the two German Missionary Societies—the Baptist and the Mennonite—which are co-operating with us, these receipts have been supporting twelve native (*i.e.,* Russian) Baptist evangelists; so that last year there were, beside the settled ministers, fifty brethren carrying on the work of evangelisation. . . .

IV.—OUR DUTIES AND TASKS.

The first and most urgent of our duties is to spead the Gospel, and therefore we must have men whose lives shall be dedicated to this work. Up to now our workers have been men with no regular theological training. But we live in an age of progress in all directions, and unless we wish to be left behind we must give our candidates for the ministry the best education in our power to qualify them to meet the demands of the time.

The need of this points out our second task, which is to found a Theological College, where students for the ministry may receive fitting preparation for their high calling. I am of opinion that for all the various tribes living in Russia we should have but one College, in which, so far as practicable, the common medium of instruction should be the Russian language; and for the place I propose Odessa. This city is in the south, where the climate is mild and healthy; while in it and its environs are numerous congregations, both Russian and German, young members of which, desirous of studying for the ministry, would thus have the opportunity of properly qualifying themselves to enter it.

Our third duty is to produce and circulate a healthy literature, Christian and denominational, and for this purpose we must establish an adequate institution, that shall send good and pure thoughts in print through the length and breadth of the land.

The fourth thing we have to do is to establish a Building Society to furnish funds for the erection of chapels, a need which is everywhere most keenly felt. Nor must we forget those of our ministers who are invalided, but must maintain a fund for their support also.

Our Union has resolved to build a Mission-house in St. Petersburg, where our Brother Fettler has already gathered together a flock; but he needs an adequate building in which to publish our Saviour's words to thousands of eager listeners. As we of Russia are still but a young Church, and our resources are very limited, we trust that our elder brethren, the Baptists of England and America, will aid us in carrying out all the objects above-named. There are over a hundred tribes in Russia stretching out their hands to us for the Bread of Life, and crying to us, "Give us to eat!" And our Master's command is, "Give ye them to eat!" Up, then, brethren! Up, and to the work.

17.5 Report on Russian Baptists, 1928

In his report on Russian Baptists at the Baptist World Alliance meeting of 1928, P. V. Ivanov-Klyshnikov reviewed the history and current situation of Baptists in the Soviet Union. He could not have anticipated the crisis of renewed persecution which befell Russian Baptists in 1929, but his report does show deep concern for the evangelization of that vast land. The report concludes with a Macedonia call for help from the West. Within a year the Soviet government put such severe restrictions upon Baptists that they could not maintain much contact with Baptists in the West, much less receive any aid from them. *Source:* Baptist World Alliance, 1928, 75-78.

The second address was given by the Rev. P. V. Ivanov-Klyshnikov, secretary of the Baptist Union of the U. S. S. R. His theme was

THE WORK AND TASKS OF BAPTISTS IN THE U.S.S.R.

1867 is a year never to be forgotten in the history of the religious life of many millions of Russian people; in that year, in the city of Tiflis, Nikita Isaevitch Voronin was baptised in water. He was the first Russian Baptist and the founder of the Baptist movement in Russia. The beginning in Russia is interesting for its independence. Independent of any outside propaganda, independent of the efforts of any missionary, but solely by the study of the written Scripture in response to the deep inward longing for truth, N. I. Voronin avowed himself a sinner, confessed his belief in the redeeming sacrifice of Jesus Christ and arrived at those fundamental convictions and views, that compose the distinguishing features of our Baptist faith. He received Christ and received an unction from the Holy One and this unction taught him everything (1 John, 2.27). This fact from the history of the Russian brotherhood of Baptists is a new and most wonderful confirmation of the truth of one of our principal views on the sufficiency of the Scripture for salvation.

During the sixty years of its existence in Russia our brotherhood has achieved wonderful results with which can be compared the achievements of no other religious movement. We can boldly state, that already in 1905—the year of the first World Congress—among the socalled sects in Russia, the Baptists were the foremost in point of numbers, the firmest in defence of the purity of their teaching, the bravest during the heavy repression of the tzarist regime and the most ardent in zeal of spirit and soul in the great work! And that is what we are now! . . .

From the very beginning of the work of the Baptists in our country was undertaken by natives of Russian. Foreign Baptist missionaries did not work in Russia. But during the entire period of our history we have had obstinately to defend the pure principles of the Baptist faith in view of the work of sojourning foreign missionaries of other religious currents.

At the present time the communities of our brotherhood are scattered throughout our great country: from Leningrad to the Japanese Sea, from the northernest point in Murmansk on the Arctic Ocean to lonely villages along the Persian and Turkish frontiers. Scattered over such an enormous territory we represent a firmly united living people, and although in our songs may often be heard notes of tears and sadness, like the sighs of snowdrifts on the boundless Russian plains, nevertheless, there is also always in them the note of thanksgiving and a double joy or rest and labour:—rest in God and labour for God!

Our organization in Russia is not complete, but we are gathering statistics from the associations and churches that are fully organized. So far as we can find, there are 200,000 members; there may be some others where churches are not fully organized, but not great numbers. There are also other groups that hold principles like those of Baptists, but they are much smaller than the Baptists. Our brotherhood is united in the Federative Union of Baptists of the U. S. S. R., which reflects the unity of the people of God throughout our country.

The Constitution of our country decrees and realizes in practice the complete separation of the church from the state—a principle of peculiar value for Baptists at all times. Further, in accordance with the Constitution of the Soviet Republic, every citizen can propagate any religion. Religious freedom and anti-religious propaganda is the right of all citizens. The freedom of worship with any religious rites is guaranteed, in so far as they do not violate social safety and do not involve infringements on the rights of citizens of the Soviet Republic. In view of this, we have the full right to hold meetings and teach in them the Word of God, and our evangelistic work has already spread beyond the confines of the Russian people and is gradually spreading among the heathen and Mohammedans living in our country. Further, we have the possibility of publishing our periodicals (the Magazines "Baptist" and "Baptist of Ukraine") and the Books of Holy Scripture, and also received in 1927 the official authority to open in Moscow a Preachers' School, dedicated in celebration of the sixty years' existence of the Baptist Brotherhood in Russia.

Such are our achievements. However, these achievements have laid upon us such duties and have placed before us such gigantic tasks, as we cannot ourselves fulfil, but before which we have no right to retreat; and of these I must tell the Baptists of the entire world. In order to understand what I have to say, it is absolutely necessary to give some figures. Our country occupies a territory of 21,352,572 square kilometres, and stretches from the west to the east for 9,000 kilometres, and from the north to the south for 4,000 kilometres. It is inhabited, according to the last census of 1926, by 147 million people. Of these the town population represents 26 millions, and the rural 121 millions. According to religious profession this population is divided as follows: the main body of 114 millions is composed of Orthodox, about 14 millions are Mohammedans, about 5 millions heathen and semi-heathen; the rest are attached to various groups.

Of this large mass less than one per cent. accept the Baptist faith. It is clear from this that the Gospel hardly touches the Russian people. In many places the inhabitants have never heard of Christ's teaching. Even in the big cities, and above all in Moscow with its about 3,000,000 inhabitants, the people still know very little about the Baptists. In a territory of 100,000 square kilometres, that is, on an area equal to two and one half times the area of Switzerland, we have but one preacher. For 4,000 churches and groups we have about 900 preachers, and 3,100 churches are totally without Baptist workers. With 5,000 preaching places, we have only about 400 buildings which we own, and about 800 hired; the rest of the meeting places, *i.e.*, 3,800 are in private flats and houses.

It is under such hard and difficult conditions that our work is carried on in U. S. S. R.

Meanwhile the Russian people is an exceptional people for the depth of their religious frame of mind and religious seekings. It represents the most fruit-bearing spiritual ground among the peoples of the whole world. It is a people of God-seekers, of God-bearers, . . .

In the spiritual cravings of the people we observe signs of the approach of a great awakening, and a sensitive ear can already hear the noise of this approaching awakening, "the sound of a going in the tops of the mulberry trees."

Besides the work among the Russian nation, before us has opened a path to work among the peoples of the national minorities—among the heathen and semi-heathen, and particularly among the Mohammedans, living in our country. Beginning from 1925 our Union has started a systematic work among the national minorities, and this will reap good harvests, although, perhaps, not in the nearer future.

Together with this great evangelising problem we stand before not less important tasks in our churches in the matter of inner educational work. The Russian people over a period of many centuries have fought stubbornly with the forests and swamps of their country, giving all their strength to the hard preparatory work for civilization. Very much like this the pioneers of the Russian Baptist movement, during tens of years have directed all their strength in work among wild spiritual weeds, among thick forests of spiritual unsociableness and swampy marshes of corrupted morals. It is natural that our communities, carved from these wild rocks, drawn out from this deep pit, are still in need of great educational work in order to be really irreproachable as "a city set on a hill."

This, therefore, will explain the tasks that arise from our activities. They are as follows: In the first place, to evangelize our country with its tremendous population of different tribes and nationalities; secondly, to carry out educational work in our churches. These tasks are very great, and in our position, who have not yet recovered from the very heavy blows inflicted upon us by the World War and Civil War, they are beyond our strength.

Therefore, we stand in sore need of the help of our brothers, who are in better material conditions than we.

We stand in need, before all, of support to equip our Preachers' School and continued aid for the maintenance of the School. Secondly, we need means for publishing books of Holy Scripture; thirdly, we need aid in order to erect houses of prayer in the large centres of our country, and first of all, in Moscow and Kharkov; finally, and fourthly, we need help for evangelists. . . .

And if the motto of today are the words: "Come over into Macedonia and help us,"— it is this collective Macedonian, many-featured, many-millioned, that stands there on the great Russian plains, with one foot in Europe, and the other in Asia, and that cries to you: "Come over and help us!"

17.6 A Survey of Russian Baptist History Since 1929

The year 1929 marked a great turning point for Baptists in the Soviet Union. The "golden decade" of relative freedom after the Revolution of 1917 came to an end, and Baptists faced a time of persecution which in its intensity rivaled anything the ancient caesars did to the church. The selection below cites major historical developments among Soviet Baptists since 1929. It is particularly helpful in clarifying the "Letter of Instruction" of the All Union Council of Evangelical Christians-Baptists (AUCECB) of 1960, and the subsequent schism of the Council of Churches of Evangelical Christians-Baptists (CCECB). *Source:* From *Vestnik spaseniia,* No. 3 (1967), 24- 29, trans. by PDS. As printed in Paul D. Steeves, *Church and State in the U.S.S.R.: A Sourcebook,* 136-138.

In 1929, in the presence of the law on freedom of religion, there was published the Resolution of the Central Executive Committee and the Sovnarkom, "Concerning Religious Associations," which reduced religious freedom to nil. Already by the summer of this year the publication of the journals, *"Khristianin"* and *"Baptist",* was forbidden, which have heretofore not been revived. At the same time congregations were closed. Atheists sought the possibility of deposing the church through their actions on the leadership of the fraternal unions. Many brethren workers of the union applied all their energies to preserve the brotherhood's faithfulness to the Lord and to all suggestions of cooperation with the authorities and curtailment of preaching the Gospel they answered: "We submit unconditionally to all governmental laws, if they do not violate our convictions. If you promulgate laws that we, believers, must not preach the Gospel to anyone, then such a law for us is not binding, since the law of God is above the laws of the state. If you publish a law that people not believe in God, then also that law is not binding for us."

For such faithfulness to the Lord they all, with few exceptions, accepted imprisonment, and several, such as Odintsov, Bukreev, Kostiukov, Vins, and many others, gave their lives. . . .

In 1935 the Union of Baptists was closed and the Union of Evangelical Christians also curtailed its spiritual activity. Societies of Evangelical Christians and Baptists everywhere were closed and prayer houses were confiscated.

But the year 1937 was especially hard for our brotherhood. It is difficult to determine the number of believers who were imprisoned in those years and who died through torture in the severe conditions of Siberia, the Far East, and on Solovki Island. The terms of imprisonment were so long that for many they seemed to be for life. Thrown into the wild taiga forests, deprived of the right of correspondence, tormented by hunger and weakened by labor, the true children of God died by the thousands. Only a few of those condemned returned home as invalid, old men, after the nightmares they experienced. . . .

The Church of Christ in those years went through a long, deathly darkness. In 1940, in all the country, there remained only a few open congregations. To enemies of the work of God it seemed that religion had already ceased. In reality, the Church continued to live even in these improbable conditions. In the congregations where sin did not rule, the following picture was observed: the presbyter was arrested; the church elected another for leading meetings; he was taken; a third was elected. And so on until all were awarded bonds. The modest, wretched apartments of believers, the forests and ravines were the places of worship services. Many expected deliverance from the Lord, which they saw in the imminent advent of Christ for the church.

Thus passed the mournful path of the Church of Christ in our country. This was a period of cruel persecutions in the life of our brotherhood in all of its hundred years' existence. From these tears the Lord also delivered His elect.

The same ruler under whom believers were suppressed so unimaginably, according to the will of God, at the end of the last war permitted the opening of prayer houses.

The ensuing period of the life of our brotherhood was a period of new revival. . . . In October, 1944, the All-Union Council of Evangelical Christians and Baptists was formed. Into its founding entered the workers of the former unions who had been freed from the places of confinement, after they had given consent to form the Union on specified conditions.

For the supervision of the life of the churches the AUCECB named its commissioners, the so-called senior presbyters. In 1947, the work of registration of the congregations was begun, after which few churches received official permission for conducting services. Societies and groups of believers who did not manage to organize themselves in this short period began to be refused registration by local organs of the state for various pretenses. After 1948 registration of congregations was completely ceased, as a result of which a significant part of the congregations suffered persecution. . . .

The church languished under such violence from the secular authorities, and workers of the AUCECB and the senior presbyters everywhere taught that such obedience was pleasing to God, seducing the weak and unstable souls who accepted the interference of outsiders in the inner life of the church as the will of the Lord. The vigilent children of God saw that the actions of the authorities and of the workers of the AUCECB coincided. It became clear to them that the persecutors who had become convinced of the futility of persecutions and repression had decided to suppress the Church using for this purpose its own ministers.

But the life of Christ found a place in the midst of the sorrowing people of God. "Philips" were found who baptized new converts, despite bans. There were found good pastors, who in secrecy from the leadership of the congregation visited believers in their homes and established them in the faith, encouraged and exhorted them to renewed prayer for the work of God. There were also benefactors who found the means for support of the needy. Meetings for young people and for exhortation were held without the knowledge of the presbyter. The children of God did all of this, subjecting themselves to danger, and many of them had to accept bonds for their zeal. There were also separate groups and whole congregations who did not want to be reconciled with apostasy and began independent services, protecting themselves from every kind of influence from the AUCECB. It was this way in Baku, Tashkent, Khar'kov, Kiev, Voronezh, Simferopol, Ordzhonikidze, and elsewhere.

In 1960, the AUCECB, to please the authorities, worked out the infamous "Situation of the Union of ECB" and the Letter of Instruction to the senior presbyters which strengthened the spiritual restrictions which existed earlier in the life of the church. On the strength of these documents our brotherhood was artificially divided into registered and unregistered societies, since the AUCECB turned from the latter and they were doomed to suffering under the intensified repressions. The ministers of these societies were falsely accused of parasitism and exiled. . . .

In August 1961, [several ministers] formed the Initiating Group for the Calling of an all-Union Congress of ECB Churches and accused the ministers of the AUCECB of conscious apostasy from the evangelical truth and, having given the initiative for a congress, called the people of God to intensified prayers and fasts on Fridays for the sake of revival in the country. Their call was accepted by numerous groups of believers and separate congregations. In support of the initiative for a congress, thousands of petitions were sent to the government. . . .

From 1961 to 1963 was a difficult period for our brotherhood. In meetings there was little room for preaching the pure gospel. Preachers of the registered congregations, distorting the Word of God, represented the revival that was beginning as displeasing to God. . . .

The awakened churches suffered intensified persecution. Their meetings were broken up, believers were summoned to organs of authority with the demands that they renounce petitions concerning the congress, searches were conducted in their apartments, and children were taken away from their parents for religious education. At this time, on false charges, around 200 brothers and sisters were convicted, and in the courts senior presbyters and ministers of registered congregations frequently represented the adherents of the movement for the congress as enemies of the state. . . .

17.7   Coerced Mergers Affecting Russian Baptists

The generic term "Baptist" does not mean exactly the same thing in the Soviet Union as in most Western countries. In the 1940s the Soviet government forced Baptists to merge with several other evangelical groups, resulting in one major denominational "union" which the government could more effectively control. These "shotgun marriages" were never completely happy, but Baptists have tried to make the best of them. Selection A describes the forced merger in 1944 of Baptists and Evangelical Christians, which united Baptists and several groups of near Baptists. *Source:* Walter Sawatsky, *Soviet Evangelicals Since World War II* (Scottdale, Penn.: Herald Press, 1981), 475-476. Used by permission. Selection B shows the 1945 inclusion of Pentecostals into that coerced merger. All sides had to give up cherished emphases in this union, but Pentecostals found it especially galling to speak against their own practices. It seems hard to imagine how article 11 could be carried out in sincerity in light of restrictions in articles 6-9. *Source:* Ibid., 477-478.

A.   The Merger of Russian Baptists and Evangelical Christians, 1944

Statute of Unity, October 27, 1944

1

From two unions—the Union of Evangelical Christians and the Union of Baptists— one union for the entire territory of the USSR is established: the Union of Evangelical Christians and Baptists.

2

The leading organ of the Union of Evangelical Christians and Baptists is the All-Union Council of Evangelical Christians and Baptists—AUCEC+B.

3

The following are to be elected from the members of the All-Union Council of Evangelical Christians and Baptists: Chairman, two vice-chairmen *(Tovarishchyi),* secretary and treasurer, who form the presidium of the council

4

The All-Union Council of Evangelical Christians and Baptists has its seal on which is written "All-Union Council of Evangelical Christians and Baptists" and the words on the inner circle: "One Lord, one faith, one baptism."

5

Evangelical Christians and Baptists existing as separate unions before the amalgamation are now fused into one society. Congregations, existing separately, as congregations either of Evangelical Christians or of Baptists, now enter into one union.

6

Each congregation, entering the Union of Evangelical Christians and Baptists, bears the name: (some specific) Congregation of Evangelical Christians and Baptists.

7

All congregations of Evangelical Christians and Baptists must if possible have ordained presbyters and deacons in accordance with the Word of God: Titus 1:5, Acts 6: 1-6; and 1 Tim 3:1.

8

In each congregation baptism, communion, and marriage are performed by ordained presbyters. In the absence of such, these activities may also be performed by unordained members of congregations, however only by charge of the church.

9

Baptism and marriage performed with the laying-on of hands, or without laying-on of hands on those baptized and married, has equal force. But to attain full unity in church practice, it is recommended that the performance of marriage and baptism be done with the laying-on of hands, interpreting this action as a form of festive prayer for blessing. Further, in the event of more than two baptismal candidates, the laying-on of hands is performed by raising the hands above the candidates while pronouncing a prayer for them.

10

The Lord's Supper or the breaking of bread may be conducted either by breaking the bread into many little pieces, or else by breaking it into two or three or several larger pieces.

Bread and wine are received by the members of the congregations standing, thereby expressing our reverence for the command to break bread.

B. Merger of Russian Baptists and Pentecostals, 1945

The August Agreement, 1945

The following twelve points were agreed to as a basis of union between the Christians of Evangelical Faith (Pentecostal) and the Union of Evangelical Christians and Baptists. Repeated requests for a revision of the Agreement has not resulted in any changes.

1

The congregations of the Christians of Evangelical Faith unite with congregations of Evangelical Christians and Baptists into one union.

2

The single union has its general executive center in the city of Moscow as well as a single treasury.

3

Representatives of Christians of Evangelical Faith are also included in the headquarters staff.

4

The spiritual workers of the Christians of Evangelical Faith remain in their spiritual calling which they bore before uniting with Evangelical Christians and Baptists, that is, senior presbyters, presbyters, and deacons.

5

Both sides recognize that the fullness of powers from on high, spoken of in Acts 1:8, may be manifested through the sign of other tongues as well as without this sign (Acts 2:4; 8:17, 39; 10:46; 19:6).

6

Both sides recognize, on the basis of Holy Scripture, that diverse tongues are one of the gifts of the Holy Spirit, not given to all but to some (1 Cor. 12:4-11).

This is supported by the words of verse 30 of this chapter: "Do all have the gifts of healing? Do all speak in tongues? Do all interpret?"

7

Both sides recognize that unknown tongues without interpretation is fruitless, concerning which the Apostle Paul explicitly states: 1 Cor. 14:6-9; 1 Cor. 14:28: "If there be no interpreter, then keep silent in the church." Both sides uphold this as a rule given by God, through the Apostle Paul.

8

Considering the word of the Apostle Paul about the fruitlessness of unknown tongues in the absence of an interpreter, both sides agreed to abstain from unknown tongues in general meetings.

9

Recognizing that, along with the operation of the Holy Spirit in the services, there may be manifestations leading to the destruction of the decency and decorum of the service (1 Cor. 14:40), both sides agreed to conduct an educational program against this type of manifestation, remembering that God is not a God of confusion, but of peace (1 Cor. 14:33).

10

In view of the fact that the Evangelical Christians and the Baptists do not practice foot washing, the present agreement recommends that the Christians of Evangelical Faith conduct an educational program designed to achieve a common understanding with the Evangelical Christians and Baptists on this question, aiming toward unity and the uniformity of public worship.

11

Both sides are to utilize all measures, so that among the Evangelical Christians and Baptists on the one hand, and the Christians of Evangelical Faith on the other, the most sincere fraternal and mutual relations will be established for reciprocal joy and blessed joint labor.

12

After signing the present agreement, both sides will announce the unification event to their congregations and will call for a prayer of thanksgiving for the great and praiseworthy matter of unity of all Christians in our country, who have been born again by faith.

17.8 The "Letter of Instruction" from the AUCECB, 1960

In 1960 the leaders of the All Union Council of Evangelical Christians-Baptists in the USSR issued a "Letter of Instruction" to Baptist pastors. Many of the pastors interpreted the Letter as a complete capitulation to government pressures, and felt the church could not continue to be a true church if it caved in to these unChristian demands. This Letter stirred resentments against the Union that were already present among many Baptists, and led to an organized movement of rebellion against Union leaders. The protesters in 1961 organized a rival Baptist Union in Russia, the Council of Churches of Evangelical Christians-Baptists (CCECB), a schism that still exists. They refused to accept the instructions in the Letter and refused to register their churches with the government. They also developed name-calling to a literary science in their description of Union leaders whom they regarded as traitors to the cause of Christ. The full Letter was never made public by the AUCECB, and was, in fact, rescinded in 1966. However, it is still regarded by many Baptists both within and outside the USSR as a primary example of complete capitulation of religion to government. *Source:* Paul D. Steeves, *Church and State in the U.S.S.R.: A Sourcebook,* 131-135.

TO ALL SENIOR PRESBYTERS OF THE AUCECB

Dear Brothers in God:

In sending you these new statutes of the AUCECB, we wish to give you some practical pieces of advice and instruction which you would do well to observe in your work.

The General Tasks of the Senior Presbyters of the AUCECB

1

The basic tasks of the senior presbyter of theAUCECB is verifying the observance of the statutes of the AUCECB in all their paragraphs and points and also of Soviet legislation concerning cults, in the parishes located within the borders of the territory served by him. . . .

3

The senior presbyter should understand thoroughly and remember that the main goal of the religious service at the present time is not the attraction of new members but the satisfaction of the essential spiritual needs of believers.

4

It is the duty of the senior presbyter to check unhealthy missionary manifestations, called by the Apostle Paul zeal for God without judgment (Romans 10:21), such as individual ministers and groups of believers who are hastily trying to attract people into the congregations, including people who are not educated or who are not confirmed in the basics of our doctrine; or in some congregations those who arrange recitations, poetry reading, and choir holidays having the character of a concert with the use of instruments which are foreign to our practice, such as guitars, mandolins, balalaikas, accordions and other similar instruments, and in this way violate the reverence of our religious services. . . .

6

It is necessary for the senior presbyter to watch very carefully over the acceptance of new members and over the strict observance of the probation period of not less than 2 to 3 years which has been established by the statutes of the AUCECB in order to eliminate in our congregations the unhealthy practices of a drive for numbers of members. . . .

The Ministry of the Local Presbyter

The presbyter of the congregation of Evangelical Christians-Baptists should be a tactful and attentive minister of the church, carrying out his work in accordance with the statutes of the AUCECB, and strictly observing Soviet legislation on cults.

1

Every presbyter is a minister only of his own parish and should not carry out any spiritual work outside of its borders, and he should not permit such activity on the part of other members of the congregation. . . .

3

The presbyter should not allow a tendency in the direction of hasty attraction of new members or the arrangement of concert choir performances, the use of orchestras, the reading of poems, and other forms of service not listed in the statutes of the AUCECB.

Concerning Members of the Congregation

1

Every member of the congregation of Evangelical Christians-Baptists should know that all of his spiritual needs may be satisfied only in the location of the registered society, and for that reason he should not take part in any other religious services organized outside of the society.

2

In satisfying his spiritual needs the member of the society should not organize any religious services in his own quarters. . . .

3

Members of the congregation should be worthy citizens of the Socialist Homeland. They have the same duty as all citizens of the USSR to work honorably and to follow a healthy, Christian life. Narrow views which are still encountered among believers concerning art, literature, movies, radio, television and so on should be decisively set aside.

Acceptance of New Members

1

The approach to the acceptance of new members of the ECB society should be made carefully. From the time of application for acceptance to the examination, not less than 2 to 3 years should elapse, so that our congregations will not get clogged up with weeds, as Christ says in his sermon on weeds (Matthew 13:24-27). . . .

2

The testing of those entering the congregation is carried out by the executive organ, and this is done carefully so that people unworthy of being members of our church are not received into the congregation. The drive for numbers of believers in our congregations should be decisively done away with, and more attention paid to the education of our members; for that reason the presbyters of the church should strictly observe the 2-3 year period for those to be baptized and also the age of those accepted in the church, attempting to hold the baptism of youth from the age of 18 to 30 to the very minimum, accepting into the church only those really confirmed in their belief and well-proven. Applications for church membership from individuals serving in the armed forces should not be accepted until they have finished their training or military service. . . .

6

On the occasions when baptism does not take place in a pool or prayer house but outdoors in a river, a sea or any other kind of body of water, it is necessary to insure that large crowds do not gather around the baptism and that everything be carried out in calm and quiet.

Baptism in the open should take place only during the summer and with the knowledge of organs of the Soviet state. . . .

> With brotherly greetings,
> The All-Union Council of
> Evangelical Christians-Baptists

17.9 Statutes of the Union of Churches of Evangelical Christians-Baptists (Dissidents) in Russia

Many of the stricter sort of Russian Baptists never approved the All Union Council of Evangelical Christians-Baptists, formed by the coerced mergers of the 1940s. The AUCECB further alienated many by its effort to work cooperatively with the government, despite severe persecution. The infamous "Letter of Instruction" of 1960 seemed to many to be the final capitulation of the church to government domination, and led to a schism in which more militant Baptists formed their own rival group, the Union of Churches of Evangelical Christians-Baptists (UCECB). The selection below gives the founding documents of that dissident union. *Source:* G. Keith Parker, *Baptists in Europe* (Nashville: Broadman Press, 1982), 258-266.

I. The UCECB

1. General Information
   1) The Union of Churches of Evangelical Christians-Baptists is a voluntary association of independent and equal churches, confessing the Evangelical Baptist creed, which is based upon the Holy Scriptures—the Books of the Old and New Testaments (canonical).
   2) The only statutes for the spiritual activity of the UCECB is the Word of God (the Bible). The present statutes are a collection of rules necessary for the conduct of those aspects of the activity which relate to the civil and legal norms of life.
   3) On the basis of the principle of the separation of church and state, the Union of Churches of ECB, its administrative organs and departments, and its member churches are completely free in their spiritual and internal activity and are associations of like-minded believing citizens which are independent of the state.

2. Goals and Tasks of the Union

"I press toward the mark for the high calling" (Phil. 3:13-14). "After ye have done the will of God, ye might receive the promise" (Heb. 10:36).
   4) The Union of Churches of ECB sets before itself the goals and tasks established by the Lord for His disciples:
      a) to preach the Gospel of Jesus Christ to all people (Mark 16:15-16);
      b) to achieve a higher spiritual level of holiness and Christian piety for all the people of God (Rev. 22:11; 2 Tim. 3:17);
      c) to achieve the association and unity of all churches and of all ECB believers, on the basis of purity and holiness, in a single brotherhood in Christ (John 17:21; Eph. 4:13).

3. The Composition and Structure of the Union

"From whom the whole body fitly joined together and compacted by that which every joint supplieth, according to the effectual working in the measure of every part, maketh increased of the body unto the edifying itself in love" (Eph. 4:16).
   5) The Union of Churches of ECB unites all legally registered and unregistered local ECB churches active on all the territory of the USSR, Religious associations of other denominations, which are similar in faith, may be received into the body of the Union of Churches of ECB on the condition that they recognize the doctrines of the Evangelical Christians-Baptists and are governed by the Word of God in life, ministry and activity.
   6) A local church informs the governing organ of the Union (The Council of Churches of ECB) of its decision to join the Union of Churches of ECB) of its decision to join the Union of Churches of ECB, by declaration.
   7) Each local church enjoys the right to withdraw from the Union of Churches of ECB freely.
   8) The Union of Churches may have fraternal fellowship with ECB churches and associations of other denominations of similar faith that are not members of the Union of Churches of ECB, provided that they are governed by the doctrines of the Evangelical Christians-Baptists.

4. Leadership of the Union

"Without counsel, purposes are disappointed: but in the multitude of counsellors they are established" (Prov. 15:22). "And the apostles and elders came together for to consider this matter" (Acts 15:6).

9) The highest governing organ, determining all the activity of the union, is the All-Union Congress of Evangelical Christians-Baptists.

10) For the execution of the decisions of the congress and the conduct of the activity of the Union in the period between congresses, the All-Union Congress elects a Council of Churches of Evangelical Christians-Baptists (CCECB), composed of 15-17 ministers of ECB churches.

11) The Council of Churches of ECB organizes departments: evangelists, publication, etc.

12) The regular All-Union Congress is called once every three years. The standards of representation at the All-Union Congress, and also the place and time of its convocation, are determined by the Council of Churches of ECB.

5. Ministry and Activity of the Council of Churches of Evangelical Christians-Baptists
"The care of all the churches" (2 Cor. 11:28). "And whatsoever ye do in word or deed, do all in the name of the Lord Jesus" (Col. 3:17).

13) The ministry and activity of the Council of Churches of ECB are determined by the goals and tasks, established by the congress and expressed in the present statutes, and they should be carried out in full accordance with the teachings of Jesus Christ.

14) The Council of Churches is responsible for:
   a) giving spiritual and organizational help to local churches, and the district and inter-district fraternal councils. The CCECB maintains ties with them both through correspondence and through visitation by its representatives;
   b) publication and supply for the ECB churches of the necessary religious literature;
   c) organization of Bible and choir directing courses and seminars;
   d) conduct, within the limits of the law, of external representation of the ECB churches both in the USSR and abroad. . . .

6. Finances of the Union
"Praying us with much intreaty that we would receive the gift, and take upon us the fellowship of the ministering to the saints" (2 Cor. 8:4).

18) The finances of the Union consist of:
   a) voluntary assignments and contributions of local ECB churches;
   b) voluntary contributions of individual persons;
   c) other income received.

19) Auditing of the finances of the Union is carried out by an Auditing Commission, elected by the Congress and composed of three persons. The commission reports the results of its audit to the regular All-Union Congress of representatives of Evangelical Christians-Baptist Churches.

7. Termination of the Activity of the Union

20) A resolution concerning the termination of the activity of the Union is accepted exclusively by the All-Union Congress of representatives of ECB churches, as the highest governing organ of the Union of Churches of ECB. . . .

III. The Local ECB Church

"That thou mayest know how thou oughtest to behave thyself in the house of God, which is the church of the living God, the pillar and ground of the truth" (1 Tim. 3:15).

8. Objectives and Tasks of the Local Church

26) The ECB Church is an association of believing citizens of the Evangelical Baptist creed, united for joint satisfaction of their spiritual needs and having the goal of the preaching of the Gospel of Jesus Christ for the salvation of sinners and the achieve-

ment of holiness and Christian piety by believers, expressed in love for God and neighbor (Mark 16:15-16; 1 Thess. 4:3; Mark 12:30-31).

27) For the accomplishment of these stated objectives the ECB church conducts meetings for the preaching of the Gospel, prayer, study of the Holy Scriptures and other spiritual requirements. Congregational and choral singing, with musical accompaniment, is an integral part of divine worship.

28) All citizens, including children, are guaranteed free attendance at worship services.

29) Worship services of local ECB churches are conducted on Sundays, Christian holidays, and on other days of the week according to the authorization of the church.

30) The premises for worship services of the ECB church may be granted both by the state and by private individuals.

31) The ECB church participates in district (territorial), inter-district, and all-union conferences and congresses of ministers of ECB churches and is linked with other local ECB churches both in its own district and beyond its boundaries; by its participation it comprehensively supports the activity of the Council of Churches of ECB.

9. Relationship to the Government

"My kingdom is not of this world"(John 18:36).

"Render therefore unto Caesar the things which are Caesar's; and unto God the things that are God's" (Matt. 22:21).

32) The local ECB church is an association of likeminded believing citizens, completely free and independent of the state.

33) The election and dismissal of ministers, the reception of members and their excommunication, the conduct of religious rites, general and members' meetings are conducted by the church in observation of the principle of the separation of church and state. Registration of the ECB churches with the organs of government should not serve as an occasion for violation of the principle of the independence of the church from the state.

10. Composition of the Local Church and the Obligations of the Members of the Church.

"For we are his workmanship, created in Christ Jesus unto good works, which God hath before ordained that we should walk in them" (Eph. 2:10).

34) Each person who has believed in Christ as his personal Saviour, has turned to God in repentance, has received water baptism upon profession of faith, and is guided by the Word of God in his life may be a member of the ECB church.

35) Guided by the Word of God, the member of the church is called:

—to grow in knowledge of the Lord Jesus Christ (2 Pet. 3:18).

—to witness regarding Christ by word and life (Rom. 1:16).

—to act in his relationship with people according to the teaching of Christ: (Matt. 7:12), and do not do toward others what you do not wish for yourself (Acts 15:20).

—to labor conscientiously, "doing with his hands the thing that is useful, so that he will have something to give to him who is in need" (Eph. 4:28), for it is said in the Scripture: "if anyone does not wish to work, he shall not eat" (2 Thess. 3:10).

—to take active part in the life of the church, and to perform service according to his calling (Rom. 12:6-11); not to miss meetings (Heb. 10:25) and to bear responsibility for the spiritual condition of the church and its members (Gal. 6:1-2).

—to manifest concern for relatives and to be a model in the family, to preserve peace and holiness (Heb. 12:14), to educate his children in the teachings and admonition of the Lord (Eph. 6:4), and to strive to serve the Lord with all his house (Josh. 24:15).

—to manifest submission to the civil laws according to the teaching of Jesus Christ: 'render to Caesar what is Caesar's, and to God what is God's (Mark 12:17), and to pray for the government, that it will exercise the authority entrusted to it in accordance with the will of God in order to preserve peace and justice (Rom. 13:5,7; Titus 3:1; Acts 5:20; 1 Tim. 2:1-4).

11. Administration of the Local Church

"Take heed therefore unto yourselves, and to all the flock, over the which the Holy Ghost hath made you overseers, to feed the church of God which he hath purchased with his own blood" (Acts 20:28).

36) The highest organ of administration of the local ECB church is the members' meeting of the given church.

37) All important questions, such as reception of members, excommunication, election of ministers, and others, are decided by the members' meeting of the church.

38) For conduct of the daily ministry and spirtual education of the members, the church elects a presbyter, deacons, and a church council comprised of as many members as the church itself stipulates. In their activity, the presbyter, deacons and church council are responsible to the members' meeting.

39) All church institutions, such as baptism, marriage, burial, prayers for the sick and prayers for children are conducted by the presbyter and ministers elected for this by the church.

40) Both members of the given church and ministers of other churches, on authorization of the church council, may participate in preaching and worship services.

41) The presbyter of the given church bears the chief responsibility for the conduct of worship services.

42) External representation of the local church in matters relating to registration, conclusion of agreements for the use of property, etc., are carried out by three members of the church, elected by the church. The final decision of questions related to registration and relations with governmental organs resides in the members' meeting of the church.

12. Finances of the Local Church

"Every man according as he purposeth in his heart, so let him give; not grudgingly, or of necessity; for God loveth a cheerful giver"(2 Cor. 9:7).

43) Finances of the local church consist of the voluntary contributions of believers and are disbursed for the needs of the work of God under supervision of the church itself.

44) The local church keeps an inventory book, in which is entered the property received from the state as well as that which has been purchased and donated.

45) An audit of the finances and material valuables is conducted by an auditing commission, elected by the church, comprised of three members. The commission notifies the church of the results of its audit.

13. Closing of a Local Church

46) The activity of a local ECB church may be terminated only upon decision of the members' meeting of the given church.

Council of Churches of Evangelical Christians-Baptists

November 30, 1965   Translated from the Russian

17.10 Efforts to Heal the Schism Among Russian Baptists

The schism which divided Soviet Baptists in 1961 has had reverberations far beyond Russia as each side has tried to win support for its views. However, efforts to heal the painful schism have surfaced from time to time. In time, leadership passed from those who actually provoked the schism to those who had only read about it, and both sides modified their previous harsh statements. In October 1975 the AUCEBC approved a statement composed by A. I. Mitskevich to seek reconciliation with the rival CCEBC. Mitskevich emphasized that any reasons for the schism had long since passed; the documents that caused the schism had been revoked, and leaders who most offended the strict Baptists were no longer in power. The AUCECB offered to take a more aggessive stance in urging the government to grant basic civil rights to believers, and they noted that the registration of churches had become easier. For all its conciliatory tone, however, this overture had little discernible impact upon the dissident group. By the late 1980s conditions had changed further and reconciliation seemed much more likely. *Source:* "Concerning the State of the Work of Unity in the Evangelical Baptist Brotherhood," RCDA-Religion in Communist Dominated Areas, 16, 4-6 (1977): 64-67. Used by permission.

Concerning the State of the Work of Unity in the Evangelical Baptist Brotherhood

[Subheadings inserted by RCDA]

Dear brothers, ministers in the Lord's vineyard!

I have been charged with making the report on the state of the work of unity and the course which we must take for overcoming the schism in our evangelical Baptist brotherhood.

In this connection, I wish to begin my report with the words: "But now there are many members, yet but one body. And the eye cannot say unto the hand, I have no need of thee: nor again the head to the feet, I have no need of you. Nay, much more those members of the body, which seem to be more feeble, are necessary. And those members of the body, which we think to be less honourable, upon these we bestow more abundant honour; and our uncomely parts have more abundant comeliness; that there should be no schism in the body" (1 Cor. 12:20-25). And again: "Honour all men. Love the brotherhood. Fear God. Honour the king" (1 Pet. 2:17).

In connection with the fact that there are in our midst various views concerning our further work in the matter of the achievement of unity, I wish to recall what was said in letters and decisions of the All-Union congresses of the Evangelical Christians-Baptists, inasmuch as we all should be executors of the decisions of our highest organ, which made the decisions on the basis of the Word of God.

At the All-Union Congress of 1963, the "Statutes" and "Letter of Instructions" were abolished and a new Constitution was adopted. In the fraternal letter of the congress it was said: "We extend the hand of brotherly love to all who love the Lord . . . We open wide the doors of our churches for all who thirst for unity in Christ . . .

All to whom the work of the Lord is dear, we, the ministers of Christ, call in meekness to lay at the feet of Christ all offences and pains and to rally into one fraternal family of Christ, so that He may be the Shepherd of His one flock—the people of God." This spirit of love and reconciliation resounded in the other congresses.

At the Congress in 1966 the following call to all ECB believers was adopted:

To cease mutual insults (Pr. 15:1).

To pray fervently for one another (Jam. 5:16).

To come to mutual reconciliation on the basis of unity in Christ (Jn. 15:6).

The All-Union Congress calls all separated brothers and sisters to recognize profoundly that we are children of One Father, and to strive to be in one family of the people of God. The doors of our churches are opened wide for them—all that is necessary is mutual forgiveness; 'even as Christ forgave us, so also do we' (Col. 3:13).

The All-Union Congress of 1969 also charged the All-Union Council of Evangelical

Christians-Baptists to strengthen even further the unity among the redeemed children of God.

Thus, beginning from 1963, we have not changed our deep striving—with great long suffering and with love we have continued our call and work for unification. And after the 41st Congress, we will strive to fulfill the High Priestly Prayer of the Saviour: "May they all be one."

The All-Union Council of Evangelical Christians-Baptists has frequently sent its responsible workers to local churches to continue the labor on the matter of unification of the children of God, and on May 29, 1975, for the fourth time, it sent an invitation to the CCECB for a meeting and discussion, but to this, as also to the invitations sent earlier, and answer was not forthcoming. . . .

Of course, it is impossible to expect that the question of unification can be decided immediately, but, regardless of the attitude on the part of the Council of Churches, we should continue our discussions and, as it is said, "shew ye to them, and before the churches, the proof of your love" (2. Cor. 8:24).

The CCECB, for example, declares that only the leaders of the Council of Churches insisted in 1961 upon the necessity of the convocation of an All-Union Congress of ECB and of a change in the Statutes and Letter of Instructions of 1960. However, existing documents demonstrate that in 1961, in discussion of these questions, they were not the only ones who spoke for the necessity of the convocation of a congress.

Status and Letter of Instructions abolished in 1963

In 1961, 1962, and 1963, the AUCECB sent to the offices of the government documents with a petition for the convocation of an All-Union Congress of Evangelical Christians-Baptists. The All-Union Congress was held in 1963, at which the "Statutes" and "Letter of Instructions" were abolished and a new Constitution adopted.

The All-Union Council of ECB, in meekness, recognized the lack of soundness of these documents and expressed repentance at the 1963 Congress, affirming this at the 1966 Congress, and this was brought to the attention of all our brotherhood by means of the journal, *Bratsky Vestnik,* and in letter No. 2850 of the AUCECB, dated September 3, 1969.

We have done almost everything in order to correct this abnormal situation. The facts show that the Council of Churches, in the course of all its 15-year activity, has also made mistakes, but we do not see among them any meekness and repentance.

The CCECB, apparently, does not wish to liquidate the schism, which is what all their activity demonstrates. Unfortunately, some of the believers and leaders of groups which left local churches maintain this; some, on the basis of a misunderstanding of the actions of the Council of Churches, are leading not to the realization but to the destruction of unity; others are frightened by the threat of excommunication, by accusations of "treason," "betrayal," and the like. The majority of them, unfortunately, having been deceived, have a distorted opinion about the real activity of the AUCECB and our local churches at the present time. . . .

One of the causes of the continuing division in various places is the fact that many of our ministers of the churches of God do not always, by any means, enlighten the believers regarding the many-faceted activity of the AUCECB and the changes which have occurred both in the composition of the AUCECB and in its activity, and they do not point out the danger for the work of the Lord in the calls of the Council of Churches: not to go along the path of reconciliation and rapprochement, not to attend the services of our churches, not to pray together, not to tolerate the conduct of services in the

AUCECB houses of prayer because of fear, so that the congregations will not appear to be in the hands of the AUCECB *Bratsky Listok,* No. 4, 1975, article 8).

Nevertheless we cannot fail to note that the believers in the CCECB congregations are oppressed by such a situation and they treat the calls of the CCECB rather coldly and they seek ways for legalization. According to existing reports from various places, more than thirty congregations have decided to be registered, despite the prohibition by the CCECB.

The CCECB strives to keep the believers under its influence and to do this they continue to defame our dear brotherhood. . . .

Seeing that many believers are changing their attitude toward the AUCECB to a better light, the CCECB in its *Fraternal Leaflets* has again condemned the AUCECB, casting a shadow over the decisions of the congresses and plenums, and even on the work of our Bible Courses.

Full separation of Church and State

We must here declare firmly that on the basis of the principles of our brotherhood we, Evangelical Christians-Baptists, at all times have affirmed and now affirm the freedom of conscience of all people. We confess that freedom of conscience can be guaranteed only in conditions of full separation of the Church from the State. The Church, in its spiritual activity, is independent of the State; it does not enjoy its support and it does not participate in government and political affairs. But Evangelical Christians-Baptists have never called for anarchy: "For there is no power but of God; the powers that be are ordained of God" (Rom. 13:1).

Holy Scriptures determine for the Church activity that is exclusively spiritual: to preach the great news of the Gospel—eternal salvation, peace and love to all far and near (Eph. 2:17; Mark 16:15-16), to educate its members in the attainment of holiness and Christian piety, expressed in love for God and neighbor (Jam. 1:27; Eph. 5:27), and all of this is expressed in our ECB Constitution. In this, in the main, the students in the Bible Courses are trained.

But, on the other hand, we are obliged to train believers correctly to relate to outsiders according to the Word of God, since each member of Christ's Church, as a citizen of his fatherland, has also his civil rights and obligations with respect to the government and authorities. . . .

Each Christian must be an exemplary citizen, love his nation, and sincerely care for its welfare and the flourishing of his native country. . . .

All-Union Council wants to overcome the schism

We as ministers of ECB churches stand on the principles: freedom of conscience, separation of church and state, and non-intervention in the spiritual and internal activity of the churches. If these principles are violated anywhere, then in these cases we defend our freedom of belief guaranteed by the Constitution.

Indeed, even the leadership of the CCECB declares that it is loyal to the organs of authority, and at the same time it accuses us of sin in the observance of the legislation.

Dear brothers! We must fervently explain to the believers the mortal danger of separation as the cause of great delusion in our families and among those around us. No one can guarantee that the believers who have been torn from our brotherhood may not gradually be influenced not only by hostility but also by various teachings that do not conform to Holy Scripture. Such phenomena have already been observed.

We have already pointed to the incorrect teachings of the CCECB concerning "saving" and "non-saving" churches; concerning excommunications declared by the

CCECB of ministers who were not their members, in their absence, and without any kind of conservations with them; and concerning their claim that only the persecuted Church is the true Church, etc. . . .

Dear brothers! We must continue, with prayer, to work on the matter of reconciliation and the achievement of concrete steps for the restoration of unity. Senior presbyters and presbyters of local churches, where there are separated brothers and sisters, must give them information regarding the sincere desire of the AUCECB not to return railing for railing (1 Pet. 3:9), but with brotherly love to disclose to them the will of God concerning the necessity of reconciliation and unity for redemption by the precious blood of Christ.

The All-Union Council of Evangelical Christians-Baptists is ready to do everything necessary in order to overcome the schism and it regrets that it meets stubborness on the part of the CCECB. . . .

In conclusion, turning to the present high meeting of ministers of the Lord, I want to say that, speaking about the achievement of unity, we will have more success if we devote serious attention to the condition of our local churches and help them in the matter of discipline and the achievement of high spiritual level. . . .

May our churches shine as clear lights of the love of Christ, drawing many hearts and also the brothers and sisters who are still not with us. "God is love."

May the Lord help us in this.

17.11   European Baptist Statistics, 1980

Statistics on religion are notoriously difficult, none more so than those behind the Iron Curtain. However, there is some value in forming at least a general idea of the relative size of various Baptist groups in both eastern and western Europe. Some of the Baptist unions there enjoy more religious freedom, and thus can report their statistics with greater accuracy. Other unions remain under severe government pressure, and some find it better not to report much growth lest they call down upon themselves even greater government restrictions. The statistical reports of Baptists in the USSR, for example, have not varied for a generation. *Source:* G. Keith Parker, *Baptists in Europe* (Nashville: Broadman Press, 1982), 278-279.

STATISTICS 1980

Taken in part from 1980 Baptist World Alliance Statistics with permission

Country/Union	Churches	Church Members	Publications	Youth Work	Women's Work	European Baptists Mission Society (EBM)	Foreign Missions	Home m./Evangelism	Social Ministry	Sunday Sch./Education	Baptist World Alliance	Bible School/Seminary
1. England (Baptist Union of Great Britain and Ireland)	2,091	174,578	X	X	X		X	X	X	X	X	X
2. Scotland (Baptist Union of Scotland)	157	14,429	X	X	X			X	X	X	X	X
3. Wales (Baptist Union of Wales)	638	37,770	X	X	X		X	X	X	X		X
4. Ireland (Baptist Union of Ireland)	90	7,676	X	X				X	X	X	X	X
5. Germany, Democratic Republic (Union of Evangelical Free Churches in the GDR)	215	21,193	X				X	X				X
6. Germany, Federal Republic (Union of Evangelical Free Churches in the FRG)	356	68,012	X	X	X	X	X	X	X	X	X	X
7. Switzerland (Union of Baptist Churches in Switzerland)	15	1,425	X		X	X	X		X	X	X	X (Int.)
8. Austria (Baptist Union of Austria)	9	691						X			X	
9. The Netherlands (Union of Baptist Churches in the Netherlands)	81	11,951	X	X	X	X		X	X		X	X
10. Denmark (Baptist Union of Denmark)	41	6,362	X	X	X	X	X	X	X	X	X	X
11. Norway (Norwegian Baptist Union)	64	6,299	X	X	X	X	X	X	X	X	X	X

		Churches	Members														
12.	Sweden (Baptist Union of Sweden)	422	21,651	X	X		X	X		X	X	X	X	X	X	X	X
13.	Sweden (Orebro Mission)	234	19,000	X	X	X	X			X	X	X						X
14.	Finland (Finnish Baptist Union, Finnish-Speaking)	10	771	X	X	X				X						X		
15.	Finland (Swedish-Speaking Baptist Union of Finland)	24	1,712	X	X	X				X						X		
16.	Italy (Baptist Christian Union of Italy)	80	4,200	X	X			X	X	X	X	X	X	X	X	X		
17.	Spain (Baptist Evangelical Union of Spain)	61	4,800	X	X	X	X	X	X	X	X	X	X	X	X	X	X	X
18.	Portugal (Portuguese Baptist Convention)	52	2,800	X	X	X	X	X	X	X	X	X	X	X	X	X	X	X
19.	France (Federation of Baptist Evangelical Churches)	28	2,997	X	X	X	X	X	X	X	X	X	X	X	X	X	X	X
20.	Belgium (Union of Evangelical Baptist Churches)	8	512	X	X	X	X			X		X	X	X		X	X	
21.	Evangelical Association of French-Speaking Baptist Churches	26	2,000	X						X		X						
22.	Greece	1	28															
23.	Soviet Union (All Union Council of Evangelical Christians-Baptists)	5,000	545,000	X						X		X				X	X (Corr.)
24.	Poland (Polish Baptist Christian Union)	55	2,539	X			X											
25.	Hungary (Baptist Union of Hungary)	200	12,000	X	X	X	X			X		X	X	X	X	X	X	X
26.	Czechoslovakia (Baptist Union in Czechoslovakia)	28	3,978	X								X						
27.	Yugoslavia (Baptist Union of Yugoslavia)	61	3,484	X	X	X	X	X		X		X	X	X	X	X	X	X
28.	Romania (Baptist Union of the Republic of Socialist Rumania)	662	160,000	X	X	X	X			X		X	X	X	X	X	X	X
29.	Bulgaria (Union of Baptist Churches in Bulgaria)	10	650	X														
30.	Europe (European Baptist Convention-EBC, English Language)	43	3,847	X				X		X					X			

Editorial Note: The figures for the Baptist Union of Wales do not include South Wales and North Wales area figures which are already included in those for the Baptist Union of Great Britain and Ireland.

Index